CHANGING INEQUALITIES AND SOCIETAL IMPACTS IN RICH COUNTRIES

CHANGING INEQUALITIES AND SOCIETAL IMPACTS IN RICH COUNTRIES

Thirty Countries' Experiences

Edited by

BRIAN NOLAN, WIEMER SALVERDA, DANIELE
CHECCHI, IVE MARX, ABIGAIL McKNIGHT,
ISTVÁN GYÖRGY TÓTH, AND
HERMAN van de WERFHORST

OXFORD
UNIVERSITY PRESS

OXFORD
UNIVERSITY PRESS

Great Clarendon Street, Oxford, OX2 6DP,
United Kingdom

Oxford University Press is a department of the University of Oxford.
It furthers the University's objective of excellence in research, scholarship,
and education by publishing worldwide. Oxford is a registered trade mark of
Oxford University Press in the UK and in certain other countries

Published in the United States of America by Oxford University Press
198 Madison Avenue, New York, NY 10016, United States of America

British Library Cataloguing in Publication Data

Data available

Library of Congress Control Number: 2013955766

ISBN 978–0–19–968742–8

Printed and bound in Great Britain by
CIP Group (UK) Ltd, Croydon, CR0 4YY

FOREWORD

···

INCOME inequalities, with their many causes, including labour market polarization, financial sector deregulation, loopholes in tax systems and weakening of the Welfare State, are increasingly being viewed as a factor that has contributed to the on-going economic and social crisis and that makes recovery more difficult.

The Europe 2020 Strategy addressed this issue by stressing that growth cannot be smart or sustainable unless it is also inclusive. The targets of a 75 per cent employment rate and of lifting at least 20 million people from the risk of poverty or social exclusion were intended to shape the EU's socio-economic development model precisely towards the vision of a more inclusive growth.

I have therefore taken a keen interest in the Growing Inequalities' Impacts project from its beginning in 2010, and I am pleased to now see its final product coming to fruition.

This book offers a unique comparative analysis across 30 EU and OECD countries covering economic inequality developments over the last 30 years. Such breadth of coverage, building on a well-designed analytical approach commonly applied to the individual country analyses, allows for the identification of common patterns as well as divergences. And this is precisely what this book does: it takes the reader country by country through a similar analytical process from long-term patterns of economic inequalities and their determinants, to their social, political and cultural impacts, to the role of national policies and institutions in the moderation or amplification of inequalities.

The individual country profiles are complemented by summary chapters, which draw on the rich data available and provide useful policy conclusions. Hence, we obtain confirmation of a general long-term rising trend in income inequalities, albeit with important country variations or occasional trend reversals. We see for instance how health outcomes display strong income, educational or social gradients; and how coordinated wage-setting mechanisms and minimum wages appear to contribute to reducing income inequalities.

The Commission has benefited from the GINI project to inspire its in-house analytical work on inequalities and the future of the Welfare State, as summarized in various chapters of the Employment and Social Developments in Europe reviews for 2011 and 2012. But more than that, we have drawn on the GINI research in the preparation of key policy initiatives such as the Employment Package of 2012 and the Social Investment Package of 2013.

There is a clear need for proactive public policy to improve opportunities and transitions at the lower end of the labour market while correcting excesses at the top. This need is well-summarized in the concept of social investment, which should, in our view, guide the design of twenty-first century Welfare States aiming to support inclusive growth. Taxation obviously also needs to catch up, and recent moves against tax avoidance on both sides of the Atlantic offer some renewed hope.

Much of the action obviously needs to be taken at national level. I therefore hope that when implementing labour market, social protection or taxation reforms, governments will benefit from the lessons of the GINI analysis as much as possible.

László Andor
European Union Commissioner for Employment, Social Affairs and Inclusion

Preface by the Editors

This volume is the product of a most extensive and fruitful scientific collaboration across countries and disciplines, focused on issues of central importance to modern societies. It is a core output of the *Growing Inequalities' Impacts—GINI* research project, funded by the European Commission under the Socio-Economic Sciences and Humanities theme of the Seventh Framework Programme. This project has addressed pressing questions about the evolution of inequalities in income, in wealth, and in educational outcomes and opportunities; and the social, political and cultural impacts these may have, as well their policy context and implications. In doing so, it has drawn on the expertise and commitment of over 150 social scientists, drawn from the disciplines of economics, sociology, political science and public health, and covering a total of 30 countries—25 of the 27 European Union Member States (the exceptions being Cyprus and Malta), Australia, Canada, Japan, Korea, and the USA. This exceptionally wide span is an essential component and strength of the scientific endeavour. This book presents one central element of the product of this collaboration, in the form of individual country studies presenting an overview of the evidence on the evolution of inequalities and their impacts in the country in question over the last three decades. The other core output, reflecting both the findings from comparative analysis and the key messages from the country experiences detailed here, is also being published by Oxford University Press under the title *Changing Inequalities and Societal Impacts in Rich Countries: Analytical and Comparative Perspectives*.

The GINI research project has been structured around six core research partners, with their teams, in the Amsterdam Institute for Advanced Labour Studies (AIAS) and the Amsterdam Centre for Inequality Studies (AMCIS), both at the University of Amsterdam, the College of Human Sciences and Geary Institute at University College Dublin, the Herman Deleeck Centre for Social Policy at the University of Antwerp, the Work, Training and Welfare interdisciplinary research centre (WTW) at the University of Milan, the Centre for Analysis of Social Exclusion (CASE) at the London School of Economics and Political Science, and TÁRKI Social Research Institute, Budapest. These coordinated the work of another 20 country teams that were joined later by the Korean team, which volunteered to participate in the project with the support of the National Research Foundation of Korea in December 2011. The work has generated substantial Country Reports that provide the background to the chapters of the present volume. Twenty-three individual research associates committed themselves to the project from the start, while in the course of the project many other experts accepted our invitations to contribute in their fields, which have resulted in 80 GINI Discussion Papers. The full listing of contributors (country team members and individual experts), their reports and the papers can be found on the website of the project: <gini-research.org>. As project coordinators and as editors of this volume, we are extremely grateful to all these participants for their intensive engagement throughout the project, and owe a particular debt here to the authors of the country chapters presented in this volume for the spirit in which the enterprise was brought to a successful conclusion.

The project has also benefited greatly from the input and advice of its Advisory Board, comprising Professors Tony Atkinson (Nuffield College Oxford), Gøsta Esping-Andersen (Pompeu Fabra University, Barcelona), John Hills (CASE at the LSE), Suzanne Mettler (Cornell University), Haya Stier (Tel Aviv University), Jane Waldfogel (Columbia University and LSE), Richard Wilkinson (University of Nottingham), and Marco Mira d'Ercole (OECD). We are very grateful to them for their thoughtful advice and their involvement in guiding what has been a particularly complex project, both in terms of structure and range of challenging topics to be investigated, and the contribution of their own views at the meetings that we have organized.

The substantial funding provided by the European Commission's programmes for international scientific collaboration was an essential underpinning to a multi-year, multi-country study of this type.[1] We have received extremely helpful guidance and support from Ronan O'Brien and Marie Ramot of the Commission's Directorate General for Research and Innovation, and also very helpful input from Georg Fisher, Director for Analysis, Evaluation, and External Relations, in the Directorate General for Employment, Social Affairs and Inclusion.

Finally, we have been in good hands throughout with Oxford University Press, and wish to express our deep appreciation for the support received from its commissioning editor, Adam Swallow, from the outset, which has been critically important, as well as to Aimee Wright and colleagues in shepherding the volume through the production process.

The research project on which this book is based has been challenging but highly rewarding, and we trust that the broad-ranging findings will deepen understanding, act as a springboard for further research, and inform policy in relation to inequality and its impacts, crucially important for the development of our societies.

Brian Nolan (Dublin), Wiemer Salverda (Amsterdam), Daniele Checchi (Milano), Ive Marx (Antwerp), Abigail McKnight (London), István György Tóth (Budapest) and Herman G. van de Werfhorst (Amsterdam).

[1] The 7th Framework Programme in the field of Socio-Economic Sciences and Humanities awarded grant No 244592 to the GINI proposal, submitted in January 2009 and very favourably reviewed by the Commission's independent and anonymous referees, whom we thank for their support. The GINI project started in February 2010 and concluded in July 2013.

Contents

List of Figures

LIST OF TABLES

LIST OF CONTRIBUTORS

All authors are listed by their country teams, including the editors of this volume (see Ireland, Netherlands, Italy, Belgium, UK, and Hungary).

Australia

Peter Whiteford is a Professor in the Crawford School of Public Policy at The Australian National University, Canberra. His work encompasses pension and welfare policies. He has also worked on child poverty, family assistance policies, welfare reform, and other aspects of social policy, particularly ways of supporting the balance between work and family life.

Austria

Nina-Sophie Fritsch is a Research Associate and PhD candidate in the Department of Sociology at the University of Vienna. Her main research topics comprise education, labour market research, social inequality and poverty.

Roland Teitzer (Mag.) is a recipient of a DOC-fellowship of the Austrian Academy of Science in the Institute of Sociology at the University of Vienna. His research interests are social inequality and poverty, democracy, and labour market research, as well as methods in social science.

Tobias Troger is a PhD candidate in the Department of Sociology at the University of Vienna. His main research interests are in the field of comparative welfare state research, the nexus between family, gender and employment, as well as poverty and social inequality.

Roland Verwiebe—country team coordinator—is Full Professor of Social Stratification Research and Quantitative Methods at the University of Vienna and Head of the Department of Sociology. His main research interests cover social inequality, migration, labour market and European integration.

Laura Wiesböck is a PhD candidate in the Department of Sociology at the University of Vienna. Her research interests are mainly in the field of migration, transnationalism, social inequality, exclusion and poverty.

Baltics (Estonia, Latvia and Lithuania)

Kerly Espenberg (PhD) is Deputy Head of the University of Tartu's Centre for the Social Sciences. Her main research area is labour economics.

Anu Masso (PhD) is a Senior Research Fellow at the Institute of Journalism and Communication, University of Tartu, Estonia. Her main research areas are personal social space, cultural distances, geo-cultural mobility and the role of language communication in creation of social space. She has participated in various national and international research projects.

Jaan Masso (PhD)—country team coordinator—is a Senior Research Fellow at the University of Tartu, Estonia. His main research areas are labour economics, foreign direct investments, innovation economics, and science policy. He has participated in various national and international research projects (EU FP, ILO, World Bank, OECD).

Inta Mieriņa (PhD) is an Assistant Professor at the Institute of Sociology, University of Warsaw, and funded by an ERC Starting Grant for 'Public Goods through Private Eyes: Exploring Citizens' Attitudes towards Public Goods and the State in East-Central Europe'. She is also a researcher at the Institute of Philosophy and Sociology, University of Latvia. She has been a visiting researcher at the Aarhus University, the University of Illinois at Chicago, and GESIS EUROLAB.

Kaia Philips (PhD) is an Associate Professor at the University of Tartu. She is an experienced researcher and evaluator in the fields of labour market and social policy, effectiveness of labour and social policy measures, industrial relations, employment and unemployment, workers displacement and social security, migration, wages, and income inequality.

Belgium

Ive Marx—country team coordinator—is an Associate Professor at the University of Antwerp and Chair of the Department of Sociology. He coordinates research on poverty and income distribution, labour, and migration at the university's Centre for Social Policy Herman Deleeck. He is a political and social scientist and an economist. The main focus of his research is poverty and minimum income protection. He coordinated the policy work package of the GINI project.

Tim Van Rie is a sociologist and was a junior researcher in the Herman Deleeck Centre for Social Policy, Antwerp, during the GINI project.

Bulgaria

Bogdan Bogdanov (PhD) works at the National Statistical Institute as head of Households, Income and Expenditure Statistics Department. He has authored many academic papers and co-authored books on social and economic topics.

Petya Ivanova is an Associate Professor at the Tsenov Academy of Economics, Svishtov, Bulgaria. She also works as a project coordinator in the Institute of Scientific Research of the University and as an expert at the Bulgarian Chamber of Education, Science and Culture. Her main research interests are sustainable development, mediation, tourism safety and security, and the economics of services.

Silviya Panteleeva (PhD) is Chief Assistant at the D. A. Tsenov Academy of Economics. Her research interests are in the area of pension insurance, labour market and unemployment, problems of poverty, and the minimum wage.

Vassil Tsanov—country team coordinator—is a Professor in the Economic Research Institute of the Bulgarian Academy of Sciences and at the University of Veliko Tarnovo. His research interests are in the field of the labour market, incomes and income policy, inequality and poverty. He participates as an expert in international projects of the EU and ILO.

Canada

Robert Andersen—country team coordinator—is Distinguished Professor of Social Science and Chair, Department of Sociology at the University of Toronto. His teaching and research interests are in political sociology (especially the social bases of attitudes and political actions), social stratification, applied statistics, and survey methods. Most recently, he has been exploring the contextual factors associated with national differences in social and political attitudes and civic participation.

Mitch McIvor is a PhD candidate in Sociology at the University of Toronto. His research interests include social stratification (especially the rise of personal debt levels) and the sociology of mental health. His dissertation research explores how student debt influences the labour market decisions and outcomes of recent university graduates.

Denmark

Ioana Neamtu is a PhD candidate in the Department of Economics and Business, Aarhus University.

Niels Westergaard-Nielsen—country team coordinator—is a Professor in the Department of International Economics and Management at the Copenhagen Business School. Until recently, he was a Professor and Director of the Centre for Corporate Performance at the Aarhus Business School, Aarhus University. He is a Research Fellow of IZA. His major research interests are wage formation at the individual and firm levels, unemployment and employment, matched worker and firm data, personnel economics and health economics.

Finland

Jenni Blomgren (PhD) is a Senior Researcher at the Social Insurance Institution of Finland (Kela). Her current research interests include quantitative analyses of e.g. use of sickness-related social insurance benefits, care arrangements for older people, social determinants of health, and regional differences in well-being.

Heikki Hiilamo (2 PhDs) is a Professor of Social Policy at University of Helsinki. He is a former Professor at the Social Insurance Institution of Finland (Kela) and a leading scholar on poverty and inequality in Finland. He is an Adjunct Professor in social and health policy at the University of Tampere and in welfare sociology at the University of Eastern Finland. He was a Visiting Professor at the University of California and San Francisco.

Olli Kangas (PhD)—country team coordinator—is Research Director at the Social Insurance Institution of Finland (Kela). He has been Visiting Professor in Stockholm, Beijing, Sydney, Budapest, Bremen, and Umeå. In 2012, he occupied the H.C. Andersen Professorship at the University of Southern Denmark. He has Adjunct Professorships in Social Policy (Helsinki and Turku), in Sociology (Stockholm and Tampere) and in Political Science (Odense). His research interests revolve around the comparative political economy of the welfare state—institutional designs, causes and consequences in terms of legitimacy, inequality, and poverty.

Mikko Niemelä (PhD) is a Senior Researcher at the Social Insurance Institution of Finland (Kela), and an Adjunct Professor in sociology at the University of Turku and at the University of Eastern Finland. His current research focuses on the mechanisms of institutional change in welfare states, public perceptions of the causes of poverty, and on cross-national differences in public attitudes towards the role of government. Other areas of research include the measurement of poverty and the intergenerational transmission of poverty.

France

Nicolas Frémeaux holds PhD from the Paris School of Economics under the supervision of Thomas Piketty. He currently works on the dynamics of inequality and, more especially, on the role of the family in the persistence of inequality across generations.

Thomas Piketty is Professor of Economics at the Paris School of Economics, of which he was the founder and first director. He has done major historical and theoretical work on the interplay between economic development and the distribution of income and wealth. In particular, he is the initiator of the recent literature on the long-run evolution of top income shares in national income and the corresponding World Top Incomes Database.

Germany

Giacomo Corneo is Professor of Public Finance and Social Policy at the Free University of Berlin, and a Research Fellow of CEPR, London, CESifo, Munich, IMK, Düsseldorf, and IZA, Bonn. He has published in the fields of public economics, labour economics, comparative economics, industrial organization, and growth theory.

Reinhard Pollak (PhD) is Head of the Project Group, "National Educational Panel Study: Vocational Training and Lifelong Learning," at the Social Science Research Center (WZB), Berlin. He studies trends and mechanisms of social mobility, educational inequality, and gender segregation from a cross-national comparative perspective.

Sonja Zmerli is a Researcher at the Institute of Sociology at the Goethe University, Frankfurt am Main, and at the Institute of Political Science at the Technische Universität Darmstadt. Her research interests focus on inequality, social capital, political attitudes, political participation, and welfare state regimes.

Greece

Margarita Katsimi (PhD) is an Associate Professor of Economics in the Department of International and European Economic Studies, Athens University of Economics and Business (AUEB), and a Research Fellow at CESifo. Her research focuses on issues of macroeconomics, political economy, unemployment, European economic integration, applied economics, and public economics.

Thomas Moutos—country team coordinator—is Professor of Economics at the Athens University of Economics and Business (AUEB) and Director of the Executive MSc Programme in European Studies, and a Research Fellow of CESifo. His main fields of interest are labour economics and international economics.

George Pagoulatos is Professor of European Politics and Economy in the Department of International and European Economic Studies, Athens University of Economics and

Business, and a Visiting Professor at the College of Europe in Bruges. He was Senior Advisor and Director of Strategic Planning to the Prime Minister, Lucas Papademos. His research focuses on the EU, Southern European and Greek political economy.

Dimitri Sotiropoulos is an Associate Professor in the Department of Political Science and Public Administration of the University of Athens. He has studied law and obtained his PhD in sociology from Yale (1991).

Hungary

Zoltán Fábián PhD in sociology, is a Senior Researcher at TÁRKI Social Research Institute Inc., Budapest. His fields of research are political behaviour, and social and cultural stratification.

András Gábos PhD in sociology, is a Senior Researcher at TÁRKI Social Research Institute Inc., Budapest. His fields of research are family and social policy, fertility, child poverty and well-being.

Marianna Kopasz PhD in sociology, is an economist-sociologist. Her research focuses on child poverty, regional inequalities, labour markets, business networks, social capital and trust.

Márton Medgyesi (PhD) is a Senior Researcher at TÁRKI Social Research Institute since 1997 and regularly lectures on social policy at the Corvinus University. His main research interests are income distribution, private and public intergenerational transfers, and redistribution.

Péter Szivós Dr. Univ., is an economist-statistician, Managing Director and project leader at TÁRKI Social Research Institute Inc., Budapest. His fields of research are income distribution and inequalities, social exclusion, and poverty.

István György Tóth—country team coordinator—is a sociologist and Director of TÁRKI Social Research Institute, and Docent, Department of Sociology, Corvinus University, Budapest. He is also an Advisory Board Member of the Luxembourg Income Study. He coordinated the Political and Cultural Impacts work package of the GINI project together with Herman van de Werfhorst, and built the GINI database of income inequality and poverty.

Ireland

Emma Calvert is a Lecturer in Sociology at Queen's University, Belfast. Before joining Queen's, she held research positions at University College Dublin, the ESRC Centre for Population Change, University of Southampton and the Economic and Social Research Institute, Dublin.

Tony Fahey is Professor of Social Policy in the School of Applied Social Science in University College Dublin. His main fields of research are family patterns and family policy, child well-being, demography and housing.

Deirdre Healy is a Lecturer in the UCD Institute of Criminology. Her research interests include desistance, community sanctions, victims and the criminal justice system. She has recently published *The Dynamics of Desistance: Charting Pathways through Change* (Routledge, 2012).

Aogán Mulcahy teaches in the School of Sociology at University College Dublin. His main research interests lie in the area of criminology, and he is author of *Policing Northern Ireland* (Willan/Routledge, 2006) and co-author (with Ian Loader) of *Policing and the Condition of England* (Oxford, 2003).

Bertrand Maître is a Research Officer at the Economic and Social Research Institute, Dublin. His research focuses on multi-dimensional approaches to poverty, social exclusion and quality of life, the distribution of income and earnings, and the development and use of measures of deprivation.

Michelle Norris is a Senior Lecturer in social policy at University College, Dublin. Her research examines housing policy and urban regeneration in Ireland and from a comparative perspective. Her latest book, *Social Housing, Disadvantage and Neighbourhood Liveability* will be published by Routledge in 2013.

Brian Nolan—country team coordinator—is Professor of Public Policy in the School of Applied Social Science and Principal of the College of Human Sciences, University College Dublin. He is an economist and has published widely on income inequality, poverty, public economics, social policy, and health economics. He acted as the research coordinator of the GINI project and coordinated the Social Impacts work package of the project together with Abigail McKnight.

Ian O'Donnell is Professor of Criminology at University College Dublin and Adjunct Fellow of Linacre College, Oxford. His most recent book is *Coercive Confinement in Ireland: Patients, Prisoners and Penitents* (with Eoin O'Sullivan) published by Manchester University Press.

Nessa Winston is a College Lecturer in the School of Applied Social Science, University College Dublin. Her research focuses on the linkages between social policy and sustainable development, with recent publications on housing provision in Europe, the Irish house price boom and bust, and policies and practices promoting the development of sustainable communities.

Christopher T. Whelan is an Emeritus Professor in the School of Sociology, University College Dublin, and a Senior Fellow at the Geary Institute, and also a Professor of Sociology at the School of Sociology, Social Policy and Social Work, Queen's University Belfast. His research interests include the causes and consequences of poverty and inequality, quality of life and social mobility, and inequality of opportunity. He has published extensively on these topics and also on economic and social change in Ireland.

Italy

Gabriele Ballarino is Professor of Economic Sociology at the University of Milan. His research focuses on the relations between educational systems, labour markets and social stratification.

Michela Braga is a Postdoctoral Fellow at the Department of Economics of the University of Milan and Researcher at the Fondazione Rodolfo DeBenedetti (fRDB). Her main research interests are in labour economics, education, and development economics.

Massimiliano Bratti (PhD) is an Associate Professor of Economics at the University of Milan, where he teaches labour and education economics. His main research topics are female labour force participation and fertility decisions, pecuniary and non-pecuniary (mainly health) returns to education, the effect of parental health on children's outcomes and the determinants of firms' innovation performance.

Daniele Checchi—country team coordinator—is Professor of Labour Economics at the University of Milan. He has published on the role of labour market institutions, on intergenerational mobility and, more recently, on educational reforms. He coordinated the Drivers of Inequality work package of the GINI project together with Wiemer Salverda.

Antonio Filippin (PhD) is Assistant Professor at the University of Milan, where he teaches behavioural economics, and a Research Fellow at IZA. His research interests encompass educational choices and inequality, and concentrate mainly on experimental methodology as far as the empirical analysis is concerned.

Carlo Fiorio (PhD) is Associate Professor of Public Finance at the University of Milan. His research interests focus on inequality measurement, tax and benefit simulation and empirical public economics, and labour economics.

Marco Leonardi (PhD) is Associate Professor of Economics at the University of Milan. He was a Visiting Scholar at the MIT Department of Economics, UC Berkeley, and Georgetown University, and he worked at IZA, Bonn. His research interests are in labour economics with particular reference to wage inequality, earnings mobility, and unemployment.

Elena Meschi is an Assistant Professor at Cá Foscari University of Venice, Department of Economics. Her main research interests are in labour economics, education, trade, and applied micro-econometrics. Recently, she has focused on the trade and technology related determinants of income inequality and on several aspects of educational inequality.

Francesco Scervini (PhD) is a postdoc at the University of Milan. His research interests focus on inequality and its relationship with public choice with regard to redistribution and within the educational framework. He received the Aldi Hagenaars award from the Luxembourg Income Study for the paper 'Empirics of the Median Voter: Democracy, Redistribution and the Role of the Middle Class', *Journal of Economic Inequality*, 2010.

Japan

Miki Kohara (PhD) is an Associate Professor in the Department of Comparative Public Policy, Osaka School of International Public Policy (OSIPP), Osaka University. Her research interests include inequality, labour supply, time allocation, household behaviour, and within-family transfers.

Fumio Ohtake—(PhD) country team coordinator—is a Professor in the Institute of Social and Economic Research, Osaka University. His research topics are labour economics, income distribution, applied economics, public finance/monetary economics, and economic policy. He was awarded several prizes for his book *Inequality in Japan* (2005).

Korea

Byung You Cheon —(PhD) country team coordinator—is a Professor at Hanshin University. He received his PHD in economics at Seoul National University, and has worked as a research fellow at the Korea Labor Institute for 10 years. He has published books and articles in the research areas of labour economics and social policy, including political sociology, social welfare, social inequalities, social movements, and civil society.

Jiyeun Chang is a Research Fellow at the Korea Labor Institute (KLI). She earned her PhD in sociology from the University of Wisconsin, Madison. Her research interests include: the female and elderly labour market, work-life balance, and income inequality. She is currently working on the issues of poverty and social assistance program in Korea. Her recent publications are *Globalization and Asian Women* (2007) and *Compatibility between Labor Market Structure and the Social Security System in Korea* (2011).

Gyu Seong Hwang (PhD) is a Research Professor at Hanshin University. He received his PhD in Politics at Sungkyunkwan University. His recent publications are *Social Policies and Welfare State in Unified Germany* (2012) and *Structured Reproduction of Disparities in Korea* (2012).

Shin-Wook Kang (PhD) is a Research Fellow at the Korea Institute for Health and Social Affairs (KIHASA). He received his PhD in Economics from Seoul National University. His main research areas are income distribution, income mobility, and policies for social inclusion. He is co-author of several books and policy reports, including *Understanding Korean Economy* (2013), *Developing Social Cohesion Index in Korea* (2012), *Economic and Social Polarization in Korea* (2007–2009).

Hyun Joo Kim is a Research Assistant at the Academy of Democratic Society and Policy. She received her master degree at Sungkyunkwan University. Her dissertation is Taxation in the Park Chung-Hee regime: political origins of the regressive tax structure (2012).

Byung-Hee Lee (PhD) is a Research Fellow at the Korea Labor Institute (KLI). He earned his PhD in economics at Seoul National University. His recent publications are *Low Wages and Policy Options in the Public of Korea: Are Policies Working* (2012) and *Non-Regular Employment and Labour Market Segmentation in the Republic of Korea* (2007).

Jin-Wook Shin (PhD) studied sociology at Yonsei University in Seoul, South Korea, and received his PhD in sociology at Free University of Berlin in 2003. He has been teaching at Chung-Ang University in Seoul as Professor of Sociology since 2005. He has published books and articles in research areas of political sociology, social welfare, social inequalities, social movements, and civil society, including: *Modernisierung und Zivilgesellschaft in Südkorea* (2005), *From Symbols to Mobilization: Cultural Origins of Democratization Movements in South Korea* (2007, co-author), and *Citizen* (2008).

Luxembourg

Alessio Fusco is a research economist at CEPS/INSTEAD (Luxembourg). His research interests, which mainly involve the use of household surveys, are on applied micro-economic topics related to the analysis of income and non-income poverty as well as on the measurement of various concepts such as multiple deprivation, income polarization or social polarization.

Philippe Van Kerm—country team coordinator—is a researcher at CEPS/INSTEAD, and recently acted as its interim director. His interests are in social welfare and inequality with particular reference to income dynamics. Currently, he is working on the measurement of discrimination, poverty persistence, and wage inequality.

Aigul Alieva, Fanny Etienne-Robert, Anne-Catherine Guio, Kristell Leduc, Philippe Liégeois, Maria-Noel Pi Alperin, Anne Reinstadler, Eva Sierminska, Patrick Thill and Marie Valentova are researchers at CEPS/INSTEAD. **Luna Bellani and Denisa Sologon** are postdoctoral fellows at CEPS/INSTEAD. **Iryna Kyzyma** is a PhD candidate at CEPS/INSTEAD and at the Bremen International Graduate School of Social Sciences. **Bogdan Voicu** was a visiting scholar at CEPS/INSTEAD.

Netherlands

Christina Haas was a Research Masters student of sociology and junior researcher at the Amsterdam Institute for Advanced Labour Studies for the GINI project, and is currently a Research Associate at the Integrative Research Unit on Social and Individual Development (INSIDE) of the University of Luxembourg. Her research interests concern inequality, educational inequality, and school-to-work-transitions.

Marloes de Graaf-Zijl (PhD) is a scientific researcher at CPB Netherlands Bureau for Economic Policy Analysis. She studies the labour market of older workers and income inequality over the life cycle. She was a postdoctoral researcher at AIAS, contributing to the GINI project.

Bram Lancee (PhD) is a Senior Researcher in the research unit, 'Migration, Integration, Transnationalization' at the Social Science Research Center Berlin (WZB). From 2010 to 2011, he was a postdoctoral researcher at the University of Amsterdam, Department of Sociology. His academic interests include social capital and social participation, ethnic inequality in the labour market, attitudes towards immigrants, ethnic diversity, and quantitative research methods.

Natascha Notten was a postdoctoral researcher at the University of Amsterdam for the GINI project and currently works as an Assistant Professor in the Department of Sociology at the Radboud University Nijmegen. Her research focuses on the intergenerational transmission of inequality in various domains (e.g. cultural consumption, health, and education), particularly the causes and consequences of parental media socialization.

Wiemer Salverda—country team coordinator—is Emeritus Director of the Amsterdam Institute for Advanced Labour Studies (AIAS) at the University of Amsterdam. He is a labour economist and his research focuses on the low-wage labour market and earnings inequality from an international comparative perspective. His work also targets comparative employment performance, top incomes, ageing, and the evolution of youth labour. He was the overall coordinator of the GINI project and coordinated its Drivers of Inequalities work package with Daniele Checchi.

Herman van de Werfhorst is Professor of Sociology, and Director of the Amsterdam Center for Inequality Studies (AMCIS) at the University of Amsterdam. He works on the role of education in issues of inequality, in terms of social stratification and political outcomes. He coordinated the Political and Cultural Impacts work package of the GINI project with István Tóth.

Poland

Michał Brzeziński is an Assistant Professor in the Faculty of Economic Sciences, University of Warsaw. His research interests include measuring poverty and inequality in Central and Eastern European countries and modelling income/wealth distributions.

Barbara Jancewicz is a PhD Student at the Institute of Sociology, University of Warsaw, Poland. Her PhD thesis, 'Measures of Inequality and Individual Income Inequality Evaluations', focuses on the analysis of people's perception of inequality and its relationship with inequality measures. Her research interests include mathematical aspects of income inequality measures, income inequality perception, and multidimensional scaling.

Natalia Letki—country team coordinator—is the Principal Investigator of the ERC Starting Grant 'Public Goods through Private Eyes. Exploring Citizens' Attitudes towards Public Goods and the State in East-Central Europe", hosted by the Institute of Sociology, University of Warsaw. Previously, she was a Post-Doctoral Prize Research Fellow at Nuffield College, Oxford. She researches political behaviour, attitudes towards public goods and law-abiding behaviour, with a particular emphasis on the effect of institutional context.

Portugal

Isabel Andrade (PhD) has lectured in Quantitative Methods and Econometrics ISEG—Lisboa School of Economics and Management/University of Lisbon, and is a member of CEMAPRE —the Centre for Applied Mathematics and Economics. She has undertaken research in diverse areas of economics and has recently published 'Monetary Poverty, Material Deprivation and Consistent Poverty in Portugal' with Carlos Farinha Rodrigues.

Carlos Farinha Rodrigues—country team coordinator—is a Professor of Economics at ISEG, School of Economics and Management University of Lisbon, and an adviser to the Portuguese Statistical Office in the field of household statistics. He is a member of CEMAPRE—the Centre for Applied Mathematics and Economics. His research interests focus on income distribution, poverty and inequality, social policy and the evaluation of its redistributive effects, and microsimulation.

Romania

Iuliana Precupetu (PhD)—country team coordinator—is a Senior Researcher in the Research Institute for Quality of Life, Romanian Academy. She specializes in quality of life issues, social policy, social inequality and the methodology of social research. She currently coordinates the research project, Quality of Life and Social Inequalities in Romania in a European Comparative Perspective: Twenty Years of Social Transformation, funded by the Romanian National Authority for Scientific Research.

Marius Precupetu (PhD) is a university teacher (Reader) in the Political Science Department at the National School of Political Studies and Administration (SNSPA), Bucharest. His fields of teaching, research and expertise include the methodology of social and political research, education studies, the sociology of public opinion, and democratization studies. He has researched the democratization process in post-communist countries and higher education.

Slovakia and the Czech Republic

Martin Guzi (PhD) is a postdoctoral researcher at Masaryk University in Brno, Czech Republic, and Research Fellow at the Central European Labour Studies Institute (CELSI). His research interests are labour economics and applied econometrics, with a focus on welfare-driven migration, the relationship between immigration and well-being in Europe, and the analysis of work incentives created by social welfare systems.

Martin Kahanec (PhD)—country team coordinator—is an Associate Professor at the Central European University in Budapest, Visiting Research Fellow, Deputy Programme Director, 'Migration', leader of the research sub-area EU Enlargement and the Labour Markets, former Deputy Director of Research (2009) at the Institute for the Study of Labor (IZA) in Bonn, Germany, and co-founder and Scientific Director of the Central European Labour Studies Institute (CELSI), Bratislava, Slovakia. His main research interests are labour and population economics, ethnicity, migration, and reforms in Central Eastern European labour markets.

Monika Martišková is a researcher and journalist at Central European Labour Studies Institute (CELSI) and a PhD candidate at the Institute of Economic Studies at Charles University in Prague, Czech Republic. Her research concentrates on labour markets, active labour market policies, regional development and regional differences within the EU.

Zuzana Siebertová (PhD) currently works as a Senior Analyst at the Council for Budget Responsibility in Slovakia. Previously, she worked as an Assistant Professor at the Comenius University in Bratislava. Her research interests include labour economics and micro-econometrics.

Slovenia

Maša Filipovič Hrast—country team coordinator—is a researcher and Assistant Professor in the Faculty of Social Sciences, University of Ljubljana. She has been involved in several international and national research projects, mostly on vulnerable groups and their inclusion in various aspects of social life. She has also been a member of international networks such as European Homelessness Observatory and European Network of Experts on Gender, Social Inclusion, Health and Long Term Care.

Miroljub Ignjatović is a researcher and Assistant Professor in the Faculty of Social Sciences, University of Ljubljana. His research activity concerns the labour market (employment, unemployment, flexibilization), vocational education and training, social policy, postmodern society.

Spain

Ada Ferrer-i-Carbonell—country team coordinator—is a tenured scientist in the Institute for Economic Analysis (IAE-CSIC) in Barcelona and Research Fellow at IZA, Barcelona GSE, and MOVE, and an associate editor of the *Journal of Economic Behavior and Organization*. Her current interests are welfare analysis (through subjective well-being measures), including health, inequality, and risk attitudes. She published (with Bernard Van Praag) *Happiness Quantified: A Satisfaction Calculus Approach* (Oxford University Press, 2004).

Mónica Oviedo is a PhD candidate in applied economics at the Universitat Autònoma de Barcelona. She is member of the research network, 'Economics of Inequality and Poverty Analysis' (EQUALITAS), and the 'Economics, Public Policy and Citizenship' research group at the Universidad Nacional de Colombia. Her research focuses on inequality, institutional quality and public support for redistributive policies. In addition, she has worked on public policy evaluation from the perspective of inequality of opportunity.

Xavier Ramos is an Associate Professor of Economics at the Universitat Autònoma de Barcelona, Research Fellow of IZA, and member of EQUALITAS. He is on the Board of Editors, and is Book Review Editor of the *Journal of Economic Inequality*. Currently he works on equality of opportunity and on inequality aversion. He has worked on the measurement, causes and impacts of inequality and poverty from static and dynamic perspectives.

Sweden

Jennie Bacchus Hertzman (BSc Applied Social Research/Sociology) is a researcher at CHESS (Centre for Health Equity Studies) at the Stockholm University and Karolinska Institutet.

Olof Bäckman is an Associate Professor of Sociology and a researcher at the Swedish Institute for Social Research (SOFI) and at the Department of Criminology, Stockholm University. He is the author of several articles and book chapters on poverty and social exclusion in affluent countries.

Ida Borg MSc Applied Sociological Research/Sociology, is a PhD Student in Human Geography in the Department of Human Geography at Stockholm University.

Tommy Ferrarini is an Associate Professor of Sociology in the Swedish Institute for Social Research (SOFI), Stockholm University. His research covers comparative studies on welfare state development, in particular, family policy institutions, political economy, gender and class. Recent work has focused on the development of family policy institutions in post-war welfare democracies.

Johan Fritzell—country team coordinator—is Professor of Sociology at the Centre for Health Equity Studies, Stockholm University/Karolinska Institutet (CHESS). He has published extensively on the determinants and distribution of welfare in Sweden, as well as on comparative income distribution and poverty. Recent books include *Changing Social Equality: The Nordic Welfare Model in the 21st Century* (co-editor) and *Health Inequalities and Welfare Resources* (co-editor), both published by Policy Press.

Kenneth Nelson is an Associate Professor of Sociology in the Swedish Institute for Social Research (SOFI), Stockholm University. He is the director of several comparative research projects focusing on social policy, poverty and indicator construction. He has published on various topics, including the measurement of redistribution, the European social inclusion process, social assistance and social insurance.

United Kingdom

Abigail McKnight (PhD)—country team coordinator—is a Toyota Senior Research Fellow in the Centre for Analysis of Social Exclusion (CASE), London School of Economics, and an economist specializing in labour economics. Her research interests include low-wage employment, earnings inequality and mobility, wealth inequality and asset-based welfare, evaluation of active labour market programmes, and the economics of education. She coordinated the Social Impacts work package of the GINI project with Brian Nolan.

Tiffany Tsang contributed to GINI as a Research Officer at the Centre for Analysis of Social Exclusion (CASE), London School of Economics. She currently works as a researcher at The Work Foundation.

United States

Lane Kenworthy is Professor of Sociology and Political Science at the University of Arizona. He studies the causes and consequences of living standards, poverty, inequality, mobility, employment, economic growth, social policy, taxes, public opinion, and politics in the United States and other affluent countries. His books include *Progress for the Poor* (2011) and *Should We Worry About Inequality?* (with Christopher Jencks, forthcoming).

Timothy Smeeding is the Arts and Sciences Distinguished Professor of Public Affairs and Economics at the University of Wisconsin-Madison and Director of the Institute for Research on Poverty. His research interests are in the economics of public policy: especially, social policy and at-risk populations; poverty and income distribution, income transfers and tax policy; social and economic mobility; the economics of ageing; the economics of non-money income, non-wage compensation and income from wealth; inequality in income and consumption; housing and the Great Recession; social statistics; comparative international social policy; health care finance; education finance and policy.

CHAPTER 1

....

INTRODUCTION

....

BRIAN NOLAN, WIEMER SALVERDA, DANIELE

CHECCHI, IVE MARX, ABIGAIL McKNIGHT,

ISTVÁN GYÖRGY TÓTH, AND HERMAN van de WERFHORST

THIS book is about economic inequality and its impacts on the richer countries of the world. This topic has come to the fore as a matter of pressing societal concern over the past few decades as inequality has deepened in some of the major economies, and the economic crisis from 2007/8 has served to sharpen that focus. The fact that anti-austerity demonstrators adapt slogans such as 'We are the 99 per cent!' serves to highlight the central role that issues of income inequality and perceived fairness are playing in responses to the crisis. Well before that crisis, the way the industrialized economies were evolving was seen to be putting their societies under increasing strain. A contrast was being drawn, especially, but not only, in the USA, between the lengthy period after the second World War when the benefits of sustained economic growth were widely shared in increasing living standards throughout the income distribution, versus the more recent decades when growth has been patchy but with an increasing proportion of it accruing to the top of the distribution and with little improvement for ordinary workers and families. The extent to which increasing inequalities of that kind risk exacerbating a variety of ills in society, potentially undermining political processes and social cohesion, is now a central issue for these societies.

To see whether these concerns are well-founded and, if so, what can be done about them, one needs a clear picture of what has actually been happening to economic inequality and what are the possible drivers of its evolution, an understanding of the complex causal channels through which it could potentially impact on social, political and cultural behaviours and outcomes, and evidence about whether such impacts are to be seen at this stage. This is central to the contribution that research can make and to the aim of this book, which examines the experiences of thirty countries within a common framework to amass and assess new evidence about inequality and its impacts. A large international research project, funded by the European Union's Framework Programme for internationally cooperative scientific research, has enabled a set of countries to be covered, comprising 25 European Union countries (all 27 except Cyprus and Malta) together with Australia, Canada, Japan, Korea,[1] and the United States, the leader of the pack for the size of its economy as well as the level of its income inequality.[2] As we shall see, this research design, where individual country experiences are examined by national experts familiar with the local context but applying a common analytical framework and approach, proves to be extremely fruitful.

The main endeavour of this book, in 27 out of its 30 chapters,[3] is to present the stories of inequalities, impacts and policies for each of these countries. It purports to show the richness of, and variation in, national experiences, adopting a uniform template for telling the story, so that each individual chapter can offer food for thought. It is particularly the unique, comparable collection of country studies in large number that serves to provide valuable input for further research, as international comparison can often provide insights that tend to be overlooked at the national level. Such thoughts and research can be found especially in the companion volume *Changing Inequalities in Rich Countries* (Salverda *et al.*, 2013) to the present book. That other volume proposes a transversal scrutiny of a) inequalities, which looks at income, labour earnings, wealth, and education separately; b) impacts, distinguishing between social and political/cultural impacts; and also c) policies, where it considers both enhancing and mitigating effects. That scrutiny builds on the country experiences that are reported here, and is combined with insights from research that has focused on these transversal issues. The cross-country contribution of the present book, in Chapter 2, is that it brings together from the country chapters the data on the evolution of income inequality and poverty and compares trends between countries. It also contrasts this new dataset to existing ones based on the work of the OECD and the Luxembourg Income Study (LIS). The concluding Chapter 30 highlights the distinctive contribution of the country studies, identifies some of the key findings when they are taken together as a set and discusses some key implications which are among the issues taken up in the companion volume.

In the remainder of this introductory chapter we first discuss, but only summarily given the companion book, why recent trends in economic inequality, in terms of income distribution and educational attainment and opportunities, have been the focus of such interest and concern. Next, we describe in more detail the approach behind this book and the framework within which the various elements of the country analyses are organized.

1. ECONOMIC INEQUALITY AND ITS IMPACTS

Economic inequality has long been one of the major themes of socio-political debate, on which a very substantial body of research from a variety of disciplinary perspectives has been produced in recent years, building on the potential of improved data and focused on clarifying concepts and measures, capturing trends, and understanding the causal processes

---

[1] FP7 Contract No 244592 (2010–2013). The Korean team joined the international project with the help of National Research Foundation of Korea Grant NFR-2011-330-B00052.
[2] Except four Eastern European Union countries—Bulgaria, Latvia, Lithuania, and Romania—all are also members of the OECD.
[3] The three Baltic countries are covered in one chapter and so are the Czech Republic and Slovakia.

at work. The recent upsurge in academic interest in inequality can be linked to both inequality trends themselves and the policy environment in which research is carried out. For some years, levels of inequality were sufficiently stable for one analyst to describe tracking them as about as exciting as 'watching the grass grow' (Aaron, 1978), but this changed as the post-World War II boom petered out. The 1980s saw a dramatic widening in the dispersion of wages and overall income inequality in both the UK and the USA, giving rise to a sustained and wide-ranging investigation into why this was happening and whether it was confined to those two countries or pervasive throughout the industrialized world. The title of recent studies by the OECD encapsulates current understandings and concerns: *Growing Unequal* (2008) and *Divided We Stand: Why Inequality Keeps Rising* (2011). Evidence has also been accumulating that the share of household income going to the very top of the distribution has increased markedly in many rich countries (e.g. Atkinson and Piketty, 2007). At the other end of the scale, poverty and social exclusion have remained stubbornly high even before the onset of the economic crisis. At the same time, and closely related to incomes and the labour market, aspects of the changing educational landscape may be giving rise to increasing inequalities in educational outcomes and opportunities, and intensifying stratifying effects.

A complex set of forces, including technological change and globalization, may be contributing to these trends in inequality, posing new challenges for Welfare States (including their educational systems). The distribution of income among households, which is at the core of economic inequality, is influenced most importantly by the earnings from work accruing to different household members. This reflects in turn the position of these individuals in the labour market, their skills and opportunities and the returns they receive, together with patterns of family formation and how earners cluster together with others in households. Labour market institutions, with employers and often also unions as key actors, and the State, in regulating minimum wages in particular, exert an important influence on the distribution of earnings. Another important component of household income is income derived as a return on capital—interest, dividends and rent, as well as capital gains and profits. Though less important in family income for most households than earnings, its effect in explaining the changes of inequality may be strong and also growing, due to its higher concentration. This is particularly the case for the top one per cent and, in many countries, seems to be fuelled by a growing distaste by governments for taxing capital and capital income, which may be another sign of the powerful elite influencing policy to their advantage. This relates to the distribution of wealth, and to the relationship between that distribution and other elements of household income. Another significant element in household income, the main or only source of income for many households, is social protection cash transfers received from the State. Private pensions, paid from occupational schemes or as a result of personal investment rather than from the social security system, are also important. The way income tax, often progressive, on the one hand, and social security contributions, in many cases regressive, on the other hand, are structured is also an important influence on the shape of the income distribution. The shift towards indirect taxation, clearly witnessed during the current economic crisis, exerts a regressive effect along the income distribution on the actual spending out of income. More broadly, institutional structures, and the political economy considerations they may reflect, are also a major force when considering the overall impact of the Welfare State on economic inequality.

The picture with respect to educational institutions/policies and educational inequalities is equally complex. Educational institutions may be designed and operated in a fashion that favours inclusion (in the sense of bringing up the bottom of the educational distribution) or they may promote (meritocratic) selection (i.e. supporting high achievers to do more, raising the upper tail of the distribution). However, enhanced income inequality may also skew access by widening gaps in the resources available to parents for investment in their children's education, especially if at the same time fees are raised and grants lowered, as they have been at tertiary level in a number of countries. Participation in secondary schooling has been successfully expanded in almost all countries, but with varying degrees of success in incorporating the tail, while major differences have emerged in strategies for expansion of tertiary education and access to it. As well as differences in the distribution of qualifications/attainment, substantial differences across countries are now evident in educational achievement assessed by standardized achievement tests. Educational systems differ significantly between countries and over time in various dimensions: notably the extent to which students are separated in clearly distinct educational curricula during secondary education (commonly known as 'tracking') and the age at which that occurs; in the extent to which education meets the same standards nationwide in terms of curricula, teacher quality, resources across schools, and exit examinations; and in the extent to which there is vocational orientation in the upper secondary school system with strong links to the labour market. When considering average student performance and its dispersion, a trade-off between equality and efficiency would emerge if higher performances coincided with larger dispersions. Braga, Checchi and Meschi (2013) bring out the way that institutional features like pre-primary education, age of compulsory schooling, and expansion of university admission may affect both the average level of attainment and skill acquisition and the dispersion around that average. This in turn can have fundamental implications for life chances and their distribution. Bol and Van de Werfhorst (2013) have shown that early tracking is associated with larger inequalities between children of different social classes, whereas tracking is unrelated to average performance. So, in that instance, in line with Hanushek and Wössmann (2005), there is no evidence for a trade-off between equality and efficiency in skill formation: the greater inequality associated with tracking does not achieve a higher average skill level.

Inequality in incomes, education, and life chances more broadly is something about which many people feel strongly, simply as a matter of fairness: indeed, its extent can be seen as a defining characteristic of a society. However, there is also a manifest instrumental basis for concern about growing inequality in terms of its potential consequences for a variety of economic, social and political outcomes of central concern ranging from health status and life expectancy to crime and community breakdown, political alienation and the lack of trust, and increased inter-generational immobility and the transmission of poverty from one generation to the next. If inequality influences such outcomes, with the potential to generate negative feedback to inequality (for example increased concentration of wealth at the top skewing political decision-making in a way that reinforces that concentration) and to undermine economic growth and living standards, then understanding the linkages and their significance is clearly a core task for research.

Research has indeed looked at each of the very wide and diverse range of areas in which such impacts could potentially arise, including health, poverty and deprivation, crime, the family, political participation, social cohesion, and social capital. Wilkinson and Pickett's

(2009a), *The Spirit Level* has been particularly effective in generating a wide-ranging debate about the over-arching issue of the potentially harmful impact of inequality. It argues that income inequality is harmful to society by virtue of its relationship to many different undesirable outcomes: societies with higher income inequality have lower levels of social cohesion, exemplified in outcomes such as more social problems, higher crime rates, higher mortality rates, worse health, higher dropout rates from schools, lower social trust, and lower political involvement. Socio-economic gradients in health have been intensively researched for many years (Acheson, 1998, Mackenbach, 2008 Marmot, 2005), but the scale and breadth of effects of income inequality *per se* on health outcomes and health inequalities have been a particular recent focus (Kondo *et al.*, 2009, Pop *et al.*, 2012, Erikson and Torssander, 2007, Torssander and Erikson, 2010, Wilkinson and Pickett, 2009b). The manner in which income inequalities may influence social outcomes, and the channels through which such impacts would operate, have also been hotly debated (see, for example, Leigh, Jencks and Smeeding, 2009). Wilkinson and Pickett place considerable emphasis on the 'psychosocial' implications of status differences in more unequal societies, with low social status and perceptions of inferiority understood to produce negative emotions such as shame which directly damage individual health through stress reactions (see also Siegrist and Marmot, 2004, Marmot and Wilkinson, 2006, 2009), as well as undermining supportive community and social relations. In contrast, the neo-materialist perspective emphasizes the role of different levels and distributions of resources available within societies related to differential levels of investment in social and institutional infrastructure (Davey Smith and Egger, 1996, Lynch *et al.*, 1998, 2004). Increasingly, these perspectives are being seen as complementary rather than competing (Elgar and Aitken, 2011, Layte, 2012). Inequality can be seen as having a causal impact on such outcomes due to both differential resources and the psychosocial consequences.

In this context, Goldthorpe (2010) makes the important point that social stratification cannot be seen as one-dimensional, one cannot for example treat 'class' and 'status' as essentially synonymous (see also Chan and Goldthorpe, 2007), and the relationships between economic inequality and other forms of stratification are contingent. The processes mediating objective social inequalities and the manner in which they are subjectively experienced are also highly complex (see for example Merton *et al.*, 1950, Runciman, 1966/1972, Jasso, 1999). This means that analyses focusing on the impact of income inequality have to take into account the complexities of its relationship with social status and social class in developing their understanding of the processes and mechanisms through which negative social outcomes may arise. Distinct dimensions of stratification relating to income, education, social class and status may operate rather differently, and indeed this may vary between men and women (Erikson and Torssander, 2008, Torssander and Erikson, 2010). Erikson and Torssander also highlight the way that, in the health domain, general risk factors associated with income or social class are likely to interact with specific ones, so that particular causes of death are related to distinct features such as consumption patterns, lifestyles and exposure to dangerous and hazardous conditions rather than simply location on a social gradient as such; this clearly has broader relevance for other domains as well as health.

The complexities of the channels through which inequality may impact on social, political and cultural outcomes are matched by the methodological difficulties in establishing with any degree of certainty the scale of such impacts and the causal relationships involved. For example, given indicators of various social outcomes for different countries, one can look at whether variation in these outcomes appears to bear any relationship to variation in a summary measure of income inequality such as the Gini coefficient. Wilkinson and Pickett (2009a) have plotted a variety of such bivariate relationships, and a good deal of (at times acrimonious) debate in the research community and among the wider public has focused on questions such as the impact on observed associations of the range of countries included in the analysis, the particular outcomes on which the analysis focuses and the extent to which what is involved is average effects across societies or effects observed at variable levels of social stratification (Saunders 2010, Snowdon, 2010, Wilkinson and Pickett, 2010). However, irrespective of such issues, the causal interpretation of such a relationship (when observed robustly) presents formidable difficulties. More sophisticated statistical techniques such as the use of multi-level models can assist in controlling for a range of societal characteristics that may be correlated with income inequality but, as Van de Werfhorst and Salverda (2012) emphasize, causal interpretation of the consequences of inequality also requires deductive theory building and hypothesis formulation and testing. This constitutes what Goldthorpe (2001) has labelled 'causation as a generative process', aiming to explain empirical regularities by specifying hypotheses that are derived from a 'causal narrative' at the level of individual actions, which can then be put to empirical test. For an association between inequality and outcomes to be interesting from a scientific perspective there needs to be good theoretical arguments about why inequality could be related to such outcomes, and, naturally, these arguments have to be substantiated with empirical evidence.

While strict causality is obviously impossible to establish, a variety of methodological approaches can usefully be applied in seeking to enhance our understanding of inequality and its impacts, and these are best seen as complementary with one another. Economists, sociologists and political scientists study income inequality from a purely theoretical perspective, intensively investigate patterns in the empirical data, and seek to estimate theory-driven models at macro- and micro-levels, and a similar range is seen when it comes to assessing and understanding impacts. We go on in the next section to describe the particular approach adopted in this book and where it seeks to make its contribution.

2. The Contribution, Approach and Structure of this Book

The point of departure for this book, as outlined above, is the very active debate in both the research literature and, more broadly, among policy-makers, the politically-engaged and concerned citizens more generally, about increasing inequalities and their potential social, political and cultural impacts. The book aims to contribute to the research literature, and to this broader debate, by examining in depth the experiences of thirty countries in a common broad analytical framework. This allows us to collect and scrutinize an extensive range of new evidence about inequality and its impacts, which focuses primarily on research from the disciplinary perspectives of economics, sociology, political science and (social) policy analysis.

Looking at a wide range of countries both increases the number of observations on which analysis can rest and provides a way of avoiding the risk that patterns and relationships observed in a given country or small set of countries arise for idiosyncratic reasons specific to those countries. International comparison can also help detect factors and effects that may go unnoticed at the national level. Comparative analysis of such topics is commonly carried out by amassing datasets of variables measured in an as-much-harmonized-as-possible fashion and applying more or less sophisticated statistical methods to explore patterns of association, either in a purely cross-sectional context or pooling multiple observations for a set of countries over time. This type of methodological approach is extremely valuable, and plays a major role in the companion study (Salverda *et al.*, 2013). One of the significant challenges for such comparative analyses, though, is not to lose sight of the contextual factors and specific experiences of each country, which can only be properly understood by in-depth analysis and may be crucial in understanding the patterns observed.

The distinctive approach adopted here is that the individual experiences of the 30 countries are examined by expert teams who are familiar with the local context, institutions, data and research, but applying a common framework and approach to addressing the same set of topics and questions from one country to the next. The framework is aimed primarily at ascertaining comparable coverage of fields of analysis and periods of time. The broad fields concerned are, first, the drivers of inequality, and, second, the social impacts and the political/cultural impacts of inequality already mentioned, but, third, also policies and institutions mitigating or compensating inequality but possibly also enhancing it. The approach is squarely based on interdisciplinary cooperation, especially between economists, sociologists and political scientists, and it views the collection of data as deserving significant attention in itself. It retains analytical flexibility and does not impose a singular analytical approach, however, for different reasons. First, analyses of inequality itself abound but that is much less the case for impacts in relation to inequality, and imposing a specific approach would have been arbitrary and premature. Second, possible impacts span a broad range of fields and can be usefully studied from different disciplinary perspectives. Third, the analytical flexibility allows also for possible vital variation in country experiences as well as disciplinary views. Fourth, full-fledged comparative research for so many countries using microdata seems beyond the possibilities of available data (presence, comparability, quality, and timing) and beyond the efforts allowed by the available funding. To this can be added, finally, that the fields where the impacts of inequality are sought may be subject to important other societal changes apart from shifts in income or educational inequality. These five considerations provide important caveats for the results that are presented here. However, the approach combines with an improved understanding of inequality beyond what a single measure such as the Gini coefficient can offer, by distinguishing more distributive detail (e.g. bottom/middle/top, and very top) and, particularly, by looking also at gradients of income, social class and also education across individuals in relation to impacts. As a result the prime aim is to compare developments in different areas, inequalities, impacts, and policies; and look at their timing and possible interactions. The methodological aspects of this are further elaborated in the companion volume to this book.

This research design produces individual country studies with a striking degree of specificity, national 'stories' that are of very significant interest in themselves, going well beyond the local. Crucially, bringing these together then provides a unique set of insights into what has actually been happening to economic inequality across most of the richer countries and evidence about whether the negative social, political and cultural impacts that have been debated are to be seen at this stage. Such a broad-ranging approach cannot hope to assess causal relationships in a rigorous manner, in the way that a strongly focused investigation of a specific hypothesized relationship—between income inequality and crime, for example— might hope to do. It can, however, present and examine trends in inequality and in social, political and cultural outcomes in each country, assess the extent to which inequalities have actually increased, examine which amongst various outcomes deteriorated over time as, or after, inequality increased, consider the contributions made by policies and institutions, and draw on the findings of national research about these trends and relationships. Note that the chapters in this book draw on comprehensive country reports, which provide more detail including discussion of data limitations or problems of method.[4]

We now begin, in Chapter 2, with an overview of the trends in inequality revealed by the country studies brought together, and then proceed to the individual country chapters. Each country chapter sets the scene in terms of key features of the local context, and then looks at what has been happening to inequalities in income and education over the last three decades or so, depending strongly on data availability. The factors underpinning these trends, as brought to light in the available research, are also discussed. The evolution of key indicators of social, political and cultural outcomes are then described and placed in the context of inequality trends. Central features of social expenditure, taxation and related policies, which frame and influence trends in inequality and its impacts, are then discussed, and the conclusions brought together. Each chapter seeks to bring out the distinctive national 'story' which the national teams identify and describe. The final chapter of the book then brings together the key findings taking an overview across the country studies.

Inequality and its impacts are a core concern for society as a whole, and the style of presentation employed in this book is designed to be non-technical, aiming at dissemination of the analysis and findings to the widest possible audience. The complexities of the underlying relationships and the research seeking to tease them out should not stand in the way of an informed and wide-ranging debate about some of the most important features of the way many of the rich countries are evolving and how to respond to them.

REFERENCES

Aaron, H. (1978), *Politics and the Professors*, Washington D.C.: Brookings Institute.
Acheson, D. (1998), *Independent Inquiry into Inequalities in Health*, London: Department of Health.
Atkinson, A.B. and Piketty, T. (2007), *Top Incomes Over the Twentieth Century, A Contrast Between Continental European and English-Speaking Countries*, Oxford: Oxford University Press.
Bol, T. and van de Werfhorst, H. G. (2013), 'Educational Systems and the Trade-off Between Labor Market Allocation and Equality of Educational Opportunity', *Comparative Education Review* (forthcoming).
Braga, M., Checchi D. and Meschi, E. (2013), 'On Institutional Reforms and Educational Attainment in Europe: A Long Run Perspective', *Economic Policy* (forthcoming).

---

[4] The Country Reports can be found at <http://www.gini-research.org/cr>. The website also provides more detail about the research project as a whole and the many (often cross-country) Discussion Papers treating specific aspects of inequality, impacts, or policy.

Chan, T.-W. and Goldthorpe, J.H. (2007), 'Class and Status: the Conceptual Distinction and its Empirical Relevance', *American Sociological Review*, 72, 512–532.

Davey Smith, G. and Egger, M. (1996), 'Commentary: Understanding it All—Health, Meta Theories and Mortality Trends', *British Medical Journal*, 313 (No 7072), 1584–1885: 5.

Elgar, F. and Aitken, N. (2011), 'Income Inequality, Trust and Homicide in 33 Countries', *European Journal of Public Health*, 21(2): 241–246.

Erikson, R. and Torssander, J. (2008), 'Social Class and Causes of Death', *European Journal of Public Health*, 18.5: 473–478.

Goldthorpe, J.H. (2010), 'Analysing Social Inequality: A Critique of Two Recent Contributions from Economics and Epidemiology', *European Sociological Review*, 26,6: 731–744.

Hanushek, E.A. and Wössmann, L. (2006), 'Does Educational Tracking Affect Performance and Inequality? Differences-in-Differences Evidence Across Countries', Economic Journal, 116 (510), C63–C76.

Jasso, G. (1999), 'How Much Injustice is there in the World? Two New Justice Indices', *American Sociological Review*, 64: 133–168.

Kondo, N., Sembajwe, G., Kawachi, I., van Dam, R.M., Subramanian, S.V., and Yamagata, Z. (2009), 'Income Inequality, Mortality and Self-Rated Health: Meta-Analysis of Multilevel Studies', *British Medical Journal*, 339 (10), b4471.

Layte, R. (2012), 'Association Between Income Inequality and Mental Health: Testing Status Anxiety, Social Capital and Neo-Materialist Explanations', *European Sociological Review*, doi.org.10.1093/esr.jce012.

Leigh, A., Jencks, C. and Smeeding T. (2009), 'Health and Inequality' in W. Salverda, B. Nolan, and T. Smeeding (eds.), *The Oxford Handbook of Economic Inequality*, Oxford: Oxford University Press, 384–405.

Lynch, J.W., Kaplan, G.A., Pamuk, E., Cohen, R.D., Heck, K., and Balfour, J.L. (1998), 'Income Inequality and Mortality in Metropolitan Areas of the United States', *American Journal of Public Health*, 88 1074–1080.urbeu.

Lynch, J., Smith, G.D., Harper, S., Hillemeier, M., Ross, N., Kaplan, G.A., Wolfson, M. (2004), 'Is Income Inequality a Determinant of Population Health? (Parts 1 and 2)', *Milbank Quarterly*, 82, 5–99 and 355–400.

Mackenbach, J. P, Stirbu, I., Roskam, A., J. R., Schaap, M. Menvielle, G., Leinsalu, M., and Kunst A.D. (2008), 'Socioeconomic Inequalities in Health in 22 European Countries', *The New England Journal of Medicine*, 358: 2468–2481.

Marmot, M. (2002), 'The Influence of Income on Health: Views of An Epidemiologist: Does Money Really Matter? Or is it a Marker for Something Else?' *Health Affairs* 21(2): 31–46.

Marmot, M. (2005), 'Social Determinants of Health Inequalities', *Lancet* 365: 1099–1104.

Marmot, M.G. and Wilkinson, R.G. (2006), *Social Determinants of Health*, Oxford: Oxford University Press.

Merton, R.M. and Kitt, A.S. (1950), 'Contributions to the Theory of Reference Group Behaviour', in R.K. Merton and P.F. Lazarfeld (eds.), *Studies in the Scope and Method of the American Soldier*, Glencoe: The Free Press.

OECD (2011), *Divided We Stand: Why Inequality Keeps Rising*, Paris: OECD.

Runciman, W.G. (1966/1972), *Relative Deprivation and Social Justice: A Study of Attitudes to Social Inequality in Twentieth Century England*, Harmondsworth, Middlesex: Penguin.

Saunders, P. (2010), *Beware False Prophets: Equality, the Good Society and the Spirit Level*, London: Policy Exchange.

Siegrist J, and Marmot M. (2004), 'Health inequalities and the psychosocial environment—two scientific challenges', *Social Science and Medicine* 58(8):1463,73.

Snowdon, C. (2010), *The Spirit Level Delusion: Fact-checking the Left's New Theory of Everything*, Democracy Institute/Little Dice.

Torssander, J. and Erikson, R. (2010), 'Stratification and Mortality—A Comparison of Education, Class, Status and Income', *European Sociological Review*, 26,4: 465–474.

Van de Werfhorst, H.G. and Salverda, W. (2012), 'Consequences of Economic Inequality: Introduction to a Special Issue', *Research in Social Stratification and Mobility*, 30: 377–387.

Wilkinson, R. and Pickett, K. (2009a), *The Spirit Level*, London: Routledge.

Wilkinson, R. and Pickett, K. (2009b). 'Income Inequality and Social Dysfunction', *The Annual Review of Sociology*, 33: 493–511.

CHAPTER 2

....

REVISITING GRAND NARRATIVES OF GROWING INEQUALITIES: LESSONS FROM 30 COUNTRY STUDIES*

....

ISTVÁN GYÖRGY TÓTH

1. INTRODUCTION

....

A number of narratives about the development of income inequality are present in the large and rapidly growing income distribution literature (for overviews see Atkinson and Bourguignon (eds.), 2000; Salverda, Nolan and Smeeding, 2009). Two major 'stories' are:

A: 'Within country' inequalities have been increasing in OECD countries, at least until the Great Recession (OECD, 2008, 2011, Brandolini and Smeeding, 2009).
B: The intertemporal variance of 'within country' inequality is smaller than the cross-country variance of 'within country' inequality, at least until the first half of the nineties (Li, Zou, Squire, 1998).

These narratives provide a useful starting point for this book's focus on 25 EU countries and five other developed countries in the rest of the world: Australia; Canada; Japan; Korea

* The author wishes to thank, first and foremost, Brian Nolan and Wiemer Salverda for their continued support and immensely useful suggestions on various versions of the draft. Special thanks are due to Herman van de Werfhorst for his support in the computation and interpretation of the multivariate analysis of Gini increases over the GINI country universe. Insightful comments on the first version of this paper from Francesco Bogliacino, Michael F. Förster, Virginia Maestri and Ive Marx are especially acknowledged. Special thanks to Katalin Molnarfi and Anna B. Kis who provided assistance in all sorts of preparatory work while gathering the data and drafting the report. Also gratefully acknowledged is the patience of many of the country teams while clarifying the data in their reports. Remaining errors are all mine.

(South); and the USA. Other scenarios come to mind if one moves beyond these OECD countries, which will not be discussed here.[1]

In this chapter, I first discuss some results of inequality research for a selection of European countries and some non-European icons/benchmarks. This is followed by a presentation of the inequality data that have been gathered in the *GINI Inequality and Poverty Database* and a discussion of how the overall patterns and trends it reveals fit these two narratives.

Next we leave the grand picture behind and 'zoom in' on the results by country groupings, periods, etc., together with a discussion of methodological and data issues, including a comparison with other available comparative inequality datasets. Since the famous *bon mots* of Simon Kuznets in *Economic Growth and Income Inequality*, referring to his own findings as 'perhaps 5 per cent empirical information and 95 per cent speculation, some of it possibly tainted by wishful thinking' (Kuznets, 1955:26), the empirical foundations of inequality research have improved beyond recognition.[2] Data brought together by the OECD[3] and the Luxembourg Income Study (LIS) are now central to the debate, and here we compare them to the newly collected GINI series and also draw on them where that is helpful. First, we consider inequality and, second, poverty.

---

[1] From a global perspective, for example, the World Bank concludes that inequalities between countries (international inequality) decreased recently—as a result of GDP convergence between the (formerly called) developed part of the world—see World Bank (2005). Milanovic (2005) shows that inequalities between individuals around the world fluctuate despite GDP convergence, due to increasing income dispersion within the countries concerned. When focusing on specific regions the overall inequality growth is not the major narrative. For example, recently it is shown that there is a fall of 'within country' inequalities in some countries formerly having a bad record of a high level of segregation and seemingly unchangeable income distribution (mostly Latin American countries—see Cornia, 2012, Bourguignon, Ferreira and Lustig, 2005).

[2] Although datasets proper for these exercises still need much improvement, there are many, which are now widely available. Already, back to the early seventies, a great improvement of international comparisons was achieved when Adelman and Morris (1973), Paukert (1973) tested the Kuznets curve hypothesis. Later analyses on development and inequalities were summarized in Adelman and Robinson (1989). A new wave of data collection was the setting up of the Deininger-Squire database within the World Bank (Deininger and Squire, 1996, 1997, 1998), and the setting up the World Bank LSMS surveys (used in this context by Milanovic, 2002, 2003, 2005) and the Luxembourg Income Study dataset (Atkinson, Rainwater and Smeeding, 1995, Förster and Mira D'Ercole, 2005). In addition to these, the UNU-WIDER dataset on World Income Inequality Dataset (WIID, revised, corrected and updated version of the Deininger and Squire dataset) has been maintained under the direction of Cornia (Cornia and Court, 2001, Cornia, 2005) and most recently improved and updated by F. Solt (see Solt, 2009). They, Atkinson, Rainwater and Smeeding (1995), Förster and D'Ercole (2005), Förster and Pierson (2002), Smeeding (2002), and many other studies using WIID and LIS, measure inequalities and publish data out of the above-mentioned datasets. Recently, the World Bank Poverty Monitoring database has also provided a useful source for researchers (see for example Ravallion, 2004). Probably one of the most influential of the datasets and of the publications is the OECD income distribution series, see most recently OECD, 2013, in addition to OECD, 2008, OECD, 2011, and others. For the European countries, an undoubtedly most important recent exercise (following the previous attempts like the European Community Household Panel Study) is that of the Eurostat, called European Statistics on Incomes and Living Conditions (EU-SILC), which, unlike the other sources that rely on post-collection data harmonization, seeks, to some extent, to harmonize pre-collection survey instruments. Publications from this include Atkinson and Marlier (eds.) 2010, Ward *et al.* (eds.) 2009, Nolan and Whelan, 2011.

[3] And, also, the online OECD inequality database at <www.oecd.org/social/inequality-database.htm>

2. TREND SPOTTING: THE GENERAL NARRATIVE OF THE EVOLUTION OF INEQUALITIES

Influential OECD comparative studies on income inequality include Atkinson, Rainwater and Smeeding (1995) and culminate in the recent landmark analyses of *Growing Unequal* (2008) and *Divided We Stand* (2011). These start from a thorough analysis of within-country inequality measures, especially the Gini coefficient (or Gini for short). This measures the dispersion in incomes from a value of 0 representing complete equality across all units up to a value of 1 when all income goes to a single unit, and compares their evolution over various periods of observation, mostly over 5- and 10-year periods. Based on the observed pattern of increases and decreases in these measures, conclusions are drawn about how income inequality has evolved. OECD (2011) concludes that, until the onset of the Great Recession, 'inequality [was] on the rise in most OECD countries', and that in a large majority of OECD countries, the income of the richest 10 per cent of households has grown faster than that of the poorest 10 per cent. The Gini coefficient increased on average from 0.29 in the mid 1980s to 0.316 in the late 2000s. Seventeen out of the 22 countries for which a long time-series is available have witnessed increasing inequality. For seven of these, the Gini coefficient rose significantly by more than 4 points over the period. In only five of these countries did inequality not increase, or even decline. The results represent a clear warning of a world growing more and more unequal—as reflected in the title of OECD (2008).

The OECD's income inequality data collection is based on a broad network of country correspondents who produce detailed and harmonized sets of tables at regular intervals on the income distribution in their countries (there is more about this and further methodological development and details on the underlying datasets in OECD, 2013, as well as OECD, 2008, and OECD, 2011). These tables are cross-checked with other sources, validated and continuously improved, and the network of correspondents is regularly contacted seeking improvements. A very valuable feature of the OECD database is the substantial and systematic efforts aimed at achieving consistency over time in the data series, to the greatest extent possible.

As well as this and the LIS database, other influential discussions of inequality developments have been based on a collection of a large number of inequality measures from all over the world. A wave of data collection has grown out of the Deininger-Squire database originally started by the World Bank (Deininger and Squire, 1996, 1997, 1998), and maintained and developed further by UNU-WIDER (Cornia and Court, 2001, Cornia, 2005) and most recently improved and updated by Solt (2009). An early analysis of that dataset asked (among other questions) whether inter-temporal variation or cross-country variation is the most marked characteristic of income inequality. Li, Zou and Squire (1998) analysed 573 observations spanning 47 years in an unbalanced panel of 49 countries and concluded that inequality itself and the significant cross-country variation of inequality are both remarkably stable over time (at least until the mid nineties, the period they were able to cover). They attribute the stable cross-country patterns to structural constraints embedded in the various country experiences—most notably related to the political economy of inequalities and to capital-market imperfections due to institutional constraints. All in all, the suggestion is that countries do not really change regimes of inequality—in a sense this argument seems very similar to that found in the literature on welfare regimes (Esping-Andersen, 1990).

The core question of this chapter is what support these two visions find in the new GINI database. Before addressing that question, we first discuss the data and methods employed.

3. The Origin and Structure of the GINI Database

The focus of the GINI project is inequalities in income, wealth and education, together with their social, political and cultural impacts. The research carried out under this project endeavours to exploit differences between and within countries in inequality levels and inequality trends in order to understand their impacts and tease out the implications for policy and institutions. The research design includes in-depth case studies for the 30 participant countries, which include 25 of the 27 EU countries (the exceptions being Cyprus and Malta), three non-European, Anglo-Saxon countries (US, Australia and Canada), and two Far Eastern representatives of rapid development and integration into the world economy: Japan and Korea. The 30 countries are covered in 27 chapters in this book and in the more detailed *Country Reports* on which they draw (since the three Baltic states are combined into one, as are the Czech Republic and Slovakia). Each study was undertaken by a team of national experts, including leading figures in the profession internationally and nationally.

The country case studies followed a pre-agreed template[4] specifying the most important variables to be monitored over a 30-year time span (from 1980 to 2010). The groups of variables included:

- Measures of inequality (of incomes and earnings, wealth, and education).
- Indicators of variables measuring the social impacts of inequality (such as monetary and non-monetary poverty, material deprivation, various measures of social cohesion, crime, and inequalities or gradients in fields such as health and housing).
- Indicators of political and cultural impacts in the country (such as political, civic and social participation, attitudes to welfare and redistributive policies and to immigrants, etc.).
- Indicators of policies aimed at controlling or mitigating inequalities (data on taxes and transfers, on wage-setting institutions and policy measures such as the minimum wage, etc.).

The database presented and analysed in this chapter has been derived from a transversal reading and analysis of these country studies. For some of the variables, it was possible to create a systematic collection of indicators and the database seems a promising starting

---

[4] For the detailed template, the readers may consult <http://gini-research.org/articles/cr>.

point for a further development into a new and extensive set of data on inequality in a major rich country grouping with a real value added compared to existing inequality datasets. Currently, the database provides rather comprehensive coverage of income inequality from about 600 observations of Gini coefficients and over 550 of relative poverty levels, all related to the GINI universe of countries, and in this chapter we use these to analyse trends in income inequality and income poverty.

For Gini coefficients and relative poverty, the aim is to present time series aligned as close as possible to pre-agreed consistent definitions (Nolan, Marx and Salverda, 2011; for income concepts and definitions see also Canberra Group, 2011). For both Gini coefficients and poverty, the preferred income concept is net/disposable household income, equivalized to take differences in household size/composition into account. This is consistent with common practice in the measurement of income inequality and poverty, for example by the European Union. The income-sharing unit is the household while the unit of analysis for the computation of various indices is the individual member of the household. Household resources are assumed to be shared among household members, and a correction for economies of scale of the household is assumed and implemented by means of equivalization. No preferred equivalence scale is specified, leaving open the choice between the increasingly common square root of the number of persons in the household, the modified OECD scale that takes the number of adults versus children in the household into account, or a national set of equivalence scales. Applying a strictly uniform scale would have required access to microdata in all countries. Relative poverty is defined following common usage as the proportion of individuals in households having less than 60 per cent of the median equivalized household income in the country in question. In each case the figures refer to national coverage and thresholds rather than, e.g., regions or specific social groups. For most of the countries and for most of the data points these requirements are met, but for some this was not possible as will be explained later in the chapter, at which point we will also assess how severe a constraint such non-uniformity is for comparative purposes.

This GINI database is a secondary dataset after all and despite its promise may suffer some of the potential 'pitfalls' of such datasets as highlighted in, for example, Atkinson and Brandolini (2001, 2006). First and foremost, in many cases the microdata behind the figures are not available for public use, so the database relies on the judgements of the country experts. In direct communication with them potential methodological problems were clarified and uncertainties about the data were sorted out insofar as possible. The current state of the database makes the most of what can be achieved without direct access to microdata. Second, in certain cases there are breaks in the series, some of which create the risk of confusing artefacts of sampling and data collection with genuine changes, as will be mentioned where appropriate. Finally, the data is still unbalanced in many respects, notably in terms of time period and country coverage, but this is unavoidable and one has to accept such limitations and work within them.

In spite of these significant caveats, it can be emphasized that the GINI database has great potential for the analysis of the evolution of income inequalities over time in 30 rich countries over up to 30 years, generally with annual data and validated by scholars familiar with the data for their own country.

4. The Evolution of Inequality in the GINI Country Universe

For a general impression of the evolution of income inequality in the 30 countries in question consider Figure 2.1. It looks complicated at first sight, but serves as a good starting point.

We find 19 countries whose first data point is no later than 1983. Among them, the Gini ranges between 0.20 (in Sweden) and 0.33 (in the USA) in the whole sample, and 0.31 (Italy) if we restrict our attention to European countries only. At the end of the period there are 29 countries whose last data point is 2008 or later.[5] Now the Gini ranges between 0.23 (in Czech Republic) and 0.38 (in the USA). The most unequal European country at the end of the period appears to be Latvia (with a Gini of 0.37).

Regarding our first overarching question about the general trend in inequality, on this basis we can make the following preliminary statements:

- In general, there has been an upward shift in the range of Gini coefficients measured (from between 0.20–0.33 to between 0.23–0.37). This means that inequalities have indeed, on average, increased in our country sample (which represents a large proportion of the high- and medium-high-income countries of the world).
- The heterogeneity of countries with respect to their inequality levels also increased: at the beginning of the period the countries were more similar to each other than they were at the end of the period.
- In this respect, however, it should be noted that the sample was even more heterogeneous at the beginning of the nineties—a fact due to the asynchronicity between inequality developments in the West and in the East (i.e. many, though not all, transition countries witnessed an unprecedented rise in inequality in the early 1990s).

As a point of comparison, the corresponding figures for the same selection of countries, based on the OECD income distribution database[6] and on the Luxembourg Income Study database,[7] are presented in Figure 2.2. Figure 2.2a presents Gini coefficients for those countries in our GINI study which had a sufficiently long series to be in the sample both at the beginning and at the end of the period. As the countries with extreme values at both the start and the end of the period are present in the group having the longest series, the presentation of this balanced panel shows the same results as above in terms of trends.

---

[5] Although there is a long term series of Gini coefficients of gross incomes also for Japan, the Gini of net disposable household incomes is available only for 5 datapoints in the thirty years period, 2004 being the latest. Details of data availability are set out in the Japan country chapter of this book.

[6] Downloaded from <www.oecd.org/social/inequality-database.htm>

[7] Retrieved from the LIS key figures search engine available at <http://www.lisdatacenter.org/data-access/key-figures/inequality-and-poverty/> The Luxembourg Income Study (LIS) collects household income surveys from a large number of countries (currently 39). The data is ex post harmonized and then made available to users all over the world. The careful harmonization of variables (especially that of the income and labour market variables) makes insightful analyses possible on a wide range of issues. In addition, key figures are made readily available via the website of the Centre. We utilize these key figures for our purpose in this chapter.

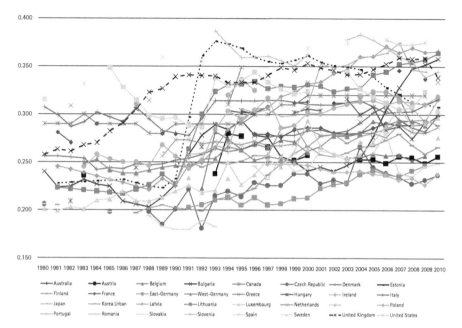

FIGURE 2.1 The evolution of inequality in 30 countries (Gini coefficients)

Note: For these and the subsequent charts, sources and definitions are shown in the Annex.

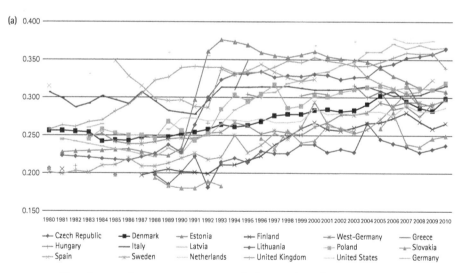

FIGURE 2.2 The time and country coverage of Gini, LIS and OECD income inequality data. (a) GINI database (countries with sufficiently long series starting no later than 1983 and ending no earlier than 2008); (b) OECD database; (c) LIS database

Note: data from GINI in the 2b panel contain real panel of the GINI countries having sufficiently long series to cover the whole period. From OECD and from LIS database, data for the GINI country universe was chosen

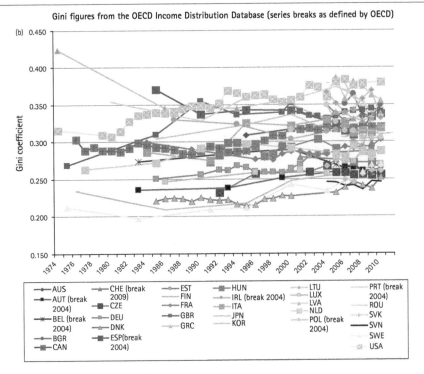

Gini figures from the OECD Income Distribution Database (series breaks as defined by OECD)

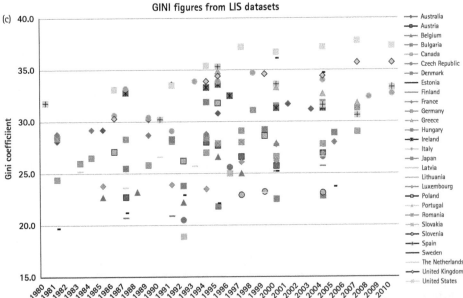

GINI figures from LIS datasets

FIGURE 2.2. (Continued)

The OECD data in Figure 2.2b shows a similar time-trend (with the exception that the first data point for Spain differs considerably from the one we included in our series, based on the LIS estimate). Except for the latter figure, the general upward-moving tendency in inequality can be seen together with some increase in heterogeneity. However, less is found on the country specific time trends in the OECD database.

The LIS database (Figure 2.2c) covers fewer countries at the beginning of the period (because LIS started operating in 1985 and focused mostly on getting most recent data in the database first) and also towards the end (because 'Lissifying' new datasets takes time and countries submit their datasets to LIS only after producing their own publications). Nevertheless, both the range of Ginis and the overall time-trend look similar to what we found with the GINI database.

A point relating to the period on which the analysis focuses should be noted here. At the beginning of the period, the early eighties were specific in the sense that the post-dictatorship Mediterranean countries had already experienced a decline in inequality in the 1970s, while the then socialist countries in Central and Eastern Europe still had particularly low levels of inequality. Therefore, the low 'average' level of Gini can be attributed to this asynchronicity. Regarding the end of the period, it should be observed that for some of the countries the effect of the economic crisis may be transitory. However, even taking this into account, the overall pattern of increasing inequality seems to be clear.

Importantly, neither the LIS nor the OECD income inequality database (as yet) allows one to follow yearly time paths in the data for individual countries.[8] The capacity of the GINI database to do so makes a more detailed analysis here worthwhile.

5. Tracking Changes Over Time in Various Country Groupings—Caveats

In what follows, we investigate the developments in income inequality over time in various country groupings, presented in Figures 2.3–2.8. Before analysing the data some further methodological remarks have to be made.

First and foremost, it has to be acknowledged that all Gini figures (in fact all international comparisons, not only ours) are estimates from samples. Due to sampling and non-sampling errors (further complicated by sometimes hidden or unknown sample design features in secondary datasets[9]), there is variability in the estimates which may not reflect real societal changes. With no microdata to hand, we have to apply some rule of thumb to decide what can be considered a real 'change' over time. Arbitrarily, a difference of a magnitude of 1 point in the Gini from one year to the next will be considered as a 'no-change', especially if it is followed by movement in the other direction. However, if in a series of subsequent years there is a monotonic change (in consistent manner), then small year-to-year changes may cumulate into a 'spell': consistent year-to-year changes of even half a point can accumulate to a five-point change in Gini or more over ten years, a substantial change indeed. The length of a 'spell' is also difficult to define a priori, so as a working definition we define a spell as lasting at least 3–4 years during which time the series changes in a consistent manner. Finally, the length of a spell is not capped: there may be good reasons to assume that there is a long-term

---

[8] The OECD plans to include in its database indicators of income inequality on the basis of the most regular/frequent basis and for some indicators they plan to do this retrospectively for a dozen countries.

[9] See on this Biewen and Jenkins, 2006, for example.

tendency in either direction, and, as we will see, in the case of some countries (such as the Nordic group or the Netherlands, for example) there are quite long spells of this type.

Secondly, using the Gini coefficient to track changes over time carries the risk of missing some important changes 'inside' the income distribution. As the coefficient is less sensitive to changes in the tails of the distribution, the picture we get from Gini comparisons will give more weight to changes in the middle, and important features of where inequality is changing—such as increases in top income shares, for example—will not be obvious.

Thirdly, breaks in series pose a serious challenge for cross-country comparisons as well as for intertemporal tracking of inequality, as already noted (Atkinson and Brandolini, 2001, OECD, 2013). A break in a series may provide an obvious basis for suspicion if accompanied by a sudden change in the level of inequality, which subsequently does not continue in the same direction. However, in other cases one must rely on expert judgements as to whether such breaks have in fact masked an underlying change in inequality. We refer the reader to the data description at the end of this chapter, in Tables A1 and A2 in Annex 1.

Finally, decisions need to be taken on how best to classify countries into meaningful groupings. We essentially use a geographical (North-South-West-East-Centre) classification, which roughly corresponds to the standard welfare regimes typology (Esping Andersen, 1990, Bonoli, 1996, Ferrera, 1997). An alternative approach to classification would have been based on similarities and dissimilarities in observed over-time patterns/paths of inequality developments. However, as we will see, the alternative would in fact not have made very much difference, so clarity and convenience suffice to justify the groupings employed here.

We discuss the evolution of inequality in the set of 30 countries[10] according to six groupings:

- Five Continental European welfare states
- Four Nordic countries and the Netherlands
- Five English-speaking liberal countries
- Four Mediterranean countries
- Two Asian countries
- Ten Central and Eastern European countries.

Comments are derived from the country chapters (in this book) and reports (prepared within the GINI project).

6. TRACKING CHANGES OVER TIME IN VARIOUS COUNTRY GROUPINGS—RESULTS

To get more insight into the magnitude in the trend in inequality, we model the trend in Gini coefficients as shown in Figure 2.1, using fixed effects for country, allowing country-specific intercepts. Table 2.1 shows linear models with and without control for GDP per capita (PPP in

---

[10] With Germany being given a slight overweight as long term series are provided for East and West as well as for the whole country.

Table 2.1 Linear trend in Gini coefficients with country-fixed effects

	1	2	3	4	5	6	7	8
	All countries	All countries, GDP controlled	English-speaking	Nordic (incl. NLD)	Continental	Medi-terranean	Central and Eastern Europe	Baltic States
Year	0.245*** (22.60)	0.433*** (16.89)	0.146*** (8.65)	0.256*** (18.38)	0.121*** (6.40)	0.015 (0.69)	0.303*** (14.42)	0.537*** (14.51)
GDP per capita		-0.000*** (-9.46)						
Country fixed effects	Yes	yes	yes	yes	yes	yes	yes	

~ p < 0.10, * p < 0.05, ** p < 0.01, *** p < 0.001
Notes: t statistics in parentheses
Source: Data from country chapters of this volume.

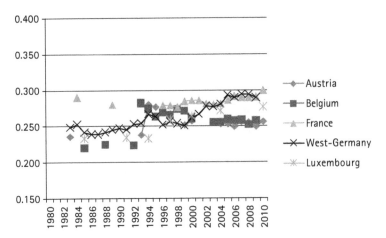

FIGURE 2.3 The evolution of inequality in European Continental Welfare States

current dollars, taken from the Worldbank, <http://data.worldbank.org>). Table 2.1 shows that the linear trend is definitely upward, with 0.25 points increase each year, or 0.43 points if controlled for GDP per capita. Over the thirty-year window of the data the increase thus equals 7.35 points, more than half of the 'within year' range of Gini coefficients between countries.

Table 2.1 also shows linear trends for separate groups of countries. Interestingly, the English-speaking countries do not stand out in terms of inequality trends; the average growth in inequality is 0.15 Gini points, not much higher than in Continental Europe (0.12 Gini points per year). The trend in the Nordic countries is much larger, with 0.26 Gini points per year on average, and in Central and European countries (0.30 Gini points) and the Baltic States (0.54 Gini points per year). In all groups of countries, except in the Mediterranean countries, inequality has been on the rise.

However, as will become clear below, there are large discrepancies in inequality trends between countries within these groups.

The overall patterns for the **Continental European Welfare States** (Belgium, France, (West) Germany, Luxembourg and Austria) are mixed, as illustrated in Figure 2.3. In general, the year-to-year changes are not very large, where they exist at all. In Austria and France there has been considerable stability in inequality over the years. For Austria this can be attributed to the effectiveness of the Welfare State in tackling inequalities, as brought out in the Austrian country chapter, although 2000–2004 sees a major break in series which prevents us from drawing strong conclusions for later years.

The French case is different. Inequalities declined between the beginning of the eighties and the end of the nineties, followed by a U-turn and increasing income dispersion later on. For Germany we have a separate series for the East and for the West, motivated by the fact that the time span of our analysis covers the decade before the collapse of the Berlin Wall. It is clear that in Germany there has been a considerable increase in inequality, especially between 1985 and 2007, with an especially large shift between 2000 and 2005. The substantial increase in market income inequality after reunification was tackled by strong Welfare State provisions throughout the nineties, so the effect on inequality in disposable incomes was modest. However, after 2000, inequalities increased, probably because of the weak performance of

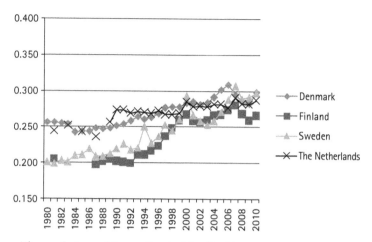

FIGURE 2.4 The evolution of inequality in Nordic EU countries and the Netherlands

the labour market, with rising unemployment combining with lower capacity in the tax and transfer system to mitigate market income inequality (as discussed in the German country chapter). Altogether in this period, a five-point increase in the Gini occurred. In Luxembourg there was also a gradual growth in inequality, of a smaller magnitude than in Germany. The Belgian data series have a break in data source between 1992 and 1993 and between 2000 and 2003, so the large jump in the Gini between these two years should not be given too much weight; Belgium can be classified as a 'no-change' country, alongside with France and Austria. This is clearly a puzzling phenomenon as one can point to many reasons why inequality might have grown there: increased regional disparities (between Flanders and Wallonia), the strong decentralization of various state activities and services, as well as the openness of the country to globalization in general and foreign trade and migration in particular. The reasons for the stability in income inequality appear to be found in the strong Welfare State and in the complex and elaborate institutional framework, including compulsory voting and settings that promote union membership, as discussed in the Belgium country chapter.

The second group presented here are the **Nordic countries** (Denmark, Finland and Sweden) **together with the Netherlands** (Figure 2.4). There is a gradual increase (with no real interim spells) in inequality in all four of these countries, albeit to a differing extent. The largest growth in inequality is experienced in Sweden (amounting to a ten point increase in Gini, this being the largest increase among the 'old' EU member states). The Swedish data series seems to show considerable volatility (which may be partly due to the way income inequality data is constructed from tax and other administrative records). Nevertheless, the Swedish country chapter highlights the way that behind the substantial increase in inequality, one first observes a strong rise of top incomes and most recently also a widening gap at the bottom tail. Most changes can be associated with policy changes, including the loosening of the net of social policies in Sweden and retrenchment following the 1990s financial crisis and recession.[11]

---

[11] In Sweden, data volatility is due mostly to policy changes, rather than series breaks. For example, when we see a data break in 1990–1991, there is no apparent 'jump' in the trend, However, the larger jumps in the data series are due, in 1994, to changes in the taxation of realized capital gains while the

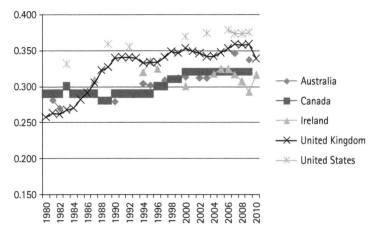

FIGURE 2.5 The evolution of inequality in English-speaking liberal countries

A similar steep increasing trend can be observed in Finland (altogether a 6–8 point increase over the period for which statistics are available). The immediate reasons appear to be an increase in the share of capital incomes in total income on the one hand and the decreasing effectiveness of the various redistributive tools in reducing inequalities on the other hand. A more modest, but still pronounced, increasing trend is witnessed by the Dutch (especially between 1987 and 1990) and the Danes (throughout the period). This is a striking phenomenon: Figure 2.4 suggests that we need to revise the commonly-held view about the stability of inequality rankings across countries and regimes—or, at a minimum, this group serves as a counter-example. The magnitude of the cumulative increase in inequality in Sweden and in Finland has certainly exceeded the average of the countries for which comparable data are available for the entire period. It is also worth noting that while there was slow or negative growth in the first half of the eighties, three of the four members of this group (Denmark, Finland and the Netherlands) saw declines in inequality. By the end of the period, however, the level of inequality in this group puts them into the same bracket with the first category of the Continental European Welfare States. Whether this shift means a real regime change or not is an important topic for further research.

For the third grouping, the **English-speaking liberal countries** (USA, UK, Ireland, Canada and Australia), we observe substantially diverging trends (Figure 2.5). The USA had the highest level of inequality at the beginning of the period and has remained in this position as inequality rose (with the Gini increasing from 0.33 to 0.38). In Australia, the trend was very similar to the USA, in fact the increase in the Gini was even larger (from 0.27 in to 0.34). In the UK, the substantial increase in inequality of the Thatcher years was followed by fluctuating inequality spells, resulting a Gini of 0.34 in 2010. The trend for Ireland was rather flat, a remarkable finding for a country that experienced such pronounced volatility in economic conditions (continued stagnation in the 1980s, the Celtic Tiger period in the

bumps in 2000 and 2007 and the decrease in 2001 and 2008 are at least partly to do with changes in the stock market. For more on this see, for example, Fritzell *et al.*, 2012.

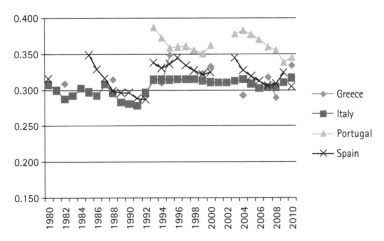

FIGURE 2.6 The evolution of inequality in Mediterranean European countries

second half of the 1990s, and the largest GDP decline after the financial crisis, all of these being major shocks).[12] Interestingly, as the Irish country chapter highlights, the particularly deep great recession has initially had an equalizing, rather than a disequalizing effect—similar, by the way, to the Netherlands during its deep recession in the early 1980s. Finally, Canada seems to be moving towards a higher level of inequality over time, step by step. Developments in this group in particular warrant further study of institutions and policies to understand why in certain contexts inequality is on the rise while in other contexts it remains unchanged though the macroeconomy is in a state of flux.

For some of the **Mediterranean countries**—the fourth country grouping—it was the period just before the start of our observations that witnessed major changes (see Figure 2.6). Getting rid of political dictatorships in the seventies appears to have led to equalization in the income distribution in Spain, Portugal and Greece. After the initial periods of these transitions, however, the pattern is rather unclear, mostly because of series breaks. To some extent, the clearest case is Portugal, where in the last couple of years seem to show a robust reversal of the previous increase in inequality. The problem of series breaks seems to be most serious in Spain[13] but the Greek series also seems to suffer from the same type of problems.

The Italian story is different, however. While, at the beginning of the period, Italy was the most unequal European country in our sample, at the end, by 2010, Italy was only moderately unequal in relative terms, due to a stagnant Gini while inequality in other countries increased. Underneath the surface, however, as the Italian chapter highlights, one may observe substantial changes—most importantly with respect to labour market

[12] There is, however, a considerable volatility in Gini measures over time in Ireland. Consider, for example, the sudden jump in the value of Gini in 1995 and in 2010—after an apparent decline. The latter change can, obviously, be related to the impact of the economic crisis. (See the chapter on Ireland in this book.)

[13] The periods of various data sources for Spain between 1985–1992, 1993–2000, 2001–2002 and 2003–2009 seem to show consistent stories in themselves but the large jumps in between the four are significant. The chart does not include the clearly outlier 2000–2001 estimates. (For more, see the chapter on Spain in this book.)

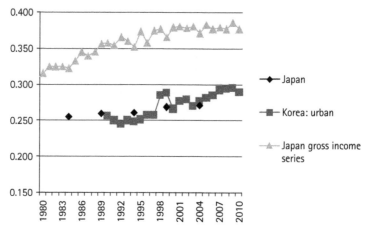

FIGURE 2.7 The evolution of inequality in Japan and Korea

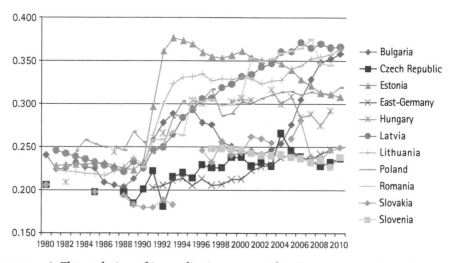

FIGURE 2.8 The evolution of inequality in post-socialist European transition countries

segmentation—with major implications for the opportunities facing younger generations in particular.

The two **Asian countries** present in the database show levels of inequality, which would rank them in the middle range, among the Europeans. Figure 2.7 shows that the prolonged stagnation in Japan (the country report calls it the 'Lost Two Decades'), together with the pronounced ageing of Japanese society, has been associated with no change in inequality levels (in terms of net incomes), according to the country report.[14] For Korea, both economic conditions and inequality trends are different, with the Gini increasing from 0.245 in

---

[14] As far as gross incomes are concerned, there is a slowly moving upward trend in inequality in Japan as well. Unfortunately, it is not possible to show such long trends for the net incomes.

1992 to 0.295 by 2009. (The 1998–1999 figures seem to be local outliers.) However, it should be emphasized that for Korea there are no distributional data for the country as a whole; the available statistics apply only to urban households with 2 or more members. This is clearly a major limitation, both in capturing overall inequality in the country and perhaps also for trends over time, though the latter is difficult to judge.

We have left the analysis of inequality trends in the transition countries of Central and Eastern Europe until last. This group displays very substantial volatility over the observation period, and merits a separate treatment in the section to which we turn now.

7. EFFECTS OF TRANSITIONS IN THE CENTRAL AND EASTERN EUROPEAN COUNTRIES

For a start we consider the trends in Figure 2.8. While the **post-socialist group** of transition countries was very homogeneous during the eighties, at least as far as the differences in their inequality levels are concerned, the first half of the nineties saw remarkable changes and

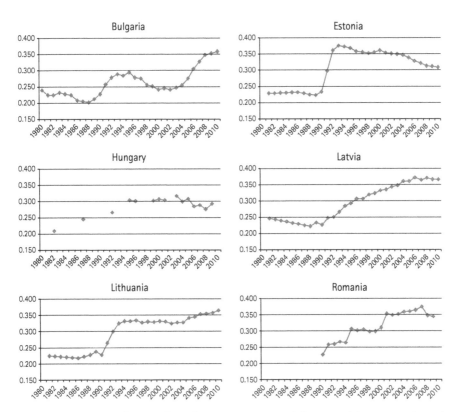

FIGURE 2.9 Patterns of inequality change in post-socialist transition countries where the Gini growth was 10 points or more

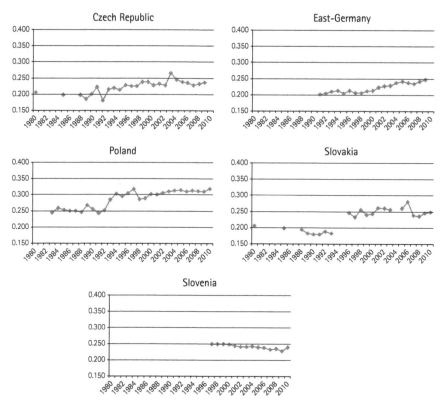

FIGURE 2.10 Patterns of inequality change in post-socialist transition countries where the Gini growth was less than 10 points

great divergence in their inequality level. This resulted in the evolution from a seemingly uniform country grouping stagnating behind the 'Iron Curtain', with Gini figures between 0.20–0.25, to a very heterogeneous group with Gini figures ranging from 0.23 to 0.37. This means that by the time these countries joined the EU in the 2000s, they already represented different inequality regimes (see Tóth and Gábos, 2005).

They have followed two markedly different trajectories. A cluster of six countries— Bulgaria, Estonia, Lithuania, Latvia, Romania and Hungary—experienced a large (over 10 Gini points) increase in inequality in just a few years, as shown in Figure 2.9. Estonia and Lithuania underwent the largest shocks, with a close to thirteen point Gini increase in Estonia just over two years between 1990 and 1992—warranting caution and requiring further analysis of the underlying data—and an almost ten point Gini increase in Lithuania between 1990 and 1993. Several factors make these extreme changes more plausible than they might seem at first sight. The most fundamental difference between these countries' stories concerns the speed of the transition to a market economy. The Baltics country report emphasizes that the transition was exceptionally fast in Estonia—followed by the largest inequality increase among the three countries. The differences in speed of privatization and liberalization were reflected in labour market developments although the largest unemployment shock occurred in Latvia, which had the highest level of industrialization in the Soviet era, leading to major shocks in redundancies when transforming into a market economy. Finally, its exceptionally low educational premium before the transition (with the higher educated at only 108 per cent of the national average wage while the lower educated were at 97 per cent) was changed by an exceptionally fast differentiation of pay by education in the first half of the nineties. Equally interesting, though, is the divergence between the inequality paths of the three countries after they had reached their local peaks. In Estonia, a consistent inequality decline set in, but Lithuania witnessed a continued increase albeit at a reduced pace. Latvia, compared to the other two Baltic states, has climbed up rather gradually from the position of being one of the most equal European countries around 1990 to the most unequal by 2010 (see Baltics country report).

Both in Bulgaria and (to a lesser extent) in Romania, the increase in inequality has taken place in two waves. In Bulgaria, the dynamics of this process derive from a complex interplay of GDP growth and decline, incomes and pensions policies and migration, as described in the Bulgaria country report. The peculiar pattern of Romania is associated with non-transparent privatization practices, state capture, corruption and shadow economy activities,[15] together with effects exerted by migration on inequality, while at the same time social policies are inefficient in tackling increases in inequality. The Hungarian story of inequality development is, different from the rest, like its transition. Given that the transition, at least in terms of liberalization of the economy, started earlier than in other countries (Tóth, 2008), the transition shock seems to be smaller, at least for the final outcomes for inequalities. It seems that the inequality effects of the exceptionally harsh labour market adjustment (due to very tough bankruptcy laws) were mitigated by various social policies, which resulted in a long-term financing of inactivity in the country as highlighted in the country chapter. The effect was a smoother increase in inequality (Figure 2.9).

It is worth emphasizing that in some of these countries clear spells of declining inequality occurred: Bulgaria between 1995 and 2001, Estonia since 1994–5 or Hungary between 2003 and 2008. Inequalities are not always on the rise, which is an important general point to make in view of the forces that may be at work.

Figure 2.10, the last figure of this series, presents trends in the rest of the transition countries, the cluster following the second trajectory. East Germany is shown here as being of some interest in itself, without attempting to interpret it in any way in the same frame as the others. The five-point increase in the Gini could simply be considered as a delayed reaction to unification, following an increase of similar magnitude in the western part of the country. The cases of Slovenia and of the Czech Republic deserve special attention. The two countries were able to avoid large inequality shocks throughout the transition process.[16] To understand the immediate reasons, one has to understand the economic and social policies adopted and also the way the process of transition has proceeded. The Slovenian chapter emphasizes that the low inequality is largely attributable to the relatively efficient tax and social policy measures in redistributing incomes. The Czech chapter also emphasizes the role of tax and transfer policies—the transfers of the pension system for the older

---

[15] Normally, the shadow economy should not directly appear in net incomes, of course. However, if there is an variance over time in the way the various surveys can capture these items, this volatility can be reflected in the inequality trends as well.

[16] There is a series break in Slovenia between 2004 and 2005—with no effect on trends. (Figure 25.2 in the Slovenian country chapter.)

population and taxes for the working-age population. For Poland, the transition resulted in an inequality increase but the magnitude of 5 Gini points remains relatively modest by 'eastern standards'. The Slovak development parallels the Czech one, albeit with a break in the series that lifted inequality onto a higher level.

We conclude that large social transformations (like the socio-economic transition in CEE countries) have had very significant effects on inequality developments. However, the magnitude of the impact depends heavily on country-specific factors, the study of which will be a very important subject for further research. Inequality is part of the story in each case, but it is not simply an inevitable consequence of some exogenous shock (as highlighted in the Hungarian chapter but also in the Slovenian and Czech ones). To broaden the scope of this comparison, it will be very interesting to compare the post-transition periods of the former Mediterranean dictatorships to those of the former socialist countries. A hypothesis that the transition to democracy had an equalizing effect in one set of the countries while in another set democratization and rapid privatization led to soaring inequalities seems worth serious study. Related to this, an important distinction can be made between economic regime (and economic liberalization) and political regime (and democratization). One might hypothesize that the secular effect of democratization may be equalizing while a change of economic regime can be disequalizing, so that the joint effect would be uncertain.[17]

8. INEQUALITY AND POVERTY—FURTHER METHODOLOGICAL CAVEATS

The GINI database also covers relative poverty rates. As already mentioned, 60 per cent of median equivalized household income is used as the poverty cut-off point. Not all countries were able to report it: Japan, for example, does not have a government publication series on this basis, so figures with the 50 per cent of median threshold were used instead. In Korea, as was the case for the Gini figures, poverty rates are available for urban households having 2+ members only. However, while these differences are potentially very important in studying the incidence of poverty by various socio-economic characteristics, they constitute less of a problem for the cross-country comparison of time series.[18] For the comparative analysis of trends in inequality, Ginis, and poverty rates that we present below, however, the issue of consistency between these two series raises some serious concerns. A quick look at the series presented in Figure 2.11 gives a flavour of the nature of the problem. The GINI database as a whole contains ten per cent fewer observations for poverty than for Gini (roughly five hundred and fifty poverty rate observations as compared to roughly six hundred Ginis), and poverty rates are non-randomly missing. Figure 2.11 shows that they are missing particularly for the earlier part of our observation period, which is especially problematic for

---

[17] Some available papers on this issue (see Nel, 2005, Galbraith, 2012) suggest a disequalizing effect of democratization but without the above-mentioned distinction.

[18] For European comparisons of relative poverty rates, the 60 per cent thresholds is the most common (and also preferred by the various European reporting systems, see Atkinson and Marlier, 2012, Nolan and Whelan, 2011).

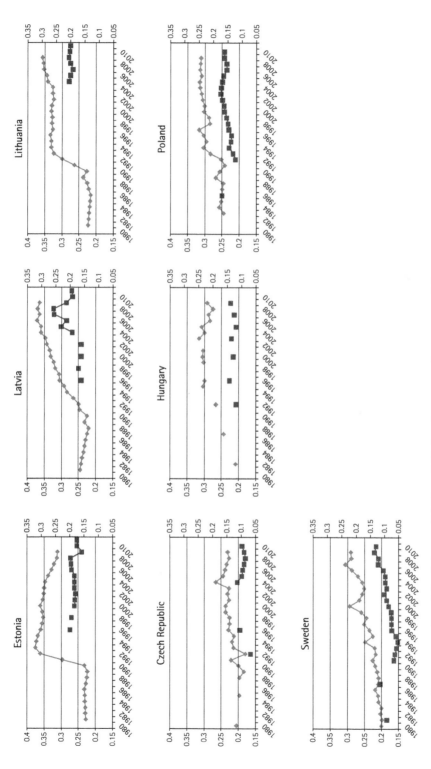

FIGURE 2.11 Some examples of the joint availability of Gini and poverty data: potential for Gini-to-poverty comparisons

those countries where there was an inequality shock in those years, while poverty data are available only for the after-shock period. This is a serious constraint and means that particular care must be taken in making any generalizations.

Finally, until now we have not explored variations in the equivalence scales applied across the countries. For Ginis this is less of a substantial problem. The value of Gini at the country level is sensitive to the choice of equivalence scale (Tóth and Medgyesi, 2011) but the variance attributable to this is not prohibitively high. For the poverty rate, however, the choice of equivalence scale matters much more, even at the level of country aggregates (Coulter, Cowell and Jenkins, 1992). Depending on the equivalence scale chosen, cross country comparisons might easily show different rankings/images, due to differential demographic structures in various societies. Therefore, in what follows, we concentrate on the issue which is less troublesome, as the same equivalization is applied to both sides at the country level: the development of the relationship between the Gini and poverty over time—with due attention paid to caveats mentioned above.

9. Inequality and Poverty—Some Results

The study of the interrelationships of poverty and inequality is an issue of importance in itself. The political debate about what should come first: the reduction of (absolute) poverty or the taming of inequality is a major question in research, and in policy as well (see for example the influential debates about poverty and growth, mostly in developing country contexts and mostly instigated by various World Bank publications—see Dollar and Kray, 2002, Ravallion 2001, 2004, 2005, Ravallion and Chen, 1997, Chen and Ravallion, 2001, etc). We leave out this whole debate as no absolute poverty data are available in the GINI database (at least not for a sufficiently large number of countries for which a proper international comparison could have been presented). The more general interrelationship between inequality, (relative) poverty (and growth) is the focus here (see Figure 2.12). Following the formulation of Bourguignon (2004) and Ferreira and Ravallion (2009), we assume that the relationship between relative poverty and inequality (even when controlled for income growth) is not trivial. It depends on the shape of the distribution (most importantly in the lower tail but also at the other end). Empirically, a change in relative poverty may move in the same direction as a change in inequality, but in many cases the magnitude of change can differ substantially. Furthermore, in certain conditions, the changes may not even go in the same direction (Förster and Vleminckx, 2004). The reasons behind that have to be found in economic trends and in policy choices as well.

Among the 30 countries we noticed three different patterns.

In some of the countries, the relationship between poverty and inequality seems to run parallel to each other, e.g. Belgium, France and Italy—and presumably in other countries experiencing no change in inequality. Poverty in these countries (which is an aspect of the lower tail of the distribution) does not change when there is no change in inequality, provided there are no major underlying polarization trends in the society (Alderson, 2005 and Alderson and Doran, 2013).

A second pattern shows interesting combinations of rising inequality and falling or unchanging poverty in three English-speaking liberal countries (UK, USA and Canada).

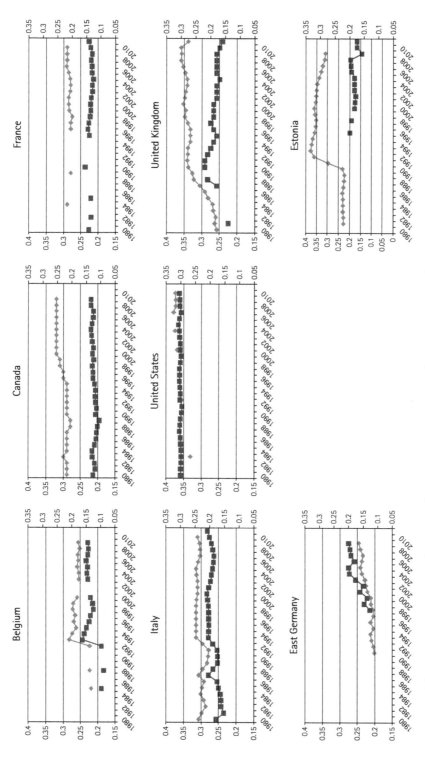

FIGURE 2.12 The joint movement of Gini and poverty—some exemplary patterns under growing, declining and unchanged inequality scenarios

Table 2.2 Change in inequality levels (Gini coefficient values) during three periods

Gini coefficients	1980–1984	1996–2000	2006–2010
above 0.350		Estonia, Portugal, Romania, United States	Latvia, Lithuania, Portugal, Romania, United Kingdom, United States
0.301 to 0.350	Greece, Spain, United States	Australia, Bulgaria, Canada, Greece, Hungary, Ireland, Italy, Korea, Latvia, Lithuania, Romania, Spain, United Kingdom	Australia, Bulgaria, Canada, Estonia, Greece, Ireland, Italy, Korea, Poland, Spain
0.251 to 0.300	Australia, Canada, Denmark, France, Germany (West), Italy, Japan, United Kingdom	Austria, Belgium, Denmark, France, Germany and Germany (West), Japan, Luxembourg, Poland, Netherlands, Sweden	Austria, Belgium, Denmark, Finland, France, Germany and Germany (West), Hungary, Korea, Luxembourg, Netherlands, Sweden
up to 0.250	Austria, Bulgaria, Czech Republic Estonia, Finland, Hungary, Latvia, Netherlands, Lithuania, Slovakia, Sweden	Czech Republic, Finland, Germany (East), Slovakia, Slovenia	Czech Republic, Germany (East), Slovakia, Slovenia
no data	Belgium, Germany (East), Ireland, Korea, Luxembourg, Portugal, Romania, Slovenia		Japan

How and why this is the case here is a subject for further investigation and further study of the country experiences. Also, the magnitude of the changes merits further scrutiny, for example in the UK where a large increase in top incomes coincided with increased efforts by subsequent governments to implement anti-poverty measures (see UK chapter).

Finally, in some other cases (Estonia and East Germany, for example) a third pattern of converging trends emerges. The changes in inequality and poverty go in a different direction: an inequality decrease is associated with growing poverty in these countries. For these countries, it is probably the changing relationship (and share) of the middle classes to the increasingly marginalized poor which holds the key to the puzzle. Any further analysis will, however, come from further close inspection of the data in detail—especially if longer poverty series could be constructed, at least for some of the crucially important country cases.

10. CONCLUSIONS

In this concluding section, we return to our initial question: is inequality on the rise and if so is it on the rise in a uniform manner over the time period (1980–2010) being studied?

Our analysis shows that inequality has indeed increased on average across the countries included in the analysis, with the whole range of Gini coefficients being at a higher level at the end of the period (from 0.228 to 0.373) than it was at the beginning (from 0. 20 to 0.33).

Second, the growth in inequality was far from uniform. In certain countries (such as Austria, Belgium, France, Italy, Ireland, Slovenia) the level of inequality remained largely unchanged or fluctuated around the same level, while in others it increased substantially. The most dramatic increase in inequality was experienced by some transition countries (Bulgaria, Estonia, Lithuania, Latvia, Romania and Hungary) and, to a lesser but still significant extent, by the Nordic countries, most notably Sweden and Finland. In some of these countries, the increase was sudden and large (like in the Baltics, Bulgaria and Romania); in others it accumulated gradually over time (the Nordic group, Netherlands).

Third, the pattern of change in inequality does not always point upwards. There are countries where inequality has been declining for shorter or for longer periods. Such spells of decline were also observed in Estonia, Bulgaria and Hungary, for example, after, sometimes, sharp increases.

Fourth, over time it seems possible, indeed, that countries do shift between inequality regimes. This means that the variance over time can be large enough for countries at the end of the period to belong to a different segment of the international league from the one they belonged to at the beginning of the period. One example is the Nordic countries. This group of countries has long been celebrated for having the lowest levels of inequality in Europe. After decades of gradual but constant increases in inequality, they no longer belong to the lowest division of the inequality 'league table'. Also, some of the transition countries like the Baltics, Romania or Bulgaria witnessed very large changes that have put their inequality levels in a different range.

The resulting picture of the inequality scene is summarized in Table 2.2. It shows the countries in terms of their inequality levels during three different parts of the 30-year period scrutinized here: 1980–1984, 1996–2000 and 2006–2010. To smooth out measurement uncertainties and cyclical trends, values for the Gini coefficient are averaged for these periods. The table shows a clear upward trend in general. No country had a Gini above 0.35 in the first period, whereas five countries had reached this level of inequality in the latest period, three of them belonging to the post-communist bloc. There were nine countries in the first half of the eighties with a Gini value below 0.25, but the number of countries with this low level of inequality then declined considerably, so that only the Czech Republic, Slovakia and Slovenia (and Eastern Germany) were at that level in the latest period. The Nordic countries by then cluster together with the Continental European Welfare States in the 0.25–0.30 range of Gini coefficients.

The aim of this chapter was to present and discuss trends in income inequality in the OECD (and EU) countries that can be drawn from the GINI Inequality and Poverty Database that is derived from the 30 country studies. While the resulting picture, we believe, contributes to a better understanding of the 'whats' of income distribution, there are many questions, mostly related to the 'whys', that remain for further research. Modelling and understanding the causal factors underpinning the variation in income inequality across countries and over time remains a major challenge for research (Brandolini and Smeeding, 2009). The diverging paths seen in various countries (especially those having similar starting-points and/or histories) suggest that the development of inequalities is not simply driven by exogenous forces: political and institutional processes, societal institutions and policies matter, as will be brought out in the detailed country case studies that follow.

REFERENCES

Adelman, I. and Morris, C. T. (1973), *Economic Growth and Social Equity in Developing Countries*, Stanford, CA: Stanford University Press.

Adelman, I. and Robinson, S. (1989), 'Income distribution and development', in H. Chenery, and T.N. Shrinivasan, (eds.), *Handbook of development economics*. Vol. 2, Elsevier Science Publishers B.V, pp. 949–1003.

Alderson, A. S. (2005), 'Exactly How Has Income Inequality Changed? Patterns of Distributional Change in Core Societies', *International Journal of Comparative Sociology* 46(5-6): 405–423., <http://cos.sagepub.com/cgi/doi/10.1177/0020715205059208>.

Alderson, Arthur S. and Doran Kevin (2013), 'How Has Income Inequality Grown? The Income Distribution in LIS Countries', in Janet Gornick, and Markus Jantti (eds.), *Economic Disparities and the Middle Class in Affluent Countries*, Stanford, CA: Stanford University Press, pp. 51–74.

Atkinson, A. and Marlier, E. (2010), *Income and living conditions in Europe*, Luxembourg: Eurostat.

Atkinson, A.B. and Rainwater, L. and Smeeding, T.M. (1995), 'Income distribution in the OECD countries', *Social Policy Studies*, No. 18, Paris: OECD.

Atkinson, A.B. and Bourguignon F. (eds.) (2000), *Handbook of Income Distribution*, Amsterdam: Elsevier Science B.V, especially pp. 1–58 ('Introduction').

Atkinson, Anthony B., and Brandolini, Andrea (2001), 'Promise and Pitfalls in the Use of "Secondary" Data-Sets: Income Inequality in OECD Countries', *Journal of Economic Literature* 39(3): 771–799.

Atkinson, Anthony, B. and Brandolini, A (2006), 'On Data: a Case Study of the Evolution of Income Inequality Across Time and Across Countries', *Cambridge Journal of Economics*, 2006, Vol. 33(3), pp. 381–404.

Biewen, M. and Jenkins, S. P. (2006), 'Variance Estimation for Generalized Entropy and Atkinson Inequality Indices: the Complex Survey Data Case', *Oxford Bulletin Of Economics & Statistics*, 68(3), 371–383.

Bonoli, Giuliano (1997), 'Classifying Welfare States: A Two-Dimension Approach', *Journal of Social Policy* 26: 351–372.

Bourguignon, F., and Ferreira, F., and Lustig N. (2005), *The Microeconomics of Income Distribution Dynamics in East Asia and Latin America*, Washington DC, World Bank and Oxford University Press.

Bourguignon, F. (2004), 'The Growth-Inequality-Poverty Triangle', *Indian Council for Research on International Economic Relations Working Paper* 125, March, (download from here: <http://www.icrier.org/pdf/wp125.pdf>)

Brandolini, Andrea and Smeeding, Timothy, M. (2009), 'Income Inequality in Richer OECD Countries', in Wiemer Salverda, Brian Nolan, and Timothy M. Smeeding (eds.), Oxford: Oxford University Press, p. 71–100.

Canberra Group (2011), *Canberra Group Handbook on Household Income Statistics*, United Nations, New York and Geneva.

Chen, S. and Ravallion, M. (2001), 'How did the World's Poorest Fare in the 1990s?' The Review of Income and Wealth Volume 47, Number 3, September 2001, pp. 283–300 (18).

Cornia, G. A. (2012), 'Inequality Trends and their Determinants, Latin America over 1990-2010', *UNU-Wider Working Paper* No 2012/09.

Cornia, G. A. (2005), 'Policy Reform and Income Distribution', *DESA Working Paper No. 3*. See: <http://www.un.org/esa/desa/papers/2005/wp3_2005.pdf>.

Cornia, G.A. and Court, J. (2001), 'Inequality, Growth and Poverty in the Era of Liberalization and Globalization', *Policy Brief* No. 4. Helsinki: UNU/WIDER .

Coulter, F. and Cowell, F. and Jenkins, S. P. (19920, 'Equivalence Scale Relativities and the Extent of Inequality and Poverty', *The Economic Journal*, Vol. 102, September 1067 –1082 .

Deininger, K. and Squire, L. (1996), 'A New Data Set Measuring Income Inequality', *The World Bank Economic Review*, Vol. 10. No. 3, pp. 565–591.

Deininger, K. and Squire, L. (1997), 'Economic Growth and Income Inequality. Reexamining the Links', *Finance and Development*, March, 1997. pp. 38–41.

Deininger, K. and Squire, L. (1998), New Ways of Looking at Old Issues', *Journal of Development Economics* 57, pp. 259–287.

Dollar, D. and Kraay, A. (2002), 'Growth is Good for the Poor', *Journal of Economic Growth* 7(3) 195–225.

Esping-Andersen, Gosta and Myles, John (2009), 'Economic Inequality and the Welfare State', in Wiemer Salverda, Brian Nolan, and Timothy Smeeding (eds.), *The Oxford Handbook of Economic Inequality*, Oxford: Oxford University Press, pp. 639–664.

Esping-Andersen, Gosta (1990), *The Three Worlds of Welfare Capitalism*, Princeton, NJ: Princeton University Press.

Ferrera M. (1996), 'The Southern Model of Welfare in Social Europe' *Journal of European Social Policy* 6(1): 17–37.

Ferreira, Francisco, and Ravallion, Martin (2009), 'Poverty and Inequality: The Global Context', in Wiemer Salverda, Brian Nolan, and Timothy M. Smeeding (eds.), *The Oxford Handbook of Economic Inequality*, Oxford: Oxford University Press, p. 599–635.

Förster, M. and d'Ercole, M. M. (2005), 'Income Distribution and Poverty in OECD Countries in the Second Half of the 1990s', *OECD Social, Employment and Migration Working Papers* No. 22. Paris: OECD, at: <http://www.oecd.org/dataoecd/48/9/34483698.pdf>(6 July 2005).

Förster, M. and Pearson, M. (2002), 'Income Distribution and Poverty in the OECD Area: Trends and Driving Forces', *OECD Economic Studies*, No. 34. Paris.

Förster, M. and Vleminckx, K. (2004), 'International Comparisons of Income Inequality and Poverty: Findings from the Luxembourg Income Study', *Socio-Economic Review* (2004) 2, 194–212.

Fritzell, J., Bäckman, O., and Ritakallio, V.-M. (2012), 'Income Inequality and Poverty: Do the Nordic Countries still Constitute a Family of their Own?' in J. Kvist, J. Fritzell, B. Hvinden and O. Kangas (eds.) *Changing Social Equality. The Nordic Welfare Model in the 21st Century?* Bristol: Policy Press.

Galbraith, J. K. (2012), *Inequality and Instability: A Study of the World Economy Just Before the Great Crisis*, New York: Oxford University Press.

Kuznets, S. (1955), 'Economic Growth and Income Inequality', *American Economic Review* Vol. 65, pp. 1–25.

Li, H., Zou, H., and Squire, L. (1998), 'Explaining international and intertemporal variations in income inequality', *The Economic Journal* 108: 26–43. At: <http://www.worldbank.org/research/inequality/pdf/squire.pdf>.

McKnight, Abigail and Nolan, Brian, 'Social Impacts of Inequalities', *Intermediate Report No 4. of the GINI project. At:* < http://www.giniresearch.org/system/uploads/391/original/Intermediate_Work_Package_4_Report.pdf?1351592931>.

Milanovic, B. (2002), 'True World Income Distribution 1998 and 1993: First Calculation Based on Household Surveys Alone' *Economic Journal*, January 2002.

Milanovic, B. (2003), *Can We Discern the Effect of Globalisation on Income Distribution?* World Bank, Washington, Development Research Group.

Milanovic, B. (2005), 'Global Income Inequality: What it is and Why it Matters?' *World Bank Policy Research Working Paper* 3865, March 2006.

Nel, P. (2005), 'Democratization and the dynamics of income distribution in low- and middle-income countries', *Politikon*, 32(1), 17–43.

Nolan, Brian, Marx, Ive and Salverda, Wiemer (2011), 'Comparable Indicators of Inequality Across Countries' *GINI Discussion Papers* No 9, downloadable from here: http://www.gini-research. org/system/uploads/246/original/DP_DP9_-_Position_Paper_1_-_Nolan_Marx_Salverda. pdf?1301588126.

Nolan, B. and Marx, I. (2009), 'Inequality, Poverty and Social Exclusion', in W. Salverda, B. Nolan, and T. Smeeding (eds.), *Oxford Handbook of Economic Inequality*, Oxford: Oxford University Press.

Nolan, B. and Whelan, C. T. (2011), *Poverty and Deprivation in Europe*, Oxford: Oxford University Press.

OECD (2008), *Growing Unequal? Income Distribution and Poverty in OECD Countries*, Paris: OECD.

OECD (2011), *Divided We Stand. Why Inequality Keeps Rising*, Paris: OECD.

OECD (2013), *Jobs, Wages and Inequality. Quality Review of the OECD Database of Household Incomes and Poverty and the OECD Earnings Database*, Paris: OECD.

Paukert, F. (1973), 'Income distribution at different levels of development', *International Labour Review*, August–September.

Ravallion, M. (2001), 'Growth, Inequality and Poverty: Looking Beyond Averages', *World Development*. Vol 29.n11, November, pp. 1803–1815.

Ravallion, M. (2004), 'Pro-Poor Growth: A Primer', *World Bank Policy Research Working Paper* 3242.

Ravallion, M. (2005), 'A Poverty-Inequality Trade-Off?' Research Working Paper 3579 Development Research Group, World Bank.

Ravallion, M. and Chen, S. (1997), 'What can the data tell us about recent changes in distribution and poverty?' *World Bank Economic Review* 11(2): 357–382.

Salverda, W., Nolan, B., and Smeeding, T. M. (eds.) (2009), *Oxford Handbook of Economic Inequality*, Oxford, UK: Oxford University Press.

Solt, Frederick. (2009), 'Standardizing the World Income Inequality Database', *Social Science Quarterly* 90(2):231–242.

Tóth, I. Gy. (2008), 'The reach of transition in Hungary: assessing the effects of economic transition on income distribution, 1987–2001', in Lyn Squire, and Jose Maria Fanelli, (eds.), *Economic Reform in Developing countries: Reach, Range and Reason*, Cheltenham UK: Edward Elgar.

Tóth, I. Gy. and Gábos, A. (2005), 'Income inequality and poverty in the EU: a macro level comparative analysis' in *Social Situation Observatory Annual Report 2005* (mimeo)

Tóth, I. Gy. and Medgyesi, M. (2011), 'Income distribution in new (and old) EU member states' in *Corvinus Journal of Sociology and Social Policy* Vol 2 No 1 2011 pp. 3–31.

Ward, Terry, Orsolya, Lelkes, Sutherland, Holly, and Tóth, István György (eds.) (2009), *European Inequalities. Social inclusion and income distribution in the European Union*, Budapest: Tárki Social Research Institute, available at: <http://www.tarki.hu/en/publications/EI/>

World Bank (2005), 'Equity and Well-Being', in *World Development Report 2006. Equity and Development*.

ANNEX 1

DEFINITIONS AND SOURCES

Definitions: unless otherwise stated, the calculation of the Gini coefficient and of poverty rate is based on the following:

Gini:
 - population: individuals living in non-institutionalized households
 - income concept: net disposable household income
 - equivalization: yes, but the elasticity may vary

Poverty rate:
 - population: individuals living in non-institutionalized households
 - income concept: net disposable household income
 - equivalization: yes, but the elasticity may vary
 - poverty threshold: 60 per cent of the median equivalent household income

Table 2.A1 Country specific cities for Gini coefficients

Country	Years and original data source	Gini coefficients	
		Publication quoted in country report	Comment or alteration to the above definitions
Austria	1983–1999: Microcensus and OECD (2011a); 2004–2010: Statistics Austria, EU-SILC, calculations by the GINI team of Austria; LIS: 1994, 1995, 1997, 2000	Biffl (2008); OECD (2011a)	1983–1999: disposable household income (monthly average), equivalized using the square-root of the number of persons in the household; 2004–2010: disposable household income (per year): equivalized using the modified OECD scale.
Australia	1981: LIS, 1982, 1986, 1990: Johnson and Wilkins (2002, 1990–2010: ABS estimates	Johnson and Wilkins (2002)	Modified OECD equivalence scale. Values are in 2009–10 dollars, adjusted using the Consumer Price Index.
Belgium	1985, 1988, 1992: SEP1993–2000: ECHP2003–2009: EU-SILC	Horemans, Pintelon et al. 2011, updated to 2009	95% conf intervals also published
Bulgaria	1980-2010: SWIID, Version 3.1	S. Frederick, 2011	Equivalent net income per household member.

(Continued)

Table 2.A1 Continued

		Gini coefficients	
Country	Years and original data source	Publication quoted in country report	Comment or alteration to the above definitions
Canada	1980–2009: Statistics Canada's CANSIM database		
Czech Republic	1988: Atkinson and Micklewright (1992); 1989–1994 Cornia (1994); 1995–2002 Transmonee (2004), 2003 Transmonee (2005), 2005–2010 country team calculations based on EU-SILC; 2004: LIS	Atkinson and Micklewright (1992); Cornia (1994); Transmonee (2004); Transmonee (2005)	Unit of analysis is household (after 1993) or person (up to 1992). Household income equivalized since 2005. Income defined as disposable income (monetary disposable income before 1989).
Denmark	1980–2010: Statistics Denmark		Includes imputed rents and has, as base-line, the primary income. Income concept: equivalized (OECD modified).
Estonia	1981–2010: SWID		Disposable equivalized household income.
Spain	1980: LIS, 1985–1992: ECPF, 1993–2000: ECHP, 2001–2002: ECPF, 2003–2009: EU-SILC, 2010:EPF		Equivalent Disposable Income (Modified OECD).
Finland	1981, 1987–2010: Income Distribution Statistics, Statistic Finland		
France	1984, 1989, 1996, 1999, 2000, 2002, 2005, 2007–2010: INSEE1990,1995: OECD1995, 1998, 2001, 2004, 2006, 2011: EU-SILC	Insee-DGI, enquêtes Revenus fiscaux 1970 à 1990; Insee-DGI, enquêtes Revenus fiscaux 1996–2000; DGFiP; Cnaf; Cnav; CCMSA, enquêtes Revenus fiscaux et sociaux 2005–2009	There is a break in data series for the EU-SILC in 2001.

(Continued)

Table 2.A1 Continued

Country	Years and original data source	Gini coefficients Publication quoted in country report	Comment or alteration to the above definitions
West-Germany	1983-2009: SOEP, calculations of the German GINI team		
East-Germany	1991-2009: SOEP, calculations of the German GINI team		Equivalent net household income.
Greece	1982, 1988, 1994, 1999: HBS; 1981, 1983-87, 1989-1993, 1996-1998, 2001-2006, 2008-2009: EU-SILC; 1995, 2000, 2007, 2010: LIS	Mitrakos and Tsakloglou (2012)	Important feature of the Greek HBS: contains data about the presumptive spending of households. Income concept: disposable income. Modified OECD scale, which gives a weight of 1.0 to the head of the household, 0.5 to all other members above 13 years old, and 0.3 to children up to the age of 13.
Hungary	1982, 1987: Hungarian Central Statistical Office income survey; 1992, 1995, 1996: Hungarian Household Panel; 1999-2009: TÁRKI Household Monitor, EU-SILC	Tóth (2005, 2010).	
Ireland	1987: ESRI survey, 1994, 2000: Living in Ireland survey, 1995, 1996: LIS, 2004-2010: EU-SILC		Equivalized disposable income.
Italy	1980-2010: The Bank of Italy's survey of household income and wealth (SHIW-HA)		Disposable household income, equivalized using OECD square root rule, weighted using household weights.
Japan	1984, 1989, 1994, 1999, 2004: CSLC; NSFIEGross income series: 1980-2010: Japan GINI team calculations, using data from CSLC, MHLW		The upper series of the figure is for gross incomes calculated from CSLC, (Comprehensive Survey on Living Conditions). The lower series is for net incomes, calculated from National Survey of Family Income and Expenditure (NSFIE). All calculations by Japan GINI team.

(*Continued*)

Table 2.A1 Continued

		Gini coefficients	
Country	Years and original data source	Publication quoted in country report	Comment or alteration to the above definitions
Korea	1990–2010: Korea National Statistics Office, Household income and expenditure survey		Data refers to urban households with 2+ members.
Latvia	1981–2010: SWID		Disposable equivalized household income.
Luxembourg	1985, 1991, 1994, 1997, 200, 2004: LIS,; 2010: PSELL3/EU-SILC		Modified OECD equivalence scale.
Lithuania	1981–2010: SWID		Disposable equivalized household income.
The Netherlands	1981, 1985, 1989–2010: IPO of DutchStatistics; LIS: 1983, 1987		Net-equivalized household income.
Poland	1983–1989: Atkinson and Micklewright (1992), 1990–1992: Szulc (2000), 1993–2010: Brzezinski *et al.*	Atkinson and Micklewright (1992), Szulc (2000), Brzezinski *et al.*, Brandolini (2007)	Before 1989: per capita incomes, then equalized household incomes. Original OECD equivalence scale, which assigns the weight of 0.7 to every adult household member beyond the first one and the weight of 0.5 to every child. Two breaks in the series: in 1993 and in 1997.
Portugal	1993–2010: ECHP, EU-SILC and communication with C. F. Rodriges		Incomes are equivalized using the OECD square root of the number of persons in the household scale.
Romania	1990–2009: NIS		
Sweden	1980–2010: Statistics Sweden (2012)		From 1980: old household definition. From 1991: new and improved household definition. Equivalent disposable income. Equivalence scale: gives a weight of 1 of a single-person household, a weight of 1.51 to a couple, an additional factor of 0.6 for other adults, 0.52 for the first child and additional weights of 0.42 for subsequent children. All realized capital gains that are taxable are included in the income concept.

(Continued)

Table 2.A1 Continued

Country	Years and original data source	Gini coefficients	
		Publication quoted in country report	Comment or alteration to the above definitions
Slovenia	1997–2010: SORS		Disposable net household income. Before 1997: there is no official data on Gini coefficients.
Slovakia	1980, 1985, 1988 Atkinson and Micklewright (1992); 1989–1992: Cornia (1994); 1993: Milanovic (1998), 1996–2002: Transmonee (2004); 2003: Transmonee (2005); 2005–2010 calculations by the GINI team of Slovakia, based on EU-SILC	Atkinson and Micklewright (1992), Cornia (1994), Milanovic (1998), Transmonee (2004), Transmonee (2005)	Unit of analysis is the person, income defined as disposable income (monetary disposable income before 1989). Household income equivalized since 2005.
United Kingdom	1980–2009: Office for National Statistics data, UK HBAI series		Net disposable household income (ETB series). GINI ROI uses McClements' scale. It is assumed that income is shared equally between all household members.
United States	1983, 1989, 1992, 2000: 2003, 2006–2009: Thomson and Smeeding (2012)	Thomson and Smeeding (2012)	Net household income, adjusted for household size differences, square root equivalence scale.

Table 2.A2 Country specific cities for poverty rates

| Country | Poverty rates | | |
	Years and original data source	Publication quoted in country report	Comment or alteration to the above definitions
Australia	1982–2009: Calculated from ABS Income Distribution Surveys and Surveys of Income and Housing, various years. 1981: LIS.		
Austria	1983, 1993, 1999: Microcensus and OECD (2011a); 1987, 1994, 1995, 1997, 2000: LIS, 2004–2010: Statistics Austria, EU-SILC.	Biffl (2008)	Microcensus: without self-employed. EU-SILC: total incomes.
Belgium	1985, 1988, 1992: SEP; 1993–2000: ECHP; 2003–2009: EU-SILC.	Horemans, J., Pintelon, O. & Vandenbroucke, P. (2011)	
Bulgaria	1998–2010: National Statistical Institute, EU-SILC.		
Canada	1980–2009: Statistics Canada.		50% of the median after-tax income
Czech Republic	1992, 1996, 2004: LIS; 2006–2010: Czech Statistical Office.		
Germany	1981, 1983, 1984, 1989, 1994, 2004, 2007: LIS; 1990, 1995, 2000, 2005: OECD, database on income distribution and poverty.		
Denmark	1980–2006: Eurostat.		
Estonia	1996, 1998: Trumm 2010, Lace 2006; 2000–2011: Statistics Estonia.	Trumm 2010, Lace 2006	
Spain	1980, 2010: LIS, 1985–1992 Canto et al (2003), 1993–2001: Barcenas & Cowell (2006); 2003–2009: EUSILC, Eurostat.	Canto et al. (2003), Barcenas & Cowell (2006)	
Finland	1981–2010: Income Distribution Statistics, Statistic Finland.		
France	1980–2010: INSEE, except: 1982, 1990, 1995: LIS.		

(Continued)

Table 2.A2 Continued

Country	Poverty rates		
	Years and original data source	Publication quoted in country report	Comment or alteration to the above definitions
West-Germany	Data from the draft report of the German government on Wealth and Poverty.		
East-Germany	Data from the draft report of the German government on Wealth and Poverty.		
Greece	1982, 1988, 1994, 1999, 2008 Eurostat and Mitrakos and Tsakloglou (2012); 1995, 2000, 2004, 2007, 2010: LIS.	Mitrakos and Tsakloglou (2012)	The poverty estimates are significantly lower than those obtained from LIS. The reason for difference is inclusion of own produced agricultural produce and house rent.
Hungary	1992, 1996, 2000: HHP/ TÁRKI Monitor; 2001–2009.		
Ireland	1987: Brian Nolan, 1994, 1997-: Living in Ireland, 2004–2010 EU-SILC, except 1995, 1996: LIS.		
Italy	1980-2010: The Bank of Italy's survey of household income and wealth. (SHIW-HA), Italian GINI team calculations.		
Japan	1984, 1989, 1994, 1999, 2004: calculations of the GINI team of Japan, using microdata of NSFIE.		50% of median hh income (this is the official Japan publication for relative poverty).
Korea	1990–2010: Korea National Statistics Office, Household income and expenditure survey.		Long series only available for urban hholds with 2+ members.
The Netherlands	1983, 1987: LIS, other years: calculations of the GINI team of The Netherlands.		
Lithuania	2000: Trumm 2010, Lace 2006; 2005–2010: Statistics Lithuania.	Trumm 2010, Lace 2006	
Luxembourg	LIS:1985, 1991, 1994, 1997, 2000, 2004; 2010: PSELL3/ EU-SILC) data, computation of the GINI team of Luxembourg.		

(Continued)

Table 2.A2 Continued

Country	Years and original data source	Publication quoted in country report	Comment or alteration to the above definitions
		Poverty rates	
Latvia	1996–2002: Trumm 2010, Lace 2006; 2004–2010: Latvijas Statistika.	Trumm Lace 2006	
Poland	1986, 1992: LIS, 1993–2010: Brzeziski *et al.*		
Portugal	1993–2010: EU-SILC, communication with C.F Rodriges.		
Romania	1995, 1997: LIS; 2000–2010: MLFSP 2010, NIS data.		
Sweden	1981, 1987: LIS, 1991–2010: Socialstyrelsen (2010).		
Slovenia	1997–2010: SORS.		
Slovakia	1992, 1996: LIS, EU-SILC: 2005–2011.		
United Kingdom	1980–1995: FES UK, 1995–1997: FRS GB, 1998–2010: FRS UK.		
United States	1980–2009: Smeeding and Thompson (2012); DeNavas-Walt, *et al.* (2012).	Smeeding and Thompson (2012); DeNavas-Walt, *et al.* (2012)	

ANNEX 2

COMPARING INEQUALITY MEASURES IN GINI DATABASE TO THOSE OF THE OECD AND OF THE LIS DATABASES

OECD and GINI comparisons (for Gini coefficients)

- In cases where we have data from both sources, the indicator generally shows a similar pattern. However, there are some exceptions: in the Czech Republic (for 1992,1996, 2002, 2006–2008) and Italy (for 1993, 1995, 2000, 2004, 2008) the OECD inequality indicator shows substantially higher values than the GINI database. There are also substantial deviations for other countries, but for fewer years: for Belgium (for 1995 and 2000), Greece (for 1994 and 2004), Japan (1994) and the Netherlands (1981 and 1985).

- Also, there are many other minor differences in the values in the majority of the given countries, especially in Denmark (for 1985–2007) and Sweden (for 1980–2008) and Hungary (for 1995, 2000, 2005, 2007 and 2009) where our database shows higher values, and in the Netherlands (for 1989–1999), Austria (for 2004, 2006 and 2007), Spain (1985, 2000) where the OECD indicator has higher values. In the case of Finland, the trends shown from the GINI database seem to be steeper than the one shown by the OECD database. This comes from the fact that in the first half of the period (for 1987–1992), we have lower values, and higher values for the second half (for 1999, 2000, and 2007).
- The highest level of coherence between GINI and OECD databases could be traced in the case of Australia (for 1997), France (for 1984), Germany (for 1983), USA (for 2000).

LIS and GINI comparisons (for Gini coefficients)

- In cases where we have data from both sources, the indicator generally shows a similar pattern. However, there are some exceptions. For the years 1996 in the Czech Republic, 1992 in Denmark, 2004 in Greece, 1986 in Poland, 2010 in Spain, 1992 in Sweden (due to higher coverage of capital incomes in the Socialstyrelsen data), 1993, 1998, 2004 in Italy, the LIS inequality indicator shows substantially higher values than our database.
- Also, there are many other minor differences in the values in the majority of the given countries, especially in the United States, The Netherlands, Spain, Finland, Denmark and Belgium, but also in Canada, Hungary, Ireland, Luxembourg and Slovenia.
- The lowest degree of deviation could be traced in the case of Austria, Romania and Slovakia.

CHAPTER 3

···

AUSTRALIA: INEQUALITY AND PROSPERITY AND THEIR IMPACTS IN A RADICAL WELFARE STATE

···

PETER WHITEFORD*

1. INTRODUCTION

···

OVER the past two decades Australian households have enjoyed the second highest increase in average real disposable income in the OECD (OECD, 2011).[1] But, over the same period, income inequality increased—while the poorest 10 per cent of Australians experienced the 5th greatest increase in their incomes, the richest decile had the largest increase of any OECD country (OECD, 2011). Rising inequality and rising prosperity are therefore characteristic of Australia's recent experience.

While Australia is not currently considered to be a particularly low inequality country, this has not always been the case. Egalitarianism has long been a significant issue in Australian political debate. Garnaut (2002, pp. 12–13) argues that the Australian concern for equity lasted the entire 20th Century, and that no important policy change is feasible if it violates broadly supported conceptions of equity, whichever political party is in power.

Since the early 1970s—and accelerating in the 1980s—Australian economic policy has been subject to wide-ranging reforms by successive governments. These included reducing high protective tariffs on imported goods and removing non-tariff barriers, floating the Australian dollar, deregulating the financial services sector, increasing efficiency between federal and state governments, privatizing government-owned industries, deregulating the labour market, and reforming the tax system, including introducing a Goods and Services

* I am grateful for comments from Rob Bray, Francis Castles, Matt Cowgill, Murray Goot, Gerry Redmond and Sue Regan. I am responsible for any errors.

[1] Australian income growth up to 2008 was only exceeded by Ireland, which started from a much lower level. Moreover, between 2008 and 2010 household disposable income in Ireland dropped by close to 10 per cent, compared to 1.5 per cent in Australia.

Tax (a VAT) and cutting marginal income tax rates (Freebairn, 1998). These reforms are often seen to reflect a newly dominant neo-liberal agenda (Quiggin, 1999), or what in Australia has been called 'economic rationalism' (Pusey, 1991).

The benefits of these reforms took time to appear. Gregory (1993) labelled the period 1970 to 1990 as 'the disappointing decades': from the mid 1970s to 1990 Australian real wages stagnated, unemployment increased fourfold and the male full-time employment-population ratio fell by 25 per cent. Gregory (1993) also pointed to the widening dispersion of male wages, job losses from the middle of the earnings distribution and job growth mainly for those with low earnings. Some family changes such as the growth in lone parenthood reinforced these negative trends, and Australia developed an extremely high concentration of joblessness in households with no adults in paid employment.

Since the 1990s, this situation has reversed, and Frijters and Gregory (2006) more recently wrote of a new 'golden age' in the Australian economy. This has turned Australia into one of the fastest growing advanced economies in the world (Goot, 2013). Following a fall in GDP in 1990–91, Australia has enjoyed uninterrupted economic growth, accelerating after the late 1990s (Edwards, 2006).

For most developed countries, the recent Global Financial Crisis (GFC) resulted in the steepest decline in economic activity since the Great Depression. Australia, Poland and Korea were the only OECD countries to escape negative real GDP growth in the 2008–9 year[2] with respective GDP growth of 1.4 per cent, 1.8 per cent, and 0.2 per cent,[3] and since then real GDP has grown by more than 8 per cent.

Indicative of the changes in Australia's economic performance, Figure 3.1 shows Federal Reserve Bank of St Louis estimates that between the early 1950s and 1970, Australian GDP per capita in purchasing power terms fluctuated at around 95 per cent of the US level, but after 1970 it fell to around 85 per cent of the US level and fluctuated at between 80 and 85 per cent until 2000. In contrast, between 2000 and 2010, Australian GDP per capita rose from 81 per cent to 106 per cent of US levels, although in part this reflects a slowing of GDP growth in the USA after 2001.

Despite this remarkable turnaround in economic fortunes, Garnaut (2002) notes that 'the history of the period after 1983 was and is seen by some as a comprehensive retreat from the values and policies through which Australians in the early Federation had primarily defined their nationality' (2002, p. 7). A strong element of the criticisms made of this economic reform agenda is its perceived impact on income disparities, with arguments that overall the record of the Labor Government in 1980s even compared unfavourably with that of the Thatcher government in UK in the comparable period.[4]

[2] The Australian fiscal stimulus package was the third highest in the OECD over the period 2008 to 2010; only the USA and Korea spent more on discretionary stimulus (OECD, 2011). The spending component (compared to tax cuts) of the fiscal stimulus was higher in Australia than any other OECD country.

[3] A number of non-member OECD countries managed relatively strong growth throughout the GFC. Among the significant non-member OECD countries in 2009, China and India had the strongest performing economies with annual growth of 8.7 per cent and 5.7 per cent. These countries are amongst Australia's most important destinations for exports.

[4] See Whiteford (1994) for a summary and critique of these arguments.

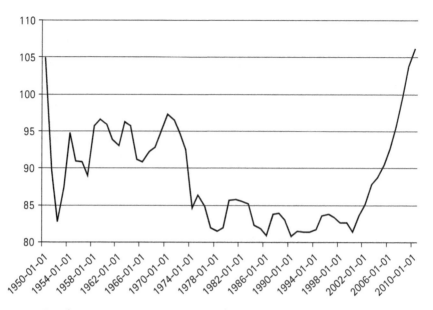

FIGURE 3.1 Purchasing power parity converted to GDP per capita relative to the United States, at current prices for Australia (USA=100)

Source: FRED Economic data, <http://research.stlouisfed.org/fred2/categories/32291>, 23 January 2013.

2. INEQUALITY AND ITS DRIVERS

The Australian Bureau of Statistics (ABS) has conducted household income surveys since the late 1960s, although only surveys since 1982 are comprehensive and available for public analysis. There have been major changes in methodology over time, giving rise to diverse estimates of inequality.

Recent changes are most significant. In 2007–8, the ABS revised its household income statistics following the adoption of new international standards.[5] In summary, these changes mean that measured income is more comprehensive and better captures the full extent of income inequality. However, increases in income levels and in income inequality in recent years are exaggerated, although this means that inequality was higher in previous years than previously measured.

---

[5] Implementation of the broader income measure in 2007–8 resulted in an $85 increase in mean weekly gross household income, compared to the previous definition, a difference of roughly 5 per cent. The inclusions affected 3.4m households in total (43 per cent). Most of the impact was on employment income, which increased by $89 per week on average. The inclusion of non-cash employment benefits and bonuses had the most impact ($43 and $32 per week respectively). In 2007–8, the Gini coefficient on the new basis was 0.331, which is higher than that compiled on the former basis (0.317). This reflects that most of the changes have been at the higher end of the income distribution i.e. the fourth and highest quintiles.

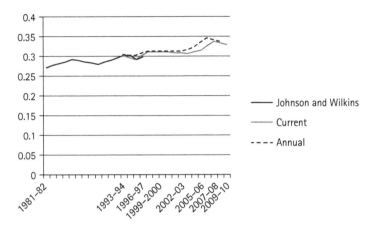

FIGURE 3.2 Longer run trends in income inequality in Australia, 1981–2 to 2009–10
Gini Coefficient

Source: Johnson and Wilkins (2006); ABS (various years).

Figure 3.2 shows inequality trends estimated by Johnson and Wilkins (2006) from 1981–2 to 1996–7, and official ABS figures from 1994–5 to 2009–10.[6] Despite differences in income measures and equivalence scales, the long run trend is clear. There are periods in which inequality fell, but overall the Gini coefficient rose from around 0.27–0.29 in the 1980s, to 0.30–0.31 in the 1990s and early 2000s, and 0.32–s0.34 in the mid and late 2000s.[7]

Figure 3.3 shows that real mean equivalized incomes rose by around 0.5 per cent per year between 1981–2 and 1996–7, with falls between 1989–90 and 1993–4 and between 1994–5 and 1995–6 (Johnson and Wilkins, 2006). Since 1996–7 real mean incomes grew by at least 2 per cent per year up until 2002, then by between five and eight per cent per year up until 2007–8, after which they declined by about 1.5 per cent. Trends in real median incomes follow a simi-lar pattern, with lower increases after 2003.

Figure 3.4 shows trends in real incomes at different decile points from 1994–5 to 2002–3, from 2002–3 to 2007–8 and between the latest two surveys. In the first period, real incomes grew least for the lowest decile, but averaged between 10 and 15 per cent for other income groups. After 2002–3, real incomes grew by between 25 per cent at P10 and 36 per cent at P90, with households between P20 and P50 doing better than those just above the median. Following the GFC, real incomes fell slightly or remained unchanged for most of the income distribution, with a small real increase for P10 and minor changes at P60 and above.

---

[6] Both series are based on current income recorded in the surveys, although the equivalence scales differ—Johnson and Wilkins (2006) use the square root of family size, while the ABS uses the 'modified OECD equivalence scale'.

[7] A further source of information on income inequality trends is the Household, Income and Labour Dynamics in Australia (HILDA) Survey, a household-based panel study which began in 2001. In broad terms the series are quite similar, although the ABS surveys show somewhat higher levels of inequality over most of the period since 2001.

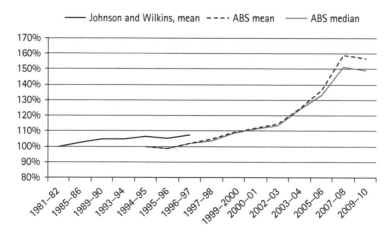

FIGURE 3.3 Trends in real mean and median income unit incomes in Australia, early 1980s to late 2000s

Johnson and Wilkins: 1981–2=100; ABS: 1993–4=100

Source: Calculated from ABS Surveys of Income and Housing and Johnson and Wilkins (2006).

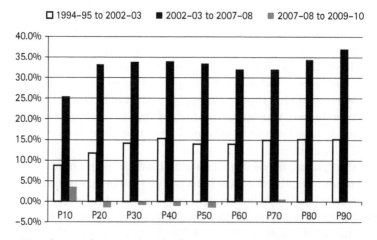

FIGURE 3.4 Trends in real incomes at decile points in Australia, mid-1990s to late 2000s

Cumulative percentage change in period

Source: Calculated from ABS Surveys of Income and Housing.

Trends in Income Poverty

Australia has no official poverty line. Since the 1980s, Australian poverty studies have tended to use 50 per cent of the median equivalent income as the relative poverty line. Figure 3.5 shows estimates of trends in poverty headcounts between 1981–2 and 2009–10 (Redmond,

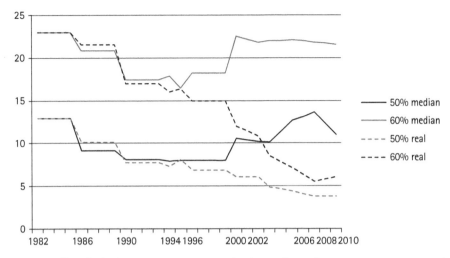

FIGURE 3.5 Trends in income poverty rates in Australia, 1981–2 to 2009–10 per cent of income units in poverty

Source: Calculated from ABS Income Distribution Surveys and Surveys of Income and Housing, various years.

Patulny and Whiteford, 2013), using a 50 per cent and a 60 per cent of median income poverty line, and the same lines in 1981–2 held constant in real terms.[8]

Relative poverty fell over the 1980s, was fairly stable in the early 1990s, but then started to rise, before falling at the end of the period, with both the rise and the subsequent fall being greater at the 50 per cent of median income level than at the 60 per cent level. Since 2000, the 'at-risk-of-poverty rate' using the 60 per cent of median income line has remained around 22 per cent, while the poverty rate using the 50 per cent line has varied between 10 per cent and 14 per cent. Poverty rates using the 50 per cent line were lowest in the mid 1990s at around 8 per cent and highest in 2007–8 at around 14 per cent.

Poverty levels where the poverty line is held constant in real terms initially show a similar trend, falling up to 1990, then flattening out, but continuing to fall from 1996, so that by the end of the period the proportion of the population estimated to be in poverty ranges from 4 per cent to 6 per cent depending on the line used.

The main explanation for these trends flows from the earlier picture of trends in median incomes. Real median income increased very little between the 1980s and the mid 1990s, so reductions in relative poverty reflect the fact that the poverty line did not increase in real terms. In contrast, after 1996 real median incomes rose very strongly—by around 50 per cent in real terms, so that progress against poverty became much more difficult.

There are broad similarities in trends between the poverty rates for older people and the overall population, but the fluctuations are more marked, and poverty rates tend to be higher except in the mid 1990s. Trends in poverty rates among families with children are

---

[8] Incomes are equivalized using the modified OECD equivalence scale. The income measure is current income of income units, and using a consistent measure over time, i.e. stripping out the effects of the ABS improvements to income measures, as discussed in the text.

similar—falls in relative poverty over the 1980s, a flattening out in the early 1990s, followed by an increase.

In summary, relative income poverty rates fell during the 1980s, but in the context of close to stagnant median incomes. Relative poverty rates rose between the mid 1990s and 2007–8, but in the very different context of rapidly rising real median incomes.

Debt and Wealth Inequalities

Total debt rose from around 40 per cent of disposable income in the late 1970s to around 60 per cent in the mid 1990s, but then the rate of growth accelerated to reach 156 per cent of household disposable income in 2007. Debt has subsequently fallen slightly to around 150 per cent of household disposable income.

Most household debt is housing-related, with the share having increased from around 70 per cent in the 1970s and 1980s to over 80 per cent in the 1990s, and is currently around 90 per cent. Home-ownership rates in Australia have been high throughout most of the post-war period, climbing from 53.4 per cent in 1947 to around 70 per cent by 1960 and remaining around this rate for the past five decades.

While debt has grown, so have assets. Total assets grew from 390 per cent of disposable income to 850 per cent in 2007, before falling back to around 710 per cent on the most recent figures. While housing remains the largest share of assets, financial assets have grown from 30 per cent to 42 per cent of total assets.

The rapid growth in assets has meant that household net worth (assets minus debt) has grown significantly. The ratio of household net worth to real household disposable income roughly doubled between 1977 and 2007, but then fell significantly at the time of the GFC; there was then a sharp but brief increase, before the ratio of household net worth to income fell again.

According to the 2012 *Credit Suisse Global Wealth Report*, in US dollar terms, Australian wealth per adult in 2012, at USD355,000, was the second highest in the world—after Switzerland and ahead of Norway. Its median wealth of USD 194,000 is the highest in the world. The level of real assets per adult in Australia is now the second highest in the world after Norway, reflecting high urban real estate prices. Compared to the rest of the world, very few Australians have a net worth that is less than USD10,000. This reflects factors such as relatively low credit card and student loan debt. The proportion of those with wealth above USD 100,000 is the highest of any country—eight times the world average.

When households are ranked by net worth, wealth is much more unequally distributed than disposable income, and increasingly so—the Q5 to Q1 ratio increasing from around 42 to 1 in 2003–4 to 62 to 1 in 2009–10. A very different picture appears, however, when households are ranked by disposable income—that is when the joint distribution of net worth and income is considered. Overall, when ranked by disposable income the Q5 to Q1 ratio for net worth is around 3.2 to 1; which is less unequal than disposable income. The main reason is that owner-occupied housing accounts for about half of all net worth, and the Q5 to Q1 ratio for housing is only around 2 to 1. This reflects the life-cycle accumulation of assets, so that many low-income older people own their homes outright, while younger and higher income groups are still acquiring assets and thus have more substantial debts.

While the distribution of net worth ranked by disposable income is less unequal than the distribution of disposable income, there is evidence of growing inequality since 2003–4. Two factors seem important—an increase in disparities of financial assets and reduced disparities in liabilities, which therefore reduce the net worth of higher income groups less than in the past.

Inequality Drivers

The single most important source of household income is wages and salaries—in 2009–10 around 61 per cent of all households had wages and salaries as their main income source (ABS, 2011). For families of working age, earnings (including self-employment) account for more than 90 per cent of all market income (Whiteford and Redmond, forthcoming).

In the period 1982 to 1997–8, Johnson and Wilkins (2006) found that approximately half the growth in private income inequality was due to changes to the distribution of income unit types, labour force status and demographic characteristics. However, changes in labour force status (i.e. shifts between employment, unemployment and non-participation) by themselves acted to increase market income inequality by the full amount attributed to all the characteristics examined. Changes to the income unit composition of the population also increased income inequality, while changes in the distribution of demographic characteristics, such as age, education and migrant background offset the effect of changes in income unit composition.

Whiteford and Redmond (forthcoming) point to the importance of employment and earnings for trends in inequality among those of working age. From 1982 to the mid 1990s, female earnings were the most unequally distributed income source within the overall distribution, as women with earnings tended to be the partners of men with higher earnings. Since the mid 1990s, female earnings growth has tended to reduce inequality, primarily because the growth benefited lower-income families. Male earnings inequality increased over the first half of the period and peaked around 2000, after which its contribution declined. Overall, market income inequality among people of working age peaked in 2000 and started to decline thereafter, with the main reason for this being earnings growth in the lower half of the income distribution, mainly associated with higher employment.

Austen and Redmond (2008) analyse trends in women's incomes relative to men, finding that in 1982 women of working age received 31 per cent of all income of people in this group, but by 2006 this had increased to 38 per cent; virtually all of this increase had occurred by 1995–6, while in the decade to 2005–6 women's share of total income changed little. Whiteford and Redmond (forthcoming) find this was due to divergent trends in male and female earnings in the first period. Between 1982 and 1995–6, real earnings for men fell in the second to seventh deciles of working age households, so that in aggregate real male earnings in 1995–6 were only 2 per cent higher than in 1982. Men in the third decile had aggregate real earnings that were 30 per cent lower in 1995–6 than in 1982, and most others below the median were 15 per cent worse off in real terms. This was an employment effect rather than a wage rate effect. In the same period, overall real earnings for working-age women increased by 37 per cent, with the increases being greatest towards the bottom of the house-hold income distribution, largely the result of greater hours of employment. The narrow-ing gap between aggregate male and female earnings was thus due to lower employment among men and higher employment among women. In contrast, in the period 1995–6 to 2007–8 average real male earnings increased by 47 per cent, while average real female earn-ings increased by 54 per cent, so the gap remained stable.

Income from property and investments shows wide variations in its contribution to inequality, being lower than most of the main income sources up to 2003, and then increas-ing dramatically to be the most unequally distributed income source in 2007–8. Close to 40 per cent of investment and property income is held by the richest decile. Whiteford and Redmond (forthcoming) find that very high incomes show much greater volatility in lev-els of inequality. However, income from property and investments increased from around 6.5 per cent of disposable income of working age families in 1982 to around 10 per cent in 2007–8, so even though it is very unequally distributed its low weight in overall household income means that it has less of an effect on overall income inequality than changes in the distribution of earnings.

A further factor is trends in inequality among people 65 years and over. The relative incomes of older people have increased significantly—until the late 1990s the average equivalized income of households with a head 65 years and over were around 60 per cent of those of the total population, but since the late 1990s this ratio has risen to around 70 per cent. This was associated with a very large increase in inequality among older people. The Gini coefficient for couples aged 65 years and over increased from 0.236 in 2000–1 to 0.339 in 2007–8, or from about 75 per cent of the level for the whole population to more than 100 per cent (ABS, various years). For single older people the increase in inequality was not quite so dramatic but still very large—from 0.231 in 2000–1 to 0.298 in 2007–8, then falling to 0.259 in 2009–10 (ABS various years). Rising inequality among older peo-ple appears to be related to trends in capital income, with very high-income people over 65 benefiting most.

An important component of the Australian population is indigenous. In 2011, there were nearly 550,000 people or around 2.5 per cent of the population who identified as being of Aboriginal and/or Torres Strait Islander origin and counted in the Census. Indigenous households are over-represented by two to one in the lowest income quintile. Between 1991 and 2001 the average equivalized gross income of indigenous households fell from 64 per cent to 62 per cent of that of non-indigenous households, but remained stable between 2001 and 2006 (ABS, Cat. No. 4713.0, various years). Indigenous people living in very remote areas are even worse off, with average income being only 43 per cent of those of non-indige-nous households in the same area.

Earnings Disparities

Australia's industrial relations institutions (discussed below) appear to have had a major influence on earnings inequality in Australia. Even in the late 1990s, Australia had a less unequal distribution of earnings than most OECD countries. This was associated with relatively high minimum wages, a narrow gender wage gap and a smaller share of low pay than many other countries. The most likely explanation for this was the legacy of

Australia's wage fixing institutions, which continued to compress wage differentials. However, since the mid 1990s wage disparities have widened, so that Australia has moved to the middle of OECD countries in terms of rankings. Nevertheless, disparities in earnings in Australia are more similar to those in European countries than they are to the USA.

In 1985 Australia had the highest minimum wage in the OECD relative to the median (65 per cent), whereas in 2011 it was the sixth highest (54 per cent).[9] In 2010 the 90/10 ratio for full-time male and female workers was the sixteenth lowest ratio of 28 OECD countries, a considerable fall down the OECD rankings, from 11th lowest in the 1990s.

Between 1975 and 2010, the minimum wage rose by 10 per cent in real terms, and the 10th percentile wage rose by 14 per cent. Real wage growth was much greater at higher income levels—the median rose by 38 per cent in real terms and the mean by 50 per cent; while the 90th percentile wage was 72 per cent higher in real terms.

As a result, since 1975 the 90/10 ratio for full-time non-managerial employees has increased from around 2 to 1 to just over 3 to 1. The increase in inequality was slightly greater in the top half of the earnings distribution than below the median.

Employment, Unemployment and Underemployment

In addition to widening wage disparities, and in common with many other OECD countries, the Australian labour market deteriorated seriously from the 1970s onward. Figure 3.6 shows trends in unemployment from 1978 to 2012: the recessions of the early 1980s and 1990s are clearly observed. After its peak in 1993, unemployment declined, and by February 2008 unemployment was just below 4 per cent, its lowest level since 1974. Unemployment then started to increase, reaching 5.8 per cent in August 2009 before declining to 5 per cent in December 2010, but increasing to 5.4 per cent by late 2012. While the increase in unemployment since the beginning of 2008 has been significant, this is well below the increases in most other OECD countries.

The Australian workforce is characterized by a very high share of part-time work. In 2012, around 30 per cent of total employment was part-time, 45 per cent for women and 16 per cent for men. Seventy per cent of part-time employment is female, but male part-time employment has doubled since 1990.

Reflecting high levels of part-time employment, Australia also has a high level of underemployment—people who want to work longer hours than they do. In fact, Australia has the highest head count rate of underemployment in the OECD (OECD, 2012), with the result that labour force under-utilization in Australia is close to the OECD average. There was a very large increase in underemployment in the recession of the early 1990s, reaching a peak for women of close to 10 per cent of the employed labour force. There was a slight downward trend in unemployment after 2003, but a sharp increase at the time of the GFC.

---

[9] Australia did not have a statutory national minimum wage until 2006, so this estimate is based on the lowest minimum rate contained in awards prior to this date.

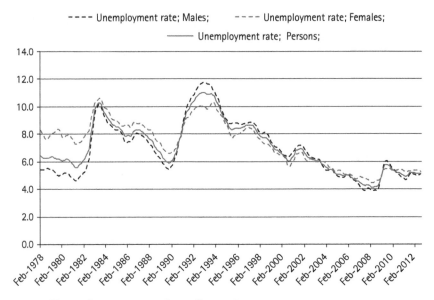

FIGURE 3.6 Unemployment rate, Australia, 1978 to 2012

Source: Australian Bureau of Statistics, Labour Force Survey.

Australia has also seen a growth in casual employment. Casual employees are those who are not entitled to paid holiday or sick leave but who may receive a higher rate of hourly pay to compensate for this.[10] In addition, casual employees do not qualify for protection from unfair dismissal and have no right to notice of employment termination. The proportion of casual employees has grown over the last two decades from 17 per cent in 1992 to 20 per cent in 2009 (ABS, 2010).

There is another area in which Australia's employment performance is very weak. On standard measures of individual unemployment, Australia ranks 7th lowest in the OECD and is 6 percentage points below the OECD average. When looking at the share of working age people living in jobless households, Australia is the 5th highest in the OECD and more than 4 percentage points above the OECD average. For jobless households with children, Australia is the 5th highest in the OECD and 5.5 percentage points above average. The ratio of family to individual joblessness in Australia is more than twice the OECD average (Whiteford, 2009). To a significant extent, the concentration of household joblessness among families with children is related to low employment rates among lone parents.

Overall, the combined impact of changes in earnings and employment status has been a significant widening in earned income disparities. For full-time workers, earnings gaps have increased, but more importantly, the share of all employment that is full-time has fallen from 85 per cent to 70 per cent, with a concomitant increase in part-time work as well as casual employment. However, it has been the concentration of joblessness in families where no one has paid work that appears to be the major contributor to overall earnings

---

[10] Casual loadings are set by industry awards and workplace agreements and may very between 23 per cent and 25 per cent.

inequality. As noted above, a full-time worker at the 90th percentile earns about three times as much as a full-time worker at the 10th percentile. However, a family at the 90th percentile of the distribution for working-age households had earnings in 2009–10 that were 50 times greater than households at the 10th percentile (Whiteford and Redmond, forthcoming) because earnings in low income households are negligible—around $2,000 a year.

Educational Inequality

Educational attainment is a major influence on socio-economic circumstances in Australia (ABS, 2012a). In 2010, people aged 20–64 years were more likely to be employed if they had attained Year 12 (school leaving qualification) than those who had not (81 per cent compared with 72 per cent). The gap is maintained throughout most of the life course.

Young adults are more likely to have attained Year 12 if they live in major cities compared with inner or outer regional areas and remote or very remote areas. There is considerable variation across states and territories, with the proportion ranging from 59 per cent in the Northern Territory to 86 per cent in the Australian Capital Territory. Indigenous people have far lower rates of Year 12 attainment than non-Indigenous Australians. In 2008, less than one-third of young Indigenous people had attained Year 12 compared with three-quarters of non-Indigenous 20–24 year olds. Between 2002 and 2008, there was a small, but not statistically significant, increase in the proportions of Indigenous people aged 20–24 years with Year 12 (from 28 per cent to 31 per cent).

People who have attained Year 12 are more likely to be working in 'white collar' jobs than those who had not. People aged 20–64 years who have personal gross weekly income in the highest quintile are far more likely to have attained Year 12 (70 per cent) than those who had not (30 per cent). Leigh (2008) estimates that the increase in hourly wages from raising educational attainment by one year is in the order of 8–11 per cent, with the largest gains being for grade 12 completion and Bachelor degree completion. When participation effects are taken into account, the benefits of education and training are larger still, with the annual earnings increase from completing year 12 estimated to be 30 per cent.

Over recent decades there has been a significant increase in the level of educational attainment (ABS, 2011). Between 1984 and 1992, the proportion of students continuing through to Year 12 increased from 45 per cent to 77 per cent. Since decreasing slightly in the early 1990s, the apparent retention rate[11] remained relatively stable (at around 75 per cent) from 2002 to 2008, before rising to 78 per cent in 2010—83 per cent for female students and 73 per cent for males.

Despite the increase in educational attainment, there is a good deal of concern about educational inequalities (Review of Funding for Schooling, 2011). Results from PISA for 2009 show that Australia has a higher degree of performance inequality than the OECD average. In the reading literacy domain, the gap between Australian students from the highest and

---

[11] The apparent retention rate is calculated by dividing the number of full-time students in Year 12 by the number of full-time students in the base year and converting the figure into a percentage.

lowest quartiles was equivalent to almost three years of schooling. Year 12 attainment rates for students from low and medium socio-economic backgrounds are 56 and 62 per cent respectively, compared to 75 per cent for students from high socio-economic backgrounds. In 2010, the university access rate for students from low socio-economic backgrounds was around half (17 per cent) that of students from high socio-economic backgrounds (35 per cent) (Review of Funding for Schooling, 2011).

3. SOCIAL IMPACTS

Material Deprivation

Azpitarte (2012) measures social exclusion in the domains of material resources, employment, education and skills, health and disability, social connection, community quality and personal safety, with individual scores varying between 0 and 7. Between 2001 and 2010 income poverty remained stable at around 20 per cent, but the level of marginal exclusion (a score between 1 and 2) fell from 25 per cent in 2001 to 18.6 per cent in 2008, rising to 20 per cent in 2010. The rate of deep exclusion (scores above 2) dropped from 7 per cent to 5 per cent in 2006, and remained stable thereafter. Rates of deep exclusion are higher for women (5.5 per cent) than for men (4 per cent). Around 10 per cent of Aboriginal Australians are deeply excluded, a rate which changed little over the decade. Deep exclusion is higher for those with long-term health conditions or disability but fell from around 20 per cent to 14 per cent over the period. Rates of deep exclusion are high for those who have not completed year 12, above 10 per cent for most of the decade. Public housing tenants show very high but variable levels of deep exclusion—dropping from 25 to 15 per cent between 2001 and 2008, and rising to 20 per cent thereafter.

Health

Although the overall level of health of Australians is relatively high, there are significant disparities in health outcomes. Relating trends in health outcomes to trends in inequality is not straightforward, as inequality trends are measured using household incomes and the most common measure used in Australian studies of health impacts is locational. People who live in poorer areas have worse health, higher levels of disease risk factors and lower use of preventative health services than people from more advantaged areas. Around 16 per cent of Australians rate their health as only fair or poor but almost 25 per cent of people in the most disadvantaged areas do, compared with 10 per cent in the least disadvantaged areas. There are clear gradients for arthritis, ischaemic heart disease, and diabetes across quintiles of disadvantage, as well as for cancer, mental and behavioural problems, and disability (ABS, 2012b).

Gaps in life expectancy at birth are estimated to be 11.3 years and 9.5 years for Aboriginal and Torres Strait Islander males and females respectively compared to total males and females. Sixty-two per cent of Indigenous Australians live in areas in the bottom two quintiles of socio-economic disadvantage, and those living there are 1.4 times more likely to report their health as fair or poor compared with non-Indigenous Australians in these areas.

The prevalence of health risk factors varies with socio-economic disadvantage. In 2007–8, people living in the most disadvantaged areas were more likely to be current smokers (30 per cent) compared to those in the least disadvantaged areas (12 per cent). One-third of people in the most disadvantaged areas were categorized as obese compared to 19 per cent in the least disadvantaged areas, with a clear gradient as levels of disadvantage increased. In contrast, the proportion of people who consume alcohol at a level considered risky to health is slightly lower in the most disadvantaged areas (10 per cent) compared with the least disadvantaged areas (13 per cent).

Turrell and Mathers (2001) analyse trends between the mid 1980s and the mid 1990s in mortality across areas ranked by levels of disadvantage. Their results show complex trends by age and sex and causes of mortality. For most age groups and mortality types, age-standardized mortality rates fell over this period.[12] As with studies elsewhere, widening inequality was found to be due to greater declines in mortality among higher SES areas than among lower SES areas, with the exception of diabetes mellitus and asthma/emphysema among both sexes and lung cancer among women, where there were actual increases in mortality among the most disadvantaged quintile.

Clarke and Leigh (2011) carried out the first Australian study analysing the relationship between household income and longevity. They find that the relative risk of mortality between the poorest and richest income quintile translated into a life expectancy gap (at age twenty) of six years. Having more than twelve years of education was also associated with a significantly lower risk of death, translating into a gap of 4.6 years of life. Area-based measures of socio-economic disadvantage, however, were smaller (2.6 years) and not significant after controlling for individual-level factors.

Punishment and Crime

Over the last fifteen years, Australia, like most OECD countries, has experienced a continuous rise in its prison population, with the imprisonment rate roughly doubling since the early 1980s. At 129 prisoners per 100,000 population, Australia in 2008 had the 12th highest prison rate out of 30 OECD countries. There are very large differences in imprisonment rates by states. In 2011, the Northern Territory had the highest imprisonment rate at 762 prisoners per 100,000 adult population (or around the same as the USA, although the Northern Territory has a very small population).

The imprisonment of Indigenous Australians is a major issue of concern. In June 2009, the age standardized imprisonment rate for Indigenous prisoners was 1,891 per 100,000 adult Indigenous population compared to 136 non-Indigenous prisoners per 100,000 adult non-Indigenous population. Twenty-five per cent of all prisoners in Australia in 2009 were Indigenous (ABS, 2012).

---

[12] The exceptions were for deaths due to drug dependence and suicide among 15 to 24 year olds, diabetes among 25 to 64 year olds and suicide among men aged 25 to 64 years, as well as for deaths due to respiratory diseases among males and females aged 25 to 64 years.

The rise in imprisonment rates appears to be related to policy choices, as crime rates have shown declines over the last decade. Since 1996, the rate of assault in Australia has been far higher than any other type of violent crime. At its peak in 2007, the assault rate was 840 per 100,000 persons, but by 2010, the rate fell to 766 victims per 100,000. The homicide rate is 1.2 per 100,000 people (compared to an OECD average of 2.1). The rate of sexual assault has been declining since 2006. Since 2004, robbery has declined, while the rate of motor vehicle theft has been falling since 2001 at a rapid rate. In 2010, the rate of unlawful entry with intent was 971 per 100,000, an overall decline of 56 per cent since 1996. Overall, the number of property crimes has decreased across all locations since 2005.

The level of crime experienced by Aboriginal and Torres Strait Islander peoples is also very high in comparison to the rest of the Australian population. In 2008, around one-quarter of Indigenous people aged 15 years and over reported being a victim of physical or threatened violence in the last 12 months, and one in seven (15 per cent) had experienced at least one episode of physical violence in the previous year (ABS 2012).

4. Political and Cultural Impacts

Political Participation

In Australia, voting is compulsory and, at 95 per cent, Australia has the highest turn-out in the OECD (compared to an average of 70 per cent), remaining a little higher than Belgium and Luxembourg, which also have compulsory voting. Voter turnout for Federal Parliamentary elections has generally been very high since the 1970s. There was some variation over this period, with an increase in the mid-1980s and a decline between 2007 and 2010, but varying between 93 per cent and 96 per cent over this period.

Over the period since the 1980s, a number of minor parties have emerged and then shrunk. One Nation, a right-wing nationalist party founded in 1996 gained more than 22 per cent of the state-wide vote, translating into 11 of 89 seats, in the 1998 Queensland election. Federally, the party peaked at the 1998 election at 9 per cent of the nationwide vote, electing one Senator. The party has never approached these heights again, and while it nominally still exists it attracts a negligible percentage of the vote. There have also been a number of parties which could be regarded as extreme right-wing, but their support level has been negligible.

Trust in Institutions and Social Trust

Trust in institutions has declined in Australia over the last 30 years, particularly between 1983 and 1995, most for the federal government, the legal system, the press, churches, the public sector and major Australian companies (Papadakis, 1999), but not including trade unions (Reed and Blunsdon, 2002). Blunsdon and Reed (2010) found that confidence in institutions declined dramatically from 1983 to 1995. It increased slightly by 2005 but this increase was not statistically significant, and confidence remained low compared to the 1980s.

Between 1983 and 2005 general social trust displayed different patterns, declining slightly from 1983 to 1995, but by 2005 trust was back at 1983 levels (Blunsdon and Reed, 2010). The greatest decline in confidence was for banks and financial institutions during a period of financial deregulation. The period of the greatest decline in trust in institutions coincided with the period of slowly increasing inequality and slowly increasing real incomes. The period of more rapidly rising real incomes and faster increases in inequality coincided with a stabilization in levels of institutional trust. What may be relevant here is trends in market income inequality, which increased most significantly between the early 1980s and the mid 1990s and stabilized thereafter.

Attitudes to Redistribution and the Welfare State

The proportion of Australians who think that it should be the responsibility of the government to provide health care for the sick was broadly stable between 1985 and 2006, at around 90 per cent (Bechert and Quandt, 2009). Respondents who think that it should be the responsibility of the government to provide a decent standard of living for the unemployed were a much lower percentage and more variable—rising from around 55 per cent in 1985 to a little over 60 per cent in 1996, before falling again to around 50 per cent in 2006. There was also a decline from 50 per cent to 40 per cent in the proportion agreeing that it is a government responsibility to provide a job for everyone who wants one, although there was higher and increasing support—from 75 per cent to 80 per cent for increases in government financing to create jobs.

Over the two decade period there was an increase from 50 per cent to 55 per cent in those who thought that government should reduce income differences, which is much lower than in many other countries, but a little higher than in New Zealand and the United States. Support for increasing taxes on the rich increased from around 62 per cent to 65 per cent. There was a fall from around 55 per cent to 45 per cent in those favouring less government regulation, and a large fall in those in favour of cuts in government spending from around 70 per cent to 40 per cent. There was high and increasing support for more money for health care (from 60 per cent to over 85 per cent) and in support for education (60 per cent to 75 per cent).

5. POLICIES

A distinctive feature of Australian social arrangements has been the role of institutions for workplace relations. A Commonwealth Court of Conciliation and Arbitration was established in 1904, and the basic legal character of this system remained unchanged over the subsequent 85 years. The system developed into a mechanism for establishing and implementing minimum labour standards, including wage rates, hours of work, annual leave, sick leave[13], allowances and notice of termination payments. Among the most visible

---

[13] Paid sick leave entitlements were introduced in 1921. See Castles (1992) for a discussion.

manifestations of this at different periods were national hearings to determine the adjustment of wages in relation to inflation and productivity changes. Up until the middle of the 1980s, the basic terms and conditions of more than 80 per cent of the employed workforce were governed by the awards and determinations of the state and federal tribunals.

Castles (1985) has described Australia as a 'wage earner's welfare state'. The key features of this approach were high minimum wages, and in the post-World War II period, extremely low unemployment, easy access to owner-occupied housing (Castles, 1998) and a targeted system of Welfare State benefits that was almost wholly non-discretionary in character. Those in work were not poor because arbitrated wages were (at least, in principle) sufficient to support a working husband, a wife who stayed at home and at least two children. The presumption was that wage-earners were males and the prevailing pattern was an extreme version of what has come to be called the 'male breadwinner state'.

This relatively egalitarian wage structure (for men) and the provision of social protection through employment were not associated with strict employment protection legislation: the level of employment protection in Australia only exceeds that in the other English-speaking countries of Canada, Ireland, New Zealand, the United Kingdom and the United States (OECD, 2013).

Changes to wage setting institutions took place over time. Since the late 1980s, there has been a shift in the level at which bargaining takes place towards a hybrid system emphasizing agreements at the enterprise and workplace level. Following the 1996 *Workplace Relations Act* for the first time agreements could be struck directly between employers and workers, without union intervention if desired. Major changes came with the Workplace Relations Amendment Act in 2005, popularly known as Work Choices. Work Choices dispensed with unfair dismissal laws for companies with fewer than 100 employees. It also significantly compromised a workforce's ability to legally go on strike, requiring workers to bargain for previously guaranteed conditions without collectivized representation, and restricted trade union activity. The laws were strongly opposed by the Opposition and the trade union movement, and were a major issue in the 2007 federal election. The new government repealed the Work Choices legislation shortly after assuming office. The Federal Fair Work Act came into effect from 1 July 2009. The main features of the Fair Work Act include: increased protection from unfair dismissal; minimum employment conditions; standards for good faith collective bargaining; assistance in bargaining for low paid workers; clear rules governing industrial action; widened provisions for unpaid parental leave; and rights to request flexible working arrangements.

Social Security and Taxation

The Australian social security system differs markedly from those in other OECD countries. In Australia payments are flat-rate and financed from general taxation revenue, and there are no separate social security contributions. Benefits are also income-tested or asset-tested, so payments reduce as other resources increase. Payments are not time-limited and continue for as long as people remain entitled.

In 2012, social expenditure in Australia was estimated to be 18.7 per cent of GDP compared to an OECD average of 21.7 per cent, a level lower than the United States and

Japan, and the tenth lowest in the OECD (OECD, 2013). With taxes at about 27 per cent of GDP in 2008 compared to an OECD average of close to 35 per cent, Australia is the sixth lowest-taxing country in the OECD. Because of the absence of social security contributions, income tax takes a higher share of total tax revenue than in many other countries, averaging 55–60 per cent of total revenue since 1980, compared to an OECD average of around one-third.

Australia is often regarded as the epitome of the 'liberal' or residual welfare state. Esping-Andersen (1990) found Australia to have the lowest score on his de-commodification index, while Korpi and Palme (1998) described Australia as the only example of a targeted (rather than basic security) welfare state. These characterizations are disputed by Castles and Mitchell (1993) who argue that Australia is one of a distinctive 'radical' group of nations, focusing its redistributive effort through instruments rather than high expenditure levels.

The characterization of Australia as a 'radical' welfare state is apt. Australia is the strongest example of a country using the 'Robin Hood' approach to the Welfare State, relying more heavily on income-testing and directing a higher share of benefits to lower-income groups than any other OECD country. The poorest 20 per cent of the population receives nearly 42 per cent of transfer spending; the richest 20 per cent receives only around 3 per cent. As a result, the poorest fifth receives twelve times as much in cash benefits as the richest fifth, the highest ratio in the OECD and about 50 per cent more than the next most targeted country, New Zealand (Whiteford, 2010).

Australia also has one of the most progressive systems of direct taxes of any OECD country (OECD, 2008). However, the progressivity of taxes in Australia is not due to particularly high taxes on the rich, but reflects the fact that lower-income groups in Australia pay much lower taxes than similar groups in most other countries. This is a result of the low level of direct taxes on social security recipients; effectively, any individual fully reliant on a social security payment will pay no income taxes.

The welfare state has been subject to major reform since the 1970s. Some periods saw retrenchment of social security support, while others saw increased targeting and generosity to the poor, or retrenchment for some groups and improvements for favoured categories. Overall, social spending rose from just over 10 per cent of GDP in 1980 to an estimated 18.7 per cent in 2012 (OECD, 2013). The growth in spending reflects a range of factors, including the deterioration in the labour market, increased generosity for some groups such as the aged, and the extension of new payments in other periods.

Since the early 1980s the tax and transfer systems have varied in their impact on inequality. Overall, the redistributive impact of the social security system is more than twice as great as the impact of the direct tax system. Between 1981–2 and 1995–6, the tax and transfer systems offset around 43 per cent of the increase in private income inequality (Johnson and Wilkins, 2006). It is also worth noting that while the tax and transfer system offset only part of the rise in income inequality, the increase in transfer spending and targeting of tax cuts between 1982 and 1995–6 was sufficient to compensate households below the median for the loss in real earnings associated with higher unemployment and reduced participation. The third decile were most adversely affected by the recessions in this period, with their real market income falling by around $73 per week or 25 per cent in 2007–8 terms between 1982 and 1995–6. This was completely offset by increased transfers of \$64 per week and reduced taxes of around \$10 per week (Whiteford and Redmond, forthcoming).

Official ABS income inequality figures do not give private or gross inequality trends. However, OECD (2008) and Whiteford and Redmond (forthcoming) find that redistribution peaked in the mid 1990s and fell thereafter: in the mid 1990s benefits and taxes reduced inequality by close to 34 per cent: this reduced to 33 per cent around 2000, 32 per cent in 2003 and 28 per cent by 2007–8. The social security system became less effective as private incomes from employment rose strongly in this period, but the main impact was due to reductions in tax levels from 2003 onwards.

Table 3.1 shows a broader measure of the impact of welfare state arrangements in Australia, including the effects of government non-cash benefits (health, education, child care etc.) and indirect taxes in 2009–10. For example, the lowest quintile of equalized disposable income receive only 3.3 per cent of all private income (including imputed income from owner-occupied housing) but they are paid more than 36 per cent of all cash benefits, so that their share of gross income doubles to 6.6 per cent. They also pay only 1.2 per cent of all direct taxes (while the richest quintile pay 56 per cent of direct taxes), increasing their share of disposable income to 7.5 per cent. Health benefits are approximately equal across the distribution, but education benefits are more value to lower income groups. Together with all other non-cash benefits (e.g. child care, housing, utility subsidies) they raise the share of disposable income plus benefits in kind for the lowest quintile to 10.8 per cent. Indirect taxes are regressive in that the poorest quintile pays 12.5 per cent of all indirect taxes (although their share of disposable incomes is 7.5 per cent). Overall the share of final income of the lowest quintile increases to 11.3 per cent. In aggregate, the Australian welfare state reduces the Q5/Q1 ratio from 13.7 to 1 to 3.1 to 1, or by 77 per cent.

Table 3.1 Distribution of income, social expenditures and taxes by income quintile, Australia, 2009–2010. Share (%) of total by equivalized disposable income quintile

	Lowest	Second	Third	Fourth	Highest	Ratio Q5/Q1
Private income	3.3	9.1	16.5	25.0	45.0	13.71
Cash benefits	36.5	34.7	18.9	7.8	2.5	0.07
Gross income	6.6	11.6	16.7	23.3	40.8	6.21
Direct taxes	1.2	5.2	12.4	23.3	56.2	48.73
Disposable income	7.5	12.7	17.5	23.3	38.2	5.10
Health benefits	21.0	25.0	20.0	18.0	16.1	0.77
Education benefits	24.1	22.1	22.4	17.8	13.8	0.57
Disposable income plus social transfers in kind	10.8	15.0	18.0	22.1	33.5	3.12
Indirect taxes	12.5	15.1	19.0	23.2	30.1	2.41
Final income	11.3	15.1	17.6	21.3	34.7	3.08

Source: Calculated from ABS, Government Benefits, Taxes and Household Income, 2009-10, Cat. No. 6537.0.

6. CONCLUSIONS

There is a tendency in discussing inequality to treat it as if it is a single phenomenon, but Australian experience shows that developments in inequality are the consequence of a wide range of causal factors varying over time. Apparently similar trends in inequality in different periods may actually be associated with different outcomes, so that in understanding the impacts of rising inequality it is important to focus on differing causal factors in different periods.

Many of the most negative social impacts of inequality may be symptoms of other underlying trends—the decline in labour force participation after the recessions of the 1980s and the 1990s and the apparent entrenchment of family joblessness. In this sense, disentangling what is an impact of rising inequality from what is a cause is not straightforward.

There is also an important policy lesson to be drawn—one of the major causes of increasing inequality over the last 30 years has been periods of recession, both in terms of the immediate job loss among lower paid workers and the patterns of employment growth in recovery which have tended not to favour those who lost employment earlier in the recession. It took nearly 15 years of sustained economic growth to get the level of family joblessness in Australia by 2008 back approaching the level it had been in the early 1980s. The costs of recessions are profound and long-lasting.

One factor that seems to have operated continuously to increase inequality in Australia since the early 1980s is increases in wage disparities. This is likely to be partly explained by changes to Australia's wage fixing institutions, although other factors are also involved, since the trend is observed in other countries with different institutional settings.

It is significant that in the 1980s and early 1990s, the effectiveness of government redistribution policy increased and moderated the rise in market income inequality, and also compensated for losses in real market incomes. From the mid 1990s to 2008, government policies became less effective, partly because there was less need during a period of strong employment and income growth, but also due to deliberate government policy decisions, particularly tax cuts that favoured higher income groups.

The social security system also became less effective at reducing inequality. In part this was a reflection of positive trends—as reliance on welfare payments fell after 1997 the transfer system automatically contracted. However, an important factor in this contraction is that payments for the unemployed are indexed to prices and therefore did not keep pace with rising wages and household incomes. Unless policy changes, this effect can only worsen over time as wages and community incomes rise in real terms, with the inevitable result that working-age social security recipients will fall further behind community living standards.

As discussed earlier, Australia has been characterized in the past by overseas commentators as a 'residual welfare state', whereas in terms of its redistributive profile it has been argued that it is more appropriate to view Australia as having been a 'radical welfare state' (Castles and Mitchell, 1993; Whiteford, 2010). However, policy changes starting in the 1990s and accelerating more recently suggest that working-age welfare recipients are increasingly in danger of being seen as the undeserving poor.

The rising tide of employment has lifted many but not all boats—a small minority have remained jobless and as welfare recipients for much of the last decade. While the size of the group in this position appears to have shrunk their distance from the median has widened. Growth in real incomes across the income distribution is not inconsistent with the impoverishment of those left behind.

The prospects for future inequality trends are unclear. Wage disparities have continued to widen for most of the last 30 years, and there is little reason to think that this trend will cease. Underemployment continues to exacerbate earnings disparities, and was slow to improve during the period of strong employment growth after 2000. Even though there are some signs of positive change, indigenous disadvantage remains profound. Growing educational attainment may have positive impacts for some time to come, and further reducing educational inequalities is high on the policy agenda.

The prospects for income growth and future prosperity are also unclear. Considering the rise in Australian GDP per capita from 81 per cent to 106 per cent of the US level in the decade from 2000, it seems highly unlikely that this trend can continue on the same trajectory. The issue will be whether this new found prosperity reverses itself or stabilizes, whether at its current peak or somewhere lower—and how much lower.

To date, Australia has largely escaped the consequences of the Great Recession and has maintained the enormous increase in economic prosperity enjoyed since 2000, but uncertainty about the global economy remains widespread. A major challenge for Australian society in coming decades will be to seek to ensure that the benefits of prosperity are widely shared if economic growth continues, but be ready to offset negative consequences if there is a downturn.

References

Austen, S. and Redmond, G. (2008), 'Women's Incomes' in Australian Bureau of Statistics (ABS) (2008), *Australian Social Trends, 2008* Catalogue No. 4102.0, ABS, Canberra.

Australian Bureau of Statistics (ABS) (2012a), *Year Book Australia, 2012*, Catalogue No. 1301.0, ABS, Canberra.

Australian Bureau of Statistics (ABS) (2012b), *Australian Health Survey: First Results, 2011–12*, Catalogue No. 4364.0.55.001, ABS, Canberra.

Australian Bureau of Statistics (ABS) (2012c), *Prisoners in Australia, 2012*, Catalogue No. 4517.0, ABS, Canberra.

Australian Bureau of Statistics (ABS) (2011), *Australian Social Trends, 2011*, Catalogue No. 4102.0, ABS, Canberra.

Australian Bureau of Statistics (ABS) (2010), *Australian Social Trends, 2010*, Catalogue No. 4102.0, ABS, Canberra.

Australian Bureau of Statistics (ABS) (2010b), *Measures of Australia's Progress, 2010*, Catalogue No. 1370.0, ABS, Canberra.

Australian Bureau of Statistics (ABS) (various years), *Survey of Income and Housing*, Catalogue No. 6523.0, ABS, Canberra.

Australian Bureau of Statistics (ABS) (various years), *Population Characteristics, Aboriginal and Torres Strait Islander Australians*, Catalogue No. 4713.0, ABS, Canberra.

Bechert, I and Quandt, M. (2009), *Attitudes towards the Role of Government*, ISSP Data Report No. 7, GESIS—Leibniz-Institut für Sozialwissenschaften.

Blunsdon, B. and Reed, K. (2010), Confidence in Australian Institutions 1983–2005, *Australian Journal of Social Issues*, v.45, no.4, Summer 2010, p.445–458.

Castles, F. G (1992), 'On Sickness Days and Social Policy', *Australian and New Zealand Journal of Sociology*, 28 (1): 29–44.

Castles, F. G. and Mitchell, D. (1993), Worlds of Welfare and Families of Nations. In F. G. Castles (ed.), *Families of Nations: Patterns of Public Policy in Western Democracies*, Aldershot: Dartmouth, 93–128.

Castles, F. G. (1998), 'The Really Big Trade-Off: Home Ownership and the Welfare State in the New World and the Old', *Acta Politica*, 32: 5–19.

Clarke, P. and Leigh, A. (2011), 'Death, Dollars and Degrees: Socio-economic Status and Longevity in Australia', Economic Papers, 30(3): 348–355.

Edwards, J. (2006), *Quiet Boom: How the Long Economic Upswing Is Changing Australia and Its Place in the World*, Lowy Institute for International Policy, Sydney.

Freebairn, John (1998), 'The effects of microeconomic reforms on product and factor markets', pages 49-64 in Productivity Commission, *Microeconomic Reform and Productivity Growth* (Canberra, Ausinfo).

Frijters, P. and Gregory, R. G. (2006), 'From Golden Age to Golden Age: Australia's Great Leap forward', *Economic Record*, June, 82, 2, 207–225.

Garnaut, R (2002), 'Equity and Australian development: Lessons from the First Century' Paper presented at the Melbourne Institute and The Australian Conference, *Towards Opportunity and Prosperity*, 2002 Economic and Social Outlook Conference, Melbourne, April.

Goot, M. (2013), 'The New Millennium', in Stuart Macintyre and Alison Bashford (eds.), *The Cambridge History of Australia*, Volume 2, Cambridge: Cambridge University Press.

Gregory, R. (1993), 'Aspects of Australian and US Living Standards: The Disappointing Decades 1970 to 1990', *Economic Record*, March, pp. 61–76.

Johnson, D. and Wilkins, R. (2006), *The causes of changes in the distribution of family income in Australia, 1982 to 1997–98*, Social Policy Research Paper Number 27, Department of Families, Community Services and Indigenous Affairs, Canberra.

Korpi, W. and Palme, J. (1998), 'The Paradox of Redistribution and Strategies of Equality: Welfare State Institutions, Inequality, and Poverty in the Western Countries', *American Sociological Review*, Vol. 63, No. 5 (Oct., 1998), 661–687.

Leigh, A. (2008), 'Returns to Education in Australia,' *Economic Papers, The Economic Society of Australia*, 27(3), 233–249, 09.

OECD (2008), *Growing Unequal? Income Distribution and Poverty in OECD Countries*. OECD, Paris.

OECD (2011), *Divided We Stand: Why Inequality Keeps Rising*, OECD, Paris.

Papadakis, E. (1999), 'Constituents of Confidence and Mistrust in Australian Institutions', *Australian Journal of Political Science*, 34, 75–93.

Pusey, M. (1991), *Economic Rationalism in Canberra: A Nation-Building State Changes its Mind*, Melbourne: Cambridge University Press,.

Quiggin, J. (1999), 'Globalisation, Neoliberalism and Inequality in Australia', *The Economic and Labour Relations Review* 10(2), 240–259.

Redmond, G., R. Patulny and P. Whiteford, (2013), 'The Global Financial Crisis and Child Poverty: the Case of Australia 2006-2010', *Social Policy and Administration*, Vol. 47(6), pp. 709-728, December.

Reed, K. and Blunsdon, B. (2002), 'Declining Trust in Australian Companies', paper presented at the Australia, New Zealand Academy of Management Conference, Victoria.

Review of Funding for Schooling (2011), *Final Report*, Department of Employment, Education and Workplace Relations, Canberra.

Turrell, G. and Mathers, C. (2001), 'Socioeconomic Inequalities in all-Cause and Specific-Cause Mortality in Australia: 1985–1987 and 1995–1997', *International Journal of Epidemiology*, 30, 231–239.

Whiteford, P. (1994), 'Income Distribution and Social Policy under a Reformist Government: the Australian Experience', *Policy and Politics*, 22(4), October, pp. 239–255.

Whiteford, P. (2009), 'Family Joblessness in Australia', a paper commissioned by the Social Inclusion Unit of the Department of the Prime Minister and Cabinet, Canberra, January 2009.

Whiteford, P. (2010), 'The Australian Tax-Transfer System: Architecture and Outcomes', *Economic Record*, 86 (275), 528–544.

Whiteford, P. and G. Redmond, (forthcoming), 'Polarization and Income Inequality among Working-Age Households in Australia', mimeo, Australian National University, Canberra.

CHAPTER 4

....

AUSTRIA—THE BASTION OF CALM? STABILITY AND CHANGE IN INEQUALITIES IN TIMES OF WELFARE STATE REFORMS AND EMPLOYMENT FLEXIBILIZATION

....

ROLAND VERWIEBE, TOBIAS TROGER, LAURA WIESBÖCK,

ROLAND TEITZER, AND NINA-SOPHIE FRITSCH

1. Introduction and Context: The Austrian Economic and Welfare Model

....

INCOME inequality among households is much less pronounced in Austria than in most other OECD countries. From an international perspective, Austria appears to be a model of success which guarantees the population as a whole a very high standard of living. Macro indicators paint a generally positive picture: Austrian per-capita income is one of the highest among EU-27 countries. In 2010, its GDP amounted to over €34,000 per inhabitant, 40 per cent above the European average[1] and constantly increasing since the early 1980s (see Table 4.1). Moreover, Austria is typically characterized by a comparatively low unemployment rate. In 2010, it was 4.2 per cent by ILO definitions, compared to an average of about 10 per cent in the EU-27 as a whole. This puts Austria near full employment: among EU countries, such a high level of employment has in recent years been typical only in the Netherlands. In addition, Austria's level of social expenditures is one of the highest in the

---

[1] Measurement in Purchasing Power Parities (PPP); a comparable standard of living can be found in countries like the Netherlands or Sweden, which had a per-capita income of about €35,000 in PPP in 2010.

Table 4.1 Background statistics for Austria, 1980–2010

	1980	1985	1990	1995	2000	2005	2010
GDP per capita, PPP in Euro	7,700	12,000	16,900	23,000	26,000	29,800	34,100
Unemployment rate (ILO)	-	-	-	4.5	4.3	3.8	4.2
Unemployment rate (national definition)[2]	1.9	4.8	5.4	6.6	5.8	7.3	6.9
Social expenditure as % of GDP	22.4	23.7	23.8	26.5	26.6	27.1	28.8
Public debt as % of GDP	35.3	47.9	56.2	68.2	66.2	64.2	72.0

Source: Eurostat (2012a), OECD (2012b), Statistics Austria (Statistik Austria 2012a, c) *as a percentage of whole population.

EU. In 2010, it reached almost 29 per cent of GDP—well above its level in the 1980s and '90s (see Table 4.1).

Welfare State: Design and Restructuring

European welfare states have in recent years faced tremendous social, economic and political challenges. They are under pressure from a tough economic environment, unfavourable socio-demographic development, and the advancing processes of globalization and flexibilization. Austria is no exception to this trend.

A particularity of the Austrian welfare state is its strong orientation toward labour market participation, as well as the design of its social insurance programmes in accordance with traditional family forms. Austria has 'a highly developed, albeit mainly employment-related, social security system strongly based on the idea of wage-earners' status preservation' (Obinger and Tálos 2009: 101). This is characteristic of what international comparative Welfare State research knows as conservative Continental Welfare States (Castles, 1993; Esping-Andersen, 1990; Sainsbury, 1999). Comparable Welfare State structures and labour market regulation are found, for example, in Germany and France.

When one traces the development of the Austrian social model over the past three decades, a series of specific characteristics become evident. During the post-war decades, Austria was characterized by a large state sector, far-reaching regulation of the market, and a strong role for the social partners within a coordinated market economy (Hermann and Flecker, 2009: 42). During the past 20 to 25 years, this model has been revamped multiple times. As in many other Western societies, the starting point was a transformation in the economy at the end of the 1970s and the beginning of the 1980s, wrought primarily by two oil shocks and the liberalization of trade and capital markets. While Austria was not affected as strongly by these developments as other conservative-corporatist countries— which were more exposed to international trade, such as Belgium and the Netherlands—it

---

[2] The national definition is based on the share of unemployed persons as a share of the employed workforce (age group: 15–64 years). According to the international definition, employed *and* self-employed people make up the workforce (age group: 15–74 years).

suffered the negative effects more than larger countries like Germany and France (Unger and Heitzmann, 2003: 384).

In particular, the second oil crisis (1978–79) and the high interest rates which accompanied it had negative consequences. Until the mid 1980s, the problems that arose in the course of internationalization of the labour market were met by social and industrial policy measures (Unger and Heitzmann, 2003: 376). Through labour hoarding in highly subsidized national-ized industries, labour market participation could be maintained at a high level. Generous early-retirement provisions constituted an important policy tool to counter rising unemploy-ment rates. This notwithstanding, between 1980 and 1995, the share of unemployed increased according to national statistics (see Table 4.1, Row 3); however, compared to other OECD countries, unemployment remained at a rather low level in Austria even during this period. Growing pressure on labour markets and political countermeasures—together with the afore-mentioned factors—led to an increase in public expenditure and a corresponding increase in public debt. As Row 5 in Table 4.1 clearly shows, and this is important to notice, the success of the Austrian model came at the cost of growing public indebtedness. Between 1980 and 2010, the national debt more than doubled; today, it amounts to 72 per cent of annual GDP.

During the mid 1980s, the Austrian social model entered a period of crisis in the opinion of many social-scientific observers (Hermann/Flecker, 2009: 26). In the wake of this pro-cess, a paradigm shift occurred in Austrian social and employment policies. In light of a growing budget deficit, the goal shifted from full employment to budget consolidation. The period between 1987 and 1999 is characterized as a period of retrenchment (Obinger and Tálos 2009: 121). A significant event during this period was Austria's joining the EU in 1995. The Maastricht criteria required a strict policy of budget consolidation. Facing growing fis-cal pressures, Austria privatized state enterprises, reduced public-sector employment and turned away from its course of social policy expansion. In particular, benefits were cut in the area of unemployment insurance and early retirement (Unger/Heitzmann, 2003: 367–377). The restructuring of the Austrian Welfare State reached its zenith in the years 2000 to 2006 (Obinger and Tálos, 2009: 121). The statutory pension and unemployment insurance schemes in particular were reformed. The principle of status preservation no longer applies to workers with atypical occupational careers. Unemployment benefits were cut and activa-tion incentives for the unemployed were increased (Obinger and Tálos, 2009: 113).

In the past few years, an end of retrenchment and a return of corporatism can be detected. With regard to the reforms of recent decades, Obinger and Tálos describe Austria as a 'partially defrosted' Bismarckian Welfare State (2009: 102). Whereas some traits of the Bismarckian Welfare State were reinforced, in the last three decades, new principles were introduced as well, e.g. in the areas of pension and unemployment policies. Obinger and Tálos suggest that this could lead to a higher degree of inequality over the long run. Despite having been restructured multiple times, it should be noted here that the Austrian Welfare State continues—compared to international standards and trends—to exhibit considerable redistributive potential.

Labour Market: Structure, Reforms, Flexibilization

One key fact about the Austrian labour market, noted earlier, is the low level of unemploy-ment (Auer 2000; OECD 2009). Over the course of the last 15 years, the unemployment rate

Table 4.2 Characteristics of the Austrian labour market

	Dependent employees	Self-employed	Labour force participation, men	Labour force participation, women	Average working hours	Part-time quota	Freelancers, self-employed no employees	Fixed-term contracts
1995	3,137.7	487.2+	–	–	38.9	14.0	–	6.3
1998	3,265.1	497.0	77.0	58.8	38.8	15.7	–	–
2000	3,266.5	477.5	77.3	59.6	38.5	16.4	–	7.9
2004	3,528.0	562.0	76.4	61.6	39.8	19.7	326.4	9.6
2008	3,198.5	487.2	78.5	65.8	38.6	23.3	336.4	9.7
2010	3,265.1	497.0	77.1	66.4	37.9	25.2	341.6	10.0

Source: Own calculations based on Statistics Austria, Microcensus 1995–2010; dependent employees, self-employed, freelancers, self-employed, not employees in 1000; part-time quota: working time <35 h/week; fixed-term contracts as % of the total labour force; +1996; earlier information on freelance work is not available for the Austrian labour market; labour force participation is based on <www.eurostat.ec.europa.eu>.

has ranged—by the ILO definition—between 3.7 (1995) and 4.4 per cent (2010). This low level of unemployment is a peculiarity of Austria and somehow related to its traditionally strong social partnership and high union density. The low unemployment rate is the result of a focus on what was long the most important and prevailing economic policy goal: to keep unemployment low. The labour market remained regulated for a longer period of time than elsewhere, and labour market issues were displaced into other policy realms. This affected pensions above all, where the instrument of early retirement was able to reduce unemployment among older workers (Heitzmann and Österle 2008).

With growing pressure on the national labour market and changed economic conditions, a liberalization and flexibilization of the labour market was set in motion in Austria as well (Biehl, 2008; Hawlik and Vötsch, 2006; Mühlberger, 1999; Obinger and Tálos, 2009; Tálos, 1999). A substantial increase in atypical employment was the result (compare Table 4.2). However, the Austrian labour market is (still) quite strongly regulated with relatively stable institutional structures and, by international standards, high job security. It is important to notice that processes of deregulation and liberalization started later in Austria than in most Western societies. The first reform initiatives were not enacted by the Austrian government until the late 1980s and early/mid 1990s—for example, laws on temporary agency employment (1988) and on contract work (1996).

Besides the persistently low level of unemployment over the past 15 years, the period between 1995 and 2010 also saw modest average annual growth in employment (4 per cent) and self-employment (2 per cent), driven mainly by an increasing number of Austrian women entering the labour market (Jaumotte, 2003; Mairhuber and Papouschek, 2010). While female labour force participation grew from 58.8 per cent in 1998 to 66.4 per cent in 2010—trailing only the Scandinavian countries and the Netherlands—male labour force participation remained unchanged (Table 4.2, columns 4 and 5). The underlying dynamic of these changes in the structure of the Austrian labour market is—as in most other Western economies—an expansion of nonstandard forms of employment, which accounts for most of the job growth (Barbieri, 2009: 624; DiPrete et al., 2006). Part-time work, in particular, although already quite high compared to other countries, has become more widespread (OECD, 2010: 214; Tálos, 1999: 258). Its share in the total labour force increased from 14 per cent in 1995 to 25 per cent in 2010. Freelance work, temporary agency work as well as fixed-term contracts have also become more widespread in Austria, while over the same period, the number of individuals in standard employment has decreased (Fasching et al., 2011: 57).

In sum, compared to other European countries, the Austrian labour market is still quite regulated with relatively stable institutional structures. Nevertheless, over the last 20 years, major changes have been observed in employment flexibilization. Above all, part-time employment and fixed-term contracts have been rising to a remarkable extent. What effects theses changes in the labour market structures have on inequality patterns will now be discussed.

2. PATTERNS OF INEQUALITY

Income and wage inequality are less pronounced in Austria than in most other OECD countries (OECD 2011: 27–29). Their development over time is intriguing. While it is true that

Table 4.3 Household income inequality in Austria, 1983–2010

		1983	1993	1999	2004	2010
Gini coefficient	Disposable income (employees*)	0.236	0.238	0.252	0.253	0.256
	Disposable income	-	-	-	0.258	0.261
	Net income	-	-	-	0.263	0.267
	Market income incl. pensions	-	-	-	0.340	0.351
	Market income	-	-	-	0.386	0.434
P-ratios (employees*)	P90/P10	2.94	3.04	3.35	3.06	3.12
	P90/P50	1.70	1.66	1.71	1.72	1.75
	P10/P50	0.58	0.55	0.51	0.56	0.56
Income shares (employees*)	Bottom 10%	4.0	4.0	3.4	3.9	4.0
	Bottom 20%	9.8	9.7	8.8	9.6	9.7
	Top 10%	19.2	19.5	19.7	21.2	21.5
	Decile 8-10 (upper)	46.0	46.3	46.9	47.1	47.4
	Decile 4-7 (middle)	37.6	37.3	37.6	36.4	36.1
	Decile 1-3 (lower)	16.4	16.4	15.5	16.5	16.5
Poverty	At risk of poverty° (employees*)	11.4	13.7	15.6	12.4	12.1
	At risk of poverty°	-	-	-	12.8	12.1

Source: 1983–1999: Biffl (2007, 2008) based on Microcensus, 2004–2010: Statistics Austria, EU-SILC, own calculations; income concept: 1983–1999: disposable household income (monthly average) equivalized using the square-root of the number of persons in the household, 2004–2010: disposable household income (per year) equivalized using the modified OECD scale; *employee household = main earner employed, °at risk of poverty = less than 60% of national median equivalized income.

since the middle of the 1980s, income inequality has steadily increased, this growth has been less steep than in Germany, the UK or Sweden. Wage inequality has increased more sharply than income inequality across households. The following sections will examine inequalities in household income, wages and returns to education.

Household Income Inequality

The data available for Austria show a slight yet continuous rise in income inequality among employee households between 1983 and 2010 (see Table 4.3), which is especially driven by an increase of inequality in the 1980s and 1990s (Gini coefficient: 0.236 in 1983, 0.252 in 1999). [3]

[3] For a long-term analysis of household incomes in Austria, two data sets are most useful: the Microcensus and the EU-SILC data (Biffl 2008). In contrast to the EU-SILC, the Microcensus contains no income data for self-employed persons. The calculations based on the EU-SILC data thus refer to two groups: first, the general population, and second, households whose primary breadwinners are not self-employed. A comparison between the Microcensus and the EU-SILC is possible only to a limited extent, however, due to divergent survey concepts. In order to limit data discontinuity, our study utilizes the Microcensus, an approach taken in comparable studies (Biffl, 2008; OECD, 2011).

Between 2004 and 2010, the EU-Statistics on Income and Living Conditions (SILC) data reveal only a slight growth of income inequality between households (Gini coefficient: 0.253 in 2004, 0.256. in 2010). Including dependently employed and self-employed households in the analysis, inequality was seen to be somewhat higher: the Gini coefficient for the population as a whole in 2010 was 0.261. However, in Western Europe, only the Nordic countries (with the exception of Denmark) and the Netherlands experienced a lower level of household income inequality in this time period (Eurostat, 2012a).

The picture of a slight increase in household income inequality is also underlined by other indicators. Table 4.3 shows various percentile ratios which are sensitive to different parts of the income distribution. It makes it clear that from 1983 to 1999, shifts occurred in all parts of the distribution. The lower end of the income spectrum lost ground compared both to the middle (P10/P50) and the top (P90/P10). A different story is evident for the period after 1999. The bottom of the income distribution caught up to a degree, while the middle lost ground relative to the top (P90/P50).

Further insight into the unequal distribution of income is provided by an examination of various income groups' share in total population income. The highest income decile increased its share of total income steadily from 19.2 per cent in 1983 to 21.5 per cent in 2010. Consolidating the income deciles into three groups (1–3, 4–7, 8–10), it is also clear that upper-income households were able to increase their shares continually between 1983 and 2010. This development redounded to the disadvantage of households in the middle-income range foremost, while the situation of households with a low income—similar to the findings above—first worsened and then improved.

A similar picture is seen with the at-risk-of-poverty rate. Between 1983 and 1999, it increased from 11.4 to 15.6 per cent (see Table 4.3). According to EU-SILC data, by 2004, the share of people living at risk of poverty had fallen back to 12.4 per cent (not counting self-employed households). Thereafter, the number of persons at risk of poverty remained relatively constant. In 2010, 12.1 per cent of all Austrians were at risk of poverty, slightly more than in 1983. The unemployment rate could play a crucial role in this regard. The share of unemployed persons increased in the 1980s and 1990s, going hand in hand with a growth in the at-risk-of-poverty rate. From a comparative point of view, it still remained at low levels, as did the degree of household income inequality.

A further major explanation for the moderate increase in household income inequality at comparatively low levels is the still quite intact redistributive function of the Austrian Welfare State. The increase in market income inequality between 2004 and 2010 (Gini coefficient: 0.386 and 0.433 respectively) was compensated largely by the pension system and to a smaller degree also by the taxes and transfers system, keeping net income inequality almost stable. Overall, market income inequality is considerably reduced by the Austrian Welfare State. The degree of inequality in primary incomes—including earnings, capital income and pensions—decreases from 0.351 to 0.267 (2010) when taxes and transfers are taken into account. As we will see in Section 5, this is mainly due to transfers, whereas taxes and social insurance contributions have only a modestly progressive effect in Austria.

The development of inequalities also has to be considered with regard to demographic shifts. The rise in inequality in household incomes during the 1990s has been linked to a demographic shift in family employment models, as well as to a shift in earning opportunities within specific household types (Biffl, 2007). Thus, the increasing number of two-earner households contributed just as much to a widening of the income gap as did the growing earning potential of single-adult households and the diminishing earning potential of lone-parent households (cf. Biffl, 2007: 12).[4] Another source of growing inequality often mentioned in research is educational homogamy (Blossfeld and Buchholz, 2009; Blossfeld and Timm, 2003). However, for Austria, there is, as yet, only a little evidence for a rise in assortative mating (Appelt and Reiterer, 2009; Ressler, 2005).

With regard to the demographic shift, the ageing of society must also be taken into account. However, since Austria's system of old age provision is one of the most generous in Europe, demographic ageing has until now played only a subordinate role in the growing inequality of household incomes (cf. Biffl, 2008: 788). Differences in the extent of inequality between 1993 and 1999 could also be attributable to the fact that at the beginning of the 1990s, there was a strong immigration wave—mainly from areas of the former Yugoslavia— bringing people with predominately low earning potential. (cf. ibid.: 2-3).

Wage Inequality

An important source of household income inequalities are the wage differences between individuals in the labour market. Available sources indicate considerable inequality in gross wages in Austria, and that it has tended upward (Guger and Knittler, 2009; Mayrhuber *et al.*, 2010).[5] Income tax records show that in 2006 the highest quintile of employees earned 47.1 per cent—nearly half—of the country's total wage income, while the bottom quintile earned only 2.1 per cent (see Table 4.4). Since the middle of the 1990s, the bottom three quintiles have lost ground above all vis a vis the top quintile (cf. Guger and Knittler, 2009: 264–265).

Over time, and looking at all employees regardless of their employment intensity, the social insurance data report an increase in inequality during the second half of the 1980s, the second half of the 1990s, and the period from 2003 to 2005. The income tax data, which also encompass the lowest and highest incomes, show a nearly continuous rise in inequality since the mid 1990s. The Gini coefficient for all employees rose from 0.410 in 1995 to 0.448 in 2008 (cf. ibid.: 264). According to the social insurance data, inequality is somewhat less pronounced, but these data do not sufficiently cover the margins of the income distribution.

The increase in gross wage inequality should be viewed in the context of increasing unemployment and the flexibilization of the labour market (Barbieri, 2009). As indicated earlier, the unemployment rate was on the rise between 1980 and 1998. A moderate flexibilization of the labour market began at the end of the 1980s. The spread of part-time work—in particular among women—and of marginal employment are associated with low wages. If one looks only at men with year-round earnings—for whom part-time work plays only a

---

[4] In this context, the employment behaviour of couples has an important role as well. Most men work full-time, women in Austria tend to work part-time (cf. Biffl, 2008: 783; Steiber and Haas, 2010). Furthermore, women tend to work less if their partner has high earning potential. This serves to stabilize middle incomes.

[5] For the analysis of wage inequality, two sources are available: social insurance data and income tax records. Social insurance data have the advantage of longer-term comparability, for they have had only a small data discontinuity in 2000. The income tax records, in turn, are not comparable before and after 1994. In contrast to the social insurance data—which do not consider income below the marginal earnings threshold (2008: €349) and over the maximum contribution basis (2008: €3,930)—they also encompass the lowest and highest incomes (cf. Guger andMarterbauer 2007: 5). Hence both sources are used complementarily.

Table 4.4 Wage inequality in Austria, 1987–2008

		1987	1990	1995	2000	2005	2008
Wage shares by quintile (ITR*)	1st Quintile			2.9	2.5	2.2	2.1
	2nd Quintile			10.9	10.2	9.5	9.4
	3rd Quintile			17.7	17.4	17.2	17.0
	4th Quintile			24.1	24.2	24.5	24.4
	5th Quintile			44.4	45.7	46.5	47.1
Gini (ITR)	Employees			0.410	0.433	0.441	0.448
	Male employees***			0.302	0.320	0.316	0.327
Gini (SID**)	Employees	0.296	0.302	0.306	0.311	0.323	0.320
P75/P25 (ITR)	Gross			2.7°	2.9	3.2	3.3
	Net			2.4°	2.6	2.8	2.8

Source: gross wages based on income tax records and social insurance data (unless otherwise indicated data refer to all employees) (using Guger and Marterbauer 2007; Mayrhuber *et al.* 2010); *ITR = Income Tax Records, ** SID = Social Insurance Data, *** with year-round earnings, °1997.

subordinate role—wage inequality is much less pronounced. For this population, a significant increase in the Gini coefficient from 30.2 in 1995 to 32.7 in 2008 can be observed (cf. Guger and Knittler, 2009: 265). The growth in wage inequality, then, can only in part be attributed to increasing flexibilization of the labour market.

A further cause of the rise in wage inequality is assumed to lie in the large supply of insufficiently skilled workers. Although the share of low-skilled people diminished with on-going educational expansion, especially during the early 1990s, the Austrian labour market had to absorb a large number of low-skilled immigrant workers (Unger and Heitzmann, 2003: 377). Furthermore, in the wake of globalization and technological advances, the employment prospects of low-skilled workers have deteriorated considerably over the last few decades. The resulting oversupply of low-skilled workers, juxtaposed with a dearth of high-skilled workers, could explain why wage inequality in Austria has increased even during periods of strong economic growth, e.g. at the end of the 1990s and again since 2004 (cf. Guger and Knittler, 2009: 265–266).

A comparison of the gross and net earnings of wage earners reveals that the Welfare State mitigates inequality also on the revenue side (see Table 4.4, Row 9, 10). After deduction of social insurance contributions and income taxes, inequality is somewhat less pronounced. This effect has increased since 1997, so that growth in inequality has been slightly less marked for net wages than for gross wages. The overall redistributive effect of public charges on incomes (taxes and social insurance contributions) stems primarily from income taxes, which are clearly progressive, while social insurance contributions have a regressive effect (Guger *et al.*, 2009).

Returns to Education

Even after educational expansion, educational success in Austria depends largely on the social status of their parents. Whereas intergenerational educational mobility has increased somewhat in recent years, it remains much lower than in most other Western countries (cf.

Table 4.5 Returns to education by gender, 1981–2005

	Men					Women				
	1981	1989	1997	2001	2005	1981	1989	1997	2001	2005
Apprenticeship	0.14	0.17	0.15	0.14	0.15	0.13	0.13	0.13	0.12	0.13
Vocational schools	0.29	0.38	0.31	0.27	0.25	0.35	0.35	0.34	0.31	0.31
Secondary academic schools	0.53	0.52	0.43	0.38	0.37	0.66	0.50	0.42	0.35	0.34
Vocational colleges	0.70	0.62	0.50	0.46	0.49	0.84	0.59	0.47	0.42	0.42
University/polytechnic	1.03	0.89	0.70	0.72	0.75	1.18	0.88	0.66	0.67	0.69

Source: Microcensus 1981–1997 (Fersterer and Winter-Ebmer 2003), 2001–2005 (Steiner *et al.* 2007); base: compulsory schooling; all parameters are transformed by exp(β)–1; additional control variables in all regressions are experience and its square; when considering females, a part-time dummy was included; vocational college = BHS, polytechnic = Fachhochschule.

Fessler *et al.*, 2012). It is on a par with the rates in the US and Italy, and well below the rates in countries such as Denmark or Finland (cf. ibid.). The strong impact of parental resources is often attributed to the Austrian educational system. Despite being publicly run, it is characterized by an early tracking, as well as by a strong degree of segmentation among secondary schools (cf. ibid.). Thus, it is no surprise that returns to education in Austria are highly stratified (see Table 4.5). However, an analysis of the development over time shows that both for men and women, returns to education for university and polytechnic graduates declined during the 1980s and 1990s. In other European countries, too, educational degrees were devalued in the wake of the educational expansion (cf. Harmon *et al.*, 2001). In Austria this trend was driven by decreasing returns to education for employees with at least a higher secondary school certificate. The highest losses were faced by university and polytechnic graduates (cf. ibid.: 81–83). Table 4.5 shows that on average they earned more than twice as much as workers with only compulsory schooling in the early 1980s, in 1997 this figures dropped to a wage advantage for university and polytechnic graduates of circa 75 resp. 66 per cent.[6]

Decreasing returns to education for more educated workers have been related to the fact that their educational degrees were devaluated in the wake of the educational expansion (Fersterer and Winter-Ebmer, 2003; Hofer *et al.*, 2001; Steiner *et al.*, 2007). In the case of Austria, educational expansion started comparatively late. In the 1980s, especially, the increase in the share of tertiary degrees was sharp. There is some evidence that changes in the demand structure were not strong enough to compensate for a growth in relative supply (cf. Fersterer and Winter-Ebmer, 2003: 81). Increasingly, university graduates had to take positions for which they were overqualified. The losses of university graduates can be seen also in the context of diminishing employment opportunities in the public sector due to budget consolidation policies as described above (Fersterer and Winter-Ebmer, 2003: 83).

In the period after 1999, the trend of decreasing returns to education has not continued in Austria. This suggests that the excess supply of university graduates was absorbed by

---

[6] The same trend over time was reproduced in a study of (Hofer *et al.*, 2001) using a larger set of control variables in addition to the standard 'Mincerian approach' (white vs. blue collar, industry affiliation in the private sector and foreigner vs. not foreigner). The authors looked at returns to education for men between 1981 and 1993 on the basis of the same dataset.

the labour market (cf. Lassnigg and Vogtenhuber, 2009: 105). Since inequality in individual incomes can take two forms—inequality *between* and inequality *within* skill groups—changes in returns to education along skill groups have also implications for trends in earnings inequality. Despite the compensating effect of decreasing returns to education, wage inequality was already growing in the 1990s. However, since the late 1990s, slightly increasing returns to education for university and polytechnic graduates have gone hand in hand with increasing wage inequality.

3. Social Impacts

As inequality grew only moderately in Austria compared to other European countries, the question arises whether this modest increase in inequality correlates with modest changes in social outcomes that might be affected.[7]

Family Formation and Fertility

Especially in the field of family formation, there have been only fairly minor changes, given that the Austrian inequality rate has also remained quite stable over time. The more important and influential variables intervening between inequality and family formation here seem to be political direction and governance, in the form of laws, micro and macro-economic market influences, as well as the redistributional effects of the welfare state function.

For example the wedding subsidies introduced in 1972 played a pivotal role in the steady growth in marriages. It is not surprising, then, that, especially with its elimination in 1988, there has been a sharp decline, resulting also in a downward trend in marriages during the 1990s. By 2001 the marriage rate reached its lowest point ever and has stayed quite stable ever since. In 2011, a total of 36,426 couples married in Austria, which is 4.3 marriages per 1,000 population.

This trend can be observed in relation to a trend toward a lower fertility rate and higher age of first birth. Over the past 10 years, it has hovered between 1.33 (in 2001) and 1.43 (in 2011). The mean age at first birth has been increasing since the mid 1970s, when it was 26.5 years of age. By 2011 it had increased by 2 years to 28.5. Young women, who are increasingly exposed to labour-market risks and insecurities stemming from processes of flexibilization, are in particular influenced by these development in their family planning.

Social Exclusion, Material Deprivation and Consistent Poverty

Between 16 and 18 per cent of the population in Austria have recently been at risk of social exclusion (see Table 4.6). In 2008 this share increased by nearly two per cent, but then fell back to its 2007 level over the following two years. Education plays a very important role

---

[7] A table showing trends in various social, political and cultural indicators over the last three decades is included in the appendix.

in shaping poverty risks. Whereas the risk-of-poverty-rate for persons with intermediate education and higher education has been relatively stable over time, it has increased slightly among those with low levels of education. It becomes also obvious that, especially in recent years, the share of those in persistent poverty has risen. While in 2007, 5.5 per cent were persistently poor, this quota rose steadily during the subsequent three years to 6.5 per cent. Additionally, from 2007 to 2008, Austria's material deprivation rate rose from 10.1 to 13.7 per

Table 4.6 Poverty, social cohesion, quality of life and health (in %)

		2007	2008	2009	2010
At risk of poverty or social exclusion*	ISCED 0–2	20.1	23.9	22.2	22.6
	ISCED 3–4	9.5	8.9	9.6	8.8
	ISCED 5–6	6.7	6.2	4.9	6.8
	Total	16.7	18.6	17.0	16.6
Material deprivation°	<18 years	12.0	15.8	13.4	13.3
	18–64 years	9.6	13.5	11.0	10.8
	>65 years	9.8	12.1	8.0	7.5
	Total	**10.1**	**13.7**	**10.9**	**10.7**
consistently poor~	Female	7.3	6.3	7.9	7.1
	Male	3.5	4.9	4.4	5.8
	Total	**5.5**	**5.6**	**6.2**	**6.5**
Life satisfaction of employees^		82.0	82.0	79.0	79.0

Social cohesion indicators subjective health status (in %)**

	2002	2004	2006
socially inactive	37.4	31.1	28.0
socially isolated	8.7	7.8	6.0

Subjective health status– Very good subjective health (in %)***

		1991	1999	2006/07
(very) good health	Female	68.2	71.9	73.4
	Male	74.6	75.4	77.8
	Total	**71.2**	**73.5**	**75.6**

Source: *Eurostat (EU 2020 target); the indicator corresponds to the sum of persons who are at risk of poverty, materially deprived, or in households with very low employment. °Eurostat (EU-SILC); the indicator is defined as the share of the population that does not dispose of at least three of the nine components of material deprivation in the dimension 'economic strain and durables'. ~Eurostat; share of persons with a disposable median equivalized income below the poverty threshold in the current year and in at least two out of the three preceding years. The threshold value is defined as 60% of national median equivalized income (after social benefits). ^Work Climate Index; percentage of those very/fairly satisfied. **European Social Survey; socially inactive=taking part in social activities compared to others of same age less than normal; socially isolated=meeting with friends, relatives or colleagues never or less than once a month. ***Statistics Austria, Health Survey 2006/7.

cent, and has been trending downward since. Levels of reported material deprivation are higher for children than adults and are lowest for the elderly, each with a marked increase in deprivation from 2008.

Social Cohesion, Health and Quality of Life

Low social cohesion is often also considered a consequence of growing inequality (Wilkinson/Pickett, 2009). Table 4.6 shows that social inactivity and social isolation have declined over the years, when there was a moderate increase in income inequality.

When it comes to health, we see a slight improvement in self-reported health over time. While in 1991 about 70 per cent reported a good or even very good health status, this number has risen to about 76 in 2007 (see Table 4.6). As with social cohesion, this finding is consistent with the rather stable level of income inequality over this period. Nevertheless, we can find differences between certain groups; for example, men generally report better health than women. But also here, we can find no clear trend for an increasing gender gap. On the other hand, the number of Austrians who report having a chronic, i.e. long-term, illness is growing. Whereas until 2007 less than a quarter of the Austrian population was affected by an enduring health problem, in 2010 more than a third were.

Austria performs very well in overall levels of self-reported well-being compared with other countries. Nevertheless, with regard to the life satisfaction of Austrians, we find a decline in the wake of the financial and economic crisis. While in 2008 82 per cent of respondents reported that they were 'very or fairly satisfied', by 2009 this value had fallen to 79 per cent. Furthermore, there is a strong relationship between satisfaction with one's life and one's income, as well as with deprivation.

Housing

Because the residential rental market is regulated and there is a substantial share of public housing units, rents especially are relatively affordable. As a result, a higher proportion of tenants can be found in Austria (15.9 per cent) than elsewhere in Europe (11.4 per cent). The share of homeowners in Austria, however, lies below the EU average. Housing prices in Austria have risen in the last years. In particular, in Vienna, the capital of Austria, they have been rising consistently since 2004. During the first quarter of 2012, house prices in Vienna rose by 4.3 per cent. In Austria, excluding Vienna, house prices soared by 11 per cent during the first quarter of 2012. From 2005 to 2012, house prices in Vienna rose by 67 per cent, compared to a 33 per cent increase in the rest of the country.

The burden of housing costs as a share of private household incomes in Austria averages 18 per cent. Austria's EU-SILC-based study of 2007 shows that households at risk of poverty are particularly burdened by housing costs. They spend on average 38 per cent of their household income on housing. In Vienna and other cities with more than 100,000 residents, the housing cost burden for households at risk of poverty is especially high, averaging 43 per cent.

4. Political and Cultural Impacts

As with social impacts, it seems especially interesting to analyse for Austria whether a modest growth in household income inequality has been accompanied also by modest changes in the political and cultural domain. Thus, this section describes how cultural and political attitudes have developed over time in the areas of trust and perception of inequalities.

Trust in Institutions and Political Participation

In general, congruent with Austria's comparatively modest growth in household income inequality, we can also observe high stability in outcomes concerning political and cultural values. Trust in various institutions and in other people has, especially, remained relatively stable over the long term (see Table 4.7). Nevertheless, growing differences in trust can also be found in Austria. Above all, those at the bottom of the occupational hierarchy reveal a modest decline in trust (e.g. employees in elementary occupations with a 10 per cent decline in trust in parliament and justice between 1999 and 2008).

On the other hand, employees in higher occupations, (e.g. professionals) and with higher education show more stable or even slightly increasing trust towards institutions and other people. Additionally, across the entire time period under study, people in non-standard employment (e.g. part-time work) exhibit low levels of trust. High stability also can be found when it comes to approval of Austria's membership of the European

Table 4.7 Trust in parliament and justice system (in %) by occupation and working hours, 1999–2008

	trust parliament		trust justice system	
Occupation	1999	2008	1999	2008
elementary occupations	32.0	22.6	64.0	55.8
plant/machine operators	46.6	31.1	74.0	54.3
craft/trade workers	35.5	32.9	66.0	70.1
skilled agricultural workers	43.2	38.6	67.6	61.4
sales/service workers	32.6	26.9	69.1	53.8
Clerks	36.3	27.2	60.2	60.3
Technicians	45.1	32.9	70.8	73.4
Professionals	41.8	40.4	76.1	78
Managers	52.4	26.8	69.1	70.9
working hours				
part time	28.9	24.5	-	-
full time	40.6	28.5	-	-

Source: European Values Study 1999–2008; Eurobarometer 2004–2009, own calculations.

Union, which remains within a band of 30 to 45 per cent and thus far below the EU average. Furthermore, we see that in times of a modest rise in inequality in Austria, a decline
in political participation, e.g. in voter turnout, has taken place, especially between the late
1980s and 2008 (e.g. voting turnout in national elections declining from 90 per cent in 1986
to 78 per cent in 2008). Furthermore, membership and engagement in political and civic
associations showed a declining trend. For example, union density declined from about 60
per cent in 1970s and early 1980s to less than 30 per cent in 2010.

Perception of Income Inequality

Perception of social inequality is yet another crucial level of consideration for the present analysis of change in the structures of social inequality in Austria. This section
will explore the extent to which these perceptions, and their alterations, fit into the
above-mentioned findings (a slight increase in inequality following a moderate basic
level).

Although the Austrian model has been shown to provide a high standard of living—
while thus protecting its citizens quite efficiently from socio-economic risks as compared
to other European countries—we find that an overwhelming majority of Austrians perceive inequality in their country to be much more excessive compared to other European
countries. Hence, it is not surprising that the need for redistribution of income by the State
is also much more pronounced in Austria than in most other OECD member countries
(see Table 4.8).

Although a convergence of public opinion in Austria and elsewhere in the OECD has
been identified over the last two decades, these outcomes demonstrate the strong influence of this country's dominant ideology of equality (e.g. Hadler, 2005). This ideology
may be rooted in the historical significance of social accommodation by a comprehensive Welfare State and Austria´s strong tradition of corporatism (see also Section 2). One
could argue that due to this institutional basis and only moderate increases in overall
inequalities, we can observe a relatively high stability in the perception of inequality
over time in Austria. Figures from the late 1980s and the late 2000s suggest that there
have been only minor changes in the perception of income inequalities as 'too large' (see
Table 4.8). For example, in the 1990s, and thus in a phase of growing wage inequalities in Austria, income differences were seen a little less problematically than before and
afterwards. When it comes to the call for government to reduce the perceived income
inequality, in accordance with these changes in inequality perception, a clear decrease
in redistributive preferences is seen between the close of the 1980s and the early 1990s.
Since then, the general approval of state intervention that aims to reduce income inequalities has again been increasing. With a specific view on the years 1987 and 2009,
and also the years between those two time points, this illustrates substantial temporal
dynamics in Austria when it comes to inequality evaluation by its inhabitants. Especially
during the 1990s, and thus in a phase of growing wage inequalities in Austria, income
differences were surprisingly seen less problematically than before or after that decade.
Similarly, the demand for state intervention to reduce inequality was less pronounced in
this period.

Table 4.8 Perception of income inequality and opinions about measures against inequalities in Austria (% strongly agree/agree), 1987–2009

	1987	1992	1999	2009
Income differences are 'too large'				
Austria	89.9	82.1	83.3	88.3
OECD	72.3	79.3	80.6	85.1
Government should redistribute wealth/income				
Austria	80.7	69.5	69.6	74.6
OECD	61.5	63.7	65.5	72.0

Income differences perceived as 'too large' (% strongly agree/agree)
by working hours and educational attainment, 1999-2009

	1999	2009	Difference 1999/09
Working hours			
Part-time	84.7	91.0	6.3
Full-time	82.3	84.2	1.9
Educational degree			
No formal	85.1	88.5	3.4
Primary education	86.7	88.1	1.4
Lower secondary	83.9	89.5	5.6
Higher secondary	81.3	85.5	4.2
Above higher secondary	77.5	82.3	4.8
Tertiary	72.6	78.7	6.1

Source: ISSP 1999–2009, own calculations; part-time defined as working 30 hours or less per week.

Additionally, these findings and trends in the overall perception of inequality conceal substantial differences between different social groups and changes over time when it comes to group differences. For example, perceptions of whether income differences are too large vary by education. Above all, those with less educational attainment, and thus fewer returns to education, perceive income differences to be particularly problematic, while those with higher educational degrees and higher returns to education find income differences in Austria to be less problematic. We also see that differences by education have grown slightly over time (see Table 4.8, lower half). Besides, substantial differences can be observed between different labour market participants in inequality perceptions. Especially those social groups most severely affected by labour market flexibilization—in particular, those working part-time—show a more critical evaluation of income inequalities than those working in standard employment relationships. This disparity has even increased, especially over the past decade: compared to the late 1990s, part-time employees are now more strongly of the opinion that income differences in Austria are too large (Table 4.8, lower half).

From our perspective, these findings underline that although Austria is shaped by its historically rooted dominant ideology of equality, one's own objective socio-economic situation influences perceptions of social inequality as well—a finding that has already been established for most other European countries (e.g. Kluegel *et al.,* 1995).

Legitimacy of Social Inequality

Both the extent to which people find inequality to be excessive and thus problematic, and the intensity with which they regard inequality as unjust and illegitimate are particularly important factors in the evaluation of inequalities in modern societies.

In modern societies, the attribution of inequality to differences in performance and personal achievement is especially often seen as an important precondition for people to perceive inequality as being just and legitimate (Gerlitz *et al.,* 2012; Kelley and Evans, 1993; Neckel, 2008; Wegener, 1991). Thus, the perceived validity of meritocratic principles—i.e. the extent to which achievement is thought to be actually rewarded—is quite important in terms of how legitimate inequality and its correlates such as poverty, are seen in public opinion.

When Austrians are asked why people in their country live in need, most respondents attribute this to forces that can be seen as lying beyond the power and responsibility of the individual, such injustice in society and that the share of those Austrian citizens who are observing a growing injustice in society is increasing over time. At the same time, especially during the crisis, the belief that social inequality results in some people having to live in need has gained traction (Table 4.9). Hypothetically, increasing socio-economic insecurities, which in the meantime have spread to broad segments of the population including the middle classes, could have left their mark and could be reflected in attitudes toward the causes of poverty.

With this indicator, differences are also found across socio-economic groups. Over time, people who work in atypical jobs, and here again especially those working part-time, are less

Table 4.9 Legitimation of social inequality in Austria by working hours (in %), 1990–2009

	1990	1999	2009
*People live in need because of...**			
injustice in society*			
Part-time	25.0	31.2	38.0
Full-time	20.4	25.0	32.5
laziness or lack of willpower*			
Part-time	26.5	26.0	24.6
Full-time	32.2	35.0	26.7
*Getting ahead in society depends on...***			
coming from a wealthy family			
Part-time	–	30.8	33.1
Full-time	–	26.2	30.4
hard work			
Part-time	–	66.5	61.7
Full-time	–	69.5	65.1

Source: *European Values Study 1990–2008, own calculations; **ISSP 1999–2009, own calculations; part-time defined as working 30 hours or less per week.

and less of the opinion that poverty is attributable to laziness. By contrast, they increasingly believe that growing social inequality is responsible for the fact that more people are forced to live in need (Table 4.9).

Similar tendencies can be seen when it comes to the question as to what people think is important for getting ahead in society. In particular, part-time workers believe less and less that hard work is rewarded, and increasingly that getting ahead depends primarily on being born into a wealthy family (Table 4.9).

Objective Inequality and a Subjective Feeling of Insecurity

Perception of social inequality and the degree to which people legitimate inequality in general is very important in assessing how problematic inequality is seen on a subjective level. But it seems also to be essential for the subjective perception of inequality, that is, how far inequalities lead to actual subjective insecurity for people and affect their quality of life in a negative way.

Although the differences are not overwhelming, nevertheless we can see that those Austrians especially whose household income does not suffice to give them a good standard of living and who thus experience financial problems show particularly low and declining levels of life satisfaction, as well as less optimism concerning their personal future (see Table 4.10).

Furthermore, individuals working in insecure jobs—and especially those holding only temporary contracts—are less satisfied with their lives and less optimistic about their personal future than employees with permanent contracts. Looking also at trends over time, we

Table 4.10 Life satisfaction and optimism about the future in Austria by type of contract and subjective household income (means), 2002–2006

	2002	2004	2006
*Satisfaction with life as a whole**			
Type of contract			
Temporary work	7.23	7.06	7.47
Permanent contract	7.66	7.44	7.58
Feeling about household income			
Financial problems	6.41	6.14	6.28
No problems	7.84	7.59	7.70
*Optimism about the future***			
Type of contract			
Temporary work	–	–	4.07
Permanent contract	–	–	4.21
Feeling about household income			
Financial problems	–	–	4.05
No problems	–	–	4.55

Source: European Social Survey 2002–2006, own calculations; *The item is scaled from 0=extremely dissatisfied to 10=extremely satisfied; **The item is scaled from 1=not at all optimistic to 5=strongly optimistic; This item was only asked in Austria in 2006.

see on-going disadvantages for those working in fixed-term contracts compared to workers with permanent contracts.

5. Effectiveness of Policies in Combating Inequality and Underlying Demographic Patterns

A glance at other European countries reveals, however, that the Austrian Welfare State still remains comparatively generous. Austria ranks third in spending among European countries, after France and Sweden. A particularity of the Austrian welfare state is its strong orientation toward labour market participation, as well as the design of its social insurance programmes toward traditional family forms (Castles, 1993; Esping-Andersen, 1990).

Social Expenditures Since 1980

A look at social expenditure data underlines the picture drawn in the first section. The development of social expenditures, both in absolute terms and as a share of GDP, is depicted in Table 4.11. Social expenditures as a whole are seen to have risen markedly and then remained roughly stable between 1995 and 2008, when they were between 26 and 27 per cent of GDP.[8] Real annual growth in social expenditures has, nevertheless, declined considerably since the 1990s. The additional costs stemming from the ageing of society were offset by shifts in social policy emphasis and by cost-saving consolidation measures (Steiner, 2008). As a result, policy-makers were able to hold the social expenditure ratio constant over the long term, despite an ageing society. Since 2009, social expenditures have grown anew by roughly 30 per cent, and the social expenditure ratio has risen, as in other EU countries (Statistik Austria, 2012b). The primary causes of this are, on the one hand, a decline in GDP in the wake of the economic crisis, and on the other hand, the increase in unemployment (Guger *et al.*, 2009; Guger and Knittler, 2009; Steiner, 2008). Table 4.11 shows the differences between cash and in-kind benefits. This distinction indicates that spending on cash benefits reached a peak in 1995 and did not exceed this limit until 2010. In turn, in-kind benefits have increased steadily since 1985. In general, the data illustrate that cash benefits predominate in Austria.

An analysis of spending for social protection reveals that the priorities of the Austrian Welfare State lie above all in the areas of pensions, health and families. Table 4.11 depicts the development in these policy domains since the year 1980. In terms of expenditure, the pension system is the largest area of social protection in Austria. Nearly half of all social spending is devoted to old age and survivor pensions (cf. Heitzmann and Österle, 2008). The Austrian pension system consists in part of a compulsory statutory scheme whilst voluntary

---

[8] Notably, the share of social expenditures relative to GDP is not only influenced by reform measures that increase or reduce eligibility and benefit levels, but also by factors such as the prevailing demographic and economic conditions.

Table 4.11 Social expenditures, 1980–2010

	1980	1985	1990	1995	2000	2005	2008	2010
Social expenditures (in Billion Euros)	19.8	27.5	35.5	50.4	59.0	70.7	80.5	87.1
Real change in social expenditure[1]	-	-	-	3.9	1.8	1.6	2.1	1.1
Total in % of GDP	22.4	23.7	23.8	26.5	26.6	27.1	26.8	28.8
Cash benefits in % of GDP	16.4	17.6	17.1	19.1	18.2	18.4	17.7	19.2
Benefits in kind in % of GDP	6.0	5.9	6.3	7.0	7.8	8.1	8.4	9.7
Areas of social protection—% of GDP								
Old age	10.0	10.9	8.9	10.0	10.4	10.8	11.0	-
Health	5.1	4.9	5.4	5.9	6.5	6.8	6.9	-
Family	3.1	2.8	2.6	3.1	2.8	2.8	2.7	-
Disability	2.7	2.8	2.7	2.9	2.8	2.5	2.3	-
Survivor	0.7	0.7	2.6	2.5	2.3	2.1	1.9	-
Unemployment	0.4	0.9	0.9	1.3	0.9	1.1	0.9	-
Active labour market programmes	-	0.3	0.3	0.4	0.5	0.6	0.7	-
Housing	0.1	0.2	0.1	0.1	0.1	0.1	0.1	-

Source: Social Expenditures (Steiner 2008) on the basis of Statistics Austria / BMASK: ESSPROS Database of Social Statistics; for GDP: OECD SOCX (2012); 1 in % vs. previous year, inflation adjusted with Consumer Price Index of Statistics Austria, average real annual growth from 1990–1995, 1995–2000, 2000–2005 and 2005–2008.

supplemental insurance is also available from private insurers (Haydn, 2011).[9] Expenditure for old age pensions in Austria again rose between 1990 and 2008, while the share of persons younger than the retirement age (60/65) has declined. This shift in social expenditure across age groups corresponds roughly to demographic changes. This means that the system of social protection has, on the whole, responded flexibly to the ageing of society (Steiner 2008).[10]

Another important policy measure in the context of inequality reduction is unemployment protection. Preconditions for receipt of unemployment compensation are a minimum number of covered months of prior employment, as well as a willingness to work. Benefits are based on an unemployed worker's earnings during the previous year, and are paid out for a limited period of time (up to one year) (Heitzmann and Österle, 2008: 59). There was a sharp increase in expenditure for the unemployed between 1980 and 1995, a period of growing unemployment. This magnitude has never again been reached. The percentage of expenditures on active labour market policies has been increasing over the last 20 years but remains rather low compared to other European countries. Measured as a percentage

[9] According to the solidarity principle, a minimum pension is paid out in the absence of a sufficient amount of working years or level of contributions.

[10] As shown below, Austria's system of old age provision also plays an important role in the reduction of household inequalities. Demographic ageing has until now played only a subordinate role in the growing inequality of household incomes.

of GDP, expenditures levelled off at less than one per cent (OECD, 2012c) (see Table 4.11). Alongside unemployment compensation, since 1 January 2011 Austrians in need may be eligible for means-tested minimum income (in 2012, it amounted to €773.26 per month/ per adult person). Those who do not have the means to subsist on their own, and are willing to work, are eligible (Woltran 2008). The minimum income level is significantly lower than the at-risk-of-poverty threshold for a single household, which was about €1.031 in 2010 (Eurostat 2012b).

Redistributive Effect of the Welfare State and Taxation in Austria

A further major explanation for the moderate increase in household income inequality at comparatively low levels is the still quite intact redistributive function of the Austrian welfare state. Despite restructuring since the mid 1980s, household income inequality is reduced by the Austrian Welfare State to a considerable degree. As shown in Section 2.1, after taking pensions into account, inequality is much less pronounced. Austria has one of the most generous systems of old age provision in Europe (cf. Biffl, 2008: 788). Inequality is further reduced by the country's tax and transfer systems. Thus, the distribution of incomes after taxes, social insurance contributions and public benefits is markedly more equal than the distribution of primary—or market—incomes (Guger *et al.*, 2009). The redistributive effect of the Austrian Welfare State as a whole is one of the highest in OECD Countries (OECD 2012a).

Austria's tax ratio of 42 per cent, together with its government expenditure ratio of more than 48 per cent, yields considerable scope for redistribution (OECD, 2012b). In-depth analyses show that this is due mainly to public and private transfers, whereas taxes and social insurance contributions have only a modestly progressive effect in Austria (cf. ibid.). The redistributive effects on the revenue side are limited—not least because the progressive impact of the income tax system is largely counteracted by the regressive effect of social expenditure contributions and indirect taxes on goods and services. The transfer system, on the other hand, is highly progressive. Even though both universal benefits (available to all eligible persons regardless of income) and horizontal distribution predominate in the Austrian welfare state, its social protection policies clearly contribute to vertical redistribution (cf. Lunzer, 2006). Considering both monetary and real transfers (e.g. spending on education, health, childcare), the degree of progressivity has even increased over the past decade and a half. Among state expenditures, the strongest effects are exerted by unemployment benefits, social assistance and housing benefits (Guger *et al.*, 2009: 1–10).

6. Conclusion

Austria is among the small number of OECD countries in which income inequality has been increasing only modestly over the last 25 years. A detailed examination reveals a moderate increase in household income inequality, a more pronounced increase in wage inequality, and decreasing returns to education. However, the economic crisis of recent years has had social consequences in particular for material deprivation, which has grown. Additionally, we can identify a growing concern about social inequalities in reported attitudes and values. Finally, we have shown that political and civic participation has been decreasing, while trust in institutions has declined among people from lower social strata. Which societal forces have to be taken into consideration for these specific inequality structures and developments in Austria?

As discussed in this chapter, and this is the first argument, the Austrian Welfare State plays an important role in that context. This is a consequence of Austria´s corporatist tradition and a comparatively high level of social expenditure. Despite the fact that the Austrian welfare system has undergone multiple restructurings since the mid1980s, it continues to exhibit a considerable redistributive potential by international standards. The second reason, we would argue, can be identified in the specifics of Austrian labour market structures and labour market reforms: the Austrian labour market has been restructured over the past two decades, by ways of flexibilization and liberalization, to an extent that is—again—moderate in its consequences compared to other Western states. The third argument is related to the employment behaviour of couples and the educational homogamy at the household level: assortative mating is less pronounced in Austria than in other Western societies. Additionally, most men work full-time, and women tend to work part-time, especially if their partner has high earning potential. These factors tend to stabilize middle incomes and moderate the increase in inequality between households and individuals. A final important argument addresses the level of attitudes and values. Unlike in many other European countries, the restructuring of the welfare state and flexibilization of the labour market did not directly lead to a rapid and substantial increase in inequalities in Austria. But there is a remarkable increase in the attribution of inequality to injustice in society and an overall growing criticism of social inequalities amongst the population, which civil society and political actors should be aware of (from the perspective of the stability of the democratic system).

In concluding, a cautious look into the future may be permitted. In order to maintain its high level of performance, the Austrian welfare state will have to cope with a variety of challenges, e.g. in the pension system. Demographic change is exerting pressure on public spending, while from an international perspective, older people's labour market participation is exceptionally low. Key (future) discussion topics also include the tax system. High taxation of labour and low taxation of assets, high income, and legacy is a typical trait in Austria and is frequently criticized at the international level. In order to pursue a stable societal balance in the future, these challenges will need to be addressed.

References

Appelt, E. and Reiterer, A. F. (2009), 'Wer heiratet wen? Bildungshomogamie und soziale Mobilität in Österreich', *Österreichische Zeitschrift für Soziologie*, (34): 45–64.

Auer, P. (2000), *Employment revival in Europe: Labour market success in Austria*, Denmark, Ireland and the Netherlands, Geneva: ILO.

Barbieri, P. (2009), 'Flexible Employment and Inequality in Europe', *European Sociological Review*, 25 (6): 621–628.

Biehl, K. (2008), 'Starker Anstieg der geringfügigen Beschäftigung', *WISO-Wirtschafts- und sozialpolitische Zeitschrift*, 34 (3): 397–411.

Biffl, G. (2007), 'Development of the Distribution of Household Income in Austria', *WIFO Working Papers* 293, Vienna: WIFO.

Biffl, G. (2008), 'Verteilung der Haushaltseinkommen aus einer Gender-Perspektive', *WIFO-Monatsberichte* 10/2008, Vienna: WIFO.

Blossfeld, H.-P. and Buchholz, S. (2009), 'Increasing Resource Inequality among Families in Modern Societies: The Mechanisms of Growing Educational Homogamy, Changes in the Division of Work in the Family and the Decline of the Male Breadwinner Model', *Journal of Comparative Family Studies*, 40 (4): 601–616.

Blossfeld, H.-P. and Timm, A. (2003), *Who marries whom? Educational systems as marriage markets in modern societies*, Dordrecht: Kluwer.

Castles, F. G. (ed.) (1993), *Families of Nations: Patterns of Public Policy in Western Democracies*, Aldershot: Dartmouth.

DiPrete, T. A. *et al.* (2006), 'Work and Pay in Flexible and Regulated Labour Markets: A Generalized Perspective on Institutional Evolution and Inequality Trends in Europe and the US', *Research in Social Stratification and Mobility*, 24 (3): 311–332.

Esping-Andersen, G. (1990), *The Three Worlds of Welfare Capitalism*, Cambridge: Polity Press.

Eurostat (2012a), 'Statistics Database', <http://epp.eurostat.ec.europa.eu/portal/page/portal/statistics/search_database>, 5 June 2012.

Eurostat (2012b), 'Statistics Database: Activity and Activity Rates—LFS series', <http://epp.eurostat.ec.europa.eu/portal/page/portal/statistics/search_database>, 10 June 2012.

Fasching, M. *et al.* (2011), *Arbeitskräfteerhebung. Ergebnisse des Mikrozensus*, Wien: Statistik Austria.

Fersterer, J. and Winter-Ebmer, R. (2003), 'Are Austrian Returns to Education Falling Over Time?' *Labour Economics*, 10 (1): 73–89.

Fessler, P. et al. (2012), 'Intergenerational transmission of educational attainment in Austria', *Empirica*, 39 (1): 65–86.

Gerlitz, J.-Y. et al. (2012), 'Justice Perception in Times of Transition: Trends in Germany, 1991–2006', *ESR*, 28 (2): 263–282.

Guger, A. et al. (2009), *Umverteilung durch den Staat in Österreich*, Vienna: WIFO.

Guger, A. and Knittler, K. (2009), 'Entwicklung und Verteilung der Einkommen', in BMASK (Ed.), *Sozialbericht 2007-2008* Vienna: BMASK (pp. 259–273).

Guger, A. and Marterbauer, M. (2007), *Langfristige Tendenzen der Einkommensverteilung in Österreich—ein Update, WIFO*, Vienna: WIFO.

Hadler, M. (2005), 'Why Do People Accept Different Income Ratios? A Multi-level Comparison of Thirty Countries', *Acta Sociologica*, 48 (2): 131–154.

Harmon, C. et al. (2001), *Education and Earnings in Europe: A Cross Country Analysis of the Returns to Education*, Cheltenham, UK: Edward Elgar.

Hawlik, E. and Vötsch, W. (2006), 'Erwerbstätigkeit 2005', *Statistische Nachrichten* 61 (9): 808–820.

Haydn, R. (2011), 'Die österreichische Sozialversicherung im Jahre 2010', *Soziale Sicherheit*, 6 300–322.

Heitzmann, K. and Österle, A. (2008), 'Das österreichische Wohlfahrtssystem', in K. Schubert, et al. (ed.), *Europäische Wohlfahrtssysteme* Wiesbaden: VS, (pp. 47–69).

Hermann, C. and Flecker, J. (2009), 'Das "Modell Österreich" im Wandel', in C. Hermann and R. Atzmüller (eds.), *Die Dynamik des österreichischen Modells*, Berlin: Edition Sigma, (pp. 33–45).

Hofer, H. et al. (2001), 'Price and quantity adjustments in the Austrian labour market', *Applied Economics*, 33 (5): 581–592.

Jaumotte, F. (2003), 'Labour Force Participation of Women: Empirical Evidence on the Role of Policy and Other Determinants in OECD Countries', *OECD Economic Studies*, 37 (2): 51–107.

Kelley, J. and Evans, M. D. R. (1993), 'The Legitimation of Inequality: Occupational Earnings in Nine Nations', *AJS*, 99 (1): 75–125.

Kluegel, J. R. et al. (ed.) (1995), *Social justice and Political Change: Public Opinion in Capitalist and Post-Communist States*, New York: de Gruyter.

Lassnigg, L. and Vogtenhuber, S. (2009), 'Bildungserträge nach Geschlecht und Bildungsebenen', in W. Specht (ed.), *Nationaler Bildungsbericht Österreich 2009. Band 1: Das Schulsystem im Spiegel von Daten und Indikatoren*, Vienna: bmukk, (pp. 104–105).

Lunzer, G. (2006), 'Struktur und Verteilungswirkungen des österreichischen Steuersystems', *Kurswechsel*, (1): 14–24.

Mairhuber, I. and Papouschek, U. (2010), *Frauenerwerbsarbeit in Österreich. Brüche und Kontinuitäten einer begrenzten Integration seit Mitte der 90er-Jahre*, Wien: BMfF.

Mayrhuber, C. et al. (2010), *Entwicklung und Verteilung der Einkommen. Grundlagen zum Sozialbericht 2010*, Vienna: WIFO.

Mühlberger, U. (1999), 'Explaining Atypical Employment. Towards an Integrated Economic and Sociological Approach', in D. Kantarelis (ed.), *Business and Economics for the 21st Century*, Worcester: B&ESI, (pp. 281–292).

Neckel, S. (2008), *Flucht nach vorn. Die Erfolgskultur der Marktgesellschaft*, Frankfurt/Main: Campus.

Obinger, H. and Tálos, E. (2009), 'Welfare Reforms in Austria Since the 1970s', in, B. Palier (ed.), *A Long Good Bye to Bismarck. The Politics of Welfare Reforms in Continental Europe*, Amsterdam: Amsterdam University Press, (pp. 101–128).

OECD (2009), *Employment Outlook*, Paris: OECD.

OECD (2010), *Employment Outlook*, Paris: OECD.

OECD (2011), *Divided We Stand—Why Inequality Keeps Rising*, Paris: OECD.

OECD (2012a): *OECD Statistics. Income Distribution—Inequality*, <http://stats.oecd.org/Index.aspx?DatasetCode=INEQUALITY>, 1 June 2012.

OECD (2012b), *Social Expenditure Database* (SOCX).

OECD (2012c), *Special Feature: Trends in Personal Income Tax and Employee Social Security Contribution Schedules*, *OECD*, Paris: OECD.

Ressler, R. (2005), 'Wo die 'Ehe' hinfällt. Muster schichtspezifischer Homogamie bzw. Heterogamie und ihre Folgen', in W. Schulz, *et al.* (ed.), *Österreich zur Jahrhundertwende*, Wiesbaden: VS, (pp. 151–178).

Sainsbury, D. (1999), *Gender and Welfare State Regimes*, Oxford: Oxford University Press.

Statistik Austria (2012a), 'Arbeitslose (nationale Definition)', <http://www.statistik.at/web_de>, 5 June 2012.

Statistik Austria (2012b), *Ausgaben nach Sozialschutzsystemen*, Wien: Bundesministerium für Arbeit, Soziales und Konsumentenschutz.

Statistik Austria (2012c), Öffentlicher Schuldenstand, <http://www.statistik.at/web_de>, 1 September 2012.

Steiber, N. and Haas, B. (2010), 'Begrenzte Wahl—Gelegenheitsstrukturen und Erwerbsmuster in Paarhaushalten im europäischen Vergleich', *KZfSS*, 62 (2): 247–276.

Steiner, H. (2008), *Sozialausgaben Österreichs 2008, BMfA*, Wien: BMfA.

Steiner, P. M. et al. (2007), *Bildungserträge in Österreich von 1999 bis 2005, IHS*, Vienna: IHS.

Tálos, E. (1999), *Atypische Beschäftigung. Internationale Trends und sozialstaatliche Regelungen*, Wien: Manz.

Unger, B. and Heitzmann, K. (2003), 'The Adjustment Path of the Austrian Welfare State: Back to Bismarck?' *Journal of European Social Policy*, 13 (4): 371–387.

Wegener, B. (1991), 'Relative deprivation and social mobility: structural constraints on distributive justice judgments', *ESR*, 7 (1): 3–18.

Wilkinson, R. and Pickett, K. (2009), *The Spirit Level: Why More Equal Societies Almost Always Do Better*, London: Penguin.

Woltran, I. (2008): 'Auswirkungen der bedarfsorientierten Mindestsicherung auf Armut und soziale Ausgrenzung in Österreich', *WISO*, 31 (1): 71–86.

CHAPTER 5

BETWEEN ECONOMIC GROWTH AND SOCIAL JUSTICE: DIFFERENT INEQUALITY DYNAMICS IN THE BALTIC STATES

JAAN MASSO, KERLY ESPENBERG, ANU MASSO, INTA

MIERIŅA, AND KAIA PHILIPS

1. INTRODUCTION

THE Baltic States provide a very interesting case for the study of inequality, thanks to their remarkably dynamic macroeconomic environment over the past 30 years, which has had strong effects on the evolution of inequality. At the beginning of the transition, income inequality was at a fairly low level on account of the absence of both unemployment and private entrepreneurship, negligible returns to education, and low wealth inequality (e.g. the means of production were state-owned in the Soviet economy). The start of the transition was characterized by a decline in output that was deeper than in the other Central and Eastern European (CEE) countries. This was accompanied by the emergence of social problems, such as unemployment, poverty and social exclusion, and also by the introduction of various market economy institutions. All this change had profound social consequences, including on inequality and its impacts. Of all the CEE countries, the rise in income inequality since the fall of the Soviet Union has been highest in the Baltic States.

While average economic growth later on was quite strong, there has also been considerable volatility across the business cycles, as shown by the fact that the Baltic States had the highest growth rates in the EU in 2004–7, but also the deepest GDP decline in 2009.

Inequality, material deprivation, poverty, and social exclusion as social phenomena are essentially influenced by the processes going on in society. From the start of the 1990s, social and economic developments brought with them rapid growth and the spread of inequality, poverty and social exclusion, as well as a rapid rise in living standards and a significant fall in absolute poverty and material deprivation in 2003–8. The fact that poverty and material deprivation are closely related to the general economic and social development of society is also confirmed by a remarkable growth in the risk of poverty and material deprivation in the years of the Great Recession, 2009 and 2010. In terms of the drivers of the trends governing inequality, poverty and material deprivation, four periods can be discerned in Estonia (the same tendencies and drivers also largely apply to Latvia and Lithuania): a period of transitional reform; a stabilization period; a period of rapid economic development and growth of welfare; and a period of global economic crisis (Trumm, 2010). These periods will be distinguished in our analysis, too.

The aim of this chapter is to map the main developments in inequality indicators in the Baltic States, together with their social, political and cultural implications. The chapter presents the main findings of the study by Masso *et al.* (2013) in a more condensed manner. Due to the broad topic of our research, we integrate the available evidence from a large number of previous studies. Statistical data are used from both international (Eurostat and EU-SILC data) and national sources (statistical offices of the three Baltic States), and there are also microdata such as the Estonian Labour Force Survey. Unfortunately, the data are missing for some indicators such as wealth inequality, and so that has been omitted.

It is quite natural to treat the Baltic States as a single group in the analysis: as well as the aforementioned similar macro-economic trends and highly correlated business cycles, they have a similar historical background and similar institutional designs, albeit with certain important differences. Despite the various similarities, significant differences can be discerned in the dynamics of inequality and its impacts—the evolution of the Gini income inequality index has been rather different across the three Baltic States. These major changes may also provide an opportunity to analyse the consequences of increasing inequality. Yet the very dynamic macroeconomic environment also means that it is sometimes difficult to isolate the changes in inequality, its impacts or determinants (like institutional changes) from the business cycles and the changes in general income levels, because the latter often seem to dominate other developments.

2. Income Inequality in the Baltic States over the Last Three Decades

The social and economic developments that have occurred in the Baltic countries in recent decades have influenced economic inequality. During Soviet times, household income inequality in the Baltic States was modest (as indeed it was in other Soviet republics) (see Figure 5.1). This was due to the centrally planned system, which sought to achieve full employment and equality in wages and non-labour incomes (including social transfers). In this section, the main emphasis is on factors that led to differences in the evolution of income inequality in the three Baltic States during the early stages of the transition period

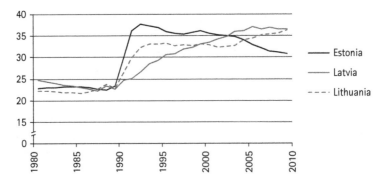

FIGURE 5.1 Dynamics of income inequality in terms of the Gini coefficient, 1980–2011

Note: Redistribution shows the percentage reduction in gross income inequality, i.e. the difference between the gross and net income inequality.

Source: Standardized World Income Inequality Database (SWIID).

and after the period of stabilization. Particular attention is paid to the early transition period, as that was when the most decisive changes occurred and when the evolutionary paths of income inequality diverged in the three Baltic States.

The early years after the states regained their independence (1991–3) were characterized by the introduction of a market economy, and the birth of entrepreneurship and capitalist market relations. These developments were rewarded with an increase in real incomes (Reuterswärd, 2003), but they also led to a rapid rise in income inequality. At the end of the Soviet period, income inequality was at the same level in all three Baltic States but since Estonia, Latvia, and Lithuania regained their independence, the development of income inequality in each has been far from uniform. In the early years of transition (1990–2), income inequality increased strongly in Estonia (the Gini coefficient rose from 0.23 to almost 0.38 in only three years), before starting to fall. In Latvia and Lithuania, income inequality also increased in the early 1990s, but more modestly. In Lithuania, where the increase was higher than in Latvia, income inequality stabilized at a Gini coefficient of 0.33 in 1994. In Latvia, income inequality increased more moderately, but more constantly, than in the other two Baltic States up to the mid 2000s.

Differences in the transition processes explain why the rise in income inequality was rapid in Estonia and more gradual (and somewhat lower) in the other two Baltic States. In Estonia, the radical economic reforms (liberalization of prices and trade, macroeconomic stabilization and privatization) were implemented very quickly, and a suitable environment for the development of a market economy was created within just four years. A comparison of net and gross inequality (Figure 5.2) clearly shows that the comparatively rapid rise in inequality in Estonia at the beginning of the 1990s was caused by the state withdrawing from its formerly large redistributive functions. In Latvia and Lithuania, by contrast, the state retained a significant role in reining in market-generated inequality. Thus Estonia moved much more decisively towards a liberal market economy. It started the privatization process earliest—in 1992—and was followed by Lithuania in 1993. In Latvia, large-scale privatization came later and was much slower. By the end of 1994, far more of Estonia's state assets (85 per cent) had been privatized than of Lithuania's (55 per cent) or Latvia's (50

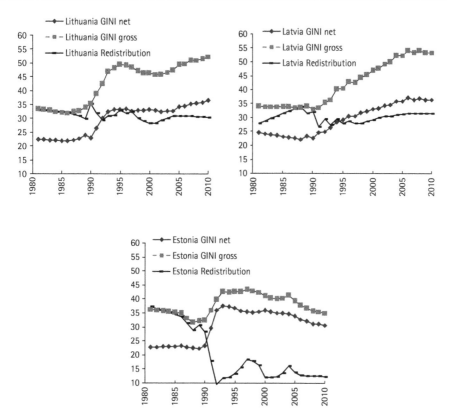

FIGURE 5.2 Gross and net Gini coefficients in Estonia, Latvia and Lithuania, 1980–2010

Source: Standardized World Income Inequality Database (SWIID).

per cent, mid 1995 data) (Milanovic, 1998). In Latvia, the process of privatizing or closing down state-owned companies and of cutting the large number of people working in the state sector was slower than in the other Baltic countries. A larger public sector means less elasticity in wages and employment, and that contributed to the slower rise in inequality in Latvia. That country's tardiness in privatizing large companies and reducing the size of the public sector slowed the growth of unemployment at the beginning of the transition, right up until 1994–5.

Moreover, the development of the market structures that supported the privatization process had an influence on the development of income inequality. Thanks to the rapid development of domestic commercial banking in Estonia, there were greater opportunities there to fund the investments needed than in Lithuania and Latvia. This supported growth, but also promoted income inequality. In Latvia, a serious banking crisis in 1995 coincided with that country's period of active privatization, which influenced its success. Also, thanks to its more favourable geographic position and its political reforms, Estonia was more successful in attracting foreign investors than were Lithuania and Latvia.

During the transition, the Baltic States witnessed large-scale employment shifts. After they regained their independence, both their activity and their employment rates fell

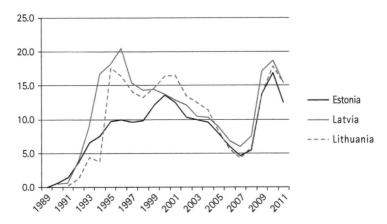

FIGURE 5.3 Unemployment rate in Estonia, Latvia and Lithuania, 1989–2011

Source: EBRD, Eurostat.

dramatically and unemployment started to rise. Latvia's slower transition to a market economy is likewise reflected in its unemployment figures: while the largest increase in unemployment in Latvia occurred in 1991–6 and in Lithuania in 1994–1996, in Estonia unemployment increased until 2000 (see Figure 5.3). During the transition period in Estonia, the rate of unemployment was lower than in the other two Baltic States, indicating its greater success with the reforms undertaken during the transition process and its higher labour market flexibility, including occupational mobility.[1] By contrast, around the middle of the 1990s, Latvia witnessed by far the highest rate of unemployment in the Baltic countries, with unemployment reaching 20 per cent in 1996. During communist times, Latvia was more industrialized than the other Baltic countries, and many people worked in manufacturing; therefore the imbalance between workers' skills and the skills needed in the new market economy following the collapse of most of the manufacturing companies was a bigger problem, and one that contributed to large wage inequality. Overall, the fact that Latvia's market inequality is the highest of all the Baltic countries can be attributed to a qualitative imbalance between labour supply and demand, as well as to big differences in regional development. The negative effects of labour market developments (structural unemployment, social exclusion) on income inequality were further reinforced by the weakness of the social insurance reforms during the transition in the Baltic States (Paas et al., 2004).

The increase in income inequality at the start of the 1990s was also partly explained by the growing differentiation in wages according to education and other individual qualifications (Reuterswärd, 2003; Fofack and Monga, 2004). The economic environment in the Soviet Union had been, in many respects, very different from that found in the advanced market economies: wages were set centrally and were not directly linked to the supply of and the demand for skills, including education. Therefore there were virtually no returns to education at that time (Philips, 2002; Leping and Toomet, 2008). As was noted by Noorkõiv et al. (1998), in 1989 the salaries of university graduates were only 8 per cent higher than

---

[1] Some 35–50 per cent of wage earners changed occupations from 1989 to 1995 in Estonia (Campos and Dabušinskas, 2009).

the national average, and the wages of workers with only primary education just 3 per cent lower. After the Baltic States regained their independence, educational wage premiums increased and the relative earnings of university graduates rose dramatically. As with the trends in inequality, the changes were very rapid, and most adjustment had occurred by 1992. While returns rose for all education groups, the increases were greatest for those with higher education. Within just five years, the wage premium for university graduates (compared to primary-educated workers) rose from 11 to 69 per cent.

As a result, the share of income going to those in the highest income decile increased markedly in Estonia, somewhat less so in Lithuania, and least of all in Latvia (Table 5.1). Whereas, at the end of the 1980s, the top decile had about a fifth of the total income in the economy in Estonia, by 1993 that had jumped by 13 percentage points and was close to a third of total income. In Lithuania and Latvia (which started from a level very close to Estonia's), the increase was approximately 10 and 3 percentage points, respectively. At the same time, the lowest decile lagged behind—again more in Estonia than in Lithuania or Latvia: whereas, at the end of the 1980s, the income of the lowest decile was 4 per cent, by 1993 it had decreased to 2.5 per cent in Estonia.

The period of stabilization (1995–99) is characterized by a rapid restructuring and a continuation of privatization, accompanied by a decline in employment and steadily growing unemployment. A feature of this period was the growth of the middle class. Rapid economic growth and restructuring of the economy brought a differentiation of incomes and a widening gap in material inequality, which remained high throughout the period under consideration. A clear-cut vertical stratification emerged, with younger people and people with a higher level of education generally the ones who managed to adapt. The same can be said of people whose social activity and enterprising spirit were not hampered by an inadequate command of the official language, poor state of health, or family commitments. Long-term unemployment was mostly a feature of rural areas, and it was not at all unusual for practically the entire working-age population of a region to be unemployed.

Whereas, in Estonia and Lithuania, income inequality remained stable during that time, in Latvia it continued to increase. The aforementioned structural changes and

Table 5.1 The income share of the highest and lowest decile of income distribution, 1988–2008

Country	1988	1993	1996	1998	2003	2008
Income share held by highest 10%						
EE	18.4	31.4	22.7*	29.8	27.6	N/A
LV	18.7	22.1	25.3	26.1	29.2	28.1
LT	19.0	27.8	25.6	23.7	27.6**	29.1
Income share held by lowest 10%						
EE	4.2	2.5	3.4*	3.0	2.6	N/A
LV	4.5	4.3	2.6	2.8	2.7	2.6
LT	4.5	3.1	3.1	3.4	2.7**	2.6

Note: * 1995; ** 2004.
Source: World Bank database.

reforms—consolidation of the public sector and privatization—continued in Latvia throughout the 1990s. After privatization in Latvia, redundancies at the privatized companies were slowed down for some years by protective legislation (Vipule, 2000). Unemployment continued to increase in 1995 as a result of a banking crisis, when several commercial banks went bust and depositors lost all their money.

This had the most disastrous consequences for small companies and their employees, and further contributed to the growth of poverty and inequality. The Russian crisis of 1998 especially affected the traditional sectors and geographic regions that were already struggling. Many of those who had been unable to find a job before this crisis gave up all hope of ever being employed and became economically inactive (Bičevska, 2012). The imbalance between workers' skills and the skills needed in the new market economy contributed to the large and growing unemployment and income inequality. Those who were educated and who were employed in growing sectors (such as finance, law, etc.) were sure to receive high salaries, but oversupply in the technical occupations depressed wages in manufacturing, agriculture, construction, fishing, hospitality, etc.

The period of rapid economic development and welfare growth (2000–7) considerably improved living conditions, and enhanced material, social and physical security, as well as life satisfaction and well being in the Baltic States. During that time, income inequality decreased gradually in Estonia, remained quite stable in Lithuania, and continued to increase in Latvia. In the early part of the period, high unemployment rates and weak trade unions meant there was little pressure to increase wages, but in later years (2004–7), with the highest growth rates in Europe and a tight labour market (unemployment close to natural rates), wage growth accelerated and outstripped the growth in productivity, which damaged the countries' competitiveness in the open sector, and also created a growing labour share (e.g. in Estonia from 44 per cent in 2003 to 48 per cent in 2007). Alongside decreasing returns to education (Rõõm, 2007), the somewhat declining wage inequality related to the housing boom, and the growing outward migration of (mostly low-skilled) people, may explain the lower inequalities in Estonia. Yet in Latvia and Lithuania, despite similar developments, overall income inequality continued to increase, perhaps due in part to a somewhat lower initial labour share (in 2003, 40 per cent in Latvia and 38 per cent in Lithuania). There is also anecdotal evidence that in Latvia job creation during the boom years occurred in highly paid occupations, and this might also have contributed to inequality.

The period of global economic crisis (2008–present) has been characterized by a dramatic increase in unemployment and no let-up in the decline of output. While the large share of people with a low level of education and inadequate qualifications is a continuing feature among the unemployed, those people with a higher level of education who had felt secure in the labour market are also in danger of losing their jobs. This has led to an increased risk of poverty, especially in Latvia and Lithuania (see Section 3) and also to a rise in income inequality in Lithuania. Estonia has fared relatively better, and the decline in income inequality there has continued, despite the recession. In Latvia, too, instead of rising, income inequality has fallen slightly. This is partly due to decreasing wage inequality and a comparatively large fall in income in the top income quintile (Bičevska, 2012). The important factor that has contributed to the decrease in inequality in Estonia and Latvia during the recession is that, while wages have been falling, pensions and other social security benefits have remained at practically the same level as before. Tax system changes have probably also contributed to lower inequality in Latvia, since some of the changes seem to have hit the highest income group harder than other groups (see also Section 5).

3. THE SOCIAL IMPACTS OF INEQUALITY

Distribution of Poverty, Social Exclusion and Material Deprivation

During the period of transitional reforms (1989–94) there were dramatic changes in consumption—the share of household expenditure on food in total consumption nearly doubled, and the share of expenditure on housing increased fivefold (Kutsar and Trumm, 1995). The poor economic situation was evenly distributed and collectively shared, resulting in generally low living standards and a high risk of absolute poverty. Meanwhile the rate of relative income poverty was quite modest. No clear social structure or risk factors of poverty can be discerned for that period: things were so bad that almost anyone could fall into poverty (Trumm, 2010). However, in the following years (1995–9), due to the developments in society discussed previously, clear-cut risk groups could already be distinguished among the poor: the unemployed and households with an unemployed member, families with many children and single-parent families, disabled persons and the elderly.

Thanks to positive economic growth since 2000, increased incomes and unemployment rates close to the natural rate, the structural risks of poverty decreased and the absolute poverty rate declined considerably. It can thus be concluded that, by considerably expanding their consumption opportunities and by reducing their rate of material deprivation, the positive impact of economic growth reached even those social groups with the lowest standard of living. When the economic recession hit, the unemployment rates in all the Baltic countries again rose sharply and the percentage of people living in households with low work intensity increased very rapidly in 2009—and even more rapidly in 2010. By 2010, the percentage of people living in households with low work intensity was higher than the average figure for the whole EU. In all the Baltic States, male unemployment rates soared during the years of economic recession, since those sectors hardest hit by the economic downturn employed more men than women. The share of people living in households with very low work intensity used to be lowest in the age group 18–24, but since 2006 this group has experienced the highest risk of low work intensity. People with the lowest levels of educational attainment have a higher risk of low work intensity. In the years since 2006, the number of households receiving subsistence benefit has increased immensely. The number of loan defaulters, predominantly young people with higher education and better income, has also grown rapidly. The latter have formed a new and untraditional poverty risk group. A central plank of the risk society concept—i.e. 'anyone can be affected by social risks'—is becoming a reality.

Table 5.2 describes the trends in the EU's composite indicator of people at risk of poverty or social exclusion in the Baltic States. People in Latvia and Lithuania have a higher risk of poverty or social exclusion than do their Estonian counterparts. Whereas in Latvia and Lithuania the indicator declined during the years of economic growth and then started to

Table 5.2 People at risk of poverty or social deprivation and material deprivation rate, 2005–10

	2005	2006	2007	2008	2009	2010
People at risk of poverty or social exclusion*						
EE	25.9	22	22	21.8	23.4	21.7
LV	45.8	41.4	36	33.8	37.4	38.1
LT	41	35.9	28.7	27.6	29.5	33.4
EU (27 countries)	25.6	25.2	24.4	23.5	23.1	23.4
Material deprivation rate**						
EE	26.6	17.7	15.4	12.4	17.1	22.3
LV	56.3	50.4	44.6	35.2	39.7	46.1
LT	51.7	41.4	29.6	22.2	27	36
EU (27 countries)	19.9	19	17.9	17.3	17.1	17.5

Notes: * This indicator corresponds to the percentage of persons who are at risk of poverty or severely materially deprived or living in households with very low work intensity. Persons are only counted once even if they are present in several sub-indicators. People are at risk of poverty if they have an equivalized disposable income below the risk-of-poverty threshold, which is set at 60 per cent of the national median equivalized disposable income (after social transfers). Material deprivation covers indicators relating to economic strain and durables. Severely materially deprived persons have living conditions that are severely constrained by a lack of resources: they cannot afford at least four out of nine deprivation items (see the next note below). People living in households with very low work intensity are those aged 0–59 living in households where the adults (18–59) worked for less than 20 per cent of their total work potential during the past year.

**People are considered materially deprived if they cannot afford at least three of the following: i) to pay their rent or utility bills, ii) to keep their home adequately heated, iii) to cope with unexpected expenses, iv) to eat meat, fish or a protein equivalent every second day, v) to enjoy a week of holiday away from home once a year, vi) to have a car, vii) to have a washing machine, viii) to have a colour TV, or ix) to have a telephone.

Source: Eurostat (EU-SILC).

increase again during the economic recession, in Estonia the indicator has remained almost unchanged over the period under consideration. This composite indicator shows that Estonia was less influenced by the cyclical behaviour of the economy than were Latvia and Lithuania.

Now, since the economic crisis struck, Lithuania and Latvia are also prominent among those EU countries with a particularly high share of the population at risk of poverty and social exclusion (being in third and fourth positions among the EU Member States). Around a third of Lithuania's population is at risk of poverty or social exclusion in, since they lived in households with very low work intensity or are materially deprived. According to recent Eurostat data for 2010, more than 60 per cent of people in Lithuania and almost 80 per cent in Latvia said they were unable to cope with unexpected financial outlay; these figures have increased since 2009, indicating a deepening of the problem. In Estonia, the situation is somewhat better: the share of those who have no funds to pay unexpected costs is slightly more than 40 per cent (Antuofermo and Di Meglio, 2012).

Females experience a higher risk of poverty or social exclusion in all the Baltic States: the differences were highest in 2008, though they had all but disappeared by 2010. If we analyse the risk of poverty or social exclusion by different educational groups, then we see that those with the lowest levels of educational attainment are much more likely to be at risk. Although the risk of poverty or social exclusion has decreased among those people with the lowest (pre-primary, primary or lower secondary) educational level, their share among all those at risk is still striking: in 2010 about 33 per cent in Estonia, 45 per cent in Lithuania, and more than 50 per cent in Latvia. Among university graduates these figures are much lower: about 10 per cent in Estonia and 17 per cent in Latvia and Lithuania. High-school graduates are in between these two extremes.

A comparison of different age groups shows that the risk of poverty or social exclusion is higher for (households with) children than for working-age adults (the most marked differences are observable in the case of Latvia); however, the risk of poverty or social exclusion is even higher for the elderly (bigger differences observable in Latvia and Estonia). In all the Baltic States, considerable changes were reported in 2010, when the lowest risk of poverty or social exclusion was observable in the oldest age group (65 years and over) and the highest among (households with) children. These developments are especially worrying because of the high risk of poverty and social exclusion among children (in Latvia 42 per cent and in Lithuania 34 per cent) and the lack of income to cope with unexpected expenditure. In Estonia, the situation is somewhat better: both the average figure for the risk of poverty and social exclusion and the figure specifically for children are lower.

In all three countries, two-adult households without children or with one child are best placed (Eomois, 2007): in these household types the risk of poverty or social exclusion is about 15–20 per cent in Estonia and Lithuania, though it is much higher in Latvia—about 20–30 per cent in households with a dependent child and 50 per cent in two-adult households without dependent children (though for this latter category the risk of poverty or social exclusion has decreased considerably since the mid 2000s). At the other extreme are single-person households, where the risk of poverty or social exclusion is much higher—in some years in Latvia and Lithuania close to 70 per cent. In addition, households with children and households with low work intensity belong to the risk groups. Several surveys undertaken using the Estonian data have shown that the situation is especially difficult in single-parent households. Households with old-age pensioners are not as vulnerable, since pensions have increased to some extent, even during the years of crisis. It is extremely important to realize that poverty breeds poverty in the Baltic States. Children in poor households are unable to develop in normal circumstances, do not get enough education, are unable to participate in hobby groups, and generally do not have the same conditions for development as children from households with better economic conditions.

These developments reflect the differences in the social transfer systems. While generally the social protection systems of the Baltic States are not regarded as very generous, social transfers still matter for poverty alleviation. For instance, in 2010 the at-risk-of-poverty rates before and after social transfers were respectively: 24.9 per cent and 15.8 per cent in Estonia; 29.1 per cent and 21.3 per cent in Latvia; and 31.8 per cent and 20.2 per cent in Lithuania (Eurostat figures). Another trend that merits some attention is the remarkable decrease in the absolute poverty rate in Estonia over 15 years, from 39 per cent in 1996 to 11.6 per cent in 2010 (for further details, see Masso *et al.*, 2013).

Table 5.2 also shows developments in material deprivation. These indicators of material deprivation aggregate information focused on certain key aspects of material living conditions; they do not seek to cover all dimensions of poverty and social exclusion (i.e. health, employment, education, social participation, etc.) (Guio *et al.*, 2010). Basic deprivation declined in all the Baltic States from 2005 to 2008, but then there were substantial rises in 2009 and 2010 as the recession deepened. Even so, in 2010 the levels of basic deprivation did not approach the levels seen in 2005. In the Baltic States, the Latvian material deprivation rate is highest, followed by the Lithuanian and then the Estonian. While in Latvia and Lithuania the indicator has been above the EU average in all years, the Estonian figures have not diverged much from the EU average. In all three Baltic States (though somewhat less so in Estonia) the material deprivation rate has moved about in line with the business cycle, in much the same way as have income and wage inequalities.

The material deprivation rate is higher for females in all Baltic States: the biggest differences are in Latvia and the smallest in Estonia. In all three countries, the material deprivation rates of young people (less than 18 years) and working-age adults (18–64) are almost identical, and the highest deprivation rates in Latvia and Lithuania are among older people (over 65). In Estonia, the material deprivation rate for the oldest age group was higher both before and during the years of economic growth, whereas during the years of the current economic recession it has been lower than for other age groups. In Latvia, the gap between different age groups has narrowed since 2008, while in Lithuania and Estonia it has remained unchanged over the period observed.

To sum up, different poverty, social exclusion and material deprivation indicators show different patterns and trends of inequality in the Baltic States. At the same time, indicators of income poverty and material well-being are somewhat higher, and indicators of social exclusion lower than the EU average. In Estonia, most measures of material inequality are lower than in Latvia and Lithuania. In the case of combined indicators, which also include households' work intensity, the results are fairly close to the EU average level (or perhaps a little higher), due to the relatively high rate of employment compared to other EU countries. However, polarization has increased in society during the last crisis (although it seems to have retreated somewhat in 2010/11), especially in Latvia and Lithuania.

Demographic Processes

In considering the social impacts of inequality, alongside the role of education, demographic processes and subjective estimates of well-being are central to any explanation of inequality in the three Baltic States. The data on fertility rates presented in Figure 5.4 show that during the period of transitional reform (Trumm, 2011) there was a relatively rapid decline in fertility. Although the data show a rising trend in fertility rates in Estonia and Lithuania as the transition proceeded and in the context of the countries' economic development, the

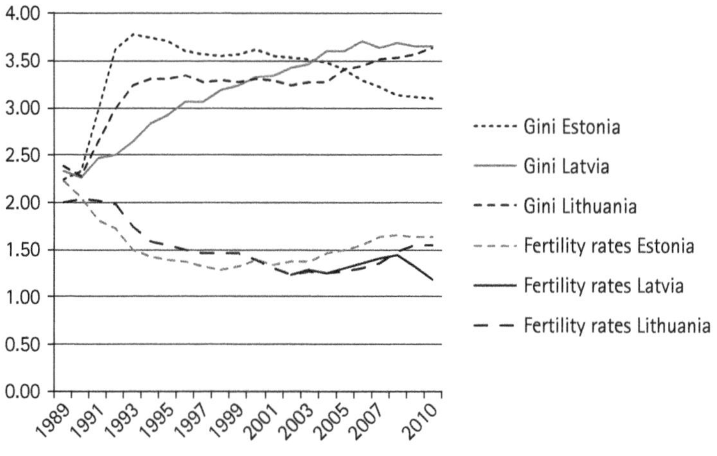

FIGURE 5.4 Fertility rates and income inequality, 1989–2010

Note: Gini divided by 10.
Sources: Eurostat, SWIID database.

rates remain below the level needed for population replacement. In present-day Latvia, following a rising trend during the years of economic growth years, there has been a sharp dip (a smaller decline is also visible in the case of Estonia). Ainsaar and Stankuniene (2011) indicate that the three Baltic States showed the most rapid population declines in the EU throughout the 1990s and 2000s—a 15 per cent drop. One reason for this population decline could be a reaction to changes in the political and social reorganization of society in the Baltic States. Other reasons behind the steadily low fertility rates would include people's perceptions of economic and social instability and modest institutional support (e.g. moderate accessibility of places at nursery school).

Besides natural processes (e.g. fertility and fluctuating mortality), emigration also helps to explain the population decrease. In the 1990s, emigration was due to the Russian-speaking population leaving for other countries of the former Soviet Union, but since the Baltic States joined the EU in 2004, outward migration to other EU countries has emerged, especially from Latvia and Lithuania. In Estonia, emigration may be rather more 'hidden': because of the country's geographical proximity to the Welfare State of Finland, commuting is more important than permanent migration. Thus, economic explanations are often regarded as uppermost in explaining emigration from transition societies, where mobility is often seen as a spontaneous process akin to the principles of gravity—individuals from lower-income countries move to higher-income countries. But alongside direct economic reasons there are also cultural explanations, such as the feeling of social alienation in a transition society—an expression of cultural trauma following rapid institutional change (Sztompka, 2004). Mobility in an ethnically diverse transition society may also be seen as an indicator of intercultural communication barriers (e.g. language policy) or an indicator of the availability of transcultural resources (e.g. contacts in other lands, openness to electronic media, etc.), at least in the case of Estonia (Masso, 2012).

Health and Subjective Well Being

Previous studies (e.g. Vihalemm *et al.,* 2011) have shown that trends over time in indicators of satisfaction and subjective well being may offer a valuable complement to non-monetary indicators of deprivation. Veenhoven (2013) indicates an increase in subjective well being over the years of economic growth in the mid 2000s and a decrease in satisfaction with life since 2009 (probably due to the feeling of instability related to the economic crisis). Previous studies (Masso, 2008) suggest that the Baltic countries differ from other European countries in terms of self-assessed life satisfaction: the overall Estonian position is quite close to the Western European mean value, whereas the mean value in Latvia is below the European average. The relatively low assessments of life satisfaction could be partially explained by the growing economic inequality inherent in the transition societies. One of the indicators underlying this inequality in self-assessed life satisfaction is the unequal social, cultural and economic status of Russian-speaking minorities: the differences in life satisfaction between the minority and the majority population in Estonia are the biggest in Europe (see Masso, 2008). Age has been another structural factor that is significant in explaining life satisfaction in the Baltic States and other transition countries (Realo, 2009). Such differences may be due to the relatively good jobs and career opportunities open to younger age groups in transition countries, at least prior to the economic crisis.

Like the subjective estimates of well being, the self-assessment of health indicates inequalities in the transition societies. Table 5.3 illustrates the variation in self-reported health for the three Baltic States by education: those with higher levels of education are much more likely to report better health. The relationship between subjective health evaluations and education is weakest in Latvia. In general, responses to this question are more negative in transition countries than in the EU overall. However, even here, significant differences

Table 5.3 Self-perceived health, by education (per cent of respondents indicating health as bad or very bad), 2004–10

	2004	2005	2006	2007	2008	2009	2010
Level 0+1 (pre–primary, primary)							
EU	27.3	33.8	32.7	29.5	29.1	29.3	26.4
EE	23.1	49.3	31.6	42.1	38.0	44.3	N/A
LV	N/A	34.1	49.4	42.2	40.0	46.9	35.1
LT	N/A					56.5	51.3
Level 2+3 (lower and upper secondary)							
EU	6.2	9.1	8.9	8.8	8.2	8.2	8.2
EE	15.6	18.3	17.5	18.4	18.5	21.0	19.8
LV	N/A	28.1	19.4	17.6	18.5	17.6	18.1
LT	N/A	19.1	15.9	16.3	18.8	19.3	20.5
Level 3+4+5 (post–secondary and tertiary)							
EU	3.0	5.2	5.2	5.3	4.7	4.8	4.6
EE	6.5	8.1	8.2	9.9	6.0	4.3	5.0
LV	N/A	13.5	16.4	11.9	12.8	12.8	15.0
LT	N/A	13.7	13.4	11.6	13.4	13.1	14.0

Source: Eurostat, EU-SILC.

may be found between the three Baltic countries, with the average perception of individual health being somewhat higher in Estonia. While in Estonia perceptions of health have changed in the period 2004–10 in a positive direction, in Lithuania the trend is reversed. One reason may be that in Lithuania (in contrast to Estonia), individuals have to pay a relatively high proportion of the cost of health care themselves, and hence certain population groups may have limited access to health care services (Ainsaar, 2011).

Previous studies (Krumins, 2011) have indicated that, from 1990 to 1995, life expectancy for both sexes fell by 2.2 years in Estonia, 2.4 years in Lithuania and 3.2 years in Latvia. Psychosocial stress was found to be the most plausible explanation for the health crisis in the Baltic States at the start of the transition. In gender terms, the significantly lower life expectancy of men can be explained by cardiovascular disease and violent death, which play a considerable role in excess mortality (Krumins, 2011). The labour market may also play a part in the differences observed in life expectancy—pressure of work may be greater for men in the Baltic States than in other European countries (e.g. highest gender wage gap in Europe, male overwork, etc.). Also, according to a 2009 survey, in approximately 94 per cent of enterprises, employees were exposed to health hazards at work (Eurofound, 2009).

Aaviksoo and Sikkut (2011) show that, thanks to health care reform, Estonia has managed to establish one of the most efficient health care systems in the Baltic States. In the 1990s it was more resolute than either Latvia or Lithuania in reforming its system of health care: it introduced a social insurance-based system of public health care, which is relatively well-funded; a strong primary care system based on family physicians; and financial autonomy for service providers. However, analysis of self-evaluated health perceptions shows that, despite the successful reform of the health care system in Estonia, individuals in a transition society may provide lower assessments of their quality of life.

Education and Inequality

The Baltic States are characterized by a relatively moderate level of public expenditure on education. The highest level of spending (percentage of GDP) over almost two decades was in Latvia, where, at the end of the 1990s and in the latter part of the 2000s, it even exceeded the average for EU countries (Masso et al., 2013). In Estonia and Lithuania, spending on education has been similar, and until the end of the 2000s was below the European average level. In all three Baltic countries there was a rapid increase in spending on education between 2006 and 2009—a period of economic change, with economic decline after rapid growth. In Estonia, expenditure on education held up nationally in the face of cuts in other fields. At the same time, education in Latvia was one of the areas that experienced the deepest cuts.

According to previous studies (Heidmets et al., 2011), the chances of going on to secondary education are relatively high in all three Baltic States (in 2008: in Estonia, 82 per cent, in Latvia, 80 per cent and in Lithuania, 89 per cent). Access to education is still limited for those groups of youngsters who drop out of school. In the Baltic countries, the proportion of early leavers from education and training is comparable to the European average (although still above the European benchmark of 10 per cent) (European Commission, 2011). Nevertheless, the proportion of early leavers is relatively high compared to other Baltic Sea countries like Finland, Sweden or even Poland, another transition country (Heidmets et al., 2011). Of the Baltic States, only Lithuania has made progress in recent years in this field.

Access to higher education has been increasing in all the Baltic States over the past two decades. The emergence of private higher educational institutions and the admission of fee-paying students to public universities have contributed to this growth, as has the high birth rate of the late 1980s (Heidmets *et al.*, 2011). Governments have been unable to cover the cost of studies of the rapidly growing student body, and so there are now two categories of students in both public and private higher educational institutions—those who fund their studies themselves, and those whose fees are paid by the state. The rapid rise in fee-paying study places has made access to higher education more dependent on the income of students' parents or the students themselves (forcing students to take a job alongside their full-time studies). During the period of economic growth in 2000–7, fee-based study was accessible to most students, thanks to the student loan system (Trumm, 2011), but since the financial crisis of 2008, access to paid higher education has decreased (e.g. due to parents' or students' unemployment, unwillingness to borrow or difficulties in taking out a student loan, etc.). In future years, the situation will change as smaller birth cohorts enter higher education. Estonia is also undertaking reform of higher education (with the aim of ensuring free tuition) and Latvia is seeking to change the model of funding studies.

4. Political and Cultural Impacts of Inequality

Participation

Even though inequality is inevitable in a market economy, it does have certain political, social and cultural consequences. The development of inequality, on the other hand, is strongly influenced by the social and political environment. In the Baltic States in particular, the political culture and habits of civic participation have played a major role. The literature suggests that among other factors, economic inequality contributes to low rates of associational membership and voter turnout (Pitchler and Wallace, 2009; Solt, 2008). After a period of massive political mobilization in the Baltic States related to the struggle for independence from the Soviet Union, in the 1990s the rates of political and civic participation—voter turnout, trade union density and membership of voluntary associations—significantly decreased (Table 5.4; Figure 5.5). Political participation rates decreased most in Estonia, where there was also the sharpest rise in inequality. Since then, Estonia has become the most equal of the three, and participation rates have been steadily recovering. In Latvia, though, as inequality continued to increase, voter turnout and the figures for membership of one or more organizations continued to fall throughout the 2000s. Some scholars blamed this on the so-called 'post-honeymoon' effect (Inglehart and Catterberg, 2002) and the loss of trust in political authority (Mishler and Rose, 2005), while others saw it as a result of declining living standards and of people being more concerned with improving their living conditions than with politics or leisure (Zepa, 1999). Of all the post-communist countries, the Baltic States experienced the biggest decline in political participation, which resulted in the lowest voter turnout and civic engagement rates in Europe. Even though there was a slight recovery from 1999 until 2008 in the membership rates of organizations

Table 5.4 Dynamics of membership of civic organizations (per cent of total adult population)

	Estonia			Latvia			Lithuania			All countries included in EVS (average)		
	1990	1999	2008	1990	1999	2008	1990	1999	2008	1990	1999	2008
trade unions	59.0	4.7	5.9	52.0	11.3	8.1	42.7	1.9	3.4	22.1	15.6	10.3
professional associations	4.2	3.6	6.5	6.2	1.4	2.6	2.7	0.5	1.6	7.7	5.3	4.8
sports/recreation	14.3	8.7	16.1	8.9	6.6	8.4	7.5	3.3	7.5	17.6	15.4	12.6
cultural activities	11.1	7.5	12.0	6.8	3.7	7.3	7.3	2.0	3.9	10.2	9.6	8.0
religious organization	3.8	7.2	7.4	3.1	5.3	7.2	3.4	5.4	4.8	13.8	13.5	9.8
political parties/groups	7.9	1.6	3.9	18.4	1.9	2.0	7.4	1.3	4.1	7.0	4.4	4.6
welfare organization	1.6	3.3	5.1	1.6	1.5	2.3	0.9	0.7	1.9	6.3	5.8	5.0
local community action	4.5	1.9	3.0	5.4	0.7	0.2	2.1	0.6	3.4	3.0	3.0	2.7
None	26.8	66.8	59.7	31.7	68.6	72.2	39.9	83.4	73.7	43.8	52.4	57.3

Source: European Values Study (EVS, 2011). Only the largest shares of participation in civic organizations are included in the table.

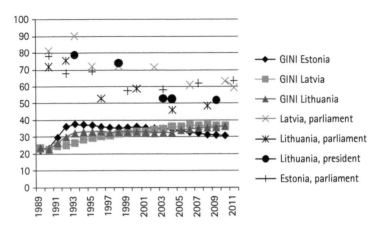

FIGURE 5.5 Voter turnout in general elections (%) and income inequality

Note: For parliamentary elections in Lithuania: turnout in the second round. Turnout in the first round is typically even lower.

Source: SWIID database, Central Election Commission of Latvia, Estonian National Electoral Committee (in Essex Database), and the Central Electoral Commission of the Republic of Lithuania.

(Table 5.4), according to the Eurobarometer data, at the end of 2010 some 70 per cent of people in Estonia, 71 per cent in Latvia, and 78 per cent in Lithuania did not belong to any NGOs or voluntary associations (European Commission, 2012a). Political organizations, in particular, have attracted very few members. Overall, the non-governmental sector in the Baltic countries is not nearly as well developed as in the Western democracies. The general scepticism about any kind of formal participation is regarded by some researchers (e.g. Howard, 2003) as one of the legacies of the communist regime that can only change with the replacement of generations.

The increase in economic inequality during the period of transition went hand in hand with an increase in political inequality. Participation rates decreased most in the poorest three income deciles of society, making it more difficult for them to articulate their interests and to be effective in influencing government policy (Howard, 2003). Currently resource-poor individuals in the Baltic States are members of far fewer associations and organizations than are people from higher strata, and they participate less in elections, too.

The lack of a strong network of NGOs (trade unions, political parties, professional associations, etc.) and low levels of political activism in the population, especially among the poor, can lead to politics being dominated by the narrow interests of certain economic and political elites at the expense of everyone else (Mieriņa, 2013). In Latvia, the weakness of civil society, accompanied by some of the highest rates of corruption in the EU (Karklins, 2005) seems to contribute to the adoption of laws that favour the wealthy and often overlook the poor (Springe, 2012), and to high levels of inequality. A better organized civil society could be one reason why only in Estonia have the levels of inequality decreased since the beginning of the 1990s, and why it is currently the most equal of the three countries. In order to reduce the large income differences in Latvia and Lithuania, it is necessary to ensure a more pluralistic policy and a balanced representation of different views and interests in the political arena. Toots and Bachmann (2010) argue that the role of labour market partners in setting social and tax policies in the Baltic States is increasing. However, the recent economic crisis, combined with the depletion of the funds that ensured the functioning of many NGOs, puts many of them in a critical position, since most are unable to survive on membership contributions. Rising membership dues would alienate the poorest from organizations, reinforcing the inequality in participation rates between different social strata.

Trust in Others and in Institutions

All Baltic countries inherited from the communist regime a 'culture of mistrust' (Sztompka, 2004). At the beginning of the 1990s levels of generalized trust in the Baltic countries were extremely low, even compared to other CEE countries. Radical liberal reforms led to a rise in poverty, inequality and social exclusion, and the rapid social and economic polarization of the society damaged trust even further (Wilkinson and Pickett, 2009). After the Baltic countries joined the EU and the economic situation improved, trust in others increased as well. By 2008, 32 per cent in Estonia, 30 per cent in Lithuania, and 26 per cent in Latvia agreed that most people can be trusted (Table 5.5). One of the reasons why people in Latvia are still among the least trusting in Europe might be the very unequal distribution of income (Wilkinson and Pickett, 2009). By contrast, in Estonia the levels of inequality during the last decade decreased and it saw the highest increase in the levels of trust.

Besides damaging social trust, inequality has a detrimental effect on confidence in institutions (Rahn and Rudolph, 2005). The high levels of corruption and the failure of governments to tackle the rapid increase in the levels of poverty and inequality during the first years of transition contributed to a large drop in the levels of political trust (Mishler and Rose, 2001). Though the political authorities became more professional, distrust continued to grow throughout the 1990s and 2000s, and has been further aggravated by the recent economic crisis. According to Eurobarometer (2011) data, currently no more than 15 per cent of people in Latvia and Lithuania trust the parliament and the government—one of the lowest levels of political trust in Europe (European Commission, 2012b). In Estonia, the crisis was handled much better, society is not so divided economically, and accordingly people have much more confidence in their political institutions: 49 per cent trust parliament and 58 per cent the government. At the same time, the fact that people in Estonia trusted their

Table 5.5 Dynamics of generalized trust (% agree that most people can be trusted)

	Estonia	Latvia	Lithuania	All countries included in EVS
1990	27.6	19.0	30.8	36.5
1999	22.8	17.1	24.9	29.5
2008	32.3	25.6	29.8	30.5

Source: European Values Study (EVS 2011).

institutions more could have contributed to the country's comparatively good economic performance during the transition and the recent economic crisis (Knack, 2002).

Political Values and Legitimacy

Political connections and bribes are still an important part of success, especially in Latvia and Lithuania. This disadvantages the poor, since the people they know are likely to be poor, too, and thus can provide little help. Moreover, they cannot afford to give bribes or to invest in connections that could later help them to get around the law, advance their interests, or receive preferential treatment (Uslaner, 2008).

The widespread perception that wealth is mostly acquired in an unfair manner originates in the 1990s: a lot of wealth was accumulated during the transition period through corruption or shady dealings (Karstedt, 2003). As a result, and also due to the communist past, most people in the Baltic States do not see the current levels of inequality as justified: 68 per cent in Estonia, 82 per cent in Latvia and 80 per cent in Lithuania think that the government should reduce differences in income levels (Figure 5.6). Since the recent economic crisis, people have become even more convinced that the government should address the issue of inequality (ISSP, 2012). In summer 2009—right before the crisis hit the Baltic countries— almost half the population of Latvia strongly agreed that it was the government's responsibility to reduce income differences. In Estonia, in summer 2010, 42 per cent agreed strongly that the government should do something to reduce income inequality.

Despite the fact that most people in the Baltic countries share social-democratic ideals, they vote for centre-right or right-wing parties. In Latvia, right-wing parties have been in a majority ever since independence was regained. It has been the same in Estonia for most of the 2000s, and currently all the Baltic countries have parliaments that are dominated by right-wing (or rather centre-right) parties. There are no strong, Scandinavian-type social-democratic parties in the Baltic countries, and votes are often cast on the basis of

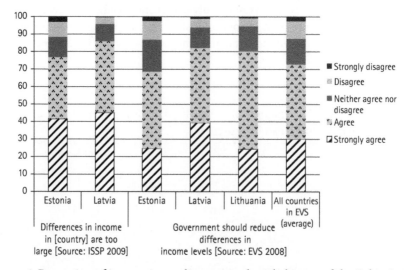

FIGURE 5.6 Perception of income inequality among the inhabitants of the Baltic States (%)

Source: ISSP (2012) and ESS (2008).

ethnic division. Analysis of the government composition (Armingeon *et al.*, 2011) reveals that the trends in inequality are not directly linked to the ideology of the governing parties. Overall, government welfare policy in the Baltic States over the past 20 years has not reflected citizen expectations, as very little money is spent on social protection—in relative terms, one of the lowest amounts in Europe (see also Table 5.8 below). One reason for this is the limited scope for the state to provide social welfare.

Yet citizens' attitudes to the state's responsibility for ensuring that everyone has a decent standard of living are changing, too. Despite the communist past, nowadays, except in Latvia, citizens of the Baltic countries do not expect more from the state than citizens of other European countries (EVS, 2011). Instead, there is an increasing tendency, especially in Latvia, to blame the poor themselves for their misery (EVS, 2011). Such attitudes are not conducive to solidarity, and can lead to social exclusion of the poor.

As well as having some of the highest levels of wealth and income inequality in the EU, citizens of the Baltic countries are further divided along ethnic lines. Because of the large influx of migrants during communist times, there is a large Russian minority in Latvia (27 per cent) and Estonia (25 per cent). Even though there is no open conflict between the two main ethnic groups, from time to time tensions do escalate. Ethnic or language group is the main basis for discrimination in the Baltic States (ESS, 2008). Some 14.6 per cent of the inhabitants of Latvia are non-citizens (Central Statistical Bureau of Latvia), who have limited political rights and opportunities for employment in public sector jobs. Poor knowledge of the national language creates additional barriers to finding a job and earning a comparable wage. Social exclusion is also more common among those who do not speak the official language (Kutsar, 1997). Thus, in a variety of ways, ethnic cleavages and social rifts undermine solidarity and can lead to social exclusion and discrimination, deepening the economic inequality.

5. EFFECTIVENESS OF POLICIES TO COMBAT INEQUALITY

Minimum Wage and Collective Labour Agreements

As general income inequality is, to a large extent, related to labour market inequalities, including earnings inequalities, it is important to know the extent to which the institutional framework that covers wage-setting lies behind the observed earnings inequalities. Minimum wages were introduced in Baltic States, together with other market economy institutions, at the beginning of the transition in 1991. The Baltic States have used a single statutory national minimum wage, which applies to all employees without distinction (Masso and Krillo, 2010). In all Baltic States, representatives of employers and of employees participate in the national minimum wage-setting process (Eamets *et al.*, 2007). Although the rise in the minimum wage may seem quite impressive in absolute terms (Table 5.7), the minimum wage/average wage ratio (Kaitz index) in the three Baltic States has not been high, converging towards the end of the 2000s at a similar level across the Baltic States. The importance of the minimum wage in terms of the proportion of full-time employees earning the minimum rate has varied around 5–6 per cent in Estonia, but the Latvian and

Table 5.6 What is important in getting ahead in life (% essential or very important)

	Estonia	Latvia
hard work	68.5	76.3
good education	77.7	73.8
knowing the right people	55.3	51.4
Ambition	48.3	56.5
well-educated parents	45.1	39.4
wealthy family	26.0	39.9
political connections	17.8	30.5
Bribes	5.7	16.2
Race	12.3	5.8
Sex	6.4	5.2
Religion	3.2	2.5

Source: International Social Survey Programme (ISSP 2012).

Table 5.7 Minimum wage (MW) and average wage developments, 1995–2011

Indicator	Country	1995	1999	2003	2005	2007	2009	2011
MW level (EUR)	EE	30.0	79.9	138.0	171.9	230.1	278.0	278.0
	LV	40.6	79.9	109.3	114.9	171.4	255.1	283.2
	LT	25.8	100.8	124.5	144.8	173.8	231.7	231.7
MW as % of average wage	EE	18.9	28.2	32.1	33.3	31.8	35.5	33.5
	LV	31.1	35.5	36.5	32.5	30.2	39.0	43.1
	LT	28.1	43.6	40.1	39.2	33.3	38.9	39.1

Source: updated version of the table in Masso and Krillo (2010), national statistical offices, Eurostat.

Lithuanian figures were, in some years, among the highest in the EU (in Latvia, 16.7 per cent in 2001; in Lithuania, 12 per cent in 2004)—quite surprising, given the modest level of the minimum wage. The number of people earning the minimum wage could be affected by the widespread phenomenon of unreported wages (so-called 'envelope wages') in the Baltic States (Masso and Krillo, 2010).

As for the effect of the minimum wage on poverty and social exclusion, Masso and Krillo (2010) showed that while in Estonia from 1997 to 2000 the absolute poverty line was higher than the minimum wage, in 2001 this was reversed, and since then the minimum wage/ poverty line ratio has increased rather rapidly, reaching 1.44 in 2006. Thus, increases in minimum wage may have had some positive effect on poverty reduction. By studying the minimum wage changes in 1995–2000 in Estonia, Hinnosaar and Rõõm (2003) found that the minimum wage increases had a relatively small negative impact on employment, while

Hazans (2007) found for Lithuania (and less so for Estonia) that the minimum wage had a positive effect on labour force participation.

The national minimum wage is more important in the Baltic States because of the relatively low density and thin coverage of trade unions. In communist times, every worker was required to be a member of a trade union, but such unions dissolved with the fall of the regime, and union density in all the Baltic States is currently the lowest in Europe. In Estonia, in 2005–10, union density was around 8–9 per cent, according to LFS data (Masso and Krillo, 2011); in Latvia and Lithuania the numbers have been higher—in 2004, 16 per cent and 14 per cent, respectively, of all employed persons. Thereafter, union membership declined considerably in both Latvia and Lithuania, reaching about 13 per cent and 8 per cent of employees, respectively, in 2008 (Carley, 2008; own calculations). In 2009, only 7 per cent of workers in Estonia, 10 per cent in Lithuania and about 15 per cent in Latvia were members of a trade union (Armingeon et al., 2011).

Coverage of collective bargaining has been somewhat higher than union density, 22–26 per cent in 2002 (Masso and Eamets, 2007). The density of employers' organizations is also low. One of the main reasons for low trade union membership is the limited awareness of both employer and employee representatives of social dialogue and collective agreements and of their advantages (Espenberg et al., 2012). There are various societal and organizational reasons for the low coverage of collective agreements, including the countries' Soviet background. Of the different levels of wage bargaining, company level is the most important in the Baltic States; the centralization of wage bargaining is among the lowest in the EU. As for the impact of unions on wage formation, even though the wages of union members have—at times—been higher than the wages of non-members (e.g. in Estonia +10 per cent in 2005, -5 per cent in 2007, +11 per cent in 2010; Masso and Krillo, 2011), it is not certain that the unions are responsible for this. At least in Estonia, the impact of unions on wages seems to be modest, irrespective of whether the information comes from statistical studies (Eamets and Kallaste, 2004/05) or from surveys of firms (Rõõm and Uusküla, 2006). Still, during the recent crisis, union members did somewhat better in terms of employment and wages (Masso and Krillo, 2011).

Taxation

The overall share of taxation and public spending as a proportion of GDP has been relatively low in the Baltic States (Masso and Espenberg, 2012). The lower share of government spending in GDP also reflects the lower GDP per capita of these countries (Staehr, 2010). The Estonian tax system, especially, has been fairly stable across the period under consideration. Since 1994, it has had a flat-rate income tax with an untaxed minimum but otherwise a uniform rate. Also social security contributions and value added tax rates have been quite stable (except that VAT was increased from 18 per cent to 20 per cent in 2009). The introduction of unemployment insurance systems (in Estonia in 2002, Latvia in 2000, and Lithuania in 2005) increased the taxation of labour somewhat. The taxation policy has been somewhat pro-cyclical—in Estonia income tax was reduced between 2002 and 2008 from 26 per cent to 21 per cent, and similarly unemployment insurance rates were reduced during the period of strong growth and increased again during the Great Recession (Masso and Krillo, 2011).

Different parts of the tax system contribute to inequality. All the Baltic States have relied more on indirect taxes since they regained their independence. Taxes on income are relatively low compared to other EU countries—both on personal income (where the rate is even decreasing) and on capital income. The tax burden on wages in Estonia has been somewhat higher than the OECD country average due to the high payroll (social security) taxes, while the tax burden on capital is lower than the EU average (Rõõm, 2003),[2] That is also reflected in the relatively high share of labour taxes and the low share of capital taxes in total tax revenue (Võrk *et al.*, 2007). Azacis and Gillman (2010) argue, on the basis of the theoretical endogenous growth model, that more balanced taxation between capital and labour would have increased welfare in the Baltic States.

All this has had important implications for income distribution and inequality. Võrk *et al.* (2007) analysed the impact of taxation policy on the distribution of the tax burden of households (measured either as the share of taxes in income, share of taxes in expenditure or the Kakwani index), using the Estonian household budget survey data from 2000 to 2007 and a micro-simulation model. The results showed that consumption taxes are highly regressive with respect to income on account of the higher savings rate among higher deciles. The share of excise duties on alcohol and (especially) tobacco in total expenditure is also lower in higher deciles (i.e. these are clearly regressive). Environmental taxes (mainly the excise duty on petrol and diesel) are rather regressive with respect to income, but are progressive with respect to consumption expenditure. Social tax and income tax are progressive with respect to income. The gradual reduction in the income tax rate in Estonia from 26 per cent in 2000 to 21 per cent in 2008 was more for the benefit of people in higher income deciles, while the increase in the tax threshold (and also the total effect) was for those in the middle deciles. In absolute terms the gains were greatest for people in the upper deciles, and thus this move has increased inequality in net incomes. Income tax deductions (household loan and student loan interest payments, educational expenditure, payments to the third pension pillar) are more for the benefit of people in the higher deciles.

A separate question that merits attention concerns the impact of the austerity measures introduced in 2009–10. Using the EU micro-simulation model EUROMOD and EU-SILC data, Leventi *et al.* (2010) studied the distributional effects of austerity measures (tax increases and benefit cuts) in four countries (Estonia, the UK, Greece and Spain) that had been hit hard by the crisis. The results showed that inequality had increased only slightly in Estonia, though the results were strongly influenced by classifying the suspension of contributions to the second pension pillar (between 1 June 2009 and 31 December 2010) as a tax cut that affected especially people in the higher income groups (Võrk, 2012). In Latvia, several changes were made to the taxation system in 2009–10: first, a reduction in personal income tax from 25 per cent to 23 per cent in 2009, and then an increase to 26 per cent in 2010; a lowering of the tax threshold; an increase in the tax rate for self-employed people; an extension of the personal income tax base to include capital income; the introduction of progressive property tax; etc. The total effect of these changes is hard to judge, but nevertheless some of the changes seem to have affected the highest income group more than other groups. Even if

---

[2] The situation has not changed much since the publication of that study.

Table 5.8 Social protection and general government expenditure as a share of GDP, 1997–2009

Country	1997	1999	2002	2003	2005	2006	2007	2008	2009
Total government budget as the share of GDP									
EE	37.4	40.1	35.8	34.8	33.6	33.6	34.0	39.5	45.2
LV	36.3	41.9	36.0	34.9	35.8	38.3	36.0	39.1	44.4
LT	49.6	39.9	34.6	33.0	33.2	33.5	34.6	37.2	43.8
EU27	48.2	46.8	46.6	47.2	46.8	46.3	45.6	47.1	51.1
Social protection expenditure as the share of GDP									
EE		15.4	12.7	12.5	12.6	12.1	12.1	14.9	19.2
LV	15.3	17.2	14.3	14.0	12.8	12.7	11.3	12.7	16.8
LT	13.7	0.0	14.0	13.5	13.2	13.4	14.4	16.1	21.3
EU27					27.1	26.6	25.7	26.7	29.5

Source: Eurostat.

they did not reduce inequality, these changes to taxation managed not to increase it; in fact, according to Eurostat GINI data, overall income inequality in Latvia decreased in 2011.

Social Expenditure

The level of social expenditure has been relatively low in the Baltic States, which reflects lower total government expenditure as a percentage of GDP (see Table 5.8). The low social protection spending is reflected, for example, in the relatively low unemployment insurance replacement rates, the lower share of pensions as a percentage of GDP, etc. In the 1990s, the term 'social dumping' was used to describe the low social protection level that was in place to promote economic growth (Masso and Paas, 2007).

Despite that relatively low level, Masso and Paas (2007) argue that the social protection systems of the Baltic States do not mimic exactly any of the four systems in Europe (Anglo-Saxon or 'liberal'; Central European or 'conservative corporatist'; Scandinavian or 'social democratic' regime; Southern European regime). As the social protection systems have undergone quite a lot of change, and as differences may be observed across the three Baltic States, it is not even possible to outline a distinct 'Baltic' social protection system. In the beginning of the transition, the Baltic States tended to follow the Central European system, but later elements of the liberal system were introduced (such as the three-pillar pension systems). In the 2000s, the elements of the Central European social protection system again became stronger thanks to the introduction of an unemployment insurance scheme. Cross-country data indicate a negative correlation between income inequality and the share of either social expenditure or tax revenue as a percentage of GDP. Thus the low levels of social expenditure and relatively high levels of inequality observed in the Baltic States are in line with that relationship (Trumm, 2010).

6. Conclusions

In this chapter we have reviewed the key patterns and impacts of the inequality dynamics in the Baltic States. We have seen that, despite their similar macro-economic background and institutions, inequality has evolved differently in each of the Baltic States since they regained their independence at the start of the 1990s. In Estonia, a very big increase in inequality at the beginning of the 1990s—a consequence of a rapid move towards a liberal market economy, the state's withdrawal from its redistributive role, privatization and the emergence of returns to education—was followed by a modest decline in income inequality across the entire period. In Lithuania, after an initial increase in the early 1990s, inequality remained stable until the mid 2000s, since when it has increased. Latvia experienced a continuous rise in inequality since it regained its independence right up until the recent economic crisis. Thus, while Estonia was the most unequal of the Baltic countries at the start of the 2000s and Lithuania was the most equal, by 2012 the situation had reversed. Since 2011, Lithuania has had the greatest income inequality of all EU Member States, closely followed by Latvia.

Certain groups have had a higher risk of poverty and unemployment during all the phases of the business cycles. The risk groups in the Baltic States' labour markets are primarily people with a lower level of education, people from the non-native population (mostly Russian speakers), and particularly those who do not have a command of the official language. Their problems originate first of all from the unequal opportunities they have in the labour market and the resulting low incomes.

Income inequality seems to be related to several social outcomes in the Baltic States: there is a negative correlation between changes in fertility and inequality; self-perceived health is strongly correlated with educational level (thus also with income due to high returns to education); and the emergence of private higher educational institutions and the admission of fee-paying students to public universities has affected access to higher education, which is now more dependent on income. Our analysis also indicates the marked associations between subjective life-satisfaction estimates and Gini coefficients—the higher the inequality in a particular country, the lower the self-reported life satisfaction.

The rapid increase in inequality during the process of transition contributed to a large drop in levels of political trust, social trust, and participation in the 1990s. The drop in participation rates was largest among the lower strata of society, and this contributed to political inequality. The network of non-governmental organizations, including trade unions, is not very well developed in the Baltic States, and civic participation rates overall are low; this limits the opportunities for society to resist implementation of reforms that encourage inequality or to achieve more socially just policies.

Taxation policies in the Baltic States have, until recently, benefited the wealthier section of society most, and this goes a long way to explain the fact that Latvia and Lithuania have the highest levels of inequality in Europe. Much of the responsibility for coping with the problems faced has been heaped on individuals, but increasingly they lack the capacity to manage these risks. The fiscal austerity measures introduced during the recent crisis (Great Recession) did not have much effect on the inequality, however. Given the characteristics of the taxation system, social protection and education, we can say that the governments of the Baltic States need to pay more attention to social problems, including the causes and impacts of the inequalities, which increase the risk of intergenerational transmission of inequality and poverty.

Given all the above, this chapter can conclude by saying that, in the case of the Baltic States, much remains to be done in the field of policies and institutions that affect inequality. It should not be taken for granted that the current policy mix and institutional setting is the best one for that purpose. It could be argued that, given their present level of development, these countries could not afford a more costly social protection system; but in fact such a system could encourage economic performance, for example through better human capital and a more cohesive society.

REFERENCES

Aaviksoo, A., Sikkut, R. (2011), *Health care policy in the Baltic countries from 1990-2010. Estonian Human Development Report. Baltic Way(s) of Human Development: Twenty Years on.* Tallinn: Eesti Koostöö Kogu.

Ainsaar, M. (2011), *Population changes, life expectancy and health. Summary. Estonian Human Development Report. Baltic Way(s) of Human Development: Twenty Years on.* Tallinn: Eesti Koostöö Kogu, pp. 65–66.

Ainsaar, M., Stankuniene, V. (2011), *Demographic costs of transition and the future of the Baltics. Baltic Way(s) of Human Development: Twenty Years on.* Tallinn, Eesti Koostöö Kogu.

Antuofermo, M., Di Meglio, E. (2012), '23 per cent of EU citizens were at risk of poverty or social exclusion in 2010', *Statistics in Focus*, Eurostat, 9/2012, 8 p. <http://epp.eurostat.ec.europa.eu/cache/ITY_OFFPUB/KS-SF-12-009/EN/KS-SF-12-009-EN.PDF>

Armingeon, K., Careja, R., Weisstanner, D., Engler, S., Potolidis, P., Gerber, M., Leimgruber, P. (2011), *Comparative Political Data Set III 1990-2009*, Institute of Political Science, University of Berne. <http://www.ipw.unibe.ch/content/team/ klaus_armingeon/comparative_political_data_sets/index_ger.html>

Azacis, H., Gillman, M. (2010), 'Flat Tax Reform: The Baltics 2000–2007', *Journal of Macroeconomics*, Vol. 32, No. 2, pp. 692–708.

Bičevska, A. (2012), 'Kā krīze ietekmēja dažādu iedzīvotāju grupu pirktspēju', <http://www.makroekonomika.lv/ka-krize-ietekmeja-dazadu-iedzivotaju-grupu-pirktspeju>

Campos, N., Dabušinskas, A. (2009), 'So many rocket scientists, so few marketing clerks: Estimating the Effects of economic reform on occupational mobility in Estonia', *European Journal of Political Economy*, Vol. 25, pp. 261–275.

Carley, M. (2008), 'Trade union membership 2003–2008', European Industrial Relations Observatory,   <http://www.eurofound.europa.eu/eiro/studies/tn0904019s/tn0904019s.htm>

Eamets, R., Kallaste, E. (2004/2005), 'The Lack of the Wage Setting Power of Estonian Trade Unions?' *Baltic Journal of Economics*, Vol. 5, pp. 44–60.

Eamets, R., Philips, K., Masso, J. (2007), 'Wages and collective bargaining in the Baltic States' in Keune M., Galgoczi, B. (eds.), *Collective Bargaining on wages—recent European experiences.* Brussels: ETUI-REHS.

Education and the Global Economic Crisis: Summary of results of the follow-up survey (2010), Education International: <http://www.eunec.eu/sites/www.eunec.eu/files/event/attachments/report_education_international.pdf>

Eomois, P.P. (2007), 'Income inequality', in *Social Inequality*, Statistics Estonia, pp. 10–23. <http://rahvatervis.ut.ee/bitstream/1/883/1/ES2007_3.pdf>

Espenberg, K., Jaakson, K., Kallaste, E., Nurmela, K. (2012), 'Kollektiivlepingute roll Eesti töösuhetes', *Sotsiaalministeeriumi toimetised* 1/2012.

ESS Round 4: European Social Survey Round 4 Data (2008). 'Data file edition 4.1', Norwegian Social Science Data Services, Norway—Data Archive and distributor of ESS data.

Eurofound (2009), 'Industrial relations in companies', <http://www.eurofound.europa.eu/eiro/surveyreports/ee1110019d/ee1110019d.pdf>

European Commission (2011), Progress towards Lisbon objectives in education and training. Indicators and Benchmarks (2010/2011), European Commission. <http://ec.europa.eu/education/lifelong-learning-policy/indicators10_en.htm> Last accessed: 3 March 2013.

European Commission (2012a), 'Eurobarometer 73.4 (2010)', TNS OPINION & SOCIAL, Brussels [Producer]. GESIS Data Archive, Cologne. ZA5234 Data file Version 2.0.1.

European Commission (2012b), 'Eurobarometer 75.3 (2011)'. TNS OPINION & SOCIAL, Brussels [Producer]. GESIS Data Archive, Cologne. ZA5481 Data file Version 1.0.0.

EVS (2011), 'European Values Study Longitudinal Data File 1981–2008' (EVS 1981–2008). GESIS Data Archive, Cologne. ZA4804 Data file Version 2.0.0.

Fofack, H., Monga, C. (2004), 'Dynamics of Income Inequality and Welfare in Latvia in the Late 1990s', *Research Working Paper* No 3336, World Bank.

Guio, A.C., Fusco, A., Marlier, E. (2010), 'Income poverty and material deprivation in European countries', *Methodologies and Working Papers*, Eurostat.

Hazans, M. (2007), 'Looking for the workforce: the elderly, discouraged workers, minorities and students in the Baltic labour markets', *Empirica*, Vol. 34, Issue 4, pp. 319–349.

Heidmets, M., Kangro, A., Ruus, V., Matulionis, A.V., Loogma, K., Ziliskaite V. (2011), *Education. Baltic Way(s) of Human Development: Twenty Years on*, Tallinn: Eesti Koostöö Kogu.

Hinnosaar, M., Rõõm, T. (2003), 'The impact of minimum wage on the labour market in Estonia: an empirical analysis', *Bank of Estonia Working Paper* No. 8.

Howard, M. (2003), *The Weakness of Civil Society in Post-Communist Europe*, Cambridge: Cambridge University Press.

Inglehart, R., Catterberg, G. (2002), 'Trends in political action: The developmental trend and the post-honeymoon decline', *International Journal of Comparative Sociology*, Vol. 43, No. 3-5, pp. 300–316.

ISSP Research Group (2012), 'International Social Survey Programme: Social Inequality IV'—ISSP 2009. GESIS Data Archive, Cologne. ZA5400 Data file Version 3.0.0.

Karklins, R. (2005), *The System Made Me Do It: Corruption in Post-Communist Countries*. London: M.E. Sharpe.

Karstedt, S. (2003), 'Legacies of a culture of inequality: The Janus face of crime in post-Communist countries', *Crime, Law and Social Change*, Vol. 40, No. 2-3, pp. 295–320.

Knack, S. (2002), 'Social Capital and the Quality of Government: Evidence from the States', *American Journal of Political Science*, 46 (4), 772–785.

Krumins, J. (2011), 'Life expectancy and mortality—achievements and challenges', *Estonian Human Development Report. Baltic Way(s) of Human Development: Twenty Years on.* Tallinn: Eesti Koostöö Kogu.

Kutsar, D. (1997), 'Multiple welfare losses and risk of social exclusion in the Baltic States during societal transition' in A. Aasland, K. Knudsen, D. Kutsar, I. Trapenciere, (eds.), *The Baltic Countries Revisited: Living Conditions and Comparative Challenges*, The NORBALT Living Conditions Project, Fafo Report 230, Oslo, Fafo, pp. 79–101.

Kutsar, D. and Trumm, A. (1995), 'Changed Situation, Remaining Needs: A Challenge for Welfare Policy in Estonia', in J. Simpura, (ed.), *Social Policy in Transition Societies. Experience from the Baltic Countries and Russia*, Helsinki, The Finnish ICSW Committee, The Finnish Federation of Social Welfare, pp. 44–59.

Leping, K. O., Toomet, O. S. (2008), Emerging ethnic wage gap: Estonia during political and economic transition', *Journal of Comparative Economics*, Vol. 36, pp. 599–619.

Leventi; C., Levy, H., Matsaganis, M., Paulus, A., Sutherland, H. (2010), 'Modelling the distributional effects of austerity measures: The challenges of a comparative perspective'. *Social Situation Observatory—Living Conditions and Income Distribution, Research Note 8/2010*.

Masso, A. (2008), Ethnic differentiations in satisfaction evaluations: Estonia's distinctions in the European context, in M. Lauristin (ed.), *Estonian Human Development Report 2008*, Eesti Ekspressi Kirjastus, pp. 81–87.

Masso, A. (2012), 'The transition from intercultural to transcultural communication: the emigration wishes of Estonian youth', unpublished conference paper presented at the IAMCR conference in Durban, 15-19 July, in Durban.

Masso, J. Espenberg, E., Masso, A., Mieriņa, I., Philips, K. (2013), *Growing Inequalities and its Impacts: Country Report for the Baltic States—Estonia, Latvia, Lithuania*, University of Tartu.

Masso, J., Eamets, R. (2007), 'Macro-Level Labour Market Flexibility in the Baltic States', in T. Paas and R. Eamets (eds.), *Labour Market Flexibility, Flexicurity and Employment: Lessons of the Baltic States*, Nova Science, pp. 101–142.

Masso, J. and Espenberg, K. (2012), 'Early application of fiscal austerity measures in the Baltic States', in D. Vaughan-Whitehead (ed.), *Public Sector Adjustments in Europe: Scope, Effects and Policy Issues*, International Labour Office, pp. 45–70.

Masso, J. and Krillo, K. (2010), 'Estonia, Latvia and Lithuania: Minimum Wages in a Context of Migration and Labour Shortages', in D. Vaughan-Whitehead, (ed.), *The Minimum Wage Revisited in the Enlarged EU*, Cheltenham, UK and Northampton, MA: Edward Elgar, pp. 113–152.

Masso, J., Krillo, K. (2011), 'Mixed Adjustment Forms and Inequality Effects in Estonia, Latvia and Lithuania', in D. Vaughan-Whitehead, (ed.), *Work Inequalities in the Crisis: Evidence from Europe, UK*, Cheltenham, UK and Northampton, MA: Edward Elgar Publishing, pp. 38–102.

Masso, J. and Paas, T. (2007), 'Social Protection Systems and Labour Market Policies in the Baltic States', in T. Paas, R. Eamets (eds.), *Labour Market Flexibility, Flexicurity and Employment: Lessons of the Baltic States*, Nova Science, pp. 143–181.

Mieriņa, I. (2013), 'The Vicious Circle: Does Disappointment with Political Authorities Contribute to Political Passivity in Latvia', forthcoming in *European Societies*.

Milanovic, B. (1998), 'Income, Inequality, and Poverty during the Transition from Planned to Market Economy', *World Bank, Regional and Sectoral Studies*. Washington, DC: The World Bank.

Mishler, W. and Rose, R. (2001), 'What are the origins of political trust? Testing institutional and cultural theories in post-communist societies',. *Comparative Political Studies*, Vol. 34, No. 1, pp. 30–62.

Mishler, W. and Rose, R. (2005), What are the consequences of political trust? A test of cultural and institutional theories in Russia', *Comparative Political Studies*, Vol. 38, No 9, pp. 1050–1078.

Noorkõiv, R., Orazem, P., Puur, A., and Vodopivec, M. (1998), 'Employment and Wage Dynamics in the Estonia, 1989-1995', *Economics in Transition*, Vol. 6, No 2, pp. 481–503.

Paas, T., Hinnosaar, M., Masso, J., Szirko, O. (2004), 'Social Protection Systems in the Baltic States', *Working Paper* No 26, University of Tartu, Faculty of Economics and Business Administration, 87 p.

Philips, K. (2002). 'The Changes in Valuation of Human Capital During the Transition Process in Estonia', Dissertatsiones rerum oeconomicarum. Universitas Tartuensis. No 6, Tartu: Tartu Ülikooli Kirjastus 2001, 290 p.

Pitchler, F. and Wallace, C. (2009), 'Social capital and social class in Europe: The role of social networks in social stratification', *European Sociological Review*, Vol. 25, No. 3, pp. 319-332.

Rahn, M. and Rudolph, T. (2005), 'A Tale of Political Trust in American Cities', *Public Opinion Quarterly*, Vol. 69, No.4, pp. 530,60.

Realo, A. (2009), 'Ptk 3.3. Eluga rahulolu ja õnnelikkus', Lauristin, M. (Toim.), *Eesti inimarengu aruanne 2008*, Tallinn: Eesti Koostöö Koda, 63–66.

Reuterswärd, A. (2003), *Labour Market and Social Policies in the Baltic Countries*, OECD.

Rõõm, T. (2003), 'Tootmistegurite maksustamine ja tööpuudus Eestis', *Bank of Estonia / Eesti Pank Working Paper* No. 5/2003, 28 p.

Rõõm, T. (2007), 'Haridus ja tööturg Eestis', *Eesti Pank / Bank of Estonia Working Paper* Series 12/2007.

Rõõm, T., Uusküla, L. (2006), Palgakujunduse põhimõtted Eesti ettevõtetes Eesti Panga Toimetised 5/2006.

Solt, F. (2008), 'Economic inequality and democratic political engagement', *American Journal of Political Science*, Vol. 52, No. 1, pp. 48-60.

Springe, I. (2012), 'The hidden side of Latvia's 'Success' story', *The Baltic Times*, 31 October 2012, <http://www.baltictimes.com/news/articles/32068/> Last accessed: 3 March 2013.

Staehr, K. (2010), 'The global financial crisis and public finances in the new EU countries from Central and Eastern Europe', *Bank of Estonia Working Paper* No. 2/2010.

SWIID (2011), 'Standardized World Income Inequality Database', version 3.1, December 2011.

Sztompka, P. (2004), 'The Trauma of Social Change: A Case of Post-Communist Societies', in J.C. Alexander, R. Eyerman, B. Giesen (eds.), *Cultural Trauma and Collective Identity*, Berkeley: University of California Press, pp. 155–195.

Toots, A. and Bachmann, J. (2010), 'Contemporary welfare regimes in Baltic States: Adapting post-communist conditions to post-modern challenges', *Studies of Transition States and Societies*, Vol. 2, No.2, pp. 31–44.

Trumm, A. (2010), Poverty in Estonia in the Context of Socioeconomic Situation. In: D. Kutsar (ed.) *Poverty in Estonia*, 2010, pp. 55–64.

Trumm, A. (2011), *Poverty in the context of societal transitions in Estonia*, Tartu: Tartu University Press.

Uslaner, E. M. (2008), *Corruption, Inequality, and the Rule of Law: The Bulging Pocket Makes the Easy Life*, New York: Cambridge University Press.

Veenhoven, R. (2013), 'Happiness in Nations'. World Database of Happiness, Erasmus University Rotterdam, The Netherlands. Accessed on 8 February 2013 at: <http://worlddatabaseofhappiness.eur.nl/hap_nat/nat_fp.php?mode=1>

Vihalemm, T., Siiner, M., Masso, A., Djackova, S., Ramonieie, M., Kello, K., Kaledaite, V., and Dabashinskiene, I. (2011), 'Language space and human capital in the Baltic States', in T. Vihalemm (ed.), *Estonian Human Development Report 2011*, Tallinn: Eesti Koostöö Kogu, pp. 116–143.

Vipule, S. (2000), 'Bezdarba attīstība un to ietekmējošie faktori Latvijā', http://www.bank.lv/publikacijas/averss-un-reverss/bezdarba-attistiba-un-to-ietekmejosie-faktori-latvija/4660?pop=1&tmpl=component>. Last accessed 3 March 2013.

Võrk, A. (2012), Personal communication, University of Tartu.

Võrk, A., Leetmaa, R., Paulus, A., and Anspal, S. (2007), 'Tax-Benefit Systems in the New Member States and their Impact on Labour Supply and Employment', *Praxis Working Paper* No 26/2007, Tallinn; <http://www.praxis.ee/data/PRAXIS_Working_Paper_26_2007.pdf>

Wilkinson, R., Pickett, K. (2009), *The Spirit Level. Why More Equal Societies Almost Always do Better*, New York: Penguin Books.

Zepa, B. (1999), *Conditions of enhancement of civic participation*, Riga: Baltic Data House.

CHAPTER 6

....

BELGIUM: WHEN GROWING BACKGROUND INEQUALITIES MEET RESILIENT INSTITUTIONS*

....

TIM VAN RIE AND IVE MARX**

1. INTRODUCTION

....

BELGIUM is one among few industrialized countries that did not experience a substantial increase in income inequalities over the course of the last three decades. This status as an international outlier is quite remarkable, considering that the country ranks consistently among the most 'globalized' countries in the world.

From a national perspective, the finding of stable income inequality is no less puzzling: since the early 1980s, the country has experienced major economic and political shifts. Belgian politics are traditionally characterized by three intercutting cleavages: linguistic; socio-economic; and religious-philosophical. As the segmentation in ideological 'pillars' gradually evaporated, the linguistic fault line came to be the dominant source of political conflict. In a process of centrifugal federalism, the Kingdom of Belgium delegated ever more competences to its communities and regions. Concurrently, European integration had a major impact on the evolving Belgian federation, arguably even preventing the federal level from disappearing (Beyers and Bursens, 2006).

* This chapter is based on a more elaborate country report prepared in the framework of the FP7 Project Growing Inequalities' Impacts. The full report can be accessed online <www.gini-research.org/CR-Belgium>

While taking full responsibility for the text, the authors would like to thank the following colleagues for topical contributions: Marjolijn De Wilde; Jeroen Horemans; Leen Meeusen; Annemie Nys; Olivier Pintelon; Pieter Vandenbroucke; Wim Van Lancker; Aaron Van den Heede; and Gerlinde Verbist. We thank Abigail McKnight and Massimiliano Bratti for helpful comments on a pre-final version of this chapter.

** Herman Deleeck Centre for Social Policy.

The constitutional reforms were all the more controversial because they coincided with a shift in the economic fortunes of the country's main regions. The past three decades saw the continued decline of heavy industry, which had been concentrated in the francophone Walloon region. Gradually, the economic centre of gravity shifted to the Dutch-speaking Flanders, which capitalized on its central geographic location to develop transport, logistics and light industry. The presence of international political organizations—NATO and a number of EU institutions have their headquarters in Brussels—contributed to the development of a service sector that is international in outlook.

Through international migration, the Belgian population became more diverse. Since 1945, net migration has been positive in all but a few years, with a clear upward trend since the early 1980s. European enlargement plays a substantial role, but there are also sizeable inflows from third countries. To a large extent, these can be linked to prior waves of labour migration (notably from Turkey and Morocco) and the colonial past (Democratic Republic of Congo) (CGKR, 2011).

While all these changes potentially have major socio-economic implications, Belgian politics are notable for a deep-rooted tendency towards stability, inertia even. In the Belgian consociational democracy, political elites are characterized by a firm commitment to consensus decision-making (Hooghe and Huyse, 2009). Government coalitions tend to seek linguistic and ideological symmetry with parties of the same political family from either side of the language border. Since 1980, there have never been fewer than four political parties in the national government. A multitude of checks and balances prevent one language group from imposing changes unilaterally. The legacy of pillarization includes an institutionalized role for actors from civil society, most notably the social partners. As expected in political theory (Tsebelis, 1995), the large number of veto players tends to be associated with policy continuity (and at times governmental instability). Crucially in terms of income inequality, the main instruments of income distribution (social security and the bulk of taxation) have largely been maintained at the central level. We argue that this combination of growing background inequalities and resilient institutions constitute the key to understanding inequality and its impacts in Belgium.

This chapter first considers the development of income inequality and its drivers. Next, it examines a number of social impacts, both in terms of trends over time and stratification of social risks. The analysis of political and cultural impacts applies a similar approach. The policy section assesses the role of cash benefits, taxes and social services in mediating inequalities. The final section concludes.

2. The Development of Inequality and its Drivers

Household Income Inequality

Survey data suggest that, while real average incomes increased, income inequality in Belgium remained fairly stable between 1985 and the late 2000s (Horemans, Pintelon *et al.*, 2011). The finding of stability is robust for inequality measures that are sensitive to different parts of the income distribution. A possible exception relates to the period between 1992

Table 6.1 Equivalent disposable household income (annual, 2009 euros) and inequality, Belgium, 1985–2009

	Average income	Gini	Theil	P90/P50	P50/P10	N
SEP						
1985	14944	0.220	0.081	1.616	1.647	18261
1988	15593	0.224	0.088	1.627	1.636	11069
1992	17154	0.223	0.084	1.632	1.654	10697
1997	17862	0.233	0.092	1.679	1.715	12184
ECHP						
1993	19926	0.281	0.138	1.781	1.939	8894
1994	19853	0.272	0.13	1.736	1.914	8616
1995	19765	0.262	0.122	1.710	1.88	8225
1996	19960	0.268	0.127	1.731	1.849	7743
1997	20180	0265	0.122	1.773	1.825	7276
1998	20665	0.273	0.141	1.693	1.786	6834
1999	21160	0.271	0.136	1.748	1.778	6455
2000	21368	0.259	0.120	1.770	1.766	5829
EU–SILC						
2003	16968	0.255	0.109	1.705	1.897	12781
2004	18021	0.255	0.111	1.676	1.845	12657
2005	18887	0.259	0.116	1.72	1.869	14169
2006	19206	0.257	0.115	1.695	1.872	15322
2007	19795	0.258	0.116	1.689	1.856	14911
2008	21042	0.252	0.109	1.681	1.843	14579
2009	21274	0.257	0,112	1.708	1.856	14621

Source: Horemans, Pintelon *et al.* (2011), updated to 2009. Incomes are equivalized using the modified OECD scale. SEP data are annualized from monthly reference period.

and 1997, which shows a relatively small but significant rise in income inequality, which mainly resulted from a stagnation of lower incomes.

A reasonable degree of caution is warranted in reading Table 6.1. Its observations are based on three distinct surveys, with breaks in series and different income concepts. While the data have been harmonized as much as possible across these sources, trends should be assessed only within each of the series, not directly across sources. Most notably, inequality measures based on the SEP survey are substantially lower than those based on ECHP and EU-SILC. At first glance, this might suggest that inequality was on the rise in the first half of our observation period. However, this gap is mainly due to differences in methods between these sources (Cantillon, van Dam *et al.*, 2003).

Similar to income inequality indicators, measures of relative income poverty suggest stability since the mid 1980s. In the late 2000s, approximately one out of seven inhabitants had an equivalized income below the poverty threshold of 60 per cent of the median.

A number of categories are at particularly high risk (see Table 6.2). Age shows a U-shaped pattern, with higher rates for children and the elderly, compared to persons of active age. In

Table 6.2 At-risk-of-poverty rates, 2009

Total		14.6
Sex	Men	13.9
	Women	15.2
Age category	<18	18.3
	18–24	14.4
	25–54	11.6
	55–64	12.5
	65+	19.4
Household type	Two or more adults, no children	11.4
	Two or more adults with children	12.4
	Single person	18.8
	Singe parent	35.3
Educational attainment (aged 18+)	Lower (secondary)	23.0
	Upper secondary	10.7
	Tertiary	5.5
Main activity status (aged 18+)	Employed	4.5
	Retired	16.1
	Other inactive	25.8
	Unemployed	30.4
Country of birth (aged 18+)	Belgium	10.8
	Other EU27	19.2
	Extra EU27	39.2

Source: Eurostat, based on EU-SILC 2010. Poverty threshold is set at 60% of the median equivalized disposable income. Incomes are equivalized using a modified OECD scale.

terms of household types, single parents are increasingly vulnerable. The poverty risk also shows regional differences, with a considerably higher rate in the Walloon region (17.7 per cent in 2009) compared to the Flemish region (10.4 per cent). Due to small sample size, no reliable point estimates are available for the Brussels region, but all the evidence suggests that the risk is higher in the capital than in the Walloon region. Moreover, there are indications that regional gaps for child poverty risk have been widening over recent years, with stability in Flanders but increases in Wallonia and Brussels (Vandenbroucke, 2012). Among adults, there are steep gradients in poverty risk according to educational attainment. Adults that did not finish lower secondary education became increasingly exposed to income poverty. Judged by international standards, the in-work poverty risk in Belgium is fairly low. Non-workers are considerably more exposed. While unemployment decreased overall, the poverty risk for unemployed has increased substantially compared to the mid 1980s (Van den Bosch, Vandenbroucke *et al.*, 2009). Finally, the poverty risk is very high among the population that was born outside the EU. This immigrant gap is considerably wider than in most other EU countries, which makes Belgium an outlier in this respect (Corluy and Verbist, 2010; OECD, 2012).

Wealth and Debt Inequality

Analyses of wealth inequality are hampered by a lack of recent data. Rademaekers and Vuchelen (1999) provide an estimate for the mid 1990s and mid 1980s. Their concept of wealth comprises financial assets, real estate (both professional and private), movable material property (both professional and private) minus debt (including mortgage debt). For 1994, the authors find a marked concentration of wealth, with the richest 10 per cent of the Belgian population accounting for nearly half of total wealth (49.6 per cent). By contrast, the first decile possessed merely 1.0 per cent. Compared to 1984, the wealth distribution had become more unequal over time.

Analysing the link between income and wealth, Van den Bosch (1998) found that in the early 1990s, the gross wealth of the income poor was about half that of the non-poor. Among the income poor, wealth was found to be very unequally distributed. Households on very low income include rather wealthy pensioners owning their home as well as other property, as well as non-home owners that possess little financial wealth.

More recently, and from an international perspective, Belgium appears to qualify as a country with rather low wealth inequality (taking into account all methodological caveats that apply to such rankings) (Keating, O'Sullivan *et al.*, 2011). These comparisons also show that the ratio of wealth to disposable income is very high in Belgium.

Labour Market Inequality

Judged by international standards, the dispersion of (net) wages among individual workers in Belgium is very low. By contrast to many other industrialized countries, there is no indication that dispersion of net wages among full-time workers increased substantially between the middle of the 1980s and the late 2000s (Horemans, Pintelon *et al.*, 2011; OECD, 2011).

One important caveat applies, however: the sizeable tax wedge appears to have stimulated the development of employer-provided fringe benefits that are fully or partially tax-exempt (OECD, 2009). These benefits, such as lunch vouchers and—most notably—company cars, tend to be strongly concentrated among the highest wage earners. Taking their value into account increases inequality substantially (Verbist and Lefebure, 2008). One of the recent crisis measures was to increase taxation on company cars.

Measures of labour market inequality that are more qualitative in nature suggest that Belgian workers are fairly secure. Part-time work has increased substantially over the past three decades, but is mostly (and increasingly) voluntary in nature. Temporary employment is on the rise, but remains low by international standards (8.1 per cent in 2010). Self-employment declined over time and contributes less to inequality compared to other countries (OECD, 2011).

While wage differences among workers are rather modest, and precarious work uncommon, labour force participation as such is highly stratified. Over the course of the past three decades, labour force participation in Belgium increased, but remained consistently below the European average (see Figure 6.1). Similar to other countries, the rise was largely due to the entry of females into the labour market. For men, the 1980s was a period of declining activity and employment rates, due to Belgium's policy of labour shedding through early retirement schemes (Marx, 2007). Unemployment, through its cyclical variations, has fallen

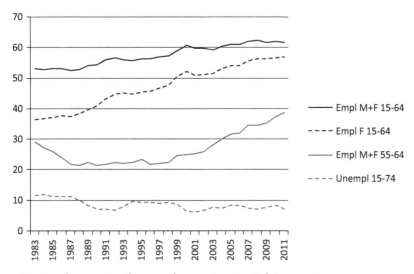

FIGURE 6.1 Employment and unemployment rates, Belgium, 1983–2011

Source: Eurostat, based on labour force statistics. Employed as a share of (a subgroup of) the population.
Unemployed as a share of the labour force (employed plus unemployed).

from approximately 12 per cent in the early 1980s to approximately 8 per cent in 2010. It tends to be rather persistent, with typically half of all unemployed having been so for over 12 months.

Labour market participation in Belgium is strongly stratified. This applies first and foremost to the life span. Belgium has fairly high employment rates at prime age (25–54) but low employment for young and, particularly, older workers. Strong gradients apply to educational attainment. In 2010, just over 60 per cent of the prime age population (25–54) with at most lower secondary education was in employment, compared to 80 per cent among those who attained upper secondary employment and 90 per cent among tertiary graduates. In addition, large regional disparities mirror the pattern observed in poverty risk: Flanders has the most favourable outcomes (employment rate of 66.3 per cent and unemployment at 5.1 per cent in 2010), followed by the Walloon region (56.7 and 11.4 per cent) and Brussels (54.8 and 17.3 per cent).

Migrants, particularly those born outside the EU, have substantially lower employment rates. The OECD has singled out Belgium as the country with a very low female employment rate among non-EU migrants. Rather worryingly, the Belgian employment and unemployment gaps for the second generation of migrants (native born offspring of migrants compared to natives) are also among the largest in the industrialized world (OECD, 2012).

Overall, the distribution of jobs across households seems to have had an equalizing effect on market incomes. Educational homogamy is relatively limited (Domański and Przybysza, 2007) and many of the new female part-time jobs came to complement workers' incomes (Van den Bosch, Van Dam *et al.*, 1999; OECD, 2011). Nevertheless, Belgium has one of the highest and most persistent rates of household joblessness amongst industrialized countries. In 2010, approximately one eighth of working age adults and children lived in a jobless household.

Educational Inequality

Belgium has experienced a major educational expansion over the previous decades. This process was accompanied by a gender switch, as tertiary attainment is now higher among women than men.

The PISA studies suggest that Belgium's 15 year olds perform significantly better than the OECD average in science, mathematics and reading literacy. Beyond this headline score, however, there are large differences. First, there are considerable gaps between the Flemish, German and French communities, which each organize their own curricula (De Meyer and Warlop, 2010). On average, Flemish students perform significantly better than their counterparts attending French-Community schools, with the German Community between both. Tracking of secondary education, in general, technical and professional streams, starts at age 12 and is a recurrent topic of political debate. International evidence suggests that such tracking may contribute to educational segregation (Brunello and Checchi 2012). Pupils' socio-economic and migrant background have a larger effect on literacy scores in Belgium, compared to the OECD average (OECD 2011).

Drivers and Interdependence Between Inequalities

Belgium's stable income inequality poses a puzzle, dubbed 'the zero-sum crisis' (Van den Bosch, Van Dam *et al.*, 1999). The explanation lies in a combination of socio-demographic trends and policy changes. Overall, the labour market and wage-setting are rather tightly regulated, which contributes to a low share of workers in precarious employment, low pay and in-work poverty. Conversely, there is quite strong stratification in labour market participation and unemployment. The household dimension has proven to be an important buffer, as the increase of female (part-time) employment complemented the single earner model, dampening increases in market inequality. Second, in terms of social policy (to be discussed in Section 5), the general approach has been to extend coverage beyond the traditional insurance-based model (including self-employed or non-contributors), whilst targeting benefits to the most needy (with family composition as a major consideration) (Cantillon, De Lathouwer *et al.*, 1999; Vleminckx, 2011).

Beyond stability, there is a recurrent pattern of risk factors across different dimensions. Both in terms of education, labour market performance and income, the Flemish north tends to have better outcomes than the mainly francophone Walloon region and Brussels. It is important to note that 'inter-regional educational discrepancies probably started in the early 50s, and preceded the socio-economic ones, known to have emerged in the 1970s and early 1980s'(Vandenberghe, 2012).

While educational expansion as such is a positive development, it also contributes to the marginalization of adults that did not complete upper secondary education. Even among 25 to 34 year olds, the less-educated represent approximately 20 per cent.

Moreover, while Belgium has been notably liberal in its migration and nationalization policies, non-natives from outside the EU tend to have lower literacy scores, less favourable labour market positions and higher risks of poverty. The data suggest that this is not just a transitory issue: there is strong socio-economic reproduction for native born offspring of migrants. The impacts sections will therefore not only consider the changes of headline rates, but also stratification linked to background inequalities.

3. Social Impacts

It has been argued that (rising) income inequalities translate into a wide range of adverse effects at the individual, household and societal level. Belgium poses a peculiar puzzle in this respect: given stable income inequalities, should one expect stability in each of these dimensions? Beyond general trends, the subsequent section considers stratification of social risks, to gauge the extent to which these correspond to background inequalities.

Material Deprivation and Housing

Over time, the share of the Belgian population that faces an enforced lack of basic necessities decreases steadily. The risk factors for material deprivation are rather similar to those of poverty risk, resulting in considerable overlap. One important exception is age: despite their high income-poverty risk rate the elderly are the least deprived (see Table 6.3).

Table 6.3 Severe material deprivation rate by a number of characteristics, 2009

Total		5.9
Sex	Men	5.7
	Women	6.0
Age category	<18	7.7
	18–24	7.1
	25–54	6.5
	55–64	4.7
	65+	2.8
Household type	Two or more adults, no children	2.6
	Two or more adults with children	4.7
	Single person	11.0
	Singe parent	18.1
Educational attainment (aged 18+)	Lower (secondary)	9.1
	Upper secondary	4.8
	Tertiary	1.7
Main activity status (aged 18+)	Employed	2.3
	Retired	3.0
	Other inactive	11.0
	Unemployed	16.1
Country of birth (aged 18+)	Belgium	3.6
	Other EU27	7.5
	Extra EU27	22.9

Source: Eurostat, based on EU-SILC 2010. Severe material deprivation is defined as an enforced lack of 4 or more items out of 9 (to pay rent, mortgage or utility bills; to keep the home adequately warm; to face unexpected expenses; to eat meat or proteins regularly; to go on holiday; a television set; a washing machine; a car; a telephone).

Compared to many other countries, the rise and promotion of home ownership by public authorities in Belgium started much earlier—in the late nineteenth century, in direct response to industrial unrest (De Decker, 2008). By the late 2000s, home ownership was clearly the norm: over 70 per cent of the population own their dwelling. While all the regions share in the increase, there remain marked regional differences: the highest ownership rates in Flanders (over 77 per cent), followed by Wallonia (73 per cent). The majority of the population in Brussels are tenants (55 per cent) (Verbist and Vanhille, 2012). Across Belgium, only 7.3 per cent of the population are tenants with reduced rent. Rent-free tenants are even less common (1.6 per cent). Immigrants are significantly less likely to own a home than natives, but appear to be neither over- nor under-represented in social housing (OECD 2012).

Tenants on the private market are particularly vulnerable to housing cost overburden. Quite possibly, there is a selection effect, where only households with considerable wealth or steady income can obtain a mortgage or acquire a home. Indeed, the poverty risk of tenants has increased steadily since the mid 1980s (Van den Bosch, Vandenbroucke *et al.*, 2009).

Family Formation and Fertility

Family life in Belgium has changed notably since the 1980s. The average size of households decreased from 2.73 persons in 1981 to 2.39 in 2001. The trend is driven mainly by an increase in single person households (who tend to be quite vulnerable socio-economically) (see Table 6.4). Flanders traditionally has larger households than Wallonia, but there has been notable downward convergence over time (Census data). Migrants tend to live in larger households, with more children, but seem to converge with native practices over time (Deboosere, Lesthaeghe *et al.*, 2009).

Declining marriage rates and rising divorce rates provide further evidence of the decline of marriage as an institution. Cohabitation has become generalized, with a growing share of extra-marital births. Single parenthood has also increased rather strongly, a notable development given the high poverty risk rates for this household type.

The total fertility rate in Belgium declined rather strongly between 1960 and the mid 1980s, from 2,5 to 1,5 children per woman over her lifetime. From the 1980s onwards, fertility has recovered somewhat, to a level nearer (but below) the natural replacement rate of 2,1. With hindsight, the decline up to the mid 1980s was linked to a pattern of delayed

Table 6.4 Household structure (% population, in private households) in Belgium, 1981–2001

	1981	1991	2001
Single, no children	8.6	11.4	13.5
Couple without children	17.4	17.6	18
Couple with children	56.2	52.8	45.6
Single parent	5.6	7.4	9.1
Other	12.2	10.8	13.8

Source: Volkstelling (census).

fertility, with women having children at later age. Fertility trends do not seem to be linked directly to income inequality trends (which are stable in Belgium). By contrast, Neels (2010) has shown how unemployment in Belgium has adversely affected birth hazards at younger ages in all socio-economic groups between 1960 and 2000, with more highly educated women recovering more strongly in years of lower unemployment.

Health

Since the 1980s, the Belgian population has made considerable gains in life expectancy. Women gained more than six life years (up to 83 in 2010), men almost eight (77.6 in 2010) (OECD Health series). Moreover, at least part of the extra life years is spent in good health.

Beyond these favourable headline rates, however, the inequalities are non-negligible. There are regional disparities, particularly among men. In the late 2000s, boys born in Flanders can expect to live three years longer than those in Wallonia, with Brussels in an intermediate position. Life expectancy at age 25 shows strong educational gradients. Between 1991 and 2001, the gap between highly and less educated has widened, particularly among women. This also applies to healthy life expectancy (Van Oyen, Deboosere *et al.*, 2011).

In terms of morbidity, the evolutions are rather diffuse. It should be noted that population ageing may possibly distort the picture, as health tends to deteriorate with age. In terms of morbidity, the trends are rather diffuse. Population ageing possibly distorts the picture, as health tends to deteriorate with age. Given that women tend to live longer, but in worse health than men, the trends reported below control for age and sex.

Subjective health improved between 1997 and 2008, despite the fact that chronic illness went up. Mental health fluctuates between 2001 and 2008, as is the case for depressive disorder. However, the use of psychotropic medication is clearly on the rise, from 10 per cent of adults in 1997 to 15 per cent in 2008. In terms of stratification, a number of recurrent patterns emerge. Controlling for age and sex, less-educated persons tend to be more vulnerable than the more highly educated. The sole exception is for allergies, which are more prevalent among tertiary graduates. For subjective health, an intergenerational analysis suggests that there is an education effect on health, independent of parental educational attainment. In regional terms, inhabitants of Flanders tend to be in better health than Walloons and the Brussels population (Van der Heyden, Gisle *et al.*, 2010).

Overall, the data suggest that the Belgian healthcare system performs rather well in providing accessible care. The share of the population reporting unmet needs for healthcare is particularly low (never more than 1,5 per cent in the late 2000s). Moreover, immigrants do not report more issues in this respect than natives (whereas in many other OECD countries, this is an issue) (OECD, 2012).

Turning to lifestyle and prevention, the headline rates once more suggest a diversity of trends, positive and negative. Smoking tobacco has declined very strongly between the early 1980s and the late 2000s, but obesity is a growing problem. Alcohol consumption among adults remains fairly stable at a high level, with some evidence that problematic use and binge drinking may be on the rise. There is a negative linear association between educational level and both smoking and obesity (controlling for age and sex). Alcohol consumption shows an inverse pattern: moderate consumption of alcohol is more common among the higher educated. The link between education and problematic drinking, however, is not clear. Regional gradients appear to be less stark: overall, French-speaking Belgians smoke more than the Dutch-speaking population, but this holds only among older age groups. Alcohol consumers are most common in Flanders and least in Brussels (Gisle, Hesse *et al.*, 2010).

Violence, Crime and Punishment

Belgium is an international outlier in terms of victimization. Against an international tendency for falling victimization rates, Belgium actually recorded an increase between the late 1980s and late 2000s (from 13.4 per cent of the population being victimized to 17.8 per cent). As a result, Belgium changed from being one of the European countries with the lowest rates to a position close to the European average (van Dijk, Manchin *et al.*, 2007).

Among the population aged 15 and over, over ten per cent (11.2) experienced violence over the course of a year (2008). Brussels (19 per cent) clearly has much higher rates than Wallonia (13 per cent) and Flanders (9 per cent). The better educated are most vulnerable to theft, burglary and robbery (Demarest, Hesse *et al.*, 2010). Belgium has a higher rate of hate crimes than the European average (4.2 per cent versus 2.8 per cent). Some twenty per cent of immigrants that live in Belgium have experienced hate crimes, which is more than double the European average (van Dijk, Manchin *et al.*, 2007).

There has been a marked increase in the prison population between the early 1990s and the late 2000s, from 67 to 82 prisoners per 100,000 inhabitants (Eurostat). The overpopulation of prisons has become a pressing political issue. Penal policy in Belgium has 'bifurcated' over time. Recent years have seen an enlarged application of non-custodial sentences such as electronic surveillance in general, but also more remand custody and longer prison sentences for drug, sexual and violent crimes (Snacken, 2007).

Life Satisfaction, Happiness and Social Cohesion

In terms of life satisfaction and happiness, Belgium is an outlier. Whereas, across countries, this level tends to be rather stable over time, there has been a noted decline among Belgians between the mid 1970s and mid 1980s. Inglehart and Klingemann (2000) linked this malaise to tension between the Flemish and Walloons. Still, one could argue that these have hardly abated since the mid 1980s. Despite the decline, Belgium still ranks fairly highly among OECD countries in terms of life satisfaction. In terms of stratification along background inequalities, there is a clear educational gradient, with higher educated adults reporting higher levels of life satisfaction.

Over eighty per cent of the Belgian population has daily or weekly personal contact with family and friends. This score puts the country firmly among the European countries that are most sociable, along with Spain, Portugal, the UK and Finland. Some 5 per cent of the population cannot turn to any friends, family or neighbours for help, which is below the European average. The data suggest multidimensional vulnerability, as persons at risk of poverty are much more likely to be isolated compared to those above the income threshold (Eurostat 2010)

Perceived social exclusion is relatively high in Belgium: the share of adults that feel left out of society, looked down upon or not recognized by others is much higher than its GDP per capita would predict. At the individual level, there is a strong link to background inequalities, with higher rates among single persons and single parents, unemployed and manual workers and persons experiencing material deprivation (European Foundation for the Improvement of Living and Working Conditions, 2010).

Intergenerational Mobility

The section on educational inequalities hinted at a strong reproduction of pupils' socio-economic background. While entry into higher education increased substantially between 1976 and 2004, little to no progress has been made in combating the social gradient. Particularly among men, the difference is very stark. In 2004, over 60 per cent of the sons of highly educated fathers participated in higher education. Among sons of fathers who had not obtained upper secondary education, participation was under 15 per cent. For girls, the gradient is less strong, but still notable (26 per cent compared to 50 per cent) (Verbergt, Cantillon *et al.*, 2009). Belgium is among the countries where intergenerational reproduction is strongest for elementary occupations (Zaidi and Zolyomi, 2007), providing additional proof that background inequalities are an important factor in understanding the national story of inequality.

4. Political and Cultural Impacts

Similar to social impacts, there is a wide range of negative political and cultural outcomes that have been (tentatively) associated with rising inequalities. Once more, the stability of income inequality in Belgium makes it a notable test case. Beyond the headline rates, stratification along background inequalities is documented wherever possible.

Civic and Political Participation

Belgium's institutional framework includes a number of features that strongly promote (formal) political participation. The vote is compulsory for nationals aged 18 and over at all political levels, (i.e. European, federal, community, regional, province and local elections). Absenteeism is in principle sanctioned by fines, but enforcement is in practice rather lenient. Since 1980, voter turnout rates have nonetheless remained within a narrow band of 85 to 95 per cent. For national elections, there appears to have been a slight downward tendency since 2000. Compared to strong declines that are observed in many industrialized countries, this drop remains limited.

One might argue that in the context of a compulsory vote, invalid votes represent a more valid measure. Participation is equally high by these standards, as typically more than 90 per cent of votes at national and European level are valid. If any, there appears to be a slight downward trend of invalid votes over time (IDEA Voter Turnout Database).

In most industrialized countries, the share of trade union affiliates among employees dwindled from the 1970s onwards, with membership falling or lagging behind job growth. Belgium bucks this trend, as its union density has remained relatively stable at some 50 per cent of employees. A number of institutional features promote participation. In many sectors, trade unions can offer a union bonus (financed by employers) to partly reimburse membership fees. In addition, and similar to some Nordic countries, Belgian trade unions are (indirectly but visibly) involved in the provision of unemployment benefits. The so-called Ghent system has been shown to promote high and resilient union density rates. In Belgium, union density is very strongly concentrated among less-educated and blue collar workers (Van Rie, Marx et al., 2011).

The only measure of formal political participation that shows a consistent decrease is political party membership. Whereas nearly 10 per cent of the electorate were members of a political party in 1978 (up from less than 8 per cent in 1961), this share has dwindled consistently to somewhat less than 6 per cent in 2007 (Deschouwer, 2012).

Survey data from the European Values Study suggests that less formal manifestations of participation are increasing rather than waning. Compared to the early 1980s, a growing share of adults claims to discuss political issues with friends. Self-reported interest in politics has also increased compared to 1990 (see Table 6.5). There is evidence of stratification: among the 'apolitical class' there is an over-representation of women, persons with low educational attainment, low-skilled blue collar workers, non-Catholics, and individuals with a materialistic value set. There is no substantial difference between Flanders and the Walloon region, although Brussels is under-represented in the apolitical class.

Between the early 1980s and 2000s, there is no clear trend in either direction for non-conventional political participation. This comprises signing petitions, taking part in demonstrations, boycotting, wildcat strikes and occupying buildings or factories. Stratification has a similar pattern to political interest: women, the less educated, blue collar workers and persons with a materialistic mindset tend to be less militant. There are regional

Table 6.5 Interest in politics among adults, 1981–2009

	1981	1990	1999	2009
Self-declared interest in politics				
Strongly interested	:	7	10	7
Somewhat interested	:	23	29	24
Not very interested	:	30	31	36
Not interested at all	:	40	30	33
Discussing politics with friends				
Regularly	5	9	13	8
Now and then	39	44	50	53
Never	56	47	37	39

Source: Abts, Swyngedouw *et al.* 2011, based on European Values Study.

differences, as Walloons tend to be significantly more militant than Flemings (with Brussels somewhat closer to Wallonia than Flanders) (Abts, Swyngedouw *et al.*, 2011). A comparison of peace protests in the 1980s and 2003 show a shift in age structure (with fewer young protesters) and education (with more tertiary educated) (Walgrave, Rucht *et al.*, 2010).

Trust

A popular line of reasoning holds that centuries of occupation by consecutive foreign powers have instilled the Belgian mindset with a deep mistrust of public authority. Recent opinion surveys suggest a different pattern. Rather than a generalized lack of confidence in all political authorities, Abts, Swyngedouw *et al.* (2011) find strong polarization. A very large majority of the Belgian population (well over eighty per cent in 2009) holds favourable opinions of the health care system, the education system and social security. By contrast, less than half of Belgians trust the main political institutions. The political parties (some 20 per cent), the government (around 30 per cent) and parliament (approximately 40 per cent) all enjoy a low degree of confidence. Recent political crises have only served to reduce trust in these institutions (ESS2002-2010). A number of other institutions hold an intermediate position: the national administration; as well as EU and NATO (each just below 60 per cent); the justice system; the army; large companies and trade unions (around 50 per cent). The police enjoy widespread trust (70 per cent), whereas the press (40 per cent), and the Church (36 per cent) do not.

While the polarization between national political institutions and welfare institutions can also be observed in neighbouring countries (France and the Netherlands), it is nowhere nearly as strong as in Belgium. This is mainly due to particularly high trust in welfare institutions among the Belgian population. One might argue that this confidence is vindicated by the stable income inequalities. On the other hand, there is a possibility that Belgians overestimate their system, for example pension entitlements. In terms of institutional trust, there is little notable stratification among the population.

Values and Legitimacy

Support among the population for democracy is both very large and rather stable over time. Less than one tenth of the population consider democracy as rather bad (8 per cent in 2009) or very bad (1 per cent). Over time there has been a shift, with a declining share considering democracy very good (49 per cent in 1999 to 37 per cent in 2009), whereas 'rather good' increases (from 41 to 54 per cent).

Quite possibly, this links to a criticism that is shared by many, namely that the practice involves 'too much talk' and indecision. This view has become slightly more common from 1999 to 2009. Indeed, the late 2000s in Belgium were a period of governmental instability and great political tension. Rejection of both the principle and practice of democracy is strongly stratified among the population. Anti-democratic views are more common among the young, among blue collar workers and persons who did not obtain secondary education. Flanders leans towards a critique of the principle of democracy, whereas Brussels and the Walloon regions report higher shares of disenchantment with its practice (Abts, Swyngedouw *et al.*, 2011).

The rise of the extremist vote is a notable development over the last three decades, particularly in Flanders. In a system of proportional representation voting, three 'traditional' political families (Christian-democrats, socialists and liberals) have dominated the electoral landscape since Belgian independence in 1831. In the early 1950s, they jointly represented 90 per cent of the vote. This share dwindled to approximately 70 per cent around the mid 1990s and 57 per cent in 2010 (Deschouwer, 2012).

The combined share of the traditional parties was mainly taken up by new actors, notably regionalist parties, ecological parties and right-wing populist parties. The extreme left is weak and dwindling in Belgium. The Belgian communist party was mainly concentrated in industrial (Walloon) areas. It has not succeeded in capturing a single seat in the Federal Parliament since 1981 (see Table 6.6).

By contrast, the rise of the extreme right is a notable development over the last three years, particularly in Flanders. Francophone Belgium has a 'Front National', with historic links to the French party of the same name. In Belgium, FN is rather marginal, representing less than 5 per cent of the Walloon electorate. In Flanders, a party named 'Vlaams Blok' (Flemish Block) has played an increasingly important role over the past three decades. It was founded in the late 1970s as a break-away radical wing of the regionalist party. In 1991, the breakthrough of this party at national level proved a major shock to the political landscape. On 'Black Sunday' (24 November), more than one tenth of Flemish votes in the national elections went to the populist right-wing party. With a programme that included unilateral secession of the Flemish region and anti-immigrant rhetoric, the party gained considerable success over subsequent elections, up to the mid 2000s. In 2004, it was convicted for the use of racist propaganda and changed its name to Vlaams Belang (Flemish Interests). That same year, it went on to claim its highest share of the vote yet, with 24 per cent in the Flemish regional elections. The subsequent dwindling success is partly a result of containment policy

Table 6.6 Share of the vote and seats for extreme parties in the national Chamber of Representatives, 1981–2010

	Vlaams Blok/Belang		Front National		KPB/PCB	
	Seats	Vote	Seats	Vote	Seats	Vote
8/11/1981	1/212	1.1%	–		2/212	2.3%
13/10/1985	1/212	1.4%	–		–	1.2%
13/12/1987	2/212	1.9%	–		–	0.8%
24/11/1991	12/212	6.6%	1/212	0.5%	–	0.1%
21/05/1995	11/150	7.8%	2/150	2.3%	–	0.1%
13/06/1999	15/150	9.9%	1/150	1.5%	–	
18/05/2003	18/150	11.6%	1/150	2.0%	–	
10/06/2007	17/150	12.0%	1/150	2.0%	–	
13/10/2010	12/150	7.8%	–	0.5%	–	–

Source: (Deschouwer 2012). Vlaams Blok/Belang and Front National are right-wing populist parties. Belgische Kommunistische Partij /Parti Communiste de Belgique was the Belgian Communist Party.

by other parties, as well as competition with the regionalist party N-VA (Nieuw-Vlaamse Alliantie, New Flemish Alliance) (Pauwels, 2011).

Vlaams Belang seems to have tapped into a powerful political current in Flanders that combines regional identification and anti-immigrant stances. In terms of socio-economic characteristics, there are no clear gradients, as the vote is quite evenly spread across educational and occupational segments (Frognier, Bol *et al.*, 2012).

Welfare

The Welfare State enjoys not only a large amount of trust, but also considerable support among the Belgian population. The support seems to be rather stable over time. A small minority consider that need is the result of laziness (less than 20 per cent). Injustice and being unlucky are much more frequent answers. Between 1990 and 2008, the view that need is a part of modern society has become more common (from one tenth to nearly a quarter of the population) (European values study).

The economic disparities between Flanders and Wallonia result in fairly large inter-regional transfers, through the individualized welfare payments. Over time, these have become a political issue, prominent on the political agenda of Flemish nationalist parties. Opinion surveys suggest, however, that splitting social security along regional lines enjoys very mixed support, even among Flemish voters (Swyngedouw and Rink, 2008).

5. THE ROLE OF POLICIES

Belgium has an extensive Welfare State, with highly coordinated wage-setting mechanisms, as well as one of the OECD's largest social expenditure budgets (relative to GDP). The austerity of the post-oil crisis decades has seen a curtailment, but no direct cuts in the overall level of welfare spending and taxes. Social services (such as health and childcare) represent a growing share of the social budget. The distributive allocation of these services suggests that they are strongly linked to a number of background inequalities.

Labour Income

Belgium has a deep-rooted tradition of centralized and coordinated wage-setting. Collective wage bargaining occurs consecutively at cross-sectoral, sectoral and company level. The former two levels are highly influential. While there has been decentralization of wage-setting over the course of the 1980s, Belgian wage setting remains highly coordinated (Plasman *et al.*, 2007). The widespread use of extension mechanisms leads to a very high coverage rate. Over 90 per cent of Belgian wage and salary earners are covered by collective wage agreements, a share that has been constant since the middle of the 1980s (Visser 2011).

Two national particularities with regard to wage formation should be noted. First, Belgium is one of few industrialized countries that applies automatic cost-of living adaptation to wages and social benefits. Concerns for wage competitiveness have led consecutive governments to reform the 'index' (including a series of indexation freezes in the mid 1980s and adaptation of the basket of goods and services in 1994). Nevertheless, the system continues to play a key role as a lower bound in wage-setting.

Second, the so-called 'Competitiveness Laws' of 1989 and 1996 institutionalized governmental intervention in wage setting when wage developments are considered harmful to competitiveness. A monitoring system was introduced, benchmarking Belgian wage developments against those in her main competitors and neighbouring countries: Germany; France; and the Netherlands. The weighted average of pay developments in these countries is considered the upper margin for negotiations, as wage increases beyond this limit trigger government intervention. Belgium's statutory monthly minimum wage applies to all private sector employees. While its real value is safeguarded by the indexation mechanism, gross minimum wages have failed to keep up with developments in average wage from the second half of the 1990s. Analyses of net wages (including certain social benefits as well) suggest that the gap between Belgian minimum wage earners and the median income widened somewhat between 1992 and 2001, but recovered slightly by 2009. For the entire period under consideration, the minimum wage has been associated with a risk of income poverty (with the 60 per cent of median disposable income threshold), at least when several household members depend on a single earner (Van Mechelen, Marchal et al., 2011) (see Figure 6.2).

Taxation

Tax revenue as a share of GDP remained fairly stable between 1980 and 2009, with fluctuation ranging between 41.3 per cent (1980) and 45.0 per cent (1998). This stability followed fifteen years of strong expansion (from 31.1 per cent in 1965 to 43.0 per cent in 1979). Taxes on income profits and capital gains are the dominant source of revenue, with social security contributions a close second. The latter increased in share from 1980 to the early 1990s.

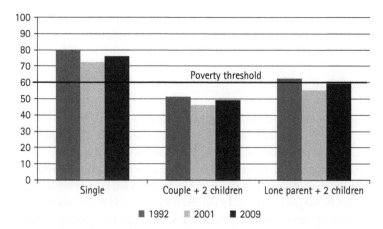

FIGURE 6.2 Net disposable income at minimum wage relative to median equivalized disposable household income (%), 1992, 2001 and 2009

Source: Van Mechelen, Marchal et al. (2011).

Taxes on goods and services have remained relatively stable as a source of revenue, and represent a fairly small share, compared to other countries. Taxes on property are a relatively modest but growing source of revenue.

From an international perspective, personal income taxes in Belgium consistently rank among the most redistributive in Europe, mainly due to the high level of the average tax rate (Verbist, 2004; Immervoll, Levy et al., 2006; Lelkes and Sutherland, 2009; Decoster, 2009). Moreover, compared to Greece, Hungary, Ireland or the UK, indirect taxes are less regressive in Belgium.

Looking at developments over time, the reform of personal income tax in 1988 (implemented 1989) reduced taxes on labour substantially, leading to a sharp drop in the average tax rate and making the PIT less redistributive (Van Cauter and Van Meensel, 2006). The reform of 2001 was fairly neutral in terms of redistribution, as the reduction in tax level that this reform entailed was offset by an increase in the progressivity of personal income taxes (Cantillon, Kerstens et al., 2003).

Social Expenditure

Public social expenditure data for Belgium reveal a pattern of stability over the longer term. Between 1980 and 2007, the share in GDP fluctuates between 23.5 and 27 per cent. There is a slight upward trend. The shares of social expenditure in GDP reported in the previous section are 'gross', i.e. they do not take into account the effect of taxes. When these are taken into account, Belgium has the third largest Welfare State in the OECD, larger than the Nordic countries, where significant amounts are reclaimed through taxation (Adema and Ladaique, 2009).

Disaggregation by function shows an increasing share of public social expenditure on health care and (to a lesser extent) old age pensions. The share of survivor's pensions and incapacity-related benefits declines, the latter particularly between 1980 and the early 1990s. No clear trend in either direction can be observed for expenditure on unemployment, active labour market policies (available from 1985), family benefits and other benefits.

The share of in kind social expenditure has increased from less than one fourth (23 per cent) in 1980 to over one third in (36 per cent) in 2007. This shift is due mainly to the increase in spending on health and child care. Within the declining branch of cash public social expenditure, the increase in pension age spending is offset by declines for incapacity-related income support and, remarkably, child benefits (family allowances) (OECD SOCX).

Benefits and Welfare

As had been mentioned earlier, wages and social benefits in Belgium are linked to price levels through automatic wage indexation. Nonetheless, when non-benefit incomes increase at a faster pace than social benefits, the latter may erode relative to overall living standards. This did indeed occur for all the social minima, from the early 1980s up to the early 2000s (see Figure 6.3).

By the mid 2000s, a rather general consensus on the inadequacy of benefit levels led to increases beyond cost of living adaptations. These concurred with the dynamic surrounding

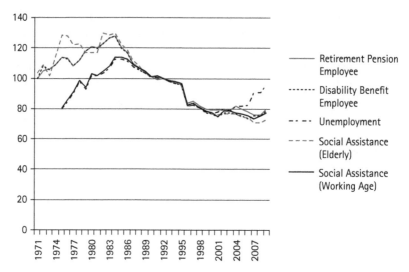

FIGURE 6.3 Social minima as percentage of net national income per capita, 1971–2009 (1991 = 100)

Source: Social indicators, Herman Deleeck Centre for Social Policy.

a so-called 'Generation Pact', which aimed at longer working lives and activation. Net income packages show a decline relative to median income between 1992 and 2001, but some recovery by 2009. Still, most benefits fall well short of the poverty risk threshold (Van Mechelen, Marchal *et al.*, 2011).

Overall, the distribution of benefits corresponds to the risk factors outlined earlier in this chapter. Cash benefits on active age generate sizeable redistributive flows from the Flemish to the Walloon (and Brussels) regions. As Flanders is ageing faster, it claims a relatively larger share of pensions, but this is not of the order to cancel out the transfers on active age (Cantillon and De Maesschalck, 2008). Migrants tend to be over-represented among benefit recipients, and particularly in social assistance (Corluy and Verbist, 2008).

The Distributional Effects of Social Services

The Belgian health care system appears to succeed rather well in terms of access (see Section 3). Belgium features a system of compulsory health insurance, administered through private, not-for-profit healthcare funds. As in other social security branches, there has been a tendency towards wider coverage. Since 2008, coverage of the self-employed was widened to so-called 'small risks' (relatively low-cost risks). In addition, protection for the most vulnerable groups was reinforced by the 'maximum bill' (Maximumfactuur/maximum à facturer). Introduced in 2002, the system aims to put a limit on the share of healthcare costs in total disposable household income. This measure reinforces selectivity of policy towards lowest incomes (Schokkaert, Guillaume *et al.*, 2008; Schokkaert, Guillaume *et al.*, 2008). The allocation of health care to income quintile suggest that the lower income quintiles claim a proportionally large share of health care expenditure (Verbist, Förster *et al.*, 2012).

Table 6.7 Distribution of expenditure on in kind education benefits by income quintile, 2007

	Q1	Q2	Q3	Q4	Q5
Total education services	17%	19%	22%	22%	20%
Compulsory education	18%	20%	22%	21%	18%
Upper secondary education	19%	21%	21%	22%	18%
Tertiary education	13%	15%	22%	22%	28%

Source: OECD (2011).

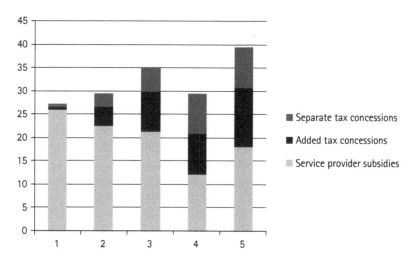

FIGURE 6.4 The social distribution of government investment in subsidized childcare, Flanders, 2005: Millions of euro, by income quintile among families with young children

Source: Van Lancker and Ghysels (2012).

Expenditure on education in Belgium as a share of GDP remained stable at 6.1 per cent of GDP between 2000 and 2007. While the Communities each organize their own educational system, compulsory schooling age is set at the national level. Study allowances and grants are a community matter, granted on the basis of family composition and income. Overall, expenditure on education services in Belgium is fairly equally distributed over the different quintiles, with a slight inverted J shape (highest share in the third and fourth quintile). Expenditure on compulsory education is concentrated in the middle quintiles, whereas expenditure on tertiary education flows disproportionally to the higher quintiles (see Table 6.7).

From a European perspective, Belgium has a fairly high coverage of child care. Provisions come both in the form of institutionalized day care centres and private but subsidized 'care mothers'. Gross fees are strongly income-related as well as partially tax deductible, rendering child care close to costless for those with the lowest incomes (Marx, 2009). Still, the use of childcare is very unequally distributed among households.

Figure 6.4 shows the total government effort, i.e. the government investment in formal child care, for Flanders in the year 2005. The very unequal distribution of public child care efforts is striking. Not only is the use of child care in Flanders biased against the lowest incomes, (scarce) government resources are allocated mostly to the households higher up in the income distribution.

6. Conclusion

Against the backdrop of growing income inequalities across industrialized countries, Belgium represents a remarkable outlier. While breaks in series and different data sources call for some degree of caution, there is no indication that disposable household income inequalities among the Belgian population have increased substantially over the past thirty years.

This stable income inequality may be considered remarkable given the political and economic context. As shown in the introduction, Belgium has experienced a number of major shifts since the early 1980s. The Belgian economy is among the most open and globalized in the world, with economic activity strongly geared towards trade and logistics. Over the last three decades, value added and (to a lesser degree) employment has shifted from manufacturing towards services. From an international perspective, such shifts have often been accompanied by skill-biased technological change and growing wage inequalities.

In terms of politics, the traditional segmentation into ideological pillars has steadily evaporated over the course of the past thirty years. The linguistic fault line, by contrast, has become ever more important. A process of federalization implied that competences have been decentralized towards the communities and regions. Whereas the social security system has largely remained at the federal level, many of the competences that relate to background inequalities (for instance education, public employment services and vocational training) are now organized at regional or community level.

The past thirty years have seen growing disparities between the more prosperous Dutch speaking Flanders in the North and Wallonia in the South. The former consistently outperforms the latter in terms of labour market participation and material living conditions. The officially bilingual Brussels Capital Region plays a remarkable role: as a major centre of economic activity (and commuting), its residential population is relatively vulnerable to unemployment and income poverty. Regional differences in prosperity are mirrored in a range of social outcomes (including housing tenure, victimization, life expectancy). In terms of a number of political variables that have been studied in this report, regional differences appear to be less pronounced. Still, the rise of the extreme right and nationalist vote in the Flemish region are particularly important in this respect.

Very significant immigration over the past thirty years represents an additional source of diversity within the Belgian population. While Belgium is considered one of the most liberal OECD countries in terms of granting nationality to newcomers, it appears that their inclusion in Belgian society has been problematic (Corluy, Marx et al., 2011). Being born outside the EU is associated with steep gradients in terms of labour market participation, material living conditions and education.

A third cross-cutting issue relates to the role of educational attainment. The past decades have seen a major educational expansion in Belgium. This implies that low levels of educational attainment (less than higher secondary education) are mainly concentrated among the older population. Still, a substantial share of the younger generations does not obtain a degree that is broadly considered the minimum to obtain stable gainful employment. Controlling for age and sex, low educational attainment is associated with many adverse health outcomes. The causality in this case can arguably be considered bi-directional. The section on political and cultural impacts has shown that low levels of educational attainment are also linked to lower interest and participation in politics, as well as more anti-democratic views. Taking into consideration the very strong socio-economic reproduction in the educational system, these findings raise concerns for a resilient dualization between the less and the more highly educated.

While these background inequalities are very strong, often significantly stronger than in many other OECD countries, Belgium also features a particularly intricate institutional framework. Some of the institutional settings have a direct effect on the impacts studied. For instance, the compulsory vote and the Ghent system play a direct role in promoting formal political participation and union membership.

In terms of policy, the Welfare State is among the largest and most regulated in OECD countries. Wage-setting is highly coordinated, including a fairly high minimum wage that arguably dampens 'market' inequalities. The Belgian Welfare State ranks among the most redistributive in the European Union and the OECD. The share of taxes in GDP has remained stable, and data suggest that their redistributive impact has proven quite resilient. Cash benefits eroded overall, but were extended in coverage and became increasingly targeted towards the most needy. Below stable headline spending, a few shifts are occurring, with social services (child care, education, health spending) taking up a larger share and cash spending waning. Some would argue that precisely such a shift is needed to directly address the background inequalities that cash transfers remediate ex post. Still, others would warn against overly optimistic assumptions in this respect, particularly given the Matthew effects that are currently observed in the take-up of tertiary education and child care.

Belgium has weathered the recent economic crisis quite well, with its automatic stabilizers playing an important role. Rather, in the late 2000s, the headlines were concerned with an on-going political crisis, including a succession of cabinets and very lengthy negotiations over coalitions and state reform. For all the stability on the surface, Belgian governance is a particularly complex and tense equilibrium, where the next (redistributive) conflict is always on the horizon. It is safe to assume that the future prospects of the country will rely to a large extent on the relative strengths of its two most salient features, namely large background inequalities and an intricate institutional framework.

References

Abts, K., Swyngedouw, M., *et al.* (2011), 'Politieke betrokkenheid en institutioneel wantrouwen. De spiraal van het wantrouwen doorbroken?' K. Abts, K. Dobbelaere and L. Voyé, *Nieuwe tijden, nieuwe mensen. Belgen over arbeid, gezin, ethiek, religie en politiek*, Leuven, LannooCampus.

Adema, W. and Ladaique, M. (2009), 'How Expensive is the Welfare State? Gross and Net Indicators in the OECD Social Expenditure Database (SOCX)', *Social, Employment and Migration Working Papers*, Paris, Organisation for Economic Co-operation and Development.

Beyers, J. and Bursens, P. (2006), 'The European rescue of the federal state: How europeanisation shapes the Belgian state', *West European Politics* **29**(5): 1057–1078.

Brunello, G. and Checchi D. (2012), 'Does school tracking affect equality of opportunity? New international evidence', *Economic Policy* **22**(52): 781–861.

Cantillon, B., De Lathouwer L., *et al.* (1999), 'De ondersteuning van het kostwinnersmodel: de beleidsverklaring voor stabiliteit', *De welvaartsstaat in de kering*. B. Cantillon. Kapellen, Pelckmans.

Cantillon, B. and Maesschalck, V. De (2008), 'Sociale zekerheid, transferten en federalisme in B. Cantillon, *De welvaartsstaat in de kering*, Kapellen, Pelckmans..

Cantillon, B., Kerstens, B. *et al.* (2003), 'Les effets rédistributifs de la réforme de l'Impôt des personnes physiques', B. Cantillon and V. De Maesschalck, Gedachten over Sociaal Federalisme. Réflexions sur le fédéralisme social, Leuven, Acco.

Cantillon, B., van Dam, R. *et al.* (2003), *Sociale indicatoren en ECHP-data. Is de armoede nu hoog maar dalend of laag maar stijgend?* Antwerpen, UFSIA/Centrum voor Sociaal Beleid.

CGKR (2011), *Migratie—Jaarverslag 2011*, Brussel, CGKR.

Corluy, V., Marx, I., *et al.* (2011), 'Employment chances and changes of immigrants in Belgium: The impact of citizenship', *International Journal of Comparative Sociology* **52**(4): 350–368.

Corluy, V. and Verbist, G. (2010), *Inkomen en diversiteit: onderzoek naar de inkomenspositie van migranten in België*. Antwerpen, UA/Centrum voor Sociaal Beleid Herman Deleeck.

De Decker, P. (2008), 'Facets of housing and housing policies in Belgium', *Journal of housing and the built environment* **23**(3): 155–171.

De Meyer, I. and Warlop, N. (2010), *PISA. Leesvaardigheid van 15-jarigen in Vlaanderen. De eerste resultaten van PISA 2009*, DOVASB, Vlaamse Overheid. Brussel, Departement Onderwijs & Vorming.

Deboosere, P., Lesthaeghe, R. *et al.* (2009), 'Monografieën van de Sociaal-Economische Enquête 2001', Nummer 4. Huishoudens en gezinnen in België Brussel, FOD Economie, K.M.O., Middenstand en Energie.

Decoster, A. (2009), 'Zijn onze belasingen (nog) progressief?' in J. Vranken, G. Campaert, D. Dierckx and A. Van Haarlem, *Armoede en sociale uitsluiting—Jaarboek 2009*. Leuven, Acco: 145–162.

Demarest, S., E. Hesse, *et al.* (2010), Enquête de santé, 2008. Rapport IV—Santé et Société. Bruxelles, Institut scientifique de santé publique.

Deschouwer, K. (2012), *The Politics of Belgium. Governing a Divided Society*, 2nd Edition, Basingstoke: Palgrave Macmillan.

Domański, H. and Przybysza, D. (2007), 'Educational homogamy in 22 countries', *European Societies* **9**(4): 495–526.

European Foundation for the Improvement of Living and Working Conditions (2010), *Living conditions, social exclusion and mental well-being. Second European Quality of Life Survey*. Luxembourg, Office for Official Publications of the European Communities.

Eurostat (2010), 'Social participation and social isolation', *Methodologies and working papers*, Luxembourg, Publications Office of the European Union.

Frognier, A.-P., Bol, D. *et al.* (2012), 20 ans d'analyse des comportements électoraux: Analyse comparée Flandre—Wallonie in A. von Busekist, *La Belgique.*, Paris: Fayard.

Gisle, L., Hesse, E. *et al.* (2010), *Gezondheidsenquête België, 2008. Rapport II—Leefstijl en preventie*. Brussel, Wetenschappelijk Instituut Volksgezondheid.

Hooghe, M. and Huyse, L. (2009), 'From Armed Peace to Permanent Crisis. Cracks in the Belgian Consultative Model', *The Low Countries. Arts and Society in Flanders and the Netherlands* 17: 227–233.

Horemans, J., Pintelon, O., *et al.* (2011), *Inkomens en inkomensverdeling op basis van Belgische enquêtegegevens: 1985-2007*, Antwerpen, UA/Centrum voor Sociaal Beleid Herman Deleeck.

Immervoll, H., Levy, H., *et al.* (2006), 'Household Incomes and Redistribution in the European Union: Quantifying the Equalising Properties of Taxes and Benefits', in D. Papadimitriou, *The Distributional Effects of Government Spending and Taxation*, New York: Palgrave/Macmillan: 135–165.

Inglehart, R. and Klingemann, H.-D (2000), 'Genes, Culture, Democracy, and Happiness'. E. Diener and E. M. Suh. *Culture and Subjective Well-Being*, Cambridge, MA: MIT Press: 165–183.

Keating, G., M. O'Sullivan, *et al.* (2011), *Global Wealth Databook 2011*, Zurich, Credit Suisse AG.

Lelkes, O. and Sutherland, H. (2009), *Tax and Benefit Policies in the Enlarged Europe: Assessing the Impact with Microsimulation Models*, Farnham, Surrey, UK; Burlington, VT: Ashgate.

Marx, I. (2007), *A new social question? On minimum income protection in the postindustrial era*, Amsterdam: Amsterdam University Press.

Marx, I. (2009), Belgium, the quest for sustainability, legitimacy and a way out of 'welfare without work', in K. Schubert, S. Hegelich and U. Bazant, *The Handbook of European Welfare Systems*, London: Routledge, pp. 49–64.

Neels, K. (2010), 'Temporal variation in unemployment rates and their association with tempo and quantum of fertility: some evidence for Belgium, France and the Netherlands', annual meeting of the Population Association of America, Dallas, Texas.

OECD (2009), *Economic Survey of Belgium 2009*, Paris: OECD.

OECD (2011), *Divided We Stand: Why Inequality Keeps Rising*, Paris: OECD.

OECD (2011), *Education at a Glance 2011*, Paris: OECD.

OECD (2011), *PISA In Focus 2011. How are schools adapting to increasing numbers of immigrant students?* Paris: OECD.

OECD (2012), *Settling In. OECD Indicators of Immigrant Integration 2012*, Paris: OECD.

Pauwels, T. (2011), 'Explaining the strange decline of the populist radical right Vlaams Belang in Belgium: The impact of permanent opposition', *Acta Politica* 2011(46): 60–82.

Plasman, R., Rusinek M. *et al.* (2007), 'Wages and Bargaining Regime under Multi-level Bargaining: Belgium, Denmark and Spain', *European Journal of Industrial Relations*, 13(2):161–180.

Rademaekers, K. and Vuchelen, J. (1999), 'De verdeling van het Belgisch gezinsvermogen', *Cahiers Economiques De Bruxelles* (164, 4ième trimestre): 375–429.

Schokkaert, E., Guillaume, J. *et al.* (2008), *Evaluatie van de effecten van de maximumfactuur op de consumptie en financiële toegankelijkheid van de gezondheidszorg*, Brussel, Federaal Kenniscentrum voor de Gezondheidszorg (KCE).

Snacken, S. (2007), 'Penal Policy and Practice in Belgium', *Crime and Justice* 36(1): 127–216.

Swyngedouw, M. and Rink, N. (2008), *Hoe Vlaams-Belgischgezind zijn de Vlamingen? Een analyse op basis van het postelectorale verkiezingsonderzoek 2007*, Leuven, Centrum voor Sociologisch Onderzoek (CeSO).

Tsebelis, G. (1995), 'Decision-Making in Political-Systems—Veto Players in Presidentialism, Parliamentarism, Multicameralism and Multipartyism', *British Journal of Political Science* 25: 289–325.

Van den Bosch, K. (1998), 'Poverty and Assets in Belgium', *Review of Income and Wealth* 44(2): 215–228.

Van den Bosch, K., Van Dam, R., *et al.* (1999), 'De zero-sum crisis: de gezinsdimensie als verklaring voor de stabiliteit', in B. Cantillon, *De welvaartsstaat in de kering*, Kapellen, Pelckmans.

Van den Bosch, K., Vandenbroucke P. *et al.* (2009), Inkomen, verdeling en armoede: over groei, stabiliteit en de kloof tussen werkenden en uitkeringstrekkers in L. Vanderleyden, M. Callens and J. Noppe, *De sociale staat van Vlaanderen 2009*, Studiedienst van de Vlaamse Regering: 113–153.

Van der Heyden, J., L. Gisle, *et al.* (2010), *Enquête de santé, 2008.Rapport I—Etat de santé*. Bruxelles, Institut scientifique de santé publique.

van Dijk, J., Manchin, R. *et al.* (2007), *The Burden of Crime in the EU*. Tilburg: Tilburg University, INTERVICT.

Van Lancker, W. and Ghysels, J. (2012), 'Who benefits? The social distribution of subsidized childcare in Sweden and Flanders', *Acta Sociologica* **55**(2): 125–142.

Van Mechelen, N., Marchal, S. *et al.* (2011), *The CSB-Minimum Income Protection Indicators dataset (CSB-MIPI)*, Antwerp, Herman Deleeck Centre for Social Policy, University of Antwerp: 104p.

Van Oyen, H., Deboosere, P. *et al.* (2011), *Sociale ongelijkheden in gezondheid in België*, Gent: Academia Press.

Van Rie, T., Marx, I. *et al.* (2011), 'Ghent revisited: Unemployment insurance and union membership in Belgium and the Nordic countries', *European Journal of Industrial Relations* **17**(2): 125–139.

Vandenberghe, V. (2012), 'Inter-regional educational discrepancies in Belgium. How to combat them?', in P. De Grauwe and P. Van Parijs (eds.), *Educational Divergence—Why do pupils do better in Flanders than in the French community?* Brussels, Re-Bel Initiative. **8**: 5–25.

Vandenbroucke, F. (2012), *The Active Welfare State Revisited*, Antwerp, Herman Deleeck Centre for Social Policy, University of Antwerp: 71.

Verbergt, G., Cantillon B,. *et al.* (2009), *Sociale ongelijkheden in het Vlaamse onderwijs: tien jaar later*, Antwerpen, UA/Centrum voor Sociaal Beleid Herman Deleeck.

Verbist, G. (2004), 'Redistributive Effect and Progressivity of Income Taxes: An International Comparison across the EU using EUROMOD', *EUROMOD Working Paper* No. EM5/04, <https://www.iser.essex.ac.uk/euromod/working-papers>, The Microsimulation Unit, Cambridge University, Cambridge, UK.

Verbist, G., Förster, M. *et al.* (2012), 'The Impact of Publicly Provided Services on the Distribution of Resources: Review of New Results and Methods', *OECD Social Employment and Migration Working Papers* Paris, Organisation for Economic Co-operation and Development.

Verbist, G. and Lefebure, S. (2008), 'The distributional impact of other non-cash incomes in Belgium', deliverable for AIM-AP Project (Accurate Income Measurement for the Assessment of Public Policies).

Verbist, G. and Vanhille, J. (2012), *Een simulatie van huursubsidies voor huishoudens in Vlaanderen. Een verdelingsanalyse*, Antwerpen, Centrum voor Sociaal Beleid Herman Deleeck.

Visser, J. (2011), *Database on Institutional Characteristics of Trade Unions, Wage Setting, State Intervention and Social Pacts in 34 countries between1960 and 2007 (ICTWSS)*. Amsterdam, Amsterdam Institute for Advanced Labour Studies.

Vleminckx, K. (2011), 'De hervorming van de Belgische verzorgingsstaat: een kroniek', *Belgisch tijdschrift voor sociale zekerheid*, **53**(3):403–456.

Walgrave, S., Rucht, D. *et al.* (2010), 'Socio-demographics: typical new social movement activists, old leftists or normalized protesters?' in S. Walgrave and D. Rucht, *The World Says No to War. Demonstrations against the War on Iraq,* Minneapolis: University of Minnesota Press: 78–97.

Zaidi, A. and Zolyomi, E. (2007), 'Intergenerational Transmission of Disadvantages in EU Member States', *Policy brief,* Vienna, European Centre for Social Welfare Policy and Research.

CHAPTER 7

··

BULGARIA: RISING INEQUALITY IN THE PERIOD OF TRANSITION AND RESTRICTIVE INCOMES POLICY

··

VASSIL TSANOV, PETYA IVANOVA,

SILVIA PANTELEEVA, AND BOGDAN BOGDANOV

1. INTRODUCTION

··

THIS chapter presents the basic country-specific characteristics of inequality development, its social and political impacts, and the role of social policy on inequality in Bulgaria over the past three decades. Broader analyses of inequality and of its impacts in Bulgaria can be found in the Bulgarian country report for the GINI project.

As a post-socialist country, Bulgaria has undergone profound political and economic reform on its journey from a centrally-planned to a market economy. The reforms started in the early 1990s and have had a considerable impact on the evolution of inequality. Over the past two decades, there has been marked fluctuation in income inequality, but the overall tendency has been for it to rise.

The socio-economic development of the country over the past 30 years has witnessed various periods of progress and stagnation. In terms of demographic development, two negative trends have appeared: population decline and ageing. The total population fell by 1.58 million between 1985 and 2011. And over the past 25 years, the proportion of children has declined more rapidly than the share of the elderly population (65+) has increased: in 2011, the number of those aged 14 years or under made up a little over a tenth of the population, while the elderly population reached a fifth. The main reasons for the demographic collapse are a decline in the fertility rate and the birth rate, a comparatively high mortality rate, and emigration. These negative processes have had an impact on the development of inequality.

The structure of the Bulgarian population with respect to labour market status has also changed over the past 25 years, with an increase in the share of economically inactive people.

In 2011, over half of the population aged 7+ was inactive. This trend is a result of economic and demographic factors.

The level of education of the population has been rising steadily. The share of people with only primary or lower education has decreased, while the proportion of those with secondary and tertiary education has increased. Despite these positive trends, ethnic differences in the level of education attained remain significant and appear to be an important driving force of inequality.

The economic development of the country between 1990 and 2011 was marked by periods of recession (1990–97), accelerated and stable growth (1998–2008), and now the current crisis (since 2009). During the seven-year recession of the 1990s, GDP fell by a quarter from the base year of 1990. The growth achieved towards the end of the decade largely restored the economic potential of the country, and stable economic development after 2001 led to a significant improvement in all macro-economic indicators.

Wages and incomes have lagged considerably behind GDP growth: taking the period as a whole, since 1990 real wages have lost about 18 per cent of their purchasing power, and the decline in real household income has been even greater. The reasons for this lag are complex, but are mostly to do with the restrictions imposed on wage growth in the first decade of the period and a declining wage share of GDP: from 54 per cent in 1990 to a little more than a third in 2011. An important point here is that even in the years of stable growth (2004–8) that share decreased steadily.

The general demographic, educational, labour and economic development of the country over the past three decades shapes the social and economic environment, the potential driving forces in income inequality, education and the labour market, and the various influences and interactions.

2. Inequality and its Development over Time

Household Income Inequality

The evolution of income inequality in Bulgaria can be charted over the longer term using the concept of the equivalized net income per household member (Figure 7.1). There have been ups and downs in the Gini coefficient (according to data from UN-SWIID, Version 3.1) over the past 30 years but, overall, inequality has increased. Fluctuations in inequality are found even before the 1980s, but at a lower level: during the 1960s and 1970s, the Gini changed within the range 0.15–0.25.

A similar picture of the dynamics of income inequality is obtained using other measures of inequality (the Theil, Atkinson, and Log variance measures) and the concept of gross income. All coefficients indicate identical trends in development over the past 15 years. Inequality declined in the period 1995–2006, but then, later, increased. Similar trends for income inequality based on the Gini coefficient (net and gross) were obtained by other studies devoted to poverty and inequality (Nikolova, *et al.*, 2011; Tzanov, *et al.*, 2006).

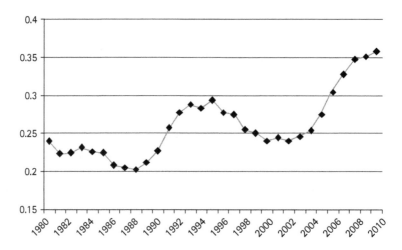

FIGURE 7.1 Evolution of income inequality, Gini coefficient, 1980–2010

Source: Frederick, S. (2009), 'Standardizing the World Income Inequality Database', *Social Science Quarterly* 90(2): 231–242, SWIID Version 3.1, December 2011.

The first wave of inequality increase (1990–95) was a direct consequence of economic development, of the reforms that were introduced (mainly in the first half of the 1990s), and of incomes policy. After 1990, there was a sizeable increase in inequality, reflecting the deepening economic crisis in the early years of the decade. As a result of growing unemployment and the reduction of social transfers, income differences within the population widened dramatically. The initial years after 1990 were marked by a rapid expansion of the private sector, which resulted in greater income inequality. A very restrictive government policy on public-sector wages and social transfers further stimulated the increase in inequality during this period.

The next wave of rising inequality (2004–10) covered a period of economic growth and the crisis. Obviously, to a great extent economic prosperity resulted in higher earnings (Zahariev, 2011). Meanwhile, the restrictions placed on public-sector incomes during the current crisis have contributed to the rise in inequality.

The continuous period of decline in income inequality (1996–2003) is associated with economic development, as well as with incomes policy and reform of the pension system. Although it is hard to evaluate the direct impact of economic growth on the decline in income inequality, growth clearly creates conditions that are ripe for active reduction policies—through processes related to economic restructuring, the state of foreign markets, foreign investment in the country, and external migration. The influence of these processes on inequality is not always one-dimensional, and income differentiation has other internal mechanisms governed by social and political factors. Fundamental among these are incomes policy, employment and taxation. In this period, the policy was to increase the minimum wage considerably, and to achieve a gradual reduction in the tax burden on wages and social security payments.

Another reflection of inequality is migration. Bulgaria has a high level of outward migration: it is estimated that around 395,000 people (roughly 5 per cent of the population) left the country in 2001–11. Most of these were young people (20–49 years of age). Migration has affected inequality in various ways. First, it has changed the size and structure of the labour force by reducing the participation rate and worsening the labour-force composition by age and level of education. Second, the outflow from the labour force has reduced labour market inequality and has therefore lowered unemployment. Third, most emigrants send money back home to their relatives, which can help reduce inequality.

Empirical research on income inequality in Bulgaria has pointed to other micro-determinants of inequality (Mintchev *et al.*, 2010). This study revealed positive net effects in the degree of urbanization and the number of employed members of households, as well as negative effects in terms of the numbers of unemployed people, children, and pensioners on all levels of income. The decomposition of inequality indices by subgroup identifies type of settlement, ethnic group, number of children, and number of unemployed as important sources of income inequality in Bulgaria.

Effects of Social Transfers on Income Inequality

The influence of social transfers on inequality in Bulgaria is evident: if all transfers and pensions are removed from the equation, income inequality clearly increases. The population of low-income groups generally consists of pensioners, unemployed, and other households that receive social aid. Among social payments, pensions are of crucial significance in reducing the level of inequality and household impoverishment.

An important peculiarity of social transfers is that they are increasing in importance in reducing inequality: according to the Gini coefficient, social transfers in 1995 reduced income inequality by approximately 20 per cent, whereas, in 2005, the figure was 28 per cent, and in 2010 approximately 40 per cent. The impact of social transfers on inequality reduction is clearest in terms of the ratio between the highest and the lowest income groups.

The reasons behind the tendency for the significance of social transfers to increase are: an ageing population; an increase in the number of people of retirement age; the emigration of young and educated people; the growing unemployment rate; and crisis trends in general economic development.

Labour Market Inequality

The lack of regular statistical information on wage distribution restricts any analysis of wage inequality in Bulgaria to two years. There have been two wage surveys carried out by the National Statistical Institute—the first in 2002 and the second in 2006.

Data on the gross wages of employees indicate that wage inequality as measured by the Gini coefficient increased over those four years by 11 per cent (Table 7.1). The quintile ratio (S80/20), however, stayed the same, while the ratio of the lowest-paid 10 per cent of employed people to the highest-paid 10 per cent increased slightly. The difference in these findings suggests that wage inequality increased as a result of greater differences in the tails of the wage distribution. Also, it is obvious that wage inequality is comparatively greater than household income inequality.

Table 7.1 Wage inequality measures, by sex, in 2002 and 2006

	Gini	S80/20	S90/10
Total			
2002	0.342	6	9
2006	0.381	6	10
Men			
2002	0.361	7	10
2006	0.404	7	11
Women			
2002	0.309	5	7
2006	0.359	6	9

Source: National Statistical Institute.

In the years between the two surveys, wage differentiation increased for both genders. The Gini coefficient and the measures of polarization (S80/20 and S90/10) have higher levels for men than for women. However, wage inequality among women is more pronounced.

Inequality in Employment

The change in employment in Bulgaria over the past three decades correlates closely with the country's economic development. In the years before the transition to a market economy, virtually the entire working-age population was employed. This model of employment changed visibly after 1990. In 1990–2000, the employment rate declined from close to 100 per cent in 1990 to 58.4 per cent in 2000. This fall in employment affected all social groups, regardless of education, gender or qualifications.

The story of employment over the last 15 years indicates that the number of employed people in the age group 25–64 began to grow after 2000. In the period 2000–8, the employment rate in the 25–64 group grew by close to 10 percentage points. Since the current economic crisis broke, employment has again declined across the spectrum of employed people, irrespective of level of education or gender.

Employment is higher among men than among women, but this is likely to even out. Therefore, there is an on-going process of inequality reduction by gender. This is not, however, a steady process. Taking the decade as a whole, the ratio of female to male employment has remained relatively stable. But as a result of the economic crisis—which has largely affected male employment—gender inequality in employment has fallen.

Inequality in Education

The past 25 years have seen a steady increase in the level of education of the population. Considerably higher growth is evident in the field of tertiary education (a rise of more than 300 per cent). The share of people with secondary education has also increased and reached

43.4 per cent in 2011. These trends show that the difference in the level of education attained is narrowing.

Despite this positive trend, there is considerable inequality when it comes to the level of education by ethnic group (Turks and Roma). In general, there has been an improvement in educational level across all ethnic groups, but the differences remain significant. The share of Bulgarians with university education reached 22.8 per cent in 2011, whereas for Turks it was 4.1 per cent, and for Roma 0.3 per cent. It is a similar story for secondary education: 47.6 per cent of Bulgarians have secondary education, 26 per cent of Turks and 6.9 per cent of Roma.

Key Determinants of Inequality in Bulgaria

On the basis of the analysis of inequality in income, wages, the labour market and education, four key determinants of inequality can be distinguished that are specific to Bulgaria: 1) the transition to a market economy; 2) the pattern of economic growth; 3) changes in policies; 4) ethnic differences.

The transition to a market economy and the reforms carried out to that end have laid the foundations for a new model of income distribution and inequality in Bulgaria. The wage-equalizing principles that were in place before the transition were scrapped and a wage-bargaining system introduced. The characteristics of the system do not facilitate a reduction in wage differentiation. The low level of union membership, coverage and density also contributes considerably to wage inequality.

Economic development during the years of recession and crisis has promoted inequality in the country, most importantly by boosting unemployment and the inactive population.

Policies—especially the incomes policy—have had a significant impact on inequality. The restrictive incomes policy with respect to the minimum wage and public-sector wages in the years of recession strongly encouraged increased wage differentiation. Also the tight fiscal policy pursued over the past two decades has led to reduced government social spending and increased inequality. The policy pursued over the past decade of reducing direct taxation and the introduction of a flat rate of tax have likewise increased income inequality.

Ethnic differences in education have been an important determinant of inequality. The relatively low educational level of the Roma minority carries over into inequality in incomes and employment. Keeping these ethnic distinctions unchanged over time leads to the reproduction of inequality and poverty in society.

3. The Social Impacts of Inequality

The purpose of this section is to examine the extent to which inequality in Bulgaria determines the development of social processes. The accent is on investigating the social impact of inequality in key aspects, such as deprivation, poverty and social exclusion, family formation, health, and housing.

Patterns and Trends in Material Deprivation, Poverty and Social Cohesion

Bulgaria has one of the highest rates of material deprivation in the EU (Figure 7.2). Despite the clear trend towards improvement on both indicators that were considered (material deprivation and severe material deprivation), material deprivation within the population remains excessively high. In 2006, seven Bulgarians in ten were materially deprived (in the sense that they lacked three of the nine items considered), whereas in 2010 the figure had fallen to five in ten. As for the severe material deprivation indicator, the decrease is more considerable.

The positive changes in material deprivation are not connected with growing income inequality, but are directly correlated with the income dynamics of this period. Real (monetary) household incomes have increased by 19 per cent, and the increase in real wages has been even more dynamic. Therefore, the decline in total material deprivation has been mainly due to the increase in the population's monetary income.

The effect of inequality is mostly expressed in the composition of material deprivation by age, income and education. Material deprivation in different parts of the income distribution indicates considerable differences in terms of both the rate and the trends: among groups with high incomes (the fourth and fifth quintiles) material deprivation is relatively low and has remained constant since 2008; by contrast, people on low incomes (the first and second quintiles) have an extremely high incidence of deprivation (though the trend has been for this to decline steadily).

There are also differences in the material deprivation rates by age: the population group aged 65+ is distinguished by having the highest incidence of material deprivation, whereas there is no significant difference in the rate for young people (under 18 years) and people aged 18–64. The material deprivation rate has tended to decline across all age groups, but particularly among the elderly.

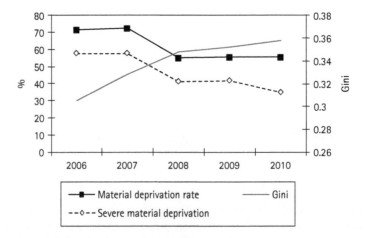

FIGURE 7.2 Material deprivation and inequality trends, 2006–10

Source: Eurostat, EU-SILC.

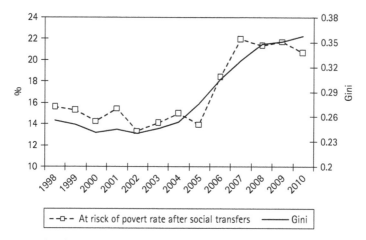

FIGURE 7.3 At-risk-of-poverty rate and inequality trends, 1998–2010

Source: National Statistical Institute, Eurostat (EU-SILC).

The trend towards a declining deprivation rate is evident for all levels of education. The difference in the trends for the separate educational levels has remained stable throughout the period in question, which could be interpreted as a lack of inequality (or its low impact). Across all education groups the decrease has been 20–22 percentage points.

In addition to its high rate of deprivation, Bulgaria has a relatively high risk of poverty. The percentage of the population considered to be poor (60 per cent of the median equivalized income) fluctuates considerably (Figure 7.3). The evolution of poverty correlates strongly with the pattern of income inequality: in the period of inequality reduction (1998–2002), the share of the poor declined by 2.2 percentage points (from 15.6 per cent in 1998 to 13.4 per cent in 2002); after 2005, the poverty rate increased (which is in line with the growth in inequality).

The variation in the pattern of social cohesion indicators cannot be associated with the rates and dynamics of income inequality, poverty and material deprivation. The tendency for income inequality to increase in recent years is matched by neither a decline in social isolation nor an increase in social activity on the part of the Bulgarian population. Nor does material deprivation have any impact on the frequency of social contact, though its decline does lead to rising social activity.

Patterns and Trends in Family Formation, Fertility and Marriage

The pattern of the Bulgarian family over the past 30 years has followed world trends: greater freedom in interpersonal relations, which has led to a variety of family formations. The basic trends in the development of the Bulgarian family are as follows: a decrease in the number of births and children in the family; a decline in marriages, along with an increase in the number of divorces; and a rise in the number of births outside marriage. These trends sketch the profile of the modern Bulgarian family.

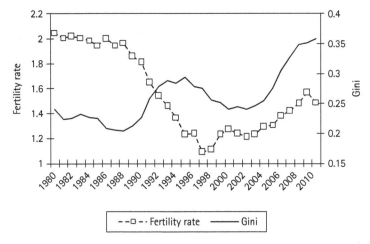

FIGURE 7.4 Fertility rate and inequality trends, 1980–2011

Source: Eurostat.

The total fertility rate of Bulgarian women over the past three decades has decreased significantly (Figure 7.4): from 2.05 in 1980 to 1.51 in 2011. This decline has proceeded with varying degrees of intensity and in various directions of development. From the early 1990s the process accelerated, so that in 1997–8 total fertility reached its lowest level (1.1 children). The fertility rate grew steadily after 1998 to reach 1.6 in 2009. The subsequent dip during the economic crisis illustrates the strong dependency of fertility on economic development and changes in living standards. This evolution in the fertility rate cannot be explained by fluctuations in the income inequality; the changes are most likely due to economic development.

In parallel with this decrease in births, there have been changes in family formation. There has been a transition from marriage-based families towards extramarital cohabitation. In the 1980s, this process was fairly negligible: the number of marriages declined, and the number of divorces also decreased, but to a lesser extent. The crude marriage rate in 1980 was 7.9 (per 1,000 population), while in 1990 it was 6.9; by 2010 it had dropped further, to 3.2. The crude divorce rate moved from 1.5 in 1980 to 1.3 in 1990. Thereafter the number of divorces remained stable.

Since 1990, the number of children born outside marriage has increased steadily, and has actually tripled: in recent years more children have been born outside marriage than within. None of these processes seem to be correlated with inequality. The basic argument is that the changes in family patterns concern all income groups equally.

Health Status and Income Inequality

The changes in life expectancy in Bulgaria over the past 50 years have been marked by periods of decrease and increase. In the 1960s, life expectancy at birth gradually increased to exceed 71 years. This growth was due to a simultaneous increase in both male and female life expectancy, though the latter was more pronounced. During the 1970s and 1980s, there was a slight dip in total life expectancy as a result of the decline in male life expectancy. The next drop in life expectancy was observed between 1990 and 1995, but since the mid 1990s life expectancy has gradually increased, and in the 15 years to 2010 it rose by 2.9 years. A similar development in the pattern of life expectancy is typical of the population at age 65.

Gender distinctions can be mapped in two ways: in terms of levels, and in terms of dynamics. Besides living longer than men, any declines in female life expectancy have been rarer and of shorter duration. Over the past 30 years, female life expectancy has increased by 3.5 years in total, while male life expectancy has increased by 1.8 years. These distinctions determine the growing gender gap in life expectancy. Whereas in 1980 the gap was 5.4 years, and in 1990 it was 6.7 years, by 2010 it had reached 7.1 years.

The trend in life expectancy has closely followed the trend in economic development over the last 20 years. The period of prolonged economic recession (1990–7) coincided with a decline in life expectancy; during the post-1998 period of rapid and constant economic growth, the greatest increase in life expectancy was to be observed. Thus the country's economic development significantly affects life expectancy.

A relatively small proportion of the Bulgarian population regards its health status as 'very poor' and 'poor'. And in the last five years the figure has steadily declined (which is not in line with growing inequality): whereas in 2006 two in ten reported bad/very bad health, in 2010 one in ten reported poor health. The majority of Bulgarians reported 'good' or 'very good' health. Their share has increased and they now make up over two-thirds of the total population.

Income inequality is a crucial factor in the differentiation by subjective health evaluation. The assessments of people in the top quintile and in the bottom quintile vary markedly in terms of poor health (and to a lesser extent in terms of good health): about a quarter of the population on a low income regard their health as 'poor', while among well-off people the figure is quite low (4–7 per cent). In both income groups there is a declining trend for people to evaluate their own health as 'poor'.

Low Impact of Income Inequality on Patterns of Housing Tenure

Most Bulgarian families live in privately owned homes. According to census data, in 1985 some 80.0 per cent of the population lived in privately owned housing. By 1992 this figure had risen to 91.3 per cent; and by 2001 to 92.1 per cent. In 2011 it stood at 87.2 per cent. Most privately owned housing is not associated with mortgages or loans. Nevertheless, in 2008–9 there was a significant expansion of mortgage loans: in 2008, 9.9 per cent of people living in privately owned housing had a mortgage or loan—up from 2.3 per cent in 2005. The economic crisis from 2009 drastically reduced the mortgage loan market, and the proportion of people with mortgage loans dropped to 1.5 per cent.

The rental market accounts for quite a small proportion of the country's population (12–14 per cent). The majority of tenants have municipal or state accommodation, with controlled rent that is generally below the market rate. Their share of the total population has remained relatively stable, with a weak tendency to decrease. The number of Bulgarians paying rent at market prices is fairly insignificant (1.7 per cent in 2011).

Distinctions in housing tenure status by income position are not significant: in 2011, 82 per cent of people at risk of poverty (below 60 per cent of median equivalized income) owned their own homes, as against 88.6 per cent of those who are not at risk of poverty. The share of people at risk of poverty with mortgage loans is negligible (0.3 per cent). Another distinctive trait of the population at risk of poverty is the great percentage of tenants who pay rent at below market prices. These people have municipal or state accommodation and pay only a nominal rent. Only 0.5 per cent of people at risk of poverty pay rent at market rates.

The distinctions in tenure status between the poor and not poor indicate that income inequality does not significantly affect tenure status in Bulgaria. Both income groups largely own their homes, and the figures have remained stable over time. Probably the impact of inequality is reflected in terms of the size and quality of the housing.

4. Political and Cultural Impacts

In this section, the analysis focuses on the political and cultural impacts of inequality. The impact of inequality is traced in terms of electoral activity, the level of trust in public institutions, attitudes towards political parties (left–right) and attitudes towards the EU and EU membership.

Political and Civic Participation

The pattern of political participation by the Bulgarian population has changed significantly over the past three decades. The dividing line was drawn in 1989, when Bulgaria's political life underwent a series of democratic changes, which came to be reflected in the introduction of a multi-party system and the institution of a presidency.

Under the old totalitarian political regime, the electoral activity of the Bulgarian population was marked by high voter turnout (over 90 per cent). The post-1990 political changes introduced free political choice and voluntary voting. The last two decades have witnessed a considerable decline in voter turnout at parliamentary, presidential and local elections (Table 7.2). Turnout in elections to the different Bulgarian institutions varies significantly. The general trend towards lower voter turnout in parliamentary elections has in the past been temporarily reversed by the appearance of a new political party (as in 2001 and 2009), but nevertheless the overall trend is downwards. And the decline in turnout is noticeably stronger at presidential and local elections.

Overall, the figures indicate political indifference on the part of a large proportion of Bulgarian citizens. This is a result of disillusionment over the failed pre-election promises of politicians and the growing number of uneducated people and people with less education (who are generally politically apathetic). An explanation can also be sought in the established tradition, according to which 'the politicization and additionally the political mobilization grow in times when democracy is unstable and limited' (Todorov, 2010).

The turnout figures for the elections to the EU Parliament that were held in Bulgaria in 2007 and 2009 do not make particularly optimistic reading: though the trend is upwards, the actual figures still remain the lowest for any elections held so far in Bulgaria.

The link between inequality and voter turnout is not clear. While the Gini coefficient fluctuated during the period under consideration (Table 7.2), voter turnout declined fairly

Table 7.2 Electoral turnout in Bulgaria (% of active voters on the electoral roll), 1991–2011

Year	Parliamentary elections	Presidential elections	Local elections	EU elections	GINI net Coefficient
1991	81.50		83.87		0.258
1992		75.90			0.278
1994	74.20				0.284
1995			57.80		0.294
1996		61.70			0.278
1997	62.90				0.276
1999			56.03		0.251
2001	66.60	54.90			0.245
2003			57.45		0.247
2005	53.80				0.276
2006		54.90			0.305
2007			43.26	29.20	0.328
2009	60.60			38.40	0.352
2011		48.09	54.29		–

Source: Todorov (2010); Central Election Commission figures for 2003, 2007, 2011 elections.

constantly, irrespective of whether inequality increased or decreased. This all suggests a lack of correlation between inequality and electoral activity. The changes in voter turnout for the various Bulgarian institutions differ greatly, and clearly other factors are at work.

Institutional Trust

The Bulgarian people have relatively little confidence in public institutions. Trust in institutions is a clear expression of the general attitude and opinion of Bulgarians towards the effectiveness of the policies pursued.

People have relatively little faith in the Bulgarian Parliament, and in the last decade this trust has declined further: in 1999 about 72.3 per cent of Bulgarians had no faith in the Bulgarian Parliament; by 2008 the figure had increased to 88.7 per cent.[1]

The Bulgarian judicial system is similarly associated with a low level of trust: the proportion of respondents who say they have full confidence in it is very small and has declined during the period under consideration, from less than a third in 1999 to less than a fifth in 2008. This decline in confidence is also evident among those sections of the population that had even less confidence in the judicial system or that distrusted it more. Lack of all trust in the judicial system is widespread in the Bulgarian population.

The level of trust in the Bulgarian government is also low, but fluctuates according to whether there is a parliamentary election: in the election years of 2005 and 2009 there was

---

[1] According to data from European Values Study (EVS) 1999, 2008.

a slight increase in trust declared by Bulgarian citizens, in contrast to years that coincided with the middle or end of government administrations. A different picture emerged in 2009, when parliamentary elections resulted in victory for a new political party (Citizens for the European Development of Bulgaria): only in that year did the share of people who were inclined to trust the government exceed the share of people who tended to distrust it.

In contrast to the serious crisis of confidence witnessed among Bulgarians towards Bulgarian institutions, confidence in the European Parliament is a great deal higher. The general European tendency towards increasing levels of confidence in the European Parliament and decreasing confidence in national parliaments held true for Bulgaria even before its accession to the EU.

Inequality in education and employment, the degree of hardship experienced by house-holds and social status—these are all fundamental factors that determine the extent to which people trust the government. There is an inverse relationship between trust and level of education: people with only primary education tend to trust institutions more than do people with a university education—perhaps because the belief is widespread among less well educated groups that the institutions can help solve their problems. People with university education are more critical of the functioning of parliament, the judicial system and the government.

Political Values and Legitimacy

According to the classical understanding of political left and right, the left covers poorer people and groups struggling for social justice, while the right attracts more affluent people who uphold the traditional Christian values and market relations. In Bulgaria, the right is keen on innovation and desires a pro-Western orientation for the country; the left is nostalgic for Russia and Russian support for Bulgarian independence. In other words, alongside the traditional characteristics of left and right, in Bulgaria these concepts contain geostrategic attitudes and orientations.

There has been an increase in the number of people who place themselves in the centre on the left–right political scale (Figure 7.5), following the collapse of the bipolar model that dominated the 1990s. The demarcation of a more clearly defined centre in Bulgaria's political space after 2000 is a result of the failed efforts by a succession of left- and right-wing governments to achieve the desired economic development and an improvement in living standards. Those who identify themselves as being on the extreme left or the extreme right are in the range 5–10 per cent. According to data from the European Values Study, in 1999 there were more extreme right-wing than extreme left-wing supporters, whereas in 2008 there were more people who identified with the extreme left. At the same time, there was an outflow from the right to the centre, while the left remained relatively stable.

The alternation of left-wing and right-wing governments was typical of the first decade of the post-socialist period (Figure 7.6). In the context of the research, we should note that the high percentage of votes cast for the Bulgarian Socialist Party (BSP) in the parliamentary elections of 1994 owed much to general dissatisfaction among the Bulgarian population with the reforms, and to people's nostalgia for the security and higher living standards that

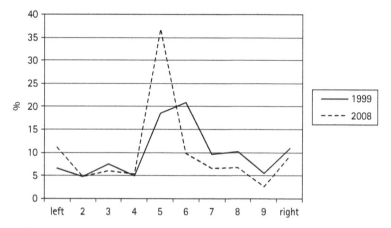

FIGURE 7.5 Political identification: left–right (% of respondents)

Source: European Values Study (EVS), 1999 and 2008.

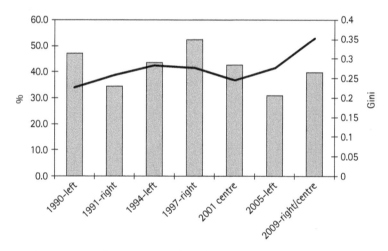

FIGURE 7.6 Percentage of votes cast for the winners in elections and inequality, 1990–2009

Source: Central Election Committee. Results from the elections in Bulgaria.

most Bulgarians enjoyed before 1989. The 'pendulum swing' from one side to the other is typical of Bulgaria and is generally quite natural in periods of transition.

If we compare the votes cast for the left, right and centre parties with the dynamics of inequality, it would seem that there is a relationship between them. In the period of growing inequality (early 1990s), more votes were cast in elections for left-wing parties. By contrast, when inequality declined, the right-oriented parties and parties in the centre triumphed in elections. Consequently, income inequality has to some extent affected the election of a government that is of the left, the right or the centre.

In terms of Europe, there is a consensus in Bulgaria: the public attitude towards member-ship of the EU is positive. Bulgarians find EU membership attractive and desirable: they are almost 20 percentage points more positive about membership than the EU average (38 per cent). Young people, people with a university education and students are the most enthusi-astic about the EU.

Values Regarding Social Policy and the Welfare State

The Bulgarian population is highly sensitive to the problems of inequality, poverty and social policy. Most Bulgarians (over 70 per cent in the period 2006–10) agreed that income inequality in the country is high.[2] The dominant opinion is that the government should reg-ulate income differences and over 80 per cent think that the government should take meas-ures to reduce income inequality.

A similar attitude is expressed in respect to poverty. Such sensitivity is a consequence of the low level of incomes and the high risk of falling into poverty, especially among people on low incomes. There is a high level of consensus that it is the function of the state to prevent people from falling into poverty: over 90 per cent of Bulgarians con-sider that government must take steps to that end. Labour incomes and the provision of employment are considered basic functions of government and legitimate grounds on which to assess the actions of the state generally. Despite the prevailing market depend-ency of incomes, the risk of poverty is regarded as a public problem, which requires gov-ernment action.

5. EFFECTIVENESS OF POLICY TO COMBAT INEQUALITY

Here the subject of analysis is the impact on income inequality of policies pursued in the spheres of income, taxation and social transfers, by attempting to answer the question of whether, and to what extent, particular policies result in a reduction or an increase in inequality.

Effects of Wage Formation and the Minimum Wage Incomes Policy

The mechanisms of wage formation, as well as government policy in this sphere, are directly related to income inequality. The minimum wage and the system of collective wage bargain-ing are the main channels of state influence.

---

[2] According to data from the European Social Survey (ESS) 2006, 2008, 2010.

The impact of bargaining on wage dynamics and inequality depends, to a great extent, on the features of the negotiation system and the relative strength of the negotiating parties. The basic characteristics are related to the type of system, its coverage, coordination between negotiating parties, and the degree of unionization.

Collective wage bargaining is not widespread in Bulgaria. It is most common in the public sector. The weak spread of collective bargaining corresponds to low union density: though statistical data on the number of union members are incomplete, they do indicate a significant decrease in the period 1998–2007. The number of union members fell by almost 83 per cent in the period 1990–2007, and union density dropped from 37.3 per cent in 1998 to 17.9 per cent in 2007 (Daskalova, 2008). The coverage of collective negotiation is also low: according to expert estimates, the proportion of employees covered by collective contracts has fluctuated as follows—33 per cent in 2007; 30 per cent in 2008; 32 per cent in 2009; and 35 per cent in 2010 (Dimitrov, 2011).

The Bulgarian system and practice of wage negotiations thus does not promote a reduction in wage differentiation. The low level of union distribution, coverage and density contributes to stimulating wage inequality.

The minimum wage dynamics has a significant influence on inequality in Bulgaria. The minimum wage is determined by the government, and its size and rate of growth are subject to government regulation.

There are two basic periods in the development of the minimum wage after 1990 that were directly dependent on government wage policy. During the first period (1990–7), a strict restrictive policy was applied with regard to wages, in order to achieve economic stability and reduce inflation. The effect of this policy was to severely erode the real minimum wage: its purchasing power declined by 78 per cent over the start of the period.

A change in policy after 1998 laid the foundations for a lengthy period of growth in the minimum wage. The minimum wage frequently rose faster than the average wage and GDP. Overall, in the period 1998–2008, the real minimum wage more than doubled. When the present economic crisis struck, wage restrictions were again imposed and the minimum wage was frozen until the middle of 2011.

If we compare the dynamics of the real minimum wage with the changes in the income inequality of households,[3] measured by the Gini coefficient, we see a remarkable interaction (Figure 7.7). The period of accelerated growth in the minimum wage (1998–2005) was accompanied by a decrease in income inequality. This increase in the minimum wage compressed the wage distribution at the bottom, contributing to a decline in wage inequality (Tzanov, 2010; 2011). A few years (1998, 1999 and 2005) particularly stand out for the extremely high growth of the minimum wage, which was accompanied by an even more considerable decrease in income inequality. A more negligible rise in the minimum wage after 2006 and its freezing after 2009 probably contributed to an increase in inequality.

The interaction between the growth in the real minimum wage and the Gini coefficient is negative. It is clear that this relationship does not take into account the impact of other factors that reduce inequality (e.g. taxation policy). Nevertheless, the minimum wage does appear to be an effective instrument for inequality reduction in Bulgaria.

---

[3] This comparison is not completely precise, but it gives an approximate idea of the connection between the minimum wage and income inequality.

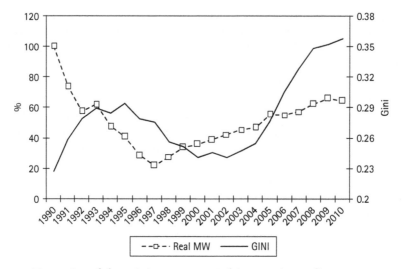

FIGURE 7.7 Dynamics of the minimum wage and income inequality, 1990–2010

Source: National Statistical Institute.

The Effects of Taxation Policy

Over the past decade, the taxation system in Bulgaria has sought to reduce direct taxes and make up the deficit via indirect taxes. In 2008, a flat-rate income tax system was introduced, and this has changed the structure of tax revenues, with even greater emphasis on cutting direct taxation. The general idea is to reduce the tax burden on labour, so as to stimulate employment and attract new investment.

Total tax revenue as a percentage of GDP has mirrored the changes to taxation policy and economic development. Total tax revenues in Bulgaria are relatively low. Over the period 1995–2010 they fluctuated within the range 28–33 per cent of GDP, and declined strongly after 2008. Bulgaria's tax revenues are much lower than those of other EU countries: in 2010 they were 12.2 percentage points lower than the EU-27 average, and even lower compared to the EU-15 (12.9 percentage points).

In the tax revenue structure, indirect revenues prevail (VAT, excise duties and other taxes on production). In the last ten years, their relation to GDP has grown by 1.4 percentage points. At the same time, their share of total revenue has increased from 44 per cent in 2000 to 55 per cent in 2010.

As a result of taxation policy, revenue from direct taxes (personal income tax, corporate income tax and others) has constantly declined. By the end of the period under consideration, direct taxes as a proportion of GDP had declined by 1.8 percentage points since 2000; and as a proportion of total revenue from 22 per cent to 18.6 per cent.

The impact of taxation on inequality can be traced as the difference between the Gini coefficients of gross and net income. The dynamics of the difference between the two coefficients indicates that taxation policy in the period 1992–97 considerably reduced inequality, but thereafter the effect gradually weakened. The downward trend in the effect of taxes on inequality corresponds to the policies of decreasing direct taxes and introducing the flat-rate tax.

Effects of Pension and Social Assistance Policy on Inequality

Differences in labour income and income from pensions and social benefits largely determine income inequality. The evolution of the ratio of the average pension to the average wage and of guaranteed minimum income (GMI) to the average wage gives some idea of income inequality in two respects: 1) with respect to the average labour income; and 2) with respect to the incomes of certain social groups.

The first indicator presents the relationship of the average pension (AV) to the average wage (AW), and shows the difference between the income of pensioners and average labour income. The second indicator represents the ratio of GMI to the average wage and explains the distinction between the average wage and the income that is defined by the state as the basis on which social benefits are determined. Of course, the latter indicator is conditional, because it does not provide the average amount of social benefits received.

The dynamics of both indicators are presented in Figure 7.8. Their development during the period under examination is quite different. The trend of the first indicator (average pension to average wage) is cyclical and corresponds to the two major economic cycles: economic decline (1990–7) and progress in the period 1998–2008. The development of the second indicator (guaranteed minimum income to average wage) shows a decreasing trend, with periods of stabilization.

The cyclical economic development strongly affected income inequality among those social groups considered. During the economic recession (1990–7), income from pensions and social benefits deviated considerably from labour income, and thus led to increasing inequality between employed people, pensioners and social benefit recipients. The differentiation is strongest between the employed and social benefit recipients. Thus the social

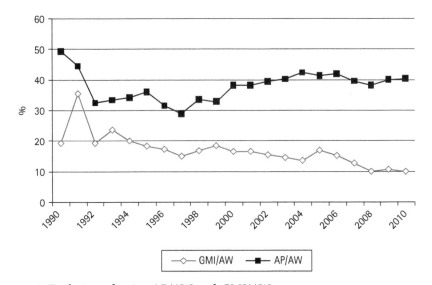

FIGURE 7.8 Evolution of ratios AP/AW and GMI/AW, 1990–2010

Source: National Statistical Institute.

transfers in this period did not decrease inequality, but rather the restrictions imposed on social transfers stimulated inequality between these social groups.

The period of accelerated and constant economic growth only favoured pensioners. They experienced a considerable decrease in inequality with respect to the average wage. The opposite was the case with social benefits. The relation of GMI to the average wage continued to decline, reaching 13.7 per cent in 2004 (though it rose to almost 17 per cent in 2005). Thus the gap between the income of pensioners and that of social benefit recipients increased significantly.

Therefore social transfers for retirement positively affect inequality, reducing the difference between labour incomes and pensions. Transfers for social assistance, however, have a negative effect on inequality. The weak adaptation of the GMI to the average wage stimulates income inequality with respect to both employed people and pensioners.

6. Conclusions

Income inequality in Bulgaria over the past three decades has grown overall, though there have been ups and downs. The evolution of income inequality is a direct result of economic development, reforms (mostly during the first half of the 1990s) and incomes policy. The increase in inequality during the 1990s was mostly a result of the development of the private sector in the economy, the continuous economic recession and the restrictive incomes policy that was pursued. The continuous period of decline in income inequality could be explained mainly by the incomes policy implemented (a considerable rise in the minimum wage) and a gradual decrease in taxes on wages and social security payments.

Labour market inequalities by gender and education have similar trends. Gender inequalities in employment and in pay have decreased. Differences in employment according to level of education attained have also declined.

There have been positive changes in the level of education of the population over the past 30 years. These changes have mostly affected the Bulgarian population, rather than the other major ethnic groups. Ethnic differences in educational attainment have remained considerable and have strongly affected inequality.

In terms of social impacts, the study reveals that in some social aspects inequality impacts indirectly on their dynamics, while in other aspects there is a direct connection. While household material deprivation has fallen in the face of rising income inequality, risk of poverty closely mirrors income inequality. The majority of Bulgarian households live in their own homes without mortgage loans or credits. The differences in the distribution of people according to tenure status and risk of poverty are not considerable.

The study finds a relatively low impact of inequality on family formation, housing and life expectancy. The changes in these social processes are mainly correlated with economic development.

In the political sphere, the impact of inequality is not strongly expressed. There is no link between inequality and political participation in elections, because voter turnout has steadily decreased while inequality has fluctuated. Also there appears to be no correlation between inequality and trust in public institutions: lack of trust in public institutions (government, parliament, judicial system) is spreading throughout the population. There does however appear to be some relationship between the development of inequality and the alternating of left-wing and right-wing governments.

Taxation policy in Bulgaria is directed towards reducing direct taxes and increasing indirect taxes. This policy restricts the impact of taxes on inequality.

Government policy and social transfers have a mixed impact on inequality reduction. Incomes policy (more precisely the minimum wage policy) has a significant effect in reducing income inequality. The pattern of taxation policy reduces revenues from taxes and limits the redistribution processes. Moreover, the introduction of the flat-rate tax has limited government interventions to combat inequality. Social transfers for old age pensions have a positive effect on reducing inequality between income from labour and pensions. Transfers via the social assistance system have a negative effect on inequality as they do not keep pace with wages.

REFERENCES

Central Electoral Commission, *Election 2003, 2007, 2011.*

Daskalova, N., *Trade union strategy to recruit new groups of workers—Bulgaria*, European Foundation for the Improvement of Living and Working Conditions, <http://www.eurofound.europa.eu/eiro/studies/tn0901028s/bg0901029q.htm>

Dimitrov, P., *Annual Review 2010 on Labour Market Relations and Social Dialog in South East Europe: Bulgaria*, Friedrich-Ebert-Stiftung, 2011, p. 12.

European Social Survey, *Exploring public attitudes, informing public policy, Selected findings from the first three rounds.*

Eurobarometer 62, (Autumn 2004), *Public opinion in European union, National Report for Bulgaria.*

Eurostat statistical book, (2012), *Taxation trends in the European union. Data for the EU Member States, Iceland and Norway, European Union.*

Frederick, S., (2009), 'Standardizing the World Income Inequality Database', *Social Science Quarterly* 90(2):231-242, SWIID Version 3.1, December 2011.

Household budgets in the Republic of Bulgaria 1995, 2003, 2010, NSI.

Mintchev, V., Boshnakov, V., Naydenov, A. (2010), 'Sources of Income Inequality: Empirical Evidence from Bulgaria', *Economic Studies*, Issue 4, 2010.

National Statistical Institute. <http://www.nsi.bg/otrasal.php?otr=41>

Nikolova, S., Markov, N., Nikolov, B., Dochev, N. (2011), 'Inequality and Public Policy: A Country Study for Bulgaria', *Working Papers*, 095, Centre for Economic and Strategic Research. The wiiw Balkan Observatory.

Solt, Frederick (2011), 'Standardizing the World Income Inequality Database', *Social Science Quarterly* 90(2):231–242. SWIID Version 3.1, December 2011.

Todorov, A. (2010), *Citizens, parties, elections: Bulgaria 1879-2009*, Sofia.

Tzanov, V., Bogdanov, B., Beleva, I. Kotseva, M., Stoyanova, K., Mircheva, D., Tzvetkov, A. (2006), *Bulgaria: the challenges of poverty*, 2003, NSI.

Tzanov, V. (2010), 'Bulgaria: A shift in minimum wage policy', in D. Vaughan-Whitehead (ed.), *The Minimum Wage Revisited in the Enlarged EU*, Cheltenham UK, Edward Elgar .

Tzanov, V. (2011), 'Inequality at work emerging in the current crisis in Bulgaria', in D. Vaughan-Whitehead (ed.), *Work Inequalities in the Crisis*, Edward Elgar.

Zahariev, B. (2011), 'Economic situation of households—tendencies, expectations, arrangement', *Open Society, Policies*, Issue 08/11, <http://politiki.bg/?cy=222&lang=1&aoi=223804&aom=readInternal&aop_id=872>

CHAPTER 8

RISING INEQUALITY AND ITS
IMPACT IN CANADA: THE ROLE OF
NATIONAL DEBT

ROBERT ANDERSEN AND MITCH McIVOR*

1. INTRODUCTION

THE goal of this chapter is to explore how income inequality in Canada evolved between 1980 and 2010, who was affected, and how governments and public opinion have responded and influenced it. Compared to many modern economies, income inequality in Canada has been relatively high since 1980 (Frenette and Milligan, 2009; Heisz, 2007). This chapter will demonstrate how this already high level grew substantially in the mid 1990s. Like many countries, much of the increase in inequality was driven by large gains for those at the very top of the income distribution. These gains made by high-income earners did not come without cost to low-income earners, however. In this respect, this is a uniquely Canadian story.

While market forces played an important role in producing higher levels of inequality than had been seen in many decades, political factors also contributed. Crucial in this regard was how Canadian governments responded to a public debt that was rapidly getting out of control. Government policy served to both increase income shares for the rich and worsen economic hardship for those at the very bottom of the income distribution. The combination of government cutbacks and a rise in market income inequality resulted in a much greater disparity between rich and poor than Canada has seen since World War II. Demographic changes—especially related to family composition and immigration—also played a role, however. Particularly important in this regard were significant increases in the number of families with two income earners and marital homogamy.

Consistent with other chapters in this volume, we start with a general description of why and how income inequality changed in Canada from 1980 to 2010. That is, we discuss in further detail the changing political, economic, and demographic context of this period.

* University of Toronto.

We then discuss the political, social, and cultural impacts of this rise in inequality. In many ways, the rise in income inequality has had less impact than would be expected based on previous findings of research in the area. We will also discuss data and methods relatively briefly, but focus on the most important developments during this period. A more extensive discussion of our data, methods and findings is found in the larger country report.[1]

2. The Evolution and Drivers of Inequality in Canada, 1980–2010

We start by exploring the pattern of income inequality in Canada from 1980 to 2010. Figure 8.1 displays trends in the Gini coefficients for household incomes during this period.[2] We see quite clearly that market income inequality has increased quite dramatically since 1980 with the biggest rise occurring in the 1990s (solid line). Government taxes and transfers largely tempered this rise in earnings inequality until 1995, after which there was also a sharp increase in after-tax income inequality (bottom dotted line). In short, government taxes and transfers failed to keep pace with the rise in market earnings inequality between 1995 and 2000. Since 2000, however, both market and after-tax income inequality have stabilized, though the vast increase in inequality experienced in the 1990s persists.

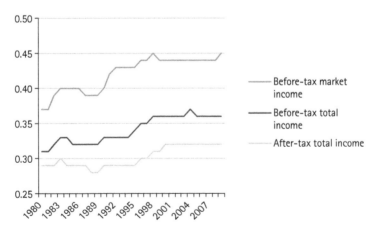

FIGURE 8.1 Gini coefficients for household income before and after taxes and redistribution[3]

Source: Statistics Canada.

[1] www.gini-research.org/CT-Canada
[2] Gini coefficients measure inequality in a country according to income dispersion wherein a score of 1 equates to maximum inequality and a score of 0 equates to perfect equality.
[3] We will overlay the Gini coefficient for 'Household After-Tax Income' on graphs of trends throughout this chapter.

Three main drivers behind the huge rise in inequality in the 1990s were: (1) globalization and a resulting restructuring of the Canadian economy; (2) a national debt crisis and
emphasis on economic initiatives that led to a decrease in government taxes and social
spending; and (3) demographic changes, including an increase in dual income earner families, greater marital homogamy, and changing immigration patterns. These factors served
to benefit top income earners, worsen the situation of the poor, and generally expand
inequality between households. We will provide more details of these factors as the chapter
progresses. We start with a general description of the economic and political climate during
this period.

Rising Public Debt and its Consequences, 1980–2010

Canadian governments became increasingly less effective at—and arguably less interested
in—redistribution from the 1990s onwards. A large body of research argues that the main
driving force behind Welfare State retrenchment was growing public debt (Greenspon and
Wilson-Smith, 1996; Minister of Finance, 2006). Extensive public spending during the 1970s
and high interest rates in the 1980s combined to create nearly unmanageable public debt by
the end of the 1980s. Figure 8.2 displays the trend in public debt (dark black line) alongside
the trend in inequality for after-tax incomes (the grey line). Public debt grew rapidly during
the 1980s and early 1990s, until finally tapering off in the late 1990s. In short, the trend in
public debt tracked fairly closely with the trend in income inequality.

The problem of rising public debt was compounded by slow economic growth. Figure 8.3
displays Canada's GDP per capita, and its growth rate, from 1980 to 2010. We see very clearly
from the top graph that the Canadian economy grew slowly between 1980 and 1985, had a
significant—but short-lived—jump at the end of the 1980s, and then levelled off again for

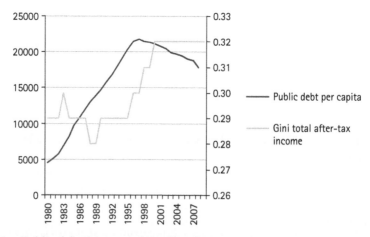

FIGURE 8.2 Public debt (per capita) in Canada, 1980–2010

Source: Statistics Canada.

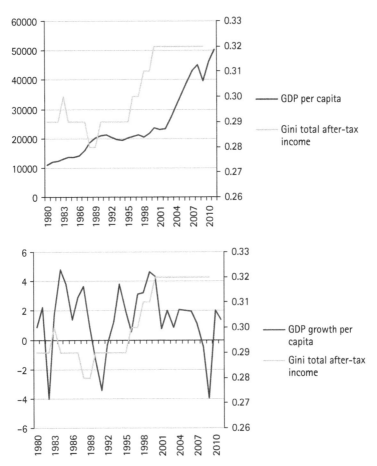

FIGURE 8.3 GDP per capita in Canada, 1980–2010

(Top) Level; (Bottom) Growth
Source: The World Bank.

about a 10-year period until around 2000. The economic slowdown in the 1990s is even more obvious in the bottom graph, which displays the annual per cent growth in GDP per capita from 1980 to 2010.

The slowdown in economic growth in the 1990s coincided with increased international competition and globalization. The North American Free Trade Agreement (NAFTA) implemented in 1994 increased Canada's international trade relations but also its competition with the US and Mexico. Increased international competition, rising national debt, and the need for economic growth all led to the rise of a neo-conservative and pro-business agenda (Banting, 1992). We will discuss how this agenda manifested in specific policy changes in Section 5, but it is important to note now that there were two general results: 1) tax cuts for business and high-income earners that were meant to encourage investment growth and 2) spending cuts to social programmes with the goal of reducing the national debt. The combination of these two factors served to further increase inequality.

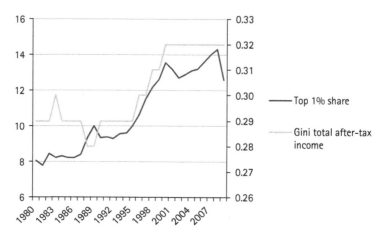

FIGURE 8.4 Top one per cent's share of total income

Source: Saez & Veal, 2003; Fortin *et al.*, 2012.

Increasing Inequality at the Top

Like the US, the rise in income inequality in Canada was largely driven by the rich getting richer (Johnson and Kuhn, 2004). Between 1980 and 2010, those in the top 20 per cent of the equivalized household income distribution experienced a significant increase in their share of total earnings, both before and after taxes. Before taxes, their share of total income increased from 40.4 per cent to 46.3 per cent during this 30-year period. Although this trend was somewhat offset by taxes, the top 20 per cent were still the only group to experience a rise in after-tax income shares as well (36.4 per cent to 39.2 per cent).

The relative gains of the top income earners are again noticeable when exploring the 80/20 ratio of equivalized household incomes—i.e. the income shares of the top 20 per cent divided by the shares of the bottom 20 per cent. In 1980, the top 20 per cent had roughly 9.5 times as much income as the bottom 20 per cent of earners; by 2010 they had 13 times as much income. As Figure 8.4 (adapted from Saez and Veall, 2003, 2005; and Fortin *et al.*, 2012) indicates, the growing advantage of the rich is even more marked for those in the top one per cent of earners. Figure 8.4 also demonstrates that the rise in incomes for the rich (the black line) followed quite closely with the rise in overall inequality as measured by the after-tax Gini coefficient (the gray line). In 1980, the top one per cent received about eight per cent of the total income in the country; by 2000, their share had risen to more than 12 per cent.

For the most part, inequality has increased primarily because the rich have become richer, and not because more people have become poor. For example, various measures of poverty indicate that material poverty has not increased in Canada over the last 30 years. The Low-Income Measure,[4] which indicates relative poverty risk, went from 12.7 per cent in 1980, to a low of 10.5 per cent in 1989, and then gradually increased to 13.3 per cent in 2009. Similarly, absolute or material poverty risk actually declined in Canada over the last 30 years

---

[4] The Low Income Measure is the percentage of population with adjusted household incomes less than 50 per cent of the median after-tax income.

as indicated by Statistics Canada's Low Income Cut-offs[5], which estimates the per cent of families spending a disproportionately large share of their household income on essentials (food, shelter, and clothing). The per cent of families in absolute poverty was 11.6 in 1980, it peaked at 15.2 per cent in 1996, then steadily decreased to its lowest total of 9.6 per cent in 2009. Finally, the per cent of households without adequate housing[6] has also decreased in recent years, falling from a high of 15.6 in 1996 to 12.7 in 2006.

This reduction in poverty, does not mean that those at the bottom of the income distribution have not been affected by increasing inequality, however. Relative Poverty risk exit rates—the per cent of people in relative poverty that moved out of poverty in a given year—went from 37.5 per cent in 1981 to 30.7 per cent in 2008. In short, cuts to government social spending have made it harder for individuals to move out of relative poverty. These rates are not replicated in absolute poverty rates, however, due to the overall drop in absolute poverty rates discussed earlier. The absolute poverty exit rate went from 33.3 per cent in 1981 to 34.1 per cent in 2008, and its entry rate went from 4.9 per cent in 1980 to 2.9 per cent in 2008. Overall, material poverty decreased, but the poor lost ground both in terms of their income relative to the rest of Canadians and their ability to escape poverty.

Increase in Dual Earner Families and Marital Homogamy

Cuts to taxation and social spending in the 1990s allowed the rich to grow richer and hurt the less fortunate, but demographic changes also played a role in the growth of inequality. In particular, increased inequality was also spurred by a growth in dual income families (Heisz, 2007). In contrast to thirty years ago when it was possible to have a relatively good living in a two-parent household with only one income earner, it has become increasingly difficult to do so today. At the same time that dual earner families have been on the rise, marital homogamy also increased significantly since 1980 (Hou and Myles, 2008; Kenworthy, 2004), with the highest levels of homogamy occurring at the highest and lowest levels of socio-economic status (Hou and Myles, 2008:361). Given that the number of dual earner families has risen (53 per cent in 1980 to 63 per cent in 2010), an increase in marriages

[5] A Low Income Cut-Off is an income threshold below which a family will likely devote a larger share of its income to the necessities of food, shelter and clothing. The approach is essentially to estimate an income threshold at which families are expected to spend 20 percentage points more than the average family on food, shelter, and clothing. The Family Expenditure Survey is used to estimate twelve different cut-offs varying by family size and region. (The different cut-offs are intended to capture differences in the cost of living between family sizes as well as rural and urban areas.) These thresholds were then compared to family income from Statistics Canada's major income survey, the Survey of Consumer Finances (SCF), to produce low-income rates (adapted from Statistics Canada Low Income Cut-off Definition).

[6] 'Acceptable housing is defined as adequate and suitable shelter that can be obtained without spending 30 per cent or more of before-tax household income. Adequate shelter is housing that is not in need of major repair . . . [and] is not crowded, meaning that it has sufficient bedrooms for the size and make-up of the occupying household. The subset of households classified as living in unacceptable housing and unable to access acceptable housing is considered to be in core housing need' (Canada Mortgage and Housing Corporation).

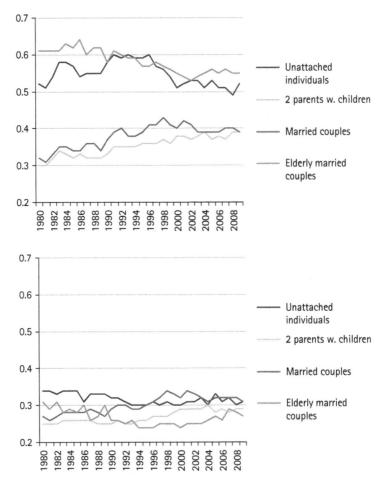

FIGURE 8.5 Before-tax (top) and after-tax (bottom) Gini coefficients for household income by household composition

Source: Statistics Canada.

between individuals with similar education and income levels serves to further increase inequality between families (see Esping-Andersen, 2007; Kenworthy, 2004).

As the top graph in Figure 8.5 indicates, between 1980 and 2010, the Gini coefficient for before-tax income inequality *decreased* for elderly married couples (0.31 to 0.27) and for unattached individuals (0.34 to 0.31). On the other hand, the Gini coefficient *grew* for both married couples (0.29 to 0.35) and for families with two parents and children (0.27 to 0.33). Although taxes and redistribution slightly mute these patterns of inequality, they do not completely remove them as is shown in the bottom graph of Figure 8.5. Since 1980, the Gini coefficient for after-tax household income again decreased for elderly married couples (0.31 to 0.27), and unattached individuals (0.34 to 0.31). Conversely, it increased for both married couples (0.27 to 0.31) and two parent families with children (0.25 to 0.29).

Historically in the traditional family arrangement of male breadwinner with a stay-at-home spouse, household income inequality among working age families was largely a function of income differences between male breadwinners. As more women entered the workforce, however, differences in household incomes became more diverse. For example, the income inequality between families with two highly educated, high-earning individuals and two less educated, lower earning individuals is potentially double what it would be if only one spouse from each family worked. Given the evidence that individuals marry similar others (Hou and Myles, 2008), the rise of dual income families partly explains why inequality has increased between married couples but not between singles and the elderly. After adjusting for household size and taxes, households in the top 20 per cent of earnings experienced an increase in their average income of $49,400 between 1980 and 2009 (from $128,500 to $177,900).[7] Conversely, during this same period, the bottom 80 per cent of households saw an average increase of only $5,450, and the bottom 20 per cent gained only $1700.

In sum, inequality in Canada has risen since 1980 with the rise occurring primarily in the 1990s. This inequality was largely driven by market forces, but government tax and social spending cuts ensured that a similar, though somewhat muted, pattern occurred for after-tax incomes as well. There is also evidence, however, that inequality was partly driven by changes to family composition. In particular, a rise in dual income earner families and marital homogamy—both along education and income lines—served to further increase household income inequality.

3. SOCIAL FACTORS IN INEQUALITY

Having described the growth in income inequality over the past few decades, we now explore how it affected Canadians. Inequality growth in Canada has affected Canadians differently along the lines of gender, education, and immigration status.

Gender

Inequality growth in Canada has affected men and women differently. Specifically, women made gains in the labour force, while men lost ground. This is evident both in terms of employment rates and incomes. For example, between 1980 and 2010, the male employment rate decreased by 5.5 percentage points (79.7 to 74.2 per cent), while the female employment rate increased 16.2 percentage points (from 52.6 to 68.8 per cent). During this same period, the unemployment rate for men surpassed the unemployment rate from women. While men's unemployment increased by 1.8 percentage points (from 7.1 to 8.9 per cent), women's unemployment decreased by 1.1 percentage points (from 8.4 to 7.3 per cent). Moreover, the percentage of women working in full-time positions increased by 11.7 (from 39.2 to 50.9 per cent), while the percentage of men in full-time positions decreased by 8.1 (from 74. to 66.5 per cent). Both men and women experienced an increase in the percentage working part-time, however. The percentage of men in part-time positions increased by 3.4 (from 5.1 to 8.5 per cent) and the percentage of women working part-time increased

---

[7] All dollar amounts are adjusted for inflation and represent values in 2009 dollars.

Table 8.1 Percentage of earners in each income category by gender, 1980 and 2009

	1980		2009		Change	
	Men	Women	Men	Women	Men	Women
Under $10k	15.6	32.8	20.7	27.7	5.1	-5.1
$10-19,999	10.4	19.5	13.5	17.1	3.1	-2.4
$20-29,999	10.3	18.7	10.7	13.7	0.4	-5
$30-39,999	12.8	14.2	11	12.2	-1.8	-2
$40-49,999	13.8	7	9.6	9.1	-4.2	2.1
$50-59,999	12.8	4.2	8	6.8	-4.8	2.6
Over 60k	24.4	3.7	26.5	13.4	2.1	9.7

Source: Statistics Canada.

by 4.7 (from 13.4 to 18 per cent). Data regarding job permanency in Canada exists only for the years 1997-2010, but during this time men's share of all permanent jobs decreased by 2.5 to a 50.1 per cent share, while women's share of permanent jobs increased by 2.5 to a 49.9 per cent share. In short, while men continue to have an advantage over women in terms of permanent full-time employment, the gap has decreased significantly over the last 30 years.

The gender gap in income also decreased in recent decades. In terms of median earnings, women in part-time employment earned only 61.9 per cent of what men earned in 1980, but by 2010, it was 87.1 per cent. Similarly, in terms of full time median earnings, women earned only 62.6 per cent of what men earned in 1980 but by 2010 it had risen to 78.4 per cent. While this convergence of incomes between men and women is largely a function of increased earnings for women, it is also a function of a decline in men's earnings. The decline in men's earnings has resulted from globalization, post-industrialism and the concomitant loss of high-paying unionized manufacturing jobs, which have traditionally been dominated by men (Duffy and Pupo, 1992). For example, McCall (2001) demonstrates that industrial cities with high-unionization have a higher gender wage gap than post-industrial cities with low unionization.

As Table 8.1 demonstrates, although much of women's gains in earnings pertain to part-time employment, major gains have also been made in high-income positions. For example, the percentage of women in jobs earning less than $40,000 has decreased by 14.5 since 1980, while the percentage of women earning over $40,000 increased by 15.4. Conversely, the percentage of men in jobs earning less than $30,000 grew by 8.6, while the percentage in jobs earning between $30,000 and $59,999 decreased by 10.8.

In summary, women have moved into the labour force and garnered a larger share of high-paying positions, which increased the wage gap between high and low skilled women (McCall, 2001). At the same time low-skilled men moved into lower paying positions as unionized manufacturing work decreased, which again increased the wage gap this time between low and high-skilled men. The result is a decrease in the gender wage gap but an overall increase in inequality between high and low skill workers, which then sets the stage for marital homogamy to further raise inequality between families.

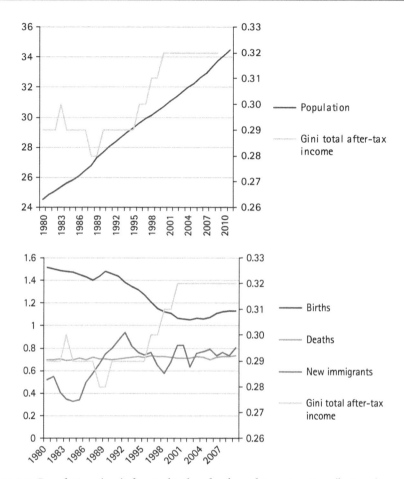

FIGURE 8.6 Population (top) due to births, death and immigration (bottom)

Source: Statistics Canada.

Immigration

With more women moving into the workforce, Canadians have waited longer to have children and tend to have fewer children generally. Yet despite the fact that the crude birth rate[8] decreased from 56.9 in 1980 to 46.7 in 2010, and the total fertility rate[9] has been below the eplacement rate of 2.1 since 1971 (Sardon, 2006), the Canadian population has steadily increased from 24.5 million in 1980 to 34.5 million in 2011 (Figure 8.6, top graph). As the bottom graph of Figure 8.6 indicates, this increase in population resulted from high immigration, especially between 1985 and 1995. Most important from the standpoint of inequality, a growing wage gap between immigrants and native-born Canadians—because the majority

[8] Number of births per 1,000 women.
[9] Average number of children born to a women in her lifetime.

of new immigrants sit near the bottom of the earnings distribution—has evolved with the growth in immigration (Aydemir and Skuterud, 2005; Li, 2001).

This growing gap between immigrants and native-born Canadians is at least partly associated with a devaluation of immigrant credentials and foreign work experience (Aydemir and Skuterud, 2005:668). Immigrants tend to be over-represented in the low-paying service economy and in non-unionized, low-paying manufacturing jobs (Sassen, 1998). Language and cultural skills also play a role, however. In particular, recent shifts in the country of origins of Canadian immigrants—i.e., from traditional European to non-traditional Asian countries—are associated with weaker language abilities among new immigrants (Aydemir and Skuterud, 2005). In general, Canada's newer immigrants tend to have less experience with Canada's official languages and/or familiarity with Canadian culture than immigrants in previous decades. These factors have occurred at the same time that the education levels of native-born Canadians have risen (Reitz, 2006), making it more difficult for employers to choose immigrants over native born Canadians.

Education

The percentage of Canadians with post-secondary credentials has increased dramatically over the past few decades. The top graph of Figure 8.7 demonstrates the relationship between employment status and education since 1990. From 1990 to 2010, the percentage of the labour force with low education—i.e., less than high school, high school, and some post-secondary—has significantly decreased. At the same time, those with a post-secondary certificate or degree have become increasingly more likely to hold a full-time job. Moreover, as the bottom graph of Figure 8.7 indicates, education and income are highly related. Compared to those with only a post-secondary diploma or certificate, holding a university degree equates to roughly a $10 per hour wage advantage. While this wage advantage remained fairly constant between 1980 and 2010, the number of people benefitting from it grew, suggesting that supply kept pace with demand.

Post-secondary education may also be contributing to inequality through student debt. The number of students taking on debt to obtain post-secondary credentials has risen dramatically in Canada—from 42 per cent in 1986 to 59 per cent in 2005. As part of the cuts to government spending that occurred in the 1990s, the percentage of post-secondary funding contributed by the government decreased from 70 per cent in 1980 to 53 per cent in 2000. On the other hand, the percentage comprised by student fees increased from 9 per cent to 20 per cent during the same period. This increase in student fees has led to average student debt at graduation increasing from $12,861 in 1990 to $24,729 in 2005 (Berger, 2009). Studies have found that the prospect of debt does not deter students from lower socio-economic status (SES) backgrounds in Canada from pursuing post-secondary education (Frenette, 2005). In a cross-national study, however, Canadian post-secondary graduates were found to have a high average monthly debt-payment-to-income ratio of 6.6 per cent (Usher, 2005)—a payment ratio of 8 per cent is considered the cut-off point for financial risk (Scwartz and Baum, 2006). In short, the roughly 60 per cent of graduates who held student debt in 2005 were at a disadvantage to graduates who had no student debt. This implies that the debt-free advantage of students from high-SES backgrounds may be another contributor to the growing

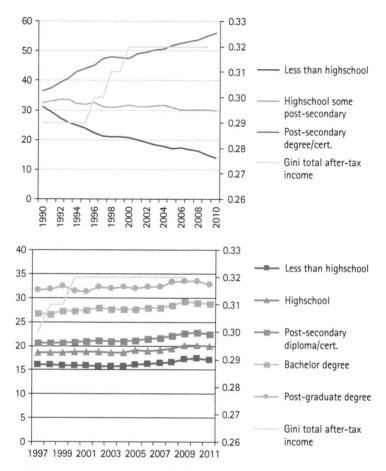

FIGURE 8.7 Educational attainment and labour force outcomes (per cent of total labour force (top) and average hourly wage (bottom))

Source: Statistics Canada.

advantage of the top income earners over the rest of Canadians. Student debt, however, is not the only type of debt to have increased between 1980 and 2010.

Debt

As Figure 8.8 suggests, there have also been significant increases in personal debt (which includes mortgage debt) generally since 1980. The debt-to-after-tax-income ratio has risen dramatically from debt equalling 86 per cent of household after tax income in 1980 to 148 per cent in 2009 (top graph). Not surprisingly, there has also been a dramatic rise in the number of consumer bankruptcies (see bottom graph). In 1980 only 21,000 people claimed bankruptcy; by 2009 the number of bankruptcies had risen to 115,000.

The rise in personal debt is largely a function of increasing house prices and the fact that Canadians have become increasingly likely to buy homes instead of rent since 1980. This

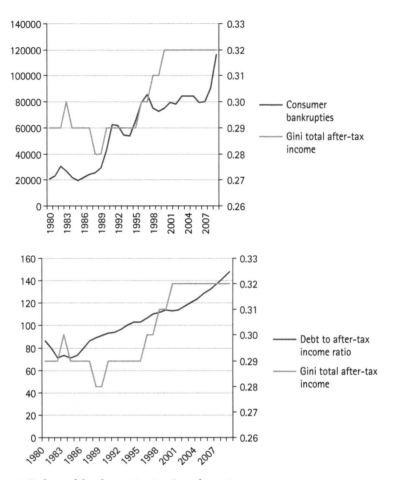

FIGURE 8.8 Debt and bankruptcies in Canada, 1980–2009

Source: Statistics Canada.

trend occurred as housing prices increased and mortgage interest rates rose (Chawla, 2011). As house prices rose, lower-income households became increasingly disadvantaged and more families began to rely on credit to purchase homes. Figure 8.9 displays house prices in Canada from 1980 to 2010. The top graph demonstrates changes in new house prices; the bottom graph displays trends in average home prices obtained from the Multiple Listing Service—a home listing service overseen by Canada's real estate boards. We see quite clearly that home prices, as a percentage of 2007 prices, increased substantially from 1980 to 1990, after which time they slightly decreased for about a decade. This slight decrease corresponded with the start of the rise in income inequality in the 1990s. After 2000, however, inequality stabilized and home prices again began to increase drastically.

During the 1990s when home prices levelled off, the Gini coefficient for market incomes jumped from 0.39 to 0.44, and median incomes adjusted for inflation slightly decreased. Moreover, the vacancy rate—the percentage of apartments vacant in metropolitan areas (over 100,000 residents)— doubled between 1985 and 1994. Later, when the trend in

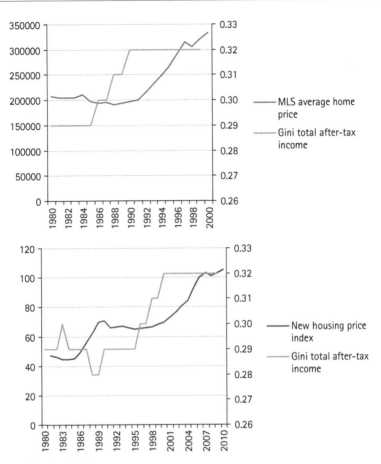

FIGURE 8.9 Housing prices

Source: Statistics Canada and Canada Mortgage and Housing Corporation.

inequality began to stagnate in the early 2000s, unemployment decreased, incomes began to rise, and market income inequality levelled off. As a result, the vacancy rate hit its lowest point since 1980 in 2001, which in turn increased home prices exponentially. These increases lead to an increase in mortgages—Canadians as a whole owed roughly 92 billion in mortgages in 1980 which rose to 1.1 trillion by 2010—and this led to lower and middle class Canadians spending more on loan interest per year. Once again, this likely contributed to the growing advantage top earners had over the rest of Canadians.

4. POLITICAL AND CULTURAL IMPACTS

Public Opinion on Inequality and Redistribution

We now turn to the relationship between growing inequality, the decline in government spending and political and cultural factors. A general finding from previous research is that the more unequal a society, the less likely people are to hold democratic 'values' (Andersen and Fetner 2008, Andersen 2012, Uslaner 2002). Previous research indicates that Canadian citizens have relatively high levels of civic and political engagement when compared to citizens of most other countries (Andersen *et al.*, 2006). It is thus of interest to assess whether this high level of participation may have been influenced in any way by the growing inequality of the 1990s. Since 1980, voter turnout at Canadian federal elections has decreased substantially from about 65 per cent of the voting aged population in 1980 to less than 55 per cent in 2010. A similar pattern is shown for the percentage of registered voters—in 1985 slightly more than 75 per cent cast votes; by 2010 less than 65 per cent cast votes. The largest decline in voter turnout took place in the 1990s at approximately the same time that the largest growth in inequality occurred. While we cannot make definitive claims from these data, the evidence suggests that the growth of income inequality may have had a negative effect on democratic engagement.

The growth in inequality may also have influenced political preferences and ideology. The percentage of Canadians who reported far left political leanings doubled (from 3 to 6 per cent) and those reporting far right leanings decreased (from 8 per cent to 5 per cent) during the period under study. The slight move to the left in Canadian public opinion is further supported in Figure 8.10, which displays trends in Canadians' attitudes towards government's role in reducing inequality. The top graph uses WVS data to show the trend in the percentage of people believing incomes should be made more equal; the middle graph uses ISSP data to show opinions towards government responsibility for reducing income differences; and the bottom graph from the WVS shows trends in the percentage who feel that the government should take responsibility for the poor.

Starting with the top graph, we see that opinions towards income inequality appear to have reacted against increasing inequality. That is, as income inequality grew in the 1990s, so too did the percentage of people who felt incomes should be more equal. Similarly, the middle graph suggests that people became increasingly more likely to think governments should reduce inequality as income inequality grew. Nevertheless, the bottom graph suggests that although public opinion became slightly more favourable to the idea that the government should be responsible for the poor as income inequality rose, it failed to keep up with the actual rise in inequality. Of course, 'the poor' is a somewhat different issue than general inequality— the former pertains to a very small group, while the latter to the vast majority—so this finding is perhaps not surprising. Moreover, the phrase 'responsible for' is rather strong. We would perhaps have slightly different findings for more moderate languages such as 'should the government 'help' the poor' but we are aware of no such data. In any event, Canadians generally responded to rising inequality by feeling that governments should do something about it.

Health and Crime

In terms of health, rising inequality seems to have been of little consequence. The life expectancy has increased in Canada for both men (75 in 1980 to 81 in 2006) and women (79 to 83) and suicide rates have been stable. Reports of self-perceived health and life satisfaction have also remained relatively stable. Only one major health indicator seems to have changed negatively while inequality rose. Specifically, the obesity rate increased from 12 per cent in 1996 to 16 per cent in 2007. Overall, however, the rise in inequality has apparently not had any serious consequences in terms of health.

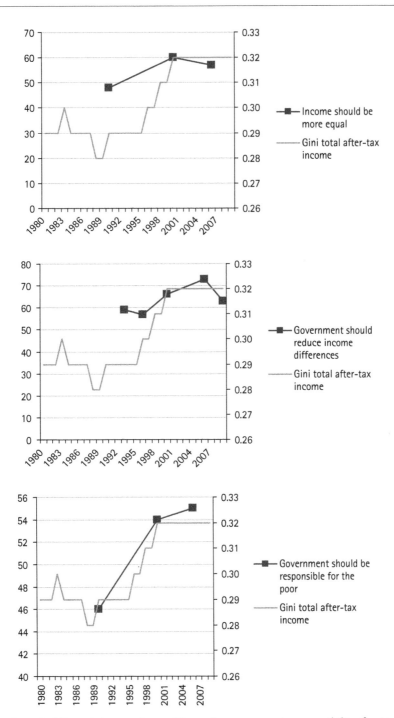

FIGURE 8.10 Public opinion on inequality and government responsibility for it

Source: World Values Survey (top and bottom graph); International Social Survey Programme (middle graph).

In terms of crime rates, rising inequality has often been linked to increasing levels of crime (Daly *et al*, 2001; Hsieh and Pugh, 1993). Rates for many crimes in Canada unexpectedly dropped in the 1990s, however, despite increasing inequality (Levitt, 2004; Mishra and Lalumiere, 2009). The overall crime rate[10] decreased between 1980 (8,832 crimes reported) and 2010 (6,969 crimes reported) although the violent crime rate, which is often more strongly correlated with increasing inequality (Daly *et al.*, 2001; Hsieh and Pugh, 1993), doubled during this same period (from 636 to 1,282 violent crimes reported). Also interesting to note is that the percentage of youth (15–24 years) deaths accounted for by homicide also doubled (3.8 per cent to 7.5 per cent) between 2000 and 2010, suggesting violent crime is increasing the most among Canada's youth. Nevertheless, the overall drop in the crime rate more likely reflects political rather than economic forces.

Over the past two decades in Canada, socially conservative parties have campaigned and won elections on platforms geared towards getting 'tough' on crime. In short, the drop in crime rates can largely be explained by increased police force sizes, more aggressive policing, and higher levels of incarceration for convicted criminals (Levitt, 2004; Mishra and Lalumiere, 2009). For example, the prison population in Canada grew exponentially from 22,502 inmates in 1980 to 38,219 inmates in 2010. Similarly, the incarceration rate rose 12 points during the same period (from 128.5 inmates per 100,000 Canadians in 1980 to 140.5 in 2010). Thus the increase in policing and incarceration may explain the decreased crime rates experienced in the face of rising inequality.

5. POLICIES

At the onset of this chapter we identified a national debt crisis in the 1990s as one of the main drivers of rising inequality in after-tax incomes. As debt grew, political discourse began to be dominated by talk of the need to balance the budget and reduce the public debt (Greenspon and Wilson-Smith, 1996; Minister of Finance, 2006; White, 1998). With compound interest on Canada's national debt growing by $85,000 a minute during the early 1990s (Greenspon and Wilson-Smith, 1996: 200–201), public sentiment shifted to favour social expenditure cuts and a refocus on economic growth. This is not to suggest that support for social programmes completely waned during this period. In fact, it remained fairly high for some time. Nevertheless, the desire for social programmes was tempered by the contradictory need for economic restraint (Banting, 1992). The result was a gradual and subtle implementation of tax and social spending cuts, leading some to characterize the movement as a 'politics of stealth' (Banting, 1992:158). Neo-Conservative ideology had risen to prominence in the 1980s—and social spending had already started to be pared away at that time—but it wasn't until the 1990s that cries for further spending cuts were increasingly pinned on the rising debt. Governments began to use the debt as a reason to cut taxes as well as spending, claiming that uncontrolled spending—which allegedly resulted in over taxation—compounded the debt problem. This was not a difficult sell considering reports surfaced that Canada's deficit had become one of the largest in the OECD (Banting, 1992;

---

[10] Crimes per 100,000 population.

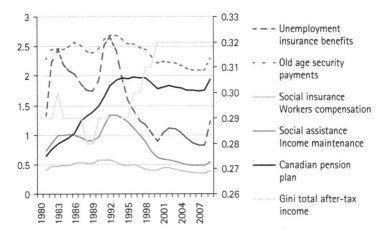

FIGURE 8.11 Trends in government expenditures

Source: Statistics Canada.

Swank 2002) and that Canada could lose its AAA credit rating if the debt did not get under control (Boothe, 1993; Martin, 1996).

Until the mid 1990s there was a gradual increase in tax revenue (from 31 per cent of GDP in 1980 to 36.4 per cent in 1991) after which tax revenue as a percentage of GDP declined progressively to 31 per cent in 2010. Tax cuts were justified by rhetoric of needing to be competitive in the international market, which created pressure to reform the tax structure and adopt a pro-business agenda (Banting, 1992). Concomitantly, tax reform focused largely on tax-cuts for businesses and corporations, which decreased overall tax revenues (Courchene, 1987; Jones and Guttsman, 2011). Also important, however, was income tax restructuring, which resulted in cuts for the top one per cent and bottom 30 per cent of families (Banting, 1992; Maslove, 1989). As mentioned earlier, this decrease in tax revenue was compensated for by spending cuts.

Total government transfers (as a per cent of GDP) decreased from 13 per cent in 1993 to 11 per cent in 2009. While seemingly only a small difference, it resulted in a $26.752 billion[11] reduction that was mostly cut from social spending. Figure 8.11 displays trends in various types of government transfers. Most notable are the marked declines in social assistance for income maintenance (i.e., welfare payments) and employment insurance payments. Both of these declines mirror quite closely the overall rise in income inequality that starts in the early 1990s. While the main story has been about increasing incomes for the richest households, we see here that those near the bottom of the income structure were drastically affected as well. While government transfers remained relatively stable between 1980 and 2010 for the top 80 per cent of earners, the bottom 20 per cent of earners saw a decrease of 7 per cent in total government transfers (a total decrease of approximately $6.163 billion).

Although we showed earlier that the number of people in absolute poverty did not rise with income inequality, the level of social assistance given to these people lessened, making their situation worse.

---

[11] All dollar amounts are in 2009 dollars.

FIGURE 8.12 Average minimum wage, absolute and relative level: adjusted hourly minimum wage (top); relative minimum wage earnings as a percentage of average earnings (bottom)

Source: Human Resources and Skills Development Canada & Statistics Canada.

Government policies regarding minimum wages also had an impact. Minimum wages are set by provincial governments in Canada. While they have been quite variable across the country over the past few decades, in all provinces they have typically been quite low when compared to the more extensive Welfare States of Europe (Murray and Mackenzie, 2007). Moreover, in the mid 1990s—the period of the greatest growth in income inequality—real minimum wages either stagnated or, in many provinces, declined. Particularly noteworthy was a sharp decline in Ontario's real minimum wage from the mid 1990s to the mid 2000s. This decline corresponds to the 'common sense revolution' of the Progressive Conservative government that implemented cuts in social spending as a way to reduce provincial debt (White, 1998). As the top graph of Figure 8.12 demonstrates, increases in the national average of the provincial minimum wages[12] lagged behind the large increase in inequality in the 1990s.

---

[12] Wages are adjusted for inflation (i.e., all values are in 2009 constant dollars).

The bottom graph of Figure 8.12 suggests that although most provinces progressively raised the minimum wage after the mid 2000s, this resulted in only a small improvement relative to the average Canadian's earnings both before and after tax. By 2009 the after-tax income of those receiving the minimum wage was only 42 per cent of the average Canadian's income.

In sum, Canada's national debt crisis of the mid 1990s was used to justify the implementation of drastic tax and social spending cuts. In line with a pro-business agenda and the perceived need to stay competitive in an international market, tax cuts occurred for businesses and top earners in an attempt to increase investment (Banting, 1992). At the same time, the national debt was reduced by cuts to social spending—particularly welfare and social assistance benefits—which were detrimental to the very poor. While the number of people in poverty did not increase, the circumstances for those in poverty worsened. Moreover, as was discussed earlier, between 1980 and 2009 relative poverty increased and the ability for those in poverty to escape it also decreased. Ultimately, then, by implementing tax and social spending cuts Canadian governments did little to stop the rising tide of inequality.

6. Conclusions

This chapter has explored the pattern of income inequality in Canada from 1980 to 2010, its political and social impacts, and how public opinion responded to it. We demonstrated that market income inequality rose significantly in the 1990s. Much of this increase in inequality was generated by top earners experiencing substantial gains in their incomes but there were also important changes at the bottom of the distribution. While globalization played a large role in this regard, it was not the only factor. Changes in family structure—especially an increase in dual-earner households and educational homogamy—also served to increase household income inequality. We further demonstrated that this rise in market income inequality was not adequately countered by redistribution policies. That is, although there was significantly less inequality in after-tax incomes than in before-tax incomes during the period under study, the difference between the two narrowed significantly in the 1990s and has not returned to previous levels. In other words, changes in taxation and social policy also played an important role. Specifically, high-income households gained, while very low-income households lost. This loss was most obvious in a decline in social assistance, unemployment benefits and poverty exit rates.

We also demonstrated that gender, immigrant status, education, and debt also played important roles in the inequality story. Women have increasingly moved into the paid work force, particularly in high paying, full time employment. This phenomenon has increased wage inequality between high and low skill women. At that same time, inequality between men also grew due to the loss of high paying unionized manufacturing work that tended to be dominated by men. Women's entrance into the workforce was accompanied by a fall in birth rates and, therefore, Canada relied on an increasing number of immigrants to meet labour force demands. For various reasons such as a shift in the source countries of immigrants, decreased language skills, and the native populations' growth in education, immigrants have tended to be located at the bottom of the earnings hierarchy. The growth in post-secondary education rates also increased inequality as rising tuition fees have led to increasing student debt levels. Other debt such as mortgages has also played a major role in inequality growth as lower and middle income families were paying more in debt interest in 2010 than ever before in Canadian history.

Perhaps just as notable as the rise in inequality and governments' inability—or unwillingness—to respond to it, was its limited impact on public opinion. A general finding from previous research is that the more unequal a society, the less likely people are to be socially tolerant (Andersen and Fetner 2008), to trust one another (Putnam 1995), and to participate in voluntary associations (Andersen *et al.*, 2006). Yet Canada experienced a large increase in social inequality with seemingly no corresponding increase in conflict. We offer three possible explanations for the low level of conflict.

First, the vast rise in inequality had little impact on the lives of the average middle-income earner, though people within the middle-income categories certainly moved around. In other words, it is true that the rich got richer, but their gains did not come at the expense of those in the middle of the income distribution. Moreover, those in poverty got poorer but the overall number of people in poverty actually decreased and conflict typically arises when poverty and not wealth increases (Nelson, 1995). It seems sensible to suggest that most Canadians perceived that their living conditions had not worsened, or that they were unlikely to worsen in the near future. In other words, while Canadians have become more likely to think the government should do something about growing inequality, the issue was not salient enough to gain political traction. The Occupy Movement in the fall of 2011 seemed to raise awareness that the top one per cent of earners were becoming even richer but, as of yet, there is no clear evidence that it has had an important and enduring influence on public opinion.

Second, it seems unlikely that inequality produced by a growth in dual income-earner families could become a political issue given the social and economic changes that have taken place over the past several decades. Most important in this regard were rising house prices and a significant increase in home ownership instead of renting. Whereas families could get by with one earner in the 1980s, two incomes are now typically required to maintain an adequate standard of living. The need for two income-earners, however, has also contributed to the increase in women's labour force involvement. Greater involvement of women in the labour force is typically seen as important in achieving gender equality. It is perhaps because of this that the need for households to have two incomes receives little political attention.

Finally, inequality may have risen without increasing conflict because of the exponential increase in debt (Hurst, 2011). Increased access to and use of debt gives the perception of wealth and allows families to obtain necessities like a home before they can afford them outright. As mentioned earlier, the average family in 2009 owed 149 per cent of their annual after-tax income in debt, which increased from 86 per cent in 1980. The inequality that may have been experienced by the middle and working classes in terms of purchasing a home or attending university, therefore, has been offset by the availability of debt.

As of 2012, the ruling Conservative Party continues to advocate a pro-market platform that promotes the need for tax cuts to 'help businesses create jobs' in a time where 'Canadians remain concerned about their jobs and their children's future' (Conservative Party Platform, 2012). The modern recession has served to further entrench pro-market policy as seen by Conservative party victories in national elections in 2006 and 2010. All indications point to the continued movement toward decreased taxes with recent federal initiatives focusing on promoting investments by corporate tax cuts (Huffington Post, 2012) and family tax cuts that will primarily benefit families with a stay-at-home spouse or with one spouse who earns significantly more than the other. These developments suggest a continued decline of total tax revenue and, therefore, at best a stagnation of social expenditure. In short, at present there is little evidence to suggest that the rising tide of inequality will begin to ebb in Canada any time soon.

REFERENCES[13]

Andersen, Robert (2012), 'Support for Democracy in Cross-National Perspective: The Detrimental Effect of Economic Inequality', *Research in Social Stratification and Mobility*, 30(4): 389–402.

Andersen, Robert, Curtis, James, and Grabb, Edward (2006), 'Trends in Civic Association Activity in Four Democracies: The Special Case of Women in the United States', *American Sociological Review* 71:376–400.

Andersen, R., and Fetner, T. (2008), 'Economic Inequality and Intolerance: Attitudes toward Homosexuality in 35 Democracies', *American Journal of Political Science* 52(4): 942–958.

Aydemir, Abdurrahman, and Mikal Skuterud (2005), 'Explaining the Deteriorating Entry Earnings of Canada's Immigrant Cohorts: 1966-2000', *Canadian Journal of Economics* 38: 641–672.

Banting, Keith (1992), 'Neoconservatism in an Open Economy: The Social Role of the Canadian State', *International Political Science Review* 13(2): 149–170.

Berger, Joseph (2009), 'Student Debt in Canada', in Joseph Berger, Anne Motte, and Andrew Parkin (eds.) *The Price of Knowledge: Access and Student Finance in Canada*, 4th ed. Montreal, QC: The Canadian Millennium Scholarship Foundation, pp. 182–206.

Boothe, Paul (1993), 'Provincial Government Debt, Bond Ratings and the Availability of Credit', in R. G. Harris (ed.) *Debt and Deficits in Canada*, Policy Forum Series No. 29. Kingston: John Deutsch Institute.

Chawla, Raj K. (2011), 'The Distribution of Mortgage Debt in Canada', *Component of Statistics Canada Catalogue no. 75-001-X, Perspectives on Labour and Income*, Statistics Canada.

Conservative Party of Canada (2012), 'Platform', retrieved 22 September 2012 (<http://www.conservative.ca/?pag eid=40>).

Courchene, T. (1987), *Social Policy in the 1990s*, Toronto: C.D. Howe Institute.

Daly, Martin, Wilson, Margo, and Vasdev, Shawn (2001), 'Income Inequality and Homicide Rates in Canada and the United States', *Canadian Journal of Criminology* 43(2): 219–236.

Duffy, Ann and Pupo, Norene (1992), *Part-Time Paradox: Connecting Gender, Work &Family*, Toronto: McClelland & Stewart.

Esping-Andersen, Gosta (2007), 'Sociological Explanations of Changing Income Distributions', *American Behavioural Scientist* 50:639–658.

Frenette, Mark, Green, David A., and Milligan, Kevin (2009), 'Taxes, Transfers, and Canadian Income Inequality', *Canadian Public Policy*, 35(4): 389–411.

Frenette, Mark (2005), 'Is Post-Secondary Access More Equitable in Canada or in the United States?' *Statistics Canada: Analytical Studies Branch Research Paper Series*, Catalogue Number 11F0019MIE—No.244.

---

[13] A full list of references and data sources can be found in the full country report for Canada (www.gini-research.org/CT-Canada).

Greenspon, Edward, and Wilson-Smith, Anthony (1996), *Double Vision: The Inside Story of the Liberals in Power*, Toronto: Doubleday Canada.

Heisz, Andrew (2007), *Income Inequality and Redistribution in Canada: 1976 to 2004*, Statistics Canada, Business and Labour Market Analysis Division, ID: 11F0019 No.298. Published by Ministry of Industry.

Hou, Feng and Myles, John (2008), 'The Changing Role of Education in the Marriage Market: Assortative Marriage in Canada & the United States since the 1970s', *Canadian Journal of Sociology* 33:337–366.

Hsieh, Ching-Chi and Pugh, M.D. (1993), 'Poverty, Income Inequality, and Violent Crime: A Meta-Analysis of Recent Aggregate Data Studies', *Criminal Justice Review* 18(2): 182–202.

Huffington Post Canada (2012), 'Business: Businesses Getting Billions in Tax Cuts Despite Rising Corporate Cash Reserves', 1 January 2012, retrieved 22 September 2012: (<http://www.huffingtonpost.ca/2012/01/01/tax-cuts-corporations-canada_n_1178382.html>)

Hurst, Matt (2011), 'Debt and Family Type in Canada', *Canadian Social Trends*, Statistics Canada: Component of Statistics Canada Catalogue no.11-008-X.

Johnson, Susan and Kuhn, Peter (2004), 'Increasing Male Earnings Inequality in Canada and the United States, 1981-1997: The Role of Hours Changes versus Wage Changes', *Canadian Public Policy/Analyse de Politiques* 30(2):155–175.

Jones, Jeffrey and Guttsman, Janet (2011), 'Canada Tories to follow tax cut, pro-business agenda', *Reuters*, 3 May 2011, retrieved 22 September 2012: <(http://www.reuters.com/article/2011/05/03/us-politics-idUSTRE73Q44720110503>)

Kenworthy, Lane, (2004), *Egalitarian Capitalism*, New York: Russell Sage.

Levitt, Steven D. (2004), 'Understanding Why Crime Fell in the 1990s: Four Factors that Explain the Decline and Six that do not', *Journal of Economic Perspectives* 18(1):163–190

Martin, Paul (1996), 'The Canadian Experience in Reducing Budget Deficits and Debt', *Economic Review* (1): 11–25.

Maslove, A. (1989), *Tax Reform in Canada: the Process and Impact*, Ottawa: Institute for Research in Public Policy.

McCall, Leslie (2001), *Complex Inequality: Gender, Class and Race in the New Economy*, New York: Routledge.

Minister of Finance (Canada), (2006), *Canada's New Government Cuts Wasteful Programs, Refocuses Spending on Priorities, Achieves Major Debt Reduction as Promised*, Ottawa: Department of Finance.

Mishra, Sandeep and Lalumiere, Martin (2009), 'Is the Crime Drop of the 1990s in Canada and the USA Associated with a General Decline in Risky and Health-Related Behavior?' *Social Science & Medicine* 68: 39–48.

Murray, S. and Mackenzie, H. (2007), 'Bringing Minimum Wages above the Poverty Line', Ottawa: Canadian Centre for Policy Alternatives, March.

Nelson, Joel I. (1995), *Post-Industrial Capitalism: Exploring Economic Inequality in America*, Thousand Oaks: Sage.

Putnam, Robert (1995), 'Bowling Alone: America's Declining Social Capital', *Journal of Democracy* 6: 65–78.

Reitz, Jeffrey (2006), 'Recent Trends in the Integration of Immigrants in the Canadian Labour Market: A Multi-Disciplinary Synthesis of Research', unpublished paper prepared for Human Resources and Social Development Canada, Ottawa.

Saez, Emmanuel and Veall, Michael R. (2003), 'The Evolution of High Incomes in Canada, 1920–2000', *NBER Working Papers*: No. 9607, 2003, National Bureau of Economic Research, Inc.

Saez, E., and Veall, M. (2005), 'The Evolution of High Incomes in Northern America: Lessons from Canadian Evidence', *American Economic Review* 95 (3): 831–849.

Sardon, Jean-Paul (2006), 'Fertility in the Developed English-Speaking Countries Outside Europe: Canada, United States, Australia and New Zealand', *Population* 61(3): 267–291.

Sassen, Saskia (1998), *Globalization and its Discontents: Essays on the New Mobility of People and Money*, New York, NY: The New Press, pp. 137–153.

Schwartz, Saul, and Baum, Sandy (2006), *How Much Debt Is Too Much? Defining Benchmarks for Manageable Student Debt*, New York: The College Board.

Usher, Alex, (2005), *Global Debt Patterns: An International Comparison of Student Loan Burdens and Repayment Conditions*, Toronto, ON: Educational Policy Institute.

Uslaner, E. M (2002), *The Moral Foundation of Trust*, Cambridge: Cambridge University Press.

White, Randall (1998), *Ontario Since 1985*, Toronto: Eastend Books.

CHAPTER 9

....

SOURCES AND IMPACT OF RISING INEQUALITY IN DENMARK

....

IOANA NEAMTU AND NIELS WESTERGAARD-

NIELSEN*

1. INTRODUCTION

....

THIS chapter gives an account of economic inequality in Denmark as it has developed from 1980 until 2010. It is based on register data for the whole population which enables us to map the entire Danish income distribution year by year for all sorts of sub groups.

The Danish income distribution after tax and transfers has, for long, been comparatively equally distributed with a relatively small difference between the lowest and the highest incomes and with a relatively high earnings mobility. However, this changes slowly towards a more unequal income distribution over the investigated years, for both household and individual incomes. It is found that the tax and transfer system have a huge impact on the distribution of incomes, reducing inequality from 0.46 to 0.30 in 2010.

There are many mechanisms in Danish society that contribute to this result and these are related to the distribution of salaries and incomes and to redistribution via the tax and benefit system but also to the policies implemented during these years.

This chapter shows an income and transfer system which is based on high redistribution which results in a relatively low, but increasing, income inequality and a society with no, or few, noticeable social, political and cultural changes in the period investigated as a result of the inequality increase. It seems that the perceived inequality by the Danish population is very low and its increase is insignificant. One of the reasons is that the increasing inequality is linked to some degree to different stages of the life cycle that all will pass through and to the increasing work participation of women, as will be demonstrated in the following.

* Centre for Corporate Performance, Aarhus University.

Another reason is the high intergenerational mobility in Denmark that allows individuals to escape the poverty trap.[1]

The chapter is organized as follows—the first section offers a brief description of the income distribution and its development since 1980 and investigates the sources of the increasing inequality by looking at contributions from men, women and marriages as well as generational sub groups. The second and the third sections concentrate on the potential social and political consequences of increased inequality in Denmark, while the final section describes the policies pursued by Denmark in order to keep inequality as low as possible.

2. The Development of the Income Distribution

In this section we will focus on both equalized household income and individual income, using all types of income available from Statistics Denmark (gross income, net income, before and after redistribution and imputed rents) in order to present a clear and detailed picture of the evolution of income inequality in Denmark since 1980.

Data

The data for this exercise comes from Danish Register data[2]. These data contain earnings after tax incomes, together with information about transfers from the public sector. The information originates from the tax register and is generally considered to be highly reliable. The income information exists in the registers for each individual. Due to a common ID-number, this information can be merged with registers for education, housing and all other relevant registers. The registers in Denmark contain detailed information on individuals, work, and earnings, down to the apartment or house address of each person. This means that households are identified as married or unmarried couples if they are registered at the same address and apartment number. Even same sex households are covered in this way. Children are also registered. As a consequence, the size of household will be revealed and can subsequently be used to calculate the income equivalence according to the normal OECD procedure. We use the OECD square root equalization method for household income, where household income is divided by the square root of the number of members in the household to net out the different consumption needs of the household.

The income variable presents a challenge as there are a small number of people (less than 0.1 per cent) with negative incomes. The main reason for this is that incomes are registered on an annual basis and there may be corrections made to the wage of the previous year. Furthermore, taxable incomes come from the tax register and, because of various tax issues, incomes can become negative in one year due to tax-deductible losses. All cases with negative incomes have been deleted from the sample.

---

[1] Bjørnskov et al., 2012.
[2] The results presented in this paper are based on own calculations, if not otherwise mentioned.

Household Income Inequality

Overall, in terms of disposable household income Denmark belongs among the most equal countries in the world. Thus, according to OECD, the Gini coefficient was 0.23 in the mid 2000s (OECD 2011). However, that distribution has changed over time due to changes in the primary distribution and in the structure of the tax and transfer system.

According to OECD (2011), Denmark has had an overall growth in household disposable income from the mid 1980s to the late 2000s of 1 per cent per annum with a growth in the bottom decile income of 0.7 per cent and a growth of the top decile of 1.5 per cent. That means that top incomes have grown much faster than incomes at the bottom. The overall growth in disposable income is towards the lower end of the OECD countries while the relative differential in growth between top and bottom incomes is higher than average in OECD countries, indicating that inequality has actually grown in the investigated period as it has in the majority of OECD countries. However, the change has been relatively modest compared to other countries.

The distribution of disposable income for households is the result of several processes. Incomes are mostly created in the labour market as earnings. On top of that, comes capital income. Both are taxed by a progressive tax that tends to equalize after-tax income. Furthermore, large groups receive pensions and other transfers from the public sector, equalizing disposable incomes even more. Figure 9.1 presents the distribution of household income in Denmark in 2006, which is chosen among other years. It shows, roughly, how unequal primary incomes are shaped by the redistribution system through taxes and transfers and transformed into disposable income. Part of the redistribution system is of course inter-generational.

Figure 9.2 shows the evolution of the Gini coefficient of household income by source of income, and brings out the importance of redistribution and taxes in shaping inequality. The top line in the graph in Figure 9.2 shows the development of the Gini coefficient for primary income, i.e. earnings before taxes and redistribution and imputed rent. It is seen that

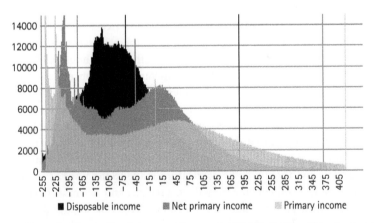

FIGURE 9.1. Household equalized income in 2006, transformation from primary to disposable income, frequencies

Source: Our own calculations using Statistics Denmark Register and Income Data (also applies to Figures 9.2–9.13 and Tables 9.1–9.5).

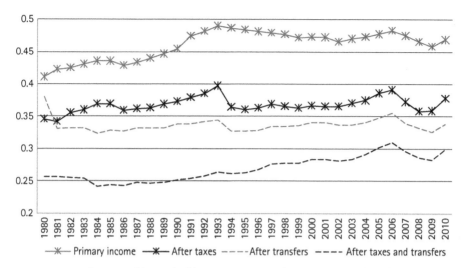

FIGURE 9.2 Evolution of household income inequality in Denmark (the Gini coeffi-cient)—decomposition by source of income

Note: All incomes include imputed rents from 1984.

the Gini coefficient reaches its highest value of 0.49 in 1993. It is remarkable that the distribution of primary income becomes more unequal in the years with low economic growth and high unemployment, 1987–1993, and becomes slightly more equal again from 1993 and until 2003 when growth starts again. After that, inequality in earnings has been rising slightly during the upswing 2004 to 2006. Finally, it should be mentioned that imputed rent from housing does not have an independent impact on the Gini coefficient before the 2000s when increasing house prices increased the imputed rent somewhat.

The next line in the graph describes the development of the Gini coefficient of incomes after tax has been paid. This line has the same overall shape as the Gini-coefficients of income before tax and transfers, but has a shift in level in 1994 due to a reform after which all transfers became taxable. After tax, Gini coefficients are substantially lower than primary income and the slightly increasing gap between them indicates a sustained increase in redistribution through the tax system since 1980. The inequality of incomes after tax decreased after 2006 as a result of a tax reform and increased again in 2010 because of a second tax reform. These will be discussed in detail in the policy section. The third line in the graph is the Gini coefficient of the income after transfer payments and before tax. This shows that the transfer system has an almost constant levelling impact until 2003, thus reducing the Gini coefficient to around 0.35. The fourth line shows the Gini coefficient of household income after both tax and transfers. It is almost con-stant and around 0.26 until the mid 1990s from where it starts climbing and reaches 0.29 in 2006. After that, the Gini coefficient falls but regains in 2010, so that 2010 is just short of the level in 2006. Including imputed rent only has an impact in more recent years where it increases the Gini-coefficient by about 0.02 units, in 2006 due to the boom in house prices.

Our results[3] are recapitulated in Table 9.1 for each kink point in Figure 9.2. It is clear from the table that redistribution levels out the Gini coefficient of primary income through

---

[3] These are higher than the ones presented in OECD, 2011.

Table 9.1 Summary of Gini coefficients of equalized household income, for specific years

	1980	1986	1993	2000	2006	2009
Primary income	0.41	0.43	0.49	0.47	0.48	0.46
Income after redistribution	0.26	0.24	0.26	0.28	0.31	0.28
Redistribution effect	0.15	0.18	0.23	0.19	0.17	0.18

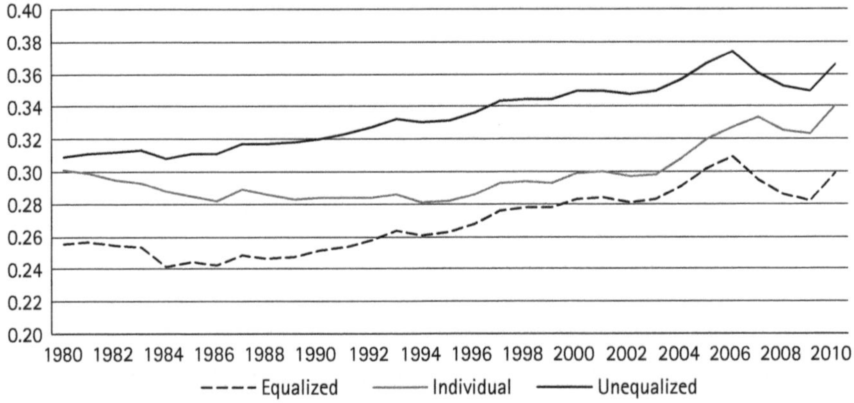

FIGURE 9.3 Comparison between household and individual income (Gini coefficient for disposable income, including imputed rents)

tax and benefits by 0.15–0.23 units every year with the result that the income after tax and redistribution has almost the same Gini-coefficient at least until 1993. Over time it has also worked as a significant levelling factor as it is found that the Gini coefficient of primary income has increased by 0.07 units from 1980 to 2006, while for income after redistribution it has increased by only 0.04 units.

These findings show that income distribution is fairly equal in Denmark. This is mainly accomplished through the benefit and tax system. These findings also point to a paradox. On the one hand, we see that primary income (before taxes and transfers) becomes slightly more equal after 1993. On the other hand, we see that income after tax and transfers has become more unequal since 1984.

In what follows we will investigate each aspect separately in order to find the culprit. We will start with equalized income and P-ratios, where we take account of household size. Then we will move to the individual level and investigate the role of the Welfare State package for old age and retired people above 65, and similarly for the young. These groups will be divided into those working and those not working. The processes at work will be investigated further by estimating a human capital function to assess whether returns to Human Capital have increased over the period. Finally, we will investigate the formation of households again and see if this in itself creates more inequality.

Equalizing incomes and P ratios. We will briefly investigate the separate effect of equalizing with the size of the household. Figure 9.3 shows that equalization lowers the Gini coefficient by about 5 percentage points and that this percentage does not change over time. So, equalization of incomes is not the culprit.

The differences in income can also be expressed by quantile ratios. Thus, the P90/P50 ratio shows that the richest 10 per cent (90th quantile) earn at least 1.7 times more than the median household. This is up from around 1.5 in the mid 1980s. Furthermore, we find that the same measure for primary income shows that the high-income earners moved away from the median until 1993, after which period the rich actually lose relative income shares. But after tax and transfers they actually earn more compared to the median. So the tax and transfer system somehow leaves the highest incomes less taxed than the median household despite its lower earnings. At the bottom of the distribution we see that the lowest 10 per-centile earns only about 5 per cent of the median before taxes but, after transfers, they earn 50 per cent of the median income. At both ends of the income distribution we see that the efficient Danish tax and transfer system smoothens out incomes. This raises the question whether the slightly upward moving Gini coefficient is felt as a factor of inequality, which will be investigated at length in sections 3 and 4.

Individual Income Inequality

The possible causes of the increasing inequality are demographic differences, education, working youth, part time versus full time employment and changes in taxation and/or transfers. Changes in household formation could also be a source of inequality or equality, as will be shown later.

Demographic changes. We have chosen to split the demographic composition of the work force into active and mainly passive age groups. Consequently, we have split the population into those below 65 and those above 64 and divided both groups according to their economic status (see Table 9.2).

The Theil coefficients for individuals between 15 and 74 years old, as reported in Figure 9.4, show that the age groups have almost the same pattern over time with an increasing Theil coefficient between and within groups, especially after 2003, though the older groups have

Table 9.2 The demographic composition of the population, 1980–2010

	1980	1990	2000	2009
15–64	3,307,822	3,470,809	3,553,458	3,622,458
Working	0.72	0.70	0.71	0.71
of which men	0.56	0.54	0.54	0.52
Women	0.44	0.46	0.46	0.48
non-working	0.28	0.30	0.29	0.29
Of which students	0.31	0.32	0.30	0.39
out of labour force	0.35	0.21	0.28	0.27
Retired	0.22	0.26	0.22	0.27
unemployed	0.15	0.22	0.10	0.10
65–74	448,343	448,343	448,343	448,343
of which working	0.00	0.10	0.09	0.14

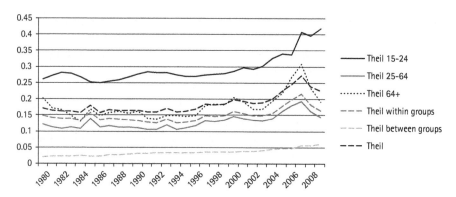

FIGURE 9.4 Theil decomposition for age groups below 75, 1980–2010

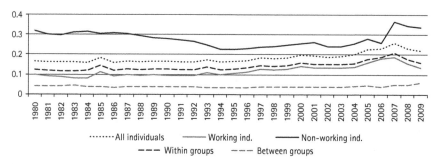

FIGURE 9.5 Theil coefficients for working and non-working individuals, 15–64 years old

a more equal distribution than the youngest group. It must also be mentioned that the share of 'between groups' inequality in total inequality has increased from 12 per cent in 1980 to 22 per cent in 2005, indicating that the increase in total inequality in Denmark can be attributed, to some extent, to the income differences that appear between age groups. Nevertheless, we conclude that the main driver of inequality is the inequality within each group, namely the elder and the very young adults, with a modest contribution of 'between groups' inequality.

We will now subdivide both groups and look at those who have mainly earnings and those who have mainly transfers, namely working and non-working individuals.

First, for the 15 to 65 age group, we find that the Theil coefficient is higher for the non-working population than for the working (Figure 9.5). Furthermore, the share of inequality between groups in total inequality has been decreasing from 25 per cent in 1980 to only 18 per cent in 2007, but started rising again as a response to the economic and financial crisis. It is remarkable that inequality between working and non-working population is so low and has been decreasing in Denmark, indicating an efficient transfer system.

In the case of individuals over 65 years old, the picture is opposite, with higher income dispersion within the working population and a low dispersion within the non-working population. Also, the share of inequality between groups in total inequality actually increases from 12 per cent in 1980 up to 20 per cent in 2005, indicating that the increase in inequality can be explained by the increase between the working and the non-working population of

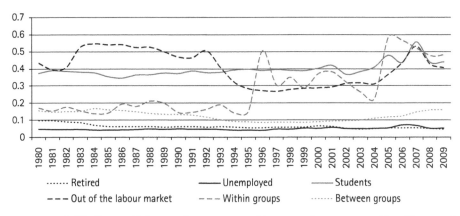

FIGURE 9.6 Theil coefficients for non-working 15–64 years old. Group-wise decomposition

Note: Data methodology change in 1994, 2002, 2007.

over 65 years old individuals. In Figure 9.6, we have drawn the Theil coefficient curves for each group of non-working individuals, age 15–64. It seems that the groups with the highest inequality are those out of the labour market and the students. 'Within group' inequality has increased dramatically after 1994, drawn by an increase in all the groups under investigation.

On the other hand, the inequality between these groups adds up to 53 per cent of total inequality of the non-working population, leading us to conclude that it is not a particular group that influences the increase in inequality but a mixture of the 'within group' and 'between group' inequality among the non-working population.

Students and youth. Students and youth constitute a special case in Denmark (as pointed out in Figures 9.4 and 9.6) because many students work in order to supplement the stipend that almost every registered student receives. Students in our context are considered to be non-working and recipients of transfers if they earn up to the allowed amount, after which deductions are made in the stipend. Students earning more than this threshold are classified as working and not as students.[4]

Figure 9.7 shows the effect of students on total income inequality in Denmark. Clearly, excluding students reduces inequality on average, by 0.04 units and the inequality between the two groups seems to be almost constant, with a slight increase in later years (after 2007). Moreover, this figure shows that total inequality is mostly due to inequality within the group and less to the income differences between the two groups. Also, it is remarkable that students lower the level but do not take away the increase in the Theil coefficient. Furthermore, the inequality between groups has decreased since 1980 until 2000 and has been fluctuating ever since.

Another similar group is youth, who have graduated from high school and start working while waiting for admission to further education. This has been common practice for years and was for a long time motivated by the admission system to further education, where applicants could earn extra points by working. These young people have been mainly taking jobs just above

---

[4] Statistical offices classify working students as part of the labour force.

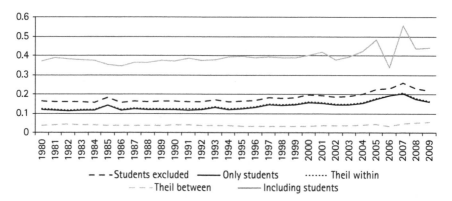

FIGURE 9.7 Theil coefficients for students and the entire population, age 15–64

Table 9.3 Composition of students in the age group 15–24

	1994	2000	2005	2009
Students with SU	37%	39%	45%	49%
Students over SU	5%	4%	5%	1%
Others	58%	57%	51%	51%

the minimum standards. The latter group is registered among the working. Table 9.3 shows that more than 50 per cent of young adults in Denmark do not participate in education (Others).

Figure 9.8 shows the decomposition of this group, dividing it into students who receive more than SU (study support), students that receive this amount or less and young adults that have their own business, work, or are on another form of government support (others). It can be seen that students earning less than the allowance are responsible for the largest within group income inequality and overall it is seen that the high inequality of this age group (15–24) comes both from within each group and also from the large income differences between groups.[5]

The large impact of students appears because students in Denmark receive a stipend and most of them work on top of that and many work to something very close to low pay. In fact students have taken over a large and increasing proportion of all low-wage jobs, (Westergaard-Nielsen, 2008).

Education. More and more Danes have acquired a further education in the investigated period, as described in Table 9.4. The increase in the numbers of upper and further educated individuals is stronger among women, being almost double in 2000, compared to 1980.

We also find that the return to education before tax and transfers has gone up from 5 per cent to 6 per cent for each year of extra education[6] as seen in Figure 9.9.

---

[5] On average, 50 per cent of total inequality is due to the between-group inequality.
[6] Return to education is calculated from a Mincer model based on primary earnings.

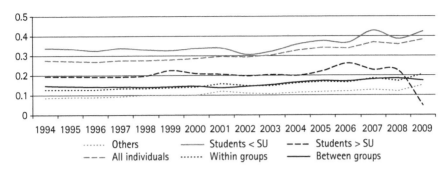

FIGURE 9.8 Decomposition of disposable income (Theil coefficients) for young adults, age 15–24, by type of activity and income earned

Table 9.4 Highest obtained education as proportion of the labour force 25–64 years old excluding students

	Basic education	Apprentice education	Gymnasium	Short further education	Bachelor level	Master level	PhD and MD
Men							
1980	34.2%	38.4%	2.7%	3.3%	8.7%	4.1%	0.9%
1990	29.0%	43.3%	3.8%	4.8%	10.7%	5.5%	1.1%
2000	22.7%	43.6%	5.4%	6.6%	12.0%	6.9%	1.3%
2009	18.4%	41.8%	5.8%	7.7%	13.1%	9.0%	1.6%
Women							
1980	45.13%	29.15%	2.13%	2.94%	13.36%	1.48%	0.30%
1990	36.05%	34.52%	3.96%	3.74%	17.29%	2.63%	0.49%
2000	23.19%	37.88%	5.97%	4.71%	21.65%	4.82%	0.77%
2009	16.36%	36.16%	5.70%	5.44%	25.46%	8.07%	1.22%

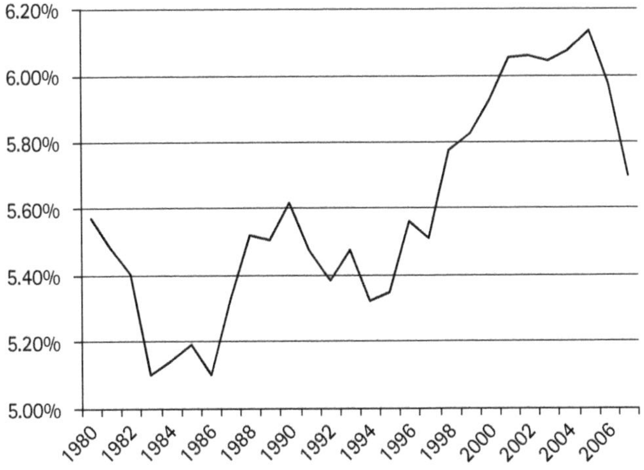

FIGURE 9.9 Return to one more year of education, 1980–2007

At the same time, we find that the return to experience on the job is actually reduced since the upswing in the mid 1980s indicating that more weight has gradually been put on formal education and less on what is learned on-the-job.

Evaluating the distributional effect of education on the income distribution is complicated. First, giving more people an education may move them from the lowest income to one that is closer to the median, which will lower the Gini coefficient. Second, increasing the educational level upwards from BA level to MA level may create more high incomes and thus produce an increase in the Gini coefficient. Third, the higher return to education and the lower return to experience indicate that people are, to a larger extent, remunerated according to their education and to a lesser degree to their experience.

The last point is illustrated by Figure 9.10, where we depicted the development of the Theil coefficient for educational groups. Generally, we find that the Theil coefficient is highest for High School graduates, MAs and PhDs, while it is low and almost identical for the other educational groups. This means that graduating more MAs and PhDs will increase the Theil coefficient, by increasing the 'within group' inequality. If the expansion happens during a brief further education, BA, or apprenticeship, the income distribution will not be affected much. The net effect of education will therefore to a large extent depend on where the expansion occurs. In our case, many more people take the low-inequality educations than the high-inequality educations, so the effect from education will probably be modest. However, the fraction graduating in the high-inequality educations has been increasing more than the low-inequality educations since 1980, so that alone will contribute to an increasing Theil coefficient. Increasing the number with top educations in the future will probably lead to an even higher dispersion. Therefore, it is remarkable that income inequality is increasing within educational groups and only modestly between educational groups, so we can (almost) rule out any particular educational group as responsible for the increasing inequality.

So far we have been able to identify two sources of the increasing inequality: students among transfer recipients, and youth working for low wages among the working group. It is obvious that both types of inequality are different from other types of inequality because they do not reflect the long-term prospects of those affected.

Family formation. Finally, we will look at the inequality that may occur when people form households either as married couples or cohabitating (which we include as married).

The Gini coefficient for married men increases from around 1984, when it was 0.22, to 2010 when it reaches 0.30. The similar curve for women starts with a much larger Gini coefficient, which falls until around 1994 from where it rises again. The fall in the female curve reflects the fact that women take up full-time work more and more, while the correlation between part-time jobs for men and their inequality is not as strong.

Figure 9.11 shows that the female income distribution of married women starts out rather unequal but becomes more equal with a falling part-time participation. Thus, females in couples seem to contribute to a more equal distribution, at the beginning of the period at least.

Based on the belief that people do not form households at random, we have reported in Figure 9.12 the annual correlation coefficient between the incomes of married men and women. This shows that there was a small positive correlation until 1991, reflecting the fact that higher-income men formed households with women earning less because of part-time jobs. That changes gradually, so that from the mid 1990s high-income men are more likely to

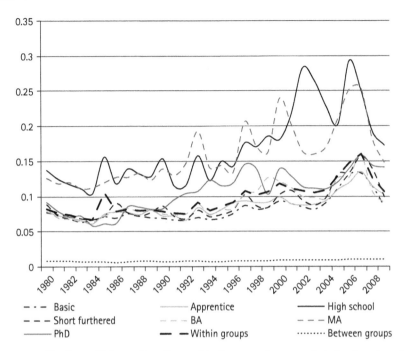

FIGURE 9.10 Theil coefficients for disposable income for completed educational levels of working population

Note: PhD also covers MD's because of their length of education.

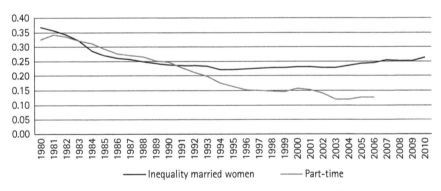

FIGURE 9.11 Gini curve for married women and their part-time frequency[7]

form a couple with high-income women, working full time. This is both a result of changed preferences for part-time work in households and a result of matching. As could be seen in Table 9.4, women attain more and more education and, as a result of that, matching is probably more and more likely to happen at educational institutions. This has obvious

---

[7] Calculated as the UI benefit per hour divided with the previous wage per hour.

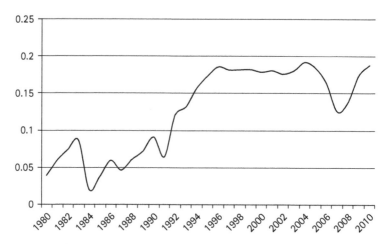

FIGURE 9.12 Correlation between income after tax and transfers for cohabiting or married couples, top and bottom 0.1 per cent of incomes deleted

Table 9.5 The composition of households

	1986	1990	2000	2010
Single households	41%	43%	45%	48%
Couples living together	59%	57%	55%	52%

consequences for the resulting household income distribution, where matching in the early period meant less income dispersion, while later means more inequality.

The resulting inequality curve for households appears consequently to increase more than it would have done if the correlations had remained at their low initial level, as shown in Figure 9.12.

Another common feature of modern society is the increased number of single households and an increase in age at first marriage. Table 9.5 shows that the Danish composition of households also exhibits an increasing proportion of single households.

The consequence is that an increasing proportion of singles will in itself increase income inequality, as seen in the USA.

3. THE SOCIAL IMPACTS OF INEQUALITY

Increasing income inequality may give rise to increases in poverty and deprivation of some sort, increasing social isolation, increasing health inequality and reductions in life satisfaction. The rationale is that increasing income inequality distribution will at some point lead to an increasing proportion of the population being deprived of material goods, or living under such bad conditions that they become socially isolated or start having health problems. It is worth remarking that data on these issues all comes from surveys, while income data came from register data. Surveys will, to some degree, also reflect the emotions of the responder while this is not case with register data. This point has to be kept in mind when comparing results from both sources.

Material Deprivation and Poverty

Material deprivation is measured as the inability of households to afford those consumption goods or activities that are typical in a society at a given point in time. For Denmark, focusing on indicators used EU-wide, more than 90 per cent of the population responds that they are not deprived of any of the specified goods and this has changed little over recent years. Figure 9.13 depicts the proportion of the population that indicates being under economic stain, deprived of one durable and housing deprivation. It is remarkable that the lack of durables is fairly constant over time with no trend.

Economic strain varies over time with no clear trend and so does housing. Most importantly, there is no upward trend and there is no immediate response to the Great Recession.

A comparison between income inequality and being at risk of poverty or social exclusion and severe material deprivation shows no clear correlation between the two indicators, while the comparison between a persistent risk of poverty and inequality have a closer connection, as shown in Figure 9.14. The persistent risk of poverty is driven by the older population (over 65 years old), but the other age groups move in the same direction. 'At persistent risk of poverty' refers to the population that is at risk of poverty (below 60 per cent of median income) for 3 out of 4 years.

Social Isolation

Social isolation can have multiple causes such as poverty, sickness, old age, depression, etc. A recent Danish Survey conducted by the Danish National Institute of Public Health

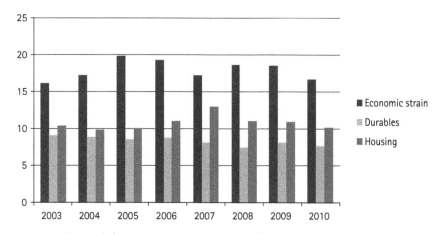

FIGURE 9.13 Material deprivation, one item in different dimensions

Source: Eurostat.

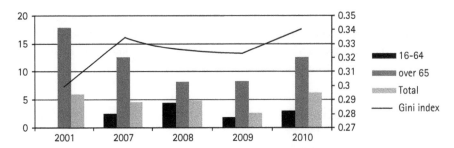

FIGURE 9.14 At persistent risk of poverty, for age groups and comparison with the Gini coefficient

Source: Eurostat.

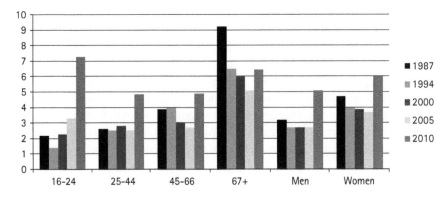

FIGURE 9.15 The proportion of people feeling alone

Source: Danish Health and Morbidity Survey.

showed that social contact with family and friends decreases slightly over time for men and women. In 1987, this percentage was quite high, but it decreased over time by 4 percentage points, for families and 3 percentage points for friends. As expected, men are more socially isolated than women, and individuals prefer meeting friends than family. A subdivision by group shows the same trend, although social isolation from family and friends increases by age. When adding a question on feeling alone there is a remarkable rise in the percentage saying that they are feeling alone among younger age groups in 2010.

The same tendency is not reflected in higher divorce rates but the number of marriages has fallen by about 15 per cent in connection with the recession. The birth rate has not, however, been affected yet. In Denmark, birth rates have been constantly increasing, from a minimum of 1.3 children per woman, on average, to 1.73 in 2010.

Health and Life Expectancy

Health has been also improving in Denmark over the entire investigated period. This shows up in improving self-reported health and in increasing life expectancy, which still

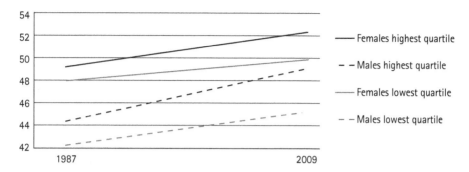

FIGURE 9.16 Remaining life expectancy for 30-year-olds in the highest and lowest educational quartiles, Denmark 1987 and 2009

Source: Diderichsen et al., 2011.

remains lower than in other European countries. However, life expectancy appears to grow more for people in the highest income quartiles than in the lower quartiles. This could be an effect of the fact that smoking has been reduced most among the more highly educated. Similarly, it is found that obesity in general is increasing, particularly for the less educated. Excess alcohol consumption, on the other hand, is increasing more among the better educated. The overall result is, however, that the less educated and those in the lower quartile of the income distribution have a lower growth in life expectancy as depicted in Figure 9.16.

As in most European countries, statistics in Denmark show an increase in the number of cancer patients for both men and women and a dramatic decrease in health problems related to the heart and circulatory system. Other studies show that mortality rates, among all age groups, have decreased but they are correlated with the level of education of individuals, so that the highest educated have the lowest rates. This indicates better self-preservation and more awareness, but also that highly skilled workers have less dangerous jobs.

Crime Statistics and Life Satisfaction

The crime statistics shows that burglary, robbery and violent crime increased somewhat over the investigated period (Figure 9.17), with a surge in the years of the Great Recession. The only exception is car theft, which has gone down over the whole period since 1996. As a consequence, the proportion of the population who are incarcerated has gone up by a small factor though the number is still relatively small.

To complete the picture, the life satisfaction of Danes actually went up in the investigated period. According to surveys by Euro Barometer and the World Dataset of Happiness, Denmark has been among the happiest countries in the world, in recent years.

To sum up, the social impacts of a more unequal income distribution is not very clear at all. Only a small increase in domestic burglary and the evolution of a persistent rate of poverty seem to show that there might be an effect from increased income inequality, but life expectancy, health and life satisfaction show no effects on the population.

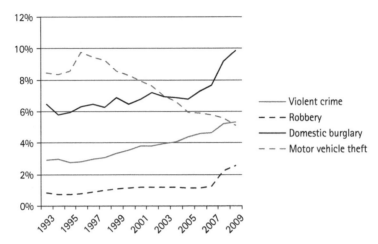

FIGURE 9.17 Trends in crimes recorded by the police, comparison with income inequality (% of total crime registered and the Gini coefficient)

Source: Eurostat.

4. THE POLITICAL AND CULTURAL IMPACTS OF INEQUALITY

Introduction

A long literature associates income inequality with social attitudes and behaviour. The key claim is that increased inequality in general has adverse social impacts. In this chapter, we therefore take a closer look at trends in Danish attitudes and social beliefs, political values and participation in civil society. We will use turnout in elections, unionization rates and strike activity as indicators of political and civic participation. We will also use trust in others and in formal institutions as indicators. Finally, we will look at political values and at the perceived legitimacy, and support for, EU institutions and membership.

Political Behaviour and Union Formation

Turnout in general elections has been quite stable from 1980 to 2011 whereas the turnout in the EP elections has increased over time and turnout in local elections has decreased slightly, as shown in Figure 9.18. In addition, it is worth noting the large increase in the turnout of the local elections in 2001. Turnout was the same in both the general and the local election but this was due to the fact that these elections were held at the same time. As such, there is no clear change in Danish turnout and the only reason for the high local turnout in 2001 is that a national election drew additional voters to the voting booth.

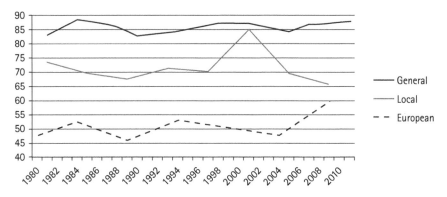

FIGURE 9.18 The electorate turnout in Denmark

Source: Bjørnskov *et al.*, 2012.

Thus, there seems to be a positive development in participation. When it comes to unionization, participation has been falling since its highest point in 1983, where the membership was 81 per cent of the labour force. In 2011 it had fallen to 68 per cent. The reason is both a general decline in manual work and a lower membership especially among the youth. Basically, it takes more years before people become members of Unions and of the unemployment insurance system.

Strike activity was low until around 1993 where a Social Democratic-lead government came to power. Then it increased sixfold. It has been falling in subsequent years with the exception of some years where new wage contracts have been negotiated. In 2009 it was back to the level of the 1980s.

Trust in Denmark

A number of studies find that Danish indicators of trust are among the highest in the world (e.g. Uslaner, 2002). This is the case for trust in parliament, government, the political parties and the legal system. All the measures shown in Figure 9.19 show high levels, except trust in government and the political parties. Although all show an ascendant trend, they start declining after 2007 and during the Great Recession. It must be noted that these results are consistent with the development of the Danish economic situation over the period investigated. In other words, trust in legal institutions is clearly pro-cyclical. Therefore, it is possible that the high level of trust reflect to a high degree the positive evolution of the economy (Bjørnskov *et al.*, 2012).

Another strong result concerning trust is that trust in other people has increased and is now at its highest level, at around 77 per cent. At the same time, Danish voters seem to have moved slightly towards the two extremes at the same time as voters in the traditional parties have been moving towards the median position. The result is ambiguous with respect to indicating what has happened to the Danish political spectrum. The issue to immigrants is a topic that has divided the population over the last 20 years. Danes at the beginning of the 1990s could agree that employers should prefer Danish employees, but this picture has changed completely in 2008, and more than 65 per cent say that Danes should not be preferred over immigrants (European Values Survey).

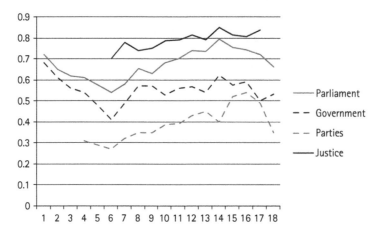

FIGURE 9.19 Trust in different institutions in Denmark

Source: Synthesis of Chapter 4, from Bjørnskov *et al.*, 2012.

Conclusion

Overall, a set of Danish measures of political and cultural attitudes and beliefs have changed for the better since the earlier 1980s. However, not all measures of institutional trust or values have changed in ways that are clearly or consistently associated with any common trend.

None of these trends are easy to associate with the development of income inequality in Denmark. Contrary to the claims in many studies (e.g. Rothstein and Uslaner, 2005), increasing inequality has not caused social or institutional trust to decrease in Denmark. Part of the explanation may be that most Danes have not perceived inequality to be on the increase, because the inequality of women has decreased significantly during the period and has only started to increase slightly in the most recent years. Likewise, causality could arguably also run the other way, such that higher trust levels increase support for redistribution and reduce rent-seeking, which subsequently affects income inequality (Nannestad, 2008).

The present exploration must therefore be interpreted with care, as it is necessarily preliminary. We nevertheless note that the increase in the correlation between inequality levels of partners and cohabitants logically seems to imply that inequality measured at the family and household level may be increasing in the years to come. Given that inequality does affect the quality of basic institutions, political participation and social attitudes and beliefs, future increases in inequality could arguably undermine some of the social cohesion of future generations in Denmark.

5. POLICIES DIRECTED TOWARDS INCOME EQUALITY

This section aims to explain some of the major sources for income distribution in Denmark. It begins with the formation of market income and continues with the policies governing taxes and transfers.

Labour Market Income

The Danish way of organizing the labour market has at face value little in common with the Central European organization of the labour market and has more in common with the North American labour markets, because of the lack of direct government intervention in rules and functioning. Furthermore, the government pays a relatively high benefit when people are out of work, and supplies training if needed. This way of organizing the labour market is often dubbed 'The Danish Model'. The key ingredient in the Danish model is that trade unions and the employers' federation (the social partners) bargain over most of the regulatory issues, and the role of the government is 'to pay the bill'. The social partners are responsible for wage bargaining and wage setting. They also make agreements concerning normal working hours, and set rules for labour protection with respect to overtime and work environment.

The role of the Danish government is to provide unemployment benefits and to re-train workers who have lost their jobs due to low productivity. The government also provides healthcare and disability pension. In other words, the government provides the safety net. This is also the case with respect to those who are not covered by unemployment insurance (UI). In general these workers are eligible for social assistance, which is equal to the UI benefit at its lowest level but with the main difference that all payments are means-tested.

Another aspect of the Danish Model is that the agreements on the labour market safeguard a certain element of flexibility, which, in principle, should ensure that workers can easily shift from one employer to another, while the government role is to provide the income security. This is often dubbed 'flexicurity'.

Trade Unions and the equality of wages have established a special 'low wage' policy in the 1980s in order to reduce the female-male wage gap. That policy culminated in parliament passing a law on equal pay for equal work. Similarly, Trade Unions have fought to reduce the wage gap between non-skilled and skilled workers but with less success. Although Denmark does not have minimum wage legislation, there is an agreement between the Trade Unions and the Employers' Federation which states that an employee covered by any type of contract cannot be paid less than a specific guaranteed hourly wage, which is 97 DKK (€13 in 2012), and must receive an extra 15 per cent as vacation pay (see Figure 9.20). The result is a de facto minimum wage of 111 DKK (€15) per hour. On top of that is a pension contribution of 7–10 per cent paid by the employer. Also, the pension system has been introduced independently of legislators, as an agreement between the parties in the labour market.

After the extension of the EU to the East European countries, Danish Trade Unions were able to prevent most under-bidding of the current wage system by demanding that Eastern European workers follow Danish 'conditions' even if there were no direct contract with the actual employers. The main reason why this worked in Denmark and not in Germany or other countries without a minimum wage legislation is an old rule allowing Trade Unions to demand a contract or start industrial action if the employers were not willing to make a contract.

Taxation

Denmark is one of the countries with the highest total tax payment in the OECD, with 48 per cent in 2010. The Danish tax system relies heavily on income tax and less on consumption

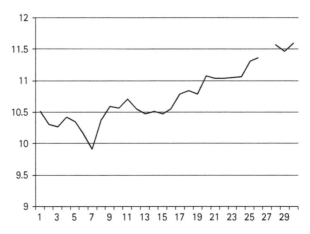

FIGURE 9.20 Minimum hourly wage in constant 2000 EUR

Source: Statistics Denmark (1980–2005), Eurostat (2007–2009).

tax as can be seen in Figure 9.21. The income tax is based on all types of income including almost all transfer income from the public sector. The tax system has a gross tax on all earnings as social security contributions of 8 per cent of all gross earnings. This is deductible against income tax. The income tax scale starts with a personal deduction of about €4000 and all income above that is taxed at 37 per cent and high incomes above €52000 are taxed at another 15 per cent. The top marginal tax including the gross tax is 55.4 per cent and that is currently paid by around a quarter of the labour force. Finally, a reduction is granted of 4.25 per cent of income if employed (in contrast to the non-employed), but the total reduction is capped at €2,000, so that helps increase the after tax income of low wage earners.

Over the years, income tax has been reformed a couple of times with the purpose of lowering the marginal tax rate. Such changes are the main reason for developments in income after tax in more recent years Figure 21. From 2005, the tax bracket for the middle tax was gradually moved upward, so that fewer were paying middle tax, and the employment allowance was introduced for low-wage earners. At the same time, the bracket for top tax was also moved upward. The result was that all incomes became less taxed, but marginal tax was not lowered. This is probably why inequality goes down in 2007–2009. In 2010, the middle tax was abandoned with the result that the marginal tax of top incomes decreases and consequently, the inequality of after tax income increased. Changes at the top have partly been balanced by higher employment allowances at the bottom.

The resulting tax wedge, i.e. the marginal tax rate, which includes all sorts of taxes irrespective of who pays them, is around 70 per cent in Denmark and places Denmark between Italy and Netherlands on an international scale (Andersen, 2012).

Social Expenditures and the Welfare System

There is a long tradition of welfare policy in Denmark. Today, Denmark provides a social safety net that means that almost all citizens who do not work for one reason or another

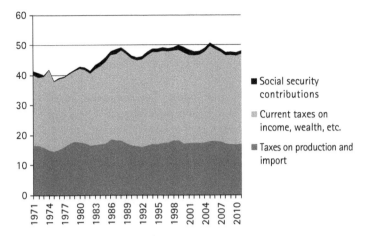

FIGURE 9.21 Taxes as a percentage of GDP

Source: Statistics Denmark.

are covered by a transfer income. This is the case for public pensions covering everyone, for sickness pay, maternity leave, disability pension, unemployment benefit[8], and welfare pay covering more or less all others. The total costs of the in-cash transfer programmes in 2012 was 18.8 per cent of GDP and all social costs including in-kind transfers were 32.5 per cent of GDP. On top of that is student support. Thirty-one per cent of the entire population is on a transfer programme on a full time basis. Of those, 60 per cent are old age related. That leaves 40 per cent among age groups who could have been in the work force. Or, put in another way, the welfare programmes give full income support to about 11 per cent of the population or 603,000 persons, or 21 per cent of the labour force, compared to a labour force of 2.8 million. These expensive transfer programmes are financed by a comprehensive tax system dominated by the income tax.

Since 1957, a universal pension system has been in effect, and everyone above the age of 67 (now 65) has the right to a minimum pension irrespective of their own income before or along with the pension. The minimum pension can be supplemented with means-tested extra benefits. Some of those are related to objective needs with respect to health, housing and heating. The major change to the pension system has been the introduction of a mild requirement for labour market experience in Denmark. Sickness insurance for the poor and mandatory work accident insurance was introduced before the turn of the century. In 1907, a law on the creation of unemployment insurance funds was passed in the parliament. This included a state subsidy and a substantial trade union influence on the management of the UI funds. Unemployment insurance has more or less remained the same over the years. The main change has been that sickness insurance has been taken over by the State and that the daily pay was increased to a maximum of 90 per cent of the previous salary but with a relatively low upper absolute ceiling in the late 1960s. These amounts have since then been

---

[8] UI benefit is in principle paid by the unemployment fund, which is formally independent of the State and unions, like in Belgium, Sweden, Finland and Iceland, though the government covers any deficit.

uprated by either a wage index or consumer price index. Now, all payments under these systems are subject to taxation. The whole system means that low-waged workers get a relatively high replacement ratio[9] in the event of unemployment or sickness. However, it also means that the incentive to seek work and get out of unemployment is relatively low for this group. At the same time, it is an important feature of the Danish system that transfer income for the normal labour market participants, who are members of the unemployment insurance system, are not means tested. Unlike unemployment benefits, all benefits for the non-insured are means tested. However, even their benefits will be paid at around the level of unemployment benefits in the short run and will be around old age pension plus supplements according to need in the longer run. The result is that the lowest level of benefits sets a minimum standard for normal pay.

Means-tested housing subsidies were introduced in 1966 and provide benefit to everyone living in rented housing according to the size of the accommodation compared to an objective need based on the size of the household and income.

For those not having a work income, nor sickness payment, nor UI payment, nor pension of some type there is the possibilities of receiving a means-tested welfare benefit. The social authorities determine the amount according to rules that are based on need. Table 9.6 shows the percentage of the labour force on different types of benefit.

After 1994 all payments under these systems are subject to taxation.

The overall result of these systems is that most people who are not in the labour force receive an income from society. This clearly means a more equal income distribution than otherwise.

Figure 9.22 shows the percentage of total governmental expenditure on education, health and social protection in the past 30 years.

Education is clearly another way that the government influences the long run income distribution, especially since almost all education is provided free of charge and with substantial stipends for students. First, the level of education has increased constantly over the past 30 years, as well as public spending on education (as a percentage of total public expenditure) and as percentage of GDP. A breakdown by level of education shows that the expenditures per GDP per capita for primary and tertiary level have decreased, especially after 1988, while the expenditure for secondary education has increased constantly. Moreover, Figure 9.23 shows a more detailed decomposition of governmental income transfers, by type of transfers, which nicely summarizes the discussions of this section.

5. CONCLUSION

In this chapter, we have shown that the tax and transfer system in Denmark does a very substantial job in redistributing income, so that a primary income distribution, which is relatively unequal, is transformed into something rather more equal. This chapter shows

---

[9] UI benefit is in principle paid by the unemployment fund, which is formally independent of the State and Unions, though the government covers any deficit.

Table 9.6 Full time equivalent persons receiving transfer income, (% of the labour force)

Per cent	2007	2008	2009	2010	2011
Registered unemployed persons, total	2.6	1.8	3.4	4.0	3.8
Persons receiving holiday benefits	0.2	0.2	0.1	0.2	0.2
Guidance and activities upgrading skills, total	1.5	1.5	1.8	2.2	1.9
Subsidized employment, total	2.6	2.8	3.0	3.4	3.7
Maternity benefits, etc. total	2.1	2.1	2.1	2.1	2.0
Retirement, total, only below 61	5.8	5.8	5.9	6.0	6.0
Other social benefits, total	5.5	5.2	5.4	5.5	5.7
Total full year equivalent persons	20.3	19.4	21.8	23.3	23.3
Number of people in labour force	2901911	2917425	2875015	2874000	2866000

Source: Statistics Denmark.

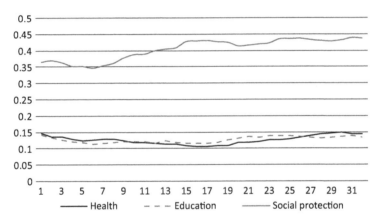

FIGURE 9.22 Expenditure on social protection, education and health (% of total governmental expenditure)

Source: Statistics Denmark.

that the overall income distribution is relatively equal but inequality has been increasing since the early 1990s.

This chapter has attempted to isolate income elements and groups that are responsible for the increasing Gini coefficient in order to see if there are explanations as to why the popular perception of income dispersion is not in line with the measured Gini coefficient. We have found that the tax and benefit system has had a large redistributional influence on incomes in all years. Furthermore, we have shown that changes in the tax structure in more recent years may explain why inequality after tax and transfers has increased in more recent years. However, there are other reasons why inequality has increased in the latter years.

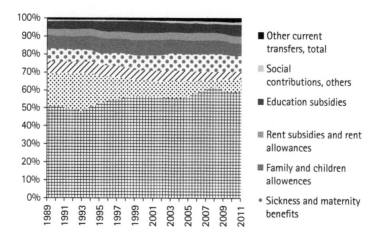

FIGURE 9.23 Decomposition of governmental income transfers, by functionality

Source: Statistics Denmark.

First, we have found that the Gini coefficient is partly increasing because a growing number of students and youth take low wage jobs before or during their studies. Second, the growing number of people with further education could have been another source of increasing inequality, but the general shift to more education is found not to have large effects on the distribution of disposable income. Only the highest levels of education contribute to more inequality, while the others do not. Finally, we have found that there is an unforeseen consequence of the increasing integration of working wives into the labour market, namely an increase in household inequality.

Overall, we have found that even when we take account of the four factors set out above, we still observe an increasing Gini coefficient in Denmark. It is, however, remarkable that we find this increase in all sub-groups we have investigated, except for the ones that affect young people and would not be expected to persist as they mature. This probably means that the increasing inequality is generally accepted in the population, and probably also explains why the qualitative measures of income distribution do not contain signals of an increasing income dispersion. Contrary to the claims in many studies (e.g. Rothstein and Uslaner, 2005), increasing inequality has not caused social or institutional trust to decrease in Denmark. Part of the explanation may be that most Danes have not perceived inequality to be on the increase, as that of women has decreased significantly during the period and has only started to increase slightly in the most recent years. Likewise, causality could arguably also run the other way such that higher levels of trust increase support for redistribution and reduce rent-seeking, which subsequently affects income inequality (Nannestad, 2008).

The present exploration must be interpreted with care, as it is necessarily preliminary. We nevertheless note that the increase in the correlation between income levels of partners and cohabitants logically seems to imply that inequality measured at the family and household level may be increasing in the years to come. Given that inequality does affect the quality of basic institutions, political participation and social attitudes and beliefs, future increases in inequality could arguably undermine some of the social cohesion of future generations in Denmark.

References

Bjørnskov, C., Neamtu, I. and Westergaard-Nielsen, N. (2012), *Growing Inequality and its Impacts: The Case of Denmark*, Gini report.

Diderichsen, Finn, Andersen, Ingelise, Manual, Celie, and the Working Group of the Danish Review on Social Determinants of Health (2011), 'Health Inequality—Determinants and Policies', *Scandinavian Journal of Public Health*.

Nannestad, Peter, (2008), 'What Have We Learned About Generalized Trust, If Anything?' *Annual Review of Political Science* 11, 413–436.

OECD (2011), *Divided We Stand: Why Inequality Keeps Rising*, OECD Publishing. http://dx.doi.org/10.1787/9789264119536-en.

Rothstein, Bo and Uslaner, Eric M. (2005), 'All for All: Equality, Corruption, and Social Trust', *World Politics* 58, 41–72.

Uslaner, Eric M. (2002), *The Moral Foundations of Trust*, New York: Cambridge University Press.

Westergaard-Nielsen, N. (ed.) (2008), 'Low-Wage Work in Denmark', *Case Studies of Job Quality in Advanced Economies*, Russell Sage Foundation, New York: Russell Sage.

···

CHAPTER 10

FINLAND: GROWING INEQUALITY WITH CONTESTED CONSEQUENCES

···

JENNI BLOMGREN, HEIKKI HIILAMO, OLLI

KANGAS, AND MIKKO NIEMELÄ

1. INTRODUCTION AND CONTEXT

···

AFTER World War II, Finland rapidly developed into an industrial country—first through wood processing and then focusing on technology. In the wake of rapid economic growth, building up universal welfare programmes began in the 1960s (Alestalo and Kuhnle, 1984; Kangas and Palme, 2005). The goal was to provide comprehensive social services and income maintenance that went far beyond emergency aid. The results were visible: in the late 1980s, relative poverty levels and income inequalities were the lowest in the industrialized world. The common belief was that the cradle-to-grave Welfare State model had solved all the poverty problems and poverty was only regarded as the nuisance of homeless alcoholics.

This development has not been stable and without problems, being characterized by up-and downturns. In the 1970s, Finland faced the first oil crisis, with a couple of zero-growth years and unemployment rates rising from the low of less than two per cent to five per cent in 1975–1977. This was followed by a decade of strong economic growth. In the early 1990s, the country was hit by a severe recession, known as the 'Great Depression'. Between 1991 and 1993, GDP declined by over ten per cent and unemployment rose from three to almost 17 per cent (see Figure 10.1). As incomes fell and public expenditure rose, national and local government fell into a financing crisis and public debt that had been virtually zero in 1990 sky-rocketed to 60 per cent of GDP in 1995.

Since 1991, governments, regardless of their colour, reacted with tax increases and cuts in public expenditure. While the gross tax rate was 40 per cent of GDP in 1985, it was close to 50 per cent in 1996. The other remedy, i.e. cuts in social expenditure, led to an end of the golden years of the Welfare State. Benefits were curtailed and plans for further expansion scrapped (Heikkilä and Uusitalo, 1997). Measured as a change in GDP, however, the depression was

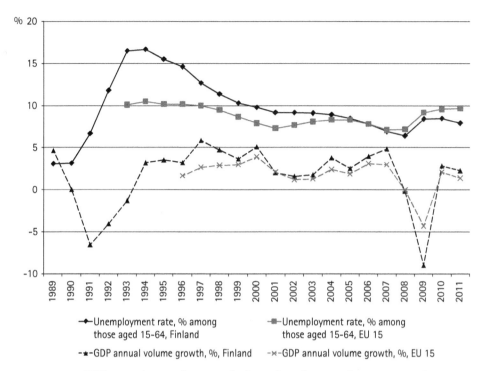

FIGURE 10.1 GDP growth rate (% annual change) and unemployment rate (% unemployed among those aged 15–64, yearly average) in Finland and EU 15 in 1989–2011

Source: Statistics Finland; Eurostat.

over fairly quickly. By 1993, GDP was rising steadily again and by the late 1990s it was higher than ever before. From 1994 to 2000, the annual GDP growth rate varied between 3.2 and 5.9 per cent and was among the highest in the Western hemisphere (Figure 10.1).

The rapid economic tide did not lift all the boats. The unemployment rate that had rapidly increased in 1991–4 was slow to fall, and only in 2000 did it again drop below ten per cent. However, some population groups remained more or less permanently excluded from the labour market. Single parents and those with little education, in particular, were exposed to persistent unemployment.

Whether the criterion is the absolute or the relative level of public debt or unemployment, the traces of the Great Depression extended into the 2000s. In particular, the minimum social benefits are now lagging behind, income inequalities are as wide as they were in the 1970s, and poverty has re-emerged as a social problem. The vicious circle has been further aggravated by the onset of the global recession in 2008. In 2009, GDP in Finland decreased even more than in the EU-15 countries on average. The unemployment rate, that in 2008 had reached a low point of 6.4 per cent, rose again, even though it remained lower than the EU-15 average (Figure 10.1). All these rapid changes reflect the fact that the Finnish economy is small, open and too one-sided and, therefore, vulnerable to international economic shocks. In such circumstances, extensive Welfare States are likely to evolve, as argued by Peter Katzenstein (1985): statutory social security acts as a buffer against the hazards of life. Finland fits well in Katzenstein's idea, and international economic crises are directly mirrored in social spending. For example, the GDP share of social expenditure in 1990 was about 25 per cent but, due to the Great Depression, it increased by 10 percentage points in three years. After the depression, the share went down to 25 per cent, but the financial crisis of 2008 led to a new increase to over 30 per cent in 2009–2010 (OECD, 2011). The increase in expenditure does not mean improved benefits, rather, it simply indicates the growth in the number of claimants.

The political appeal of the Nordic Welfare State seems to be running out of steam in Finland. The National Coalition party, demanding a leaner Welfare State and private responsibility has grown to be the dominant political party after a decades-long period of social-democratic rule. In the early 1980s, more than 40 per cent of the voters supported leftist parties in the parliamentary elections—now that proportion is about one fourth (27 per cent in 2011). No doubt, such a shift in political power constellations has left its finger-prints on the direction of the Welfare State development.

An important shift in the balance of power has also taken place in the labour market. Traditionally, employer federations and trade unions have played an important role not only in establishing a well-functioning collective bargaining system, but also in construct-ing the Finnish Welfare State. This kind of policy-making increased the legitimacy of the outcome and commitment to it. For a decade, the Employers' Federation has spoken in favour of branch or local level bargaining, instead of the centralized, top-level agreements that have been in place since the mid 1960s. The shift in emphasis mirrors the strengthening position of employers vis a vis employees. The shift in power-balance is linked to the fact that whereas employers are acting more and more in global markets and benefiting from that, trade unions are more bound into national contexts. Furthermore, there is a steady decline in the share of unionized employees, which mirrors the structural transformation of employment from manufacturing to a service economy with a low degree of unioniza-tion. Needless to say, this kind of development, attached to the shifts in the power balance in politics and labour markets, will change orientations in welfare policies. More details about the Finnish context as well as about the empirical data and methods used in the following chapters can be found in the GINI Country Report for Finland (Blomgren *et al.*, 2012).

2. The Evolution of Inequality and its Drivers

Rising Trend of Income Inequality Since the 1990s

Since the depression in the early 1990s, the increase in income inequality has been excep-tionally fast and steep in Finland (OECD, 2008; 2011). Figure 10.2 depicts Gini coefficients for different income concepts: factor/market, gross and disposable income (equalized household income, the OECD modified scale) from 1966 to 2010.[1] The development from the mid 1960s to 2010 can be divided into five periods. First, the era of Welfare State

[1] Data on Gini coefficients shown here are the same as those used by OECD (2008; 2011). Both use the official source of Income Distribution Statistics, compiled by Statistics Finland.

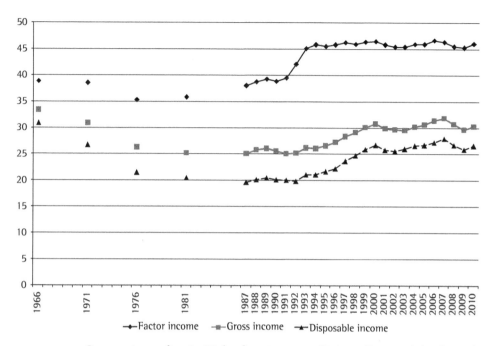

FIGURE 10.2 Income inequality in Finland, 1966–2010. Gini coefficients (%) of equalized factor, gross and disposable income (OECD modified scale)

Source: Income Distribution Statistics, Statistics Finland.

expansion in the 1960s and the 1970s decreased income inequality according to all income concepts. Second, from the mid 1970s to the economic recession of the early 1990s, factor income inequality increased but due to the income transfer system, gross and disposable income inequality remained constant. Third, the recession in the 1990s increased inequality in factor income but not in gross and disposable income. Fourth, whereas, since the mid 1990s, factor income inequality has been constant, inequality in gross and disposable income increased towards the early 2000s.

After the turn of the millennium, the development of income inequality—regardless of the measure—has been stable. This is the fifth period. In general, since the 1990s, changes in income inequality in Finland have been very much connected to the economic cycle. During past decades, the Gini coefficient grew during periods of economic growth and fell during economic downturns. The same goes for the poverty figures. Despite their growth in the past, in comparison to most other European and OECD countries, the Gini coefficient in 2010 (0.266) was still at a low level, although higher than in the 1980s (OECD, 2011).

One of the main reasons behind the rising income inequality from the mid 1990s is rapidly increasing income among high-income groups (Figure 10.3). There has been a clear divergence between the income deciles, and the highest income decile has moved well ahead of the others. Since 1990, the real median disposable income of the highest decile has increased by more than 60 per cent, while the increase in median income of the lowest decile has been 19 per cent. In absolute euro-terms, the increase in the lowest decile has been

€ (2010 currency)

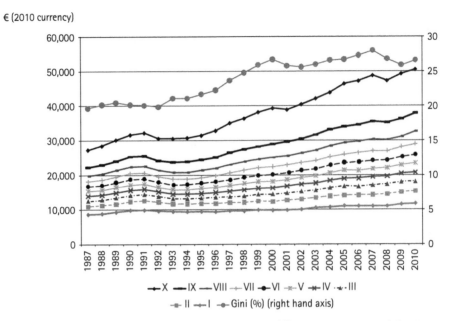

FIGURE 10.3 Median equivalized disposable income (€ in 2010 currency) by income deciles, with Gini coefficient of equivalized disposable income, 1987–2010

Source: Income Distribution Statistics, Statistics Finland.

one tenth that of the highest decile (Table 10.1). However, as Figure 10.3 shows, there has been more turbulence in the highest income decile compared to other deciles. For example, whereas the global financial crisis in 2008 immediately affected the income of the 10th decile, the lower income groups were not affected that much.

The explanation for the take-off of the highest decile is the Finnish tax reform of 1993, which introduced a dual tax system with different tax rates for work and capital income. Tax on capital income became proportional but tax on work income continued to be progressive and consequently, capital income has been taxed much lighter than other forms of income. The change in taxation created an incentive to shift work income into capital income—for example by taking out income as dividends from companies—and thus pay lower taxes. The top income earners in particular have used this financial and fiscal planning option to avoid taxes, and the development among the top one per cent of income receivers is revealing. Whereas the share of capital income of all income among the total population rose from five per cent in 1990 to 15 per cent in 2007, the share among the top 1 per cent increased from 14 to 62 per cent, respectively (Tuomala, 2009).

In conclusion, growing inequality in wages and salaries has not been the most important driver in the Finnish case. Partly due to a controlled wage bargaining system (see Chapter 5), wages and salaries in different employment sectors have developed roughly hand in hand. The rapidly rising income share of the high-income earners is largely driven by increases in capital income. As a consequence, the role of taxes in reducing inequality has diminished. This development corroded one of the main principles of the idea of progressivity.

Table 10.1 Indices of the development of median equalized disposable income by different characteristics of the households, 1990=100

	1990	1992	1994	1996	1998	2000	2002	2004	2006	2008	2010	1990–2010 increase in median, €	Median income of the group relative to the median of all households 1990	Median income of the group relative to the median of all households 2010
All households	100	97	93	97	103	107	113	121	126	130	137	6 361		
Income decile														
I	100	98	96	96	98	100	102	109	112	112	119	1 885	0.57	0.50
II	100	99	94	95	98	100	105	112	115	118	124	2 925	0.72	0.65
III	100	98	93	96	98	102	108	115	118	123	128	3 998	0.82	0.77
IV	100	97	93	96	100	104	111	118	122	126	132	5 064	0.91	0.88
V	100	96	92	96	102	106	113	121	125	129	137	6 349	1.00	1.00
VI	100	96	92	96	103	107	114	122	126	130	138	7 056	1.10	1.10
VII	100	96	92	97	105	110	115	124	129	132	142	8 539	1.19	1.23
VIII	100	96	93	98	107	112	118	127	133	135	146	10 238	1.31	1.39
IX	100	95	94	99	109	114	120	131	136	139	150	12 596	1.48	1.62
X	100	97	97	104	115	124	128	139	149	150	160	18 883	1.85	2.15
Household structure														
Single	100	99	93	98	103	108	113	121	124	127	134	4 826	0.82	0.80
Couple, no children	100	97	94	99	107	112	119	126	132	136	144	8 654	1.14	1.20
Couple with children	100	95	91	96	102	107	112	121	126	129	136	6 771	1.09	1.08
Single parent	100	101	94	97	98	101	105	110	112	119	121	3 122	0.86	0.76
Other	100	99	94	97	104	106	116	124	125	134	137	7 083	1.11	1.11
Age of the household reference person														
–24	100	86	74	73	84	90	89	90	103	105	102	285	0.79	0.58
25–34	100	91	86	90	96	102	106	115	119	124	128	5 140	1.07	1.00
35–44	100	93	89	93	99	103	112	119	123	124	139	7 424	1.11	1.13
45–54	100	95	90	93	102	103	111	118	123	123	132	6 648	1.22	1.17
55–64	100	101	100	106	116	119	129	138	144	147	154	9 438	1.01	1.14
65–74	100	108	106	113	112	122	129	136	140	150	162	8 407	0.79	0.93
75–	100	108	104	112	114	117	126	134	137	140	148	5 815	0.71	0.76

(Continued)

Table 10.1 Continued

	1990	1992	1994	1996	1998	2000	2002	2004	2006	2008	2010	1990–2010 increase in median, €	Median income of the group relative to the median of all households	
													1990	2010
All households	100	97	93	97	103	107	113	121	126	130	137	6 361		
Education of the household reference person														
Primary	100	100	95	100	103	106	110	116	119	119	123	3 469	0.87	0.78
Secondary	100	96	91	94	100	103	111	116	120	125	131	5 232	0.99	0.94
Lowest tertiary	100	94	89	96	102	108	112	120	125	130	135	7 280	1.20	1.19
Lower level tertiary	100	94	88	94	103	100	104	113	116	116	120	4 701	1.38	1.21
Higher level tertiary	100	95	94	94	102	106	112	121	128	125	133	8 777	1.56	1.51
Doctorate level	100	93	102	105	117	115	121	134	136	128	144	13 282	1.75	1.84
Socio-economic status of the household reference person														
Entrepreneurs and farmers	100	95	98	103	114	123	127	142	145	152	163	11 453	1.05	1.26
Farmers	100	97	106	105	116	121	134	133	156	162	167	11 263	0.98	1.19
Entrepreneurs	100	92	91	99	110	119	122	140	135	142	158	11 153	1.13	1.30
All employees	100	97	94	99	106	109	117	124	131	131	142	8 135	1.14	1.18
Upper white-collar	100	96	96	99	107	111	119	127	130	132	142	10 162	1.42	1.47
Lower white-collar	100	96	92	96	103	106	112	117	126	123	132	6 117	1.12	1.08
Manual workers	100	99	96	101	106	110	117	125	126	133	138	6 730	1.04	1.04
Students	100	99	105	94	108	113	116	114	120	121	133	2 776	0.49	0.48
Pensioners	100	109	107	114	116	117	127	132	136	139	150	6 469	0.76	0.83
Unemployed	100	109	102	102	98	97	98	105	105	103	114	1 477	0.64	0.53
Other	100	114	105	97	100	95	95	99	102	112	112	1 409	0.66	0.54
Household tenure status														
Owned	100	98	95	101	108	112	119	127	132	135	145	8 342	1.09	1.15
Rented	100	95	87	90	92	97	99	104	105	109	112	1 733	0.84	0.69

Source: Income Distribution Statistics, Statistics Finland.

The average tax rate of the top income earners has decreased more than the average tax rate of the total population—among the top one per cent from 42 per cent in 1990 to 28 per cent in 2007. The corresponding figures for the total population are 25 to 24 per cent (Tuomala, 2009).

Those who Have and Those who Have Not: Increasing Income Poverty

Increasing income inequality has brought about increases in at-risk-of-poverty rates. The trend in the at-risk-of-poverty rate (the proportion of persons living in households with less than 60 per cent of the national median equalized disposable income, the OECD modified scale) has a pattern similar to what was demonstrated for income inequality above. From the mid 1960s to 1990, income poverty decreased from 18 to 8 per cent. During the recession of the 1990s, the poverty threshold decreased and at-risk-of-poverty rate continued to fall. Despite mass unemployment and the severe economic difficulties of households, relative income poverty was at its historically lowest level in the middle of the recession (Figure 10.4)—mainly because the median income of the total population fell. Similarly with income inequality, the latter part of the 1990s witnessed an increase in relative income poverty: from 1993 to 2000 at-risk-of-poverty rate increased from 6 to 11 per cent. Following the trends described above in income inequality, the relative poverty level has been rather

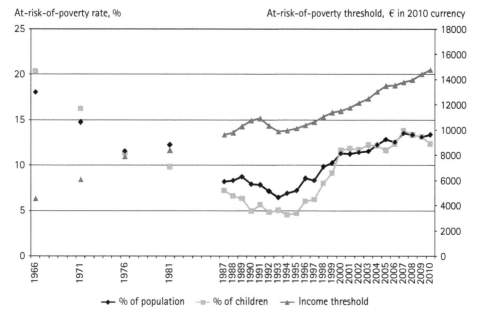

FIGURE 10.4 Trends in at-risk-of-poverty rate (%) of total population and children (aged under 18) and at-risk-of-poverty threshold (equalized € in 2010 currency) in Finland 1966–2010

Source: Income Distribution Statistics, Statistics Finland.

stable since the turn of the millennium. The increase in child poverty after the mid 1990s has been more dramatic than the increase among the total population. In 2010, the proportion of poor children was three times higher than in 1994.

In addition to changing shares of work vs. capital income, unemployment has been one of the key drivers of income inequality in Finland. After the peak (close to 17 per cent in 1994), the unemployment rate has slowly declined (7.9 per cent in 2011). Since the mid 1990s, there has been a striking divergence in the at-risk-of-poverty rates, especially between those employed and those not employed. Whereas the poverty rates among the employed have been less than 5 per cent, the rates among those not employed have risen from 15 per cent in 1990 to 36 per cent in 2010 among men, and from 9 to 30 per cent among women. Being without a job is a major risk of poverty in Finland. The most vulnerable group is the long-term unemployed living on minimum daily allowances, i.e. on basic benefits that have been lagging behind the median income. Other major low-income groups consist of students and old age pensioners who are living alone, mostly elderly women without proper employment pensions.

It is well known that poverty rates are sensitive to the choice of income threshold, but cross-national comparisons have shown that the ranking of countries does not change substantially if alternative thresholds are used. However, Finland is a deviant case in this respect. The Finnish relative income poverty rate according to the 60 per cent threshold is close to the European average. However, using the 50 per cent threshold substantially changes Finland's ranking: the Finnish at-risk-of-poverty rate is one of the lowest in Europe (Lelkes et al., 2009). In 2010, six per cent of the population were poor according to the 50 per cent threshold and as few as three per cent according to the 40 per cent income threshold. Also the increase in the at-risk-of-poverty rate since the 1990s is less dramatic for the lower income thresholds.

The at-risk-of-poverty rates say nothing about poverty gaps, i.e., the scale of transfers needed to bring the incomes of the poor up to the poverty threshold. In Finland, the gap is the lowest in the EU (13.8 per cent). For example, Norway, Sweden and the Netherlands display lower poverty rates but their poverty gaps are higher than the Finnish one. The result suggests that in Finland many people living on social benefits lay just below the 60 per cent income threshold and they would not need much additional income to rise above the line. Finnish social security may be universal but the level of benefits seems to be inadequate, at least according to the 60 per cent standard.

In accordance with rising income inequalities, inequality in wealth has also increased in Finland. From 1994 to 2009, households' net wealth increased by 115 per cent—but not surprisingly, the increase has been the fastest in the 10th decile. Inequality in wealth is larger than inequality in income. From 1994 to 2009, the Gini coefficient in net wealth increased from 0.62 to 0.67.

Despite the changes in the level of wealth, the composition of wealth in different income groups has remained rather unchanged. The role of housing is crucial in the wealth composition of the Finns: 75 per cent of households own their houses or apartments. Even though the role of housing is still important, the proportion of housing in the total wealth stock has decreased—from 80 per cent in 1994 to 76 per cent in 2009, while the proportion of financial assets increased 13 to 19 per cent. In the highest income decile, the share of assets has increased most rapidly (15 to 32 per cent, in respective years).

Labour Market Chances of the Educational Groups have Diverged

Equal opportunity has been one of the most important goals of the Nordic Welfare State and the educational system is one of the most important devices to ensure open opportunities for everybody regardless of family background. The educational level of Finns has increased substantially over the last 40 years. Whereas in 1970, most persons aged 15 and over did not have any educational qualifications, by 2010 almost 70 per cent had qualifications, and the share of those with only basic education had dropped from 70 to 30 per cent. Correspondingly, participation in higher education has increased. Less than ten (7.8) per cent of the cohort born in 1946 participated in university education, but almost twenty (17.4) per cent of those born in 1986 have studied at the university. In the wake of the expansion of university education, the gender balance has changed from male to female dominance (33/67 to 55/45) (Kivinen *et al.*, 2012).

Education is one of the most important selection mechanisms in the labour market. In Finland, the effect is significant and the gap in employment rates between educational groups is expanding. Employment rates for those with higher and secondary education have increased, while there is a decreasing trend for those with only primary education. In 2010, the gap between higher and primary educated was 44 percentage points among women and 42 percentage points among men. Employment rates at all education levels are still clearly higher among males than females (Figure 10.5).

The large differences in employment rates between those with primary education and other groups also reflect the effect of economic globalization. Jobs with lesser qualifications tend to move to countries where labour costs are lower. As a small export-oriented country without sizeable natural resources, Finland is very vulnerable to such influences. Meanwhile, migration especially from neighbouring Estonia brings workers to Finland to compete for jobs for which those with only primary education qualify. In Finland, as in many other countries, a trend towards labour-market polarization has been documented. Whereas employment is increasing in both the top and bottom occupations of the employment hierarchy, the middle strata is in relative decline (Asplund and Kauhanen, 2010; Kauhanen, 2011). Needless to say, this tendency will create a structural driver for growing inequalities and this is one reason why inequality in factor incomes has not gone down despite that fact that unemployment has decreased from nearly 17 per cent in the mid 1990s to less than ten per cent in the 2010s.

Echoing the differentiated positions of educational groups in the labour market, those with only primary education are also lagging behind measured by income (see Table 10.1). In 1990–2000, the development of the educational groups went roughly hand in hand in terms of relative changes in income, but since 2000, those with secondary or tertiary education have increased their real incomes more than those with only primary education. Strongly connected with education, socio-economic income differences have also expanded. Upper white-collar employees, entrepreneurs and farmers have had substantial increases, while the median incomes of the unemployed have increased hardly at all.

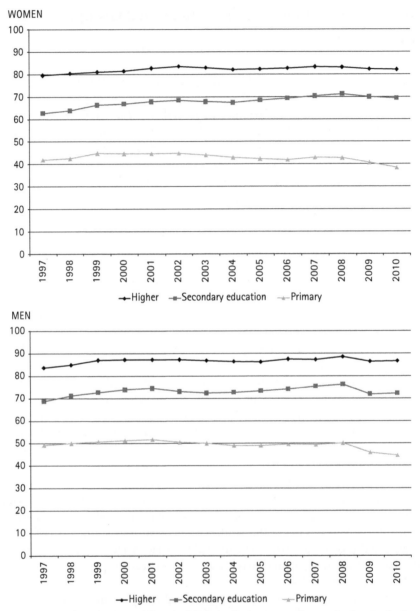

FIGURE 10.5 Employment rates for working aged women and men by level of education 1997–2010: women (upper graph) and men (lower graph)

Source: Statistics Finland.

Striving for Equal Opportunities

The Nordic vision of child education is that children from less privileged backgrounds should be enabled to receive an education on a par with children from privileged backgrounds. The educational system is crucial in explaining to what degree parental background is inherited. In that respect, Finland performs well. Students' skills are less dependent upon their family background than in most other countries. Finland scores very high in the PISA pupils' skills study, and simultaneously there is a smaller impact on the student's family background than in most countries. While in Finland the family background explains eight per cent of the student's achievement, the corresponding share is fourteen in the UK and Scandinavia and close to twenty per cent in Germany and the USA (OECD, 2010: 34).

An alternative way to evaluate the openness of the educational system, or the openness of societies at large in the spirit of John Rawls (1974), is to look at generational income mobility, i.e. the degree to which parents' income determine children's income. A strong correlation between intergenerational incomes indicates that societal institutions are not particularly open and that family background is a discriminating factor. Not surprisingly, children's incomes are correlated with the parents' incomes in all countries. However, there are substantial differences between countries. It appears that the Nordic countries are somewhat more open than most other countries. The intergenerational correlation between parents and children is less than .20 in Finland, whereas in the US and UK the corresponding figure is about .50. This result is attributed to the educational system: in Finland there are no tuition fees for university students, both secondary and upper secondary education is free of charge, and there is a universal and free grant system for students. On top of the grant, the state guarantees study loans, which allows all students irrespective of family background to finance their studies. Thus, the educational system is geared to promoting equal opportunity, and the probability of taking university education between those coming from academic homes versus non-academic homes has markedly decreased. While the odds ratio of being at university (academic vs. non-academic background) was 19.1 in 1970, it was 6.5 in 2005. The flip side of this coin is that educational mobility seems to be levelling off and the latest data show a slight increase in the impact of the childhood home (odds ratio was 6.8 in 2010; Kivinen *et al.*, 2012).

All the factors discussed above are linked to a larger societal phenomenon, i.e. social mobility. Due to the modernization and the growth of the public sector, Finnish social mobility changed rapidly during the post-war era towards greater openness (Erikson and Pöntinen, 1985; Erola, 2009) and the inheritance of social status has weakened (Erola and Moisio, 2007). One might expect that increases in other forms of inequality would inevitably impact on inequality of opportunity as well, but this seems not to be the case. During the Great Depression, the educational system was expanded to buffer unemployment and to foster social change, and the depression had no immediate effects on class mobility (Erola and Moisio, 2005). However, as indicated above, the decrease of the importance of family background in university education has levelled off and the trend may be reversing.

Today, in terms of equal opportunities, Finland seems to be a comparatively speaking open society. Intergenerational mobility in terms of occupation, income or education is cross-nationally high in Finland. Yet, as shown above, there still are clear socio-economic differences in participation in higher education and, in recent years, the impact of family background seems to have increased. Moreover, the relative significance of family background for poverty has increased after the mid 1990s. It is alarming that there is a tendency for those coming from poor childhood homes to have a significantly higher probability of being poor in their adulthood than those who are coming from non-poor backgrounds.

3. SOCIAL IMPACTS

....

It is evident that since the mid 1990s, income inequality has risen in Finland. However, it is not always straightforward whether rising income inequality has had detrimental effects on social indicators. At the general level, there may not be much change, but social gradients in many phenomena may have increased because some groups fare better but some are being left behind in the society. As will be seen, consequences in terms of social 'bads' caused by growing inequality are not clear and straightforward in Finland: they are often not visible in the averages but hidden in the margins of society. An overview of concomitant changes in income inequality and in social, cultural and political conditions is presented in the GINI country report: Finland (Blomgren *et al.*, 2012).

Material Deprivation and Cumulative Disadvantage

Despite rising income inequality and poverty rates, material deprivation has fallen in Finland. The proportion of the population suffering from 'consensual deprivation' (an involuntary lack of three or more necessities that are considered necessary by the majority of the population) has gone down from 12 per cent in 1995 to 2 per cent in 2010. The proportion of people stating that they have great difficulties in making ends meet has fallen from nine to four per cent (Ritakallio, 2010). Yet, differences between population groups are obvious. As can be seen in Table 10.2, the prevalence of financial difficulties decreased from 1996 to 2006 in all groups, but in 2006–2009 problems increased especially among the unemployed.

Even though Finnish national data show a considerable decrease in subjective deprivation and scarcity during the 2000s, EU indicators of poverty and social exclusion indicate a more stable situation. EU 2020 indicators suggest that there have not been any significant changes in the aggregate level of poverty and material deprivation during the 2000s—the level of the EU indicator for severe material deprivation hovered around three per cent in Finland in 2004 to 2010. Yet also the EU data show that relative income poverty rates are much higher than material deprivation rates.

The problem is that the overlap between different indicators is rather low (Kangas and Ritakallio, 2008). With regard to recipients of social assistance, which is the means-tested social benefit of last resort in Finland, only 36 per cent reported in 2009 that they had had financial difficulties in meeting everyday expenses. This relationship between direct and indirect measures of poverty is even weaker when we examine those who are at risk of poverty: only 24 per cent of them reported financial difficulties (Moisio, 2010). Table 10.3 confirms the findings. The table displays the proportional overlaps of various EU 2020 indicators for poverty and social exclusion. As can be seen, about half of those whose household disposable income is lower than 60 per cent of the national median are only income poor. On average, a bit more than one third of the income poor have had also low work intensity, while the overlap between severe material deprivation and being at risk of poverty is considerably lower. On the other hand, those who are materially deprived quite often also have

Table 10.2 Financial difficulties in meeting everyday expenses in Finland 1996–2009 (%)

	1996	1999	2001	2004	2006	2009
Employed	16	11	9	6	5	6
Unemployed	41	36	24	24	21	39
Student	50	30	30	26	15	18
Retired	12	12	9	11	11	9
Other	24	12	11	12	14	14
Total	21	14	11	9	8	9
Gini coeff.	0.223	0.259	0.258	0.266	0.273	0.259

Source: Moisio, 2010.

both low work intensity and low income. This overlap has increased from 21 to 48 per cent between 2004 and 2010.

Recipiency rates of social assistance follow general economic trends. There was a considerable increase in the number of persons who got social assistance during the early 1990s, and again during the global financial crises in 2008–2009. Even though the proportion of households who received social assistance in 2010 was at the same level as before the economic recession of the early 1990s (about 7 per cent), the duration of spells in social assistance has increased. While in 1990 about 22 per cent were long-term (at least six months during a calender year) claimants of social assistance, the proportion had increased to 43 per cent in 2010.

Social Cohesion

Social cohesion is often measured by two different but interlinked sets of variables. The first set of variables pertains to frequency of social contacts with other people and the second set refers to trust in fellow citizens and (inter)national institutions. When it comes to the first set, data for Finland are only available from the European Social Survey (ESS) covering years 2002 to 2010. In comparative terms, social cohesion, which is measured as the frequency of social contacts and the share of those who say that they have no close friends, is at the same level in Finland as in the other ESS-countries (8.4 per cent in Finland, about ten per cent in Europe). About every second Finn meets friends and relatives either on a daily basis or several times a week. An interesting trend is that in the early 2000s, the highest income quartile (the 4th quartile) had the most frequent social contacts and differences between quartiles were significant. By 2010, these differences had disappeared but there is still a persistent difference in the level of social contacts between those who have and those who have not met economic problems—the former group reporting significantly fewer social contacts. Over time there is no clear trend towards expanding differences. In this respect, the story is about a rather stable development throughout the 2000s regardless of economic cycles or changes in inequality.

Trust is important, not only for the economic performance of the country or for the transparency of its institutions, but it is essential for individual well being as well. Earlier

Table 10.3 The proportional shares of component overlap of EU 2020 poverty and social exclusion measures (%)

	2004		2006		2008		2010	
	Overlap, %	Relative share, %	Overlap, %	Relative share, %	Overlap, %	Relative share, %	Overlap, %	Relative share, %
At-risk-of-poverty								
Only inc.poor	4.6	50.0	4.9	47.6	6.2	55.4	5.0	44.2
Inc.poor and mat.dep	0.4	4.3	0.6	5.8	0.4	3.6	0.2	1.8
Inc.poor and work.poor	3.4	37.0	3.4	33.0	3.6	32.1	5.0	44.2
Inc.poor and mat.dep and work. poor	0.8	8.7	1.4	13.6	1.0	8.9	1.1	9.7
Total	**9.2**	**100**	**10.3**	**100**	**11.2**	**100**	**11.3**	**100**
Material deprivation								
Only mat.dep	1.8	46.2	0.9	25.0	0.8	32.0	0.6	26.1
Mat.dep and inc.poor	0.4	10.3	0.6	16.7	0.4	16.0	0.2	8.7
Mat.dep and work.poor	0.9	23.1	0.7	19.4	0.3	12.0	0.4	17.4
Inc.poor and mat.dep and work. poor	0.8	20.5	1.4	38.9	1.0	40.0	1.1	47.8
Total	**3.9**	**100**	**3.6**	**100**	**2.5**	**100**	**2.3**	**100**
Low work intensity								
Only work.poor	4.9	49.0	4.0	42.1	2.9	37.2	3.7	36.3
Work.poor and inc.poor	3.4	34.0	3.4	35.8	3.6	46.2	5.0	49.0
Work.poor and mat.dep	0.9	9.0	0.7	7.4	0.3	3.8	0.4	3.9
Inc.poor and mat.dep and work. poor	0.8	8.0	1.4	14.7	1.0	12.8	1.1	10.8
Total	**10.0**	**100**	**9.5**	**100**	**7.8**	**100**	**10.2**	**100**

Note: inc.poor = at-risk-of-poverty; mat.dep = severe material deprivation; work.poor = low work intensity.

Source: Eurostat, EU-SILC 2004–2010. We are grateful to Markus Kainu for these calculations.

studies have shown that the most important determinant of happiness and a good life is the degree of trust that individuals have. Those who have high levels of social trust enjoy a high life-satisfaction as well. Institutional trust has been and still is at a high level in Finland when compared to most other OECD countries. In particular, confidence in the police and the justice system is extremely high. The crisis of the 1990s had a huge impact upon citizens' trust in political systems and political decision-makers, in particular. Although some of the trustworthiness was regained in the 2000s, trust in political parties is even lower than trust in the EU—about which the Finns are notoriously sceptical. The morality of the story is straightforward: increasing economic problems and inequalities contributed to increasing distrust in national institutions. The situation is now more or less settled and the average levels of (dis)trust are the same as they were in 1981 as indicated by the World Value (WV) data. However, socio-economic differences in degrees of trust have expanded and they are wider than twenty-five years ago.

The story of individual trust is very much the same as that of institutional trust. Confidence in fellow citizens was at a rather high level in 1981 (60 per cent trusted in other people) but the level of trust went down in the mid 1990s, returning to the 1981 level in 2005 and many groups displayed an even higher level of individual trust in 2005 than in 1981. There were some groups that had fallen behind the 1981 levels, such as students, the unemployed and those with poor health status. Those whose self-evaluated health was bad displayed the lowest and constantly declining level of individual trust (55, 33 and 25 per cent, in respective years) (WV data).

Regardless of changes in inequality, the overall level of subjective measures of well being (happiness and life satisfaction) has remained high—some 70 per cent are satisfied with their life and about 90 per cent say they are quite or very happy (ESS). However, there is a slight tendency for bifurcation to occur. On the one hand, the shares of very happy / very satisfied respondents, and on the other hand the proportion of those who are very unhappy / dissatisfied with their lives have increased over time.

The level of criminality is one indicator of the lack of social cohesion in society. Fear of crime hollows out the trust and subjective well being of residents. No wonder, therefore, that the association between poverty (or inequality) and crime has been widely debated among social scientists. At the national level, it is difficult to find strong correlation: offences against life and health have slightly increased in the 2000s, while crimes against property have decreased steadily. The connection between inequality and crimes appears to be stronger at the municipal level. The subjective perception of crime is not completely related to the level of recorded crimes. Perception of violence decreased markedly from 1980 to 1988, after which the perception rates have remained constant. However, there has been an increase in the subjective perception of various forms of threat since 1988. This development coincided with the increase in income inequality (Blomgren et al., 2012).

Changes in Household Composition, Marriage and Fertility

Finns have become more and more secularized in their family values. Compared to earlier decades, they now tend to live alone (40 per cent of households are now single-person households), marry later or do not marry at all (mean age of women at first marriage has risen to 31 years), they have children at older ages (mean age at childbirth is 30 years) or do not have them at all (the proportion of childless women aged 35 has risen from 19 in 1990 to 27 per cent in 2010). 40 per cent of children are currently born outside marriage, largely due to increasing rates of cohabitation. Finns also tend to divorce more eagerly than in earlier times. Of marriages that were contracted in 1980, about 16 per cent were dissolved 10 years later, whereas the respective proportion for marriages contracted in 2000 was about 26 per cent. Family formation patterns are socio-economically structured: marriages are more prevalent among higher socio-economic groups (Kartovaara, 2003) and the risk of divorce is higher among those in lower socio-economic positions (Jalovaara, 2007). This gradient is influenced by income, education, occupational status, employment and housing tenure.

Rather than reflecting changes in inequality, these developments are reflections of the loosening of traditional family values, more individualistic values, establishment of a dual earner model in the labour market, and also of strong gender equality. However, these general developments may hide important differences related to socio-economic status within each household type. For example, polarization may have occurred in the employment and socio-economic situation according to family types during recent decades. There are some indications of a worsening of the situation of single and single parent households. Table 10.1 shows how real disposable income is lagging behind in single parent households in comparison to the overall trend, and accordingly, the proportion of single parent families among families with children receiving social assistance increased from 45 per cent in 1998 to 56 per cent in 2006 (Heino and Lamminpää, 2008). The poverty risks of one-adult households (both single persons and single parents) increased remarkably during 1995–2005 and have remained at the level of 25–30 per cent since the mid 2000s. An increasing share of single-person and single parent households comprises a demographical driver for rising poverty rates and widening income inequality in Finland.

However, even though couple formation has changed remarkably, there is no clear trend in the total fertility rate. The total fertility rate in Finland was 1.83 in 2011 and has fluctuated between 1.71 and 1.87 over the last 20 years. The total fertility rate has had no clear connection with income inequality, either, but it seems to have had an association with GDP growth rate: during periods of economic downturn, total fertility rate has gone up, while during periods of economic boom it has come down. Without doubt, the Finnish comprehensive and affordable day-care and supported child home care system have also contributed to maintaining high fertility rates.

Health Inequalities

After World War II, life expectancy increased in Finland faster than in many other Western countries. In 2010, life expectancy at birth was 83 years among women and 77 years among men (Statistics Finland, StatFin database). The difference in life expectancy between women and men is one of the largest in Western Europe, mainly due to a high male mortality from cardiovascular diseases. Even though population health in general has improved, socio-economic differences in health are still large and have not been significantly reduced in the golden period of the Nordic Welfare States in the 1970s and 1980s (Lahelma and Lundberg, 2009; Bambra, 2011). The issue is depicted in Figure 10.6, showing that while life expectancy at 35 among the well off has increased, the development at the bottom has been negligible, and consequently, the difference between the lowest and highest quintile has increased remarkably since the late 1980s. Among women the difference increased from 3.9 years to 6.8 years, and among men from 7.4 years to 12.5 years (Tarkiainen *et al.*, 2011; 2012). Life expectancy increased in all other quintiles but the poorest one. According to occupation-based socio-economic status, the difference grew only slightly, and the same has been observed of the life expectancy trends related to education. Thus, according to these findings, income is a more severe determinant of health than education or socio-economic status. The main reason for the stagnant life expectancy in the lowest income quintile was increasing alcohol-related mortality among those aged 35–64. Also increasing cancer mortality among women and a slow decrease in heart disease among men in this age group contributed to the differences between the quintiles. (Tarkiainen *et al.*, 2011; 2012.) Furthermore, health-related selection into the lowest income quintile has been strengthened, because benefits for those with poor health and disability have lagged more and more behind general income development.

The socio-economic gradient in reporting good or reasonably good health is also obvious: about 70 per cent of the most educated reported at least reasonably good health in 2010 while the proportion was only 55–60 per cent among the least educated. There has not been much change in reporting good health since 1999—not on average nor in the educational gradient. Overall, self-reported good health seems to be on average almost at the same level in 2010 as it was ten years earlier. Among women, a slight convergence between the educational groups has taken place (Blomgren *et al.*, 2012).

Socio-economic differences in health are linked to a number of behavioural factors—how people eat, drink and smoke—and access to health care. Without doubt, inability to combat these differences is a clear weakness of the Finnish Welfare State. For example, the socio-economic gradient in smoking has increased.

Needless to say, increasing differences in social conditions increase differences in detrimental behaviour, which fortifies the vicious cycle.

Furthermore, obesity and being overweight are important factors negatively affecting overall public health in Finland. Obesity has increased remarkably since the 1980s and about 17–18 per cent of men and women are obese. What is interesting is that the socio-economic gradient in obesity or being overweight is not always as clear as in many other morbidity or health behaviour indicators. The prevalence of overweightedness has increased in all educational groups during the last ten years, and thus no pattern connected with increasing inequality can be observed.

4. POLITICAL AND CULTURAL IMPACTS

Political Participation

Finland was the first country to achieve universal adult suffrage in parliamentary elections (in 1906). Until the early 1980s, voting activity in parliamentary elections hovered around 80 per cent but since then there has been a downward trend towards less than 70 per cent despite some increases in turnout, as in 2011 (71 per cent). A diminishing interest in voting is

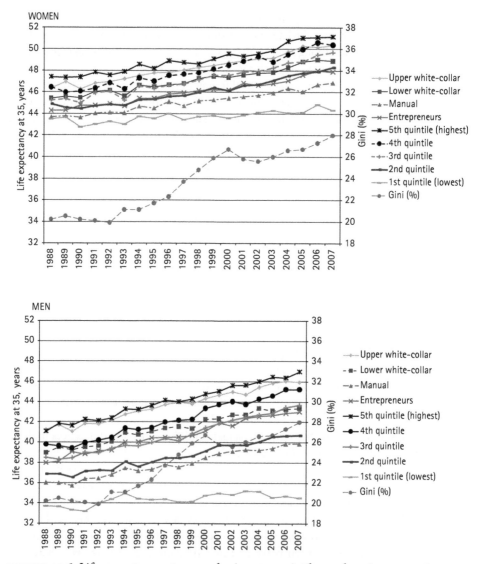

FIGURE 10.6 Life expectancy at age 35 by income quintiles and socio-economic status, with Gini coefficient of equivalized disposable income, women and men in 1988–2007

Source: Adapted from Tarkiainen *et al.*, 2011; 2012; Income Distribution Statistics, Statistics Finland.

very visible also in municipal elections—the all-time lowest electorate turnout was reached in the 2012 municipal elections when only 58 per cent cast their votes.

During the post-war period of building up the Finnish Welfare State, there were four 'big' parties in Finland: the Social Democratic Party (SDP); the People's Democratic Party (PDP, consisting of left-wing socialists and communists); the Agrarian Union/Centre Party; and the National Coalition Party (the Conservatives). A marked shift in the political power balance has taken place. In 1966 the socialists had a majority in the Finnish parliament but in 2011 elections the share of the social democrats and Left League (the former PDP) was as low as 27 per cent. The popularity of the National Coalition Party—leaning more and more towards market liberalism—has been consistently increasing. By the 2011 elections, the National Coalition Party obtained the status of the biggest party (22 per cent of the seats) and the True Finns had a phenomenal result and got 19 per cent of the votes cast, entering into the group of the 'big' four parties. In many social policy issues, the True Finns are close to the traditional left-wing pro-poor and pro-Welfare State orientation, whereas on moral questions they represent traditional conservatism, and in immigration issues they are the most anti-immigration party in Finland. In its landslide victory in 2011, the True Finns won Euro-critical votes from the SDP and notably so from the Centre.

In sum, important shifts in the political power balance have taken place in favour of right-wing policies favouring the well-off strata and employers. Needless to say, these shifts will have ramifications for the character of welfare policies implemented in the country. The policy ideals aiming at smaller income inequality and equal social conditions are evaporating.

Political Values and Legitimacy of the Welfare State

Finnish politics are based on practical compromises and grand coalitions. The strength of this kind of policy-making has been that despite deep ideological differences, coalition cabinets have been able to seek consensus and solve difficult economic and political dilemmas. One could describe Finnish political decision making as politics without politics: it is governance and muddling through. The method has been an effective device in hard times but the flip side of the coin has been the watering-down of the very role of politics, which is mirrored in turn by low voter turnout and a political frustration that was partially channelled into support for True Finns, representing pro-distribution but anti-immigration[2] attitudes. True Finns collect their votes from working-class suburbs, the countryside and mostly from people hit by the Great Depression and cuts in the Welfare State. In a way True Finns are 'a voice of forgotten people'.

There are three themes that direct Finnish policy-making: the fate of the Welfare State; immigration; and the EU/globalization. Attitudes on these issues are linked to the constituencies of different parties. Whereas the core constituency for the National Coalition Party is the upper middle class, business people and employers, the constituency of True Finns and traditionally also of the socialist parties are or have been blue-collar workers and low-income earners who regard globalization and immigration as a threat to their own employment opportunities, which explains their sceptical attitudes (cf. Rueda, 2007). The policy profile of True Finns favours redistribution among the native population and their concept of social solidarity is strongly conditional in-group solidarity. It seems to be the case that the political vocabularies of the Conservatives (being for globalization, immigration and the EU) and the True Finns are the most effective rhetorical devices in present Finnish politics.

At the first glance there seems to be a dilemma. There is strong support for welfare policies but the pendulum has turned in favour of the Conservatives who traditionally have been the

---

[2] The proportion of residents with foreign citizenships was only 0.5 per cent in 1990, and by 2011 it had grown to 3.4 per cent.

most vociferous critics of the Nordic Welfare State model. One plausible explanation to this may be the socio-economically biased electorate turnout. Well-off citizens vote more often and, as a rule, they vote for the Conservatives. Indeed, according to the European Social Survey non-voting in Finland has a strong socio-economic gradient. High-income earners, well-educated, higher and upper middle class people vote more frequently than poorer, less educated, unemployed persons and those in lower socio-economic positions. For example, among the employed, the non-voting level was about 15 per cent in 2010, whereas 29 per cent of the unemployed said that they did not vote. In 2010, the share of non-voters among the unemployed was as high as 43 per cent. The trend among those who have economic difficulties coping on their present income is very much the same as among the unemployed (ESS). This means that the 'will of the people' expressed in elections is strongly biased in favour of the 'better-offs' in the Finnish society.

Why then are the other layers of society not eager to use their political rights? One reason may be linked to the aforementioned consensual way of political decision-making. Cabinets based on grand coalitions, including both the National Coalition Party, the SDP and Left League, blur differences between parties and increase frustration among the electorate: since there are no changes in the content of policy-making, what is the point of voting? Thus, in Finnish political life there are two underpinning tensions. On the one hand, there is the socio-economic divide about who votes for whom and who does not vote at all. On the other hand, there is a deep discrepancy in opinions between the ruling political elite and a vast number of frustrated voters, which benefits the True Finns.

5. POLICIES

As described above, there have been structural drivers of inequality, such as economic cycles, changes in demography, household formation, occupational structure, and the change in income formation—as well as, directly, politics and consequently policy-related factors. The most important effects of political decision-making have been decisions on the level and coverage of social benefits and changes in the tax system.

One of the most frequently used indicators of the Welfare State effort is social spending as a percentage of gross national product (GDP). The Finnish history from the beginning of the 1990s gives an interesting testimony on the validity of the indicator. If we look at social spending in relation to GDP, the heyday of the Finnish Welfare State was 1992 to 1996 when spending exceeded 30 per cent of GDP. Thereafter there was a decline to the 'normal' level of 25 per cent. However, if we look at social spending per capita, we can see that there was a constant increase up to the year 1993, whereafter development stagnated. Since the beginning of the 2000s, there has been a steady increase in absolute spending. In 2010, Finland used 30 per cent of its GDP for social purposes, which is somewhat higher than in most other EU countries. However, these numbers perhaps conceal more than they reveal.

First, during the recession years there has been a tendency for the role of income transfers versus social services to increase. This was obvious in the early 1990s when the share of cash benefits expanded, but since then the balance has slowly shifted more towards services.

Second, the spending figures do not reveal how the levels of many social benefits were cut under the 1990s' recession, after which they have in many cases remained more or less stagnant and not followed the general development of rising incomes. Compared to the level of year 1990, the real growth in basic unemployment allowance and basic pension has been almost negligible—from 1990 to 2011 earnings have more than doubled in real terms, the cost of living index has grown by 45 per cent, but the basic allowances have increased only by less than ten per cent. This development has for its part contributed to the increase in income inequality, i.e. the redistributive effect of social policy has diminished, and more importantly, the inadequate indexation of basic benefits has contributed to the increase of relative income poverty.

In the period of austerity, and given the demographic and structural changes increasing the threat of poverty, it is difficult to raise the level of benefits high enough to eliminate poverty. Therefore, the Finnish cabinets, regardless of their political composition, have emphasized employment as the best remedy against poverty. It has been suggested that lower benefits reduce the employment threshold and create incentives to take a job instead of living on the dole. In principle this is a point well made, keeping in mind that less than five per cent of working Finns are poor but the corresponding figure for non-working is close to 40 per cent.

Also, tax reductions have been introduced to encourage employment. The gross tax rate increased in the 1990s to more than 47 per cent in 2000. During the 2000s, the tax rate has been decreasing—in 2011 it was 43 per cent of the GDP, which is among the highest among OECD countries (OECD Tax Database). Improving work incentives has been the main motivation for reducing tax on work income. These changes in taxation have diminished the redistributive effect of taxes. However, the major change was the tax reform in 1993, when taxation of capital income was changed from progressive to proportional, and which created a strong incentive to shift income towards capital income if possible. Thus, top income earners especially have used financial and fiscal planning to reduce their tax payments.

In political rhetoric, a shift has taken place from the equality of outcome towards equality of opportunities. Since education is one of the major selection mechanisms steering individuals into different socio-economic positions, open access to education is an important precondition for equal opportunities. In Finland, all education—from primary school to university degree—has historically been—and still is—free of charge. Education expenditures consist of the costs of organizing educational services as well as financial aid for students. Students' financial aid seeks to ensure subsistence during periods of study and can be paid for full-time studies after comprehensive school level, i.e. upper secondary school studies, vocational education, and higher education degree studies. The role of the free-of-charge educational system up to university degree level has been important in ensuring equality of opportunity in Finland, but as discussed above, the social inheritance of education also plays an important role, and there are some indications that the impact of family background is growing.

Due to centralized top level bargaining systems, wage dispersion in the Nordic countries has traditionally been condensed. Wages as well as social benefits in Finland were negotiated through a procedure called 'a comprehensive incomes policy solution' which often included 'social packages' including agreements on holidays, parental leaves, etc. Tripartite discussions were held between trade unions, employers' federations, and the government. Because of the reluctance of the employers' federations, the practice came to an end in 2008, and since then each trade union has negotiated separately which, together with the polarization process, i.e. the increase in top and bottom occupations and the squeezing of the middle, has contributed to growing wage inequality. Given the diminishing distributional capacity of taxes and welfare transfers, the expanding income cleavages created by the labour markets may be visible in disposable income as well.

The tripartite negotiation system had its merits in controlling wage dispersion among those inside the labour markets. However, the system has been criticized as being a machine pursuing the interests of those already well off in the society, and it has hampered many efforts to improve the social benefits of those less well off. The strong voice of trade unions has thus impeded many improvements in basic social security for labour market outsiders.

6. Conclusions

Finland is among the countries in which the rise of income inequality has been exceptionally fast and steep, even though the Gini coefficient for equalized disposable income was still comparatively low in 2010 (at 0.266). Growing trend of income inequality was seen in Finland during a relatively short period in the latter part of the 1990s. The period between 1995 and 2000 meant a dramatic increase in both gross and disposable income inequality, followed by a more stable trend during the 2000s.

Up to the early 1990s, income inequalities diminished in Finland, and at the political level there was a great deal of welfare optimism. The Great Depression Finland then experienced changed the political landscape and the context of policy-making. During the economic crisis of the 1990s, GDP fell in three consecutive years, unemployment sky-rocketed and social spending reached 35 per cent of GDP. The public budget, which used to be positive, ran into deficit, and the public debt accelerated from virtually zero to 60 per cent of GDP in 1996. These dark economic prospects formed the background for subsequent social policy-making and softened attitudes among Finns when it came to accepting retrenchment measures that otherwise would have been hard to carry through, regardless of the colour of the government. Instead of optimism and belief in the possibilities of improving social protection, persistent austerity became the mantra. Politicians wanted to move from the 'politics of redistribution' to the 'politics of responsibility'. The latter de facto meant cuts in social protection and cuts in tax rates in order to improve work incentives and to increase the consumption capacity of the population. The key idea was 'active social policy', i.e., to create work incentives. Consequently, the level of social benefits started to lag behind the development of average earnings. Since the mid 1990s, governments have emphasized tax reliefs for work income. However, reliefs did not include social benefits. Hence, taxation policy together with cuts and freezing the benefit levels have meant an increasing gap between employed insiders and those outside the labour markets (cf. Rueda, 2007). Thus, one driver for rising income inequality is the modest real income growth among low as well as middle income groups. Yet, this impact is weaker than the impact from increasing capital income and the dual taxation system.

Unlike the general trend in other OECD countries, greater inequality in wages and salaries is not the most important driver of inequality in the Finnish case. The main reason behind growing income inequality was the increase of income among high income groups, which was mainly driven by an increase in capital income. At the same time, the redistributive effect of taxes and benefits diminished. This was mainly due to the dual taxation system,

i.e. differences in taxation between capital income and earnings, which had two consequences. First, all those who could transfer their work income to capital income (usually the
upper stratum) did so. Second, opening up of the global financial markets and introduction
of new types of investment instruments from the late 1980s, combined with the ICT boom,
created totally different, circumstances for business and financial markets than before.
Consequently, the role of capital income and financial assets increased among the highest
income decile, expanding income inequality.

At the general level, growing inequality has not seemed to affect family formation patterns. Widening socio-economic differences in health are, however, a demonstration of the
potential hampering effects of widening social stratification. Already, in the early 1980s,
there were substantial differences in mental well being between the healthy and the sick, and
by the 2000s they were larger than they were two decades earlier. The same goes for differences between the unemployed and employed. The average level of subjective well being is
very high but the averages conceal a worrying trend: there are more very satisfied and happy
but on the other hand there also are more very dissatisfied and very unhappy citizens.

Neither are there strong visible consequences from growing income inequality in the
open Finnish society. Intergenerational mobility in terms of occupation, income, or education is cross-nationally high, yet there are some trends which would suggest an opposite
development. For instance, improving educational achievements are not a universal trend,
as regards social background. There are also clear but constant participatory differences in
higher education based on parents' educational background. Moreover, the relative significance of family background for poverty has increased since the mid 1990s.

The Nordic Welfare State has been often labelled a Social Democratic Welfare State. To
some extent this applies also to Finland. However, the political left seems to be losing its
appeal and the Conservatives, and recently the True Finns, are growing in importance.
Consequently, political discourse has also fundamentally changed. Up to the mid 1980s,
social policy was seen to contribute to economic growth. A positive circle between social
protection and productivity was taken for granted. Now a vicious circle is the norm. More
and more, stronger and stronger voices are demanding further cuts in taxation, lower wages
and social benefits—to compete in the global market, to make people more enterprising and
to make them take more responsibility for themselves. The stronger position of the employers vis a vis representatives of the employees contributes to that. Instead of speaking of redistribution and social justice, the legitimate political vocabulary more often contrast 'politics
of redistribution' against 'politics of responsibility', demands for social justice are equated
with envy, collective responsibility is replaced by individual blame and individual solutions,
and social problems are transformed to individual problems.

Given the increase in income inequality seen in Finland, it is fair to ask whether the
passion for equality is on the wane. The Finnish welfare model today is less universal, less
generous and more conditional than it was twenty years ago. However, the Finnish welfare model is still distinct and fares well in comparison with other Welfare State models on
most dimensions of welfare. Poverty and inequality rates are comparatively low, income
mobility—be it short-term or intergenerational—is high, and all this is combined with
high levels of subjective well being. This is very much in line with the basic Nordic ideas of
how the state should work: it should provide individuals with the resources to master their
own lives.

References

Alestalo, M. and Kuhnle, S. (1984), *The Scandinavian Route: Economic, Social, and Political Developments in Denmark, Finland, Norway, and Sweden*, Helsinki: University of Helsinki.

Asplund, R. and Kauhanen, M. (eds.) (2010), *Suomalainen palkkarakenne*, [The Finnish Wage Structure], Helsinki: Elinkeinoelämän Tutkimuslaitos, Sarja B245.

Bambra, C. (2011), 'Social Inequalities in Health: The Nordic Welfare State in a Comparative Perspective', in J. Kvist, J. Fritzell, B. Hvinden, and O. Kangas (eds.), *Changing Social Equality. The Nordic Welfare Model in the 21st Century*, Bristol: Policy Press, pp. 143–164.

Blomgren, J., Hiilamo, H., Kangas, O., and Niemelä, M. (2012), Growing Inequalities and Their Impacts in Finland. Country report for Finland. GINI Growing Inequalities' Impacts. Available at: <http://gini-research.org/articles/cr>

Erikson, R. and Pöntinen, S. (1985), 'Social Mobility in Finland and Sweden: A Comparison of Men and Women', in R. Alapuro, M. Alestalo, E. Haavio-Mannila, and R. Väyrynen (eds.), *Small States in Comparative Perspective. Essays for Erik Allardt*, Oslo: Norwegian University Press, pp. 138–162.

Erola, J. (2009), 'Social Mobility and Education of Finnish Cohorts Born 1936-75: Succeeding While Failing in Equality of Opportunity?' *Acta Sociologica* 52 (4), 307-327.

Erola, J. and Moisio, P. (2005), 'The Impact of the 1990s Economic Crisis on Social Mobility in Finland', in T-A. Wilska, and L. Haanpää (eds.), 'Lifestyles and Social Change—Essays in Economic Sociology', *Discussion and Working Papers* 11:2005. Turku: Turku School of Economics and Business Administration, pp. 11–28.

Erola, J. and Moisio, P. (2007), 'Social Mobility Over Three Generations in Finland 1950–2000', *European Sociological Review* 23 (2), 169–183.

Heikkilä, M. and Uusitalo, H. (eds.) (1997), 'Leikkausten hinta. Tutkimuksia sosiaaliturvan leikkauksista ja niiden vaikutuksista 1990-luvun Suomessa'. [The cost of cuts. Studies on the cuts in social expenditure and their effects in Finland during the 1990s.] *Reports* 208. Helsinki: Stakes.

Heino, T. and Lamminpää, K. (2008), 'Perheet ja lapset toimeentulotuen piirissä' [Families and children as recipients of income support]. Helsinki: Stakes. Available at: <http://www.stakes.fi/tilastot/tilastotiedotteet/2008/Yksinhuoltajaperheiden_tttasiakkuus_2008.pdf>, accessed 27.10.2012.

Jalovaara, M. (2007), 'The Effects of Marriage Partners' Socio-Economic Positions on the Risk of Divorce in Finland', *Finnish Yearbook of Population Research 2007*. Helsinki: The Population Research Institute.

Kangas, O. and Palme, J. (eds.) (2005), *Social Policy and Economic Development in the Nordic Countries*, Basingstoke: Macmillan.

Kangas, O. and Ritakallio, V-M. (2008), 'Köyhyyden mittaustavat, sosiaaliturvan riittävyys ja köyhyyden yleisyys Suomessa' [Measurement of poverty, adequacy of social protection and prevalence of poverty in Finland], *Sosiaali- ja terveysturvan selosteita* 61/2008. Helsinki: Kela.

Kartovaara, L. (2003), 'Miesjohtajalla ura ja perhe, entä naisjohtajalla?' [Male leaders have a career and family, what about female leaders?] *Hyvinvointikatsaus* 4/2003, Tilastokeskus. Data available at: <tilastokeskus.fi/tk/he/tasaarvo_johtajat.html>, accessed 27 October 2012>

Katzenstein, P. (1985), *Small States in World Markets: Industrial Policy in Europe*, Ithaca: Cornell University Press.

Kauhanen, M. (2011), 'Muuttuvien työmarkkinoitten haasteita', [Challenges from changing labour markets], *Talous ja Yhteiskunta* 4, 32–38.

Kivinen, O., Hedman, J., and Kaipainen, P. (2012), 'Koulutusmahdollisuuksien yhdenvertaisuus Suomessa', [Equality of educational possibilities in Finland]. *Yhteiskuntapolitiikka* 77 (5), 559–566.

Lahelma, E. and Lundberg, O. (2009), 'Health Inequalities in European Welfare States', *European Journal of Public Health* 19 (5), 445—446.

Lelkes, O., Medgyesi, M., Tóth, I., and Ward, T. (2009), 'Income Distribution and the Risk of Poverty', in T. Ward, O. Lelkes, H. Sutherland, and I. Gy. Tóth (eds.), 'European Inequalities. Social Inclusion and Income Distribution in the European Union', Budapest: TÁRKI, pp. 17–44.

Moisio, P. (2010), 'Tuloerojen, köyhyyden ja toimeentulo-ongelmien kehitys' [Development of income inequality, poverty and financial difficulties], in M. Vaarama, P. Moisio, and S. Karvonen (eds.) *Suomalaisten hyvinvointi 2010*, Helsinki: Institute for Health and Welfare, pp. 180–196.

OECD (2008), *Growing Unequal? Income Distribution and Poverty in OECD Countries*, Paris: OECD.

OECD (2010), *PISA 2009 Results: Overcoming Social Background—Volume II*, Paris: OECD.

OECD (2011), *Divided We Stand. Why Inequality Keeps Rising*, Paris: OECD.

Rawls, J. (1974), *A Theory of Justice*, New York: Basic Books.

Ritakallio, V-M. (2010), 'The State of Poverty in Finland—Preliminary Findings of a 2010 Finnish PSE Survey', paper presented to a seminar on poverty and social exclusion, Finnish Social Policy Association, Helsinki, 24 August 2010.

Rueda, D. (2007), *Social Democracy Inside Out: Partisanship and Labor Market Policy in Industrialized Democracies*, Oxford: Oxford University Press.

Tarkiainen, L., Martikainen, P., Laaksonen, M., and Valkonen, T. (2011), 'Tuloluokkien väli-set erot elinajanodotteessa ovat kasvaneet vuosina 1988–2007', [Disparity in life expectancy between income quintiles, 1988–2007], *Suomen Lääkärilehti* 66 (48), 3651–3657a.

Tarkiainen, L., Martikainen, P., Laaksonen, M., and Valkonen, T. (2012), 'Trends in Life Expectancy by Income from 1988 to 2007: Decomposition by Age and Cause of Death', *J Epidemiology and Community Health* 66 (7), 573–578.

Tuomala, M. (2009), 'Income Inequality in Finland. Past and Future', lecture presented at the Social Insurance Institution of Finland, Helsinki, 27 October 2009.

CHAPTER 11

FRANCE: HOW TAXATION CAN INCREASE INEQUALITY

NICOLAS FRÉMEAUX AND THOMAS PIKETTY

1. INTRODUCTION

In this chapter, we describe the evolution of inequality in France and its impact on social, political and cultural outcomes. Three points make France distinctive with respect to other rich countries. First, the increase in inequalities in France occurred later than in many countries. More specifically, income inequality declined during the 1980s. Then, inequality started to rise at the end of the 1990s and this offset the decrease observed at the beginning of the period. Second, this difference in terms of timing also influences the study of its effects since it may take time for changing inequalities to lead to social, political or cultural impacts. Third, the role of taxation is rather important in France. The absence of progressivity in the tax system has contributed to the recent increase in income inequality. The content of this chapter will detail these three specificities. An in-depth analysis of the evolution of inequality, its impacts and of the policies implemented to fight inequalities is however beyond the scope of this chapter, and more detail is presented in the Gini project country report.

By way of introductory background it is important to know that France experienced several periods of slow growth between 1980 and 2010: between 1980 and 1985; during the mid 1990s; and since 2008. Significant changes have also affected demographics (population growth, ageing and the rise of single-parent families), labour market structure (feminization, an increasing dual labour market, and high unemployment rates) and also the economy (with a decrease in the wage share in GDP since 1985 and increasing private wealth).

2. The Evolution of Inequality in France: A Late Increase

The starting point of the GINI project is that inequality has gone up in many countries since 1980. Therefore, the first and main question we want to address in this chapter is: has inequality also grown in France during the past decades and, if yes, by how much? We focus on several dimensions: income; wealth; earnings; and education. Income and wealth are evaluated at the household level while earnings and education are examined on an individual basis. For each field, we use several data sources (national or international surveys, tax returns, national accounts…), several definitions (primary, gross, net, equivalized…), and several inequality indicators (the Gini coefficient, inter-decile ratios, Theil, top shares…). We take a long-run overview, especially for household income, by going back to the 1970s.

The main distinctiveness of France relates to the timing of this evolution. In contrast to many countries, income inequality decreased in France during the 1970s and the 1980s. The rise in inequality only started in the end of the 1990s. This recent growth has cancelled the decrease observed in the 1980s. Thus, France was above the average level of income inequality in OECD countries during the 1970s and the 1980s. At the end of the 2000s the country is just below the average and close to countries from continental Europe like Germany, Estonia, Poland or Switzerland. This group of countries is itself between the Anglo-Saxon (US, UK, Australia and Canada) and Nordic countries. In order to fully describe the evolution of inequality, we will begin with a focus on income and more specifically on net equivalized disposable income. Then, we will analyse the trends during the same period for wealth, earnings and education. We will finish this section by providing evidence why inequality has recently increased in France.

Income Inequality

The starting point of the analysis about income is the evolution of net equivalized disposable income.[1] In other words, we are focusing on income after tax and transfers, standardized across types of households for their composition (number of adults and children) by means of equivalization. This is maybe the most important definition of income because it measures the standard of living of households.

Figure 11.1 depicts the evolution of inequality from 1970 to 2010, measured by the Gini index. There is an unambiguous decline in inequality during the 1970s and 1980s, then a period of relative stability in the 1990s and an increase during the last decade of the period

---

[1] Disposable income = earnings (wages, salaries and mixed income) + pensions (unemployment and retirement) + capital income (from financial and non-financial assets) + welfare payments (housing and family benefits + social assistance) + alimonies—taxes (personal income tax + housing tax). Capital gains, because they are not taxable, are excluded. In order to go from disposable income to standard of living, we take into account household composition through the OECD-modified equivalization scale.

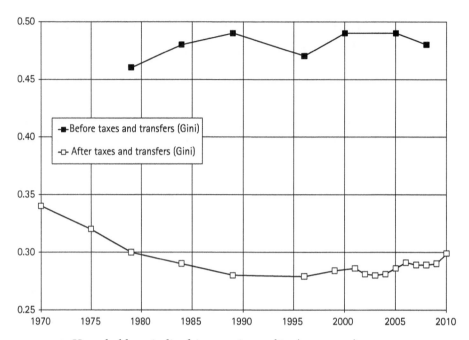

FIGURE 11.1 Household equivalized income inequality (1970–2010)

Note: The inequality index we use here is the Gini coefficient.

Source: INSEE (Insee–DGI, enquêtes Revenus fiscaux 1970–1990; Insee–DGI, enquêtes Revenus fiscaux 1996–2005; DGFiP; Cnaf; Cnav; CCMSA, enquêtes Revenus fiscaux et sociaux 2005–2010).

of observation. The 2008 recession does not modify this upward trend. In the end, the rise starting in the late 1990s cancels the decline of the 1980s. However, the evolution is not the same across all indices. More specifically, the inter-decile ratios present differences in terms of evolution. Most of the decline happens during the 1970s but the ratio P90/P10,[2] sensitive to changes in the middle of the distribution, decreases by 30 per cent between 1970 and the mid 1980s, while the ratios P90/P50 and P50/P10 only diminish by around 15 per cent. Similarly, the increase in income inequality during the 2000s is sharper for indices sensitive to the middle of the distribution like the Gini coefficient.

In this figure, we also present the evolution of inequality for household income before taxes and transfers.[3] We observe a slight increase during the 1980s but then a period of relative stability. Thus, primary income inequality seems to follow only partially the pattern of disposable income. More importantly, it indicates that the recent evolution has not been only caused by market income evolutions but also by taxes and transfers.

Changes in the overall distribution are mainly driven by variations at the tails. As a consequence, it is essential to look at the bottom and the top of the income distribution.

---

[2] With this ratio we compare the income of the lower limit of the top 10 per cent with the upper limit of the bottom 10 per cent.

[3] Until 1990 and particularly during the 1970s, capital income was not taken into proper account. If we exclude all capital income, the same decline appears until 1990.

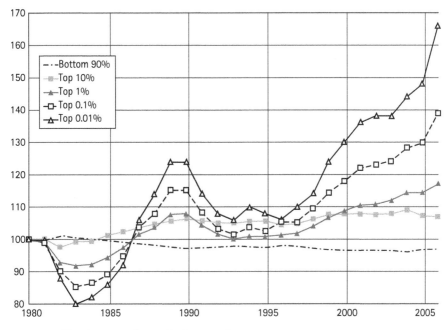

FIGURE 11.2 Top income shares (1980–2006)

Source: World Top Income Database (index = 100 in 1980).

In Figure 11.2, we decompose the income distribution in order to study in detail the evolution of the top income shares.[4] The moderate rise in income inequality since 1990 hides a boom in the top 1 per cent income share. In 1980, the top 10 per cent of income distribution received 30.7 per cent of total income while in 2006 it had 32.8 per cent (+ 7 per cent). During the same period, the increase is equal to 17 per cent for the top 1 per cent, to 39 per cent for the top 0.1 per cent and to 66 per cent for the top 0.01 per cent. The figure also shows that most of this increase happens between 1998 and 2006. In other words, there has been a transfer from the bottom to the top of the distribution, given that the share of the bottom 90 per cent of the population has decreased by 2 percentage points since 1980. This recent increase is mainly due to the rapid growth of capital income, particularly concentrated at the top of the distribution but also to a greater dispersion of labour income inequality. From this point of view, France might be beginning to converge on the Anglo-Saxon model's increase in incomes captured by the top of the distribution.

Income composition is crucial in understanding the evolution of economic inequalities because all types of income have not experienced the same evolution. A major determining fact is that the share of capital income (interest, dividend, rent…) in household income is positively correlated with total income. Besides, this link is even stronger for income from

---

[4] Here, the definition of income is different from the disposable income described above. Piketty (2003) only considers taxable income. As a consequence, the welfare payments and some capital income, which do not directly appear in personal tax returns, and are not imputed by the author, are excluded.

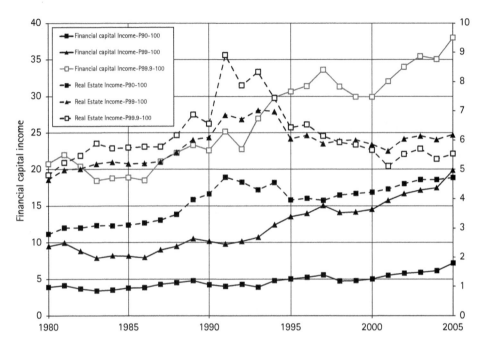

FIGURE 11.3 Share of income from financial and non-financial assets for top fractiles (1980–2005)

Source: World Top Income Database.

financial assets. Figure 11.3 illustrates this evidence and indicates that the contribution of capital income to the top income shares has increased. This evolution has been caused by a rapid increase in capital income over the period. Landais (2009) provides evidence of the income growth by type of income over the period 1998–2005. At the aggregate level, wages have grown by 0.7 per cent per year, rents by 2.2 per cent and financial capital income (interests, dividends...) by almost 4 per cent (+31 per cent in 8 years). Capital income is unequally distributed and, as a consequence, its growth is even larger if we only focus on the sub-sample of households who have a strictly positive capital income. For them, the rise equals 53 per cent between 1998 and 2005.

It is also interesting to do a symmetric analysis and look at the bottom of the distribution. About 3.6 million households were considered to be poor[5] in France in 2010, corresponding to more than 8.2 million individuals. The poverty rate has declined by more than 30 per cent between 1970 and 1985, from almost 18 per cent of households to 14 per cent. The proportion of poor households follows the evolution of unemployment. Thus, we can notice two peaks, in the mid 1990s and after 2008. Poverty gaps follow the same pattern as poverty rates. What are the main characteristics of poor people in France? First, single households and single-parent families are over-represented among poor people. In

---

[5] A person is a situation of monetary poverty if his/her income is below 60 per cent of the median income.

2010, these types of household represent 37 per cent of overall deprived households and their poverty rate is respectively equal to 18.1 and 32.9 per cent (according to the 60 per cent definition). Second, among households with only one adult, the household head is a woman three times out of four. Third, the inactivity of at least one of the two parents is positively correlated with poverty. Among the households with two parents, 60 per cent of one-earner couples are deprived households. Even if employment is negatively correlated with poverty, it does not prevent people from being poor. The number of working poor is highly correlated with economic cycles. Workers with a low level of education and/or with a temporary contract are much more likely to be poor even though they are employed. In 2010, 10.7 per cent of workers with primary education were poor while this share was only 2.9 per cent for workers with tertiary education. The effect of the type of contract goes in the same direction.

The study of the tails of the income distribution presents interesting differences. The reduction of inequality between 1970 and 1990 went with a decline in poverty while the recent increase in inequality has been caused by a rapid growth of the share held by top incomes.

Wealth Inequality

Before turning to individual aspects of inequality, we are going to study the long run history of wealth in France. Piketty (2011) uses national accounts to describe the evolution of household wealth. During the last 30 years, the ratio net private wealth/national income[6] has almost doubled, going from 298 per cent in 1980 to 552 per cent in 2009. If we put into perspective this large increase, we note that the levels reached in the late 2000s are similar to the values reached before World War I. A large part of this increase is due to price effects but long-run mechanisms also explain this evolution. More specifically, the returns to capital are larger than income growth since the beginning of the 1980s. In this context, past wealth and inheritance are bound to play a key role for aggregate wealth accumulation and the structure of lifetime inequality.

What are the consequences in terms of distribution? Has this rise benefited everybody or only a small fraction of the population? Using wealth surveys, we see that wealth is very unequally distributed, much more than income. Over the period 1992–2010 we observe an increase in wealth inequality that mostly arises between 2004 and 2010. Even if the Gini index has been stable at 0.64–0.65 over the period, the inter-decile ratios and the top shares have almost all grown. Besides, the amount of wealth held by the top one per cent has increased by 36 per cent (from 12 to 17 per cent), and the share of the top 10 per cent by 4.8 per cent. Households in the top quartile are 40 times richer than households in the bottom quartile in 2010. Cordier *et al.* (2006) decompose wealth inequality in order to identify its

---

[6] Aggregate private wealth is defined as the market value of all tangible assets (in particular real estate assets) and financial assets owned by private individuals (i.e. households), minus their financial liabilities. We use national income instead of GDP because we want to compare aggregates (wealth and income) that are both net of depreciation. The other difference between GDP and national income is about the income flow between France and the rest of the world. This difference is close to zero for France so using GDP would not significantly modify the evolution.

major determinants. Income and social positions jointly explain half of household wealth. Age also plays a key role in wealth accumulation. Only two factors explain a bigger share in 2004 than in 1992: inherited wealth and house ownership.

Fiscal data reveal that the level of inequality as provided by surveys is underestimated because of sampling and non-sampling errors. Piketty *et al.* (2006) use national samples of estate tax returns. They show that the share of wealth held by the top 10 per cent of the wealth distribution was equal to 60.9 per cent in 1994, and the share held by the top one per cent is slightly more than 21 per cent. Furthermore, the 2011 *Global Wealth Report* produced by Crédit Suisse indicates that there are more than 2.6 million dollar millionaires living in France. This makes France the top European country of residence for millionaires. The evolution of real estate prices, the low level of debt of French households and higher wealth inequality explain this concentration of rich households.

One very crucial dimension of wealth inequality is the source of wealth. There are basically two ways to become rich: either through one's own work or through inheritance. Piketty (2011) demonstrates that inheritance is back in France. More specifically, this paper relies on recent evidence about the long-run evolution of inheritance as a fraction of aggregate wealth. Piketty states that 'modern economic growth did not kill inheritance'. In France, the annual flow of inheritance was around 20–25 per cent of national income between 1820 and 1910, down to less than 5 per cent in 1950, and back up to about 15 per cent by 2010.[7] This result demonstrates that, in France at least, the structure of modern economic growth does not seem to lead to meritocracy but it rather favours past wealth.

Labour Market Inequality

So far, income and wealth have been measured at the household level. We now turn to the individual components of these two variables: labour income and education. These fields are interesting in and of themselves because they might be drivers of social and political impacts but also because they are drivers of household income inequality.

Before examining the extent of earnings inequality, we need to determine the significance of labour market earnings for household income. Though correlated negatively as a share, labour income is still very important for the top of the distribution. If we compute the share of total labour income (wages, salaries and pensions + farm, business and non-business incomes) the importance of labour income is even more striking. It represents more than 90 per cent of total income for the top 10 per cent and still around 80 per cent for the top one per cent. As a consequence, the significance of labour-market earnings for household income inequality is crucial.

The evolution of inequality strongly depends on the sample that is chosen. In most studies regarding wages, only full-time wage-earners are observed. In France over the period 1980–2009, the level of inequality among full-time wage-earners has decreased during the

---

[7] We use national income instead of GDP because we want to compare aggregates (wealth and income) that are both net of depreciation. The other difference between GDP and national income is about the income flow between France and the rest of the world. This difference is close to zero for France so using GDP would not significantly modify the evolution.

1980s and 1990s and has been stable since. The ratio between P90/P10 was 3.3 in 1980 and is now equal to 2.9. This reduction in inequality mainly comes from the bottom of the wage distribution since the ratio P50/P10 is the only one decreasing over the period (from 1.7 to 1.5). Contrary to many OECD countries, the minimum wage is high and it has increased in France over the period. More specifically, it has grown more quickly than the mean wage between 1970 and 1985 and in the mid 2000s.

Focusing on full-time wage-earners can only be misleading because it hides the increasing duality of the French labour market (and as a consequence the role of working hours) and it excludes the self-employed. In OECD (2009), the Gini coefficients for earnings are provided for different samples. In 2000, for full-time wage-earners only, the coefficient is equal to 0.30; it rises to 0.345 if part-time workers are included. Self-employed people make this coefficient grow to 0.358. For these two extended definitions of workforce the Gini coefficient has increased by 6 per cent between 1984 and 2000. In France, almost 50 per cent of earnings variation is explained by variation in working hours, the other half by variation in wage rate. Last, labour market participation is decisive for a full picture of labour market inequalities. Unskilled workers and clerks are much more affected by unemployment than people in intermediate or managerial positions. The unemployment ratio between managers and unskilled workers is between 2.5 and 3.5.

As for income, the analysis of top wage shares is important because it allows us to focus on specific parts of the sample that are crucial to understanding the dynamics of inequalities over time. The slow growth of mean wages[8] hides important disparities along the distribution. Piketty (2003), Landais (2009) and Godechot (2012) demonstrate that there is a transfer of 2 points from the bottom 90 per cent of the wage distribution to the top 10 per cent. Within the top one per cent, wages are booming: +21 per cent for the top 1 per cent and +335 per cent for the top 0.01 per cent.

The evolution described in this section shows that changes in wage inequality during the last decade led to a major break in France. Indeed, the relative stability of the wage hierarchy over the twentieth century has been replaced by an increase in inequality through a transfer to the very top of the distribution. This rise is more modest compared with the evolution in Anglo-Saxon countries[9] but it has contributed to the rise in inequality since the late 1990s.

Educational Inequality

As in many other countries, the educational attainment of French people has increased rapidly over recent decades. More specifically, in 2010, among the 25–34 years olds, the proportion of men who completed tertiary education reached 38.3 per cent as compared to 18.7 per cent for men aged between 55 and 64. The rise for women is even more dramatic since these proportions are 47.2 per cent and 17.8 per cent, respectively. Human capital is probably the main factor explaining the differences of incomes between individuals. As a consequence, whether this increase in educational attainment has benefited everyone is a key question in understanding the mechanisms behind economic inequalities.

[8] Between 2000 and 2009, the annual growth rate of net wages for full-time workers equals 0.49 per cent (source: INSEE).

[9] See Piketty and Saez (2003).

We measured the Gini index for the inequality of years of education by cohort. We observed a continuous decline in the level of inequality across cohorts: from 0.23 for the cohort born before 1930 to 0.122 for the cohort born after 1980. This evolution is representative of the general trend in developed countries (see Meschi and Scervini, 2010).

However, this overall increase in educational attainment must be put into perspective with the role of social background. Albouy and Wanecq (2003) study how the probability of graduating from tertiary education, and more especially from French elite schools, depends on social background. For university (short or long degree course), the authors establish a reduction in the gap between men with opposite social origins. However, for the elite schools, we note a sharp decline in this gap for men born in the 1920s and 1930s but an increase in the role of social background for younger cohorts. As a consequence, the democratization of the French system is partial.

A last aspect we can look at is the link between education and employability. The effect of education on access to jobs is large: the employment rate of men with tertiary education is on average 30 percentage points higher than that of men with primary education. There is no convergence or divergence over the period (1983–2010). However, the recent recession has led to a decrease by 3 percentage points in the low-skilled employment rate. For women, the overall employment rate has grown by 10 percentage points since 1983 (from 50 to 60 per cent). The gap between low-skilled and high-skilled women is slightly larger than that of men but there is a divergence. Better-educated women have seen their employment chances increase while these chances for low-skilled women have remained flat. This contrasts with men who witnessed a decline for the low skilled and a stable rate for the tertiary educated.

After this description of the evolution of inequality for income, wealth, earnings and education, it is important to understand the mechanisms behind this evolution in France since 1980. We have seen that the apparent stability of income inequality at the two endpoints of the period hided a decrease in inequality during the 1980s followed by an increase since the end of the 1990s. Several factors can explain this evolution.

First, examining the evolution of labour market earnings is important because it is the major source of income for a large majority of the population. Between 1980 and 2010, women's labour market participation increased. Moreover, the growth of the minimum wage has been higher than the growth of the mean wage. The decrease of the capital share in GDP between 1974 and 1985 is also a factor in income equalisation. The combination of these effects has contributed to reducing the level of income inequality during the first half of this period (especially at the bottom of the distribution) and it partly explains why the inequality growth started later in France. However, the increase in wage inequality since 1998 tends to indicate that these factors were not sufficiently strong to counter the growing income dispersion. Most classical explanations, like skill-biased technological change or international trade, do not fit with a boom in the top one per cent of the earnings distribution. As other explanatory factors, we would propose a change in social norms concerning the definition and the setting of top wages (higher shares of bonuses and profit-sharing) and also higher tolerance regarding inequalities. Another potential cause relates to Gabaix and Landier's interpretation of the compensation of top CEOs (superstars model[10]). Godechot

---

[10] In a context of strong competition between firms, these are ready to offer high compensations to attract the best CEOs because of their positive impact on the firm's results.

(2012) by contrast emphasizes the role of finance at the very top (0.1 per cent) of the wage distribution.

However, we have seen that the evolution of wage inequality was smoother compared with that of total income. The role of capital income is crucial in this evolution and enables us to explain this gap. The unequal distribution of capital and its growth with respect to the other sources of income helps to understand the upward trend in income inequalities observed since the end of the 1990s. As explained *supra*, wages have grown by 0.7 per cent per year, rents by 2.2 per cent and capital income by almost 4 per cent.

The conclusion of this chapter could be that the non-meritocratic aspects of income, wealth or even education—together with social background—drive inequality. More importantly, they play a stronger role today and can explain part of the recent increase in inequality. Before going on to an in-depth analysis of the effect of the French tax system on the evolution of inequality, we review the impact of inequality on social, political and cultural outcomes.

3. The Impact of Inequality on Social, Political and Cultural Outcomes

The effect of the evolution of inequalities on social, political and cultural outcomes is a key issue of this chapter. The case of France is interesting because of the timing of inequality growth. The increase in income inequality only started at the end of the 1990s. Therefore, the potential impact on these outcomes could only be observed recently. Besides, the reduction of inequality observed during the 1970s and the 1980s, when the trend was upward in many countries, makes the study of its impact even more interesting.

The analysis of social outcomes in developed countries cannot be reduced to a few items. Many fields must be taken into account and among them different indicators and dimensions must be considered. Thus, nine fields are studied in the Gini report: material deprivation; cumulative disadvantage of poverty; social isolation; family; health; housing; crime; well being; and intergenerational mobility. The core result relates to the link between the evolution of these outcomes and the evolution of inequality. But, the role of social gradients (education or income) at any time, as well as the identification of the channels through which inequality could affect these outcomes, matter as well.

We can divide our results into two categories. First, there is an absence of correlation for several social outcomes. Crime, intergenerational mobility and, to a lesser extent material deprivation and family changes, seem to be rather uncorrelated to changes in inequality. The crime rate in France has slightly increased over the period since it was around 50 (per 1,000 inhabitants) in 1980 and it equals 60 in 2010. But this increase hides a sort of cyclical evolution with a peak every ten years. If we only focus on some types of crimes (property crime for instance) or if we use subjective indicators (feeling of safety), the correlation with the evolution of inequality does not become clearer. There are several socio-economic approaches to estimating intergenerational mobility: comparison of parents' and children's occupations;

income or wealth elasticity between parents and children... In France, economic and social mobility seem to have been rather stable over the past decades while income and wealth inequalities have fluctuated. Poverty is multidimensional and can be measured on a monetary basis (see Section 2) or through a more materialistic approach. Thus, it emerges that material deprivation seems less correlated with inequality than monetary poverty. During the 1970s and the 1980s, both income inequality and poverty have decreased. Since 1985, the poverty rate has remained stable and material deprivation has declined—while income inequality has started to rise since the end of the 1990s. For the outcomes regarding family, the statement regarding the absence of correlation must be moderated. Indeed, the reduction of marriage and fertility rates since 1980 are continuous but the growth of single-parent families (from 720,000 in 1968 to 1.76 million in 2005) explains part of the compositional changes at the bottom of the income distribution. Indeed, the working and living conditions of single-parent families are less stable and more difficult. More specifically, 13.9 per cent of single parent families were poor in 2006 while this share equals 6.2 per cent for other couples with children.

Secondly, several outcomes like health, well being, or housing seem to be slightly more correlated. Health indicators like life expectancy or self-reported state of health are subjected to a continuous improvement over the period 1980–2010 but they are very sensitive to social gradients. However, the gap in life expectancy across categories of workers seems to react to changes in inequality with a delay (Table 11.1). The growing gap in life expectancy between unskilled and high-skilled workers during the 1990s (when income inequality was stable) may be seen as the consequence of the high level of inequality in the 1970s and the 1980s. Symmetrically, the current deterioration of the quality of life of unskilled workers, partly caused by economic factors, could affect life expectancy in the coming years. For well being, people with more education report a higher degree of satisfaction with their lives and the gap with respect to the bottom of the distribution has grown slightly over the past decade. Other indicators of well being, like the suicide rate or alcohol consumption, indicate an improvement over the past decades but we cannot cross these evolutions with social gradients. For housing, the mechanisms are complex. The share of owners in the overall population has increased by 5 points between 1985 and 2008 (from 52.9 per cent to 57.8 per cent) but it has declined by 12 points for the bottom quartile of the income distribution partly because of a change in the composition of this population. Moreover, since 1996, housing expenses have increased for all households but more rapidly for low-income households. This may negatively affect the other items of their budget: travel; leisure; but also health and education. Nevertheless, even for this category of outcomes, the magnitude of the effect is rather limited and the transition from correlation to causality is unclear.

The weak correlation in time should not be interpreted as a total absence of impact of inequality on these social outcomes. For all the outcomes, social gradients do play a role. People at the top of the income distribution or with a high level of education are healthier, happier and live in high quality housing. They are also at less risk of poverty and less affected by social isolation. However, this study shows that the existing gap in 1980 has not significantly evolved during the past decades.

Two effects can explain this relative absence of correlation: timing and magnitude. First, contrary to many countries, the increase in inequality in France is very recent. The problem for our analysis is that it takes time for inequality to have an effect on social outcomes especially on dimensions like health or family. The second explanation is about the magnitude

Table 11.1 Life expectancy at 35 by sex and social category

	High-skilled, Executive [1]	Intermediate job	Farmer	Tradesman, shopkeeper and business owner	Clerk	Unskilled worker [2]	Out of LF (excl. retired)	All	Gap [1–2]
Men									
1976–1984	41.7	40.5	40.3	39.6	37.2	35.7	27.7	37.8	6.0
1983–1991	43.7	41.6	41.7	41.0	38.6	37.3	27.5	39.2	6.4
1991–1999	45.8	43.0	43.6	43.1	40.1	38.8	28.4	40.8	7.0
2000–2008	47.2	45.1	44.6	44.8	42.3	40.9	30.4	42.8	6.3
[2000–2008]–[1976–1984]	5.5	4.6	4.3	5.2	5.1	5.2	2.7	5.0	
Women									
1976–1984	47.5	46.4	45.7	46.0	45.6	44.4	44.3	45.0	3.1
1983–1991	49.7	48.1	46.8	47.4	47.4	46.3	45.4	46.4	3.4
1991–1999	49.8	49.5	48.8	48.8	48.7	47.2	47.1	48.0	2.6
2000–2008	51.7	51.2	49.6	50.3	49.9	48.7	47.0	49.4	3.0
[2000–2008]–[1976–1984]	4.2	4.8	3.9	4.3	4.3	4.3	2.7	4.4	

Source: Permanent demographic sample (INSEE), extracted from Blanpain (2011).

of inequality. The recent upward trend of income dispersion has 'just' cancelled the decrease observed during the 1980s and it does not make France a very unequal country even if this growth is substantial. This characteristic probably leads to an absence of strength in the links we are trying to identify.

4. POLITICAL AND CULTURAL OUTCOMES

The relationship between inequality and political or cultural outcomes is probably even more complex to determine. On top of the timing and magnitude effects already described for social outcomes, we can add the role of institutions as another difficulty in interpreting the results we obtained. The political indicators we look at are political and civic participation, the share of unionized workers and trust in institutions. To describe the values of French people, we use the vote for extreme parties, the opinion regarding immigration and inequalities as proxies.

For political participation, we note a decreasing trend for local elections but a relative stability for general elections. More specifically, for general elections the turnout has been stable at around 70–80 per cent and it reached a peak for the 2007 presidential elections. For local polls, there is a downward trend for the cantons and regions (especially in 2010 and 2011) but stability for municipal elections. Another way to express political opinions is to be member of a union. The share of unionized workers, low in France, has decreased continuously over the past decades and it reached 7.6 per cent in 2008. Trust in institutions (Table 11.2) is complementary to political and social participation because it measures how much people believe in the institutions that are supposed to represent them. The level of confidence follows a sort of U-shaped curve between 1980 and 2008, whatever the institutions we consider (parliament, justice, government, political parties...). Inequality may affect political and civic participation in two ways: by discouraging and by encouraging citizens. Even if the first channel seems more plausible (high inequality may make people believe that politicians cannot help them), inequality can also lead to political action (not necessarily peaceful when it reaches an unacceptable level). The relative stagnation of the French economy (high level of unemployment, slow growth of income...) maybe fits more with this 'discouragement' channel. But the economic situation of France only explains part of political outcomes. Culture and institutions are at least as important. As a consequence, the results are quite difficult to interpret because the discouragement motive we could invoke does not fit the results.

The analysis of political values leads to a similar interpretation about the weak relationship between the evolution of inequality and the different outcomes that are studied. More specifically, the vote for extreme political parties has been fairly stable since 1990 but it significantly varies depending on the type of elections. During the same period, opinion about immigration has improved, whether we measure it by views about immigration policies or, more generally, from the impact of immigrants on the economy or on the country. However, the satisfaction and, to a lesser extent, the degree of trust about the EU have declined (from 61 per cent of satisfaction in 1973 to 46 per cent in 2011). Finally, opinion relative to inequalities has remained roughly similar. In 1990 and 2008, around 40 per cent of French people thought that incomes should be made more equal than they are; one respondent in six is

Table 11.2 Trust in others and in institutions by education (1981–2008)

Trust in institutions	All				Q1				Q2				Q3				Q4			
	1981	1990	1999	2008	1981	1990	1999	2008	1981	1990	1999	2008	1981	1990	1999	2008	1981	1990	1999	2008
Parliament																				
Complete trust	6.7	4.8	2.8	3.9	9.1	9.4	2.4	3.2	7.2	0.5	3.7	3.0	7.1	1.4	2.3	2.3	3.8	8.6	3.2	6.8
Quite a lot	49.5	43.5	37.7	47.5	52.2	35.9	37.0	40.2	52.6	39.9	33.4	45.9	47.1	47.1	34.8	49.6	46.8	46.4	46.1	53.8
Not very much	30.8	34.5	36.1	36.3	27.8	29.2	33.5	40.9	25.3	38.0	30.1	36.0	33.4	39.1	37.6	39.6	36.2	33.2	36.9	29.5
None at all	13.0	17.3	23.4	12.3	11.4	25.5	27.1	15.6	14.9	21.6	26.8	15.1	12.4	12.4	25.3	8.5	13.2	11.8	13.9	9.9
Government:																				
Complete trust	–	–	–	2.1	–	–	–	2.9	–	–	–	2.1	–	–	–	0.9	–	–	–	2.5
Quite a lot	–	–	–	32.0	–	–	–	32.7	–	–	–	29.1	–	–	–	32.2	–	–	–	34.2
Not very much	–	–	–	38.8	–	–	–	33.8	–	–	–	38.7	–	–	–	4.9	–	–	–	40.6
None at all	–	–	–	27.1	–	–	–	30.7	–	–	–	30.1	–	–	–	25.1	–	–	–	22.7
Political Parties:																				
Complete trust	–	–	–	0.8	–	–	–	0.8	–	–	–	0.7	–	–	–	0.5	–	–	–	1.3
Quite a lot	–	–	–	15.4	–	–	–	18.8	–	–	–	13.5	–	–	–	12.9	–	–	–	16.8
Not very much	–	–	–	52.8	–	–	–	38.9	–	–	–	53.7	–	–	–	59.9	–	–	–	58.2
None at all	–	–	–	31.0	–	–	–	41.8	–	–	–	32.1	–	–	–	26.7	–	–	–	23.7

Distribution of years of education

Table 11.2 Continued

Trust in institutions	All 1981	All 1990	All 1999	All 2008	Q1 1981	Q1 1990	Q1 1999	Q1 2008	Q2 1981	Q2 1990	Q2 1999	Q2 2008	Q3 1981	Q3 1990	Q3 1999	Q3 2008	Q4 1981	Q4 1990	Q4 1999	Q4 2008
Justice system:																				
Complete trust	8.4	7.4	5.3	7.1	8.3	13.6	7.2	8.6	12.2	5.8	4.2	4.6	7.0	3.0	6.7	7.3	6.1	8.0	3.6	8.1
Quite a lot	48.0	50.1	40.5	48.5	44.6	43.0	39.1	45.6	49.6	45.3	35.0	47.2	49.2	51.3	39.2	47.4	48.1	59.3	48.7	53.5
Not very much	34.2	31.6	34.7	35.5	37.7	27.1	32.4	32.5	28.6	35.6	37.3	37.3	35.1	36.7	35.8	39.1	35.8	26.6	33.0	33.2
None at all	9.5	10.9	19.5	8.9	7.4	16.4	21.3	13.3	9.6	13.3	23.6	10.9	8.8	13.8	25.1	9.1	10.1	6.2	14.7	5.2
Others:																				
Most people can be trusted	24.0	22.8	22.2	27.2	13.2	10.6	12.7	13.0	20.0	18.0	19.3	24.6	24.1	25.1	21.7	30.7	38.9	36.1	35.2	39.8
Can't be too careful	76.1	77.2	77.8	72.8	86.8	89.4	87.3	87.0	80.0	82.0	80.8	75.4	75.9	74.9	78.3	69.3	61.1	63.9	64.8	60.2

Distribution of years of education

(Continued)

Note: the population is ranked by quartiles of years of education with Q1 the lowest quartile.
Source: European Values Study 1981–2008 Longitudinal Data File. GESIS Data Archive.

in favour of a complete equalization of incomes. According to Björklund and Jäntti (2011), tolerance about inequalities is much lower in France than in Nordic or Anglo-Saxon countries. This summary of results indicates that political values depend not only on the level of inequality but also on what people think causes it.

Once again, social gradients like income or education play a role since rich/educated people are more politically active (through their vote or their participation in associations) and tend to trust institutions more but also the other members of society. Moreover, opinions regarding immigration or the level of trust in EU institutions is more positive for educated/rich people while less educated people are more frequently in favour of income equalization.

The general conclusion of these sections is that the impact of the evolution of inequality on social, political and cultural outcomes in France has been rather limited. Some outcomes are more affected than others but for all of them social gradients matter. The timing, but also the magnitude of this increase in inequality, may explain the weak correlation we observe.

5. EFFECTIVENESS OF POLICIES IN COMBATING INEQUALITIES

Labour market policies are crucial for inequality issues given the importance of labour income for most households. The minimum wage partly explains the evolution of inequality and notably the decline of inequality between 1970 and 1990. More specifically, from 1970 to 1983, the minimum wage increased by 70 per cent while the average wage only grew by 35 per cent.

The general evolution of the French labour market tends to indicate that employment protection has decreased over the past decades. In the late 1980s, some policies have average undermined the rigidities of the labour market by favouring part-time jobs, short-term contracts and temporary jobs. As a result, the French labour market became more and more dual, with a large share of protected jobs (85 per cent) and a minority of flexible jobs.

Other policies have affected the French labour market over recent decades. During the last 20 years, the main goal of labour market policies in France was to enrich the labour content of growth. In the 1990s, policy-makers tried to fulfil this aim through tax cuts for low-wage workers (300,000 jobs created), for personal workers (100,000 jobs) or for part-time jobs. At the end of the 1990s, the socialist government in power decided to enrich the job content of growth through sharing labour and through public jobs. Firstly, they created 200,000 public short-term contracts (5 years) to increase youth employment. Secondly, they reduced the number of hours worked per week from 39 to 35 (350,000 jobs). During the 2000s, the niche job markets became the main target. Thus, the government created tax cuts for personal workers (no detailed evaluation), for firms in special urban areas (10,000 jobs created but at a high unit cost), short-term contracts for workers above 55 (no impact), tax cuts for extra hours or new status for the self-employed ('auto-entrepreneurs'). These policies have led to a rapid decrease of unemployment (from 8.9 per cent in 2004 to 7.4 per cent in 2008) but these solutions have been inefficient in fighting unemployment during the economic crisis.

Taxation is the main political and economic tool for fighting inequality because it enables a correction of income differences due to inequality in initial endowments and market forces, while preserving the role played by the price system. As a consequence, taxation may considerably affect disposable income. The levels and types of taxes, but also the deductions and subsidies, must be considered in order to evaluate the redistributive effect of a country's tax system. In this chapter, we present a detailed analysis of the redistributive characteristics of the French tax system. More specifically, we provide estimates of the average tax rate for each part of the income distribution.

The historical importance of taxation in France probably makes the study of its tax system and of its redistributive aspects more relevant than for many other countries. More specifically, the ratio 'tax revenue / GDP' was 44.2 per cent in France in 2011.[11] France is the third-ranked OECD country in terms of the importance of tax revenue, ahead of Finland and Belgium but behind Sweden and Denmark. Since 1965, the amount of tax revenue (expressed as a percentage of GDP) has considerably increased. Most of this evolution occurred between 1975 and 1985. During this decade, total tax receipts grew by 8 percentage points from 35 to 43 per cent. Since 1985, we observe a relative stability: the slight rise by 3 points between 1985 and 2000 has been compensated for by a decline of 2 points during the last decade.

The decomposition of tax revenues by origin enables us to have a first intuition of the redistributive characteristics of the French tax system. Indeed, all types of taxes do not have the same effect on income redistribution and as a consequence the weight of each type of taxes is an indicator of its degree of progressivity. According to the OECD tax database, employers' and employees' social security contributions (SSC) account for 40 per cent of the overall tax receipts; taxes on goods and services account for 26 per cent; and taxes on income, profits and capital gains for 20 per cent. The remaining 15 per cent is explained by taxes on property, payroll, workforce, and other taxes. The structure of the French tax system has been fairly stable over the last three decades. One important change occurred in 1997 when part of the SSC (financing health and family benefits particularly) was replaced by personal income taxes. Concretely, the government increased by 4 points the 'Contribution Sociale Généralisée[12]' (CSG), a proportional income tax created in 1990, in order to reduce SSC. Therefore, a specificity of the French tax system is that the income tax is actually composed of two taxes: the 'original' progressive tax (created in 1914) and a proportional tax (created in 1990). One of the differences between these two taxes regards the tax base (much larger for the proportional tax). As a consequence, in 2010, the revenues of the proportional tax—with a flat rate of 8 per cent—are twice those of the progressive tax, which has a top marginal rate of 41 per cent. Actually, one could even divide the progressive tax into four or five types of taxes, given the differences in the rules applied to each kind of income (earnings, capital gains, dividends, interests...).

If we compare France with other OECD countries we note the large weight of SSC in overall tax receipts, the highest among the OECD countries. The revenues coming from indirect

---

[11]   OECD tax database

[12]   This income tax is proportional and affects all sources of income: earnings (7.5 per cent); unemployment and social security benefits (6.2 per cent); retirement and invalidity pensions (6.6 per cent); capital income (8.5 per cent); and lottery/winnings (9.5 per cent).

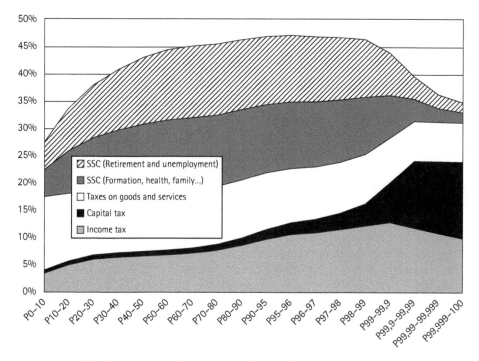

FIGURE 11.4 Effective tax rate (in % of gross income) per income fractile

Source: Landais, Piketty and Saez (2011).

taxes are also more important than the average, while the direct taxes (personal and corporate taxes) are lower than the average. More specifically, in many countries, the tax revenues coming from personal income tax are two to three times bigger than in France. A last particularity of the French tax system is about the implicit tax rate on labour income, one of the highest in the European Union (Eurostat, 2011).

The progressivity of the French tax system has been extensively studied by Landais, Piketty and Saez (2011). The objective of this analysis is to consider all types of taxes in France and to estimate the effective tax rate for different levels of income. A parliamentary report estimates that the average rate of income taxation is below 20 per cent for the top one per cent of the income distribution. However, this is the first study that tackles this issue by considering all types of taxes and all tax deductions and exemptions.

Figure 11.4 depicts the main result: the French tax system is not progressive. More specifically, when we consider SSC, income and capital taxes, as well as indirect taxes like taxes on goods and services and local taxes, the average tax rate (as expressed as a percentage of national income) is 49 per cent. More precisely, if we consider total income before taxes and if we rank the French population[13] from the poorest individual to the richest we note that for the bottom 50 per cent of the distribution (with a gross monthly income less than €2,200), the effective tax rate goes from 41 to 48 per cent and is on average 45 per cent. The following

---

[13] Given that our focus is at the individual level, we have to make some assumption for income measured at the household level. That is why we present an example of a married couple for whom capital income is measured at the household level and not individually. Precisely, we use a married

40 per cent of the distribution has a tax rate between 48 and 50 per cent. Actually, for a large middle class with a gross monthly income ranging from €1,700 to €6,900, the tax rate is stable. Then, for the top 5 per cent and even more for the top one per cent of the income distribution, the effective tax rate declines sharply and falls to 35 per cent for the top 0.1 per cent (which is 50,000 individuals out of 50 million).

This illustration can also show the role played by each tax. Taxes on goods and services are regressive since the proportion paid by the poorest categories is higher (15 per cent for P0–P90 against 5 per cent for P99–P100). The result is similar for the SSC (25 per cent against 5 per cent) and this is explained by the larger share of the self-employed at the top of the distribution. Nevertheless, the case of the SSC is noteworthy because some of these contributions finance social benefits received by workers (retirement or unemployment pensions). The fact that only labour income contributes to this spending may make sense because workers only can benefit from these transfers.[14] However, SSC also finances universal benefits (like family or health allowances) that are open to all French residents. A priori, there is no reason for this last category of allowances to be financed only by labour income.

The regressivity of these taxes should be compensated by the progressivity of taxes on income and capital. We do observe a progressivity from taxes on capital[15] (corporate, real-estate, wealth and inheritance taxes). However, this is not the case for income, mainly because of the accumulation of fiscal deductions and exemptions. More specifically, a large part of capital income is not included in the progressive schedule of income taxation. Most capital income is subject to the proportional tax rate. Thus, individuals receiving the same income can pay a different amount of tax because the nature of the income differs. As a consequence, the tax system, which is the main tool for fighting socio-economic inequality, does not even reach its minimum objective of proportionality in France.

Bozio *et al.* (2012) extend this analysis by studying the evolution of progressivity over the last fifteen years. The French tax system was already regressive in 1997, especially because of the weakness of the progressive income tax in the entire tax system and because of the importance of indirect taxes and SSC. However, the authors demonstrate that the tax reforms introduced between 1997 and 2012, and especially between 2002 and 2007, have reinforced this lack of progressivity. During this period, the overall tax rate, expressed as a percentage of national income, fell by 0.6 points but the decrease amounted to 3.6 points for the top one per cent of the income distribution. The consequences in terms of inequality are of course very serious and it could also lead to a tax revolt. This study clearly shows that the rise in the inequality of taxation on disposable income since the end of the 1990s is not only due to a greater dispersion in market incomes but also to a failure of the French tax system.

More precisely, we can decompose the period 1997–2012 into three sub-periods (following the changes of government): 1997–2002; 2002–2007; and 2007–2012. Between 1997

---

couple, whose individual capital income is equal to half the household capital income. The results presented in this chapter relate to the population aged between 18 and 65, working at least 80 per cent of the full time standard. This sample is the most relevant to estimate permanent income inequality and also the progressivity of the tax system. Estimates based on different samples provide similar results (see appendix to Chapter 1 <www.revolution-fiscale.fr>). Landais *et al.* (2011).

[14] However, the retirement contributions of low-wage workers subsidises the retirement pensions of high-skilled workers because of the gap in life expectancy across workers.

[15] Even if in 2007 both wealth and estate tax were cut.

and 2002, several major changes in the tax system were implemented: the reduction of the weekly working hours to 35; the decrease in social security contributions for low-paid jobs; the switch of part of SSC to income tax; the reduction in VAT; and several modifications to income tax. During this period, the overall tax rate decreased from 47.7 per cent to 46.3 per cent, partially driven by rapid economic growth. This decline was more significant at the bottom of the distribution, mainly because of the reduction in SSC for low-paid jobs. However, the impact of this policy on workers' purchasing power has been limited since the decline in SSC went together with the reduction of working hours, and therewith earnings. At the top of the distribution, the slight growth of the tax rate is essentially due to the increasing receipts from corporate tax driven by the cyclical rise in profits.

The second five-year period explains almost all the general increase in regressivity in the French tax system over the period 1997–2012 and yet, there many fewer reforms than between 1997 and 2002. The average tax rate (on primary income) was stable. However, the implementation of a tax shield[16] (a maximum tax rate) and the fall in income tax benefited the top of the distribution. Thus, all the population above the median of the primary income distribution experienced a reduction in the tax rate but the decline was much more significant for the top one per cent (which fell by more than 2 percentage points).

From 2007 to 2012, a multitude of tax reforms were implemented but part of them were cancelled during the period or compensated for by other reforms. More specifically, the fiscal shield was reinforced (to 50 per cent instead of 60 per cent) but then cancelled; the same happened for the tax deductibility for mortgage interest payments. The proportional income tax (CSG) was increased and a tax on high incomes was created, tax cuts were implemented for extra working hours and in the restaurant industry…But, all these reforms cancelled each other out and the authors do not detect any effect on the redistributive aspect of the tax system when they compare the endpoints of the period. However, this apparent stability hides contradictory evolution, depending on the source of income: capital or earnings. Indeed, the massive cuts in wealth tax have been partially compensated by rises of taxes affecting the top of the income distribution. In the end, households at the top of the distribution in terms of wealth but not in terms of earnings are the main winners of these reforms, whereas households with high earnings but no wealth are the main losers. The timing of the implementation of these reforms also matters. It would be misleading not to take into account the length of time over which these policies were in place. Indeed, all the tax reforms that negatively affect the top of the distribution were implemented during the last months of the five-year period (essentially in 2011 and 2012). So, the tax cuts have been in place for almost all the five-year period.

A project of the newly elected government was to increase the marginal tax rate for individuals earning more than €1 million to 75 per cent. This bill has been held to be as unconstitutional and a new law will be proposed in 2013. In any event, this new tax bracket is not likely to change the lack of progressivity of the tax system. Indeed, most capital income (dividends, interests, capital gains…) is exempt from this tax and it will be computed at the individual and not at the household level. The government estimates that the tax will only affect 1,500 people with a total tax receipt of €210 million per year. More generally, the new socialist government cancelled part of the fiscal policies

---

[16] The amount of tax paid by a taxpayer cannot be greater than 60 per cent of his/her income in taxes.

implemented by the previous government, especially the cuts on wealth and inheritance taxes. Without recent data it is difficult to know precisely if the tax system has become more progressive. However, income tax has not been deeply modified and the tax base remains the same.

The failure of the tax system has important consequences for inequalities since taxation increases market income dispersion. More importantly, it can also lead to distrust for the system of taxes and transfers and, more generally, for the political institutions, especially in France where tolerance for inequality is low.

Do social expenditures compensate for the failure of the French tax system regarding its redistributive effect? Social expenditures are the other side of transfers and they may play a key role in the fight against inequalities and poverty by targeting populations at risk and/or provide highly redistributive goods or services. Even if the overall expenditure does not enable us to capture the aims of social policies, it is a rather good indicator of government's willingness to pursue redistribution. The impact of social expenditures on inequality depends on two factors: its progressivity (a transfer is progressive if it proportionally decreases when income increases) and its weight in the overall household income. Thus, every social expenditures, means-tested or not, reduces inequality.

Total expenditures have increased by 9 per cent between 1980 and 2010, going from 26 per cent of GDP in 1985 to 28.4 per cent in 2010. Most of the increase is imputable to the old age pension (+46 per cent) and health care (+34 per cent). By contrast, the share of unemployment benefits and social welfare, disability benefits and survivor pensions has decreased over the period. The causes of increases or decreases vary a lot from one item to another. For old age pensions, health care, as well as survivor pensions, the changes are mainly due to demographic forces. The 'boom and bust' of economic growth mainly explains the variations in unemployment benefits.

Not all social expenditure is means tested in France. For instance, family benefits, health care or survivors' pensions—around 40 per cent of total social spending—do not depend on the household's or individual's income. On the other hand, social assistance, housing benefits and disability benefits are means tested. Last, in order to be eligible for unemployment or old age pensions, people must have contributed for a certain period of time. The main reforms affecting social expenditure since 1980 relate to unemployment and old age pensions[17]. In these two fields, the balance between rights and duties has changed in order to reduce budget deficits. More specifically, the recent reform of unemployment insurance have reduced the length and the amount of the benefit. Moreover, the duty to look for work has been strengthened. Since 1990, the pension system has been affected by similar reforms since successive governments have modified two parameters, in particular: the minimum contribution period (from 150 quarters for the 1934 cohort to 164 for the 1952 cohort) and the normal pension age (from 60 to 62, when the retiree reaches full entitlement). Other modifications have been introduced, such as a reduction in the pension rate where there is a missing quarter, the lengthening of the reference period for the benefit calculation (from 10 to 25 years in the private sector), and a stronger link between the pensions of civil servants and workers in the private sector.

---

[17] Describing all reforms related to social policies is beyond the scope of this chapter. The country report provides more detailed information.

Cazenave *et al.* (2011) show that social spending[18] explains, overall, 66 per cent of the reduction of income inequality in 2010 (against 34 per cent because of taxation). Family benefits represent 26 per cent of this diminution, housing benefits 19 per cent and the different components of social assistance (minimum income, minimum pension for the elderly and disabled, etc.) 17 per cent. The authors also demonstrate that the progressivity of social expenditures has decreased between 1990 and 2010. Most of this evolution has been caused by the way transfers have evolved each year. Indeed, most of them follow inflation but, over the period, incomes have grown faster than inflation. As a consequence, even if the purchasing power of the beneficiaries has not fallen, the gap with respect to average income has grown. The evolution of social policies seems to go hand in hand with that of taxation, since its overall progressivity has declined during the past decades.

6. Conclusions

In this chapter, we have seen that France is distinctive for several reasons. First, the timing of inequality growth in France has been different from many countries, since income inequality started to rise only at the end of the 1990s. One of the consequences is that the effect on social, political and cultural outcomes has been more recent and rather limited. The magnitude of the change in inequality may also contribute to the weak correlations we observe. Last, but not least, the role of taxation of France is noteworthy. The importance of tax revenue is very large, but more importantly, the overall tax system is not progressive, since people at the top of the distribution pay (proportionally) less taxes than people at the bottom. This feature, that has been reinforced during the 2000s, partly explains the rise in inequality and especially the growth of top income shares.

References

Albouy, V. and Wanecq, T. (2003), 'Les inégalités sociales d'accès aux grandes écoles', *Economie et Statistique*, vol. 361, p. 27–52.

Björklund A. and Jäntti M. (2011), 'SNS Välfärdsrapport: Inkomstfördelningen i Sverige', *SNS förlag*.

Blanpain, N. (2011), 'L'espérance de vie s'accroît, les inégalités sociales face à la mort demeurent', INSEE Première, vol. 1372.

Bozio, A., Dauvergne, R., Fabre, B., Goupille, J. and Meslin, O. (2012), '*Fiscalité et redistribution en France 1997-2012*, Paris: Institut des Politiques Publiques.

Cazenave, M.-C., Duval, J., Eidelman, A., Langumier, F., and Vicard, A. (2011), 'La redistribution: état des lieux en 2010 et évolution depuis vingt ans', *INSEE France Portrait Social* 2011, 87–101.

---

[18] The definition of social expenditures is different from the OECD classification. In Cazenave *et al.* (2011), social spending based on an insurance mechanism (old age pensions, health and unemployment) are accounted for beforehand with the other sources of income (labour and capital). Here, we focus 'only' on social expenditures with the aim of reducing inequality: housing; family; social assistance, etc.

Crédit Suisse. (2011), *Global Wealth Report,* Zurich, Credit Suisse AG.

Eurostat (2011), *Taxation Trends in the European Union,* Luxembourg: Eurostat, European Commission.

Gabaix, X. and Landier, A. (2008), 'Why has CEO pay increased so much?', *Quarterly Journal of Economics,* vol. 123 (1), 49–100.

Godechot, O. (2012), 'Is finance responsible for the rise in wage inequality in France?' *Socio-economic Review,* vol. 10 (2), 1–24.

Landais, C. (2009), 'Top incomes in France (1998-2006): Booming inequalities?', *PSE working paper.*

Landais, C., Piketty, T. and Saez, E. (2011), *Pour une révolution fiscale—Un impôt sur le revenu pour le XXIème siècle,* Paris: Editions du Seuil.

Meschi, E. and Scervini, F. (2010), 'New Dataset of Educational Inequality', *GINI Discussion Paper* No. 3.

OECD (2009), *Divided We Stand—Why Inequality Keeps Rising,* Paris: OECD.

Piketty, T. (2003), 'Income inequality in France, 1901-1998', *Journal of Political Economy,* vol. 111 (5), 1004–1042.

Piketty, T. (2011), 'On the long-run evolution of inheritance: France 1820-2050', *Quarterly Journal of Economics,* vol. 61 (3), 1071–1131.

Piketty, T., Postel-Vinay, G. and Rosenthal, J-L. (2006), 'Wealth concentration in a developing economy: Paris and France, 1807-1994', *American Economic Review,* vol. 96 (1), 236–256.

Piketty T., and Saez, E. (2003), 'Income inequality in the United States, 1913-1998', *Quarterly Journal of Economics,* vol. 118 (1), 1–39.

CHAPTER 12

....

GERMANY: RISING INEQUALITY AND THE TRANSFORMATION OF RHINE CAPITALISM

....

GIACOMO CORNEO, SONJA ZMERLI,[*] AND

REINHARD POLLAK

1. INTRODUCTION[1]

....

In the 1980s, Germany consisted of two separate states with different economic systems: the Federal Republic of Germany (FRG), a member of NATO with a population of almost 62 million; and the German Democratic Republic (GDR), a member of the Warsaw Pact with a population of about 17 million. In the following, we only deal with the FRG during the 1980s and with both the East (the former GDR and West Berlin) and the West (the rest) after reunification—which occurred on 3 October 1990.

The economic system of the FRG during the 1980s can be described as a corporatist variant of capitalism, referred to as Rhine capitalism. It has two distinctive traits. The first is cooperative industrial relations, both at the firm level—with work councils and co-determination in large firms—and at the national level—with comprehensive industry-wide wage agreements struck between employer representatives and trade unions. The second is a highly developed social security system of the Bismarckian variety, strongly relying on the equivalence principle, and strongly determined by the work history and family circumstances of the insured. In conditions close to full employment, as they prevailed

[*] Sonja Zmerli wishes to express her gratitude to Ylva Norén Bretzer and to the School of Public Administration at Gothenburg University who generously hosted her as a guest researcher during fall 2012, and where parts of the first version of this chapter were prepared.

[1] This chapter is based on the corresponding GINI German country report which encompasses a multitude of further in-depth analyses and can be downloaded at www.gini-research.org/CR-Germany.

in Germany during the three decades after World War II, Rhine capitalism was successful in providing insurance against income shocks and restraining long-term income disparities.

Since reunification, the German economic system has undergone far-reaching changes, involving the hybridization of the corporatist model inherited from pre-reunification FRG with elements that are borrowed from the Anglo-Saxon world of capitalism: de-unionization; privatizations; minimum wages in some sectors; a kind of earned income tax credit; declining public pensions; subsidization of private retirement savings; and a stronger emphasis on shareholder value. As we will show in this chapter, this transformation has come with a substantial increase in income inequality that came to the fore during the first half of the last decade. At the same time, political disenchantment, social intolerance and demands for redistributive policies have become more common.

The FRG of the 1980s was one of the most affluent and egalitarian countries in the world. Average income was higher in West Germany than in France or in the Netherlands and only the Scandinavian countries exhibited a more even income distribution. The integration in 1990 of the GDR into the political structure of the more affluent FRG implied that reunified Germany was starting with a lower level of per-capita GDP than West Germany had in 1990. Still, at the beginning of the 1990s, reunified Germany had a higher level of per capita GDP in current prices than France and the Netherlands. Reunification also produced an immediate effect on income inequality: on the one hand, the population of West Germany was merged with a poorer population, which tended to increase inequality; on the other hand, that poorer population had more evenly distributed incomes, which tended to reduce inequality. As a result, just after reunification, Germany still exhibited an income distribution that was quite egalitarian by international comparison.

After reunification, the macro-economic performance of Germany has been on the whole rather poor until about 2006. German GDP growth has been low, not only as compared with former decades but also by international standards. In terms of GDP per capita in current prices, reunified Germany has been surpassed by Austria, Belgium, and the Netherlands, and it has been caught by France. The disposable income of private households, except for some growth years in the second half of the 1990s, has stagnated most of the time. In real terms, median household equivalent net income in 2008 was only 5 per cent higher than in 1991.[2]

A high unemployment rate accompanied slow economic growth in the fifteen years that followed reunification. The unemployment rate, measured according to the official German definition, increased from 7.3 per cent in 1991 to 13 per cent in 2005.[3] Since then, however, unemployment has substantially declined and reached again the level it had at the time of reunification.

The number of working people in 2005 was about the same as it was in 1991. After 2005, employment grew rapidly. In 2010, there were about 1.6 million working people more compared to 2005,[4] employment in Germany has thus increased by about 4 per cent from 1991 to 2010. However, since average work hours per employed person have substantially decreased,

---

[2] Own calculation based on German SOEP data. Unless stated otherwise, all statistical facts mentioned in this chapter appear in publications of the German Federal Statistical Office.

[3] Unemployment measured according to the harmonized OECD definition is lower, but its evolution is similar.

[4] The entire employment growth occurred in the service sector.

total working hours have actually declined by 4 per cent from 1991 to 2010. The evolution of employment was very different for the employees and the self-employed: while the number of employees increased by only 2 per cent, the number of self-employed persons increased by more than 25 per cent. Moreover, the labour market underwent a dualization process, entailing the rise of a large segment of badly-paid and unstable jobs, most of them in the service sector.

Labour's share in German national income declined between 1991 and 2010 from 71 per cent to 66.3 per cent, the bulk of the decline occurring in the period 2000–2007. Correspondingly, entrepreneurial and property income increased. In real terms, employees' compensation increased very modestly between 1991 and 2010. Average gross hourly wages increased in real terms during the 1990s, as employees in the regions of the former GDR reduced the pay gap that separated them from their counterparts in the West. Since 2000, average real hourly wages have stagnated in Germany.

The structure of aggregate demand has changed significantly since the beginning of the 2000s: while consumption and investment, both private and public, have stagnated, the current account has thrived. Since 2004, a trade surplus of the order of 5 to 6 per cent of GDP has been common for Germany. The share of German production that is sold abroad almost doubled during the last two decades: exports represent now about 50 per cent of GDP, while they represented only about 26 per cent of GDP in 1991.

The share of GDP obtained from services has increased, while the shares of agriculture and manufacturing have declined. However, as compared to other countries, the relative decline of manufacturing has been less pronounced in Germany and its share of GDP is high by international standards. Manufacturing is directly responsible for about one quarter of all jobs in Germany, for most of the exports and for Germany's current account surplus. German manufacturers often specialize in high-technology productions, invest heavily in R&D and benefit from a wide range of government programmes to support scientific research and innovation. Large companies act as multinational enterprises with substantial foreign direct investment (FDI) across the entire globe. Most value added in German manufacturing comes, however, from small and medium-size enterprises. They are often deeply rooted in the territory where they produce and, at the same time, have successfully outsourced part of their production to producers in Eastern Europe and Asia.

Typically, industrial relations in manufacturing firms are peaceful and characterized by a cooperative attitude. In large companies, co-determination is mandated by law. The strong performance of German manufacturing relies upon institutions that favour the rise and durability of a network of long-term relationships based on mutual trust. In particular, the banking sector is characterized by the strong presence of local public and mutual savings banks that support the expansion strategies of small and medium-size enterprises. Furthermore, German manufacturers benefit from a dual system of education that combines schooling with vocational training in firms. This system has proven to be an effective way to foster human capital investment, limit youth unemployment and provide firms with the skilled workforce they need in order to be internationally competitive in post-fordist high-tech industry.

Globalization has affected Germany also in terms of the composition of its resident population. Over the last fifty years, the share of foreigners living in Germany has strongly increased, starting from a very low level. Today, the Turks are the largest group of resident foreign population, its large size going back to the policy of actively recruiting 'guest-workers' in the 1960s. Many immigrants were also recruited from Southern Europe, in particular Italy and Yugoslavia. Contrary to official expectations, most 'guest-workers' did not return to their countries but stayed to live in Germany and started their own families. German integration policy began relatively late and has not been very successful yet. After the demise of the Soviet empire, there has also been a large inflow of people from Eastern Europe, in particular ethnic Germans.

A main policy concern during the last two decades has been the convergence of living standards and productivity in the regions of the former GDR to those in West Germany. Starting from less than half of the West German level in 1991, real GDP per employed person in the East has increased to about 80 per cent of the West German level in 2009; the strongest increase took place in the first half of the 1990s. The average gross monthly wage of full-time employees in the East was just 46.5 per cent of the corresponding wage in the West in 1991. Five years later, the East-West ratio had already climbed to 73.2 per cent. In 2009, it amounted to 76.5 per cent. Convergence was on its way also with respect to average household disposable income: the East-West ratio increased from 59.2 per cent in 1991 to 78.3 per cent in 2008.

Where convergence has failed is with respect to employment. Over time, the unemployment rate in the East has remained at roughly twice the level of the West. The atrophy of Eastern employment as compared to employment in the West is matched by its worse demographic evolution. From 1990 to 2008, the population living in the East declined by 11.7 per cent, while the population of the West grew by 6.5 per cent. The decline of the population in the East went along with a massive increase in the average age of its resident population.[5] This was due to a dramatic decrease of fertility, an increase of longevity, and large outflows of young migrants, especially women.

2. INCOME INEQUALITY

German income inequality was rather stable during the 1980s. After reunification, the inequality of market incomes and the inequality of earnings at the bottom of the distribution began to increase. The increase of inequality at the level of primary incomes accelerated in the years 2000–2005 and that inequality stayed roughly constant afterwards. By contrast, the distribution of disposable income did not become significantly more unequal during the 1990s. Inequality of disposable income, poverty, and income concentration at the top of the distribution rapidly grew in the years from 2000 to 2005 and has stood at that higher level since.

Inequality among Households

Household income is a key determinant of the standard of living. In order to take household size and composition into account, we make multi-member household income equivalent

---

[5] For Germany as a whole, the median age of the resident population increased from 36.4 years in 1980 to the current 44.3 years.

to one-person household income using the modified OECD equivalence scale. The evolution of household income inequality in Germany since 1983 is depicted in Figure 12.1. It shows the Gini coefficients for the distributions of net and gross income, separately in the West and the East of Germany. The evolution of the Gini coefficients for Germany as a whole is very similar to the evolution for West Germany.

Figure 12.1 shows that the Gini coefficient of the cross-sectional distribution of net household income in West Germany was slightly less than 0.25 in the early 1980s and about the same level of inequality prevailed at the end of the century. After 1999, inequality rapidly grew over six years, reached a level of about 0.28 and approximately stayed at that higher level afterwards. In contrast to net incomes, gross incomes are computed before taxes and public transfers and those incomes had already became more unequal during the 1990s. It is apparent from Figure 12.1 that the tax transfer system substantially reduces cross-sectional income inequality in Germany.

The evolution of income inequality in the East has been similar to the one in West Germany, albeit less stable. In particular, the rise in inequality of gross income was more pronounced in the East. In terms of inequality levels, there is a striking difference between the two regions: gross incomes are distributed more unequally in the East but, thanks to general governmental redistribution, net incomes are distributed more evenly there. However, during the last few years inequality has become more similar in the two regions.

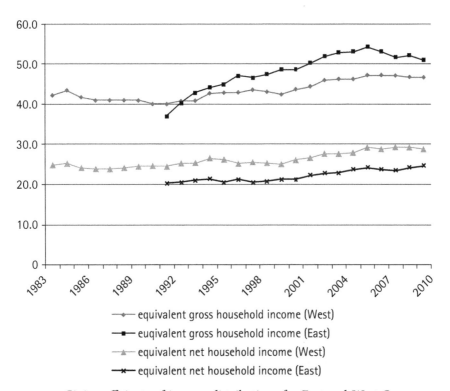

FIGURE 12.1 Gini coefficients of income distributions for East and West Germany

Source: SOEP, own calculations; annual incomes, with frequency weights.

The growth of income inequality has affected both households with relatively high incomes and households with relatively low incomes, as indicated by increasing 90/50 and 50/10 percentile ratios.

The evolution of poverty rates has been similar to the evolution of the Gini coefficient. After taxes and transfers, the poverty rate—with the poverty line at 60 per cent of the median net equivalent household income—exhibited no distinguishable trend until the end of the century. The poverty rate rapidly increased during the first half of the 2000s and then hardly changed in the second half.

Among groups, lone mothers and the unemployed often live in poverty. More than half of all households headed by an unemployed person or by a lone mother receive incomes below the poverty line. Especially for the unemployed, the decade of the 2000s substantially increased their poverty risk: it rose from about 41 per cent to more than 56 per cent. Also households headed by a person without a licence from an advanced secondary school (*Abitur*) or by someone younger than thirty are subject to a severe poverty risk. That risk moderately increased for both groups during the 2000s. Households living in the East face a greater poverty risk than the rest of the population and that difference has increased during the 2000s. This is a contrast with the 1990s, a decade during which the poverty rates in the East and in the West were converging. The incidence of poverty over the last decade was rather stable in the case of foreigners—defined as individuals who were not born in Germany, independently of their ethnic origin. Perhaps surprisingly, in Germany neither blue-collar workers nor the elderly exhibit a poverty rate that substantially differs from that of the overall population.

Unfortunately, the SOEP data contains too few households with very high incomes to accurately portray the very top of the income distribution. Bach *et al.* (2013) have merged individual tax returns data from administrative data with the SOEP. Their income concept is household income after taxes and transfers; in contrast to the previous analysis, they do not use an equivalence scale. They show that the share of total income received by households in the top percentile grew from 6.78 per cent in 1992 to 7.91 per cent in 2005. It is noteworthy that the income increase in the top percentile was very unequal, with the very top of the distribution increasing its incomes at a much faster pace than the rest.

In contrast to the U.S., top managers represent in Germany a relatively minor fraction of the very top of the income distribution. The overwhelming majority of the economic elite of Germany—defined as the top 0.001 per cent fractile—consists of individuals whose main income sources are business activity and financial capital (Bach *et al.*, 2009). In line with this finding, the increase in income concentration in Germany has been paralleled by a decline in labour's share of national income.

An important aspect of the rise of inequality after reunification is the increasing role of the self-employed. Income from self-employment is distributed more unequally than income from dependent employment and the share of the self-employed in the workforce has strongly increased during the last two decades.

Because of data problems, the analysis of German wealth distribution has been hitherto subject to severe limits. However, some interesting facts can be established. First, the ratio of household net wealth to household yearly income is about 3.5 in Germany and that ratio has been increasing over the last three decades. Second, wealth is distributed more unequally than income, and wealth inequality has increased between 2002 and 2007. Third, households in the East own substantially less wealth than households in the West. The inter-regional wealth gap is substantially more pronounced than the inter-regional disparity in income levels: household wealth in East Germany is only about 40 per cent of household wealth in West Germany. Fourth, wealth is more unequally distributed in East Germany than in West Germany. As wealth produces income, this contributes to explain why market incomes are distributed more unequally in the East than in the West. Also, in the case of wealth, there is a tendency for the Gini coefficients in the two regions to converge.

Labour Market Inequality

Because of its large relative size, labour income is a major direct determinant of income inequality. The picture of the evolution of labour income inequality in Germany over the last three decades is complex. Using social security records, Dustmann *et al.* (2009) find that cross-sectional wage inequality was already increasing in West Germany in the 1980s, but only in the top half of the distribution. They also find that in the early 1990s inequality started to rise for the entire wage distribution. Using data from the German Socio-Economic Panel (SOEP) and the German Income and Expenditure Survey (EVS), Fuchs-Schündeln *et al.* (2010) confirm the rise of wage inequality in West Germany after reunification, the upward trend of inequality being mainly driven by an increase in inequality after the year 2000. By contrast, they find that inequality did not noticeably increase during the 1980s. Also using the SOEP data, Gernandt and Pfeiffer (2007) find that inequality of wages for prime-age male employees was stable in West Germany between 1984 and 1994 and increased thereafter. In the period of increasing inequality they find a significant positive gap between high-tenure and low-tenure workers in terms of respective wage growth rates. They suggest that the adjustment of wages to worsening labour market conditions mainly concerned entrants into the labour market. For all workers in West Germany, they find that real wage growth at the tenth percentile has been slightly negative since the mid 1990s. Becker (2006) uses the SOEP to compare 1998 and 2003 in terms of inequality of hourly wages. She finds that workers without a full-time job suffered from wage stagnation and that overall inequality increased, with a low-pay sector already developing before the labour-market reforms of the Hartz legislation. By contrast, 'within group' wage inequality did not change significantly between 1998 and 2003.

Bach *et al.* (2009) investigate the distribution of individual market incomes for the entire adult population living in Germany. Market income includes, along with wage income, income from self-employment and from capital. They find a steady increase of the Gini coefficient in the period from 1992 to 2003, from 0.616 to 0.652.

Two remarkable developments in earnings inequality occurred over the last two decades. First, a very rapid decline of earnings inequality at the bottom of the distribution took place just in the wake of reunification. This was mainly due to a partial catching up of wages in the regions of the former GDR. Those wages started from a low level and were raised in a few years to levels close to three-quarters of comparable West German wages. Second, there was a substantial increase in earnings inequality at the bottom of the distribution during the first decade of this century.

Unemployment has been a major crux for the German economy during the last three decades. The unemployment rate trended upwards in Germany until 2005 and started declining afterwards. After reunification, the level of unemployment has systematically been much higher in East Germany. The incidence of unemployment has been especially high for the individuals with low educational attainment.

The rise of unemployment in West Germany from the mid 1970s to the mid 1990s is usually attributed to the institutional rigidity of its labour market, which resisted a downward wage adjustment in spite of competitive pressure resulting from globalization and skill-biased technological change. The rise of unemployment is therefore seen as the price for keeping a low level of wage dispersion—the counter-example being the US, where in the same period the unemployment rate was kept under control at the price of increased wage dispersion.

The exceptionally high unemployment rates in the region of the former GDR mirror several factors, most prominently: mistakes in economic policy that led to accelerated de-industrialization;[6] the absence of an entrepreneurial class with a network of long-standing relationships; an excessive wage push during the years when Eastern Europe was experiencing an economic breakdown; and a dramatic fall in public employment.[7]

The pool of the unemployed is heterogeneous. Along with people that remain unemployed for a short duration and then find a new job, there is a group of long-term unemployed people. These are often older persons and persons with serious health problems who cannot work longer than a few hours. Since the Hartz reforms, there has existed a large group of people who at the same time have an official job and receive transfers under the same programme as the one for the unemployed. It is estimated that, as of today, about 1.3 million people combine low market wages with such public transfers.

The German labour market shares a secular trend with all other advanced economies: the rising participation of women. The female activity rate has steadily increased over the last three decades and is approaching the rather stable activity rate of men. Part-time employment is much more common among women (45.8 per cent) than among men (9.2 per cent). Overall, the share of workers in part-time employment has increased in Germany from 14 per cent in 1991 to 26.5 per cent in 2009. Some of that increase occurred because of a shortage of full-time jobs. According to EU-LFS, in 2011 some 17.1 per cent of those individuals would have preferred full-time work. SOEP data indicates that the gap between the desired number of working hours and the actual number of hours worked by part-time employees has increased since the second half of the 1990s (Holst and Seifert, 2012). In terms of overall female labour-market participation, Germany takes a middle position among OECD countries.

Labour market inequality is intertwined with the decline of both trade unions and collective bargaining. Trade unions used to play a key role in the wage formation process in the FRG. Industrial relations were characterized by industry-level wage negotiations, typically led by the metal working industry. This system has been weakened after reunification when in many cases firm-level bargaining replaced industry-level bargaining, and opening clauses in collective agreements allowed for plant-level derogation. The unionization rate, which was about 36 per cent at reunification, has steadily declined to about half that level.

---

[6]   In the East, employment in manufacturing dropped between 1991 and 1993 by 60 per cent and kept declining until 1997. The public agency in charge of privatizing the former GDR firms (*Treuhandanstalt*) operated until the end of 1994, and then bequeathed the German government a financial loss of about 240 billion German Marks.

[7]   From 1991 to 2009, the public administration narrowly defined lost about half of its staff in the East.

Furthermore, especially in East Germany, many firms have begun to set their wages unilaterally, without any formal agreement with unions or worker representatives.

Another major institutional change has been the rise of fixed-term employment contracts. The share of employees in temporary jobs has risen from about 10 per cent to almost 15 per cent today in the last fifteen years. Temporary workers typically receive low wages and face a high unemployment risk.

Why has Inequality Grown?

In Germany, income inequality was rather stable during the 1980s. After reunification, the inequality of market incomes and the inequality of earnings at the bottom of the distribution began to increase. The increase of inequality at the level of primary incomes accelerated in the years 2000–2005 and inequality stayed roughly constant afterwards. By contrast with primary incomes, post-fisc incomes did not become significantly more unequal during the 1990s. Inequality of net income rapidly grew in the years from 2000 to 2005 and stood at that higher level afterwards.

There are three prominent features of the evolution of German inequality that need an explanation:

1. The rise in the inequality of primary incomes since reunification
2. The stability of the distribution of net incomes during the 1990s, despite the above element
3. The rise of overall inequality in 20002005.

The rise of inequality of primary incomes since reunification. To a substantial extent, the long-run rise of inequality in the distribution of market incomes in Germany mirrors the growing numbers of the unemployed and pensioners, i.e. individuals with zero or very low market incomes, in the overall population.

In Germany, the earnings distribution and the wage distribution showed a slight increase in inequality after the economic downturn of 1992–1993. This mainly occurred through a relative worsening of the pay received by the new entrants into the labour market (Gernandt and Pfeiffer, 2007; Fuchs-Schündeln *et al.*, 2010). The main drivers behind those changes were: skill-biased technological change in the upper half of the distribution; immigration shocks from Eastern Europe; and the decline of unions in the lower half of the distribution (Dustmann *et al.*, 2010). It is likely that large privatizations and the outsourcing of low-skill tasks by the public sector contributed to the growth of a low-wage sector in Germany.

The long-run rise of inequality in equivalent gross household income was also due to compositional effects, in particular the increased share of pensioner households and the reduced average household size. Between 1991 and 2008, the population of Germany increased by 2.6 per cent, while the number of one-person households increased by 33.2 per cent. According to Peichl *et al.* (2012), the increased inequality of gross household incomes is strongly related to changes in household structure that have occurred in Germany during that period.

The stability of the distribution of net incomes during the 1990s. The redistributive performance of the German tax transfer system strengthened in the 1990s, as the distribution of post-fisc income changed little, despite an increasingly unequal distribution of pre-fisc income. The generosity of unemployment benefits remained relatively high during the 1990s. With respect to old age pensions, the retirees were still benefiting from the reforms introduced in the late 1970s. That expansion was characterized by relatively high replacement rates and generous early retirement provisions (Bönke et al., 2010). Pensioner households in the East benefited from having work histories with no unemployment spells and a high labour-market participation of women.

In the years 1996–98, the burden of personal income tax was reduced for low-income households (Corneo, 2005a). The average income tax rate for individuals with low income fell substantially as compared to 1995, which helped to offset zero or even negative real wage growth in the lowest quartile of the distribution. Furthermore, there were strong increases in the child benefit, starting in 1996, that reduced the poverty risk for families with children.

The rise of inequality in 2000–2005. The impressive acceleration of the rise in inequality after 1999 occurred during a period of weak economic growth and high unemployment levels. To a great extent, the rise of inequality was caused by the poor performance of the German labour market. Growing unemployment mainly hit low-skilled workers and exerted a downward pressure on their wages, especially in the case of new entrants into the labour market. In a context of vanishing union power, of firms rejecting industry-wide wage agreements, and of increasingly privatized public services, there were few institutional barriers to resist such a pressure. After 2003, the Hartz-reforms are likely to have contributed to put even more pressure on the low-skilled and to foster low-pay employment. As a result, wage and earnings inequality at the bottom of the distribution increased.

This time, the German tax transfer system did not generate the progressive effects that would have stabilized the distribution of post-fisc incomes. With regard to transfers, current pensioners continued to benefit from relatively generous arrangements stipulated in the past, and their poverty risk hardly changed. By contrast, the poverty risk of the unemployed increased substantially—as one would expect from the substantial increase in earnings inequality even without any change occurring in unemployment benefits. In fact, the Hartz-reforms are likely to have contributed to a higher poverty rate among the unemployed. The increased incidence of poverty among the unemployed in 2000–2005 can also be related to the high unemployment rates that prevailed in Germany from the mid 1990s. In contrast to those who were unemployed in the mid 1990s, the people who were unemployed during the early 2000s had often already been unemployed for a long period and were thus entitled to lower benefits.

Turning to the German tax system, during 2000–2005 it actually became less progressive, especially as a consequence of the income tax reform enacted in various steps by the government of Chancellor Schröder (Social-Democrats and Green Party) from 1998 to 2005 (Corneo, 2005b). The substantial reduction of the top marginal tax rate, along with cuts in corporate taxation and lasting effects from the demise of the personal wealth tax in 1996/7, contributed altogether to increasing the concentration of net income at the top of the distribution. Tax policy is likely to have also spurred the increase in gross incomes at the top of the distribution, e.g. by encouraging top managers to demand pay increases. Fabbri and Marin (2012) document a massive increase in CEO pay in Germany, especially in 2005 and 2006, just after a substantial cut in the top marginal rate of income tax and consistently with theories of compensation bargaining.

Using a decomposition analysis, Biewen and Juhasz (2012) have attempted to quantify the strength of various potential drivers of inequality in Germany from 2000 to 2006. They find that the main drivers were rising unemployment, rising inequality in market returns, and changes in the tax system. Each one of those three factors is found to account for about one quarter of the overall increase in inequality of disposable equivalent household income in Germany in that period.

3. THE IMPACT OF INEQUALITY ON SOCIAL INDICATORS

Rising income inequality in the early 2000s went along with an increase in poverty rates, at least for some sub-groups of the population. These monetarily defined measures may find their consequences in changing living conditions, in worsening health conditions, in a lack of social interaction, and in an eroding subjective well being. However, these consequences are not deterministic. Some indicators of daily life experiences and conduit may be immune to moderate changes in income inequality; other indicators may be affected after a considerable delay. This section provides a description of the development of social indicators and relates it to income inequality.

Material Deprivation

Households with significant income losses may be able to maintain their material living standard for a certain amount of time by exploiting existing resources, for example using an existing car or TV. Hence, we would expect a gradual increase in material deprivation as a consequence of growing income inequality and unemployment. Using SOEP data from 2001–12.2007, we find an increase in material deprivation for the entire observation period (Figure 12.2).[8] The level of material deprivation is higher in East than in West Germany, and the increase is more pronounced in East than in West Germany as well. Andreß (2006) shows that the amount of material deprivation parallels the development of unemployment rates, with a strong increase in material deprivation after the turn of the century. In the most recent years, material deprivation has been declining (Engels et al., forthcoming). Thus, material deprivation seems to correlate more with developments in unemployment rates than with income inequality.

The increase in material deprivation varied across social groups. Households with tertiary educated members hardly experienced an increase in material deprivation. Households without academic degrees have been increasingly confronted with cuts in the standard of

---

[8] The index of material deprivation is based on eleven items: possession of a colour TV; phone; car; replacement of old furniture; good condition of the residential building; good neighbourhood; ability to paying rent/mortgage on time; to put money aside for emergencies; to go on vacation once a year for one week; to invite friends to dinner at least once a month; and the ability to eat a hot meal with meat, fish or poultry at least every other day. Households are considered to be materially deprived if at least four of those items are not affordable.

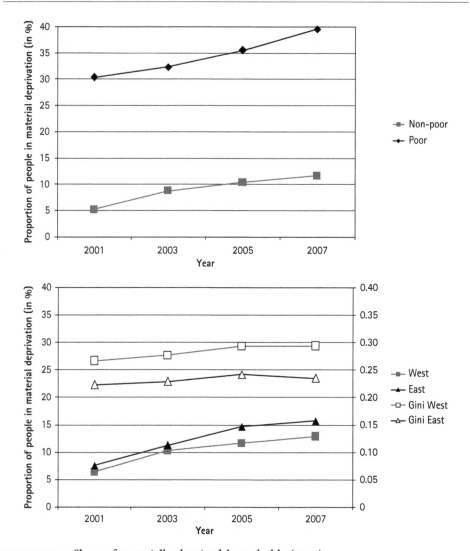

FIGURE 12.2 Share of materially deprived households (as %)

Source: SOEP, own calculations.

living. For poor people, the rate of materially deprived poor households jumped from about 30 per cent to 40 per cent. The remarkable increase for this group suggests that poor households increasingly suffer from their financial situation.

Social Interactions

Growing inequality and poverty rates may result in forms of social deprivation as well. People could be less willing, less inclined or less able to see other people and interact with them on a daily base. Using data from the SOEP, the ISG research institute (forthcoming) summarizes the frequency of contacts with friends, relatives and neighbours. On average, between 21.5 and 23.6 per cent of the population do not have contacts with their peers at least once a month. For the first decade of the 2000s, there is no clear trend in these numbers. We find somewhat higher rates of social exclusion for poor people and for less-educated people. The higher numbers for less privileged people raise questions about the capacity of our society to avoid alienation for these groups.

Subjective Well Being

In contrast to the previous social indicators, measures of subjective well being are more prone to react instantaneously to changes in income inequality. The SOEP data provide measures of an individual's satisfaction with life in general, with her or his health and with household income. The long-term trends of these measures exhibit some fluctuations between 1995 and 2009 (Figure 12.3). For the time period between 2000 and 2005—the period of growing income inequality—we find a decline in life satisfaction, health satisfaction and income satisfaction. However, the variation in these satisfaction measures before and after the rise of income inequality does not speak to a systematic correlation of income inequality and satisfaction.

On average, people in West Germany are more satisfied with aspects of their life than people in East Germany. The difference is about 0.3 and 0.8 points on an 11-point-scale. People with secondary or primary education are less satisfied with their situations than tertiary educated people. Again, a stark contrast exists between poor people and non-poor people. The average difference between these groups ranges between 0.4 points for health and 2.2 points for income satisfaction. Poor people show little tendency for health satisfaction, especially not at the beginning of the millennium. Life satisfaction, however, declined in the first years of the 2000s. Even more pronounced is the development of income satisfaction during that time. Income satisfaction plummeted for this group by about 0.8 points. The drop after 2003, in particular, suggests that this development may be related to the newly introduced labour market reforms and the reforms in social assistance (see Section 5).

Social Mobility

An increase in cross-sectional inequality may be less damaging to the social fabric if it is accompanied by increased mobility. Using SOEP data, Goebel *et al.* (2011) present income dynamics out of income quintiles within a 4-year period. As shown in Figure 12.4, about 66.5 per cent of people from the highest income quintile in 1985 remained in this quintile at least until 1988. Likewise, about 57.3 per cent of the people from the lowest income quintile in 1985 remained in this quintile at least until 1988. The trends over time show remarkable stability for people in the highest quintile. The finding for the bottom of the distribution is markedly different. After 2000, the proportion of people who were not able to leave low-income conditions rose to 65.2 per cent. Thus, the rise in cross-sectional inequality in Germany was not accompanied by more income mobility but rather by an increased difficulty in escaping poverty.[9]

---

[9] Bartels and Bönke (2013) have studied income volatility, taking the changes over time in the composition of the SOEP into account. While they do find an increase in earnings volatility at the bottom of the distribution, they do not find much change in the volatility of net household income.

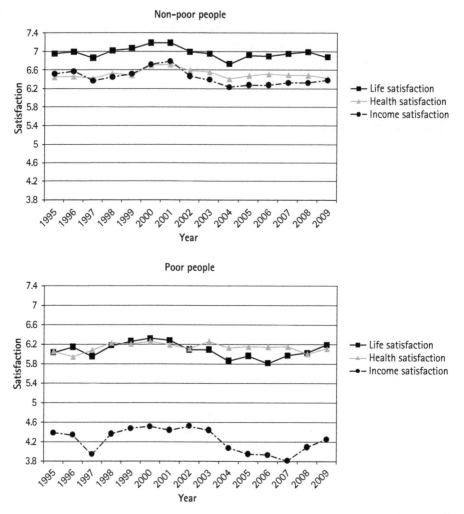

FIGURE 12.3 General and domain-specific satisfaction for non-poor and poor people (11-point-scale)

Source: SOEP, own calculations.

Overall, we find little support for correlations between income inequality dynamics and the development of social indicators. For material deprivation and social interactions, there is little evidence of concomitant trends. For life, health and income satisfaction, we find trendless fluctuation in the long run. However, we do find short-term trends of declining satisfaction that parallel the increase in income inequality in the early 2000s. The most prominent findings concern the poor. Material deprivation rises for the poor and the increase in cross-sectional poverty rates at the beginning of the millennium is not matched by an increased likelihood of climbing up the income ladder.

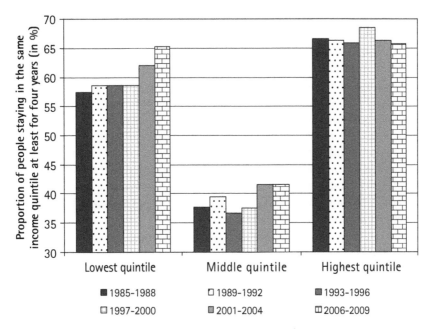

FIGURE 12.4 Income dynamics for selected income quintiles

Source: Goebel *et al.*, (2011), own graphical display.

4. POLITICAL AND CULTURAL IMPACTS

Income inequality poses a challenge to social cohesion and political stability. High levels of inequality induce corruption, social distrust, bad governance, and weak political support (Newton and Zmerli, 2011; Rothstein, 2011; Uslaner, 2008, 2011). The latter is a prerequisite upon which the legitimacy of democratic regimes depends. Aspects of social cohesion and institutional settings are intrinsically related to the fabric of social structures. Individual political attitudes are not only shaped by personal experiences but by collective socio-tropic perceptions (Kumlin, 2004). These perceptions relate to macro-level phenomena such as economic performance, unemployment and income inequality.[10] Notwithstanding, some economic theory or philosophical schools of thought would argue in favour of inequality, pointing either to its function as an economic incentive or to the rightfulness of benefiting from one's own endowments (Roemer, 2011).

The following analysis mainly focuses on behavioural and attitudinal trends in East and West Germany during the previous ten years, the period of time covering the most pronounced increase in inequality.

---

[10] These arguments are derived from Castillo and Zmerli (2012).

Voting

As the official statistical data on voting depict, turnout in German national elections was high throughout the first three decades after the Second World War and reached its peak at the beginning of the 1980s, with a turnout of nearly 90 per cent at the national election in 1983 (Figure 12.5).[11] Since then, a steady decline in turnout has set in, resulting in a difference in turnouts of nearly twenty percentage points from 1983 to the most recent national election in 2009. The process of German unification does not appear to account for this pronounced downward trend. In both parts of the country, turnout during the most recent national election was at an all-time low, although East Germans have consistently had lower turnout rates than West Germans in preceding elections. Taking the trends of the last twenty years into consideration, the drop in the percentage share of voters which occurred during the most recent election in 2009 is particularly striking.

An investigation of the five waves of the European Social Survey data (ESS, 2002 to 2010) substantiates the notion of diverging voting behaviour between East and West German citizens. Differentiating by educational degree reveals for both regions that turnout rates of people with a tertiary educational degree have been the highest and most stable over the first decade of the 21st century. While turnout rates for citizens with primary schooling have been lowest and fluctuating over time, the initially high turnout rates of citizens with secondary schooling have declined since 2002. Overall, a widening participatory gap between citizens with tertiary education and citizens with primary and secondary schooling can clearly be discerned.

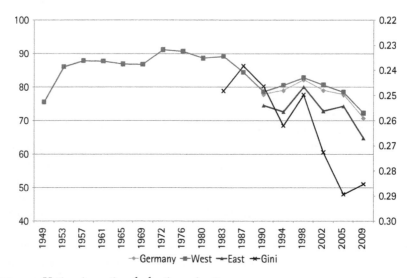

FIGURE 12.5 Voting in national elections, in %

Source: Federal Statistical Office; Der Bundeswahlleiter, 2009a, 2009b.

---

[11] In order to better present the expected relationship between inequality and political involvement, most of the subsequent GINI scales on the secondary y-axis are depicted in reversed manner.

Trust in Others and Political Institutions

We investigate the trends of political trust using data from the German General Survey (ALLBUS), which covers the period between 1984 and 2008. The empirical results are complemented by the five waves of the ESS.

As shown by ALLBUS, trust in the legal system has been remarkably stable over time with the exception of a decline in the course of the 1980s. The comparison between the former GDR and FRG discloses a pronounced perceptual divide. While nearly fifty per cent of West Germans steadily express trust in the legal system, East Germans are somewhat less inclined to do so.

Inspecting trust attitudes by educational level based on ESS data reveals for both parts of the country a significant decrease amongst people with the lowest educational achievement. The same holds true for secondary degree holders, albeit to a lesser extent. Tertiary education degree holders experience an outstanding boost in trust in the legal system—in particular in the eastern part of the country. Rising levels of inequality, which disproportionally affect lower and middle class households, could be related to these remarkable developments.

Trust in the German national parliament (*Bundestag*) has been expressed by less than one third of the German population since the beginning of the 1990s, according to data drawn from ALLBUS. The East/West comparison reveals another significant perceptual divide. While a little less than a third of West Germans express trust in the German Bundestag, less than one fifth of East German citizens share the same trustful attitude. In addition, as the West German cross-educational-level analysis of ESS data suggests, the three categories maintain observable 'between group' differences, with the primary education degree holders as the least trustful citizens (Figures 12.6 and 12.7). For East Germany, a particularly sharp drop in trust can be observed for the least educated with only approximately one tenth

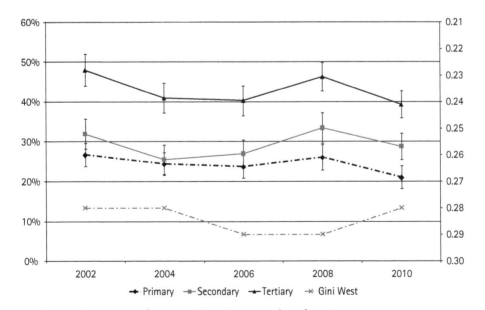

FIGURE 12.6 Trust in parliament, West Germany, by education

Source: ESS (also Figures 12.7–12.11).

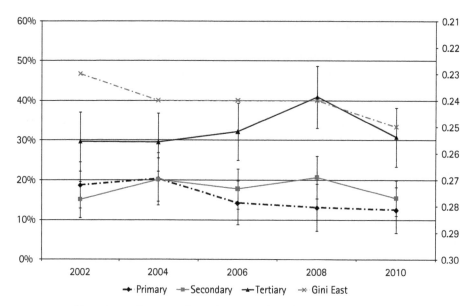

FIGURE 12.7 Trust in parliament, East Germany, by education

of citizens expressing a trustful attitude. Citizens with a tertiary education degree contrast this consistent trend of declining trust levels. Considering potential sources of this disturbing development, increasing levels of inequality could provide one part of the explanation.

Turning to Germans' levels of social trust, the ESS data depict how levels and trends of social trust differ across educational degrees (Figures 12.8 and 12.9). In both regions, tertiary degree holders are the most trustful. In addition, East Germans with tertiary degrees experience the highest percentage share increase over time resulting in a remarkable cross-educational 'trust gap'. A similar diagnosis also applies to West German citizens despite different underlying trends. While people with tertiary schooling, by and large, maintain their high percentage shares of trust, secondary and primary degree holders become increasingly distrustful over time. A concomitant development with rising levels of inequality could be one potential explanatory factor.

Political Values and Legitimacy

With regard to attitudes of social tolerance, a quite small percentage share of Germans *strongly* opposes immigration of people of different race according to the five surveys of the ESS.[12] Apart from some fluctuations in 2004 and 2006, only a slight increase amongst the entire German adult population can be observed. However, this increasing trend in 2004, and high levels in 2006 coincide with patterns of increasing inequality accompanied by pessimistic

---

[12] The question wording in the ESS reads: 'How about people of a different race or ethnic group from most of Germany's people?' (The previous and related question wording was: 'Now, using this card, to what extent do you think Germany should allow people of the same race or ethnic group as most of Germany's people to come and live here?')

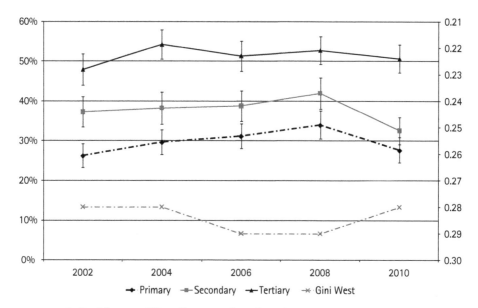

FIGURE 12.8 Social trust, West Germany, by education

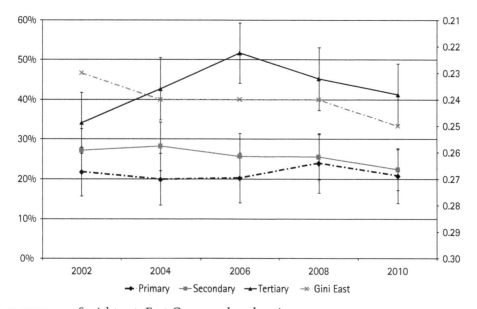

FIGURE 12.9 Social trust, East Germany, by education

prospects for the unemployed. The observable decrease from 2008 onwards with concomitant decreasing unemployment rates could represent another indicator of this inter-relatedness. The comparison between East and West Germans depicts societal attitudinal differences. While in both parts of the country noteworthy fluctuations can be discerned, only East Germans tend to reject immigrants of different race in 2010 more than they did a decade before.

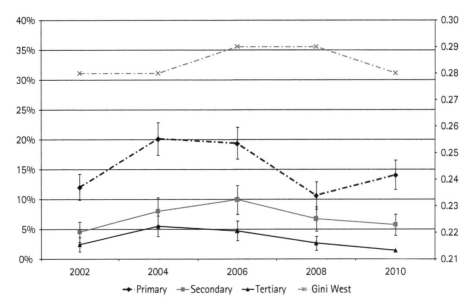

FIGURE 12.10 Don't allow different race, West Germany, by education

From a cross-educational-level perspective, remarkable differences between educational categories emerge in both parts of the country (Figures 12.10 and 12.11). In West Germany, a considerable gap exists between citizens with primary education who have rising levels of dismissive attitudes, and the two other educational categories that have declining levels of strongly opposing views. A slightly different pattern prevails in East Germany, where a remarkable gap exists between citizens with primary and secondary education, depicting increasing levels over time, on the one hand, and citizens with tertiary education with decreasing shares of strongly opposing views, on the other. Rising levels of inequality and high rates of unemployment, which disproportionally affect lower and middle class households could be related to these developments.

Values about Social Policy and Welfare State

In line with increasing levels of inequality in Germany, the percentage share of Germans who *strongly* believe that income differences are too large in their country has doubled from 1987 to 2009, as data derived from different waves of the International Social Survey Programme (ISSP) indicate (Figure 12.12). Nevertheless, there is no steadily increasing trend but considerably fluctuating shares of corresponding responses. The same holds true for the East/West German comparison: in both parts of the country, there are strongly fluctuating percentage shares of strong believers in the presence of too large income differences which ultimately result in a remarkable increase after a time period of more than fifteen years. Particularly noteworthy is another strong perceptual difference between East and West Germans, which varies from twenty to thirty percentage points.

Breaking down these attitudes by levels of educational attainment reveals the strongest increases in percentage shares for citizens with primary and secondary educational degrees

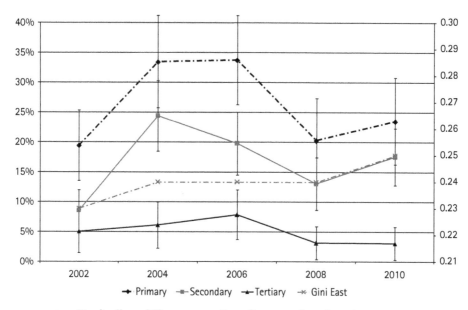

FIGURE 12.11 Don't allow different race, East Germany, by education

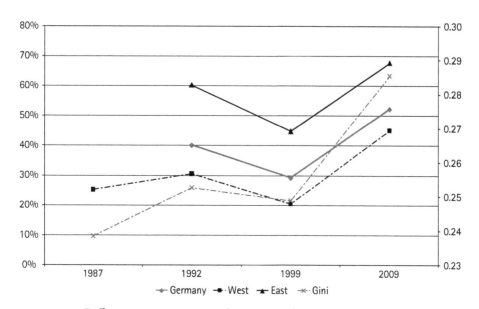

FIGURE 12.12 Differences in income too large, strongly agree, ISSP

in both parts of the country. East German citizens with a tertiary education degree, by contrast, are the only group category with decreasing shares of strong affirmative respondents.

According to ISSP data, hardly one fifth of the (West) German population in 1987 strongly agreed with the government's responsibility to reduce income differences (Figure 12.13). Despite some fluctuations over time, the corresponding percentage share of citizens rose to approximately

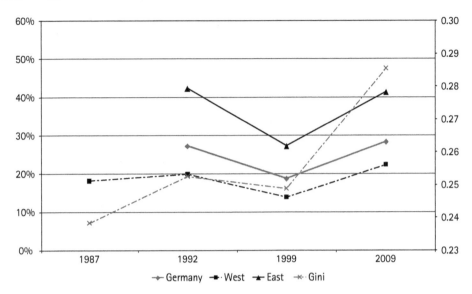

FIGURE 12.13 Government's responsibility to reduce differences, strongly agree, ISPP

thirty per cent in 2009. The East/West comparison, however, stresses the persisting intra-societal divide. From the outset of the unification process, East Germans attributed a significantly greater role to the federal government in reducing income differences than West Germans did.

Turning to the interrelatedness between educational degree and one's assessment of government's responsibility in West Germany, the ISSP data reveals upward trends during the period of the strongest increase in inequality for all three categories. As expected, people with the lowest educational attainment, and the potentially highest risk of being dependent on redistributive policies, have twice the probability of strongly agreeing with this statement than people holding the highest educational degree. East Germans, by contrast, follow a slightly different pattern. Citizens holding tertiary education degrees appear to be the least affected by the encompassing upward trends. As a result, the corresponding attitudinal gap between the lowest and middle-range educational degree holders and people with the highest level of schooling is increasingly widening.

5. THE ROLE OF POLICY

The Hartz Reforms

The Hartz-reforms of the labour market were introduced by the second Schröder government in four steps from 2003 to 2005 and mainly followed the approach of 'negative activation', with benefit cuts for the unemployed and a tightening of the sanction regime. They also included fiscal inducements for small jobs and self-employment, a deregulation of temporary work and a re-organization of the public agencies in charge of the unemployed.

In 2003, the Hartz I and Hartz II laws were passed. In particular, they involved: a tightening of the obligation to work for transfer recipients (obligation to take up a job even if it differs from own profession); the establishment of agencies to place people in temporary employment and deregulation of temporary employment; the broadening of minor employment by means of social security exemptions (Mini- and Midi-Job schemes, a kind of earned income tax credit); a financial support for mini entrepreneurs (so called 'Me Inc.').

The Hartz III law of 2004 further tightened the sanction regime for the unemployed and created distinctive public offices of job search for the unemployed (*Jobcentre*) that concentrated tasks previously dispersed across various institutions. Another law in the same year reduced the maximum duration of unemployment benefits. The duration for which a dismissed worker can receive unemployment benefits reduced remarkably for almost all age groups. Also the time period a person has to have been employed, subject to social security contributions, in order to gain a right to unemployment benefits, was raised: from a minimum of six months to twelve months. Several of these measures either presented formal constitutional deficiencies or produced politically unacceptable results so that they had to be amended or abolished altogether. In part, this also applies to the final and most prominent piece of the labour-market reforms, the Hartz IV reform.

In 2005, with registered unemployment approaching the 5 million bar, the Hartz IV reform was introduced. Prior to that law, the benefit system consisted of three layers: unemployment insurance; unemployment assistance; and social assistance. The second layer implied that unemployed individuals received means-tested earnings-related unemployment assistance after the exhaustion of unemployment-insurance benefits. The duration of unemployment assistance was basically indefinite. Hartz IV abolished unemployment assistance and basically substituted it with social assistance.[13] Those who would have received unemployment assistance in the old system had now to apply for the new, means-tested, unemployment benefit II (*Arbeitslosengeld II*).[14] In most cases, the resulting transfer income is significantly lower than in the previous system. However, the new system entails stronger incentives for transfer recipients to supplement the transfer by taking up some work, although the implicit marginal tax rates on the earnings after the threshold of disregard remain high.

Overall, the Hartz reforms entailed a significant rejuvenation of active labour market policy in Germany. In terms of participants, the most successful programme has been the public job creation II scheme (*1-Euro-Jobs*). That programme is mainly targeted at long-term unemployed people who receive means-tested social assistance. In order to re-integrate them into the labour market, they must accept to work for non-profit employers under some conditions. The Federal Employment Agency pays them a small amount, which is not credited against their social assistance.

The consequences of the Hartz legislation for labour market outcomes and income inequality are not yet entirely understood. There is a consensus that they have contributed to the substantial increase in so-called atypical employment (e.g., marginal part-time work partially exempted from social security contributions). By 2011, only two thirds of employees in Germany were subject to social security contributions and, hence, eligible for

---

[13] There is however a supplementary temporary benefit for up to two years after transiting from unemployment benefits into social assistance.

[14] Currently, about 70 per cent of the unemployed receive that benefit.

unemployment benefits (Bundesagentur für Arbeit, 2011). Marginal part-time work is now a major form of employment in the retail, cleaning, and the hospitality sectors. It is likely that the Hartz reforms contributed to increasing the labour supply of low-skilled workers. In turn, that increase in supply is bound to exert a downward pressure on the wages of the low-skilled. Benefit abuse is thought to have become less frequent, while bureaucratic load, heavy controls and legal disputes before the courts have increased. The official unemployment rate has substantially decreased in the wake of the Hartz reforms.

Tax Policy

During the last two decades, German tax policy has often been framed in terms of reaction to mounting international tax competition. The corporate tax rate stood at 56 per cent in the 1980s in the FRG. It was subsequently reduced in several steps, especially during the years of the Schröder government. Since 2008, the corporate tax rate in Germany has been merely 15 per cent.

Corporations, especially banks, strongly benefited from the total abolition of capital gains taxes on the sales of large share blocks, decided on by the Schröder government in 2000. This occurred at a time when the German company network centred around major banks was already eroding. The exemption of capital gains from taxation accelerated its dissolution, which in turn led top management to assign higher priority to shareholder value. Companies carefully exploited the timing of the tax reform to first deduct capital losses from their tax liabilities and then realize tax-free capital gains. The fiscal losses to the public budget were severe.

Germany had a personal wealth tax until 1996,which, in that year, generated a revenue equivalent to about €4.6 Billion. That tax was declared unconstitutional by the federal constitutional court because different kinds of wealth were being treated too differently. Since 1997, the personal wealth tax has not been levied.

The inheritance tax is a long-standing element of the German tax system. Some items of the bequeathed estate benefit from special exemptions and evaluation methods that lead to a severe erosion of the tax base. This holds true in particular for business wealth, which is almost tax-exempted.

Personal capital income was taxed until 2008 within the progressive tax on personal income. Since 2009 this has no longer been the case, as a kind of dual system of taxation has been introduced. Incomes from interests, dividends, and financial capital gains are now subject to a 25 per cent flat-rate withholding tax and are exempted from personal income tax. By contrast, the top marginal tax rate on remaining personal incomes is 45 per cent. Both taxes entail an additional solidarity surcharge of 5.5 per cent of the tax liability, which enhances the progressivity of taxation.

While regressive tax reforms were often blamed on international tax competition, the German government did not generate much international cooperation to fight tax evasion and avoidance. In contrast to other countries, Germany steadily refuses to provide bank information automatically to foreign tax authorities, if the recipient of interest income is a foreigner.

Table 12.1 displays the effect of the income tax reform of the Schröder governments from 1998 to 2005 on the real net incomes of single taxpayers, as calculated from the evolution of statutory tax rates. It shows that for the bulk of taxpayers, the reform directly increased real net incomes by roughly five per cent. The income gains were much higher for taxpayers in the top percentile of the income distribution. By way of an example, somebody with an annual taxable income of €500,000 experienced a net income increase of about twenty per cent.

The reform of 1998–2005 also affected the tax basis of the income tax. While the decrease of effective average tax rates has been across the board, it has been especially pronounced for households with very high incomes. By way of an example, the average tax rate for the top 0.001 per cent group dropped from 43 per cent in 1998 to 31 per cent in 2005 (Bach *et al.*, 2013).

Taxes and transfers substantially reduce cross-sectional income inequality in Germany: the Gini coefficient is reduced by roughly 40 per cent when one shifts from the distribution of gross income to the distribution of net income—see Figure 12.1. The inequality-reducing impact of the tax transfer system increased during the second half of the 1990s, whereas it became slightly weaker during the 1980s and the 2000s. The success of policy in combating inequality during the second part of the 1990s is partly due to two measures that were implemented in 1996: a substantial increase in the basic allowance for the personal income tax and a substantial increase in child benefit. Both measures had been called for by the Federal Constitutional Court.

Table 12.1 Effect of the income tax reform 1998–2005

Taxable income	Real net income growth
10,000	4.94
20,000	5.27
30,000	4.77
40,000	4.34
50,000	4.44
60,000	5.15
70,000	6.78
80,000	8.36
90,000	9.65
100,000	10.72
200,000	16.41
300,000	18.43
400,000	19.69
500,000	20.4
1,000,000	21.87

Source: Corneo (2005b).

6. CONCLUSIONS

In terms of cross-sectional income inequality, the FRG of today is quite different from the FRG of the 1980s. In the 1980s, the FRG was one of the most egalitarian countries in the world. Inequality of pre-fisc incomes began to rise after the economic downturn of 1992–1993, and kept growing until the mid 2000s. The distribution of post-fisc income changed little during the 1990s. In the period 2000–2005 it became substantially more unequal and the level of inequality did not significantly change in the subsequent period. This overall tendency for inequality to grow was paralleled by a mutation of the German socio-economic compact: its traditional corporatist model imported a number of elements from the Anglo-Saxon one, giving rise to an original hybrid model. By international comparison, Germany still has a relatively egalitarian income distribution, but during the 2000s inequality has mounted more rapidly than in most other OECD countries.

In the 1980s, the pressure exerted by globalization and skill-biased technological change did not lead to significantly more wage inequality in Germany but rather to increased unemployment. Thanks to the short-lived post-reunification boom, inequality did not rise in the first few years after reunification. In the sequel, equality-preserving institutions like trade unions, industry-level bargaining, regulated labour markets and public ownership were to decline irreversibly, allowing for a gradual increase of wage dispersion. The adjustment of the earnings distribution left core workers relatively unaffected and mainly hit entrants to the labour market. In that respect, the workforce in East Germany constituted a huge group of entrants. Since reunification, collective wage agreements have covered a substantially smaller share of the workforce there than in the West. Since about the mid 1990s, market incomes have been distributed more unequally in the East than in the West of Germany.

Reunification and the worldwide demise of 'real existing socialism' also implied a changed tone in the political discourse, which became more receptive to free market ideology. However, in the first years after reunification, no far-reaching neoliberal reforms could be introduced despite a centre-right government. Meanwhile, additional factors were making the distribution of market incomes in Germany more unequal. At the bottom of the distribution, a large inflow of migrants from Eastern Europe into the German labour market put pressure on the wages of low- and medium-skilled workers. At the top of the distribution, the rise of shareholder value, financial markets, and markets for superstars drove an increase in income concentration. Changes in the age structure of the population and the erosion of traditional family arrangements further contributed to generate a more unequal distribution of market incomes.

The resilience of equality in terms of post-fisc income during the 1990s—despite increased pre-fisc inequality—can be traced to the delayed effects of social policy measures, e.g. generous rules for computing pension benefits. Furthermore, the Federal Constitutional Court repeatedly exhorted the government to adjust the tax transfer system so as to guarantee that the disposable income of individuals did not fall short of a minimum threshold. The subsequent hikes in child benefit and in the basic allowance of personal income tax contributed to combat inequality.

The government launched two main waves of reforms: a tax reform starting in 1998 and the Hartz legislation for the labour market in 2003–2005. Empirical studies indicate that the tax reforms strengthened the rise of inequality but the evidence on the effect of the labour market reforms is less clear-cut. In perspective, the pension reform of 2001, which significantly reduced future pension rights, is likely to increase inequality.

Growing income inequality has not gone unnoticed by Germans. Most noticeably, people at the poorer end of the income distribution face increasing difficulties in overcoming their precarious situation. They experience more material deprivation and social exclusion. For the main part of the population, however, social indicators fluctuate over time without any systematic correlation with trends in income inequality. Political disenchantment, social intolerance and demands for redistributive policies, however, show a concomitant trend to the rise of inequality. East Germans' and less educated people's attitudes seem to be especially affected by these developments. In sum, the repercussions of rising levels of income inequality seem to have already impaired citizens' relationship with the democratic state.

References

Andreß, H.-J. (2006), 'Zur Entwicklung von Lebensstandard und Deprivation in Deutschland von 1996 bis 2003', *Vierteljahreshefte zur Wirtschaftsforschung* 75/1, 131–149.

Bach, S., Corneo, G. and Steiner, V. (2009), 'From Bottom To Top: The Entire Income Distribution in Germany, 1992-2003', *Review of Income and Wealth* 55/2, 303–330.

Bach, S., Corneo, G. and Steiner, V. (2013), 'Effective Taxation of Top Incomes in Germany', *German Economic Review* 14/2, 115–137.

Bartels, C. and Bönke, T. (2013), 'Can Households and Welfare States Mitigate Rising Earnings Instability?' *Review of Income and Wealth*, forthcoming.

Becker, I. (2006), 'Effektive Bruttostundenlöhne in Deutschland. Eine Verteilungsanalyse unter Aspekten der Leistungsgerechtigkeit und besonderer Berücksichtigung des Niedriglohnsegments', *Arbeitspapier* Nr. 2 des Projekts „Soziale Gerechtigkeit", J. W. Goethe Universität Frankfurt a. Main.

Biewen, M. and Juhasz, A. (2012), 'Understanding Rising Inequality in Germany, 1999/2000–2005/06', *Review of Income and Wealth*, 58, 622-647.

Bönke, T., Schröder, C. and Schulte, K. (2010), 'Incomes and Inequality in the Long Run: The Case of German Elderly', *German Economic Review* 11/4, 487–510.

Bundesagentur für Arbeit (2011), *Der Arbeits- und Ausbildungsmarkt, Monatsbericht Mai 2011*, Nürnberg.

Castillo, J. C. and Zmerli, S. (2012), 'Income Inequality and Political Support. How Objective and Subjective Income Inequality Affect Latin American Democracies', conference paper submitted to the (cancelled) Annual Meeting of the American Political Science Association, 30th August—2nd September 2012, New Orleans.

Corneo, G. (2005a), 'The Rise and Likely Fall of the German Income Tax, 1958-2005', *CESifo Economic Studies* 51, 159–186.

Corneo, G. (2005b), 'Verteilungsarithmetik der rot-grünen Steuerreform', *Schmollers Jahrbuch* 125, 299–314.

Der Bundeswahlleiter (2009a), Heft 1, *Ergebnisse und Vergleichszahlen früherer Bundestags-, Europa- und Landtagswahlen sowie Strukturdaten für die Bundestagswahlkreise*, Wahl zum 17. Deutschen Bundestag am 27. September 2009, Informationen des Bundeswahlleiters. Wiesbaden.

Der Bundeswahlleiter (2009b), Heft 2,*Vorläufige Ergebnisse nach Wahlkreisen*, Wahl zum 17. Deutschen Bundestag am 27. September 2009, Informationen des Bundeswahlleiters. Wiesbaden.

Dustmann, C., Ludsteck, J. and Schönberg, U. (2009), 'Revisiting the German Wage Structure', *The Quarterly Journal of Economics* 142/2, 843–881.

Engels, D. *et al.* (forthcoming), 'Wahrnehmung von Armut und Reichtum in Deutschland: Primärerhebung und Sekundäranalyse der repräsentativen Befragung' *ARB-Survey 2011*, Institut für Sozialforschung und Gesellschaftspolitik und aproxima Gesellschaft für Markt- und Sozialforschung Weimar mbH im Auftrag des BMAS.

Fabbri, F. and Marin, D. (2012), 'What Explains the Rise in CEO Pay in Germany? A Panel Data Analysis for 1977-2009', *CESifo Working Paper* 3757.

Fuchs-Schündeln, N., Krueger, D. and Sommer, M. (2010), 'Inequality Trends for Germany in the Last Two Decades: A Tale of Two Countries', *Review of Economic Dynamics* 13/1, 103–132.

Gernandt, J. and Pfeiffer, F. (2007), 'Rising Wage Inequality in Germany', *Journal of Economics and Statistics* (Jahrbuecher fuer Nationaloekonomie und Statistik), 227/4, 358–380.

Goebel, J., Habich, R. and Krause, P. (2011), 'Einkommen—Verteilung, Angleichung, Armut und Dynamik', in Statistisches Bundesamt (ed.): *Datenreport 2011. Zahlen und Fakten über die Bundesrepublik Deutschland*, Bonn: Bundeszentrale für politische Bildung, 162–172.

Holst, E. and Seifert, R. (2012), 'Arbeitspolitische Kontroversen im Spiegel der Arbeitszeit-wünsche', *WSI Mitteilungen* 2, 141–149.

Kumlin, S. (2004), *The Personal and the Political: How Personal Welfare State Experiences Affect Political Trust and Ideology*, New York: Palgrave.

Newton, K. and Zmerli, S. (2011), 'Three Forms of Trust and their Association', *European Political Science Review* 3, 169–200.

Peichl, A., Pestel, N. and Schneider, H. (2012), 'Does Size Matter? The Impact of Changes in Household Structure on Income Distribution in Germany', *Review of Income and Wealth*, 58/1, 118–141.

Roemer, J. E. (2011), 'The Ideological and Political Roots of American Inequality', *GINI DP* 8.

Rothstein, B. (2011), *The Quality of Government. Corruption, Social Trust, and Inequality in International Perspective*, Chicago: University of Chicago Press.

Uslaner, E. M. (2008), *Corruption, Inequality, and the Rule of Law: The Bulging Pocket Makes the Easy Life*. New York: Cambridge University Press.

Uslaner, E. M. (2011), 'Corruption, the Inequality Trap, and Trust in Government', in Zmerli, S. and M. Hooghe (eds.), *Political Trust. Why Context Matters*, Colchester: ECPR Press, 141–162.

CHAPTER 13

....

GREECE: THE (EVENTUAL) SOCIAL HARDSHIP OF SOFT BUDGET CONSTRAINTS

....

MARGARITA KATSIMI, THOMAS MOUTOS, GEORGE

PAGOULATOS, AND DIMITRI SOTIROPOULOS[*]

1. INTRODUCTION

THIS chapter examines the evolution of inequality in Greece and its broader socio-economic, political and policy implications.[1] Greece stands out as a country case study mainly for three reasons. First, through the overall period 1974–2009, Greece exhibits a significant reduction of inequality. Second, the catch-up with the EU15 levels of social spending was not followed by a proportionate effectiveness of welfare state institutions and policies in reducing overall inequality; indeed, in certain cases, a regressive function of these institutions and policies is observed. Third, the lack of fiscal soundness and economic viability of the Greek economic and social 'model' engendered the steep, abrupt and on-going decline of the social accord and living standards since 2009, following the end of *soft budget constraints*[2] and the concomitant bursting of the debt bubble. The content of this chapter will further elaborate on these and other relevant features.

[*] We wish to thank: Manolis Chrysakis, Theo Mitrakos, and Panos Tsakloglou for making available to us their data; Tasos Palaiologos, Yannis Panouris, and Dimitra Tsingou for research assistance; and Wiemer Salverda for comments and suggestions.
[1] For more details about the issues covered, the methodology, data, and references, the interested reader may consult the country report, available at <www.gini-research.org/CR-Greece>.
[2] The term is borrowed from Kornai (1980), who discusses in detail how soft budget constraints can come into existence, and how they can affect agents' behaviour. In the Greek context it can be understood as the belief by public and private agents that deficits can be financed forever since permanently higher growth rates will ensure the sustainability of government and private debts.

The Politico-Economic Context: An Unsustainable Growth Model Terminated in 2010

In this section we provide the politico-economic context that was instrumental in shaping the evolution of inequalities in Greece over the last four decades. We discern three phases, and in what follows we describe the main events and economic outcomes which made each period a distinct era.

Starting with the 1974 transition to democracy, Greece began its long socio-economic convergence with the advanced EU countries. The first phase (1974–1981) involved fast economic growth, low and declining unemployment, but slow progress regarding social integration. The second phase (1982–1994) showed considerable progress towards increasing opportunities and capabilities for disadvantaged social groups, mainly through the large public sector expansion. This period was marked by the rise to power of the socialist PASOK party and EC accession (both in 1981), and ended with Greece's decision to seek to join the European Monetary Union (EMU). The rather haphazard public sector expansion, and the careless macro-economic management during most of this period, led to economic stagnation, rising unemployment, and an increase in public debt (still domestically held) to dangerously high levels. The third phase (1994–2009), saw a further expansion (and some rationalization) of the Welfare State and rapid economic growth. With hindsight, we know that the 'growth model' of this period was seriously flawed, being predicated on excessive borrowing from abroad. The global financial crisis terminated this phase, and ushered in the Greek Great Depression, sending the unemployment rate in 2012 to 25 per cent and reducing (real) GDP per capita to about the level of 2001.

In terms of GDP per capita, Greece began at 43.9 per cent of the EU15 average in 1960, and reached 72 per cent by 1978. Income convergence was reversed in the 1980s, and in 1990 the ratio was 57.6 per cent. Convergence resumed again, and from 57.7 per cent of the EA12 average in 1995, Greece reached 70.1 per cent in 2009. In 2012, however, the country's GDP per capita relative to the EA12 is expected to be less than 60 per cent. The large gyrations in Greece's economic activity were reflected in large fluctuations in real compensation per employee. Indeed, between 1970 and 2009 there was an increase in real compensation per employee by about 80 per cent. However, it is expected to drop in 2013 to levels previously experienced in the late 1970s. It is important to our perspective on inequality trends that there were two periods in which there was a clear upward trend in real compensation per employee: from the mid 1970s to the mid 1980s, and from the mid 1990s to 2009.

These developments in employee compensation were matched by movements in the adjusted wage share (compensation per employee as a percentage of GDP at market prices per person employed). From 56 per cent in 1973, the wage share reached a peak of 66 per cent in 1983. After 1983, it started declining towards the 55 per cent mark—where it hovered until 2009, falling sharply with the Great Depression, to 52.4 per cent in 2010, and 48.5 per cent in 2011. The rise in real compensation per employee and in the wage share from the mid 1970s to the early 1980s, were principal factors behind the large decrease in income inequality during this period.

The gross national saving rate posted a steep decline, from 28.8 per cent in the 1970s to 3.5 per cent in 2010–2011. This huge decline in the gross saving rate meant that in the 2000s net national saving (equal to gross national saving minus depreciation) became negative, i.e. (in the absence of valuation changes) national wealth started decreasing. The development is wholly attributable to the decline in the private sector's gross saving rate (from 27 per cent in 1988 to 11 per cent in 2008), and it led to large current account deficits after 1997, which took Greece's net foreign assets position from -3 per cent in 1997 to -86 per cent of GDP by the end of 2009 (Katsimi and Moutos, 2010). At that point, investors started to question the government's ability (and/or willingness) to service its debt to foreigners, since it became clear that the Greek government faced a 'mission impossible': on the one hand, to make public debt sustainable, the economy should grow so as to increase tax revenue; on the other hand, to make net foreign debt sustainable, the economy should contract so as to eliminate the huge current account deficit. Under these conditions, foreign creditors started demanding interest rates that embodied a high probability of default, thus forcing the government to resort to the official bailout mechanism to avoid the impending default.

This brought an end to the large expansion of Greek living standards (since 1995), an expansion which was sustained by the availability of private foreign credit and allowed both the private sector and the government to operate under a regime of soft budget constraints. This growth-on-(foreign credit)-steroids allowed large expansions in compensation per employee: the cumulative increase over the 1994–2009 period in (gross) nominal private sector wages (excluding the banking sector) was 137 per cent, whereas the cumulative increase in public-sector wages was 291 per cent, and in publicly-owned enterprises it was 356 per cent (Fotoniata and Moutos, 2010). In economies unable to borrow excessively from abroad—something Greece, as part of the euro, was able to do—such increases in public-sector wages would be associated with higher tax rates, thus crowding out private employment, and forcing an end to the unsustainable public spending spree.

The seemingly unlimited access to credit which the Greek economy enjoyed until 2008 allowed the private sector to develop along with the public sector, thus enabling private-sector employees to experience after-tax real wage increases as well. The elimination of the soft budget constraints post-2009 has produced unprecedented declines in private employment and wages (for all employees), thus setting the stage for large, though as yet unrecorded, increases in inequality.

2. EVOLUTION OF INEQUALITY AND ITS DRIVERS

This section discusses the trends in various inequality and poverty measures, examines the major factors (drivers) behind these trends, and analyses how these developments have been related to various social gradients.

Income Inequalities

Unlike most other OECD countries, Greece experienced a decline in almost all inequality indices during the last three decades. During the first phase, the fast-rising living standards produced a large decline in inequality and the Gini coefficient was reduced by 19 per cent. This reduction in inequality, albeit from a high level relative to the richer EU countries, was underpinned by minimum wage increases of about 20 per cent in real terms from 1974 to 1981, business-sector productivity increases of about 17 per cent, and unemployment rates below 4 per cent. The rising tide of economic activity lifted the boats of middle- and lower-income households by more than the affluent ones. During the second phase, the economy stagnated, real minimum wages were, in 1994, about 20 per cent lower than in 1982, whereas the unemployment rate had risen to 9 per cent. Inequality remained roughly constant during this period—despite the decline in real minimum wages—due to the expansion of an idiosyncratic Welfare State. During the third phase, growth resumed, minimum wages started increasing, and inequality decreased as well—but not nearly as much as during the first phase. Since 2010, GDP has plummeted, the real value of the minimum wage has dropped by over 25 per cent, unemployment has soared, and social welfare spending has been seriously curtailed. These changes make it highly probable that inequality has also risen back to the level it was three decades ago.

Figure 13.1 depicts the aggregate inequality indices (Gini coefficient and the Atkinson index for values of the parameter capturing the aversion to inequality equal to $\varepsilon=0.5$ and $\varepsilon=2.0$). During 1974–82, equivalized household disposable income inequality declined by between 19 per cent (Gini) and 36 per cent (Atkinson, $\varepsilon=0.5$). From 1982 to 1999, income inequality remained roughly constant.[3] It is reassuring that these changes in inequality

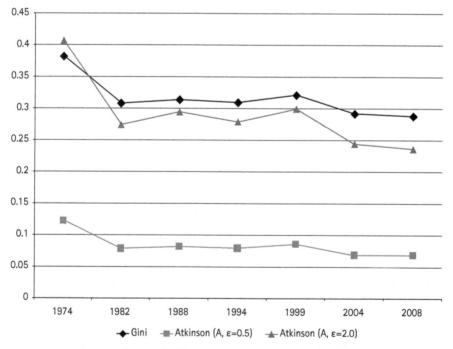

FIGURE 13.1 Evolution of Household Income Inequality Indices, 1974–2008

Source: EU-SILC, Mitrakos and Tsakloglou (2012).

[3] In what follows, unless otherwise stated, we report equivalized inequality measures according to the modified OECD scale, which gives a weight of 1.0 to the head of the household, 0.5 to all other members above 13 years old, and 0.3 to children up to the age of 13..

Table 13.1 Income shares by population deciles

Decile	1974	1982	1988	1994	1999	2004	2008
1 (poorest 10%)	2.3	3.2	3.0	3.1	3.0	3.5	3.7
2	4.0	4.9	4.8	4.8	4.7	5.1	5.2
3	5.1	6.0	6.0	5.9	5.9	6.1	6.2
4	6.1	7.0	7.0	7.0	6.8	7.1	7.1
5	7.2	8.0	8.0	8.1	7.9	8.1	8.2
6	8.4	9.1	9.1	9.3	9.0	9.3	9.3
7	9.9	10.4	10.5	10.6	10.4	10.6	10.5
8	12.0	12.2	12.3	12.3	12.1	12.2	12.1
9	15.3	14.8	15.0	14.9	15.0	14.7	14.6
10 (richest 10%)	29.7	24.3	24.4	24.0	25.1	23.2	23.3

Source: Mitrakos and Tsakloglou (2012).

Table 13.2 Decile ratios (D9/D1, D5/D1, D9/D5)

Ratios	1974	1982	1988	1994	1999	2004	2008
D9/D1	6.7	4.6	5.0	4.8	5.0	4.2	3.9
D5/D1	3.1	2.5	2.7	2.6	2.6	2.3	2.2
D9/D5	2.1	1.9	1.9	1.8	1.9	1.8	1.8

Source: Mitrakos and Tsakloglou (2012) and authors' calculations.

are similar across the three indices. The next significant decline in inequality took place between 1999 and 2004, and it declined very little—in effect, it remained constant—from 2004 to 2008. The indices showing the biggest drop in income inequality during this period are those more sensitive to changes at the extremes of the distribution (i.e. the Atkinson indices).

The decline in income inequality is also reflected in the rising proportion of total household income accruing to the poorest decile, according to the Greek Household Budget Surveys (HBS). The poorest population decile increased its share of total income from 2.3 per cent in 1974 to 3.7 per cent in 2008. In contrast, the share of the richest decile declined from 29.7 per cent in 1974 to 23.3 per cent in 2008. The rise in income shares from 1974 to 2008 was experienced by the seven lowest deciles, whereas only the two highest deciles had any discernible fall in their income shares (Table 13.1).

Table 13.2 reveals that the ratio of the income share accruing to the second richest decile to the income share of the lowest decile (D9/D1) declined from 6.7 in 1974 to 4.6 in 1982. This drop in the D9/D1 ratio tallies well with Gini's decline. This ratio hovered around 5 until 1998, and then declined to 4.2 in 2004, and to 3.9 in 2008. The same qualitative movements are observed for the D5/D1 and D9/D5 ratios as well. This implies that the poorest registered gains in their relative income standing not only relative to the rich, but relative to middle incomes as well. OECD (2011) calculates that the growth in real household incomes for the bottom decile from the mid 1980s to the late 2000s was equal in Greece to 3.4 per cent per annum, while the corresponding growth rate for the top decile was 1.8 per cent, compared to

OECD average corresponding growth rates of 1.3 per cent for the bottom decile and 1.9 per cent for the top decile.

The evolution of poverty has followed a similar pattern to the evolution of income inequality. Employing Eurostat's *relative* poverty line, which corresponds to 60 per cent of median (equivalized) income according to the utilized HBS, 15.6 per cent of the Greek population was below the relative poverty line in 2008, i.e. the poverty rate was 15.6 per cent. In the same year, the poverty *gap*—defined as the income that would be needed to raise the incomes of all persons classified as poor to the relative poverty line—was 3.4 per cent of aggregate augmented income. Between 1974 and 2008, the drop in the poverty rate was 23.3 per cent and the reduction in the poverty gap was 47.6 per cent, whereas the drop in the Foster-Greer-Thorbecke (a=2) (FGT2) index was 63.8 per cent. The largest drop in the FGT2 index, sensitive to situations of extreme poverty, indicates considerable progress in reducing extreme poverty. The biggest drop in poverty also took place between 1974 and 1982—a 45.7 per cent decline in the FGT2 index. Poverty remained roughly constant from 1982 to 1999, and it declined again considerably from 1999 to 2008, with the percentage decline in the FGT2 index being 45.2 per cent during this latter period.

For a country like Greece, with extensive owner-occupied housing among lower-income households, and a large agricultural sector, the effect of different non-monetary factors (incomes in-kind) on income inequality is significant. According to Koutsabelas and Tsakloglou (2012), drawing on HBS data 2004/5, the importance of incomes in-kind—which they define as the sum of imputed rent, education-related and health-related public transfers, and other in-kind incomes—is far more important for the lower quintiles, than for the higher quintiles of the distribution. For the lowest quintile, disposable income represents only 51.4 per cent of augmented income (which includes incomes in-kind), whereas for the top quintile the corresponding share is 84.4 per cent. We note also that for the poorest quintile, whose non-monetary income is about half of the total, most of this income is due to public transfers (29.1 per cent of the total), whereas private incomes in-kind represent 19.6 per cent of the total. As we climb up the income distribution, the relative importance of public transfers becomes smaller; indeed, for the richest quintile, private incomes in-kind represent 8.5 per cent of augmented income, whereas public transfers in-kind represent only 7.1 per cent of augmented income.

Also significant were the effects of in-kind public transfers, and in-kind private incomes (we use the term non-monetary incomes for these incomes, hereafter) on inequality. Koutsambelas and Tsakloglou (2012) find the provision of publicly-funded health services to be the factor with the strongest influence in reducing inequality: the percentage reduction in inequality ranges from 10.9 (Gini index) to 23.3 per cent (Atkinson index with e=1.5). Imputed rent and publicly-funded education have also had an impact, with the reduction in inequality ranging between 5.3 and 13.3 per cent for the first, and between 6.4 and 12.1 per cent for the second. The joint influence of the above non-monetary sources of income (including private incomes and transfers in-kind, consisting of own-consumption of agricultural and non-agricultural goods, in-kind employment benefits, and in-kind private transfer) is impressive, resulting in percentage reductions in the inequality indices between 22.1 and 41.8 per cent.

Consumption Inequalities

The evolution of household consumption inequality has followed a similar pattern to income inequality. Figure 13.2 indicates that the indices showing the largest drop in inequality are the ones dependent on changes at the tails of the distribution. The largest drop in consumption inequality took place during 1974–1982. From 1982 to 1999, the indices remain roughly constant, whereas a significant drop takes place during 1999–2004. The last period (2004–2008) shows a very small rise in consumption inequality. Consumption inequality has always been smaller than income inequality.

Keeping the poverty line fixed in terms of real purchasing power, the decline in the poverty rate in terms of household consumption spending has been impressive: the poverty rate declined over the whole period by 87.8 per cent, the poverty gap by 93.3 per cent, and the FGT2 index by 95.8 per cent. Almost all of these declines happened in two batches: the first from 1974 to 1982; and the second from 1999 to 2004.

Group Differences in Inequality Patterns

How has the reduction of inequality and poverty during 1974–2008 been distributed among various socio-economic groups on the basis of their exposure to poverty risk (FGT2 index)?

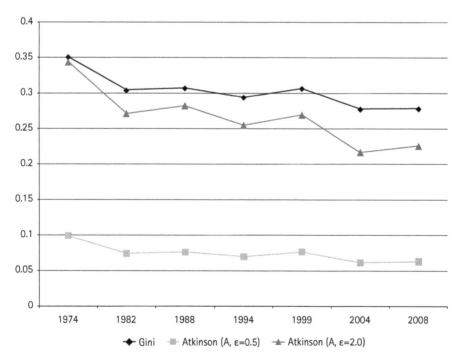

FIGURE 13.2 Consumption Inequality Indices, 1974–2008

Source: Mitrakos and Tsakloglou (2012).

All the groups usually considered to be at high risk of poverty, with the exception of house-holds headed by a pensioner and couples without children, were still facing a relatively high poverty risk in 2008. For persons aged over 65 and living alone, as well as for households headed by a pensioner, the relative poverty risk declined considerably from 1974 to 2008—from 4.36 to 1.39 for the first group, and from 1.93 to 0.49 for the second. By contrast, for households with three or more children under eighteen, the relative poverty risk increased from 1.50 to 3.64, making this group the one with the highest poverty risk in 2008. However, this group's contribution to aggregate poverty is not large, hovering around 10 per cent during the entire period. Residents of agricultural areas have always had the largest contribution to aggregate poverty—yet, this contribution declined steadily from 56.9 per cent in 1974, to 28.7 per cent in 2008: this group's relative poverty risk has remained roughly constant during this period. Single-parent family members, a group at high risk of poverty in many European countries, experienced a rise of poverty risk, especially after 1982, but the group's contribution to the aggregate poverty rate remains small. Of possibly greater importance is the rise in poverty risk for members of households headed by a farmer, whose poverty risk increased continuously, and reached 2.91 in 2008. This group's contribution to total poverty declined throughout the whole period (given the declining share of farmers in the population) but it retained its importance for aggregate poverty, contributing 18.5 per cent.

The reduction in aggregate (income, and consumption) inequality was accompanied by a reduction in 'within group' inequality. For all socio-economic groups, the reduction in overall income (and, consumption) inequality was accompanied by far larger reductions in 'within group' inequality than in inequality between groups. Given that, in Greece, the largest part of aggregate inequality is 'determined' from differences that exist within different socio-economic groups (rather than between groups) this has been a welcome development.

Wealth Inequality

According to the Credit Suisse (2011) *Global Wealth Databook 2011*, wealth inequality is low in Greece relative to most European countries. Credit Suisse (2011) calculates the Gini for wealth inequality in 2011 among adults at 70.3 in Greece against a European average of 82.9. The proportion of Greek adults with wealth less than 1,000 USD is only 1.6 per cent, compared to a European average of 20.4 per cent. The high European average is a result of the low wealth levels of some post-communist countries. Yet, there exist some high-income European countries for which a high proportion of their adult population has wealth below 1,000 USD: 13.6 per cent of the adult population in Germany, 12.5 per cent in the Netherlands, and 7.1 per cent in the UK. It is also of interest that 48.3 per cent of adults in Greece have wealth between 10,000 and 100,000 USD, compared to a European average of 28.2 per cent.

Labour Market Inequality

One of the salient features of the Greek economy is the differential labour market outcomes between males and females. The differences between the sexes in employment and participation rates were enormous up to the early 1990s: in 1992, the participation rate for males was 76.4 per cent, whereas for females it was only 41.8 per cent. The difference in employ-ment rates was also large in 1992—72.3 per cent for males and 36.2 per cent for females. By 2008, both the employment and participation gaps between the genders had closed con-siderably, mainly by increasing female participation and employment rates, which had increased to 55.1 per cent and 48.7 per cent, respectively, thus bringing the participation gap to 24 percentage points (from 34.6 p.p. in 1992), and the employment gap to 24.6 percentage points (from 36.1 p.p. in 1992).

The improvements in the integration of females in market activities coincided with a large expansion of employment rates for people with upper-secondary and post-secondary non-tertiary education level qualifications. The employment rate for these persons rose from 52.3 per cent in 1992 to 61.2 per cent in 2008, but it still remained far lower than the employment rate for people with tertiary education, which was 82.1 per cent in 2008. On the other side of the educational spectrum, persons with less than a high-school diploma did not experience rising employment rates, possibly as a result of the economy shifting from agricultural activities to the more skill-intensive service sector.

The decline in income inequality during 1999–2008 coincided with a large reduction in the unemployment rate for females with upper-secondary and post-secondary education, from 23.8 per cent in 1999 to 13.2 per cent in 2008. The rise in female employment rates cannot be attributed to any increases in part-time employment, which in 2008 remained at a very low 5.4 per cent of total employment. The rise in female employment rates should rather be attributed to the expansion of the service sector (from the demand side), a rise in the marrying age of women, and much-increased educational attainment of women (from the supply side).

Wages and salaries remained throughout the period the most important factor in the for-mation of aggregate income inequality, their trendless contribution ranging from 34.7 per cent to 46.9 per cent. This is due to labour income being the single largest source of income in the aggregate (34.7 per cent of total income—the self-employed are included in a differ-ent category), but also due to the large correlation coefficient between this source and total income. Incomes from self-employment (excluding agricultural income) and from capital ownership each contributed around one quarter in 2008. The rise in importance of income from pensions during this period (from 8.4 per cent in 1974 to 13.2 per cent in 2008) mostly reflects its rise as a share of total income (from 8.6 per cent in 1974 to 18.3 per cent in 2008).

Inequality in the distribution of net hourly earnings in Greece is rather high relative to other European countries. Based on ECHP data (2000 and 2001), Cholezas and Tsakloglou (2007) found that among the thirteen countries examined, Greece has the second most unequal distribution of hourly earnings.

Educational Inequality

Educational inequalities in Greece are strongly linked with income inequalities, with higher levels of educational attainment strongly associated with higher earnings and household income. Educational inequality is of overwhelming importance for determining differences in income inequality. Contrary to other factors (region of residence, urbanization, type of household, employment category of household head) whose importance in explaining inequality between groups has tended to decline from 1974 to 2008, the education of the household head has retained its prominence. A possible explanation could be assortative mating and the high participation rate of educated spouses.

This strong link between educational and income inequalities has been mediated through increasingly differentiated employment and participation rates across educational groups; indeed, unlike the economy-wide trends of rising employment rates, persons with less than a high-school diploma did not experience rising employment rates. Similarly, the declines in the unemployment rates for people (females, especially) with upper secondary and post-secondary education were far more pronounced than for persons of lower-educational achievement—a result of the re-orientation of economic activity away from agricultural (and industrial) activities, and towards the service sector. Linkages between income and educational inequalities may create a vicious circle: income inequality, in the absence of equal education opportunities, reinforces educational inequality, which, in turn, leads to higher income inequality. This adverse effect has been kept in check in Greece through a significant expansion of educational opportunities, especially through the large expansion of the tertiary sector. Nevertheless, this expansion did not manage to reduce inequality in accessing higher-educational institutions (especially universities) for lower-income groups. As education is an important factor in the intergenerational transmission of economic status, the reduction in inequality observed during the last four decades may not be sustainable once some of the other factors behind the decline in inequality exhaust their influence.

Since the 1970s, there has been a large increase in educational attainment, a result of a latent demand in Greek society for further expansion of higher education. The proportion of students admitted to tertiary education rose from about 15 per cent of high-school graduates in 1974 to about 40 per cent in 2008. The synthetic indices of education level and dispersion (Meschi and Scervini, 2010) indicate a large rise in the percentage of the population with a tertiary education and a decline in educational inequality. Less than 6 per cent of the population born between 1920 and 1924 in the EES sample has attained tertiary education but the corresponding percentage increases to over 43 per cent for individuals born in the 1982–1984 period. The Gini index was 0.299 for the 1920–24 birth cohort but it fell to 0.117 for the 1982–84 cohort.

Yet, despite the significant expansion of tertiary education, which lessened the competition for available places, lower-income families still faced considerable hurdles in gaining access to higher education. This is because private spending on tutors and crammer schools preparing students for the national exams has increased, from an estimated 2.15 per cent of household budgets in 1974 to 4.41 per cent in 1999, and to 5.09 per cent in 2005 (Kanellopoulos et al., 2003; KANEP, 2009). It can reach up to one fifth of household income for lower-income families.

From 1984 to 2004, the children of white-collar employees enjoyed a slight increase in their over-representation as first-year students in Greek universities; the inequality indicator for this group went from 2.01 in 1984 to 2.18 in 2004.[4] By contrast, the inequality indicator for a student whose father was a blue-collar worker declined from 0.90 in 1984 to 0.62 in 2004, whereas for farmers' children the indicator went from 0.53 in 1984 to 0.32 in 2004. During the same period, first-year university students with an unemployed

---

[4] An inequality indicator above (below) 1 indicates that a particular category is over- (under-) represented in tertiary education.

father were continuously and significantly under-represented in the student body, despite the improvement observed in the indicator, from 0.07 in 1984 to 0.26 in 2004 (Chrysakis *et al.*, 2009).

The worsening prospects for children whose fathers are either blue-collar workers or farmers, with respect to university education, were not reflected in better access opportunities in the (lower-ranked) Technological Educational Institutes (TEI). For blue-collar workers, the inequality indicator dropped from 1.21 in 1984 to 1.00 in 2004, whereas for farmers it went from 0.75 to 0.50 during the same period. Again, surprisingly, the relative access of children with unemployed fathers improved, the indicator rising from 0.07 in 1984 to 0.47 in 2004. A possible explanation could be the gradual emergence of a two-earner family in Greece, enabling families with unemployed fathers to be able to finance the expenses needed to succeed in the entrance examinations with the mother's earnings.

Drivers of Inequality Decline

Despite the large decreases in inequality, and the rise in the corresponding measures in most EU15 countries, Greece had a Gini coefficient of disposable income in 2008 higher than the EU15 average: the disposable income Gini coefficient in that year was 0.3065, and it was lower than the Ginis for Italy, Portugal, Spain, and the UK. Regarding inequality of extended income (which includes in-kind benefits from public services), the Gini coefficient in Greece in 2008 was 0.288, with Portugal being the only country among the EU15 which had a higher Gini coefficient (OECD, 2011). We may thus conclude that, as far as inequality is concerned, Greece had, by 2008, partially converged with the EU15 average.

The large decline in inequality between 1974 and 1982 was strongly connected with the cumulative rise in the real value of the minimum wage (MW), which increased by 52 per cent from 1974 to 1982 During the same period the cumulative rise in real compensation per employee was 39 per cent. To appreciate just how large this increase was, we note that the real value of the MW started declining after 1984, and its subsequent rise did not return it to its 1982 level until 2009, subsequently dropping to levels prevailing in the late 1970s. Unlike the MW, real compensation per employee did not suffer a strong and protracted fall after 1982, and was 28 per cent higher in 2008 than in 1982. Between 1982 and 1999, when income inequality increased slightly, real compensation per employee increased by 6 per cent, but the real value of the MW declined by 15 per cent. Between 1999 and 2008, when inequality declined again, both the real MW and real compensation per employee rose by 17 per cent and 21 per cent, respectively. Thus, rises in real compensation per employee are not, by themselves, able to explain the evolution of income inequality in Greece—the behaviour of the MW is. Increases in the real value of the MW (1974–1982 and 1999–2008) have been associated with declines in inequality. Declines in the real value of the MW wage (1982–1999), which went in tandem with increases in real compensation per employee, have been associated with (albeit small) increases in inequality.

To further appreciate the importance of the MW for the large decline in inequality from 1974 to 1982, we compare the monthly MW with the poverty line (equivalized disposable income) for 1974 and 1982. A MW employee was earning 28 per cent above the poverty line in 1974; by 1982, the MW employee was earning 43 per cent above the poverty line. Since no significant changes in taxation took place between 1974 and 1982, this rise in the 'premium' of the MW over the poverty line appears to have contributed to the significant decreases in inequality and poverty that took place during this period.

Another factor that has contributed to the decline in inequality is the increasing prevalence of two-earner families. Females massively entered the labour market in the 1980s, as a result of changes in family attitudes and/or the expansion of employment opportunities in the public sector. Not only were conditions of public-sector employment less demanding on female employees also burdened with their traditional household duties; they were also more lucrative (in current wages and future benefits) than private-sector jobs, thus providing an added incentive for labour market participation. Of crucial importance in this expansion of employment opportunities for females was that it did not take the form of part-time jobs, since a rise in part-time employment tends to increase inequality.[5]

3. Social Impacts

The absence of a sufficiently long time-series on relevant variables in Greece does not allow us to identify with confidence many of the social impacts of changes in income inequality. We will now briefly review these social outcomes and discuss whether or not they appear to be associated with inequality changes.

Material deprivation represents the inability to afford some items considered by most people to be desirable or even necessary in order to lead an adequate life. Available evidence suggests that levels of material deprivation have moved broadly in line with average income (or better, real compensation per employee), and naturally, are dependent on economic status. Severe material deprivation has fallen significantly between 2003 and 2009.

Perhaps surprisingly, social exclusion does not seem to be strongly associated with income inequality. Unlike poverty, which is a distributional outcome, social exclusion refers to a process of declining participation, solidarity, and access. Andriopoulou et al. (2010) find that poverty and social exclusion are not closely linked, since more than half of the people considered to be at high risk of social exclusion are not poor. Households headed by females face a significantly higher risk of social exclusion, with the relative risk for females being almost twice as high as for males. However, there is a close linkage between labour market inequality and the risk of social exclusion. This is made apparent by the fact that, compared to household heads who are full-time employees, the risk of social exclusion is about two and a half times larger for household heads which are part-time employees, and about four times larger for unemployed household heads. A strong association also exists between educational inequality and social exclusion. The risk of social exclusion is about eight times greater for household heads with primary education than for graduates of tertiary institutions. People with the lowest educational qualifications make up more than 60 per cent of the population with a high risk of social exclusion.

Changes in the rates of family formation and breakdown have reflected the expansion of tertiary education opportunities more than the inequality trends. Family formation and

---

[5] There was no rise in overall part-time employment in Greece, which ranged between 4 per cent and 6 per cent of total employment. Female part-time employment in 2008 was lower than in 1983.

breakdown rates have moved closer to the EU15 average, through a rise in the divorce rate and a decrease in the marriage rate. Fluctuations in income inequality do not seem to be strongly linked with patterns of fertility and living arrangements for children either. The declines in the total fertility rate, which lasted until the early 2000s, were reversed later (though they still remain significantly below most EU countries) probably due to the influx of immigrants but also due to the rise in labour incomes, which started again in the late 1990s. In contrast to other European societies, births out of wedlock did not increase and lone parenthood was still a rather rare instance. Greece remains a relatively traditional society as far as family formation and family structure are concerned. The same holds true with respect to the intergenerational mobility of income, since paternal occupation and education exercise the strongest influence on the poverty risk of the children when they become adults.

The rising life expectancy in Greece reduced, but it did not eradicate, the difference in self-perceived health status across income quintiles, with members of the bottom quintile still (2008) being three times as likely to report a very bad/ bad health status as members of the top quintile. The differences in health status across educational groups became wider, with persons of only primary education being between two and eight times as likely in 2008 to report a very bad/ bad health status as persons with more education.

The high rate of owner-occupier status among the poor in Greece has not prevented the existence of the highest severe housing deprivation rate among the EU15, which, despite declining from 8.2 per cent in 2004 to 7.6 per cent in 2010, was still the highest among the EU15, and higher than some new EU Member States. In 2009, Greece also had a higher over-crowding rate[6] than all other EU15 countries. Contrary to other EU15 countries though, there was not much difference in overcrowding rates between the poor and the non-poor.

Crime has also increased since the mid 1990s, partly reflecting the influx of undocumented migrants, but also the social transformation of Greek society, namely its urbanization, as crime is less frequent when people live in rural areas (European Sourcebook of Crime and Criminal Justice Statistics, 2003 and 2010). Trends in both crime and prison population do not correspond to shifts in inequality.

Reported levels of overall life satisfaction in Greece have remained below the EU average, have been very responsive to the economic cycle, and, naturally, have plummeted to unprecedented levels since 2008.

As argued earlier, most of the decrease in inequality in Greece took place from the mid 1970s to the early 1980s, with only small declines in inequality taking place in the 2000s. It is thus not surprising that we have not seen improvements in many of the socio-economic indicators examined in this section, since most of the available data on social outcomes cover only the last 10 years. To some extent the inability of inequality decreases to impact positively on social outcomes has to do with failures of social policy in Greece. But it also reflects the changes in social and economic structure that took place during the last two decades. Chief among them has been the movement of the population from rural areas to urban centres, and the large influx of immigrants.

---

[6] This is the proportion of people living in an overcrowded dwelling, as defined by the number of rooms available to the household, the household's size, as well as its members' ages and family situation.

4. POLITICAL AND CULTURAL IMPACTS

It is very difficult to identify any specific impact of inequality on political and cultural outcomes. While other EU societies have experienced high-income inequalities, which had a negative political and cultural impact, in Greece income inequality is not clearly associated with political participation, levels of institutional trust, political values or values about social policy and welfare. Between 1974 and 2012, Greece had an overall stable two-party system, where the centre-right ND and the socialist PASOK alternated in power, usually forming strong majority governments. Instead of income-group based political cleavages, divisions in Greece reflected: first, party conflict between the right and the left associated with past dramatic moments of political history (the Civil War, break-down of democracy); second, political contests to 'colonize' the state, a preponderant actor in the Greek economy and society; and, third, a contradictory value system containing modern and traditional aspects associated with Greece's position on the periphery of Europe. It is in the light of these patterns that Greece's high political participation, negative levels of trust, and endurance of traditional values can be better understood (Mouzelis and Pagoulatos, 2005).

Political party identification was so strong that high and low income earners voted on the basis of family tradition (whose side the voter's family was on during the Civil War) and personal political socialization (whether the voter had shaped his or her value system in the post-war period or during the Colonels' regime or the transition to democracy that followed). Political participation was also positively affected by the expansion of secondary and tertiary education.

Owing to this tradition of conflict and polarization, extended participation in elections was not reflected in patterns of trust towards democratic institutions. Except for the legal system, i.e. the courts, which were relatively trusted by Greeks, the parliament, the government and the political parties did not enjoy the stable confidence of citizens and lost this confidence altogether by the start of the crisis in Greece (2010). Indeed, the decrease in trust in Greek political institutions was so dramatic, that we can claim that political trust in Greece collapsed after 2010.

In contrast to many other advanced democracies, the extreme right was negligible until the 2012 elections which were preceded by the economic crisis, and usually failed to obtain parliamentary representation. The extreme left was comparatively stronger. The Greek party system still includes one of the last remaining pro-Soviet communist parties in Western Europe, while other extreme left factions have been visibly present in universities and some public sector unions.

It appears that the two main push factors of political extremism in the late 2000s have been the large inflows of non-documented immigration, which from the second half of the 2000s acquired prominence in the public debate, and the on-going deep economic and political legitimacy crisis that erupted in 2010. The crisis has also been received as a failure of the party-political status quo, fuelling anti-system sentiment. It can well be argued that economic hardship and the rise of unemployment and poverty rates since 2010 are fuelling the extremist vote (in the 2012 elections the newcomer extreme racist Golden Dawn party came second after the radical left SYRIZA in the voter group aged 18–34). However, the time span of the data is too short to provide sufficient backing for any clear association of the changing rates of inequality with political extremism.

Opinion polls reflect a tension between, on the one hand, the progressive Europeanization of Greek public debate over issues concerning social values and civil rights and, on the other, the spreading societal insecurity and xenophobia vis a vis the growing waves of non-documented immigration (V-PRC, 2008, Public Issue, 2009). Contradictions abound also with regard to values about social policy and the Welfare State. Traditional Greek atomism, manifested in low trust in interpersonal relations and low levels of voluntarism, coexists with the highest propensity in the EU-27 to call on the government to redistribute wealth in a fair way to all citizens, and the lowest level of agreement in the EU-27 with the idea that people, rather than the government, should take responsibility for providing for themselves (EKKE, 2010).

Despite the very limited presence of unions in the overwhelmingly small sized private enterprise sector—traditional union bastions being government, public enterprises and banks—the acceptance of the need for strong trade unions has been broadly shared. In the early 2000s, Greece registered one of the highest cross-European rates of agreement with the statement that strong unions are needed to protect the working conditions and wages of working people. Finally, public opinion approval rates of EU membership from the 1980s to 2009 have been higher than the EU average, among the highest in the Union. Greek approval rates of the EU are positively correlated to those in other EU member states, and to the domestic economic cycle. There does not seem to be any association of EU public acceptance with inequality trends.

5. POLICIES

Successive Greek governments have responded to the timeless wishes of the electorate for the government to redistribute wealth in a fair way to all citizens by 'throwing money' at the problem. However, the rise in social spending in Greece has failed to reach the categories of the population that receive minimum or no social protection. The Greek welfare system has created 'insiders' (such as the relatively well-protected members of liberal professions, employees of state-owned enterprises and civil servants) and 'outsiders' (private sector employees, particularly those working in small enterprises, or employed on fixed-term contracts or other types of temporary employment). Among the outsiders, those who fare worst are: a) young people, who always suffer the most from unemployment (unemployment rates in excess of 25 per cent have been typical for 18–24 year olds, and they currently stand at over 50 per cent); b) the long-term unemployed left on their own after the 12-month long period of unemployment benefits expires; c) women who are hired last and fired first and who also leave the labour market after they get married or after they bear their first child; and d) migrants who are employed by business owners paying them under the table and also refraining from paying social insurance contributions.

Labour market institutions do not reduce the various types of income inequality either. None of the categories of outsiders noted above are represented in Greece's trade unions, which mostly defend the interests of the civil servants or the employees of state-owned enterprises and the larger private businesses. It is also telling that until 2012, Greece still remained one of the only two among the EU15 countries (the other is Italy) without a minimum income guarantee programme at the national or regional level.

The rest of this section will examine these themes in more detail by focusing on the respective institutions and social policy instruments.

Labour Market Institutions

When it comes to labour market institutions, MW legislation has, in effect, through the years substituted for the lack of a well-developed Welfare State. Both the cumulative increase in productivity and in the real value of the MW was substantial from 1970 to 1980 (although the rise in the MW was only half as large as the rise in productivity), whereas during the 1980s the real value of the MW kept rising but labour productivity fell. Since the early 1990s, there has been a significant rise in labour productivity (by about 40 per cent up to 2005), while most recent increases in the real value of the MW failed to match the rise in labour productivity. There is a clear association between the large increase in the real value of the MW between 1974 and 1982 and the substantial decline in income inequality during the same period.

The MW in Greece is determined at national level and sets the floor for all wage settlements in the country, with the exception of wages in the public sector (which are policy determined). The level of the MW used (until 2010) to be the outcome of negotiations between the social partners, represented by third-tier organizations of employees and employers. Increases in bargained wages were usually higher than the MW and resulted in a continuous fall in the ratio of minimum to average wages from 1995 to 2004—a trend reversed afterwards. Nevertheless, the continuous rise in the real value of the MW, along with the rise of participation and employment rates for women of lower educational attainment, appears to have succeeded in lowering inequality during this period.

Structure of Taxation

The rise in the share of government revenue in GDP in Greece in the 1980s lagged behind the rise in government spending. While government spending relative to GDP rose by 18 percentage points in the 1980s, government revenue rose by only 5 percentage points (from 26 per cent in 1980 to 31 per cent in 1990). More adjustment in government revenue occurred in the 1990s, when its GDP share rose by 11 percentage points (from 31 per cent GDP in 1990 to 43 per cent in 2000). This brought Greece's general government revenue less than 3 percentage points below the EU15 average, but by 2009 total government receipts in Greece (38.2 per cent GDP) had again fallen way below the EU15 (44.7 per cent) and even the peripheral four (comprising of Greece, Ireland, Portugal, and Spain) average (39.3 per cent).

The significance of indirect taxes declined from 40 per cent of government revenue in 1988 to 30 per cent in 2011. Given the non-progressive nature of these taxes, it is not surprising that the decline in their relative significance was followed by reductions in inequality. Social security contributions, which provided 26 per cent of government revenue in 1976, rose to represent 35 per cent of revenue in 1989, and had dropped to 31 per cent in 2011. In 1981, the rate for employer social security contributions stood at 18.75 per cent, whereas the

Table 13.3 Decomposition of tax receipts by main tax components

	% of GDP				% of total taxation			
	1995	2000	2005	2010	1995	2000	2005	2010
	Taxes on consumption				Taxes on consumption			
Euro area	10.9	11.1	10.8	10.7	27.4	27.1	27.3	27.5
Greece	12	12.4	11.3	12.1	41.3	36	35	38.9
	Taxes on labour				Taxes on labour			
Euro area	21.5	21.3	20.5	20.8	54.1	52	51.9	53.4
Greece	10.5	12.4	13.1	12.4	36.1	35.9	40.5	39.9
	Taxes on capital				Taxes on capital			
Euro area	7.5	8.7	8.3	7.6	18.8	21.1	21	19.5
Greece	6.6	9.8	7.9	6.5	22.6	28.3	24.5	21.1

Source: Eurostat.

employee rate was 10.25 per cent. By 2008, these rates had risen to 28 per cent for employers and 16 per cent for employees.

The Greek state has traditionally relied on consumption taxes to support its functions. Table 13.3 demonstrates this, comparing Greece with the EA17. From 1995 to 2005, there has been a fall in the share of consumption taxes to total tax revenue in Greece, bringing it closer to the EA17 average. This trend was reversed in 2010, as the EU/IMF conditionality programme of May 2010 involved significant increases in VAT tax rates. Tax revenue sourced from labour incomes was also raised from 1995 to 2010, contrary to the EA17 trend.

The worldwide trend in reducing the top statutory tax rates was observed in Greece as well. From 2000 until 2002, the top statutory income tax rate decreased from 45 per cent to 40 per cent, and remained at that level until 2009. The 2010 conditionality programme restored a 45 per cent tax rate.

The outline of the Greek tax system shows that Greece has significantly lower tax revenue (including social security contributions) than the other EU15 countries and even lower ones than the other periphery countries (except Ireland). In comparison to EU15, the shortfall of total government revenue, and of tax revenue, relative to GDP has been in the range of 6 or 7 per cent of GDP in recent years. In addition, the Greek tax system remains replete with serious drawbacks. These have arisen because the tax system has been changing frequently in ad-hoc fashion to comply with EU regulations, to generate additional revenue, and to reverse (or, sometimes foster) real or perceived inequities of the tax system.

Both equity and efficiency are adversely affected by the main problem bedevilling Greek public finances, i.e. tax evasion. The distributional implications of tax evasion in Greece have been found to largely offset some of the progressive elements of the tax system. Matsaganis and Flevotomou (2010) have found that tax evasion causes the poverty rate and the poverty gap to rise above what it would have been under full tax compliance, in spite of the fact that in their calculations the poverty line was allowed to rise to reflect higher disposable incomes with tax evasion.

In addition to the large rates of income tax evasion, Greece faces very high rates of payroll tax evasion, estimated to have increased through the years, from around 13 per cent of revenues in the early 1990s to about 16 per cent in 2003, and to 20 per cent in 2005 (POKOPK, 2005). IKA estimated that employers in 10 per cent of all firms inspected in 2008 failed to pay social contributions, while 27 per cent of all workers remained unregistered (Matsaganis *et al.*, 2010).

Social Expenditure

In 1970, government spending was 23 per cent of GDP in Greece and 34 per cent in EA12, whereas, in 1980, the corresponding figures were 30 per cent for Greece and 43 per cent for EA12. After a huge public sector expansion in Greece in the 1980s, government reached 44 per cent of GDP in 1999 (EA12: 48 per cent). After acceding to the euro, Greek policy-makers apparently became even less vigilant in their efforts to curb government spending, and by 2008 government spending stood at 48 per cent, climbing to 53 per cent of GDP in 2009.

The growth in government spending in Greece is largely accounted for by the growth in social transfers, which rose from 8 per cent of GDP in 1970 to 21 per cent of GDP in 2009, and in the compensation of public employees, from 8 per cent in 1976 to 12.7 per cent of GDP in 2009. The growth in transfers (mainly to households) is partly explained by the fact that as late as 1980 Greece spent only 11 per cent of its GDP on income transfers (EU15 average: 17 per cent).

The most important category among income transfers in Greece is old age benefits—the fastest growing category of social spending, and the biggest risk in the sustainability of Greek public finances. Government spending on old age benefits (essentially—over 95 per cent—pensions) rose from 9.5 per cent of GDP in 1995 to 11.3 per cent in 2009. A significant rise was also observed during the same period in public expenditure on sickness/health care, which rose from 5 per cent of GDP in 1995 to 8 per cent in 2009. All other categories of social spending (invalidity payments, unemployment benefits, family/ children benefits, housing benefits) remained below 2 per cent GDP during 1995–2009. We note that with the exception of old age benefits (pensions), Greece spends less (per cent GDP) than the EA17 on all other categories of public social expenditure.

From 1980 to 2007, the growth in cash payments and in payments in kind was large—both types of public social expenditure doubled as a share GDP (from 6.9 per cent to 13.9 per cent, and from 3.6 per cent to 7.3 per cent, respectively). This increase has brought government spending on these items close to the EU15 average. Thus, whereas in 1995 total public spending on social protection (as per cent GDP) was 7.2 percentage points lower in Greece than in the EU15, by 2009 the difference was only 1.8 percentage points (Greece: 27.3 per cent, EU15: 29.1 per cent).

The importance of non-means tested social expenditure has increased, whereas means-tested expenditure has remained roughly constant as a percentage of GDP. Thus, the total of non means-tested benefits increased from 18.1 per cent in 1995 to 25.4 per cent in 2009. We note that most of the increase in non means-tested benefits during this period was in benefits in kind: from 5.2 per cent in 1995 to 9.0 per cent in 2009. Although means-tested benefits were still, in 2009, significantly lower in Greece than in the EU15, the pan-European trend for the rising (relative) importance of means-tested benefits was also observed in Greece.

Active labour market programmes is the type of government expenditure where Greece still lags significantly behind other EU countries. Although Greece had higher unemployment rates during the last three decades than most of the EU15, public expenditure on active labour market programmes never exceeded 0.4 per cent GDP—most of the time it was less than 0.25 per cent, whereas many of the EU15 spent more than 0.8 per cent on such programmes, with some countries (Denmark, Netherlands) regularly spending over 1.2 per cent GDP.

Education

Education has been a most important route to social mobility in Greece. Public expenditure on education increased from 2.9 per cent of GDP in 1993 to 4.1 per cent in 2005—still significantly lower than the EU27 average of around 5 per cent. Despite the increased public spending, the gross enrolment ratio in pre-primary education has not shown any marked improvement. However, for a brief period in the late 1990s, it remained roughly constant at about 67 per cent, compared to an average in other EU15 countries above 80 per cent in the late 1990s, even reaching 93 per cent in 2007. Much of the increased spending was used to lower the student to teacher ratios in primary and secondary education—from 11.4 in 2001 to 8.6 in 2007. These ratios were the lowest in the EU15 (where ratios close to 15 are not the exception), and may reflect, in addition to geography (many small islands), inefficiency in resource allocation.

An increase by 65 per cent in the number of students in tertiary education from 1999 to 2010 meant Greece had the highest number of students in tertiary education per capita among the EU15 countries in 2010. Given the relatively low public expenditure on education, this implies a very low public spending level per student (even when normalized by GDP per capita) compared to all other EU15 countries.

Based on the HBS of 2004/5, Table 13.4 displays measures of intergenerational educational mobility in Greece classified according to the household's income status. Among the poor (defined as those with income less than 60 per cent of the median equivalized income), the proportion of those which achieve the same level of education as their father was 31.5 per cent, whereas the corresponding proportion among the non-poor was 22.4 per cent. (Due to assortative mating, the relative proportions if the mother's education was the reference point were similar.) Upward educational mobility (a person's educational achievement

Table 13.4 Intergenerational educational mobility: educational mobility measures from father's to children's generation (%)

Measures of educ. mobility	Poor	Non-poor
Educational stagnation	31.5	22.4
Upward trend in educational mobility	62.5	72.3
Downward trend in educational mobility	6.2	5.0

Source: ELSTAT.

Table 13.5 Distribution of beneficiaries of third-level education by household income quintile

	Quintile				
	Bottom	2nd	3rd	4th	Top
All beneficiaries	17.6	24.8	20.7	19.6	17.3
Excl. students living away from parental home	9.2	17.0	22.3	25.7	25.8

Source: Callan *et al* (2008).

higher than his/her father) was experienced by 62.5 per cent among the poor, and by 72.3 per cent among the non-poor. The high proportion of upward educational mobility among the poor may just reflect the previous generation's high proportion of very low educational achievement (less than primary or just primary education).

In many European countries, about half of Welfare State transfers consist of in-kind benefits such as education, health insurance, child care, elderly care and other services. Regarding tertiary education, Callan *et al.* (2008) have estimated that, in Greece, the proportion of beneficiaries of (publicly-funded) tertiary education do not vary greatly across household income quintiles, ranging between 17.3 per cent (of the total population) for the top-income quintile to 24.8 per cent of the second-from-the-bottom income quintile (Table 15.5). This is common across many European countries. However, the distribution of beneficiaries changes markedly if the sample excludes students living away from the parental home. In this case, the beneficiaries belonging to the lowest-income quintile are only 9.2 per cent of the total. The proportion of beneficiaries rises gradually as we move to higher-income quintiles, with those belonging to the highest-income quintile representing 25.8 per cent of the total number of beneficiaries. Given that in Greece most tertiary education students live with their parents (and are thus counted as part of their parents' household in the HBS), the distribution excluding students living away from the parental home is a more appropriate metric for the incidence of in-kind educational transfers. It thus appears that the incidence of these transfers is regressive.

A FRAGMENTED AND INEFFECTIVE SOCIAL MODEL

The effects of social transfers on poverty risk demonstrate both the inefficiency and the inter-generational character of Greek social policy. During the period 2004–2010, the average reduction in the at-risk-of-poverty rate was 3.0 percentage points for the whole population, and 4.9 percentage points for those aged over 65, compared to an average of 10.0 and 4.0 percentage points for the EU15 respectively. These data not only underscore the inability of the Greek state to use social policy effectively (Greece *does* spend on social policy comparable sums to the EU15 average), but they also reflect the willingness of Greek policy-makers to cater to special interest groups.

Old age pensions illustrate the haphazard way in which the disbursement of social welfare was administered. From the mid 1970s to the mid 1980s the pensions-to-GDP ratio almost doubled. The lowest pensions increased considerably, uninsured old age persons started receiving a social assistance benefit, and pensions (along with social security coverage) were granted even to groups that had not paid any contributions (e.g. to Greek repatriates from the former Soviet Union and other Eastern European countries). Yet, the system remained fragmented, with pension funds serving 'special interest' groups managing to maintain their privileged position—usually achieved by receiving indirect subsidies from the government (often by imposing taxes on third parties). Such unequal treatment of pensioners, which was underpinned by the use of public funds, was also responsible for the higher incidence of poverty among pensioners compared to the total population. It is thus ironic that social transfers (excluding pensions) in Greece were very effective in reducing the high (relative to EU15) at-risk-of-poverty rate for persons older than 65, while at the same time government policy was responsible for creating the high poverty risk among pensioners by over-subsidizing through scarce public funds the more 'affluent' pension funds.

Some efforts at improving some of the inequities and inefficiencies of the social welfare system were made in the 1990s and in the first decade of the new millennium. These efforts, usually underpinned by the belief (or, the pretext) that social and economic reform should be the result of social dialogue, did not produce the hoped-for social concertation and were abandoned by successive governments. The conditionality programmes of 2010–12 finally introduced, in a top-down and pro-cyclical manner, many of the necessary pension reforms that had been eschewed by reluctant governments over the previous two decades.

5. Conclusion

During the period 1974–2009, Greece managed to converge on the EU average and significantly reduce overall inequalities. However, the persistent shortcomings of welfare institutions and policies, and the failures and omissions of macro-economic management, contributed to patterns of social expenditure that were both of low effectiveness and, eventually, financially unsustainable.

The effects of the previous three decades of soft budget constraints and social policy inefficiencies are most likely to be long-lasting social hardship. ELSTAT's (2013) analysis of EU-SILC data indicates dramatic deterioration since 2009 in many of the variables that are drivers of inequality and poverty developments. For example: the proportion of jobless households increased from 9.1 per cent in the fourth quarter of 2009 (2009Q4) to 17.7 per cent in 2012Q3; the unemployment rate increased from 9.3 per cent in 2009Q3 to 24.8 per cent in 2012Q3; the at-risk-of-poverty rate after social transfers increased from 19.7 per cent in 2009 to 21.4 per cent in 2011 (despite the drop in the at-risk-of-poverty threshold); the proportion of people with material deprivation increased from 23.0 per cent in 2009 to 28.4 per cent in 2011; and the Gini index with respect to the equivalized disposable income increased from 0.331 to 0.336 during the same period. Given the continuing deterioration in the economic environment since 2011, these developments are an unwelcome portent. The decision taken by decree in February 2012 to reduce the minimum wage by 22 per cent for those aged over 25, and by 32 per cent for the rest, and the large (and still on-going) reductions in real compensation per employee, will, most likely, lead to a dramatic rise in poverty rates if previous patterns re-emerge and the social welfare budget is increasingly starved of funds (as it is planned it will be).

References

Andriopoulou, E., Papadopoulos, F., and Tsakloglou, P. (2010), 'The portrait of social exclusion in Greece: Analysis and determinants', mimeo (in Greek).

Callan T., Smeeding, T., and Tsakloglou, P. (2008), 'Short-run distributional effects of public education transfers to tertiary education students in seven European countries', *Education Economics*, vol. 16(3), 2008, pages 275–288.

Cholezas I. and Tsakloglou, P. (2007), 'Earnings inequality in Europe: Structure and patterns of inter-temporal changes', *IZA Discussion* Paper,

Chrysakis, M., Balourdos, D., and Capella, A. (2009), 'Inequalities in Access to Tertiary Education in Greece: An Approach Based on the Official Statistics (1984–2004)', *Social Cohesion Bulletin* 2/2009, National Centre for Social Research, INSPO.

Credit Suisse (2011), *Global Wealth Databook 2011*, Credit Suisse Research Institute, Zurich.

EKKE (2010), *European Social Survey/ EKKE (2010), Greece—Europe: Society, Politics, Values*, November (in Greek).

ELSTAT (2013), *Living Conditions in Greece*, available at: <http://www.statistics.gr/portal/page/portal/ESYE/PAGE-livingcond/content/LivingConditionsInGreece_0113.pdf> .

European Sourcebook Group (2003), *European Sourcebook of Crime and Criminal Justice Statistics*, available at: <http://www.europeansourcebook.org/esb2_Full.pdf>.

European Sourcebook Group (2010), European Sourcebook of Crime and Criminal Justice Statistics (2010), available at: <http://europeansourcebook.org/ob285_full.pdf>.

Fotoniata, E. and Moutos, T. (2010), 'Greece: Neglect and Resurgence of Minimum Wage Policy', in D. Vaughan-Whitehead (ed.), *The Minimum Wage Revisited in the Enlarged EU*, Geneva: Edward Elgar and International Labour Office.

Kanellopoulos, C., Mitrakos, T., and Mavromaras, K. (2003), *Education and Labour Market*, Centre for Planning and Economic Research, Athens (in Greek).

KANEP-GSEE (2009), *Main figures of Greek education*, Centre for the Development of Education Policy, GSEE, Athens (in Greek).

Katsimi, M. and Moutos, T. (2010), 'EMU and the Greek crisis: The political-economy perspective', *European Journal of Political Economy*, 26, 568–576.

Kornai, J. (1980), *Economics of Shortage*, Vols I and II, Amsterdam: North Holland.

Koutsabelas, C. and Tsakloglou, P. (2012), 'The Distribution of Full Income in Greece' *IZA Discussion Papers* 6396, Institute for the Study of Labour.

Matsaganis, M. and Flevotomou, M. (2010), 'Distributional Implications of Tax Evasion in Greece', *Hellenic Observatory Papers on Greece and Southeast Europe*, Paper No. 31, The Hellenic Observatory, LSE, London.

Matsaganis, M., Benedek, D., Flevotomou, M., Lelkes, O., Mantovani, D., and Nienadowska, S. (2010), 'Distributional Implications of Income Tax Evasion in Greece, Hungary and Italy', *MPRA Paper* 21465, Munich Personal RePEc Archive.

Meschi, E. and Scervini, F. (2010), 'A new dataset on educational inequality', *GINI Discussion Paper* 3, Amsterdam Institute for Advanced Labour Studies (AIAS), University of Amsterdam.

Mitrakos T. and Tsakloglou, P. (2012), 'Inequality, Poverty and Material Welfare: From Regime Transition to the Current Crisis' in Bank of Greece, *Social Policy and Social Cohesion in Greece under Conditions of Economic Crisis*, Athens (in Greek).

Mouzelis N. and Pagoulatos, G. (2005), 'Civil Society and Citizenship in Postwar Greece', in F. Birtek and Th. Dragona (eds.) *Citizenship and the Nation State in Greece and Turkey*, Abington and New York: Routledge, 2005, pp. 87–103.

OECD (2011), *Divided We Stand. Why Inequality Keeps Rising*, OECD: Paris.

Public Issue (2009), *Immigration Survey, 2009*, <http://www.publicissue.gr/wp-content/uploads/2009/07/immigration-survey-2009.pdf> (in Greek).

V-PRC (2008), *Public Opinion in Greece*, Athens: Livanis (in Greek).

CHAPTER 14

HUNGARY: A COUNTRY CAUGHT IN ITS OWN TRAP

ZOLTÁN FÁBIÁN, ANDRÁS GÁBOS, MARIANNA KOPASZ, MÁRTON

MEDGYESI, PÉTER SZIVÓS, AND ISTVÁN GYÖRGY TÓTH

1. INTRODUCTION AND BACKGROUND

BEFORE the transition to a market economy, Hungary and other countries with a socialist economic system were characterized by relatively low levels of income inequality—approximately at the level of Scandinavian societies (Atkinson and Micklewright, 1992; Flemming and Micklewright, 2000). This has changed in many transition economies and has led, in most cases, to significant increases in inequality and poverty. This chapter describes how this evolution occurred in Hungary. It also argues that the evolution of inequality is not merely a product of developments in supply and demand for skills. Rather, policies to tackle inequalities—and politics of instrumentalization—are just as important.

General Historical Background

Although the 1956 revolution clearly marked the end of the Stalinist era in Hungary, the following decades were characterized by attempts on the part of the political regime to consolidate its power through measures to improve general living standards. A serious commitment to full employment, wage control measures, restrictions on wealth accumulation, and various steps to boost social mobility all contributed to the fact that income inequality declined substantially in the post-war period, right up until the start of the 1980s.

As the socialist regime[1] proved inflexible and unprepared to adjust to the world economic challenges of the 1970s, maintaining the economic and political regime became very costly,

---

[1] See Kornai (1980; 1992).

and that led to a steep rise in the country's indebtedness. All in all, it found that it could not deliver on its declared aims. Under the circumstances, the Hungarian political leadership (unlike many other Eastern European regimes) chose to relax the regulations and partially liberalize the economy. This led to a rise in inequality as early as at the beginning of the 1980s: the period 1982–87 witnessed a widening of the difference between the top decile and the bottom, as well as an increase in the Gini coefficient (Tóth, 2008a).

The transformation of the system brought about early privatization (in both spontaneous and more managed forms), together with one of the toughest bankruptcy laws in the region, contributing to heavy job losses (over 20 per cent of jobs were lost in the few years after 1990). As this happened in parallel with an extension of welfare provisions (relatively generous unemployment benefits, various ways of effecting an early exit from the labour market, social assistance benefits and fairly widespread and long maternity provisions), the income structure of households suddenly shifted and a large segment of the population became dependent on various social transfer schemes. This is the starting point for the story of the evolution of Hungarian inequality in the decades since the late 1980s.

Major Socio-Economic Trends between 1980 and 2010

Certain other characteristics of the socio-economic background are also of importance from 1980–2010.[2] In terms of demographic structure, the Hungarian population was ageing in this period. Also, it declined: the population in 2010 was about 94 per cent of the figure in 1980. This decline was mainly due to high mortality and a fall in fertility rates at a time when there was only a very modest increase in average life expectancy. The generational balance shifted significantly from the younger to the older generations: whereas in 1980 almost 22 per cent of the population were in the 0–14 age bracket, by 2011 the share of children (thus defined) had declined to less than 15 per cent; in the same period, the share of the 65+ population rose from 13.5 per cent to almost 17 per cent. The average household size declined from almost 2.8 to below 2.5 in this period, and this was accompanied by a drastic change in the composition of the population by living arrangements: the share of those living in one-person households increased from less than one fifth of the total population to slightly above 30 per cent. Much of this shift was due to later first marriages (the average age at first marriage went up from 24.5 (men) and 21.8 (women) to 31.4 and 27.7 in this period), as well as to the differential life expectancy of men and women. The share of all household types with more than three members declined.

If we look at education, the structural changes reflect improvements in the level of education in the first half of the period and a significant expansion in education thereafter. The share of those in the 18+ age bracket, who had completed at least secondary schooling, grew from 23.6 per cent in 1980 to 49.3 per cent in 2011, while the proportion of those completing tertiary education went up from 6.5 per cent in 1980 to 18.9 per cent in 2011. This change was the result of a large (from 80.4 to 98.3 per cent) increase in the secondary school enrolment rate within the 16–17 age cohorts and an even more significant (from 17.5 to 25.1 per

---

[2] Here (and later) all figures not indicated otherwise will come from the Hungary country report of the GINI project (Tárki, 2012). Detailed references to original data are to be found there.

cent) increase in the tertiary education enrolment rate in the 18–22 age cohort between 2000 and 2010.

For income distribution, probably the most significant change to be observed is in employment structure. The share of those employed declined from 47.3 per cent to 36.2 per cent of the total population between 1980 and 2001, and thereafter showed only a very modest increase (to 38.1 per cent in 2005). Naturally, this also meant a decline in the tax base. At the same time, the share of recipients of various state redistribution programmes (mostly old age and invalidity pensioners) increased dramatically (from 20.6 per cent to 36.5 per cent) by 2001, with only a slight decline (to 35.1 per cent) by 2005. The number of those dependent only on household resources declined.

In what follows, we present the trends and drivers of inequality change (in Section 2). This is followed by an account of social cohesion, demography and political changes (Section 3). Finally, together with an overview of major tax/transfer policy changes (Section 4), we conclude with an attempt to produce an integrated summary and a reflection on the 'big picture' of the Hungarian inequality story (Section 5).

2. Evolution of Inequality and its Drivers

The studies reviewed here show a substantial increase in income inequality between 1987 and 2005, followed by a moderate decline in inequality towards the end of the 2000s, at least until the economic crisis broke. Since 2007, inequality has been on the rise again, as has income poverty. This section starts by introducing the trends; there then follows an account of potential drivers.

Trends in Income Inequality

As mentioned in the general introduction, income inequality decreased between 1962 and 1982, during which period the Gini index of per capita household income fell from 0.26 to 0.21. According to data from the Hungarian Central Statistical Office (HCSO) Income Surveys,[3] that is the lowest level of income inequality recorded over the past fifty years. Inequality began to increase a couple of years before the start of the transition, with the Gini index reaching 0.24 back in 1987.

As revealed by data from the Tárki Household Monitor survey, the rapid increase in inequality continued into the first years of transition, and the Gini index of equivalent household income reached the range of 0.30 by the mid '90s (see Table 14.1). Changes in inequality

---

[3] Survey data are better at capturing income from undeclared work compared to data from tax authorities or social security registers. This is important in the case of Hungary, since estimates of the size of the informal economy range from 15 to 30% of GDP (Elek *et al.*, 2009). Surveys, on the other hand, are biased towards middle incomes, since they are unable to represent the very bottom and the very top of the distribution.

Table 14.1 The distribution of equivalent incomes between 1987 and 2009, as measured by indicators sensitive to different segments of the income distribution

	1987	1992	1996	2000	2003	2005	2007	2009
Indices sensitive to the top of the distribution								
P90/P50	1.690	1.860	1.900	1.920	1.920	1.910	1.740	1.810
GE(2)	0.116	0.168	0.236	0.207	0.261	0.260	0.205	0.155
A(0.5)	0.046	0.059	0.071	0.072	0.078	0.073	0.064	0.062
Indices sensitive to the middle part or symmetrically sensitive to bottom and top								
S10/S1	4.550	5.520	6.620	6.630	7.300	6.680	6.000	6.350
P90/P10	2.800	3.100	3.600	3.500	3.580	3.420	3.160	3.530
GE(0)	0.092	0.119	0.143	0.147	0.156	0.145	0.127	0.128
GE(1)	0.097	0.127	0.156	0.155	0.175	0.163	0.14	0.128
Gini	0.236	0.263	0.290	0.292	0.302	0.291	0.271	0.272
A(1)	0.088	0.112	0.133	0.137	0.144	0.135	0.119	0.120
Indices sensitive to the bottom of the distribution								
P10/P50	0.600	0.590	0.540	0.550	0.540	0.560	0.550	0.510
A(2)	0.164	0.219	0.244	0.294	0.259	0.243	0.228	0.233

Note: Equivalent income (Y_{eq}) was calculated with e=0.73 parameter ($Y_{eq}=Y_H/N^e$), where Y_H means household income, and N is the number of individuals living in the household.

Source: Tóth (2010a). 1987: HCSO Income Survey; 1992, 1996: Hungarian Household Panel; 2001–09: Tárki Household Monitor.A(x)=Atkinson index with ε=0,1,2, G(x) = Generalized Enthropy Index with α=0,1,2 parameters. PX= Xth percentile value. SX = share of the xth decile from total incomes.

were smaller in the period 1995–2005. There was a slight increase during this period, with the highest Gini being observed in 2003, when the index was at 0.302. In the second half of the past decade, inequality started to decrease, with a notable decline between 2005 and 2007. The drop in inequality came mainly from a fall in top incomes, as shown by the trend of the P90/P10 index. With regard to changes between 2007 and 2009 (partly related to the economic crisis), various inequality indices seem to imply different trajectories. The S10/S1 index and the P90/P10 index increased, while the GE(1) index fell, and other indices remained pretty stable. Among the indicators sensitive to the lowest segment of the distribution, however, the P10/P50 also shows a decline in the position of those at the lower end of the income scale. Results from the most recent survey in 2012 show a significant increase in income inequality, with the Gini index rising to 0.29 (Medgyesi and Tóth 2012).[4]

Data from the EU-SILC study are also available for the most recent years. Based on 2011 data, this study shows Hungary with a Gini index of 0.27, which is close to that of Austria and Luxembourg and well below the EU average (0.307). A comparison of data from EU-SILC and the Tárki Household Monitor for the most recent years shows higher Gini indices estimated by the Tárki Monitor (approximately 2 Gini points higher) for four of the five overlapping years (the exception being 2005, when there was a sudden jump in the EU-SILC

---

[4] Medgyesi and Tóth, 2012.

estimate). Based on Tárki Household Monitor data, Hungary would position around the median of the country ranking, with a Gini close to that of Germany and Cyprus.

The poverty rate, following the trend of general income inequality, rose sharply during the transition years: whereas in 1987 the at-risk-of-poverty rate (estimated for a threshold set at 60 per cent of the median equivalent income)[5] was 10 per cent, in 1996–97 it exceeded 14 per cent (Tóth, 2008a). According to this data series, the risk of poverty reached its peak in 1996; then, after a long period of slight ups and downs, it started to increase again slowly in the second part of the 2000s, rather in line with what was observed in the case of the P90/P10 ratio.

Hungary is among the European countries with a relatively low overall risk of poverty. According to EU-SILC data, the at-risk-of-poverty rate of the overall population in Hungary was 13.8 per cent in 2011; that is 3 percentage points lower than the EU-27 average. Countries having a similar level of overall at-risk-of-poverty rate are Slovenia, Finland, France, and Sweden.

During the transition years, the percentage of both the poor and the rich has increased, but the rise in the percentage with less than half of the median is more pronounced (from 4 to 12 per cent). At the same time, we see the percentage of those in the middle range declining during the period 1987–96. Only minor changes can be discerned during the period 1996–2007. The beginning of the economic crisis brought about a further polarization of the income distribution (Tóth and Medgyesi, 2011).

Components of Inequality

One way to study the components of inequality and inequality change is to examine the importance of income differences between certain population sub-groups, e.g. men and women or those with less and more education. Some inequality indices are decomposable, which means that total inequality can be expressed as the contribution of income differences between population sub-groups and the contribution of income differences within groups. Here we show the results of decomposition of the MLD index (Shorrocks, 1980). The grouping variables considered here are: gender of the household head (male/female); age of the household head (below 35 years, 35–59 years, over 60 years); settlement type (Budapest, city, village); level of education of the household head (primary, vocational, secondary, tertiary); employment status of the household head (head is the only working adult in the household, head and other adult working, head inactive, head retired, head retired with other working adult); and number of children in the household (0, 1, 2, 3 or more).

As Figure 14.1 shows, the single factor accounting for the highest fraction of total inequality is the education of the household head. The importance of income differences between groups by education level rose steeply during the early years of the transition period—from 8 per cent of total inequality in 1987 to 25 per cent in 1996—and it has remained at around that figure for the past 15 years. The factor accounting for the second-highest fraction of total inequality is employment status of the household head: 10–15 per cent of total

---

[5] See note above, Table 14.1.

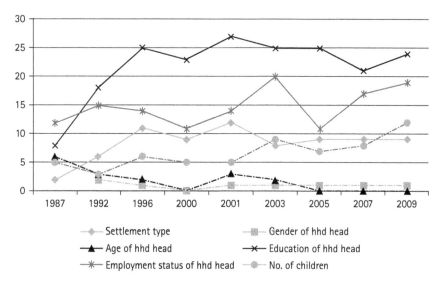

FIGURE 14.1 Evolution of between-group inequality as a percentage of total inequality, according to different household attributes

Note: The percentages of between-group inequalities were calculated by univariate decompositions of the MLD index, so between-group percentages should not be added together.

Source: Data from Tóth (2010a).

inequality in most years of the period and 20 per cent in 2003, 2007, and 2009. The differences in income between those living in different settlement types gained in importance during the initial years of transition: in 1987, this factor accounted for only 2 per cent of total income inequality, but since 1996 the figure has been around 10 per cent. Income differences between households with different numbers of children also account for approximately 10 per cent of total inequality, but the importance of this factor has been rising steadily throughout the period. Income differences between groups by gender and age of the household head account for only a small fraction of total inequality.

Drivers of Inequality Change: Structural Adjustment, Technological Advancement and Educational Expansion

Explanations for the increase in inequality during the transition emphasize structural change and the role of technological modernization of the economy. The first period of economic transition in the early 1990s was indeed characterized by structural change. Due to the collapse of trade among the old socialist countries, mega-enterprises in mining or heavy engineering went bankrupt, while new enterprises mainly sprang up in the service sector. This period was marked by a decline in the country's GDP between 1990 and 1993 and by dramatically falling employment: the workforce dropped by 1.2 million. The decline in employment was reflected in a rapid increase in the unemployment rate and (more importantly in the long run) a rise in the economically inactive population, with the proportion of inactive people of working age growing from 23 per cent in 1990 to 35 per cent in 1996.[6]

Structural change of the economy has contributed to rising income inequality by shifting the composition of incomes: the proportion of self-employment incomes, entrepreneurial incomes and capital incomes has risen, while the share of labour income has fallen. This is partly due to the decrease in employment, but a further element is the emergence of the private sector (World Bank, 2000). The removal of legal restrictions on private ownership and entrepreneurship has led to the emergence of new small, private firms in industry and services. Privatization of formerly state-owned firms has resulted in the formation of national economic elite of corporate business owners. This has contributed to increasing income inequality, since self-employment and entrepreneurial income is more unevenly distributed than wages. Moreover, these activities often depend on an individual's access to assets (property, but also information), which thus reinforces initial inequalities.

The rise in income inequality is related not just to the shifting composition of incomes, but also to increasing inequality among workers. As with income inequality, so inequality in labour earnings had started to increase even before the political transition: the P90/P10 ratio increased from 2.6 in 1986 to 3.07 in 1989 (Figure 14.2). The increase in inequality continued during the years of transition, and the P90/P10 index peaked in 2000 at 4.66. After 2000 we see a fluctuation in earnings inequality, with the P90/P10 index varying between 4 and 4.5

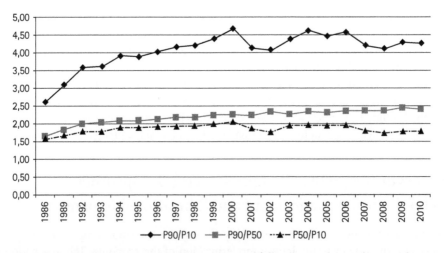

FIGURE 14.2 Inequality in gross monthly earnings of full-time employees (men and women)

Note: Data are gross monthly earnings of full-time employees in May of each year. Data source: Enterprise survey (Survey of Individual Wages and Earnings). Before 1994, workers in private enterprises with fewer than 20 employees were not included. Since 1994, the sample has also covered enterprises with 10–20 employees. Data exclude enterprises with 5–9 employees. Data include 1/12 of non-regular payments from the previous year.

Source: OECD Earnings Database.

---

[6]   Working age is 15–59 years for men and 15–54 years for women.

Figure 14.2 also shows how inequality evolved in the lower and upper parts of the earnings distribution. In the upper part, we see a steady increase in the P90/P50 ratio: the value of this index was 1.64 in 1986, 2.00 in 1992, and 2.43 in 2009. The path of the P50/P10 index followed the same trend up to 2000, but it declined between 2000 and 2002 (meaning that low earnings came closer to the median). A similar phenomenon occurs from 2006.

One major aspect of rising inequalities in the Hungarian labour market is the increased importance of education in determining labour market prospects (See Table 14.2). The education gradient of employment rates is considerable. Among men in the 15–64 age group, the employment rate among tertiary graduates was 83 per cent in 2009, while for men with only a primary education, the employment rate was only 29 per cent. The employment rate among those with least education is among the lowest in the OECD area (OECD, 2009).

The wage premium associated with higher education increased markedly during the period of transition. In 1989, graduates had earnings that were 57 per cent higher than those of employees with only primary education; by 1995 the wage premium had risen to 70 per cent, and by 2002 it was 92 per cent.[7] The wage premium of secondary school (leading to a leaving certificate) also increased during these years: in 1989, people with a leaving certificate as their highest educational award earned 24 per cent more than those with primary education, while in 1999 the figure was 35 per cent more. Since 2002, the wage premium

Table 14.2 Returns to education: results from Mincer–equations, 1989–2002

	1989	1992	1995	1999	2002
Female	-0.222	-0.154	-0.132	-0.142	-0.127
Experience	0.028	0.025	0.021	0.022	0.017
Experience squared	-0.000	-0.000	-0.000	-0.000	-0.000
Vocational school	0.117	0.129	0.106	0.122	0.097
Secondary school	0.238	0.300	0.297	0.354	0.313
College	0.572	0.663	0.697	0.872	0.918
Industry dummies	Yes	Yes	Yes	Yes	Yes
Region dummies	Yes	Yes	Yes	Yes	Yes
City-town-village dummies	Yes	Yes	Yes	Yes	Yes
Constant	8.77092	8.30731	8.40765	10.1015	10.9588
Observations	145,198	131,745	153,112	164,706	137,713
R2	0.44	0.45	0.43	0.45	0.44

Notes: Left-hand side variable: log of deflated after-tax earnings. Right-hand side variables: female dummy; potential labour market experience (difference of age and modal age at highest completed education) and its square. All regressions contain 2-digit industry dummies, 7 region dummies, and 4 city-size dummies (Budapest, other city, small town, and village).

Source: Kézdi (2005). Data source: Wage Surveys, employees between 16 and 65 years of age.

---

[7] Bukodi and Goldthorpe (2010) draw attention to the fact that tertiary qualifications no longer produce the same returns in terms of access to higher social class for individuals of different social origin. The chances of someone with higher education but from a relatively disadvantaged background entering the professions have worsened, while individuals without such qualifications but with a better class of parental background have had a better chance after the transition to capitalism.

of tertiary degree holders and secondary graduates has broadly stagnated. The wage premium of college education over primary school has fluctuated between 90 and 100 per cent. There is, of course, a considerable heterogeneity in the wage premium according to field of study: diplomas in social sciences (including economics and law) and technical education appear to realize the highest earnings (Galasi, 2007). The wage premium for secondary education has been stable at around 35 per cent since 2002. The labour market value of vocational education, on the other hand, has not increased over the past 20 years: the wage premium associated with this level of education (relative to primary schooling) has remained roughly stable, at around 10 per cent throughout the period.

The importance of education in determining employment probabilities and wages has risen, despite the significant expansion of education that occurred in Hungary after the political transition. In the 1990s, the proportion of young people attending secondary school and higher educational institutions increased. In 1989, only a fifth of those completing elementary school continued their studies at grammar school and only 27 per cent at a secondary technical school. By the end of the 1990s, a total of 70 per cent of all pupils who completed elementary school continued their studies at a secondary school to take the leaving-certificate exam. At the same time, the proportion of those who went on to a vocational school dropped significantly, by some 20 percentage points (Loboda *et al.*, 2007).

Given an increased supply of educated labour, the educational wage premium can only rise if the demand for educated labour also expands rapidly. After the period of the transformational recession, the country enjoyed a decade of prosperity between 1997 and 2006, with the level of GDP growth reaching 4–5 per cent annually. Foreign direct investment played a major role in kick-starting and accelerating this growth, which brought about a significant technological modernization of production processes. Technological change increased demand for young educated labour, while employment prospects worsened for the poorly educated and older cohorts with obsolete human capital.

3. The Social and Political Spheres: Generational Change and Political Polarization in a Low Social Capital Context

Hungary is a country with a traditionally low level of social capital. Probably the root causes of this extend well back into the past, but the trend was reinforced by communist rule, and there has been no change in the past two decades. From the beginning of the 1980s to the present day, we can even detect a declining trend: according to European Values Survey data, a third of Hungarians were trustful[8] in 1982, but by 2008 this share had fallen to a fifth. There is a deficit of social capital of both the formal and the informal kind. Very few people participate in voluntary organizations (such as clubs or trade unions), and even informal

---

[8]   Agreeing to the statement that most of their fellow citizens can be trusted.

ties to family and friends became weaker during the transition. Generalized trust is lower than the EU-27 average; in this respect, Hungary belongs to those countries where family ties (strong ties or informal social capital) are stronger than formal social capital (participation in formal associations, trade unions and other civic activities) (Pichler and Wallace, 2007). At the same time, the ethos in Hungary regarding getting ahead in life was very individualistic, attaching primary importance to diligence and effort (though nepotism, rule avoidance and favouritism are also regarded as necessary for advancement). Parallel to that, poverty (at least the poverty of other people) was seen as a result of individual failure or laziness (Tóth and Keller, 2012). The low level of social cohesion in Hungary and the high level of perceived conflict between different social groups may be a result of social inequality and lack of effective social policy measures. At the same time, the lack of trust and altruism may be a cause of social segregation and growing inequality. Further research is required to clarify the direction of causality.

Poverty and Social Exclusion

Rising inequalities in the first half of the 1990s resulted in a sharp increase in the risk of poverty. While only one Hungarian in ten was at risk of poverty in 1987, the rate peaked at over 14 per cent in 1996–97. Since then, a long succession of slight ups and downs has been followed by an increasing risk of poverty in the second half of the 2000s (though different data sources are ambiguous and do not reveal clear trends). The risk of poverty seems to have started rising again as a consequence of the economic crisis. Moreover, the recent increase in the financial vulnerability of households (shown by the material deprivation indicator) foreshadows an even higher level of poverty and social exclusion in the coming period. According to the 2009 Tárki data, the overall risk of poverty got close to the 14 per cent peak of the mid 1990s, and even higher in 2012 with its 17 per cent.

While the main driver of this increased risk at the beginning of the period was the sharp decline in employment, the highest attained level of education of the household head plays the most important role, even when other factors (like labour market attachment or household structure) are controlled for (Gábos and Szivós, 2010). In the case of the most vulnerable, level of education is strongly correlated with other characteristics (e.g. persistent unemployment or inactivity, region, type of settlement), which gives a lasting complexity to the problem of poverty and social exclusion.

At high risk from all these factors, the Roma population is the most vulnerable social group in Hungary (Gábos and Szivós, 2010). Their labour market opportunities are few on account of their low level of education and the fact that they characteristically live in settlements (mainly villages) and regions that offer little scope for employment. Although more Roma now have elementary education than used to be the case, when it comes to secondary schooling or higher education, the differences between Roma and non-Roma have widened (Kemény and Janky, 2006). Analysing factors behind the severe employment disadvantage of the Roma, Kertesi and Kézdi (2011) found that one-third of the gap is explained by the lower level of education. The number of children is a significant factor in the female employment gap, while geographical location seems to be less important in explaining differences in employment rates.

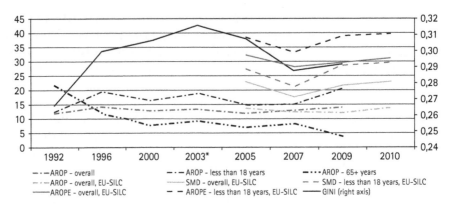

FIGURE 14.3 The risk of poverty and social exclusion among young and elderly, Hungary, 1992–2010

Note: AROP—at-risk-of-poverty rate; SMD—severe material deprivation rate; AROPE—population at risk of poverty and social exclusion (composite EU 2020 poverty target indicator). Right-hand scale for Gini.

Source: 1992–2009: Tárki Household Monitor Survey; 2005–10: EUROSTAT. Years are shown according to the income reference period. Indicators based on household income are unreliable in the case of Hungary for 2006 (2005 income reference year).

The sharp increase in income poverty in the early 1990s took place alongside a significant generational shift (see Figure 14.3). The welfare level of elderly people and children, of small and large families started to diverge strongly after the political and economic system changed. At the beginning of this period, the elderly had the highest risk of poverty; since then their relative position has steadily improved. By contrast, the position of families with children—and particularly of large families—deteriorated markedly in the first half of the 1990s, levelled off for a while, and then started to worsen again in recent years. Childbearing became an important driver of income mobility, reflected in diverging life trajectories across social status. On the one hand, a low level of parental education and weak labour market attachment are associated with a higher than average number of children: apart from Ireland and the United Kingdom, Hungary occupies the worst position in the European Union in terms of the share of children in jobless households (EU Task-Force, 2008; Tárki-Applica, 2010; Tárki, 2011). On the other hand, the practice of putting off having children and the decrease in completed fertility have shown themselves in the post-communist era to be strategies that allow women (mostly better educated) to pursue a career and to obtain a better income (Spéder and Kamarás, 2008).

As for the elderly, the pension system has provided a robust safety net against poverty throughout the period, though the overall income position of older people has not improved substantially in absolute terms, even though they have been important beneficiaries of the budget cycle (see Section 4).

The increasing vulnerability of children in recent years is also revealed by other indicators of social exclusion, like the indicators of material deprivation, the composite Europe 2020 poverty target indicator, or the at-risk-of-poverty rate anchored at a fixed moment in time. According to all of these indicators, the position of families with children has deteriorated and they seem to have been severely hit by the recent economic and financial crisis (Gábos and Szivós, 2010).

In general, the Hungarian population is at high risk of poverty and social exclusion, as defined by the Europe 2020 strategy's poverty target indicator (European Commission, 2010). Almost one Hungarian in three is affected by income poverty, by severe material deprivation or by living in a low work-intensity household. While the extent of income poverty is below the EU average, Hungary is a poor performer when material deprivation and household joblessness are considered.

Demographic Behaviour and Health

Demographic change (e.g. of household size and composition, age structure) is a major background factor to income inequality (see Figure 14.4). In Hungary, demographic behaviour started to align itself with the Northern and Western European trends even before the political and economic system changed. Fertility in Hungary has been marked by a strongly fluctuating (but basically declining) trend in the post-war period. Strict policy measures— first and foremost a ban on abortion (1953–56, 1973–76), but also housing policy and generous family benefits—brought about high peaks (the baby-boom generations of the mid 1950s and mid 1970s) in an otherwise declining fertility trend. The early 1980s constituted a turning point, with strong social-psychological and policy consequences: since 1981, Hungary has experienced a population decline. The declining fertility trend is attributed to an enduring process of demographic transition and to political regime changes—the communist takeover after the Second World War and then the political and economic upheaval at the end of the twentieth century (Spéder and Kamarás, 2008). From the early 1990s onwards, the total fertility rate declined each year, dipping below 1.3 in 1999. Following a period of stagnation in the 2000s, the total fertility rate stood at 1.32 in 2009. Since then, fertility figures have reached even lower levels—in 2011 the rate was only 1.23, among the very

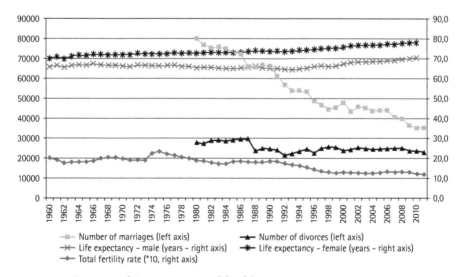

FIGURE 14.4 Demographic processes and health, 1992–2011

Source: HCSO.

lowest in Europe. The proportion of live births outside marriage in Hungary has more than tripled, from 13.1 per cent in 1990 to 42.3 per cent in 2011.

The alarming levels of fertility and the desire to reduce excessive labour supply have combined to impact strongly on institutional arrangements. Maternity and child care benefits are quite generous and provide a strong incentive for mothers to stay at home with their child for three years (Bálint and Köllő, 2008). This is further reflected in day-care enrolment rates: only 9 per cent of children under the age of 2 are in formal child care. It also has an impact on female labour market participation, and consequently on overall inequality.

Trends in couple formation and dissolution have played an important role in the evolution of fertility processes. Since the mid 1970s, the number of marriages in Hungary has declined. The greatest fall has occurred over the past two decades: between 1990 and 2011 the figure dropped by 46.2 per cent. The crude marriage rate in 1990 was 6.4 (per thousand inhabitants), whereas it was 3.6 in 2011, one of the lowest in the EU. The number of divorces in Hungary grew slowly between 1980 and 1987, while during the 1990s and 2000s there was no substantial change. However, the frequency of divorce (measured by the total divorce rate) shows an unfavourable tendency: in 1990, the total divorce rate stood at 31 per cent; by 2007 it had soared to 45 per cent, indicating that almost half of all marriages end in divorce. In a European comparison, Hungary is close to the upper end of the range in this respect.

While the overall health of the Hungarian population—at least at the level of averages—has improved over the past two decades, there remains a disturbingly strong social gradient of mortality. Life expectancy at birth declined slightly between 1968 and 1993, but since 1994 it has been rising—by 5.7 years for men and 3.9 years for women in the period between 1994 and 2010. Educational attainment has an effect on life expectancy, healthy life years, and mortality as well (HCSO, 2007; Mackenbach et al., 2008). Education-related inequality in mortality is higher than in Europe as a whole. In line with findings elsewhere in Europe, the education gradient of mortality is steeper for men than it is for women: in Hungary, the relative index of inequality for men is greater than 4, indicating that the rate of death (from any cause) differs by a factor of more than 4 between the lower and the upper end of the education scale (Mackenbach et al., 2008). The disparity between social strata increased during the 1990s, largely because of a lack of improvement in the high mortality rate of poorly educated citizens (Leinsalu et al., 2009).

Based on data from the EU-SILC, the share of those reporting bad or very bad health is among the highest in the EU. In 2009, 17.5 per cent of Hungarians reported poor health, compared to 9.4 per cent in the EU as a whole. The share of those judging their health status to be poor is extremely high among those with only primary education. Subjective health reports show that the proportion of those in poor health is higher in all income quintiles than in the EU as a whole. Generally, those with higher incomes tend to report better health. Nevertheless, income inequality in health status shows a slight downward trend in Hungary between 2005 and 2010.

Housing

There are a number of reasons why housing may be important in determining inequality trends. First, the presence of a widely accessible rental sector is essential to facilitate geographical and social mobility. Hungary has a very high rate of home ownership (90 per cent in 2010, compared to the EU average of 71 per cent). This high proportion of ownership has its roots in the privatization process: between 1989 and 1997, 15–20 per cent of the housing stock moved from state ownership to the owner-occupied sector. Tenant status is associated with low social status: the share of tenants decreases as income rises (Beck *et al.*, 2010), while the public rental sector caters for families with low incomes (Rózsavölgyi and Kovács, 2005). The market rental sector is exceptionally low by international standards (2.9 per cent of the total housing stock in 2011), and is concentrated regionally, mostly in larger towns, which imposes a severe constraint on regional mobility.

Second, the high and increasing risk of material deprivation among Hungarians is related to the indebtedness of households. While indebtedness is still far below the level of developed economies, households spend almost the same proportion of their income on loan repayments (Holló, 2007). Housing loans accounted for about 52 per cent of total household credit in June 2011. Indebted households (including those with housing loans) spent on average 19 per cent of their net income on repayments in 2007. As a consequence of high unemployment and the higher interest costs on Swiss Franc-denominated mortgages, the household debt service ratio—the ratio of debt payments to disposable income—rose dramatically to 32 per cent in 2010. In 2007, the household debt service burden tended to decrease with an increase in household income. But the tendency was less clear-cut in 2010 when households in the second income quintile had by far the highest debt service ratio (Central Bank of Hungary, 2010).

Demand for Redistribution and Attitudes Towards the Welfare State

In the 1980s, Hungary was an egalitarian country, according to both the measures of income distribution and the public's attitudes toward income differences.[9] Cross-national comparative studies found a dynamic change in attitude right after the transition in former communist Central European countries like Poland and Hungary. By the end of the 1990s, Hungarians and Poles tolerated greater wage differentials than most Westerners thought right. Together with greater tolerance of income inequality between groups, in recent decades the gap has widened in Hungary between perceived and acceptable levels of inequality: people could *accept* that a factory chief executive was paid ten times more than a blue-collar worker, but they *perceived* a much higher difference than they thought was legitimate.

The International Social Survey Programme (ISSP) Social Inequality survey data shows that the growing intolerance of income inequality is far from universal in the ex-communist countries.[10] The trend has been declining in Bulgaria, the Czech Republic, Eastern Germany and Slovakia. Bulgaria was an extreme case in 1992, but by 2009 its position had been usurped by Hungary. In 2009, 78 per cent of Hungarians 'agreed strongly' and an

[9] This in no way contradicts what we said earlier about individualistic values. See an early account of this 'half-way' modernization of value systems in Hankiss (1983) and also Tóth (2010b) on distrust, feelings of injustice and paternalism.

[10] Although Medgyesi (2013) finds that, in general, opinions about inequality in ex-communist countries have become more similar to opinions in other developed countries.

additional 20 per cent just simply 'agreed' that the range of income differentials exceeded an acceptable level.

Growing demand for government redistribution went hand in hand with a growing level of perceived and unacceptable income differences in Hungary. At the beginning of the democratic transition (1987–92), about a third of Hungarians agreed strongly that government should reduce differences, but by 2009 this figure had grown to 55 per cent.

Hungarians tend to underestimate the value of public services in terms of the tax burden those services place on society (Csontos et al., 1998; Tóth, 2010b). They expect more from public services than the state (the government or its agencies) is able to deliver. Low tax consciousness, in addition to many other things (see Tóth and Keller, 2013) could be an explanation for the higher demand for redistribution in Hungary than in other countries.

How do individuals perceive the determinants of getting ahead in life? Looking at the rankings of EU countries, it turns out that Hungary has the lowest rate (33 per cent) of people who consider that getting a good education is important in getting ahead in life (Lannert, 2009: 147). On the other hand, almost a third of Hungarians (31 per cent) thought that a wealthy family background was important for an individual's career—the highest rate among EU countries in 2007. This latter belief may be related to observed patterns and to the low level of social capital in Hungary, as Hungarians rated family background higher than Americans and West Germans did even back in the 1980s, under state socialism.

Interestingly, as Table 14.3 shows, intergenerational occupational mobility did not change between 1983 and 1992, but it did decrease from 1992 to 2000. During the whole period, the total mobility rate (which shows the percentage of those in an occupational category that was different from that of their father) decreased from 73.4 per cent to 65.8 per cent in the case of men. The total mobility rate also decreased in the case of women, albeit to a somewhat lesser extent. It is worth highlighting the fact that occupational mobility seems to be lower than in other EU countries. Zaidi and Zólyomi (2007) found a high rate of transmission of advantages and disadvantages between generations in Hungary, compared to other European states.

Table 14.3 Evolution of total occupational mobility rate

	1983	1992	2000
20–69 years			
Men	73.4	72.2	65.8
Women	77.5	76.1	73.9
20–34 years			
Men	66.4	65.5	60.5
Women	74.0	72.3	73.4

Note: Mobility rates are based on a 7*7 mobility table with occupational categories: manager, professional, clerk; routine non-manual; self-employed; self-employed agriculture; skilled worker; unskilled worker; worker in agriculture.

Source: Bukodi (2002).

According to Albert Hirschman's (1973) 'tunnel effect' hypothesis, anticipated individual mobility chances have an impact on demand for government redistribution. As Tóth (2008b: 1083) concluded, analysing Hungarian data: 'Perceptions of (levels of and changes to) actual incomes and confidence in the future development trajectories of respondents' households play an important role. In other words, the belief that things will get better in the future decreases the redistributive expectations of even those who may be currently in need of help.' A similar conclusion was reached by Ravallion and Lokshin (2000) for Russia in the 1990s.

The Political System

The communist history explains much about Hungarian society, which is more atomized and less participatory than the majority of European countries. Still, the political institutional settings of Hungary that were established as a result of negotiations between the various political forces in 1989 did create what has been a stable party system for the first two decades of new democracy. The value of this stability is, however, rather questionable in light of the 2010 landslide election. The country was politically paralysed between 2006 and 2009, when an unpopular government faced a strong, combative opposition: the government was unable to execute social and economic reforms, and the opposition could not bring about early elections. This apocryphal party-system stability is based on a complex, mixed-type electoral system, which combines majority-system elements with the characteristics of a proportional representation system.

After a fluid period between 1990 and 1998, by the turn of the millennium, Hungary had developed a party system with a strong ideological polarization in terms of the electorate being 'left' or 'right' and a high level of consolidation—i.e. the players (parties) were stable and no new parties entered the competition until 2010. For example, aggregate volatility[11] was rather modest (8.2 per cent) from 2002 to 2006, well below the European average at that time. Parties exercise overwhelming control over the political processes, but they fulfil few social functions and their reputation is low compared to other institutions (see the low membership rates and low level of trust in parties) (Enyedi and Tóka, 2007). The latest parliamentary elections held in 2010 resulted in an absolute majority for the conservative party alliance of Fidesz-KDNP, which had been in opposition for eight years. Despite the efforts of the two major incumbent parliamentary forces (the socialist-liberal coalition in government and the centre-right coalition in opposition) to monopolize the political arena, in 2010 two new parties crossed the 5 per cent parliamentary threshold, both of them protest parties. The green, ecological LMP got 7.5 per cent of the vote—its full name means 'politics can be different'. The extreme-right Jobbik got 16.7 per cent of the vote. Its name contains a double meaning and is a play on words—'rightist' and 'better'.

As in some European countries, voter turnout rates are higher in Hungary in parliamentary elections than in local or municipal polls, with European Parliament elections being

[11] The electoral volatility index (Pedersen, 1979) measures the stability and change in party systems in terms of percentage change of votes cast for winning parties. This index has a theoretical range of 0 to 100. If there is no change in the share of votes for each party from election to election, then the index value is 0. If no old party receives any votes in the subsequent election (just new ones) the index is 100.

the least mobilizing events. Turnout rates at referendums—there were six between 1989 and 2011—ranged from 14 to 58 per cent.

As was mentioned above, the most recent general parliamentary election in Hungary was in 2010. This proved to be a 'critical election' that altered some fundamental features of the party system. The Fidesz-KDNP coalition gained an absolute majority in the legislature, and the extreme right-wing Jobbik party secured 16.7 per cent of votes on its party lists. The ideology of Jobbik can be described as anti-establishment, anti-EU and nationalistic. However, its core issue is the Roma minority, as the party expresses deep concerns about 'Roma criminality' and public safety. There is virtually no immigration to Hungary from outside Europe, unlike in other parts of the continent: the share of the foreign-born population is one of the lowest in the EU, and the influx of foreigners is not on a large scale. Anti-Roma attitudes in Hungary function in the same way as anti-immigrant feelings and anxiety do in extreme rightist discourse in countries like France, Germany or Norway. The context of debates about Roma policies is also about whether the Roma are 'deserving'—should a particular group (immigrants, minorities like the Roma) be entitled to welfare provisions, and under what conditions should the public at large, or local communities, support such groups? Welfare chauvinism was successfully associated with anti-Roma attitudes by Jobbik, and they have managed to attract the attention of the mass media by claiming 'ownership' of the issue of so-called 'Roma criminality' and by the establishment of Magyar Gárda (Hungarian Guard), a paramilitary organization that used symbols associated by many with pre-1945 extreme right-wing movements.

An earlier study found support for the European Union and further integration to be dependent on national identity, economic anxiety and trust in national institutions and satisfaction with national democracy (de Vries and Van Kersbergen, 2007). In Hungary, all these factors changed after 2002 in a direction that weakens support for the EU. Moreover, fewer people felt that the country was benefiting from its EU membership: in 2008 and 2009,

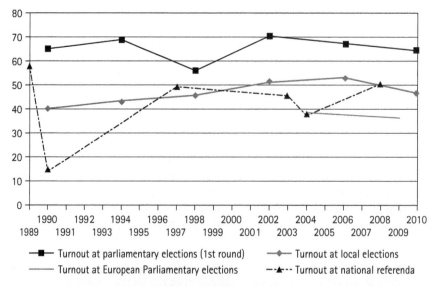

FIGURE 14.5 Voter turnout in Hungary, 1989–2010 (%)

Source: Angelusz and Tardos (2005) and National Election Office (www.valasztas.hu).

the share of those who thought that Hungary was profiting from integration was extremely low (36 per cent), compared to other new Member States. The European Union has become part of Hungary's political system, and attitudes toward the EU are presumably determined to a large extent by the country's economic and governmental performance.

4. Policies as Causes and Consequences of Inequality Trends

To recap on some of the contextual factors surrounding redistribution: there are large numbers of economically inactive people, a generally low level of tax awareness, and widespread demand for redistribution. This complex of factors has been very well exploited by political forces in the past decade. The political agenda has gradually become dominated by competition over the votes of large segments of the economically inactive (most recently there have been attempts to pit the claims of various recipient groups against one another).[12] While, for example, pensioners have traditionally been strong supporters of the socialists, a massive populist campaign by Fidesz-KDNP has caused a fundamental shift in the voter base of both parties over the last decade. The socialists introduced large rises in public sector wages (in 2003), as well as in pensions and social benefits (partly to secure their traditional voter base), but this led to an over-indebtedness of general government, which left very little 'wiggle room' when the crisis broke. While initial attempts (between 2006 and 2008) to balance the general government budget had an income-equalizing effect (since they were primarily based on tax rises), this brought the electorate little long-lasting political satisfaction. Rather, as tax rises proved insufficient to balance the budget, the need arose to cut back on benefits. In 2009 a sort of caretaker, socialist-backed government introduced sweeping cuts in pensions and family benefits. However, this completed the process of erosion of the socialists' voter base: the 2003 public sector wage rise had evaporated by 2009; the 'thirteenth-month' pension introduced earlier was cut back again; the tax rise for the upper middle classes remained; and large elements of child-related benefits were taken away from families with children. All of this further contributed to the political landslide of 2010.

Budget Cycles

The path of Hungarian GDP evolution differs from that in the other countries of the region. While the annual 3–4 per cent growth for the decade around 2000 was high by Western European standards, it was fairly low in comparison with other new EU Member States. Furthermore, whereas in other countries of the region the economic slowdown started later and was a consequence of the Great Recession, the steep decline in Hungarian GDP began earlier and was a result of an unfortunate sequence of expansionary fiscal policies and

---

[12]   To some extent, this represents a break with the welfare policy of the 1990s; it has been described by Vanhuysse (2006) as a policy of 'divide and pacify'.

austerity measures. The budget deficit of previous years had reached unsustainable levels, especially in the election years of 2002 and 2006, and, since 2007, budget consolidation has been the top priority for the various administrations, which have applied a wide range of measures that have affected the country's tax/benefit system.

The general political volatility is also manifested by strong budget cycles. Government deficits were especially high in 1998, 2002 and 2006 (8, 8.9 and 9.4 per cent of GDP, respectively). There is also an asynchronicity in the development of the government deficit: during the recession, other European governments tended to stimulate their economies by spending, and thus went deeper into deficit but, in Hungary, deficit reduction had to be continued because of the dangerous imbalances and international financial difficulties.[13]

While the overall size of government may also be important for the formation of inequality, our focus is restricted here to (macro) redistributive elements and leaves out secondary effects on incentives, macro-economic balances, growth impact, etc.

Hungarian tax revenue relative to GDP declined between 1991 and 2011 (from 45.5 per cent to 35.7 per cent, with an interim peak of 46.1 per cent in 1993). A sharp decline between 1993 and 1996 (from 46 per cent to 40 per cent) was followed by a stagnant ratio of tax receipts to GDP at around or below 40 per cent until 2009. Since then, the available statistics have again shown a sharp decline.

Around a fifth or a quarter of GDP is consistently allocated to public social expenditure—a level that is in line with the OECD average but well below the Western European welfare states. Two periods stand out as exceptions: between 2000 and 2007, expenditure increased by almost 3 percentage points; and a new trend emerged recently, with a 3 percentage-point decline over the short period between 2009 and 2012. This latter seems to be unique in Europe.

In Hungary, splitting total expenditure into more homogeneous elements reveals three distinct groupings by spending level: two main areas of expenditure are 'high'; two are 'medium'; and the rest are 'low'. With 9 per cent of GDP in 2009, 'old age' (pension) is the biggest item and is on the rise (it accounts for three-quarters of the increase in social expenditure); 'health' is the second biggest, with 5 per cent, but is more or less stable. In the mid-range are 'family' (3.6 per cent) and 'incapacity' (2.7 per cent), both of them constant as a percentage of GDP. No clear trend is visible among the lower-ranked functions.

In Hungary, the share of cash expenditure is larger than that of expenditure in kind. The largest functions are 'old age' (mainly cash) and 'health' (mainly in kind); therefore these have the biggest influence on the patterns of type of expenditure.

Minimum Wage

The minimum wage, as a labour market instrument, may influence the lower tail of wage distribution in two ways: on the one hand, by directly censoring the lower part of the distribution; and on the other, by having an impact on labour supply and demand, especially in the low-wage segment. The effect of the minimum wage on the Hungarian wage distribution

---

[13]   In 2011, Hungary even produced a surplus, thanks to one single measure: the nationalization of private pension funds. This is an important characteristic that provided the framework for tax and benefit measures in these years. However, it has become a determining factor in the years since 2010, when the government priority shifted more markedly to deficit reduction.

has been pronounced, especially after the major shock-like increase of 2002. It was seen to represent an effective wage floor—at least for legally 'clean' wages. It should be noted, however, that in Hungary the hidden economy (of which non-registered employment and income are an important part) is put at around 24 per cent of GDP (Schneider, 2011).

The path of minimum wage development has two abrupt turning points. During 2001 and 2002, the minimum wage was doubled, in two steps. While average wages also grew, the relative level of the minimum wage increased from 0.29 to 0.41 within this short period. Since then it has been stable. This kind of shock sheds light on the complex effect of a minimum wage increase. On the one hand, it is an instrument for the social protection of employed people; on the other, it is a barrier to labour market participation, as it increases the cost of labour. According to a study by Köllő (2008), the immediate negative effect of doubling the minimum wage was to significantly reduce employment in the small-firm sector and adversely affect the probability of low-wage workers losing their jobs and of finding a job. These effects appear to be stronger in low-wage segments of the market and in depressed regions, where the minimum wage bites deeper into the wage distribution.

5. Conclusions

In Hungary income inequality started to increase in the eighties, there was a marked increase during the first years of transition, followed by a period of stability, and from 2004–2008 inequality decreased but was still significantly higher at the end of the period than at the outset. The rise in inequalities in Hungary has been driven by a multitude of factors. First, education has been a major component of inequality trends: the gap between the better educated and the less well educated has widened both in terms of monetary returns to education among the employed and in terms of employment chances by category of education. Second, differential re-employment chances (also a clear failure of the education system) and continued low activity levels have contributed to a 'freezing' of the original employment differentiation that resulted from the transition shocks around the time the political and economic system changed.

Third, state redistribution policies have also been important—not just in the sense that the operation of the progressive tax/benefit system has contributed to smaller after-tax-and-transfer inequalities, but also in the sense that the politics of redistribution started to dominate the political discourse in the second half of the observed period.

Political science emphasizes how personal wealth and its distribution can result in biased politics that favour influential groups. In the Hungarian experience, though this type of manipulation by the rich cannot be excluded, another hostage-type situation emerged. The country seemed to descend into a downward spiral: this began with a badly managed labour market shock; carried on through the implementation of various instruments of social policy; and then significant sections of Hungarian society were excluded from the labour market over the long term.

The institutionalization of financed inactivity, together with specific features of the Hungarian political system, has resulted in a 'benefit auction' at election time, with no strong countervailing institutional factors to limit volatile budget deficits. The political cycle has produced a series of unbalanced growth periods, followed by spells of austerity. This has further eroded trust in the political system as a whole and in political actors in particular.

Reinforced distrust—much of it already inherited from the communist past—leads, paradoxically, to further pressure on governments to follow unsustainable paternalistic policies.

The methodological and theoretical conclusion of the Hungarian story, therefore, is that we cannot simply speak of a linear causality 'from inequality to various social impacts'. Rather, the country's story seems to show a situational logic. At the start of the game, the parameters include a number of societal and political conditions, as well as initial inequality. When this inequality starts increasing, the collective reactions will depend very much on the portfolio of societal assets (as well as the actual distribution of income and wealth, we might mention social and political trust, ability to pull together and experience of cooperation, etc.), all with an impact on the evolution of inequalities and poverty in a country. Hungary is a case in point.

REFERENCES

Angelusz, Róbert and Tardos, Róbert (2005), 'Választási részvétel és politikai aktivitás' in R. Angelusz and R. Tardos (eds.), *Törések, hálók, hidak. Választói magatartás és politikai tagolódás*, Budapest: DKMKA, p. 323–384.

Atkinson, A.B. and Micklewright, J. (1992), *Economic Transformation in Eastern Europe and the Distribution of Income*, Cambridge: Cambridge University Press.

Bálint, M. and Köllő J. (2008), 'The labour supply effects of maternity benefits', in K. Fazekas, Zs. Cseres-Gergely and Á. Scharle (eds.), *The Hungarian Labour Market, 2008: Review and Analysis*, Budapest: Institute of Economics, HAS Hungarian Employment Foundation, p. 53–71, available at: <http://econ.core.hu/english/publications/lmyb.html>

Beck, T., Kibuuka, K. and Tiongson, E. (2010), 'Mortgage finance in Central and Eastern Europe: Opportunity or burden?' *Institute for the Study of Labor (IZA) Discussion Paper* No. 4758.

Bukodi, Erzsébet, (2002), 'Társadalmi mobilitás Magyarországon, 1983-2000', in Tamás Kolosi, István György Tóth, and György Vukovich (eds.), *Társadalmi Riport 2002*, Budapest: Tárki, p. 193–206.

Bukodi, E. and Goldthorpe, J.H. (2010), 'Market versus meritocracy: Hungary as a critical case', *European Sociological Review*, vol. 26: 655–674.

National Bank of Hungary (2010), *Jelentés a pénzügyi stabilitásról*, [Report on Financial Stability], Budapest: MNB

Csontos, L., Kornai, J., and Tóth, I. Gy. (1998), 'Tax awareness and the reform of the welfare state. Hungarian Survey Results', *Economics of Transition*, 6(2): 287–312.

De Vries, Catherine E. and van Kersbergen, Kees (2007), 'Interests, Identity and Political Allegiance in the European Union', *Acta Politica* 42(2-3): 307–328.

Elek, P., Scharle, Á., Szabó, B., and P.A. Szabó (2009), 'A fekete foglalkoztatás mértéke Magyarországon', in A. Semjén and I. J. Tóth (eds.), *Rejtett Gazdaság*, Budapest: MTA KTI.

Enyedi, Zsolt, and Tóka, Gábor, (2007), 'The only game in town: Party politics in Hungary', in Paul Webb and Stephen White (eds.), *Party Politics in New Democracies*, Oxford: Oxford University Press, p. 147–178.

European Commission (2010), *Europe 2020—A European strategy for smart, sustainable and inclusive growth*, <http://ec.europa.eu/eu2020/pdf/COMPLET%20EN%20BARROSO%20%20%20007%20-%20Europe%202020%20-%20EN%20version.pdf>, 15 July 2010.

EU Task-Force on Child Poverty and Child Well-Being (2008), *Child poverty and child well-being in the EU. Current status and way forward*, Brussels: European Commission,

Directorate-General for Employment, Social Affairs and Equal Opportunities, Social Protection Committee.

Flemming, J.S. and Micklewright, J. (2000), 'Income distribution, economic systems and transition' in A. Atkinson and F. Bourguignon (eds.), *Handbook of Income Distribution*, Volume I, Amsterdam: Elsevier Science pp 843–918.

Gábos, A. and Szivós, P. (2010), 'Jövedelmi szegénység és anyagi depriváció Magyarországon', in T. Kolosi and I. Gy. Tóth (eds.), *Társadalmi Riport 2010*. Budapest: Tárki, 58–81.

Galasi, P. (2007), 'Earnings of Higher-Education Graduates: The Role of Education, Type of Education and Under/Over Education', in K. Fazekas and G. Kézdi (eds.), *The Hungarian Labour Market 2007*, Budapest: Institute of Economics.

Hankiss, Elemér (1983), *Diagnózisok*, Budapest: Magvető.

Hirschman, Albert O. (1973), 'Changing Tolerance for Income Inequality in the Course of Economic Development', *Quarterly Journal of Economics* 87(4): 544–566.

Holló, D. (2007), 'Household Indebtedness and Financial Stability: Reasons to be Afraid?' *Hungarian National Bank Bulletin*, November.

Hungarian Central Statistical Office (2007), *Egészségesen várható élettartamok Magyarországon,2005* [Healthy life expectancy in Hungary, 2005], Budapest: KSH .

Kemény, I. and Janky B. (2006), 'Roma population of Hungary 1971–2003', in I. Kemény (ed.), *Roma of Hungary, East European Monographs*, New York: Atlantic Research and Publications.

Kertesi, G. and Kézdi, G. (2011), 'Roma employment in Hungary after the post-communist transition', *Economics of Transition* 19(3): 563–610.

Kézdi, G. (2005), 'Education and Earnings', in K. Fazekas and J. Varga (eds.), *The Hungarian Labour Market 2005*, Budapest: Institute of Economics.

Kornai, J. (1980), *Economics of Shortage*, Amsterdam: North-Holland.

Kornai, J. (1992). The Socialist System. The Political Economy of Communism. Princeton: Princeton University Press

Köllő, János (2008), 'Hungary—The consequences of doubling the minimum wage' in Daniel Vaughan-Whitehead (ed.), *The Minimum Wage Revisited in the Enlarged EU*, Geneva: ILO.

Lannert, Judit (2009), 'Value of knowledge: skills, competences, opinions', in István György Tóth (ed.), *Tárki European Social Report 2009*, Budapest: Tárki Social Research Inc., p. 133–150.

Leinsalu, M. *et al.* (2009), 'Educational inequalities in mortality in four Eastern European countries: Divergence in trends during the post-communist transition from 1990 to 2000', *International Journal of Epidemiology* 38: 512–525.

Loboda, Z., Lannert, J., and Halász, G. (eds.) (2007), *Education in Hungary 2006*, Budapest: Hungarian Institute for Educational Research and Development.

Mackenbach, J. P. *et al.* (2008), 'Socioeconomic Inequalities in Health in 22 European Countries', *New England Journal of Medicine* 358:2468–2481.

Medgyesi, M. (2013), 'Increasing income inequality and attitudes to inequality: a cohort perspective', *GINI Discussion Paper* (forthcoming).

Medgyesi M. and Tóth, I. Gy. (2012), 'Long term determinants of income inequality in Hungary', (in Hungarian) in: T. Kolosi and I. Gy. Tóth (eds.), *Társadalmi Riport 2012*. Budapest: Tárki, 19–40.

OECD (2009), *Education at a Glance*, Paris: OECD.

Pedersen, Mogens N. (1979), 'The Dynamics of European Party Systems: Changing Patterns of Electoral Volatility', *European Journal of Political Research* 7(1): 1–26.

Pichler, F, and Wallace, C. (2007), 'Patterns of Formal and Informal Social Capital in Europe', *European Sociological Review* 23(4): 423–435.

Ravallion, Martin, and Loskhin, Michael (2000), 'Who Wants to Redistribute? The Tunnel Effect in 1990s Russia', *Journal of Public Economics* 76: 87–104.

Rózsavölgyi, R. and Kovács, V. (2005), 'Housing Subsidies in Hungary: Curse or Blessing?' *ECFIN Country Focus*, Vol. 2, Issue 18.

Schneider, Friedrich (2011), *The Shadow Economy in Europe, 2010*, Linz: Johannes Kepler University.

Shorrocks, Anthony (1980), 'The Class of Additively Decomposable Inequality Measures', *Econometrica*; vol.48(3): 613–625.

Spéder, Zs. and F. Kamarás, (2008), 'Hungary: Secular fertility decline with distinct period fluctuations', *Demographic Research* 19(18): 599–664.

Tárki (2011), 'Child well-being in the European Union—Better monitoring instruments for better policies', report prepared for the State Secretariat for Social Inclusion of the Ministry of Public Administration and Justice, Budapest; <http://www.tarki.hu/en/research/childpoverty/tarki_chwb_mainreport_online.pdf>

Tárki/Applica (2010), 'Child Poverty and Child Well-Being in the European Union', report for the European Commission, Budapest and Brussels.

Tárki (2012), 'Country report on growing inequality and its impacts in Hungary', research report with GINI Project, mimeo.

Tóth, I. Gy. (2008a), 'The reach of transition in Hungary: assessing the effects of economic transition on income distribution, 1987–2001', in Lyn Squire, and Jose Maria Fanelli, (eds.), *Economic Reform in Developing Countries: Reach, Range and Reason*, GDN Series, Edward Elgar Publishing,

Tóth, I. Gy. (2008b), 'The demand for redistribution. A test on Hungarian data', *SociologickýCasopis*/Czech Sociological Review, 2008, Vol. 44, No. 6: 491.509

Tóth, I. Gy. (2010a), 'Jövedelemeloszlás 2007–2009 között', in *Jövedelem egyenlőtlenség és szegénység Magyarországon 2009*, Tárki Háztartás Monitor 1. kötet elemzések, available at: <http://www.tarki.hu/hu/research/hm/monitor2009_teljes.pdf>.

Tóth, I. Gy. (2010b), 'A társadalmi kohézió elemei: bizalom, normakövetés, igazságosság és felelősségérzet—lennének...', in T. Kolosi and I. Gy. Tóth (eds.), *Társadalmi Riport 2010*, Budapest: Tárki, 254–287. p.

Tóth, I. and Keller, T. (2013), 'Income Distribution, Inequality Perception and Redistributive Preferences in European Countries', in Janet C. Gornick and Markus Jäntti (eds.), *Economic Inequality in Cross-National Perspective*, Palo Alto CA, Stanford University Press.

Tóth, I. Gy. and Keller, T. (2012), 'Az újraelosztás iránti kereslet Magyarországon és nemzetközi összehasonlításban', in *Földobott kő? Tények és tendenciák a 21. században*, Budapest: Akadémiai Kiadó, p. 124–154.

Tóth, I. Gy. and Medgyesi, M.(2011), 'Income distribution and living difficulties in the midst of consolidation programmes and crises in Hungary', in K. Fazekas and Gy. Molnár (eds.), *The Hungarian Labour Market—Review and Analysis 2011*, Budapest: Institute of Economics, (170–186.)

Vanhuysse, P. (2006), *Divide and Pacify. Strategic Social Policies and Political Protests in Post-Communist Democracies*, Budapest: Central European University Press.

World Bank (2000), *Making Transition Work for Everyone. Poverty and Income Inequality in Europe and Central Asia*, The World Bank, Washington D.C.

Zaidi, Ashgar and Zólyomi, Eszter (2007), 'Intergenerational transmission of disadvantages in EU member states', Vienna: European Centre for Social Welfare Policy and Research.

ANNEX

Table A1. Summary table on macro data

	GDP 1990 = 100%	per capita income 1990 = 100%	government deficit	gross MW to average wage	total tax revenue as % of GDP	taxes on income, profits and capital gains as % of GDP	SSC as % of GDP	social expenditure as % of GDP
1990	100.0	100.0						
1991	87.9	98.4			45.5	12.5	16.2	
1992	85.3	94.7			45.2	9.8	17.5	
1993	84.4	90.2			46.1	9.5	17.9	
1994	87.0	92.7			43.5	9.1	16.8	
1995	88.7	87.8		0.306	41.5	8.7	14.7	
1996	88.9	84.9		0.305	40	8.7	13.5	
1997	91.6	84.9		0.292	38.4	8.2	12.8	
1998	95.4	86.9		0.283	38.1	8.4	12.5	
1999	98.4	87.8	-5.4	0.291	38.9	8.9	11.5	21.2
2000	102.6	89.8	-3	0.291	39.3	9.3	11.3	20.3
2001	106.4	93.9	-4	0.386	38.4	9.7	11.3	20.1
2002	111.2	100.4	-8.9	0.408	38	10.0	11.4	21.3
2003	115.5	105.7	-7.3	0.364	37.9	9.3	11.5	22.4
2004	121.0	108.6	-6.5	0.364	37.7	8.8	11.2	21.6
2005	125.8	112.7	-7.9	0.360	37.3	8.8	11.7	22.6
2006	130.7	114.3	-9.4	0.365	37.3	9.1	11.9	22.9
2007	130.9	109.0	-5.1	0.354	40.3	10.0	13.0	22.9
2008	132.0	107.3	-3.7	0.347	40.1	10.4	13.0	na
2009	123.0	103.3	-4.6	0.358	39.9	9.6	12.5	23.9
2010	124.6	100.4	-4.2	0.363	37.6	7.7	11.9	22.6
2011	126.5	102.9	4.3	0.366	35.7	6.1	12.3	21.8
2012	124.8		-1.2	0.424				21.1

CHAPTER 15

···

IRELAND: INEQUALITY AND ITS IMPACTS IN BOOM AND BUST

···

BRIAN NOLAN, CHRISTOPHER T. WHELAN, EMMA CALVERT,

TONY FAHEY, DEIRDRE HEALY, AOGAN MULCAHY,

BERTRAND MAÎTRE, MICHELLE NORRIS, IAN O'DONNELL,

AND NESSA WINSTON

1. INTRODUCTION

IRELAND's remarkable macro-economic fluctuations make it a particularly interesting case study into what has been happening to inequality in recent decades, and the impact this may have on social, political and cultural outcomes. Having experienced prolonged economic stagnation for much of the 1980s, Ireland had the fastest economic growth rates in the OECD during the first part of the so-called 'Celtic Tiger' boom period from the mid 1990s, with sustained strong though more modest growth from 2000 up to the onset of the crisis. This was followed by a post-crisis recession, which had a more negative impact on national output in Ireland than in any other OECD country. Against this background, it is particularly revealing to explore what happened to income and educational inequalities and their impacts, and that is the focus of this chapter. We first describe the contours of the political economy within which economic and social changes are taking place. We then document the macro-economic context, distinguishing a set of critical sub-periods which differed from each other, often dramatically so. We then turn to the way income inequality, poverty and educational inequalities evolved over these years, distinguishing where possible the same sub-periods. Next we focus on trends in the key social, political and cultural outcomes that might have been affected, inter alia, by inequalities in income and education. Finally, we discuss the policy context and major innovations before summarizing core findings.

Ireland's Macro-Economic Roller-Coaster

The political economy context within which economic and social change unfolded in Ireland had distinctive features. One of the most open economies in the world, Ireland can be located clearly within the Anglo-American model of capitalism (Hall and Soskice, 2001). As Dellepiane and Hardiman (2012) observe, its openness provided Ireland with substantial incentives to actively manage its economic fortunes, giving it something in common with a range of small European states. The preferred strategy combined tripartite centralized bargaining at the national level with considerable autonomy for employers at the workplace level. O'Riain and O'Connell (2000) note that the Irish state has played a significant role both in shaping development outcomes and in negotiating the distribution of the associated rewards and costs. The state played a central part in upgrading industry and expanding the educational system, and a two-tiered welfare state has maintained a basic level of social citizenship supplemented by middle and higher income groups, while a distinctive version of what Rhodes (1997) labels 'competitive corporatism', which prioritizes competitiveness, macro-economic stability and employment creation but downplays the 'equity' objective of more traditional 'golden age' forms of corporatism.

Ireland in 1980 faced a sustained period of stagnation in economic growth after misguided pump-priming policies in the late 1970s had attempted to force recovery from the oil price crisis. Taxation rose by 10 percentage points of GNP in seven years, while unemployment soared to 16 per cent of the labour force, emigration to 1 per cent of the population, and government debt to 130 per cent of GNP by 1986. From 1987, though, the marked tightening of fiscal policy produced a remarkably rapid improvement in government borrowing and the debt ratio. While giving rise to debates about whether this constituted a case of 'expansionary fiscal contraction', the contribution of greatly improved external conditions was very significant. Once economic activity started to pick up, tax receipts rose, allowing the government to lower tax rates, structural fund grants from the EU also came at an opportune time, but the major contribution to demand growth came from exports, due to greater competitiveness and foreign direct investment (Bradley and Whelan, 1997).

Economic growth was erratic and unemployment stubbornly high until 1994, from which point the remarkable take-off to 'Celtic Tiger' status was seen. From 1994 to 2000, the average annual increase in real GNP was 7 per cent, among the highest in the OECD. Growth dipped in 2001–2 but then returned to 4–6 per cent per annum up to 2007, at which point Ireland's GNP per capita was among the highest in the European Union, having more than doubled over the previous twelve years in purchasing power terms.[1] Real median household incomes adjusted for household size increased by 116 per cent over the same period. The numbers employed expanded dramatically, from 1.2 million in 1994 to 1.7 million by 2000 and 2.1 million by 2007. Unemployment declined very rapidly, from 16 per cent in 1994 to 4 per cent by 2000, staying at that level up to 2007, and the long-term unemployment rate fell from almost 11 per cent in the late 1980s to just over 1 per cent in 2001. The employment rate for women rose from 40 per cent to 60 per cent, and migration was also important in the expansion of the workforce. There was a wave of return migration by Irish people who had

---

[1] Gross Domestic Product is problematic as a measure of domestic income (rather than output) in the Irish case, since Foreign Direct Investment is particularly important and generates profits which flow out of the country, not directly impacting on domestic household incomes.

left in the 1980s, followed by substantial numbers from other EU countries, particularly after the 2004 enlargement, so that by 2006 about 10 per cent of the population was foreign-born.

The latter part of the economic boom was accompanied by an unbridled property boom and very rapid increase in levels of household debt. The tax base became highly unbalanced, with income tax cuts being offset by revenue from stamp duties and other taxes on property development and sales. The global financial crisis and the bursting of the domestic property bubble then led to an unprecedented contraction in national output and income in 2008–9, together with a collapse in asset values and a banking crisis of unprecedented proportions. Unemployment rose to 14.5 per cent, with the unemployment rate for men aged 20–24 soaring from 8 per cent to over one in three, and net emigration also returned, both of Irish citizens and recent arrivals from Eastern Europe.

The rate of individuals in households characterized by very low work intensity (VLWI) in Ireland, employing the measure incorporated in the EU Poverty and Social Exclusion Target, increased from 15 per cent of people under age 60 in 2004 to 22 per cent in 2010. The rate in Ireland is currently more than double the rate in other EU countries. The reason for the very high VLWI rate is partly due to the high joblessness rate among adults, but also due to the fact that jobless adults are less likely in Ireland to live with working adults and more likely to live with children (Watson *et al.*, 2012).

The recession had a profound impact on the government's fiscal position, with the fiscal deficit and debt to GDP ratio soaring. By late 2010, despite substantial increases in taxation and expenditure cuts, the deficit including support provided to the banking system reached 32 per cent and the government had to avail itself of a 'bail-out' by the EU and IMF, entailing a programme of public spending cuts and tax increases intended to bring the deficit down to three per cent by 2014. The effects of this domestic austerity combined with weak external growth continue to play out as the economy 'flatlined' with no increase in GDP, export growth being offset by very weak domestic demand, and with unemployment no higher only because of the scale of emigration.

The scale of the bust, boom and subsequent recession experienced since 1980, accompanied by sharp swings in taxation and public spending, make Ireland an outlier in terms of macro-economic fluctuations, and the country is likely to be particularly illuminating as a case study on their impact on the distribution of income and on poverty. In pursuing this investigation throughout the chapter, it is worth keeping in mind the discrete sub-periods which may be distinguished in macro-economic terms as follows:

- 1980–86: recession, high unemployment and emigration
- 1987–1993: significant recovery but limited employment growth and unemployment stubbornly high
- 1994–2000: fastest growth in the OECD with employment increasing dramatically, long-term unemployment almost disappearing, and significant immigration
- 2001–2007: growth, employment expansion continuing but fuelled by credit expansion and construction/property boom
- 2008–now: banking and fiscal crises, a property crash, collapse in national ouput, soaring unemployment.

2. INCOME INEQUALITY, EDUCATIONAL INEQUALITIES AND SOCIAL MOBILITY

Analysis of levels and trends in income inequality and poverty relies mostly on microdata from large-scale household surveys, notably the ESRI's 1987 survey,[2] the Living in Ireland Surveys (LII) carried out by the ESRI from 1994 to 2001 as part of the European Community Household Panel,[3] the survey carried out by the Central Statistics Office (CSO) annually since 2003 as part of the EU-SILC data-gathering framework,[4] and the Household Budget Surveys carried out every 5–6 years or so by the CSO. Data from the administration of the income tax system also provide a perspective on trends towards the top of the income distribution. In the early part of the period data are only available for the years 1980 and 1987, whereas from 1994 onwards there is some survey data for each year except 2002 due to the gap between the LII/ECHP and SILC.

The overall degree of income inequality is conventionally summarized using measures such as the Gini coefficient, and Table 15.1 shows the available estimates from different sources, national and comparative, over the years from 1987 based on disposable income equivalized to take household size and composition into account. The estimates for individual years sometimes vary, due to differences in the underlying survey, in the equivalence scale employed, or for other reasons investigated in a number of studies (notably Nolan and Smeeding, 2005) but not elaborated on here, where our focus is on the overall picture of inequality and how it changed over time.

Figures on this basis are available only from 1987, but estimates for 1980 drawn from the Household Budget Survey carried out that year suggest a level of inequality similar to 1987.[5] Looking then at the period from 1987 to 1994 or 1995 in Table 15.1, the Gini coefficient appears to have been relatively stable, at somewhere between 0.31–0.33, depending on the source/equivalence scale. Inequality at that point was thus above the average in the then EU-15, similar to the level seen in the UK, Spain and Greece, and also above average in an OECD context but similar to most of the other countries in the Liberal welfare regime in which it would customarily be placed, including Australia, Canada and New Zealand as well as the UK. This was consistent with relatively low social protection spending (as a proportion of national income) and a low redistributive impact of income transfers together with direct taxes, arising in particular from low spending on public pensions, in turn reflecting both a low share of older persons in the population and the flat-rate nature of the social security pension system. Despite the economic fluctuations from 1980, inequality appears to have been more influenced by those underlying structural features than even the major macroeconomic fluctuations seen over the period.

This turns out to have remained the case, in broad terms, over the years of the 'Celtic Tiger' boom. As Table 15.1 shows, the Gini coefficient may have declined somewhat in the first half of the boom before increasing towards the latter part (though some sources do not

---

[2] See Callan, Nolan *et al.* (1989).
[3] See Nolan, O'Connell and Whelan (2000).
[4] See for example CSO (2013).
[5] The available estimates for 1980 employ the household as unit of analysis, whereas all the figures in Table 15.1 are based on the individual with each person attributed the equivalized income of their household.

Table 15.1 Summary income inequality measures, equivalized disposable income among persons, Ireland 1987–2011

	National			Comparative		
	ESRI Surveys*	SILC*	Household Budget Survey	Growing Unequal**	LIS**	EU SI Indicators***
1987	0.31			0.33	0.33	
1994	0.32				0.33	
1995			0.30**	0.32	0.34	0.33
1996					0.33	0.33
1997	0.32					0.33
1998						0.34
1999						0.32
2000	0.30		0.30**	0.30	0.31	0.30
2001	0.30					0.29
2003						0.31
2004		0.32			0.31	0.32
2005		0.32	0.32*	0.33		0.32
2006		0.32				0.32
2007		0.32				0.31
2008		0.31				0.30
2009		0.29				0.29
2010		0.32	0.32*			0.32

* National' equivalence scale (1/0.66/0.33)
** Square root equivalence scale (square root of number of persons in the household)
*** Modified OECD equivalence scale (1/0.5/0.3)
Sources: 1987 ESRI Survey calculated directly from microdata; 1994–2001 Living in Ireland Survey calculated directly from microdata; 2003–2010 SILC published by Central Statistics Office from annual SILC survey, most recently in CSO (2012); HBS 1994–95 and 1999–2000 estimated from microdata, 2004–2005 published in CSO (2007) p. 19, 2009–2010 in CSO (2012) p. 29; Growing Unequal see OECD (2008); LIS from 'Key Figures' downloadable from LIS website; EU SI Indicators from Eurostat website Income and Living Conditions Data Main Tables' 'Income Distribution' 'Gini Coefficient'.

show even that much change), but by 2007 inequality was back at very much the same level as in the mid 1990s. This is remarkable given the extent of the increase in employment, the virtual disappearance of long-term unemployment, and the reduction in direct taxes seen over the period as described in the next section.

Turning to the period from the onset of the economic crisis, the immediate impact of the recession was equalizing rather than disequalizing, indeed quite considerably so, with income inequality falling in 2008 and especially in 2009.[6] This reflected in particular a decline in the share of total income going to the top and an increase in the share going to the bottom half.

---

[6] Note that EU-SILC income data for most EU countries use the previous calendar year, so inequality figures labelled '2009', for example, come from the 2009 round and actually refer to 2008 incomes. Ireland uses the 12 months prior to the interview date as the period for measuring household incomes, with interviewing carried out throughout the year.

Table 15.2 Decile shares, equivalized disposable income (among persons, 1/0.66/0.33 equivalence scale)

Decile	1994	2000	2004	2005	2006	2007	2008	2009
	%	%	%	%	%	%	%	%
Bottom	3.7	3.2	3.3	3.3	3.4	3.5	3.6	2.8
2	4.7	4.5	4.7	4.7	4.9	5.1	5.3	4.8
3	5.5	5.5	5.6	5.7	5.7	5.9	6.1	5.7
4	6.4	6.9	6.8	6.8	6.6	6.8	7.0	6.5
5	7.6	8.0	8.0	7.9	7.7	7.9	8.1	7.5
6	9.0	9.3	9.3	9.2	9.0	9.1	9.2	8.9
7	10.7	10.8	10.6	10.6	10.6	10.4	10.6	10.2
8	12.6	12.7	12.3	12.2	12.3	12.2	12.3	11.9
9	15.4	15.6	14.7	14.6	15.1	14.7	14.8	15.2
Top	24.4	23.6	24.9	25.9	24.8	24.5	23.3	26.6

Source: Calculated from Living in Ireland Survey and EU-SILC microdata.

Declines in profits and income from capital and self-employment at the onset of recession would have impacted most heavily towards the top, while (as discussed in more detail in the policy section) increases in direct taxation implemented at this point were rather progressive in character. In 2010, the Gini rose to 0.32 before falling to 0.31 in 2011. For the period 2008–11 the mean Gini was 0.307 compared to an average of 0.321 for 2004–8. Thus rather than the recession leading to an increase in inequality, the opposite was the case. However, it is an open question whether such an outcome can be sustained in an extended period of austerity.

Summary measures may mask important changes occurring in different parts of the income distribution, so it is worth also looking at decile shares—the share of total income going to those in the bottom 10 per cent, next 10 per cent etc. Comparable figures based on the LII survey from 1994 to 2001 and SILC from 2004 are shown in Table 15.2. These suggest some decline in the share going to the top 10 per cent over the first half of the boom, followed by an increase to the mid 2000s. However, SILC shows larger shares going towards the top than the Household Budget Survey, and the comparison between LII and SILC could overstate the increase in share for that part of the distribution after 2001.

Household surveys may have particular difficulty right at the top of the income distribution, so trends in that respect may be better captured by data from the income tax system. Large increases in top income shares have been revealed by recent studies based on this data source, being particularly pronounced in countries such as the USA and the UK but by no means confined to them. Estimates of the share of total income going to the top 1 per cent in Ireland, derived from data produced by the Revenue Commissioners, suggest a sharp increase over the 1990s, from about 6 per cent to 10 per cent (Nolan, 2007). This appears to have continued through the latter part of the boom, with the share of the top 1 per cent reaching 12.5 per cent in 2006, before falling back with the onset of the recession.[7]

---

[7] An updating of the estimates in Nolan (2007), together with a methodological note, are now on the World Top Incomes Database <http://g-mond.parisschoolofeconomics.eu/topincomes/>

Table 15.3 Percentage of persons below 60 per cent of median relative income poverty line, Ireland 1994–2010

	1994	2000	2004	2007	2008	2009	2010	2011
Below line	%	%	%	%	%	%	%	%
All	15.6	21.9	18.0	16.5	14.4	14.1	14.7	16.0
Children (<18)	24.6	23.7	21.2	19.9	18.0	18.6	18.4	18.8
Working Age	12.2	16.4	17.6	15.0	13.5	13.0	14.2	15.9
Older (65+)	6.0	38.4	27.1	16.5	11.1	9.6	8.7	9.7

Equivalence Scale 1/0.66/0.33
Source: Analysis of LII and SILC microdata, published SILC Reports.

As well as overall income inequality and top incomes, trends affecting incomes towards the bottom are of particular interest. This is often examined in terms of numbers falling below relative income poverty lines—included among the EU's social inclusion indicators as the 'at-risk-of-poverty rate'—with a threshold of 60 per cent of median equivalized income in the country being a commonly-used reference point. On this measure, between 1987 and 1994 the relative income poverty rate rose quite sharply, despite improved economic circumstances. Unemployment remained high, and while the lowest social transfer rates were increased, this brought recipients closer to but not quite up to the income threshold (so depth-sensitive poverty measures of the Foster-Greer-Thorbecke type fell).[8] As shown in Table 15.3, relative income poverty measured in this fashion then increased further in the earlier years of the Celtic Tiger boom. This was despite sharply rising levels of employment and incomes from work, and reflected the fact that those who remained reliant on social transfers fell behind. This ground was made up in the latter part of the boom, so that by 2005–7 Ireland's relative income poverty rate was back to the level seen in the mid 1990s, which was above the EU and OECD averages but not an outlier.[9] The rate for older people fluctuated particularly sharply, peaking at 38 per cent in 2000 as social pensions fell behind rapidly-increasing incomes from work but falling very sharply thereafter as they were increased substantially in the latter years of the boom.

The immediate impact of the economic crisis from 2008 was to reduce this at-risk-of-poverty measure, from 16.5 per cent per cent to an average of 14.4 per cent for 2008–10, partly because median income and thus the poverty threshold declined. In 2011, however, the percentage of persons falling below this relative threshold rose to 16 per cent. This increase was concentrated among working age adults and older people while the rate for children was stable.

Given the decline in the relative income threshold, it is also important to look at what happened to poverty measured vis a vis a threshold held constant in purchasing power terms. The percentage of people falling below the 60 per cent median threshold anchored at 2007 fell from 16.5 per cent to an average of 15 per cent for 2008–9 as the recession hit,

---

[8] See Nolan, O'Connell and Whelan (2000).
[9] See Nolan, Maitre and Whelan (2007), Nolan, Russell and Maitre (2010).

and then rose very sharply to 19 per cent in 2010 and 21.2 per cent in 2011. Before the crisis, the pattern was very different: given the scale of increases in real income, a poverty threshold anchored at the 60 per cent of median threshold in the mid 1990s, and subsequently indexed to prices, would have seen poverty virtually disappear by the peak of the boom.

The dispersion in earnings among individual employees is another significant factor in overall income inequality, whose evolution it is important to understand. Wage bargaining was centralized at the national level from 1987 up to the onset of the economic crisis through a process known as social partnership, in which the government, employers and unions concluded agreements on wage levels in both private and public sectors, together with a wide range of economic and social policies. Mean and median earnings rose rapidly in real terms throughout the boom period, with average earnings increasing by 38 per cent and the median going up by 34 per cent between 1994 and 2007. Public sector pay rose relatively rapidly in the period from about 2000 but was reduced in 2009 as the economic and fiscal situation worsened dramatically. The introduction of a national minimum wage for the first time around the mid-point of the boom, in 2000, was an important institutional change. Table 15.4 shows the level of earnings at different percentiles as proportions of the median, together with the ratio of the top to the bottom decile. We see that P90/P10 fell very sharply indeed from 1997 to 2000, from 4.8 to 3.6, primarily because the bottom decile moved closer to the median in 2000. From then, up to 2007, the top quartile and especially the top decile rose more rapidly than the median, while the bottom decile moved broadly in line with the median, so that by 2007 the P90/P10 ratio had risen back up to 4. The immediate impact of the recession on earnings dispersion was not substantial.

Decomposition analysis by Voitchovsky, Maître and Nolan (2011) shows that declining returns to both education and work experience from 1994 to 2000 were key to the narrowing dispersion over those years, associated with the substantial immigration of relatively highly skilled workers. By contrast, from 2000 to 2007 the change in returns produced some increase in dispersion, as did changing workforce characteristics. The introduction of the minimum wage in 2000 appears to have been important, anchoring the bottom of the distribution at a higher proportion of the median from then onwards, with P10 and the minimum wage evolving in a very similar fashion up to 2007. When recession hit, the minimum wage was cut by €1 but this was reversed after a change of government.

Ireland's bust, boom and bust cycle may well have had deep-seated effects on the distribution of wealth, but microdata to capture this are not available. Wealth held in forms other than housing is highly concentrated, in Ireland as elsewhere, but the house price bubble was a central feature of the boom and bust period. Investment in housing (including buy-to-let) fuelled by the ready availability of credit and low interest rates became very widespread as a means of wealth accumulation in the boom. After the bust, with house prices down to half their 2007 peak levels, substantial numbers of families were left in negative equity; overall the recession may have seen the distribution of wealth among wealth holders become more unequal, while the gap between those with and without wealth may have narrowed. A distinctive feature of the current recession, particularly in Ireland, has been the scale of debt problems (Russell *et al.*, 2012). In Ireland the level of mortgage lending per capita increased tenfold over the period 1995–2008, the level of credit card debt rose by just over 700 per cent, and the ratio of household debt to disposable income rose by 270 per cent between 1995 and 2008. After the bust, with house prices down to half their 2007 peak levels, many households, as noted above, were in negative equity. In 2002 the ratio of liabilities to disposable

Table 15.4 Distribution of hourly earnings, all employees, 1994–2009

| | As proportion of median | | | | Top decile/ |
	Bottom decile	Bottom quartile	Top quartile	Top decile	Bottom decile
1994	0.49	0.69	1.53	2.35	4.77
1995	0.50	0.70	1.54	2.27	4.54
1996	0.49	0.69	1.50	2.24	4.62
1997	0.50	0.71	1.52	2.33	4.64
1998	0.51	0.67	1.45	2.12	4.16
1999	0.51	0.73	1.45	2.15	4.21
2000	0.59	0.75	1.44	2.10	3.56
2001	0.58	0.74	1.44	2.09	3.62
2002			*No data available*		
2003	0.56	0.73	1.46	2.04	3.67
2004	0.58	0.74	1.46	2.12	3.65
2005	0.57	0.73	1.46	2.11	3.67
2006	0.56	0.71	1.50	2.18	3.92
2007	0.56	0.72	1.50	2.26	4.00
2008	0.57	0.71	1.50	2.23	3.93
2009	0.56	0.71	1.50	2.20	3.88

Source: Calculated from Living in Ireland Survey and EU-SILC microdata.

income was close to 1, but by 2007 it had risen to 2.3. Despite the evidence that indebtedness is highly structured in socio-economic terms, the debt issue together with increased and more progressive taxation and cuts in public sector pay have led to a focus in popular discourse on notions of 'middle class squeeze'.

As far as educational attainment and inequalities are concerned, Ireland underwent an education revolution from the introduction of free compulsory schooling in the 1960s through to the mass expansion of higher education during the 1990s and 2000s. Between 1984 and 1993, the proportion of young people completing second-level education increased from 67 per cent to over 80 per cent, and reached 84 per cent by 2007 (Smyth and McCoy, 2011). While 72 per cent of young people completing secondary education entered the labour market directly in 1984, this fell to 43 per cent in 2004. Participation in higher education grew from 20 per cent in 1980 to 44 per cent in 1998, and 55 per cent by 2004.

This was reflected in an increase in participation in higher education by most social groups, with the rate for those coming from families of unskilled manual workers increasing from 3 per cent in 1980 to 21 per cent in 1998, and for skilled manual, other non-manual and semi-skilled groups from about 10 per cent to over 30 per cent. However, over the same period the higher professional social class increased its participation rate from just under 50 per cent to near saturation.[10] While the participation rates of some of the lower socio-economic groups did continue to increase subsequently, a steep gradient persisted,

[10] Clancy and Wall (2001) also report a social-economic gradient with regards field of study and institution (the higher professional group was most strongly represented in the university sector and in subjects such as Medicine, Law, Dentistry and Veterinary).

and widening participation in higher education for students from disadvantaged backgrounds has continued to be a major focus of educational policy.

The linkage between inequalities in income and educational inequalities in a cross-section context is pronounced in the Irish case, with higher levels of educational attainment strongly associated with higher earnings and household income, and low levels of attainment and skills being key predictors of welfare receipt and dependency. Changes in income inequality and education over the period from 1980 do not appear to have weakened these interdependencies. With average levels of educational attainment increasing substantially, the decreasing proportion of the age cohort failing to complete secondary school is at an ever-greater disadvantage in the labour market. The linkage between welfare recipiency and education also remained deep-seated during the economic boom, in relation not only to unemployment but also welfare payments associated with disability and lone parenthood. The increase in non-employment with the recession was disproportionately concentrated among younger age cohorts, despite their relatively high levels of education. However, within age groups, those with low levels of education saw a particularly marked increase.

Macro-economic conditions and income/educational inequalities may also have implications for social mobility and inequality of opportunity. Ireland has long been seen as test case in relation to such mobility processes because of the lateness and rapidity of its industrialization (Whelan and Layte, 2002). Analysis of survey data from 1973 to 2000, using the 7-category CASMIN social class schema, reveals a significant reduction in the level of absolute immobility for men, except for those originating in the professional and managerial class. For most classes, there was a substantial increase in movement into the professional/managerial class, including a doubling of the flow from the non-skilled manual and farming classes, and there were also increased flows into the routine non-manual class. Changes in the class profile of the population—notably increases in the size of the professional/managerial and routine non-manual classes—account for most of this increase, but the limited changes in relative mobility—in the odds of movement from one class versus another—appear to have been in the direction of increased openness, especially toward long-range upward mobility. In a period of rapid educational expansion, there was no evidence of a weakening in the scale of educational advantage conferred by class origins, as illustrated in Whelan and Layte (2006). However, the capacity of such qualifications to guarantee access to more favoured classes was reduced. Educational expansion was also key to promoting economic growth in the first place, and the major changes in the class structure that accompanied it. So while it did not entail increased meritocracy (in the sense of a decrease in the origin-education relationship and a strengthening of the education-destination relationship), both the longer-term up-grading of the class structure and the tightness of the labour market in the boom appear to have promoted greater absolute mobility and, to a much more limited extent, greater equality of opportunity (see Figure 15.1).

The Irish evidence is consistent with the conclusion by Breen and Luijkx (2004) that there is evidence of significant variation in social fluidity across countries and over time but not of a systematic nature and that, in circumstances where policies in advanced industrial societies have shown an increasing tendency to diverge, increased social fluidity may arise as a consequence of highly variable economic and social policies. It also confirms the need to distinguish clearly between inequality of opportunity as captured by indices of social fluidity and changes in absolute levels of mobility shaped by changes in opportunity structures.

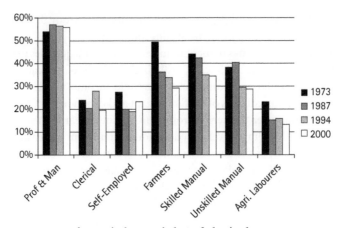

FIGURE 15.1 Percentage of sons 'achieving' their father's class

Source: Whelan and Layte (2002).

3. SOCIAL IMPACTS OF INEQUALITY

We now turn to the potential impact of inequality in income and education, and more particularly changes in those inequalities, on social, political and cultural outcomes, attitudes
and practices. Such impacts are by their nature difficult to identify, and in the Irish case
this is exacerbated by the fact that annual income inequality estimates are available only
from 1994, but the dramatic fluctuations in macro-economic conditions described earlier
do make Ireland a particularly interesting setting to examine such potential effects.

Focusing first on social outcomes and on deprivation and exclusion in particular,
non-monetary indicators of deprivation have been developed and used especially intensively in Ireland so there is a good deal of research to draw on.[11] At the official level, the poverty reduction targets incorporated into Ireland's anti-poverty or social inclusion strategies
since the mid 1990s have prioritized those in 'consistent poverty', in other words those both
below (relative) income poverty thresholds and reporting significant levels of basic deprivation. Levels of consistent poverty measured this way declined substantially over the first half
of the economic boom and continued to fall to 2008; the rate then was below 5 per cent but
rose almost 7 per cent by 2011 as the recession deepened. Levels of basic deprivation themselves fell dramatically in the first half of the economic boom, from 24 per cent in 1994 to 9.5
per cent in 2000 (Table 15.5). The EU-SILC survey then shows that basic deprivation (with
a somewhat different set of items and threshold) was broadly unchanged from 2003 to 2008
but increased markedly thereafter, going from 13.6 per cent in 2007 to 24.5 per cent in 2011.
Material deprivation is generally higher for households with children and lowest for the
elderly. Those at the lowest part of the income distribution are much more likely to report
severe material deprivation: those in the second income quintile from the bottom saw particularly sharp increases in the recession. Likewise, those with low levels of educational

---

[11] See for example Nolan and Whelan (1996), Whelan & Maître (2007).

Table 15.5 Trends in numbers above basic deprivation thresholds

	%
Living in Ireland Survey	
Basic Deprivation 1 +	
1994	24.0
1997	14.6
1998	12.4
2000	9.5
EU-SILC	
Basic Deprivation 2 +	
2004	14.1
2005	14.9
2006	13.8
2007	11.8
2008	13.8
2009	17.3
2010	22.5
2011	24.5

Sources: National-level data (LII, EU SILC IRELAND).

qualifications are much more likely to report severe material deprivation and those with tertiary education report the lowest levels of material deprivation, although even this comparatively protected group saw its rate approximately treble between 2006 and 2011. More generally, deprivation and exclusion across a range of dimensions continued to be highly structured in income and social class terms throughout the period. However, the key driver of levels over time appears to have been changing average income rather than its distribution: deprivation and exclusion fell especially rapidly when average income was growing during the boom years, even if income inequality trended upwards in the latter half of the Tiger years. It rose again when average income fell in the crisis, though increasing inequality may then have also played some role.

The EU's poverty reduction target for 2020 has framed the target population—labelled as 'at risk of poverty or social exclusion'—as being below the 60 per cent relative income threshold, or above a threshold in terms of material deprivation, or in a working-age household with 'low work intensity'. The size of this target group was relatively stable from 2004 to 2007 but has risen in the recession; those with the lowest levels of educational attainment are much more likely to be in this group than others, and saw a particularly large increase since the onset of the crisis.

Turning to the family, Ireland saw major legislative changes over the period, from contraceptive availability to the legalization of divorce during the 1990s. The number of births peaked in 1980, declined by one-third to 1994, then recovered so that in 2008 the total exceeded 1980 and marked a new high for births in Ireland since the nineteenth century, although recession saw a slight downturn in 2009. The total fertility rate fell from 3.23 in 1980 to 1.85 in 1994 and then rose to 2.10 by 2008, but the key driver was the increase of over one-third in the number of women of childbearing age. Births outside marriage rose for almost two decades after 1980, but this trend then levelled off. The annual number of marriages fell by 40 per cent between 1980 and 1995 but rose back to the levels of the early 1980s by 2007–8. Cohabitation became more common, with the proportion of all couples cohabiting rising from 4 per cent in 1996 to 12 per cent in 2006. Divorce was introduced only in 1996, while various forms of legal and informal separation had been on the rise prior to the advent of this legislation, but from a low base. Subsequently, Ireland did not experience a pronounced spike in divorce rates and the upward trend in marital breakdown (counting both separation and divorce) seemed to level off at a low rate by European standards early in the 2000s (Lunn *et al.*, 2009).

The extent of lone parenthood has been particularly high in Ireland for many years, increasing from 7 per cent of all families with children in 1981 to 21 per cent in 2006 (Fahey and Field, 2008). Most such families are headed by women and, in the 2006 Census, 60 per cent had never been married, 35 per cent were separated or divorced and 6 per cent were widowed. Lone parenthood is heavily stratified by socio-economic position, women with incomplete second-level education being 10 times more likely to be unmarried lone parents by age 25–27 than women with third level qualifications (Lunn *et al.*, 2009). Relationship instability also has an effect in reducing fertility—lone parent families tend to have fewer children than two-parent families. The fertility-reducing effect of lone parenthood has a disproportionate impact among lower socio-economic categories where a higher incidence of lone parenthood occurs and this has tended to mute the once strong association between lower social status and higher fertility found in Ireland in the past (Fahey *et al.*, 2012). The association between lone parenthood and poverty is stronger in Ireland than most other EU countries (Whelan and Maître, 2010), and children in Irish lone parent households have one of the highest poverty risks in the EU (Watson *et al.*, 2012). While patterns of household formation and composition can have a substantial effect on indicators of poverty and income inequality, a causal impact of trends in inequality on fertility and family structures has not been established.

Inequalities in health and access to health services in Ireland are deep-seated, with a two-tier system of access to services and consistent socio-economic differentiation in objective and subjective indicators of health. Health status as measured by life expectancy has improved markedly since the 1980s, with much of the increase occurring during the last decade, bringing average life expectancy substantially above the EU average for both men and women. Socio-economic inequality in mortality rates is pronounced, with analysis of deaths for the ten-year period 1989–1998 finding that a standardized mortality rate for the lowest occupational class was 235 per cent higher than the rate in the highest occupational class. This cannot be reliably compared with other countries due to differences in the socio-economic categorization, and trends over time in mortality differentials across socio-economic groups are also not clear. Perinatal mortality rates have been declining over the last three decades, but very substantial differentials on the basis of the mother's socio-economic circumstances remain. Based on data from the late 1980s, Nolan and Magee (1994) estimated that the unskilled manual socio-economic group in Ireland had a 99 per cent higher risk of perinatal mortality compared to professional and intermediate non-manual groups. Layte and Crimins (2010) recently revisited this and found that, after adjusting for demographic changes, this differential appeared to have fallen to about 88 per cent.

In terms of self-reported health, comparative data from EU-SILC show relatively higher proportions reporting good health in Ireland at both high and low incomes, but the gradient across the income distribution and across education levels is not distinctive. Overall, people with no formal educational qualifications are only half as likely to report having excellent, very good or good general health as those with third level education qualifications, but no clear trend over time in this gradient has been established. Self-reporting of obesity has increased among women from 10 per cent in 1998 to 13 per cent in 2007 and among men from 12 per cent to 16 per cent (OECD), but daily smokers as a proportion of the population have decreased from 32 per cent (females) and 37 per cent (males) in the mid eighties to 27 per cent (females) and 31 per cent (males) in 2007. This may be partly attributed to the ban on smoking in pubs and restaurants in 2004. Alcohol consumption per head of the population aged 15 years plus has increased from 10 litres to 13.4. Overall, improvements in health status coincide with improved living standards when income inequality was stable or increasing modestly While socio-economic gradients in health and health-related behaviours are pronounced, the very limited data available on a consistent basis over time does not allow trends in these inequalities to be related to potential drivers.

Turning to housing and housing-related inequalities, home ownership had for long risen in Ireland, reaching almost 80 per cent in 1991. However, active government promotion of home ownership was scaled back during the 1990s and the credit-fuelled housing boom that then set in was strongly driven by buy-to-let investors rather than owner-occupiers. By 2002, home ownership had fallen back to 77 per cent of the housing stock and it fell below 70 per cent by 2011, with private renting being the big growth sector (it grew from 9 per cent to 19 per cent of the housing stock in the period 1991–2011). This sharp reversal of the long-term trend towards home ownership is likely to have important effects on wealth distribution and housing costs for households but it will take time for its full impact to become clear. The overall housing stock expanded very rapidly in the economic boom, by about three-quarters between 1991 and 2006. Local authorities had previously provided the vast bulk of social housing, much of which fed into the home ownership sector through heavily subsidized tenant purchase schemes (Norris and Fahey, 2011), but their contribution fell below 10 per cent of total output in the 1990s (compared with 20–30 per cent previously). A central feature of the boom and subsequent 'bust' was the dramatic increase and then collapse of house prices, which rose by 270 per cent between 1996 and the peak in 2006 (when consumer prices rose by only 30 per cent), and then fell by about half. In terms of affordability, the proportion of household expenditure which private renters devoted to housing increased from 13 per cent in 1973 to 23 per cent in 2004, while for owners with a mortgage it increased from 7 per cent to 11 per cent and for those renting social housing from 7 per cent to 9 per cent. Social housing rents in Ireland are very low and are pegged progressively to income, but increasing proportions of low-income households are housed in the private rented sector where rents are much higher and tenure rights are limited. Housing allowances for private sector tenants are available but are limited to non-employed households and produce poverty traps. Public policy is experimenting with new ways of supporting the provision of low-income housing. In addition, the scale of borrowing for house purchase at inflated prices in the boom has left many recent house-purchasers in negative equity and struggling to meet their housing costs.

As in the majority of EU countries, Ireland has seen its trade union density decline over recent decades. However, Ireland differs from other liberal market economies in that trade unions had a central role in the neo-corporatist social partnership agreements in place from the late 1980s through the period of economic recovery and then boom, before collapsing in the crisis (Wallace, 2003). Trade union membership is strongly structured by sector, with older more traditional sectors having higher rates and, during the boom, unions faced particular challenges in organizing the new migrant workforce. More generally, in terms of other forms of association, the 2008 European Social Survey reports that 16.5 per cent of Irish people were involved in an association in the past year.

Attitudes to migrants must be seen in the context of Ireland's distinctive experience. Long a country of substantial out-migration, the economic boom saw significant in-migration from the mid 1990s. Following EU Enlargement large numbers of migrants came to Ireland from the new member states, but from the onset of the crisis substantial net emigration has been seen, with Irish nationals constituting the largest group among the emigrants. The ISSP in 2002 found that 70 per cent of respondents felt that different ethnic groups abused the social welfare system, but a majority also reported positive attitudes, for example that the authorities should do more for minorities. The European Social Survey in 2002 found that six per cent of Irish people agreed with the statement 'no further immigrants should be allowed into the country', and this had risen to eleven per cent in 2008.

Going beyond material deprivation and circumstances, the impact of the economic boom on social cohesion and 'social capital' has been debated in the Irish case, especially in the context of the housing boom and the potential impact of developing peripheral suburban neighbourhoods with long commutes and limited infrastructure. Relevant aggregate indicators as well as in-depth studies of particular suburbs (Corcoran et al., 2007) do not suggest dramatic change. Indicators of satisfaction/subjective well being provide another valuable social indicator. In terms of overall life satisfaction, figures from Eurobarometer surveys show (Figure 15.2) that the proportion reporting themselves to be 'very satisfied' with their lives in Ireland fell in the mid 1980s in the depths of that prolonged period of economic stagnation. Levels of satisfaction recovered in the boom, and were considerably higher than the average across the EU. Reported levels of overall subjective life satisfaction are highly structured by education. Focusing specifically on financial circumstances, in the recession there was a very marked decline in the percentage reporting that their financial situation was good. Once again, changes in general macro-economic conditions rather than in inequality appear to be the key driver of change over time.

Crime is often thought to be linked to economic conditions, but changes in the way recorded crime data have been gathered and reported over the period mean charting long-term trends in recorded crime is problematic. Homicide rates are least affected by such changes and increased steadily between 1994 and 2007 but then stabilized. Since 2003, when the Irish crime classification system was changed substantially, property offences such as burglary and theft have remained relatively stable or begun to rise. (Recent media coverage of childhood sexual abuse may have increased reporting rates for these crimes, temporarily inflating recorded sexual offence figures.) Overall, reported crime rates for most offence types in Ireland are below the European average. However, victimization surveys provide an alternative perspective. The International Criminal Victimization Survey 2005 found that victimization rates in Ireland were the highest in Europe at 22 per 100,000 of population, and the International Self-Report Delinquency Survey showed Ireland with one of the highest rates of youth delinquency among participating countries. Irish surveys have found that reporting to the police for individual crimes varied widely and depended on perceptions of police willingness or capacity to provide a remedy. Comparable data over time are limited,

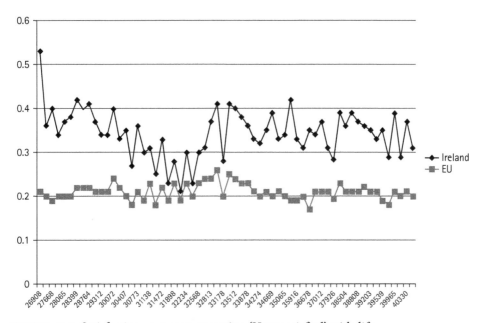

FIGURE 15.2 Satisfaction: per cent reporting 'Very satisfied' with life

Source: Eurobarometer (GESIS).

but the Garda (Police) Public Attitudes Survey showed a decline in victimization between 2001 and 2007 from 12 per cent to 9 per cent. While Irish crime rates have experienced ebbs and flows over the past thirty years, prison and probation populations have increased steadily. Sentenced committals to Irish prisons rose from 3,060 per year in 1980 to 10,865 by 2009 and the probation population also grew. While Ireland's rate of imprisonment remains low by international standards, the gap is closing. There are recent signs of a shift towards more non-custodial sanctions, but it is too soon to say what impact this will have on the prison population.

4. POLITICAL AND CULTURAL IMPACTS

We now turn to potential impacts of inequality on political and cultural attitudes and practices. The configuration of the Irish political system is distinctive, with two centre parties dominating but the more leftward-leaning Labour Party having a key role in coalition governments for a significant period, notably from 1981–7, 1993–7, and in the government which was elected with an overwhelming majority during the current economic crisis. Voter turnout in national elections has declined markedly since 1980, with a low towards the height of the economic boom in 2004. Ireland has one of the lowest average rates of voter turnout in the EU for general elections over the course of the last three decades. Turnout at European elections largely reflects whether they are tied into national elections, but there has also been a decline in turnout there, to below the EU average. Voting behaviour with regard to national elections is less structured by education/socio-economic characteristics than the European elections, where those with lower levels of education are much less likely to vote.

Ireland's positive stance with regards to the EU fell below the member states' average during the 1980s, but since then Ireland has maintained a higher than average percentage responding favourably in surveys in relation to membership. Despite this, the percentage voting in favour of successive Treaty changes in an EU context has declined markedly over time, even before the onset of the economic crisis, with changes in the constitution required to implement changes initially rejected in referenda. The crisis itself, leading to the situation where Ireland had no alternative but to seek a 'bail-out' from the EU and IMF, has led to the EU occupying a much larger role in national debate than heretofore, with implications that are difficult to predict at this point.

The European Values Survey (EVS) shows levels of trust in other people at 41 per cent in 1981 and 39 per cent in 2008. Those in the upper part of the educational distribution report higher levels of trust than those in the lower end, but there has been little change over time even for the latter. The EVS also indicates that membership of clubs, etc. increased from just over 3 per cent in 1990 to approximately 7 per cent in 2008, while involvement in youth work was around 9 per cent in 1981, fell to 6 per cent in the 1990s, but rose again to 9 per cent in 2008. The European Social Survey shows a slight increase in the percentage reporting themselves to be socially inactive (from around 33 per cent in 2002 to 37 per cent in 2008) and a larger increase in the percentage socially isolated (from just under 8 per cent in 2002 to 11 per cent in 2008), with those with tertiary education being much less likely to report a lack of social connectedness.

Trends in trust in government in Ireland over the last decade have been remarkable. While levels of trust in government found in social surveys were above the EU average during the boom, they have fallen spectacularly with the onset of the financial and economic crisis, with the percentage 'tending to trust' declining from about 40 per cent at the peak of the boom to half that by 2010. Trust in parliament also fell, from just over 30 per cent in 2002 to nearly 23 per cent in 2008, although it then rose slightly in 2010.

One of the most striking features of Ireland's experience over the past thirty years or so, in terms of political attitudes and values, has been the dramatic collapse in levels of trust in government and the political system in the aftermath of the economic and financial crisis. The scale of public dismay at the extent and consequences of the economic crisis was reflected in the results of the general election of February 2012. Fianna Fáil, the leading party in the previous coalition government, suffered the worst defeat of a sitting government in the history of the Irish state. Its share of the vote at 17.4 per cent was less than half of its first preference vote in 2007. Its number of seats fell from 77 when the election was called, to 20. Its coalition partner, the Green Party, lost all six of its seats. Fine Gael and the Labour Party, which formed the new coalition government, increased their number of seats from 71 to 113. Sinn Fein and other left wing parties saw their representation increased from 5 to 20 seats. Since the election, the need to implement austerity measures on a unprecedented scale, the continuing difficulties relating to sovereign debt, persisting difficulties with the banking system, and the scale of personal debt problems have been associated with striking declines in the opinion polls in the popularity of both government parties.

The fact that the latter part of the economic boom is now widely perceived to have been mismanaged, with the property boom and bust and near-collapse of the banking system greatly exacerbating the impact of the international financial crisis and recession, has meant that the political system as a whole—and aspects of Ireland's Eurozone and EU membership—are being questioned in a manner that would have been unimaginable as recently as 2007. While perceptions of trends in inequality and potential linkages with the political system may have contributed to evolving attitudes during the boom, the most distinctive feature of the Irish experience has been in the bust, where concerns about protecting the vulnerable from the worst effects of the recession have been to the forefront.

5. POLICIES AND STRATEGIES

Policies and strategies to combat inequality and its effects take many forms and have an extremely wide range of direct and indirect effects, in Ireland as elsewhere. The structure and parameters of the tax and social transfer systems and the level and pattern of social expenditures on health, education, housing and personal social services are key, but other forms of public spending, the overall level of taxation and public expenditure as a proportion of national income, the design of the Welfare State and how it interacts with the labour market, are all relevant. Here we first discuss the labour market, including minimum wages and the structure of collective agreements potentially affecting dispersion in wages, before broadening out to address policies of redistribution in terms of taxation and social expenditure.

Ireland introduced a National Minimum Wage (NMW) for the first time in 2000, shortly after the UK did so; until that date there had been minimum rates set only for very specific occupations and sectors. On introduction, it was set at a rate that is estimated to have affected up to 4–5 per cent of private sector employees. The NMW comprises a full adult rate per hour and reduced rates for younger workers or those with little experience; these rates are set by the relevant government Minister following consultation with employers and trade unions, and are not formula-based or explicitly linked to wages or prices. Since its introduction, the NMW has been increased on a number of occasions and appears to have kept pace with median hourly earnings up to the crisis. The NMW was reduced during the crisis in 2010, but this was reversed when the government changed shortly afterwards. The minimum wage for an experienced adult worker had reached €8.65 per hour at that point. Recent studies based on large-scale surveys suggest that the NMW has effectively underpinned the earnings distribution since introduction, with the lower parts of the distribution keeping pace with the median (Voitchovsky, Maître and Nolan, 2011).

Turning to wage bargaining, in Ireland centralized wage bargaining at the national level was adopted in 1987 in response to the economic stagnation experienced through the 1980s. In a social partnership process, government, employers and unions concluded agreements on wage levels in both private and public sectors, together with a wide range of economic and social policies. The contribution of these agreements to the economic boom, and indeed the extent to which they represented successful social corporatism, is debated, though wage restraint does seem to have contributed to enhanced competitiveness in the earlier part of the boom. The centrally bargained increases generally set a floor, with more profitable firms—particularly in the multinational sector—often giving greater increases. Public sector workers received substantial additional increases from 2002 via a 'benchmarking' process aimed at preventing public sector workers from falling behind rapidly rising private sector wages. Kelly, McGuinness and O'Connell's (2008) study suggests that the public sector premium over equivalent private sector workers grew substantially from 2003 to 2006 and was then greater than in other industrialized countries.

Turning to taxation, Ireland experienced an unusual degree of variation over the past three decades in the overall share of tax revenue in national income/output. Very low economic growth for much of the 1980s and the stringent measures required to close the persistent fiscal deficit saw the share of taxation rise sharply, though it started to fall as economic growth returned. This was followed by very substantial declines as the economy boomed in the late 1990s. During the second half of the boom, substantial cuts in income tax in particular were implemented and taxes on property continued to be low throughout. The onset of the economic crisis was reflected in a yawning fiscal deficit and, as measures are taken to close that deficit, the overall level of taxation as a proportion of national income is rising sharply.

There were significant changes in the tax structure over the period, with five income tax rates ranging from 25 per cent up to 60 per cent in 1980 reduced to only two rates, of 22 per cent and 44 per cent, by 2000. The personal allowances deducted before tax liability is computed almost doubled between 1980 and 1987, but were then increased only marginally to 1994, then increased much more rapidly. In 1999 there was a major change in the way allowances operated, as part of a move towards a tax credit system. Tax bands were not increased in line with incomes through the 1980s and into the 1990s, so the numbers paying tax at the higher rates rose very substantially, and scope to transfer bands between spouses was restricted from 2000 as part of a move towards greater individualization of the system. Income tax rates then fell modestly in the second half of the economic boom. In responding to the economic crisis, the main emphasis has been on the system of income 'levies' and social insurance contributions, with the introduction of a substantial new income levy subsequently restructured with social insurance contributions as a Universal Social Charge.

Overall levels of public expenditure as a proportion of national output have fluctuated substantially over the period, strongly influenced by the very dramatic changes in macro-economic conditions. Their share of national output peaked in the recessionary years of the early 1980s, as high unemployment boosted social transfers while GDP stagnated. It fell back as public spending was cut back and modest economic growth returned in the late 1980s, and fell further in the second half of the 1990s as the very rapid pace of economic growth exceeded that in spending, with a very rapid fall in expenditure on cash social transfers for the unemployed as the number of recipients fell (see Figure 15.3). From about 2000, though, public spending rose significantly more rapidly than GDP. This expansion in spending occurring across the board, but was particularly marked in health, pensions and family-related transfers (i.e. the universal Child Benefit payment, which was increased very substantially). This increase was seen in both cash transfers and other aspects of public spending, with rates of income support (notably on social pensions) and health spending increasing rapidly. Nonetheless, public spending as a share of national output remained below the EU average. The economic crisis then meant sharply increasing unemployment-related transfers and a remarkably large decline in GDP.

A substantial body of research has been carried out on the distributional impact of changes in the structure and parameters of the income tax and social transfer systems in Ireland using a tax-benefit simulation model based on microdata developed in the Economic and Social Research Institute. Research on this basis suggests that the very considerable fluctuations in tax and welfare levels and rates during the 1980s and 1990s produced

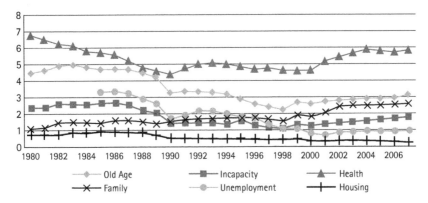

FIGURE 15.3 Public expenditure by type as percentage of GDP

Source: OECD SOCX.

or permitted a redistribution of income from the bottom of the distribution towards the top, though maintaining a social protection floor. In particular, the strategy of cutting tax rates towards the latter part of the period, continued in the early years of the twenty-first century, favoured higher incomes. In the crisis, by contrast, the nature of the changes in direct taxes and cash transfers has been highly progressive (Callan, Nolan and Walsh, 2011; Callan, Keane and Walsh, 2012). This reflects the fact that the direct tax increases required to help close the fiscal deficit affected upper income groups more in proportionate terms, while rates of social welfare transfers were cut for those of working age but not for pensioners, significantly insulated older people who comprise a substantial proportion of those on relatively low incomes.

These substantial changes over time are to be seen in a context where the share of public spending in the Irish economy has remained relatively low in comparative terms if measured against GDP, though it is close to the EU average if measured against GNP. Irrespective of how the size of Irish public spending is measured, the Irish experience illustrates the crucial role that tax/welfare structures play in ameliorating or reinforcing market income inequalities.

6. CONCLUSIONS

Ireland represents a very interesting case study on inequality trends and impacts given the remarkable macro-economic roller-coaster of recession, boom and bust experienced over the past 30 years. Through the recession of the 1980s and the first part of the economic boom income inequality was above the average in the EU-15 but was stable, with some increase towards the latter part of that boom. In the recent economic crisis income inequality has fluctuated. Levels of educational attainment have risen rapidly, but this left those failing to complete secondary school at an ever-greater disadvantage in the labour market, and in the recession young people with low levels of education saw a particularly marked increase in unemployment and inactivity.

Among key social indicators, levels of material deprivation moved broadly in line with average income over the period, falling substantially in the boom but increasing sharply in the recession. Inequalities in health and access to health services remained deep-seated, with a two-tier system of access to services and persistent socio-economic differentiation in objective and subjective indicators of health. The housing market played a central role in the economic boom and bust, with particularly dramatic effects on those who borrowed towards the height of the boom. Home ownership has fallen back in relative terms since the early 1990s and access to affordable housing for low-income households continues to be highly problematic. Reported levels of overall life satisfaction are highly structured by education but relatively stable over time, whereas in the recession there was a very marked decline in the percentage reporting that their financial situation was good. Social class position remains strongly associated with educational qualifications despite the major expansion in numbers going to tertiary level.

One of the most striking features of Ireland's experience over the period has been the dramatic collapse in levels of trust in government and the political system in the aftermath of the economic crisis. The latter part of the economic boom is widely perceived to have been mismanaged, with the property boom and bust and near-collapse of the banking system greatly exacerbating the impact of the international financial crisis and recession, so the political system as a whole—and aspects of Ireland's Eurozone and EU membership—are being questioned in a manner previously unimaginable. The crisis has given rise to intense public debate on government accountability and confidence, as well as about who is—or should be—bearing the brunt of the fiscal reforms undertaken in its wake.

Levels of Irish public social expenditure as a proportion of national output have fluctuated substantially over time, strongly influenced by the changes in macro-economic conditions. Changes in tax and welfare levels and rates over much of the period reduced the extent of redistribution from the top half, though maintaining the social protection floor, while in the current crisis changes in direct taxes and cash transfers have been progressive. Tax and welfare structures continue to play a crucial role in ameliorating market income inequalities.

Overall, the period since the early 1980s is often portrayed as an era of widening social and economic inequalities in rich countries, but this does not adequately characterize the Irish experience. During the economic crisis of the 1980s social disparities did not increase markedly, and the benefits of the subsequent economic boom in terms of living standards, employment, educational attainment and health were large and widely shared. Since the advent of economic crisis, employment and incomes have suffered, but serious efforts have been made to protect the least well off. If Ireland has not shown a whole-hearted commitment to a highly egalitarian society, social partnership and a catch-all party system have maintained a social protection floor while promoting absolute opportunities in relation to educational advancement and social mobility. Current efforts to put the public finances on a stable basis require major structural reform but unprecedented economic contraction and austerity has so far provoked little in the way of social disruption or conflict. There is, however, still some way to travel on the austerity path, in the most difficult of circumstances, and sustaining the capacity for constructive social dialogue and maintaining social cohesion and political legitimacy constitute a formidable challenge.

REFERENCES

Bradley, J. and Whelan, K. (1997), 'The Irish Expansionary Fiscal Contraction: A Tale from One Small European Economy', *Economic Modelling*, 14: 175–201.

Breen, R. and Luijkx, R. (2004), 'Conclusions' in R. Breen (ed.), *The Comparative Study of Mobility*, Oxford: Oxford University Press.

Callan, T., Keane, C., and Walsh, J. (2012), 'Distributional Impact of Tax, Welfare and Public Sector Pay Policies: 2009-2012', special article in *Quarterly Economic Commentary*, Winter 2011/Spring 2012, Dublin: ESRI.

Callan, T., Nolan, B., Whelan, B.J., Hannan, D.F., and Creighton, S. (1989), 'Poverty, Income and Welfare in Ireland', *General Research Series Paper* No. 146, Dublin: The Economic and Social Research Institute.

Callan, T., Nolan, B. and Walsh, J. (2011), 'The Economic Crisis, Public Sector Pay and the Income Distribution', in H. Immervoll, A. Peichl and K. Tatsiramos (eds.), *Who Loses in the Downturn? Economic Crisis, Employment and Income Distribution, Research in Labor Economics*, 32: 207–225.

Central Statistics Office (2013), *Survey on Income and Living Conditions (SILC) 2011 and Revised 2010 Results*, Cork: CSO.

Clancy, P. and Wall, J. (2001), *Social Background of Higher Education Entrants*, Dublin: Higher Education Authority.

Dellepiane S. and Hardiman, N. (2012), 'Governing the Irish Economy: A Triple Crisis', in Hardiman N (ed.) *Irish Governance In Crisis*, Manchester: Manchester University Press.

Fahey, T. and Field, C.-A. (2008), *Families in Ireland. An Analysis of Patterns and Trends*, Dublin: Department of Social and Family Affairs.

Fahey, T., Russell, H. and Whelan, C.T. (eds.) (2007), *The Best of Times? The Social Impact of the Celtic Tiger*, Dublin: Institute for Public Administration.

Layte and Clyne, B. (2010), 'Did the Celtic Tiger Decrease Socio-Economic Differentials in Perinatal Mortality in Ireland?' *Economic and Social Review*, 41, 2: 173–199.

Lunn, P., Fahey, T. and Hannan, C. (2009), *Family Figures. Family Dynamics and Family Types in Ireland, 1986-2006*, Dublin: Economic and Social Research Institute.

Nolan, B. (2007), 'Long-Term Trends in Top Income Shares in Ireland', in A.B. Atkinson and T. Piketty (eds.), *Top Incomes over the 20th. Century: A Contrast Between Continental European and English-Speaking Countries*, Oxford: Oxford University Press.

Nolan, B. and Magee, H. (1994), 'Perinatal Mortality and Low Birthweight by Socio-Economic Background: Evidence for Ireland', *Economic and Social Review*, 25, 4:, 321–342.

Nolan, B., O'Connell, P. and Whelan, C.T. (eds.) (2000), *Bust to Boom: the Irish Experience of Growth and Inequality*, Dublin: Institute for Public Administration.

Nolan, B., Russell, H. and Maître, B. (2010), 'Monitoring Poverty Trends in Ireland 2004-2007: Key Issues for Children, People of Working Age and Older People', *Research Series* 17, Dublin: The Economic and Social Research Institute.

Nolan, B. and Smeeding, T. (2005), 'Ireland's Income Distribution in Comparative Perspective', *Review of Income and Wealth*, 54, 4: 537–560.

Nolan, B. and Whelan, C.T. (1996), *Resources, Deprivation and Poverty*, Oxford: Clarendon Press.

Norris, M. and Fahey, T. (2010), 'From Asset Based Welfare to Welfare Housing: The Changing Meaning of Social Housing in Ireland', *Housing Studies*, 26, 3: 459–469.

O'Riain, S. and O'Connell, P. (2000), 'The Role of the State in Growth and Welfare', in B. Nolan, P. O'Connell and C. T. Whelan (eds.), *Bust to Boom?: The Irish Experience of Growth and Inequality*, Dublin: Institute of Public Administration.

Rhodes, M. (1997), Globalization Labour Markets and Welfare States: a Future of 'Competitive Corporatism'. in M. Rhodes, & Y. Meny (eds.), *The Future of European Welfare: A New Social Contract?* London: Sage.

Russell, H., Maître, B. and Whelan, C. T. (2012*)*, 'Economic Vulnerability and the Severity of Debt Problems: An Analysis of the Irish EU-SILC 2008', *European Sociological Review*, doi: 10.1093/esr/jcs048.

Smyth E. and McCoy, S. (2011*)*, 'The Dynamics of Credentialism: Ireland from Bust to Boom (and Back Again)', *Research in Social Stratification and Mobility*, 29, 1: 91–106.

Voitchovsky, S, Maître, B., and Nolan, B. (2013), 'Wage Inequality in Ireland's Economic Boom', *Economic and Social Review*, 43,1: 99–133.

Watson, B., Maître, B. and Whelan, C.T. (2012), *Work and Poverty in Ireland*, Dublin: Department of Social Protection and ESRI.

Whelan, C. T. and Layte, R. (2002), 'Late Industrialisation and the Increased Merit Selection Hypothesis', *European Sociological Review*, 18, 1: 35–50.

Whelan, C. T. and Layte, R. (2006), 'Economic Boom and Social Mobility: The Irish Experience', *Research in Social Stratification and Mobility*, 24, 2: 193–208.

Whelan, C. T., Layte, R., Maître, B., Gannon, B., Nolan, B., Watson, D., and Williams, J. (2003), 'Monitoring Poverty Trends in Ireland. Results from the 2001 Living in Ireland Survey', *Policy Research Series* Number 51, Economic and Social Research Institute, Dublin.

Whelan, C. T. and Maître, B. (2007), 'Levels and Patterns of Multiple Deprivation in Ireland: after the Celtic Tiger', *European Sociological Review*, 23, 2: 139–156.

Whelan, C. T. and Maître, B. (2010), 'Poverty in Ireland in Comparative European Perspective', *Social Indicators Research*, 95, 1: 85–104.

CHAPTER 16

....

ITALY: HOW LABOUR MARKET POLICIES CAN FOSTER EARNINGS INEQUALITY

....

GABRIELE BALLARINO, MICHELA BRAGA, MASSIMILIANO

BRATTI, DANIELE CHECCHI, ANTONIO FILIPPIN,

CARLO FIORIO, MARCO LEONARDI, ELENA MESCHI, AND

FRANCESCO SCERVINI

1. INTRODUCTION

....

COMPARED to other developed societies, Italy is characterized by peculiarities that represent distinguishing features of the country and its socio-economic status. In particular, two dimensions are crucial to understanding the way income inequalities and their impact are structured in Italy: the geographical disparities and the weakness of the state. On the one hand, Italy suffers from a sharp division between a more developed North and a backward South. This division has been a feature of the country since the birth of the Italian national state in 1861 and it is still a central topic in the political and public debate today. On the other hand, the state as institution suffers from an intrinsic weakness, as demonstrated by a long series of ineffective, unimplemented or poorly-timed reforms. Such weaknesses have generated a clear dichotomy between the country's formal constitution (the laws of the state) and its material constitution (the way society and the economy actually work).

Both features are useful in order to explain the relatively high level of inequality experienced by Italy compared to countries with a similar level of development. The country is typically classified among the coordinated market economies, but the European social model of relatively low social inequality does not fit the Italian context well, since inequality and intergenerational mobility in almost all social dimensions are more in line with the Anglo-Saxon economies than with the Continental ones. In particular, the weakness of the state does not facilitate the implementation of redistributive policies that would be effective in reducing all types of inequality. Furthermore, it indirectly increases social inequality because it enhances individualistic behaviour and it strengthens the power of particular social groups, first, the family, followed by interest associations, which makes it very difficult to implement reforms to increase equality of opportunity among citizens.

The data on income inequality show an increase at the time of the 1992 currency and financial crisis, and stability thereafter. Furthermore, they do not show a particular increase in the recent recession: the effect of the current economic downturn on inequality seems to be mild compared to the effects of the previous recession of 1992, which caused a steep increase in all measures of inequality. In most countries this smoothed effect has been attributed to government's redistributive policies and stimulus packages. In Italy, a high stock of private savings and diffused house ownership together with extended (but not universal) measures of short-time work and wage integration, which avoided mass lay-offs (*cassa integrazione guadagni*[1]), as well as the family network have played a substantial role in smoothing the impact of recession.

The overall stability of inequality hides substantial changes underneath it: over the last decades, in line with other countries with a similar level of development, Italy experienced an increase in life expectancy, educational levels, and female labour force participation. Such a pattern is not homogeneous within the country: regional disparities did not disappear and in some dimensions they increased. The flexibilization at the margin of the labour market reinforced its two-tier nature and this change mainly hits younger generations. Consumption increased steadily in the previous decade and was partly independent of wage dynamics (which were hardly affected by the 1993 wage freeze agreement). However, starting from the current decade, per capita consumption stagnated, clearly indicating that something in household behaviour had changed.

By spreading job opportunities among a larger group of labour market participants, two-tier reforms increase earnings inequality. This does not necessarily imply that the household income distribution becomes more unequal, because this also depends on the distribution of job opportunities within families. However, it is likely that increased income variability translates into a greater perception of insecurity, which induces greater savings in order to achieve consumption smoothing. One should also consider that Italian families may have resisted the decline in income opportunities by running down assets during the previous decade, but now they may have reached the limit of desired indebtedness, and therefore may have reverted to a lower consumption path.

In Section 2 we describe the nature of inequality and its evolution over time. We also focus on the interactions with education inequality and labour market reforms. In Section 3 we look at the impacts of inequality on various dimensions such as poverty, health, and social cohesion and we introduce the role of the family. In Section 4 we look at the impact of inequality on political and civic participation. Section 5 describes the main policies adopted in combating inequalities and stresses the weak role of the state and the lack of attention to the younger generations. Finally in Section 6 we summarize and give an interpretation of the causes and consequences of the evolution of inequality in Italy in the past decades and identify some likely patterns for the future.

---

[1] See below, Section 5 (Policy), for details of this institution.

2. The Evolution of Income and Educational Inequalities

Income Inequality

Compared to other OECD countries, Italy appears to be among the most unequal in terms of income distribution. Apart from some developing countries (like Mexico and Brazil) and the United States, Italy is among the most unequal economy in the OECD area together with the United Kingdom. The Gini index for household equivalent income of Italy stands at 0.35 while the value for the UK is 0.33 and the OECD average is 0.30.

Historical reasons are certainly important in these patterns. Italy is among the latecomer countries in terms of capitalistic development. This process typically requires a strong upgrade of the skills of the labour force in order to permit socio-economic development. The delay in the transition is confirmed by the lack of a robust industrial structure, the large share of small firms and self-employment, the large share of employment in the service sector (exceeding 50 per cent). All these elements are underlying forces that tend to create and perpetuate inequality in income distribution. In addition, Italy is characterized by a relatively limited power of the state, partly due to its relatively recent unification, which took place in 1861. It also exhibits a very low rate of tax compliance and a huge public debt, compared to similar countries. Both elements reduce the ability of the public administrations to redistribute incomes and provide adequate safety nets.

While perceived inequality is currently at its highest in Italy, empirical evidence is more controversial in this respect (Fondazione de Benedetti, 2011). Since the end of the 1970s, inequality decreased for about twenty years, but largely increased at the beginning of the 1990s with the 1992 economic and financial crisis, to remain rather stable afterwards at levels similar to those seen before the 1970s. The year 1992 is a crucial year because it also saw the final abolition of the automatic system of wage indexation—the *Scala Mobile*—that contributed to wage compression in previous years. This pattern emerges from Figure 16.1 irrespective of the inequality index used and whether or not incomes from self-employment and/or imputed rents are included: two factors which are crucial for Italy, since the rate of self-employment and house ownership are very high compared to the EU average (respectively 25 per cent of total employment and 80 per cent of house owners). We use both equivalized and non-equivalized household income to account for large families with cohabiting children who may work on temporary jobs. Although the level of the inequality index depends on the measure of income used, the overall trend is roughly consistent whatever income definition is used.

A Few Comments on Decomposing Changes in Inequality

1) Decomposing inequality by deciles, most of the action over time occurs in the bottom part of the distribution, below the median. Wage compression due to the *Scala Mobile* occurred mostly at the bottom of the distribution and its abolition in

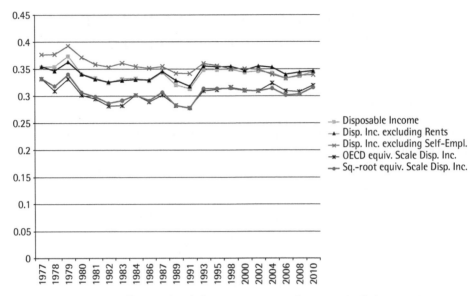

FIGURE 16.1 Gini coefficients for different measures of income in Italy

Source: SHIW.

1992 penalized mostly workers at the bottom of the distribution. The effect of two of the drivers, self-employment income and pensions, is also concentrated at the bottom of the distribution. However, the Italian income distribution also experienced a significant change at its very top (top 1 per cent). Therefore, when inequality is measured focusing on the top 1 per cent of the distribution, it shows some increasing trend.

2) Decomposing the inequality trends of household inequality by main geographical areas (North, Centre and South) we find that changes of inequality in Italy at the end of the 1990s can be largely accounted for by changes in the distribution of household income within the South (Fiorio, Leonardi and Scervini, 2012), with the offsetting effects of self-employment and labour income (which tend to increase inequality) and the opposite effects of pension income (which tend to decrease inequality). The Gini index within regions of the South is above 0.35 while the Gini in the North is around 0.3. Inequality between the South and the rest of the country has increased somewhat since the early 1990s. The economic differential in terms of economic activity and infrastructure, together with a much lower internal migration since the 90s, could be responsible for the stable gap and the recent divergence between the South and the rest of the country.

3) Among the possible causes of household inequality trends, demographic changes (household composition) are found to be relatively unimportant, as opposed to female labour force participation. In particular, labour force participation increased largely for women of high-income families while it did not change substantially for women from families at the lower deciles of the income distribution. The implication is that the increase of female labour force participation tended to increase household income inequality (Fiorio, 2011).

4) The difference between the average income of young and old workers has increased, most likely because of the increased instability of incomes for young workers due to the recent changes in the labour market and the diffusion of temporary contracts, which—on average—affected elderly and young workers differently. No major difference is found between prime age and older workers' average incomes. Most likely these results are due to three factors: the increased coverage of the welfare system since the early 1980s; the larger share of pensioners among Italians; and the fact that pension income has an equalizing effect on the overall distribution.

5) The role of self-employment income in explaining inequality trends in Italy is important: changes in self-employment income account for a similar proportion as changes in employment income, even though the total contribution to national income of the former is about one third of the total contribution of the latter. The incidence of self-employment is related to issues of tax evasion and the structure of the labour market, which will be addressed in the next sections.

Finally the data on consumption inequality provide a complementary picture. The evolution is similar to the one for income but with reduced volatility: it shows a decline in the 80s; an increase in the 90s; and stability thereafter. Consumption is a better indicator than current income of household living standards in the longer run. In the early 1990s, inequality in income rose sharply while consumption inequality did not because consumers smoothed transitory variations in earnings with savings and new debt. This brings us to wealth distribution.

Wealth and Debt Inequality

Italy is a country of high net private wealth but also of high public debt. The net total wealth increased over the whole period between 1965 and 2009, though faster between 1985 and 1993 and between 1996 and 2007. The wealth of families experienced also negative growth in real terms in 1977, when it reduced by over 4 p.p. and between 1981 and 1985, when it reduced by about 8.3 p.p., and between 1993 and 1994 when it reduced by about 5 per cent. Only in 2008 did the increasing trend of per capita net wealth slow down, reflecting both the progressive reduction in the growth rate of Italian GDP and the progressive reduction of private savings (D'Alessio, 2012).

Interestingly, the ratio of net wealth to GDP also presents an increasing trend, which is reasonable, as GDP has also largely increased over the same period. Notwithstanding the flatter trend, the net wealth over GDP ratio is roughly doubled, showing that Italy has increased its wealth more than its production. This shows the growing relevance of wealth as opposed to income, which has important implication in terms of overall inequality. Figure 16.2 also presents some inequality indices (p90/p10 and p95/p5) for net wealth, highlighting the fact that the distribution of wealth became increasingly unequal across the last two decades, reinforcing the trend that we have observed for the case of income.

It has to be noticed that while the net private debt of households has grown in most countries in recent decades, in Italy it reached much lower levels with respect to other countries. For example in 2006 it was 68.8 per cent of disposable income while it was at 174.9 per cent in the UK. The per capita average value of house loans was €5.100 in Italy against €28.800 in the UK. This is due to the higher house ownership ratio in Italy and also to a less developed

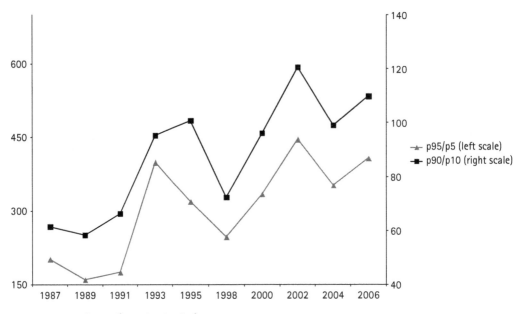

FIGURE 16.2 Quantile ratios in Italy

Source: SHIW.

financial market. In any case the low level of private debt helped make the impact of the recession less serious.

Finally an important issue for Italy is the relationship between the wealth of families and the total public debt, which indirectly is a liability of Italian citizens. In the period considered, Italian public debt largely increased. In 1965 the total amount of the public debt corresponded to an average per capita debt of about €2,700 (at 2009 prices) and it is more than ten times larger in 2009, reaching €29,500. Therefore families have weathered the crisis and inequality has not grown thanks to private wealth but the price is paid through a higher public debt.

Labour Market Inequality

The Italian labour market displays major differences across gender and age groups. According to EU-LFS data, the employment and participation rates for men are stable at around 70 per cent and 75 per cent respectively, in line with most European countries. However, labour market participation and employment are particularly weak for women, with the participation and employment rate respectively slightly above and slightly below 50 per cent. The mean hides regional differences: while women in the North have an employment rate of around 56 per cent, in the South it is around 30 per cent: a large portion of females, mainly in the Southern regions, do not participate in the labour market. There are also major differences between women with and without children: approximately 15 per cent of employed women quit their jobs after giving birth and do not come back to work. The two greatest factors of employment inequality in Italy are the gender and the regional dimension. Furthermore employment rates for the young and the elderly are low compared to many other countries.

A major factor of inequality in the Italian labour market is the diffusion of temporary contracts since the so-called Treu Law of 1997 and the Biagi Law of 2003 (see, for a description of the reforms, Cappellari, Dell'Aringa and Leonardi, 2012). The stock of temporary contracts of various types reached 13 per cent of total employment after 2005. Temporary workers, mainly young and females, have lower wages on average and a volatile employment attachment. Figure 16.3 shows that among female workers aged 15 to 24 the rate of temporary contracts has reached 50 per cent of employment in 2010 (only slightly less for males). The figure also shows that temporary employment has a clear generational gradient, as the percentage of temporary contracts decreases rapidly to 10 per cent of total employment among workers aged 15 to 65.

The incidence of temporary contracts in employment is in line with other European countries. However, other contractual arrangements exist, through which firms can use the labour services of external workers. As in many other countries there are temporary work agencies supplying labour services upon the payment of an agency fee. Additionally, and this is mostly an Italian peculiarity, firms can use collaboration contracts. These contractual arrangements provide an employment framework for individuals who are not formally employees of the firm but they perform duties similar to those of normal employees. Thanks to a reduced regime of compulsory pension contributions, and to lower labour costs compared to regular employees and lower unisation rates, many employers, mostly in the tertiary sector, including the PA, use them extensively. Finally, with the same intent of saving on labour costs, firms may simply outsource tasks to single individuals, who act formally as

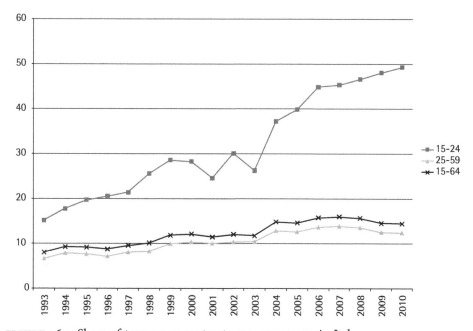

FIGURE 16.3 Share of temporary contracts among women in Italy

Source: LFS.

external supplying firms but actually have an exclusive relationship with the firm, thus being in all respects economically dependent on it.

The peculiarity of the Italian labour market concerns the possible inclusion of a part of formally self-employed workers (i.e. collaborators and external suppliers) in the group of temporary employees. In Italy, 10 per cent of those aged 15 to 24 are self-employed compared to 4 per cent on average in the EU (OECD 2010). Understanding how many of these are not really self-employed but 'economically dependent' on a single firm is not an easy task and depends on the interpretation and the definition of 'economically dependent'. The best estimate of 'economically dependent' self-employment is probably around 1.5 million workers, i.e. those who work exclusively at the principal office. In this sense, the inclusion of this type of worker in the category of temporary employees makes their incidence substantially higher in the Italian labour market than in other European countries, increasing the share of temporary contracts from 13 per cent to 19 per cent of the employed population aged 15–64 and from 50 per cent to 70 per cent of the employed population aged 15–24.

Educational Inequality

In line with the global trend, educational attainment in Italy increased substantially over the last century. In about fifty years, the average years of education almost doubled, increasing from around 7 for the cohort born in the first half of the 1920s to around 13 for the 1975–79 cohorts.

The same pattern emerges when educational attainment is measured in terms of school level completion rates. While in the oldest cohorts only 30 per cent of people completed lower secondary education, in the younger cohorts this percentage is close to 100 per cent. Similarly, the completion rate of upper secondary education grew from around 16 per cent to 65 per cent and the completion rate of tertiary education has also grown but it is still quite low compared to other OECD countries. The rapid expansion of schooling started in the 1950s after the Second World War in response to the extraordinary growth rates and the new economic and socio-political conditions. During the 1960s governments implemented several reforms to create a more democratic and universalistic school system. The first reform in this vein was implemented in 1962 and created a unique and comprehensive lower secondary school, de-stratifying the previous tracked system. A second reform in 1969 significantly reduced restrictions to access tertiary level education by allowing graduates of vocational secondary schools to enrol in all university faculties. These institutional changes produced a major expansion in schooling and a substantial reduction in educational inequality. For example, microdata from the European Social Survey indicate that, starting from the cohort born in 1920, while the average years of education doubled between 1920 and 1924 and 1975 and 1979, inequality of years of schooling steadily decreased (see Figure 16.4).

Inequality in education can also be evaluated through its distribution across social groups and evaluating intergenerational mobility in school attainment, that is, the weight of parental background in determining pupils' attainment. Evidence for Italy suggests that educational inequality has declined over time, as the importance of family background has decreased. However, while the impact of parental occupation has significantly decreased

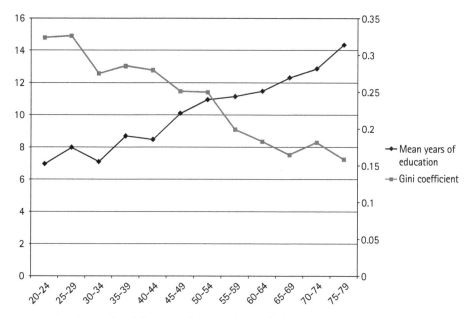

FIGURE 16.4 Educational levels and inequality in Italy

Source: Meschi and Scervini (2010).

over cohorts, that of parental education seems to be quite stable over time (Ballarino and Schadee, 2008; Ballarino *et al.*, 2009).

Drivers and Interdependence Between Inequalities

The substantial stability of income inequality during the last twenty years masks significant changes within the distribution associated with labour market transformations. The increased flexibilization of labour market regulations has mostly affected the young component, who remain a source of additional incomes within pre-existing families, indicating a reinforced role for the family as income shock absorber. This is interesting, as reforms intended to increase employment, and thus to diminish the role of the family compared with the market in providing economic opportunities to individuals, have had exactly the opposite effect.

The high level of private wealth has allowed families to sustain an extended period of economic crisis. However, the data on household wealth growth and distribution indicates that households may be challenged in maintaining this role in the future, since an increasing fraction of them has begun to run down previous savings (as indicated by data on wealth inequality).

Finally, data on educational attainment provide a basis for some optimism, because education is expanding and the impact of family background is reducing in more recent cohorts, thus improving intergenerational mobility. However, this is a situation common to all advanced countries, and Italy is in fact among those where such a reduction has been lower (Breen *et al.*, 2009).

3. Social Impacts

Having analysed the dynamic of income inequality over the last decades, it is important to see how it relates to other features of social life at individual, household and social level. A general point is in order before entering into the detail: we do not find clear correlations over time between the pattern of the Gini index (and of other indices) and most of the social phenomena of interest. This reflects a number of factors. First, we have seen that the Gini index in Italy has been relatively stable over the last two decades. Second, the Gini index is a statistic, which can hide important internal changes in the distribution, which offset each other. Finally, and perhaps more importantly, the transmission from income inequality to various forms of social inequality can take time, intervening variables can weaken the impact itself, and the observation window available for most of the outcomes of interest is relatively short. Given these general problems, in this section and in the following we will limit ourselves to describing the relevant patterns of Italian social inequality over time and in comparison with the other European countries.

Consistently with higher income inequality, Italy is characterized by a relatively large fraction of materially deprived families. Risk of poverty is also higher, at 18.3 per cent against a EU-15 average of 12.8 per cent (Eurostat data). Moreover, the geographical distribution of (income) poor families, which in the south are six times more frequent than in the north, gives an impressive picture of how unequal are life chances in the country. While the family acts as a shelter against individual poverty, Italian families are changing as elsewhere in Europe, albeit with some time-lag due to cultural factors, related in turn to the importance of the Catholic Church and its influential stance in promoting the traditional family. For instance, the percentage of single households was 5.7 per cent in 1983, and increased to 16.2 per cent in 2009 (Istat data). Declining marriage rates and increasing divorce, combined with the increased number of single-parent families, the decline in fertility and increasing births outside marriage, all indicate a reduced capacity for families to attenuate income volatility and deprivation risks. Individuals tend to postpone their marriage, and age at childbearing increases accordingly.

However, familism still emerges as one of the most recurring attitudes among Italian families, as the country scores comparatively low in all measures of social capital based on trusting others (OECD, 2001) as well as on social participation (Eurostat, 2010). Concerning the latter, it is interesting to note that Italy ranks among the countries with the highest frequency of contacts with friends and relatives: the concept of 'amoral familism' (Banfield, 1958) seems still useful to describe the way many Italians feel about their social relations. This general situation, coupled with the historical weakness of the Italian state in providing protection against risk, makes for a quite pessimistic forecast concerning the future evolution of both poverty risk and inequality therein.

Besides low fertility, the other main features of the Italian demography are relatively high levels of life expectancy, a negative natural increase and a positive balance between immigrants and emigrants, with persistent regional variability. Such patterns are typical of Southern European states, while the strong and persistent regional variability is typically Italian. Health status as measured by life expectancy and infant mortality rate has improved markedly over the twentieth century. The median life expectancy during the last forty years increased by 8 years for men and 12 years for women, and is now at 78.3 and 84.1 years (Istat data). A similar improvement can be seen in the number of deaths per 1000 live births. Both indicators display a similar trend for men and women. We do not observe a clear improvement in individual health status over the last twenty years for specific diseases. Hypertension and diabetes have increased both for males and females. Breathing problems decrease for males and are fairly stable among females, while cardio-vascular problems decline among females and are stable among males. This gender gap might be possibly related to unhealthy habits in eating, drinking and smoking, more frequent among men.

Housing is a powerful channel for inequality reproduction in Italy. With almost 4/5 of the population owning their home, after having received it as gift/inheritance from the previous generation in 3 out of 5 cases, the deprived families tend to be those who cannot obtain a mortgage loan and are forced to live on (increasing) rents. Moreover, a clear social class gradient can be seen in rates of home ownership: the cumulative structure of inequality is quite clear in this case, as well as the low capacity of the state to provide help to the social groups more in need. Social housing, which had been quite important from the early 20th century up to the 80s, has in fact almost disappeared for a couple of decades.

The general trend of all recorded crimes is increasing up to the early 1990s, when it peaks, probably related to the internal Mafia wars that ravaged the South during that period. Then we observe a stable situation, with some signs of a declining trend in the last years. The downward trend is particularly strong for homicides, also in international comparison. In 1980, the homicide rate in Italy was about double that of the other big western EU countries: the figure per 100,000 inhabitants was 1.9, compared to 1.0 in the UK, Spain and France. In 2006, the Italian rate went down to around 0.7, compared to 1.4 in Spain (2004), 0.8 in France (2004), 0.4 in the UK.[2] This general pattern has probably to do, as elsewhere, with the changing demography: while young males are the social group more prone to crime, their weight in the total population has decreased during the last decades.

Life satisfaction is declining, after a long rising trend: its long-term pattern over time is quite close to that of GDP and of life expectancy, while the recent decrease might be related to increasing inequality. Italians are slightly less satisfied with their life than their Northern neighbours, but the rising trend has been stronger in Italy than elsewhere (Veenhoven, 2011). Inside the country, there is something puzzling in the interaction between dimensions of life satisfaction and the geographical split: in fact, while economic satisfaction is higher in the richer part of the country (the North), social satisfaction is higher in the poorer and more unequal regions of the country. A further puzzle is observed when one takes into account data on crime rates: while the latter have been declining lately, while life satisfaction was also declining, they are typically higher in the Southern regions, where life satisfaction (at least from a social point of view) is higher.

---

[2] Eurostat data. The figure for the US is 10.5 for 1980 and 5.8 for 2004 (Barbagli and Colombo 2011).

4. Political and Cultural Impacts

When considering political participation, Italy ranks quite high, despite the relatively high level of income inequality that has been documented in the previous sections. It has to be recalled that voting is compulsory under the Italian Constitution, although this 'civic duty' has never been systematically enforced and legislation in the 90s has de facto cancelled it. However, there are three issues that should concern Italian policy-makers: first, voting turnout has declined since the early 90s, even if the level is still very high (from more than 90 per cent to around 80 per cent);[3] second, turnout decreases dramatically among younger cohorts (more than 6 p.p. of difference) and low educated individuals (almost 6 p.p.); third, and more relevant, the correlation between the two issues is increasing over time (Scervini and Segatti, 2012a). The joint effect is that, while the elderly cohort experienced a universal and equal political participation, younger cohorts are becoming much more divided, with very high participation rates among more educated and richer individuals and significantly lower voting turnouts among low educated and poorer individuals. In turn, this may result in a worse representation of such disadvantaged classes (see Scervini and Segatti, 2012a, for more details).

By contrast, participation in civic activities, proxied by being a member of any kind of organisation (social services, religious groups, sport and recreation activities and so on), in Italy is lower than in many European countries. Moreover, there is a significant difference between rich and poor (more than 27 p.p. of difference in 1990) and between men and women (around 10–15 p.p., stable over time). With respect to the trend, it is interesting to notice that, after a period of expansion, the share of people participating in civic activities slightly decline in the last decade, with a drop of more than 5 p.p. among women.

The loss of confidence in the government and the disillusionment with political representation may also be responsible for the convergence towards the centre in political self-assessment (see Figure 16.5). In particular, since the early 1970s, the share of people declaring themselves to be of the extreme left declined steadily, without differentiation by gender and education (also due to the breakdown of the Soviet Union). On the other side, Italy experienced an increase of people declaring themselves to be of the extreme right (from 5 per cent in 1976 to 10 per cent in 2008). In this case, however, the increase is much higher among low-educated individuals (7 p.p. of increase, with respect to about 2 p.p. for high-educated ones). Related to this is the increase of xenophobia and the intolerance toward immigrants and foreign workers (in 1981–84, only 3 per cent of Italians would not like an immigrant as a neighbour, while the share was at 16 per cent in 2008–10).

The final evidence we provide concerns the puzzling data about support for redistribution. Among the poorest of three classes of individuals, there is a significantly higher share of individuals believing that the poor are lazy and opposing the role of the State in supporting poor individuals (Figure 16.6). Moreover, the support for redistribution from poor interviewees has declined over time, despite the increasing inequality in the aggregate. However, the poor also believe that incomes should be made more equal. Therefore, those who would

---

[3] A dramatic fall of participation (75.2 per cent) took place in the last election, on February 2013. Scervini and Segatti, (2012a) explain also the impact of the abolition of compulsory voting on electoral turnout.

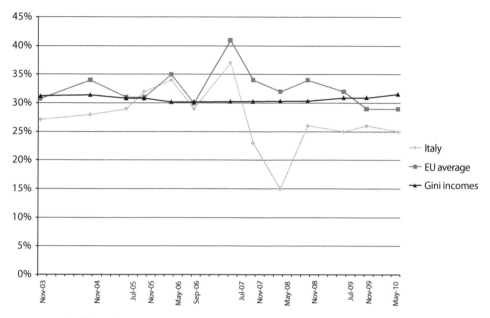

FIGURE 16.5 Trust in government

Source: Eurobarometer.

benefit more from a strong government, which could redistribute wealth and opportunities effectively, do not believe in this possibility. Only rich families exhibit more awareness of the changed economic situation (Scervini and Segatti, 2012b, for more details).

The evidence we presented concerning the cultural and political impact of inequality is in general consistent with the evidence on its social impacts, as presented in the previous section. On this basis, we would suggest that the weakness of the state has left Italian individuals and families on their own in trying to absorb employment shocks, which are the main source of income and worked hours' variability. Moreover, being embedded in relatively weak social ties (as witnessed by comparative low levels of social capital), they feel abandoned by their leaders, and have therefore lost interest in policy. This is particularly clear amongst the young generation. Unsurprisingly, poor individuals seem to lose interest and hope in the redistributive role of the state, while educated/rich individuals exhibit the opposite belief. We have seen how changes in the political system contributed to this feeling of helplessness: in particular, the weakening of political parties and of their partisan ideology resulted in a reduction in the social and cultural support available to individuals. Not surprisingly, racism and intolerance are on the rise, with right-wing extremism diffusing, and thereby reinforcing, the very same feelings it grew from.

Of course, persistently high income-inequality does not help in solving the problem, because it exacerbates social distances (thus making the production of social capital more difficult), as well as pushing people back within their homes. Moreover, we have seen that a vicious circle is operating: the economically worst-off people, who would benefit more from state redistribution promoted by the political system, are the very same ones who participate less in the political system. This is a phenomenon widely diffused in contemporary democracies, especially in the US, where the level of electoral participation is particularly

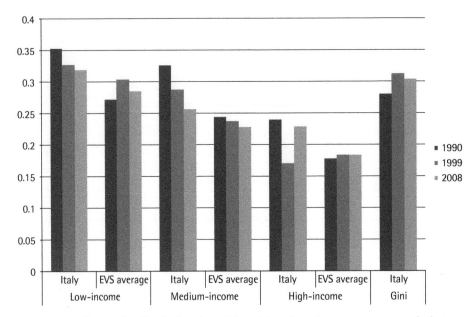

FIGURE 16.6 Share of individuals who self-positioned as 8–10 on a 1–10 scale between the extreme statements: 'The state should take more responsibility to ensure that everyone is provided for' (8–10) and 'Individuals should take more responsibility for providing for themselves' (1–3)

Source: EVS.

low. However, in the Italian case, the vicious circle appears to be increasingly important, because of the historical weakness of the state, augmented by the loss of legitimacy of the whole political system, following the collapse of the traditional parties in the early 90s. The parties that have substituted for the old ones have been not able, at least up to now, to stop the decline of interest and trust in politics on the part of the Italian public, especially amongst the lower classes and the social groups more at risk of poverty.

Some cause for hope emerges from the observed correlation between educational attainment and civic participation: since education is expanding and educational inequality is declining, as was documented above, this may partially counteract any further detachment from social participation. We now move to another key topic for the patterns of inequality in Italy, namely the impact of policies aimed at the reduction of inequality.

5. POLICY

Social Expenditure

Italy spends approximately as much as other European countries on social benefits, but the internal composition of this expenditure is biased against the young generation.

Expenditure in unemployment benefits and housing appears compressed to leave room for expenditure towards the elderly, through the pension system. (See Figure 16.7.)

Over the past thirty years social expenditure has risen by 7 p.p. of GDP, 5 of which are accounted for by the increase since the mid 90s. The bulk of Italian social expenditure goes on pensions. The increasing burden imposed by old age pensions, and the unsustainable social security system of the 80s, motivated several reforms that have been introduced in Italy by governments since the 90s.

Social expenditures that are likely to benefit younger people and families—whose job security was sensibly reduced by the recent labour market reforms—are very low and stable over time. Branches such as family, unemployment, and active labour market policies account for less than 2 per cent of GDP each. Unemployment benefits (in particular the *cassa integrazione guadagni*) tend to protect more those who lost a job than first-time job seekers, and youth unemployment rates in Southern Italy are among the highest in Europe, both factors meaning that there will be pressing needs in the future for adequate forms of income support for young unemployed people and families.

Taxation

On the revenue side, apart from the highest incidence in GDP, the tax burden is unequally distributed (leaving considerable room for indirect taxation). Italy is one of the countries in the EU with the highest level of taxation. Its tax burden has increased significantly since the currency and fiscal crisis that hit it in 1992, as a key component of the more general social and political crisis. Since 1998, total tax burden has remained at about 2 percentage points higher than the EU averages. If social contributions are also taken into account, labour income is taxed much more (around 20 per cent of GDP and 50 per cent of total tax and social contribution revenues) than consumption and capital (each about 10 per cent of GDP and about 25 per cent of total revenues). (See Figure 16.8.)

Tax evasion in Italy is estimated to be over 25 per cent of total tax revenues, a very large share compared to the EU27 average, and it could significantly alter the distribution of incomes, if only it were seriously tackled by policy-makers. Tax evasion is much stronger among self-employed workers such as entrepreneurs, professionals, owners of small shops and businesses: this difference may have played a part in the increase of inequality among self-employed workers, which we have seen, in the first section, to have been significantly higher than among dependent workers.

Benefits and Welfare

With respect to fighting inequality and social exclusion, the main problem is the lack of measures against poverty regulated at the national level. The existence of regional programmes minimizes any redistributive aim of these initiatives. Benefits in kind are still a minimal part of public support for the needy, while pensions remain the main channel of monetary transfer. Italy does not have measures against poverty that are defined and regulated at the national level (Kazepov, 2011): those who are in a situation of economic distress are not covered by generalized national measures of social protection, but only by local-level

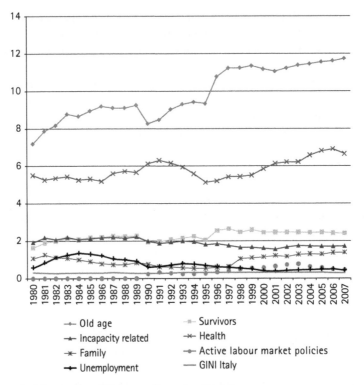

FIGURE 16.7 Public total social expenditure by branch

Note: The figure reports public total social expenditure (all types) by branch as a percentage of nominal GDP.
Housing and other social policy areas always account for o per cent of GDP.

Source: OECD—SOCX database.

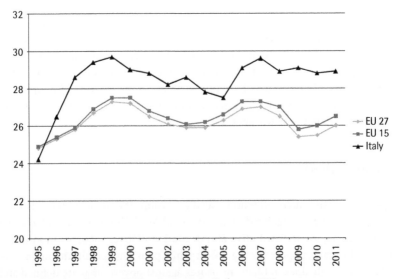

FIGURE 16.8 Tax burden as GDP percentage, Italy vs. EU average

Source: Eurostat.

ones, with a strong variation between territories. The only exception to this situation is a national programme to support the income of individuals aged more than 65 who do not have an occupational pension or have one that comes under a given threshold. This programme, called *pensione sociale* up to 1995 and *assegno sociale* thereafter, is managed by the national pension fund (INPS).

Between 1999 and 2000 a centre-left government attempted to introduce a universal income support programme for those under a giving income level, modelled on the French *revenu minim d'insertion*: besides income support, the programme provided assistance in job search, re-training and other active labour market policies. The programme was piloted in a selection of municipalities, but unfortunately there has been no systematic evaluation of its outcomes. After the end of the experimentation, the programme was due to be rolled out nationwide, but it was not, because of a change of government.

As is typical of Mediterranean versions of 'Conservative' welfare regimes (Esping-Andersen, 1999; Ferrera, 2006), the core institution providing care to those in need is the family: most of the assistance to children and the elderly is carried out by unpaid female members of the households.

Pensions still constitute most of the social transfers in Italy but their internal composition has changed. Low pensions are increased by a kind of benefit ('integration'), whose amount has fallen over time while pensions for the disabled have increased significantly. It has to be noted that the latter include transfers to close family of the disabled people (called *indennità di accompagnamento*, or 'attendance allowance'). This programme is managed at the local level, and is often criticized as its management involves a lot of discretion on the part of its managers, who are typically controlled by local government. This frequently makes this kind of pension a matter of political commerce and an important resource in the building of clienteles on the part of local politicians (Madama and Ferrera, 2006), especially in the poorest areas.

In the conclusion, we shall come back to social transfers and their effectiveness, giving a general picture of the extent of redistribution provided by the Italian government.

Labour Market and Active Labour Market Measures

Historically, Italy has always spent very little on active labour market policies compared to other European countries, around 0.5 per cent of GDP, half of other countries, such as France and Germany. The definition of active policy, however, is quite contested, because many of the policies that are considered 'passive' contain some form of activation, in the sense of being contingent on labour market search. However, this is not the case in Italy, where unemployment benefits are not conditional on job search. Also the definition of an active policy is subject to some caveats, in as much as it contains policies like public job creation.

Most Italian expenditure on labour market policy is allocated to passive policies (early pensions and unemployment benefits). Historically, they constitute around 60 per cent of total expenditure on labour market policies, but during the crisis this share went up to 78 per cent, as payments to the short time work programme soared. The *cassa integrazione guadagni*[4] is similar to the German *Kurzarbeit* but usually—unlike the German case—puts

---

[4] Literally: wage integration counter.

workers on total suspension from work, while in Germany the system more often implies a partial suspension. But this makes a big difference: while the German system allows firms to increase their internal flexibility, pushing them to redistribute tasks and workloads among employees, the Italian system increases external flexibility. In fact, it incentivizes firms to substitute older dependent workers (with standard employment contracts), who exit via *cassa integrazione* or early pension schemes (*prepensionamenti*), with younger workers hired with the new 'atypical' fixed-term contracts. But in this way the Italian policy, besides reducing labour costs to the firm, also weakens the relation between firm and workers and thus the propensity of both parts to invest in human capital, with negative outcomes on the propensity to innovate. The very different performance of Italian and German firms observed during the last years is probably related to the different labour market reforms experienced by the two countries.

Labour market institutions should be inequality reducing, but the decline in union membership and coverage (union density went from above 50 per cent at its 70s peak to around 33 per cent, still high in comparison), coupled with the absence of a minimum wage scheme raises strong doubts about the effective ability to prevent further increases in earning inequality. On the contrary, the outcome of neo-corporatist bargaining (*concertazione*) from the early 90s has produced a new split, between younger and more mature workers, that adds to the already existing inequalities.

Italy does not have a legal minimum wage, but has a system of collective bargaining agreements based on two levels: the first or centralized level where firms and trade unions define wage and employment levels and general working conditions, and the second or firm-level bargaining where the firm and the local unions bargain over the rents produced at establishment (or firm) level. Italy is a country with little decentralization of contracts, as only a little more than 15 per cent of firms (especially large firms) have a firm-level bargaining system. It is unclear whether these institutions had a direct impact on inequality. Given that, as we have seen above, inequality in Italy has increased in the crises of the early 90s, but has been stable since then, it is likely that institutions have had a minor effect on the trend in inequality but may have had an important effect in this discontinuity. As recalled above, in that year the entire system of wage indexation rules was reformed.

Schooling Institutions

Among the policies that may help in combating and reducing inequalities, the design of the educational system certainly plays a prominent role. The Italian school system is unified and comprehensive until age 14, when pupils have to choose between academic and vocational tracks.

In this sense, the Italian system is less stratified compared to many other European countries, where the age of first selection for school tracking is lower (e.g. at age 10 in Austria and Germany, 11 in the Czech Republic, Hungary and Slovakia, 12 in Netherlands and Belgium). Nevertheless, Checchi and Flabbi (2007) argue that in Italy (compared to Germany) parental education is more relevant than ability in determining the choice of different tracks, which tends to reinforce intergenerational persistence. This depends on the mechanisms allocating 14-year-old pupils to the different tracks: in Germany this allocation depends to a great extent on teachers, whose indications are binding in most of the German Länder; in Italy the allocation depends almost exclusively on the family, whose choice is not constrained by the school. Thus, ability does not play a big role in this process, while family aspirations and motivation do.

In Italy, pre-primary education lasts 3 years and is given to children from 3 to 6 years of age. The pre-primary level is part of the education and training system, yet it is not compulsory. The state took over complete responsibility in the sector of pre-school education only in 1968, when it recognized its educational value. Since then, even if not compulsory, pre-primary education has been provided free of charge by the state, and the only things families have to pay are small contributions, from which low-income households are exempted, towards transport and canteen services. Over the last 10 years, several laws have stressed the objective of making the offer general and achieving a widespread attendance of pre-primary school. In this spirit, the reform of the education system in 2003[5] provided for the full introduction of pre-primary education in the education system. As a result of these policies, participation in pre-primary education has increased substantially reaching a participation of around 100 per cent.[6]

Other dimensions that may affect educational inequality are related to the school admissions arrangements and school competition. Public school admissions can be broadly organized around two models of school provision: i) neighbourhood-based systems, where admission is purely determined by where pupils live, typically with rigidly defined catchment areas; ii) choice-based systems that are meant to give parents a wider choice not limited to neighbourhood schools. Choice-based systems are found to increase social stratification of schools along lines of ability, ethnicity and socio-economic status, since families with higher socio-economic status benefit at the expense of the poor, given they are advantaged in their ability to exercise choice, being better equipped at making good decisions, and they are also less constrained by transport costs (see for example Gibbons and Silva, 2006). In Italy, enrolment in state schools doesn't depend on catchment areas and the families can choose whether to enrol the pupil at the school of the area of residence or in any other school they may prefer, provided a place is available. When available places exceed demand, priority is given to those who live in the local area.

Related to the question of school competition, the proportion of private school enrolment, which implies that public schools face more competition, is found to increase the effect of students' social origins on their school performance, thus reducing social mobility (Ammermuller, 2005). This problem is not relevant to Italy, which has a relatively small private school sector. Moreover, Italian public high schools are associated on average with better performance than private schools that appear to focus more on the recovery of less brilliant students than on a high quality education (see Bertola and Checchi, 2002).

[5] Law no. 53 of 28 March 2003.
[6] Gross enrolment ratio is defined as the percentage of pupils enrolled in pre-primary education, regardless of their age, over the population of the age group which officially corresponds to that level of education. Since pre-primary schools also accept early enrolments (pupils aged less that 3), this percentage can potentially be higher than 100 per cent.

6. Conclusions: Appraisal of the Interdependence and the 'National Story' of Inequality Drivers in Relation to Policies (Causes and Effects)

There is a well-established consensus among economists that inequality in Italy has been stable over time since 1992. In 1992, a significant institutional change was implemented. After a severe economic recession, the wage indexation mechanism (*Scala Mobile*) was abolished. As a result, inequality jumped upwards and has remained there ever since. The overall stability hides changes within the distribution.

Two powerful dimensions of inequality are gender and the geographical divide. In the Italian case, gender inequality is falling over time, as women's labour force participation increases. However, it is still higher compared to other countries, especially the Northern ones. However, this trend is fully in line with the global trend and we do not expect the Italian case to be significantly different from other countries that experienced an earlier process of the equalization of labour market opportunities between genders. By contrast, the geographical split has not changed over time: GDP per capita in the Southern region is stable at 65 per cent of the North.

The main recent driver of inequality in Italy has been labour market reforms, which worsened the relative position of the younger generation. Labour market inequality increased with the implementation of the Treu Law in 1997 and the Biagi Law in 2003. On the one hand, these reforms increased employment and slightly reduced informal work (still significant in Southern regions, especially for females). On the other hand, the reforms have increased the diffusion of temporary contracts among younger workers (50 per cent of females and 40 per cent of men aged 15–24 in 2010). These reforms increased earnings inequality and instability, in particular among the younger cohorts (Cappellari and Leonardi, 2006; Comi and Grasseni, 2009; Ballarino and Barbieri, 2012). Italian policy-makers should be more worried by the widespread use of self-employment instead of dependent contracts than by the incidence of temporary employment. If added to the number of temporary contracts, the 1.5 million self-employed with characteristics similar to dependent employees would dramatically increase the number of young people at risk of precarious work and would push Italy to the top of the incidence of temporary employment in Europe (along with Spain).

Another crucial dimension of inequality in contemporary Italy is related to workers' position as employees and as self-employed: self-employment is a key factor in explaining the growth of inequality. On the other hand, it is not clear how institutions, such as unions and collective wage bargaining, have affected inequality. Given that inequality in Italy has been stable since 1992, it looks like those institutions have had a minor effect on the trend in inequality but may have had an important effect in the discontinuity of 1992. After that date, inequality went back to the levels observed before the 1970s.

Finally, the almost stable level of inequality could depend on the distribution of net wealth in the Italian population. Italy has a very high saving rate that has buffered the transitory volatility of income and guaranteed stable consumption. The distribution of wealth is very unequal but a peculiarity of the country is the large diffusion of home ownership (80 per cent of households) and this has also guaranteed stable consumption. However, high savings and house property are typical of individuals in the central part of their life and the situation may be radically different for the younger generations with temporary contracts, low saving and an inability to buy houses.

To conclude the chapter, we present a summary assessment of the effectiveness of Italian public policies in reducing inequality. In fact, there is a strong negative cross-country correlation between social transfers and indicators of income inequality. Figure 16.9 reports, for instance, a cross-plot of the Gini coefficient versus spending in social transfers as a percentage of GDP. The graph shows a negative correlation: countries that spend more have lower inequality.

However, this association could be interpreted in two ways. On the one side, it may suggest that countries with high inequality lack the economic and political means to fund social programmes, the so-called 'Robin Hood paradox', according to which redistribution is lacking where it is most needed (Lindert, 2004). It is a macro version of the 'vicious circle' cumulative mechanisms we have repeatedly described in this report.

On the other hand, the same association could be interpreted as evidence that social transfers are effective in reducing inequality. In general, it is difficult to establish a clear causal link in this direction, without exogenous variation either in inequality or in social expenditures. This argument, applied here for social expenditures, can be generalized or expanded to the other components of policies aimed at reducing inequality.

According to the OECD, in Italy income taxes and cash benefits contributed in the late 2000s to reducing inequality by close to 30 per cent, which is higher than the typical OECD

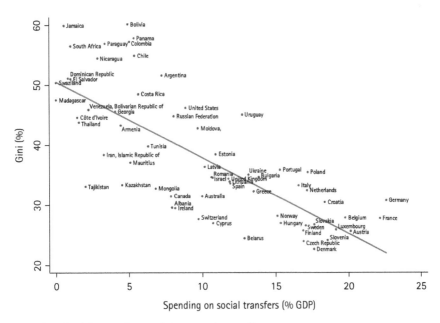

FIGURE 16.9 Social transfers and income inequality

Note: OECD countries are shown in red

Source: Prasad (2008).

country in which the corresponding figure is about 25 per cent (OECD, 2011). This is shown in Figure 16.10. Moreover, the effectiveness of the tax-benefit system at fighting inequality increased over time. Indeed, while only half of the rise in market income inequality was offset by taxes and benefits prior to the mid 1990s, the rise in inequality since then was completely offset. However, we have seen that during the last two decades, the relative stability of income inequality went along with an increase of wealth inequality and of consumption inequality.

OECD (2011) also states that the contribution of social expenditure to the reduction in income inequality in Italy was close to 20 per cent in 2007, a level similar to that of many OECD countries. This figure declined after 2000, when the contribution of social expenditure was about 25 per cent.

At first glance, the evidence reported in Figure 16.10 represents good news for the capacity of the Italian state to reduce, via taxation, the income inequality produced by the market. OECD (2011) itself, in fact, puts this interpretation to the forefront. From this point of view, that may seem to be at odds with much of what we have observed and commented on concerning the weakness of the Italian state and its socio-economic implications. However, the figure also confirms what we observed earlier, namely that in Italy income inequality, be it pre- or post-taxation, is among the highest of OECD countries, and, a fortiori, among European countries.

How can those two, somehow opposite, interpretations be brought together? One could say that a strong Italian state is able to significantly reduce a relatively high level of income inequality produced by a very anti-egalitarian market. However, this interpretation ignores

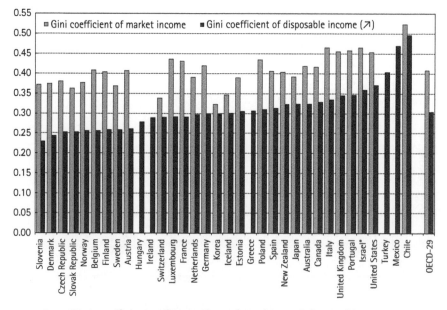

FIGURE 16.10 Gini coefficients of inequality of market and disposable incomes, persons of working age, late 2000s

Source: OECD (2011).

the fact that the role of the state in the economy is not limited to taxation. The state also regulates the economy, in two ways: directly, via laws and administrative regulations concerning economic life; and indirectly, via the provision of incentives which shape the behaviour of economic actors. Considering this, one could first observe that the Italian state regulates the economy in such a way that the market produces more inequality than it does elsewhere: even more than in the US, according to the OECD figures.

So, despite being very high, the tax burden weighing heavily on Italians can eliminate only a relatively small part of the large income inequality produced by the market, because the state is unable to regulate it so as to produce a level of inequality similar to those of the other European countries (with the exception of the UK). Thus, this reduction, despite being relatively large, comes at a substantial cost in terms of tax-paying citizens, who feel the burden of heavy taxation without getting its benefits in terms of the provision of services and efficiency in administration.

REFERENCES

Ammermüller, A. (2005), 'Educational Opportunities and the Role of Institutions', *ZEW Discussion Paper*, No. 05–44.

Ballarino, G., Barbieri, P. (2012), 'Disuguaglianze nelle carriere lavorative', in D. Checchi (ed.) *Disuguaglianze diverse*, Bologna: Il Mulino.

Ballarino, G., Bernardi, F., Requena, M., Schadee, H. (2009), 'Persistent Inequalities? Expansion of Education and Class Inequality in Italy and Spain', *European Sociological Review*, 25, 1, pp. 123–138.

Ballarino, G., Schadee, H. (2008), 'La disuguaglianza delle opportunità educative in Italia, 1930–1980: tendenze e cause', *Polis*, XXII, 3, pp. 373–402.

Banfield, E. (1958), *The Moral Basis of a Backward Society*, New York: The Free Press.

Barbagli, M., Colombo, A. (2011), *Rapporto sulla criminalità in Italia—2010*, Rome: Ministero degli interni—ICSA.

Bertola, G. and Checchi, D. (2002), 'Sorting and Private Education in Italy', *CEPR Discussion Papers* 3198, Centre for Economic Policy Research.

Breen, R, Luijkx, R., Müller, W. and Pollak, R. (2009), 'Non persistent Inequality in Educational Attainment: Evidence from Eight European Countries', *American Journal of Sociology*, 5, pp. 1475–1521.

Cappellari L. and Leonardi M. (2006), 'Earning instability and tenure', *IZA Discussion Papers*, n. 2527.

Cappellari L., Dell'Aringa C. and Leonardi M. (2012), 'Temporary Employment, Job Flows and Productivity: A Tale of Two Reforms', *The Economic Journal*, 122(562), F188–F215.

Checchi, D., and Flabbi, L. (2007), Intergenerational Mobility and Schooling Decisions in Germany and Italy: The Impact of Secondary School Track, *IZA Discussion Paper* No. 2876, Institute for the Study of Labour (IZA).

Comi S. and Grasseni, M. (2009), 'Are Temporary Workers Discriminated Against? Evidence from Europe, *CHILD Working Papers*, n. 17.

D'Alessio, G. (2012), 'Ricchezza e disuguaglianza in Italia', in D. Checchi (ed.) *Disuguaglianze diverse*, Bologna: Il Mulino.

Esping-Andersen, G. (1999), *The Social Foundations of Post-industrial Economies*, Oxford: Oxford University Press.

Eurostat (2010), *Social Participation and Social Isolation*, Luxembourg: Publication Office of the European Union.

Ferrera, M. (2006), 'L'analisi delle politiche sociali e del welfare state', in M. Ferrera (ed.) *Le politiche sociali*, Bologna: il Mulino, pp. 11–51.

Fiorio, C.V. (2011), 'Understanding Italian Inequality Trends', *Oxford Bulletin of Economics and Statistics*, Vol. 73, pp. 255–275.

Fiorio, C.V., Leonardi, M. and Scervini, F. (2012), 'La diseguaglianza dei redditi in Italia', in D. Checchi (ed.) *Disuguaglianze diverse*, Bologna: Il Mulino.

Fondazione de Benedetti (2011), *The Great Recession and the Distribution of Household Income*. mimeo.

Gibbons, S. and Silva, O. (2006), 'Competition and Accessibility in School Markets: Empirical Analysis using Boundary Discontinuities', in Gronberg, T.J. and Jansen, D.W., (eds.), *Improving School Accountability: Check-ups or Choice. Advances in Applied Microeconomics*, Oxford: Elsevier, pp. 157–184.

Kazepov, Y. (2011), 'Le politiche socio-assistenziali', in U. Ascoli (ed.) *Il welfare in Italia*, Bologna: Il Mulino, pp. 103–144.

Lindert, P.H. (2004), *Growing Public*, Cambridge: Cambridge University Press.

Madama, I. and Ferrera, M. (2006), 'Le Politiche di Assistenza Sociale', in Ferrera M. (ed.) *Le Politiche Sociali*, Bologna: Il Mulino, pp. 227–286.

Meschi, E. and Scervini, F. (2010), 'A New Dataset of Educational Inequality', *GINI Discussion Papers* n.3, AIAS, Amsterdam Institute for Advanced Labour Studies.

OECD (2011), *Economic Outlook*, Paris.

Prasad, N. (2008), Policies for Redistribution: The Use of Taxes and Social Transfers, *International Institute for Labour Studies*, Discussion Paper 194.

Scervini, F. and Segatti, P. (2012a), Education, Inequality, and Electoral Participation, *Research in Social Stratification and Mobility*, vol. 30, pp. 403–413.

Scervini, F. and Segatti, P. (2012b), 'Disuguaglianza dei redditi e propensione alla redistribuzione', in D. Checchi (ed.) *Disuguaglianze diverse*, Bologna: Il Mulino.

Veenhoven, R. (2011), *World Database of Happiness*, Erasmus University, Rotterdam.

CHAPTER 17

....

RISING INEQUALITY IN JAPAN: A CHALLENGE CAUSED BY POPULATION AGEING AND DRASTIC CHANGES IN EMPLOYMENT

....

MIKI KOHARA AND FUMIO OHTAKE

1. INTRODUCTION

....

INEQUALITY has attracted considerable attention in Japan over the past two decades. The degree of inequality in any period is closely related to the economic situation at that time. Inequality in Japan increased slightly during the 1980s, when the economy fell into a recession because of the deteriorating profitability of exports that resulted from the appreciation of the yen after the 1986 Plaza Accord. In an attempt to recover from the recession caused by the strong yen, Japan initiated expansionary financial policies, which led to an increase in the price of assets such as stocks and housing, a rise in real GDP growth in the 1990s, and a decline in unemployment rates from the late 1980s to the early 1990s. During this period, inequality remained around the same level.

At the same time, however, Japan faced economic challenges such as a rapid rise in asset prices and an overheating of economic activity, often referred to as a bubble economy. This led the government to tighten the money supply, and as a result, stock prices dropped sharply in 1991 and house prices started to fall, leading to the eventual collapse of the bubble. Japanese financial institutions faced the problem of non-performing loans. After the bubble burst, there was a lengthy process of adjustment from excessive capital stocks, loans, and employment, caused by the bubble economy. In addition to the economic recession that persisted in the wake of the collapse of the bubble, the Asian financial crisis in 1997 and the economic recession from 1998 aggravated economic conditions, which led to large-scale unemployment. Inequality increased rapidly and remained at a high level.

During the 2000s, the fall in the value of the yen contributed to the revitalization of export-driven industries and this led to the continuous growth of real GDP, but this economic recovery was interrupted by the crisis that followed the collapse of Lehman Brothers. Inequality has continuously increased in the 2000s.

As a consequence of the increase in inequality over the past 30 years, Japanese society has experienced several important social changes. For example, the crime rate increased in the 2000s. The wider income gap has also affected people's health, including their mental health. Japan has one of the highest suicide rates in the world, even though life expectancy has increased over the past two decades and is now the highest in the world. Growing economic inequality may be related to greater inequalities in health.

There are two main causes of the long-term upward trend in inequality in Japan. The first is population ageing, stemming from longer life expectancy and lower fertility rates. In the 1980s, people aged 60 years and over comprised 9.1 per cent of the total population, but this rose to 22.5 per cent in 2010. At the same time, the percentage of people aged 15 years and under fell from 23.5 per cent in 1980 to 14.3 per cent in 2010. Because inequalities are generally higher among older people, and because the elderly tend to have lower income, the increase in a portion of the elderly in society led to an increase in inequalities in the entire society, even if inequality within the elderly did not become larger. As we will see in later sections, inequalities within the elderly have not increased, whereas inequalities are becoming more marked among the young. Not only has there been an increase in inequality but there has also been a rise in the poverty rate among people aged 20–39 years and those aged ten years and under.

Another feature of the increase in Japan's inequality is the growing number of people in lower wage groups. In response to the economic recessions described above, many Japanese companies avoided employing full-time employees and instead hired non-standard employees, because of the sizeable cost of employment adjustments if full-time staff are laid off. In the working-age population, the male employment rate has declined and male non-standard employment, such as part-time, contract, and casualized work, has dramatically increased. This change is apparent even among men in their prime earning years. Because the average earnings of non-standard employees are lower than those of full-time employees, increases in non-standard employment and labour market segmentation have created a widening distribution of income.

These two factors, population ageing and drastic changes in employment, caused the upward trend in Japan's inequality from the 1980s to the 2000s. Despite this increase in inequality in society, Japanese attitudes toward political activities or income redistribution policies have not changed significantly. In addition, there is a wide generational difference in voting rates in Japan. The voting rate of people aged 55 years and over is 25 per cent higher than that of people aged 35 years and under. The higher absolute numbers of elderly people and their higher voting rates mean that the elderly receive considerable political attention, which might have undesirable consequences in policy formation. In the past, many elderly people were in lower-income groups but, at present, poverty is more prevalent among adults aged less than 40 years and their children.

In Section 2, historical changes in Japan's inequality and their causes are examined. The social, political, and cultural impacts of widening inequality are summarized in Section 3, and the effectiveness of policies is discussed in Section 4. Conclusions are presented in the last section.

The Nature of Inequality and its Development over Time

General trends in Japan's inequality

According to the OECD (2008), Japan's Gini coefficient is close to the OECD average; it is at a similar level to that of Korea, Canada, Spain, and Greece, lower than that of the United States (US) and United Kingdom (UK), and higher than that of France and the Nordic countries. It is noted, however, that caution must be used when making comparisons of the Gini coefficient between countries where different household groups are targeted and different income measures are used for its measurement.

In the case of Japan, measurement of the Gini coefficient is usually based on three large data sets compiled by the government: (1) *National Survey on Family Income and Expenditure* (*NSFIE*) compiled by the Statistics Bureau, Ministry of Internal Affairs and Communications; (2) *Comprehensive Survey on Living Conditions*, compiled by the Ministry of Health, Labour, and Welfare; and (3) *Income Redistribution Survey*, also compiled by Ministry of Health, Labour, and Welfare. The first two data sets contain large samples—*NSFIE* covers more than 55,000 households every five years, and the *Comprehensive Survey on Living Conditions* covers about 50,000 households every year—while the *Income Redistribution Survey* covers about 5,000 households.

Figure 17.1 shows the long-term trend in Japan's household income inequality over the past three decades, based on the three sources of data for pre-tax income and as measured by the Gini coefficient. The calculation of the Gini coefficient based on the *NSFIE* includes households regardless of the employment status or employment type of the household heads, but excludes single-person households. The Gini coefficient using the *Comprehensive Survey on Living Conditions* is calculated based on income class data reported by the government (income quartile before 1985 and income quintile after 1986). It may be upwardly biased because we use income-group data, although single-person households are included in the calculations. The Gini coefficient based on the *Income Redistribution Survey* is also reported by the government.[1]

Generally, the *Income Redistribution Survey* shows much greater inequality than the other two data sets because the sample covers a larger proportion of aged people. The other two data sets show different levels but the same trend of inequality. The Japanese government now provides the OECD with inequality measures as measured by the *Comprehensive Survey on Living Conditions*, although it formerly provided them from the *NSFIE*. The differences between the two data sets arise partly because the sample coverage is different.[2]

Using either the *Comprehensive Survey on Living Conditions* or the *NSFIE*, we can say that income inequality has been increasing gradually, but not dramatically, since around 1980. Note, however, that income inequality has several shortcomings when used as an indicator of true household welfare. Income statistics are affected greatly by fluctuations in temporary income, but a change in temporary income does not always result in a change in

---

[1] For the *Comprehensive Survey of Living Conditions*, we use income group data, but not the data reported by the government, because the Gini coefficient was not reported before 1992.

[2] Because the *NSFIE* surveys detail daily consumption, households in the tails of the income distribution may not be covered by the survey.

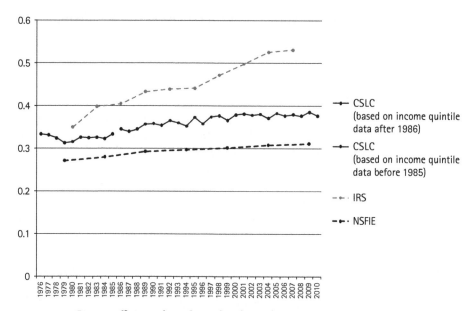

FIGURE 17.1 Gini coefficients based on the three data sets

Note: The dotted lines in the figure are drawn simply by connecting each of the data points.

Source: Authors' calculation based on:

Gini coefficients from *Comprehensive Survey on Living Conditions* (*CSLC*), calculated using before-tax income quartile data before 1985, and before-tax income quintile data after 1986, both of which are reported by Ministry of Health, Labour and Welfare (MHLW).

Gini coefficients from *Income Redistribution Survey* (*IRS*), calculated using before-tax income, reported by MHLW.

Gini coefficients from *National Survey of Family Income and Expenditure* (*NSFIE*), calculated using before-tax income for all households with two or more household members, reported by the Statistics Bureau.

household welfare. In addition, income statistics do not reflect lifetime welfare. Because elderly people have more asset holdings but less income, income inequality does not properly measure the gap in social welfare, especially in a country such as Japan where the ageing population comprises a large share of the total population. Thus, we want to show inequality based on a different measure of welfare, namely, consumption expenditure. Unlike income, consumption expenditure can reflect an individual's welfare over the long term. Individuals consume more if they have sufficient money to survive and if their lifetime income is higher. Fortunately, in Japan, the *NSFIE* reports household consumption expenditure in detail. Therefore, in the following parts, we attempt to show outcomes using consumption inequality as well as income inequality based on the *NSFIE*.

Figure 17.2 shows the change in Gini coefficients, calculated from before-tax income, after-tax income, and consumption expenditure, using microdata (household and individual data) in the NSFIE. Note that the microdata of the NSFIE include both single households and households with more than two household members. All types of income, including labour income, agricultural income, rent, pensions, other social security payments, income from dividends, interest, and occasional work, are included in the definition of income. To obtain the Gini coefficient for after-tax income, we need to calculate the amount of tax each household pays. Because the NSFIE (and any other microdata with

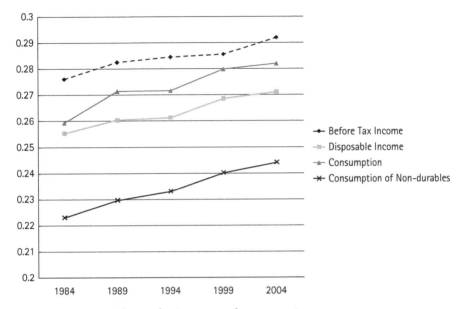

FIGURE 17.2 Gini coefficient for income and consumption

Note: We used an equivalence scale for the number of household members. That is, each household income and consumption expenditure is divided by the square root of the number of household members.

Source: Authors' calculations using individual and household data taken from the NSFIE.

large samples in Japan) does not contain information on individuals' tax payments, we need to calculate them using information on household and individual characteristics. By comparing observed characteristics such as family type, age of family members, working status, and types of income in the NSFIE with the taxation system in the corresponding year, we estimated tax payments and disposable income for each household. The details of the estimation are given in the GINI Japan country report. For the calculations of Gini coefficients, we divided all values of income and consumption by the square root of the total number of household members.

The figure shows that between 1984 and 2004 there was an overall upward trend in inequality. Inequality rose between 1984 and 1989; the rate of increase then slowed between 1989 and 1994, after which it increased significantly. A look at each measure shows that the Gini coefficient based on before-tax income is the highest. After excluding tax payments, which means after redistribution, the Gini coefficient for disposable income is lower. The Gini coefficient for consumption expenditure is somewhat higher than that based on disposable income. This is unusual, but it may be because our disposable income is not the reported data for tax administration but the estimated data by our tax calculation program based only on the observed characteristics. The important difference is the one between before-tax income inequality and consumption inequality. This can be significant in a country with an ageing population, such as Japan, because the elderly may not have high incomes but may possess considerable assets. Inequality as a whole can be overestimated when using income measures only. This figure suggests that even consumption inequality has increased slightly over the past 30 years.

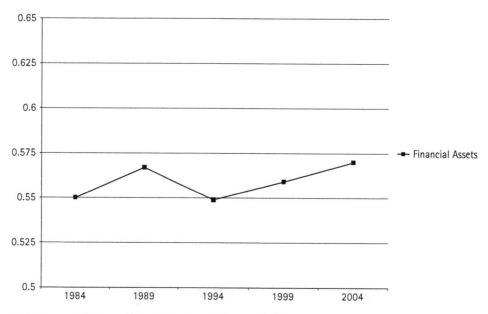

FIGURE 17.3 Gini coefficient for financial asset holdings

Source: Authors' calculations using microdata of the NSFIE.

Figure 17.3 shows changes in wealth inequalities in Japan. The Gini coefficients are calculated using total household asset holdings (excluding the value of real estate) in NSFIE divided by the same equivalence scale as before. The figure shows a similar trend of inequality as income and consumption inequalities. That is, wealth inequality increased between 1984 and 1989, it decreased between 1989 and 1994, and it expanded after 1994. Sudo, Suzuki, and Yamada (2012) also report the same trend: inequality of financial wealth, like that of wage income, grew rapidly from 1984 to 1989, fell for a decade, and again grew moderately from 1994 until 2009. The increase in inequality was driven by high-wealth households, say the top 5 per cent.

Who is suffering from this increase in inequality? Figure 17.4 shows the Gini coefficients based on consumption expenditure by age groups (within the same generation). The most prominent feature in this figure is that the Gini coefficient is high in older age groups. The dynamics over age tell us that within-age group inequalities increase after the age 35. In fact, income inequality among the elderly is high because of their high labour force participation rates in Japan. High labour force participation rates among the elderly could have led to a reduction in the income distribution among them if the elderly in the low-income group work and those in the high-income group are retired. In Japan, however, the elderly in the higher income group are continuously working even after the mandatory retirement age, for example in the re-employment scheme. Because inequalities in earnings are higher than those in pensions and because the gap between wage income and pensions is large, inequality among the elderly is high in Japan.[3] We can say that one of the causes of the increase in Japan's inequality is the enormous increase in the proportion of the elderly in society, whose

---

[3] We suspect that dropping families with zero income from the calculation of Gini underestimates inequalities among the aged 30–34, 35–39 and 40–44 in Figure 17.4. But, employment rates among

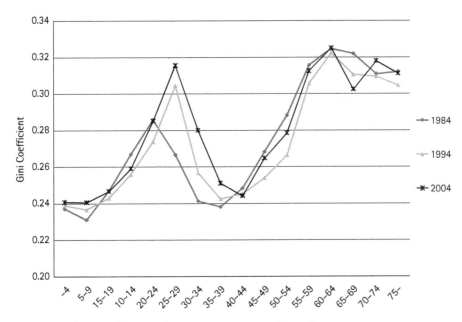

FIGURE 17.4 Gini coefficient of consumption expenditure by age group

Note: For the calculation, household income and consumption are divided by the square root of the number of household members.

Source: Authors' calculations using microdata taken from the NSFIE.

within-age inequality is high compared with younger groups. Ohtake and Saito (1998) argue that inequality in the 1980s and 1990s can be explained mainly by population ageing. Second, in Figure 17.4, the inequality in consumption expenditure is high and increasing for children aged less than 20 years and for their parents' age group of 25 to 49 years. There is no significant change in consumption inequality for the group aged over 50 years. In the age group 35–49 years, a wider consumption inequality is observed.

The same pattern is observed when measuring poverty using disposable income and consumption expenditure (see Figure 17.5). That is, the poverty rate for the elderly, as measured by consumption expenditure, dropped from the mid- to late-1980s and has not changed much since then. However, poverty rates for those aged 25 to 35 years and under 10 years continued to rise throughout the 1990s. Thus, the three groups with the highest poverty rates are those over 70 years old, those in their 20s and 30s, and those aged under 10 years. The rise in the poverty rate is especially large for children aged five years and under.

Within-age inequality and the poverty rate among the elderly show declining trends, but they still remain at a high level compared with other age groups. The rapid increase in the proportion of the elderly in the population makes poverty rates appear high in the older age groups. However, a striking feature of the changes in recent years is the emergence of new poverty-stricken groups: children aged under 10 years and their parents in the 25–35 years age group. The serious situation of younger households must not be overlooked, even in an ageing society.

these age groups are quite high in Japan, so excluding families with zero income seems not to affect the measurement of inequality.

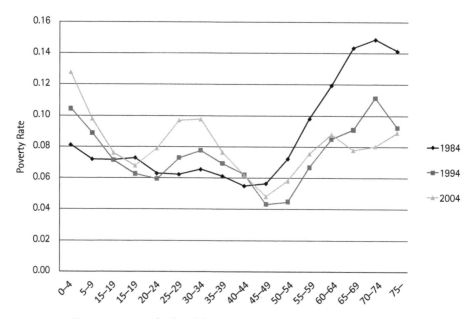

FIGURE 17.5 Poverty rates calculated by consumption

Note: The figure shows the proportion of people whose consumption expenditure is less than or equal to half of the national median. For the calculation, household consumption is divided by the square root of the number of household members. Note also that the limited number of cases for those aged 75 and over gives unstable results in this group, so we focus on the figures for groups below 75 years of age.

Source: Authors' calculations using microdata taken from the NSFIE.

Causes of the widening income/consumption gap

As suggested in the previous section, population ageing is one of the reasons for widening inequality in Japan—but what is the cause of the widening distribution among working-age people? Figure 17.6 shows the wage differentials for men under 60 years of age. The wage in this figure is based on a census data on establishment, which is not exactly same as the household disposable income shown in the previous figures, but describes the trend of wage earnings in the entire country. We can examine the background behind the increase in inequalities, focusing on workers' earnings.

As seen in Panel A, the log wage difference between the 90th and 50th percentiles of wage distribution decreased or remained unchanged until the middle of the 1990s. Panel B shows a similar pattern for the difference between the 50th and 10th percentiles. However, since 1997, the 50th–10th percentile wage gap has apparently expanded, whereas the 90th–50th percentile gap has been relatively stable. In other words, widening wage differentials among higher-income groups were rarely observed before the late 1990s, while the increase in Japan's wage inequality since the mid 1990s has coincided with an increase in the number of people in lower wage groups.

Noting that the top wage groups have not increased since the mid 1990s, according to Moriguchi and Saez (2008), who analysed historical changes in the Japanese top income share, stated that the top wage income shares in Japan have remained relatively stable, unlike the sharp increase in wage income inequality observed in the United States since 1970. Sudo, Suzuki, and Yamada (2012) reported that the income levels of lower-income groups started

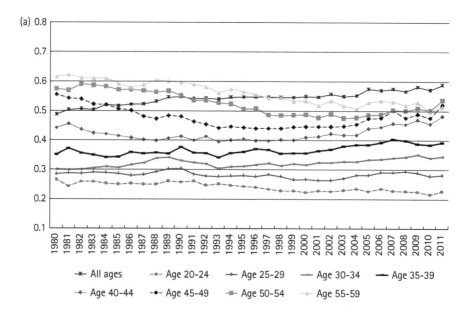

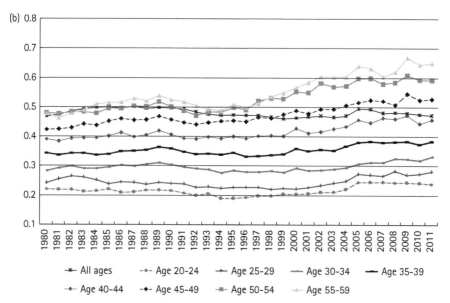

FIGURE 17.6 Log wage differences: (a) for men between the 90th and 50th percentiles; (b) for men between the 50th and 10th percentiles; (c) for women between the 90th and 50th percentiles; (d) for women between the 50th and 10th percentiles

Note: The figure depicts the average log wages across all industries and education-level groups, separately by birth cohort. Because the reported age categories in the original data set differ across years for those aged 60 and over, here we list figures only for those aged less than 60 years. All ages show the average for all ages including those aged 60 and over, which is not shown in the figure, so the figures for All ages may be higher than those for other age groups.

Source: *Basic Survey of Wage Structure* (Ministry of Health, Labour, and Welfare).

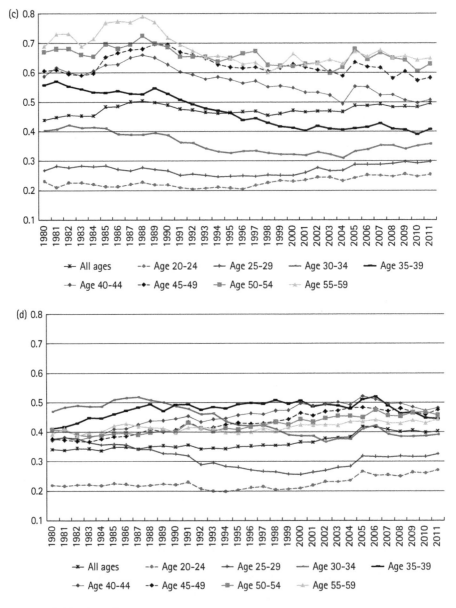

FIGURE 17.6 Continued

to decline from the mid 1990s and, accordingly, that the income gap has grown significantly since the early 2000s.

For females, the trend for the upper group is different. The 90th–50th percentile wage gap decreased dramatically after 1987, and continued to follow a downward trend or remained unchanged after 1995. This is attributed to the Gender Equal Employment Opportunity Law promulgated in 1986. The 50th–10th percentile wage gap has been rather stable, but increased gradually from the mid-1990s, as it did for males. To summarize the trend in male and female wage inequality, an increase in wage gap is not observed among upper wage groups, while it is among lower groups.

We note here that wage inequality related to educational attainment remained relatively stable in Japan over the period 1980–1990. This is in sharp contrast to the findings in the UK and the US since 1980. The growing inequalities in wage income observed in these countries are often characterized by a widening income gap related to educational attainment and an increase in the incomes of higher-income groups (Autor, Katz, and Kerney, 2006; Lemieux, 2006; Piketty and Saez, 2006). This does not mean that skill-based technological change (SBTC) has not affected Japan substantially over time. Kawaguchi and Mori (2008) showed that both the demand for and supply of skilled workers have increased because of SBTC, a rise in the number of college-educated workers following education policy changes, and the ageing of the population. Because the shifts in demand and supply were similar, the changes had no impact on the skill price, which has been stable. They pointed out that the industries that underwent rapid computerization also experienced an upgrading of workers' skills.

Thus, differentials in wages between education-level groups have been relatively constant for the past three decades in Japan. Note, however, that inequality within education-level groups may have widened. Figure 17.7 shows how wage inequality has changed among college or university graduates since 1980. The figure shows log wage difference for male college graduates between the 90th and the 10th percentiles. The inequality is quite high for senior groups especially after 60 years old, which is the mandatory retirement age in most Japanese companies. There is a stark difference in wage between those who remained at the firm on the board of directors and those who work in part time jobs after mandatory retirement age.

According to this figure, wage inequality within the same educational groups became larger after 1990 for almost all age groups except those aged 60-64. Kambayashi, Kawaguchi, and Yokoyama (2008) also explained that the increase in the within-group variance contributed to the wage disparity for males in the late 1990s. Thus, the expansion of wage inequality within college/university groups, but not between educational groups, led to a larger wage gap after the mid 1990s in the entire country.

There are two possible causes of the growth of lower-wage groups. The first is an increase in unemployment, especially among mid-life men. In the early 1990s, the male employment rate for those aged 25–34 was about 95 per cent, but this declined to about 90 per cent in the 2000s. Kohara and Ohtake (2006) pointed out that the growing income dispersion in Japan in the late 1990s was associated with an increase in income and consumption inequality within the unemployed, especially among those aged 45 and over.

Second, even among the employed, the ratio of non-standard employees, such as part-time, contract, and dispatched workers, to total workers has increased considerably. Figure 17.8 shows this trend. As seen, the proportion of non-standard employees was 15.3 per cent in 1984 and reached 35.1 per cent in 2012. Among men, a dramatic change in the proportion of non-standard employees occurred around the mid 1990s. Before 1995, this proportion was stable at roughly 8 per cent, but it started to increase after 1996 and reached about 18 per cent in 2005. This change is pronounced even among men in their prime earning years. That is, for men aged 25–34 years, the proportion of non-standard employees started to increase in 1996, reaching 13 per cent in 2005, while for men aged 35–54 years it started to increase in 2000, reaching about 8 per cent by the mid 2000s.

Figure 17.9 shows the income inequality between part-time and full-time employees. During the period from 1980 to 2002, the hourly wage rate for part-time employees declined

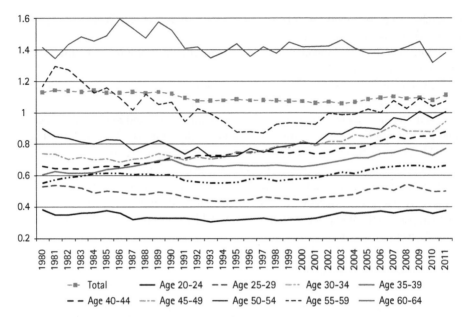

FIGURE 17.7 Log wage difference for male college graduates between the 90th and 10th percentiles

Note: The dotted line indicates average log wages across all age groups.

Source: *Basic Survey of Wage Structure* (Ministry of Health, Labour, and Welfare).

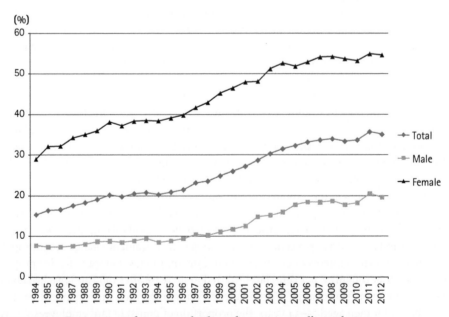

FIGURE 17.8 Proportion of non-standard workers among all employees

Note: The figure shows the ratio of non-standard workers to employees, excluding executives of companies or corporations. Non-standard workers include part-time workers, contract employees, and dispatched workers.

Source: *The Special Survey of the Labour Force Survey* (1984–2001), and *Labour Force Survey* (2002–present) (both by Ministry of Health, Labour, and Welfare).

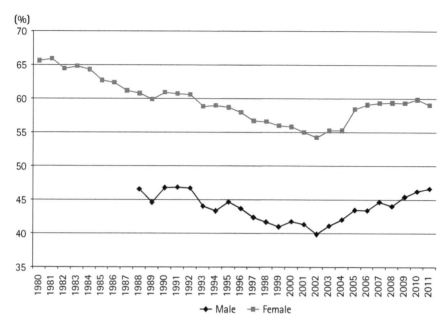

FIGURE 17.9 Proportion of hourly wage for part-time workers compared with full-time workers

Note: The ratio of hourly wage includes bonuses for part-time workers relative to full-time workers.

Source: *Basic Survey of Wage Structure* (Ministry of Health, Labour, and Welfare).

continuously compared with that for full-time employees. In the 2000s, part-time hourly wages appeared to increase slightly, but male part-time employees are still paid only half as much as full-time employees, whereas female part-time employees receive 60 per cent of full-time employees' wages. This slight increase has not sufficiently mitigated the large increases in the proportion of non-standard workers, for either men or women.

The increase in the rate of male non-standard employment is attributable to the employment adjustment that started in earnest in 1995 after the economic bubble burst. Full-time permanent employees benefit from a high level of job security, whereas employment adjustments targeting non-standard workers can be made relatively easily in Japan. During the economic recessions of recent decades, many Japanese companies avoided employing full-time employees, instead hiring part-time employees because of the sizeable cost of any subsequent employment adjustment if full-time staff are laid off. Because non-standard employees' average earnings are lower than those of full-time employees, the increases in non-standard employment and labour market segmentation have led to a widening of the income distribution.[4]

---

[4] Wage inequality between males and females in Japan has been steadily decreasing from the 1980s to the 2000s: the ratio of monthly contract earnings for female regular employees to those for males was 0.56 in 1985, and it increased up to 0.75 in 2011, both of which are calculated using *Basic Survey of Wage Structure* (Ministry of Health, Labour, and Welfare). A decline in the gender wage gap may have contributed to lower inequality in the country. See Figure 2.19 for details in the corresponding GINI Japan country report.

3. SOCIAL, POLITICAL AND CULTURAL
IMPACTS OF INEQUALITY

Family structures have changed considerably in Japan over the past three decades, which is not only a cause but possibly also an effect of inequality. Increases in the numbers of relatively poor older singles (or couples), relatively poor young singles, and single-parent households have led to greater income inequality between households.

Crime is often associated with increasing inequality. Figure 7.10 shows that the total crime rate increased during the serious recession in the 1990s, but decreased consistently in the 2000s. Negative economic shocks and increased inequality may cause crime rates to rise, although statistics on youth crime indicate that offenders are not always from poor families. According to Ohtake and Kohara (2010) and Kawashima (2012) which examines a causal effect of inequality on crimes, removing unobserved heterogeneity, producing a possible reverse causality, increases in inequality during the 1970s and the 1990s led to higher crime rates in Japan.

Inequality can also have a negative impact on health. Although increases in Japanese life expectancy is now the highest in the world, health as measured by an active healthy life or a subjective measure of health can deteriorate during an economic downturn. One serious health issue is an increase in mental health problems, reflected by an increase in

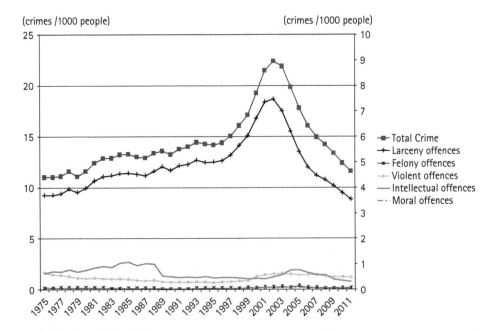

FIGURE 17.10 Crime rates

Note: Total penal code crimes and larceny offences are measured on the left axis, while felony, violent, intellectual, and moral offences are measured on the right axis.

Source: *Criminal Statistics* (National Police Agency).

suicide rates. Suicide rates in Japan are higher than in other countries. During the recession between 1995 and 2005, they increased rapidly among the middle aged and elderly; since 2005, suicide rates have been increasing among young people. This coincides with the fact that the severe economic conditions after the Asian financial crises affected the employment of middle-aged people and the recent recession beginning in 2007 affected the employment of young people.

A similar picture emerges on households' subjective well being. In the *Comprehensive Survey on Living Conditions*, respondents are asked: 'How would you describe your living conditions?' Possible answers are 'very hard,' 'hard,' 'not hard but not easy,' 'easy,' or 'very easy'. Figure 17.11 shows that subjective measures of living conditions, based on this question, deteriorated from 1992 to 2004. The number of households that answered 'not hard but not easy' decreased, whereas the number answering 'hard' or 'very hard' increased sharply. Other statistics in the same survey showed that the number answering 'very hard' or 'hard' increased more significantly in lower-income groups than in higher groups, and were more apparent among single-parent households and those who worked as fixed-contract employees. The disparity in subjective well being might become larger than the actual inequality in observed well being, such as levels of income and consumption.

It might be expected that, when inequality increases, more people will participate in political activities to redress deteriorating differentials in a society. The statistics, however, show no significant increase in political activities in Japan. The labour unionization rate has declined significantly over the past four decades, led by a change in Japan's employment conditions, that is, that the number of regular full-time workers has decreased and that of non-standard part-time workers has increased since the late 1990s, as seen in Section 2.

The voting rate has also continuously declined since World War II. Data on Voter Turnout in Visual Form reports that the average electoral turnout in general elections

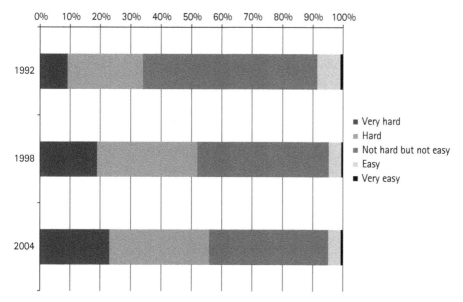

FIGURE 17.11 Living conditions

Source: Comprehensive Survey on Living Conditions (MHLW, 2010).

has been on a downward trend for both the House of Representatives and the House of Councilors. There is also a very large gap in voting rates between age groups. Figure 17.12 summarizes the feature of Japanese voting behaviors, reported by OECD Social Indicators (2011). Panel a of Figure 17.12 shows a large difference between older people and young people in Japan compared with other countries. This difference is much more marked than the insignificant difference in voting rates between highly educated and less educated people, shown in Panel b.

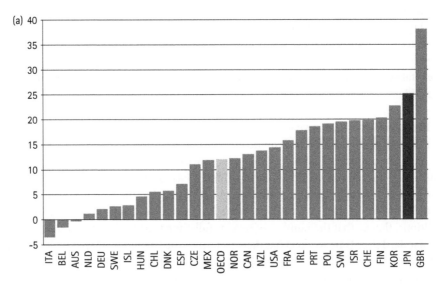

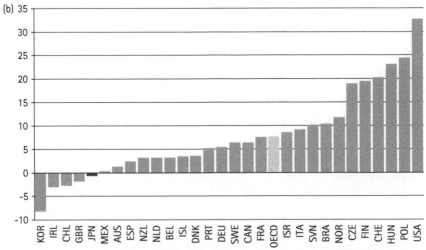

FIGURE 17.12 Percentage differences in voting rates (most recent election)

(a) Between those aged 55+ years and those aged 16–35 years (b) Between people with high and low education levels.

Note: The original figures for Panels a and b are numbered CO4.2 and CO4.3, respectively, in the source data.

Source: Society at a Glance: OECD Social Indicators (OECD, 2011; <http://www.oecd-ilibrary.org/social-issues-migration-health/society-at-a-glance-2011_soc_glance-2011-en>).

This age gap in voting rate is an important factor to consider when discussing policies that target inequality. Although inequality is becoming a more serious problem among the young relative to the elderly, the policy changes required to address inequality-related problems may not be adopted if differentials in voting between the young and the old do not reduce.

How have Japanese political values changed over time? It is said that more than 80 per cent of Japanese people have already recognized that income inequality is too large. At the same time, however, more than 70 per cent agree that 'the poor are lazy'. As a result, there is limited support for income redistribution, with 62 per cent supporting income redistribution and more than 30 per cent neither supporting nor not supporting it, although the number of people supporting redistribution increased during the 2000s.

4. EFFECTIVENESS OF POLICIES FOR COMBATING INEQUALITY

The increasing political power of the elderly and the minimal change in attitudes toward income redistribution policies indicate a failure to implement efficient policies to reduce income inequality. Consequently, it is among adults aged less than 40 years and children aged ten years and under that the rate of inequality is growing and poverty is more prevalent.

Japan's minimum wage rates have been rising consistently since 2007. However, the relative level of the minimum wage to the average wage in the country—the Kaitz index—has not changed greatly. Figure 17.13 shows the Kaitz index for men and women. For men, the

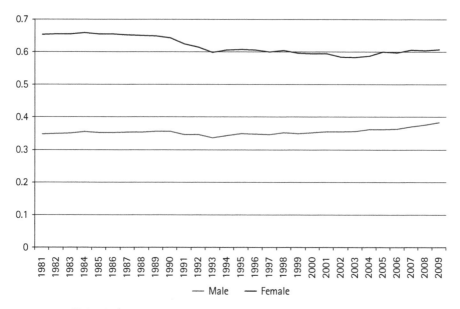

FIGURE 17.13 Kaitz index

Source: *Handbook on Minimum Wage Settings* (Roudou Chousakai, 'Sitei-Chingin-Kettei-Yoran').

minimum wage level was unchanged during the 1980s, decreased between 1990 and 1993, and then slightly increased. For women, it was unchanged during the 1980s, decreased markedly between 1990 and 1993, stayed at the same level until 2004, and then increased after that. That is, throughout the entire period from 1980 until 2009, the relative level of the minimum wage remained the same. The increase in the minimum wage is thought to have had only a small effect on alleviating existing levels of income inequality (Kawaguchi and Mori, 2009).

The impact of income redistribution policies through income tax has also been small. The maximum income tax rate was cut and the progressiveness of income taxes as a whole was reduced in the late 1990s. Tax revenue as a percentage of GDP has been on a continuous downward trend since 1990. The government has created debt to combat persistent recessions and to finance expenses in the ageing society. Government debt as a percentage of GDP was about 230 per cent in 2011, which is extremely high globally.

The Japanese government has increased fiscal spending on social security for the elderly. Figure 17.14 shows the upward trend of total expenditure as a percentage of annual real GDP, which is shown by bars in the figure. Looking at the composition of the payments, amounts related to population ageing, such as social security payments for the elderly, and for health and medical care, have increased. As another type of expenditure related to population ageing, Japan started public mandatory long-term care (LTC) insurance in 2000. People aged over 40 must pay LTC insurance, and can receive benefits when they actually need long-term care in principle (depending on ADL). The LTC payments have continuously increased since 2000 as the population has aged.

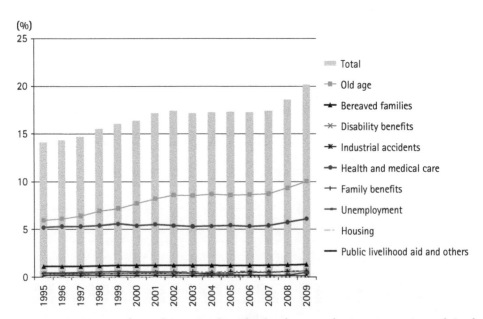

FIGURE 17.14 Ratio of social security benefits by functional category to Annual Real GDP (%)

Source: The Cost of Social Security (National Institute of Population and Social Security Research).

(*100%)

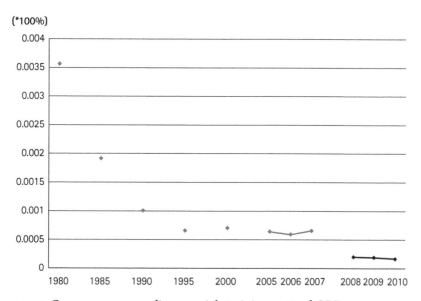

FIGURE 17.15 Government expenditure on job training as % of GDP

Note: Government expenditure on job training includes general job training, job training especially for young people, and for disabled people, which is reported by Ministry of Health, Labour and Welfare. Because the components of all expenditure related to unemployment and job training have changed significantly since 2008, the line is disconnected. The statistics are shown every five years before 2005.

Source: The White Paper on Labour and Economy 2012 (Ministry of Health, Labour and Welfare).

Figure 17.15 shows that government expenditure on job training as a percentage of GDP is low. Looking at the changes, expenditure on job training has been on a downward trend for a long time. Although it increased from 1995 through 2000 when the labour market was in a severe condition following the bursting of the economic bubble and the Asian financial crisis, it has not increased since the 2008 crisis that followed the collapse of Lehman Brothers. The unemployed are given unemployment insurance, but not much job training. People participate in job training at their own expense in many cases.

In response to the serious economic conditions and austere budget conditions since the late 1990s, government expenditures on basic education, which are financed mostly by local governments, peaked in 1995, and have been decreasing since then (Figure 17.16). National government expenditures on education, which are mostly for college and university education, have also fallen since 1995, regardless of the increase in the number of people entering higher education. The burden of expenditure on education is mostly imposed on each household in Japan. As economic inequality increases more, educational inequality may increase between households who can and cannot afford education costs. This tendency might be stronger if less educated parents who have lower incomes tend to invest less money on child's education.

Thus, we can say that fiscal spending on the elderly has been increased in response to population ageing, whereas fiscal spending on the working population, such as subsidies for job training and education, is quite limited. As seen in Section 2, there is an urgent need for efficient policies that address the needs of lower-income groups, which consist mainly of younger people, but for financial and political reasons the government has failed to formulate and implement such policies.

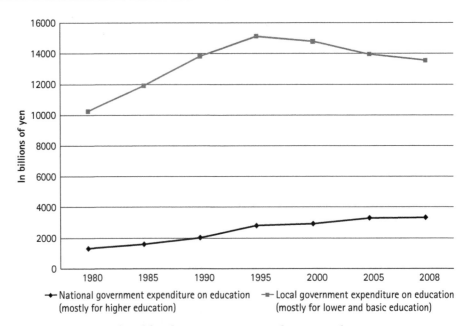

FIGURE 17.16 National and local government expenditure on education

Note: National government expenditure is mainly on college and universities, while local government expenditure is mainly on kindergartens, elementary schools, and secondary schools.

Source: National government expenditure is from *Basic Survey on Schools*, and local government expenditure is from *Survey of Local Educational Expenditure* (both are reported by Lifelong Learning Policy Bureau, Ministry of Education, Culture, Sports, Science and Technology).

5. POLICIES AND STRATEGIES

Income inequality in Japan started to increase gradually in the 1980s; it then increased significantly during the late 1990s and has been on a slower upward trend since the turn of the century. This trend is seen not only in income, but also in consumption expenditure and asset holdings. There are two distinctive features of Japan's inequality. The increase in income dispersion in the late 1990s was accompanied by a smaller share of income for low-income groups. The poverty rate also rose during this period especially among people aged 20–39 years and children aged ten years and under, whilst the poverty rate among the elderly has declined. Income and wealth inequality has become more serious recently among the young.

The increase in Japan's inequalities is mainly attributable to population ageing. Moreover, a large increase in inequalities since the late 1990s is attributable to growing gaps in wages and employment within generation and education-level group together with the effects of long-term trends in population ageing. Wage inequality related to educational attainment remained relatively stable over the period 1980–1990, in contrast to countries such as the UK and USA.

The situation for lower-income groups has become worse because of a change in Japan's employment environment. Since the late 1990s, male employment rates in the working-age population have fallen and male non-standard employment has increased. The increase in the rate of male non-standard employees has occurred because of employment adjustments that started in earnest in 1995 after the asset-inflation-fed economic bubble burst. In Japan, full-time permanent employees benefit from a high level of job security, whereas employment adjustments targeting non-standard workers can be made relatively easily. In response to the economic recessions, many Japanese companies avoided employing full-time employees and instead hired part-time, contract, and dispatched workers, because of the sizeable cost of employment adjustments. Because non-standard employees' average earnings are lower than those of full-time employees, the increases in non-standard employment and labour market segmentation have caused the income distribution to widen.

With the widening inequality due to the growth in size of lower-income groups after the late 1990s, Japanese society experienced several important social changes. First, the crime rate increased, particularly the rate of violent offences rose in the late 1990s. Second, the suicide rate has increased since the late 1990s and remains at a high level.

Most Japanese people recognize that inequality has been growing. However, Japanese attitudes toward income redistribution policies did not change in the 2000s. This is also reflected in low participation rates in political activities and low voting rates. One of the features of Japanese society is a wide generational difference in voting rate: the voting rate is much higher among people aged 55 years and over than among people aged 35 years and under. The higher absolute numbers of elderly people and the higher voting rate of the elderly will increasingly strengthen their political power.

The increasing political power of the elderly and the minimal change in attitudes toward income redistribution policies mean that young people in Japan are receiving little political attention, even though poverty is more prevalent and the extent of income inequality is the highest among adults aged less than forty years and children aged ten years and under. Despite evidence of an urgent need for efficient policies to address those lower-income groups, which consist mainly of younger people, the government has failed to formulate and implement such policies.

References

Autor, D. H., Katz L. F., and Kerney M. S. (2006), 'The Polarization of the U.S. Labor Market', *American Economic Review* 96, No.2, 189–194

Kohara, M. and Ohtake F. (2006), 'Unemployment and Inequality in Japan', *JCER Economic Journal, Japan Center for Economic Research*, No.55, pp.22–42. (in Japanese)

Kambayashi, R., Kawaguchi D. and Yokoyama I. (2008), 'Wage Distribution in Japan, 1989-2003', *Canadian Journal of Economics*, Vol. 41, No.4, pp. 1329–1350.

Kawaguchi, D. and Mori Y. (2008), 'Stable Wage Distribution in Japan, 1982-2002: A Counter Example for SBTC?', *RIETI Discussion Paper Series*, 08-E-020.

Kawaguchi, D. and Y. Mori (2009), 'Is Minimum Wage an Effective Anti Poverty Policy in Japan?' *Pacific Economic Review*, Vol. 14, No. 4, pp. 532–554.

Kawashima, H. (2012), 'Labor Markets, Poverty and Crime', *OSIPP Discussion Paper*, DP-2012-J-007.

Lemieux, T. (2006), 'Postsecondary Education and Increasing Wage Inequality', *American Economic Review*, Vol. 96, No.2, pp. 195–199.

Moriguchi, C. and Saez, E. (2008), 'The Evolution of Income Concentration in Japan, 1886-2005: Evidence from Income Tax Statistics', *The Review of Economics and Statistics*, MIT Press, Vol. 90, No.4, pp. 713–734.

Ohtake, F. and Saito M. (1998), 'Population ageing and consumption inequality in Japan', *The Review of Income and Wealth*, Ser.44, No.3, pp. 361–381.

Ohtake, F. and Kohara M. (2010), 'The Relationship between Unemployment and Crime: Evidence from Time-series Data and Prefectural Panel Data', *Japanese Journal of Sociological Criminology, Japanese Association of Sociological Criminology*, No.35, pp. 54–71.

Piketty, T. and Saez E. (2006), 'Evolution of Top Incomes: A Historical and International Perspective', *American Economic Review*, Vol. 96, No.2, pp. 200–205.

Sudo, N., Suzuki M. and Yamada T. (2012), 'Inequalities in Japanese Economy during the Lost Decades', *CIRJE Discussion Paper*, CIRJE-F-85.

CHAPTER 18

....

KOREA: THE GREAT U-TURN IN INEQUALITY AND THE NEED FOR SOCIAL SECURITY PROVISIONS

....

BYUNG YOU CHEON, JIYEUN CHANG, GYU SEONG HWANG,

JIN-WOOK SHIN, SHIN-WOOK KANG,

BYUNG-HEE LEE, AND HYUN JOO KIM

1. INTRODUCTION

....

EVER since the 1960s, Korea has had one of the fastest growing economies in the world. In only five decades, Korea has transformed itself from a poor country into a developed one. Its rapid export-oriented growth, combined with a long political dictatorship up to 1987, caused structural changes that have been accompanied by polarization and dualization across all sectors.

For years, Korea's strong economic growth, which was based on an expanding population and massive investment, created jobs and educational opportunities for all. These factors were able to contain the negative effects of growing inequality in the market without recourse to a social security system.

However, since 1980, Korea has experienced great economic and social upheaval. It joined the OECD in 1996, and the Asian financial crisis hit the country the following year. From the mid 1980s, with political democratization and the activation of trade unions, and with relatively strong economic growth based on consistent government-led industrial policies and expanding domestic demand, there was a decrease in inequality. But in the mid 1990s there came a great U-turn in inequality in Korea: the full-fledged opening up of the economy and political liberalization in the wake of the Asian financial crisis transformed both the economic structure and the social system. As a natural consequence of this, inequality expanded.

The jobs crisis lay at the heart of this growing inequality. While the Korean economy bounced back from the economic crisis of 1997, the jobs crisis continued, as the quantity and quality of jobs deteriorated. Though regular employment rates have not increased, work in small companies and non-regular work has. Even though the impact of the 2008 global financial crisis was felt relatively weakly in Korea (compared to other OECD countries), the jobs crisis and growing inequality have continued.

At this point, it is no longer possible to curb social unrest and meet welfare needs by creating jobs and expanding educational opportunities. Growing inequality has led to higher crime and suicide rates, lower fertility and marriage rates, and reduced social mobility. All this has undermined the social system that has supported the high level of growth. For further sustainable development to take place in Korea, labour market performance must be improved (in terms of both quantity and quality) and an inclusive social security system needs to be established. Accordingly, reducing non-regular jobs and expanding welfare provision were major issues in the Korean presidential election of December 2012.

In this chapter, we attempt to highlight specific features of national inequality, on the basis of the Korean country report in the GINI research project. We will address the trends and drivers of growing inequality (Section 2), the social impacts of increasing inequality (Section 3), the political and cultural impacts of inequality (Section 4), policy responses to combat inequality (Section 5), and provide a conclusion (Section 6).

2. Growing Inequality and its Drivers

Specific Features of Inequality in Korea

One striking feature of Korean inequality is that the overall level of household income inequality is relatively low, while individual labour market income inequality is among the highest in the OECD. According to the OECD (2008: 358; 2011a: 87), in 2006 wage inequality in Korea was the highest after the United States, and the share of low-wage workers (below the median wage) was 26–27 per cent—the highest in the OECD. On the other hand, comparisons with other countries indicate that Korea's household market income dispersion is well balanced (Figure 18.1).

The discrepancy between individual wage inequality and household income inequality suggests that active labour market participation among the class with the lowest income off-sets the inequality of individual labour income. If a relatively high number of household members from the low-income brackets participate in the labour market, then household income may be distributed equally, even if the labour market is unequal. In reality, Chang (2012b) found that, although the number of labour-income earners in the lowest income quintile in developed nations was 0.3 to 0.7 people per household, in Korea an average of 1.4 people per household participate in labour activities in that same quintile. This is also related to the fact that the Gini coefficient of hourly wages is higher than that of total wages. Low-wage workers compensate for their lower hourly pay by working longer hours (see more details in the GINI Korean Report, 2012). That is, the high rate of growth of the Korean

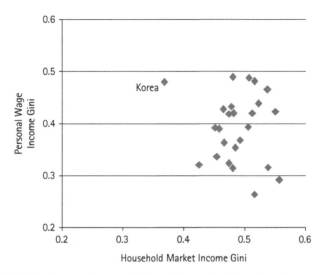

FIGURE 18.1 Individual wage income Gini and household market income Gini

Source: Luxembourg Income Study (LIS) data, mid 2000s. Korea's 2006 Household Income
and Expenditure Survey data were submitted to LIS.

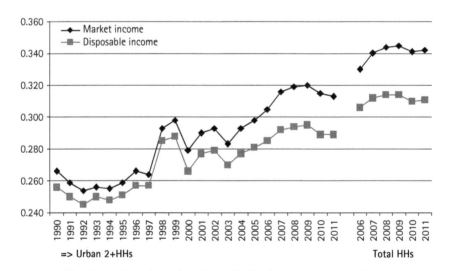

FIGURE 18.2 Trends in Gini for urban households (Korea, 1990–2011)

Notes: 2+HHs = household with two or more members.

Source: Korea National Statistical Office, Household Income and Expenditure Survey.

economy could mitigate inequality by creating jobs for low-income households, and there
was no need for a social security system—at least before the mid 1990s.

The other distinctive feature of Korean inequality is the relatively small gap between the
Gini coefficients of gross and net income (Figure 18.2), which implies that income redistribution policies (such as public transfers and taxation) contributed little toward mitigating

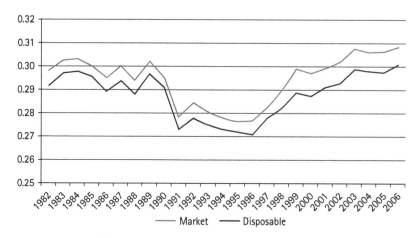

FIGURE 18.3 Gini coefficient trends (1982–2006): urban household with two or more members

Note: Calculations by Dr Roh Dae-Myung (Korea Institute for Health and Social Affairs).

Source: Korea National Statistical Office, Household Income and Expenditure Survey.

inequality in Korea, at least before the 2000s. Although the gap between market and disposable income has since increased, the redistribution system does not function as well in Korea as in other developed countries: this will be explained in more detail in Section 5.

A time series approach to income inequality shows that inequality declined significantly in the late 1980s, before escalating again in the mid 1990s (Figure 18.3). The changes coincide with a series of labour strikes in 1987 and the financial crisis of 1997. The high-growth system did not work well after the mid 1990s, when there was a great U-turn in inequality, and the downward trend in inequality changed to an upward trend.

Moreover, inequality has worsened in the lower levels of income distribution rather than in the upper levels, as is shown by the trends for P50/P10 and P90/P50 in Figure 18.4. One caveat is that the top income is not well represented in the survey data. While the income share of the top 1 per cent is 6–8 per cent if it is calculated on the basis of the National Survey of Tax and Benefit (Korea Institute of Public Finance) or the Survey of Household Finance, it is more than 16 per cent according to National Tax Service data (Park, 2012); this may lead the P90/P50 to be underestimated.

Growing inequality is related to the great economic and social changes that occurred in the mid 1990s, including the re-establishment of diplomatic ties with China in 1992, joining the OECD in 1996, and the Asian financial crisis of 1997. Since the mid 1990s, the Korean economy has been opened up fully to the world, and the manufacturing sector has continued to grow thanks to expanding exports. Its employment share has, however, fallen dramatically, and this has resulted in the growth of joblessness and labour market dualization.

Moreover, the financial crisis required economic restructuring, and the decline in the economic growth rate was accompanied by a fall in both the population growth rate and the fertility rate. All of this has damaged labour market performance. Employment was particularly hard hit by the financial crisis, and while the economy recovered to its previous levels very rapidly, employment did not. Though the self-employed sector began shrinking rapidly and the proportion of wage-earners increased, the share of labour in the national accounts

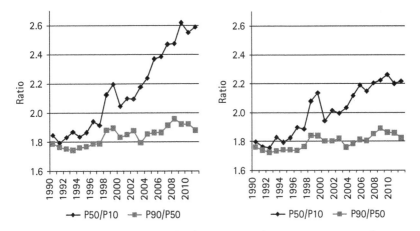

FIGURE 18.4 Gini coefficient trend of urban HHs with two or more members
(Market Income) (Disposable Income)
Source: Korea National Statistical Office. Calculated from data on kosis.kr

has been decreasing or stagnating since 1996. This stagnation may be due to a deterioration in the quality of jobs, since non-regular and low-wage work has expanded. The poor performance of the labour market in terms of both quantity and quality has been the main driver of growing inequality in Korea.

Drivers of Growing Inequality in the Labour Market

Growing household income inequality has coincided with worsening labour market inequality. The Gini coefficient of wage inequality is higher than the coefficient of income inequality; it decreased more rapidly up to the mid 1990s and increased faster after that period (Figure 18.5). The decomposition of increasing income inequality over a 15-year period (GINI Korean Report, 2012) showed that increasing inequality in wage earning was a major factor behind the rise in inequality. Furthermore, the increase in income inequality in households of working age explains inequality best, while the effect of the increasing proportion of elderly households is secondary. Stagnating employment performance after the financial crisis of 1997 would also have made earning inequality in the entire working-age population higher than individual wage inequality. Access to employment for less well educated individuals has decreased since 1999, particularly in the male labour force, so that the unequal mitigating effects of relatively good access to the labour market for low-skilled workers have been reduced (for more details see the GINI Korean Report, 2012).

The GINI Korean Report (2012) analysed changes in the difference in household income between the highest and the lowest income groups in the period 1996–2011, and found that the unequal mitigating effect of a higher labour supply in lower-income households has been reduced. Labour market participation among low-income women used to offset the wage inequality among household heads around the time of the 1997 Asian financial crisis (Lee, 2008), but analysis of the past 15 years shows that this effect has evaporated. Given that

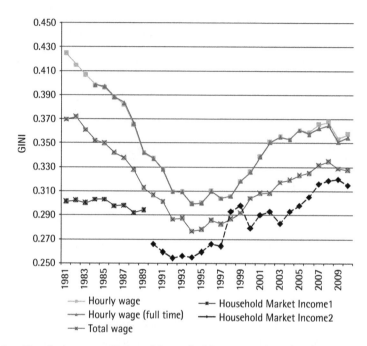

FIGURE 18.5 Trends in wage Gini and household income Gini (Korea, 1981–2010)

Trends in Gini coefficient (1981–2010)

Notes: Calculations by Dr Roh Dae-Myung (Korea Institute for Health and Social Affairs); Korea National Statistical Office. Household Income and Expenditure Survey.

Source: Ministry of Employment and Labour, Basic Wage Structure Survey.

the labour market participation rate among the spouses of high-income household heads in Korea is lower than in developed countries, it is unlikely that the inequality-reducing effects of household labour supply patterns will continue.

Moreover, Kim and Shin (2008) has shown that the inequality-reducing effect of female labour participation lessened between 1998 and 2005, due to the increased incidence of assortative mating, the dualization of the female labour market, and a relatively high rate of increasing female participation in the upper levels of spouse-income distribution.

The key factors in growing labour market inequality are education, firm size, and employment type. The wage premium for higher education began to rise at around the same time as the enrolment rate for tertiary education began to increase (in 1993) (Figure 18.6). Skill-biased technological change, like information technology, has been counted as a driver of wage inequality.[1] Many studies show that the very rapid expansion of trade with China has increased demand for highly skilled workers, has destroyed medium-skilled jobs, and has increased wage inequality (Ahn et al., 2007; Nahm, 2010; Ok et al., 2007). The ratio of foreign trade (sum of export and import) to GDP has a very similar shape to the Gini coefficient—it was 78.9 per cent in 1980, at its lowest of 55.5 per cent in 1993, and was 105.5 per

---

[1] Korea is one of the most rapidly growing countries in IT manufacturing and consumption.

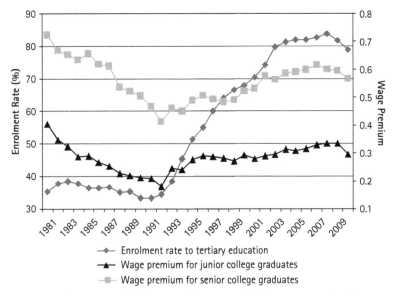

FIGURE 18.6 Trends in enrolment rates for tertiary education and educational wage premium (1981–2010)

Note: Wage premium is calculated from Mincer-type wage equations in the form of: *Log(hourly wage)* = α + *β1*Male(dummy)*+ *β2*Age*+ *β3*Age*+ *β4*Ten*+ *β5*Tensq*+*β6*Establishment Size(dummy)*+ *β7*Manufacturing Sector(dummy)*+ *β8*Production Occupation (dummy)*+*β9*Senior College (dummy)*+ *β10*Junior College(dummy)*+ *β11*High School(dummy)*+ ε.

Source: Korea National Statistical Office. Ministry of Employment and Labour of Korea, Basic Wage Structure Survey.

cent in 2010; the trade structure has changed dramatically from a US to a Chinese orientation (for more details see the GINI Korean Report, 2012). OECD (2011a: 89, Figure 1.3) reveals that Korea has the most rapidly increasing intensity of trade with developing countries. Nahm (2010) explains that the growing wage inequality is a kind of opportunity cost for the change in trade structure from a country with an abundance of low-skilled workers to a country that has an abundance of highly skilled workers and that enjoys increased trade with China.

Growing wage inequality, however, cannot be fully explained by labour demand and supply. Labour market institutions are also important factors in the growing inequality. Even within the same educational group, inequality has been increasing, while this is not the case within companies of the same size. Company size, tenure (job stability), and employment type (regular or non-regular employment)—all variables related to labour market institutions—operate as important factors in the deteriorating level of wage inequality. To clarify matters, the changes in economic and industrial structure— the dualization of large export-oriented firms and small domestic market-oriented firms, and labour market flexibilization, with more and more non-regular jobs—are becoming significant. Extending educational opportunities is not enough to curb growing wage inequality in Korea.

Educational Inequality

Between 1960 and 1990, Korea came to be regarded as successful in its so-called 'shared growth' (growth without inequality) policy of extending opportunities for universal education. The average length of education in 1980 was only 7.6 years, whereas by 1990 this had risen to 9.5 years. And in 2010 it stood at 11.6 years. That year, for the 20–29 age group, the figure was 14.1 years—the highest educational attainment level in the world. This growing educational attainment has led to a more equal distribution in the labour force in terms of level of education. The Gini coefficient for educational attainment was 0.221 in 1994, but 0.185 in 2010.

Nevertheless, education no longer seems to be very effective at reducing inequality in Korean society. Even though, in terms of quantity, educational opportunity has long been extended throughout society, differentials in educational expenditure by income have also grown since 1993, when the enrolment rate for tertiary education started to increase. Together with growing wage inequality by level of education, this has served to aggravate inequality by widening differentials in the quality of education.

3. The Social Impacts of Growing Inequality

Job creation and the extension of educational opportunities were major pillars of the growth-driven economy of Korea. Creating more jobs through economic growth and expanding educational opportunities for lower-income groups restrained social instability, which could have been unleashed by high levels of labour market inequality. Yet it is becoming more difficult these days for such strategies to work as devices to reduce inequality and mitigate social instability.

Since the mid-1990s and the turning point for inequality trends, Korea has experienced very dramatic social changes: increasing rates of crime, suicide and divorce; declining rates of fertility and marriage; a higher persistence of poverty; and lower social mobility. The rise in inequality has exposed the poor and less well educated to more social risks than the rich and better educated face in terms of family dissolution, crime, suicide and social immobility.

Family Dissolution

The decline of the family as an institution—with increased numbers of single-parent families, higher divorce rates, and falling marriage rates—seems to have a high correlation with growing inequality. The figures for single-person households and for families with a female or divorced head of the household have increased since the mid1990s (Table 18.1). The poverty rate among families with a female head of the household is higher than the average household poverty rate, which itself has started to increase more rapidly since 2000.

The share of divorce related to economic problems in particular has shown similar trends to the Gini (Figure 18.7). Ki Won Jung (2004) and Chang-Mu Jung (2008) have shown that

Table 18.1 Changes in family formation indicators

	Average number of family members	Single-person household	Family with a divorced head of household	Single-parent family	Family with a female head of household	Relative poverty rate of families with a female head of household (absolute poverty)
1980	4.5	4.8	0.9	9.3	14.7	
1985	4.1	6.9	1.1	8.9	15.7	
1990	3.7	9.0	1.5	7.8	15.7	
1995	3.3	12.7	2.1	7.4	16.6	
2000	3.1	15.5	3.9	7.9	18.5	14.7 (7.4)
2005	2.9	20.0	5.7	8.6	21.9	19.1 (9.4)
2010	2.7	23.9	7.3	9.2	25.9	20.1 (10.0)

Source: Korea Women's Development Institute (2011), Gender Statistics in Korea.

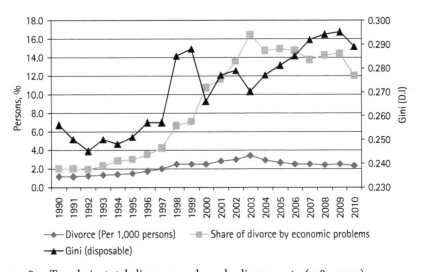

FIGURE 18.7 Trends in total divorces and crude divorce rate (1989–2011)

unemployment among male heads of household has contributed significantly to an increasing crude divorce rate. It is certain that the employment crisis that followed the financial crisis of 1997 had significant effects on increasing divorce rates and family breakdown. The employment crisis had a very close relationship with growing inequality.

By 2006, Korean fertility rates had declined to 1.12—the lowest in the world. Various factors may have played a part: for example, the country's birth control policy has been highlighted as a major cause in the 1970s and 1980s. Since the 1990s, however, factors related to low fertility rates have usually been analysed in terms of an increased child care burden that

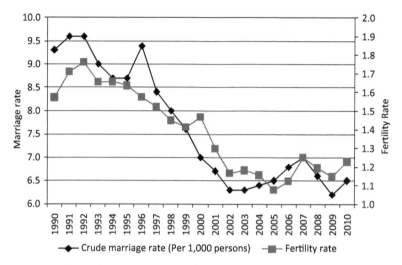

FIGURE 18.8 Trends in fertility and marriage rates (1990–2010)

Source: Korea National Statistical Office. Calculated from data on kosis.kr

is due to rising living costs, the growing number of families where both parents work, and poor provision of child care facilities.

As Figure 18.8 shows, the number of young married people has declined rapidly, particularly since the financial crisis of 1997. The drivers of the low fertility rate also seem to contribute to the declining number of marriages, especially after 1997. The age of first marriage has also increased, which seems to reflect economic and cultural change. Among other factors, youth unemployment has made the economic position of young people worse, leading them to put off getting married. While family structure is influenced by cultural and historical factors, the Korean family has broken down for socio-economic reasons since the 1997 crisis; this is closely related to changes in the labour market and their subsequent effects on inequality.

Crime and Suicide Rates

Since the 1990s, Korea has moved from being a society with low crime and suicide rates to being one with high rates. As we can see from Figure 18.9, crime and suicide have increased rapidly since 1992 and have a strong correlation with growing inequality. It is still not clear whether the increasing rates are due to the deterioration in income distribution or only reflect long-term trends according to economic development. However, in their analysis of the causal relationship between crime rates and socio-economic variables between 1966 and 2007, Park et al. (2009) showed that the unemployment rate and the Gini have a significant effect on the rate of economically motivated crimes, controlling for the economic growth rate, the number of people per police officer, and the authority-regime index. A more compelling finding is that the period variable (1998–2007) has significant negative effects even when controlling for all other variables, which means that the crime rate would not have increased without the financial crisis and its aftermath. The jobs crisis and worsening

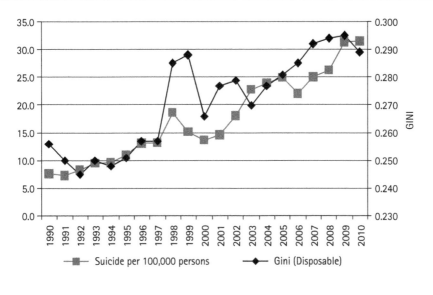

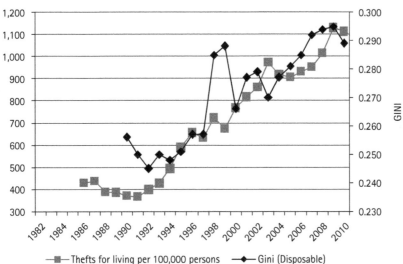

FIGURE 18.9 Crime rate, suicide rate and Gini

Source: Korea National Statistical Office.

inequality in the wake of the financial crisis seem to have had a significant effect on the crime rate.

Social Mobility

Korean society used to be characterized by considerable social mobility in the age of industrialization. Rapid modernization in the latter half of the twentieth century transformed Korea from an agrarian society into an industrial one, opening up the possibility of upward

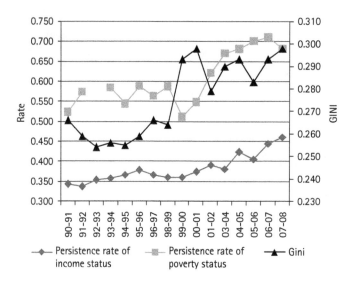

FIGURE 18.10 Trends in income mobility (one-year persistence rate) and Gini (disposable income)

Data: Korea National Statistical Office, Household Income and Expenditure Survey, each year.

Source: Kang (2011).

mobility to almost everyone. As inequality has grown, however, so the persistence of poverty has risen and income mobility and generational mobility have declined.

One feature of poverty in Korea is its recurring nature (Hong, 2004; Lee and Jung, 2002). The figures for people escaping from poverty are fairly high, but the figures for people slipping back into poverty are also not low. Around 50–60 per cent of all those in poverty escape absolute poverty within one year and over 30 per cent escape relative poverty (below 50 per cent of median income). The three-year poverty persistence rate is estimated at 14 per cent (Hong, 2004), and the five-year rate is put at 16 per cent (Kim and Noh, 2009). Although the rates are not as high as in other countries, the poverty persistence rate has been increasing since 2000 (Figure 18.10).

Income mobility in Korea is relatively high compared to other countries (though it has been declining since 2000) (Figure 18.11). Moreover, intergenerational income elasticity (the correlation between the income of children and of their parents) is 1.5–2, the lowest level in the OECD. However, Yang (2012) re-estimated the results, controlling for sample selection bias, and came up with a figure of 3.5–4. This is around 0.5 lower than for other developing countries, but not much lower than for other OECD countries (around 0.4 lower than for the United States and 0.3 lower than for the European Union), which suggests that the opportunities for status advancement have gradually declined as inequality has grown.

The increasing breakdown of the family, falling fertility and marriage rates, increasing suicide and crime rates, and reduced social mobility all mean that social risks and social costs are increasing in Korea as well. Such costs are also related to growing inequality; thus, they cannot be cured by economic growth and job creation alone. More policies to reduce dualization and inequality in the market, and more resources for redistribution, are urgently needed to reduce these risks.

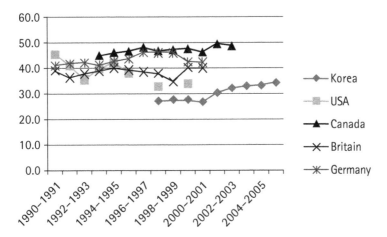

FIGURE 18.11 Trends in the share of individuals maintaining their income class (one-year persistence rate)

Sources: Chen (2009) and Lee (2009). The Cross National Equivalent File (Cornell University) 2005 and the Korea Labour and Income Panel Survey (the Korea Labour Institute).

4. POLITICAL AND CULTURAL IMPACTS OF GROWING INEQUALITY

Inequality and its Political and Cultural Impacts in a Developmental Context

During its rapid growth between the 1960s and the late 1980s, it was said that the Korean political economy was a 'developmental state', that it had a 'developmental dictatorship' and that it experienced 'mobilized modernization' (Cho, 2007; 2010; Pirie, 2008; Woo-Cummings, 1999). In fact, the Korean industrialization pattern entailed political, economic and socio-cultural features that were closely interwoven: political authoritarianism; state direction of the economy (dirigisme); ideological manipulation of development as a supreme national objective; and mass mobilization to that end. This provides the context for the way in which socio-economic inequalities were addressed. Although income inequality during the developmental period is hard to estimate because of insufficient reliable data, socio-economic inequalities did not threaten the social system; that is not to say that Korean society was equal, but its unique mechanism prevented inequality from emerging as a serious problem.

First, export-led growth based on competitive pricing required low wages and accordingly the suppression of labour movements; this resulted in a low labour share in the national accounts of around 40 per cent in the early 1970s (Korea National Statistical Office). The fact that most people had low wages in common meant that inequality was felt less acutely. Second, the 'elevator effect' (Beck, 1986) accompanied by 'shared growth' (World Bank, 1993) worked. A gradual but overall improvement in living conditions through growth made inequality a less sensitive issue, despite the fact that it persisted (or even worsened). Third, ideology has a role in inequality. The state succeeded in manufacturing mass consent to a deliberately devised developmental ideology. The state-imposed collective enthusiasm for development made most Korean people endure today's pain for tomorrow's gain. In sum, whether or not inequality had an explosive potential, it was effectively kept in check.

Nonetheless, this pattern of modernization and inequality management came at a price. First, the authoritarian power monopolized the vehicle by which inequality was managed. A strong state left little room for civil society to develop inequality-coordination mechanisms, such as industrial or corporatist wage bargaining. Second, keen competition in pursuit of success brought about low trust in others and in society. On the relentless—and militant—march to industrialization, most Korean people were driven to a fierce race in their everyday lives—for higher education, good jobs, promotion, etc. Under the circumstances, people could hardly be expected to cultivate tolerant attitudes. Third, the developmental ideology created subordination of 'the social' to 'the economic'. Almost all resources were allocated to economic growth at the expense of other values; this partly explains why social policy was underdeveloped until recently.

Still, challenges to this system came thick and fast: political democratization in 1987; economic liberalization from the 1980s on; and the economic crisis of the late 1990s. These developments were a litmus test for whether the traditional model could survive; they forced it to move on. Inequality and its political and cultural impacts keep encountering one another in different guises from the past.

Inequality and its Impacts on Political Participation and Values

Political participation. When procedural democracy was introduced in 1987 after a long period of military dictatorship, the turnout in the presidential election was 89.2 per cent— the highest for three decades. Since then it has declined steadily, reaching 63 per cent in 2007. The relationship between inequality and political participation is difficult to establish but, because the Great U-turn occurred in the mid 1990s, Schattschneider's hypothesis that inequality would reduce participation holds true only for the second half of the last three decades.

An examination of turnout by income, education and age reveals some compelling points (see Table 18.2). While income and education have no linear effect on participation, age has a clear-cut correlation with electoral turnout: older people are more participatory than their younger compatriots. While 90.1 per cent of older people (60 and over) visited the polling booths in the 2007 presidential election, for those under 29 the figure was only 63.8 per cent (Korean General Social Survey). Older people, who mostly lived in the developmental period, are supposed to be more inclined to take part in national events because of their conservative patriotism. By contrast, it is logical for the younger group—who benefited from the extension of educational opportunities, but who have witnessed (or suffered from) the unstable labour market—to view politics with more scepticism. We see here a coexistence of lasting political activism for the less well-educated older people, and fresh political cynicism for their better educated younger compatriots. It seems that inequality in Korea has different political impacts along generational lines.

Table 18.2 Percentage of voting by income, education and age in Korea

	Subgroup	Presidential		National Assembly		Local	
		2002	2007	2004	2008	2006	2010
income	lowest 20%	83.9	81.7	77.6	68.1	70.5	69.4
	20–40%	81.9	73.6	74.0	57.6	62.4	59.8
	40–60%	87.6	77.9	73.8	66.6	64.8	63.1
	60–80%	83.8	75.5	79.8	67.8	65.9	67.5
	highest 20%	84.2	82.6	84.3	66.4	74.9	74.4
education	less high	90.2	83.7	82.5	77.4	77.1	75.9
	high	83.4	74.8	75.1	59.5	63.8	58.3
	junior college	78.7	79.5	67.1	59.3	58.8	54.5
	college	81.3	76.6	78.8	65.1	66.3	68.0
age	19–29	67.9	63.8	59.1	43.5	46.5	43.5
	30–39	82.8	74.8	73.5	60.5	59.1	61.4
	40–49	88.9	81.3	82.6	71.0	71.6	68.3
	50–59	91.9	87.1	85.3	77.0	77.7	76.3
	60+	90.7	90.1	85.6	82.5	83.5	79.1

Source: Korean General Social Survey.

Civic culture and trust. In the 2000s, Korea failed to escape from the old low-trust society. In 2007, only 46.2 per cent of people (well below the OECD average of 58.6 per cent) expressed a high level of trust in others, ranking Korea among the least trusting countries (OECD, 2011b). Only around half of the people expressed trust in their society in the 2000s. Even though we cannot identify long-term trends, it can be reasonably inferred that growing inequality, combined with increased labour market instability and dualization, has caused trust to deteriorate.

The race to success had grown more and more intense when a new phenomenon arose: the general 'elevator' stopped and was replaced by a 'paternoster lift' (Butterwegge, 2009: 141)—as one individual moves up, another moves down. This phenomenon was mostly caused by a slowing of the trickle-down effects, growth without employment, and worsening employment quality.

Political values, social policies and the welfare state. Rising inequality may punish political conservatives, who are usually averse to redistribution. As expected, the number of those identifying themselves as conservatives has declined slightly from 38.1 per cent in 2003 to 30.5 per cent in 2010, and self-reported liberals increased from 28.7 per cent to 31.2 per cent in the same period. But the third competing group is made up of those who declare themselves to be 'neither liberal nor conservative'. At 32.9 per cent, this group constituted the largest faction in the political landscape of 2010 (Korean General Social Survey). This remarkable level of political hedging hints at a further degree of political cynicism, which, combined with the apathy of younger people, poses a major political challenge for the existing political parties.

Korean people are regarded as sensitive to inequality and are supposed to have a strong orientation towards equality. Some nine people in ten found the state of income distribution either 'very unfair' or 'somewhat unfair' in 2009. Rising inequality plus rising instability since the late 1990s has led to collective interest in social policy. Korea has long lagged behind as far as the welfare state is concerned. However, discussion about welfare state expansion—hardly mentioned in Western societies in recent years—is currently much in vogue in Korea. Three-quarters (74.7 per cent) of people in 2009 regarded income distribution reduction as a government responsibility (Korean General Social Survey). We can discern a very clear break with the past here. The old developmental state employed growth strategies without social policies, and achieved success. But the expiry date for this prescription is approaching—or has perhaps passed. The Korean socio-economic structure has changed too profoundly in recent decades for that model to survive. Furthermore, developmental ideology, which used to comprise institutional complementarities, has lost its effectiveness in the changing circumstances. The inequality-management methods of the past are giving way to other indispensable social policies. If 'consolidated democracies require a set of socio-politically crafted and socio-politically accepted norms, institutions, and regulations' (Linz and Stepan, 1996: 11), these must include social policies and a welfare state in the case of Korea.

5. POLICY RESPONSES TO GROWING INEQUALITY

Because the 'jobs crisis' is the main reason for increased income inequality (Section 2), labour market policies (such as the minimum wage) could be important in reducing inequality. The Minimum Wage Act was passed in 1987 and entered into force in 1988. The minimum wage began to catch up with the average wage after the crisis of 1997. However, it has not been successful in raising the relative wage level of low-waged workers, because the minimum-wage regulations are not strictly enforced or complied with. The share of workers earning below the minimum wage increased from 4 per cent in 2000 to more than 10 per cent of wage workers in 2009. It has also been argued that the minimum wage is not very effective in reducing household income inequality, because it may assist low-wage workers in high-income households. The rigorous enforcement of the minimum wage, however, could prove a very powerful device to reduce the high level of labour market inequality in the midst of widespread low-wage jobs. Moreover, the minimum wage policy could be a very effective way of supporting low-income families by preventing any wage reduction among low-skilled workers as a result of a greater supply of low-skilled labour following the introduction of earned income tax credit—a measure enacted in 2008 and set in motion in 2009.

The redistributive effects of tax and income transfer in Korea fall short of those in developed countries. The fact that Korea's social policies are not effective in lowering income inequality has been revealed by previous studies and explained by the paucity of social spending (Kim, 2004; Yeo, 2009; Yeo and Song, 2010). As we saw in the Gini coefficient trend, however, the effect of redistribution policies has been slowly increasing of late (Figure 18.2). In particular, their poverty-reducing effects show an upwards trend (Figure 18.12).

The poverty-rate reduction effect of each income-transfer programme is provided in Table 18.3. Public assistance is the most effective programme in reducing poverty; pensions come next. The Korean social assistance programme—known as the National Basic Livelihood

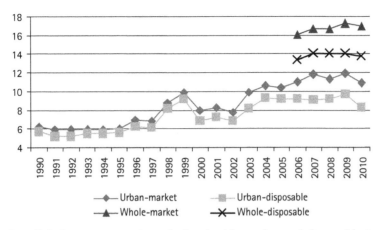

FIGURE 18.12 Relative poverty ratios calculated with market and disposable incomes

Notes: Since 2006, HIES has provided information on all households, including non-urban households. Urban household data cover households with two or more family members whose heads are wage and salary workers. Since 2006, HIES has provided information on all households with only one person and on households whose heads are non-wage workers.

Relative poverty ratio means the proportion of persons with income below 50 per cent of equivalized households median income.

Source: Korea National Statistical Office, Household Income and Expenditure Survey (1990–2010).

Security System (NBLSS)—was initiated straight after the Asian financial crisis of 1997, when the number of poor and unemployed had increased rapidly; thus, an expansion of the social safety net was urgently required. NBLSS is the largest income-transfer programme and it has had strong poverty-reducing effects, even though controversy persists over its labour-supply effects.

Old age pensions in 2010 accounted for only 1.82 per cent of GDP, which is a relatively low figure for the OECD countries. The immaturity of the public pension scheme and the relatively young population structure largely explain the low level of pension expenditure. Although Korea is one of the most rapidly ageing societies, it has a relatively young population structure compared to other developed countries. Because the national pension scheme was introduced in 1988, the proportion of pension recipients among the elderly population is still low, since there is a requirement to have at least 20 years of contributions. As a consequence, the old age poverty rate is about 45 per cent, the highest in the OECD countries. To counteract this problem, the Basic Old Age Pension was introduced in 2010 to provide means-tested benefits for 70 per cent of those aged 65 and over. However, the benefits are quite small—less than US$100 a month—and are fixed at 5 per cent of the average pre-retirement earnings of the claimant.

Korea's Employment Insurance System (EIS) and its unemployment benefits scheme (UB) were launched in 1995 and have undergone several refinements to reinforce their effectiveness as a safety net for the unemployed. During the last economic downturn, caused by the global financial crisis, more than 40 per cent of the unemployed in 2009 received benefits. Even though the monthly average number of UB recipients and the proportion of the unemployed who receive it have gradually increased since it was initiated, many workers with non-regular jobs in small companies are still not covered.

Table 18.3 Poverty-rate reduction effect, by income-transfer programme

Country	+ 0	+ Demo-grant	+ Pension	+ Unemployment benefits	+ Other social insurance benefits	+ Public assistance	+ Overall public income transfer
Korea	12.1	12.1	11.0	12.0	11.9	10.0	8.5
Germany	15.8	14.8	12.4	14.1	13.9	14.0	5.2
Sweden	17.3	16.4	16.2	14.5	8.8	15.8	3.0
UK	21.0	20.0	20.3	20.9	18.8	11.5	5.4

(Header span: Market income)

Note: Relative poverty = household with income below 40 per cent of the median income. Households included in the analysis are limited to those with heads aged between 15 and 64.

Source: Yeo and Song (2010). Original source: Korea's data from Welfare Panel Study 2008, data for other countries based on LIS data for mid 2000s.

Table 18.4 Subscription to and receipt of national pension by non–wage workers

	Employers	Self-employed small business owners	Total
Workplace-based subscribers	40.3	6.7	15.4
Region-based subscribers	33.2	34.7	34.3
Recipients (eligible persons)	4.8	14.3	11.9
Non-subscribers	21.8	44.3	38.4
Total (1,000 persons, %)	1493.7 (25.9%)	4265.9 (74.1%)	5759.6

Source: Korea National Statistical Office, Economically Active Population Survey Supplementary Survey, August 2009.

It is very important to understand why income inequality has increased in the last few decades in spite of the rapidly expanded social insurance and public assistance programmes. First, although it has increased in recent decades, the volume of social expenditure itself as a percentage of GDP is still inadequate: just 7.5 per cent in 2010. This is partly due to the fact that the public old age pension plan has not yet matured. The second and more noteworthy feature of public transfers is that they depend greatly on the social insurance system, under which low-income and high-risk populations are less likely to be covered (Chang, 2012a). In particular, national pension and employment insurance provide some income security, but the coverage of those two programmes is still low (people may be institutionally not covered, or else institutionally covered but actually not covered).

First, let us look at the self-employed (Table 18.4). Among all employed persons, wage workers account for about 70 per cent; the remaining 30 per cent consist of employers, the self-employed, unpaid family workers, and other non-wage workers. Social insurance contributions for wage workers (who contribute through the workplace) are split evenly between the employers and the employees, whereas non-wage workers (region-based subscribers) must shoulder 100 per cent of the contributions themselves. Employment insurance is not compulsory for the self-employed, and this has led to low take-up by self-employed people and the owners of very small businesses. The 2009 Supplementary Survey on Non-Wage Workers, conducted as part of the Economically Active Population Survey, had questions on the national-pension subscription and found that 21.8 per cent of employers and 44.3 per cent of business owners with no employees did not contribute to the national pension. We can surmise that in all likelihood the owners of very small businesses remain beyond the protective reach of the safety net that is provided through social insurance.

Wage workers, too, are sometimes overlooked, remaining unprotected by the social safety net (Table 18.5). Among all wage workers, 27.1 per cent do not contribute to the national pension, while for employment insurance the excluded and non-contributors account for 33.4 per cent of all wage workers. Lower-wage groups require more help from the social safety net provided by state welfare when they experience an interruption in their wage income,

Table 18.5 Wage worker social insurance subscription rates (%)

All		National pension (+special occupational pension)			Employment insurance			
		U	WB	CB	CS	S	Ex	U
Wage workers		27.1	65.6	7.3	7.7	58.9	8.6	24.8
Wage group	Low-wage	60.0	30.0	10.0	0.3	33.6	16.4	49.8
	Mid-wage	22.0	69.7	8.3	3.4	67.2	6.8	22.6
	High-wage	4.4	92.6	3.0	21.5	69.5	4.0	5.1
Employment type	Regular	16.8	78.6	4.6	10.9	67.2	1.5	20.4
	Irregular	48.0	39.3	12.7	1.3	42.1	22.8	33.9
	Contingent	31.7	60.9	7.4	2.1	63.8	12.3	21.9
	Part-time	81.4	8.4	10.2	0.7	10.0	37.6	51.7
	Atypical	57.8	21.4	20.8	0.1	28.1	36.8	35.1

Notes:

U = unsubscribed, WB = workplace-based, CB = community-based, CS = civil servants and others, Ex = legally excluded, S = subscribed.

For wage groups, 'low-wage' is less than two-thirds of the median hourly wage, 'high-wage' is at least 1.5 times the median value, and 'mid-wage' is between two-thirds and 1.5 times the value.

Irregular = contingent, part-time and atypical; Contingent = fixed-term and repeat contractual; Atypical = temporary employment agency, independent contractor, home-based and daily workers.

Data: National Statistics Korea, Economically Active Population Survey March 2010 (Supplementary Survey on Employment Type).

but the reality is that these groups are not able to subscribe to social insurance programmes. Of the low-wage workers who earn less than two-thirds of the median wage, 60 per cent are not covered by the national pension and 66.2 per cent are not protected by employment insurance.

Korea also introduced the earned income tax credit in 2008, in response to the growing number of working poor. Although it is still too early to evaluate its effects, since it is supposed to be extended in the future (e.g. to the self-employed in 2015), some researchers have argued that its poverty-reducing effect is not beneficial. Yoon (2012) maintains that the policy targeting is not accurate because the government is unable to determine income. According to the analysis of Cho *et al.* (2011), however, the reason for its ineffectiveness lies in its initial design—small in scope and with fairly low benefit levels. Its budget is only one-twentieth that of the National Basic Livelihood Security System, and it covers only a third as many people as the NBLSS.

In sum, although public transfers and taxation have worked positively to reduce income inequality in the past 15 years, the redistribution effect of social expenditure in Korea is far from adequate. In 2006, the Gini coefficients of market income and of disposable income for Korea were 0.368 and 0.311, respectively. After adding publicly transferred income to household market income and subtracting tax and social security contributions, the Gini coefficient is reduced by only 15 per cent in Korea, whereas in all Nordic and Western European countries the reduction is 40 per cent or more. Two reasons for the less effective redistribution policies can be identified. First, even though it has increased in past decades, the volume of social expenditure itself as a percentage of GDP remains inadequate. Second, public income transfers are disproportionately dependent on the social insurance system, which still lacks coverage. The low-income population is also less likely than others to be covered by social insurance.

6. CONCLUSION

A distinctive feature of Korean inequality is that labour market inequality has tended to be higher than household income inequality, for the simple reason that members of lower-income households have tended to have a greater level of economic participation. However, this tendency appears to have altered since the mid 1990s, when there was a reversal of inequality trends in Korea. Previously, Korea's high economic growth could alleviate inequality by creating jobs for low-income households; there was little need for social security. However, the jobs crisis and labour market dualization since 1997 and the Asian financial crisis have made this much more difficult.

Growing inequality has been driven by deteriorating labour market conditions (increased wage inequality among the heads of household), and inequality has worsened in the lower levels of income distribution. The expansion of educational opportunities (such as the unparalleled growth in enrolment to tertiary education) could no longer curb the increasing inequality.

Since the mid 1990s, growing inequality has been related to various economic and social changes. As well as the opening up of the economy and growing trade with China, the rise of information technology, changes in industrial organization and in the labour market, we have witnessed an increasing breakdown of the family, lower fertility and marriage rates, increasing suicide and crime rates, and reduced social mobility. All these factors are closely related to growing inequality in Korea. At this point, the social risks and social costs cannot be covered by the traditional mechanism of economic growth-driven job creation and expanding educational opportunities alone.

The traditional link between inequality and politico-cultural impacts has swung between path dependence and path shaping. In the face of growing inequality, since the 2000s the low-trust society has been sustained (at best) or has even got worse. Changes in the validity of inequality-management methods are most striking. The old model of inequality management—characterized by doing without strong social policies—is no longer workable. Korea will have to expand its social policies if rising inequality is to be addressed.

The Korean government did act after the 1997 crisis—by introducing and boosting public income assistance, launching a national pension programme, initiating unemployment insurance, and pursuing other policies like earned income tax credit. However, these policies have not been enough to hold down the rising inequality in the market, and very many people in need are still not covered by public policies either in principle or in reality. Therefore, it is essential not only to expand social expenditure, but also to improve the labour market. An important task facing the Korean government is to learn how to develop well-designed economic and social policies that combine an expansion of social programmes with the creation of 'good' jobs.

References

Ahn, Sanghoon, Kyoji, Fukao and Keiko, Ito (2007), 'Outsourcing in East Asia and Its Impact on the Japanese and Korean Labour Markets', *OECD Trade Policy Working Paper* 65.

Beck, Ulrich (1986), *Risikogesellschaft*, Frankfurt am Main: Suhrkamp.

Butterwegge, Christoph (2009), *Armut in einem reichen Land*, Frankfurt am Main: Campus.

Chang, Jiyeun (2012a), 'Labour Market Dualism and Social Insurance Coverage in Korea', *e-labour News* 119, Seoul: Korea Labour Institute.

Chang, Jiyeun (2012b), 'Level of Inequality According to Various Strata of Income Definition and Constituting Factors', *Trends and Outlooks* 85: 131–163 (in Korean).

Chen, Wen-Hao (2009), 'Cross-national Differences in Income Mobility: Evidence from Canada, the United States, Great Britain and Germany', *Review of Income and Wealth*, 55/1: 75–100 (in Korean).

Cho, Hee-Yeon (2007), *Park Chung-Hee and Developmental Dictatorship Era*, Seoul: Yeoksabipyeongsa (in Korean).

Cho, Hee-Yeon (2010), *Mobilized Modernization*, Seoul: Humanitas (in Korean).

Cho, Sujoo et. al. (2011), *Evaluation of EITC's Effects by Gender*, Seoul: Korea Women's Development Policy Institute.

Hong, Kyung Zoon (2004), 'Analyzing the Length of Poverty Spells', *Korean Journal of Social Welfare Studies* 24: 187–210 (in Korean).

Jung, Chang-Mu (2008), 'Exploring the Relationship Between Divorce Rate and Socio-Economic factors in Korea', *National Land Planning* 43/3: 81–90 (in Korean).

Jung, Ki Won (2004), 'Socioeconomic Conditions and Divorce Rate in Korea: An Analysis of Time-Series Data, 1970-2002', *Korean Population* 7/1: 57–80 (in Korean).

Kang, Shin-Wook (2011), 'Income Mobility of Urban Laborer Household of Korea Since 1990', *Studies of Economic Development* 17(1): 1–28 (in Korean).

Kim, Jin-Wook (2004), 'An Empirical Study on Income Transfer System in Korea: Focusing upon Income Inequality and Poverty Reduction Effects', *Social Welfare Policy* 20: 171–195 (in Korean).

Kim, Kyo-seong and Noh, Hye-jin (2009), 'An Empirical Study of Poverty Exit and Duration: Life Table Analysis and Hierarchical Generalized Linear Analysis', *Social Welfare Policy* 36: 185–212 (in Korean).

Kim, YoungMi and Shin, KwangYoung (2008), 'Labour Market Dualization of Marriage Female and Changes in Household Income Inequality', *Economy and Society* 77: 79–106 (in Korean).

Lee, Byunghee and Jung, Jaeho (2002), 'An Analysis of Poverty Structure, Repeat Poverty and its Relation to Employment', *Trends and Prospects* 52: 128–150 (in Korean).

Lee, Chul-Hee (2008), 'Rising Household Income Inequality: 1996-2000', *Korean Journal of Labour Economics*, 31/2: 1–34. (in Korean).

Lee, Keunbum (2009), Income Mobility in Korea, *Korean Studies of Economic Development*, 15(2), 55–77 (in Korean).

Linz Juan and Stepan, Alfred (1996), *Problems of Democratic Transition and Consolidation*, Baltimore: Johns Hopkins University Press.

Nahm, PyeongTak (2010), 'International Trade and Wage Inequality in Korea', *Journal of Economic Studies* 28/3: 253–278 (in Korean).

OECD (2008), *Growing Unequal? Income Distribution and Poverty in OECD countries*, Paris: OECD Publishing.

OECD (2011a), *Divided We Stand: Why Inequality Keeps Rising*, Paris: OECD Publishing.

OECD (2011b), *Society at a Glance 2011: OECD Social Indicators*, Paris: OECD Publishing.

Ok, Wooseok, Jeong Seeun and Oh Yonghyup (2007). 'Trade, International Division of Labour, Skill-Demand Structure and Wage Inequalities: With a Focus on the Korea-China Trade', *The Analyses of Korea's Economy* 13/3: 73–135 (in Korean).

Park, MyungHo (2012), *International Comparison of Characteristics of Top-Income Earners, Tax and Finance Brife*, Seoul: Korea Institute of Public Finance. (in Korean).

Park, Sunghoon, Jang Anshik and Lee, Jaekyung (2009), 'Social Changes and Crimes rates in Korea 1966-2007', *Social Studies* 18/2: 45–72. (in Korean).

Pirie, Iain (2008), *The Korean Developmental State*, London: Routledge.

Woo-Cumings, Meredith (ed.) (1999), *The Developmental State*, London: Cornell University Press.

World Bank (1993), *The East Asian Miracle*, Oxford: Oxford University Press.

Yang, Jaejin (2012), The Origin of Low Tax Rate and Tax Boost Politics in Korean Welfare State, presented paper in Joint Conference of Korean Social Policy 2012. Hansin University (in Korean).

Yeo, Yu-Jin (2009), 'Redistributive Effects of Public Transfer Programmes', *Korean Social Security Studies* 25: 45–68 (in Korean).

Yeo, Yu-Jin and Song, Chi-Ho (2010), 'Redistributive Effects of Public Transfer Programmes: A Cross-National Analysis', *Korean Social Security Studies* 26: 95-119 (in Korean).

Yoon, Heesook (2012), 'Problems of Welfare Decision Making Process; Case of EITC', *KDI foucs* 24 (in Korean).

CHAPTER 19

···

LUXEMBOURG: HAS INEQUALITY GROWN ENOUGH TO MATTER?[*]

···

ALESSIO FUSCO, PHILIPPE VAN KERM, AIGUL ALIEVA,

LUNA BELLANI, FANNY ETIENNE-ROBERT, ANNE-CATHERINE

GUIO, IRYNA KYZYMA, KRISTELL LEDUC, PHILIPPE LIÉGEOIS,

MARIA NOEL PI ALPERIN, ANNE REINSTADLER,

EVA SIERMINSKA, DENISA SOLOGON, PATRICK THILL,

MARIE VALENTOVA, AND BOGDAN VOICU

1. INTRODUCTION

···

LUXEMBOURG has experienced remarkable economic performance and employment growth since the middle of the 1980s. After the restructuring of the steel industry from the 1980s onwards, the primary engine of economic growth in Luxembourg was the financial sector, together with other service activities (e.g., in information and communication

[*] This book chapter was prepared by CEPS/INSTEAD for the 'Growing Inequalities' Impact (GINI)' FP7 research project funded by the European Commission. It was also supported by core funding from the Ministry of Higher Education and Research of Luxembourg and by the Luxembourg Fonds National de la Recherche through funding of FNR CORE projects *PersiPov* for A. Fusco, *WealthPort* for E. Sierminska and *InWin* for P. Van Kerm and through AFR Doc and Post-Doc Grants for L. Bellani, I. Kyzyma and D. Sologon. This Chapter derives from a GINI country report in which further details or elements not covered in the present chapter can be found. The authors would like to thank Tom Dominique, John Haas, Vincent Hildebrand, Jérôme Hury, Serge Krippler, Julien Licheron, Caroline Lieffrig, Guillaume Osier, Günther Schmaus, Marianne Scholl, Michèle Wolter and Paul Zahlen for their help in gathering statistical or background information or retrieving them from miscellaneous data sources. In addition, comments by Jacques Brosius, Reinhard Pollak, Donald Williams, Sonja Zmerli,

technologies). Between 1985 and 2007, the average annual GDP growth in Luxembourg (5.3 per cent) was more than twice as high as that of the EU15 area (2.3 per cent) (Zahlen, 2012a). The average annual growth over the period 2008–2011 has however been zero, the same as the EU15 average (Zahlen, 2012a).

According to the International Monetary Fund (2000) or Schuller (2002), the key factors explaining this economic success are a central location in Europe, a stable political and social environment and a multilingual and skilled domestic labour force. In addition, successive governments put in place a favourable fiscal and regulatory framework that attracted foreign financial institutions and investors, laying the foundations for the creation of the international financial centre for which Luxembourg is known. This positive situation created a virtuous circle (Annaert, 2004). High growth generated high revenues from corporate taxes which allowed Luxembourg to maintain low levels of income taxation, to contain real labour costs at acceptable levels and to keep excellent public finances. In turn this constituted the roots of a generous Welfare State.

Following the crisis in the steel industry in the 1970s, Luxembourg experienced a phase of stagnation and a decline in its employment. It is only since the mid 1980s that employment has known an exceptional growth with significant structural changes. Labour demand in the industry declined while the service sector began an exceptional development. Domestic labour supply soon failed to match demand. The country needed to attract foreign labour and, since 1985, the share of migrants and cross-border workers (residing in France, Belgium and Germany) increased continually. Luxembourg now has an unusual domestic labour force composed of three large groups: Luxembourg nationals; foreign national resident workers; and non-resident cross-border workers (Berger, 2005). At the end of the 2000s, cross-border workers represented 43.8 per cent of domestic employment. However, since cross-border workers are not covered by the sampling frame of national survey data on income, they will not be analysed here: it is inequality *among residents* that is considered in this chapter.

The high level of migration is one of the main distinguishing characteristics of Luxembourg. The share of foreign residents in total employment has been fairly constant between 1994 and 2011 (28.1 per cent and 26.9 per cent) while the share of foreign residents in the population increased from 26.3 per cent to 43 per cent between 1981 and 2011 (Zahlen, 2012b). The percentage of foreigners in the total population is the highest among OECD countries. Different types of migrants joined the country at different points in time. As mentioned by Alieva (2010), Luxembourg had (as many other European Union (EU) countries did) an active labour migration policy until the 1970s, which resulted in a high inflow of low-skill migrants, mainly from Southern Europe. This has formed a large proportion of today's second- and third-generation immigrant population. Finally, there is an intensified highly-skilled migration, which followed the development of the financial sector, the installation of EU institutions and more recently, the European Union enlargement. Migrants are nowadays mainly European, young, highly skilled, in good health and with high employment rates. All these inflows have generated a highly heterogeneous immigrant population with heterogeneous earnings capacity, which impacts the income distribution in complex ways.

one anonymous referee and the GINI core teams are gratefully acknowledged. None of these persons should, however, be held responsible in any way for the results and views presented in this chapter.

The high economic growth in Luxembourg over the period 1985–2010 led to a massive increase in the average living standards of the resident population (Osier, 2012). The median net income per adult equivalent is now the highest among European countries. But according to the OECD (2011a, 2012), during the same period, income inequality increased too. Even if the level of inequality is still low by international standards, this trend is a potential source of concern if, as argued, e.g., in Wilkinson and Pickett (2009), inequality has detrimental impacts on individual outcomes such as health or education or creates the conditions for insecurity and distrust that might lead to social or political conflict. The purpose of this chapter is to document trends in inequality in Luxembourg across various dimensions and to link these trends to social and political developments. The Luxembourg case is interesting in this respect because alongside the rising dispersion of incomes, levels of living have increased substantially. The question is then whether the positive effects linked to the increase of overall living standards (and also the development of effective welfare institutions that it helped finance), have prevailed over the potential negative effects of the increase in income inequality when considering the evolution of a set of social outcomes.

This chapter is organized as follows. Section 2 documents trends in several dimensions of inequality. Section 3 considers the potential social impacts of the observed inequality trends while Section 4 considers political and cultural impacts. Section 5 discusses the effectiveness of policies in combating inequality, while Section 6 concludes.

2. THE EVOLUTION OF INCOME AND EDUCATIONAL INEQUALITIES

Income Inequality Trends

We document trends in income inequality from the *Socio-Economic Panel 'Liewen zu Lëtzebuerg'* (PSELL). This representative household survey is based on the annual collection of data on income and living conditions of individuals and private households residing in the Grand Duchy of Luxembourg. PSELL consists of three independent and consecutive panels: PSELL1 (1985–1994), PSELL2 (1995–2002) and PSELL3/EU–SILC (2003 onwards).

We use here the harmonized version of the data included in the *Luxembourg Income Study* (LIS) database for the years 1985, 1991, 1994, 1997, 2000, and 2004 and original PSELL3/EU-SILC data for 2010.[1] We focus on the resident population and the unit of analysis is the individual. Despite efforts at data harmonization, trends over time must be interpreted cautiously. Differences in underlying data (PSELL1 vs. PSELL2 vs. PSELL3/EU-SILC) are likely associated with variations in the sampling frame, in data collection

[1] The first three years are covered by PSELL1, the following two by PSELL2 and the other by PSELL3/EU-SILC (see Allegrezza et al, 2004). Note that, in PSELL1 and PSELL2, only incomes net of income taxes and social security contributions are recorded so that each component is also net. The implications are that household disposable income is the sum of net income from labour, net income from capital and net transfers. The impact of tax policy on inequality cannot be assessed. By contrast, both gross amounts and net amounts are collected in PSELL3/EU-SILC. In that case, household disposable income is the sum of gross components minus taxes and social contributions.

Table 19.1 Income inequality 1985 to 2010

	1985	1991	1994	1997	2000	2004	2010
Average real household net income, 2005 prices	28700	45000	46950	47000	50200	57100	56700
Gini Coefficient	0.233	0.234	0.233	0.259	0.264	0.271	0.276
Theil index generalised entropy (parameter=1)	0.091	0.096	0.091	0.115	0.118	0.129	0.137
generalised entropy (parameter=2)	0.104	0.121	0.103	0.141	0.141	0.170	0.191
generalised entropy (parameter=0)	0.089	0.089	0.088	0.111	0.113	0.124	0.130
p90/p50	1.732	1.710	1.724	1.782	1.908	1.809	1.798
p10/p50	0.617	0.608	0.601	0.569	0.582	0.537	0.535
poverty rate (in %)	8.6	9.6	9.8	12.3	11.7	13.5	14.5

Source: LIS (1985-2004) and PSELL3/EU-SILC (2010) data, authors' computation. Negative income values or values equal to zero have been excluded from all computations. Poverty threshold is set at 60 per cent of the median equivalent income. Inequality indicators are based on single-adult equivalent income (modified OECD equivalence scale).

methods and/or in details of income components definitions. While income data in the LIS dataset are constructed according to harmonized definitions, such ex post construction may not fully control for differences in underlying data collection, especially in the early period of analysis. Our conclusions about trends in inequality are therefore based on changes *within* the three periods covered by different data instruments rather than *between* the three periods.

The high economic growth over the period 1985–2010 led to an increase in average living standards. According to computation from the LIS and PSELL3/EU-SILC data (see Table 19.1), average household real disposable income (in 2005 prices) increased from €28700 in 1985 to €56700 in 2010. The increase in real household average income was steep between 1985 and 1991, which was a period of high economic growth; it was then regular between 1991 and 2004, and remained stable afterwards until 2009 before a small decline afterwards (see also Osier, 2012).

Between 1985 and 1994, which is the period covered by the PSELL1 dataset, income inequality was stable. Between 1997 and 2000, the period covered by PSELL2, income inequality increased. A further increase in inequality occurred from 2004 onwards, the period covered by PSELL3/EU-SILC. Overall, comparison of the inequality level of 2010 with that of 1985 suggests that inequality increased substantially in Luxembourg, as reported by OECD (2011a). Yet given the important caveat of the jumps *between* survey instruments (between PSELL1 and PSELL2 in particular), the reliability of such an estimate of the magnitude of the total increase is open to question. Nevertheless, the observation of an increasing trend in inequality is confirmed if we consider the inequality changes *within* each sub-period, specifically during the period covered by PSELL2 and PSELL3/EU-SILC.

Income source decomposition analysis (see Country Report) reveals that the relative contribution of paid employment income to total inequality increased over time. This reflects major labour market evolutions: (i) the expansion of the high-wage financial sector;[2] (ii) an increase in the female employment rate, mainly married women; as well as (iii) an increase in earnings inequality (see Country Report). The increase in earnings inequality is corroborated by the evolution of hourly wage inequality estimated from administrative data from the General Inspectorate of Social Security in Luxembourg (IGSS). According to this alternative source (which also covers cross-border workers), wage inequality measured by the Theil index for the entire working population in Luxembourg increased by around 20 per cent between 1988 and 2009.[3] The recent upward trend in the unemployment rate also coincided with a period of increasing inequality. Finally, changing educational inequalities and the change in skills required by the structural change from a heavy industry based society to a high value-added service society also influenced income inequality (as discussed below).

Educational Inequality

The share of highly educated residents has been increasing significantly over time: more men and women have a tertiary degree (22 per cent in 2010 vs. 5 per cent in 1985) while the share of less educated residents remained stable. As in other post-industrial societies, women appear to have benefited most from this educational expansion. The rapid increase in tertiary education was also fuelled by the immigration of highly skilled workers.

The earlier immigration wave in Luxembourg attracted mostly manual workers with a lower educational level while recent immigrants are more likely to be highly educated and are filling professional and managerial positions. The distribution of educational skills among the adult population according to individuals' citizenship therefore changed dramatically over time. As underlined by Amétépé and Hartmann-Hirsch (2011), the share of highly qualified foreigners is currently higher than the share of highly qualified nationals.[4] However, the share of immigrants with low educational levels remains high, resulting in a heterogeneous population with very different human capital and earnings capacity. This is reflected in much higher within-group wage inequality among immigrants than among Luxembourg nationals or even among cross-border workers (see Country Report).

---

[2] For example, the OECD (2012:43–4) evaluated that 'a one percent rise of the share of the financial sector among the working population increases the interdecile gap by 0.3 per cent in Luxembourg as in many other countries'. In 2010, this sector represented 11 per cent of the overall employment in Luxembourg compared to a 3 per cent average in the Euro area.

[3] The impact of the cross-border workers on the overall income distribution cannot easily be evaluated since, by definition, cross-border workers are not part of the population among which income inequality is assessed. Yet, they impact the labour market. Also, the contribution of both migrants and cross-border workers to the tax system is high given their high employment rate, which contributed to maintaining a low level of personal income taxation and social contributions and, in turn, to build and expand a generous welfare system for all residents. On the other hand, the age structure of the migrants and cross-border workers implies that most of them are not entitled yet to pensions and that their need, say, in healthcare is on average lower.

[4] Amétépé and Hartmann-Hirsch (2011:200) even suggest that there could be 'a reversal of the usual hierarchical relations between nationals and migrants, with a group of highly qualified foreigners and foreign managers positioned above the national elite'.

Unsurprisingly, with positive and substantial labour market returns to education, educational, earnings and income inequality followed correlated trends. The increase in the share of highly educated residents from the 1990s onwards, fuelled by the inflow of highly skilled migrants, corresponded to the period of increase in inequality in both household equivalent income and wage inequality.

Intergenerational Transmission

Over the longer term, intergenerational transmission mechanisms appear to be factors for sustained inequality in Luxembourg. Family background has been shown to be an important determinant of wealth inequality, especially through inheritance (see Country Report). Recent research by the OECD (2010a) shows that Luxembourg has one of the highest correlations between characteristics of parents and the income of the descendants. The penalty for growing up in a less educated family in Luxembourg is found to be around 16 per cent relative to wages earned by individual raised in a better-educated family. Educational achievements are also strongly correlated to family background in the country and the situation of youth currently at school raises concerns about the persistence of inequalities in the long run. Results from the OECD PISA 2000 study of 15-year old students revealed that the average student performance is below OECD average, with significant gaps persisting for families with lower educational, economic, and cultural resources.

The education system in Luxembourg, as e.g. in Germany, is based on early tracking: after primary school, children are assigned to various educational tracks on the basis of their academic record and teachers' recommendation. Another crucial condition, which makes the Luxembourgish system particularly rigid, is fluency in both languages of instruction: German and French. Therefore, transition from primary to secondary school becomes decisive for future educational and occupational outcomes, of which 11-year-old children are not likely to be fully aware (see also OECD, 2010b, 2012).

Research has documented that stratified educational systems are more likely to reinforce socio-economic inequalities, and the OECD PISA 2009 results reported in Figure 19.1 support these findings. With the exception of Hungary, it is countries with differentiated school programmes that have stronger associations between achievement and family background.

OECD (2012) also stresses that students from disadvantaged families in Luxembourg are more likely to attend schools with fewer educational resources, schools that experience teacher shortages, or schools with a lower share of teachers with tertiary education (OECD 2012).

As a result, Luxembourg has among the lowest share of resilient students—those who are in the bottom quarter of the PISA index of economic, social and cultural status and perform in the top quarter across students from all countries after accounting for socio-economic background. Immigrant-origin students in Luxembourg frequently come from disadvantaged background—according to PISA 2009 76.8 per cent of 15-year-old immigrant students are at the bottom of the socio-economic scale. The difference from other countries is immense, with Switzerland being the second country with highest share (44 per cent).

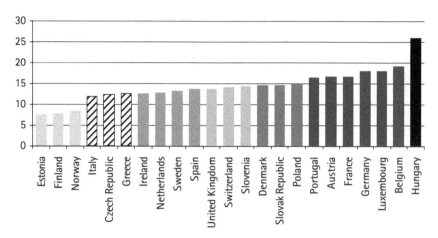

FIGURE 19.1 Proportion of variance in PISA 2009 test explained by social, cultural, and educational resources of family

Source: OECD 2010b.

3. SOCIAL IMPACTS

In this section, we analyse whether the increasing trend in income inequality observed over the period 1985 to 2010 has been correlated with the trend of a set of social outcomes, namely material deprivation, health, life satisfaction, criminality and generalized trust.

Life Satisfaction

According to data from the European Values Study (EVS), between 1999 and 2008 the level of happiness was stable and high: more than 90 per cent of the Luxembourgish residents considered themselves at least 'quite happy'. Eurobarometer data provide a long term perspective on the evolution of life satisfaction in Luxembourg. Since the beginning of the 1980s, life satisfaction has been fairly stable at a high level. On average, the proportion of individuals at least fairly satisfied is higher than 90 per cent. Peaks occurred in 1991 and 2004 when more than 50 per cent of the population declared themselves very satisfied. Over the period, the proportion of individuals not at all satisfied remained very low. The analysis of this first social outcome suggests that the modest increase in inequality did not substantially affect the level of happiness and life satisfaction in Luxembourg.

Material Deprivation

In order to complement the income poverty figures and to better reflect differences in actual standards of living, the EU portfolio of commonly agreed social indicators includes measures of material deprivation (MD), conceived as an enforced lack of a combination of nine items depicting material living conditions (see e.g. Fusco, Guio and Marlier, 2011). On the basis of the EU Statistics on Income and Living Conditions (EU-SILC), the standard MD rate is defined as the proportion of people living in households who cannot afford at least 3 of the 9 items.[6] Severe MD is defined as the proportion of people living in households who cannot afford at least 4 of the 9 items.

A low proportion of individuals suffer from deprivation in Luxembourg, i.e. around 4 per cent lack 3 items or more, and less than 1 per cent lack 4 items or more. At the EU level, in 2010, these percentages reach 17.4 per cent (standard MD) and 8.1 per cent (severe MD), respectively.[7]

The increase in inequality over the period does not seem to be correlated with an increase of material deprivation. This is unsurprising since the items of material deprivation included in the EU measure capture absolute levels of resources. The low average level of material deprivation hides some diversity between population subgroups, however (with immigrant sub-populations observed in less favourable situations; see Hildebrand et al., 2012).

Health

The health status of the population improved over the last three decades. Life expectancy at birth increased steadily from 75.6 years in 1980 to 83.5 years in 2010 for women, and from 70 years up to 77.9 years for men. In 1998, men's life expectancy in Luxembourg (73.7) was lower than that of the Euro zone average (74.7) while in 2009, it was higher (78.1 vs 77.8). Since 2004, statistics on 'healthy life expectancy' (HLE) have been available. The HLE indicator shows that, in 2010, a man could expect to spend 64.5 years (of the 77.9 years of his life) without activity limitations due to health problems (this represents 83 per cent of his total life). For women, the life expectancy in good health is 66 years (79 per cent of total years of life expected at birth). Between 2004 and 2010 men gained five years of life expectancy free of health limitations, compared to nearly six years for women. The increase in life expectancy in good health between 2004 and 2010 is faster than the increase in total life expectancy, so that the share of healthy life in the lives of individuals is also growing. Individuals live not only longer but also live healthier lives, despite the increase in income inequality.

The number of deaths per 100,000 residents in Luxembourg has decreased drastically from 1500.4 (1533) in 1980 to 768.8 (812.6) in 2009 for women (men). This decrease can be associated with more efficient treatments, a better social security system and disease prevention campaigns, as well as with the inflow of a relatively young immigrant population.

The perception of individuals about the quality of their health also improved over time.[8] In general terms, the percentage of individuals considering their health status as good or better has increased between 1996 and 2010. During the whole period (from 1996 to 2010),

---

[6] The nine items depicting material living conditions are the ability to: 1) face unexpected expenses; 2) afford one week annual holiday away from home; 3) pay for arrears (mortgage or rent, utility bills or hire purchase instalments); 4) afford a meal with meat, chicken or fish every second day; 5) keep the home adequately warm; 6) have a washing machine; 7) have a colour TV; 8) have a telephone; 9) have a personal car.

[7] On the same ground, the level of housing deprivation was globally stable during the recent period and far less problematic than at the EU level.

[8] Assessment is made on the basis of answers to the following question: 'How is your health in general? "Very good," "Good," "Fair," "Bad" or "Very bad"' (OECD, 2011b).

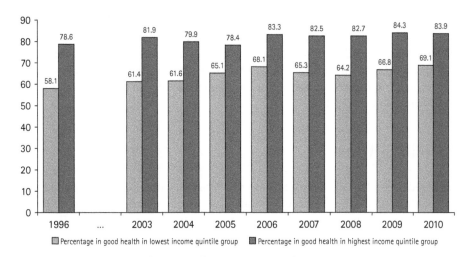

FIGURE 19.2 Perceived health status by income quintile

Source: OECD (2011b), OECD Health Data: Selected Data, OECD Health Statistics (database).

the percentage of men declaring their health as being good or better is higher for males than females. However, this gap is being reduced over time.

An income gradient in self-reported health is observed (see Figure 19.2). When dividing the residents of Luxembourg by income quintiles, the proportion of individuals belonging to the richest quintile declaring that their health status good or better (83.9 per cent in 2010) is higher than the proportion of individuals belonging to the poorest quintile (69.1 per cent). This gap is however declining over time from 1996 (78.6 per cent for the highest quintile versus 58.1 per cent for the lowest quintile) and 2003 (81.9 per cent versus 61.4 per cent).

Besides these favourable health outcomes, there is a concern regarding the increasing trend in being overweight and in obesity. Being overweight (defined as a BMI between 25 and 30 kg/m^2) has increased among females (resp. males) from 22.8 per cent (37.9 per cent) in 1997 to 28.3 per cent (43.5 per cent) in 2011. Obesity (defined as a BMI of 30 kg/m^2 or more) has increased from 14.9 per cent (14.8 per cent) to 22 per cent (24.7 per cent) for females (males). These indicators are alarming since obesity is associated with a higher risk of developing different types of health problems such as certain types of cancer, heart diseases, stroke and diabetes (Pi Alperin and Berzosa, 2011).[9]

Crime and Punishment

The total number of crimes recorded by the police initially decreased from 1994 on but rose dramatically between 2001 and 2005. This increase is mainly linked to drug trafficking.

---

[9] Since 1995, the percentage of individuals with none or only a primary school level having some degree of overweight is more important than for those having secondary or post-secondary studies. In 2008, 66.8 per cent, 53.8 per cent and 44 per cent of individuals with none or primary, secondary, and post-secondary level of school are overweight or obese, respectively.

Following a similar pattern, the number of individuals in prison increased from around 400 in 1993 to almost 700 in 2009. In 1999, the prison population per 100,000 thousand inhabitants was 90.3 and it increased to 137.6 per 100,000 inhabitants in 2009. This increase is directly linked to the increase in the number of crimes—especially drug trafficking. The steep increase in crime records does not seem to be associated with the slow inequality trend observed in income inequality.[9]

Generalized Trust

Generalized trust, although among the lowest in Western Europe, is relatively high as compared to other parts of the World. The overall image therefore includes average to high levels of social capital expressed by membership in associations and social trust. They exist in a multicultural environment, which is also shaped by large immigrant stocks. Figure 19.3 provides information on the evolution of social trust as recorded by two measures.[10] The left hand side indicates no difference in 2008 as compared to 1986, although the numbers for 1999 indicate slightly lower levels of trust. The right-hand side of the figure indicates a marginal increase of social trust in 2007 as compared to 2003 and 2004, followed by a reversion towards initial values in 2010, probably under the impact of economic recession.

As elsewhere, better-educated and higher-income people display higher levels of trust. From this point of view, Luxembourg is no different from other societies (Paxton, 2007). Looking at differences within the local society, it is striking that immigrants' level of trust is higher as compared to the natives, and the relative difference is one of the largest in Western Europe (Voicu, 2012). EVS 2008 data indicate that 27 per cent of the natives in Luxembourg display trust in others, according to the dichotomous measurement. The corresponding figure for foreign-born residents is 34 per cent.

This may raise some questions about the sources of social trust in Luxembourg, particularly when considering the country's high ethnic heterogeneity. On the one hand, Blau's theory of intergroup relations (Blau and Schwartz, 1984) implies that when in contact with various different groups, there will be more gratifications to develop cross-group relations. Such relations are said to build trust (Putnam, 2001). Apparently, Luxembourg does not fit this description, which leads to Putnam's (2007) 'hunkering down' hypothesis on the disruptive effects of fractionalization on social trust. However, such effects appear only under specific conditions, including high segregation (Uslaner, 2011) or high-income inequality (Kesler and Bloemraad, 2010). Luxembourg is quite far from being segregated. The increase in inequality in the past decades is not followed by decreasing levels of generalized trust, as

---

[9] Note that a break in the series occurred between 2004 and 2009 (see http://epp.eurostat.ec.europa.eu/statistics_explained/images/archive/3/3a/20121214153659!Prison_population%2C_1999-2009.png. Last accessed February 15, 2013).

[10] Social trust is differently measured in different surveys. The most common measures are the dichotomous item ('most people can be trusted' vs. 'can't be too careful in dealing with people') or using a 10-point scale with the two choices from the dichotomous item as labels for the ends of the scale. In Luxembourg, the dichotomous item was applied in the 1999 and 2008 waves of the value surveys, as well as in the 1986 Eurobarometer. The ten-point scale is part of ESS02-2004, of the Eurobarometer 74.1 (August-September 2010), and of the EQLS waves from 2003 and 2007 (EQLS 2011 data will be available in spring 2013). Although the measures are not fully comparable, we use both of them in order to be able to assess existing trends.

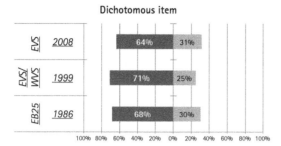

Dichotomous item

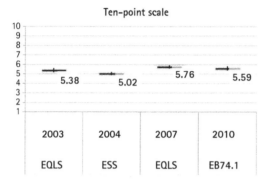

Ten-point scale

FIGURE 19.3 Dynamics of social trust

Source: Eurobarometer, European Social Survey and European Quality of Life Survey (see footnote 10).

the above data show. In addition, the stock of immigrants has continuously risen, but generalized trust has not decreased.

Summary

Luxembourg is a special case in terms of social impacts. We started this section by asking whether the positive effects linked to the increase of overall living standards, but also of the development of generous welfare institutions, have prevailed over the potential negative effects of the moderate increase in income inequality when considering the evolution of a set of social outcomes. To date, the increase in income inequality does not seem to have had a strong impact on most of the social outcomes considered in this project. Material deprivation in Luxembourg is among the lowest in Europe, generalized trust maintained its level, the level of happiness and life satisfaction is stable at high levels and the overall level of health has improved. The outcomes that worsened over time are obesity, the level of crimes and of population imprisoned, which has only recently increased. Overall, the results suggest that the moderate increase in inequality in Luxembourg over the last decades was not high enough to matter in this country, given the increase of the overall living standards.

4. POLITICAL AND CULTURAL IMPACTS

After social outcomes, this section considers trends in political or cultural indicators, in particular political and civic participation, confidence in institutions, political values and attitudes towards the welfare state.

Political and Civic Participation

Political stability in Luxembourg is an important asset. Over the past four decades the conservative party has almost always provided the Prime Minister, the shares of votes for the right and left have been virtually unchanged, and participation in voting, as compared to registered voters, has remained the same. However, an increasing part of the population—the non-citizens—has no right to vote in national elections, and seems reluctant to participate in local elections either.[11]

As in most European countries, membership of labour unions declined over the past four decades. However, in the Luxembourg case, the decrease was quite smooth. Currently, union coverage is 37 per cent of wage and salary earners. This is much lower than in Scandinavian countries or Belgium, but is higher than in almost all other EU member states. The labour unions negotiate contractual conditions for a little under two-thirds of the total wage or salary earners.

Luxembourg is one of the countries in Europe with the highest civic participation. Half of the adult population is a member of at least one voluntary association. There is a stable trend of a slight decrease in participation in traditional associations (political parties, religious organizations, trade unions), but it is compensated by the growing presence of newer associations and social movements. Participation is higher among the better-educated and better-off Luxembourgers, reflecting a regularity to be found in most societies (Wilson, 2000). The same pattern is found when analysing data from the beginning of the 2000s (Lejealle, 2003).

---

[11] In Luxembourg, voting in national elections is compulsory for all citizens. As compared to registered electors, since 1945, the national voter turnout remains stable around 90 per cent. This is only slightly lower than the similar figure for Belgium, where voting is also mandatory. If considering all residents of voting age, the turnout has fallen sharply since 1960s. The peak was registered in 1959, then in 1974, when 74 per cent of the residents expressed their option during national elections. Since then, there is an obvious negative trend. The high immigration flow combined with the residency of EU nationals has led to such a decline. The voting age population increased much more sharply as compared to registered voters, and the impact is reflected in electoral participation. Luxembourg faces today the risk of a turnout of less than 50 per cent. This might be seen paradoxical in a country where participation to voting is reinforced by law, and contributes to high discrepancies in rights between citizens and non-citizen residents.

Confidence in Institutions

Confidence in institutions was stable over the past decade and is remarkably high compared to other European countries, particularly when considering political institutions. The long-term stability of political systems, lack of major scandals, and low corruption make Luxembourgers one of the most trustful of Europeans when considering their political parties, and the executive and the legislative branches. In 2010s, only Scandinavia and the Netherlands had as high levels of confidence in these three institutions. The dynamic seems to have no connection with the evolution of inequality. Instead, it follows the same pattern to be found elsewhere (Tufiş, 2012): confidence in institutions is boosted immediately after elections and falls during the electoral cycle.[12]

Luxembourg is a founding member of the EU. European integration is beneficial for the country. It offers a way to become a cross-border metropolis (Sohn, 2012) providing easier access to the labour force in neighbouring countries (mainly France, Germany and Belgium). Various incoming migration waves, mainly from European countries, shaped the Luxembourgish social composition (Fetzer, 2011). A common European space allows faster connections to the origin country, particularly for the important communities of Portuguese and (second generation) Italians. On the other hand, EU regulations were not easy to accommodate for the banking industry, which for a long while was the main local resource. Troubles in the European economy and financial market are reflected in the decreasing trend of confidence in supranational institutions. However, high confidence in EU institutions is enduring (see also below).

Political Values and Legitimacy

Luxembourgers exhibit strong support for democracy as a way to organize society. According to the 2008 EVS wave, 59 per cent rejected authoritarian leaders, 50 per cent rejected technocratic governance, 93 per cent rejected army rule, and 85 per cent supported democracy as the best system for governance. As compared to EVS/WVS 1999, the figures reflect a slight tendency to increased support for democracy and to consider the mentioned alternatives as bad. This makes the Grand Duchy closer to Western Europe average attitudes. Considering the 2008 data, support for democracy is higher when education is higher, and lower when income is lower. Being a native or immigrant makes no significant difference when considering supporting democracy.

In many Western countries, the cultural shift towards post-modern values and the globalization has triggered retreats towards traditional values in some groups, and led to the rise of extreme-right parties in the 1990s (Ignazi, 2006). This was not the case in Luxembourg, where building the EU (and slightly weakening the national sovereignty) and hosting more and more immigrants was done in an era of increasing growth. The second half of the 1900s was prosperous enough to maintain low unemployment and to lead to levels of GDP per capita much higher than anywhere in the EU.

[12] This level of confidence is valid for other institutions as well. See Country Report.

EU membership approval has always been strong in Luxembourg. It has fluctuated between 70 per cent and 85 per cent in the last four decades with no noticeable trend, except for a smooth decline during recession. The attitudes towards the EU should also be considered in the context of Luxembourg as a multi-ethnic nation, with a society that incorporates a high number of immigrants, many of them born in other EU countries.

In 1999, 48 per cent of Luxembourgish respondents to the EVS/WVS considered that when jobs are scarce employers should give priority to Luxembourgish people over immigrants. The figure was among the lowest in Europe and the world, the Grand Duchy's tolerance being next just to Sweden, Denmark and the Netherlands. The EVS 2008 figure is 41 per cent. Only 8 per cent in 1999, and 14 per cent in 2008, mentioned immigrants and foreign workers among undesirable neighbours, placing Luxembourg among the most tolerant societies in Europe. Older, lower educated, and native people tend to be less tolerant, but even in their cases, the share of those avoiding immigrants as neighbours is no larger than 20 per cent using 2008 data. The pre-War tradition of attracting immigrants, particularly Italians and Germans at the beginning of the twentieth century (Fetzer, 2011; Scuto, 2012), has continued. Portuguese is the main nationality to set up here, but asylum seekers have also been numerous. Their flow peaks at 2000 refugees in 1993, and 4600 persons in 1999 (Blau, 2005). One may notice that incoming migration is mostly European, i.e. easier to integrate, and less different as compared to the native population. This may also contribute to the lower impact of extreme-right parties (Golder, 2003).

Frequent contact with both cross-border workers and immigrants could lead to more tolerant values and attitudes (Blau and Schwartz, 1984). Considering all marriages involving Luxembourgish citizens, the share of mixed ones (a spouse is Luxembourgish, the other is of another nationality) in the total number of marriages involving at least a Luxembourgish was 9 per cent at the beginning of the 1990s, and increased to 19 per cent in 2003 and to more than a third (34 per cent) in 2008 (own computations based on Blau, 2005 and STATEC, 2010). At the same time, considering the marriages in which at least one partner is not Luxembourgish, the share of those involving a Luxembourgish spouse is currently 51 per cent (it used to be 60–70 per cent during the 1970s and 1980s, when the number of immigrants was low, and 37–40 per cent in the early 1990s, after the 1986 relaxation of naturalization laws, when many immigrants received Luxembourgish nationality). One should also consider that many of the Luxembourgish spouses are in fact second-generation migrants. However, their number is large enough to offer hints of a relative tolerance to immigrants.

Prosperity, a tradition of receiving immigrants, the fact that incoming migration has consisted mainly of Europeans, as well as the presence of a mild nationalism promoted by the smallest mainstream party meant that extreme-right activities have lacked popular support in the past four decades. The extreme-left was virtually non-existent except for a short while during the 1970s.

Attitudes to Social Policy and the Welfare State

When asking individuals 'Why are there people in this country who live in need?', the EVS data show that the perception of the main drivers behind being in need have changed between 1999 and 2008. In concrete terms, in 2008 there are fewer people who consider luck as the most important reason for being in need than in 1999. The percentage dropped from 32.4 per cent in 1999 to 24.5 per cent in 2008. On the other hand, we observe a growing tendency to see people in need as an inevitable element of modern society, thus as something that cannot be avoided. The percentage indicating this in 1999 was 18.1 per cent of respondents, whereas in 2008 it was 24.1 per cent.

EVS also provides information on what people think about the distribution of income and about the individual's as against state's responsibility to provide for themselves. The results of our analysis reveal that, in 2008, the Luxembourg residents tended to agree slightly more with the statement pleading for a more equal distribution of income than they did in 1999. The difference between 1999 and 2008 concerning the people's views on the individual's responsibility to provide for themselves was negligible. It became also apparent that, in general, Luxembourg residents support the arguments for individual responsibility more than the belief that incomes should be made more equal.

Summary

The increase in inequality seems mostly unrelated to the issues that we have described in this section. Political and civic participation, confidence in institutions, support for extreme parties all changed their levels or maintained the same intensity independently of changes in income distribution, in educational attainment, or of the increasing share of immigrants. The same is true for approval of the EU and attitudes toward immigrants. The main driver here seems to be perceived prosperity, which remained stable and unaffected by inequality dynamics and the increasing share of immigrants in the country. In fact, the immigrants, mostly European and better educated than immigrants to other European countries, may have also prevented a deterioration in social cohesion and support for democracy which might otherwise have been triggered by the slight increase in inequality levels.

5. POLICY

In this section, we finally analyse the way in which policies may have contributed to shaping the trend in income inequality, upward or downward. To this end, we present time series on policy variables related to economic inequality, especially income inequality.

Wage Policy

The Luxembourg labour market is one of the most regulated within OECD countries (Hartmann-Hirsch, 2010). Bargaining processes between social partners (trade and employer unions) have shaped wages considerably. Bargaining at corporate, tripartite or—more recently—through bipartite meetings with a single social partner and the government, is not only part of what is often referred to as Luxembourg's social model (Allegrezza et al, 2003; Thill, Thomas 2009), but is also embedded in a legal framework dating back to the steel crisis in the 1970s when tripartite instruments were designed as a means of tackling unemployment and restoring competitiveness. This model constituted an element in Luxembourg's successful transition from a steel industry-based economy to a financial industry-based one, since it provided a consensual decision-making environment.

Luxembourg is one of the few countries that still uses a full and automatic linking of salaries to changes in prices (STATEC, 2003) similar to that applied to wages in Belgium.[13] Luxembourg also has a high statutory minimum wage, which is tied to inflation. Figure 19.4 displays its evolution relative to mean and median earnings of full-time employees. Minimum wages increased over time and remained between 30 per cent and 35 per cent of the mean wage of full-time employees, thereby providing an evolving 'floor' that compressed the bottom of the wage distribution.

Taxation

Taxes have a considerable impact on final disposable household income, and hence income inequality. Tax revenue as a share of GDP in Luxembourg experienced little fluctuation between 1990 and 2010. During a first period, the burden increased from 33.4 per cent in 1991 up to 39.7 per cent in 2001. Then, the share of tax revenue in GDP was reduced, reaching 35.5 per cent in 2009, before rising again. On average over the 1990–2010 period, the tax burden was comparable in Luxembourg (37.2 per cent of GDP) and Germany (36.3 per cent), but lower compared to Belgium (43.8 per cent) and France (43.5 per cent).

The composition of the tax burden remained fairly stable over the 1990–2010 period. Luxembourg has in general concentrated more on taxes on income, profits and capital gains than the neighbouring countries. Corporate tax revenues are however much higher in

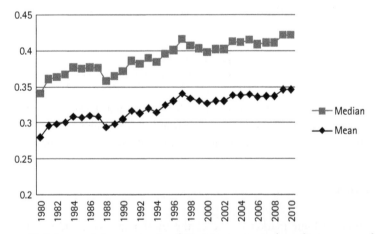

FIGURE 19.4 Statutory minimum wage relative to mean and median wages of full-time workers

Source: OECD. http://stats.oecd.org/Index.aspx?DatasetCode=MIN2AVE.

[13] If living costs (measured through the half yearly average of the retail price index) increase by 2.5 per cent, wages and salaries in the public and private sectors are automatically inflated by 2.5 per cent.

Luxembourg: 16 per cent of total revenue in 2010 (16 per cent in 1990, 18 per cent in 2000), against between only 4 per cent and 7 per cent in the other three countries. On the other hand, social contributions are moderate: 30 per cent of tax revenue in Luxembourg in 2010 versus 39 per cent in Germany.

It is often argued that the tax structure in Luxembourg is attractive in its taxation of labour income (Annaert 2004) or, more generally, personal income. Such a scheme would have 'contributed to containing the rise in labour income while guaranteeing high net incomes…' Altogether, taxes on income, profits and capital gains (out of corporate tax) as well as social contributions represent a share of 51 per cent of the tax burden in 1990, 44 per cent in 2000 and 50 per cent again in 2010, to be compared to a fraction ranging from 54 per cent and 65 per cent in neighbouring countries over the same period, even if the gap was significantly reduced during the last decade, especially by comparison with France.

Several tax reforms have been implemented during the period 1990–2010, which might be roughly summarized in three stages: a fall in the maximum marginal tax rate on personal income from 50 per cent in the early nineties (it had culminated at 62.70 per cent in 1984–1985) down to 38 per cent in 2001–2002 (then 39 per cent since 2011); an important tax reform in 2001–2002; and, more recently, several changes regarding households with children. The tax reform of 2001–2002, besides a drop in marginal tax rate from 46 per cent to 38 per cent, also included an enlargement of the first tax bracket. Overall this reform benefited mainly the richest: a 9 per cent increase of mean equivalized income was observed when considering the highest decile compared with less than 1 per cent for the lowest decile (Liégeois et al, 2011). More recently, several adaptations have been adopted. For example, Luxembourg has a system of compulsory joint taxation (income splitting) for married couples. Cohabiting couples under the 'partenariat' law can also be taxed jointly since 2008. In the same year, a child bonus was introduced to replace the tax credit for children, hence benefiting all households fulfilling the eligibility conditions and no longer taxable households only. This reform mainly benefited households (with children) with the lowest taxable income.

Capital income, which had been taxed at a rate of 25 per cent since 1994 (15 per cent earlier) has been 'better' treated since 2002 (back to a tax rate of 20 per cent) and even more so since 2007 (15 per cent) (Elvinger, 2008). Personal wealth tax was abolished in 2006.

Social Expenditures

Since 1901, Luxembourg has had a Bismarckian insurance model. It was able to develop a broad system of social protection providing, e.g., generous unemployment benefits and old-age pensions. Hartmann-Hirsch (2010) explains how, thanks to the massive presence of foreigners in the private sector, the Luxembourg system of social security has been able over the last twenty years to expand and improve its insurance provision and benefits—including universal benefits.

Among the new insurances and benefits introduced, one can mention parental leave (1999), care insurance (1999) ('assurance dependence'), an education allowance (2002), a minimum income scheme for disabled persons (2003), a child bonus to replace a tax credit (2008) and in-kind benefits to help finance childcare (2009); see IGSS, 2011. In addition to the introduction of these transfers, the generosity of some measures has been substantially improved.

A minimum guaranteed income (Revenu Minimum Garanti (RMG)) was introduced in Luxembourg in 1986 (Amétépé, 2012). It was at that time granted under conditions of age (30 years at least), residence (10 years in Luxembourg over the previous 20 years) and income. These eligibility criteria have changed: in 1999, the age condition was set at 25 years, and the residence period reduced to 5 years; even this last condition disappeared in 2001 for EU-citizens. These changes have led to an increase in the eligible population.

Policies in favour of the elderly but also for families with children are extremely generous. According to IGSS (2011:25) or Kieffer (2012), the gross pension replacement rate increased substantially to more than 80 per cent for all income groups following the 1991 and 2002 pension reforms. Child benefits in Luxembourg are among the highest in the European Union. Considering spending (in cash and in kind) on families with children and taking into account tax expenditures (expressed in per cent of GDP), Bradshaw and Chzhen (2009) find that Luxembourg is the second most generous OECD country. When expressing the spending per child as a proportion of spending per old person, they find that spending on children compared with the elderly has increased strongly in Luxembourg between 1980 (around 30 per cent) and 2003 (around 90 per cent). In the same way, STATEC (2003:185) notes that 'the increasingly important role played by various benefits and allowances for families with dependent children also becomes apparent when we consider the rate of increase of expenditure on the various functions. From 1985 to 2000, they rose by 338 per cent, while pensions spending only doubled'.

The social security administration has had a positive budgetary balance since the beginning of the 1990s, even during the recent crisis. This situation is mainly the result of the continued growth of the domestic labour market attained through the inflows of migrants and cross-borders workers. The current number of insured individuals contributing directly to the funding of social protection through social contribution and tax exceeds the number that would actually be necessary to sustain the system (Allegrezza et al, 2005, Amétépé and Hartmann-Hirsch, 2011 or IGSS, 2011). The net gain in pension and healthcare insurance is based on the contribution of foreigners and cross-border workers who are on average younger, better educated and with higher employment rates than the nationals. However, as already mentioned, the ageing of the population might create sustainability problems when this 'over-contribution' will end due to the mass retirement of these two groups (Amétépé and Hartmann-Hirsch, 2011).

Old age and health are the two functions with the highest expenditures. As for STATEC (2003:183), this suggests that 'the solidarity established by the social welfare system is not so much between rich and poor as between those in employment and those retired, and between those who are healthy and those who are sick'. Spending on unemployment has increased since 2000, but remains quite low. Universal family allowances are continuously growing since 1980 and went from an 8 per cent share of the total spending to a 15 per cent share in 2007. While the share of cash public social expenditure in overall expenditure over time has decreased, the share of in kind social expenditure has increased. In 1980, the latter represented 25 per cent of the overall social expenditure while in 2007, they amounted to almost 40 per cent. This increase is mainly due to the increase in health care spending. In-kind family benefits have not accounted for a high share since the 1980s but this has probably changed recently, however, as one major childcare reform has been introduced (Reinstadler, 2011).

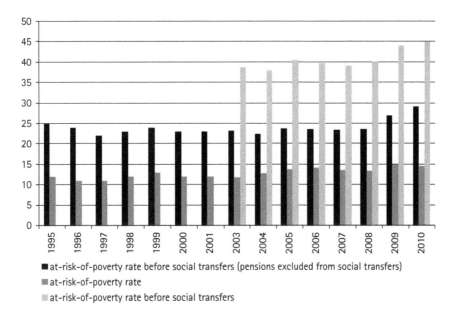

FIGURE 19.5 At-risk-of-poverty rates, before and after social transfers, 1995-2010

Source: Eurostat for at-risk-of-poverty rate and at-risk-of-poverty rate before social transfers (excluding pensions). STATEC for the at risk poverty rate before social transfers 2003-2010.

In 2010, Luxembourg is among the countries displaying the highest reduction of the Gini coefficient before and after taxes and transfers (OECD, 2012). Figure 19.5 shows that the poverty rate after transfers (using a 60 per cent of the median equivalent income poverty threshold) is consistently lower than the poverty rate before transfers. However, as observed by the OECD (2012), the reduction in poverty is less than in other countries such as Denmark or Sweden where social spending expressed as a share of national income are comparable. This may be explained by the fact that the main components of the social system such as pensions or family benefits are 'designed mainly to tackle specific social issues and are not primarily designed for redistribution [...]. As a result, the progressivity of cash transfers is rather low in international comparison' (OECD, 2012:47).

Summary

The Luxembourg labour market is one of the most regulated of the OECD countries with a strong regulatory framework within the Luxembourg 'social model', that is a strong social dialogue between unions, employers' representatives and the government. There is an automatic indexation of salaries to inflation that applies to all wages and to the minimum wage. The minimum wage relative to average wages also increased over time contrary to what happened in other countries. This feature of the labour market, together with the generous welfare state (in particular the pension system and family-related policies) contributed to raising the floor of the income distribution and therefore contributed 'from the bottom' to achieving a comparatively low level of inequality. On the other hand, trends in a relatively low personal income taxation since the 1980s generally benefitted higher income recipients.

6. CONCLUSIONS

The purpose of this chapter was to document trends in inequality across various dimensions and to link these trends to social, cultural and political developments in Luxembourg for the period 1985–2010. The situation described is a 'success story', which saw Luxembourg successfully transition from a steel-based industrial economy to a high value-added services-oriented society. While the average standard of living increased substantially, not all Luxembourg residents benefited equally from this growth since the income distribution became more dispersed. The analysis of the evolution of a set of social, political and cultural outcomes suggests, however, that the (moderate) rising trend in inequality did not appear to impact strongly on the society or was offset by the benefits of increasing living standards and a generous Welfare State that expanded over the period thanks to the continued economic growth.

Of course, not everything is perfect. First, the main conclusion of our study is based on the evolution of average trends. Where possible, we also analysed the evolution of trends at a subgroup level, which revealed how some less-skilled populations do lag behind. Second, some inequalities at a subgroup level appear to be sustained by an educational system that tends to reproduce social disadvantage across generations. Finally, the period covered by this report was a period of great economic expansion, which has slowed down in recent years. Dependence of the economy on the financial sector is now perceived as a vulnerability and the country is facing the challenges of an ageing population, rising unemployment, fiscal consolidation, and difficulties in the social dialogue that threatens the social model in place since the industrial transition and the capacity of the country to maintain its generous Welfare State.

REFERENCES

Alieva, A. (2010), *Educational Inequalities in Europe: Performance of Students with Migratory Background in Luxembourg and Switzerland*, Frankfurt am Main: Peter Lang.

Allegrezza S., Brosius J., Gerber P., Hausman P., Langers, J., Schuller G., Zanardelli M. (2005), 'Emploi, production, rémuneration et transferts courants des salariés frontaliers', *Cahiers Economiques* n°100, STATEC, Luxembourg.

Allegrezza, S., Heinrich, G. and Jesuit, D. (2004), 'Poverty and Income Inequality in Luxembourg and the Grande Région in Comparative Perspective', *Socio-Economic Review*, Vol. 2, pp. 263–283.

Allegrezza, S., Hirsch, M., Kunitzki, N. (2003), *L'histoire, le présent et l'avenir du modèle luxembourgeois*, Luxembourg: Institut d'études européennes et internationales du Luxembourg.

Amétépé F. (2012), 'The Effectiveness of Luxembourg's Minimum Guaranteed Income', *International Social Security Review*, 65, 1/2012.

Amétépé F., Hartmann-Hirsch C. (2011), 'An Outstanding Position of Migrants and Nationals: the Case of Luxembourg', *Population Review*, vol. 50, 1, pp. 195–217.

Annaert J.L. (2004), 'A Bright Spot in the Heart of Europe: What Can we Learn from the Luxembourg Success Story?', *ECFINI Country Focus*, Volume 1. Issue 15. 1/2012, pp. 99–116.

Berger F. (2005), 'Développement de l'emploi transfrontalier au Luxembourg et portrait socio-démographique des frontaliers', *Population and Emploi* N°8, CEPS/INSTEAD, Luxembourg.

Blau, L. (2005), *Histoire de l'extrême-droite au Grand-Duché de Luxembourg au XXe siècle*, Esch-sur-Alzette: Éditions Le Phare.

Blau, P.M. and Schwartz, J.E. (1984), *Crosscutting Social Circles: Testing a Macrostructural Theory of Intergroup Relations*, New York, NY: Academic Press.

Bradshaw J., and Chzhen Y. (2009), 'Child Poverty Policies across Europe', *Zeitschrift für Familienforschung*, 21. Jahrg., Heft 2/2009, S. 128–149.

Elvinger A., (2008), 'Regards sur un demi-siècle d'histoire de l'impôt au Luxembourg', in *Droit fiscal luxembourgeois, Livre jubilaire de l'IFA Luxembourg*, Bruylant, Bruxelles, 3–38.

Fetzer, J.S. (2011), *Luxembourg as an Immigration Success Story. The Grand Duchy in Pan-European Perspective*, Lanham, Boulder, New York, Toronto and Plymouth: Lexington Books.

Fusco A., Guio A.-C., Marlier E. (2011), 'Income Poverty and Material Deprivation in European Countries', *CEPS/INSTEAD Working Paper* n°2011-04, CEPS/INSTEAD, Luxembourg.

Golder, M. (2003), Explaining Variation in the Success of Extreme Right Parties in Western Europe, *Comparative Political Studies* 36(4): 432–466.

Hartmann-Hirsch C. (2010), 'The state of the Luxembourg welfare state: the effects of the crisis on a corporatist model shifting to a universalistic model', *CEPS/INSTEAD Working paper* n°2010-44, CEPS/INSTEAD, Luxembourg.

Hildebrand, V., Pi Alperin M.N. and Van Kerm, P. (2012), 'Measuring and accounting for the deprivation gap of Portuguese immigrants in Luxembourg', *CEPS/INSTEAD Working Paper* n°2012-33, CEPS/INSTEAD, Luxembourg.

Ignazi, P. (2006), *Extreme Right Parties in Western Europe*. Oxford: Oxford University Press.

IGSS (Inspection Générale de la Sécurité Sociale) (2011), *Rapport Général sur la Sécurité Sociale au Grand-Duché de Luxembourg*, Ministère de la Sécurité Sociale, Luxembourg.

IGSS (Inspection Générale de la Sécurité Sociale) (2012), <http://www.isog.public.lu/gbe/pkg_isgbe5.prc_show_dokument?p_aid=28881772&p_uid=statsecu2007&sprache=D&p_lfd_nr=1&p_dokumente=0> (last accessed October 2012).

IMF (International Monetary Fund) (2000), 'Why is Luxembourg Growing so Fast?' in Luxembourg: Staff Report for the 2000 Article IV Consultation—Selected issues, pp. 6–14.

Kesler, C., Bloemraad, I. (2010), 'Does Immigration Erode Social Capital? The Conditional Effects of Immigration-Generated Diversity on Trust, Membership, and Participation across 19 Countries, 1981-2000'. *Canadian Journal of Political Science* 43(2): 319–347.

Kieffer R. (2012), 'Avis du Président de la Caisse Nationale d'Assurance Pension concernant le projet de loi portant réforme de l'assurance pension', Caisse Nationale d'Assurance Pension (CNAP), Luxembourg.

Lejealle, B., (2003), 'Participation à la vie associative au Luxembourg en 2001', *Population and Emploi n°1*, CEPS/INSTEAD, Luxembourg.

Liégeois Ph., Berger F., Islam N. and Wagener R. (2011), 'Cross-validating Administrative and Survey Datasets through Microsimulation and the Assessment of a Tax Reform', *International Journal of Microsimulation*, 4(1), 1–18.

OECD (2010a), *Economic Policy Reforms—Going for Growth*, Chapter 5, Paris: OECD.

OECD (2010b), 'PISA 2009 Results: Overcoming Social Background—Equity in Learning Opportunities and Outcomes, Volume II, Paris: OECD.

OECD (2011a), *Divided We Stand: Why Inequality Keeps Rising*, Paris: OECD.

OECD Health Statistics (2011b), http://stats.oecd.org/index.aspx?DataSetCode=HEALTH_STAT#.

OECD (2012), *Economic Surveys of Luxembourg*, OECD: Paris.

Osier G. (2012), 'L'évolution du revenu des ménages depuis le milieu des années 80', *STATEC, Collection le Luxembourg 1960-2010*, Luxembourg: STATEC.

Paxton, P. (2007), 'Association Memberships and Generalized Trust: A Multilevel Model across 31 Countries', *Social Forces*, 86(1):47–75.

Pi Alperin M.N. and Berzosa G, (2011), 'A fuzzy logic approach to Measure Obesity'. *CEPS/INSTEAD Working Paper* n°2011-55, CEPS/INSTEAD, Luxembourg.

Putnam, R.D. (2007), 'E Pluribus Unum: Diversity and Community in the Twenty-first Century', *Scandinavian Political Studies* 30(2):137–174.

Putnam, R.D. (2001), *Bowling Alone. The Collapse and Revival of American Community*, Touchstone.

Reinstadler Anne (2011), 'Luxembourg and France: Comparable Family Benefits, Comparable Fertility Levels?' *CEPS/INSTEAD, Working Papers* n°2011-65, CEPS/INSTEAD, Luxembourg.

Schuller G. (2002), 'Des déterminants du développement économique du Luxembourg: Tendances et perspectives', *Forum*, n°221, pp. 16–23.

Scuto, D. (2012), *La nationalité luxembourgeoise (XIXᵉ-XXIᵉ siècles). Histoire d'un alliage européen*, Bruxelles: Éditions de L'Université de Bruxelles.

Sohn, C. (2012), 'La frontière comme ressource dans l'espace urbain globalisé. Une contribution à l'hypothèse de la métropole transfrontalière', *CEPS/INSTEAD Working Paper* No 2012-25, CEPS/INSTEAD, Luxembourg.

STATEC (2003), Economic and Social Portrait of Luxembourg, Luxembourg.

STATEC (2010), Nuptialité et Divortialité au Luxembourg (1994-2008), *Bulletin du STATEC*, n°2.

Thill P. and Thomas A. (2009), 'Le "Modèle social luxembourgeois" au défi de la crise, *Gouvernance et Emploi*, n°12, CEPS/INSTEAD, Luxembourg.

Thill P. and Thomas A. (2011), 'The End of Consensus? The Effects of the Economic Crisis on Industrial Relations in Luxembourg' in Baglioni M., Brandl B. (eds.), *Changing Labour Relations Between Path Dependency and Global Trends*, Labour, Education and Society, Vol. 24, Frankfurt am Main: Peter Lang,

Uslaner, E.M. (2011), Trust, Diversity, and Segregation in the United States and the United Kingdom', *Comparative Sociology* 10(2):221–247.

Wilkinson, R. and Pickett, K. (2009), *The Spirit Level: Why Inequality is Bad for Everyone*, Allen Lane, UK.

Wilson, J. (2000), Volunteering, *Annual Review of Sociology* 26: 215–240.

Zahlen P. (2012a), 'L'évolution économique globale du Luxembourg sur la longue durée', *Collection le Luxembourg 1960-2010*, Luxembourg: STATEC.

Zahlen P. (2012b), '50 ans de migrations', *Collection le Luxembourg 1960-2010*, Luxembourg: STATEC.

CHAPTER 20

....

THE NETHERLANDS: POLICY-ENHANCED INEQUALITIES TEMPERED BY HOUSEHOLD FORMATION

....

WIEMER SALVERDA, MARLOES DE GRAAF-ZIJL,

CHRISTINA HAAS, BRAM LANCEE, AND

NATASCHA NOTTEN[*]

1. INTRODUCTION

....

In this chapter we first scrutinize the evolution of inequalities in the Netherlands in terms of income, employment, educational attainment, and wealth—on a household basis for income and wealth, and on an individual basis for employment and education, linking the former to the latter whenever relevant and possible. This provides the basis for studying the impacts of inequalities in the next section and also raises various questions about policies, which are then addressed.

It is important to realize that the Dutch economy went through a deep recession in the 1980s by international comparison, as GDP per capita fell by almost 7 per cent from peak to trough (quarterly) and the employment rates of young (15–24) and older (55–64) men fell by a fifth to a quarter. This has strongly affected policies—of government, unions and employers—and outcomes in many fields. In addition, the labour market (rapidly rising part-time and female employment), demographics (dwindling population growth, growing minorities), and household formation (quadrupling of singles) have changed radically. Real GDP almost doubled but grew by only 5 per cent per household. Real net-equivalized

[*] There is more detail in GINI *Netherlands Country Report* (<http://www.gini-research.org/CR-Netherlands>). Valuable comments were made by Daniele Checchi, Olli Kangas, Abigail McKnight, Paul de Beer, and Matthijs Kalmijn.

household income increased by 24 per cent though, affected by the shift towards single headed households.

2. Inequalities: Sharp and Persistent Wage-Driven Growth

Since the late 1970s inequalities have increased strongly for income and employment and decreased for education; the wealth picture is more complex. Market incomes, household behaviour, and policy, together with educational attainment, have driven changing inequalities.

Income is key to household inequalities. The Gini coefficient of equivalized incomes shows a 12 per cent rise between 1985 and 1990, followed by a stable level over the 1990s and a small 2 per cent rise over 2001–2011 (Figure 20.1). This coefficient, published by Statistics Netherlands, will serve as the inequality indicator when looking at impacts and policies in the next sections. In this section, we discuss this outcome against the background of the effects of taxation, transfers, equivalization and the evolution of market incomes with the help of deciles of the distribution. This helps highlight changes in the tails of the distribution, which are given less weight in the Gini coefficient. The S10:S1-ratio of the sums of

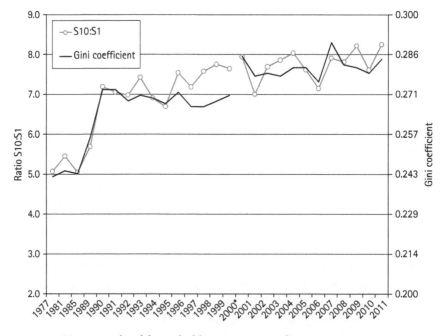

FIGURE 20.1 Net equivalized household income inequality: two measures, 1977–2011

Note: Series break in 2000, still subject to scrutiny by Statistics Netherlands; 2007 peak due to one-time tax measure for business ownership (see Country Report).

Source: Statistics Netherlands, specially provided tables (authors' calculations).

incomes in the top and the bottom deciles, rises more sharply up to 1990 (+42 per cent) and also after that (+10 per cent, accounting for the break). It lends weight to the small increase in the Gini[1].

The basic accounting is simple: real equivalized incomes of the bottom decile fall by 21 per cent until 2000, recover 12 per cent of this until 2007 but fall back to a 19 per cent loss in 2011. By contrast, the top decile grows by 39 per cent until 2007 and falls back to 26 per cent in 2011. The middle follows the top with a 28 per cent rise until 2007 and only a small decline to 25 per cent after that.

Transfers, Taxation and Equivalization

Equivalized household incomes and their inequality result from the interaction of market incomes, social transfers, taxation, and household equivalization. These correspond with four common income concepts: market, gross, disposable, and equivalized incomes.[2] The effects of each are demonstrated using a fixed ranking of households by gross incomes.[3] Figure 20.2 compares real average decile incomes between 1977 and 2011. Clearly, in all four cases the upper decile leaves the rest behind, gaining between €17,000 and €35,000 depending on income type. Conversely, market incomes decline significantly in the middle of the distribution, but gross and disposable incomes do so only very little and equivalized incomes show a small gain and are flat for most of the distribution. Surprisingly, the first decile gains in terms of market income but loses on equivalized income. Evidently, important composition shifts are behind the changes in the middle and at the bottom.

The gaps between the curves indicate the effects of redistribution through transfers, and income taxes and social security contributions respectively, and of equivalization. The corresponding level of inequality (Figure 20.3) declines with each step, pointing to the continued strength of redistribution and equivalization. Over time, however, inequality grows at all three levels and more strongly with each step: +33 per cent for gross income, 49 per cent for disposable income, and 35 per cent for equivalized income.[4] The fixed ranking implies that the rather flat Gini's of Figure 20.1 incorporate a significant effect of re-ranking, meaning that households starting from their gross income experience a larger decline in their distributive positions.

The ratios rise sharply until 1990 with substantial mutual differences (23, 37 and 42 per cent) while the subsequent evolution is more gradual (8–9 per cent) and largely concentrated in the 2000s. In the year 1989–1990, the effective tax rate on the first decile shows a 14 per cent hike, then increases further up to 1998, when its rate almost equals that of the middle of the distribution, and shrinks after the tax revision of 2001. Thus taxation is an

---

[1] The ratio is highly correlated with the Gini (0.92), which encourages its use below where the Gini is not available. The correlation for P90:P10 is much less.

[2] For indirect taxation and in-kind subsidies see Section 4.

[3] The usual comparison of distributions shifts the ranking criterion and includes the effect of household re-ranking in its results. Note that data used here are largely corrected for the 2000 series break, adapting the later data to the earlier definitions, and therewith, unfortunately, underestimating the level of inequality (see *Country Report*).

[4] Gross-income ranking spreads households differently than net-equivalized ranking (Figure 20.1) resulting in a lower but more strongly growing S10:S1 ratio.

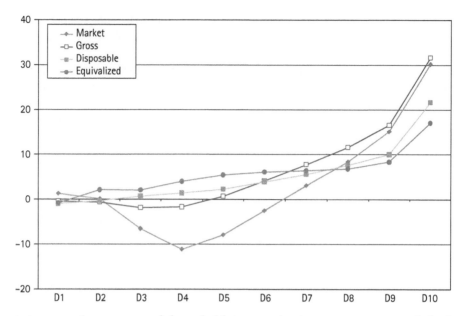

FIGURE 20.2 Average annual household income by income concepts and deciles, always ranked by gross incomes, absolute changes 1977 to 2011 (1000s of euros—prices at 2011)

Source: Statistics Netherlands, specially provided tables (authors' calculations).

important contributor to the evolution of inequality. It also becomes clear that equivalization, which rests on household formation, affects inequality at least as much as taxation and social security contributions.

The reduction due to equivalization is almost nil for the first decile, as households are mostly singles, but 20–30 per cent for the tenth decile where only 5 per cent are singles. Income levels differ significantly across household types, age and ethnicity. The number of households expands strongly, from 4.7 million to 7.4 million and singles make up 70 per cent of the expansion. This affects the middle as it brings them up to higher deciles—especially pensioners.[5]

Market Incomes from Labour and Enterprise, and Top Incomes

Figure 20.3 does not include the S10:S1 inequality ratio for market incomes, which is at a much higher level than the three ratios just discussed and is also highly volatile—varying between 50 and 180. This is due not to top incomes but to first-decile incomes. These are very low and small absolute changes, which, over time or from primary to gross income,

---

[5] Occupational pensions, though based on wage payments and capital returns, are treated as transfers by CBS.

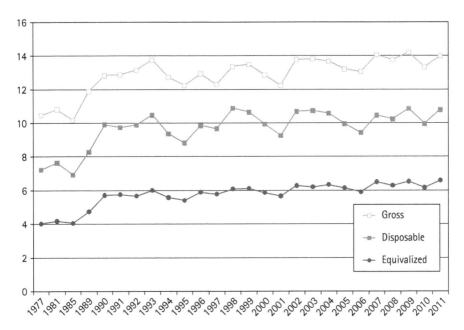

FIGURE 20.3 S10:S1 inequality ratios for household incomes, always ranked by gross incomes, 1977–2011

Source: Statistics Netherlands, specially provided tables (authors' calculations).

translate into large relative effects. Market incomes originate from three sources that behave very differently (Figure 20.4). Almost 90 per cent of households receive income from wealth, or suffer a loss. The amounts of wealth income are often negative or very small and hardly increase over the income distribution.[6] Household wage and enterprise incomes diverge strongly from this and from each other. Wage incomes are received by 70 per cent of households, enterprise incomes by 10 per cent.[7] The inequality (S10:S1) of earnings almost doubles up to 1989, and contributes significantly to the increase in inequality found in Figure 20.1. It falls back to half the initial level but rises structurally from the mid 1990s, also during the financial crisis. By contrast, enterprise incomes show no structural change.[8] Top-decile wage incomes exceed enterprise incomes in virtually all years. The top-decile share in total market income[9] rises from 28 per cent to 33 per cent, mainly driven by top shares from earnings (21 to 29 per cent) as the enterprise top share almost halves (6.1 to 3.5 per cent). The rising share of top earnings partly reflects a growing presence of wage earners in the top decile.

---

[6] Income from wealth includes imputed rent and is after deduction of mortgage interest. The 2000 data break adds more than 1 million (very) small wealth incomes.

[7] This regards *any* wage or enterprise income. At least about 15 per cent of households with market income receive both.

[8] First-decile wage and enterprise incomes separately are stable, suggesting that the decile is not an arbitrary residue of the distribution, outside the realm of analysis, as implied by inequality measures that ignore negative values.

[9] The focus is households not tax units as in common top-income shares (Atkinson and Piketty, 2007) but the starting point in gross incomes is the same.

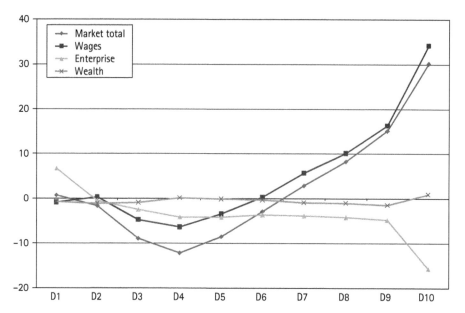

FIGURE 20.4 Average annual household income levels by types of market income and deciles, ranked by gross incomes, absolute changes 1977–2011 (1000s of euros—prices at 2011)

Note: Market-income households only.

Source: Statistics Netherlands, specially provided tables (authors' calculations).

As wages are a core determinant of rising income inequality, the analysis of labour market developments and their effects on household incomes is essential for a proper understanding. In 2011, 5.1 million households received a labour income, 3.9 million of them as the *main* income. 8.2 million persons were employees or self-employed. The common *individual* employment rate (employed individuals as a percentage of working-age population) trends solidly upward (55 per cent → 67 per cent).[10] The *full-time* individual employment rate stagnates at around 42 per cent, implying that all employment-rate growth is in part-time jobs. This makes working hours an important new dimension of (unequal) job access and earnings inequality. Part-time work is concentrated in low-skill jobs and carries a pay and career penalty.[11] At the same time, the *household* employment rate[12] moves up less and only during the second half of the 1990s (68 per cent → 74 per cent). Joint household labour supply (two-earners are a majority among couples) explains the difference between the two rates. The shift away from single-earner couples largely coincides with the increase in part-time employment, and today in 90 per cent of the two-earner households at least one of the partners works part-time.

[10] International definition, including small jobs (<12 hours/week; >10 per cent of employees) left out in Dutch statistics.

[11] E.g., Salverda (2011).

[12] The share of households aged below 65 with *main* income from labour. Other households may have a small labour income.

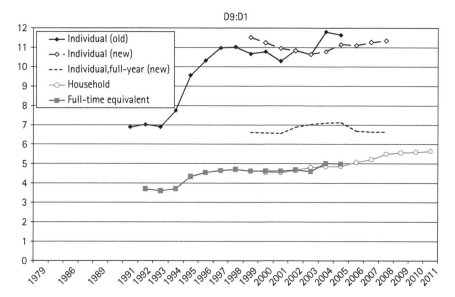

FIGURE 20.5 Inequalities (P90:P10-ratio) of individual annual earnings and labour-household annual incomes, 1991–2011

Note: New series replaces old one. Households are with main income from wages.

Sources: Calculated from Statistics Netherlands wage and household income statistics.

The growth of part-time jobs exerts an important effect on the inequality of individual *annual* earnings (Figure 20.5). The P90:P10-ratio almost doubles from seven to almost twelve between 1993 and 1997. Of the new high level almost 40 per cent is due to the inequality among part-year wages, witness the gap with individual full-year earnings (P90:P10 ratio around seven). Another 40 per cent is due to hourly wage inequality: the P90:P10 ratio of the full-time equivalent series is close to five. The remaining 20 per cent (between 'full-year' and 'full-time equivalent') point to the lower pay of part-time jobs among full-year earners. Household earnings inequality is between four and six, far below individual inequality. Clearly, household joint labour supply compensates for a large part of individual labour-market income inequality.[13]

Nevertheless, there still is a strong rise in inequality among households with *any* wage income across gross-income deciles, and also among households with their main income from labour. Over 1990–2011 the latter's gross-income inequality rises by 50 per cent, and disposable-income inequality by 30 per cent.[14] Surprisingly, their equivalized-income inequality rises by 5 per cent only. Apparently, the composition of labour-households has shifted in a way that takes away most of the remaining effects of the increase in labour market inequality. This contrasts with the population as a whole where equivalization adds little as the trends in equivalized-income inequality and disposable-income inequality are equally flat.

[13] Households with main income from earnings; individual earnings concern any wage.
[14] Increasing by 24 per cent for market incomes over the 2000s (not gross ranked), unknown earlier.

Educational Inequalities

The educational attainment of the population has become more equally distributed with a 26 per cent decline in the corresponding Gini coefficient of individuals' years of education over 1920–84 cohorts (Meschi and Scervini, 2010). This is a great accomplishment. The share of the working-age population[15] having tertiary education has risen from 6 per cent in 1971 to 28 per cent in 2011, the primary level share falls by almost two thirds and the junior secondary share by more than one third. The change is much stronger for women who initially lagged behind but are now on a par with men.

However, strong cross-section inequalities have grown along the educational dimension. An analysis of the role of education in the evolution of household income inequality is available for 1979–1999 only (SCP, 2003). The Theil index increases from 0.090 to 0.164, mostly over 1987–1995. Inequality within educational groups doubles, while between/group-inequality hardly changes. This seems consistent with the growth of part-time employment and under-utilization of education, which both enhance the spread of (annual) earnings.

Inequalities in education are more visible in the labour market. The employment rate increases with educational attainment. This gradient is extremely steep for women, a 50 percentage-points gap exists between best and least educated, and is undiminished by their rapid employment growth. For men, a similar gap starts to grow in the 1980s, bringing the least educated 30 points below the best educated in a few years' time. The common view is that the less educated adapt their skills insufficiently to the upgrading of employment resulting from technological change. However, they certainly lose out significantly in the competition with the growing mass of the better educated for jobs which are suitable for them. Least-skill occupations surprisingly retain their employment share of around 7 per cent, whereas jobs at the next-higher level suffer a blow (-9pcpt). The growth at the highest occupational levels lags the sharp increase in labour supply of the better educated.[16] Increasing numbers are found in jobs at lower skill levels, reflecting bumping down along the educational dimension. Thus better-educated persons are increasingly under-utilized in their jobs, and low-skill jobs have more over-skilled occupants—e.g. 80 per cent of the least skilled jobs have a better-educated occupant (Salverda, forthcoming). The average rate of under-utilization is now 28 per cent, only slightly up (+1pcpt) for women compared to 1990 but strongly up (+8pcpt) for men, diminishing the gender gap. It is consistent with the above increase of inequality within educational groups.

A large (10 per cent) share of Dutch employment is in small jobs (<12 hours/week), not included above and concentrated strongly in low-wage low-skill jobs. Their inclusion dampens the employment gap of the low-skilled somewhat but also reinforces working hours as a dimension of educational labour-market inequality. The lower the educational level of an employee or the occupational level of a job, the shorter are the hours. The prolonged stays in education and later entries into the labour market implied by higher attainment reinforce this. The participation in full-time education grew among teenage youth (ages 15–18) from 75 to → 93 per cent, 1980–2010: it doubled from 27 to 55 per cent for older youth (19–24).

---

[15] Lack of microdata and limited number of educational levels prevent using a formal measure of educational inequality. Instead we rank by level corresponding to ISCED 0-1, 2, 3-4, and 5-7.

[16] CBS job-level classification links directly to educational levels.

However, in the Netherlands a large overlap has grown with labour-market participation: two-thirds of those in education also have a job, mostly a small low-skill one. This adds fiercely to the job competition experienced by the less well-educated. The part-time, often over-skilled employment of second earners in couples is another contributor.

The conclusion must be that the inequality of educational attainment falls while simultaneously educational inequalities in the labour market grow.

Poverty

Poverty, a core indicator in the European inequality debate, provides a specific focus on social inequality. It rises and deepens significantly in the wake of the 1980s recession and remains well above the initial level. Poverty is measured for equivalized incomes as the percentage of persons living in poor households, defined as having a household income below 60 per cent of equivalized median income (Europe 2020). The incidence is shown following Statistics Netherlands (CBS) (Figure 20.6). This evolution largely mimics that of income inequality (Figure 20.1). In 2011, 11.2 per cent of households and 10.4 per cent of persons live in poverty. The OECD's poverty database tells a similar but less detailed story, at a higher level,[17] and enables an international comparison. The Dutch rate increases much more rapidly, from half the average for available GINI countries in 1985 to the average in the early 1990s, and decreases to 80 per cent after that.

Poverty differs strongly between social groups. Singles (21 per cent), single parents (29 per cent), and youths (26 per cent) run high risks, as do ethnic minorities (29 per cent). The poverty gap tends to widen for these groups in the 2000s. The evolution of absolute poverty stands in stark contrast: increasing rapidly before 1985 and falling equally rapidly first and, interrupted by periods of stagnation during the recession of the early 1990s and after the dotcom crisis, falling ultimately well below the initial level. The first sign of a rise is found in 2011.

Wealth

Total gross wealth of private households has grown rapidly since 1977, from 220 per cent of GDP to 350 per cent (CPB, 2012). Gross self-owned housing wealth doubled relative to GDP, but net housing wealth grew from 90 per cent of GDP to 104 per cent only as most was debt financed. Net other wealth (mainly financial)[18] grew from 100 to 120 per cent. As a result, the growth of net wealth (34 per cent of GDP) was far exceeded by total debt growth (100 per cent).

The distribution of net wealth over households is highly skewed, much more than incomes ('income' bars, left-hand panel of Figure 20.7).[19] The first wealth-decile is always

---

[17] Dutch Statistics leaves out students and part-year incomes.
[18] Also including real estate (not own home) and other property, and enterprise ownership.
[19] Derived from CBS tabulated decile-based wealth data without a generalized measure of inequality. Claessen (2010) mentions a Gini coefficient for wealth inequality of 0.82 for 2009.

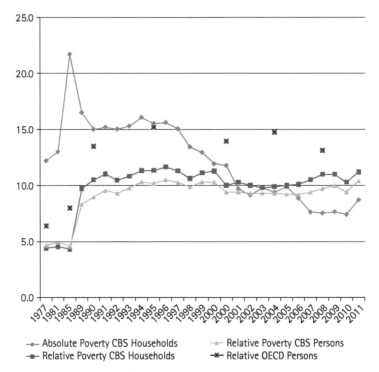

FIGURE 20.6 Incidence of poverty below 60 per cent of median equivalized income and absolute poverty* (national and OECD sources, 1977–2011*)

Note: Anchored at the purchasing power of the social assistance level for a single person in 1979.

Sources: Statistics Netherlands/Statline and OECD. Preparation courtesy of Paul de Beer.

negative (2-4 per cent), deciles 2 to 5 have virtually no wealth, and around 90 per cent of all wealth is concentrated in the top-3 deciles (right-hand panel).

The inequality of wealth over the distribution of (disposable) income is much flatter (wealth bars, left-hand panel) and a higher income does not always imply greater wealth. This adds important nuance to the study of wealth inequality. In 2011, the first income-decile owns a significant 4 per cent of net wealth—more than the second or third decile—mostly concentrated in the top wealth-decile. The top income-decile receives 25 per cent of all incomes and owns 33 per cent of all wealth. The top wealth-decile owns 60 per cent of all wealth and only one third of these households are also in the top income-decile. Financial wealth is more unequally spread over both income and wealth deciles than housing wealth: the top income-decile owns 44 per cent, the top wealth-decile 70 per cent.

Since 1993, the wealth distribution over income has grown steeper, especially for financial wealth, in contrast to the distribution over wealth. House ownership has grown strongly, from 42 per cent of all households in 1993 to 57 per cent in 2011—the lower the income decile the stronger that expansion. The importance of mortgage debt for financing house ownership shows in the rapid growth of house ownership in the first, negative wealth decile: from only 83,000 households in 1993 to 300,000 at the start of the financial crisis, and 684,000 in 2011. These are spread over all ten income-deciles. Net housing wealth can be negative as traditionally mortgages were allowed to exceed the value of the

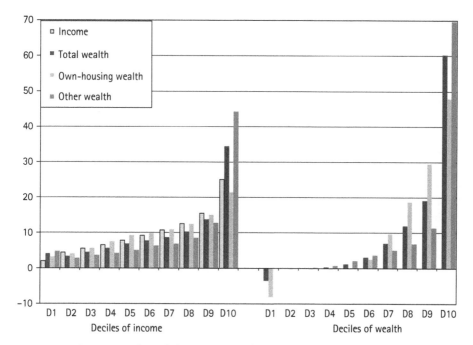

FIGURE 20.7 Income and total, housing, and financial net wealth: per cent distribution over deciles of income and of wealth, 2011

Source: Statistics Netherlands and special tables at request.

house,[20] making debt even more sensitive to declining house prices. Couples with dependent children and households with a prime-age main earner are largely over-represented among those with negative wealth, and this has increased quickly in recent years.

The very top of a steady 250,000 households is found in the overlap of the top wealth (> € 400,000) and the top income decile (>€ 59,000). Their share of net wealth declines over the 1990s (28 → 21 per cent) but swings back to 29 per cent after 2006 (except 2009: 27 per cent). Financial wealth is especially concentrated in their hands (39 per cent), and also determines the decline and increase of their aggregate wealth. The share in net housing wealth hovers around 16 per cent, that in debt around 11 per cent.

3. IMPACTS OF INEQUALITY: INCREASED EDUCATIONAL GRADIENTS

An important issue in the literature and the public debate is that the growth of inequality may negatively impact on social, political and cultural outcomes. Section 2.1 deals with

---

[20] This helps to pay for transaction tax as well as investments in the house. This practice is disappearing rapidly.

social impacts, Section 2.2 with the rest. The previous section has shown rising income inequality particularly in the second half of the 1980s, and to a lesser extent after that. After 2000, equivalized household income inequality rises by 2 per cent only, while the inequality of gross, disposable and equivalized income rises by 8 to 9 per cent (Figure 20.3). As the composition of income and educational groups and household types has changed over the past decades we need to remain cautious in interpreting the numbers and the figures below.

Social Impacts

Wilkinson and Pickett (2009) suggest that growing inequality leads to serious social impacts. As status differences increase with income inequality, societal cohesion decreases, accompanied by an increasing social distance between groups. Another theory explains similar outcomes from the unequal distribution of resources (Lynch *et al.* 2000). We discuss possible impacts in eight areas: material deprivation; poverty risk; social isolation, family formation; health; housing; crime; and life satisfaction. The analysis is hampered by the availability of data in most areas for recent years only; thus the sharp 1980s increase in inequality cannot be taken into account.

Material deprivation, poverty risk and social exclusion. Figures 20.1 and 20.6 suggest that the rapid growth in inequality of the 1980s is reflected in a strong rise in relative poverty among households. It grows first over the 1990s (+7 per cent) when the Gini stagnates, and again over 2000–2011 (+12 per cent), when the Gini grows only modestly (+2 per cent). Simultaneously, absolute poverty falls in several steps to its lowest level in 2010 but shows an increase in 2011 for the first time in many years. Material deprivation, defined as inability to afford consumption goods and activities that are typical in a society at a given point in time (Whelan and Maître, 2012), decreases between 2005 and 2009 and increases in 2010–2011 (Eurostat, 2013). This is largely in line with the national absolute measure, less with the Gini coefficient, and can be understood also from economic development putting pressure on incomes across the board, similar to the 1980s. The stratification of material deprivation by educational level and household type remains stable: single parents and less-educated persons face the largest risk (SCP, 2011; *Statistics Netherlands*, 2012). The percentage of households with arrears in payments increases over the last ten years, also more strongly among less-educated and low-income households, which is in line with poverty growth (*Statistics Netherlands*, 2012).

Social (dis)connectedness. According to both the psycho-social and the resource explanation (Allport, 1979; Wilkinson and Pickett 2009), rising inequality may lead to feelings of social disconnectedness due to rising distance and decreasing trust between social groups (Putnam, 2000). Over the past two decades, the percentage of people feeling isolated or socially disconnected has remained stable (about 10 per cent of the population). While it increased among less-educated people, it decreased among single parents (*Statistics Netherlands*, 2012; SCP, 2011). Summing up, no general decline in social connectedness is observed with the rise in (relative) poverty but there is an increasing gap along educational lines.

Family formation and breakdown, lone parenthood and fertility. As in other advanced societies, family formation and living arrangements have changed dramatically during the most recent decades. These developments relate to changing gender roles and are affected more by economic development than by rising income divergence. Yet, family formation differs strongly by level of education (NIDI, 2013). Women's growing independence, increasing educational attainment, and more active roles in the labour market led to both a decline in the average number of births per woman and an increase in woman's age at first childbirth (Beets, Verweij and Sanderse, 2012; Liefbroer and Corijn, 1999). Postponement of childbirth and voluntary childlessness occur especially among more highly educated women (Agtmaal-Wobma and Van Huis, 2008; Keizer *et al.*, 2008).

The divorce rate also seems more sensitive to economic development than to income inequality (NIDI, 2012). Up until the early twentieth century, persons from higher social classes, especially those in higher cultural groups, were more likely to divorce than people from lower socio-economic backgrounds, pointing to cultural hindrances to divorcing. In the post-war decades, when divorces became more common, the association between education and divorce turned negative, with the less-educated currently having a higher risk of divorce than the better-educated (De Graaf and Kalmijn, 2006; Kalmijn, Vanassche and Matthijs, 2011).

There is also a sharp increase in the proportion of single-person households, whereas the percentage of two-person households decreases, in particular those with children living at home (from 44 per cent in 1981 to 27 per cent in 2011; *Statistics Netherlands*, 2012 and SCP 2011). The proportion of single-parent households remains at a stable 6 to 7 per cent between 1981 and 2011. Summing up, no direct impact of inequality on family formation patterns can be found. Yet, a divergence in family-formation patterns by education (and consequently by income) evolves, which can reinforce the inequality of living conditions and life chances of the next generation.

Health inequalities. Both from the psycho-social and the resource perspective the higher educated are expected to have a better health (Wilkinson and Pickett, 2009). They live in superior material circumstances and tend to have healthier lifestyles with lower numbers of smokers and overweight people (Huijts, Monden and Kraaykamp, 2010; RIVM, 2010)[21]. The expected healthy lifespan of tertiary-educated persons at age 25 is around 17 years longer compared to primary educated. Over recent years this gap has increased by around one year (*Statistics Netherlands*, 2012). The percentage of overweight individuals doubled from 5 per cent in 1981 to almost 12 per cent in 2009 (Statistics Netherlands, 2012). The educational gradient is considerable: about 60 per cent of the low educated are overweight compared to approximately 40 per cent of the tertiary educated.

Housing. In line with growing equivalized household incomes, home-ownership increases during the 1990s (VROM, 2003; Van Kempen and Priemus, 2002). The financial crisis strongly lowers this growth in 2009–2011 but does not entirely take it away. The higher educated are more often homeowners compared to the less-educated, and this difference increases significantly over the period 1992–2003 (Tolsma and Wolbers, 2010). Social renting increases among the lowest income-deciles, especially during the 1980s, and decreases in higher income groups, resulting in a more homogeneous low-income group of social renters (Schutjens *et al.*, 2002). Compared to other European countries, Dutch housing costs are quite high (Haffner and Dol, 2011). Housing costs amount to about 47 per cent of disposable income for those in the lowest income quintile, compared to 22 per cent in

---

[21] Some studies of health effects on inequality, like education and labour market success (e.g., Haas, 2006), suggest reverse causality.

the top quintile (Özdemir and Ward, 2009). Since 1992, housing expenditure has slightly increased for renters but remained stable for homeowners (*Statistics Netherlands*, 2012)[22]. As housing expenditures are considered relative to income and renting is more likely among low-income households, this finding is not surprising.

Investigating the relationship between inequality and housing in Europe, Dewilde and Lancee (2012) find that income inequality is related to a higher incidence of housing deprivation among low-income households, but that inequality has no effect on housing affordability over and above available resources. Again, it is difficult to directly link increasing inequality and the housing situation. Yet, home ownership may reinforce wealth inequality due to the intergenerational transmission of homeownership (Tolsma and Wolbers, 2010; Smits and Mulder, 2008).

Crime and punishment. Because they lack material or cultural resources, as well as for psycho-social reasons (Wilkinson and Pickett, 2009), crime involvement is highest among disadvantaged groups. The number of criminal acts reported by the police increases between 1977 and 2010, reflecting an overall trend in inequality, poverty and crime rates (*Statistics Netherlands*, 2012). However, particularly for the 2000s crime rates and inequality seem unrelated, as crime rates decrease for both property and violent crimes. While it has been argued that higher levels of perceived inequality are accompanied by feelings of threat and anxiety (Wilkinson and Pickett, 2009), the percentage of crime victims and people who feel unsafe, related to their perception of crime (which differs from fear of crime), remains rather stable (Statistics Netherlands, 2012).

Subjective measures of well-being, satisfaction, happiness. Life satisfaction has remained stable since the 1970s: about 90 per cent of the population reports being happy (*Statistics Netherlands*, 2012; Eurostat, 2012)[23]. The higher the level of education attained, the happier one is. This gradient increases over time, which may be explained by an increasing role of education as a determinant of economic success. Reduced labour market opportunities for the less-educated may lead to dissatisfaction as others get ahead while their mobility chances remain constrained (De Jonge, Hupkens, and Bruggink, 2009). As employment chances by educational level become more unequal, opening up a significant gap between least and best educated, reinforced by a strong educational gradient for working hours (Section 1.3), the divergence by education in life satisfaction may also be an indirect impact of income inequality since the late 1990s.

Political and Cultural Impacts

Rising income/wealth inequalities, and stable or declining educational inequalities, may have severe repercussions on outcomes in the sphere of politics and values. The question is whether we can explain trends in the sphere of political and cultural values with developments in inequality.

---

[22] Housing costs defined as a percentage of total expenditure of disposable income of owner-occupiers and tenants on housing, after allowing for benefits and costs like energy and tax.

[23] These findings are challenged by Veenhoven (2011) who finds an increase in the overall level of happiness and life satisfaction between 1973 and 2010.

Electoral turnout. Turnout rates in elections have declined steadily since abolition of compulsory voting in 1970. Turnout for elections to the national parliament drops from close to 100 per cent in 1969 to around 80 per cent in the 2010 elections. Solt (2010) finds that in US states with higher income inequality compared to other states or earlier, citizens are less likely to vote. This can be explained with Schattschneider's hypothesis of increasing differences between the rich and poor. Solt (2010: 285–286) summarizes this as follows: 'As the rich grow richer relative to their fellow citizens, they consequently grow better able to define the alternatives that are considered within the political system and exclude matters of importance to poor citizens. Poorer citizens, less and less able to place questions of concern to them on the agenda, increasingly stay away from the voting booth.' Hence, with rising inequality, we expect the general turnout to drop. More importantly, we expect differences across groups to increase over time. However, Hakhverdian *et al.* (2011), analyse the intention to vote and show that differences across groups do not change much over time.

Unions. Since unions bargain for better labour conditions for their own group, one would expect more benefits of membership with rising levels of inequality.[24] With higher income inequality the bottom groups lag behind, making it more beneficial to unite and fight for their interests. Similarly, groups at the top, under conditions of higher inequality may have a stronger incentive to protect their interests.

Until the end of the 1970s, the union membership rate is fairly stable at 35 per cent, with a sharp decline to 27 per cent until the mid 1980s. This is consistent with a decline in income inequality in the same period: when inequality decreases, differences across groups become smaller, potentially providing less reason to protect one's own interests. From 1988 to 1992 membership rates increase to 30 per cent. These are the years in which inequality rises most sharply. Over the 2000s, inequality edges upwards and union membership decreases. This decline is not in line with the idea that with rising inequality people would protect themselves from possible marginalization by becoming a union member. It could be that, as suggested by Wilkinson and Pickett (2009), inequality reduces trust, solidarity and increases status competition. Rising inequality fuels a more individualistic mentality, which causes people to perceive their interests to be represented by not a collective, but rather as an individual endeavour.

Civic and social participation. Cross-national research suggests that in countries where inequality is high, social and civic participation are low (Lancee and Van de Werfhorst, 2012). Civic participation[25] derived from the Dutch Election Survey (Hakhverdian *et al.*, 2011) shows an upward trend between 1977 and 1989 and a roughly flat continuation until 1998, almost identical to the evolution of inequality. This does not agree with previous findings. A possible explanation is that most studies are cross-national, comparing levels across countries and not within countries over time. A more substantial explanation might be that with rising inequality, frustration rises, and together with that the motivation to change things, resulting in increasing participation.

Figure 20.8 plots satisfaction with democracy. The percentage of people that is fairly satisfied has risen since the 1970s, the share that is not very satisfied has declined, suggesting

---

[24] Usually unions are thought to affect inequality; however, in the analysis of impacts the opposite is at stake.

[25] An index comprising modes of civic behaviour, such as joining a demonstration, civic action group, being active in political parties and so on.

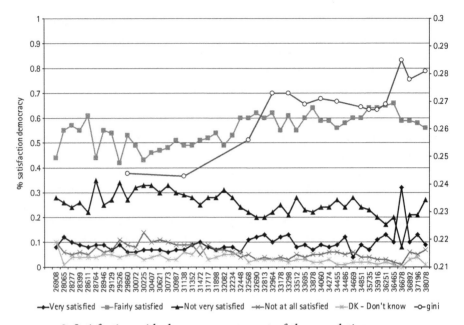

FIGURE 20.8 Satisfaction with democracy, per cent of the population

Note: 1 to 6% do not know.

Source: Eurobarometer (Eurostat, 2011).

that satisfaction with democracy has (modestly) grown until approximately the year 2000. In 2002, the political debate changed radically and populist parties entered the parliament with great electoral success (Van der Brug, 2003). There seems to be a weak correlation with the Gini coefficient, in the sense that in the years when the Gini goes up satisfaction also goes up. It could hence be that people evaluate politics at least partly based on the distribution of income.

Political values and legitimacy. In so far as 'left' orientations stand for more government intervention and more redistribution, one would expect with rising inequality that more vulnerable groups would shift towards the left because more redistribution can provide insurance against the higher risks that inequality implies. Groups in society that profit from higher inequality (for example, because their income grows disproportionally) are more likely to favour a smaller role for government, so as to avoid paying more taxes. As can be expected (De Vries *et al.*, 2011; Hakhverdian *et al.*, 2011), lower levels of education are positioned more on the right. The trend seems to be slightly declining, meaning that the population on average is becoming more left-oriented. However, this changes in the year 2002, when the educational levels move closer together, and the higher educated become more right oriented.

It could be that, as inequality rises and pressure on resources rises too, this translates into more negative attitudes towards immigrants. The mean xenophobic attitude[27] of people for several educational levels seems to trend downward: a sharp decline in the 1980s, a rise in

---

[27] The variable summarizes three items: whether in case of a promotion at your work, the position should go to a Dutch person or to an immigrant, whether if somebody has to be fired it should be an

the late 1980s and early 1990s, followed by a hovering but gradually less xenophobic attitude (Figure 20.9). If inequality triggers anxiety and stress, which subsequently translate into blaming the out-group, this may be in line with the trend in inequality and xenophobic attitudes in the Netherlands: in the period that inequality rose (1985–1990) attitudes towards immigrants became more negative. In the years before 1985, when inequality fell, we also find a decrease in xenophobia.

Values about social policy and welfare state. As inequality rises, one would expect attitudes towards redistribution to change as well. Larger differences could give the bottom income groups a stronger incentive for desiring redistribution, as they would benefit from it. One would not expect this to happen at the top of the income distribution, as this would imply paying more taxes. Figure 20.10 plots attitudes towards redistribution and income inequality. From the beginning of the 1980s until the beginning of the 1990s, fewer people think that income differences are too large, and fewer people think that income differences should be smaller. From 1992 approximately, this trend reverses with more people agreeing that income differences are too large. Around 2005, this increase levels off and stabilizes. Agreement with the statement declines with educational attainment.

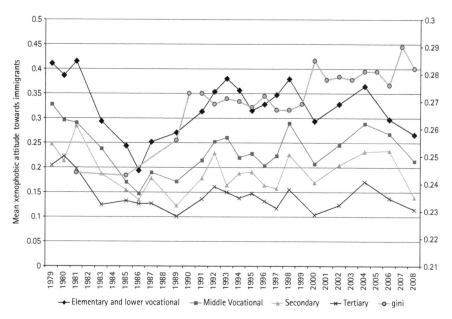

FIGURE 20.9 Mean of xenophobic attitude by educational level, 1979–2008
Source: Survey Cultural Changes (1979–2008).

immigrant or a Dutch person, and whether if there is social housing available this should go to an immigrant or a native.

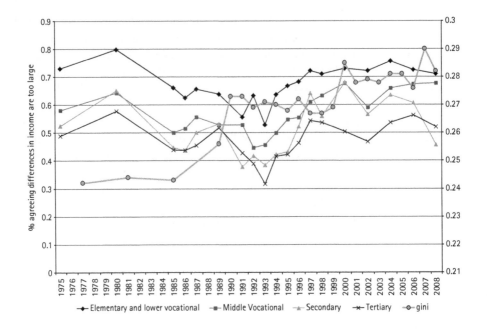

FIGURE 20.10 Percentage of people agreeing that income differences are too large, by educational level, 1975–2008

Source: Survey Cultural Changes (1975–2008).

4. POLICIES: MINIMUM WAGES, TRANSFERS AND TAXATION REDUCE INEQUALITY LESS THAN BEFORE

For many years income redistribution was barely an issue in Dutch politics, but it was at the core of the government formation in 2012. The social-democratic party aims to achieve income redistribution to support the lower end in bearing the cuts deemed necessary to better balance the government budget in the current economic crisis. In the past recessions, that lower end suffered severely from budget cuts. Declining minimum wages and cuts in benefit levels—meant to achieve budget balance in the crisis of the 1980s and early 1990s—had long-lasting effects on the income distribution. In addition, structural changes were implemented in the tax and benefit system, mostly aimed at activating citizens to work. This section discusses the evolution of public policies affecting the income distribution over the last three decades.

Policies Affecting Market Incomes

Households earn their primary incomes on the labour and financial markets. Inequality of wage incomes has grown fastest of all income types (Section 1.2). The government can influence the market-income distribution directly or indirectly but when the option of a general wage intervention was de facto abolished,[27] only the statutory minimum wage has remained as a universal instrument. It applies from the age of 23 and has a long tail of special, low minimum wages for youths, which stimulates inequality between young and adult workers. Minimum wage growth is legally indexed to the average growth of collectively agreed wages but this rule was breached during each previous recession. Nominal reductions during the 1980s and a prolonged freeze were followed by new freezes in 1993–1995 and 2004–2005. As a result, real minimum wages declined strongly between 1980 and 1997 (-23 per cent) and have regained only very little since (+4 per cent until 2011) (Salverda, 2008). The evolution of the minimum wage largely explains the strong growth in wage inequality between 1981 and 1989. It has lost most of its labour-market significance and the possible compressed effect on the wage distribution (Koeniger *et al.*, 2007) has been weakened. In the current crisis, the minimum wage has been left untouched so far, but indexation has been weak.

The government affects labour-market outcomes also as a major employer, of 27 per cent of all employees, directly for the administration and at arm's length for the rest of the public sector (local government, education and health care). In times of recession public sector wages are a key instrument for reducing government spending and are also seen as a tool for bringing about general wage moderation. In the 1980s they underwent the same 3 per cent nominal reduction and prolonged freeze as the minimum wage. This turned a public sector pay premium into a penalty (Berkhout and Salverda, 2012). In the 1990s free wage negotiations were introduced and decentralized within the public sector. Since then negotiated wages have developed largely in parallel with the private sector. In the current economic crisis, the government has endorsed a freeze for the administration for some time already (by refusing negotiations) and aims to prolong this until 2014. Importantly, wage inequality in the public sector has declined (-10 per cent) and since 1989 has been smaller than in the private sector, where it has grown substantially (+28 per cent).

Indirect government influence in the labour market stems primarily from consultation with the social partners and the legal extension of collective labour agreements, key elements of the labour relations system. Though union density has declined, the coverage of collective agreements remains high at over 80 per cent. The exemplary result of consultation is the well-known *Wassenaar Accord* of 1982, when the unions agreed to wage moderation in exchange for shortening working hours and the early retirement of older workers. In 1992–1993, another agreement on wage moderation was concluded. Under government pressure the *Tabaksblatt* governance code for private sector top wages was introduced for stock exchange listed companies in 2003 but its enforcement is still voluntary. The government has sought a moderation of top incomes in the public sector ('no salary higher than

---

[27] Intervention was permanent until the early 1960s. It was 'if demanded by the state of the national economy' (8 times in 12 years) until the early 1980s; and has possible been only in case of national emergency since.

the prime minister'), on a voluntary basis in 2006 and recently by law. Another indirect means of government influence on market wages runs through quantity effects on labour supply. Stimulating educational attainment, increasing the retirement age, expanding employment in health care, and introducing activating measures in the tax and benefit system, all affect the distribution over socio-economic groups (paid labour, retirement, school, (un)employment).

Transfer and Tax Policies

Social transfers and (direct) taxes redistribute income from rich to poor households. Contrary to the OECD average, cash public transfer spending has declined as a share of GDP over the last three decades (Figure 20.11). Social Assistance, National Insurance (old age, survivors, family benefits) and Employee Insurance (unemployment, disability, sickness)[28] make up most of the cash transfers. Subsidies for pupils/students and housing make up the rest. The decline in disability-related benefits is responsible for most of the decrease in spending.

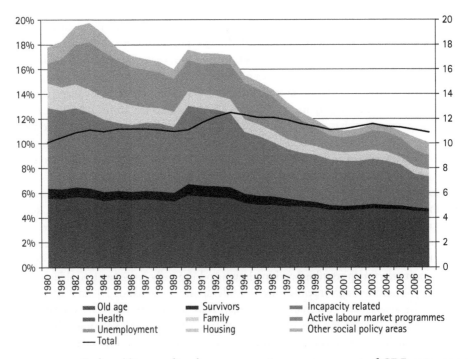

FIGURE 20.11 Cash public spending by expense category as per cent of GDP, 1980–2007

Source: OECD SOCX.

---

[28] All residents are by law subject to National Insurance, all employees to Employee Insurance.

As elsewhere, social assistance and public old-age pensions account for most of the redistribution (Caminada *et al*, 2012). Social assistance is means tested and therefore has a targeted redistributive effect. Old age pensions are of course targeted at the elderly, many of whom used to have little other income. Benefit levels are indexed to average collectively negotiated wage growth and their minimum level was legally coupled to the minimum wage (net after taxes) in 1974 but has increasingly lagged behind 'to make work pay'. Benefits have declined significantly in real terms as during the 1980s recession they followed the 3 per cent lowering and freeze of the minimum wage. The resulting decoupling of wages and benefit levels was the main source of growing income inequality during that period (Gradus and Hendrix, 1999). Since the early 1990s ad hoc decoupling is no longer allowed. Instead there is a law stipulating a decoupling of benefits from wage developments only if the ratio of the inactive-to-active population becomes too high.

The contribution of unemployment benefits to redistribution is cyclical by nature, while disability and sickness benefits show a more stable trend. Since 1985, all three employee benefit schemes have been subject to structural reforms. To reduce spending, but also enhance the activating nature of the benefit system, benefit levels have been cut,[29] durations shortened,[30] entry conditions strengthened (for unemployment benefits and especially disability pensions[31]), and benefits made conditional on job search and participation in active labour market programmes. Thus entitlements relative to previous earnings have been reduced. Sickness benefits were privatized in 1996, shifting entirely from social security to employers, aimed at stimulating them to combat sick leave and act as an effective gatekeeper to the disability scheme. Due to decentralization, municipalities now bear full financial responsibility for social assistance, aimed at stimulating them to actively reduce the number of benefit recipients. These policy changes are structural and aimed at incentivizing citizens to work and save on public expenditures.

As to taxation, two important changes have been made: the Oort revision in 1990 and the Zalm/Vermeend overhaul of the tax system in 2001. Both reduced the number of tax brackets and lowered top marginal rates, thus reducing the taxation of higher incomes. Taken together, the top marginal rate shrunk from 72 to 52 per cent. The Oort revision effectively also hit the lower deciles by increasing the tax burden of singles who are mostly found in these deciles. Thus the Oort reform reduced redistribution through taxation substantially (Gradus and Hendrix, 1999). Zalm/Vermeend replaced unequal deductions at the marginal rate with tax credits of equal value to the taxpayer irrespective of income. This benefited the bottom decile but had little effect on the rest of the distribution as lower top tariffs went together with diminished deductibles. The main idea was to stimulate employment by reducing income taxation, while special tax credits added targeted instruments for that.[32]

---

[29] Employee benefits were cut from 80 per cent to 70 per cent of last earnings in 1985.

[30] Maximum duration of unemployment benefit has been subject to recent policy interventions. It was reduced substantially to three years—still long compared to other countries and government intends to further reduce this.

[31] This was meant to cure the 'Dutch disease' of 10 per cent of the potential labour force in disability schemes.

[32] Employment stimulating are a general tax credit for people in work and special credits for those in work and having young children, for people entering the labour market, for elderly people continuing to work, for parents taking parental leave.

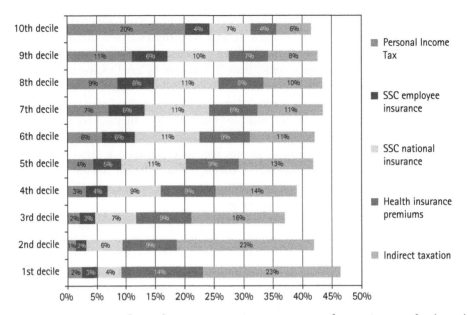

FIGURE 20.12 Taxes and social security premiums, per cent of gross income, by (gross) income decile, 2010

Source: CBS Statline, own calculations.

Dutch social security contributions are not progressive. They are paid on earnings below certain thresholds. Taking personal income tax and social security contributions together with health insurance premiums and consumption taxes, the tax system is neither progressive nor regressive (Figure 20.12). The progressive effect of personal income taxation is neutralized by taxes on consumption and health insurance premiums, which are more significant for lower incomes than for higher incomes. Health insurance premiums were made flat rate in 2006, when a personal duty to take insurance and compulsory acceptance by the insurer were introduced, aimed at enhancing the cost-sensitivity of demand for health care. Households receive an income-dependent health-care allowance to make up for part of the higher fixed costs. Nevertheless, the bottom spends the highest share of its income on health insurance.

Internationally, Dutch social policy is neither the most nor the least redistributive, with a tax and transfer system that lowers market-income inequality by approximately 30–40 per cent (Immervoll and Richardson, 2011; Jesuit and Mahler, 2010; Caminada *et al.*, 2012) (Table 20.1). According to OECD data, the redistributive effect of taxes and transfers has declined since the mid 1980s, especially for households with working-age heads (not shown). However this conclusion is not shared by Caminada *et al.* (2012), who come to a different conclusion based on LIS-data.[33] All agree that the redistributive effect fluctuates over time, but due to the use of different data sources, different conclusion are reached regarding the increase or fall of redistribution since the 1980s. Since the LIS-data for the Netherlands

[33] For the Netherlands, LIS uses a rather diverse set of surveys over time, and results of Caminada *et al.* (2012) conflict with those of Caminada and Goudswaard (2001).

Table 20.1 Redistributive effects of Dutch taxes and transfers from the mid-1970s to the late 2000s

	mid 70s	mid 80s	around 1990	mid 90s	around 2000	Mid 2000s	late 2000s
All households (OECD)							
Gini coefficient before tax and transfers	0.426	0.473	0.474	0.484	0.424	0.426	0.426
Gini coefficient after tax and transfers	0.263	0.272	0.292	0.297	0.292	0.284	0.294
Redistributive effect of taxes and transfers	0.163	0.201	0.182	0.187	0.132	0.142	0.132
All households (Caminada et al., 2012)							
Gini coefficient before tax and transfers		0.435	0.405	0.420	0.373	0.459	
Gini coefficient after tax and transfers		0.260	0.226	0.257	0.231	0.264	
Redistributive effect of taxes and transfers		0.175	0.139	0.163	0.142	0.195	

Source: OECD database, Caminada et al. (2012).

for 2004 are based on EU-SILC, whose representativeness and quality of income information are criticized by many, we are inclined to trust the OECD conclusion more.

Finally, demographic changes, combined with policies aimed at the young and the old
have significantly affected transfers. The last three decades have witnessed important benefit
growth especially for the elderly. The expansion of capital-funded occupational pensions
that have now started to pay out[35] has lifted pensioners up the deciles. An expansion of transfers to students and children in the first decile has shifted transfers down the distribution.
Overall, the evolution of redistribution since 1977 rests on a complex interaction between
demographic change, a shrinking of employee benefits, and the growth or establishment
of new institutions such as for pension funding, student grants, youth disability, and health
care insurance. Without the student grants and the growth of youth disability benefits introduced in 1998, the first decile might have suffered even more.

In-Kind Benefits and Consumption Taxes

Tertiary income is defined as disposable (= secondary) income plus the indirect subsidies that
households receive through government services and goods, minus indirect taxes they pay on
consumption. Consumption taxes capture a larger share of household income for the poor
than for the rich making tertiary incomes in principle more unequal than secondary incomes
(Figure 20.12). The effect of in-kind subsidies is harder to establish, especially for true public
goods, such as the signposts and street lamps which are left out here. The lowest income groups
receive a higher share of their net income from in-kind subsidies, especially for education,
which is not surprising since students make up a large part of the lowest decile (Table 20.2).[36]
Social housing is also important for redistribution, just like social services and health care. In
absolute terms the highest decile receives most subsidies, but relative to disposable income the
lowest decile receives most. In-kind subsidies thus reduce tertiary income inequality.

In-kind public social spending is an important element of the in-kind subsidies of
Table 20.2. According to OECD SOCX data, Dutch in-kind public social spending has
increased as a share of GDP, mostly because of the increased expenditures on health care.
The OECD does not account for education subsidies. These are an important source of
in-kind social spending, and have fallen as a share of GDP. As a result, total in-kind spending is now more or less at the same level as in the early 1980s.

5. CONCLUSIONS

For the Netherlands, the Gini coefficient for equivalized disposable household income rises
sharply up to 1990 (+13 per cent) and slowly (+2 per cent) over the 2000s. The ratio of top to

---

[35] See footnote 7. Occupational pensions are left out in the OECD social security database and by
Caminada *et al.* (2012).
[36] SCP uses a peculiar concept of households, in which students living with their parents are identified
as separate single households. This has an important effect on the composition of the lowest decile.

Table 20.2 Households' receipt of public services, per cent of disposable income, 2007

	1st decile	2nd decile	3rd decile	4th decile	5th decile	6th decile	7th decile	8th decile	9th decile	10th decile
Housing	8.0%	17.7%	11.8%	8.3%	5.9%	5.3%	4.8%	4.6%	4.3%	3.4%
Education	82.9%	11.4%	8.9%	7.3%	7.6%	9.0%	10.4%	9.1%	8.8%	5.6%
Public transport	5.2%	1.3%	1.4%	1.5%	1.4%	1.5%	1.8%	1.8%	1.9%	1.3%
Culture and recreation	8.1%	2.4%	2.3%	1.9%	2.0%	1.9%	1.8%	1.8%	1.6%	1.0%
Social services	2.4%	11.4%	7.0%	4.4%	2.7%	2.1%	1.5%	1.6%	1.5%	0.8%
Health care	6.8%	9.6%	8.9%	6.7%	4.0%	3.4%	0.8%	-0.8%	-1.4%	-0.8%
TOTAL	113.4%	53.9%	40.4%	30.2%	23.6%	23.3%	21.0%	17.9%	16.6%	11.3%
TOTAL in Euros	6.900	12.900	15.000	16.800	18.800	20.900	23.500	26.700	31.700	54.600

Source: Pommer *et al.* (2011), own calculations. Social services include care for elderly and newborn.

bottom-decile total incomes (S10:S1), which accounts better for developments at the tails, underlines this, rising by 42 per cent and 10 per cent over these periods respectively. This sharp rise is caused by both rapid growth in top labour market incomes and reduced redistribution to low incomes. Persistent growth in wage-earnings inequality—incomes from enterprise or wealth play remarkably little role—and secular decline in the minimum wage and social transfers push up inequality after 1990. A 2001 tax revision provides some relief to the very bottom but not a full reversal. Relative poverty roughly follows the same course, but absolute poverty moves in the opposite direction.

Nevertheless, cash transfers and taxation still reduce market-income inequality considerably, but have not compensated fully for strong market-income inequality growth. The equivalization of incomes for household composition significantly lowers inequality, especially for wage-earning households, who are prime-age and have children. Joint household labour supply mitigates the effects of individual wage inequality.

A major decline in educational inequality is accompanied by a strong increase in the educational gradient in employment access, and thus in wage incomes. An inverse relationship between part-time hours and educational attainment and occupational level enhances these effects.

Finally, inequality in the distribution of wealth is strong, particularly for financial wealth. It declines over the 1990s and increases over the 2000s. Growing house ownership flattens this distribution but its large debt financing poses a significant risk. There is certainly not a one-to-one correspondence between income and wealth. High incomes and large wealth come together for a small fraction only: 3.5 per cent of households own 29 per cent of wealth and more than 40 per cent of financial wealth.

Descriptive statistics suggest mostly no direct social impacts of rising inequality. Even where a common evolution of inequality and a social indicator is observed, this may still be due to other factors such as cultural change or economic development. Bivariate analysis and the limited time series available do not permit strong conclusions as to whether rising inequality is a main driver of changes within Dutch society. Yet, it is also clear that there is an increasing gradient of inequality along educational levels and income groups in various impacts fields, e.g. arrears in payments, social disconnectedness, fertility, healthy life expectancy, house ownership, life satisfaction. It implies that education attainment increasingly affects individual life chances and well being. These correlations also need to be interpreted with caution, though, as the effect of low education may be confounded with (old) age.

We described the trends for several 'political and cultural' impacts in terms of attitudes and behaviour. Bearing in mind the difficulties with the data, some trends in indicators might be interpreted as in line with the developments in inequality. Union membership, civic participation and attitudes towards distribution seem linked to the increasing inequality in the second half of the '80s. Attitudes towards immigrants follow a somewhat similar pattern to the changes in income inequality. The changes in educational gradients could in general not be linked to developments in income inequality.

Dutch social policy brings about a sizable income redistribution and reduction in welfare inequality, if we look at taxation, cash transfers and non-cash benefits over the full life cycle (Ter Rele, 2007). However, three decades of social policy reforms indicate that social policy is particularly cyclical. Repeatedly, during recessions policy changes (minimum wage, benefits), serving the purpose of balancing the government budget, were detrimental to lower incomes. In addition, structural reforms, implemented during the economic boom of the late 1990s and early 2000s, were aimed mainly at enhancing the activating nature of the welfare state by restricting eligibility, shortening duration, privatizing sickness benefit). Two tax reforms (1990, 2001) lowered top rates and introduced working tax credits in order to stimulate employment. Overall, this reduces the redistributive effect of social policy, though if it effectively stimulates a net employment gain for those (otherwise) on benefits it may enhance labour incomes. At the same time, significant demographic benefits growth, especially for the elderly, makes redistribution much more important to the middle of the distribution than before.

We conclude that inequality in *market* incomes has grown strongly, that policy making has shrunk its efforts to reduce that inequality and that demographic shifts have played an important role in containing income inequality. Though equivalized income inequality edged up only slightly after 1990 this partly rests on a re-ranking of households and may underestimate people's experience of decreasing redistribution and taxation. Educational inequalities have decreased but an increasingly strong gradient in social, political, and labour-market inequalities by education is seen.

References

Agtmaal-Wobma, E. and van Huis M. (2008), *De relatie tussen vruchtbaarheid en opleidingsniveau van de vrouw*, Centraal Bureau voor de Statistiek, Voorburg/Heerlen.

Allport, G.W. (1979), *The Nature of Prejudice*, Cambridge, MA: Perseus Books.

Atkinson, A.B. and Piketty. T. (eds.). (2007), *Top Incomes over the Twentieth Century: A Contrast Between Continental European and English-Speaking Countries*, Oxford: Oxford University Press.

Beets, G.C.N., Verweij, A. and Sanderse, C. (2012), 'Wat waren de belangrijkste ontwikkelingen in het verleden?' In *Volksgezondheid Toekomst Verkenning*, Nationaal Kompas Volksgezondheid, Bilthoven: RIVM.

Berkhout, E. and Salverda, W. (2012), 'Development of the Public-Private Wage Differential in the Netherlands 1979–2009', *Discussion Paper 71*, SEO, Amsterdam.

Caminada, C.L.J. and Goudswaard, K.P. (2001), 'Trends in inkomensongelijkheid en sociaal beleid', *Tijdschrift voor Politieke Ekonomie*, 22(4), 55–69.

Caminada, C.L.J., Goudswaard, K.P. and Wang C. (2012), '*Disentangling Income Inequality and the Redistributive Effect of Taxes and Transfers in 20 LIS Countries over Time*', LIS Working Paper No. 581.

Claessen, J. (2010), 'Vermogensverdeling en vermogenspositie huishoudens', *Sociaal-economische Trends*, 2010 nr 2, 7-12. CBS, Voorburg.

CPB: Centraal Planbureau (2012), *Tabel: Vermogens van gezinnen (miljard euro's) 1970-2011* (Provided on request).

De Jonge, T. Hupkens, C. and. Bruggink, J.W. (2009), *Living a Happy, Healthy and Satisfying Life*, Statistics Netherlands, Voorburg/Heerlen .

De Vries, C. E., Hakhverdian A. and Lancee, B. (2011), 'The Dynamics of Voters' Left/Right Identification: The Role of Economic and Cultural Attitudes', paper presented at the ECPR Conference, Reykjavik.

Dewilde, C. and Lancee B. (2012), 'Income Inequality and Access to Housing in Europe', *GINI Discussion Paper 32*. Amsterdam, AIAS (accepted for publication in *European Sociological Review*).

Eurostat (2013), 'Material Deprivation Rate—Economic Strain and Durables Dimension', database retrieved February 2013, from <http://epp.eurostat.ec.europa.eu/portal/page/portal/statistics/search_database.>

Eurostat (2012), <http://epp.eurostat.ec.europa.eu/portal/page/portal/statistics/search_database> (retrieved August 2012).

Eurostat (2011), *Eurobarometer Surveys.* <http://ec.europa.eu/public_opinion/cf/index.cfm?lang=en> (retrieved 20 June 2013).

Gradus, R.H.J.M. and Hendrix, P.C.M. (1999), 'De inkomensverdeling ontleed', *Economisch Statistische Berichten*, 8 4210, 484–489.

Haas, S. A. (2006), Health Selection and the Process of Social Stratification: The Effect of Childhood Health on Socioeconomic Attainment. *Journal of Health and Social Behavior*, 47(4):339–354.

Haffner, M. and Dol K. (2011), *Internationale vergelijking van woonuitgaven met EU-SILC*, Eindrapport: Ministerie van BZK / WWI.

Hakhverdian, A, W., Van der Brug, W and De Vries, C. (2011), 'The emergence of a "diploma democracy"? The political education gap in the Netherlands, 1971-2010', paper presented at the AMCIS Year Conference, 30 January Amsterdam.

Huijts, T., Monden, C.W.S. and Kraaykamp, G. (2010), 'Education, Educational Heterogamy, and Self-Assessed Health in Europe: A Multilevel Study of Spousal Effects in 29 European Countries', *European Sociological Review*, 26: 261–276.

Immervoll, H. and Richardson, L. (2011), 'Redistribution Policy and Inequality Reduction in OECD Countries: What has Changed in Two Decades?', *OECD Social, Employment and Migration Working Papers*, No. 122,OECD Publishing.

Jesuit, D. and Mahler, V. (2010), 'Comparing Government Redistribution Across Countries: The Problem of Second-Order Effects', *Social Science Quarterly*, 91(5): 1390–1404.

Kalmijn, M., Vanassche, S. and Mattijs, K. (2011), Divorce and Social Class during the Early Stages of the Divorce Revolution: Evidence from Flanders and the Netherlands. *Journal of Family History*, 36(2):159–172.

Keizer, R., Dykstra, P.A. and Jansen, M.D. (2008), 'Pathways into Childlessness: Evidence of Gendered Life Course Dynamics'. *Journal of Biosocial Science*, 40(6), 863–878.

Koeniger, W., Leonardi, M. and Nunziata, L. (2007), Labor Market Institutions and Wage Inequality, *Industrial and Labor Relations Review*, 60(3): 340–356.

Lancee, B. and Werfhorst, H. Van de (2012), 'Income Inequality and Participation. A Comparison of 24 European Countries', *Social Science Research* 41 (5): 1166–1178.

Liefbroer, A.C. and Corijn, M. (1999), 'Who, What, Where, and When? Specifying the Impact of Educational Attainment and Labour Force Participation on Family Formation', *European Journal of Population*, 15(1):45–75.

Lynch, J. W., Smith, G.D., Kaplan G. A. and House, J.S. (2000), 'Income Inequality and Mortality: Importance to Health of Individual Income, Psychosocial Environment, or Material Conditions', *British Medical Journal*, 320: 1200–1204.

NIDI: Netherlands Interdisciplinary Demographic Institute (2012), 'Trouwen en scheiden in tijden van voor- en tegenspoed', *Demos Bulletin over Bevolking en Samenleving*. 28: May.

NIDI: Netherlands Interdisciplinary Demographic Institute (2013), 'Kinderen willen en kinderen krijgen', *Demos Bulletin over Bevolking en Samenleving*,29:1. Information retrieved from <http://publ.nidi.nl/demos/2013/demos-29-01-debruijn.pdf>.

Özdemir, E. and Ward, T. (2009), Research note no.1: 'Housing and Social Inclusion', European Commission, Network on Income Distribution and Living Conditions of the European Observatory on the Social Situation and Demography.

Pommer, E., Jonker, J-J. van der Torre A. and Kempen, H. van (2011), *Minder voor het midden, Profijt van de overheid in 2007*, SCP-publicatie 2011-11, The Hague: Sociaal Cultureel Planbureau.

Putnam, R. D. (2000), *Bowling Alone. The Collapse and Revival of American Community*, New York: Simon and Schuster.

RIVM: Rijksinstituut voor Volksgezondheid en Milieu (2010), *Gezondheid en determinanten.* Deelrapport van de VTV 2010. Van gezond naar beter. Bilthoven.

Salverda, W. (2008), 'The Netherlands: Minimum Wage Fall Shifts Focus to Part-Time Jobs', in Vaughan-Whitehead, D., *The Minimum Wage Revisited in the Enlarged EU*, Geneva: International Labour Office-Edward Elgar.

Salverda, W. (forthcoming), 'Merit en werk in 1960–2010: Effecten van de Nederlandse onderwijs- en deeltijdtsunami's', in Werfhorst, H. van de and Ganzeboom, H. (eds.), *Kerende Kansen. Hoe lager en hoger opgeleiden steeds meer op elkaar gaan lijken*, AMCIS-bundel, Amsterdam University Press.

Schutjens, V., Kempen, R. van and Weesep, J. van (2002), 'The Changing Tenant Profile of Dutch Social Rented Housing, *Urban Studies*, 39(4): 643–664.

SCP: Sociaal en Cultureel Planbureau (2003), *Inkomen Verdeeld*, The Hague.

SCP: Sociaal en Cultureel Planbureau (2011), *De Sociale Staat van Nederland 2011*. The Hague.

Smits, A. and Mulder, C.H. (2008), Family Dynamics and First-Time Homeownership, *Housing Studies*, 23 (6): 917–933.

Solt, F. (2010), 'Does Economic Inequality Depress Electoral Participation? Testing the Schattschneider Hypothesis', *Political Behavior* 32(2): 285–301.

Statistics Netherlands (Centraal Bureau voor de Statistiek) (2012), information retrieved December 2012 from <http://www.cbs.nl>

Ter Rele, H. (2007), 'Measuring the Lifetime Redistribution Achieved by Dutch Taxation, Cash Transfer and Non-Cash Benefits Programs', *Review of Income and Wealth*, 53: 335–362.

Tolsma, J. and Wolbers, M. (2010), *Naar een open samenleving? Recente ontwikkelingen in sociale stijging en daling in Nederland*, Den Haag: Raad voor Maatschappelijke Ontwikkelingen (RMO).

Van der Brug, W. (2003), 'How the LPF Fuelled Discontent: Empirical Tests of Explanations of LPF-Support', *ActaPolitica* 38(1): 89–106.

Van Kempen, R. and Priemus, H. (2002), 'Revolution in Social Housing in the Netherlands: Possible Effects of New Housing Policies', *Urban Studies*, 39(2): 237–253.

Veenhoven, R. (2011), *Distributional Findings on Happiness in Netherlands (NL)*, World Database of Happiness, Erasmus University Rotterdam, The Netherlands. Accessed on 2 January 2012 at <http://worlddatabaseofhappiness.eur.nl.>

VROM (2003), *Beter thuis in Wonen*. Kernpublicatie WoonBehoefte Onderzoek (WBO) 2002. Information retrieved at http://www.rigo.nl/nl-NL/Publicaties/Publicatie/_p/itemID/1453/Beter-thuis-in-wonen.aspx

Whelan, C.T. and Maitre, B. (2012), 'Understanding Material Deprivation in Europe: A Multilevel Analysis', *GINI Discussion Paper* 37. Amsterdam, AIAS.

Wilkinson, R. G. and Pickett, K.E. (2009), *The Spirit Level. Why More Equal Societies Almost Always do Better*, London: Allen Lane.

CHAPTER 21

···

THE RISE OF INEQUALITIES IN POLAND AND THEIR IMPACTS: WHEN POLITICIANS DON'T CARE BUT CITIZENS DO

···

NATALIA LETKI, MICHAŁ BRZEZIŃSKI, AND

BARBARA JANCEWICZ

1. INTRODUCTION

···

In 1989, Poland was the first country in Eastern Europe to start transformation, and while the political reforms were initially gradual and negotiated, the economic reforms were so radical they were termed the 'shock therapy'. The cost was paid by the most vulnerable groups in the society (the less skilled, the elderly, and most of all—children) (Harwin and Fajth, 1998). It resulted in the loss of support for the new democratic government, and an early election in 1993, which brought the post-communist party to power. Throughout the 1990s and 2000s Poland was considered an example of a success story of political and economic transformation, although it was sometimes criticized for the lack of control over corruption. Even in the face of a recent economic crisis, Poland has had economic growth, and its bank sector has remained stable.

The case of Poland is typical for a country in transition from a command to a market economy, where the major policy focus has been on promoting deregulation and economic growth, at the expense of growing social and economic disparities and the marginalization of certain groups. In comparison with some other post-communist countries, Poland is used as an example of a gradual growth of inequalities accompanied by at least some policy attempts to adjust the safety net accordingly, which is in stark contrast with cases such as Russia, where the 'explosion of inequality' was only marginally corrected by delayed policy measures (Mitra and Yemtsov, 2006). On the other hand, the initial welcome of inequalities as a sign of successful economic reforms turned into a deep disenchantment and dissatisfaction with the new economic landscape of Polish society (Grosfeld and Senik, 2010). Social polarization resulting from the rise of inequalities became one of the main social costs, next to unemployment, of an economic transformation that has been negatively evaluated by the public.

In this chapter we show the post-1989 trends in the key types of inequalities: income, wealth, and educational. We also show Poles' perceptions of the income and inequality changes that have taken place since the beginning of economic transformation. We later discuss key social and political impacts of the growth of inequalities. Finally, we turn to an overview of policies that might have had a corrective effect on inequalities in Poland, but frequently made them worse.[1]

2. EVOLUTION OF INEQUALITY AND ITS DRIVERS IN THE POLISH TRANSITION

The collapse of Communism in Central and Eastern Europe (CEE) had a profound effect on income distribution, although even under communism in the 1980s, income inequality in Poland was similar to that of the USSR and clearly higher than in Hungary or Czechoslovakia (Flemming and Micklewright 2000, p. 866–870). The Gini coefficient for individual per capita income in the mid 1980s was slightly higher or comparable to that of Scandinavian countries and Belgium. However, the Gini index was on average lower by seven percentage points than in OECD countries.

This picture changed soon after the economic transformation was initiated. In what follows, data from the Household Budget Survey (HBS) conducted yearly by the Polish Central Statistical Office (CSO), and from the European Social Survey (ESS) are used to illustrate the evolution of income, wealth and educational inequality in Poland between 1993 and 2010. We present our estimates of income inequality indices independently for the 1993–1997 and 1998–2010 periods because of the change in methodology of data collection that took place in 1998 (this break is marked on relevant figures using a dashed vertical line).[2] All welfare measures used in this chapter are expressed in real terms after correcting for changes in the level of prices. If not otherwise stated, all calculations and figures in this section are based on the HBS data.

Household Income Inequality

We start with an overview of changes in household income inequality using several measures, which show different sensitivity to differences in various parts of income distribution.

---

[1] Analyses presented in this chapter are based on the GINI country report for Poland, by the same authors. For detailed data, information and analyses not covered by this chapter, see the country report.

[2] In 1998, HBS changed the definition of household disposable income and some other categories. We have used information from the CSO to adjust income data for 1993–1997 according to new income definitions from 1998. However, our estimates show a large drop in inequality from 1997 to 1998, which may be in part a statistical artefact related to the changing income definitions.

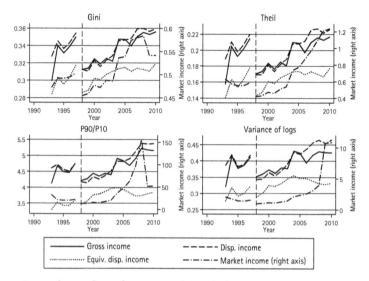

FIGURE 21.1 Inequality indices for various household income concepts

Source: Own calculations using the HBS data.

Figure 21.1 presents four commonly used inequality indices computed for four household income concepts: 1) market income (before taxes and redistribution); 2) gross income (market income plus transfers); 3) net disposable income (gross income minus taxes); and 4) equivalized net disposable income.[3]

The major conclusion, which is robust for most of the inequality measures and income concepts used, is that for both sub-periods (1993–1997 and 1998–2010) there was a moderate, but steady growth in inequality in Poland. For example, in the case of equivalized net household income, inequality as measured by the Gini index increased in both sub-periods by about 10.5 per cent.

Inequality of market income is much higher in Poland than inequality in terms of other income concepts. For example, the Gini index for market income was 0.54 in 2010, while it was 0.36 for disposable income. Figure 21.2 shows that for all inequality measures used, and for most of the time-span analysed, there is little difference between these two series, which suggests that the transfer system, rather than taxes, has helped to reduce market income inequality in Poland. Figure 21.2 also shows the role of household income equivalization. For all inequality measures used, inequality of equivalized income is significantly lower than inequality in terms of unequivalized incomes. The gap between the two series visibly increases between 1998 and 2010. The Gini index for unequivalized disposable income rose by 15 per cent, and for equivalized income by only 10.5 per cent. The reason for this difference is the changing composition of households. For example, the average number of children for households in the first decile fell from 1.07 in 2005 to 0.86 in 2010 while in the ninth

---

[3] We use the original OECD equivalence scale, which assigns the weight of 0.7 to every adult household member beyond the first one and the weight of 0.5 to every child. The modified OECD scale, which is recommended by Eurostat, may be less appropriate for Poland and other CEE countries because of lower economies of scale than in Western countries.

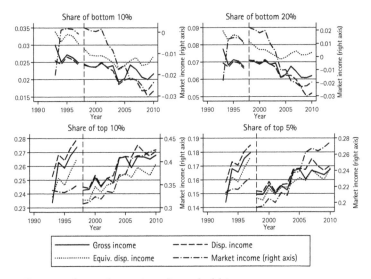

FIGURE 21.2 Income shares for various household income concepts

Source: Own calculations using the HBS data.

decile it increased from 0.31 to 0.37. The share of singles in decile 1 increased from 11 per cent in 2005 to 17 per cent in 2010, while in decile 10 it fell from 30 per cent to 28 per cent.

Income shares of the bottom 10 per cent and 20 per cent of the population declined for all income definitions. For example, in the case of household equivalized disposable income the share belonging to the bottom 10 per cent decreased from 3 per cent in 1998 to 2.7 per cent in 2010. Simultaneously, top income shares were rising fast, especially over the 1998–2010 period. Using household equivalized disposable income, we estimate that the share of income going to the richest 5 per cent of the population increased from 14.6 per cent in 1998 to 16.8 per cent in 2010. The share of market income going to the richest 5 per cent grew exceptionally fast: by about 42 per cent between 1998 and 2010, but this increase was reduced by the tax and transfer system to 15 per cent.[4] Therefore, there is clear evidence for a gradual rise of economic polarization of the Polish society.

Household consumption expenditure inequality measures grew moderately. The Gini index for household equivalized consumption increased from 1993 to 2010 by 14 per cent, while the increases for the Theil index and decile ratio were, respectively, 31 per cent and 21 per cent. In general, the dynamics of consumption inequality is similar to the dynamics of income inequality—both types of measures show that inequality was rising steadily, but slowly.

Figure 21.3 presents trends in absolute and relative poverty rates for household equivalized disposable income. Absolute poverty rates are computed with a quasi-absolute poverty line equal to the 60 per cent of median income in 1993, while relative poverty rates—with a poverty line equal to 60 per cent of median income in a given year. In general, absolute

---

[4] The share of income going to the middle 60 per cent of the population (not shown in Figure 2) fell from 54 per cent in 1998 to 52 per cent in 2010.

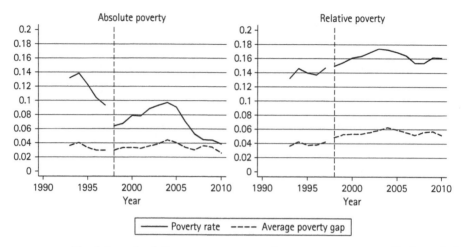

FIGURE 21.3 Absolute and relative poverty rates and average poverty gaps for household equivalized disposable income

Source: Own calculations using the HBS data.

poverty declined from 13.2 per cent in 1993 to 3.9 per cent in 2010. However, between 1998 and 2004 absolute poverty increased from 6.4 per cent to 9.7 per cent due to slower economic growth and worsening labour market conditions. Since 2004, when economic growth in Poland was particularly strong and the unemployment rate plummeted, absolute poverty has been falling very fast. The situation is different with relative poverty rates, which in fact may be considered as a dimension of inequality applying to the lower part of the income distribution. It was increasing up to 2004, but later declined from 17.2 per cent in 2004 to 16.1 per cent in 2010, and these changes follow the evolution of income and consumption inequality. The average poverty gaps behave in a similar way to poverty rates.

Wealth and Debt Inequality

Available comparative data on the wealth and debt of Polish households produce contradictory results. For example, according to the Survey of Health, Ageing and Retirement in Europe (SHARE) project, which gives socio-economic information on Europeans aged 50 and over, 14 per cent of Polish respondents reported zero or negative wealth. The bottom half of the elderly Polish population owns 6 per cent of total wealth, while the top 10 per cent and 5 per cent own, respectively, 62 per cent and 53 per cent. The Gini index for wealth is 0.75, and the wealth inequality among the Polish elderly is the highest in the SHARE sample of countries (Skopek *et al.* 2011). On the other hand, Global Wealth Report (GWR) data by Credit Suisse shows that the Gini index for wealth inequality in Poland increased from 66.8 per cent in 2010 to 74.9 per cent in 2011, and 75.3 per cent in 2012 (Davies *et al.*, 2012). According to GWR, this is significantly lower than the European average.[5] Finally,

---

[5] The GWR estimates of wealth inequality for Poland were constructed by rescaling data on income distribution taken from World Development Indicators or the World Income Inequality Database

according to Yemtsov (2008), who approximated wealth distribution by the distribution of housing stock using HBS data, Poland emerged as the least unequal country (in comparison with Russia and Serbia).

There are no data we could use to reconcile these findings; however, we can estimate changes in wealth measured by income and tenure status based on the HBS data. Shortly after the economic transition begun, percentages of those not living in their own apartments were roughly similar across income quintiles (disposable equivalized income). Since then the share of wealthier households living in their own housing has been growing, while the percentage of the poorest living in not-owned accommodation has remained approximately the same. Therefore, inequality in terms of housing has increased, as those with higher incomes have been more likely to acquire houses and apartments they live in. However, these purchases seem to have been financed mostly through mortgages. Thus the rise in housing inequality does not translate directly into wealth inequality, since those new property owners will be burdened with mortgage payments for years to come.

Labour Market Inequality

The CSO data show that between 1998 and 2005 the percentage of households with income from the labour market declined from 58 per cent to 52 per cent.[6] After 2005, due to the fast rate of economic growth and declining unemployment rate, labour market participation increased.

A substantial increase in earnings inequality in the early period of transition (1989 to 1993) was followed by stabilization between 1993 and 1998, and a steady growth since then. The Gini index for monthly earnings increased in this period by almost 17 per cent. The inequality increase in the case of gross earnings was even higher.[7] As stressed by Magda and Szydłowski (2008), most of this increase came from the lower part of the earnings distribution. They suggest that the worsening of the lower tail of the distribution can be attributed to the fall of in the real wages of low-skilled workers during the recession of 2001–2002 and to the decreasing relative minimum wage during this period. After 2006, all available sources show stabilization and even some decline of the levels of earnings inequality.

The growth in gross income inequality for labour households was, especially in recent years, smaller than the growth in market income inequality, which suggests that the Polish transfer system did have a moderating effect on inequality. Deducting taxes (net household income) makes little difference to the trend of income inequality, so it seems that the Polish tax system has little effect on income inequality.

(details not provided in the GWR) by estimates of average wealth. The extent of error introduced by various simplifications and approximations in this approach is unknown and, in our opinion, does not allow for a meaningful assessment of trends in wealth inequality in Poland over such a short time period.

[6] This group of households excludes farmers' households, households of self-employed, households of retirees and pensioners and households living on unearned sources.

[7] The increase was the highest according to decile ratio (P90/P10), which rose by about 30 per cent between 1998 and 2006.

Educational Inequality

Data from ESS by birth cohort show that the generations that matured after World War 2 are better and less unequally educated than their predecessors (in terms of the years of education). (Figure 21.4). This equalization continued for some years, yet it gradually lost its impact, stabilized and even reversed for those born between 1965 and 1979. Educational inequality among the youngest cohort (1980–1984) fell radically. Educational attainment in general has improved significantly over the last two decades. The share of tertiary graduates has almost doubled since 1997 (rising from 7.7 per cent to 13.8 per cent in 2008). Current governmental policy promotes higher educational attainment, so we can expect that new cohorts will continue this trend.

Optimistic conclusions about falling educational inequality in terms of education level and duration are undermined by the fact that inequality measured in terms of a dependency between one's background and achieved level of education did not decrease after 1989 (Domański and Tomescu-Dubrow, 2008).

Why has Economic Inequality Grown?

Economic inequalities in Poland have increased substantially since the mid 1980s. The major factors that explain this inequality growth are related to the process of transition from socialism to a market economy. It seems that the single most important factor is the rise in earnings inequality caused by increasing educational premia for highly-qualified workers employed in highly-skilled occupations, coupled with a worsening of the relative position of workers employed in low-paying occupations. Returns to university education were

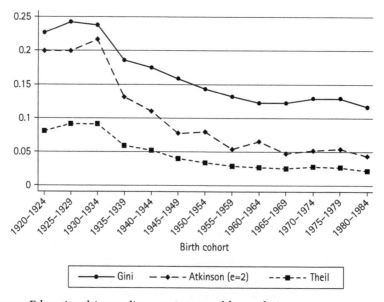

FIGURE 21.4 Educational inequality: 25–64-year-old population

Source: ESS.

non-existent or low under socialism and started to grow significantly during the transition period, eventually reaching levels similar to those of advanced market economies. The change from centrally-planned to decentralized wage setting and radical structural and technological changes have shifted labour demand from the public to the private sectors and from manual workers to professionals and highly-qualified workers (Keane and Prasad, 2006, Newell and Socha, 2007).

Changes in income inequality in Poland can also be associated with labour market performance. In the initial phase of the transition, the unemployment rate increased from nearly zero in early 1990 to 14.4 per cent in 1994 and fluctuated strongly afterwards.[8] Some of these shifts coincided with pronounced changes in income inequality. In particular, much of the inequality growth after 1998 occurred during the period of increasing and persistent unemployment (1998–2005) as well as increasing absolute poverty. After 2005, when the labour market situation improved radically, the level of income inequality stabilized.

The Subjective Measures of Inequalities' Growth: Poles on Income and Income Inequality

Early literature on the rise of inequalities in the CEE posited that the increase in inequalities may be welcome by post-communist citizens, who will see such changes as carrying legitimacy (Kelley and Zagórski 2004). However, Grosfeld and Senik's study (2010) has shown a 'growing aversion to inequality' in Poland in the late 1990s and in the 2000s.

Figure 21.5 shows that the shares of respondents who evaluate their household financial situation negatively has fallen substantially since 1992.[9] The patterns for evaluations of one's household economic situation roughly follow the objective measures of Poland's financial situation, such as GDP. At the same time, people's perceptions of the levels of inequality in Poland are changing in accordance with the changes in Gini index. The percentage of respondents who believe that income inequalities in Poland are too large has risen steadily from 80 per cent in early 1990s to 91 per cent in 2010, following Gini very closely.[10] Summing up, Poles have been deeply aware of the changes in income levels and the rise of inequality throughout the entire period. Most importantly, however, they have shown increasing disapproval of the growth of inequality despite their favourable evaluation of their own economic situation.

[8] It fell to 10.7 per cent during the 1994-1998 period, increased rapidly to 19.9 per cent over the 1998–2002 period, decreasing dramatically to 7.1 in 2008 and slowly rising again since 2008.

[9] Estimated by respondents reporting an insufficient income or an income that is much lower than that of an average household and describing their financial situation as rather bad, bad or very bad.

[10] To explore the causality between income inequality and political outcomes, we have employed various lags of Gini. Whenever there seems to be a relationship visible, it is always for a 3 or 4 years lag, suggesting that changes in income inequality take about 3 to 4 years to have an effect on political outcomes. Also in this case, the relationship is most visible when Gini lags by 4 years.

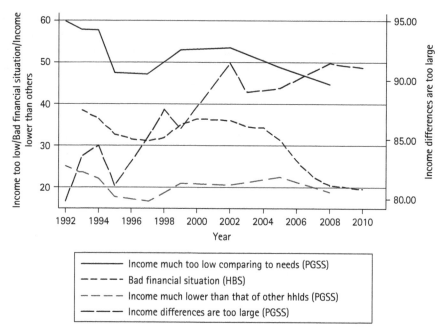

FIGURE 21.5 Households according to their income self-assessment and opinions about levels of inequality in Poland

Source: Polish General Social Survey (PGSS), HBS.

3. SOCIAL IMPACTS

In the previous section we have shown that income, wealth and labour market inequality in Poland has gradually grown in the 1990s and 2000s. We have also shown that these changes have been reflected in Poles' perceptions of inequality levels. In this section we look at material deprivation, social relations and social cohesion, crime rates, and subjective well-being, as they have been identified as inequality's most important social impacts (Wilkinson and Pickett, 2009). In the Polish transitional context, we would expect these impacts to be effected by a number of interrelated factors, thus the precise impact of inequalities' growth may be difficult to assess. On the other hand, if positive changes are observed, we should be able to conclude that they could not have been brought about by increasing inequalities.

Material Deprivation

The first measurement of material deprivation based on the EU-SILC definition was carried out in Poland in 2005 and it showed that over half of the population was living in materially deprived households and one third in severely materially deprived households. In the following years, this situation improved radically but Poland is still far behind the Euro area countries. Comparing with 26 other countries monitored by Eurostat since 2005, Poland ranked 25th in 2005 and 24th in 2010 in terms of material deprivation, and 26th in 2005 and 24th in 2010 in terms of severe material deprivation.

In 2005, 45.3 per cent of the EU-SILC Polish sample was considered at risk of poverty or social exclusion, which subsequently fell to 27.8 per cent in 2010. The reduction of the numbers of people at risk of poverty was initially of a great magnitude, but it slowed down and stopped between 2009 and 2010, which is likely to be linked to an increase in income inequality in 2010s.

In 2005, almost one third of the population was considered severely housing deprived, but by 2010 this share had fallen by 16.4 per cent (to only 13.3 per cent) and the gap between Poland and Europe's average narrowed to 5 per cent. Overall, an increase in income inequalities has been concurrent with the decline of material deprivation, at least since 2005.

Well-being and Satisfaction with Life

Data on satisfaction with life and well-being show a positive trend, despite a concurrent growth of inequalities: while income and wealth inequalities were growing, levels of satisfaction with one's life, work and with the life/lifestyle of one's family were growing as well. Poles have been most satisfied with their work: the share of those who claim they are happy with their work increased from 61 per cent (in 1994) to 78 per cent (in 2009). The number of respondents declaring they are happy with their life increased from 53 per cent (in 1995) to 68 per cent (in 2012). Finally, the economic dimension of well-being assessments— satisfaction with the lifestyle of one's family—increased as well, as in 1992 only 11.5 per cent of respondents declared that their family lives well or very well, while in 2001 this group of respondents was as large as 40.3 per cent (CBOS 2011, CBOS 2009). It is clear that this increase in life satisfaction should be attributed to a growing satisfaction with one's income (c.f. Figure 21.4) and generally rising living standards, rather than the increasing economic polarization of Polish society.

Health

Although there has been a significant improvement in the overall levels of Poles' health since 1989, measured both in absolute (e.g. rising life expectancy for both men and women) and relative (self-assessed health) terms, inequalities in access to health care deepened due to rising income inequality and the expansion of the private healthcare sector. The first private health clinics were created in the 1990s and soon they started introducing private health insurance that was bought by private firms for their employees. Since then, the range of paid healthcare services available both in private and public clinics has widened significantly.

The relationship between educational attainment and self-assessed health fluctuated throughout the 1992–2008 period without a clear trend (PGSS data, Figure 21.6). However, the financial situation (self-assessed) has had an increasing influence on people's health self-assessment. Since the beginning of the 1990s, changes in the correlation between satisfaction with a household's financial situation and its health status have followed changes in the Gini coefficient for income. This suggests that the larger the income inequalities, the

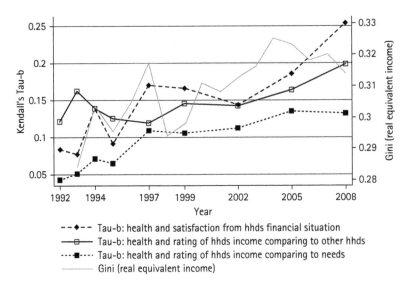

FIGURE 21.6 Relationship between self assessed health and other variables (Kendall's Tau-b)

Source: PGSS.

more strongly a person's health self-evaluation was linked to satisfaction with their household's financial situation.

Social Cohesion

One of the negative aspects of a rapid social and economic transformation, such as the processes taking place in Poland since 1989, is the breakdown of social ties. Due to a rapid differentiation of social structure, people are expected to withdraw from social life, losing social and support networks. Therefore, societies in transition, such as Poland, are expected to be poor in terms of social capital and to experience a decline in social cohesion (Uslaner and Brown 2005, Wilkinson and Pickett 2009).

Data series on socializing with family, friends and neighbours in Poland are short, covering only 10 years from 1992 to 2002 (PGSS). There was no major change in sociability during that time, as only socializing with neighbours declined by under 5 per cent (from 61.5 per cent of respondents meeting socially with neighbours at least once a month to 56.3 per cent).[11] This small change could be linked to an increasing spatial mobility, where ties with one's old neighbourhood are broken, and new ties have not yet been established. It seems that an increase of income inequality has not had a profound impact on either strong or weak ties.

---

[11] Meeting with family and friends at least once a month fluctuated around 66 per cent and 59 per cent, respectively.

Family Formation and Fertility

The fall in fertility rates and marriages that took place in Poland over the last couple of decades seems to follow patterns seen in the countries of Western Europe. However, most of these changes begun as early as in the 1970s and are, therefore, difficult to link to the changes in inequality levels taking place since mid 1990s.[12]

Similarly to many Western countries, Poland has experienced prolonged education, the postponement of marriage[13] and childbearing, and an increased percentage of out-of-wedlock births (from 5 per cent of all births in 1985 to 20.6 per cent in 2010). Cohabitation and divorce still seem to be rather infrequent in Poland in comparison with Western Europe. Marriage rates were falling constantly up to 2002; since then they have risen, followed by an increasing birth rate.

The last 'baby boom' in Poland reached its peak of 2.4 fertility rate in 1983 and, until 2003, fertility rates had fallen constantly (Pociecha, 2003). They then rose slightly and reached 1.4 in 2009, mainly due to a higher birth rate in urban areas. As in Western Europe, such a fall in fertility can be partially explained by women postponing their decision about having children.[14] This trend applies mostly to women with non-tertiary education, as the number of children born between 2008 and 2010 by mothers with upper secondary and post-secondary non-tertiary education fell from 232 thousands to 209 thousands, while mothers with tertiary education gave 141 thousand births in 2008 and 167 thousand births in 2010.[15] In terms of income inequality this might be a good sign, since it is a divergence from a classic model, where the rich and well educated have few children and the poor and poorly educated have many, causing the inequality to increase.

The main impact of inequality on family formation has been through childcare and educational policy. Public childcare that was widely available under the communist regime was significantly reduced after 1989, as fewer places at public kindergartens, nursery schools and crèches were available, and their cost to parents is rising. This discourages the employment of young women, putting them and their families at a disadvantaged position. It also excludes children from poor backgrounds from pre-schooling.

Crime and Punishment

The change of political system marks itself clearly on the patterns of prison population and the number of recorded crimes. During the communist time, the number of inmates fluctuated markedly, partially due to mass protests, militia actions and amnesties (1974, 1977, 1983 and 1984 after the period of martial law in Poland, 1986 and 1989). A high prison population

---

[12] All figures quoted in this section come from the Central Statistical Office.

[13] Since 1989, the average age of females at their first marriage rose steadily from 22.8 to 24.7 in 2004 and the most common age of marrying couples shifted from 20–24 to 25–29 years (Kotowska et al. 2008).

[14] The mean age of women at their first childbirth was 23.6 in 1989 and rose by 2.7 years within the next two decades, to 26.3 in 2009.

[15] Controlling for the share of all women with tertiary education (according to estimates by LFS), there has been a decrease in fertility per capita among those with ISCED 3–4 by 7.8 per cent and by 1.8 per cent among females with ISCED 5–6.

was accompanied by a low number of recorded crimes. After the transition, the situation changed dramatically: the number of crimes rose rapidly and the prison population diminished. In the last two decades, the number of inmates corresponded to the number of recorded crimes, which should be considered as a normal situation. Income inequality can hardly be considered as a factor driving changes in crime rates since the main fluctuations in inequality levels happened later than the increase in crime rates.

4. Political and Cultural Impacts

There is a growing body of literature showing that income inequality and social polarization resulting from it have a negative effect on citizens' political engagement and attitudes, and that perceptions of excessive inequality undermine political legitimacy and may lead to withdrawal from social and political life (Solt, 2008; Uslaner and Brown, 2005). In what follows we look whether this has also been the case in Poland over the past 20 years.

Trust in Others and in Institutions

Confidence in political institutions is traditionally considered to be the key aspect of system legitimacy, which is likely to suffer when citizens experience declining economic returns, or when they perceive the dominant economic order as unjust. Given the patterns presented earlier—rising levels of disapproval for income inequality—we should expect a strong negative relationship between Gini levels and confidence in political institutions.

Indeed, this seems to be the case. The percentage of respondents expressing confidence in parliament dropped from 40.1 per cent in 1992 to 21 per cent in 2010, and confidence in government started at 37.9 per cent in 1992, peaked at 64 per cent in 1997, and dropped to 31 per cent in 2010 (PGSS). It seems that the relationship between inequality and political confidence has been particularly pronounced since the late 1990s, as an increase in inequality has been accompanied by a steady and significant decrease of confidence in political institutions.

PGSS data indicate also that confidence in government and parliament is stratified by education, and that changes in levels of institutional trust are of a different magnitude depending on the educational level. In general, over time respondents with low educational qualifications have become less and less trusting, while the opposite has been true for respondents with high educational qualifications. This has resulted in the convergence of attitudes towards political institutions.

Generalized trust, however, shows a pattern that implies a positive relationship with income inequality. After an initial decline in early 1990s, social trust has been steadily rising, despite the growth of income inequality (PGSS, CBOS 2010b), which is in stark contrast with findings from stable Western democracies (Uslaner and Brown, 2005). As with happiness and well-being, it is difficult to propose mechanisms linking increasing social and economic polarization with rising levels of social trust, other than to refer to processes concurrent with the growth of inequalities under conditions of political and economic transformation, such as economic growth and the rise of living standard associated with it.

Civic and Political Participation

Voting turnout since 1989 has been low in Poland: national elections mobilized more voters than local and EU elections but, even in national elections, turnout has never exceeded 54 per cent. In the first free elections in 1991, the turnout was a low 43.2 per cent, then it increased to 52.08 per cent two years later, and has declined since then, with some recovery in late 2000s (National Electoral Commission). It seems that an increase in Gini is concurrent with a decrease in voting turnout, despite growing economic and general life satisfaction. Such a negative relationship between social and economic polarization and voting turnout should be interpreted as a further evidence (on top of declining political trust) of income inequality undermining political system legitimacy.

We do not see, however, a similar negative effect from inequalities' growth on non-political participation. Donating to charitable causes and Gini have an almost identical pattern (which is best visible when Gini is lagged by about 4 years), while associational membership remains at a lower level than donating, but instead of declining it fluctuates around 20 per cent for most of the period (CBOS 2010b). We link increasing levels of charity-oriented behaviour with a growing number of people in need, due to the increase of inequalities.

Union membership shows a clear negative relationship with income inequality. Between 1991 and 1997, declared trade union membership fell from 19 per cent to only 10 per cent. As inequality was rising in the 2000s, membership was falling further to as little as 6 per cent in 2009 (CBOS 2010c). There are several possible factors explaining this decline, which are also linked to inequality. First is the growth of the private sector, where levels of unionization are significantly lower than in the public sector. The second relevant factor is the shift from stable full-time employment to more temporary and more flexible forms of employment. Finally, growing long-term unemployment also depresses unionization rates.

Political Values and Legitimacy

Since the growth of inequalities has been noticed and disapproved of by Polish citizens, and it can be linked to attitudes towards political institutions and to political and civic participation, we expect it to influence people's policy preferences. For example, since the early 1990s Polish society has consistently expressed an overwhelming support for integration with the EU. Growing inequality, poverty, and other economic ills have usually been associated with the actions of the Polish government and political elites: EU membership is in this context perceived as an external source of economic stability and a remedy to social and economic problems.

Poles' expectations about the government's social policy are also associated with the growth of inequalities. Typically for a post-communist society (Gijsberts and Nieuwbeerta 2000), Poles express high levels of support for governmental regulation and redistribution. As inequalities were increasing, support for government intervention in the distribution of income grew from 72 per cent in 1992 to 85 per cent in 2008. It subsequently dropped back to the level from early 1990s (PGSS) in 2010, but based on Polish General Electoral Survey (PGSW) results this was only a short reversal, as in 2011 80.9 per cent of

PGSW respondents agreed that 'Government should undertake actions to reduce income differences.'

5. Effectiveness of Policies in Combating Inequality

In this section, we look at the interrelations between changes in economic inequalities and various socio-economic policies that have been implemented in Poland since the process of transition to the market economy started in 1989. We also briefly discuss economic ideas held by policy-makers implementing inequality relevant policies in Poland.

Minimum Wages

The first minimum wage legislation in Poland was introduced in 1956, and since then the way it is set has changed several times. From 1986 to the mid 1990s, the minimum wage served as a base for the wage rate schedule for all labourers, even those earning higher wages. This mechanism was abandoned in late 1990s. Up to 2002, the level of minimum wages was set unilaterally by the government. Since 2003, the minimum wage is set annually in the process of negotiation between the government and the Tripartite Commission for Social and Economic Affairs (TCSEA), which is composed of representatives of the government, employees and employers.[16] The minimum wage rate is uniform with the exception that workers in the first year of employment receive 80 per cent of the full rate.

Figure 21.7 compares changes in the net minimum wage (NMW)[17] with the evolution of poverty lines (social minimum calculated by the Institute of Labour and Social Studies in Warsaw) and the corrected social minimum (CSM)[18] for 1990–2003 (Szulc 2008). The differences between CSM and NMW were rather small up to 2007, but since 2008 the NMW has been significantly higher than the CSM. However, NMW is substantially lower than the original SM up to 2008. Overall, it seems that, at least until 2008, earning a minimum wage in Poland was equivalent, in the case of a single-earner household, to living in—or on the brink of—poverty.

[16] The minimum wage level proposed by the government for the following year has to be equal to at least the current minimum wage adjusted by the CPI forecast for the following year plus the two thirds of the projected GDP growth for the following year.

[17] The net minimum wage is calculated assuming that the income taxes and social insurance contributions applying to the minimum wage did not change over 1990–2010 period.

[18] Szulc (2008) shows that the social minimum calculated by the Institute of Labour and Social Studies was seriously biased. We therefore present also his estimates of the corrected social minimum (CSM) for 1990-2003, updated since 2004 using changes in the overall CPI.

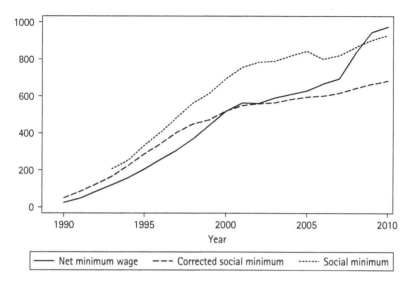

FIGURE 21.7 Net minimum wage and poverty lines (Polish zlotys)

Source: ILSS, Szulc, 2008.

Taxation

Poland introduced a modern tax system in the early 1990s. Before that, most of the budgetary revenues were collected from state-owned companies. Personal income tax (PIT) and corporate income tax (CIT) were introduced in 1992 and value added tax (VAT) was introduced in 1993. The total tax revenue declined by as much as 7 percentage points between 1993 and 2009, due to the lower tax rates for PIT and CIT (Figure 21.8).

In 2009, the total tax revenue was about 31.8 per cent of GDP, which is noticeably lower than the average for the OECD countries (33.8 per cent). The main sources of tax revenue in 2009 were VAT (36.8 per cent), social security contributions (35.7 per cent) and taxes on income, profits and capital gains (21.8 per cent). The most significant difference between Polish tax revenue structures and the OECD average is a much smaller contribution from income taxes, which is 11 percentage points lower for Poland.

The CIT rate fell rapidly from 40 per cent in 1992 to 19 per cent in 2004. PIT rates decreased as well, although more slowly: at first they increased over the 1994–1997 period (from 20, 30 and 40 to 21, 33 and 45, respectively), and then they returned to their initial level in 1998 (with a small reduction for the lowest bracket). In 2009, the number of brackets was reduced to two with a very significant reduction (8 percentage points) of marginal tax rate for the richer.[19] The top marginal tax rate of 32 per cent set in 2009 is among the lowest in the OECD

---

[19] Morawski (2009) uses a tax-benefit microsimulation model to show that this reform has primarily benefited the richest households, while the incomes of many low-income households have not changed. Domitrz *et al.* (2012), using the same approach estimate that, as a result of the 2009 reforms, income inequality measured by the Gini increased in 2009 by 0.4 percentage point. The inequality-increasing effect of tax changes in this year was somewhat reduced by inequality-decreasing effect of growing family benefits.

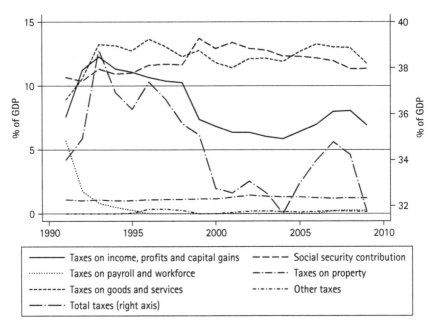

FIGURE 21.8 Tax revenue by origin as percentage of GDP

Source: OECD Tax database.

group (the lower rate was set at 18 per cent). Turning to effective tax rates, we can observe an even smaller progression. The top effective tax rate dropped from 29.4 per cent in 1994 to 22 per cent in 2010, and the difference between effective tax rates paid by persons facing different tax brackets was only 8 percentage points. Throughout the period under study, the lowest tax bracket applied to over 90 per cent of taxpayers, and in 2008 this number was as high as 98 per cent. The level of personal allowance has been continuously low and did not play an important redistributive function.

A tax change with important redistributive consequences occurred in 2007, when a non-refundable and rather generous child tax credit was added to the PIT system. The credit is available to all families paying PIT, irrespectively of their income. The policy introduced was not intended as a redistributive mechanism, but rather as a tool to 'counteract the approaching demographic crisis' (Morawski and Myck, 2011). Because the credit is non-refundable (that is its amount is limited by the amount of income tax paid) and available to all families, the biggest relative gains from it go to middle-class families in deciles 5–7 (Morawski and Myck, 2011). The families in the first decile gain only about 4.7 PLN per month or 0.4 per cent of their disposable income.

Despite a positive rate of economic growth and frozen tax thresholds (over the 2001–2006 period), the share of taxpayers in the highest tax bracket and their share of tax collected did not increase between 2004 and 2007. The reason for this was a 2004 tax reform, introduced by a post-communist left-wing party, which lowered the CIT rate from 27 per cent to 19 per cent and introduced a flat 19 per cent PIT tax rate for persons who had already been conducting non-agricultural business activities or who wanted to start a new business. Effectively, PIT taxpayers were offered a choice between the standard progressive rate system and a new flat rate tax. In effect, in order to avoid the higher standard PIT tax rate many high-earners moved to self-employment. This explains why the share of tax paid by persons facing the highest tax bracket has fallen so much (about 9 percentage points) in 2004.

Using the corrected HBS data Aksman (2010) shows that the redistributive effect of PIT has been progressive but rather small. Changes in the D index[20] show that income inequalities measured by Gini were reduced by 2.4 per cent and 6.3 per cent in 1997 and 2004, respectively. The trend in the D index was increasing over the 1996–2004 period and have fallen since 2004, which is a reflection of the 2004 tax reforms described earlier.

Overall, the redistributive effect of PIT in Poland has been low due to both low average effective tax rates and the low progressivity of tax rates. Policy-makers, even from the left-wing parties, have rarely considered PIT as a redistributive mechanism. Rather, a flat (or proportional) income tax system has been advocated, which according to its supporters would enhance the rate of economic growth. These ideas motivated the 2009 tax reform, which brought the progression of PIT to a very low level.

VAT was introduced in Poland in 1993 with a standard rate of 22 per cent and reduced preferential rates set at 0 per cent, 3 per cent and 7 per cent.[21] A recent study by Dobrowolska and Cmela (2012), using the HBS 1995–2010 data, concludes that the Polish tax system is regressive. The ratio of VAT paid to the net income of households was 5.7 per cent in 1995 and 9.3 per cent in 2010, which means that it grew by 63 per cent over that period. There are, however, important differences for households in different income decile groups. In general, the incidence of VAT (ratio of VAT paid to the net household income) has been declining as we move from the first to the tenth decile group. For example, in 1995 the VAT incidence for the first decile group was 7.1 per cent, while for the tenth decile group it was 5.2 per cent. In 2009, the VAT incidence was 11.6 per cent and 7.9 per cent for the first and the tenth decile groups, respectively. The preferential VAT rates were increased several times for a number of goods and services categories since 1995, which made the system more regressive (Dobrowolska and Cmela, 2012).

Social Expenditure

In this part we draw on social expenditure data from the internationally comparable OECD SOCX database, which for Poland covers the period between 1990 and 2007. The database includes statistics on public and private (mandatory and voluntary) social expenditure broken down by the following categories of spending: old age; survivors; incapacity-related benefits; health; family; active labour market programmes; unemployment; housing; and other social policy areas.

---

[20] The D index is the proportionate difference between the Gini index calculated for net disposable incomes and for gross incomes.

[21] The standard rate was increased in 2011 (for a period of two years) to 23 per cent, while the two reduced rates (3 per cent and 7 per cent) were increased to 5 per cent and 8 per cent, respectively.

Total Expenditure

The evolution of social expenditure (total, cash and in-kind) between 1990 and 2007 is shown in Figure 21.9. All three kinds of expenditure rose in the early transition period of 1991–1992. However, their starting level in 1990 was rather low. The rise over the 1991–1992 period was a policy response to the large drop in real wages, pensions and agricultural incomes when price liberalization, trade deregulation and other free-market reforms were introduced. However, the level of cash social expenditure was gradually decreasing between 1992 and 2000, recovered somewhat during the 2000–2003 period, and has been declining since then. The total social expenditure followed the same pattern as in-kind expenditure. Overall, total social expenditure fell by about 5 percentage points between 1992 and 2007. The fall in the total level of social spending was in line with the fall in total taxes collected, which fell by about 4 percentage points between 1993 and 2007.

Breaking the cash and in-kind social expenditure down by expense category reveals that the major reason for the decline in total social expenditure since 1992 has been the fall in three categories: incapacity-related benefits; unemployment benefits; and family benefits. The biggest decline was noted in incapacity-related expenditure, which includes sickness, disability and occupational injury benefits.

On the other hand, we observe a large increase in old age pensions, especially after 1999. The effect of this increase was, however, erased by the combined effect of the decrease in three types of cash benefits discussed above. In-kind social expenses contribute significantly less to total social expenditure than cash expenses. The most important category of in-kind expenditure—spending on health—declined significantly between 1992 and 2000, but recovered after that and in 2007 returned to its initial level.

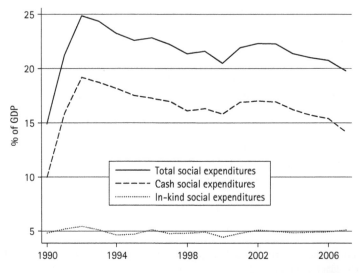

FIGURE 21.9 Total, cash and in-kind social expenditure (per cent of GDP)

Source: OECD SOCX database.

Unemployment Benefits and Social Assistance

Free market reforms introduced in 1990–91 resulted in a large increase in unemployment levels. According to the Act on Employment, introduced in 1989, the unemployed were entitled to benefits if the labour office did not succeed in finding them a job offer or training. The amount of the benefit for the first three months of unemployment was 70 per cent of the last remuneration, 60 per cent over the next six months and eventually 40 per cent after that. There was no restriction on the period of unemployment benefit collection. However, the scale of unemployment in early 1990s soon made this generous programme unsustainable. In 1990–92, a series of reforms made the programme significantly more restrictive. In the following years, other reforms reduced the amount of benefits and the coverage of the programme even further. The average unemployment benefit since 1998 has fallen to about 20 per cent of the average wage. In the mid 1990s, about 50 per cent of the unemployed received the benefit (Podkaminer, 2006), but in 2004 the share of the unemployed receiving the benefit was 14.4 per cent, and in 2010 it was 16.7 per cent.

The social assistance system has undergone several changes since 1989. In the early 1990s, the assistance directed to the poor accounted for about 20 per cent of all social expenditure, while in 2003 it was about 10 per cent (Staręga-Piasek *et al.* 2006). In general, transfers directed to the poor include social assistance benefits, family benefits and housing benefits.

Despite growing prices and cost of living, the income threshold above which persons and families are eligible for social assistance, permanent and temporary allowance was not changed between 2006 and 2011. As a result, the coverage of these programmes fell substantially. The number of persons receiving monetary social assistance dropped from 2.62 million in 2006 to 1.76 million in 2010. The share of the population receiving monetary or in-kind social assistance fell from 13.2 per cent in 2005 to 9.8 per cent in 2010.

Similarly to many other countries, Poland has gradually shifted her labour market policy from passive measures (unemployment benefits and early retirement programmes) to active measures (support for employment and rehabilitation, employment incentives, training, etc.). Since 2002, expenditure related to passive labour market policy has fallen radically (from 1.16 per cent of GDP to 0.34 per cent of GDP in 2010), while spending on active measures increased from 0.22 per cent of GDP in 2002 to 0.69 per cent in 2010. Expenditure on active measures in Poland is close to the OECD average, but expenditure on the passive measures is much lower than the OECD average of about 1 per cent GDP).

Disability Benefits

Incapacity-related expenditure, which includes sickness and disability benefits, accounted for a significant fraction of total social expenditure in the 1990s, which had been stable over time. Between 1990 and 1999, the population of disability benefits recipients increased from 2.2 million to 2.7 million. Until 1997, the eligibility for disability benefits was decided on the basis of disability evaluation and not on the basis of assessment of incapacity to work. This relatively easy access to disability benefits (and old age pensions) was provided by early reformers and later backed up by various political parties in order to gain the political support of the older electorate, which was perceived to be more disciplined than the younger voters (Golinowska, 2010).

In reaction to the high cost of the system, a reform of disability pensions was introduced in 1997. The most important changes included the separation of disability evaluation for non-insurance purposes from the evaluation of incapacity to work. The eligibility for the benefits was restricted to persons completely or partly incapable of work. As a result, the number of disability pensioners fell radically, from 2.7 million in 1999 to 1.2 million in 2010.

Mandatory social security contributions to disability insurance were reduced by 7 per-centage points over the 2007–2008 period. The employees' contribution was reduced by 4 per cent, while the employers' contribution was reduced by 3 per cent. The uniform rate of reduction resulted in more substantive gains for those with a larger income share coming from earnings. It is, however, difficult to distinguish the distributional effect of this reform from the effects of other tax and benefit reforms implemented in the same period (Domitrz *et al.* 2012).

Old Age Pensions

Expenditure on old age pensions increased substantially in the first years of the transition, then stabilized in the mid and late 1990s and increased again over the 1999–2002 period. In the early 1990s, old age pensions, together with disability benefits, became a safety net mechanism through which older or less fortunate workers, who faced unemployment and economic uncertainty, could secure some stable moderate income flows (Keane and Prasad, 2002). The easier access to pensions was provided through granting early retirement for the unemployed. Moreover, in 1995 pre-retirement allowances and benefits were introduced. The allowances were suspended after 2001.

The population of old age pensioners (excluding farmers, who are under a separate old-age pension system) increased by 4 per cent in 1990, by 18 per cent in 1991, and by 7.5 per cent in 1992. The replacement rate (average pension divided by the average wage) rose from about 52 per cent in 1988–1989 to 65 per cent in 1991 and remained above 60 per cent through to 1997. It may be argued that the old age pension system played an important role in mitigating inequality growth during early transition years, which did not happen in countries with more restrictive and less generous pension systems (Keane and Prasad, 2002, Mitra and Yemtsov, 2006). The standard age of entitlement to old age pensions was 65 years for males and 60 years for females, which was close to the OECD average. However, various special regulations for certain occupational groups (e.g. miners, the military), usually with a much lower age eligibility criteria, brought the effective retirement age in 1995 down to 59 for men and 55 for women, which was lower than the OECD average by, respectively, 3 and 6 years. The overall cost of the pension system (including disability benefits) in the mid 1990s was around 10–15 per cent of GDP, which was among the highest in the OECD. The system was based on a defined benefit[22] financed by the Pay-As-You-Go (PAYG) method. The system was redistributive as the formula for calculating the amount of pension con-tained a 'social' component equal for all contributors.

---

[22] Benefits are based on a formula taking into account workers' earnings and their overall time of work.

In order to reduce the cost of the pension system and to react to worsening demographic trends, the existing system was replaced in 1999 with a three-pillar one consisting of a notional defined contribution plan (with contributions invested in individual accounts funded on a PAYG basis); a mandatory system of privately managed pension funds for contributors aged 30 and less, with the option of joining for contributors under 50 years old; and a voluntary pillar.

The replacement rate under the new system is expected to drop on average by one third to about 50 per cent. Another feature of the reform was the elimination of the redistribution in the pension system as the benefit is calculated solely on the basis of individual accounts. In the following years, the smaller revenues of the first pillar had to be compensated by increasing the budget deficit and accumulating public debt. The government reacted to this problem in 2011 by partially reversing the 1999 reform. Overall, these reforms tend to weaken the redistributive effect of the old age pension system.

Health Care

Public health care expenditure represented 5.3 per cent of GDP in 2009, 1.6 percentage points lower than OECD average, but it was consistent with Poland's level of development. Until 1999, Polish health care system was fully funded from the general taxes. A decentralized public health insurance system was introduced in 1999 with 16 regional Sickness Funds providing management and finance. Another reform in 2003 merged the Sickness Funds into the National Health Fund (NHF) responsible for financing health care services.

About 98 per cent of the population is covered by public health care insurance (Boulhol *et al.*, 2012). However, the self-assessed quality of care is among the lowest in Europe, probably due to relatively low accessibility of new technologies and lengthy waiting times for specialized care. Other problems include non-means-tested co-payments for medicine and only basic dental care coverage by public insurance. Private financing of health care (e.g. medicine, appointments with specialists) is done mainly by out-of-pocket expenses. The share of the private sector in the total health care system grew from 10.6 per cent in 1997 to 22.2 per cent in 2009. It might be argued that a two-tier health care system operates in Poland, with the public NHF providing medical services for all insured persons and the private sector providing much more accessible, yet expensive services to wealthier persons (Podkaminer, 2006). These 'large persistent inequalities' (Boulhol *et al.*, 2012) in access to specialist care are likely to affect economic inequalities in income and wealth, both in the intra- and intergenerational context.

Family Benefits

The eligibility criteria for family allowances for families with dependent children have changed several times since 1989. Initially, the family allowance was not means tested and set to 8 per cent of the average wage. Since 1993, the benefit has been conditional on income. Between 1993 and 2002, the threshold for family allowance eligibility was 25 per cent of the average wage. Since 2002, the threshold has been regulated by the family benefits law. In 1997–2005, the size of the family allowance was determined by the number of children, but since 2005, eligibility has required the presence of a dependent child. From 2006 on, the amount of the benefit depends on the age of the children. This last change raised the average amount of the benefit by about 30 per cent (Domitrz *et al.*, 2012). The threshold below which families are eligible for family allowance was frozen from 2004 to 2011, which resulted in a substantial decrease (by about 800,000) in the number of children receiving the allowance. In 2006, a universal grant for each newborn child was introduced.

6. Conclusions

In this chapter, we have shown that by most accounts inequality has grown moderately but steadily in Poland since the early 1990s. Absolute poverty declined from 13.2 per cent in 1993 to 3.9 per cent in 2010, and although the relative poverty rates were increasing up to 2004, subsequently they fell as well. A decline in labour market participation was accompanied by a substantial increase in earnings inequality caused by the increasing divergence between the position of highly-qualified workers and those employed in low-paying occupations. At the same time, however, educational inequality declined and educational attainment has improved significantly.

Inequality's Impacts

There are several dimensions to the Polish story of inequality's impacts. First, there has been a significant decline in material deprivation in Poland, both by objective and subjective standards. The quality of housing has improved significantly, and the number of Poles living in deprived accommodation halved since 2005. Despite the growth of inequalities, subjective measures of well-being show that health quality in Poland has significantly improved, and life expectancy has increased. This was accompanied by an increase in life satisfaction. However, the relationship between income and health strengthened over time, closely following changes in the Gini index.

Patterns of family formation and breakdown can hardly be linked to growth of inequalities, as the decline in natality and postponing of marriage had started before the transition. However, increasingly restricted access to public childcare and its growing cost have negatively impacted lower-income families. The increase in crime and punishment rates that took place after 1989 should be linked to reporting policy rather than to changes in inequalities, and informal sociability seems to be largely unaffected by the growth of inequalities.

Overall, it seems that the effect of the growth of inequalities on social factors identified by literature as the key social impacts (Wilkinson and Pickett, 2009) has been at best modest since where negative trends were expected positive changes or no change were noted. The story looks different, however, when we look at political impacts, as growth in inequalities has been concurrent with the decline of confidence in political institutions, and accompanied by a declining voting turnout, and radically declining levels of unionization. With the growth of inequalities, Poles increasingly expected the government to do something about it. But they were also trying to compensate for it individually, supporting those in need through charitable contributions. They were also declaring increasing levels of trust in others. It seems, therefore, that the growth of inequalities has had a profound negative effect on politics and system legitimacy in Poland after 1989, but did not have the same effect on social capital and social trust.

Policies Affecting Inequality

When discussing how policy affected inequality in Poland over the last 20 years, it is important to note that among Polish elites (intellectuals, politicians, media personalities) the dominant economic worldview has been that of economic liberalism, focusing on stimulating economic growth and encouraging entrepreneurship (Kochanowicz, 1997).[23] According to the economic ideas prevailing among Polish policy-makers, economic growth will eventually 'lift all boats', not only increasing average incomes but also the incomes of the poor. Inequality may rise substantially during this process, but the absolute situation of the poor will be improved. Therefore, it is not surprising that there are hardly any examples of socio-economic policies in Poland being shaped by concerns about inequality. Despite the dominance of economic liberalism, a group of early reformers was concerned with the impact of free market reforms on unemployment, levels of incomes and ultimately on poverty. As a result, an extensive system of social transfers, including generous unemployment benefits, social welfare benefits and relatively easy access to retirement and disability benefits, was introduced in the early 1990s. This system was primarily concerned with reducing absolute poverty, but it limited inequality growth as well. However, since the mid 1990s, the system has gradually become less redistributive. A number of other important policy changes, often with serious distributional implications, were driven mostly by a mix of free market ideas and budgetary as well as demographic objectives. These would include lowering PIT tax rates in 2009, the introduction of children tax credit in 2007, various changes in the VAT system, reduction in amounts and coverage of several social benefits and the reforms of the pension system implemented in 1999 and 2011. These policies affected economic inequality in indirect and often unintended ways, and their overall effect is hard to measure. It seems, however, that most of them reduce the degree of redistribution in the Polish tax-benefit system, which may increase inequality in the years to come.

When Politicians don't Care but Citizens do...

Summing up, the case of Poland shows how a mismatch between politicians' priorities and the public's expectations may undermine system legitimacy in vulnerable times. The policy emphasis on economic growth has resulted in growing living standards and declining poverty, which have been reflected in citizens' increasing satisfaction with the household's economic situation and life in general. But the political neglect of inequalities' growth (combined with other transitional maladies, such as corruption) has undermined the legitimacy of the very same political class that delivered economic growth and all its positive consequences.

---

[23] Economic liberalism is understood here as a general support for the free market capitalism.

References

Aksman, E. (2010), *Redystrybucja dochodów i jej wpływ na dobrobyt społeczny w Polsce w latach 1995-2007*, Warszawa: Wydawnictwa Uniwersytetu Warszawskiego,

Boulhol, H., Sowa, A., Golinowska, S., Sicari, P. (2012), 'Improving the Health-Care System in Poland', *OECD Economics Department Working Paper 957*.

CBOS (2009), 'Zadowolenie z pracy i mobilność zawodowa', Komunikat z badań BS/156/2009.

CBOS (2010a), *Aktywność Polaków w organizacjach obywatelskich w latach 1998-2010*, Komunikat z badań BS/16/2010.

CBOS (2010b), 'Zaufanie społeczne', Komunikat z badań BS/29/2010.

CBOS (2010c), 'Związki zawodowe i naruszenia praw pracowniczych', Komunikat z badań BS/109/2010.

CBOS (2011a), 'Polacy o swoim szczęściu i pechu oraz zadowoleniu z życia', Komunikat z badań BS/06/2011.

Davies, J., Lluberas, R., Shorrocks, A. (2012), *Credit Suisse Global Wealth Databook*, Zurich: Credit Suisse Research Institute.

Dobrowolska, Bogusława and Cmela, Piotr (2012), 'The redistribution consequences of taxing the consumption of Polish households with Value Added Tax in the years 1995-2009', in A. Jaeschke and W. Starzyńska (eds.), *Statistical methods in regional and social analyses under integration and globalization*, Łódź: Statistical Office in Łódź, pp. 151–173.

Domański, Henryk, Tomescu-Dubrow, Irina (2008), 'Nierówności edukacyjne przed i po zmianie systemu' in Domański, Henryk (ed.), *Zmiany stratyfikacji społecznej w Polsce*, Warszawa: IFiS PAN.

Domitrz, A., Morawski, L., Myck, M., Semeniuk, A. (2012), 'Dystrybucyjny wpływ reform podatkowo-świadczeniowych wprowadzonych w latach 2006-2011', CenEA Microsimulation Report MR01/12.

Flemming, J. S. and Micklewright, J. (2000), 'Income distribution, economic systems and transition', in Atkinson, A.B. and Bourguignon, F. (eds.), *Handbook of Income Distribution*, vol.1, pp. 843–918. North-Holland: Elsevier.

Gijsberts, Mérove and Nieuwbeerta, Paul. (2000), 'Class Cleavages in Party Preferences in the New Democracies in Eastern Europe: A Comparison With Western Democracies', *European Societies* 2(4): 397–430.

Golinowska, S. (2010), 'Polityka wobec ubóstwa i wykluczenia społecznego w Polsce w minionym dwudziestoleciu', *Polityka Społeczna*, 9, pp. 7–13.

Grossfeld, Irena and Senik, Claudia (2010), 'The Emerging Aversion to Inequality. Evidence from Subjective Data', *Economics of Transition* Vol. 18 (1), pp. 1–26.

Harwin, Judith and Gaspar, Fajth. (1998), 'Child Poverty and Social Exclusion in Post-Communist Societies', *IDS Bulletin* Vol 29 (1):66–76.

Keane, M. P. and Prasad, E. S. (2002), 'Inequality, Transfers, and Growth: New Evidence From The Economic Transition in Poland', *Review of Economics and Statistics*, vol. 84(2), pp. 324–341.

Keane, M. P. and Prasad, E. S. (2006), 'Changes in the Structure of Earnings during the Polish Transition', *Journal of Development Economics*, vol. 80(2), pp. 389–427.

Kelley, J. and Zagorski, K. (2004), 'Economic Change and the Legitimation of Inequality: The Transition from Socialism to the Free Market in Poland and Hungary, 1987–1994', *Research in Social Stratification and Mobility* 22: 319–364.

Kochanowicz, J. (1997), 'Incomplete Demise: Reflection on the Welfare State in Poland after Communism', *Social Research*, vol. 64(4), pp. 1477–1501.

Kotowska I.E., Jóźwiak J., Matysiak A., Baranowska A., (2008), 'Poland: Fertility Decline – A Response to Profound Societal Change and Transformation in the Labour Market?' *Demographic Research* 19, Article 22, pp. 795–854.

Magda, I. and Szydłowski, A. (2008), 'Płace w makro i mikroperspektywie', in Bukowski, M. (ed.) *Zatrudnienie w Polsce 2007*. Warszawa: Ministerstwo Pracy i Polityki Społecznej, pp. 71–110.

Mitra, P. and Yemtsov, R. (2006), 'Increasing Inequality in Transition Economies: Is there More to Come?', *Policy Research Working Paper Series* 4007, The World Bank.

Morawski L., Myck M. (2011), 'Distributional Effects of the Child Tax Credits in Poland and Its Potential Reform', *Ekonomista*, No. 6, 815–830.

Newell, A. and Socha, M. W. (2007), 'The Polish Wage Inequality Explosion', *Economics of Transition*, vol. 15, pp. 733–758.

Polish General Social Survey 1992-2010, ISS UW (<http://pgss.iss.uw.edu.pl/index.php?show=cytowanie.html>), downloaded 10 December 2012.

Pociecha J., ed. (2003), *Ekonomiczne i społeczne konsekwencje osiągania wieku emerytalnego przez generacje powojennego wyżu demograficznego*, Wydawnictwo Akademii Ekonomicznej w Krakowie, Kraków.

Podkaminer, L. (2006), 'Distributional Effects of Evolving Spending and Tax Policies', in Post-Socialist Poland', in Papadimitriou, D. B. (ed.), *The Distributional Effects of Government Spending and Taxation*, Houndmills: Palgrave Macmillan, p. 166–175.

Skopek, Nora, Buchholz, Sandra and Blossfeld, Hans-Peter (2011), 'Wealth Inequality in Europe and the Delusive Egalitarianism of Scandinavian Countries', *MPRA Paper* 35307, University Library of Munich, Germany.

Solt, F. (2008), 'Economic Inequality and Democratic Political Engagement', *American Journal of Political Science*, 52(1), 48–60.

Staręga-Piasek, J., Matela, P., Wóycicka, I., Piotrowski, B. (2006), *Rescaling Social Welfare Policies in Poland*, Warsaw. European Centre for Social Welfare Policy and Research.

Szulc, A. (2008), 'Checking the Consistency of Poverty in Poland: 1997–2003 Evidence', *Post Communist Economies*, 20(1), p. 33–55.

Uslaner, E. and Brown, M. (2005), 'Inequality, Trust and Civic Engagement', *American Politics Research*, Vol. 33 no. 6 868–894.

Wilkinson, Richard G. and Pickett, Kate E. (2009), *The Spirit Level. Why More Equal Societies Almost Always do Better*, London: Allen Lane.

Yemtsov, R. (2008), 'Housing Privatization and Household Wealth in Transition', in Davies, James B. (ed.), *Personal Wealth from a Global Perspective*, Oxford: Oxford University Press, p. 312–333.

CHAPTER 22

PORTUGAL: THERE AND BACK
AGAIN, AN INEQUALITY'S TALE

CARLOS FARINHA RODRIGUES AND ISABEL ANDRADE

1. INTRODUCTION AND CONTEXT

SINCE Portugal became a member of the European Union in 1986, the Portuguese economy has gone through substantial changes that have significantly altered its mechanisms and incentives for economic agents. The increased economic integration, reflecting both EU membership and the intensification of the globalization process, was followed by the profound financial integration required by joining the euro. In a period characterized by increased global competition, augmented external financing capacity due to the removal of the foreign exchange risk, and structurally lower interest and inflation rates, the Portuguese economy changed rapidly.

Between 1986 and the end of the nineties, Portugal went through a significant convergence process with the EU: GDP per capita increased from about 34 per cent to 55 per cent of the EU average. However, this process slowed considerably during 2000–9 and was reversed in 2010, reflecting the current economic crisis.

The weak performance of the Portuguese economy during the noughties was characterized by feeble economic growth, rising unemployment, falling domestic savings, and increased private sector indebtedness, which contributed to a significant increase in the balance of payments deficit. Simultaneously, the consistently high budget deficit led to a severe deterioration in the public sector finances. The poor condition of the Portuguese economy at a time of turmoil in the international financial markets, particularly in the euro zone, dramatically reduced the possibility of financing public debt in those markets. Eventually, Portugal had to ask for EU and IMF financial support and subscribe to a programme of economic and financial adjustment.

It is not yet possible to evaluate and quantify the impact of the current economic crisis, or of the policies implemented within the agreement with the Troika, on inequality in Portugal. Nevertheless, what has already been implemented and announced actually suggests a reversal of the process of falling inequality that had been observed in recent years.

This chapter is organized as follows. In Section 2, the evolution of income, earnings, wealth, and educational inequalities in recent decades is analysed. Section 3 evaluates the social impacts of inequality, followed by its political and cultural impacts in Section 4. Section 5 discusses the effectiveness of policies in combating inequality, and Section 6 concludes the chapter.[1]

2. EVOLUTION OF INEQUALITY AND ITS DRIVERS

The objective of this section is to analyse the changes in income, earnings, wealth, and education inequalities that have occurred in Portugal in recent decades. Three main datasets are used: the five Portuguese Household Budget Surveys (HBS) for 1990–2011, which differentiate between monetary and total (monetary and non-monetary) household income;[2] the annual ECHP/EU-SILC surveys for 1994–2009; and the annual *Quadros de Pessoal* for 1985–2009, which has detailed information on the wages and earnings of all employees except public servants.

Household Income Inequality

Between 1989 and 2009, Portuguese monetary equivalized disposable income increased by about 72 per cent in real terms while total income increased by about 76 per cent. This growth was not identical over the two decades: in the nineties, monetary equivalized income increased by about 4.6 per cent per year, but only by about 1 per cent in the noughties.

The Gini coefficient reported in Figure 22.1 shows how non-monetary income has an equalizing effect in Portugal, as discussed in Rodrigues (2007, 2012): the monetary income distribution reveals inequality levels one to three percentage points above that of total income.

The evolution of monetary and total income also diverged. Between 1989 and 1994, both distributions identified a substantial increase in inequality, with the Gini rising by about three percentage points. However, between 1994 and 2005, while the monetary income Gini continued to increase, that of total income initially remained largely unchanged and then decreased. Most recently, in 2005–9, both Gini coefficients showed a decrease in inequality.

The equalizing effect of non-monetary income is confirmed by all the inequality indices in Table 22.1. They also reveal a rise in inequality between 1989 and 2009, whichever

---

[1] This chapter is based on *Growing Inequality and its Impacts—Country Report: Portugal* (2012) available at www.gini-research.org/CT-Portugal where a detailed discussion of these issues, datasets, methodologies, and further references can be found.

[2] Non-monetary income includes households' produce for their own consumption, services derived from owner-occupied dwellings, and transfers in kind. In 2009, over 75 per cent of the total non-monetary income corresponded to estimated rents of owner-occupied dwellings and rent-free tenants. Non-monetary income accounts for 19.4 per cent of total income in the 2010/11 HBS.

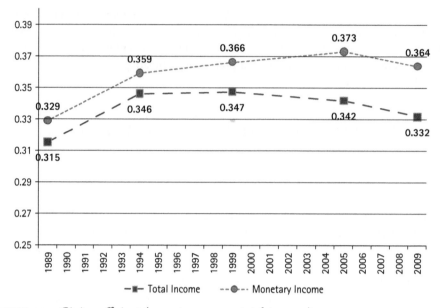

FIGURE 22.1 Gini coefficient (monetary versus total income)

Source: INE Statistics Portugal, Household Budget Surveys.

Table 22.1 Inequality indices

	1989	1994	1999	2005	2009
Total Income					
Gini Index	0.315	0.346	0.347	0.342	0.332
MLD	0.168	0.201	0.200	0.195	0.180
S80/S20	5.1	5.9	5.8	5.5	5.2
S90/S10	7.9	9.4	9.3	8.8	8.2
S95/S05	11.8	14.2	14.1	13.7	12.2
P90/P10	4.3	4.8	4.8	4.4	4.3
P95/P05	6.7	7.8	7.7	7.2	6.9
Monetary Income					
Gini Index	0.329	0.359	0.367	0.373	0.364
MLD	0.186	0.218	0.226	0.235	0.220
S80/S20	5.6	6.4	6.6	6.5	6.2
S90/S10	8.8	10.5	10.8	11.0	10.1
S95/S05	13.4	16.8	17.0	17.9	15.8
P90/P10	4.7	5.1	5.2	5.0	4.9
P95/P05	7.5	8.4	9.0	8.9	8.4

Note: Income refers to disposable household income corrected for household size using the OECD square root of the number of persons in the household scale.

Source: INE Statistics Portugal, Household Budget Surveys.

Table 22.2 **Changes in inequality**

	1989-94	1994-99	1999-2004	2005-09
HBS–Total Income	+ +	- +	-	- -
HBS–Monetary Income	+ +	+	- +	- -
ECHP/EU-SILC Monetary Income	n/a	- -	+ +	- -

Note: A positive (negative) sign indicates an increase (decrease) in inequality. '+' ('-') indicates that the magnitude of the change is less than 3 per cent, and '+ +' ('- -') that it is higher; '- +' indicates that the indices vary in opposite directions.

Source: INE Statistics Portugal, Household Budget Surveys, Eurostat EU-SILC.

Table 22.3 **Trends in real household income by income group**

	Average annual change, in percentage				
	1989-94	1994-99	1999-05	2005-09	1989-05
Bottom 5%	3.6	4.4	0.7	3.2	2.8
1st Decile	3.7	4.0	1.2	2.6	2.8
2nd Decile	3.6	3.7	1.5	1.6	2.6
3rd Decile	3.7	3.7	1.1	1.1	2.4
4th Decile	4.3	3.5	0.5	1.4	2.4
5th Decile	4.2	3.5	0.4	1.2	2.3
6th Decile	4.3	3.5	0.3	1.3	2.3
7th Decile	4.6	3.3	0.6	1.4	2.4
8th Decile	4.9	3.4	0.8	1.1	2.5
9th Decile	5.3	4.0	0.9	1.0	2.8
10th Decile	7.3	4.5	1.5	0.4	3.5
Top 5%	8.2	4.6	1.7	- 0.1	3.6
All	5.3	3.9	1.0	1.0	2.8

Note: Income refers to disposable household monetary income corrected for household size and deflated by the consumer price index (CPI).

Source: INE Statistics Portugal, Household Budget Surveys.

distribution is chosen. The fall in inequality in recent years was not sufficient to compensate for its substantial increase during 1989–94. Furthermore, inequality decreased in periods when the living standards of lower income households improved.

Comparing the inequality indicators based on HBS data with those based on ECHP/ EU-SILC data in Table 22.2, two periods can be identified when all the indicators move together: one, in 1989–94, characterized by a strong increase in inequality; the other, 2004– 9, by a consistent decrease. The 1994–2004 period is more difficult to interpret, with contra- dictory evidence in Table 22.2. However, there is a suggestion of constancy in the inequality indicators in the second half of the nineties, followed by a rise in inequality in the first half of the noughties.

Table 22.3 shows that, throughout this period, all income groups recorded an improvement in real income and that equivalized disposable income grew at an annual average rate of 2.8 per cent. As discussed earlier, this growth was not homogeneous over time and neither was it homogeneous across income groups. The period of highest inequality increase (1989–94) is characterized by strong gains in the 10th decile, which is the only decile with an annual rate of growth above the average (7.3 per cent versus 5.3 per cent). The 'top 5 per cent' was even larger at 8.2 per cent. The first eight deciles show rates of growth that are both below the average and inversely proportional to their ranking in the income scale. The rate of growth of the 1st decile corresponds to only about two thirds of the average rate. Thus, the inequality increase in this period is connected to the stronger growth in the highest incomes.

Conversely, the 2004–9 period shows a decrease in inequality and stronger growth in the lower incomes. The first decile records an annual rate of 2.6 per cent compared to the 1 per cent average; and the 5 per cent poorest record 3.2 per cent. This remarkable achievement is closely associated with the introduction of two means-tested benefits—'Social Integration Income' (RSI) and 'Solidarity Supplement for the Elderly' (CSI)—which will be discussed in Section 5. The divergent results obtained earlier for 1994–99 may be partially explained by the strong average growth of both the 5 per cent wealthiest and the poorest, which exceeded 4 per cent in this period. Finally, 1999–2005 is characterized again by stronger growth of the highest incomes and a subsequent increase in inequality.

Household Expenditure Inequality

The analysis of household income inequality can be complemented by that of household expenditure inequality using data from the HBS. Figure 22.2 shows a marked fall in the Gini coefficient for monetary expenditure between 1995 and 2006, in marked contrast to the increase in the income Gini coefficient in the same period already discussed.

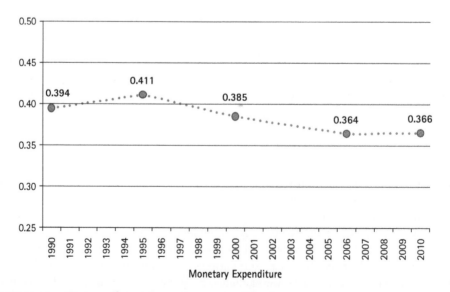

FIGURE 22.2 Gini coefficient (monetary expenditure)

Source: INE Statistics Portugal, Household Budget Surveys.

Wealth and Debt Inequality

Another important dimension of household inequality concerns wealth. The gross house-hold savings rate has fallen steadily in Portugal since the 1980s, from a maximum of 22.0 per cent of disposable income in 1982 to 9.7 per cent in 2011. It was influenced by the deregulation of the financial system (which led to an unprecedented availability of easy credit) and the introduction of the euro and low stable interest rates, but more recently it has reflected the increased indebtedness and financial difficulties of households. The main component of household wealth is housing, although its importance has considerably decreased from about 70 per cent of the total to around 50 per cent since 1996. Still, the composition of households' portfolios is quite conservative, if progressively more diversified, revealing a strong preference for low risk assets: cash and deposits represented about 70 per cent of the portfolio until 1987 and still more than a third in 2011.

The Household Financial Situation Survey of 2010 reveals substantial wealth inequality, as reported in Table 22.4. Net wealth (median and average) increases strongly with monetary income: the average net wealth of the 10 per cent highest income households is over seven times that of the 20 per cent lowest income ones. The average net wealth of the 10 per cent wealthiest is more than 240 times that of the 25 per cent less wealthy households, revealing an even more asymmetrical distribution than for income.

Non-financial assets represent 88 per cent of total household assets, with little difference across the net wealth percentiles. The main home is its most important component, but its relative importance decreases with net wealth: the less wealthy own very little other real estate, whereas it represents only 29.6 per cent of the wealthiest non-financial assets. Over 70 per cent of Portuguese households own their main home and a motorized vehicle.

Table 22.4 Private household net wealth, 2010

	Median net wealth	Average net wealth
Net Wealth Percentiles		
< 25	2.3	3.3
25–50	47.3	47.1
50–75	106.3	110.5
75–90	204.2	213.3
90–100	482.4	805.1
Monetary Income Percentiles		
< 20	42.6	69.7
20–40	49.0	84.0
40–60	69.5	107.8
60–80	93.0	144.7
80–90	129.3	207.2
90–100	231.0	511.0

Note: Values in 10^3 euros.

Source: INE Statistics Portugal, Household Financial Situation Survey (ISFF).

Costa and Farinha (2012) find that 37.7 per cent of households are in debt, with a median value of €30.7 thousand. Household indebtedness is dominated by mortgages on the main home: 80.3 per cent of total debt on average, and highest in the 25–50 percentile of net wealth. Finally, the median of the ratio debt repayments/monthly monetary income is equal to 16 per cent, but for 13 per cent of indebted households this ratio is higher than 40 per cent (considered its critical value). Naturally, the ratio decreases with income, but a massive 57.9 per cent of households in the lowest income percentile are above the critical 40 per cent level. This proportion decreases rapidly to 25.4 per cent of the households in the second lowest percentile, but highlights the financial difficulties of the poorest families.

Labour Market Inequality

The *Quadros de Pessoal* data allows for the measurement of earnings inequality. The results in Table 22.5 show that there is an increase in earnings inequality over the period: the Gini coefficient increases steadily until 1994 (0.344), then decreases slightly, but increases again to reach a maximum in 2005 (0.351), before returning to its 1994 value in 2009. The Atkinson Index with ε=0.5, the more sensitive to changes in higher earnings, has the highest increase (about 54 per cent) linking the increase in earnings inequality to the variation in the highest earnings. Increases in the indices more sensitive to the lower end of the distribution, Atkinson ε=0.2 and DML, also reveal increasing inequality for lower earners.

The period up to the mid nineties saw an increase in earnings inequality, followed by a decrease until the end of that decade. Then, between 2000 and 2005, most indices register a sustained increase, both for the lowest and highest earners. The following years register a decrease in inequality.

Educational Inequality

A final dimension of inequality is given by educational access and attainment. There has been a determined and consistent effort by successive governments to improve the level of education of the Portuguese population in general. The proportion of pupils and students

Table 22.5 Earnings inequality indices

	Gini	Atkinson ε=0.5	Atkinson ε=1.0	Atkinson ε=2.0	MLD
1985	0.284	0.067	0.123	0.215	0.131
1989	0.300	0.075	0.135	0.223	0.145
1994	0.344	0.100	0.173	0.270	0.190
1999	0.336	0.096	0.166	0.258	0.182
2005	0.351	0.105	0.179	0.277	0.198
2009	0.344	0.101	0.173	0.267	0.190

Source: Quadros de Pessoal, MSSS/GEP, Rodrigues et al. (2012).

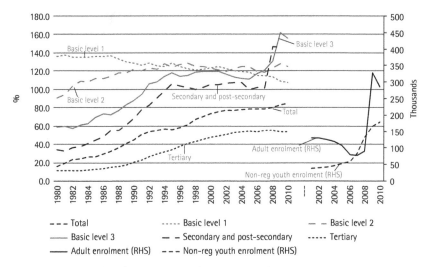

FIGURE 22.3 (Gross) Enrolment rate and return to education

Source: GEPE/ME, GPEARI/MCTES, INE Statistics Portugal.

has increased significantly over the years, exceeding 20 per cent of the population since 1983, with substantial rises in pre-school, secondary and tertiary education since the late 1980s. Recently this effort has been particularly significant in improving the educational attainment and qualifications of the adult population and early school leavers, in line with the Lisbon 2000 recommendations.

The (Gross) Enrolment rate[3] has increased steadily in Portugal from 15.4 per cent in 1980 to 85 per cent in 2010, as shown in Figure 22.3. There has been a significant increase in secondary school enrolment (basic level 3 and secondary) leading to rates above 100 per cent from 1992 and 1996, respectively. Tertiary education enrolment rate has increased from 10.7 per cent to 53.8 per cent in 2010 (consistently above 50 per cent since 2002).

The sharp recent increase in the number of pupils enrolled in both basic level 3 and secondary shown in Figure 22.3 is explained by the impact of the 'New Opportunities' programme of adult education, whereas the number of pupils of 'regular' age has remained largely unchanged since the mid nineties. Initially, these 'back to school'/'lifelong learning' initiatives were limited to dedicated adult evening classes: the recurrent learning scheme. Building on its success, the 'New Opportunities' courses are specifically designed for older pupils or/and the recognition and validation of their professional skills and experience. The latest EU report (Hawley *et al.* (2010)) includes Portugal in the group of countries that has 'a high degree of development' and a significant level of take-up of 'return to education' opportunities.

---

[3] The (Gross) Enrolment Rate is defined as the proportion of pupils and students enrolled at each level of education, irrespective of their age, over the total resident population of normal age to be enrolled at that level of education. In the Portuguese education system, pupils and students who do not achieve a pre-defined minimum standard have to re-take the year, and therefore gross enrolment rates above 100 per cent are shown in Figure 22.3.

Another important aspect of these initiatives applies to youths that have abandoned school early, but are still within school age. There are various types of (secondary level) courses that lead to enrolment in post-secondary professional and tertiary levels of education. Enrolment has increased particularly on professional courses.

Notwithstanding these significant improvements, according to the OECD Education at a Glance, in 2009 only 30 per cent of Portuguese 25–64 year olds had attained at least secondary level education, although that rate was highest, 48 per cent, in the younger 25–34 olds sub-group. Furthermore, the percentage of 15–19 year olds that stay in education has increased from 73 per cent in 1997 to 85 per cent in 2010, whereas that of the next age group (20–24) remains rather unchanged around 39 per cent, reflecting the reduction in the duration of university degrees from the traditional five academic years to four and then to three with the introduction of the Bologna scheme.

Continuous improvement in the (maximum) education attainment levels is also reflected in the educational attainment of the labour force. The percentage of employees with 'no or basic education' has decreased in the younger age groups, but there is an increase in that of the 35–44 and 45–64 groups with attained basic level 2 education. This possibly reflects the success of the adult 'back to school' initiatives, plus the natural ageing of the population. In the higher levels of education there is less relative difference amongst the age groups, except the oldest age group (officially retired, 65+ years old) that suggests that it is the older, less educated, who keep on working past retirement age. The unemployment rate has a similar evolution for all levels of education, but perhaps surprisingly, it was the 'no education' group that had the lowest rate until 2008. As the crisis struck, this place was taken by the tertiary educated group.

The analyses of the distribution of households according to the education level attained by their head reveals a clear improvement: 14 per cent of the heads had attained equally secondary or post-secondary professional and tertiary in 2009, up from 9 per cent and 7 per cent respectively in 1993. This educational attainment by the head was reflected in the level of the relative mean household income: higher education achievement is rewarded with higher income, as discussed in detail in the country report.

Interdependence Between the Above Inequalities over Time

The evolution of inequality in Portugal measured by the Gini coefficient is given in Figure 22.4 using both the income distribution (from HBS) and wage asymmetry (from *Quadros de Pessoal*).

Combining the information from both household and wage inequality enables the clear identification of three sub-periods—1985–1994, 1994–2005, and 2005–2009—when the behaviour of the different distributions indicates a more consistent pattern for the evolution of inequality. In the first period there is a steep increase in inequality, whichever distribution is chosen. Conversely, in the third period there is a significant reduction in the Gini coefficient across the distributions, although not sufficient to compensate for the earlier increase in inequality. The intervening period is more complex: HBS monetary income points to a significant rise in inequality (about two percentage points in the Gini coefficient) which is contradicted by both HBS total income and EU-SILC monetary income, and wage data.

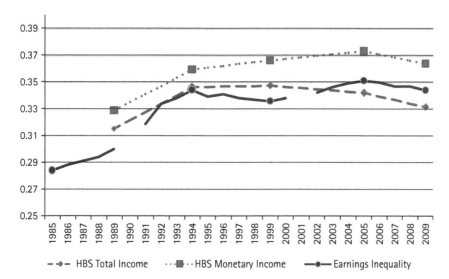

- ◆ - HBS Total Income   ··· ■ ·· HBS Monetary Income   —●— Earnings Inequality

FIGURE 22.4 Changes in inequality (Gini index)

Source: INE Statistics Portugal, Household Budget Surveys,
Quadros de Pessoal, MSSS/GEP, Rodrigues *et al.* (2012).

The Nature of Inequality

During this period Portugal remained one of the most unequal countries in the EU and, simultaneously, recorded real growth of the equivalized income of all economic groups. Except in 1989–94, the real rate of growth of the first two deciles of the distribution was higher than that of average income, thus its share of the total income was not reduced. The implementation of a number of means-tested policies aimed at the more vulnerable sectors of the population, which started in the second half of the nineties, had a prominent role in this achievement. However, the substantial rise in the earnings of the higher wage distribution deciles, together with the relative depreciation of the minimum wage (discussed in Section 5) led to increased wage inequality. The analysis of wealth inequality, although confined to 2010 due to data consistency limitations, confirms the high levels of inequality in the Portuguese economy and society.

Finally, the role of education attainment and qualification levels is fundamental in this analysis as Alves (2009), Rodrigues (2007), and Rodrigues *et al.* (2012) found that it is the main explanatory variable of inequality. The latter estimates that the level of education attained by the reference individual explains more than 25 per cent of the household inequality measured by the MLD. The recent marked improvement in educational attainment and qualification levels of the Portuguese population should have an important attenuating role on future inequality.

The deep economic crisis and the policies adopted by the economic authorities resulting from the agreement with the Troika will inevitably lead to a new increase in inequality. A first look at the still provisional EU-SILC 2011 data recently released suggests an increase of 1.5 per cent in the Gini coefficient (0.337 in 2009 to 0.342 in 2010) and a rise in the S90/S10 index from 9.2 to 9.4, as the gap between the wealthiest and poorest Portuguese increases a bit further. Another indication is given in Callan *et al.* (2011) using the Euromod micro-simulation model. They found that the first effects of the 'austerity packages' imply a reduction of around 3 per cent of the pre-austerity total disposable income. Of all the countries analysed, Portugal is the only one where the implemented measures generated 'a clearly regressive distribution, with percentage losses that are considerably larger in the first and second decile groups than higher up the distribution'.

3. SOCIAL IMPACTS

The objective of this section is to evaluate the impact the changes in inequality observed during recent decades had on the living standards of the population. Different aspects of those will be considered, such as poverty and social exclusion, deprivation, health, housing, social cohesion, and criminality. The aim is to expand inequality into a wider concept of the well-being of individuals, when inequality and monetary poverty are considered as only two of the components of a larger and multidimensional picture.

Poverty Indicators

This study, like most recent studies of monetary poverty in Portugal, follows the Eurostat methodology, which takes as a benchmark a poverty line defined as 60 per cent of the equivalized median income. However, to ensure compatibility with the analysis of income distribution, the main poverty indicators were calculated using the OECD square root of the number of persons in the household scale. Figure 22.5 shows the poverty rate for the period 1989–2009.

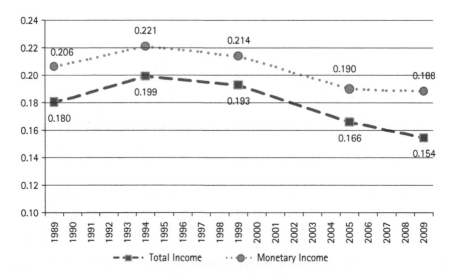

FIGURE 22.5 Poverty rate (monetary versus total income)

Source: INE Statistics Portugal, Household Budget Surveys.

Table 22.6 Poverty indices

	1989	1994	1999	2005	2009
F_0 Poverty Incidence	0.206	0.221	0.214	0.190	0.188
F_1 Poverty Intensity	0.059	0.063	0.060	0.051	0.046
F_2 Poverty Severity	0.024	0.026	0.024	0.021	0.018
F_0 Children	0.193	0.235	0.224	0.201	0.232
F_0 Elderly	0.453	0.431	0.408	0.336	0.258

Source: INE Statistics Portugal, Household Budget Surveys.

The comparison between monetary and total (monetary and non-monetary) income confirms the importance of the non-monetary resources of the households in limiting the poverty risk, together with the equalizing effect in the income distribution already identified. Figure 22.5 also emphasizes the initial increase in the poverty rate in 1989–94, which coincided with the inequality increase already discussed, followed by a clear decrease between 1994 and 2009.

The monetary poverty indices in Table 22.6 record an increase up to 1994 followed by a reduction to the end of the period. The incidence of poverty decreased from 0.221 to 0.188 between 1994 and 2009, poverty intensity from 0.063 to 0.046, and poverty severity from 0.026 to 0.018. Particularly revealing is the evolution of the elderly poverty intensity that decreased from 0.453 in 1989 to 0.258 in 2009. However, children's poverty intensity showed no comparable evolution. Starting from a much lower initial level in 1989 (0.193), it increased to 1994 more considerably than the national average, followed the general decrease to 2005, but returned to close to its highest level in 2009.[4]

Table 22.8 (to be found at the end of this section) highlights how the evolution of the poverty indices follows closely that of income inequality. This close relationship is particularly evident in periods of strong increase (1989–94) or decrease (2005–09) in inequality.

The austerity policies adopted in Portugal since 2010 have also had serious repercussions on the poverty level. The EU-SILC 2010 data shows that for the first time since income data has been collected, the poverty line fell by about 3 per cent in nominal and 4.4 per cent in real terms year on year, as a result of the fall in household income. Rodrigues (2012) shows that the poverty incidence would be equal to 19.6 per cent in 2010 (a rise of 9.5 per cent) if the poverty line had remained unchanged in real terms from 2009. Callan et al. (2011) obtain a similar estimate.

Material Deprivation

The material dimension of poverty, or material deprivation, is defined as the inability to attain certain basic standards of living and consumption, in particular, the enforced lack of

---

[4] Unlike what was found earlier in the analysis of the evolution of inequality, the main trends in the evolution of poverty do not differ significantly when different datasets are used. The evolution of the poverty indicators calculated using either HBS or ECHP/EU-SILC data coincide, though the former gives slightly higher poverty levels.

at least any three of the nine items defined by the EU. Severe material deprivation is defined as the enforced lack of at least any four of those. In 2010, 22.5 per cent of the Portuguese were materially deprived, a percentage that has not changed much from 21.7 per cent in 2004, with a minimum of 19.9 per cent in 2006 and a maximum of 23.0 per cent in 2008.

If age is taken into consideration, there was a considerable decrease in the deprivation rate of the elderly (31.1 per cent in 2004 to 24.4 per cent in 2010), reflecting the success of the social policy measures for this age group. However, there was an increase in the deprivation rate of the youngest age group (less than 18-years-old), which has become the most deprived group (27.5 per cent in 2010).

Severe material deprivation has decreased from 9.9 per cent in 2004 to 9 per cent in 2010, keeping a similar age group pattern as material deprivation. Those in the 1st income quintile are the most severely deprived, but with a significant decrease from 26.5 per cent in 2004 to 21.5 per cent in 2008. This decrease has not been matched by the 2nd quintile (12.9 and 12.1 per cent respectively), perhaps reflecting a stronger presence of the elderly in the 1st quintile.

Cumulative Disadvantage and Multidimensional Measures of Poverty and Social Exclusion

It is a curious fact that not all people at risk of poverty see themselves as lacking a sufficient number of items so that they are considered materially or severely materially deprived, or conversely, that many not at risk of poverty see themselves as materially deprived, as discussed in Rodrigues and Andrade (2012). A more inclusive definition is that of being consistently poor (both at risk of poverty and materially deprived), which has decreased marginally over the 2004–10 period (9.2 per cent to 8.5 per cent of the population). A stronger sign is given by the consistent poverty rate using the severe material deprivation concept—it has decreased consistently from 5.4 per cent to 4.0 per cent. Finally, the broader concept of 'at risk of poverty or social exclusion' has decreased very slightly (from 26.1 per cent to 25.2 per cent over the period) with the already discussed decreases of two of its components ('at risk of poverty' and 'severe material deprivation'). However, its third component, 'living in a household with low work intensity' has increased since 2008 and had a negative impact on the final rate.

Indicators of Social Cohesion

A key indicator of social isolation is the inability to get help when needed from family and/ or friends, as investigated in the ad hoc module about social participation within EU-SILC 2006. Portuguese people, like most Southern Europeans, have strong family ties: 38.5 per cent meet relatives daily plus an extra 34.5 per cent meet them every week. They also have strong friendships: 44 per cent meet their friends daily and 32.5 per cent every weekly. Remote contact is less frequent than personal contact, and is more frequent with relatives than friends.

The frequency of contacts by those at risk of poverty is similar to those who are not, except for lower remote contact with friends, perhaps reflecting cost concerns. Furthermore, the 'ability to ask any relative, friend or neighbour for help' was marginally lower for those at risk of poverty (90.7%), than for those not at risk (92.8%). Although the Portuguese keep strong regular social contacts, they do not tend to participate in social groups or organizations. The highest level of participation by far is in religious activities: 45.9 per cent of those at risk of poverty compared to 42.4 per cent not at risk, with a higher intensity in the older age group (65+). 'Helping others' is a distant second (20.8 per cent and 30.1 per cent respectively), but there is little participation in 'political parties or trade unions', 'professional associations', 'recreational groups or organizations', or 'charitable organizations', and even less (almost always below 5 per cent) by those 'at risk of poverty'.

Demographics, Health, House Tenure, and Crime

Since the early 1980s there has been a steady decline in the Portuguese birth rate, from 16.2 births per thousand total population in 1980 to 9.6 per thousand in 2010, together with a noticeable increase in the average age of the mother at the birth of the first child (27.2 years in 1991 to 30.6 in 2010), reflecting a higher participation of women in higher education and in the labour market. This is confirmed in Távora (2012), who finds high rates of female full-time employment that co-exist with traditional gender values in a unique way in Southern Europe.

Simultaneously, the significant increase in the health budget has contributed to a substantial fall in the infant mortality rate (from 24.3 per thousand in 1980 to 3.1 per thousand in 2011) and a rise in life expectancy at birth from 71.7 years in 1980 to 79.5 in 2010. The mortality rate has remained around 10 per thousand throughout the same period, but the main causes of death have changed. 'Circulatory system diseases' is still top, but it has fallen by about one quarter to 317.7 per 100,000 in 2010 with a parallel rise in deaths caused by tumours (235.0) and respiratory diseases (111.0).

Nevertheless, the Portuguese are never very happy about their health, as can be judged from their self-reported health status in the National Health surveys. The percentage of Portuguese reporting their health status as 'good' or 'very good' is low in this context, though it increased from 47.0 per cent in 1998–9 to 53.2 per cent in 2005–6; those that consider it 'bad' or 'very bad' fell from 16.5 per cent to 14.1 per cent. Important factors are gender and age group: women, particularly as they grow older, are more pessimistic than men. This picture is reinforced by the 2005–6 survey data on self-reported diseases. Most are associated with old age: high blood pressure; rheumatism; chronic pain; or, particularly with older women, such diseases as osteoporosis. Many are gender invariant, such as diabetes, kidney stones or emphysema/bronchitis, whereas depression and anxiety are much more often self-reported by women.

Another Portuguese particularity relates to (a very imperfect) housing market. House rents have been frozen for decades, leading to a virtually non-existent modern rental sector and a substantial proportion of home ownership and mortgages, as shown in Table 22.7. It may also have prevented a house market bubble, although the easier access to credit following the deregulation of the financial sector contributed to the increased mortgaged ownership in the noughties. As discussed earlier, the main home is the main asset of most households and mortgage repayments are a heavy burden, particularly in low income/ wealth households. Furthermore, the substantial home ownership explains the significant

Table 22.7 Housing Tenure (%)

	1990	1995	2000	2006	2010
Owned outright	49.2	57.0	54.1	50.4	48.4
Owned with mortgage	9.8	9.2	14.4	25.4	24.6
Rented	32.2	26.0	25.0	17.8	19.2
Other	8.8	7.5	6.5	6.4	5.9

Source: INE Statistics Portugal, Household Budget Surveys.

difference between monetary and total income already discussed: imputed rents are the main component of non-monetary income.

The number of offences per 1,000 population recorded by all police forces in Portugal over the period 1998–2011 varied between 33.7 per thousand and 39.0 per thousand. The most common type of recorded criminal offences are those 'against property' (thefts/burglaries) in 2011, of which those associated with motor vehicles and 'muggings' are the most significant. Of all crimes 'against people' the most significant is 'assault' with 5.7 per thousand in 2001, 'against society' is 'driving under the influence of alcohol', with 2.2 per thousand, and 'under other legislation' is 'driving without a valid licence' with 1.6 per thousand.

Subjective Measures of Well-Being, Satisfaction, 'Happiness'

It is very clear from the Eurobarometer bi-annual survey that the Portuguese are not very happy with their life either: on average, over the period for which data is available (November 1985–May 2012) only 4.95 per cent of the Portuguese respondents were 'very satisfied', whereas 8.95 per cent were 'not very satisfied'. More strikingly, before the start of the current financial crisis, the Portuguese were already frankly pessimistic. What causes this Portuguese pessimism? The respondents can choose the two most important issues affecting their country and over the period 2003–12 these have consistently been related to the economic situation: the most important has always been unemployment, followed by either the economic situation in general or inflation. Even security issues like crime (chosen by only 8 per cent of the respondents in 2012), terrorism, education, or the environment virtually did not register as main concerns. Portuguese expectations are not positive at all. What worries us most is the economy: 'unemployment'; 'the economic situation'; 'rising prices/inflation'. Again these worries were already there in 2003.

Intergenerational Mobility

There is evidence of intergenerational mobility in Teixeira (2010) using data from the ad hoc module on intergenerational transmission of poverty of EU-SILC 2006. She finds that 52.8 per cent of the 25–65 Portuguese age group attained higher education levels than their parents, 44.7 per cent achieved the same and only 2.4 per cent did worse, reflecting the improvement in the Portuguese education system already discussed. Gender is important: 52.1 per cent of those that did better were women. Class is also important: considering a four class partition, 72.5 per cent of the children of parents in the highest class attained secondary or higher education levels, but only between 18 per cent and 21 per cent of the children in the other classes did as well.

Wall *et al.* (2001) found less evidence of mobility in their analysis of informal support networks using data from a 1999 survey of families with children. Informal support actually reinforced existing social inequalities: it was mostly the better-off parents (particularly the wife's mother) of the better-off families who helped with child care, financial support, household tasks, or even advice and emotional support. Working-class mothers working full time actually received little informal support from their families and less from their friends and had poor access to (expensive) child care facilities.

Appraisal of the Interdependence and the 'National Story' of Inequality Drivers and their Social Impacts

Wilkinson and Pickett (2009) suggest that an increase in inequality has a negative impact on different social indicators. The analysis in this chapter does not completely validate this statement, as there is no clear indication of a direct relationship between the evolution of inequality and the portfolio of indicators used to ascertain the social situation of the Portuguese population, as can be seen from Table 22.8.

Two facts make it particularly difficult to establish a causal relationship between inequality and the social indicators throughout this period in Portugal: one is that the inequality levels remained particularly high compared to the rest of the EU countries; the other is that the equivalized real disposable income increased for all economic groups, though at different rates.

Table 22.8 Trends in inequality and select indicators of social impact

	1990-95	1995-00	2000-05	2005-10
HBS–Total income	↗	↔	↘	↘
HBS–Monetary income	↗	↗	↘	↘
At-risk-of-poverty rate	↗	↘	↘	↘
Severe material deprivation				↔
Population at risk of poverty and severely materially deprived				↘
Population at risk of poverty and social exclusion				↘
Crime rates			↗	↔
Fertility rates	↘	↗	↘	↘
Life expectation	↗	↗	↗	↗

4. POLITICAL AND CULTURAL IMPACTS

The aim of this section is to analyse whether living in a society with high inequality levels, compared to the EU average, influences the attitudes and perceptions of the Portuguese.

Political Participation and Trust in Institutions

Measured by the abstention rate, political participation in Portugal has dropped considerably over the years: this rate has increased from 8.3 per cent in 1975, the first free elections after 48 years of dictatorship, to around 40 per cent abstaining in the late 1990s and 42 per cent in the most recent (2011) general elections. Using survey data about participation in the 1999 parliamentary elections, Magalhães (2001) found that 'social inequality does not translate directly into political inequality in an electoral (participation) sense', only indirectly through, for example, interest in politics and political opinions.

Union Membership has also declined significantly. Using Visser's ICTWSS data, Sousa (2011) shows that union density decreased from more than 60 per cent in the late seventies to about 30 per cent in the late eighties, and has then stabilized around 20 per cent since 2000 (19.3 per cent in 2010). He also emphasizes the high level of union creation, extinction and restructuring: between 1975 and 2000, 438 unions were created and 279 disappeared or merged. There were 331 legally recognized unions in 1975 and 490 at the end of 2010. This is an important specific characteristic of the pluralist union system adopted in Portugal, which undermines the effectiveness of the unions and their ability to attract and consolidate a membership.

Furthermore, the trust Portuguese people place in their institutions is not high, according to the results of the Eurobarometer surveys. Less than half of the Portuguese 'tend to trust' the national government, parliament, and political parties. This negative view has increased significantly in the current crisis: 79 per cent, 76 per cent and 82 per cent do not trust them in 2012, respectively. However, this lack of trust for the traditional institutions and political parties has not led to the adoption of extremist views (until now): there are no significant extremist parties or organizations.

Sedes' survey of the quality of the democratic regime, analysed in Magalhães (2009), shows that this lack of trust derives from believing that the political system lacks responsiveness. More than 70 per cent of the respondents felt that politicians are neither concerned with what people 'like me' think, nor that public opinion can influence government policy. Perhaps even more damaging, 75 per cent feel that politicians 'always seek to further their own personal interests'. The fundamental characteristics of a democratic system that were chosen more often were 'an economic system that ensures a fair plentiful income for everyone' and 'a justice system that treats everyone equally'.

Magalhães (2005) found that the prevailing political attitude in Portugal is 'democratic disaffection', characterized by 'low levels of participation in political elections, conventional political activism, and unconventional civic activism', which summarizes this section well. Although much less prevalent, 'democratic dissatisfaction' increased particularly in the second half of the nineties, which was a period of stable government but also of economic growth and a fall in inequality, as already discussed.

Values About Social Policy and Welfare State

The stress on a 'fairer' economic system also comes through in the results of the 2010 Eurobarometer *Poverty and Social Exclusion Report*. It shows strong support for social policies: almost 60 per cent of the Portuguese respondents agreed totally (more than 90 per cent also adding the 'tend to' answers) that poverty is a problem that needs urgent action by the government and that income differences are far too large. A slightly lower percentage, close to 50 per cent, agrees totally with wealth re-distribution and higher taxes for the wealthier (again around 90 per cent when the second 'tend to' answer is considered). However, and perhaps expectedly, the institutions the Portuguese trust more 'with regard to their action combating poverty' are NGOs and charities (60 per cent), religious institutions (59% per cent), and the EU (48 per cent), but not their national government (only 26% per cent). This higher trust in the EU is perhaps surprising in a country that has seen the approval rating for its EU membership decline from a high of 79 per cent of the Eurobarometer respondents rating it 'a good thing' in March 1991 to only 39 per cent in May 2011, with 26 per cent considering it 'a bad thing'.

Immigration

Lages *et al.* (2006) analyses the attitude of the Portuguese to immigration, using data from a 2002 survey. It shows that about three quarters of the Portuguese do not agree with the arrival of more immigrants be it from Africa, Brazil or Eastern Europe. However, the answers are influenced by the educational attainment and age of the respondents: those with a basic level education and the older disagree more. Nevertheless, most respondents have a very positive attitude about the rights of immigrants, in particular 93 per cent agree that they should be entitled to be re-joined by their families, 84 per cent that the naturalization process should be made simple, and 79.7 per cent that the process of legalization of illegal immigrants should be made easier. This favourable attitude to the rights of immigrants is confirmed by the Portuguese scores in the MIPEX III index, which analyses existing migrant integration policies and their implementation. Portugal comes in second place (only behind Sweden) with overall scores of 76 per cent and 81 per cent in 2007 and 2010, respectively. It scores best in labour market mobility, family reunion, anti-discrimination, and access to nationality policies.

The Social Climate Index

The social climate index published by Eurobarometer since 2009 does not allow for a direct comparison with the past evolution of inequality in Portugal, for which definitive data is only available up to 2009. It is however an important indicator of the perceptions of the Portuguese about the impact of the current deep economic and social crisis and the policies that have been implemented to address it. The Portuguese overall index varies between -2.3 in 2009 (ranked 22nd amongst EU countries) and -3.2 in 2012 (24th). The only positive score is for the 'area people live' in. 'Neutrality' could only be argued for 'life in general', 'personal job situation', and 'relations between people', but all suffered sharp declines in 2012. The most negative perceptions are those about the national economic and employment situation, with scores between -5.8 and -6.7 throughout the period.

Appraisal of the Interdependence and the 'National Story' of Inequality Drivers and their Cultural and Political Impacts

The relationship between political and cultural impacts and inequality does not come through in a direct form, but is obviously behind the attitudes and perceptions of the Portuguese population. When asked about poverty and inequality, more than 90 per cent of the respondents show that they are aware of, and concerned about, the Portuguese situation and support the need for change and a reduction in inequality. However, there seems to be a simultaneous complete lack of credibility in the national political institutions, particularly in the national government, and its capacity or political will to redress the situation which co-exists with a significant decline in the positive valuation of the advantages of EU mem-bership, though the majority view is still positive.

After decades when Portugal has consistently been one of the most unequal EU countries, trust in public institutions is seriously dented, as revealed by high levels of electoral absten-tion and the lack of trust in most public institutions. Furthermore, the current social and economic crisis, which has led to a sharp increase in inequality and a drop in the income and living standards of the poorest population, spreading into large sectors of the middle classes, may lead to a profound change in the attitudes and perceptions of the Portuguese, as some of the results above already suggest.

5. EFFECTIVENESS OF POLICIES IN COMBATING INEQUALITY

Policies aimed at reducing inequality can take different forms and generate vast effects, both direct and indirect. As labour income is the main component of the income of most Portuguese households, this section will start by analysing state intervention in the labour market, particularly the setting of the minimum wage, and union density.

State Intervention in the Labour Market

The minimum wage was first introduced in Portugal in May 1974, and fixed at about 50 per cent of the average wage. Its steady increase in nominal terms translates to a sluggish evolution in real terms, and in 2009 it was equal to only 37.2 per cent of the average wage. This depreciation has certainly contributed to the rise in wage inequality since 1985, as discussed in Section 2. An indirect way of assessing its regulating role and influence on wage inequality is given in Rodrigues *et al.* (2012) by comparing the minimum wage with a low wage threshold (defined as 2/3 of the median wage). It has dropped steadily from 104 per cent in 1985 to about 90 per cent in 2009.

The regulation of the labour market has been a hot political discussion topic in Portugal in recent years. According to some, the labour market was too regulated and the legislation too protective of workers' rights. Hence, the labour market has been gradually deregulated, with increased speed after the Troika agreement. The impact of these changes on wage and household inequality is so far impossible to estimate, but expected to be non-negligible.

The drop in union membership may have contributed significantly to the increase in wage inequality. Sousa (2011) shows that union membership dropped from just under 1.49 million workers in 1978 to just under 740 thousand in 2010, corresponding to a fall in union density from 60.8 per cent to just below 20 per cent.

Taxation

The structure and parameters of the fiscal system play a fundamental part in the definition of the resources available to households. An important indicator of the depth of state intervention in the economy is given by the proportion of taxes and social transfers in GDP. However, their effects on inequality depend on the level and the progressivity of the fiscal system.

Since 1960 there has been a very significant increase in the Portuguese tax burden. Tax revenue as a percentage of GDP increased from 6.8 per cent to 20.1 per cent of GDP in 2010 (21.0 per cent in 2007). Starting in the 1980s from a value of about 10 per cent and well below the OECD average (as shown in Figure 22.6), the Portuguese rate increased much faster during the 1990s and equalled that average at about 19 per cent in 2000. It has continued its upward progression, further increasing to about 23 per cent compared to an OECD average hovering just below 20 per cent.

The biggest increases in Portuguese taxation as a percentage of GDP have been in taxes on 'goods and services' (7.6 per cent in 1965 to 13.7 per cent in 2006, but 12.4 per cent in 2010), taxes on 'income, profits and capital gains' (3.9 per cent in 1965 to 9.3 per cent in 2008, but 8.6 per cent in 2010), and social security contributions (5.2 per cent in 1974 to 9.0 per cent in 2010).

Table 22.9 reports the redistributive effect and progressivity of the fiscal system on the income distribution and inequality level using a methodology similar to Verbist (2004). It is affected however by the lack of information about gross incomes in the 2005 and 2010 HBS, which had to be supplemented by information from the EU-SILC surveys. Although the change in the databases will have an effect on the results, the main trends should not be significantly affected.

The redistributive effect is given by the difference between the Gini coefficient of the gross and net income distributions, whereas the vertical equity index gives the variation in inequality that would occur if there were no re-ranking effect between gross and

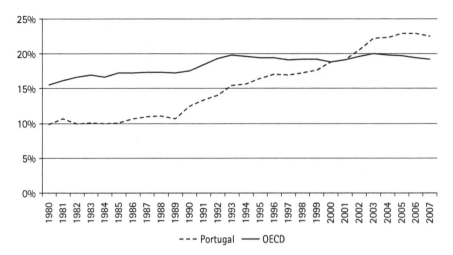

FIGURE 22.6 Tax revenue as percentage of GDP, Portugal and OECD

Source: OECD.

Table 22.9 Redistributive effect of direct taxes

	1989	1994	1999	2006	2009
G_G–Gini Gross Income	0.352	0.388	0.394	0.415	0.380
G_N–Gini Net Income	0.329	0.359	0.367	0.370	0.338
RE–Redistributive effect	0.023	0.028	0.028	0.046	0.043
RE as % of G_G	6.5	7.3	7.0	10.0	11.2
VE–vertical equity	0.025	0.030	0.030	0.048	0.046
PI–progressivity	0.186	0.190	0.174	0.174	0.182
t–tax level	0.118	0.138	0.147	0.217	0.201

Note: Income refers to disposable household income, corrected for household size using the OECD square root of the number of persons in the household scale.

Source: INE Statistics Portugal, Household Budget Surveys (1989–94–99), Eurostat, EU_SILC (2006–10).

net incomes. The progressivity index is defined in Kakwani (1977) and gives the difference between the tax concentration index and the gross income Gini coefficient.

The results in Table 22.9 suggest a continuous increase in the redistributive capacity of the fiscal system, which is based on an increase in the fiscal level rather than on significant changes in its level of progressivity.

Notwithstanding the sharp increase in the taxation level, the redistributive ability of the Portuguese fiscal system is still hampered by serious problems that limit its efficacy in reducing inequality. A recent study (CEAFGEA (2008)) calculates that the informal economy represents more than 20 per cent of GDP, and Rodrigues *et al.* (2012) estimate that only 75 per cent of households pay taxes.

Social Expenditures

Social security expenditure as a percentage of GDP is given in Figure 22.7. It increased sub-stantially in the period following the 1974 revolution (local maximum of 7.7 per cent in 1977, then affected by the financial difficulties and budget cuts of the late 1970s), followed by a sus-tained, if irregular, growth to 10.3 per cent in 2001. A period of intense growth is observed between 2007 and 2010 (12.7 per cent to 18 per cent).

By type and as a percentage of GDP, the two biggest shares of expenditure are 'old age' and 'health', which have increased considerably from just above 3 per cent each in 1980 to 9.2 per cent and 6.6 per cent, respectively, in 2007. As already discussed, the ageing of the Portuguese population has necessarily increased public expenditure on both pensions and health care, but there have also been several social policy initiatives directed at the elderly to take them out of the most severe poverty.

Again the comparison with the OECD average reveals the considerable increase in Portuguese public expenditure (in cash) since 1980, catching up with the OECD average quickly during the 1990s, and overtaking it in the noughties. Although Portuguese 'benefits in kind' have grown, they are still trailing the OECD average, and diverging down from 'cash benefits'.

Starting in the second part of the 1990s, the implementation of specific means-tested benefits aimed at fighting poverty and social exclusion has introduced a new redistributive component into Portuguese social policy, which has a direct effect on levels of inequality. Two of the most important measures are the RSI and the CSI, already mentioned in previous sections in connection with the detected falls in inequality and poverty, particularly of the elderly.

The evaluation of the efficacy of social transfers in reducing inequality is given in Table 22.9 by calculating the Gini coefficient at different stages of the sequence from market to disposable income. Redistributive Effect 1 measures the percentage change in the Gini

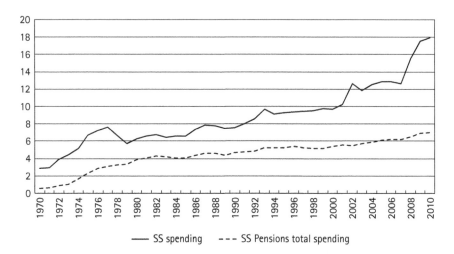

FIGURE 22.7 Social security expenditure and pensions (cash) as percentage of GDP
Source: INE—Statistics Portugal/BP *Contas Nacionais Anuais* and IGFSS/MTSS.

Table 22.10 Redistributive effect of social benefits

	1989	1994	1999	2006	2009
Gini Market Income	0.418	0.469	0.496	0.499	0.513
Gini Market Inc. + Pensions	0.334	0.371	0.382	0.393	0.389
Gini Disposable Income	0.329	0.359	0.366	0.373	0.364
RE—Redistributive effect 1	-20%	-21%	-23%	-21%	-24%
RE—Redistributive effect 2	-2%	-3%	-4%	-5%	-6%

Note: Income refers to disposable household income corrected for household size using the OECD square root of the number of persons in the household scale.

Source: INE Statistics Portugal, Household Budget Surveys (1989–94–99), Eurostat, EU SILC (2006–10).

coefficient due to the inclusion of social pensions, whereas Effect 2 measures the change due to other social benefits.[5]

The redistributive effect of social pensions is higher and growing slightly, thus reflecting the ageing of the population and the increasing level of pensions. However, the growing importance of Effect 2 highlights the importance and efficacy of means-tested benefits in addressing inequality. These results are consistent with Rodrigues (2009) who estimates that the joint effect of the CSI and RSI reduced the Gini coefficient by about 3 per cent in 2003.

Using EU-SILC 2006–8 data, Gouveia (2011) argues that social benefits have lower efficacy in Portugal than in other EU countries, a view not shared by Alves (2012). He shows that their lower relative efficacy (in 2009) is mostly related to the low level of social transfers rather than to a lack of redistributive efficiency. However, the results in Table 22.10 suggest a growing level of efficacy of social policies in Portugal.

Education

Together with the health and social security spending already discussed, the largest share of public social expenditure is education. Spending in all three increased massively following the 1974 revolution, with education and health booming as required by a young growing population, while social security (biggest share—pensions) grew at a much slower rate. As birth and fertility rates fell and the population aged, education expenditure flattened and even decreased, health expenditure was probably allocated more and more to old(er) age ailments and social security increased dramatically. From being the highest, at 3.0 per cent of GDP in 1977, education expenditure became the lowest at 5.0 per cent in 2010. Conversely, health rose from 1.5 per cent to 5.7 per cent and social security from 1.1 per cent to 6.8 per cent respectively. The lower rises in 2010 and falls in 2011 are an obvious consequence of the current budget cuts.

[5] Ideally, social benefits should be divided into contributive and non-contributive, but the data currently available does not have enough detail. The sequence adopted here follows closely that of Eurostat's poverty risk rate before and after social transfers.

Expenditure on educational institutions showed an increasing trend from 1998 to 2003 (from 5.7 per cent of GDP to 5.9 per cent), but it was not continued and fell to 5.2 per cent in 2008. By level of education, there has been a sustained, if small, increase in expenditure on pre-school education; expenditure in all basic levels and secondary education has decreased (from 4.2 per cent to 3.4 per cent), also reflecting the decrease in pupil numbers; finally tertiary expenditure has increased (from 1.0 per cent to 1.6 per cent). Further cuts have been announced as part of the current austerity measures.

Appraisal of the 'National Story' of Policies Affecting Inequality

The steady devaluation of the minimum wage relative to the average wage, the considerable drop in union density, and the deregulation of the labour market have all contributed to the increase in wage inequality. Conversely, the significant growth in the tax level has increased the redistributive capacity of the fiscal system, although its progressivity level has remained virtually unchanged.

The rise in social expenditure in the last two decades in Portugal has undoubtedly had an impact on the income distribution and inequality levels. The implementation of social policy measures designed to fight poverty and social exclusion impacted on the resources and income of the poorest households, and significantly improved their living standards

As the current economic and social crisis deepens, all social policies are losing ground, both through the increased difficulty in access and the lower benefits awarded. The substantial recent effort to increase the average level of educational qualifications of the population has also been reversed as a result of the implementation of the budget cuts. The joint impact of all these measures will inevitably result in higher inequality and, above all, increased poverty.

6. Conclusions

Portugal has remained one of the countries with the highest inequality levels in the EU and OECD over the last decades. Nonetheless, and allowing for the use of different data sources and breaks in the statistical series, it was possible to identify different sub-periods in the evolution of Portuguese inequality. Portuguese membership of the EU in 1986 and the ensuing fast growth and economic integration processes generated a significant rise in economic inequality that would not be fully reversed in subsequent years. Between 1989 and 1994, the Gini coefficient increased by more than 10 per cent, and other inequality indices recorded even higher increases.

The two following sub-periods, 1994–9 and 1999–2005, showed relatively stable inequality levels with mixed evidence provided by the different data sources on the magnitude and direction of their changes. During the second half of the noughties, between 2005 and 2009, there was an unequivocal reduction in inequality, irrespective of the data source or inequality index chosen. However, the magnitude of this reduction was not sufficient to take inequality back to the initial level of 1989.

Another important element of the 'national story of inequality' is the non-matching evolution of household and earnings inequalities. Earnings inequality is one of the main drivers of household inequality. However, its growth dynamics are much more structural than those of household inequality, as the latter can somehow be offset, or even reversed, by social policies aimed at the most excluded or disadvantaged sectors of the population.

The progressive expansion of the Portuguese Welfare State in recent years, building on a relatively fragile base and clearly inferior to that of the majority of the European developed countries, has played an important role in limiting and even mitigating the rise in inequality. Throughout this chapter, the crucial role that means-tested policies, designed to fight poverty and social exclusion, played until 2009 to mitigate inequality was highlighted.

This co-existence between high levels of inequality and real income growth, between an improvement in social policies and the reduction of poverty, makes it more difficult to establish a clear causal relationship between inequality and the different dimensions of the Portuguese social, political and cultural reality that were analysed in this chapter, as suggested by Wilkinson and Pickett (2009). This chapter also highlighted how education attainment and qualification levels are fundamental in the analysis of inequality in Portugal. Their recent marked improvement should have an important attenuating role on future inequality.

The relationship between the political and cultural impacts and inequality does not come through in a direct form, but is obviously behind the attitudes and perceptions of the Portuguese population. The very clear way that the deepening economic crisis, general impoverishment of the population, weakening of the middle classes, and return to higher levels of poverty and inequality are changing the expectations of the Portuguese may perhaps become an additional element to validate Wilkinson and Pickett's thesis. The progressive deterioration of the credibility of the political system and of many of its institutions and the massive reduction in the positive view of EU membership are clear symptoms that the new cycle of increasing inequality into which Portugal seems to be sinking will have strong political and social effects.

Finally, the serious economic crisis that has been afflicting Portugal since 2010, together with the tough austerity policies implemented by the Portuguese government, as a result of the aid agreement signed with the European authorities and the IMF, appear to be taking the country back into a period of sharp increases in social and economic inequality. Although the available statistical data does not yet allow for a detailed evaluation of the redistributive effects of the successive austerity programmes, the available evidence so far points to the start of a new cycle of increasing inequality in Portugal.

REFERENCES

Alves, N. (2009), 'New facts on poverty in Portugal', *Banco de Portugal Economic Bulletin*, Spring, 125–154.

Alves, N. (2012), 'A view on income redistribution in Portugal and in the EU', *Banco de Portugal Economic Bulletin*, Winter, 41–58.

Callan, T. *et al.* (2011), 'The Distributional Effects of Austerity Measures: A Comparison of Six EU Countries', *Euromod Working Paper EM6/11*, Essex.

CEAFGEA (2008), *Economia Informal em Portugal*, Centro de Estudos de Gestão e Economia Aplicada, UCP, Porto.

Costa, S. and Farinha, L. (2012*)*, 'Inquérito à Situação Financeira das Famílias: Metodologia e principais resultados', *Banco de Portugal Occasional Papers*.

Eurobarometer, *Eurobarometer Interactive Search System*, available at: <http://ec.europa.eu/public_opinion/cf/index_en.cfm>.

Eurobarometer (2012), *Social Climate Report*, EBS 391.

Eurostat, *ECHP, EU-SILC*.

GEPE/Department of Education, *Estatísticas da Educação*.

Gouveia, M. (2011), 'A eficiência das políticas contra a pobreza em Portugal', *Revista Brotéria*, 173.

GPEARI/Department of Science, Technology and Higher Education, *Estatísticas*, available at: <http://www.gpeari.mctes.pt/stat>.

Hawley, J., Otero, M.S., and Duchemin, C. (2010), *2010 Update of the European Inventory on Validation of Non-formal and Informal Learning—Final Report*, Cedefop.

INE Statistics Portugal, *Household Budget Surveys*.

INE Statistics Portugal, online database available at: <www.ine.pt>.

Kakwani, N. (1977), 'Measurement of Tax Progressivity: An International Comparison', *Economic Journal*, 87, 71–80.

Lages, M., Policarpo, V.M., Marques, J.C., Matos, P. Lopes, and António, J. H.C. (2006), Os imigrantes e a população portuguesa: imagens recíprocas. Lisbon: ACIME.,

Magalhães, P. (2001), 'Desigualdade, Desinteresse e Desconfiança: A abstenção nas eleições legislativas de 1999', *Análise Social*, 157, 1079–1093.

Magalhães, P. (2005), 'Disaffected Democrats: Political Attitudes and Political Action in Portugal', *West European Politics*, 28, 973–991.

Magalhães, P. (2009), *A Qualidade da Democracia em Portugal: A Perspectiva dos Cidadãos*, SEDES, Lisboa.

MSSS/GEP (Statistical Department of the Portuguese Ministry of Solidarity and Social Security), *Quadros de Pessoal*, Data in magnetic media.

OECD (2008), *Growing Unequal? Income Distribution and Poverty*, Paris: OECD,.

OECD (2011), *Divided We Stand—Why Inequality Keeps Rising*, Paris: OECD.

OECD, *Education at a Glance*, several issues, available at: <http://www.oecd.org/edu/highereducationandadultlearning/>.

Pordata, online database available at: <www.pordata.pt>.

Rodrigues, C.F. (2007), *Distribuição do Rendimento, Desigualdade Pobreza: Portugal nos anos 90*, Almedina, Coimbra.

Rodrigues, C.F. (2009), 'Efficacy of Anti-poverty and Welfare Programs in Portugal: The Joint Impact of the CSI and RSI', *Economics Department Working Paper 42/2009*, ISEG, Lisboa.

Rodrigues, C.F. (2012), 'Pobreza e Desenvolvimento Económico', *Conferência Portugal em Mudança*, ICS, Lisboa.

Rodrigues, C.F. *et al.* (2012), *Desigualdades Económicas em Portugal*, FFMS, Lisboa.

Rodrigues, C.F. and Andrade I. (2012), 'Monetary Poverty, Material Deprivation and Consistent Poverty in Portugal', *Notas Económicas*, 35, 19–39.

Sousa, H.J. (2011), 'Sindicalização: A Vida por detrás das Estatísticas (alguns problemas metodológicos)', *Projecto Sociedade Civil e Democracia Working Paper*, FCSH-UNL, Lisboa.

Távora, I. (2012), 'The Southern European Social Model: Familialism and the High Rates of Female Employment in Portugal', *Journal of European Social Policy*, 22, 63–76.

Teixeira, C. (2010), 'Transmissão Intergeracional da Pobreza', in *About Poverty, Inequality and Material Deprivation in Portugal*, INE, Lisboa.

Verbist, G. (2004), 'Redistributive Effect and Progressivity of Taxes: an International Comparison across the EU using EUROMOD', *Euromod Working Paper EM5/04*, Essex.

Wall, K., Aboim, S., Cunha, V. and Vasconcelos, P. (2001), 'Families and Informal Support Networks in Portugal: the Reproduction of Inequality', *Journal of European Social Policy*, 11, 213–233.

Wilkinson, R., and Pickett, K. (2009), *The Spirit Level: Why More Equal Societies Almost Always do Better*, New York: Penguin Books.

CHAPTER 23

ROMANIA: HIGH RISING INEQUALITY OVER TWO DECADES OF POST-COMMUNIST TRANSFORMATION*

IULIANA PRECUPETU AND MARIUS PRECUPETU

1. INTRODUCTION AND CONTEXT

The Socio-Economic Background

IN Romania, during the post-communist transition, inequality increased tremendously. While, in 1990, the value of the Gini coefficient placed this country at the level of Sweden, by 2007 Romania had become the most unequal country in Europe according to the same coefficient. Although Romania was an egalitarian country under communism, it was characterized by equality at a very low level of income and the population was generally poor and impoverished. Today, the country displays high levels of inequality while incomes continue to remain very low.

The recent history of GDP growth can generally be described as having an up and down pattern. Economic recession started in the mid 1980s, became established and became further aggravated during the first years of transition. The year 1991 registered a record low of a 12 per cent contraction in economic output. The economy slowly started to recover in 1993 and a relative stabilization was noticeable, but only for four years. The output expansion was reversed by renewed economic turmoil in 1997 and 1998. In 2000, a new period of economic growth began, which seemed at the time to be on a more robust and sustainable path: in 2008, GDP registered a record high of 9.6 per cent growth. However, the positive

* We would like to thank the reviewers in the GINI project who contributed to the improvement of this paper as well as to Professors Ioan Mărginean and Cătălin Zamfir, who kindly made comments and suggestions.

trend ended abruptly in the economic crisis, as GDP contracted in 2009 by 8.4 per cent. The following years brought a certain stagnation. By and large, consumption, which is generally low in Romania, followed the same pattern as GDP, recording the most dramatic decline in 1991 (15 per cent by comparison with the previous year) and then twenty years later when, in 2011 it recorded a contraction of 11.2 per cent, much more severe than that of GDP.

Real wages remained low for the entire transition period. They declined dramatically in the early 1990s and, despite a small positive trend during 1994–6, they largely tracked the evolution of GDP and recovered to their 1990 level only in 2007. Employment fell significantly in the 1990s due to the economic restructuring, the slow process of job creation, and early retirement schemes. The number of employees in the economy fell from 8.1 million in 1990 to 5.9 million in 1996 and to 4.4 million in 2010 (NIS data). The dismantling of socialist agriculture and the consequent land restitution resulted in the formation of a sizeable subsistence agriculture in which a large part of the former industrial labour force has been immersed. However, agriculture today conceals a large group of the unemployed. Informal employment is very high, estimated at between 1 and 2 million people.[1] In relation to educational composition, 29.4 per cent of the active population have attained ISCED levels 0–2 and 57.6 per cent levels 3–4. Although tertiary education expanded a lot during the transition, the proportion of graduates in the active population is still the lowest in the EU (13 per cent) (Eurostat data).

The government consolidated gross debt (percentage of GDP) has been on the increase, from 6.6 per cent of GDP in 1995 to 33.3 per cent in 2011, currently still being one of the lowest in the EU.

Romania has been through a demographic decline that started during the early 1990s. In the past, the pro-birth policy introduced in the mid 1960s by the communist regime, led to a demographic expansion that reached its peak in 1990 when the population was 23.2 million. The last census of 2012 recorded a total population of 20,254,866 (NIS, census provisional data 2012). The sharp decline is due to a fall in the fertility rate owing to the unfavourable economic and social circumstances of transition. Emigration, currently estimated at 3 million (OECD, 2012), with its more recent form, emigration for work, also contributed to the population decrease. The composition of the population by nationality shows that 88.6 per cent is represented by Romanians, 6.5 per cent by Hungarians, 3.2 per cent by Roma, while the remaining 1.4 per cent is represented by other ethnic groups.[2] (NIS, census provisional data 2012). Ageing affects Romania along with the other European countries: between 1990 and 2011, the proportion of the population over 65 years old increased from 10.4 per cent to 15 per cent, whereas the proportion of those aged 0–14 fell from 23.6 per cent to 15.1 per cent.

The Context of Transition: Shaping Long Lasting Inequalities

The communist regime aimed at comprehensive development and an egalitarian society. However, although aiming at social equality, communism only managed to generate a process of 'homogeneity in poverty' (Márginean, 2004: 64). During the transition from

---

[1] MLFSP, Strategic national report regarding social protection and social inclusion, 2008–2010
[2] The remaining 0.3 per cent is represented by those who do not declare their ethnicity.

communism to democracy and capitalism, important drivers of inequality have been generated. Economic restructuring, consisting of a substantial process of deindustrialization and privatization of agriculture coupled with the fall of former communist markets, largely defined the first decade of economic transition. It is largely acknowledged that Romania embarked on a slow and painful path of transformation. The structural reforms have been gradual and have been accompanied by high social costs. Poverty and inequality increased to a large extent. (Table 23.1 presents socio-economic indicators on Romania.)

During the first decade of transition, absolute poverty rose tremendously from 5.7 per cent[3] in 1990 to 35.9 per cent in 2000 when it reached its peak. Income inequality also grew greatly and by 2000 it had risen by more than 70 per cent above its 1990 level. Romania went from a relatively egalitarian country to one of the most unequal countries in Europe. Employment decreased due to economic restructuring and early retirement schemes, and the number of employees fell from 8.1 million in 1990 to 4.6 million in 2000 (NIS data).

As part of the general strenuous reform, privatization of large state assets was intricate, lingering and not transparent. In fact, it was characterized at the time as 'insider privatization', 'asset stripping' and '*nomenklatura* privatization' (Tanzi, 1998). The transfer of ownership from state to private owners created important opportunities for the concentration of resources in the hands of a small elite. This has been one of the major factors leading to the formation of large private wealth. Corruption plagued the process of privatization and continued to diversify and amplify during transition in many spheres of society, turning it into a factor that contributed to deepening inequality. 'State capture' (Hellman *et al.*, 2000) created unjustified privileges and produced unbalanced outputs in society. Public positions have been abused many times and people occupying these positions legislated in favour of specific interests or overlooked the legal requirements in order to fulfil private interests (Precupetu, 2012). Well into transition, legislating in favour of special interests took many forms, like passing special pieces of legislation for special pensions, for creating advantages in the process of privatization or for awarding contracts or licences. Privatization of agriculture has generated a favourable distributional impact (Cornia, 2003). However, land restitution, usually small parcels of land, has led to the emergence of a large, unproductive, fragmented agricultural sector dominated by a subsistence type of farming. Agriculture accounts today for about 30 per cent of total employment[4] (NIS data) while the rural population is 45 per cent. Nevertheless, subsistence agriculture served as a safety valve for numerous households, both for the rural population and for those coming from urban areas who lost their jobs during the restructuring process of industry. The great agricultural potential of the country has not been realized yet and the subsistence model perpetuated down to today. The role of subsistence agriculture is to be seen in the high proportion of own consumption and in the dampening effect that it has on inequality.

The informal economy grew considerably and was estimated in 2001 at 25–28 per cent of GDP[5] (Albu 2004). Between 1 and 2 million people were estimated to work in the shadow economy[6] in 2008. Subsistence agriculture and the informal economy constituted, at

[3] MLFSP, 2010, HBS data.

[4] Involvement in small scale farming might be under-reported.

[5] Estimations vary a lot according to source and measurement method. Estimations go up to as much as 37.4 per cent of GDP (Schneider, 2005).

[6] Strategic national report regarding social protection and social inclusion, 2008–2010.

Table 23.1 Basic socio-economic background statistics on Romania

	1990	1995	2000	2005	2010	2011
Population						
Ages 0–14 (% of total)	23.6	20.5	18.4	15.6	15.2	15.2
Ages 15–64 (% of total)	66.0	67.5	68.1	69.6	69.9	69.8
Ages 65 and above (% of total)	10.4	12.0	13.4	14.8	14.9	15.0
Population, total	23201835	22684270	22442971	21634371	21438001	21390000
GDP						
GDP per capita (constant 2000 US$)	1896	1741	1651	2260	2637	2633
GDP per capita growth (%1990)	100	91.8	87.1	119.2	139.1	138.9
Consumption						
Household final consumption expenditure per capita (constant 2000 US$)	1315	1245	1304	1981	2660	2362
Household final consumption expenditure per capita growth (%1990)	100	94.7	99.1	150.7	202.4	179.7
Debt						
Government consolidated gross debt (% of GDP)		6.6	22.5	15.8	30.5	33.3
Real wages						
Index of real wages (%1990)	100	66.5	59.4	89.5	123.6	
Unemployment						
Unemployment rate		9.5	10.5	5.9	7	7.7
Education composition of active population (ISCED)						
Levels 0–2				33.3	30.3	29.4
Levels 3–4				57.6	57.8	57.6
Levels 5–6				9.1	11.9	13

Sources:
GDP, Population: WDI
Real wages: NIS, Statistical Yearbook
Unemployment rate: NIS, Statistical Yearbooks
Government consolidated gross debt (% of GDP)
Education: Eurostat.

individual and household level, successful survival strategies for those affected by recession. 'Informal cash earnings have deepened inequality, however; in the informal sector, the rich are becoming richer, while the poor are only managing to obtain the bare necessities' (Zaman and Stanculescu, 2007, 24). In the short and long term, the informal economy means, especially for the poor, less security as regards their future earnings at retirement.

Emigration, and especially its more recent form, emigration for work, produced heavy imbalances in the workforce. Currently, it is estimated that 3 million people work abroad (OECD, 2012). Emigration is selective in terms of education and regions. Data suggest that the percentage of university graduates who have left Romania for good rose from 6 per cent in 1990 to 23 per cent in 2000, while, with regard to regions, migration was concentrated more in the western and eastern regions of the country (UNDP, 2005). Although generally contributing to increasing life standards, emigration also exacerbated the existing inequalities.

In the case of Roma, the transition process affected this population to a greater extent than the majority. Being less educated and less qualified, they were among the first to lose their jobs in the economic restructuring. Enrolment in education decreased while the emerging segregated patterns of schools did not help their social inclusion. The lack of opportunities on the labour market, their traditional but outdated occupations, the cultural models and the discrimination they are subject to, all contributed to a trend of social marginalization of Roma.

Through the difficult times, social policy did not compensate for the negative effects of transition. On the contrary, over the periods of crisis/recession in the first decade of transformation, social expenditure tended to fall and 'the public sector seemed the first one to be sacrificed' (Zamfir et al., 2010, 15).

All these factors either created new inequalities or contributed to the deepening of the existing ones. Today, a series of inequalities characterize Romania: inequalities between a small elite of very rich and a large group of poor people; between several large developed cities and the rest of the country; between rural and urban areas; between big cities and small, former mono-industrial small towns; between large villages and small, poor, aged, peripheral villages; as well as between various regions of the country. Moreover, transition created new opportunities for some categories while considerably lowered prospects for others. A certain stratification of life chances by age, education, and employment status has emerged and has widened over time. Currently, inequalities seem to be deeply entrenched and tend to perpetuate themselves; there is no evidence that the existing gaps tend to be reduced.

2. Evolution of Inequality and its Drivers

Household Income Inequality

In 2010, Romania had a median equivalized income of €2,037, which was the smallest in the EU and around ten times smaller than that of some of the foremost western countries like the Netherlands (€20,292), Austria (€20,618) or France (€20,046), and less than half of the NMS12 average (€4,431) (Eurostat data). Even though very poor, in 2010 Romania ranked fifth in the EU with regard to income inequality. With a Gini coefficient of 33.3, Romania was placed among the most unequal countries in EU, having a level of income inequality lower only than Lithuania (36.9), Latvia (36.1), Spain (33.9), and Portugal (33.7) and significantly higher than the EU27 average (30.5) (Eurostat data). In time, income inequality grew considerably. In 1990, immediately after the fall of communism, Romania was characterized by a low level of inequality, being in the group of countries less unequal in Europe, like

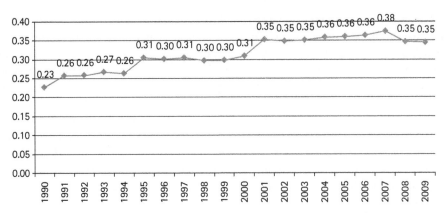

FIGURE 23.1 Distribution of per capita household net income: Gini coefficient, 1990–2009

Source: Transmonee, based on NIS data.

Sweden or Hungary. After only a decade of transition, Romania went into the group of the most unequal countries in EU, like the UK or Portugal.

The early 1990s saw a moderate increase in the Gini coefficient at a time of economic recession (Figure 23.1). [7] In the second part of the 1990s, with the start of modest economic growth, the Gini coefficient registered another increase, followed by a relatively stable period. The most significant increase in the Gini coefficient occurred after 2001, when the economy entered a path of more robust growth. The Gini coefficient maintained a very high level all through the time of economic growth and reached a peak in 2007 when Romania ranked the highest in the EU in regard to income inequality (Eurostat data). Only starting with 2008, for the first time after 1990, the Gini coefficient recorded a significant decrease although the country still remains one of the most unequal in the EU.

The income quintile ratio (S80/S20) depicts approximately the same picture of income inequality as the Gini coefficient. In 2010, the S80/S20 ratio was 6, which ranks Romania fourth in the EU, after the countries with the most unequal income distribution, represented by Spain (6.9), Lithuania (7.3) and Latvia (6.9), and higher than the EU27 average (5). The highest ratio was registered in 2007, when it reached 7.8 (Eurostat data).

Trends in Poverty Risks

Poverty continues to remain one of the crucial problems of the country.[8] In 2010, Romania ranked the second highest in the EU with regard to relative poverty rates. According to

---

[7] Here we use Transmonee data as it is the most complete series available for the Gini coefficient. International comparisons are based on Eurostat data, which start the series in the year 2000. The Eurostat measure is the Gini coefficient of equivalized disposable income using the modified OECD scale and the Transmonee refer to the distribution of population by per capita household net income.

[8] At-risk-of poverty rates come from Eurostat, EU SILC data, absolute poverty rates come from MLFSP, 2010, HBS data.

Eurostat data,[9] the at-risk-of-poverty rate was 21.1 per cent, second after Lithuania (21.3), higher than the EU27 average (16.4 per cent) and much higher than in countries like the Netherlands (10.3 per cent) or France (13.5 per cent). It is also worth mentioning that Romania has one of the lowest poverty thresholds in the EU. Relative poverty, calculated by using a threshold fixed at 60 per cent of the national annual median disposable income, shows little change since 2000. Despite a period of economic growth from 2000 to 2008, which led to an increase, in time, in incomes and consumption, the poverty rates remained rather stable as the median income also changed. The relative poverty measure does not capture the dynamics of poverty. For this reason, another measure of poverty was calculated nationally that is able to reflect the changes in the level of welfare, against an absolute poverty line anchored to a minimum consumption basket.

The absolute poverty measure is based on a national methodology, developed by NIS, government experts, researchers, and the World Bank. This methodology uses a consumption-based welfare indicator, and an absolute poverty line based on the cost of a basic needs method. The consumption-based welfare indicator includes own consumption. The poverty line is absolute, including a food component plus an allowance for essential non-foods and services. The food component is defined as the cost of a food basket preferred by individuals from the second and third deciles. The equivalence scale is *empirical*, taking into account economies of scale and the relative cost of children over adults (each adult = 1, each child = 0.5, economy of scale parameter = 0.9) (World Bank 2007). Absolute poverty rose sharply after 1990 (Figure 23.2), along with the economic recession, until 1995, when it began to fall for two consecutive years as the economy seemed to recover to a certain extent. Once again, with a new economic recession, starting in 1997, absolute poverty rose again abruptly up to 2000, when economic growth re-launched more robustly, and continued to fall until 2010 when the effects of the economic crisis were strongly experienced by the population. In 2000, the number of persons affected by absolute poverty was 8,045,000, while in 2010 the number fell to 1,110,000.

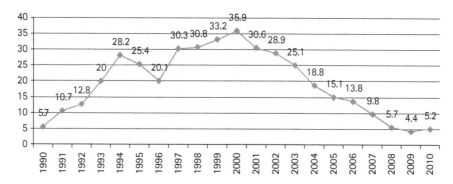

FIGURE 23.2 Absolute poverty rates, 1990–2010

Source: MLSFP, 2010, NIS data.

[9] The figures for the at-risk-of-poverty rate slightly differ between Eurostat and NIS data based on HBS. Here, we used Eurostat for international comparisons and NIS national data for trends in time.

The relative poverty measure is well suited for international comparison and for under-standing the position that various social groups hold relatively to the national standard of living.

We will detail the various inequalities by the social and individual characteristics that are highlighted by the relative poverty measure, and we will complete the picture with absolute poverty data only when the latter better highlights disparities. Essentially, poverty profiles based on the relative poverty measure and the absolute poverty measure are very similar.

Most exposed to poverty risks are children, youths, households with dependent children (especially those having three or more children), single persons and single persons with dependent children, the unemployed, the self-employed in agriculture and less-educated people. In 2010, the risk of poverty for persons under 18 was almost two times higher than that of persons of 65 years and over. Children and youths (under 30) represent almost half of the number of people in absolute poverty. Households with dependent children face a sig-nificantly higher risk of poverty than those without children. Most exposed to poverty are households of two adults with three or more children and in 2010 the at-risk-of poverty rate for households with three or more dependent children was the second highest in Europe after Bulgaria and was more than twice the EU27 average. Unemployed people face a risk of poverty almost three times higher than the employed and maintain high and relatively stable risks over time. However, the self-employed in agriculture seem to be most exposed to absolute poverty.

Inequalities are marked not only by individual and household characteristics but also by rural/urban and development region. In 2010, the gap between rural and urban areas was important since absolute poverty was four times higher in rural than in urban areas. Pockets of poverty are concentrated mostly in rural areas, as 76.7 per cent of the poor are living there and only 23.3 per cent live in urban areas. In time, the gap between the two areas tended to deepen: in 2000, absolute poverty in rural areas was less than twice than in urban areas, while in 2010 it was four times higher. The pattern (Zaman and Stanculescu, 2007) was that, even though the rural population has been less affected by recession, the urban population has tended to gain to a greater extent from recovery. Important disparities appear between regions. The poorest region (North-East) has poverty rates five times higher in comparison to the richest one (Bucharest-Ilfov). The ratio is even greater (eightfold) according to abso-lute poverty rates. Some of the disparities have deepened in time, even in times of economic growth, when poverty fell. For example, in the period 2003–2006, the West region regis-tered a 62 per cent drop in the number of the poor, in the South the number of the poor was reduced by more than half, while in the Centre region the decrease was much lower, at only 34 per cent. The differences in the pace of poverty reduction have led to increasing regional disparities (World Bank 2007).

There are also important disparities associated with ethnicity. The Roma population rep-resent a deep pocket of poverty, as in 2010 their absolute poverty rate was 31.4 per cent in comparison to that registered in the case of the Romanian population (4.4 per cent) and of the Hungarian minority (2.4 per cent). The gap between Roma and the Romanian popula-tion gradually increased in time: in 2003 the Roma poverty risk was 3 times higher than the Romanian poverty risk, whereas in 2010 it was more than 7 times higher (MLFSP 2010, NIS data).

Labour Market Inequality

Employment rates are low: in 2011 the total employment rate (15–64 years old) was 58.5 per cent, well below the EU 27 average (64.3 per cent) and much lower than leading western countries like the Netherlands (74.9 per cent), Sweden (74.1 per cent) or Denmark (73.1 per cent). Employment rates were similar to those in Italy (56.9 per cent) and Bulgaria (58.5 per cent).

From 1997 to 2001, employment rates declined continuously and fell more abruptly in 2002, to remain rather stable to the present. The declining employment rates in the early 2000s were due to the accelerated reforms and economic restructuring, coupled with early retirement schemes. The older age groups (55–64), women and those with less education experienced the greatest declines in employment rates, while for the younger work force (15–24) the decline was rather steady.

In term of regions, employment rates vary from a low 53.5 per cent in the Centre to a high 64.3 per cent in Bucharest-Ilfov region, reflecting once again disparities in development of the various regions and therefore the different capacity to absorb the work force.

The Roma employment rate is much lower than the national average, being only 35.5 per cent, while inequalities are related to gender, education, age and basic abilities (reading and writing). The employment rate is significantly higher for men (44.3 per cent) than for women (27.4 per cent), for the better-educated (67 per cent) in comparison to the less-educated (33.6 per cent), and significantly lower for younger age groups (16–24) (28 per cent) in comparison to those between 25 and 54 years old (39.3 per cent) (Preoteasa 2012). A combination of factors contribute to the particularly difficult situation of Roma: their low level of education; low level of qualifications and skills; the tradition of specific jobs which do not match the current conditions on the labour market; and the discrimination faced from employers who generally offer less qualified jobs to Roma (Cace et al., 2010).

Looking at unemployment in 2011, unemployment rates were moderate (7.7 per cent) and lower than the EU average (9.7 per cent). High unemployment rates are found among the youth, the less-educated, males in comparison to females, urban areas in comparison to rural ones. An interesting case is represented by the better-educated since over the three years 2009–2011 their unemployment rate has almost doubled. They seem to have been impacted more during the economic crisis. This can be explained by the higher graduation rates from tertiary education and the incapacity of the labour market to absorb the more educated labour force during the crisis. Higher unemployment rates for males than females probably originate in the economic restructuring process, which affected the male workforce to a greater extent. In urban areas, unemployment is considerably higher than in rural areas, as agriculture accommodated an important segment of the jobless. However, in the agricultural sector there is also substantial hidden unemployment (Zaman and Stanculescu 2007).

Wages Inequality

Real wages suffered a dramatic reduction during the transition since in 1996 they reached 56.2 per cent of their 1990 level. It was 17 years (1990–2007) into the transition before they recovered their value from the first year of transition. Moreover, wages are among the most unequal in EU: in 2006, the P90/P10 wage ratio was 5.5 in Romania while in other countries of the EU, the ratio was as low as 2.1 in Sweden, 2.3 in Finland and 2.4 in Denmark. Wages represent an essential source of income at household level although their contribution to total income of households remains low, at about half of total income. Their contribution to household income is important for the employed, for those living in urban areas, and for the most affluent households. Disparities in wages are found between economic sectors, public and private sectors and by gender.

Education Inequalities

A series of inequalities characterize education, among which those determined by income, residence and ethnicity are crucial. Income introduces an important divide in education, even though public education is free. The costs associated with education (transportation, clothing, meals, sometimes textbooks, etc.) introduce a divide between low-income families and the rest of the population in regard to access to school. Income becomes important also when looking at the quality of education. Private tutoring, a widespread model in Romania, supplements low-quality education in some schools or disciplines, and prepares the children for evaluations and admissions etc. Consequently, those who cannot afford private tutoring and rely on the public education system are disadvantaged in comparison to the others.

Another important divide is the omnipresent rural/urban disparity. While schools in urban areas generally have a better infrastructure, higher qualified staff and provide better opportunities for their students, those in rural areas tend to illustrate the opposite. Participation in education is significantly higher in urban than in rural areas and is especially strong for higher levels of education: upper; secondary; and tertiary. Participation rates in higher education are more than double in urban (56.3 per cent) than in rural areas (27.2 per cent). Rural residence seems to provide lower educational opportunities to children all along their educational path. Rural populations also have a generally lower education, which further impedes their development: in 2009, only 4 per cent of population living in rural areas had a university degree, while the percentage was 25.4 in urban areas.

Roma children are disadvantaged in comparison to others. In 2011, 20 per cent of the Roma children (6–16 years old) were not enrolled in school. Illiteracy affects 25 per cent of the Roma aged 16 and older, being higher in rural areas, in Roma compact communities and among women. Educational attainment is very low among Roma, as almost half either have no formal education or graduated from primary school, around one third graduated from lower secondary education while only 15 per cent have upper secondary education. Only 1 per cent have a university degree (Tarnovski, 2012). Other vulnerable groups of children face significant problems in regard to participation in education: children coming from disadvantaged families; HIV infected children; or children with special educational needs (Preda, 2009).

Transition to the labour market is rather difficult and is evident in the high unemployment rate of the young population, which, in 2011, was 23.5 per cent for the age group 15–24, much higher than the 7.4 per cent rate at national level (NIS 2012). There is a sort of asymmetry between the education system and the modern requirements of the labour market, as the education system is not flexibly adapted to its needs. This misfit contributes the low participation in adult training in comparison with other European countries. The skills gap in the labour markets comes also from the emphasis placed for a relatively long time on vocational education at the secondary level, and the relatively modest coverage of higher education (World Bank, 2008).

Romania is characterized by low returns on education and, even though an increasing trend in time is noticeable, the growth is still modest. Returns to schooling are low for those with less-than-tertiary education, especially for the graduates of vocational secondary schools who are working in the private sector. Poor children are more likely to be directed into low-return education paths (namely vocational schools), while wealthy children are more likely to attend general secondary and tertiary education institutions. This has obvious implications for the reproduction of inequality. For tertiary education, returns on education are higher, but they are still significantly lower than in other countries (World Bank, 2008).

3. Social Impacts

Even though it is difficult to assess the impacts that inequality has had in the social realm, and this relationship cannot be tested directly in this analysis, we can still observe the various disparities that characterize Romania across a range of social dimensions. The goal is to scrutinize whether the increasing income inequality during the past two decades has been accompanied by a rise in negative social impacts as some scholars have proposed (Wilkinson and Pickett 2009). This relationship is not tested as such, but, rather, we look at trends over time and rely on data and literature to understand the divisions between social groups that characterize the social set up of Romania in the main social domains. However, while analysis of the social dimensions generally describes a poor situation in Romania, it did not worsen during the time described by the data as income inequality rose. It is clear though that inequalities are accompanied by social features, which are long lasting: 'low social trust, corruption, decline of state authority are here to stay and most probably will not disappear during the life time of current generations' (Zamfir *et al.*, 2010, 11).

Material Deprivation

Material deprivation looks at a multi-dimensional perspective on poverty by going beyond the limited income measure and capturing the inability of people to participate in their society due to lack of resources. This perspective is especially fruitful when using a comparative approach and particularly when aiming to describe living standards across countries which are very diverse in term of affluence, as is the case in the EU (Whelan and Maitre, 2012). Material deprivation comprises the enforced lack of items that are customary in a certain society at a certain point in time; that people would like to possess (have access to) but cannot afford. The material deprivation rate was calculated for Romania, starting with 2007, when EUSILC was implemented in this country (Eurostat, 2010). When looking at the levels of material deprivation in comparison to EU averages, Romania has the second highest deprivation rate in the EU, after Bulgaria: around half of the population lacks at least three of the items that are customary in a modern society and that people would like to possess but cannot afford. Although, between 2007 and 2010, the deprivation rate slightly decreased, Romania still maintains its top ranking in the EU: the material deprivation rate is almost three times the average of EU27 and around four and a half times that of more advanced countries, like Germany (11.1 per cent) or Austria (10.7 per cent). This indicator speaks of the low standard of living as well as of the low degree of modernization in this country: with a high proportion of underdeveloped rural countryside, it is likely that this makes an important contribution to the high material deprivation rate.

The period described by the data was, at the household level, a time of accumulation (especially between 2007 and 2009) for a population that was generally materially deprived in comparison to the standard of other developed countries. The gap that separates Romania from the developed countries of the EU still remains huge.

The data presented below include rates for severe material deprivation (Figure 23.3). The indicator of severe material deprivation is defined in terms of households being deprived of any four of nine items. This measure has been included, along with the risk of poverty and jobless households, as one of the Europe 2020 headline targets to indicate progress towards reducing poverty and social exclusion. The severe material deprivation rate is lowest for the age category between 18 and 64 years old. Over time, a slight but significant fall in severe deprivation rates has been registered for those over 65 years old.

Couples with three or more dependent children, single persons and single persons with dependent children are most exposed to severe material deprivation. Couples with three or more dependent children seem the most vulnerable and rates increased for them, even though severe deprivation rates generally fell over time from 2007 to 2010. Even the most affluent households (fifth quintile) face high deprivation levels and they barely situate themselves at the level of the total material deprivation rates of the developed countries in the EU. As expected, the poorest households (first quintile) face extremely high deprivation levels, reaching 60 per cent in 2010. Also, in 2010, Romania had the third highest proportion in the EU of people in arrears of payment, at 29.8 per cent.

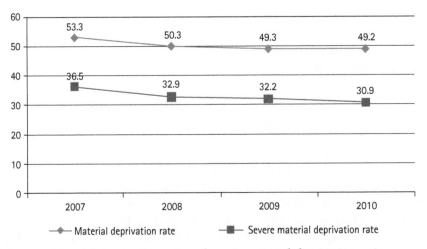

FIGURE 23.3 Material deprivation rate and severe material deprivation rate

Source: Eurostat (EU SILC).

Social Cohesion and Social Capital

Social relationships have been shaped by a communist heritage characterized by high levels of distrust of others outside their primary groups, of social institutions, and by subsequent social isolation. In regard to social relationships, Romania has been described as a country characterized by 'bonding' relations, mainly developed within the family and kinship groups, being thus a rather traditional country in this respect (Precupetu, 2007). 'Both involvement in networks of friends and trust in people, minority groups or institutions display lower levels in comparison to other European societies. Moreover, networks of useful relations are rather scarce' (Voicu 2005, 159).

Voicu (2010) tested the influence of the communist past on bridging social capital in Eastern European countries. The author confirmed through his analysis the presence of a certain negative effect of communist rule on the frequency of meeting friends and trust in institutions. He discovered that the residents of the Eastern European countries tend to meet their friends less often than Western Europeans, while they also have a lower level of trust in institutions.

Generalized trust placed Romania among other countries in the 2008 EVS study[10] in the EU with low trust in people: Bulgaria (18 per cent): Hungary (21 per cent): and Portugal (20 per cent). Only 18 per cent declared that most people can be trusted, while in Western countries generalized trust in people is more widespread and goes up to 76 per cent in Denmark and 70 per cent in Sweden. It should be noted though, that trust varies to a great extent for Western countries, while in Eastern European countries the levels of trust tend to be more consistently low.

The frequency of social contacts is also low (Figure 23.4), with a significant increase only in the recent past (from 2003 to 2010), which was a little bit more prosperous economically.

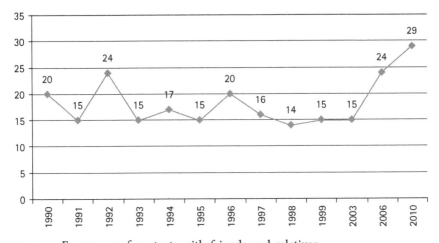

FIGURE 23.4 Frequency of contacts with friends and relatives

Source: Quality of Life Diagnosis.

---

[10] Source: EVS 2008, GESIS.

Membership of associations is also low: only 8 per cent of Romanians were part of at least one association, this being the lowest proportion of participation in Europe[11]. This can be explained by a series of factors, among which are: poor structural opportunities for participation; a weak tradition of non-governmental organizations; as well as poor individual resources.

Romania is a country with no historical tradition of civil society and has tried during transition to build this sector from scratch. 'Communist period furthered atomisation processes, cultivated suspicion and lack of transparency, while social order was based not on trust but on institutional fear. Socialism acted as a factor of anti-modernization' (Sandu, 1999). In fact, Romania shares the model of the other post-communist countries, which also exhibit low levels of bridging social capital (connecting relationships, outside the primary groups).

Health Inequalities

Population health is rather poor and aggregate indicators (life expectancy, infant mortality, mortality) show that a big gap separates Romania from the foremost countries in the EU in regard to health status. Furthermore, a series of inequalities characterize health.

In 2010 life expectancy was 73.8 years, the third lowest in the EU after Latvia (73.7) and Lithuania (73.5). When compared to Western societies, Romania lags far behind countries like Sweden where people live on average for 81.6 years or Ireland where life expectancy is 81 years. Over time, life expectancy increased slightly, with a more significant rise of 2.6 years from 2000 to 2010 (Figure 23.5). The gap between women and men grew greater over time: in 1980, women lived on average 5.3 years longer than men; in 2010 the gap grew to 7.5 years. The gender disparity is a universal feature and studies have shown that women live longer but they also spend more days in poor health and they run greater risks of a number of chronic illnesses, whereas men are more exposed to fatal illnesses like vascular diseases (Alber and Kohler, 2004). Beside the gender gap, there are also other inequalities, which are evident in life expectancy data. Life expectancy varies by urban-rural and development region. Life expectancy is higher in urban, in comparison to rural, areas (1.7 years difference), as well as in developed regions in comparison with less developed ones (differences of up to 2.1 years) (NIS data). Life expectancy is ten years shorter, while infant mortality rates are 40 per cent higher, among Roma than among the general population (Cace and Vladescu, 2004).

Disparities in self reported health and in access to health services arise from the socio-economic situation as well as from the general development of the country and the specific set up of the health system (between rural and urban, between development regions or localities of various size). Access to health care is significantly stratified by income and inequalities in access are pronounced in terms of the costs of seeing a doctor, which seems the most difficult aspect of care for those with low incomes. People in rural areas find access more difficult, mostly to hospitals: the costs of seeing a doctor prove to be the most difficult aspect of access for those in rural in comparison to urban areas.

---

[11] EVS/WVS 1999–2002.

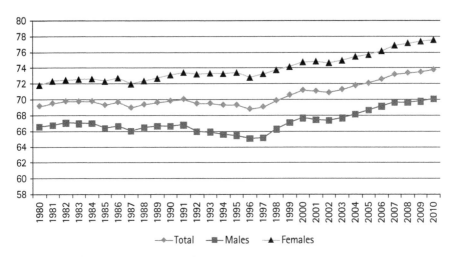

FIGURE 23.5 Life expectancy by gender

Source: Eurostat.

Life Satisfaction

Low levels of life satisfaction are generally recorded in Romania. According to Eurobarometer[12] data in 2011, Romania ranked the second lowest in Europe in regard to life satisfaction, after Bulgaria. Only 40 per cent of the population declared themselves either very satisfied or fairly satisfied with life, in comparison to the high levels of satisfaction that are present in leading countries like the Netherlands and Finland (both 96 per cent) or UK (92 per cent). Romania ranks close to Bulgaria (37 per cent), traditionally the most dissatisfied country in the EU, and Greece (46 per cent) also ranking constantly low in satisfaction. National level data shows significant variations over time in life satisfaction (Figure 23.6). The lowest level was registered in 1991 when the economy experienced the most dramatic contraction during transition, as GDP fell by 12.1 per cent in comparison to the preceding year. Life satisfaction also fell significantly in the 1990s. In 1990, at the very beginning of transition, some reparatory measures were taken aimed at increasing the very low standard of living imposed during communism. However, the second year of transition with its abrupt economic contraction was the turning point in which it became evident that the social costs of transformation to be born by the population would be very high. This explains the very low satisfaction registered in 1991.

In the following years, life satisfaction extended to about one third of the population. At the macro level, the process of economic decline continued and brought about further deterioration in living conditions. Moreover, the newly built social protection system was not broad enough and did not create safety nets for the people affected by the new social realities, among which economic restructuring and increasing unemployment made a powerful mark on peoples' lives. However, a certain adaptation process (Headey and Wearing, 1992) is visible in life satisfaction data and the period 1992–1996 can be considered as one of survival and adaptation as people began to learn how to shape their lives and adjust to the grim social

---

[12] Standard Eurobarometer 2011, spring wave.

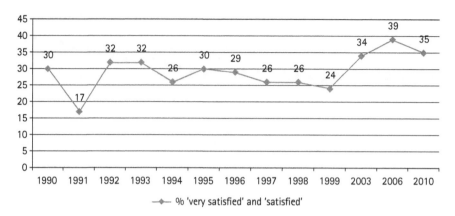

FIGURE 23.6 Life satisfaction

Question: Taking all things into consideration, how satisfied would you say you are with your life? 1. Very satisfied, 2. Satisfied, 3. Not satisfied, nor dissatisfied, 4. Dissatisfied, 5. Very dissatisfied.

Source: Quality of life Diagnosis, 1990–1999, 2003, 2006, 2010.

realities of the early 1990s. The following years saw a steadily fall in levels of satisfaction reaching a new low in 1999, associated with the economic decline, political instability and culminating with the social conflicts of 1999. The period after 2000 was characterized by ten years of economic recovery and, for the first time during transition, this had visible consequences in living conditions and was accompanied by a significant increase in levels of life satisfaction. However, the economic growth abruptly ended in 2010 and in 2011 a significant fall in life satisfaction was revealed by Eurobarometer data.[13] Life satisfaction decreased from 46 per cent in 2010 to 40 per cent in 2011(2011, spring wave).

4. POLITICAL AND CULTURAL IMPACTS OF INEQUALITY

As an essential component of a democratic regime, the participation of Romanians in civic and political affairs, together with people's behaviour, values, attitudes and evaluations in relation to politics and social life are worth scrutinizing through the lens of inequality present within the Romanian society.

Turnout in Elections

Participation in elections is falling (Table 23.2). Parliamentary elections saw a sharply declining turnout after their separation from the presidential competition in 2008. The

---

[13] Eurobarometer uses a different scale for life satisfaction (4 point scale) than Quality of life Diagnosis (5 point scale).

Table 23.2 Turnout in elections (%)

	Parliamentary Elections	Presidential Elections	Local Elections	EP Elections
1990	86	86		
1992	76	76	65	
1996	76	76	56	
2000	65	65	51	
2004	58	58	54	
2007				29
2008	39		51	
2009		54		28
2012	42		56	

Source: Permanent Electoral Authority of Romania, own calculations.

presence of Romanians in the voting booths in presidential and local elections, although on the same declining path, remains at levels of over 50 per cent of the total electorate. Less than 30 per cent of citizens have voted so far in the only two elections that took part for the European Parliament.

Trust in Institutions

In Romania, we can speak of a prevalence of distrust displayed by people in relation to political institutions (Figure 23.7). From the three political institutions analysed here, the most trusted, in general, in the last 8 years, is that of government (having an average trust of 24 per cent), followed closely by the National Parliament (with an average trust of 20 per cent) and political parties (14 per cent average trust). We have to notice, though, the rather low level of trust: in Romania, over the last eight years, the level of trust ranged between 10 per cent and 43 per cent in the case of government, 9 per cent and 35 per cent for parliament and from 8 per cent to 22 per cent for political parties.

The lowest point of trust for Romanian political institutions (10 per cent for government, 9 per cent for parliament and 8 per cent for political parties) was November, 2011, a time marked by the effects of the global economic crisis, prolonged social protests, and political instability, which eventually, in the spring of the next year, led to a change of government due to the centre-right administration losing support in parliament in favour of a centre-left coalition. Probably related to this, the more recent data (from the spring of 2012) indicate an increase in trust for political institutions.

As a general conclusion, trust in major political institutions (national parliament, national government, and political parties) is heavily influenced by the logic of electoral cycles. Every election and the formation of a new government is followed by an increased level of trust. In time, as the new administration unfolds, trust enters a declining path— until the moment of new elections approaches. The pattern is of a relatively high level of

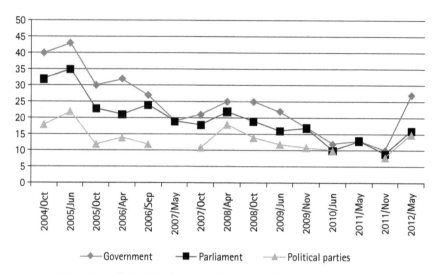

FIGURE 23.7 Trust in political institutions (2004–2012)

Source: Eurobarometers.

trust close to the beginning of each cycle, registering a more or less pronounced erosion of this capital of trust during the electoral cycle.

Satisfaction with Democracy

More than for other types of political regime, the persistence and consolidation of a democracy is profoundly dependent on citizens' support. Support given by the members of the polity appears as a variable that connects the political system to its broader social environment.

In Romania there is a strong acceptance of the democratic values and principles, as demonstrated by numerous studies (Precupetu, 2006, Precupetu, I. and Precupetu, M. 2004). In contrast to people's high commitment to democratic values and to democracy as an appropriate form of government, the functioning of democracy is evaluated as poor by the majority of Romanians (an average of only 24 per cent, over time, of people are satisfied with the way democracy works in their country) (Figure 23.8).

Even if people are dissatisfied with the functioning of the democratic regime, their attachment to the values and principles of democracy means that they care about the fate of their democracy and are interested in improving its performance. The rather low specific support for democracy was not converted into attitudes and actions directed against democracy itself. Instead, people's discontent with the functioning of democracy was driven inside the democratic system through a majority vote in favour of the political opposition. As a result, change in power took place in four (out of a total of seven) general elections. The absence of extremist parties in Romania is another characteristic of its political life that favours the persistence and consolidation of democracy.

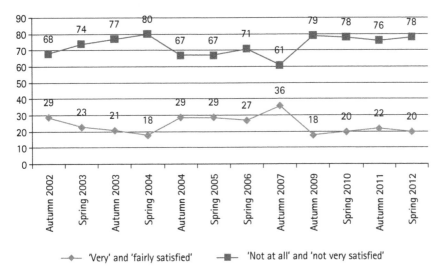

FIGURE 23.8 Satisfaction with the way democracy works in Romania

Source: Eurobarometers.

Attitudes towards Inequality and Redistribution

According to Eurobarometer data (Figures 23.9 and 23.10), in 2010 an overwhelming majority of the population, 91 per cent, totally agreed that income differences between people are far too large in Romania. This seems a largely shared, consensual perception in society. The percentage situates Romania close to EU27 average (88 per cent). In the EU, the percentage of those sharing this belief varied between 65 per cent in Denmark and 97 per cent in Latvia and Slovenia. The general agreement in Romania can be explained by the special circumstances of the country, where large amounts of wealth have been accumulated often through non-transparent, illicit means. The general rise in inequality during the transition, as well as the economic crisis at the time of the survey in 2010, might have added to this widely shared belief.

In 2010, 88 per cent of people believed that government should ensure that the wealth of the country is redistributed in a fair way to all citizens, while the EU27 average was 85 per cent. The lowest share of people sharing this belief was in the Czech Republic (67 per cent) while the largest was in Greece (97 per cent). On the other hand, only 32 per cent of respondents in Romania believed income inequalities are necessary for economic development, below the EU27 average (44 per cent). The least support for this idea was in Greece (24 per cent), while the highest was in Denmark (70 per cent).

During the transition in Romania, especially its first decade, the government role in welfare has been weak and mostly inefficient. Moreover, within the welfare mix, where government, the market economy and civil society should all play their role in ensuring the well-being of the population, the market economy failed in its role in this respect. Civil society, underdeveloped at first and with no tradition in Romania, picked up only later, with much external pressure and help, in gaining a certain stance in providing social services. Consequently, it is rather easy to understand today the strong support that the population gives to the idea that the government should ensure redistribution. Rather than being the expression of a communist mindset (as also shown by Voicu, 2005), it is the result of a

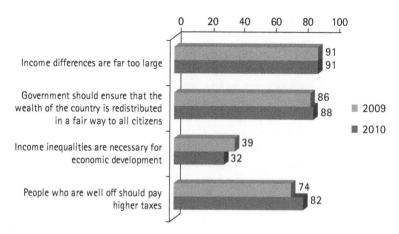

FIGURE 23.9 Attitudes towards inequality and redistribution

Source: EB 72.1, EB 74.1.

process of social learning during transition, where people saw, on the one hand, rapid afflu-ence being accumulated by unfair means and, on the other hand, that no mechanisms com-pensated efficiently for unemployment, poverty and rising inequality.

A large majority of the population (82 per cent) believed in 2010 that people who are well off should pay higher taxes, placing Romania around the EU27 average (79 per cent). The proportion of the population sharing this view varies between 67 per cent in Poland and Denmark and 96 per cent in Greece.

Between 2009 and 2010, the support for the idea that income inequalities are necessary for economic development decreased to a certain extent while the view that the well off should pay higher taxes gained stronger support. This might be explained by the fact that in 2010, at the time of the survey, the effects of the economic crisis started to have a powerful bearing on people's lives, through salary cuts in the state sector and the consequent effects in the economy (e.g. lowered consumption). When looking at the country's perceptions of welfare respon-sibilities, it is evident that a much more important role is placed at the level of government than at the individual level. Romania shares this model of belief with the majority of Eastern European countries, as well as other countries like Ireland, Greece, Italy, Spain, Portugal and former Eastern Germany. Finding the same pattern for the first decade of transition in Romania, Voicu (2005) concluded that the 'collective mentality does not encourage passive expectations towards the state, but rather promotes the idea of welfare based on workfare, where both individual and the state play an active role' (Voicu 2005, 67). In the EU, in 2010, the countries where the balance of views leaned towards a more important role for the individual in comparison to government are Sweden, the UK, Denmark, the Netherlands and Lithuania.

5. POLICIES

Social policy only partly compensated for the negative effects of transition. In difficult times, people relied more on kinship networks, and the subsequent inter-family transfers, on sub-sistence agriculture or immersion in the informal economy.

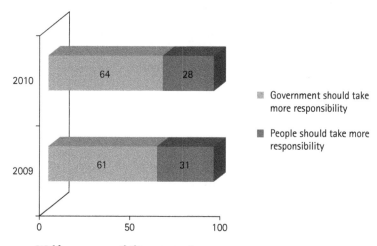

FIGURE 23.10 Welfare responsibility strategies

Source: EB 72.1, EB 74.1, own calculations.

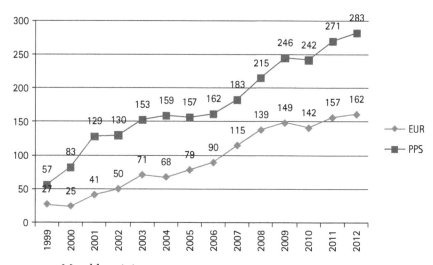

FIGURE 23.11 Monthly minimum wages

Note: Minimum wages as valid in January of each year

Source: Eurostat.

Minimum Wages

In January 2012, the monthly minimum wage in Romania was €162 (Figure 23.11). In the EU, minimum wages varied from €138 gross per month in Bulgaria to €1801 gross per month in Luxembourg. When expressed in Euros, minimum wages in Romania are nine times lower than those in Ireland or the Netherlands. The gap lowers when looking at minimum wages in PPS, as they represent in Romania almost a fifth of their amount in the Netherlands. However, Romania still has the second lowest minimum wage in EU after Bulgaria. During the period covered by the data minimum wages registered a significant increase.

The level of minimum wages varied during the time described by data between 21 per cent and 33 per cent of the average monthly gross earnings in industry and services. In EU countries, in 2010, minimum wages went from the lowest share in Romania to as high as 47 per cent of the average monthly gross earnings in industry and services in Slovenia.

Taxation

In 2010, the overall tax-to-GDP ratio was 28.1 per cent, much lower than the EU-27 average (39.6 per cent). The level of taxation is higher than that of Latvia (27.5 per cent), Lithuania (27.4 per cent), and Bulgaria (27.4 per cent) and comparable to the level of Slovakia (28.3 per cent) and Ireland (29.8 per cent). Between 1999 and 2004, the tax-to-GDP ratio declined, then picked up until 2007 as GDP registered higher growth (Figure 23.12). During the following two years, the tax ratio fell again, due mainly to a decrease in VAT revenue. Even though, in 2009, GDP dropped by 6.6 percentage points compared to 2008, the increase in excise duty rates in 2009 and VAT standard rate in 2010 (from 19 per cent to 24 per cent) ensured higher revenues from indirect taxes, which compensated for the drop in revenues from direct taxes and social contributions. The following year, 2010, the overall tax-to-GDP ratio increased by 0.3 percentage points with respect to the year before (Eurostat 2012).

There is a flat rate tax system with the rate set at 16 per cent. The system was introduced in 2005 and replaced the previous progressive four-bracket system, with tax rates ranging from 18 per cent to 40 per cent. The rate of 16 per cent applies to income from independent work activity, royalties, income from movable and immovable property (e.g. rents), but also to short-term capital gains on listed shares. Interest income is also subject to a final withholding tax of 16 per cent. Social security contributions are payable at a combined rate (31.3 per cent) for the employer and the employee. The rate, starting in 2009, is levied on employees with normal working conditions at 10.5 per cent. Employers contribute at a rate of 20.8 per cent. Higher rates for employers apply for special working conditions. Furthermore,

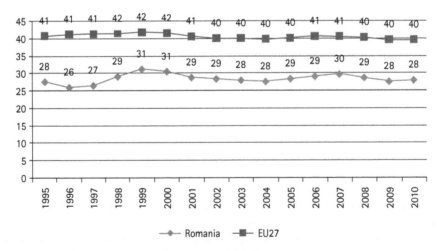

FIGURE 23.12 Tax revenue as a percentage of GDP

Source: Eurostat.

both employees and employers contribute to the health insurance fund and to the national unemployment fund. All social contributions are deductible for income tax purposes. The revenue shares received by social security funds account for 31.9 per cent, two percentage points above the EU-27 average (29.9 per cent) (Eurostat, 2012). The policy of the flat rate tax was implemented in 2005 in an attempt to increase the tax base by reducing tax avoidance and evasion. The adoption of the flat 16 per cent corporate profit and income tax was assessed as not being successful enough in encouraging formal employment expansion, as the still high social contributions might have offset its positive effect. On the other hand, it was considered that the flat rate, enhanced the flexibility, though limited, of the labour market. The flat rate, coupled with the revision of the labour code in 2005 (including more emphasis on active labour market policies and the simplification of company registration) has had beneficial effects and has resulted in increased employment and lower unemployment (Daianu, 2006). A study by Voinea and Mihaescu (2009) investigated the effects of flat-rate tax on inequality by using the Household Budget Survey data, through comparing the period before and after the introduction of flat-rate tax. Their research showed that the gains from the flat rate tax were unequally distributed, with 10 per cent of employees gaining 40 per cent of the total returns from the tax. As a general model, the higher the incomes, the bigger the benefits of the flat tax and the larger the household, the smaller the gains were.

The benefits from flat-rate tax represent 3.3 per cent of the net income of households in the upper part of the distribution and 2.4 per cent of the net income of households in the lower part of the distribution. But, for the 1 per cent of top income households, the returns from flat-rate tax represented 10 per cent of their net income. Overall, only the richest 20 per cent were the winners from the flat-rate tax (Voinea and Mihaescu, 2009). The authors' estimation is that the vast majority of gains went into consumption, especially in the case of rich households and only a small part went into savings.

Social Expenditure

In 2009, Romania had the third lowest social protection expenditure in the EU as a percentage of GDP (17.9 per cent), after Latvia (16.8 per cent) and Bulgaria (17.2 per cent). This means less than two thirds of the EU average (29.5 per cent) and only about half of the social protection expenditure of countries like Denmark (33.4 per cent) and France (33.1 per cent). When looking at the breakdown of social protection expenditure by function as a percentage of GDP, the largest function is old age, followed by health care (Figure 23.13). All of the functions maintained low, stable levels, with the exception of old age that grew more markedly after 2007.

Education

In 2009, Romania allocated 4.2 per cent of GDP for education, representing the second lowest share allocated to education in the EU after Slovakia (4.1 per cent). This share of GDP corresponds to less than half of what Denmark spends annually (8.7 per cent) and places Romania well below the average of EU countries (5.4 per cent). Despite some increase

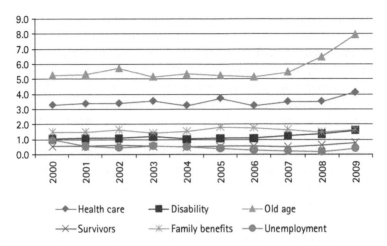

FIGURE 23.13 Social protection expenditure by function as percentage of GDP

Source: Eurostat, ESSPROS system.

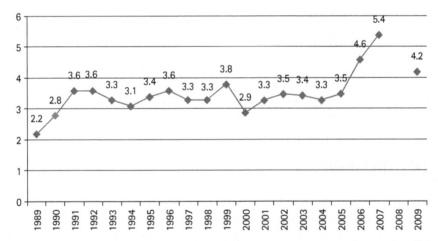

FIGURE 23.14 Total public expenditure on education as percentage of GDP, for all levels of education combined

Source: Transmonee 1989–2007, Eurostat 2009.[14]

since 2005, expenditure remained at very low levels during the time described by the data (Figure 23.14).

For the past 22 years, Romania's education system has been under perpetual reform, either deep-seated or less significant, depending on the objectives of various governments and political moments. These reforms have placed considerable pressure on all the actors involved in the educational process: policy-makers; teachers; parents; and students.

---

[14] Data for 2008 is not reported.

Changes have translated into a continuous instability that affected long-term plans for students and their families, as well as career plans for teachers. Moreover, it was explained (Márginean and Precupetu, 2010) that this instability turned, at individual level, into a perception that the education system is not accessible to all. The reforms, starting with the 1990s, aimed at decentralization of the education system with the purpose of lessening the financial pressure on central authorities and transferring partial or total funding responsibilities to local levels. However, for a country with an economy affected by successive crises and with a long tradition of centralization, the process proved to be very difficult. Moreover, given the disparities between development regions, urban/rural, and even at county level, decentralization has the potential to contribute to the deepening of educational inequalities (Neagu, 2005).

During the recent financial and economic crisis, in 2010, the effects of the economic downturn and pressures on the public finances became very pronounced and Romania applied salary cuts to public employees in order to restore the budget balance. The reduction consisted of a 25 per cent cut implemented since July 2010, which impacted heavily on teachers' salaries, which were already generally low and has had negative effects on the education system as such.

6. CONCLUSIONS

Two decades after the beginning of post-communist transformation, Romania stands out as one of the most unequal countries in the EU. While, in 1990, the value of the Gini coefficient placed this country at the level of Sweden, by 2007 Romania had become the most unequal country in Europe according to this measure. In 2010, Romania ranked fifth highest in the EU in regard to income inequality. Although Romania was an egalitarian country under communism, it was characterized by equality at a very low level of income and the population was generally poor and impoverished. Today, this country displays high levels of inequality while the incomes continue to be very low.

Currently, Romania has the lowest median equivalized income in the EU, less than half of the EU12 average and around ten times smaller than that of some foremost Western countries like the Netherlands or Austria. Poverty continues to remain one of the crucial problems of the country.[15] In 2010, Romania ranked second highest in the EU as regards its relative poverty rate, after Lithuania. In 2010, absolute poverty affected 1,110,000 people.

Inequalities are accompanied by low scores on the main social aspects. Romania has the second highest rate of material deprivation in the EU, after Bulgaria: around half of the population lacks at least three of the items that are customary in a modern society and that people would like to possess but cannot afford. In Romania, the populations' health is rather poor and aggregate indicators (life expectancy, infant mortality, mortality etc) show that a big gap separates Romania from the developed countries in the EU as regards health status. In 2010, life expectancy was 73.8 years in Romania, the third lowest in the EU. Social capital levels are poor and characterized by low level of trust in others outside primary groups, or

---

[15] At-risk-of-poverty rates come from Eurostat, EU SILC data. Absolute poverty rates come from MLFSP, 2010, HBS data.

in social institutions, and a poor involvement in associative life. Life satisfaction is generally low in Romania, revealing at the individual level that people's needs are not fully satisfied and, at the macro level, the low quality of structural circumstances and opportunities that are provided to people in order for them to fulfil their goals and live according to their values and aspirations.

The main dimensions of the political and cultural domains also display a rather meagre picture. Participation in elections is declining, trust in political institutions is especially low while the actual functioning of democracy is evaluated as poor by the majority of Romanians. Objective indicators suggest that Romania is an unequal society, and it is perceived as such by the majority of the people in their subjective assessments. A very large majority consider that there are huge disparities between incomes and that the fairness of redistribution should be ensured by the government.

Social policy compensated for the negative effects of transition only partly. In difficult times, people relied more on kinship networks and the subsequent interfamily transfers, on subsistence agriculture or immersion in the informal economy.

In Romania, existing inequalities became deeply seated during transition, a relatively short period of time and, in the absence of mechanisms that are able to target them, there is no evidence that the existing gaps will narrow.

References

Alber, Jens and Köhler, Ulrich (2004), *Health and care in an enlarged Europe*, Luxembourg: Office for Official Publications of the European Communities.

Albu, Lucian-Liviu (2004), *Estimating the Size of Underground Economy in Romania*. Accessed 10 July 2012. <http://papers.ssrn.com/sol3/papers.cfm?abstract_id=1569577>

Cace, Sorin, Preoteasa, Ana Maria, Tomescu, Cristina and Stanescu Simona, (eds.) (2010), *Legal şi egal pe piaţa muncii pentru comunităţile de romi [Legal and equal in the labour market for Roma communities]*, Bucureşti: Expert.

Cace, Sorin, Vlădescu, Cristian (eds.) (2004), *The health status of Roma population and their access to health care services*, Bucureşti: Expert.

Cornia, Giovanni Andrea (2003), 'The impact of liberalization and globalization on income inequality in developing and transition economies', *CESIFO Working paper* no 843. January 2003. Accessed 22 May 2012: <http://www.cesifo-group.de/portal/page/portal/DocBase_Content/WP/WP-CESifo_Working_Papers/wp-cesifo-2003/wp-cesifo-2003-01/cesifo_wp843.pdf>.

Dăianu, Daniel (ed.) (2006), *Romania just before EU accession. Sustaining growth and fostering jobs in an emerging economy. Fourth Report*. Bucharest: GEA. Accessed 20 June 2012. <http://www.gea.org.ro/ro/geastudii.htm>

Eurostat (2010), *Income poverty and material deprivation in European countries*, Luxembourg: Publications Office of the European Union.

Eurostat (2012), *Taxation trends in the European Union*, Luxembourg: Publications Office of the European Union. Accessed 20 June 2012. <http://ec.europa.eu/taxation_customs/taxation/gen_info/economic_analysis/tax_structures/index_en.htm>

EVS, GESIS (2011). *EVS 2008—Variable Report. GESIS-Variable Reports 2011/9*. Accessed July 2, 2012. <http://www.europeanvaluesstudy.eu/>

Hellman, Joel S., Jones Geraint, Kaufmann Daniel and Schankerman Mark (2000), 'Measuring Governance, Corruption, and State Capture. How Firms and Bureaucrats Shape the Business Environment in Transition Economies', *World Bank Policy Research Working Paper* 2444: 1-41. Accessed 12 February 2009. <http://courses.essex.ac.uk/EC/EC330/lecture_notes/Hellman%20State%20Capture.pdf>

Mărginean, Ioan (2004), *Studii de sociologie, calitatea vieţii şi politici sociale [Studies in sociology, quality of life and social policy]*. Piteşti: Universitatea din Piteşti.

Mărginean, Ioan, and Precupeţu Iuliana (eds.) (2010), *Calitatea vieţii în România 2010 [Quality of life in Romania 2010]*. Bucureşti: ICCV. Accessed 14 June 2012. <http://www.iccv.ro/node/190>

Ministerul Educaţiei, Cercetării şi Inovării [Ministry of Education, Research and Innovation] (2009), *Raport asupra stării sistemului naţional de învăţământ Bucureşti*. Accessed 14 June 2012. <http://administraresite.edu.ro/index.php/articles/12926>

MLFSP (Ministerul Muncii, Familiei şi Protecţiei Sociale) [Ministry of Labour, Family and Social Protection] (2010), *Raport privind incluziunea socială în România [Report on social inclusion in Romania]*. Accessed 12 June 2012. <http://www.mmuncii.ro/ro/articole/0000-00-00/raportul-privind-incluziunea-sociala-in-romania-in-anul-2010-2533-articol.html.>

Neagu, Gabriela (2005), 'Cheltuielile cu educaţia. Analiză comparativă ['Education expenditure. A comparative analysis']'. *Calitatea vieţii* XVI (3–4): 359–371.

NIS (Institutul Naţional de Statistică) [National Institute of Statistics] (2012a), *Ocuparea şi şomajul în anul 2011 [Employment and unemployment in 2011]*, Labour Force Survey (AMIGO). Accessed July 20, 2012 www.insse.ro/cms/files/statistici/comunicate/com.../somaj_2011r.pdf

NIS National Institute of Statistics [Institutul Naţional de Statistică] (2012b), *Ocuparea şi şomajul în anul 2011 [Employment and unemployment in 2011]*, Labour Force Survey (AMIGO). Accessed July 20, 2012, <www.insse.ro/cms/files/statistici/comunicate/com.../somaj_2011r.pdf>

NIS (Institutul Naţional de Statistică) [National Institute of Statistics], (2012c). COMUNICAT DE PRESĂ, 2 februarie 2012 privind rezultatele provizorii ale Recensământului Populaţiei şi Locuinţelor—2011 [Press communiqué on provisional results of Population and Housing Census—2011]. Accessed 10 June 2012. <http://www.recensamantromania.ro>

OECD (2012), *International Migration Outlook 2012. Romania*. DOI 10.1787/migr_outlook-2012-en: <http://www.keepeek.com/Digital-Asset-Management/oecd/social-issues-migration-health/international-migration-outlook-2012_migr_outlook-2012-en>.

Autoritatea Electorală Permanentă [Permanent Electoral Authority] (2008), *Cartea Albă a alegerilor parlamentare din 30 noiembrie 2008 [White Book of parliamentary and presidential elections from November 30, 2008]*. Accessed 10 July 2012. <http://www.roaep.ro>

Precupeţu, Iuliana (2012), 'Systemic Factors of Corruption in Romania. Evidence from Discourses on Corruption', in Taenzler, Dirk, Maras, Konstandinos and Giannakopoulos, Angelos (eds.) *The Social Construction of Corruption in Europe*, pp. 125-219, Farnham: Ashgate.

Precupeţu, Iuliana (2007), *Strategii de dezvoltare comunitară [Strategies of community development]*, Iaşi: Lumen.

Precupeţu, Marius (2006), *Democratizare postcomunistă şi integrare europeană [Post-communist democratization and European integration]*, Bucureşti: Editura Academiei Românăe.

Precupeţu, Iuliana, and Precupeţu, Marius (2004), 'Mechanisms of Democratic Consolidation in Romania', *Central European Political Science Review*. Vol. 5, No. 18: 88–104.

Preda, Marian (ed.) (2009), *Riscuri şi inechităţi sociale în România. Raportul Comisiei Prezidenţiale pentru Analiza Riscurilor Sociale şi Demografice [Risks and social inequities in*

Romania. The report of the presidential commission for the analysis of social and demographic risks]. București: Polirom.

Preoteasa, Ana Maria (2012), 'Specificity of employment of Roma in Romania', in Tarnovschi Daniela (ed.), *Roma situation in Romania 2011, Between social inclusion and migration 22–36*, Bucharest: Soros Foundation Romania.

Sandu, Dumitru (1999), *Spațiul social al tranziției*, Iași: Polirom.

Tanzi, Vito (1998), 'Corruption Around the World. Causes, Consequences, Scope, and Cures', *IMF Staff Papers*, Vol. 45, No. 4 (December 1998).

UNDP (2005), *National Human Development Report Romania 2003–2005*, UNDP publishing. Accessed 15 June 2012, <http://www.undp.ro/publications/nhd.php>

Voicu, Bogdan (2010), *Capital social în România începutului de Mileniu: Drumeț în țara celor fără de prieteni? [Social capital in Romania at the beginning of the Millennium: Traveller in the no-friends land?]* Iași: Lumen.

Voicu, Bogdan (2005), *Penuria Pseudo-Modernă a Postcomunismului Românesc*. Volumul II Resursele *[The penury of Romanian Postcommunism. Volume II. Resources]* Iasi: Expert Projects.

Voicu, Mălina (2005), *Ce fel de bunăstare își doresc românii? [What kind of welfare do Romanians want?]* Iasi: Expert Projects.

Voinea, Liviu, and Mihăescu, Flaviu (2009), 'The impact of the flat tax reform on inequality—the case of Romania', *Romanian Journal of Economic Forecasting* 4: 19–41.

World Bank (2007), *Report No. 40120-RO Romania: Poverty Assessment Analytical and Advisory Assistance Program: First Phase Report, Fiscal Year 2007*, Washington DC: The World Bank.

World Bank (2008), *Report No. 47487—RO Romania Poverty Monitoring Analytical and Advisory Assistance Program: Labor Market Vulnerabilities in Romania*, Washington DC: The World Bank.

Whelan, Christopher T. and Maître, Bertrand (2012), 'Understanding Material Deprivation in Europe: A Multilevel Analysis', *Research in Social Stratification and Mobility*, Vol 30, Issue 4, December 2012, pp. 489–503.

Wilkinson, Richard G., and Pickett, Kate E. (2009), *The Spirit Level. Why More Equal Societies Almost Always do Better*, London: Allen Lane.

Zaman, Constantin, and Stănculescu, Manuela Sofia (2007), 'The social dimension in selected candidate countries in the Balkans: country report on Romania', Enepri Research Report no 40. Accessed 12 June 2012. <http://ec.europa.eu/employment_social/social_situation/index_en.htm>

Zamfir, Cătălin, Stănescu, Iulian and Ilie Simona (eds.) (2010), *Raportul social al ICCV. După 20 de ani: opțiuni pentru România [Social report of ICCV. After 20 years: Options for Romania]*, București: ICCV.

CHAPTER 24

....

SLOVAKIA AND THE CZECH REPUBLIC: INEQUALITIES AND CONVERGENCES AFTER THE VELVET DIVORCE*

....

MARTIN KAHANEC, MARTIN GUZI, MONIKA MARTIŠKOVÁ,

AND ZUZANA SIEBERTOVÁ

1. INTRODUCTION

....

THE roots of inequalities in the Czech Republic and Slovakia date back to the times even before the establishment of Czechoslovakia in 1918, when northern parts of the Austrian Empire—the present-day Czech Republic—and northern parts of the Kingdom of Hungary—present-day Slovakia and Carpathian Ruthenia—united in a new state.[2] The two parts of the newly established state differed in a number of aspects, including the degree of industrialization, urbanization, education and literacy (Slovakia being the less-industrialized part) and preferences (Slovakia being the more conservative and religious part). Within pre-war and post-war Czechoslovakia the two parts converged in many aspects, whether as a consequence of deliberate policies or as a by-product of mingling populations and economic and social interactions under one umbrella.

* We thank Wiemer Salverda, István György Tóth, an anonymous referee and the reviewers from Tárki and the GINI project for useful comments on earlier drafts of this chapter as well as the 'GINI Country Report: The Czech Republic and Slovakia' on which this chapter draws (available at www.gini-research.org/CT-Czech-and-Slovak). We also thank Michal Páleník and Filip Pertold for their indispensable contributions to that report, as well as Daniel Munich for providing some inequality data for the Czech Republic. We are indebted to Matúš Konečný for his excellent editorial support. Remaining errors are ours.
[1] Most of Carpathian Ruthenia ceased to be part of Czechoslovakia after World War II.

The coup d'état in 1948, followed by four decades of communist rule, deeply affected the Czech and Slovak societies, with scarring effects that lasted well beyond the 1989 Velvet Revolution. One of the key policy doctrines during the communist period was reduction of inequality, which the communist regime often enforced using rather harsh methods, such as the 1953 currency reform.[2] After the Velvet Revolution, deep economic, social, and political reforms were implemented, leading to democratization and economic liberalization in Czechoslovakia. On 1 January 1993, the so-called Velvet Divorce resulted in two successor states to Czechoslovakia—the Czech Republic and Slovakia.

While some of these legacies have withered away (both Slovakia and the Czech Republic are now similarly non-agricultural), others have affected and still affect inequalities in the two independent republics (Slovakia, for example, remains more conservative). Understanding those legacies is thus crucial in interpreting inequalities and their impacts in the Czech Republic and Slovakia.

This chapter's main objective is to provide a comprehensive account of changing inequalities in income, wealth or education over time and their social, political and cultural impacts in the Czech Republic and Slovakia. This includes elaboration of country-specific narratives and interpretations linked to national policies and institutions, but also comparative accounts illuminating the variation observed between the two countries. Data permitting, the chapter primarily covers the period from 1980 to present, mainly focusing on the 1990s and 2000s. We offer a comprehensive description of the driving forces behind inequalities and their impacts, rather than extensive statistical evidence of all trends.[3]

To this end, Section 2 of this chapter depicts the nature of inequality and its development over time. Facing severe data limitations and measurement challenges, every effort is made to define and measure inequality over time and across the two countries as uniformly as possible, applying a common methodology. Sections 3 and 4 are dedicated to analysis of the social, political and cultural impacts of changing inequalities. The policy context is discussed in Section 5. Section 6 comparatively evaluates the experience of the two countries and offers conclusions. This chapter draws on the *GINI Country Report: The Czech Republic and Slovakia* (Kahanec, Guzi, Martišková, Paleník, Pertold and Siebertová, 2013).

2. THE NATURE OF INEQUALITY AND ITS DEVELOPMENT OVER TIME

The process of economic and political transformation at the beginning of the 1990s released economic and societal processes that provided drivers for rising income inequalities in the Czech Republic and Slovakia. Prior to 1989, the Czech and Slovak societies in Czechoslovakia had felt some income inequalities, but their extent had been modest, and they manifested in different ways. For example, some inequalities expressed themselves

---

[2] Other redistribution mechanisms included price subventions and regulations as well as wage interventions (Mareš, 1999).

[3] These are provided in the underlying report Kahanec *et al.*, (2013), available online at <www.gini-research.org/CR-Czech-and-Slovak>.

in terms of the accessibility of goods. After the fall of the communist regime, the Czech Republic and Slovakia, along with many other post-socialist countries, went through a series of major political, social and economic changes. The formerly centrally-planned economy collapsed, resulting in various shocks to the economy. Producers lost their customers, unemployment grew, inflation hit savings, and former business and social ties were broken. In this chapter, we concentrate on the development of income and educational inequalities in the Czech Republic and Slovakia, especially during and after the transformation period of the 1990s. We reveal the drivers and the reasons for the observed developments as well as their consequences and social impacts, focusing on changes in the economy, labour markets, and education.

Has Inequality Grown?

Both the Czech Republic and Slovakia are considered to belong to the group of countries where inequalities grew significantly during the 1990s (OECD, 2011). However, in comparison with some other transition countries, income inequalities remained modest.[4] In Figure 24.1 we observe a steady decline before the Velvet Revolution, a steep increase during the 1990s, and a levelling off during the 2000s. It appears that the observed variation has

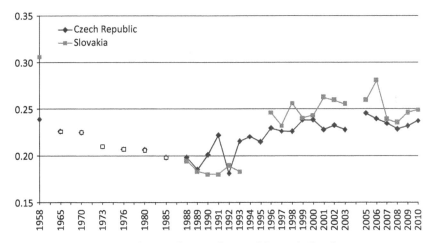

FIGURE 24.1 Income inequality in the Czech Republic and Slovakia

Notes: Gini coefficient in Czechoslovakia (hollow square), Czech Republic (diamond), Slovakia (square). Gini coefficient measures the dispersion among frequency distribution of incomes. It ranges from 0, which represents absolute equality, to 1 representing absolute inequality in society. Gini coefficients based on disposable income. The income sharing unit is the household. Equivalization: household per capita until 1992; none 1993–2004; equivalized since 2005.

Sources: 1958–1988 Atkinson and Micklewright (1992); 1989–1992 Cornia (1994); 1993–2002 Transmonee (2004) except for 1993–1995 for Slovakia; 1993 for Slovakia from Milanovic (1998); 2003 Transmonee (2005); 2005–2010 own calculations based on EU Survey of Income and Living Conditions.

---

[4] For example, according to Transmonee (2004), the Gini coefficient in the Baltic states rose by about 0.1 over the 1990s, from about 0.25–0.30 to as high as 0.35–0.40. Compare to Figure 24.1.

been greater in Slovakia than in the Czech Republic, but data limitations do not permit a definite conclusion in this respect.

The growth of inequalities is primarily attributed to the increase in incomes in the top decile, as well as changing patterns of remuneration, where education gained an exceptional position as a key determinant of earnings. However, redistributive policies have partially mitigated the consequences of the economic transformations on inequalities.

Rising inequalities in the 1990s mostly affected middle-income groups. As claimed by Mysíková (2011), the distribution of income in the Czech Republic has shifted towards the tails of the density function, shrinking the middle section. This phenomenon, also called 'hollowing out the middle', suggests that the middle-income group shrank while income groups in both tails of the distribution grew. A possible explanation is offered by Sirovátka and Mareš (2006), who claim that the expensive redistributive policies were paid for mostly by the middle-income groups, lowering the levels of poverty rates at the cost of a lowered net income for the working population.

Despite the changes in the composition of income, growth of income inequalities remained relatively low compared to other transforming countries. This is mainly because wage differences were not high before the 1990s. In addition, the Czech Republic and, especially, Slovakia have moderate average wages and social benefits do not fall far short of the minimum wage. The combination of these factors results in a higher density of low-income workers and families and lower inequality overall.

The changes in the distribution of income in the 1990s can be linked to the changes in the remuneration schemes of employees, which themselves reflected changing demand for and supply of various types of labour and skills, as well as changing institutional contexts. In the Czech Republic, workers' characteristics, such as age and number of children have lost much of their importance since the 1990s. More recently, they do not explain much of the income variation, whereas education and position at work gained significance (Večerník, 2001). The changes in the composition of low-income households between 1988 and 1996 can serve as an example of the changing inequality patterns. According to Večerník (2001) the lowest-income households in the Czech Republic were composed of retirees receiving only social transfers in 1988 while, eight years later, low-income households were mostly families with children.

Instruments of redistribution play an important role in lowering income inequalities in both countries.[5] For instance, in Slovakia, the Gini coefficient for income before taxes and transfers for the age group over 65 is around 0.80, while after redistribution it is circa 0.20.[6] Similarly, in the Czech Republic redistribution in this cohort lowers the Gini coefficient from 0.85, before, to 0.19, after, taxes and transfers.[7] Tax redistribution also lowers inequality for the working population, but we can observe some additional dynamics in Slovakia. In the mid 2000s taxation was significantly decreasing inequalities (from 0.40 to 0.23) while in the late 2000s taxation contributed significantly less to the income redistribution of the working population. A key factor was the introduction of a flat tax rate in 2004, which had positive impacts on high-income groups, but a neutral effect on low-income populations.[8]

---

[5] See also Garner and Terrell (1998).

[6] Based on OECD Social and Welfare statistics, late 2000s.

[7] Based on OECD Social and Welfare statistics, late 2000s.

[8] OECD Social expenditures database. For details see Figure 2.9 and the related discussion in Kahanec *et al.* (2013).

Labour Market

Growth of income inequalities in both countries in the 1990s was mostly determined by the growth of earnings inequalities, which in turn reflected the manifold changes in the labour market. The earnings distribution illustrates these changes. At the end of the 1980s in the Czech Republic, the 90th to 10th decile ratio of wages was 2.4. This ratio increased rapidly in the 1990s, with 90th decile wages three times higher than the 10th decile wages in 1999. The corresponding figure for 2009 was 3.19.[9] In Slovakia, the corresponding ratio for gross earnings increased from 1.89 in 2002 to 2.00 in 2004, and has oscillated around that figure since.[10]

The overall number of self-employed individuals in the Czech Republic increased between 1993 and 1998 by 4 percentage points, or 130,000 people. In 2010, 17.7 per cent of households declared self-employment as their main source of income.[11] In Slovakia, the number of self-employed rose from 6 per cent of workers in 1998 to the current value of 16 per cent, near the EU average. According to Garner and Terrell (1998), the impact of self-employment gains in income redistribution within three years after 1989 was more visible in Slovakia then in the Czech Republic, comprising an 11.4 per cent share on Gini in Slovakia, compared to 9.2 in the Czech Republic.

Another new phenomenon in the labour market appeared in the late 1990s, when alternative forms of employment contracts, such as part-time work or temporary work, became available. Since 1997, the share of part-time workers has persistently fluctuated at around 5 per cent of the working population in the Czech Republic and around 4 per cent in Slovakia.[12]

An important variable, where the two countries have differed markedly, is the unemployment rate. One of the key factors behind the diverging unemployment rates were the historically given differences in the industrial structure in the two economies, including the large share of heavy industry built up in Slovakia before the Velvet Revolution. In the Czech Republic the unemployment rate has fluctuated around 7 per cent since the mid 1990s (see Figure 24.2). By contrast, in Slovakia, it steeply increased from 12 per cent in the first quarter of 1998 to 19.1 per cent in the second quarter of 2000, stayed at about that level for four years, and then sharply decreased to 8.9 per cent in the fourth quarter of 2008.[13] The effects of the Great Recession dramatically worsened the labour market situation in 2009, pushing the unemployment rate to 14.1 per cent within this year, at which point it has approximately levelled off since.

Educational Inequality

The role of education in the changing distribution of wages was essential in the 1990s in both republics. According to Mysíková (2011), in the Czech Republic education contributed the most to the deepening of income inequalities during the transition period. Filer *et al.* (1999) estimate the impact of an additional year of education on wages using the standard Mincer

---

[9] Eurostat.   [10] OECD.
[11] Labour Force Survey, Eurostat; Kahanec et al. (2013), Table 2.6.
[12] Labour Force Survey, Eurostat.   [13] Labour Force Survey, Eurostat.

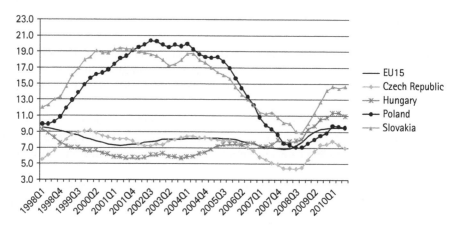

FIGURE 24.2 Unemployment rates in the Visegrad countries

Source: own calculations based on EU Labour Force Survey.

equation, finding an effective 12 per cent increase to wages of an additional year of education between 1995 and 1997, from 8.4 to 9.4 per cent. In 2010, tertiary-educated people in the Czech Republic had on average 62 per cent higher median yearly wages than primary-educated people; in Slovakia they earned 77 per cent more.[14] The increasing importance of education also impacted the labour market position of people with different educational attainment. In the Czech Republic, the employment rate of tertiary-educated people is the highest, reaching 80 per cent (compared to the population average of 60 per cent).[15] On the other hand, people with only primary education have difficulties finding a job, and compose more than two thirds of all unemployed.

In Slovakia, employment statistics clearly show that the situation there is similarly stacked against less-educated individuals.[16] Although the employment rate of people with diplomas dropped from 85.2 per cent in 1998 to 73.2 per cent in 2011, this group is still the best paid and most employed.[17] In contrast, less-educated individuals (ISCED 0-2) have significantly lower probabilities of labour force participation, employment, permanent contract or full time contract than their more educated counterparts (Brožovičová *et al*, 2012).

A lamentable phenomenon that remains largely sidelined by the political elites is the social exclusion of some vulnerable groups. This is of especial concern for the Romani people, but also for the elderly or single-parent families with more children. In the Czech Republic, for the Roma population aged 15–64, the employment rate is 31 per cent and the unemployment rate is 39 per cent; the corresponding figures for Slovakia are 15 and 70 per cent.[18] Among the Roma, females and young cohorts seem to suffer from even worse employment prospects.

[14] Eurostat and authors' calculations.
[15] Eurostat, for details see the Figure 2.15, Kahanec *et al.* (2013).
[16] EU Labour Force Survey and authors' calculations.
[17] Kahanec *et al.* (2013), Figure 2.19.
[18] UNDP 2011.

3. THE SOCIAL IMPACTS OF INEQUALITY

The effects of inequality go beyond economic categories. According to a 1990 survey, the shares of 'objectively poor' were 3.7 per cent in the Czech part and 5.9 per cent in the Slovak part of the then Czechoslovakia (Večerník, 1991). The poverty rates are still lower in the Czech Republic compared to Slovakia today. Figure 24.3 shows that the shares of people in poverty or social exclusion exhibit a declining trend in both countries, with Slovakia reducing this rate quite sharply from 32 per cent in 2005 to about 20 per cent in 2011, and the Czech Republic reducing it from about 20 per cent to slightly above 15 per cent during the same period. The figures indicate that the economic boom before the economic recession substantially reduced the risk of poverty and material deprivation, but the Great Recession has stopped or even reversed this trend.

Low education is a strong predictor of poverty, as it is often associated with low levels of income and a higher risk of unemployment. Our findings based on the EU SILC confirm the declining trend of poverty rates for all educational groups. However, as of 2010, the risk of poverty was four times higher among groups with little education compared to persons with tertiary education.

Household structure is another key factor, and has effects on income inequality. Statistics from national statistical offices document a substantial increase in the number of single-earner households with children. This trend is mainly driven by the rising number of single-person households accompanied by the rising number of newborns to non-married couples. As single-earner households with children exhibit the highest risk of poverty, the continuation of this trend may pose a significant disadvantage for children growing up in incomplete families.

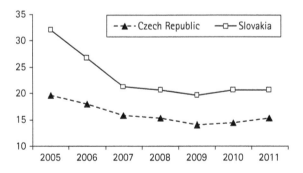

FIGURE 24.3 People at risk of poverty or social exclusion (per cent of total population)

Notes: this indicator corresponds to the sum of persons who are: at risk of poverty; or severely materially deprived; or living in households with very low work intensity. At risk-of-poverty are persons with an equivalized disposable income below the risk-of-poverty threshold, which is set at 60% of the national median equivalized disposable income (after social transfers). Severely materially deprived persons have living conditions severely constrained by a lack of resources who experience at least 4 out of 9 deprivations items. People living in households with very low work intensity are those aged 0–59 living in households where the adults (aged 18i59) work less than 20% of their total work potential during the past year.

Source: Eurostat (EU–SILC).

The most visible evidence of high concentrations of poverty and material deprivation is among the Roma minority. A recent World Bank (2012) study estimates a population of 320,000 Roma living in Slovakia. A World Bank survey shows that the vast majority of Roma in Slovakia—87 per cent of those households interviewed—live in poverty. Slovak Roma rank among the poorest communities in the EU (World Bank, 2012). In the Czech Republic, Gabal (2006) identifies over 300 socially excluded Roma communities often characterized by low levels of education, high long-term unemployment rates (90 per cent to 100 per cent) and high inactivity. Davidová *et al.* (2010) report that more than 60 per cent of the Roma minority attain only primary education. From interviews with members of Roma communities, the authors draw a conclusion that the motivation to pursue education is extremely low because of anticipated labour market discrimination. The number of Roma living in unbearable conditions in rural communities and devastated central city zones represents a potentially very serious social and economic problem in both republics. Inter-ethnic tensions between the majority population and this significant minority have caused many problems in the past. Moreover, such tensions undermine the creation of inter-ethnic social ties and social cohesion.

The indicators of social cohesion approximated by the frequency of meetings with friends, relatives or colleagues have visibly improved between 2002 and 2010. Based on the 2010 European Social Survey, one in ten individuals reported meeting with their peers less than once a month in the Czech Republic. Social isolation has dominated among individuals older than 60 years. This category of elderly people often live alone and face the greatest risk of no or rare contact with their peers. One in five elderly reports meeting with their peers less than once a month. Even higher social isolation is observed among the elderly population in city areas. The figures for Slovakia are very similar, the only difference being that the elderly population shows a higher rate of exclusion in villages than in cities.

The housing market in both countries has been characterized by high homeownership rates, a growing number of mortgages (especially in the early 2000s), increasing housing prices until 2008 followed by moderate decline, and wide regional price disparities. In particular, developments of regional housing disparities have contributed to wealth and income disparities. Due to the expected weaker economic growth in the early 2010s, a rise in the over-indebtedness of low-income households can be expected. This may further increase the difficulties of low-income households in meeting their obligations. In 2008 and 2009, this risk was 2.4 times higher among the 20 per cent of households with the lowest equivalized income than among the richest 20 per cent (Czech Statistical Office based on EU–SILC calculations).

Concerning health inequalities, the overall health status of people remained rather stable in the Czech Republic and has somewhat deteriorated in Slovakia since 2005. Figure 24.4 shows that the positive long-run development is specific only to high-income and highly-educated people. In 2011, Eurostat estimates from EU-SILC showed that about 31 per cent of people reported long-standing illness or health problems in each country. In the Czech Republic, an interesting tentative pattern is observed, whereby the generally decreasing trend in the share of people reporting health issues reversed around the same time as the crisis started. A similar pattern is observed in Slovakia among groups with low and medium education. This could have been caused by worsened living conditions or increased unemployment during the crisis.

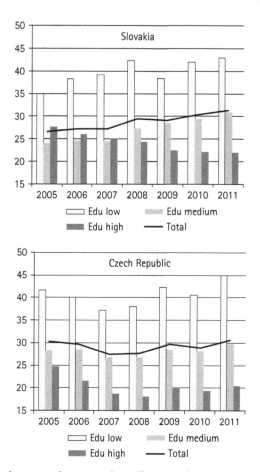

FIGURE 24.4 People having a long-standing illness or health problem

Notes: In per cent of adult population. Edu low: pre-primary, primary and lower secondary education (ISCED-97 levels 0–2); Edu medium: upper secondary and post-secondary non-tertiary education (ISCED-97 levels 3 and 4); Edu high: first and second stage of tertiary education (ISCED-97 levels 5 and 6).

Source: Eurostat (EU–SILC).

Crime in the Czech Republic is characterized by a continuous fall in the crime rate, while surprisingly the number of prisoners has been steadily increasing in the last ten years. This outcome is driven by the recent changes in criminal law that increased the duration of the mandatory minimum prison sentence (Dusek, 2012). While 95 per cent of prisoners are men and 70 per cent are younger than 40 years, they are almost exclusively less-educated individuals.[19] In Slovakia, the crime rate has also been falling for most of the studied period, except for the years 2000–2004, when it steeply increased.[20] The number of prisoners in Slovakia increases in the long term but the development is cyclical. The highest

---

[19] Information is taken from yearbooks of the Prison Service of the Czech Republic.
[20] Eurostat.

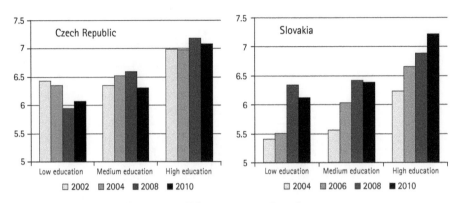

FIGURE 24.5 Average subjective well-being ratings by education

Notes: Adults aged 16 and over were asked: 'Overall, how satisfied are you with your life nowadays?' Possible answers are on the scale from 0 to 10. For the definitions of Low, Medium and High level education see Figure 4.

Source: Own calculations based on ESS Cumulative file 1–4 (2011). Weighted by design weight.

number was recorded in 2004, after which it experienced a decrease and has been rising again since 2008.

Education is one of the main drivers of intergenerational social mobility. The education of parents plays a crucial role in both educational choices and the educational performance of children. The former is partially determined by the early tracking of children into different types of secondary school. Drnáková (2007) points to the strong influence of parental education on the choice of school for their children. The influence of parental background on student test score (PISA) achievements is analysed in OECD (2010) study. International comparisons put the Czech Republic and the Slovak Republic into the group of countries in which the influence of family plays a major role.

An important component of national well-being is the subjective well-being of individuals, which is measured by finding out how people think and feel about their own lives. Well-being in seven eastern European countries at the very beginning of the transformation process is analysed by Hayo (2007), using New Democracy Barometer 1991 data. The highest national happiness levels in Eastern Europe at that time were observed in Czechoslovakia. The recent development of life satisfaction in the Czech Republic based on ESS shows a drop of life satisfaction levels after the start of the economic recession in 2009. A closer look reveals that reported levels are very stable for the group with the highest education, while the aggregate drop in life satisfaction is mainly driven by less-educated workers (see Figure 24.5). In the case of Slovakia, the satisfaction levels rose in recent years and the drop in 2009 for groups with less education was milder. Interestingly, although Slovakia recorded visibly lower satisfaction levels than the Czech Republic in 2004, the average satisfaction was slightly higher in Slovakia at the end of 2010.

To conclude, social indicators discussed in the text show divergent patterns across groups defined by education. This particularly concerns health status and crime. Several trends are identified that constitute a risk of increasing inequality in the future, such as the increasing number of single-earner households with children and persistently low intergenerational educational mobility. Recent developments show an increasing divide in subjective well-being levels between less- and highly-educated individuals, particularly in the Czech

Republic. This may be at least partly attributed to the worsening labour market conditions during the economic crisis.

4. Political and Cultural Impacts

After the Velvet Revolution and Velvet Divorce, the political system in the Czech Republic quickly consolidated and stabilized, and two newly emerged political parties—the conservatives and social democrats—became the major players in Czech politics. Another phenomenon in the Czech political scene is the gradual amalgamation of the Communist Party (KSCM) into the political mainstream. The KSCM has an important position in the party system, although it has never entered any governmental coalition. The explanation for the success of the Communist Party (compared to other neighbouring post-communist countries) can perhaps be linked to a historical tradition of *Sozialstaat* ideas in the Czech Republic, as well as the relatively straightforward transformation after 1989.

In Slovakia, the early transformation period has been considerably more complicated. The situation especially deteriorated during the coalition under Prime Minister Mečiar, who, with a short intermission, led the country from 1992 to 1998. His government employed a populist, nationalist rhetoric and threatened democratic institutions in Slovakia. In 1997, Slovakia was excluded from the first accession round to the European Union. In the election year 1998, the political situation became highly polarized and the mobilized masses in the democratic (mainly centre-right but also reformed left) segment of the political spectrum succeeded in ousting Mečiar's cabinet. These events determined the nature of the political system in Slovakia, with a group of heterogeneous parties sharing a more democratic vision on the centre-right and a single dominant party with some pendants on the centre-left.

After 1998, the political situation in Slovakia consolidated under the first Dzurinda cabinet (1998–2002). The second Dzurinda government (2002–2006) passed major structural reforms, such as the introduction of a flat-rate tax system and reform of the pension system. However, the true effect of economic reforms became visible only later, and citizen discontent with social policy and labour-code reforms resulted in a change of the government in the 2006 elections. The reform efforts have stalled since the mid 2000s, mainly due to a lack of will on the left and lack of cohesion on the right sides of the political spectrum.

Democracy in the two republics is currently confronted with an increasing gap between political parties and citizens. In both countries the lack of interest in public matters is reflected in falling voter turnouts. In the Czech Republic, this can be attributed to the power-sharing agreement—the so-called 'opposition contract'—established after the 1998 elections by the two major political parties. This mutual cooperation has been perceived as a breach of the pre-election promises of both parties, leading to lower turnout rates in subsequent elections (Linek, 2011).

The Slovak elections in 1998 were exceptional as the political situation at that time was highly polarized and led to 84 per cent turnout. After 2002, turnout rates in parliamentary elections in both countries dropped markedly to a relatively stable level of 55 to 65 per cent.[21]

---

[21]   Statistical Office of the Czech Republic, Statistical Office of the Slovak Republic.

In both countries parliamentary elections attract the largest shares of voters, and regional and European election exhibit the lowest turn-out rates, with municipal elections somewhere in between. Voters with a higher socio-economic status have the highest participation in parliamentary elections in both countries. Similarly the observed participation in civic organizations is higher among more educated and wealthier people.

During the communist regime, there was *de facto* (although not *de iure*) obligatory membership of trade unions. Following the change of the political regime, union density (i.e. the proportion of employees who are union members) dropped from more than 60 per cent in 1993 to only 17 per cent in 2009 in each of the countries.[22] Union coverage, defined as the share of employees whose contract is regulated by wage bargaining agreements, stabilized at around 40 per cent in recent years. A detailed analysis of trends and an historical overview of union membership can be found in Myant (2010).

Social inequality affects not only civic and political engagement but also the degree to which people trust other people and society as a whole (see Table 24.1). The Czech Republic exhibits higher levels of social trust (i.e. trust in other people) among Central and Eastern European (CEE) countries. Sedláčková and Šafr (2008) report that the level of social trust in the Czech Republic has been relatively stable over the last 20 years. Opinion polls from the Public Opinion Research Centre[23] in the years 1998–2006 show that the level of institutional trust in the Czech Republic was relatively stable over that period, along with the ordering of institutions based on the observed levels of public confidence. Stachova *et al.* (2008) confirm that the president was the most trusted institution in the Czech Republic in 2004 (trusted by 74 per cent of respondents). Other institutions with a high level of trust are municipal (61 per cent) and regional (42 per cent) councils. National institutions, such as the parliament (23 per cent) and government (32 per cent) have much lower levels of trust. These results are in line with Mishler and Rose (2001) who show that distrust in post-communist societies is greatest for political institutions, especially parliaments and parties.[24]

The level of trust in national institutions in Slovakia is generally low from the European perspective. Using the ESS surveys, Lovaš (2010) observes that the Slovak people report higher trust in international institutions such as the European Parliament and the United Nations than in national institutions. In particular, trust in the Slovak judiciary is amongst the lowest in the European Union. Bojarski and Koster (2012) argue that the public generally does not have trust in the impartiality of its judges, believes the judiciary is corrupt, and complains about the lengthiness of legal procedures. On the other hand, trust in the Slovak government and parliament has increased. Based on the Eurobarometer surveys, the share of people trusting the Slovak parliament and government steadily increased from 23 per cent in 2005 to 40 per cent in 2010. Trust in justice remained stable over the same period, at about 30 per cent. The reported trust varies little by educational attainment, yet people with the lowest levels of education report slightly higher trust in national institutions. Our analysis of the data from the ESS shows that one in three respondents in 2010 agreed that most people can be trusted in both countries. Individuals with higher education and those

---

[22] Figures on union density and union coverage are taken from ICTWSS database (<www.uva-aias.net/208>).

[23] Public Opinion Research Centre, Sociological Data Archive IS CAS CR, <http://archiv.soc.cas.cz>.

[24] Based on New Democracies Barometer survey conducted in 1998 in Belarus, Bulgaria, the Czech Republic, Hungary, Poland, the Russian Federation, Romania, Slovakia, Slovenia and Ukraine.

Table 24.1 Trust indicators, political values and values about social policy (per cent of total population)

	Czech Republic						Slovakia					
	2005	2006	2007	2008	2009	2010	2005	2006	2007	2008	2009	2010
Trust in others and in institutions												
Institutional trust (Government)	24	31	21	20	28		23	27	42	43	39	
Institutional trust (Parliament)	17	22	17	16	21		25	30	38	39	40	
Institutional trust (Justice)	34	37	33	34	41		28	33	28	32	31	
Interpersonal trust				38		35	28			27		31
Political values and legitimacy												
EU membership approval	50	52	48	51	45	30	55	57	65	65	71	59
Agreeing no further immigrants to be allowed to country (from poorer countries)				22		26	13			15		20
Values about social policy and welfare state												
Income differences are too large in the country					53						61	
Government should reduce differences	63			54		63		74		68		77
Consider the social welfare situation as good	35	41	35				12	20	24			
Poor are lazy					28	25					23	19

Note: For more details see Kahanec *et al.* (2013).

Source: Authors' calculations based on ESS, ISSP and Eurobarometer surveys.

in richer households report higher levels of trust in people and the observed gap is larger in Slovakia.

The Czech and Slovak societies also differ markedly when it comes to their support for, and the benefits they perceive to come from, the European Union. While the Czech Republic can be characterized by growing Euro-scepticism, support for the European Union and approval of EU membership remain strong in Slovakia. In the Czech Republic, public criticism of the European Union has grown, and faith in its benefits and institutions has eroded. In general, the Czech population appears to be either indifferent or mildly supportive of pessimistic beliefs about the future of the European Union.

Interestingly, despite the adverse effects of the current economic crisis, both countries have exhibited declining support for extremist parties since the late 2000s. In the Czech Republic, the aggregated support for extremist parties reached its pinnacle in 1992 and then again in 2002, and since then it has dropped to 12.4 per cent. In Slovakia, the aggregated support for extremist parties culminated in 2006 at 15.8 per cent, since which time it has dropped to just above 7 per cent in the 2010 and 2012 elections, with no extremist party making it into the parliament in 2012.

One has to approach these positive developments with due caution. When asked about right and left preferences,[25] a relatively stable share of Czechs, 16 to 19 per cent, identify themselves with extreme political views on the left-right spectrum, whereas the corresponding share in Slovakia increased from 16 per cent in 2004 to 22 per cent in 2010. In both countries, the gradients by education and income are negative for the support of left-extreme parties, and positive for the support of right-extreme parties; and in the case of education they are significantly more pronounced in the Czech Republic than in Slovakia.[26]

These concerns are confirmed by the statistics on tolerance toward immigration, which has declined in both countries, more steeply and to somewhat lower levels in the Czech Republic. This latter observation may be linked to the relatively high recent inflow of immigrants in the Czech Republic (but not in Slovakia). In 2010, on average one in four respondents of ESS in the Czech Republic opposed the immigration of either different ethnic groups or those from poorer countries outside Europe, while the corresponding rate in Slovakia was one in five.[27] In both countries the education and income gradients of tolerance to immigration are steeply negative. On average, people with higher education oppose immigration half as often as less-educated individuals.

The negative perceptions of the existing income inequalities have been declining in both countries, from significantly higher levels in Slovakia. In both countries, the educational and income gradients of these perceptions are negative. Support for governmental redistribution of income is significantly stronger in Slovakia than in the Czech Republic, with both countries sharing negative gradients by education and income. Satisfaction with the social situation is higher and stable in the Czech Republic, and one in three respondents in the

[25] Political self-identification is based on the question in ESS 'In politics, people sometimes talk of "left" and "right." Where would you place yourself on this scale, where 0 means the left and 10 means the right?' Answers 0 and 1 are treated as 'extreme left' while 9 and 10 as 'extreme right'.

[26] Kahanec *et al.* (2013).

[27] The number is the share of ESS respondents who agree that no further immigrants should be allowed to come and live in the country.

ESS survey consider the social situation as good or very good. In Slovakia, based on the ESS, popular satisfaction with the social situation has doubled between 2005 and 2007, with one in four respondents expressing satisfaction in 2007. The educational and income gradients concerning this variable are rather flat in both countries.[28]

The two countries do not differ much in how the important factors for getting ahead in life are perceived, although in Slovakia getting a good education, working hard, knowing the right people, or being smart are, compared to the Czech Republic, viewed as relatively more important than coming from a wealthy family or being lucky.[29] On the other hand, a somewhat higher share of people in the Czech Republic than in Slovakia think that people live in poverty because of laziness and lack willpower.

5. ARE PUBLIC POLICIES EFFECTIVE IN COMBATTING INEQUALITIES?

In this section, we study the main features of public policies in the Czech Republic and Slovakia that have affected or potentially could affect socio-economic inequalities. The role of trade unions notably conditions these linkages. In both countries, as in most of Central Europe, the power of trade unions declined dramatically in the 1990s. Unionization in the two republics is lower than the EU average in spite of an economic structure relatively favourable to unions, with a large share of manufacturing and middle-sized firms. To illustrate, in Slovakia the actual coverage rate is estimated at 40 per cent, and only a few sectors in the economy preserve collective bargaining.[30]

The general weakness of unions is similarly reflected in other important domains. The last change to the minimum wage in the Czech Republic took place in 2007, and its current level is about 33 per cent of the average wage.[31] In Slovakia the minimum wage had fallen to 35 per cent of the average wage by 2000. In the early 2010s, the minimum wage was once again at about 40 per cent of the average wage, with 5.4 per cent of employees earning the minimum wage.[32] Due to its relatively low and declining relative value the minimum wage did not affect many workers especially in the Czech Republic. The overall effect of the minimum wage is not clear, however. On the one hand, a relatively low minimum wage facilitates employment of low-skilled employees, enabling firms to hire them at affordable costs. On the other hand, low levels of minimum wages create conditions for the emergence of a stratum of working poor in the labour market, although the underlying cause has more to do with the inefficient educational system and labour market mismatches.

---

[28] Kahanec *et al.* (2013).

[29] Figures come from the Eurobarometer 2006 survey which asked its respondents to identify two important things for getting ahead in life.

[30] Source: Database on Institutional Characteristics of Trade Unions, Wage Setting, State Intervention and Social Pacts (ICTWSS), <www.uva-aias.net/208>.

[31] Source: Czech Statistical Office. For detailed data see Table 5.1 in Kahanec *et al.* (2013).

[32] Source: SOSR, authors' calculations. For detailed data see Table 5.2 in Kahanec *et al.* (2013).

In the 1990s, the number of self-employed workers grew rapidly in most of Central Europe, necessitating a hastened adjustment of the legislative framework, sometimes with unforeseen consequences. Both the Czech and Slovak labour markets feature a special regime for self-employed workers entitling them to pay lower social security and health insurance contributions than comparable employees have to pay. While this reduces the cost of their labour and may have enabled some workers to find a job—often as dependent self-employed—the lower social security contributions for self-employed workers result in lower future social entitlements and threaten stable social development in the future. Indeed there already is a group of retired self-employed who need to be supported by additional social transfers because they are only entitled to very low pensions.

The Czech tax system consists mainly of income taxes and taxes on production. According to Eurostat, the share of taxes on production reaches around 60 per cent of the total tax receipt and has been increasing. Restructuring the tax burden from income to production and consumption taxes has shifted the tax burden onto lower-income households. The most important recent change in the income tax system was the introduction of the flat-rate tax in 2006, which slightly reduced the tax burden for all income groups. The development over time suggests that after its introduction the level of redistribution increased compared to 2005.[33] Effective as of 1 January 2013, a second tax rate of 22 per cent is applied to income over CZK100,000 per month. Although this implies a slight increase in the degree of redistribution, the Nečas government is also increasing consumption taxes, which can be expected to have an adverse effect on the relative well-being of low-income households.

Until the mid 2000s, Slovakia had progressive tax brackets for income taxes. One of the milestones in taxation policy was the introduction of a flat income tax rate in 2004. The tax reform also included changes in value added tax (VAT) and in taxes on capital. In income taxation, instead of a progressive scheme, a single tax rate was introduced together with a system of deductions. An analysis by the Ministry of Finance claimed a 'not negative' impact on low-income groups, a slightly negative impact on middle-income groups and a strictly positive impact on high-income groups (MF SR, 2005). However, the potentially positive effect on low-income groups of the increase of tax deductibles was in part countermanded by the simultaneous introduction of a flat VAT rate, which effectively increased the VAT tax rate on some basic goods and services. Overall, the new taxation system in Slovakia seems to be less redistributive than the former one (Brook and Leibfritz, 2005; Moore, 2005). Most recently, the second Fico government has introduced a tax of 25 per cent on income over €39,600 per annum. This formally increases the progressiveness of the tax system, but it is expected to affect only about 1 per cent of taxpayers.

Both the Czech Republic and Slovakia impose high social security contributions on labour.[34] These significantly increase labour costs and may result in unemployment. The problem appears to be more severe in Slovakia, which suffers from some of the highest long-term unemployment rates in Europe.

As Jurajda and Münich (2011, 2012) point out, in the Czech Republic in the late 2000s around 27 per cent of all expenditures on employment policies were spent on active labour market

---

[33] Source: Eurostat. For detailed data see Table 5.4 in Kahanec *et al.* (2013).

[34] The Czech Republic and Slovakia have the highest labour costs among the Visegrad countries (OECD, 2006).

Table 24.2 Social expenditures

	2000	2001	2002	2003	2004	2005	2006	2007	2008	2009
Czech Republic										
All functions	18.2	18.1	18.8	18.8	18	17.8	17.4	17.5	17.5	19.8
Sickness/health care	6.1	6.2	6.6	6.7	6.3	6.3	6	5.9	5.8	6.4
Invalidity	1.4	1.4	1.5	1.5	1.4	1.4	1.5	1.4	1.4	1.5
Old age	7.1	6.9	7.1	6.9	6.6	6.8	6.8	6.9	7.3	8.3
Survivors	0.8	0.8	0.9	0.8	0.8	0.8	0.7	0.7	0.7	0.8
Family/children	1.5	1.5	1.5	1.4	1.5	1.3	1.3	1.6	1.4	1.4
Unemployment	0.6	0.6	0.6	0.8	0.7	0.6	0.6	0.6	0.6	1.1
Housing	0.1	0.1	0.1	0.1	0.1	0.1	0.1	0.1	0.1	0.1
Social exclusion	0.5	0.5	0.5	0.5	0.5	0.5	0.5	0.2	0.2	0.2
Slovakia										
All functions	18.8	18.4	18.5	17.8	16.6	15.9	15.7	15.4	15.5	18.2
Sickness/health care	6.5	6.4	6.3	5.7	5.0	4.8	4.8	4.7	5.1	5.8
Invalidity	1.4	1.5	1.6	1.6	1.3	1.3	1.3	1.3	1.4	1.5
Old age	6.0	6.1	6.2	6.3	6.1	6.2	6.1	5.9	5.8	6.8
Survivors	0.9	0.9	0.9	0.9	0.9	0.9	0.9	0.9	0.8	1.0
Family/children	1.7	1.5	1.5	1.5	1.7	1.7	1.6	1.5	1.5	1.7
Unemployment	0.9	0.7	0.8	1.0	1.0	0.5	0.5	0.6	0.6	1.0
Housing	0.1	0.1	0.1	0.1	0.0					
Social exclusion	1.2	1.2	1.1	0.8	0.5	0.5	0.6	0.5	0.4	0.4

Note: In per cent of GDP.

Source: Eurostat.

policies. In Slovakia, the expenditures on active labour market policies were low and even fell from 16 to 14 per cent of all expenditures on employment policies between 2004 to 2010.[35]

In the Czech Republic, 17.5 per cent of GDP was spent on social expenditures in 2008 but with the crisis, this increased to 19.8 per cent in 2009 (See Table 24.2). In Slovakia, according to the OECD SOCX database, social expenditures expressed as a percentage of GDP were near the OECD average in 1995, but considerably lower in 2007—the OECD average was 19.2 per cent of GDP, whereas for Slovakia it was 15.7 per cent.[36] The current discussion about social policies in the Czech Republic and Slovakia alike is centred around their negative effect on incentives to seek employment, especially for individuals with lower productivity. Such distortions could negatively affect income distribution, driving less productive workers into long-term unemployment or the inactivity trap. On the other hand, the potential enabling and empowering effects of social benefits and services are habitually ignored in the debate.

Old age pensions are one of the biggest long-term challenges for the sustainability of public finances in both the Czech Republic and Slovakia. In Slovakia, the reform introduced in

[35] Eurostat database on Labour market policies (LMP)
[36] For detailed data see Table 5.7 in Kahanec *et al.* (2013).

2004 changed the former pay-as-you-go pension system to a three-pillar system. The first pillar retained the features of the former PAYG system (i.e. non-funded pillar and mandatory), the second pillar is fully funded and mandatory, and the third pillar is fully funded but voluntary. The reforms were intended to strengthen the link between the contributions and benefits as well as to create a more stable pension system based on diversified sources (Melicherčík and Ungvarský, 2004).

The Czech Republic has a pay-as-you-go (PAYG) public pension system, although there have been several attempts to reform the system and maintain sustainability with respect to demographic challenges such as an ageing population. Recently, however, measures were undertaken to make early retirement less attractive; the statutory retirement age has been increased each year; and a new second pillar will be established in 2013.

In Slovakia, the accessibility of health services is in general satisfactory, although the level of services provided varies. Moreover, the health sector generates a considerable share of public debt. Verhoeven et al. (2007) found that health care efficiency is rather low compared to western European standards. As the main source of inefficiency, they identified the low private contributions and high number of consultations and visits to doctors. During the 2000s, some reforms, such as privatization of city hospitals and the introduction of co-payments by patients, were introduced. However, their level was rather low and the expected result—the decrease of unnecessary visits at the doctor—was not achieved. The co-payments were abolished in 2006 when the first Fico government took office. None of the reform measures implemented in 2003 and 2004 resolved the problem of systemically generated debt in the sector.

The health-care system in the Czech Republic functions relatively well, with formally equal access for the whole population.[37] It is publicly funded, but the government recently established several policy changes that increased private co-payment into the system. First, there are gradually increasing co-payments for prescribed medication. The second change dates back to 2008 when the Czech government imposed co-payment for each visit to a general practitioner, prescriptions, and days of hospitalization. The reform did not change the behaviour of the most vulnerable groups of patients. The increasing trend of utilization by older individuals persists, and thus they carry a larger financial burden.[38]

The Czech and Slovak education systems are notoriously under-financed and in need of structural reforms, yet there have been few signs of improvement. Teachers' wages at all educational levels are too low to be competitive in the labour market. However, there has been significant improvement in the accessibility of tertiary education in both countries. In the Czech Republic, the number of university students increased by 68 per cent from 2001 to 2010. In Slovakia, the increase over the same period was 63 per cent.[39] The increased number of tertiary educated people has the potential to reduce earnings inequalities by eroding the skill premium.[40] However, the inflated numbers of university students put significant

---

[37] Hromadkova and Zdenek (2012).

[38] Hromadkova and Zdenek (2012).

[39] Own calculations, Eurostat Data Explorer (educ_itertp).

[40] See Kahanec and Zimmermann (2009) for an argument on how increased supply of skilled workers can reduce the Gini coefficient.

pressure on the capacity of tertiary education to provide quality. Moreover, university programmes often fail to meet the demand for skills in the labour market.

Secondary education in both republics is based on the early tracking of children into different types of schools. There is a strong sorting of students based on their background into the *gymnázium* (secondary grammar school), vocational schools and apprenticeships. In fact, the pool of children is fairly homogeneous within school types. This is an important source of inequality, as those students who choose the 'wrong' type of school are disadvantaged in access to further education and ultimately to the labour market.

To conclude, there have recently been a number of institutional developments, some of which decreased and some of which increased the degree of redistribution in the two republics. The two countries in fact shared a very similar pattern and contrary to the preceding decade in the 2000s it was Slovakia which introduced a number of key reform measures first.

Among the measures that decreased the degree of redistribution could be considered the shift to consumption and production taxes such as the VAT, the introduction of the flat tax rate, the introduction of the funded pension pillar in Slovakia (with a similar reform planned in the Czech Republic), the stricter conditionality of access to and decreased generosity of social security, and the introduction of co-payments in the health care sector. The weakening of trade unions in both republics and diminishing minimum wage in the Czech Republic provides for additional impacts on inequalities.

On the other hand, some of these reforms have resulted in a greater degree of redistribution. Among the primary examples are the higher taxation of income over certain thresholds, weakening of the funded pension pillar, and discontinuation of some co-payments in Slovakia. More accessible tertiary education can be expected to lower income inequalities in the future. In addition, the positive effects of reforms on employment and labour market participation provide for more equitable access to labour income.

6. Conclusions and Implications: A Comparative Perspective on Inequality in the Czech Republic and Slovakia

The two nations under scrutiny shared one state from 1918 until 1992, with a de facto exception in the period between 1939 and 1945 during World War II. Even after their independence on 1 January 1993, the two republics underwent broadly similar social, economic and political transitions. This history of shared institutions and similar transformations can be expected to manifest itself in similar inequalities with similar development.

On the other hand, the two nations differed in many aspects as well. While, in 1918, the Czech, Moravian and Silesian Lands emerged as a rather industrialized part of the Austrian part of Austria-Hungary, Slovakia entered the newly established Czechoslovakia with a legacy of underdeveloped institutions and a predominantly agrarian population from the Hungarian part of Austria-Hungary. While, by European standards, Czech society is traditionally very secularized, religiosity—primarily Roman Catholic—is rather high in Slovakia. The Czech Republic started as a vigorous reformer in the 1990s, slowing down a bit in the 2000s. Slovakia lagged behind its neighbours in the 1990s, but has reformed at a very high pace since 1998, especially up to the mid 2000s. In some important aspects, such as the introduction of the flat-rate tax regime, funded pension schemes, and introduction of the Euro it was even ahead of its western neighbour.

Such differences resulted in some divergences in the development of inequalities in the two countries. Inasmuch as we can interpret historical data from several sources, the two republics shared a general pattern of decreasing income inequality until just after the fall of the Iron Curtain, increasing inequality until the late 1990s, and rather trendless, or slightly decreasing, inequality since then. In both countries, increasing inequality during the early transition period can be ascribed to the massive transformations that the two nations went through at that time. These primarily involve price liberalization, introduction of hard budget constraints, privatization, labour market reforms, and changes in the social security system. Another related development is the increase in the share of rather unequally distributed non-labour income in people's total income in both countries, as self-employment and private ownership were legalized after the Velvet Revolution. After the initial transformation turmoil of the 1990s subsided, it appears that in each country income inequalities stayed relatively stable. Taxation and transfers have mitigated income inequalities significantly.

Although the data do not permit a decisive conclusion on whether inequality rose more in Slovakia than in the Czech Republic over the 1990s, it appears that more vigorous reforms in the Czech Republic in that period did not lead to larger, but rather to perhaps smaller, increases in income inequality. On the other hand, the reforms implemented during the late 1990s and early 2000s in Slovakia do not appear to have increased income inequality in Slovakia, excepting perhaps an initial shock in late 1990s. However, the long run effects of the flat-tax rate, funded second pillar of the pension systems, and decreasing social security benefits may lead to increased inequality in the two countries in the future.

In spite of these similarities, the two countries differ markedly in their experience with the labour market. While the unemployment rate has been rather high and varying in Slovakia, it has been moderate and stable in the Czech Republic.[41] As concerns labour force participation rates, they have been rather high and at about the same levels in the two countries for prime-age workers, increasing for elderly workers and decreasing for the youth.[42] The last trend can be explained by steeply increasing university enrolment rates, underscoring the importance of a marketable education for the younger generations, who are trading off expected returns to human capital investment for the labour income forgone during their studies.

Current inequalities are also driven by the sectoral restructuring through which the two countries have gone since the fall of the communist regime. Both countries exhibit a relatively large and growing service sector, although the gap relative to the EU15 has declined only moderately. Even more remarkable is the decline of the agricultural sectors in the two countries, attaining the levels typical for the EU15.[43] From the historical perspective, and for the interpretation of our findings, it is important to note that the legacy of an agricultural, less-industrialized Slovakia from the earlier 20th century has been obliterated during the last few decades. Slovakia now has the largest service sector and smallest agricultural sector, measured by employment, among the

---

[41] Own calculations based on EU LFS. See Figure 6.2 in Kahanec *et al.* (2013).
[42] Own calculations based on EU LFS. See Figures 6.3-5 in Kahanec *et al.* (2013).
[43] Own calculations based on EU LFS. See Figures 6.6–7 in Kahanec *et al.* (2013).

Visegrad countries. The relative size of the agricultural sector in Slovakia has recently declined below the level of the Czech Republic and below the EU15 average.

In both countries we observe significant positive gradients of educational attainment and labour market success, whether measured by earnings or employment probabilities.[44] With the steeply increased university enrolment rates, we can expect attenuation of these gradients and inequality when these larger cohorts of university graduates enter the labour market. This may also happen through the decreased quality of overcrowded institutions of higher education.

While inequalities have affected the whole Czech and Slovak populations, some of the sub-populations have been more affected than others. In both countries, women, the elderly and the young, the less educated, and those living in less-developed regions are among the most affected. Most of the Roma people are affected by severe social exclusion and poverty.

The effects of inequality go well beyond economic categories. People at the bottom of the income distribution often suffer from material deprivation. In both countries, the gains from the robust economic performance in the recent decade appear to have trickled down to the poorer echelons of the society, as the rate of material deprivation fell significantly in each of the countries. This decrease appears to have stalled during the crisis. Among those most affected by material deprivation are women, the Roma people, less-educated people, and people living in less-developed regions.

The two countries also shared a diminishing rate of poverty or social exclusion in the 2000s. While Slovakia was reducing its rate of poverty or social exclusion faster, it also started at higher levels. In both countries, young people appear to be more likely to find themselves in poverty or social exclusion, and to some extent this is the case also for the elderly, especially women, in Slovakia. In contrast, in the Czech Republic the elderly appear to be in a better position than any other age group.

Household structure is a key factor, and effect, of income inequality. Both countries under scrutiny suffer from an ageing population and low fertility rates, declining through the 1990s and slightly recovering during the 2000s. Both countries have experienced a significant increase of age at first marriage during the last two decades and a decrease in the number of marriages, excepting the first half of the 2000s.

The two countries share similar developments in the housing market: high homeownership rates, increasing housing prices and fast-growing numbers of mortgages prior to the Great Recession, as well as large regional disparities in housing prices. These regional disparities in housing prices have contributed to wealth and income disparities and, combined with credit constraints, impeded labour migration.

The overall perceptions of health status have improved in both countries, although fewer females than males report good or fairly good health. During the last decade crime has been in decline in the Czech Republic, but the number of people in prison has been growing. The same holds for Slovakia, excepting the early 2000s.

A key variable reflecting people's participation in the political life of the society is electoral turn out. We observe similar patterns in the Czech Republic and Slovakia, urban or rural: the turn-out rates increase from regional and European elections through municipal elections up to the highest rates for parliamentary elections. Unlike in Slovakia, the impact of education on inequality in electoral participation in the Czech Republic is rather high.

---

[44] SOSR 2010, Eurostat, and own calculations.

Civic participation is somewhat higher in the Czech Republic, which also exhibits a steeper gradient by education and to some extent also by income. Both nations have experienced rather similar patterns of declining union density and union coverage. In both countries trust in other people has been generally increasing since the early 2000s, with Slovakia enjoying a considerably more significant improvement in this measure of trust, although still at somewhat lower levels than in the Czech Republic. The educational and especially income gradients are steeper in Slovakia.

Institutional trust has also been improving in the two countries, although remaining relatively low by the standards observed in Western Europe. Slovakia belongs to the countries with a robust support for European Union institutions, whereas the Czech Republic exhibits a higher degree of Euro-scepticism.

The two countries differ significantly when it comes to voters' preferences for extremist parties. While, in Slovakia, the majority of votes for extremists go to right-wing parties, in the Czech Republic they go to the left extreme of the spectrum. The underlying explanatory factor may be a higher degree of conservatism in Slovak society. Quite remarkably, in spite of the adverse effects of the Great Recession, both countries, especially Slovakia, have exhibited declining support for extremist parties since the late 2000s. On the other hand, the shares of people identifying with extreme political views on the left-right spectrum remained significant in both countries. In the same vein, tolerance toward immigration has declined in both countries.

The negative perceptions of existing income inequality have been declining in both countries, from significantly higher levels in Slovakia. The approval of governmental redistribution of income is significantly stronger in Slovakia than the Czech Republic, with both countries sharing negative gradients by education and income. While satisfaction with the social situation is higher and stagnating in the Czech Republic, it is growing in Slovakia.

The future prospects of inequalities are largely determined by the quality of health care and education. Public expenditures on health care have been relatively high and increasing in the Czech Republic, whereas in Slovakia they have been stagnating. When it comes to education, both countries share the trend of decreasing numbers of pupils but increased participation in tertiary education, an early-tracking educational system, and limited life-long learning. Against this background, both countries also experienced decreasing expenditures on education until 2008, with a slight increase in 2009. While part of this development can be explained by strong GDP growth prior to 2008 and a decline in 2009, these trends still signify a decreasing priority given to education and result in several problems, including a deteriorating quality of education and negative selection into teaching occupations. All these factors combined to provide for increased inequalities in the distribution of human capital. With the declining capacity of the welfare state to dampen their impacts, these fundamental inequalities will, in both countries, manifest themselves in increasing inequalities in terms of most socio-economic variables, including income, poverty, political and civic participation, or crime.

References

Atkinson, A. B. and Micklewright, J. (1992), *Economic Transformation in Eastern Europe and the Distribution of Income*, Cambridge: Cambridge University Press.

Bojarski, I. and Koster, W.S. (2012), *The Slovak Judiciary: Its Current State and Challenges*, Bratislava: Open Society Foundation.

Brook, A.-M. and Leibfritz, W. (2005), 'Slovakia's Introduction of a Flat Tax as Part of Wider Economic Reforms', *OECD Economics Department Working Papers*, 448.

Brožovičová, K., Fabo, B., Kahanec, M., and V. Messing (2012), 'Overview of the Labour Market Situation of Low-Educated and Roma Population and Regulation Affecting their Employment'. *NEUJOBS State of the Art Report* No. D19.1.

Cornia, G. A. (1994), 'Income Distribution, Poverty and Welfare in Transitional Economies: A Comparison between Eastern Europe and China'. *Journal of International Development*, 6(5): 569–607.

Davidová, E. *et al.* (2010), *Kvalita života a sociální determinant zdraví u Romů v České a Slovenské republice*, Praha: Triton.

Drnáková, L. (2007), 'Determinants of Secondary School Choice in the Czech Republic', *CERGE-EI Working Paper* No. 341.

Dušek, L. (2012), *Kde hledat příčiny přeplněných věznic*, Praha, IDEA 4/2012

Filer, R. K., Jurajda, Š., and Plánovský, J. (1999), 'Education and Wages in the Czech and Slovak Republics during Transition', *Labour Economics*, 6(4), 581–593.

Gabal, I. (2006), *Analýza sociálně vyloučených romských lokalit a absorpční capacity subjektů působících v této oblasti*, Praha, MPSV CR.

Garner, T. I., and Terrell, K. (1998), 'A Gini Decomposition Analysis of Inequality in the Czech and Slovak Republics During the Transition', *The Economics of Transition*, 6(1): 23–46.

Hayo, B. (2007), 'Happiness in Transition: An Empirical Study on Eastern Europe', *Economic Systems*, 31(2), 204–221.

Hromádková, E., and Zdeněk, M. (2012), 'Demand Side Cost-Sharing and Prescription Drugs Utilization: Evidence from a Quasi-Natural Experiment', mimeo.

Kahanec, M., and Zimmermann, K.F. (2009), 'International Migration, Ethnicity and Economic Inequality', in Salverda, W., Nolan B., and Smeeding, T.M. (eds.), *Oxford Handbook on Economic Inequality*, Oxford: Oxford University Press, 455–490.

Kahanec M., Guzi, M., Martišková, M., Paleník, M., Pertold, F. and Siebertová, Z. (2013), *GINI Country Report: The Czech Republic and Slovakia*, GINI Country Report available at <http://www.gini-research.org/CT-Czech-and-Slovak>.

Linek, L. (2011), 'Proč se měnila úroveň účasti ve volbách do Poslanecké sněmovny v letech 1996–2010?' ['Why Did Voter Turnout in the Czech General Elections Change between 1996 and 2010?'], *Czech Sociological Review*, 47(1), 9–32.

Lovaš L. (2010), 'Politické postoje', in: Výrost J. a kol., *Európska sociálna sonda (ESS) 4.kolo na Slovensku*, Košice: UNIVERSUM.

Mareš, P. (1999), Sociology of Inequality and Poverty, Prague: Sociologické nakladatelství.

Melicherčík, I., and C. Ungvarský. (2004), 'Pension Reform in Slovakia: Perspectives of the Fiscal Debt and Pension Level', *Finance a úvěr*, Czech Journal of Economics and Finance, 24(9-10), 391–404.

MF SR. (2005), *Podklad k Daňovej reforme*, Ministerstvo financií SR. Retrieved on August 25, 2012, from <http://www.finance.gov.sk/Default.aspx?CatID=3996>

Milanovic, B. (1998), 'Income, Inequality, and Poverty during the Transition from Planned to Market Economy', *World Bank Regional and Sectoral Studies*, Washington, D.C.: The World Bank.

Mishler, W., and Rose, R. (2001), 'What are the Origins of Political Trust? Testing Institutional and Cultural Theories in Post-Communist Societies,' *Comparative Political Studies*, 34(1), 30–62.

Moore, D. (2005), *Slovakia's 2004 Tax and Welfare Reforms*, IMF WP/05/133.

Myant, M. (2010), Trade Union Influence in the Czech Republic since 1989, *Czech Sociological Review*, 6, 889–911.

Münich, D., and Jurajda, Š. (2011), *Quarterly Report from the SYSDEM Correspondent*, Czech Republic, European Employment Observatory, Birmingham.

Münich, D. and Jurajda, Š. (2012), *Quarterly Report from the SYSDEM Correspondent*, Czech Republic.

Mysíková, M. (2011), 'Personal Earnings Inequality in the Czech Republic', *IES Working Papers*, 11.

Sedláčková, M., and Šafr, J. (2008), 'Social Trust and Civic Participation in the Czech Republic', in Lewandowski, J. D., and Znoj, M. (eds.), *Trust and Transition*, Newcastle upon Tyne: Cambridge Scholars Publishing, 213–236.

Sirovátka, T. and Mareš, P. (2006), 'Poverty, Social Exclusion and Social Policy in the Czech Republic', *Social Policy and Administration*, 40(3), 288–303.

Sirovátka, T., Hora, O., and Kofroň, P. (2008), 'Příjmová chudoba a materiální deprivace v České republice', *Fórum sociální politiky, Praha, Výskumný ústav práce a sociálních věcí*, 2(5), 2–8.

Stachová, J., Čermák, D., and Vobecká, J. (2008), 'Institutional Trust in the Regions of the Czech Republic', in Mayerová, V. (ed.) *Venkov je náš svět, Countryside—our World*, Praha: Česká zemědělská univerzita.

TransMonee (2004), A database of socio-economic indicators for CEE/CIS/Baltics, Florence: UNICEF International Child Development Centre. Online database: <http://www.unicef-irc.org/databases/transmonee/>.

TransMonee (2005), A database of socio-economic indicators for CEE/CIS/Baltics. Florence: UNICEF International Child Development Centre. Online database: <http://www.unicef-irc.org/databases/transmonee/>.

UNDP (2011), 'Data on Roma': <http://europeandcis.undp.org/data/show/D69F01FE-F203-1 EE9-B45121B12A557E1B>, last accessed 25 January 2013

Večerník, J. (1991), 'Úvod do studia chudoby v Československu [Introduction into study of poverty in Czechoslovakia], *Sociologický Časopis* [Czech Sociological Review], 577–602.

Večerník, J. (2001), *Mzdová a příjmová diferenciace v České republice v transformačním období*, Sociologický ústav Akademie věd České republiky.

Verhoeven, M., Gunnarsson, V., and Lugaresi, S. (2007), 'The Health Sector in the Slovak Republic: Efficiency and Reform', *IMF Working papers*, WP/07/226.

World Bank (2012), *Policy Advice on the Integration of Roma in the Slovak Republic*, Washington D.C: The World Bank.

CHAPTER 25

SLOVENIA: AN EQUAL SOCIETY DESPITE THE TRANSITION

MAŠA FILIPOVIČ HRAST AND MIROLJUB IGNJATOVIĆ

1. INTRODUCTION

IN this chapter, we look at trends in inequality in Slovenia over the past 20 years. The changes have been significant in this period since it covers the country's transition to democracy and to a market economy after it gained its independence in 1991. At the beginning of the 1990s, GDP growth was negative (-8.9 per cent in 1991) on account of the loss of the markets in the former Yugoslavia and the aforementioned transition to a market economy. However, GDP then grew rapidly until 1995, after which time it remained relatively stable until 2008. The global economic crisis subsequently had a significantly negative impact on the GDP growth rate: the decline was similar to that observed at the start of the 1990s (Figure 25.1).

The turbulence caused by the transition to a market economy also affected the country's labour market. Slovenia experienced substantial job losses, a decline in labour force participation and employment/population ratios, the growth of structural unemployment and a particularly steep rise in unemployment rates, as registered unemployment increased from 15,000 in 1987 to 129,000 in 1993. From 1993 onwards, the situation started to improve until the end of 2008, when it again deteriorated due to the economic crisis.

We will look at inequality trends and juxtapose these with the trends in poverty and social exclusion in the period of transition (and subsequent consolidation) of the Slovenian state. Specific emphasis will be placed on the emerging vulnerabilities and vulnerable groups. One would expect transitional turbulence to have a significant impact on inequality in society. Yet, despite the significant changes, inequality in Slovenia has been quite stable and low. Several activities undertaken by the state have been important in maintaining this stability. In addition, we will link the issue of inequality to its social impacts, such as the problems of poverty and social exclusion, as well as to political and cultural impacts. However, we will observe only certain aspects of the social and political impacts. For further information and more detailed data, please refer to the Slovenian Country Report prepared within the Growing Inequalities' Impacts (GINI) project.

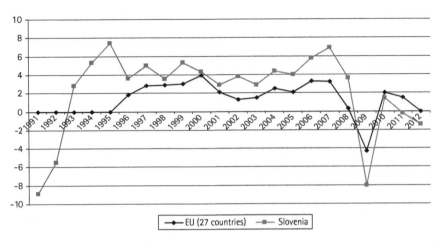

FIGURE 25.1 Real GDP growth rate—volume (percentage change over previous year)

Source: Eurostat.

2. INEQUALITY TRENDS—SLOVENIA IN COMPARATIVE PERSPECTIVE

According to various studies (Čok, 2003; Čok *et al.*, 2011; Fuest *et al.*, 2009; Stanovnik and Verbič, 2012a) and the available data (SORS,[1] IMAD,[2] Eurostat, OECD), inequality in Slovenia remained relatively stable and low[3] in the period from independence in 1991 up to the end of 2008 (see Figure 25.2), when the current economic crisis finally hit the country. Furthermore, according to OECD (2011), in the late 2000s Slovenia was the most equal of the OECD countries, with a Gini coefficient of 0.24.[4] The current economic crisis has increased inequality somewhat, but it still remains relatively low, due largely to the state's increased redistributive activity. This has been achieved mainly through social transfers, which have had the effect of increasing state spending (and consequently also state debt).

Regardless of the increase in 2010, the Slovenian Gini coefficient[5] is still much lower than the EU-27 average provided by Eurostat. In fact, the Slovenian Gini coefficient in 2010 was the lowest of the European countries (Figure 25.3), with countries such as Sweden, Hungary, the Czech Republic, Finland and the Netherlands having slightly higher GINIs.

---

[1] Statistical Office of the Republic of Slovenia.

[2] Institute of Macroeconomic Analysis and Development.

[3] The reasons for such low inequality may be found in the country's relatively long socialist history (which accentuated low inequality as one of the most important objectives) and related values that became embedded in Slovenian society and which are still present today in the form of more egalitarian expectations.

[4] Slovenia became an OECD member relatively late on, and thus data on the Slovenian Gini index are available only from the mid 2000s onwards.

[5] The calculations made by the Statistical Office of the Republic of Slovenia are based on annual disposable net household income. Official data are available from 1997 onwards.

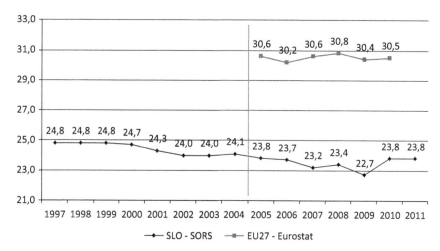

FIGURE 25.2 Gini coefficient—Slovenia and the EU-27 average

Note: Between 2004 and 2005 there was a break in series.

Source: SORS, Eurostat.

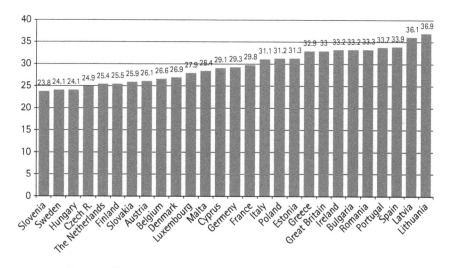

FIGURE 25.3 Gini coefficient in EU countries, 2010

Source: Eurostat.

While all these other countries have similarly high-income equality, they represent two specific European regions—Northern and Central Europe that have very different standards of living and a very different historical background. As Figure 25.4 shows, the GDP per capita in the northern European countries (Finland, Netherlands, Sweden, Denmark) is twice that of Central Europe (Hungary, Slovakia, the Czech Republic and Slovenia).

The data above also show that Slovenia, unlike most other developed countries during the pre-crisis economic boom, managed to avoid increased income disparities within the population, despite some fiscal reforms that made income tax slightly less progressive.

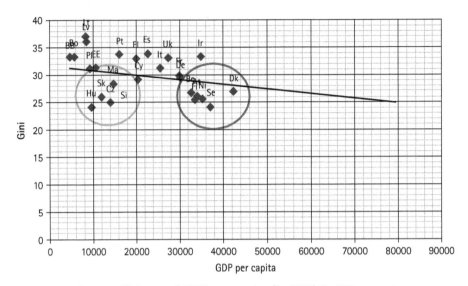

FIGURE 25.4 Gini coefficient and GDP per capita (in PPP) in EU countries, 2010

Source: Eurostat.

One of the most important factors influencing income inequality in Slovenia is, of course, the labour market (or, more precisely, the individual's position and activity in the labour market). The labour market increases inequality in Slovenian society through two processes: 'flexibilization' and labour market segmentation. One of the most important features of the Slovenian labour market is its relatively rapid 'flexibilization', especially over the past decade, when student work (one of the peculiarities of the Slovenian employment landscape)[6] and fixed-term contracts boomed. The relatively secure position of employees with permanent contracts means that fixed-term contracts and student work have come to be widely used by employers to reduce the costs of production and to increase the organizational and labour force flexibility of companies. Such an employment pattern produces, among other things, a strong bifurcation and segmentation of the labour market, with the younger workforce found predominantly in flexible (and generally precarious) forms of employment, and the older workforce in more secure, permanent employment.

Taking the Gini coefficient as the relevant indicator, Stanovnik and Verbič (2012b) found that employee income inequality had increased somewhat in the period 1991–2009. Though the increases in income inequality were moderate, some non-negligible changes did occur at the very top of the income distribution, i.e. in the top 5 per cent and top 1 per cent of employees.[7] But income inequality in employees' net income remained fairly stable throughout this

---

[6]   Student work holds a unique position in the Slovenian labour market that differs from its place in other EU countries. In Slovenia, students and pupils occupy a special labour market segment that is covered by Student Service Agencies, which offer temporary and occasional work only to students and pupils who are in need of work or are willing to work as well as study.

[7]   'Thus, according to data source A, the share of total gross income accruing to the top income quintile group has increased by 2.38 percentage points in the 1993–2008 period. A large part of this increase accrued to the top one percent of employees, whose income share increased by 0.89 percentage points' (Stanovnik and Verbič, 2012b: 11).

Table 25.1 Structure of educational attainment of Slovenian population (15 and over) in 2010 (%)

| | total | Age group (years) | | | | | | |
		15–24	25–34	35–44	45–54	55–64	65–74	75+
No education, incomplete basic	4.2	1.7	0.7	1.0	1.9	3.7	10.1	20.1
Basic	20.7	40.0	5.9	13.3	17.4	24.3	26.6	28.9
Short-term vocational, vocational upper-secondary	23.6	10.4	20.2	26.2	30.7	27.7	25.5	22.1
Technical, general upper-secondary	32.7	44.6	42.0	32.5	30.1	28.5	22.9	19.5
Tertiary	18.7	3.3	31.3	26.9	19.9	16.5	14.9	9.4
Total	100	100	100	100	100	100	100	100

Source: SORS 2010, statistics yearbook, LFS data.

period. In other words, changes in the personal income tax (PIT) regime largely damped down the effects of increasing inequality in the distribution of employee gross income.

One of the most important factors influencing someone's position in the labour market and in society is that person's education or educational attainment. Slovenia has experienced some important changes in the structure of educational attainment over recent decades. Some of this could be attributed to the increased aspirations of the new cohorts, and some to the explicit activities of the state, which has set some ambitious objectives for wider access to tertiary education and to that end has steadily reformed the system.

The structure of educational attainment of the Slovenian population in 2010 shows growing shares of technical, general upper-secondary and tertiary education in younger cohorts (Table 25.1).

Educational attainment, of course, has an important influence on a person's ability to find and keep a job in the labour market. Figure 25.5 clearly shows the differences in the employment rates, according to the educational attainment of the workforce.

There is a very strong negative correlation between the educational inequality measured by the education Gini and the average number of years of schooling. This means that a higher education attainment level in the population leads to greater education equality (Flere *et al.*, 2004).

The inequality indices (Čok, 2003) show the highest inequality among the less well-educated: in 1983 and 1997/98, it was to be found in the subgroups with *primary school* education, whereas, in 1993, it was in the category *upper-secondary school*. Conversely, the lowest inequality is found among well-educated people: in the subgroup *higher education* (V+VI) in 1983, in the subgroup *university or more* in 1993, and in the subgroup *non-university higher education* in 1997/98.

Despite substantial educational expansion at the tertiary level, obtaining post-secondary or tertiary qualifications still pays off, especially in terms of occupational status. With their ranks dwindling in the course of educational reform, those individuals with primary education or less are the losers in market transformation. They get the lowest-quality jobs, require a long time to find their first significant job, and are the most likely then to lose it.

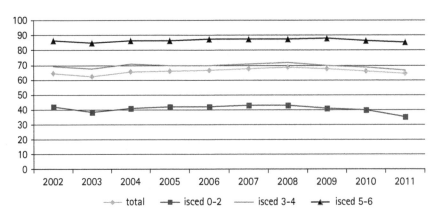

FIGURE 25.5 Employment rates by education level (15–64) in Slovenia (%)

Source: Eurostat.

Another part of the 'inequality story' can be told using data on wealth and debt inequality. However, such data—especially data on debt inequality—are relatively scarce and are not collected systematically for Slovenian households. Here we present the available data on household borrowing and on the burden on household income.

According to Ferk (2009), data from the beginning of the 1990s show a gradual increase in household borrowing up until 1999, when there was a marked increase in the purchase of cars (ahead of the introduction of a different tax, VAT). After 2000, indebtedness slowed down, though it began to rise again in 2004—a trend that continued until the end of 2008. On the other hand, according to Noč (2011), household debt in Slovenia is among the lowest in the countries of the euro zone. At the end of 2010, Slovenian household debt amounted to 31 per cent of GDP (only in Slovakia it is lower, at 26 per cent of GDP).

Furthermore, 70 per cent of Slovenian households reported that they had no repayments of instalments in 2007: payments by instalment and consumer loans represented a heavy burden for 11 per cent of all households, though the proportion was greater in the third income quintile. In addition, housing costs were very burdensome for nearly a third of all households, and for nearly half of households in the first (poorest) income quintile (see Table 25.2).

All the data presented indicate that inequality has remained low in Slovenian society even after the transition. In the next sections, we will sketch some of the social and political context to give a clearer view of conditions after transition.

3. SOCIAL IMPACTS

The transitional period brought with it significant changes in certain social areas (such as housing), while in other areas there was greater continuity with the period before transition (e.g. health, social networks). We present the trends in some of these areas, and also try to identify the groups that are (becoming) more vulnerable in Slovenian society, despite the generally low inequality trends.

Table 25.2 Burden on households with loans and missed payments, Slovenia, 2007 (%)

	Size of the burden on households: purchases by instalment or other non-housing loans			Households that have missed repayment of instalments or non-residential loans in past 12 months for financial reasons		Size of the burden on households: housing costs			
	Heavy burden	Average burden	Not a burden	Yes	No	Heavy burden	Average burden	Not a burden	Household did not have instalments
Total household income	11	16	3	4	26	31	56	13	70
1.quintile	11	7	1	5	14	49	42	9	81
2.quintile	13	16	2	5	26	36	55	9	69
3.quintile	14	18	2	4	29	29	60	11	66
4.quintile	11	22	4	3	34	22	63	15	63
5.quintile	5	22	6	3	30	13	64	23	67

Note: Households are classified according to the total income in the five quintiles. The first is the poorest 20 per cent, while the fifth is the wealthiest 20 per cent of households.

Source: Statistical Office of Republic of Slovenia–EU–SILC.

General Trends in Poverty, Material Deprivation and Social Exclusion

In the previous section, we dealt with inequality trends in Slovenia. Here we would like to link the data on inequality to the data on poverty, material deprivation and social exclusion, as these indicators tell another part of the story. Is Slovenia a society that is equal in poverty, or is it equal in wealth, and what are the trends?

At the European level, Slovenia has a low at-risk-of-poverty rate: it keeps company with almost the same group of countries as it did in the case of the Gini coefficient – the Czech Republic, the Netherlands, Luxembourg, Hungary, Austria, France, Denmark and Sweden (Figure 25.6).

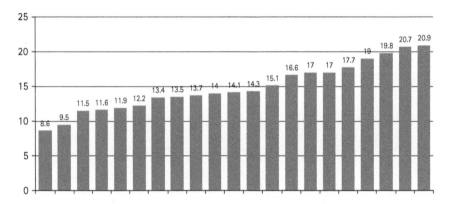

FIGURE 25.6 At-risk-of-poverty rates in EU countries, 2011 (%)

Source: Eurostat.

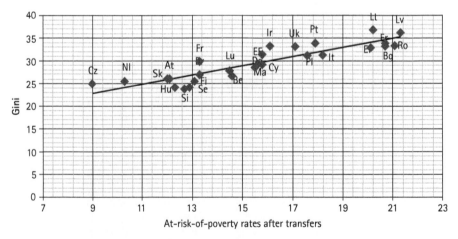

FIGURE 25.7 Correlation between Gini coefficient and at-risk-of-poverty rate in EU countries, 2011

Note: Calculated correlation between Gini coefficient and at-risk-of-poverty rate is Corr.=.899**; *p*=0.000

Source: Eurostat.

A quick analysis of the correlation between the Gini coefficient and the at-risk-of-poverty rate shows (Figure 25.7) a positive correlation, meaning that countries with a lower Gini coefficient also have a lower at-risk-of-poverty rate.

At the national level, the at-risk-of-poverty rate was quite constant from 2000 to 2009 (Figure 25.8). From 2009 there has been a slight increase in the at-risk-of-poverty rate—evidence of the negative effect of the economic crisis.

Poverty indicators should also be combined with indicators that illustrate material deprivation and other areas of quality of life. Here we will use the indicators commonly used in social exclusion research, i.e. material deprivation, severe material deprivation and social exclusion. Unfortunately, the official indicators of material deprivation, social exclusion and the composite indicator 'social exclusion or poverty' are only available from 2005 onwards, and so we are unable to observe the trends from the beginning of the transition.

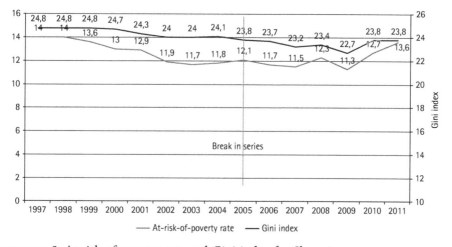

FIGURE 25.8 At-risk-of-poverty rate and Gini index for Slovenia

Source: SORS.

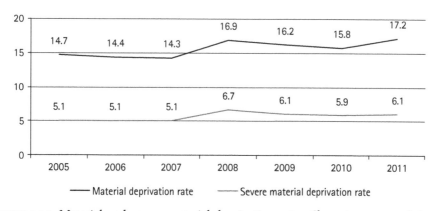

FIGURE 25.9 Material and severe material deprivation rates, Slovenia, 2005–11 (%)

Source: Eurostat, Income and Living Conditions data.

These indicators also show a relative stability in Slovenia that corresponds to a low at-risk-of poverty rate. There is a peak in 2008 in both material deprivation and severe material deprivation, indicating the impact of the economic crisis on people's material circumstances (see Figure 25.9).

However, the cumulative indicator—the share of people at risk of poverty or social exclusion (according to the definitions of Eurostat, Europe 2020)—was quite constant from 2005 to 2010; the economic crisis had not (yet) had any significant effect (see Table 25.3).

Family Formation and Social Cohesion

Slovenia is like other European countries facing demographic change, i.e. ageing of the population, decreasing birth rates, and the associated increasing number of single-person households and households without children. From 2005 to 2010, the number of single-person households increased from 180,000 to 223,800; the number of households with two adults without children increased in the same time period from 268,500 to 318,200 (Eurostat). The number of marriages fell steadily from 6.5 per 1,000 persons in 1980 to a low of 2.9 in 2005, since when the figure has been slowly rising, reaching 3.2 in 2010 (SORS). The fertility rate has dropped from 2.11 in 1980 to 1.57 in 2010.

These changed family circumstances also influence the social networks and support networks among family members, neighbours, friends and others, which can be observed as an indicator of the level of social cohesion. Research on social networks indicates that there have been some relatively minor changes over the past 20 years in the composition of networks, though generally speaking these are quite stable. The research done by Hlebec *et al.* (2010) on social networks and a comparison of them in 1987 and 2002 showed that the effect of time on network composition is relatively weak, while the effects of age and marital status (as well as of gender, in some cases) are stronger. However, the effect of time is relatively strong when it comes to the proportion of co-workers and neighbours in the networks, which was considerably higher in 1987 than in 2002. It therefore seems that discussion partners have become less numerous and more intimate, which might be linked to the transition and the changes it wrought on society, or else to other, more general societal changes, such as a trend towards individualization (Hlebec *et al.*, 2010).

Table 25.3 Cumulative disadvantage in Slovenia (per cent of population)

People at risk of poverty or social exclusion

2005	2006	2007	2008	2009	2010
18.5	17.1	17.1	18.5	17.1	18.3

Note: The indicator of people at risk of poverty or social exclusion corresponds to the sum of persons who are: at risk of poverty or severely materially deprived or living in households with very low work intensity.

Source: Eurostat, Income and Living Conditions data.

General Trends in Health and Housing

In general, Slovenia can be described as a country with a well-developed system of health-care, with an extensive public network of health institutions. Access to healthcare services is through compulsory health insurance. Even though the public healthcare system remains the strongest, the past decade has seen increasing privatization of health services. The consequence of this may be greater inequality in accessing health services, as only some can afford the private services and so jump the long waiting lists that are characteristic of public health services.

Life expectancy in Slovenia is steadily increasing: it rose for both men and women by approximately three years from 2004 to 2010. However, male life expectancy is still lower than female (76 years for men and 83 years for women in 2010). It also differs according to social class and level of education. The data show that life expectancy in Slovenia for men with the highest level of education across all observed age groups is lower than for women with the lowest level of education something that is true of only a few European countries (Corsini, 2010, in Buzeti et al., 2011).

Subjective indicators of health also show a positive trend. The share of those who evaluated their health as 'very good' has been slowly increasing since 2005, and almost 18 per cent of people rated their health as 'very good' in 2010. However, the difference between those with lower and higher education is significant: among those with higher education (level 5 and 6), more than 24 per cent rate their health as 'very good' (Eurostat data for 2010), whereas among those with only primary education (level 1), the figure is only 4 per cent (see Table 25.4).[8] In addition, the share of those reporting a long-standing illness or health problem is consistently higher among those with lower income in the observed time period (2005–10). In all income groups in the year 2008 (i.e. the year of the crisis), there was an increase in reported problems.

Table 25.4 Self-rated health (percentage of very good), by education

	2005	2006	2007	2008	2009	2010
Total	14.8	15.9	15.8	16.4	17.2	17.9
Pre-primary education (level 0)	4.0	12.2	5.0	:	:	:
Primary education or first stage of basic education (level 1)	11.0	8.6	4.3	4.6	3.5	4.1
Lower secondary or second stage of basic education (level 2)	3.5	17.2	11.9	12.2	11.9	13.5
Upper secondary education (level 3)	16.1	16.8	16.3	17.0	17.8	18.2
Post-secondary non-tertiary education (level 4)	17.6	13.5	:	:	:	:
First stage of tertiary education not leading directly to an advanced research qualification (level 5)	22.6	24.2	22.3	21.9	24.3	24.0
Second stage of tertiary education leading to an advanced research qualification (level 6)	25.0	25.1	28.6	30.4	20.7	27.6

Source: Eurostat.

---

[8] Eurostat data on population and social conditions, Health, EU-SILC Survey, 2006. Definition: The percentage sum of people reporting bad or very bad health.

The transition has brought about significant changes in the field of housing. Before the transition, housing was guaranteed by the state, but there was also a significant share of 'self-help building' (individual building of houses). However, since the transition, housing has seen the most noticeable decline in the role of government. The denationalization and privatization of housing have been the most important policies (see Mandič and Filipovič Hrast, 2008). Due to the privatization of housing during the transition, there has been a significant shift in housing tenure: the public rented stock diminished and the tenure structure changed from 32 per cent in public rental in 1990 to approximately 9 per cent in 1994. This was solely due to an increase in the number of owner-occupiers, from 65 per cent in 1990 to 89 per cent in 1994. The private rental sector stayed practically the same, with approximately 3 per cent (Mandič, 2000). The situation has changed little since 1994: according to public census data, only 9 per cent of dwellings were rented in 2011 (this figure includes both private and public rentals) (SORS, 2011).

The rise in home ownership has increased the wealth of those people who bought their dwellings at favourable prices and who, in other circumstances, would not have been able to become homeowners. This could therefore be seen as a process that reduced inequality. However, the consequences of this are not entirely positive. While privatization has improved the housing opportunities for those households that have managed to buy their homes, the housing prospects of other groups waiting to be housed—particularly vulnerable low-income and single households—have worsened because of the reduced accommodation that is available for rent. In addition, the negative impacts of privatization can be viewed through a long lens: such redistribution presents some cohorts with a historically unique opportunity to amass public resources (as in the case of tenants' 'right to buy' rented housing) and leaves later cohorts with fewer opportunities even to rent (Mandič and Filipovič Hrast, 2008). Consequently, their chances of receiving not-for-profit rented housing are minimal, as this kind of housing is not widely available. Even though it was envisaged that this sector would gradually develop, this has not happened.

Furthermore, the quality of housing is generally lower in Slovenia (and other Central and Eastern European countries) than in Western European countries. The dwellings are generally much smaller, so that the overcrowding rate in Slovenia is much higher than the EU average. In this, Slovenia is similar to other Central and Eastern European countries. The trend is, however, a positive one, as the share of those living in an overcrowded dwelling has dropped from 42 per cent in 2005 to 35 per cent in 2010 (Eurostat, EU-SILC).

As with the indicators of inequality, so too the indicators of poverty, housing and health show Slovenia to be relatively successful in ensuring the well-being of its citizens. However, no link between inequality and the observed impacts can be confirmed on the basis of the data given here.

Specific Vulnerable Groups

Regardless of the fairly egalitarian nature of current Slovenian society, there are certain groups that are at greater risk of falling into material deprivation, poverty or social exclusion. These groups are more dependent on the different activities of the state and the growing number of non-governmental organizations.

One of the most important characteristics that increase the risk of falling into an unfavourable position is the labour market status of the person or household. The at-risk-of-poverty rate broken down by activity status shows that there are groups that are more affected, especially the unemployed and inactive. During the past decade, certain changes—especially a tightening up of the eligibility criteria and the 'activation principle'—have contributed to a reduction in the share of unemployment benefit recipients: in 1992, 45.0 per cent of all registered unemployed received unemployment benefit or unemployment assistance; in 2000, the figure was only 29.1 per cent; and by 2008 it had dropped to 22.7 per cent (Employment Service of Slovenia, 2012). This can be seen as part of the explanation for the increasing poverty rates among the unemployed.

Aside from the classic division between activity and inactivity in the labour market, where unemployed and inactive persons[9] are more 'prone' to greater risk, there is growing differentiation among active persons as well. While permanent, full-time workers enjoy a relatively secure position in the labour market, there is a growing segment of flexibly employed people with positions in the labour market that could be described as precarious or insecure. Here, as already mentioned, the age of the employed person is the main point of differentiation—younger generations (at least those younger than 30 years of age) are predominantly to be found in the flexible forms of employment.

With the economic crisis, vulnerable groups have already been faced with a further deterioration in their position. Unemployed persons have the highest at-risk-of-poverty rate in the population (36.2 per cent in 2007, rising to 43.5 per cent in 2009).[10] We can see very large differences across society: it is clear that an individual's living standard depends heavily on his or her activity status in the labour market (Figure 25.10).

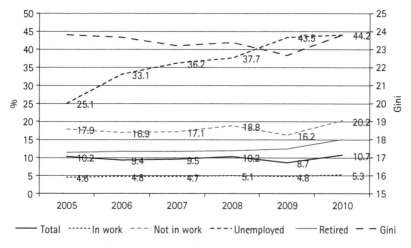

FIGURE 25.10 At-risk-of-poverty rates by most frequent activity status, Slovenia, annually

Source: SORS—Statistics data portal.

[9] As regards the most frequent activity status, unemployed persons (44.1 per cent) and retired persons (18.3 per cent) were the most vulnerable. The at-risk-of-poverty rate was also high for women aged 65+ (27.1 per cent) and for tenants (27.6 per cent).

[10] In the SILC survey of 2009, Eurostat changed the methodology for collecting data about the monthly status of people in the income reference year. The changes mean that inactive persons are

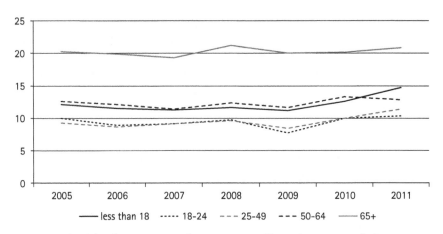

FIGURE 25.11 At-risk-of-poverty rate by age group, Slovenia, 2005–11 (%)

Source: Eurostat, Social inclusion data.

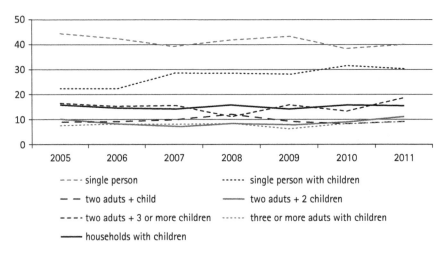

FIGURE 25.12 At-risk-of-poverty rate by household type, Slovenia, 2005–11 (%)

Source: Eurostat, Social inclusion data.

However, retired people and the elderly (over 65) are also particularly vulnerable. They have a much higher at-risk-of poverty rate than the overall average for the population (see Figure 25.11). Particularly vulnerable are elderly women living alone, as those households

classified into each category in more detail than is included in the administrative sources, and data from administrative sources are combined with data from the questionnaire. The status of the other inactive persons from administrative sources (housewives, unable to work, students, other inactive) is determined by their answers to the questionnaire (prior to 2009, the sources of data were administrative sources). Because of this methodological change in 2009, there is a higher proportion of the unemployed and a lower percentage of other inactive persons among all persons classified by most frequent activity status.

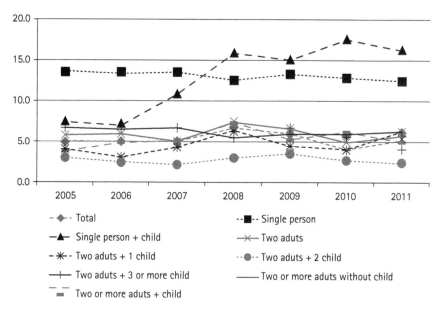

FIGURE 25.13 Severe material deprivation, by household type, Slovenia, 2005–11 (%)

Source: Eurostat, Income and Living Conditions data.

have especially high poverty rates. Due to the ageing of the population and the changing patterns of family formation, the number of single households is rising rapidly and therefore this particularly vulnerable group is growing in society.

Another vulnerable group is single parents. Here the trend is a negative one, as the at-risk-of poverty rate for this group has increased from 22 per cent in 2005 to 30.8 per cent in 2011 (Figure 25.12). Similar trends for this group are indicated when we look at severe material deprivation, which has also increased significantly, from 7.6 per cent in 2005 to 16.4 per cent in 2011 (Figure 25.13).

The data show that in Slovenia, despite low inequality, specific groups are becoming more vulnerable and have increasing at-risk-of poverty rates, especially since the economic crisis of 2008.

4. Political and Cultural Impacts

Political and Civic Participation

When speaking of political circumstances in Slovenia, we need to go a little way back into history—to the socialist revolution and the subsequent changes that led to the transition to democracy. In Slovenia, the socialist revolution was autochthonous, accomplished without any direct help from the Soviet Union, unlike other countries of Central and Eastern Europe (CEE). Following the break between the Yugoslav and the Soviet communist party leaders in 1948, Yugoslavia opened up to the West and started making gradual changes to its social order. This was not a one-way street leading to democratization and openness: periods of liberalization (the second half of the 1960s and the 1980s) alternated with periods of repression (the beginning of the 1960s and the 1970s) (Tomšič, 2008). On the back of the intellectual, cultural and other new social movements that mobilized the public in the 1980s, a new coalition won the elections in 1990 and held a plebiscite on independence (Deželan, 2011; Tomšič, 2008). The turnout was very high (93 per cent), and 88.5 per cent voted for independence.[11]

However, this start of 'active citizenship' was followed by some disappointment in politics—a disillusionment that can be observed in lower levels of electoral turnout, decreased trust in political institutions and an increasingly negative perception of politics (Fink Hafner and Kropivnik, 2006). Malnar (2004) stated that Slovenia was, according to public opinion research (European Social Survey (ESS) 2002), one of the countries where people showed the least interest in politics, as the average evaluation of the importance of politics on a scale of 1 to 10 was only 3.18. It is not surprising, then, that the turnout at general elections has fallen from 73 per cent in 1996 to 63 per cent in 2008. By and large, general election turnout has ranged from around 60 per cent (lowest in 2004) to 85 per cent (highest in 1992). A similar turnout can be seen in presidential elections, ranging from 58 per cent (lowest in 2007) to 70 per cent (highest in 1992). The turnout in local elections ranges from 51 per cent to 72 per cent (Kropivnik, 2010). Furthermore, satisfaction with the government is quite low: in 2002–8, it was below one-third of respondents. Similarly, there is quite low satisfaction with the way democracy functions in the country: less than a third of the population was satisfied in the period 2002–08 (ESS data).

The transition to democracy has led to a revitalization of civil society. Under socialism, the previous tradition of civil society participation ceased. In the 1970s and more and more in the 1980s, the regulations became less rigorous, and civil society began forming again, with the development of new social movements (such as feminist, ecological and for peace). Many of these new movements were politically active and influenced the transition to democracy. In the 1990s, new laws and regulations in this field were adopted, and the number of civil society organizations doubled—from 11,000 in 1990 to 24,644 in 2008 (Rakar et al., 2011). However, we could still say that, in Slovenia, civic participation is developing only slowly: the share of those who had taken part in an association in the previous 12 months was only 1.6 per cent in 2008 (ESS data), which puts Slovenia among the countries with the lowest civic participation.

Moreover, after the transition union membership began to decline sharply: in 1989, 69 per cent were members of a trade union; this dropped to 58.6 per cent in 1994 and then to 42.8 per cent in 1998 (Stanojević, 2000: 39). The share of the unionized workforce dropped further in subsequent years and was estimated to be 29.7 per cent in 2008 (estimates by J. Visser). However, it should be noted that Slovenia has a higher proportion of the workforce that is unionized than other CEE countries. As noted by Crowley and Stanojević (2011), Slovenia is still exceptional in terms of its coverage rate for collective agreements, which is said to be close to 100 per cent.

---

[11] See <http://www.slovenskapomlad.si/1?id=225>

Trust in Society and Attitudes toward Inequality and the Welfare State

General trust in others has been increasing since 1990. Researchers consider this to be a normalization from the very low levels of trust of the early 1990s (only 17 per cent) that were a result of war and the transition to democracy. Low levels of trust and social capital in Slovenia are linked partly to the socialist tradition, where social instrumental reciprocity was strong, whereas more generalized trust and reciprocity were rare and limited more to the family (Iglič, 2004). It is interesting to note that levels of trust have not increased at the same pace across all social groups. Levels of generalized trust have increased most among the better educated, since they were the first to overcome the negative consequences of the economic and political transition. By contrast, the less well-educated (and therefore those of lower socio-economic class) had almost the same levels of trust in 1995 and 2000; this trust began increasing only after 2000 (Iglič, 2004).

Toš (2007) studied trust in political and civil institutions in Slovenia from 1991 to 2006. At the beginning of the transition (1991), trust in political institutions was high, while trust in civil institutions was lower. After 1993 and up until 1999, there was a decline in (and then stagnation of) trust in political institutions, while trust in civil institutions rose in the same period. In 2000, trust in institutions peaked; after 2004, there was again a decline in trust in political institutions (Figure 25.14).

There has been a clear rise in perceptions of injustice: the share of those who think that the cause of poverty is too much injustice in society has risen from 42 per cent in 2007 to 61 per cent in 2010. At the same time, the share of those who believe that the main reasons for poverty are personal (e.g. a person is unlucky or lazy) halved from 2007 to 2010 (see Table 25.5). Slovenia (and indeed Europe generally) is therefore more inclined to interpret inequality

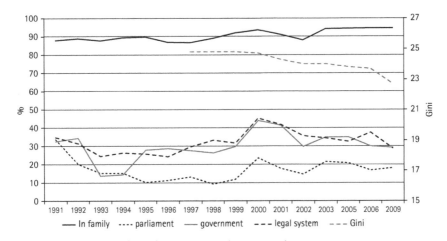

FIGURE 25.14 Trust in selected institutions (1991–2006)

Note: The question was: People must trust someone and have a feeling of reliance on themselves and others. To what extent do you trust the following…Answers: not at all, a little, a lot, and entirely. Presented are the responses 'a lot' and 'entirely'.

Source: SJM research (CJMMK FDV), cited in Toš (2007).

Table 25.5 The causes of and reasons for poverty (poverty attribution)—share of those who agree with the statements (%)

	Because they have been unlucky	Because they are lazy and lack willpower	Because there is much injustice in our society	Because it's an inevitable part of progress
2010	7.1	14.2	61.1	11.5
2009	18.2	22.8	45.3	11.6
2007	14.7	21.6	42.2	14.7
1999	10.2	32.7	34.9	17.1

Source: Eurobarometer 2007–10, 1999 SJM 1999/3 (cited in Toš, 2004).

Table 25.6 Attitudes towards redistribution

Agree that government should redistribute wealth/income (%)

2002	2004	2006	2008
83	83.7	78.9	85.5

Source: ESS.

and poverty in society in the context of structural determinants, rather than individual factors (as is more typical in the United States, for example) (Malnar, 2011). Consequently, it is not surprising that the majority of people are positively inclined towards the involvement of the state in the redistribution of wealth. The figures here are also quite constant over time (Table 25.6).

5. POLICIES AFFECTING LOW INCOME INEQUALITY, POVERTY AND SOCIAL EXCLUSION

The low income-inequality in Slovenia is largely attributable to tax and social policy measures, which have a relatively strong redistributive function in the country. Without this redistributive function of the state, inequality in Slovenia (measured either by the Gini coefficient or by the at-risk-of-poverty rate) would double, as in most other European countries. A comparison of the years 2000 and 2009 shows the effectiveness of the steps taken, as well as the improvement in overall well-being in Slovenian society. Thus, the data show that the at-risk-of-poverty rate before social transfers decreased in the first decade of the twenty-first century (from 37.2 per cent in 2000 to 22.0 per cent in 2009). Simultaneously, the at-risk-of-poverty rate after social transfers also remained relatively constant and low at 11.3 per cent in 2009 (SORS figures from 2012).

The relatively low and stable levels of inequality and the low and stable levels of poverty over the past two decades in Slovenia might lead one to claim that social policy has been quite successful in combating inequality. The social system has, to a large extent, protected established rights and benefits and reduced inequality in society. Changes were made to the social welfare system (Kolarič, 1992; Kolarič *et al.*, 2009). Here the transition coincided with general changes in welfare states that also occurred in Western European countries: the welfare state has started taking less responsibility for legislating on social rights, for the enforcement of these rights and for financing social policy and delivering services. In Slovenia, the state has kept its dominant position as a financial force, whereas the production of social services has been devolved to the private sector. In the transition from a socialist to a post-socialist society, the Slovenian welfare system has been constituted as a dual model, with elements of a conservative-corporate welfare system (a compulsory social insurance system, based on social partnership) and of a social-democratic welfare system (in which a strong public/state sector is still the dominant service provider for all types of services, to which all citizens are equally entitled) (Kolarič *et al.*, 2009).

The following measures have been the most relevant for maintaining low inequality and low poverty rates: social assistance and child benefits; unemployment benefits; and the pension system (with the disability insurance system). In addition, the Minimum Wage Act[12] and active labour market policies have played a role. The well-developed social support mechanism means that social security contributions in Slovenia are quite high.[13] According to Eurostat (2012), social security contributions in Slovenia, with a share of 40.1 per cent of total tax revenue, are the fourth highest in the EU. This figure stood at 38.5 per cent in 2001, declined steadily until 2007, and increased again in the period 2008–10 to reach its highest value since 1996. As for employees' social contributions, measured as a percentage of GDP (7.9 per cent), they are the highest in the EU—more than double the average.

Perhaps one of the most important policies for ensuring low inequality in Slovenian society has been the Personal Income Tax (PIT) system. As Čok, Urban and Verbič (2012: 2) argue: 'The overall inequality of pre-tax income in Slovenia increased as well during the last two decades…while the inequality of after-tax income remained fairly stable during 1991–2009 due to changes in the PIT system'. The PIT system remained almost unchanged from 1991 until 2005 (with five income brackets), when a new reform was launched. It introduced 'a differentiation in the taxation of individual incomes according to their character—'active' income is taxed at progressive rates applied to the annual tax base, while 'passive' income (i.e. income from interest, dividends and capital gains) is taxed at a flat rate, as in dual income systems. In 2006, the number of PIT brackets was reduced from

---

[12] When the minimum wage was introduced in 1995, it was to rise at the same pace as (or faster than) average gross pay, since it was adjusted according to the rise in inflation and partly in line with the rise in productivity or GDP. In the period from August 2004 to August 2005, the minimum gross wage reached 43.1 per cent of average gross pay, but thereafter it dropped annually to 41.1 per cent in 2008. Such trends, along with new objectives set by the Slovenian government (e.g. flexicurity and 'making work pay') and constant demands from trade union representatives for an increase in the minimum wage, brought the new Minimum Wage Act (implemented in March 2010), which set the new level of gross minimum wage. Consequently, in 2011 the number of minimum wage recipients and their share of the total number of employed persons (7.1 per cent) was more than double the figure for 2009.

[13] Social security contributions in Slovenia cover pension, health, unemployment insurance and maternity leave.

five to three and the top tax rate from 50 per cent to 41 per cent; the scheduler taxation of 'passive' income at a single 20 per cent rate was retained. In 2009, a new tax at the rate of 49 per cent was introduced, which is imposed on the income of management in companies receiving state aid' (European Commission, 2010b: 254).

As we have shown here, the elderly and retired represent one of the most vulnerable groups in society. Therefore we will look at the main policies—i.e. the pension system—that might be the reason for this. In Slovenia, the first public pillar is a mandatory earnings-related scheme, financed on a pay-as-you-go basis, which covers the risk of old age, disability and survivorship. There has been an increasingly unfavourable relationship between the final salary and the first pension. The consequence of decreasing pensions is that many pensioners have pensions that are too small to ensure an adequate standard of living and prevent them from slipping into poverty (the data on poverty among the elderly indicate how pressing this issue is in Slovenia). Within the pension and social system there are corrective factors to ensure adequate pensions, such as the right to pension assessment on the minimum pension rating base.[14] An additional social corrective in the past was the state pension, which is independent of the compulsory insurance. However, this pension was abolished under the Financial Social Assistance Act (OG 61/2010), which came into force in 2012. Pensioners on low pensions can also apply for a means-tested pension supplementary allowance.[15]

The economic crisis has affected pensions—the growth of pensions has been curtailed by the Intervention Measures Due to the Economic Crisis Act (OG RS 98/2009) and the Act of Intervention (OG 94/2010). In addition, with the recent Public Finance Balance Act (OG 40/2012), the rights of pensioners have been further affected: there has been a reduction in the supplementary allowance, a cut in those pensions that are not based on contributions, and no rise in pensions in 2012. All this goes some way to explaining the greater vulnerability of the elderly in Slovenia, as described above.

Expenditure on pensions in Slovenia is consistently below the EU-25 (27) average, and has, with minor fluctuations, been falling—from 11 per cent of GDP in 2000 to 9.6 per cent in 2008. Only in 2009 did the share rise again to 10.9 per cent (Eurostat, Social protection data). This fall in spending and the significant increase from 2008 to 2009 can be linked to pension reforms carried out in 1999 and to the changes in GDP growth.[16] From 2000 to 2008, Slovenia had constant GDP growth, but in 2009 it faced a sharp drop (Figure 25.1),

---

[14] If a person's computed pension base is lower than the minimum pension base, his/her pension is computed using the minimum pension base (Fultz, 2006).

[15] Enactment of the new Social Assistance Act in 2007 brought about a modified method of adjusting the base for supplementary rights assessment, which had a direct impact both on the number of pension support beneficiaries and on the amount of (pension) supplementary allowance. It led to the shrinking of rights (loss of allowance by a number of pensioners). Accordingly, a new Pension Support Act was passed in 2008, which regulated the right to supplementary allowance anew and defined a new base for assessing the support and the adjustment method. Its goal was to eliminate the decrease in pension supports. However, the supplementary allowance is now regulated by the new Financial Social Assistance Act (OG 61/2010), which came into force in 2012. According to this act, the recipients of supplementary allowance are long-term unemployed (or those unable to work) or elderly (for women, the age limit is 63; for men, 65 years).

[16] In 1999, the following pension reforms were introduced: (1) Accrual rates were reduced and a standard 1.5 per cent accrual rate per year replaced the general 2 per cent accrual rate and the special 3

which meant that the outflow for pensions made up a significantly larger share of GDP than in previous years.

6. Conclusions

The most important theme of the 'national story' is that Slovenia has managed over the past 20 years (thus far) to keep the main indicators of social inequality at relatively low levels. This success is also linked to the egalitarian attitude of the Slovenian public, as there is low tolerance of income inequality. There has even been an increase in the proportion of those who perceive current inequalities as too large—despite the fact that Slovenia is, according to official statistics and the Gini index, one of the countries with the lowest income-inequality. It is interesting that attitudes to this issue have generally always been in favour of reducing income inequalities: in 1975, 61 per cent of respondents felt that income differentials should be reduced, while only 5 per cent felt they should be larger; by 2009, 87 per cent of respondents felt that the differentials should be narrowed, and only 1.7 per cent were of the opinion that they should be increased (Malnar, 2011).

However, the Slovenian story is far from idyllic. The same development of Slovenian society and its institutions that enabled its convergence with more developed European countries also brought new divisions and new inequalities. For example, convergence with the modern global economy also meant relatively strong liberalization, in the shape of poorly controlled privatization of major (formerly state-owned) Slovenian companies. This enabled manipulation by the top management and produced a group of newly rich so-called 'tycoons', who have received significant media attention and can be seen as one of the reasons behind the increased popular sense of injustice and inequality in Slovenian society. Moreover, the same trends that produced more winners also produced more losers: extreme vulnerability has increased, and this is reflected in the growing number of homeless people (Mandič and Filipovič Hrast, 2008).

While inequality has remained stable and low in recent years, the current situation in Slovenia has deteriorated somewhat. This is visible in the growing vulnerability of specific groups (lone parents, the elderly, the unemployed). The current economic and financial crisis affects the whole of society through public debt, the insolvency of Slovenian banks, rising unemployment rates, and so on. The crisis has also accentuated some problems in financing various elements of the social security system, such as unemployment benefits, social assistance, child benefits and the pension system. The austerity measures adopted by the government in order to reduce public debt seriously affect the population, especially those dependent on social security benefits and other kinds of assistance and social rights, including pensions and associated benefits for the elderly and disabled.

per cent accrual rate for women with short careers; (2) The retirement age was raised to 63 years for men and 61 years for women, and incentives and disincentives (for retiring later or earlier than the prescribed retirement age) were introduced; (3) The conditions governing early retirement and the minimum contributory period were tightened. Workers with long careers (40 years for men and 38 for women) could retire at 58. The period for calculating the pension base was set to the best consecutive 18-year average of (net) wages (European Commission, 2010a).

References

Buzeti, T. *et al.* (2011), *Health inequalities in Slovenia 2011 Report*, Ljubljana: Ministry of Health Republic of Slovenia.

Čok, M. (2003), 'Income inequality during the transition in Slovenia', Available at: <miha. ef.uni-lj.si/_dokumenti/wp/DZ%20138.doc> (accessed 1 December 2012).

Čok, M., Sambt, J., Kosak, M., Verbič, M., Majcen, B. (2011), 'Distribution of personal income tax changes in Slovenia', *MPRA Paper* No. 32704.

Čok, M., Urban, I. and Verbič, M. (2012), 'Income redistribution through tax and social benefits: the case of Slovenia and Croatia', *Working Paper No. 61*. Ljubljana: Institute for Economic Research.

Crowley, S and Stanojević, M. (2011), 'Varieties of Capitalism, Power Resources and Historical legacies. Explaining the Slovenian exception', *Politics and Society*. 39. (2) 268–295.

Deželan, T. (2011), 'Citizenship in Slovenia: the regime of a nationalising or a Europeanising state?' *CITSEE Working Paper Series*. Working paper 2011/16, Edinburgh: University of Edinburgh.

Employment Service of Slovenia (2012), Available at: <http://www.ess.gov.si/trg_dela/trg_dela_v_stevilkah> (accessed 11.December 2012).

ESS (European Social Survey). Available at: <http://www.europeansocialsurvey.org/> (accessed 18 January 2013).

European Commission (2010a), *Joint Report on Pensions—Progress and Key Challenges in the Delivery of Adequate and Sustainable Pensions in Europe. Country Profiles of the Joint Report on Pensions*. <.http://ec.europa.eu/economy_finance/publications/occasional_paper/2010/pdf/ocp71_country_profiles_en.pdf.>

European Commission (2010b), 'Taxation Trends in the European Union'. Available at: <http://ec.europa.eu/taxation_customs/resources/documents/taxation/gen_info/economic_analysis/tax_structures/2012/report.pdf>.

Eurostat. Available at: <http://epp.eurostat.ec.europa.eu/portal/page/portal/statistics/search_database> (accessed 5 January 2013).

Ferk, B. (2009), *Kazalniki in merjenje (pre)zadolženosti posameznikov oz. gospodinjstev.* Paper presented at a conference, Statistični dnevi, 9–11 November 2009, Radenci: SURS.

Fink Hafner, D. and Kropivnik, S. (2006), 'Polituična udeležba v posocializmu: med deformirano modernostjo, novo modernizacijo', *Postmodernostjo. Teorija in praksa* 12 (51): 55–72.

Flere S., Barle, Lakota A., Bezenšek J., Lavrič, M. (2004), *Educational Equity and Inequity in Slovenia, Country analytical report*, Maribor: Pedagoška fakulteta Maribor.

Fuest, C., Niehues, J., Peichl, A., (2009), 'The redistributive effects of tax benefit systems in the enlarged EU'. http://dx.doi.org/10.1787/9789264119536-en.

Fultz, E. (2006), *Gender dimension of social security reform*, ii: *Case studies of Romania and Slovenia*. Budapest: International Labour Office.

Hlebec, V., Filipovič Hrast, M. and Kogovšek, T. (2010), 'Social networks in Slovenia', *European societies*, 12, 5, 697–717.

Iglic, H. (2004), 'Dejavniki nizke stopnje zaupanja v Sloveniji', *Družboslovne razprave* 20 (46/47): 149–175.

Kolarič, Z. (1992), 'From Socialist to Post-Socialist Social Policy', in Svetnik, I. (ed.), *Social Policy in Slovenia*, Ashgate: Avebury, 15–32.

Kolarič, Z., Kopač, A. and Rakar, T. (2009), 'The Slovenian Welfare System: Gradual Reform Instead of Shock Treatment' in Schubert, K., Hegelich, S., and Bazant U. (eds.), *The Handbook of European Welfare Systems*, London and New York: Routledge, pp. 444–461.

Kropivnik, S. (2010), 'Slovenski volivci na volitvah v evropski parlament 2009', in Kustec Lipicer, S. (ed). *Politične vsebine in volilna kampanija: slovenska izkušnja volitev v Evropski parlament*. Ljubljana: FDV.

Layte, R., Maitre, B. and Whelan, C. (2010), *Second European Quality of Life Survey. Living Conditions, Social Exclusion and Mental Well-Being*, Dublin: European Foundation for the Improvement of Living and Working Conditions.

Malnar, B. (2011), 'Trendi neenakosti v Sloveniji med statistiko in javnim mnenjem', *Teorija in praksa* 4, 48; p. 951–967.

Mandič, Srna, (2000), Trends in Central Eastern European rented sectors. V: Priemus, H. (ed.), Mandič, Srna (ed.). 'Special Issue: Rented housing in Eastern and Central Europe', *Journal of Housing and the Built Environment*, Vol. 15, no. 3. Dordrecht: Kluwer Academic Publishers, pp. 217–231.

Mandič, S., Filipovič Hrast, M. (2008), 'Homelessness "in Transition": A Slovenian Study', in Doherty, J, and Edgar, B. (eds.), *In my caravan, I feel like superman: essays in Honour of Henk Meert 1963– 2006*. St. Andrews: FEANTSA: Centre for Housing Research, St. Andrews, pp. 127–143.

Noč, M. (2011), *Kazalniki zadolženosti Slovenije. Statistični dnevi 2011*, SURS

OECD (2011), *Divided We Stand: Why Inequality Keeps Rising*, OECD Publishing, *http://dx.doi. org/10.1787/9789264119536-en*.

Rakar, T., Deželan, T., Vrbica S. Š., Kolarič, Z., Črnak Meglič, A., Nagode, M. (2011), *Civilna družba v Sloveniji. Uradni list RS*, Ljubljana: Ministrstvo za javno upravo.

Stanojević, M. (2000), 'Slovenian trade unions. The birth of labour organisations in post-communism', *Družboslovne razprave* 16 (32-33):39–52.

Stanovnik T., Verbič M. (2012a), 'The Distribution of Wages and Employee Incomes in Slovenia, 1991– 2009'. *IB revija* Vol. XLVI No.1 Umar, pp. 57–70.

Stanovnik T., Verbič M. (2012b), The Distribution of Wages and Employee Incomes in Slovenia, 1991–2009, *Working Paper No. 60*, Ljubljana: Institute for Economic Research.

Stanovnik, T., Verbič, M. (2008), 'Changes in the Earnings Distribution in Slovenia During Rapid Growth, 1991–2005', *MPRA Paper* no. 13101.

Stanovnik, T., Verbič, M. (2005), 'Wage and Income Inequality in Slovenia, 1993–2002', *Post-Communist Economies*, Vol. 17, No. 3, 2005, *381-397.* Available at: <http://www.tandfonline.com/doi/abs/10.1080/14631370500204412> (3 November 2012).

SORS (Statistical Office of Republic of Slovenia); <http://www.stat.si>

SORS (Statistical Office of Republic of Slovenia) (2011), 'Naseljena stanovanja, Slovenija, 1. januar 2011—začasni podatki'. Available at: <http://www.stat.si/novica_prikazi.aspx?id=4420> (5 January 2013)

Tomšič M. (2008), 'Historical Development of Slovenian Political Elite', *Innovative Issues and Approaches in Social Sciences* 1, (2): 47–65.

Toš, N. (2004), *Vrednote v prehodu 3 SJM 1999–2004*, Ljubljana: FDV.

Toš, N. (2007), '(Ne)zaupanje v institucije: potek demokratične institucionalizacije v Sloveniji (1991–2006)', *Teorija in praksa* 44 (3-4):367–395.

CHAPTER 26

....

SPAIN: WHAT CAN WE LEARN FROM PAST DECREASING INEQUALITIES?

....

ADA FERRER-I-CARBONELL, XAVIER RAMOS,

AND MÓNICA OVIEDO

1. INTRODUCTION AND CONTEXT

....

OVER the last 30 years, Spain has gone through considerable political, institutional, and socio-economic changes that started with the end of the dictatorship in 1975 and the approval of the current constitution in 1978. During these years, the country has set the basis of the current political, social, economic, and welfare structure, including the expansion of the education and health system, the building of a modern fiscal (taxes and expenditures) system, the strengthening of a Welfare State, the introduction of several very important labour market reforms, and the promotion of female participation in the labour market and in social life. In 1986, Spain became a member of the European Community and this eased and further accelerated the changes that had started less than 10 years before. These changes were, however, not always very successful in generating an increase in productivity and human capital accumulation, or in changing the productive structure of the country. This has all contributed to shaping current income and social inequalities. Although, over the studied period (1985 to date), inequality has, in contrast with most OECD countries, notably decreased, the factors contributing to this reduction are not always based on solid pillars and the current crisis may now exacerbate inequality more than in other countries. In fact, inequality reduction seems to be counter-cyclical, as it has increased only during the two recessions: notably, the one in which we are currently immersed.

GDP per capita has increased since 1985, with periods of exceptional growth. In 1987–1989, 1995, and 1998–2000, GDP per capita growth was between 4.5 and 5 per cent. Only twice has GDP per capita fallen or experienced a very small increase (1992–1993 and since 2008).[1] GDP per capita at market prices in purchasing power almost doubled from €13,400 in 1995 to €24,700 in 2011. Nevertheless, Spain has, since 2008, been immersed in a very severe recession, with high unemployment rates, considerable private household debt, and little hope for the economic situation.[2]

Spain is a large (506,000 km² and 47 million inhabitants) and very diverse country, with important economic, social, cultural, and linguistic regional differences. Spanish regions are very different in terms of their economic and productive structures, although differences have been reduced during the last twenty-five years, at a non-constant rate. De la Fuente (2001) reports larger regional convergence in terms of both income per capita and output per job for the 1975–1985 period than for the 1985–1995 period. Per capita income convergence during the latter period is largely due to differences in infrastructure investment for which the EU structural funds were used (De la Fuente, 2008).

Over the years, central government has transferred some public services (notably health, education, and some transportation) to the 17 regional governments, although tax collection has been kept centralized in Madrid, with the exception of the Basque Country and Navarra. Devolution of public services to the regions could have led to increasing regional divergence on top of the already existing historical regional differences in economic, productive, and social structure. The little available evidence, however, shows that this is not the case. For example, López Casanovas *et al.* (2005) find that regional disparities in health are not related to the decentralization of the health system. Instead, many regional differences relate to pre-existing conditions, such as in the amount of private versus public provision of health or education.

Over the period, the education and the health system were modernized to bring education and health care to all. Several reforms shaped a universal education system, increased funding and quality, and set school leaving age and tracking at 16. Despite the indisputable improvements, as discussed in Section 2, the education system performs very poorly, with meagre educational achievements and polarized outcomes. Health care has been given to everybody irrespective of their country of origin and tax contribution since 1986.

Another important feature of the economy is its peculiar labour market, distinguished by large unemployment rates and the duality between permanent workers with high employment protection and a large percentage of workers on temporary contracts. While Spain is among the countries with the highest work protection index (OECD, 2008), temporary (fixed-term) contracts cover a large share of employment and are a dead end rather than a stepping stone to permanent jobs (Dolado, García-Serrano and Jimeno, 2002). The large share of temporary employment not only has an impact on inequality, especially in times of economic downturn, as these are the most vulnerable workers, but it also generates income volatility (Cervini-Plá and Ramos, 2012).

---

[1] Eurostat data and the Spanish National Statistics Institute, INE.

[2] 99 per cent of the Eurobaromter Spanish respondents report that the current economic situation in Spain is 'bad', while only 1 per cent responds that is 'good'. http://ec.europa.eu/public_opinion/archives/eb/eb77/eb77_first_en.pdf

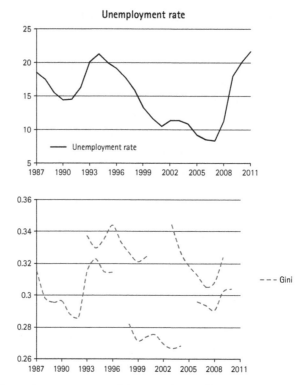

FIGURE 26.1 Unemployment rate and income inequality

Gini, own calculations (equivalized disposable income, OECD modified scale). Some inequality trends overlap for some years, as they are derived from different data sets. For the periods 1993–1996 and 1998–2000, the lower inequality trends use HBS data, while the upper inequality trend uses ECHP data (see Section 2 for further details).

Source: Unemployment rate, Spanish National Statistics Institute INE.

The traditionally high unemployment rates is the other salient feature of the labour market. As Figure 26.1 shows, the unemployment rate was at its lowest before the current crisis, but it already reached 26 per cent in the fourth quarter of 2012.[3]

As expected, unemployment affects mostly the lower tail of the distribution, thus raising earnings (and income) inequality (Pijoan-Mas and Sánchez-Marcos, 2010 and Figure 26.1). The young, the less-educated, and immigrants are over-represented among the unemployed. Although unemployment inequality across socio-economic groups is a widespread phenomenon around the Western world, the high unemployment rates in Spain make this problem more pressing.

The massive and unprecedented immigration is another striking feature of Spain's recent history, representing over 12 per cent of the population in 2011. Attracted by the economic boom of the 2000s and the relative scarcity of labour, they are now severely hit by the

---

[3] Spanish National Statistics Institute, INE.

recession, displaying, for instance, unemployment rates ten percentage points higher than the native population.

2. Evolution of Inequality and its Drivers

Income Inequality

Unlike most of the OECD countries, income inequality did not increase for most of the sample period. Over the last 25 years, has Spain experienced two periods of pronounced inequality reduction, each truncated by the arrival of a recession and followed by a period of inequality increase, which only partly offset the previous reduction. Thus, inequality seems to be lower in 2010 than in 1985—unless data breaks and gaps mislead us.[4] These trends are robust to different ways of measuring inequality (Gini coefficient, mean log deviation—MLD, half squared coefficient of variation, and variance of logs),[5] to the inclusion of imputed rents,[6] and to different equivalence scales. Figure 26.2 shows the inequality trends of two equivalent income definitions, following the OECD and the Modified OECD equivalent scales.

These inequality trends, however, have to be taken with caution, as Spain does not have a coherent series of data covering the 30-year period that ranges from 1980 to 2010. Instead, one has to rely on five different data sets.[7] All these five data sets are representative of the population but have important methodological differences, which render them not fully comparable. Also, the definition of the available income variables is not exactly the same across data sets. Hence, income inequality trends cannot be analysed in a coherent manner for the whole period of analysis, but ought to be examined within each data set. Furthermore, the trends shown by the HBS1998–2004 and the HBS2006–2010 should be taken with caution as incomes are originally reported in wide brackets and thus contain some imputation for about 80 per cent of households.[8] This helps explain why they report lower inequality than the other series.

---

[4] In addition to data consistency, we do not have reliable data for the years 2000–2003. Nevertheless, Bonhomme and Hospido (2012) report decreasing earnings inequality for this period.

[5] See Figure 2.1 in the country report (Ferrer-i-Carbonell, Ramos, and Oviedo, 2012).

[6] Including imputed rents in the definition of income does not modify the inequality trend for the period 2003–2009, as the EU-SILC is the only data set that provides information on imputed rents.

[7] The Household Budget Survey (HBS), which covers the period 1985–1996; the European Household Community Panel (ECHP), which has information on income from 1993 to 2000; the Household Budget Survey, providing information from 1998 to 2004; the European Union Survey on Income and Living Conditions (EU-SILC), with information on incomes from 2003 to 2009; and the Household Budget Survey covering the period 2006 to 2010. The first two HBS (1985–1996) and (1998–2004) are the Encuesta Contínua de Presupuestos Familiares, while the last HBS (2006–2010) is the Encuesta de Presupuestos Familiares.

[8] Precisely because of this, many scholars have not used the HBS to examine the distribution of income, see for instance Pijoan-Mas and Sánchez-Marcos (2010). Since only the HBS includes information on household consumption, the HBS income series is useful for comparing consumption and income inequality trends below.

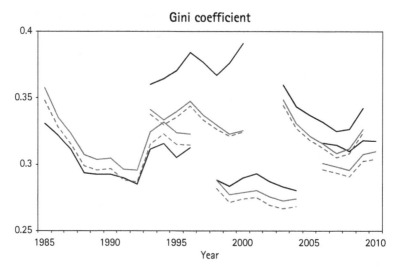

FIGURE 26.2 After-tax after-transfers income inequality trends

Legend: solid line is disposable income; dashed line is equivalent disposable income (OECD); dotted line is equivalent disposable income (modified OECD).

Source: own calculations.

The first pronounced income equalization period, which was truncated by the economic recession of 1993, has already been documented (see, among others, Oliver, Ramos and Raymond, 2001), and it has been partly attributed to wage compression and the equalizing effect of the enhanced tax and benefit system, which managed a much larger budget and increased the progressivity of the tax system (Ayala and Sastre, 2007). Due to the lack of a coherent series of data, it is not possible to pin down the beginning of this period. Notwithstanding this, the few studies, which make use of the two HBS of 1973 and 1980, find that, despite the oil shocks of the 1970s and 1980s, inequality falls slightly.

The economic recession of 1993 breaks off the long-standing decreasing inequality trend. What it is more difficult to say is whether inequality has remained constant or, rather, has increased in the years after the crisis, since the two data sets that cover the post-1993 recession period (HBS 1985–1996 and ECHP) yield inequality estimates which go in opposite directions.[9] According to the HBS 1985–96, income inequality moves erratically around a flat trend, while the ECHP data report an upward-sloping trend of rising inequality until year 2000. Taking into account the effects of family composition and scale economies through equivalent scales, however, changes the picture, as now equivalent income inequality decreases for the post-recession period.

The second period with a sharp fall in inequality has not been properly examined yet. Again, due to lack of data, it is difficult to say when this period began. The EU-SILC data starting in 2003 reports a substantial fall until 2008, when the recession hits the economy and growth contracts abruptly (2.6 pp, from 3.5 per cent to 0.9 per cent). Following the same

[9] Such differences in the overlapping years of the HBS 1985–1996 and the ECHP have already been noticed by other studies, e.g. Ayala and Sastre (2007) and Pijoan-Mas and Sánchez-Marcos (2010).

pattern as in the last crisis, after the downturn of 2008, inequality increases until 2010, the last year for which data are available.

Clearly recessions exacerbate inequality.[10] Given that unemployment behaves much the same way, one is inclined to conjecture that unemployment might be driving inequality up in such periods of hardship, as many households loose at least one of their income sources.

Changes at the top and bottom ends of the distribution seem to be partly driving the reported inequality trends. Over the two periods of strong inequality decrease, the income shares of the better-off, i.e. the top 10 and 5 per cent of the population, fall, while those of the worse-off, i.e. the bottom 10 and 5 per cent of the population, increase.

Whom has it Affected?

The overall inequality trend can be accounted for by changes in differences between mean incomes of population groups or by changing inequality for each of the groups. This section presents the results of decomposing the MLD into a 'between' component, which captures the disparities between the different population groups, and a 'within' component, constructed as a weighted average of the inequality of each group, where the weights are the population shares of each group.[11] Our decomposition analysis only uses data from the ECHP (1993–2000) and EU-SILC (2003–2009), as the HBS 1995–1996 does not contain information on the socio-economic characteristics of the household members, but only of the head of the household. It is unfortunate that we do not have information to analyse the first period of decreasing inequality, but at least we can examine the second period of falling inequality and the two post-crisis periods, where inequality increased.[12]

We partition the population in seven ways: (i) by gender: males versus females; (ii) in six age groups (defined as less than 26 years old, 26 to 35, 36 to 45, 46 to 55, 56 to 65, and over 65); (iii) for workers by age group (less than 26, 26 to 35, 36 to 55, and 56 to 65); (iv) by educational level (primary, secondary and tertiary); (v) by labour market status, that is, employed versus non-employed, the latter including unemployed and inactive individuals; (vi) by immigration status (immigrants versus non-immigrants); and (vii) by region (where regions are defined by NUTS1, i.e., Northwest, Northeast, Madrid, Centre, East, South, and Canary Islands).

The first conclusion we can draw from the decompositions is that, irrespective of how groups are defined, the 'within inequality' component follows a parallel trend to that of overall inequality. The analysis reveals that the 'between' component is quite small for most of the splits, accounting for a small percentage of overall inequality that ranges from less than 0.5 per cent for gender or immigration to 12 per cent for education groups. This means that most of the action happens inside the groups and not between them. The only distinctions

---

[10] Bonhomme and Hospido (2012) find the same counter-cyclical pattern for earnings inequality.

[11] We choose to decompose the Mean Log Deviation, and not any other index of the Generalized Entropy Family, precisely because the MLD is the only one that uses population shares to aggregate within group inequality, when computing the 'within' component—see Cowell (2011).

[12] Trends in the 'between' and 'within' components, as well as the trend of inequality within each population subgroup' are shown in Tables 2.22 to 2.24 in the companion country study (Ferrer-i-Carbonell, Ramos, and Oviedo, 2012).

that account for a relevant percentage (more than 5 per cent) of overall inequality are education groups, regions, and labour market status. We now turn our attention to these splits.

First, the 'between' and 'within' education groups inequality components track the overall inequality trend. The fall in inequality between the mean incomes of the three education groups may be the result of the similar evolution of the tertiary education premium until 2006, reported by Pijoan-Mas and Sánchez-Marcos (2010) and Lacuesta and Izquierdo (2012). Second, contrary to our intuition, inequality between employed and non-employed individuals decreases right after the recession of 1993 and increases as the recession wanes, precisely when job creation increases and unemployment falls. In the 2000s, however, disparities between employed and non-employed decrease irrespective of the business cycle. Third, while regional disparities track overall income inequality for the end of the 1990s, they are counter-cyclical for the 2000s. With regards to inequality for each of the groups it is worth noting that, while for the 2008 recession all employed age groups displayed similar inequality trends, for the post-recession period of 1993 young workers between 26 and 35 years saw their inequality increase until year 2000. Inequality for all other groups behaves much the same way as overall income inequality.

Why has Inequality Decreased? (Though it Would be Expected to Rise in The Coming Years)

The behaviour of income inequality can be explained by changes in the distribution of labour market incomes and changes in the redistributive role of the government—as other market incomes are a small share of overall household income and thus have a small effect on income inequality, despite their very unequal distribution. We discuss redistributive policies in Section 5, and consider the labour market here.

It has been argued that an important contributor to the income inequality decrease has been wage compression or wage inequality reduction, extensively documented in, *inter alia*: Bonhomme and Hospido, 2012; Lacuesta and Izquierdo, 2012; OECD, 2011, *Divided We Stand*; Pijoan-Mas and Sánchez-Marcos, 2010; Arellano, Bentolila and Bover, 2002.

Several factors may explain the evolution of earnings inequality: the changing educational composition and reduction in the skill premium; changes in the large percentage of temporary employment and its relative wages; the employment and wage effects of the demand shock that results from the construction boom and subsequent bust; increased female participation; the large immigration inflow; and the huge unemployment rates that characterize the Spanish labour market.

The reduction in the wage differential across education levels may have offset the increase of tertiary education, thus reducing wage inequality. Returns to tertiary education have fallen since the 1980s (Lacuesta and Izquierdo, 2012; Pijoan-Mas and Sánchez-Marcos, 2010; Felgueroso *et al.*, 2010).[13] This may the result of the increasing number of individuals with tertiary education and the incapacity of the productive system to absorb the more skilled labour supply. Indeed, occupational mismatch is one of the causes behind the fall in

---

[13] Even though most of the available evidence consistently points to a reduction in returns to tertiary education, some studies find the opposite. As a result, Arellano, Bentolila and Bover (2002) find that wage dispersion has increased at the top.

the wage skill premium (Felgueroso *et al.*, 2010). The fall in the wage skill premium is also explained by the increasing use of temporary employment, which reduces experience and tenure among properly-matched workers.

Temporary employment boomed as a result of the 1984 labour market reform, remaining at the very high levels of around one third of overall employment until the current economic downturn, when it dropped to one forth. The earnings gap between temporary and permanent workers narrowed from the late 1990s until the current economic downturn but widened after 2007 (Bonhomme and Hospido, 2012). The initial increase in the relative earnings and employment share of temporary employment, and the subsequent decrease of its share in the total employment have contributed to the evolution of earnings inequality. This evolution of temporary employment is very much related to employment and earnings developments in the construction sector, where about two thirds are temporary jobs. Thus the increase in the employment and relative earnings increase of construction workers contributed to reduce earnings inequality, since these workers are located at the lower-middle part of the earnings distribution (Bonhomme and Hospido, 2012).

The decrease in tenure and seniority, partly brought about by the increase in temporary employment, also contributed to reducing inequality after the mid 1990s, according to Lacuesta and Izquierdo (2012). Individuals with lower tenure have lower mean earnings, but they are also more homogeneous among themselves. Since the 'within inequality' component of this group seems to be more important than the 'between' component, the reduction in tenure helps explain the earnings reduction over the ten years before the crisis.

It is interesting to notice that while returns to education fell, returns to tenure took the opposite direction over the same period. Lacuesta and Izquierdo (2012) argue that while unions have exerted pressure to contain education-related wage differences, they did not object much to the dual labour market. This has been to the disadvantage of temporary and young employees with typically low levels of seniority and education.

The substantive increase in female participation does not seem to have contributed much to the reduction in inequality (Gradin and Otero, 2001; Lacuesta and Izquierdo, 2012). Increased female labour force participation has two effects on inequality, which operate in opposite directions. On the one hand, female mean earnings are lower than men's, which may increase inequality through the 'between inequality' component. On the other hand, since the 'within' dispersion of earnings is lower for women than for men, the increasing share of women in the labour market reduces 'within' wage inequality. These effects are mostly compositional, as the wage structure (female relative to male wages) did not change much during the period and played no role in inequality changes.

Another determinant of household (and not individual) income inequality is the role of assortative mating. If the entrance of women into the labour market disproportionally meant that richer households became two-earner households, household income inequality would have increased. This seems to be what has occurred in recent years.

In addition to changes in composition, and in the wage structure, the number of working hours has also contributed to reducing inequality, as the bottom of the wage distribution has increased the working hours while the top slightly reduced them (OECD, 2011, *Divided We Stand*).

The unprecedented immigration inflow since the beginning of the century has had a very limited effect on earnings inequality, as the native-immigrant earnings gap did not change much over the relevant period between 2000 and 2007. With the recession, the earnings gap widened but participation decreased (Bonhomme and Hospido, 2012).

Both changes in composition and in the wage structure account for the earnings inequality decrease observed from the mid 1990s to the current downturn. Moreover, Lacuesta and Izquierdo (2012) find that composition changes would have increased inequality, had there been no accompanying changes in the wage structure. The rising earnings inequality observed since the Great Recession can be accounted for solely by compositional changes.

The most important factors which shape the falling inequality trend in market incomes, are the decreasing wage premiums and the employment and earnings effects brought about by the housing boom and bust, which in turn is related to the developments of temporary employment (Lacuesta and Izquierdo, 2012; Bonhomme and Hospido, 2012).

Unemployment is another important factor when trying to understand inequality trends in Spain. As Figure 26.1 shows, unemployment and inequality trends seem to be mirror images. For instance, OECD (2011, *Divided We Stand*) argues that the high employment rate during the last economic boom accounts for near 70 per cent of the overall earnings inequality reduction. Unemployment affects job opportunities, hitting low-skilled and young individuals disproportionately. Therefore, it contributes to increasing income inequality, and again assortative mating exacerbates this effect.

Consumption and Wealth

From the mid 1980s to the early 1990s consumption inequality trends have been flatter and smoother than income inequality trends. This is the only period for which there is reliable data on both consumption and income. In the boom years at the start of the new century, consumption inequality decreases; but then increases with the recession.

Wealth inequality is also lower in Spain than in many other countries (Bover *et al.*, 2005) mainly due to the extremely high percentage—92 per cent in 2000—of house ownership, a prominent feature of the economy (Azpitarte, 2010). This has contributed to reducing wealth inequality during the period for which we have data, i.e. the last economic boom, but may accentuate inequality during the current crisis. These days, many households have large debts, over very long time periods (20–30 years), and variable interest rates, which makes them very vulnerable to financial cycles. Private (and also household) debt is currently very high and it is one of the main features of the on-going crisis.

Educational Inequality

Education has also experienced tremendous changes. As in the rest of Europe, attainment in Spain has increased significantly over the last decades, with an increase in the number of years of education. According to the data set put together by Meschi and Scervini (2010), mean years of education went from just below 5 for the 1920–1929 cohort to above 14 for the most recent 1980–1984 cohort. Such improvement results from an ever-increasing budget and several reforms, two of which are especially important. The first one, the Ley General de Educación (LGE) in 1970 extended compulsory education from 6 to 14 years old; and the second one, the Ley Orgánica General del Sistema Educativo (LOGSE) enacted in 1990, increased compulsory education further, now from 14 to 16 years old.

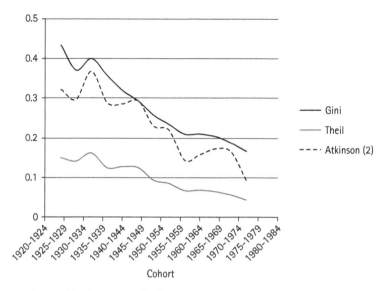

FIGURE 26.3 Inequality in years of education

Source: Meschi and Scervini (2010).

Despite all these changes and improvements in the education system and despite the clear increase in educational achievements and expenditures, Spain has generated over recent years a polarized society with a fairly large proportion of individuals—at least among the young—with tertiary education and another large proportion of drop-outs or individuals with low secondary education—low qualifications and short vocational programmes— (this is also true when looking only at the younger generations) (OECD, 2011, *Education at a Glance*). In other words, Spain is similar (although performing slightly worse) to Italy or Greece, and (performing slightly better than) Portugal in terms of individuals with at most secondary education, but it fares better than countries such as Italy, Greece, Germany, Finland, Austria, the Netherlands, and the UK, when it comes to its population shares with tertiary education. Furthermore, Spain has a very poor performance at secondary school, ranking amongst the very lowest among European countries participating in PISA (Felgueroso *et al.*, 2011).

In spite of the increased polarization of educational performance, the substantial increase in years of education has been accompanied by a decrease in educational inequality. As Figure 26.3 shows, 'within cohort' inequality has at least halved from the oldest 1920–24 cohort to the youngest 1980–84 cohort.

Tracking is an important feature of education systems, which affects inequality as well as average performance. Compared to other European countries, Spain tracks late. Such late selection may be partly responsible for the high drop-out rates at secondary education, as earlier tracking might have allowed some drop outs to successfully complete vocational training. It might also contribute to the considerable intergenerational mobility in education, relative to other European countries (see below).

The high drop-out rates and the increased numbers of individuals with low educational attainment have clear consequences for income inequality. First, since unemployment rates differ largely across education groups, job opportunities are reduced for the worse off individuals; this is especially relevant in a country with such large unemployment rates. Second, inequalities in education translate to wage disparities. This is relevant even though returns to higher education have fallen over the last years.

Intergenerational Persistence

Inequalities are considered to be especially objectionable when they persist from parents to offspring. Even though Spain usually shows larger inequality levels than most European countries, be it in terms of income, earnings or education, intergenerational persistence is relatively low compared to similar countries.

Intergenerational earnings and income mobility in Spain is similar to France, lower than in the Nordic countries and Britain, and higher than in Italy and the United States (Cervini-Plá, 2009). Cervini-Plá and Ramos (2013) find that assortative mating plays an important role in the intergenerational transmission process. On average about 50 per cent of the covariance between parents' income and a child's family's income can be accounted for by the person the child is married to.

As far as education is concerned, recent empirical evidence shows that intergenerational persistence is relatively low and decreasing over time (Schuetz *et al.*, 2008). Family background plays a smaller role in determining individuals' own education,[14] and the importance of parental education on children's educational attainment has decreased over the cohorts. Notwithstanding this, persistence is still relevant for tertiary education, as the probability of obtaining tertiary education is still remarkably larger for individuals whose parents have tertiary, and to a less extent, upper secondary education.

Intergenerational persistence in occupations is also found to be low, relative to other European countries (Raitano and Vona, 2011). However, these same authors find a larger intergenerational transmission of informal forms of social and human capital than in other EU countries, as measured by the residual correlation (controlling for child occupation and education) between parental background and children's labour income.

3. Social Impacts

Since the reestablishment of democracy, Spain has seen the development and expansion of social and welfare improving policies, such as health and education policies, the development of pensions schemes, unemployment, and to a lesser extent other social benefits for the least advantaged. Social expenditures relative to GDP have steadily increased up to the year 2000. This has certainly helped mitigate the social inequalities documented in this chapter, which go hand in hand with the fairly steady decrease of inequality over the last 25 years. It is important to keep in mind, however, that social expenditures as a percentage of GDP have

---

[14] This may be suggestive evidence of a positive effect of late tracking on intergenerational mobility (Hanushek and Woessmann, 2006).

remained throughout the entire period much below those of many other European countries and the average of the EU27 and EU25.[15]

Social inequalities have a clear socio-economic gradient, notably related to education and income. The decreasing income inequality that Spain has experienced over the recent years has certainly helped to reduce social inequalities. Education polarization, however, has increased in the last years and is an important determinant of current social inequalities. Similarly, labour market inequalities (for example if measured by the socio-economic gradient of unemployment and temporary work) have also contributed to shaping social inequalities, such as poverty and social exclusion.

In addition to the socio-economic origin of social inequalities, Spain also shows important regional differences. Although the period has been characterized by regional convergence, there are still differences generated not only by the different economic structures of the regions but also by regional differences in public finances for both tax collection and expenditures. Public service transfers to the regions, however, seem not to have contributed to increasing inequalities (López Casanovas *et al.*, 2005).

Although Spain is among the countries with the lowest percentage of individuals reporting material deprivation (EU-SILC data 2004–2010), it ranks fairly low when looking at the risk of poverty. This means that although there are many households at risk of relative poverty, this is not reflected in their reported consumption patterns. Observation of the long-term evolution of poverty is hampered by data consistency but with this limitation we can say that poverty fell from 20 per cent to less than 16 per cent in the first period of economic growth (1985–1992/3). It increased to 18–19 per cent afterwards and stayed there despite the economic boom of the 2000–2007 period. In fact, since 2004, poverty has slightly increased, to about 20 per cent, and, according to recent data for the current recession, it has increased even further, reaching levels found prior to 1985. This picture based on relative poverty is fairly consistent with the findings of Ayala *et al.* (2011), which are based on defining poverty as the proportion of households with no labour income or any social benefit. This means that while in the first period (until the 1992/3 crisis) inequality and poverty decreased together, thereafter falling inequality has not been accompanied by poverty reduction.

Eurostat data (available from 2004 onwards) indicates that social exclusion is greater than the EU15 average and has increased since 2008 with the beginning of the current economic crisis.

Poverty and social exclusion have an important education gradient, despite the wage compression experienced over the last years. For example, relative to individuals with tertiary education, the risk of social exclusion and the poverty of individuals with low levels of education is three times as large (Eurostat, 2009). Similarly, poverty has an important regional component: for instance, the region with the largest share of individuals in relative poverty (Extremadura), has a poverty rate five times higher than the region with lowest levels of poverty (Navarra).

---

[15] Spanish National Statistics Institute and Eurostat statistics.

Family, Health, and Housing

Family formation has also seen rapid change: a falling number of marriages over the last 40 years, an increasing average age at marriage, and an increasing number of family breakdowns; although the number of single mothers is very low. Spain has also seen a tremendous decrease in its fertility rate and an increase in mothers' age at birth of first child. This is related to the many social changes that have taken place, such as the increase in female labour participation and the divorce law introduced in 1981. These changes are related to the rapid social transformations that Spain has experienced since democracy. Increased female labour force participation and changes in society have accentuated changes in family formation. As argued in Section 2, these changes have had no clear impact on income inequality.

Although the Spanish National Health System (SNHS) guarantees universal health care access to everybody irrespective of their country of origin, residence status, and tax contribution, a large percentage (which varies across regions) of health services are provided privately. The use of private health services is correlated with individual income. In addition, health inequalities may arise from health behaviour that in turn correlates with income, labour market status (e.g., health at work varies across occupations), education, and origin. Another inequality dimension of health may result from regional differences. It is believed that health provision and quality vary depending on the degree of urbanization (with rural areas having worse health services) and the autonomous region. Thus, the reduction in income inequality and in regional differences experienced during the period should have contributed to reducing health inequalities. Existing data, however, do not allow us to study long-term changes and the small amount of existing empirical evidence points to the opposite. This evidence, may be partly explained by Deaton's (2002) observation that income redistribution policies are typically accompanied by other social policies that tend to benefit more individuals at higher education levels, with higher incomes and with better health.

The empirical evidence shows a clear socio-economic gradient in subjective health inequality (Blanco and Ramos, 2010; Regidor *et al.*, 2002). Using the incidence of four chronic illnesses (heart, diabetes, bronchitis/asthma, and allergies) and a measure of self-reported health, Regidor *et al.* (2002) find that health inequalities have an education and social class gradient. According to the same source, health inequality has, for some health measures, increased from 1987 to 1997. In spite of this, Van Doorslaer and Koolman (2004) found that, in 1996, Spain was among the countries with a smaller self-assessed health inequality across income groups. Comparison across regions is not straightforward as the age structure also differs largely. Nevertheless, one can fairly safely conclude that regional health disparities are large when using SNHS[16] (2006) data.

An important problem for households is their current large debts, which can bring many individuals into a very vulnerable financial situation that can lead to increasing poverty, social exclusion, and inequailty. In recent years, government policies have promoted homeownership and the international financial markets have lent money to Spain at a relatively low interest rate. The high rates of homeownership contributed to a relatively low wealth inequality (Section 2). In fact, the socio-economic gradient on homeownership is fairly negligible, except for migration status: permanent residents from non-EU15 countries,

---

[16] Spanish National Health System.

temporary residents, and undocumented inmmigrants have a lower rate of homeownership even after controling for individual and household characteristics (Amuedo-Dorantes and Mundra, 2012).

Despite the contribution of homeownership to reducing wealth inequalities in the past, current household debts on mortgages (and other credits) are unsustainable. This may explain why homeownership has fallen to less than 84 per cent, while it was 92 per cent in 2001. In the current financial crisis, many households can neither pay the mortgage nor sell the house. The housing price index (Spanish average) was 83.44 in 2011, but 100 in 2007. In addition, there are very important and large regional differences. In 2011, the index was, for example, 73.13 in Catalonia, 77.53 in Madrid, and 91.32 in Andalusia (100 in 2007). This difference in price drops can have consequences for regional differences in household income (net of wealth) inequality in the following years. The 'household overburden rate', as defined by Eurostat, which is the percentage of the population living in a household with total housing costs (net of housing allowances) larger than 40 per cent of the total disposable income, was 11.2 per cent in 2010 (in 2005 it was just above 4 per cent). Although there is no data to study recent wealth inequality, the current household debt situation and the fall in house ownership over recent years is bound to lead to an increase in wealth inequality. Since the impact of the household debt crisis varies largely across regions and has affected the richest regions more, it may contribute to a decrease in regional differences.

4. Political and Cultural Impacts

One form of political participation and social engagement is election turnout. In Spain these are a bit lower than in the rest of Western countries: turnout in general elections is just above the OECD average (OECD, 2011). As in most countries, voter turnout depends on the type of elections, being highest for general elections (70 to 80 per cent), followed by regional or municipal elections (around 65 per cent), and with the lowest turnout being for the European Parliament elections.[17]

Researchers argue that voter turnout and its evolution over time depends mostly on the political situation and other contextual variables rather than on individual characteristics, such as income or education. For example, the largest turnouts in Spain since the advent of democracy (1980) were: for the general elections of 1982, just after the failed coup of Tejero in 1981; in 2004, where, after the march bombing in Madrid, participation was greater than for the adjacent periods; and in the Catalan elections in 2012, when independence entered the political debate for the first time. Boix and Riba (2000) conclude that, in contrast to the US, an individual's decision to participate in Spanish elections depends largely on the political context (e.g., the weight one's vote has, how much interest the individual takes in the electoral campaign, or the level of social capital in the region) rather than on an individual's socio-economic characteristics, with the exception of age. OECD raw data is consistent with these results, placing Spain among the countries in which (except for age) the importance of education and income is the lowest in determining voting (OECD, 2011). In

---

[17] Spanish Ministry of Internal affairs.

fact, the OECD report 'Better Life index' reports that in Spain (together with Ireland and New Zealand) individuals in the bottom 20 per cent of the income distribution actually have a greater probability of voting than those at the top, although the difference is very small. Although there is no study linking voter turnout to income inequality, data imply that there is no clear link: the last two parliamentary elections (2008 and 2011) when the economic crisis had already hit and income inequality was increasing, were the ones with the lowest participation since the arrival of democracy (1977). The other income-inequality increasing period (around 1993) however had fairly large participation.

Political values have evolved over the years. The CIS (Centro de Investigaciones Sociológicas) produces a barometer in which respondents are asked to position themselves on a scale of 1 to 10, going from extreme left (1) to extreme right (10). The outcomes show little variation between 1996 and 2012, as the average fluctuates within the 4.5 to 5 interval only. Nevertheless, there is a tendency towards the centre, with most individuals reporting themselves as in the centre (5) or centre-left (4).

Similarly, the shares of individuals positioning themselves on the extreme right or left are very small. For example, in 2010, 3.8 per cent of individuals self-positioned on the extreme right and just a little more than 9 per cent identified themselves as extreme left-wingers. According to the EVS longitudinal data (1981–2008), medium-income households have remained fairly stable in their ideological position, while those at the bottom of the income distribution have moved slightly to the right and those at the top of the income distribution have moved towards the left. This has happened while inequality has been falling, but, for the 1993 recession period, democracy and its institutions were being developed, and a generation of individuals who had lived for 40 years under right-wing dictatorship was vanishing.

An important change for Spain was its admission to the European Community in 1986. Many citizens saw entry as the opportunity to consolidate democracy and to strengthen the institutions that would allow economic and social progress. Currently, Spain is among the countries where the percentage of individuals reporting that 'being a EU member is good' is largest.[18]

An important dimension of civic engagement and social participation is citizens' membership of other informal types of participation in political parties, unions, or other forms of associations. It is important to note that, during the dictatorship (1936–1975), trade unions, political parties, and many other forms of membership were forbidden or strictly controlled. This means that trade unions and political parties went through a difficult period dominated by illegality and the exile. Union membership in Spain has been very low, with a big increase from 1985 to 1993 (from 10 to 18 per cent of employees) and a period of stability around 15–16 per cent since then.[19] The income composition of union members has also changed considerably from a situation in the 1980s in which low-income workers were slightly over-represented among union members to the current situation in which 12 per cent of high-income workers are members of a union, whereas only 5 per cent of low-income workers are.[20] Inequalities in the labour market have contributed to the decrease of union membership, as temporary (mostly young and low paid) workers have no incentives to become

[18] Eurobarometer.
[19] OECD, Labour Force statistics.
[20] EVS (European Value Survey), longitudinal data file 1981–2008.

union members. One of the challenges of unions in the current situation is to attract these workers, as well as 'newly' arrived immigrants, a group that represents a large percentage of the working force.

In the 2006 wave of EU-SILC, respondents were asked about their participation in seven different types of associations. Spain scores around, or above, the EU15 average for participation in informal voluntary activities, professional associations, churches or other religious groups, and charitable organizations. It scores below for participation in political parties or trade unions, recreational groups or organizations, and other types of organizations. The raw data show an income gradient for individuals' participation in these associations: while poor individuals are over-represented as members of churches or other religious groups, the opposite is true for most of the other activities, although differences are fairly small except for membership of recreational groups and organizations. The EVS longitudinal data (file 1981–2008)[21] also records information about membership of various associative organizations. In this dataset, the percentage of citizens participating in various associations is much lower than the EU average. These data show, in addition, that the role of income has changed over time: in 1985, participation was similar across income groups, but the income gradient increased afterwards to again decrease significantly in recent years. Social and political engagement is nevertheless difficult to measure, as the form that it takes changes over time and differs across countries. This has led to some disagreement about the degree of social engagement. For example, while many researchers argue that civic and political participation has been low and decreasing, with the exception of an initial growth during the political transition (around 1977–1982), some find the opposite and argue that young cohorts actually participate more in some type of civic activities (Morales, 2005). This discussion is similar to the one taking place in the international literature, in which there is a debate around the decrease or not of social engagement. The current economic crisis and inequality increase seems to be stimulating social participation in the modern type of civic engagements in Spain.

Trust, Social Isolation, Immigration and Perceptions

Levels of interpersonal trust are fairly low. Although differences exist when comparing data sets, even the most favourable data places Spain below most European countries.[22] In addition, data show that these measures of trust have an income and education gradient. Citizens' trust in government and institutions is fairly large, although this percentage has fallen a lot in recent years.[23] An important political problem is corruption and citizens' ensuing distrust of politics. There is a large number of individuals (75 per cent), who perceive that corruption is widespread in business and government.[24] With the current increase in income and other inequalities, this mistrust seems to be increasing probably due to the feeling of injustice that arises when inequality increases.

[21] See footnote 19.
[22] OECD, *Society at Glance*, 2011 and EVS longitudinal 1981–2008 file.
[23] OECD, *Society at Glance*, 2011; Eurobarometer.
[24] OECD, *Society at Glance*, 2011.

The 2006 wave of the EU-SILC included a set of questions aimed at measuring social isolation in Europe.[25] This module included self-reported questions on the frequency of meeting with friends and family, or on whether respondents had someone to whom to ask for help if needed. For this type of measures, Spain comes over as one of the least isolated countries in Europe.[26] Nevertheless, social isolation is fairly correlated with poverty. The report presents the results for poor (those with an income below 60 per cent of the median of equivalent income) and non-poor separately. Spain is among the countries in which the poor, relatively to the non-poor, are more likely to be isolated: poor people are more than twice as likely to report not to have anyone (relative, friend, or neighbour) to ask for help if needed. The causal relationship however is ambiguous: it may be that poverty causes isolation (poverty hampers maintaining contacts) or that isolation causes poverty (having no ties reduces the possibility of leaving poverty). This might mean that, with the current inequality and poverty increase, social isolation might be increasing. Relative to other EU countries, Spain (together with Belgium, Italy and Portugal) scores particularly high on the frequency of meeting with family. Family ties tend to be considered stronger than friend ties. These ties are helping to overcome some of the social costs of income poverty and inequality increase that Spain has experienced in recent years.

An important and recent change in everyday life has been the massive entrance of immigrants after 2002 (see Section 1). At the same time, attitudes towards immigrants have, according to the EVS longitudinal data file (1981–2008), changed tremendously: while from 1985 until the massive entrance of immigrants in 2002, the percentage of citizens reporting not liking immigrants as neighbours increased enormously, this percentage decreased again in the later years (2008–2010). That is, it seems as if the arrival of immigrants has favoured positive attitudes towards them. People in the low-income group are more likely to dislike immigrants as neighbours than people at the middle of the income distribution, although differences are not large compared with the high-income groups. Therefore, one can also argue that the increase of positive attitudes towards immigrants is related to the economic growth and income inequality reduction that Spain has experienced over the last 25 years. This would mean that attitudes towards immigrants might change in the near future.

Another important aspect of individuals' political and social attitudes is how they perceive income inequality. Data from the ISSP[27] (1999) and the Latinobarometer (2001, 2007, 2009) show that around 85 per cent of citizens agree to some extent with statements like 'differences in income are too large' or 'the distribution of income is unfair'. This percentage has remained fairly stable over the years, despite the reduction in income inequality. This may be partly due to the fact that income inequality is larger than in other EU countries or to the fact that Spain has seen an important polarization process both in the labour market and in education outcomes, which individuals can perceive more easily than income inequalities. Iglesias et al. (2012) examine the role of individual socio-economic background on shaping preferences for equality and find that, in 1995, years of education correlated negatively with preferences for redistribution, whilst, in the mid 2000s, income and age were the variables defining preference for redistributions. This indicates that Spain has moved into the group of countries for which income equality is a luxury good. García-Valiñas et al. (2008) find

---

[25]   Eurostat report 'Social Participation Statistics'.
[26]   See footnote 9.
[27]   International Social Survey Programme.

important regional differences in preferences for redistribution, and argue that preferences for equality are larger in regions with more inequality, i.e. regional differences in taste may be related to inequality differences. The time evolution of attitudes towards the poor can be examined using EVS data. This data shows that, while at the beginning of the 1990s, 24 per cent of respondents thought that poverty was caused by laziness or lack of willpower, this percentage fell by 6 points at the beginning of the 2000s, although it has increased again at the end of this decade.

5. POLICIES

The policies that have a most important role in shaping inequality are those related to public services (notably health and education), progressive income taxation (through redistribution), transfers to alleviate poverty and social exclusion, transfers that insure against shocks and that maintain rents (given the large unemployment rates, unemployment benefits play a key role, while increasing pensions lifted incomes at the bottom), labour market reforms (labour market reforms have created a segmented labour market), and policies influencing labour income (notably minimum wage and wage bargaining policies).

The wage and earnings compression observed over the last thirty years resulted mostly from undesirable factors, such as fall in the skill premium, the large increase of construction workers, most of them with temporary contracts, located at the lower-middle part of the distribution, the increase of working hours at the bottom end of the distribution, or a centralized wage bargaining structure, which conceals differences in productivity across firms and hinders productivity growth. Still, the labour market policies that have been introduced since 1980 did not manage to correct any of these factors but, rather, were detrimental not only for the performance of the labour market but also for earnings inequality.

After the introduction of a new fixed-term contract with lower severance pay in the 1984 reform, the temporary employment share surged to one third, segmenting the labour market between temporary workers with lower pay and worse job conditions and permanent workers with better pay and higher protection. During the 1990s and the early 2000s several reforms were enacted in order to end this duality, with no success.

Wage bargaining is at the provincial industry level and covers about 90 per cent of workers. Empirical evidence shows that this intermediate level of bargaining gives rise to the largest wage increases and leads to wage compression by reducing dispersion of wages across and within skill levels. Wages, however, are not strongly related to productivity differences among sectors and occupations, and cannot adapt to economic and productivity changes (Izquierdo *et al.*, 2003). Furthermore, this lack of wage flexibility prevents firms from adapting to technological change. Although all social partners acknowledged the excessive centralization of the system back in 1997,[28] not much has been done so far to change it.

The minimum wage policy is unlikely to have contributed much to the earnings inequality decrease for two reasons. First, until 2003 it decreased in real terms, and second, given

---

[28] See the Inter-Confederation Agreement of 1997.

the relatively high wages agreed through bargaining agreements, the minimum wage bites, at most, for five per cent of the workers (Dolado *et al.*, 1996).

Further labour reforms seem to be unavoidable if we are to reduce labour market inequalities. In 2009, a group of leading labour economists issued a proposal to improve the workings of the labour market.[29] Structured in four main points, it would also increase opportunities for disadvantaged groups and help reduce inequalities. First, the introduction of a single permanent contract with severance pay that increases with seniority for new hires is recommended in order to end the segmentation in the labour market. Second, protection of the unemployed ought to be improved by raising benefits in the first months of an unemployment spell, not to discourage search and improve protection. Third, it advises the decentralization of collective bargaining down to firm-level agreements, in order to help firms to adjust labour conditions to production needs and induce productivity growth. Fourth, it advocates improving active labour market policy by focusing on low-skill workers, who suffer longer unemployment spells, and manage it together with unemployment protection.

The overall tax burden increased from 33 per cent in 1995 to 38 per cent in 2007, when it started to decrease due to the recession—in 2010 it was 33 per cent again.[30] Spain has a smaller tax burden than the EU17 and the EU27 average, which remained fairly stable at 40 per cent during the 1995–2010 period.

Direct income taxation has undergone important changes since 1980, the most important one being to allow each family member to file separately, brought about by the 20/1989 Act. Other notable modifications include: the substantial reduction in the top-to-bottom marginal tax rates gap, which narrowed down from an initial gap of 55pp in 1980 to 18pp in 2010; the notable reduction in tax brackets—28 in 1980 to only 4 in 2010—and the introduction of several allowances and deductions, especially those related to family composition and house acquisition, the latter one with clear regressive effects.

The unambiguous redistributive effect of direct income taxation has not been homogeneous over the last 30 years. It increased in the 1980s, thus contributing to further reducing inequality of disposable income, remained rather constant over the 1990s, implying a constant inequality reduction over that decade, and decreased slightly over the first decade of this century. Most of the increasing redistributive effect in the 1980s can be accounted for by the increased progressivity of the tariff brought about by the various tax reforms. The increasing tax base, due to the emergence of previously undeclared capital and professional income, and the increase in effective average tax rates had a moderate contribution. The constant redistributive effect over the 1990s is the result of a decrease in progressivity and an outweighing increase in effective average tax rates (Onrubia *et al.*, 2007). The slight decrease in redistributive effect observed over the 2000s is driven by two years. The smaller effective average tax rate brought about by the 2003 reform, reduced the redistributive effect for that year. The redistributive effect declines again in 2006, now because of a reduction in progressivity (Onrubia and Picos, 2012).

---

[29] The proposal can be found at http://www.crisis09.es/PDF/restart-the-labor-market.pdf.

[30] We use Eurostat data measuring 'total receipts from taxes and social contributions including imputed social contributions after deduction of amounts assessed but unlikely to be collected' as a percentage of GDP. There is no data available before 1995.

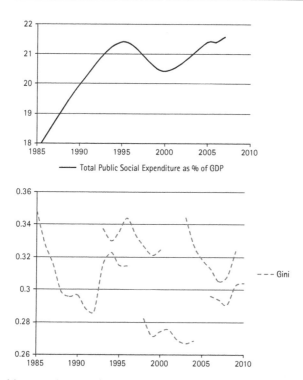

FIGURE 26.4 Public social expenditure

Gini, own calculations (equivalized disposable income, OECD modified scale)

Source: Public social expenditures, OECD.

Social expenditures—and the welfare system in general—are lower than in many European countries, although over the 1980–1995 period Spain experienced a large increase in social expenditures (Figure 26.4). A large part of these are devoted to health and to income maintenance (old age and unemployment), while expenditures on social protection are very low. Generally speaking, policies with a progressive structure, and thus a great potential to redistribute, are poorly endowed and thus doomed to have an insignificant redistributive effect. Pensions, by contrast, are designed to provide rather constant replacement rates across the earnings distribution, so their structure is not very progressive, but since the quantities involved are so huge, they stand out as the most redistributive policy (Pazos and Salas, 1997). Although no empirical study has been done, unemployment benefits may also play an important role, especially during periods of high unemployment.

Social transfers were an important factor in the inequality reduction of the 1980s, when pensions and other social transfers significantly extended their coverage and generosity. The redistributive effect of social transfers, though, reduced from the 1990s onward (Ayala and Sastre, 2007).

Since a considerable part of social spending is devoted to income maintaining expenditures (notably unemployment and pensions) and health, the high unemployment rates during the recession and the ageing population will continue to put much pressure on the welfare system.

There may be multiple reasons behind the bad education performance, notably the structure of educational expenditures, the low autonomy of the schools, and the involvement of the private sector. Although there is some evidence suggesting a weak correlation between investments in education and educational outcomes (Hanushek and Woessmann, 2010), the structure of educational expenditure is very different from many other countries'. Spain invests more in primary education and less in tertiary and upper secondary education (i.e. non-mandatory secondary education), according to Eurostat data for 1992–2010.

School autonomy and performance-related pay for teachers seem to play an important role in explaining cross-country education quality differences (Hanushek and Woessmann, 2010). Spain is one of the countries where schools have the least autonomy on deciding about teacher hiring and is one of the few not offering any type of performance pay to teachers. Thus, some economists argue that increasing school autonomy and introducing performance pay would increase educational quality (Cabrales and Felgueroso, 2011).

Another argument that has been put forward in the literature, both as a determinant of educational quality and of education inequalities, is the involvement of the private sector in education. There are three types of schools: public; private with state financial support; and entirely private with no state financial support. Public schools represent the vast majority of schools and most of the private schools receive funding from the State. For example, in 2010, out of the total number of schools offering secondary mandatory education, 67 per cent were public, 29 per cent were private with some financial support from the State, and less than 4 per cent were private not publicly supported.[31] In addition, the role of pre-primary education (which has also been highlighted as a determinant of both future education achievements and of income inequality) cannot be a cause either, as the enrolment in the pre-primary (publically provided) education system is very high, i.e. virtually 100 per cent.[32]

6. Conclusions

Since the restoration of democracy in the late 1970s, Spain has undergone many important changes, which have modernized political, economic and social institutions, and have set the basis for a new Welfare State (which improves opportunities through extending compulsory education and providing universal health care), new labour relations (which strengthen workers' rights and increase flexibility by reintroducing free trade unions, with the enactment of the workers statute, and by modifying collective bargaining agreements), and have allowed the renewal of social values and attitudes (which foster the participation of women in all life spheres). All these changes have undoubtedly increased opportunities and reduced social disparities.

In contrast with many other European and OECD countries, income inequality has decreased over the last 30 years. Nevertheless, Spain is still among the most unequal countries in the EU15, as it started from a fairly disadvantaged situation. The overall picture is fairly clear: since 1985, and with the exception of two episodes of recession, Spain has seen

[31] Spanish National Statistics Institute, INE.
[32] Eurostat.

a pronounced income-inequality reduction. During two periods of economic downturn inequality increased, but this only partly offset the previous reduction. That is, income inequality shows a countercyclical trend. Notwithstanding this, the current deep economic recession may change the picture for the coming years. These figures have to be taken with caution, as there is no coherent data for the period as a whole.

The income inequality decrease can mostly be explained by the equalizing effect of taxes and benefits and by changes in the labour market, which also channel the effects of the education level and composition.

For the labour market, earnings compression is an important factor. Such compression is brought about by reduced skill premium and collective bargaining at industry level, which favours wage compression. High participation rates and the larger increase in working hours at the bottom of the earnings distribution also help reduce earnings differentials. Having said that, the substantial increase in female labour participation did not contribute to inequality reduction. The large increase in low-productivity temporary employment, much of it related to the housing boom and bust, increased earnings in the lower middle part of the distribution, and thus reduced inequality.

The tax and benefit system contributed to the decreasing inequality trend mostly in the 1980s. Such increased redistributive effect can be accounted for by the increased progressivity of the tariff brought about by the various tax reforms, and the extended coverage and generosity of social transfers. In the 1990s and 2000s, however, the inequality reducing effect of taxes and benefits remains rather constant.

Social inequalities have decreased over the period. This is probably due not only to the inequality reduction but also to the substantial social and political transformations that Spain has undergone during this period. In Spain, however, social inequalities and social engagement (notably, poverty, health, unemployment, job conditions, and social isolation) have a clear socio-economic gradient, notably related to education and income. This means that educational polarization, the dual labour market and the economic crisis that hit Spain terribly a few years ago, will probably enhance social inequalities in the future. Political participation and attitudes instead seem to be more related to the political and social context than to the individual situation. Trust in institutions and corruption remain important unsolved issues.

Despite the falling income-inequality trend, some features of the socio-economic situation may jeopardize the well-being of Spaniards and increase income and social inequalities in the near future. These features are primarily: (i) polarization of education outcomes; (ii) duality in the labour market; (iii) high unemployment rates; and (iv) the relatively high share of low-skill workers in low-productivity industries.

Spain has gone a long way since the restoration of democracy, some thirty years ago, but needs to address these key imbalances if the country wishes to be a more prosperous and a fairer society.

References

Amuedo-Dorantes, C. and Mundra, K. (2012), Immigrant homeownership and immigration status: evidence from Spain. *IZA DP—6676*.

Arellano, M., Bentolila S., and Bover, O. (2002), 'The Distribution of Earnings in Spain during the 1980's: The Effects of Skill, Unemployment, and Union Power', in Cohen, D., Piketty, T. and Saint-Paul, G. (eds.), *The New Economics of Rising Inequalities*, CEPR, Oxford: Oxford UP,.

Ayala, L., Cantó, O., and Rodríguez, J.G. (2011), Poverty and the business cycle: The role of the intra-household distribution of unemployment. *WP 222*, ECINEQ.

Ayala, L. and Sastre, M. (2007), Políticas Redistributivas y Desigualdad. *ICE*, 837, pp. 117–138.

Azpitarte, F. (2010), 'The role of housing and financial wealth', *Hacienda Publica Española / Revista de Economía Pública*, 194: 65–90.

Blanco, C. and Ramos, X. (2010), 'Polarization and Health', *Review of Income and Wealth*, 56(1): 171–185.

Boix, C. and Riba, C. (2000), 'Las bases sociales y políticas de la abstención en las elecciones generales españolas: recursos individuales, movilización estratégica e instituciones electorales', *Revista Española de Investigaciones Sociológicas*, 90, pp. 95–128.

Bonhomme, S. and Hospido, L. (2012), 'The cycle of earnings inequality: Evidence from Spanish social security data', *IZA DP 6669*.

Bover, O., Martínez, M., and Velilla, P. (2005), 'The Wealth of Spanish Households: A Microeconomic Comparison with the United States, Italy and the United Kingdom', *Economic Bulletin of the Bank of Spain*, July.

Cabrales, A. and Felgueroso, F. (2011), 'Recortes educativos: la cuestión no es cuánto, es cómo y dónde', *NadaEsGratis* (blog), September.

Cervini Plá, M. (2009). 'Measuring intergenerational earnings mobility in Spain: A selection-bias-free approach', *Working Papers*, Departament d'Economia Aplicada. UAB (wprdea0904).

Cervini-Plá, M. and Ramos, X. (2012),'Long Term Earnings Inequality, Earnings Instability and Temporary Employment in Spain: 1993–2000', *British Journal of Industrial Relations*, 50(4): 714–736.

Cervini-Plá, M. and Ramos, X. (2013), 'Movilidad intergeneracional y emparejamiento selectivo en España', *Papeles de Economía Española*, 135: 217–227.

Cowell, F.A. (2011), *Measuring Inequality, LSE Perspectives in Economic Analysis*, 3rd edition, Oxford: Oxford University Press.

Deaton, A., 2002, 'Policy Implications of the Gradient of Health and Wealth', *Health Affairs*, 21: 13–30.

De la Fuente, A. (2008), *Inversión en infrastructuras, crecimiento y convergencia regional.*, Bellaterra (Barcelona), Spain: IAE.

De la Fuente, A. (2001), 'Regional convergence in Spain: 1965-95', *EEE120*. Fedea (Madrid, Spain).

Dolado, J.J., Kramarz F., Machin, S., Manning, A., and Teulings, C. (1996), 'The Economic Impact of Minimum Wages in Europe', *Economic Policy*, 23: 317–72.

Dolado, J.J., García-Serrano, C., and Jimeno, J.F. (2002), 'Drawing Lessons from the Boom of Temporary Jobs in Spain', *The Economic Journal*, 112, pp. F270–F295.

European Commission (2012), 'In-Depth Review for SPAIN', *Staff Working Document* SWD-159.

EVS (2010) and EVS (2008) 'Guidelines and Recommendations'. *GESIS-Technical Reports* 2010/16. Retrieved from <http://www.europeanvaluesstudy.eu/>.

EVS (2011), 'European Values Study Longitudinal Data File 1981-2008' (EVS 1981-2008), GESIS Data Archive, Cologne. ZA4804 Data file Version 2.0.0, doi:10.4232/1.11005.

Felgueroso, F., Hidalgo M. and Jiménez, S. (2010), Explaining the fall of the skill wage premium in Spain', *Working Papers* 2010-'19, FEDEA.

Felgueroso, F., Garicano, L., and Jiménez, S. (2011), 'Educación: Una chuleta para la reforma', *NadaEsGratis* (blog), 24 November, <http://www.fedeablogs.net/economia/?p=16393>.

Ferrer-i-Carbonell, A., Ramos, X., and Oviedo, M. (2012), 'Growing Inequality and its Impacts. Country Report: Spain', <www.gini-research.org/CR-Spain>.

García Valiñas, M.A., Fernández Llera, R., and Torgler, B. (2008), 'More Income Equality or Not? An Empirical Analysis of Individuals' Preferences for Redistribution', *Discussion Paper and Working Paper Series #226*. Queensland University of Technology, School of Economics and Finance.

Gradin, C., and Otero, M. (2001), 'Participación laboral femenina en España: Efectos sobre la desigualdad de la renta familiar', *Ekonomiaz*, 47: 226–247.

Hanushek, E.A. and Woessmann, L. (2006), 'School resources', in Hanushek, E.A. and Welch, F. (eds.), *Handbook of the Economics of Education*, Amsterdam, North Holland: Universidad de A Coruña, pp. 865–908.

Hanushek, E.A. and Woessmann, L. (2010), 'The Economics of International Differences in Educational Achievement'. *IZA DP* N. 4925.

Iglesias, E., Pena L. A., Sánchez, J.M. (eds.), (2012), *Evolution over Time of the Determinants of Preferences for Redistribution and the Support for the Welfare State*, Departamento de Economía Aplicada II. Facultad de Economía y Empresa. Universidad de A Coruña.

Izquierdo, M., Moral, E. and Urtasun, A. (2003), 'Collective bargaining in Spain: An individual data analysis', *Documento Ocasional*, 0302. Banco de España, Madrid.

Lacuesta, A. and Izquierdo, M. (2012), 'The Contribution of Changes in Employment Composition and Relative Returns to the Evolution of Wage Inequality: The Case of Spain', *Journal of Population Economics*, 25: 511–543.

López Casanovas, G., Costa Font, J. and Planas, I. (2005), 'Diversity and Regional Inequalities: Assessing the Outcomes of the Spanish "System of Health Care Services"', *Health Economics* 14: 5221–5235.

Meschi, E., and Scervini, F. (2010), 'A new data set of educational inequality', *Gini Working paper* 3. AIAS, Amsterdam.

Morales, L. (2005), '¿Existe una crisis participativa? La evolución de la participación política y el asociacionismo en España', in *Revista Española de Ciencia Política* (13); pp. 51-87. ['Ever less engaged citizens? Political participation and associational membership in Spain', Working Paper published in English in 2003, by ICPS (Barcelona, Spain)].

OECD (2011), *Voting in OECD, Society at Glance 2011*, OECD Social Indicators, Paris

Oliver, J., Ramos X. and Raymond, J.L., (2001), 'Anatomía de la distribución de la renta en España, 1985-1996: La continuidad de la mejora', *Papeles de Economía Española*, 88: 67–88.

Onrubia, J., Rodado, M.C., Diaz de Sarralde S., and Pérez, C., (2007), 'Progresividad y redistribución a través del IRPF español: Un análisis de bienestar social para el periodo 1982–1998', *Hacienda Pública Española/Revista de Econoía Pública*, 183(4): 81–124.

Onrubia, J. and Picos, F. (2012), 'Progresividad, redistribución y bienestar a través del IRPF español en el periodo 1999–2007', *Instituto de Estudios Fiscales, Working Paper* 1/2012.

Pazos, M. and Salas, R. (1997), 'Progresividad y redistribución de las transferencias públicas', *Moneda y Crédito*, 205: 45–78.

Pijoan-Mas, J. and Sánchez-Marcos, V. (2010), 'Spain is Different: Falling Trends of Inequality', *Review of Economic Dynamics*, 13: 154–178.

Raitano, M. and Vona, M. (2011), 'The economic impact of upward and downward occupational mobility: A comparison of eight EU member states', *Working Papers, 13*, Doctoral School of Economics—Sapienza Universita de Roma.

Regidor, E., Gutierrez-Fisac, J.L., Domínguez, V., Calle, M.E. and Navarro, P. (2002), 'Comparing Social Inequalities in Health in Spain: 1987 and 1995/1998', *Social Science and Medicine*, 54, 1.323–1.332.

Schuetz, G., Ursprung, H.W. and Woessmann, L. (2008), 'Education policy and equality of opportunity', *Kyklos* 61: 279–308.

Van Doorslaer, E. and Koolman, X. (2004), 'Explaining the Differences in Income-Related Health Inequalities Across European Countries', *Health Economics*, 13, 609–628.

CHAPTER 27

....

SWEDEN: INCREASING INCOME INEQUALITIES AND CHANGING SOCIAL RELATIONS

....

JOHAN FRITZELL, JENNIE BACCHUS HERTZMAN,

OLOF BÄCKMAN, IDA BORG, TOMMY FERRARINI, AND

KENNETH NELSON

1. INTRODUCTION

....

THE aim of this chapter is to present and examine patterns and trends in the drivers of inequality in Sweden. We highlight their relations in the social, political and cultural spheres, look at the available evidence from research, and point to the role of relevant institutions and policies in ameliorating or exacerbating those effects. In line with the overall GINI-project we focus on the changes from around 1980 onwards.[1]

A closer look at the Swedish case is of interest from several perspectives. First, Sweden tends to perform comparatively well in terms of almost all equality dimensions. The social programmes of Sweden and their chief characteristics have been seen as an archetype for a specific Welfare State model with universal systems. This involves principles in the design of social programmes, including high levels of public service provision and levels of social protection, coupled with high tax levels. The focus on equality refers not only to income or social class, but also to gender. There are, in other words, many characteristics of the model but researchers have singled out three fundamental features: comprehensive; institutionalized; and universal (Esping-Andersen and Korpi, 1987; Kildal and Kuhnle, 2005; Lundberg *et al.*,

---

[1] This chapter draws to a large extent on *Growing Inequality and its Impacts Country Report Sweden* (Fritzell *et al.*, 2012), which is the Swedish country report to the GINI-project (<http://www.gini-research.org/CR-Sweden>).

2008). At the same time, it is important to remember that the characteristics of the Swedish Welfare State model are not static but are constantly changing over time.

The Swedish experience is internationally interesting also from the perspective of the present economic crisis. Sweden experienced a deep recession in the early 1990s. The experiences and social consequences of this macro-economic development are highly relevant to our understanding of the present global economic crisis, which so far has been mild in Sweden compared to most other countries. The welfare consequences of the crisis were thoroughly investigated by the Governmental Swedish Welfare Commission (see e.g. Palme *et al.*, 2002; 2003). Over a short period of time, employment fell by over a half million people, while unemployment sky-rocketed from 1.7 to 8.3 per cent.[2] This initial economic shock led to the so-called Crisis Packages, where the right/centre government and the social democratic opposition joined forces to combat the crisis. In November 1992 the fixed exchange rate of the Swedish currency was abolished to stop speculation against the Swedish economy. The interest rate was set at 500 per cent a few days before the floating of the Swedish currency. Unsurprisingly, the government finances were in serious trouble and in the following years almost all taxes were increased and almost all benefits were reduced.

A full account of what led to the recession is of course beyond the scope of this chapter. Some important factors often mentioned in the literature are the deregulation of the credit market in 1985, not least the abolition of lending ceilings, which led to a spiral of increasing lending and prices, especially on property. The high price and wage increases of the late 1980s meant that the Swedish export industry rapidly lost market share when the international business cycle slowed at the beginning of the 1990s (see Palme *et al.*, 2002).

One of the main conclusions from the Welfare Commission was the long-term impact of the crisis. Although GDP figures would suggest otherwise, the recession continued to play a role when studying both individual living conditions and social policy. Just to mention one important aspect of this scenario, the unemployment rate has continued to stay far higher than the levels recorded of the 1980s. The low unemployment levels of the 1980s seem today just as unthinkable as the unemployment levels in 1992 would seem in the 1980s. Moreover, as we will scrutinize in more detail, while median income rapidly fell during the first half of the 1990s, income inequality did not change much. Instead, income differentials increased in the aftermath of recession in the second half of the decade.

The Swedish development is also interesting in terms of demographic profile, not least since Sweden was one of the first countries to experience the problem of an ageing population. The large number of immigrants and the heterogeneity of the Swedish population in terms of ethnicity is another development that might have a bearing on inequality and poses social policy challenges. According to Eurostat (2011) Sweden has one of the largest shares of non-native born citizens in Europe. Before the economic crisis of the early 1970s, most immigration was labour migration, something that changed from the 1970s and onwards, as a larger share of migrants has been family-related and refugees, typically from South America in the 1970s, Iran and the Middle East in the 1980s, and former Yugoslavia in the 1990s. Since then migration from African countries has increased (for a review see e.g. Gerdes and Wadensjö, 2012; Helgertz, 2010).

---

[2] According to the newer EU/ILO adjustment to the measurement of the unemployment level, the increase was actually even larger. The annual unemployment rates in the Eurostat database are 9.1 for 1993 and 9.4 for 1994 (Eurostat 2013).

Moreover the political landscape of Sweden and the politics pursued in it are changing. Sweden, the archetype for Esping-Andersen's (1990) 'social democratic' regime type, has had several right-centre governments over the last decades. New parties have also entered the parliament and, as will be shown, the politics pursued there have changed significantly since the heyday of Welfare State expansion in the immediate post-war decades. Interestingly enough, the social democratic hegemony may be less broken in terms of rhetoric. Accordingly, the right wing party (*Moderaterna*) has tried to position itself as 'the new labour party'.

This chapter is structured accordingly. First we scrutinize changes in the distribution of income in Sweden from different angles. Next, we study trends in social, political and cultural indicators, as well as the socio-economic inequalities related to these indicators. We then present the important institutional changes to the Swedish Welfare State, with obvious repercussions for income inequality. Finally we discuss our findings at a more general level.

2. Increasing Inequality

Sweden, together with the other Nordic countries, has a reputation for being one of the most equal societies in the world. In fact, when the chief characteristics of the Nordic Welfare State model are pinpointed, the relatively compressed income distribution and the successful poverty alleviation are often mentioned as key outcomes (Kautto *et al.*, 2001; Kvist *et al.*, 2012). This is also corroborated by comparative research over the years, starting off with the birth of the Luxembourg Income Study (LIS), from which it was clear that substantial cross-national variations of income inequality, redistribution and poverty existed also among rich countries. LIS data from the early 1980s show that Sweden and other Nordic countries had the lowest levels of income inequality (e.g. Atkinson, 2004). This conclusion has a bearing on our investigation, which, in time, begins with Swedish inequality numbers being much lower than in most other countries.

Has income inequality grown in Sweden since 1980? In Figure 27.1 we show trends in disposable income and factor (basically pre-transfer and taxes) income in Sweden from 1980 and 2010, as given by Statistics Sweden. Unless otherwise stated, all incomes are adjusted by an equivalence scale in order to account simultaneously for household size and economies of scale.[3] In order to cover the full period, we have to use an old imperfect household definition, but from 1991 an improved household definition has been available. We therefore also present a third curve with equivalent disposable income from 1991 and onwards.[4]

Evidently these measurement technicalities impact on the level but do not affect the trends. During the years that we can make the comparison (1991–2010), the curves almost

---

[3] The equivalence scale used in Figure 27.1, and in other figures of this chapter, unless otherwise stated, is used in most official statistics in Sweden. It gives a weight of 1 to a single-person household, a weight of 1.51 to a couple, an additional factor of 0.6 for other adults, 0.52 for the first child and additional weights of 0.42 for subsequent children.

[4] A second reason for having a curve starting in 1991 is the major Swedish tax reform in 1991, which in terms of income statistics led to a number of measurement technicalities in the definition of disposable income, which increased the Gini by around 0.02.

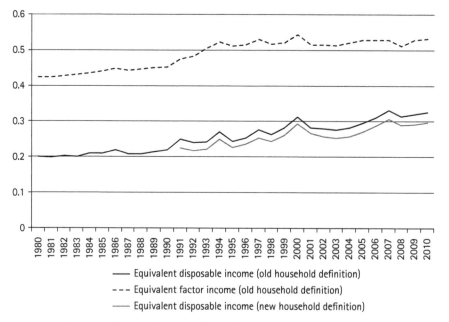

FIGURE 27.1 Gini coefficient for equivalent factor and disposable income in Sweden from 1980 to 2010. Old and new household income concept

Source: Statistics Sweden, 2012.

exactly follow each other, but the improvement in the measurement of households results in a fall in the Gini of about 0.025 in later years. We can therefore give an affirmative answer to the question above, without doubt: 'Yes, income inequality has increased in Sweden'. In fact, the recent OECD report, *Divided we Stand* (2011, p. 1) claims that, 'The growth in inequality between 1985 and the late 2000s was the largest among all OECD countries'.

Scrutinizing different time periods we find that inequality showed the most rapid increase from the mid 1990s, but Figure 27.1 also shows a modest increase during the 1980s.[5] Comparing market and disposable income inequality we can draw two conclusions. Although inequality has increased for both income concepts, the increase is sharper in disposable income, i.e. when we take transfers and taxes into account. In other words, a weakening of the redistributive system has occurred.

From earlier research we know that two, interrelated, factors are particularly important when accounting for these overall trends. First, the issue of capital income, and especially capital gains, and second, what is happening at the top of the income distribution (Roine and Waldenström, 2008; Björklund and Jäntti, 2011; Fritzell, Bäckman, and Ritakallio, 2012).

The changes at the top show quite a dramatic development. There are strong yearly fluctuations due to business cycles and changes of taxation rules, but the overall trend is clearly that 'the rich are getting richer', not only absolutely but also relatively. Accordingly, between

---

[5] The peaks we see in the figure are mostly due to ups and downs of the stock market. However, the peak in 1994 was due to a change in tax policy.

Table 27.1 Income shares (%) for the lowest (D1) and highest (D10) 10 per cent of the distribution of equivalent disposable income in Sweden, 1995 to 2010

	1995	1996	1997	1998	1999	2000	2001	2002	2003	2004	2005	2006	2007	2008	2009	2010
D1	4.0	4.1	4.1	3.8	3.8	3.7	3.6	3.9	4.0	3.9	3.9	3.8	3.6	3.3	3.3	3.3
D10	19.7	20.5	22.2	21.0	22.6	25.8	22.7	22.0	21.6	22.4	23.6	25.0	26.4	24.1	24.0	24.6

Source: Statistics Sweden 2012.

1995 and 2010, the top one per cent have increased their share of total equivalent disposable income by about three percentage points (from around four to around seven per cent) or by about 73 per cent. One driving force behind these changes was the introduction of the so-called dual income tax model (Sørensen, 1994) as part of the substantial tax reform of 1991 (Fritzell, Bäckman, and Ritakallio, 2012). The dual income tax model basically means that capital income is subject to a flat-rate taxation irrespective of labour income and that it gives high-income earners strong incentives to shift earnings to capital income. From the perspective of Swedish development, it is important to notice that the political decision to reform the tax system was made before the economic crisis. The reform had several elements, like broadening the tax base and lowering the tax rates on work and capital. While the whole reform had several rationales, the duality element was clearly related to the internationalization of capital markets.

The relative changes at the top and bottom are highlighted in Table 27.1, which gives the decile share of the highest and lowest 10 per cent of the income distribution. The increases at the top are evident here but, especially in recent times, we have seen a quite marked change at the lower end of the income distribution as well. This less widely recognized change has meant a marked reduction in the income share of the lowest decile.

To further highlight this development we present percentile ratios P10:P50, that compare the income levels at the 10th percentile with the median from 1995 to 2010 (Figure 27.2). This indicates clearly that the incomes of people in the lowest part of the distribution have not only lagged in relation to those at the top but, evidently, they have also fallen behind people with median income. In fact, since 2003 and especially during the last five years or so, there appear to be greater changes at the bottom than at the top. In other words, the common story of income inequality increases at the top driving the income distribution needs to be

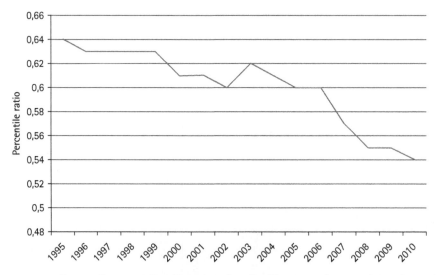

FIGURE 27.2 Percentile ratio P10/P50—in the distribution of equivalent disposable income in Sweden, 1995 to 2010

Source: Statistics Sweden (2012).

complemented by other factors when we focus on the more recent years. From an equity point of view this development is troublesome.

Given the fall in the P10/P50 ratio, the EU at-risk-of-poverty rate should have increased, as is confirmed by earlier analyses (Socialstyrelsen 2010). The sharp increase in this rate in Sweden from around 1995 is at odds with most other rich Western countries, perhaps with the most notable exception of Finland, where poverty rates seem to have increased even more (Fritzell, Bäckman and Ritakallio, 2012). However, at least until around 2005, relative poverty rates were lower in Sweden than in most other rich countries. Further, if one anchors the poverty line to an earlier year, thus having a fixed poverty threshold, poverty instead decreases. This reflects the experience of a sharp increase in average incomes over the last decades.

A main driver for changes in disposable incomes is, of course, changes related to the labour market. Basically these changes can be divided into changes in wage rates and changes in working hours. Earnings inequality among full-year, full-time employees also show an increase during the 1990s. This increase was driven by the managerial wage premium, especially in the private sector (Palme *et al.*, 2003). There is no clear continuation of this trend during the 2000s.

Thus, the development of labour income inequality for full-time full-year employed persons corresponds quite well to the general increase in income inequality during the 1990s, but not to the increased inequality in disposable income during the 2000s. However, this does not mean that the role of labour market attachment has become less important. On the contrary; for example, between 1999 and 2010, average disposable income among those employed increased by 37 per cent whereas the corresponding increase for the non-employed only is 6 per cent (Statistics Sweden 2012).

Thus the gap between insiders and outsiders in the labour market has grown considerably, a change that became particularly visible during the last five or six years. This recent change coincides with the centre-right government holding office in Sweden. In fact, this is not a coincidence, nor an unintended consequence of politics. Among other things, the present government has introduced a series of earned income tax credits (*Jobbskatteavdrag*), lowering the tax burden on employment income and also changing conditions of a number of social protection programmes (see below). This increasing gap, to a great extent policy-driven, is likely to be a key factor if we want to understand changes in the lower part of the income distribution.

A central EU-indicator of deprivation measures the proportion of the population living in jobless households. This indicator is not available in longer time series in Swedish public databases. However, we have created a similar indicator on the basis of administrative register data. The indicator differs from the EU-definition and measures the share of persons aged 20–64 who live in households where two or more adults, or one adult in a single household, have weak labour market attachment. Weak labour market attachment is defined as having an annual labour market income below one price base amount (PBA), in 2012 amounting to SEK 44,000 or approximately €5,000.[6] Figure 27.3 shows the development of this indicator from 1990 to 2008, stratified by educational level.

---

[6] The PBA is a consumer price index related tool used by the government to calculate e.g. pensions, but it is used in several other contexts as well. An annual income from a full-time job in the lowest paid occupations in the Swedish labour market approximates 3.5 PBA (Socialstyrelsen, 2010).

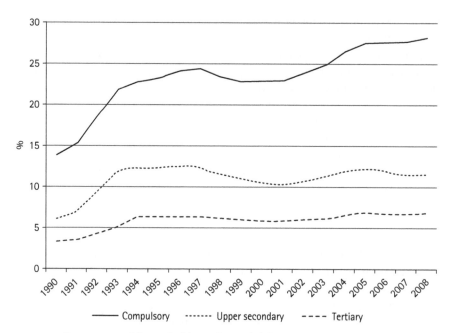

FIGURE 27.3 Percentage of households with weak labour market attachment 1990–2008 by educational level. Swedish population at 20–64 years of age

Source: Statistics Sweden's LISA database.

As could be expected, the fraction of people in households with weak labour market attachment increased during the 1990 crisis in all three educational groups. For those with upper secondary or tertiary education, this proportion seems to establish itself at a higher level. For the least educated, the increase of the proportion with weak labour market attachment stops also in the second half of the 1990s, but from 2001 undergoes a new increase which continues for the rest of the period. This differs for the other two educational groups. Thus, the international development, whereby the poorly educated find increasing difficulties in getting a foothold in the labour market, can be discerned also in Sweden.

A similar indicator used in studies of young adults is NEET (Not in Employment, Education or Training, e.g. Bynner and Parsons, 2002). Our analysis of NEET for different age groups shows to some extent a similar development for young adults (20–24) as the one observed in Figure 27.3 for those with less education. There is a rapid increase in NEET during the crisis years in the youngest age group. During the recovery period in the latter half of the 1990s the proportion of NEET falls, but for the youngest age group it remains at a level well above that of the other age groups, and after the turn of the century it begins to escalate again. Thus, a shift seems to have taken place whereby an increasing number of young adults stand at a far distance from the Swedish labour market.

We have already noted the sharp increase in income differences between non-employed and employed but, of course, also different population groups have experienced different median income changes. In particular immigrants, young adults, and single parents have had a much lower increase in median incomes over the last two decades. These three categories also started off from lower income levels. The Swedish Welfare Commission singled out these categories as the three subgroups most negatively affected by the turbulent decade of the 1990s (Palme *et al.*, 2002; Fritzell, Gähler and Nermo, 2007). One decade later, this conclusion unfortunately remains unchanged. In fact, concentrating on the developments in the 2000s, the economic situation for single mothers is especially worrisome. Although single mothers are an economically vulnerable group in all countries, they have been in a comparatively good situation in Sweden, not least due to high labour force participation rates. But their labour force participation has declined substantially over the last decade.

From a welfare perspective, and from the perspective of the intergenerational transmission of inequalities, one can make a strong argument that the distribution of wealth is a more profound factor compared to the distribution of annual disposable income. The distribution of wealth is, of course, highly skewed and for a large fraction of the population net wealth is negative or close to zero. As in most other countries, knowledge about the trends in the Swedish distribution of wealth is quite scarce. An investigation by Statistics Sweden (2000), comparing the late 1970s to the late 1990s, suggested an increase in wealth inequality. We find fairly small changes between the late 1990s and 2007 (the latest available year), but net wealth has increased both at the median and at the top. From a long-run perspective, it is also obvious that wealth has become more concentrated among those of older age than was the case three to four decades ago.

3. SOCIAL IMPACTS OF INEQUALITY

Analyses of the extent and nature of income inequality involve some important conceptual and measurement considerations. Still, describing income inequality is fairly straightforward as compared to assessing its implications for society and its members. In the following section, we discuss the potential consequences of inequality in Sweden. However, it is important to note that, we make no causal claims. The discussion is merely an exposé of potential societal and individual consequences of increasing inequality.

It is often argued that the ultimate consequence of deprivation is premature death and it has repeatedly been argued that income inequality can affect life expectancy in rich countries. Between 1980 and 2010, life expectancy at birth increased in Sweden by nearly 7 years for men and by 5.5 years for women. This improvement in life expectancy looks different when we move from an analysis of population averages to differences by socio-economic groups. In Sweden, as in the majority of affluent countries, most measures indicate that socio-economic inequalities in mortality have increased over recent decades (Socialstyrelsen 2009). These increasing inequalities are particularly salient among women. The difference in expected remaining life expectancy at age 30 between less-educated women (lower secondary education) and the highly educated (tertiary education) increased from 2 years in 1986 to 4.7 years in 2010, (Fritzell *et al.*, 2012). Inequality has increased also for lighter health impairments, such as psychological distress. Figure 27.4 shows that psychological distress has increased particularly among younger people. This analysis covers developments 1968–2000, but other studies indicate that inequality in health has continued to rise (e.g. Socialstyrelsen 2009).

Another important indicator of well-being is loneliness. People in the Nordic countries, including Sweden, are less lonely than people in southern Europe. This pattern is

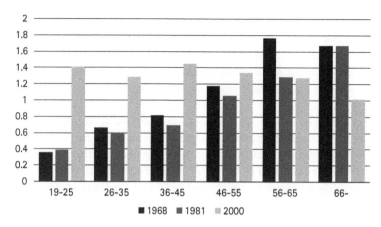

FIGURE 27.4 Psychological distress by age groups in 1968, 1981 and 2000. Odds ratios (OR) standardized by gender, country of birth, social class. Average odds = 1.0

Source: Fritzell, Lennartsson and Lundberg (2007).

particularly manifest among the elderly (Sundström *et al.*, 2009). Findings such as these have puzzled scholars for nearly two decades. A stereotype of solitary-living Swedes and intergenerational co-habiting families in the Southern Europe would suggest the reverse results. However, loneliness systematically co-varies with health and living arrangements (Holmén and Furukawa 2002). Healthy persons living with a partner are least lonesome, while single persons with poor health are most lonesome. Factors assumed to prevent lone-liness are co-residence and community ties. As argued by Wilkinson and Pickett (2009), high levels of income inequality may degrade social relations and increase social polariza-tion among citizens.

In the Swedish Living Conditions Survey some questions about contacts with family and friends are posed. In Figure 27.5, we report the fraction having no close friend, stratified by age. The proportion has diminished in all age groups. It increases with age, although the age gradient has become slightly less manifest since the downward trend for young people levels off at the turn of the century, while it continues to fall for older age groups. It would be too speculative to interpret these trends as increased social cohesion in Sweden. The concept of social cohesion is wider than that, but Swedes have undoubtedly become less lonely despite increased levels of inequality, as indicated by the Gini coefficient. We have not been able to find a definitive explanation for this reduced 'rate of loneliness' but, at least for the oldest age group, improved health and better material living conditions are strong candidates.

From a comparative perspective, material living conditions in the Nordic countries, including Sweden, are on average high. For instance, the Swedish poverty persistency rate in 2010 was 4.9 per cent, which is the lowest figure of all EU-countries. A long-term time-series of the 'persistent at-risk-of-poverty rate' for Sweden does not exist. However, one variable often used in Sweden as an indicator of precarious living conditions is take-up of means-tested social assistance benefits. Particularly long-term or extensive take-up can be used as an indicator of prolonged or particularly harsh precariousness (e.g. Bergmark and Bäckman, 2004). Social assistance benefits are granted to households where all other means of maintenance are exhausted. The benefit level is set according to a minimum basket

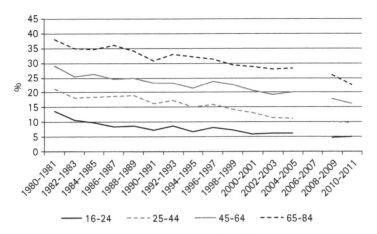

FIGURE 27.5 Proportion (%) with no close friend in four age groups. Bi-annual averages, Sweden 1980–2011

Source: Statistics Sweden (2012), Living Conditions Surveys (1980–2005)/Eurostat (2012) EU-SILC (2008–2011).

of goods, including items such as food, clothing, leisure, and so forth. Housing is covered by additional benefits outside the basic social assistance scale rates.

Social assistance caseloads were fairly stable at around five per cent of the total population prior to the 1990s financial crisis. During the crisis, this proportion increased by half to approximately eight per cent. After the crisis, take-up fell and has since stayed at levels below five per cent. The number of long-term social assistance beneficiaries also increased during the 1990s financial crisis. The proportion of people receiving social assistance for at least ten months rose by 170 per cent during the crisis, from 0.75 per cent of total population in 1990 to 2.05 per cent in 1997. This long-term social assistance beneficiary rate also fell back after the 1990s crisis, but not to pre-crisis levels. In 2008, long-term social assistance caseloads begun to increase again and, in relative terms, the number of long-term social assistance beneficiaries was twice as high in 2010 as compared to levels recorded before the 1990-crisis.

The development of long-term social assistance caseloads may indicate a widening poverty gap, in the sense that those at the bottom of the income and wealth distribution tend to get stuck in this state for longer periods than earlier. It coincides with dualization of trends in the labour market, whereby certain vulnerable groups, such as immigrants and young adults, face increasing difficulties in finding a strong foothold (Socialstyrelsen, 2010). Social assistance take-up has also increased substantially among immigrants since the 1990-crisis (Bergmark and Bäckman, 2007). It should also be noted that social assistance suffers from incomplete take-up and far from all eligible households apply for benefits (e.g. Halleröd, 1991). It is therefore important to complement the analysis by also using other poverty indicators, where material deprivation is one alternative. The Living Conditions Survey by Statistics Sweden has for several decades provided information on material living conditions. In 2006, the Living Conditions Survey was merged with the EU-SILC, something that introduced a break in the time-series. However, questions about 'no cash margin' and 'economic strain' are available for most years. Time series for these two variables, 1980–2005, are shown in Figure 27.6, stratified by socio-economic group. Both variables are strongly anti-cyclical, with high levels during economic downturns and lower levels during upswings

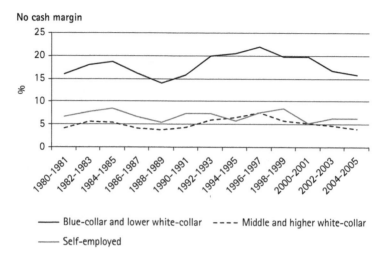

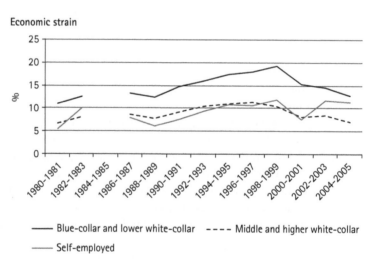

FIGURE 27.6 Proportion with no cash margin and economic strain.[7] Sweden 1980–2005, (two-year averages) by socio-economic group

Source: Statistics Sweden, Living Conditions Survey, Statistics Sweden (2012).

in the economic cycle. The effect of the mid-1990s crisis is particularly salient. The development of the economic strain indicator is fairly parallel for the socio-economic groups, whereas the cyclical effect of lack of cash margin is present only for the lower social classes. At least through the turn of the century, and at least for economic strain, the development

---

[7] The economic strain variable identifies those who during the last 12 months have had problems paying for food, rent, bills, etc. No cash margin identifies those who are unable to raise a certain amount of money for unexpected expenses. Amount 1980–81: SEK 5,000; 1982–84: SEK 7,000; 1985–87: SEK 8,000; 1988–89; SEK 9,000; 1990–91: SEK 10,000; 1992–93: SEK 12,000; 1994–95: SEK 13,000; 1996–2003: SEK 14,000; 2004–05: SEK 15,000.

for the lower classes follows the development of the Gini coefficient fairly well. Still, there is no clear tendency for disparities to increase between socio-economic groups.

Contrary to most other EU countries, both material and severe material deprivation in Sweden have declined between 2004 and 2010. Development since the mid 1990s indicates that all socio-economic groups among the employed have enjoyed these reduced risks of deprivation. Also, for indicators of material deprivation, we find that those outside the labour market have lost ground as compared to those in employment.

Another fundamental aspect of living conditions is housing. Most countries, including Sweden, have, during the past two or three decades, experienced substantial increases in house prices. In fact, Sweden has had the longest continuous increase in house prices among comparable countries since the current price boom started in 1997 (Agnello and Schuknecht, 2009). From the 1990s and onwards, housing policy in Sweden has been aimed at increasing the incentives for home-ownership by various means, tax deductions being one example (Lindbom, 2001). Meanwhile, mortgage debts have increased.

Increasing home-ownership rates may be an important and often neglected determinant of inequality. Dewilde (2011:11) has argued that the 'inclusion of housing finance into new and complex financial instruments, yielding large profits derived from assumed house price inflation' is an important driver for growing income and wealth inequalities in recent decades. Indeed, housing costs make up the single largest expenditure item in most household budgets, where outright ownership is concentrated more at the upper end of the income distribution. Ritakallio (2003) examined the role of housing costs for poverty rates, poverty gaps, and income inequality, comparing Finland and Australia. When housing costs were considered, the differences in poverty rates and in income inequality between these two countries were reduced. Thus, income-based poverty and inequality statistics that are unadjusted for housing costs may exaggerate the differences between countries. Sweden's diminishing rental sector and increasing home-ownership rates may increase the economic burden for low-income households, and increase economic inequality. Access to affordable housing in the public rental sector may be an important factor in improving the economic well-being of individuals at the lower end of the income distribution (Magnusson and Turner, 2008).

4. POLITICAL AND CULTURAL IMPACTS

It is generally accepted that there exists a relationship between socio-economic position and a whole range of political and cultural factors, i.e. a social gradient can often be observed. A bivariate relationship between these factors and economic inequalities has repeatedly been confirmed in earlier research (e.g. Wilkinson and Pickett, 2009).

We start by looking at how Swedish citizens have been involved in democratic processes, more particularly voter turnout in national elections and participation in political activities (see Figure 27.7). In both, there was a downward trend during the 1980s and 1990s. Since the turn of the millennium, however, the trend seems to have levelled off or even increased slightly.

It is important to notice that the gap between socio-economic groups (indicated by education) has increased for voter turnout since the first data point in 1988. In the latest election

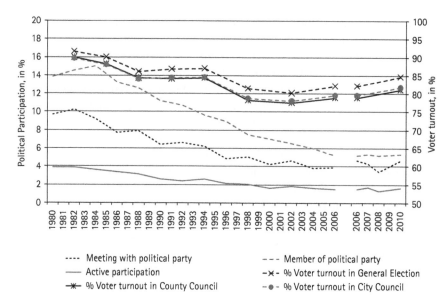

FIGURE 27.7 Voter turnouts on all three domestic levels of government and political participation, 1980–2010

Source: Statistics Sweden's Electoral Participation Survey and Statistics of Sweden's Living Conditions Surveys (ULF/SILC).

in 2010, around 79 per cent of those with compulsory education voted compared to over 94 per cent of those with tertiary education. Thus, there was a difference of over 15 percentage points between the two groups, compared to around 9 and 8 percentage points in 1988 and 1991. In other words, we find that the social gradient, at least by education, has increased in this sphere during the same period that economic inequalities increased.

A related topic is people's attitudes towards the Welfare State in general, towards economic inequalities, and towards the government's role in redistributing income, in particular. We find an increased dissatisfaction with the present economic inequalities and well-established support for a universal and generous Welfare State (Svallfors, 2011), with a redistributing responsibility. In light of the increased ethnic heterogeneity of the Swedish population, these trends challenge the hypothesis that societies with an increased ethnically differentiated population will receive less public support for a generous Welfare State model (see e.g. Alesina and Glaeser, 2004).

Political participation is an area that is associated with social capital; institutional and interpersonal trust is another one. Sweden, together with the other Nordic countries, stands out in international comparisons in these aspects, presenting high levels of trust. Results from the World Value Survey even show an upward trend between 1982 and 2006. In the latest survey almost 70 per cent of respondents stated that most people can be trusted.

There is, however, no unambiguous trend in trust during our period of measurement, instead the level has fluctuated and, by and large, trust continues to be at the same high level as measured almost three decades ago. Thus, in these aspects, there is no conformity with the development of economic inequalities during this period. However, if we take a closer look into the evolvement of trust for different socio-economic groups we find that the socio-economic gap in institutional trust has increased considerably. At the end of the 1980s there was almost no difference in institutional trust between the educational groups. During the 1990s and, especially during the economic crisis of the early 1990s, our data show a big gap between those with considerable education compared to those with less education. This gap seemed, however, to narrow somewhat in the middle of the 1990s before reaching the same high levels again. Since 2006, these high levels seem to have been fortified. Unfortunately, we lack comparable data over time for the indicator on interpersonal trust. However, two points of measurement in 1996 and 1999 show the same considerable differences between those at the highest and those at the lowest educational level. This reinforces the picture of an existing and perhaps growing social gradient within dimensions of trust.

In a comparison of public trust for 21 institutions, health care is the most trusted, closely followed by the police force. Not far behind, we find the Swedish central bank together with the universities and colleges. At the other end of the scale, among the institutions trusted least, we find the European Commission, the European Parliament and at the end, labour unions. That the European institutions have such a low degree of trust seems somewhat surprising, given the positive development of support for a Swedish EU membership, which is now fairly strong (in the latest survey, in 2010, 53 per cent had a positive attitude and 23 per cent had a negative attitude). This development is also in line with the increased voter turnout in the elections for the European parliament since 1995. A similar somewhat contradictory result goes for the low trust in the Swedish labour union movement, given the high level of labour unionization in Sweden.

The vast majority of the Swedish labour force is unionized, about 70 per cent in 2011 (Kjellberg 2010). This is a high level by international comparisons and has, at least partly, been explained by the Ghent system, i.e. the unemployment insurance being organized primarily by the labour unions. A political reform in 2007 implied that individual contributions to the funds should be related to unemployment risk. As a result, groups with high unemployment risks experienced in some cases quite substantive increases, for one group the increase was as high as 600 per cent, whereas groups with low risks could enjoy lower contribution levels. This led to members opting out of both unemployment insurance and labour unions. Between 2007 and 2008, the latter lost about six percentage points of their members. However, a slow decline in the union's density had already started in the middle of the 1980s.

Again, we note divergent development among socio-economic groups. Historically, blue-collar workers have had a higher degree of unionization compared to white-collar workers, but since around 2006 this relationship has been reversed. The gap between the groups had increased to about five percentage points in 2011. This is also visible in comparisons between the different labour unions, in which the largest organizer of blue-collar workers, the Swedish Trade Union Confederation (LO 2012), had the largest membership decline (Kjellberg, 2009).

Sweden has one of the largest shares of non-native born citizens in Europe (Eurostat 2011). Despite this, or maybe as a result, support for the reception of refugees has increased. There is now a considerably smaller proportion of respondents stating that they believe it is a good idea to accept *fewer* refugees (41 per cent in 2011) than during the crisis in the early 1990s (61 per cent). On the other hand, an 'anti-immigrant party' (the Swedish Democrats, SD) won seats in the Swedish parliament in the election in 2010. An anti-immigrant party has only been represented in the Swedish parliament once before, namely New Democracy, between 1991 and 1994. The fact that public opinion towards the reception of refugees has become more liberal at the same time that an anti-immigrant party has won enough votes to sit in the parliament, could indicate that a polarization with regard to attitudes to immigrants and immigration policy has taken place.

5. CHANGING WELFARE STATE INSTITUTIONS

We now turn to social policy and Welfare State institutions and their relationships to income inequality trends. As noted earlier, Sweden is often used as a prototypical example of the social democratic Welfare State regime (Esping-Andersen, 1990), with an encompassing system of social protection (Korpi and Palme, 1998). In some policy areas this characterization still holds but in other programmes the reorganization of the Swedish welfare state has been substantial.

Major cutbacks in replacement rates in social protection were initiated during the deep recession of the 1990s. Particularly in cash transfer schemes, this downsizing of social protection has continued well into the 2000s, not least as part of the policy package adopted by the current centre/right government to increase work incentives. Central parts of their policy package have included an earned income tax credit for those in gainful employment (*Jobbskatteavdraget*) and cutbacks in unemployment compensation and sick pay. Meanwhile, occupational and private insurance against losses in work income has become more prominent (Sjögren Lindquist and Wadensjö, 2007).

Some areas of the Swedish Welfare State have suffered less from retrenchment, either due to structural-economic factors or for ideological reasons, and sometimes a combination of the two. Examples here include education, health care and family policy. However, new governance structures have been introduced to public services, influenced by new public management ideas and quasi-markets. As a consequence, the number of private service providers has increased. In terms of minimum wages, it is difficult to find any clear trend. Sweden does not have a system of state legislated minimum wages, common to other countries. Instead wages are negotiated by the social partners, something that has its roots in the historical centralized coordinated wage agreements between employer organizations and trade unions. The most notable change is that wage increases since the 1980s have mainly been determined at industry level.

The Swedish income tax system includes municipal (including regional) taxes, state tax and employee social security contributions. State tax is only applied at above average wage levels. Along with the 1990/1991 tax reform, the highest marginal tax rate was set at 50 per cent, in the mid 1990s it was raised to 55 per cent. Another major part of the reform was the introduction of a dual income tax system, where tax levied on capital income became flat rate. Recent changes in income taxes are successive expansions of earned income tax credits (flat rate), excluding income from major social insurance programmes. Value added sales taxes (VAT) have also been changed, where VAT for restaurant services was reduced from 25 to 12 per cent in 2012. Employer social security contributions were 31.42[8] per cent of wages in 2012, but recently reductions to employer social security contributions have been introduced for people below 26 years. Similar reductions apply for people aged 65 and over. Tax deductions for costs related to renovating dwellings (ROT) were re-introduced in 2008 to counteract low demand in the construction industry. An analogous deduction was introduced in 2007 for household services (RUT), including charges for cleaning, child minding and gardening. RUT was parallel to a greater family policy package, intending to support families and increase low-skilled service sector jobs.

Sweden has not only seen a substantial lowering of income and property taxation, but wealth and inheritance taxes have also been abolished. The distributive effects of these changes to the Swedish tax system are not easy to disentangle, but as discussed earlier, the introduction of a dual income tax system is likely to be an important factor behind the rise of income inequality. Income inequality in Sweden is to a large extent linked to the rapid increase in top incomes and especially the growing importance of capital incomes. In an analysis of developments in top incomes, Roine and Waldenström (2008: 366) conclude that '[a] possible interpretation of our results is that Sweden over the past twenty years has become a country where it is more important to make the right financial investments than to earn a lot to become rich'.

Recent decades have presented new challenges to the Swedish Welfare State and often with far-reaching consequences for the organization of cash benefit programmes and public services. Since the early 1990s, the majority of changes to cash benefit programmes have been directed at reducing replacement rates in social insurance and social assistance. The 1990s cutbacks were carried out against a backdrop of fiscal constraints following the financial crisis. In the most recent decade, cash benefits have been reduced to increase work incentives. At average wage levels, unemployment insurance replacement rates have declined by more than a third between 1990 and 2010. In sickness and work–accident insurance, cutbacks to replacement levels have been only slightly less. For higher wage earners, replacement rates have deteriorated even faster, and maximum social insurance benefits have been halved since 1990. Changes to eligibility criteria and financing have also been introduced, often restricting access to social insurance (Ferrarini et al., 2012). Meanwhile, beneficiaries of social assistance and expenditure have increased (Kuivalainen and Nelson, 2012). Parallel to this decline in programmes for income redistribution there has been a growth in several other areas of public services, perhaps most prominently in family policy (Ferrarini and Duvander, 2010) and health care (Montanari and Nelson, 2013).

To illustrate the decline of social protection in Sweden, Figure 27.8 shows unemployment and sickness net replacement rates since 1990. These replacement rates refer to an average production worker in manufacturing and are an average of a single householder and a one-earner family with two dependent children, being absent from work for 26 weeks. In addition, we show the adequacy rate of social assistance, for people who lack work income or access to contributory social insurance benefits, expressed in per cent of the at-risk-of poverty threshold (below 60 per cent of median income). Thus, social insurance replacement and the social assistance adequacy rates are not strictly comparable. The social assistance benefit package includes available means-tested benefits, child benefits and housing allowances (see Nelson, 2013). For social insurance and social assistance, the general story

---

[8] Employer social security contributions in Sweden are divided into seven different categories depending on social security scheme. In total they amount to 31.42 per cent.

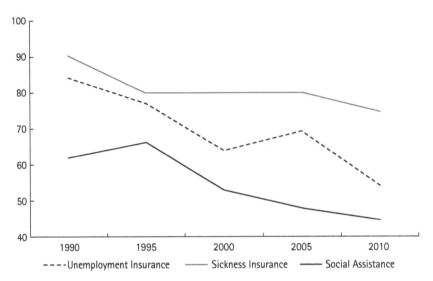

FIGURE 27.8 Unemployment and sickness insurance replacement rates and social assistance adequacy rates in Sweden, 1990–2010

Source: The Social Citizenship Indicator Program (SCIP), The Social Assistance and Minimum Income Protection Interim Dataset (SaMip) and the Social Policy Indicator Database (SPIN).

of the period is one of Welfare State retrenchment. The increase of social assistance benefit adequacy in the early-1990s is predominantly due to changes in median disposable income following the financial crisis at the time. The corresponding increase in unemployment insurance replacement rates between 2000 and 2005 is due to changes in earnings ceilings for benefit purposes.

The decline of social protection in Sweden over the most recent decades is less visible in social expenditures. One reason is of course that social spending tends to vary according to changes in welfare needs over business cycles. The Swedish unemployment insurance programme has undergone substantial changes in most recent years, concerning both replacement rates and benefit coverage. In 2005, Sweden had the second most generous unemployment insurance programme among OECD countries. In 2010, the Swedish unemployment insurance replacement rate was below the OECD average. Due to changes in the financing of unemployment insurance, including substantially increased member fees for high-risk groups, the coverage of earnings-related unemployment insurance has also been substantially reduced (Ferrarini *et al.*, 2012).

Health expenditure constitutes a large proportion of social spending. However, in per cent of GDP it declined during the 1980s and until the mid 1990s, with a slight upturn in spending following the New Millennium. Expenditure on incapacity-related programmes shows more of a roller-coaster pattern with a clear increasing trend from the mid 1980s up to the mid 2000s, whereafter expenditure levels declined. Over this period, changes were introduced to both health care and incapacity-related benefits. Private health care expenditure increased and the number of private actors providing care increased, both in health care centres and hospitals (Montanari and Nelson, 2013). In sickness insurance, we see a similar decline in replacement rates as in other major social insurance schemes. In addition, the duration of sickness insurance has been substantially reduced. In 2000, the duration of sickness insurance benefits was in practice unlimited. A few years later maximum duration was set to one year, with some exceptions. After this one-year period in receipt of benefits, a new assessment must be made. Duration of the Swedish sickness insurance scheme is now below the OECD average (Ferrarini *et al.*, 2012).

In the mid 1990s, Sweden also introduced a new pension system with a funded component. This reform introduced elements of individual risk-taking and related pension entitlements to macro-economic developments. In the Swedish premium pension (*Premiepension*), this largely involves developments of the stock market, where most individuals have their premium pension through funds. The shift from defined benefit formula in Sweden to a notionally-defined contribution formula changes generational contracts in various ways, for example, by treating different cohorts in the same way when it comes to financing of the scheme. There is also the so-called 'brake' in the pension system, which nominally reduces pensions to contain costs during slow growth and high unemployment. When the new pension system was introduced, it was assumed that the 'brake' would never be used, but it has already lowered pensions twice during the recent global financial crisis. Concerns have also been raised that the new pension system reduces income security in old age (LO, 2010).

From the early 1970s, and for nearly four decades, family policies in Sweden have increasingly been designed to support dual-earner families and more gender egalitarian patterns of care. Major reforms include parental leave, public childcare, separate income taxation, and family law. Public childcare is heavily state subsidized and, since the 1970s, it has been gradually extended to cover all children over the age of one. Children during their first year of life are usually cared for at home, when parents are on paid parental leave. Earnings-related parental leave was implemented in 1974 and subsequent reforms in 1994 and 2002 increased earmarking for fathers and extended the leave period. Maximum user fees for childcare were introduced in 2002, corresponding to 1140, 760 and 380 SEK per month for the first, second and the third pre-school child.

The family policy programme of the centre/right government initiated in 2006 introduced a more mixed system, with the declared purpose of increasing individual choice. A meagre flat-rate childcare leave benefit has been introduced, that has been criticized as supporting female home-making. Another reform, which is more in line with previous policy orientations in favour of supporting dual-earner families, is the gender equality bonus in parental leave, which is paid in cases where the earner with the highest income (typically a father) is on leave, while the other spouse is working. The bonus is designed as a tax deduction and therefore does not count as conventional social expenditure. The complicated structure of the benefit has led to fairly low take-up among eligible parents. Application procedures have therefore recently been reformed.

There is an on-going debate in Sweden concerning the organization of upper secondary school. The main lines of political conflict have concerned the role of private providers and the opportunities for students in secondary education to qualify for tertiary education. The left political opposition wants to organize upper secondary education so that all students achieve theoretical qualifications for tertiary education. The centre/right government is more in favour of tracking into academic studies or directly into employment. Adult education has been substantially reduced since the centre/right government came into power, which means that it has become more difficult to complement upper secondary school with adult education and consequently more difficult to acquire the necessary competence for tertiary level studies.

Establishment of privately-operated publicly-financed schools (*Friskolor*) has been facilitated in Sweden by the 1992 school reform. School fees are not allowed; instead each student from first grade has a school capitation allowance, which is paid directly to the school by the municipality. Primary and secondary education in Sweden is governed by local authorities under national legislation. Most school children still go to public schools run by municipalities, although enrolment in private 'free' schools has become more common. In the nine-year compulsory school system, the number of students in privately operated schools has increased from around 20,000 in 1996 to over 100,000 in 2011, nearly 12 per cent of all students. Developments in upper secondary education have been even more dramatic, with around a quarter of all students in privately-operated schools in 2011 (Skolverket, 2012). There is an on-going discussion about transferring responsibility from municipalities back to the state, not least due to concerns about wide local differences in the quality of education.

Another politically contentious issue concerns opportunities to make a profit in privately-operated education and care, where some private producers are large multinational companies. The centre/right government defends profit among private producers for ideological reasons, with the conviction that increased competition improves quality and individual choice. According to a recent evaluation it is still unclear whether strengthened private provision in education and care services has fostered efficiency, for example, in terms of reducing administration costs and increasing levels of service provision (Hartman, 2011).

6. CONCLUSION

The overall aim of this chapter was to present and examine patterns and trends of income inequality in Sweden from around 1980 onwards, highlighting their potential relationship to the social, political and cultural spheres, looking at the available evidence from research and national statistics, and pointing to the role of relevant institutions and policies. While it is, of course, impossible to draw any causal inference from just comparing income inequality trends and trends in other important social dimension, it can still be of interest in order to create reasonable hypotheses and to discuss why we find apparent associations (and why we do not). Moreover, the development of other social indicators is of course central when trying to illustrate a broader picture of developments in Sweden.

Let us first summarize some of the main findings. Sweden scored, also internationally, an all-time low of the Gini coefficient in around 1980, i.e. when we start our analysis. Since then, income inequality has increased substantially, especially from the mid 1990s and onwards. The increase in income inequality is characterized by a strong rise of top incomes and a growing importance of capital income. An important factor behind the latter is the dual income tax system that Sweden introduced in connection with the major tax reform in the early 1990s.

However, during the last five to ten years we also find a substantially increasing divergence between those at the bottom and those in the middle of the income distribution. Consequently, relative poverty increased and the P10:P50 ratio decreased. Our analysis indicates that the latter development is related to policy changes. In order to foster employ-ment several earned-income tax credits have been introduced by the centre-right govern-ment. Moreover, benefit levels in social insurance programmes have failed to keep up with wage increases and general income growth. In addition, stricter eligibility conditions have been introduced in many programmes. A markedly widening income gap between the employed and the non-employed is therefore also visible during the 2000s. Furthermore we find that an increasing proportion of young adults are neither in employment nor in educa-tion (NEET).

By and large, our analysis of the income inequality development and that of the changes in tax and benefit systems suggests a less ambitious redistributive policy focus. Rather, many policy changes, both related to taxes and benefits, seem to be drivers of increasing income inequalities.

For material deprivation, Sweden compares well from an international perspective with lower rates than most other countries. Still, we find clear differences between population groups and we can see that those outside the labour force did not experience the recovery that benefited other groups after the 1990s crisis. Take-up rates of social assistance, often used as an alternative poverty indicator in Sweden, show a strong increase during the 1990s crisis but the rate has since then fallen back to levels below the ones in 1990. However, most troublesome is the fact that long-term social assistance take-up is still considerably higher than in the pre-crisis period.

Population health in Sweden shows a somewhat conflicting development. We see a steady increase in life expectancy and a decrease in infant mortality but at the same time a notable increase in socio-economic mortality differentials. In terms of morbidity indicators, we find that the prevalence of self-reported ill health shows a more or less immediate increase dur-ing the 1990s recession. For psychological distress, the most notable change is the strong increase of ill health among younger persons.

Indicators related to forms of social capital give quite a rosy picture of Sweden. The degree of self-rated loneliness in the population has fallen substantially. The level of both institu-tional and interpersonal trust is astonishingly high throughout the period. However, we have indications of an existing and perhaps growing social gradient within dimensions of trust. The same goes for voter turnout in national elections, as well as other forms of political participation, showing a steeper social gradient, along with a general declining trend.

Also, the degree of unionization has fallen during recent decades, and this trend was rein-forced by a change in the unemployment insurance legislation in 2007. The new law, link-ing contributions to unemployment risk, led to members opting out of both unemployment insurance and labour unions. In 2006, the degree of unionization in white-collar groups for the first time became higher than among blue-collar workers and this difference has increased since then.

Sweden has one of the largest shares of non-native born citizens in Europe. Despite this, or maybe as a result, support for the reception of refugees has increased. However, this development is not unambiguous. In the 2010 national elections, an anti-immigrant party managed to win seats in the parliament. The fact that public opinion towards refugee recep-tions has become more liberal and, at the same time, an anti-immigrant party has won enough votes to sit in the parliament could indicate that a polarization with regard to atti-tudes to immigrants and immigration policy is taking place.

Another characteristic of the latter part of the period that should be noted, although it has not been the prime focus of attention in this chapter, is the growing emphasis given to private providers in public services, care and education. The long-run impact on inequality such a development may have is much debated in Sweden.

While, in many cases, we can link the increase of income inequalities to specific tax and other policy reforms, a more difficult task is to scrutinize in depth the underlying causes behind the policy changes and other drivers. One such cause could be public opinion towards inequalities and redistributive policies. We cannot but note that attitudes among the population at large do not reveal any such major changes. People's support for a redistributive Welfare State continues to be high, and a clear majority of the population thinks that income differentials are too large.

Can we then finally make a brief summary of how the trends in social, cultural and political indicators correspond to the income inequality trend? Our investigation does not reveal any unambiguous trends that we can associate with the increased income inequality. This should not surprise us since it may in many instances take much more time before such associations appear. Moreover, patterns could emerge when making more sophisticated analyses, perhaps in particular in regard to subgroups. For many social and political indicators we find increasing differences, or a more polarized pattern, when looking at educational or socio-economic groups. This is, for example, evident when looking at mortality and political participation. Such a pattern could very well be driven by increasing income inequalities but needs a more thorough analysis to be proven or falsified.

REFERENCES

Agnello, L. and Schuknecht, L. (2009), 'Booms and Busts in Housing Markets: Determinants and Implications', *ECB Working Paper*, No. 1071.

Alesina, A. and Glaeser, E.L. (2004), *Fighting Poverty in the US and Europe: A World of Difference*, Oxford: Oxford University Press.

Atkinson, A.B. (2004), 'The Luxembourg Income Study (LIS): Past, Present and Future', *Socio-Economic Review*, 2:165–190.

Bergmark, Å. and Bäckman, O. (2004), 'Stuck with welfare? Long-term social assistance recipiency in Sweden', *European Sociological Review*, 20:425–443.

Bergmark, Å. and Bäckman, O. (2007), 'Socialbidragstagandets dynamik—varaktighet och utträden från socialbidragstagande under 2000-talet', in Bergmark, Åke and Fritzell, Johan (eds.), *Välfärdens ansikte mot 2000-talet* (Socialvetenskaplig tidskrift), 14:134–152.

Björklund, A. and Jäntti, M. (2011), *SNS Välfärdsrapport: Inkomstfördelningen i Sverige*, Stockholm: SNS förlag.

Bynner, J. and Parsons, S. (2002), 'Social Exclusion and the Transition from School to Work: The Case of Young People Not in Education, Employment, or Training (NEET)', *Journal of Vocational Behavior*, 60:289–309.

Dewilde, C. (2011), 'The Interplay between Economic Inequality Trends and Housing Regime Changes in Advanced Welfare Democracies: A New Research Agenda', *Gini Discussion Paper 18*, Amsterdam, AIAS.

Esping-Andersen, G. (1990), *The Three Worlds of Welfare Capitalism*, Princeton: Princeton University Press.

Esping-Andersen, G. and Korpi, W. (1987), 'From Poor Relief to Institutional Welfare States: The Development of Scandinavian Social Policy', in Erikson, R., Hansen, E. J., Ringen, S. and Uusitalo, H. (eds.) *The Scandinavian Model: Welfare States and Welfare Research*, New York: M. E. Sharpe, Inc.

Eurostat (2011), *Migrants in Europe. A statistical portrait of the first and second generation*, Luxembourg: Eurostat, European Commission.

Eurostat (2012), 'Database' [online]: <http://epp.eurostat.ec.europa.eu/portal/page/portal/statistics/search_database> (accessed 6 September 2012).

Eurostat (2013), 'Database' [online]: <http://epp.eurostat.ec.europa.eu/portal/page/portal/statistics/search_database> (accessed 4 January 2013).

Ferrarini, T. and Duvander, A-Z. (2010), 'Earner-Carer Model at the Cross-Roads: Reforms and Outcomes of Sweden's Family Policy in Comparative Perspective', *International Journal of Health Services* 40(3):373–398.

Ferrarini, T., Nelson, K., Palme, J. and Sjöberg O. (2012). *Sveriges socialförsäkringar i jämförande perspektiv. En institutionell analys av sjuk-, arbetsskade- och arbetslöshetsförsäkringarna i 18 OECD-länder 1930 till 2010* (S 2010:04) Stockholm: Ministry of Health and Social Affairs.

Fritzell, J., Bacchus Hertzman, J., Bäckman O., Borg I., Ferrarini T. and Nelson K. (2012), *Growing Inequality and its Impacts (GINI) Country Report Sweden*, Stockholm.

Fritzell J., Bäckman O. and Ritakallio V.-M. (2012), 'Income Inequality and Poverty: do the Nordic Countries still Constitute a Family of their Own?' in J. Kvist, J. Fritzell, B. Hvinden and O. Kangas (eds.), *Changing Social Equality. The Nordic Welfare Model in the 21st Century*, Bristol: Policy Press.

Fritzell, J., Gähler, M. and Nermo, M. (2007), 'Vad hände med 1990-talets stora förlorargrupper?' *Socialvetenskaplig tidskrift* 14(2-3):110–133.

Gerdes, C. and Wadensjö, E. (2012), 'Is Immigration Challenging the Economic Sustainability of the Nordic Welfare Model?' in Kvist, J., Fritzell, J., Hvinden, B. and Kangas, O. (eds.), *Changing Social Equality, The Nordic Welfare Model in the 21st Century*, Bristol: Policy Press.

Halleröd, B. (1991), *Den svenska fattigdomen. En studie av fattigdom och socialbidragstagande*, Lund: Arkiv.

Hartman, L. (2011), *Konkurrensens konsekvenser. Vad händer med svensk välfärd?* Stockholm: SNS förlag.

Helgertz, J. (2010), 'Immigrant Careers. Why Country of Origin Matters', *Lund Studies in Economic History* 53, Lund: Lund University.

Holmén, K., Furukawa, H. (2002), 'Loneliness, Health and Social Network among Elderly People—a Follow-up Study', *Archives of Gerontology and Geriatrics*, 35 (3):261–274.

Kautto, M., Fritzell, J., Hvinden, B., Kvist, J. and Uusitalo, H. (eds.) (2001), *Nordic Welfare States in the European Context*, London, New York: Routledge.

Kildal, N. and Kuhnle, S. (2005), *Normative Foundations of the Welfare State. The Nordic Experience*, London, New York: Routledge.

Kjellberg, A. (2009), 'Det fackliga medlemsraset i Sverige under 2007 och 2008', *Arbetsmarknad & Arbetsliv*, 15:11–28.

Kjellberg, A (2010) (updated 2012), 'Kollektivavtalens täckningsgrad samt organisationsgraden hos arbetsgivarförbund och fackförbund', *Studies in Social Policy, Industrial Relations, Working Life and Mobility Research Reports* 2010:1, Department of Sociology, Lund University.

Korpi, W. and Palme, J. (1998), 'The Paradox of Redistribution and the Strategy of Equality: Welfare State Institutions, Inequality and Poverty in the Western Countries', *American Sociological Review*, 63(5):661–687.

Kuivalainen, S. and Nelson, K. (2011), 'Eroding Minimum Income Protection in the Nordic Countries', in Kvist, J., Fritzell, J., Hvinden B. and Kangas, O. (eds.), *Changing Social Equality. The Nordic Welfare Model in the 21st Century*, Bristol: Policy Press

Kvist, J., Fritzell, J., Hvinden, B., and Kangas, O. (eds.), (2012), *Changing Social Equality, The Nordic Welfare Model in the 21st century*, Bristol: Policy Press.

Lindbom, A. (2001), 'Dismantling Swedish Housing Policy', *Governance*, 14:4:503–526.

LO (2010), *Pensionsreformen i halvtid*, Stockholm: Landsorganisationen i Sverige.

LO (2012), *The Swedish Trade Union Confederation*, [online]: <http://lo.se/home/lo/home. nsf/unidView/A3E9A303B74321E5C12572E300410A32/$file/LO%20Swedish%20Trade%20 Union%20Confederation%20ENG.pdf> (accessed 6 September 2012).

Lundberg, O., Åberg Yngwe, M., Kölegård Stjärne, M., Björk, L., and Fritzell, J. (2008), *The Nordic Experience: Welfare States and Public Health. Final report from the NEWS-Project*, Stockholm: CHESS, 2008.

Magnusson, L. and Turner, B. (2008), 'Municipal Housing Companies in Sweden—Social by Default', *Housing Theory and Society*, 25:(4):275–296.

Montanari, I and Nelson, K. (2013), 'Social Service Decline and Convergence: How does Health Care Fare?', *Journal of European Social Policy* 23 (1), p. 102–116.

Nelson, K. (2013), 'Social Assistance and EU Poverty Thresholds 1990-2008. Are European Welfare Systems Providing Just and Fair Protection Against Low Income?' *European Sociological Review* 29, n. 2, p. 386-401.

OECD (2011), 'Country Note: Sweden', part of *Divided we Stand: Why Inequality Keeps Rising*. [online] <http://www.oecd.org/social/inequality.htm>

Palme, J., Bergmark, Å., Bäckman, O., Estrada, F., Fritzell, J., Lundberg, O., Sjöberg, O. and Szebehely, M. (2002), 'Welfare Trends in Sweden: Balancing the Books for the 1990s', *Journal of European Social Policy*, 12:329–346.

Palme, J., Bergmark, Å., Bäckman, O., Estrada, F., Fritzell, J., Lundberg, O., Sjöberg, O., Sommestad, L., and Szebehely, M. (2003), 'A Welfare Balance Sheet for the 1990s' Final Report of the Swedish Welfare Commission', *Scandinavian Journal of Public Health*, 60 pp7–143.

Ritakallio, V-M. (2003), 'The Importance of Housing Costs in Cross-National Comparisons of Welfare (State) Outcomes', *International Social Security Review*, 56(2):81–101.

Roine, J. and Waldenström, D. (2008), 'The Evolution of Top Incomes in an Egalitarian Society: Sweden 1903-2004', *Journal of Public Economics*, 9:366–387.

Sjögren Lindquist, G. and Wadensjö, E. (2007), 'Ett svårlagt pussel—kompletterande ersättningar vid inkomstbortfall' *ESS*, 2007:1. Stockholm: The Swedish Finance Ministry.

Skolverket (2012), *En bild av skolmarknaden. Syntes av Skolverkets skolmarknadsprojekt*, Stockholm: Skolverket.

Socialstyrelsen (2009), *Folkhälsorapport 2009*, Stockholm: Socialstyrelsen.

Socialstyrelsen (2010), *Social Rapport 2010*, Stockholm: Socialstyrelsen.

Sørensen, P. B. (1994), 'From the Global Income Tax to the Dual Income Tax', *International Tax and Public Finance*, 1:57–80.

Statistics Sweden (2000), 'Förmögenhetsfördelningen i Sverige 1997 med tillbakablick till 1975', Örebro: Statistics Sweden.

Statistics Sweden (2012), 'Statistikdatabasen' [website] <http://www.scb.se> (accessed 22 September 2012).

Sundström, G., Fransson, E., Malmberg, B. and Davey, A. (2009), 'Loneliness among Older Europeans', *European Journal of Ageing*, 6(4):267–275.

Svallfors, S. (2011), 'A Bedrock of Support? Trends in Welfare State Attitudes in Sweden, 1981-2010', *Social Policy & Administration*, 45:806–825.

Wilkinson, R.G. and Pickett, K. (2009), *The Spirit Level: Why More Equal Societies Almost Always do Better*, London: Allen Lane.

CHAPTER 28

···

DIVIDED WE FALL? THE WIDER CONSEQUENCES OF HIGH AND UNRELENTING INEQUALITY IN THE UK*

···

ABIGAIL McKNIGHT AND TIFFANY TSANG

1. INTRODUCTION

···

INEQUALITY in the UK increased dramatically over the 1980s and since then it has fluctu-ated around the level reached in the early 1990s. The UK became one of the most unequal advanced nations and this has remained the case. These changes occurred over a period of three decades, which were subject to three severe recessions: the late 1970s/early 1980s; early 1990s; and the current recession following the 2008 financial crisis. The three decades of the 1980s, 1990s and 2000s can be divided into two main periods of political governance: the Conservative Thatcher/Major government 1979–1997; and the Labour Blair/Brown govern-ment 1997–2010. In 2010, no single political party achieved an outright majority but a coali-tion government was formed between the Conservative and Liberal Democrat Parties.

Increases in household income inequality were largely driven by increases in labour mar-ket inequalities. This is not surprising as the vast majority of household original income is derived from employment. While there is no consensus on the cause of increasing earnings inequality, it is generally agreed that globalization, skill-biased (task-biased) technologi-cal change and institutional change all contributed. Changes to the supply of skills relative to changes in demand either exacerbated or ameliorated these pressures. Demographic change also played a part, such as the increase in single-headed households. Female labour force participation increased substantially but work was very unevenly distributed across

* More detail and references can be found in GINI UK Country Report (gini-research.org/CR-UK). Valuable comments were made by Ive Marx, Tim van Rie and Wiemer Salverda.

households, further contributing to increases in inequality at the household level. We examine evidence that suggests different forces dominated over these three decades, which appear to have affected different parts of household income, household wealth and individual earnings distributions.

Social policy, particularly tax and benefit policy, also played a key role in modifying these external pressures. Payment of cash benefits has a strong equalizing effect on original income inequality as cash benefits are generally targeted at low-income households. When considered together, direct and indirect taxation has had a broadly neutral effect on household income inequality since 1980. In this chapter we explore the potential impact of these key characteristics of UK inequality on a wide range of social, political and cultural factors.

2. The Evolution of Inequalities

We begin by mapping the trends in inequality in the UK since 1980. We look at trends in household income inequality, examining in detail the extent to which levels and trends are shaped by tax and benefit policy. The two main sources of market income for households are income from employment and income from investments, so we look in turn at wealth inequality and labour market inequality. Finally we look at education inequalities.

Household Income Inequality

Inequality in British household income can be characterized by two very distinct periods: a dramatic rise in the 1980s followed by two decades where inequality fluctuated around this new higher level. Estimates from the Households Below Average Income (HBAI) series (Figure 28.1) show that the Gini coefficient of equivalized disposable household income increased from around 0.26 in 1980 to 0.34 in the early 1990s, falling slightly in the mid 1990s and then increased again to 0.35 in 2000. The mid 2000s were also a period where inequality fell slightly but by 2009/10 inequality had increased to 0.36 (Jin et al., 2011). In 2010/11 inequality fell to 0.34—the largest one year fall since this series began, which seems to be driven by progressively greater falls in real income in higher household income quintiles (Cribb et al., 2012).

At the same time, real disposable equivalized household mean income doubled, but increased by only 62 per cent for the first decile compared with 147 per cent for the top decile (ONS, 2012a).

Figure 28.1 also maps changes in household income inequality and the redistributive effects of taxes and benefits since 1980 (ETB series). In contrast to the HBAI series, which is individual weighted, the ETB series is household weighted but the advantage of the ETB series is that it is possible to estimate the effects of indirect taxes. Inequality trends in these data follow the same pattern as the HBAI series. Government policy in the form of tax and welfare policy plays a significant role in terms of the distribution and redistribution of household income. Inequality in *original income*, from employment and investments, is greatly reduced by the payment of cash benefits (*gross income*), by over 10 points in the Gini

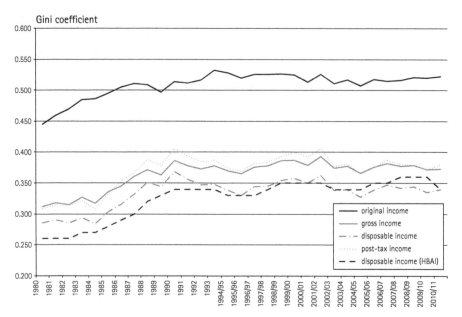

FIGURE 28.1 Household income inequality 1980 to 2010/11 (Gini coefficient)

Sources: Office for National Statistics—The effects of taxes and benefits (ETB) data series.
HBAI series—IFS, <http://www.ifs.org.uk/bns/bn19figs.xls>.

coefficient, due to the fact that cash benefits are disproportionally received by low-income families. Direct taxes reduce inequality by a considerably lesser extent (3–4 points) as the lowest income households are less likely to pay tax (*disposable income*) and while income tax is progressive amongst taxpayers, some forms of tax are regressive (for example, National Insurance). Indirect taxes (such as VAT, alcohol and fuel duty) have a disequalizing effect as lower-income households tend to spend a higher proportion of their income on goods and services liable to these taxes (*post-tax income*). Overall, tax policy (direct and indirect taxes in aggregate) since 1986 has either had no effect on gross income inequality or has had a disequalizing effect. The redistributive effects of taxation result from the ways in which tax revenues are spent rather than how revenue is raised.

The fall in the inequality of disposable and gross income but not in original income at the start of the financial crisis 2008/9–2009/10 is likely to be due to strong growth in benefits and tax credits, reflecting falling inflation (which through benefit upgrading procedures increases benefit values in real terms) and discretionary changes in benefit and tax credit rates. This meant that real income growth was greatest in the lowest income quintile (Jin *et al.*, 2011). In contrast to the HBAI series, inequality in original and gross income is unchanged 2009/10–2010/11, but inequality in disposable and post-tax income increases. This suggests that direct and indirect taxes became more regressive at the household level, which could, in part, be due to the increase in VAT from 17.5 per cent to 20 per cent in January 2011. This finding is at odds with the fall measured in the larger HBAI series, generally considered to be more reliable for measuring single year changes in inequality.

Income examined so far is measured 'before housing costs' (BHC), which is standard practice when estimates of the complete distribution of income are computed. The 'after housing costs'[1] (AHC) measure of income tends to be regarded as a better reflection of living standards (Jin *et al.*, 2011, p71) when the focus is on low-income households who are likely to have limited choice over housing cost and quality. Within the HBAI series (individual weighted) it is possible to look at income before and after housing costs. This shows that inequality, measured by decile ratios, followed the same steep increase over the 1980s for both BHC and AHC measures. The two measures record very similar levels of inequality over the 1980s but in the first half of the 1990s they diverge, so that in 1994/5 the BHC 90/10 ratio was four but the AHC ratio was five and similarly there was a greater increase in AHC income inequality between 2004/05 and 2008/09 than BHC income inequality. This suggests that the distribution of housing costs became more unequal over the income distribution.

An alternative approach estimates the share of income accruing to different groups of households. Findings from this approach show that households in the top income quintile (top 20 per cent) increased their share of equivalized disposable income from 37 per cent in 1980 to 43 per cent in 1997 and remained around this share through to 2010/11. However, the top 10 per cent and particularly the top 1 per cent increased their income share (Atkinson *et al.*, 2011; Sibieta, 2011) and this increase in concentration at the top has continued after inequality measured by the Gini coefficient levelled off in the early 1990s.

Poverty

As in the EU, UK relative poverty is typically defined as contemporary equivalized household income below 60 per cent of the median. The UK doesn't have an official absolute poverty line although the official measurement of child poverty includes a measure of absolute poverty. Between 1979 and 1989 absolute poverty, defined as income less than 60 per cent median household income fixed to the 1998/99 value, declined from around one-third to one-quarter of all households as real incomes grew, at the same time relative poverty rates increased (Figure 28.2). Poverty measured before and after housing costs, for both measures of absolute and relative income poverty, diverged between 1979 and 1996. In the second period 1994/95–2009/10 absolute poverty rates fell, reflecting the real increases in household incomes but increased rates following the 2008 financial crisis. Relative poverty continued to fall, affected by falling median incomes, which resulted in a fall in the level of income at the 60 per cent median mark and consequently fewer households were found below this level. AHC measures of poverty are higher than BHC measures, reflecting the fact that although households with lower income often receive financial support to cover housing costs, housing costs represent a much smaller share of household income among higher income households.

Looking at different population groups (Figure 28.3), single-parent households have the highest poverty rates (BHC and AHC). Since 1997, poverty rates among these households

---

[1] Housing costs include: rent (gross of housing benefit); water rates; community water charges and council water charges; mortgage interest payments; structural insurance premiums (for owner occupiers); ground rent; and service charges. There is no adjustment for imputed rent for owner occupiers.

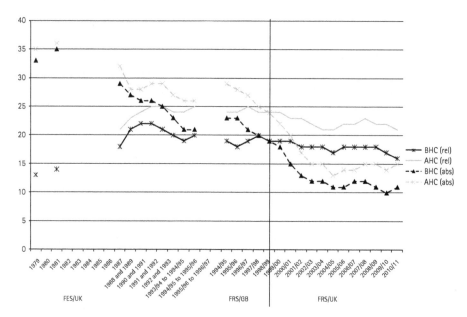

FIGURE 28.2 Population shares below 60% median household income before and after housing costs—relative (rel) and absolute (abs)

Notes: Family Expenditure Survey (FES) figures are for single and combined calendar years. Family Resources Survey (FRS) figures are for financial years. Breaks and discontinuities, as shown.

Source: HBAI series, Department for Work and Pensions/ONS.

have fallen, affected by policies aimed at reducing child poverty through tax credits and other changes to welfare benefits alongside initiatives to increase lone parent employment (such as the New Deal for Lone Parents).

Gregg, Harkness and Machin (1999) highlighted the very big increases in child poverty that occurred in Britain over the period 1968 to 1995/96. They estimate that in 1979 13 per cent of children were living in relative income poverty (AHC)[2] increasing to 33 per cent in 1995/96, with around half of these children living in households where no adult was in work. In 1999, the Labour government pledged to eradicate child poverty[3] in a generation (20 years); and later set intermediate goals, such as halving the rate in 10 years.

Figure 28.3(a) shows falling child poverty rates since 1997, from 27 per cent in 1996/97 to 18 per cent in 2010/11 for BHC estimates. The estimated rates for AHC measures are higher and have fallen by less from 34 per cent to 27 per cent (Figure 28.3(b)).

The next highest risk group shown is single female pensioner households. Falls in poverty rates for these householders have been modest, when income is measured BHC, but poverty rates halved from 40 per cent in 1997 to 20 per cent in 2005 AHC. As a result AHC poverty rates among these households were lower than BHC poverty rates in 2010/11. This suggests that housing costs have fallen for these pensioner households, consistent with increasing

---

[2] They define poverty as living below half mean equivalized household income. The estimates for BHC are lower but the increases are similar; 8 per cent in 1979 rising to 24 per cent in 1995/96.

[3] Defined as 60 per cent of median equivalized household income.

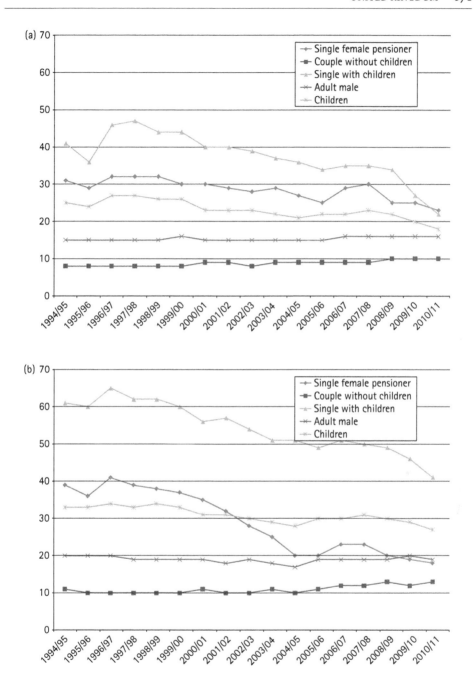

FIGURE 28.3 Population group shares below 60% median household income (a) Before housing costs (BHC) (b) After housing costs (AHC)

Notes: Figures are for the United Kingdom from 2002/03 onwards. Earlier years are for Great Britain.

Source: HBAI series, Department for Work and Pensions/ONS.

shares of pensioners owning their homes outright. Other household types without children have seen very little change in poverty rates over this 15-year period and some modest increases for individuals living in couple households.

Labour Market Inequality

Employment income is a key component of household income, typically accounting for over 80 per cent of original income. Income from employment received by a household is determined by the number of workers, their hours of work and their wage rates. A recent OECD study has shown that the two main factors that explain changes in household earnings inequality in the UK (mid 1980s to mid 2000s) are inequality in male earnings, which has increased inequality, and increases in female labour force participation, which has limited inequality growth (OECD, 2011).

Figure 28.4 maps the trends in unemployment rates since the early 1970s. Two measures of unemployment are shown, defined in terms of receipt of unemployment benefit (claimant rate) and the ILO definition.[4] These series show the deep recessions and associated high unemployment rates of the 1980s and the early 1990s and the increase in unemployment following the 2008 financial crisis. The higher ILO rates result from the fact that not all unemployed people qualify for unemployment benefit. Both numerators and denominators differ too (economically active versus claimant plus estimated workforce jobs). The gap between the two series varies over time and some of this is associated with the tightening of qualifying rules for unemployment benefit, such as a reduction in entitlement to contribution based benefits from 12 to 6 months of any unemployment spell when Jobseeker's Allowance (JSA) was introduced in 1996. Prior to 2001, where two members of a couple were unemployed, only one member claimed unemployment benefit on behalf of a household and one claimant counted in the claimant rate. Since 2001, where there are no dependent children present, most households where a couple are both unemployed are required to make a joint claim and both are required to meet the eligibility criteria. In the current recession, the rates diverge by around 2 percentage points and therefore the claimant rate now severely underestimates the true rate of unemployment, which is better captured by the ILO rate. The concern must be that unemployment unprotected by unemployment benefit has a greater negative impact on household income and this evidence suggests that the current recession is hitting household incomes hard even though unemployment rates, so far, are lower than in the previous two recessions.

Previous studies have highlighted the non-random nature of unemployment with low-skilled, less qualified, younger and older individuals experiencing more unemployment in terms of frequency of spells and duration of spells.

---

[4] The ILO defines individuals as unemployed if they are without work, want to work, have actively sought a job in the last four weeks and are available to start work in the next two weeks. Individuals who are out of work, have found a job and are waiting to start it in the next 2 weeks are also defined as unemployed. The claimant definition consists of all people claiming unemployment benefit (Jobseeker's Allowance since 1996) on a defined date. These individuals must declare that they are out of work, capable of, available for and actively seeking work during the week in which their claim is made.

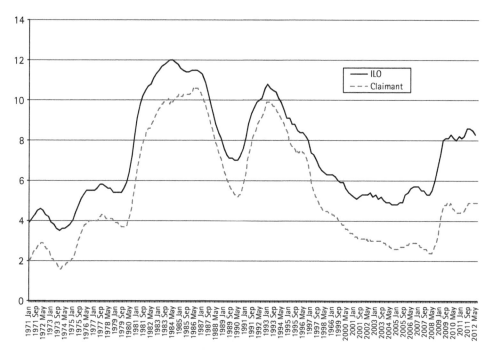

FIGURE 28.4 Trends in UK unemployment 1971–2012 (working age)—ILO and claimant rates

Source: Claimant rates derived from the ONS BCJE series based on administrative unemployment benefit claim data; ILO rates from ONS series based on LFS household data.

For those in work, rates of hourly wage inequality have consistently increased through to the mid 1990s (the 90/10 ratio increased by around one third between 1980 and 1995) after which inequality tended to level off. Overall, between 1997 and 2011, there was a slight downward trend.

Weekly earnings inequality can differ from hourly wage inequality through differences in weekly hours of work across the wage distribution. For full-time employees,[5] Pike (2012), using ASHE, finds very little change in the 90/10 ratio of gross weekly earnings between 1997 and 2011 (3.5 in 1997, 3.6 in 2011). For all employees, data from the LFS shows that, inequality is higher but also fairly stable over this period (ONS, 2011).

Bell and van Reenen (2010) show that there has been a large and sustained increase in the earnings of those at the top of the distribution (particularly between 1998 and 2008) driven by increasingly large annual bonus payments, primarily in the financial sector, which would be almost entirely missed in the more frequently analysed weekly earnings data. Inequality measured by decile ratios can also fail to pick up these big changes as they simply compare two points in the distribution. The share of total wages going to the top decile of workers has increased substantially over the last 30 years and all the gains of the top 5 per cent of workers since 1998 have resulted from substantial increases in bonus pay, much of which was in the form of bankers' bonuses.

[5] Employees on adult rates and whose pay was unaffected by absence in the pay period.

Machin (2011) concludes from his analysis that wage inequality trends can be characterized by four distinct decades: (1) the 1970s was a decade where inequality narrowed slightly; (2) the 1980s was a decade of rapidly increasing inequality; (3) more muted increases in inequality occurred over the 1990s; and (4) in the 2000s inequality increases were concentrated in the upper part of the distribution.

Over the period of increasing inequality, earnings mobility fell (Dickens and McKnight, 2008). This means that cross-sectional inequality is now more indicative of long-term differences between individuals. Coupled with evidence that intergenerational mobility fell for cohorts born between 1958 and 1970 (Blanden *et al.*, 2005) this portrays a picture of high and entrenched inequality both within a generation and between generations.

Wealth and Debt Inequality

While household income and individual earnings provide information on a current standard of living, household wealth provides additional information on past financial well-being (to the extent that savings represent the excess of income over expenditure) and an indication of future financial health. Wealth holdings are greatly influenced by the lifecycle so we start by examining the changing age profiles of net worth and its components: net financial assets and net housing assets. The age-wealth profiles in Figure 28.5 show how wealth holdings typically change with age: lower at younger ages and reaching a peak prior to retirement, although we are not able to separate time and cohort effects. We observe increases in average net worth, particularly between 2000 and 2005. Evidence on net financial assets shows falls from 1995–2000 (which could in part be a switch to housing assets and an increase in average gross financial debt), but also the effect of the dotcom market crash in 2000. In 2005, real net financial wealth is only higher than 1995 values for household heads over the age of 65. The third figure in this panel shows that the increase in net worth was driven by substantial increases in net housing equity.

Wealth is much more unevenly distributed than income or earnings (Table 28.1). This difference is due to two main factors: the much greater concentration of wealth among the wealthiest households and the significant fraction of households who are in overall debt. Overall wealth inequality fell between 1995 and 2005 since the increases in net worth were mainly concentrated in housing net worth which is more evenly distributed than financial assets. Home ownership rates increased and between 2000 and 2005 there was a rapid increase in house prices. Further analysis suggests that the increase in net housing equity and the associated fall in wealth inequality can be explained by house price rises (Hills and Bastagli, 2013) and demographic change (Cowell, Karagiannaki and McKnight, 2012). It would appear from these results that the dramatic increases in income inequality in the 1980s did not lead to increases in relative wealth inequality. In fact, inequality fell between 1995 and 2005, even when changes in house prices are taken into account, although there were big increases in the absolute gaps.

Educational Inequality

We approach the issue of educational inequality by examining the gaps between children from privileged and less privileged backgrounds defined by social class and eligibility for Free School Meals (FSMs) (a means-tested entitlement for families on low income).

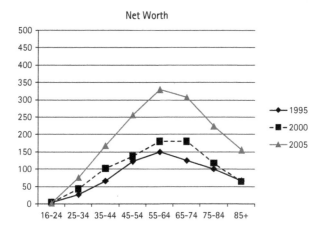

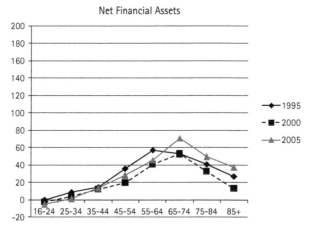

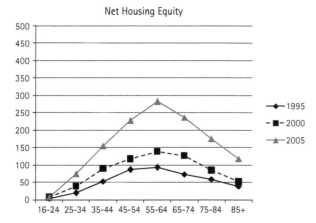

FIGURE 28.5 Age profiles in mean net worth, net financial assets and housing equity by year

Note: All monetary values are expressed in thousands 2005 Euros (Euro 16 ppp). Net worth is defined as the sum of net financial assets and net housing equity.

Source: British Household Panel Study 1995, 2000 and 2005 (Cowell, Karagiannaki and McKnight, 2012).

Table 28.1 Inequality in net worth

Year	Gini	GE(2)	P90/P50	P75/P25	P75/P50	P25/P50
1995	0.687	1.523	5.343	76.761	2.649	0.034
2000	0.655	1.099	4.822	52.732	2.343	0.044
2005	0.587	0.810	3.391	21.950	1.942	0.088

Source: BHPS 1995, 2000 and 2005 (Cowell, Karagiannaki and McKnight, 2012).

Increasing educational attainment, where attainment generally has an upper bound, will lead to falling educational inequality when measured by, for example, Gini coefficients based on years of schooling. However, even where average attainment increases there can remain important inequalities in attainment.

As in most advanced nations, educational attainment increased but there remain wide disparities according to parental background (McKnight, 2005). GCSE[6] performance (Grades A*–C) in England and Wales by parental social class widened between 1989 and 1994 due to greater relative gains made by children from more privileged backgrounds, and then narrowed 1998–2000 due to plateauing at the top and some catch-up by children from less privileged backgrounds. Over the period 2006/7 to 2010/11, the gap in the percentage of pupils attaining 5+ GCSE A*–C, with and without FSM eligibility, narrowed from 27 to 18 percentage points, but when restricted to those whose GCSEs included English and mathematics (the preferred measure of attainment) there is very little change: 27.9 percentage points in 2006/7 and 27.4 in 2010/11 (DfE, 2012).

This gap in educational achievement between more and less advantaged children is common across OECD countries but the UK performs particularly badly on these equity measures (OECD, 2010). There is also a problem of a relatively high proportion of pupils performing at a low level, described as the long tail of low achievement. Some detailed analysis of GCSE attainment data by Clifton and Cook (2012), by pupil postcode and by the performance of England's secondary schools, shows that there is a gap in attainment prior to pupils entering secondary schools, with a strong gradient in attainment tests taken at age 11 by the level of deprivation within a postcode. They also show that not only do pupils living in the most deprived areas attend poorer performing schools (in terms of the assessments made in school inspections) but within all school types (categorized according to OFSTED rating) poorer pupils' attainment is below children from more advantaged backgrounds. It is clear from this that improved educational attainment among poorer students will take more than just improving the quality of the schools they attend.

---

[6] General Certificate of Secondary Education (GCSE) examinations are taken at the end of compulsory schooling in England and Wales when pupils are aged 16.

3. Social Impacts

In this section we explore a number of social indicators to assess evidence of a relationship between their trends over time and trends in inequality. These include material deprivation, demographic trends, health outcomes and crime.

Material Deprivation

Official measurement of material deprivation is relatively new to the UK. Since 2009/10 official statistics on material deprivation for children and pensioner households have become available.

Eurostat publish a material deprivation measure based on EU-SILC but unfortunately the time series is very short: 2005–2011 (Figure 28.6). Material deprivation (deprived of at least three out of nine items[7]) is higher among children (less than 18 years of age) than the population average. In 2005, nearly one in five children in the UK were defined as materially

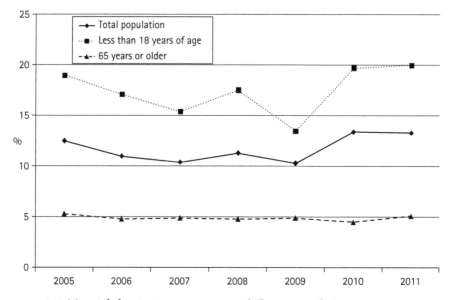

FIGURE 28.6 Material deprivation 2005–2011—different population groups

Note: The percentage of the population with an enforced lack of at least three out of nine items in the 'economic strain and durables' dimension.

Source: Eurostat, EU-SILC.

---

[7] These nine items are that the household could not afford: i) to face unexpected expenses; ii) one week annual holiday away from home; iii) to pay for arrears (mortgage or rent, utility bills or hire purchase instalments); iv) a meal with meat, chicken or fish every second day; v) to keep home

Table 28.2 Percentage of children whose parents say that they don't have because they can't afford the following items/activities by income quintile (2009/10)

	Q1	Q2	Q3	Q4	Q5	All
Outdoor space/facilities to play safely	19	13	8	5	3	11
Enough bedrooms for every child 10+ years of a different gender	30	19	10	4	3	17
Celebrations on special occasions	8	4	1	1	0	3
Leisure equipment such as sports equipment or a bicycle	16	8	3	1	0	7
At least one week's holiday away from home with family	62	48	28	14	5	36
Hobby or leisure activity	14	9	3	1	1	7
Swimming at least once a month	22	14	6	2	1	11
Have friends round for tea or a snack once a fortnight	18	10	4	2	1	8
Go on school trip at least once a term	13	8	3	1	1	6
Go to a playgroup once a week	12	7	5	1	1	6

Note: With the exception of 'Outdoor space/facilities to play safely' parents indicate whether this was something their child/ren would like to have/do but could not afford.

Source: FRS/HBAI.

deprived compared with one in twenty individuals aged 65 years or older. There is an overall downward trend in material deprivation which is driven by falls among children, consistent with the attempts made by the then UK Labour Government to reduce the incidence of child poverty.[8] As the economic crisis took hold, material deprivation increased among children, reversing the previous gains.

A more detailed examination of material deprivation among UK children using data from the 2009/10 FRS (Table 28.2) shows the overall percentage of children deprived of a range of items/activities as a result of their parents not being able to afford them. Unsurprisingly, there is a clear relationship between low income and material deprivation but not all children who are in low-income households go without these items and children in higher income households can also be deprived in this sense.

Of all the items/activities considered, one week's holiday away from home with family was least likely to be enjoyed by any of the children. There was a clear income gradient, with children living in households in the lowest income decile ten times less likely to have a holiday than children living in households in the top income decile (6 per cent compared to 60 per cent). This ratio—of ten times higher deprivation among the lowest income quintile compared with the highest—is common across many of the items/activities. There is also a very clear income gradient for a number of the items that parents reported their children did not want or need, for example a hobby or leisure activity. This causes some concern that

adequately warm, or could not afford (even if wanted to); vi) a washing machine; vii) a colour TV; viii) a telephone; ix) a personal car.

   [8] The large fall recorded in 2009 should be treated with some caution as this data point is considered, by Eurostat, to be unreliable (due to small sample size).

income-deprived parents are rationally evaluating 'need' in the light of the resources they have available and that, therefore, this measure of deprivation is underestimating material deprivation.

We now have two observations—2009/10 and 2010/11—and given the economic crisis, this is a very interesting time to observe. For nine out of ten of these items, the share of children who 'don't have because they can't afford' falls, suggesting that material deprivation fell. However, for most items there is an income gradient—the lower household income is, the more likely parents are to say that an item/activity is something that their child or children did not want or need. Further, it is of concern that the apparent fall in material deprivation is influenced by an increase in the share of parents indicating that their children did not want or need these items. All parents appear to have made a re-evaluation of what their children 'wanted or needed' as household incomes fell but this was greater among low-income households. Overall, this evidence on material deprivation raises some concern that lower income parents are more likely to say that their children don't want or need material things and an apparent fall in material deprivation as the recession hit was driven by a reassessment of need downwards by all parents but particularly by low income parents.

Family Formation, Breakdown and Fertility

Changes in inequality, particularly those associated with increases in poverty are likely to put great strain on personal relationships and could lead to family breakdown. In addition, we know from existing research that teenage pregnancy is more prevalent among young women from disadvantaged backgrounds. However, there are big societal changes taking place affecting family configuration and birth rates. Inequality and poverty can impact on families, relationships and fertility but these demographic changes can also feedback into levels and trends in inequality.

The Total Fertility Rate (TFR) is an estimate of the average number of children that a group of women would have throughout their childbearing lives if they experienced the age-specific fertility rates of the calendar year in question. The historical decline in fertility continued after 1980, albeit at a lower rate, and follows a shallow downward trend before picking up in 2001 (Figure 28.7). In 2010, the average number of children per woman rose to two; having not been this high for nearly thirty years. The increase in fertility has taken many by surprise and three possible explanations have been put forward:

- Women born in the 1960s and 1970s delayed childbearing to older ages,
- Changes in support for families (maternity/paternity leave, tax credits),
- Increases in foreign-born women with higher fertility rates (ONS, 2012b).

While it is hard to identify an effect of inequality on the TFR, falls in poverty rates among children and a levelling off in some measures of inequality may have had some bearing on the increase since 2001.

Teenage fertility rates increased between 1983 and 1990 (Figure 28.7), a period when inequality rates increased substantially. Rates then declined until the mid 1990s, increased slightly up to 1998 and substantially declined under the Labour government, which targeted the high UK teen pregnancy rate through a number of public education and health

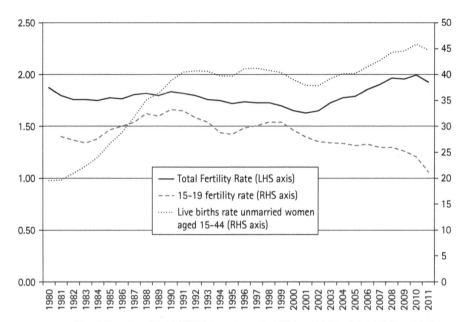

FIGURE 28.7 Total Fertility Rate (TFR), teenage fertility rate (15–19) and live births rate for unmarried women (15–44) England and Wales, 1980–2011

Source: Office for National Statistics, Birth summary tables, England and Wales 2011 (final).

initiatives but didn't meet their target, announced in 1998, of halving teen pregnancies by 2010.

Over this time period, marriage rates also fell (by at least 50 per cent) and divorce rates have remained fairly stable. Given these trends, it is not surprising that there has been an increase in the rate of children born to unmarried mothers (dotted line in Figure 28.7 above), more than doubling over this thirty year period.

Health Inequalities

Stubbornly high rates of health inequality, by socio-economic groups, have led to a number of high profile inquiries and policy reviews over the last 30 years: most recently, the Marmot Review (2010). The Acheson Report (1998) highlighted widening health gaps between different social groups and made a number of policy recommendations designed to tackle these inequalities. Progress made 10 years on, in terms of developments in tackling these inequalities, showed that while significant progress had been made in improving the health of the population, including the least advantaged, health inequalities between groups and areas persisted. Marmot concluded that sustained reduction in health inequality would require a sustainable, systematic approach across all areas of government (Marmot, 2009). A recent House of Commons report into health inequalities (2009) concluded that although the health of all groups in England was improving, health inequalities between social classes had widened over the previous ten years (4 per cent for men and 11 per cent for women) because the health of the rich improved more quickly than the health of the poor.

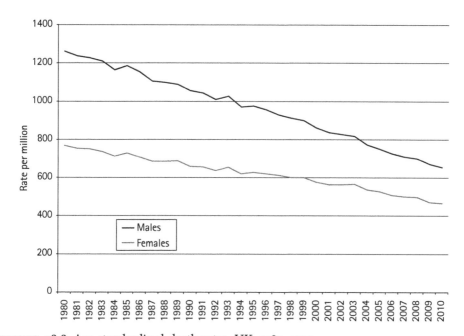

FIGURE 28.8 Age standardized death rates, UK, 1980–2010

Note: All age series. Annual rates have been standardized to the European Standard Population.

Source: Office for National Statistics.

A change in income inequality will not necessarily lead to a contemporaneous change in health inequalities—even where a causal relationship exists. In fact there could be quite long time lags as, for example, many adult health problems have antecedents in childhood circumstances (poverty, living conditions, hardship, diet, etc.). We look at mortality statistics and relate these to inequality by examining the available evidence by social class and by comparing trends directly.

Figure 28.8 shows falling age-standardized death rates for the period 1980—2010 and, while rates for men are higher than for women, the gap has narrowed: rates for men halved over this period. This fall is generally considered to be due to medical advances, with death due to circulatory diseases seeing the greatest fall (ONS, 2012b).

The ONS Longitudinal Study links data from population censuses from 1971 onwards with birth and death registrations and can be used to analyse social class differences. A recent study analysed the trends between 1986 and 2000 and examined social class[9] gradients for individuals aged 35–64 in 1993–9 shows falling mortality rates for men in all social classes but a persistent social class gradient (White *et al.*, 2003). In fact, the gap between the top two social classes (I and II) and the bottom two (IV and V) widened over this period. For women, social class gradients were not as well defined. This makes the findings harder to interpret for women and not directly comparable with men. The analysis of causes of death by social class for men showed increases in the social class gradients in ischaemic

---

[9] The Registrar General's Social Class schema, which was replaced by NS-SEC in 2001.

heart disease and cerebrovascular disease. However, while there were big increases in social class differences in respiratory disease mortality over the 1990s for men, there was a contraction for women. Social Class gradients were not found for all causes of death, in fact in some cases an inverse gradient is found, such as breast cancer and external causes of injury and poisoning in women, and prostate cancer and melanoma in men.

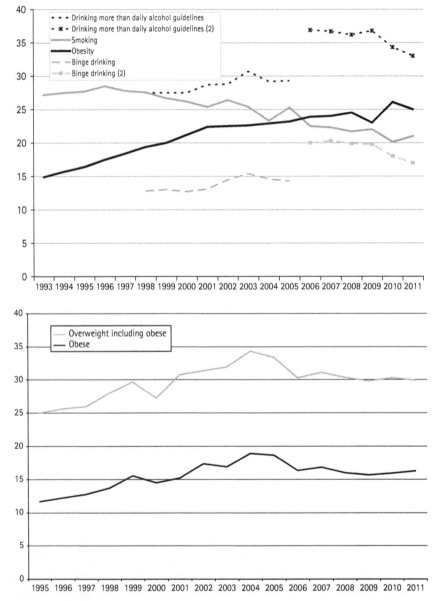

FIGURE 28.9 Trends in smoking, drinking and obesity—1993–2011 (England) (a) per cent of adult population (b) per cent of children aged 2–15 years

Note: New definitions were introduced in 2006 creating a break in the series for alcohol consumption.

Source: Health Survey England (HSE) tables, 2011.

We now turn to trends in behaviour that have a direct effect on health outcomes. Lifestyle factors that influence health inequalities are sometimes referred to as 'proximate' causes of health inequalities in contrast to the wider determinants such as poverty, housing or education. Figure 28.9(a) shows a downward trend in smoking but an upward trend in obesity. Drinking alcohol above the daily guidelines is common (one-third of the adult population) and over one in six adults binge drink. There is a break in these series in 2006 associated with a definitional change. The latest figures for 2011 show falls in drinking above daily alcohol guidelines, binge drinking and obesity but an increase in smoking. It is too early to tell how these relate to the economic crisis. Lifestyle factors such as smoking, nutrition and obesity are found to follow the same socio-economic gradient as mortality (House of Commons, 2009). Although smoking prevalence fell across the population, the decline is much greater among the most affluent groups than the poorest groups 1973–2004 (ibid.). In addition to the fact that these behaviours have a direct effect on mortality and are more prevalent among disadvantaged groups, it is also the case that, for example, people in high socio-economic classes, who smoke, live longer than those from lower socio-economic classes, who smoke (ibid.).

Figure 28.9(b) highlights the rates of children aged 2–15 living in England who are overweight or obese. These rates peaked in 2004 before declining to some extent up to 2006. Since then they appear to have stabilized. In 2011, 30 per cent of children were classified as overweight (including obese) and over 16 per cent as obese, raising concern about the healthy life expectancies these children will enjoy. There is also evidence that a social gradient exists in childhood obesity, with greater rates of childhood obesity among children from more disadvantaged backgrounds, and that these disparities increased between 1997 and 2007 (Stamatakis et al., 2010).

Crime

The relationship between crime and inequality is complex and the influences are likely to vary depending on types of crime. We start by looking at overall crime rates and homicide rates. We then focus on a number of crimes that we anticipate will be most sensitive to changes in inequality.

Annual data on Police Recorded Crime (PRC) and from the British Crime Survey (BCS) together provide the most comprehensive picture of crime in England and Wales (Figure 28.10).[10] Information from the BCS is considered to be a more accurate reflection of long-term crime trends in England and Wales—for the crime types and population it covers—than PRC, as not all crimes are reported to the police. In addition, there are differences in police recording practices over time and across local authorities; and definitions of offences can change (see 'Country Report'). However, the BCS does not cover some important offences, including homicide, fraud and victim-less crimes such as drug possession and crimes against business and other organizations (Home office 2011a: 4; Home Office 2011b: 16).

---

[10] Crime statistics are only available separately for England and Wales, Scotland and Northern Ireland as legal, judicial and police responsibilities are devolved. We focus here on England and Wales.

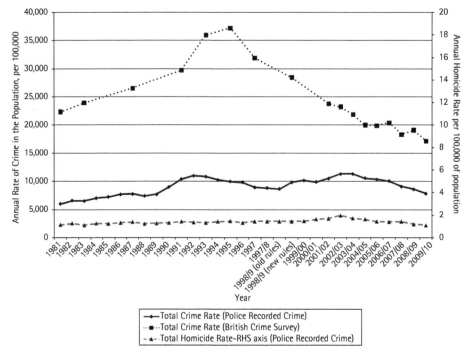

FIGURE 28.10 Overall trend in annual crime and homicide rates: PRC and BCS (England and Wales)

Source: Police Recorded Crime, Home Office; British Crime Survey.

Total annual crime rates in the PRC series exhibit a fairly steady increase over the 1980s up to 1992, falling and rising again to a peak in 2002 (this peak may be more to do with administrative changes in crime recording). PRC rates have fallen since then. Total annual crime rates in the BCS series are much higher up to the mid 2000s, show a big increase since 1981, peaking in the mid 1990s. Since then crime rates have fallen and are closer to PRC rates. The annual homicide rate also increased from 1981, nearly doubling up to 2002/3 when rates peaked before falling rapidly to below the 1981 rate in less than seven years.

A number of hypotheses have been put forward to explain the dramatic fall in crime rates since the mid 1990s:

- Improved property security;
- Economic influences;
- Social change;
- Use of CCTV;
- Other local crime reduction initiatives, and;
- Changes in policing and the wider criminal justice system (Home Office, 2011b).

Even if the increase in crime rates over the 1980s was influenced by rising inequality, these figures suggest that crime rates since 1995, and homicide rates since 2002/3, have fallen much faster and further then changes in income inequality.

Trends in specific crimes are available for a shorter period, 2002–2010. Focusing on rob-bery, burglary and vehicle-related theft, the overall rate of total thefts in the population fell by nearly one-half over this period.

Personal relationships can also be affected by financial circumstances. Domestic abuse is a measurement of the various aspects of intimate violence, combining 'partner abuse (non-sexual), family abuse (non-sexual) and sexual assault or stalking carried out by a cur-rent or former partner or other family member' (Home Office 2011c: 71). Unfortunately, only a very short time series is available from 2004/5, which excludes stalking to allow compara-bility over time. It does show a fall between 2006/7 and 2008/9 which appears to have been halted by the 2008 financial crisis.

4. POLITICAL AND CULTURAL IMPACTS

In this section we explore the relationship between trends in political and cultural variables and inequality trends. These include political engagement, political values and legitimacy, trust and values in relation to social policy and the Welfare State.

Political Participation

Voter turnout provides an indication of the extent to which citizens are actively engaged, or participating in, the political system. It is a legal requirement for UK citizens to be registered on the electoral roll but voting in elections is voluntary. Voter turnout for UK parliamentary elections in the four elections held between 1979 and 1992 was between 73 per cent and 79 per cent. In 1997 voter turnout fell to 71 per cent, from 78 per cent in 1992, and fell further to an historically low 59 per cent in 2001. Voter turnout remained low but increased to 66 per cent in 2010. In addition, the share of the eligible population who registered to vote in 2010 fell to an historic low of 93 per cent. Voter turnout in EU parliament elections is considerably lower, reaching a low of 24 per cent in 1999 and peaking at only 39 per cent in 2004.

The microdata from the British Election Study (Figure 28.11) shows the overall self-reported turnout rates[11] and a social class gradient with professional and managerial classes more likely to vote than partly-skilled and unskilled classes. It is striking that in 2005 the differences between classes widened: 67 per cent of individuals in Class V voted in the general election compared to 85 per cent of individuals in Class I. Unfortunately, at the time of writing, the microdata for the May 2010 election was unavailable. However, although not directly comparable due to differences in data collection and classification scheme, informa-tion from Ipsos MORI (who conduct many political polls) provides some evidence. In 2010, 76 per cent of individuals in higher Social Grade[12] AB voted compared with 57 per cent in

---

[11] The higher estimate of turnout in the BES seems to be due mainly to respondents who did not vote claiming to have voted, movers who are under-represented in the sample and who are less likely to have voted, along with abstainers refusing to take part in the survey and double entries in the electoral register (BES, 1983).

[12] A classification scheme favoured by a number of market research organizations.

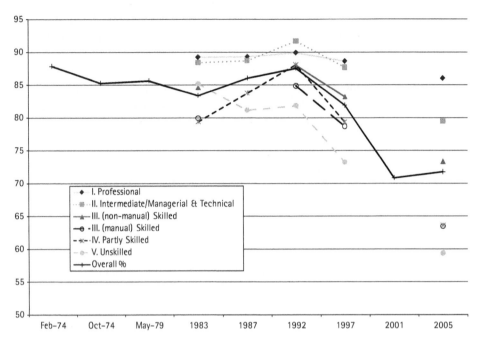

FIGURE 28.11 Self-reported voter turnout in UK general elections (1974–2005) by social class

Note: No information is available for Social Class III in 1987 as the manual/non-manual split is not available.

Source: British Election Study microdata.

lower Social Grade DE. This compares to 83 per cent and 77 per cent, respectively, in 1992: a fall of 20 percentage points for the lower Social Grades but only 7 percentage points for the higher Social Grades.

There does not appear to be a correlation between contemporaneous changes in inequality and changes in voter turnout, although turnout has been lower after 1990 than before when inequality was higher, and the social gradient in voter turnout has widened, which could, along with other factors, be a symptom of entrenched inequality leading to disillusionment with the political system and disengagement for those in less advantaged positions. This is a concerning division and trend for those who believe in democracy.

Political Values and Legitimacy

UK parliamentary elections are based on a 'first past the post' (simple plurality) electoral system which has led to the domination of a small number of political parties. The World Values Survey asks respondents to position themselves on a left-right scale by asking the following question: 'In political matters, people talk of "the left" and "the right". How would you place your views on this scale, generally speaking?' This question was asked in the UK in 1981, 1990 and 1999, and over this period individuals are increasingly likely to position themselves in the middle of the scale, alongside a general shift to the 'left' (although not the extreme left) and away from the right. This occurred during a period of increasing inequality but prior to the growth in support for the far-right groups, UKIP and BNP. However, this support is more to do with a nationalist agenda and how immigration might impinge on inequality rather than inequality per se.

Trust

The extent to which individuals trust others is likely to reflect social, demographic and economic divisions. We use information from the British Social Attitudes Survey (BSAS) from which we have four observations over a ten-year period. There is little change in the share of respondents agreeing that most people can be trusted: a slight fall from 47 per cent in 1998 to 45 per cent in 2008 (Figure 28.12) but a social class gradient exists with a much higher percentage of professionals (Social Class I) agreeing that most people can be trusted (71 per cent) than unskilled (Social Class V) (26 per cent). There is a definite reduction in the differences between social classes, mainly driven by a fall in trust among professionals and an increase in trust among unskilled people.

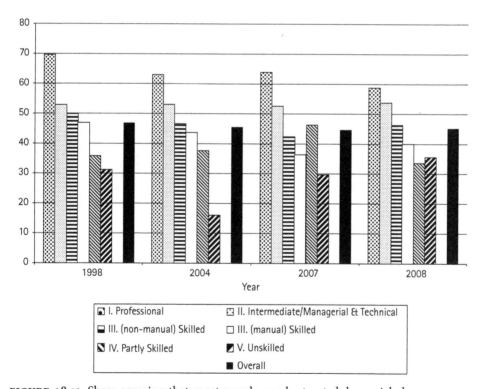

FIGURE 28.12 Share agreeing that most people can be trusted, by social class

Notes: 'Generally speaking, would you say that most people can be trusted or that you can't be too careful in life?'

Source: British Social Attitudes Surveys.

Values about Social Policy and the Welfare State

The vast majority of Britons agree that the gap between those with high incomes and those with low incomes is too large: 70–80 per cent in 1983, increasing to 80–90 per cent in 1994–1996, declining a little to 75–85 per cent by 2009. There isn't a clear social class gradient: skilled manual workers (Social Class III(M)) tend to be the most likely to think that income inequalities are too large and professionals (Social Class I) are generally the least likely to think so. Looking at the same information by highest level of educational qualification shows less difference between groups and no clear ranking. These trends mirror the time trends in inequality, increasing as inequality increased and peaking as inequality reached a high point in the early 1990s.

A smaller share of Britons agree that the government should redistribute income from the better off to those who are less well off (Figure 28.13) and, overall, we observe a downward trend in this share in the 1990s, and then fairly stable 1999–2003, with a lower share in 2004–2007, and then an increase since the start of the economic crisis. In terms of social class, Social Class I tend to be in the middle with higher shares of individuals in Social Class III, Social Class IV and Social Class V agreeing that the government should redistribute and individuals in Social Class II and Social Class III (NM) least likely to agree. There is evidence of a reduction in the differences between social classes. Individuals with the highest and lowest levels of education are more likely to agree with government redistribution than

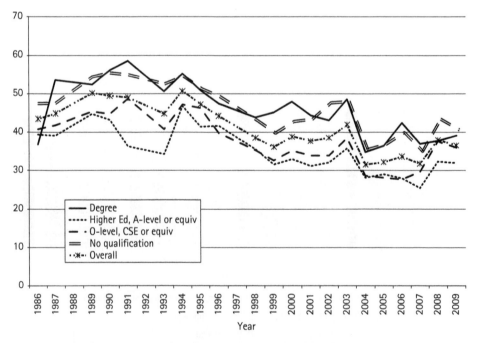

FIGURE 28.13 Share agreeing that the government should redistribute income from the better-off to those who are less well-off by education levels

Notes: 'Government should redistribute income from the better-off to those who are less well-off'
(agree and agree strongly)

Source: British Social Attitudes Surveys.

those in between; that is, the group most likely to benefit from redistribution and the group most likely to 'lose' income through redistribution.

Next we assess the extent to which people think individuals who live in poverty are poor because they are lazy or lack willpower. Respondents to the BSAS were asked why they think there are people who live in need. One of a number of potential explanations they can choose is, 'Because of laziness or lack of willpower'. We look at the percentage of respondents who indicate that this explanation comes closest to their opinion. There is evidence of a social class gradient although not strictly monotonic nor consistent across years. Individuals in Social Class I and II are least likely to think that the poor are lazy and individuals in Social Class III (M) and V are generally the most likely to think that the poor are lazy. Differences between groups are clearer when we look at education levels. With the exception of 1989, we find that higher levels of qualifications are associated with lower shares expressing the opinion that individuals live in need because they are lazy: individuals with at least degree level qualifications are consistently least likely to agree. We do find evidence that there has been an increase over time in this opinion among all education groups, mirroring the fall in the share of individuals who agree that the government should redistribute income.

5. Effectiveness of Policies

When examining the effectiveness of policies in combating inequality, it is worth distinguishing between policies capable of tackling the root causes of inequality and those designed to address the effects of inequality. As noted in the introduction, the driving forces behind increases in income inequality in the UK are thought to be a combination of skilled (or task) biased technological change, globalization and institutional changes putting pressure on wage inequality. The extent to which the supply of skills has kept up with demand has ameliorated or exacerbated the degree to which wage inequality has increased. We therefore start by looking at policies in relation to institutional change affecting wages, the distributional effects of tax and benefit policy and policies designed to raise educational attainment and tackle educational inequalities.

Trade union membership and density has fallen over this thirty-year period (membership fell from 13.2 million in 1979 to 7.3 million in 2010–11). The impact of unions on wage inequality is ambiguous where coverage is incomplete because, while unions can be effective in raising wages and narrowing differentials for those covered by wage-setting agreements, there can be an increase in the gap between the wages of insiders and outsiders. Nonetheless, de-unionization is generally associated with increases in wage inequality as unions tend to support the wages of lower waged workers. Gosling and Lemieux (2004) argue that the much steeper decline in unionization in the United Kingdom after 1983 explains why inequality increased faster than in the United States.

A National Minimum Wage (NMW) was introduced by the Labour government in April 1999. Following its introduction, initial estimates showed that it led to a small reduction in wage inequality (Dickens and Manning, 2004). A more recent study found modest spill-over effects with direct effects up to the 6th percentile of the wage distribution (Butcher, Dickens and Manning, 2012). Gosling and Lemieux (2004) find that the introduction of the NMW reduced wage inequality among women, pulling the UK female wage inequality below that observed for males.

At the other end of the earnings distribution, Bell and van Reenen (2010) find that increases in earnings inequality over the period 1998–2008 were due to large and sustained increases in the earnings of those at the top of the distribution driven by large annual bonuses made to the better off. These payments were primarily in the financial sector, mainly in the form of bankers' bonuses. It seems clear now that these bonuses were being paid off the back of practices which, while highly profitable to the banking sector, were reckless, jeopardized the wider economy and will cause hardship for many years to come. While greater banking regulation is being introduced, the UK government is opposed to EU proposals to limit very large bonuses.

Education was a priority under the 1997–2010 Labour government and large real-terms increases in the education budget moved the UK from a situation where public expenditure on education was below the EU average to above the EU average. The introduction of a National Curriculum in the late 1980s, reform of school leaving examinations in the late 1980s, the introduction of literacy and numeracy hours in primary schools at the end of the 1990s, additional resources for children with special educational needs or from disadvantaged backgrounds and elements of a programme called Sure Start, designed to help pre-school children, the introduction of Academy Schools in 2000, school inspections and published performance data, are among many initiatives that have been, at least in part, designed to narrow educational inequalities as well as raise attainment. Despite some successes in raising attainment among children from disadvantaged backgrounds, there are still wide disparities in relation to family background and some children are still leaving secondary school with very poor educational qualifications. However, a large expansion in higher education has gone some way in meeting demand and is likely to have tempered rising wage inequality.

In terms of policies designed to tackle the effects of income inequality and wage inequality, we consider the extent to which the tax and benefit system helps in the redistribution of income (effectively topping up the incomes of the low paid and those who are without work). In Section 2, it was shown that the collection of tax has, overall, a neutral effect on household income inequality but the way tax revenues are spent on cash benefits greatly reduces inequality. Statistical analysis of the impact of government tax and benefit policies provides estimates that the 1997–2010 Labour government's policies directly led to a lower level of income inequality than would have been the case if they had simply uprated the policies they inherited from the Conservative government in 1997. Uprating in line with inflation would have resulted in inequality 3.4 points higher and uprating in line with GDP would have resulted in 1.6 points higher (Adam and Browne, 2010). In contrast, the same study, estimates that the 1979–1997 Conservative government's tax and benefit policies directly led to increases in income inequality. Sefton *et al.* (2009) show the overall distributive effects of tax and benefit policies 1996/7–2008/9 by income quintile. Their analysis shows the improvements in disposable income for households in low income deciles, particularly between 2000/1 and 2004/5 as a result of changes in tax and benefit policies (relative to price and earnings indexation of 1996/7 policies) and the losses to households higher up the income distribution (due to tax credits for low-income families and slightly more progressive taxation). They show that the policy effect of these reforms over the whole period resulted in a fall in relative poverty of 4–6 percentage points overall and by 14 percentage points for lone-parent families. Increases in public spending on health and education, which is pro-poor, also benefited lower income households and it is shown that, despite the low unemployment rates, the redistributive net impact of tax-benefit and spending policies was broadly similar after 1996/7, to what was observed during the recessions of the early 1980s and early 1990s due to increases in pro-poor spending on in-work benefits and public services.

Active labour market programmes and payment of unemployment benefit have undergone a number of major reforms over the last thirty years. These policies tackle inequality to the extent that they reduce/limit unemployment and support the incomes of those who are out of work. As in many countries, the general trend over this period has been the introduction of greater conditionality in relation to unemployment benefit receipt. Two major changes in this regard were the introduction of Jobseeker's Allowance in 1996, which limited some types of unemployment benefits and increased the require-ment for benefit recipients to periodically demonstrate that they were actively searching for work. Secondly, the introduction of the New Deals from 1997 onwards offered tail-ored support for different groups of unemployed people, greater monitoring and assis-tance, and for some groups a fixed length of time in receipt of unemployment benefit before having to take up one of a number of employment or training options. Evaluation evidence has shown that JSA and the New Deals both helped to reduce unemployment in the UK (Smith *et al.*, 2000; Blundell *et al.*, 2004) but unemployment has continued to be a problem for many. In-work benefits designed to 'make work pay' for the least advantaged and to top up household income also had some success in terms of increas-ing and retaining employment but there was limited wage progression (Dickens and McKnight, 2008b).

A series of high profile reviews have highlighted the fact that while improvements have been made in health outcomes, health inequalities have remained stubbornly high. The most recent review (Marmot, 2010) has called for an approach that tackles the wider social determinants of health inequalities.

We look at behaviours affecting health outcomes that both reflect economic inequali-ties and influence future health outcomes—smoking, excessive alcohol consumption and obesity. In fact, some progress has been made in reducing them. For example, a number of policy initiatives have been introduced to tackle high and rising child obesity rates such as the Change4Life initiative in England and Wales, with similar initiatives in Scotland and Northern Ireland. These are public health programmes designed to tackle the causes of obesity by encouraging people to adopt healthy behaviours (diet, activity levels, and alco-hol consumption). As in many countries, there has been pressure to ban junk food adver-tising (with limited success), particularly during children's TV programmes, to require clearer food labelling and to improve school meals. In 2004, the Labour government announced a Public Service Agreement target to 'halt, by 2010, the year-on-year increase in obesity among children under 11 in the context of a broader strategy to tackle obesity in the population as a whole'. As was shown in Figure 28.9, this was achieved, but since 2006 childhood obesity rates have remained largely unchanged. The current government set out two national ambitions in 2011: (1) a downward trend in the level of excess weight averaged across all adults by 2020; and (2) a sustained downward trend in the level of excess weight in children by 2020.

6. Conclusions

Inequality in the UK increased dramatically during the 1980s, further and earlier than in most other European countries. Since this dramatic rise, inequality has become entrenched and while government policy seems to have had some success in protecting certain groups and tackling some of the negative impacts, it is clear that while inequality remains high, and upward pressure remains, the UK population will remain deeply divided. Divided not just in terms of financial resources but also by a range of other factors that affect the quality of individuals' lives, such as educational attainment, morbidity and mortality, well-being and life satisfaction. The division also pervades political engagement, trust and social cohesion, creating an uneven voice and representation.

Over the last 30 years, social attitude surveys have shown that people believe that inequalities are too large but they are divided on whether or not they think that the government should redistribute income from the better off to the less well off. Interestingly, it is those individuals who are either most likely to gain financially (individuals with no qualifications) and those most likely to lose (individuals with higher education) who are most given to expressing support for redistribution.

In aggregate, tax collection (direct and indirect taxation of individuals) can be seen to have a neutral effect on household income inequality but the way these tax revenues are spent in the form of cash benefits does have a significant effect in reducing household income inequality.

Increases in home ownership and a boom in house prices, particularly between 2000 and 2005, led to a fall in wealth inequality which may have softened the blow of high income inequality. However, absolute gaps in wealth, and the concentration of wealth in terms of wealth shares, suggest that there remain very large differences between households, which reflect past inequalities and will project inequalities into the future.

This is not to say that inequality is the root cause of all social 'bads' and it needs to be borne in mind that over this period real incomes have grown, average levels of educational attainment have improved and medical advances and financial investment have led to improved health outcomes reflected in longer life expectancies.

For many, life chances are highly influenced by the luck of which family they were born into and, as long as families' economic circumstances are linked to children's educational attainment and health, the ability of individuals to break the link will be severely hampered. With relatively low rates of social mobility, which fell during the period that cross-sectional inequality increased, the UK population will continue to be characterized by deep divisions that are particularly detrimental to those who are least well off but also to society as a whole.

References

Acheson, D. (1998), *Independent Inquiry into Inequalities in Health Report* (The Acheson Report), London: TSO.

Adam, S. and Browne, J. (2010), 'Redistribution, Work Incentives and Thirty Years of UK Tax and Benefit Reform', *Working Paper* 10/24, Institute for Fiscal Studies (IFS).

Atkinson, A. B., Piketty, T. and Saez, E. (2011), 'Top Incomes in the Long Run History', *Journal of Economic Literature*, 49:1, 3–71.

Bell, B. and van Reenen, J. (2010), 'Bankers Pay and Extreme Wage Inequality in the UK', *CEP Special Report*, CEPSP21, London: Centre for Economic Performance.

BES (1983), *British Election Study: Technical Details of the Survey*, ESRC Data Archive, University of Essex.

Blanden, J., Goodman, A., Gregg, P., and Machin, S. (2005), 'Changes in Intergenerational Income Mobility in Britain', in M. Corak (ed.), *Generational Income Mobility in North America and Europe*, Cambridge, MA: Cambridge University Press.

Blundell, R., Costa Dias, M., Meghir, C., and van Reenen, J. (2004), 'Evaluating the Employment Impact of a Mandatory Job Search Program', *Journal of European Economic Association*, Vol. 2, 4, 569–606.

Butcher, T., Dickens, R., and A. Manning (2012), 'Minimum Wages and Wage Inequality: Some Theory and an Application to the UK', *CEP Discussion Paper* No CEPDP1177, London: Centre for Economic Performance.

Clifton, J and Cook, W. (2012), *A Long Division: Closing the Attainment Gap in England's Secondary Schools*, London: IPPR.

Cribb, J., Joyce, R, and Phillip, D. (2012), 'Living Standards, Poverty and Inequality in the UK: 2012', *IFS Commentary* C124. Institute for Fiscal Studies.

Cowell, F. A., Karagiannaki, E., and McKnight, A. (2012), 'Mapping and Measuring the Distribution of Household Wealth: A Cross-Country Analysis', *GINI Discussion* Paper 71.

DfE (2012), 'GCSE and Equivalent Attainment by Pupil Characteristics in England, 2010/11', *Statistical First Release*, SFR03/2012, <http://www.education.gov.uk/rsgateway/DB/SFR/s001057/sfr03-2012.pdf>

Dickens, R. and Manning, A. (2004), 'Has the National Minimum Wage Reduced UK Wage Inequality?' *Journal of the Royal Statistical Society. Series A (Statistics in Society)*, Vol. 167, No. 4, pp. 613–626.

Dickens, R. and McKnight, A. (2008a), 'Changes in Earnings Inequality and Mobility in Great Britain 1978/9–2005/6', *CASEpaper 132*, London: Centre for Analysis of Social Exclusion.

Dickens, R. and McKnight, A. (2008b), 'The Impact of Policy Change on Job Retention and Advancement', *CASEpaper 134*, London: Centre for Analysis of Social Exclusion.

Gosling, A and Lemieux, T. (2004), 'Labor Market Reforms and Changes in Wage Inequality in the United Kingdom and the United States', in Card, D., Blundell, R and Freeman, R. B. (eds.), *Seeking a Premier Economy: The Economic Effects of British Economic Reforms, 1980–2000*, Chicago: University of Chicago Press.

Gregg, P., Harkness, S., and Machin, S. (1999), 'Poor Kids: Trends in Child Poverty in Britain, 1968-96', *Fiscal Studies*, Vol. 20, No. 2, pp. 163–187.

Hills, J. and Bastagli, F. (2013), 'Trends in the Distribution of Wealth in Britain', Chapter 2 in Hills, J., Bastagli, F., Cowell, F. A., Glennerster, H., Karagiannaki, E. and McKnight, A., *Wealth in the UK: Distribution, Accumulation and Policy*, Oxford: Oxford University Press.

Home Office (2011a), 'User Guide to Home Office Crime Statistics'. Available from: <http://www.homeoffice.gov.uk/publications/science-research-statistics/research-statistics/crime-research/user-guide-crime-statistics/user-guide-crime-statistics?view=Binary>

Home Office (2011b), 'Crime in England and Wales 2010/11: Findings from the British Crime Survey and Police Recorded Crime', edited by Chaplin R., Flatley, J. and Smith, K. (2nd Edition), *Home Office Statistical Bulletin*, HOSB: 10/11, Home Office, London.

Home Office (2011c), 'Homicides, Firearm Offences and Intimate Violence 2009/10: Supplementary Volume 2 to Crime in England and Wales 2009/10', edited by Smith,

K. Coleman, K. Eder, S., and Hall, P. (2nd edn), *Home Office Statistical Bulletin*, Home Office: London.

House of Commons (2009), 'Health Committee—Third Report Health Inequalities', <http://www.publications.parliament.uk/pa/cm200809/cmselect/cmhealth/286/28602.htm>.

Jin, W., Joyce, R., Phillips, D., and Sibieta, L. (2011), 'Poverty and Inequality in the UK: 2011', *IFS Commentary* C118. Institute for Fiscal Studies.

Machin, S. (2011), 'Changes in UK Wage Inequality Over the Last Forty Years', in Gregg, P., and Wadsworth, J. (eds.), *The Labour Market in Winter: the State of Working Britain*, Oxford: OUP.

Marmot, M. (2010), *Fair Society, Healthy Lives (The Marmot Review)*, Strategic Review into Health Inequalities in England post 2010, <http://www.ucl.ac.uk/marmotreview>

Marmot, M. (2009), *Tackling Health Inequalities: 10 Years On– A Review of Developments in Tackling Health Inequalities in England over the Last 10 years*, Department of Health, London:

McKnight, A. (2005), 'Education, Education, Education...: An Assessment of Labour's Success in Tackling Education Inequalities', in Hills, J. and Stewart, K. (eds.), *A More Equal Society? New Labour, Poverty, Inequality and Exclusion*, Bristol: The Policy Press, pp. 47–68.

OECD (2011), *Divided We Stand: Why Inequality Keeps Rising*, Paris: OECD.

OECD (2010), *PISA 2009, Volume 11: 'Overcoming Social Background: Equity in Learning Opportunities and Outcomes'*, Paris: OECD.

ONS (2011), 'Labour Market Statistics', 2011 <http://www.ons.gov.uk/ons/publications/re-reference-tables.html?edition=tcm%3A77-222445>

ONS (2012a), 'Tables from The Effects of Taxes and Benefits on Household Income', Office for National Statistics' <http://www.ons.gov.uk/ons/dcp171780_284709.pdf>

ONS (2012b), 'Births and Deaths in England and Wales', 2011 (Final), <http://www.ons.gov.uk/ons/dcp171778_279934.pdf>.

Pike, R. (2012), *Patterns of Pay: Results of the Annual Survey of Hours and Earnings, 1997 to 2011*, Office for National Statistics, <http://www.ons.gov.uk/ons/dcp171766_252474.pdf>

Sefton, T., Hills, J. and Sutherland, H. (2009), 'Poverty, Inequality and Redistribution', in Hills, J., Sefton, T. and Stewart, K. (eds.) *Towards a More Equal Society? Poverty, Inequality and Policy since 1997*, Bristol: The Policy Press.

Sibieta, L. (2011), 'Inequality in Britain: An Explanation of Recent Trends', presentation to the Interdisciplinary Society for International Development at University College London, <http://www.ifs.org.uk/publications/6002>

Smith, A., Youngs, R., Ashworth, K., McKay, S., Walker, R., Elias, P. and McKnight, A. (2000), 'Understanding the Impact of Jobseeker's Allowance', Department of Social Security *Research Report* No. 111.

Stamatakis, E., Wardle, J and Cole, T. J. (2010), 'Childhood Obesity and Overweight Prevalence Trends in England: Evidence for Growing Socioeconomic Disparities', *International Journal of Obesity*, 34(1):41–47.

White, C., van Galen, F., and Chow, Y. H. (2003), 'Trends in Social Class Differences in Mortality by Cause, 1986 to 2000', *Health Statistics Quarterly* No. 20, Office for National Statistics.

CHAPTER 29

THE UNITED STATES: HIGH AND RAPIDLY-RISING INEQUALITY

LANE KENWORTHY AND TIMOTHY SMEEDING

1. INTRODUCTION AND CONTEXT

THE United States is a very good test case for the hypothesis that income inequality has adverse impacts on social, political, and cultural outcomes. America's level of income inequality was comparatively high in the 1970s, and it has increased rapidly and continuously since then, leaving it at the top of the rich country inequality pyramid.

The United States is the archetypal liberal market economy and has the archetypal liberal welfare state. Non-market and extra-market institutions, such as labour unions and formalized interest group participation in policy-making, are comparatively weak. Government taxing and spending is comparatively low. From the end of the 1970s through 2007, the United States enjoyed relatively good macro-economic performance. Growth of per capita GDP and employment were stronger than in most other affluent democratic countries. In the 2000–7 business cycle, America's performance deteriorated, and in the years since the 2007–2009 recession, its recovery has been much slower than in past recessions (CBO, 2013).

We examine changes in inequality of income, wealth, earnings, and education and their social, political, and cultural impacts. While we focus on the period from 1979 to 2007, we also consider the economic crisis of 2008–9 and its aftermath. The Great Recession is important because it may have permanently and negatively altered the level and distribution of well-being in the United States.

In Section 2, we assess the level and trend in income inequality and its causes. Section 3 explores possible social, political, and cultural impacts of inequality. In Section 4 we examine policy responses to the rise in inequality. In Section 5 we summarize and offer some concluding thoughts. For more data, substantive detail, discussion of technical issues, and a full reference list, we refer readers to our country report on the United States for the GINI project.[1]

---

[1] See www.gini-research\CR-USA. The appendix to the Report contains complete definitions of each income concept and also the definitions of other measures of well-being used in this chapter.

2. EVOLUTION OF INEQUALITY AND ITS DRIVERS

High and Rapidly-Rising Inequality

Figure 29.1 shows three measures of income inequality in America. Though these measures differ in important respects, they all point to the same conclusion: long-term income inequality in the United States has been rising, is rising, and in the future will most likely rise further.

First, the US Census Bureau's Money Income measure includes cash incomes received on a regular basis (exclusive of certain money receipts such as capital gains) and before payments for personal income taxes, but gross of income transfers such as social security. This is the most commonly-referenced income measure and the longest series, dating back to 1967 for households, with adjustments for household size. This measure suggests the income inequality Gini coefficient for the United States increased from 0.37 in 1979 to 0.44 in 2007.

Second, Thompson and Smeeding (2012) calculate Net Equivalized Income (NEI). They start with gross Money Income as above. They then add near-cash transfer income not included in Money Income, such as food stamps and housing benefits, and refundable tax credits, including the Earned Income Tax Credit (EITC) and the child tax credit. They then subtract direct taxes, namely state and federal income taxes and the employee share of

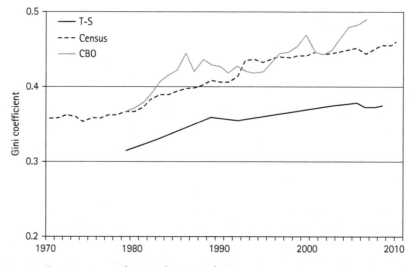

FIGURE 29.1 Income inequality in the United States

The three measures are described in detail in the text. T-S = Thompson-Smeeding Net Equivalized Income (NEI).
Data sources: DeNavas-Walt, Proctor, and Smith (2012, table A-3); Thompson and Smeeding (2012); Congressional Budget Office (2011b, Figure 11).

payroll (social insurance) taxes.[2] They then adjust for differences in household size using an equivalence scale, dividing net income by the square root of household size. This income definition is closest to the EU-SILC, Luxembourg Income Study (LIS), and Canberra definitions employed by most rich nations. But it includes income with top codes, so it misses the rapid increases in the incomes at the top of the US distribution. It also misses capital gains and employer benefits such as health insurance and pensions, which are important in the United States. According to this series, the Gini increased from 0.32 in 1979 to 0.37 in 2007.

The third measure shown in Figure 29.1 is from the US Congressional Budget Office (CBO). The CBO merges household survey data with tax records, so it gives us a more accurate picture of incomes at the very top of the distribution. The CBO income measure includes wages, salaries, self-employment income, rents, taxable and non-taxable interest, dividends, realized capital gains, cash transfer payments, and retirement benefits plus taxes paid by businesses (corporate income taxes and the employer's share of Social Security, Medicare, and federal unemployment insurance payroll taxes) and employees' contributions to 401(k) retirement plans. Other sources of income include all in-kind benefits (Medicare, Medicaid, employer-paid health insurance premiums, food stamps, school lunches and breakfasts, housing assistance, and energy assistance). Then it subtracts all federal taxes. Individual income taxes are attributed directly to households paying those taxes. Social insurance, or payroll, taxes are attributed to households paying those taxes directly or paying them indirectly through their employers. Corporate income taxes are attributed to households according to their share of capital income. Federal excise taxes are attributed to them according to their consumption of the taxed good or service. According to this measure, the Gini coefficient for household income increased from 0.37 in 1979 to 0.49 in 2007.

Because of income top-coding and the presence of a few extremely high-income households in the sample, it is difficult to use the Current Population Survey (either Census Money Income or NEI) to accurately estimate inequality at the top of the income distribution. In recent years, a number of studies have demonstrated that much of the growth in inequality since the 1970s has been isolated to the top few percentiles of the distribution. To the extent that the top few percentiles are driving inequality, Gini coefficients (or other inequality measures) calculated with the CPS using NEI or Census money income understate the level of inequality at any point in time and possibly the trend toward greater inequality over time. The Congressional Budget Office's comprehensive income measure, while only available up through 2007 (or with new definitions and methods to 2009 only, which we do not show), suggests that inequality from 1993 to 2007 was driven almost exclusively by gains in the income of the 95th and higher percentiles of households (CBO 2011b, Figure 9).

Data from the CBO for 2009 show sharp drops in top incomes and shares, but the CBO data for 2010 and 2011 are not yet available. Calculations by Saez (2013) suggest that top incomes have begun to recover.

Should we focus on inequality of consumption rather than income? This is a longstanding dispute. Exploiting the Hicks-Simons identity, consumption plus changes in net worth equals income. Fisher, Johnson, and Smeeding (2012) use this identity to construct complete and consistent measures of income and consumption inequality for the same set of

---

[2] They estimate taxes and refundable credits using the NBER TAXSIM program.

individuals using the 1985–2011 Consumer Expenditure (CE) surveys. They find that, as expected, consumption inequality is lower than income inequality. Differing from other recent research, however, they find that the trends in income and consumption inequality are similar between 1985 and 2006, with consumption inequality increasing about two-thirds as much as income inequality.

What about wealth? In the United States wealth is much more highly concentrated than income. As of the mid 2000s, the Gini for net worth was around 0.83, compared to about 0.45 for income (Wolff forthcoming, Table 1). In 2010, the top 1 per cent of households owned 35 per cent of all privately held wealth, and the next 19 per cent had 54 per cent, leaving only 11 per cent of the wealth for the bottom 80 per cent. Recent studies find the United States to have the most unequal wealth distribution among rich nations (Davies *et al.*, 2011; Bricker *et al.*, 2012). At the same time, between 1983 (the earliest year of comparable data) and 2007 there was little rise in wealth inequality. The Great Recession and its aftermath appear to have changed that. Home values, the chief asset for most middle-class Americans, collapsed and have not recovered, whereas stock values, of importance chiefly for the most wealthy, dropped sharply but recovered quite quickly. The Gini for net worth jumped from 0.83 in 2007 to 0.87 in 2010 (Wolff, forthcoming, Table 1).

Drivers

Most of the rise in income inequality in the United States is due to an increase in inequality of market incomes, especially at the top of the distribution, as changes in redistribution have played a small role. The rise in market income inequality is due mainly to changes in wage inequality and in top incomes. Demographic shifts accounted for, at most, 20 per cent of the overall change in inequality since 1980 (Western *et al.*, 2008). We organize our discussion into three parts: wage inequality (and inequality in human capital accumulation), top incomes, and redistribution.

Wage inequality. Wage inequality rose sharply in the 1980s, modestly in the 1990s, and rather sharply again in the 2000s. Figure 29.2 shows over-time developments in top-half and bottom-half wage inequality in the United States since 1979. The gap between the middle and the top increased in a relatively uninterrupted fashion, though only minimally in the 1990s. The gap between the middle and the bottom increased only in the 1980s. Since 2007 both have risen sharply.

Machin and Van Reenan (2012, Figure 4) also conclude that wage inequality in the form of the P50/P10 ratio has declined since the 1990s, suggesting that wage inequality patterns are even further polarizing than shown in Figure 29.2, and that the middle of the wage distribution is therefore falling into lower wage ranges (see also Acemoglu and Autor, 2010).

Because workers are typically part of a household unit that shares resources across several members, oftentimes including multiple earners, and because households are able to draw upon non-labour sources of income, it is important to go beyond wages or earnings and explore the level and distribution of household income as we have done above. But still, wages can be seen as the key driving factor in overall US income inequality (OECD, 2011a).

Human capital—the skill and knowledge of workers—is paramount in explaining differences in labour incomes, especially when there are rapidly changing skill demands. Employment is expanding for the best trained and falling for others. At the same time, the

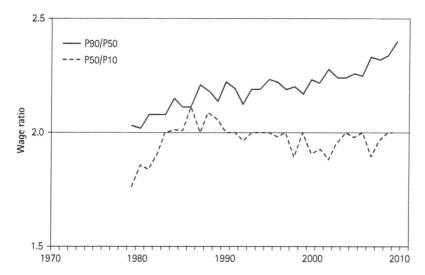

FIGURE 29.2 Wage inequality in the United States

Hourly wages for employed persons aged 18–64. Estimates adjusted to smooth over the effects of the 1993 change in CPS data collection methods. Source: Smeeding and Thompson (2011).

economic benefits of higher education have risen. In 1979, the average college graduate made 37 per cent more than the average high school graduate. The comparable figure today is 76 per cent (DeNavas-Walt *et al.*, 2012). Not everyone needs a bachelor's degree to succeed in the labour market, but all workers need better skills.

Educational attainment levels rose rapidly throughout much of the 20th century, with the college completion rate quadrupling for those born between 1915 and 1960 in the United States (especially for the generation which is today aged 55 to 64). But it has been largely stagnant since (Goldin and Katz, 2008). US college attainment levels have notably slowed in the United States compared to other nations (OECD, 2011b). Successive younger genera-tions in most other countries have increased their post-secondary educational attainment, but the United States has fallen from being the leader amongst the 55-to-64 generation to the middle of the pack for the 25-to-34 year old generation.

Wage inequality rose during the 1979–89 and 2000–7 business cycles but not during the 1989–2000 cycle. Perhaps the single most important difference is that the unemployment rate dipped to around 4 per cent in the mid-to-late 1990s. This is the only period since the 1960s when real wages in the middle and at the low end of the wage ladder increased, and many attribute this to the tightness of the labour market (Bernstein and Baker, 2003).

The decline in the real value of the US minimum wage and the weakening of unions in the United States are two institutional changes that likely also played a role in widen-ing wage inequality, but that role is hard to quantify (Levy and Temin, 2009; Western and Rosenfeld, 2011).

Immigration, both legal and illegal, has increased sharply since the 1960s, but this does not seem to have had a large impact on US inequality (Blau and Kahn, 2012). Another not-well-founded explanation is that trade with low-wage countries such as China and Mexico drove down wages and eliminated jobs for unskilled workers. Although globali-zation is the favorite hobby horse of many politicians and pundits, the evidence for trade

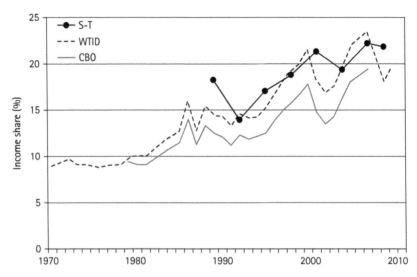

FIGURE 29.3 Top 1 per cent's share of pre-tax income in the United States

Includes capital gains. ST = Smeeding-Thompson 'More Comprehensive Income' (MCI); WTID = World Top Incomes Database; CBO = Congressional Budget Office.

Data sources: Congressional Budget Office (2011a); Smeeding and Thompson (2011); Alvaredo *et al.* (2012).

causing the majority of the change in inequality is weak. As Autor, Dorn, and Hanson (2012) show, Chinese imports account for at most 25 per cent of the jobs lost in US manufacturing over the past 30 years.

Top incomes. Figure 29.3 shows the share of income going to the top 1 per cent of US households (taxpaying units) since the early 1970s. The data comes from three sources: the CBO, the World Top Incomes Database (WTID), and Smeeding and Thompson (2011). All three tell a similar story: Americans at the top of the ladder have been collecting the lion's share of economic growth in recent decades.

The CBO measure is likely to be more accurate than the WTID measure, as it includes more sources of income and more reliable information for households below the top. But even the CBO data excludes the vast majority of capital income that is not realized in a given year, such as imputed rent on owner-occupied homes as well as accumulated financial and business wealth. Smeeding and Thompson (2011) use data from the Survey of Consumer Finances (SCF) to calculate a 'More Comprehensive Income' (MCI) measure that combines standard income flows with imputed income to assets. According to the CBO data, the top 1 per cent's share of income increased from 13 per cent in 1989 to 19 per cent in 2007. According to the Smeeding-Thompson MCI data, the rise was from 18 per cent to 22 per cent.

What accounts for this spectacular rise in pre-tax incomes and income share at the top of the distribution? We have many hypotheses but as yet few solid answers. Possible contributing factors include changes in market competition, technology, the financialization of the economy, business influence on policy-makers, the demand for high-end talent, corporate governance practices, and norms (see, e.g., Gordon and Dew-Becker, 2008; Atkinson, Piketty, and Saez, 2011).

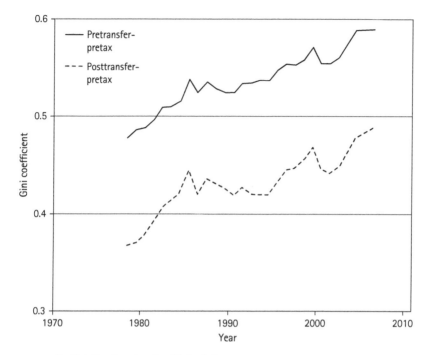

FIGURE 29.4 Redistribution in the United States

Gini coefficients for pretransfer-pretax income and post-transfer post-tax income.

Data source: Congressional Budget Office (2011b, Figure 11).

Redistribution. Redistribution in the United States stayed more or less constant from 1979 through 2007. Figure 29.4 shows Congressional Budget Office calculations of inequality for market income post-tax and market income with transfers added and federal taxes subtracted. Transfers and taxes reduce the level of income inequality at any given point in time, but neither has altered the upward trend in inequality since the 1970s.

The Great Recession and Beyond

Though the 2008–9 economic crisis was deeper in the United States than in many other rich countries, GDP and per capita GDP have rebounded to or beyond their pre-recession heights, corporate profits are at an all-time high, and the stock market has recovered more than 98 per cent of its earlier peak value (US Department of Commerce, 2012a; 2012b; Thompson and Smeeding, 2012). The labour market, however, is a long way from true recovery.

More than eight million jobs were lost. Employment is still three percentage points below its 2007 peak, more than three years after the official end of the Great Recession in summer 2009. Over 14 million Americans now seek work, are involuntarily working part-time, or have left the labour force as discouraged workers. Long-term unemployment is still far above its 2007 levels and is recovering only slowly. The good news for job creation is that the American population is growing older and retirements at the rate of 100,000 per month are expected, hence reducing the need for as much job creation. But that still leaves the United States about 11 million jobs below pre-recession employment levels. With population growth, the US is three or more years away from a 6.5 per cent unemployment rate at current rates of job growth (Greenstone and Looney, 2012).

While unemployment in the United States has been cyclical in recent decades, the cyclical change has been more pronounced for those with less education all the way back to the early 1980s. Even among college graduates, the unemployment rate jumped from 2.4 per cent in 2006 to 5.6 per cent in 2010, and among those with advanced degrees it rose from 1.5 per cent to 3.5 per cent in the same period. But the largest increases and greatest pain—in absolute terms—were felt by younger workers with the lowest levels of education. Unemployment among workers with only a high school degree jumped from 5.3 per cent to 12.2 per cent between 2006 and 2010, and among those lacking a diploma it climbed from 8.6 per cent to 17.4 per cent. The youngest workers (aged 18 to 24) saw their unemployment rate quickly shoot up from 9 per cent to 17 per cent, while the unemployment rate for somewhat more experienced workers (those aged 25 to 35) went from 4.3 per cent to 9.7 per cent.

The official unemployment rate excludes 'discouraged' workers who have ceased looking for work. Declining labour force participation has been most prominent among younger and less-educated workers. Participation fell by 0.7 per cent among college graduates and 0.2 per cent among those with advanced degrees, but it dropped by roughly 2 per cent for all workers with education below the bachelor's degree level (US Bureau of Labor Statistics, 2011, Table 8.A2).

Capital markets and executive pay have recovered faster than wages or jobs, as they have in past recessions. Middle and lower-income households—those relying on earnings to provide essentially all of their income, those whose primary asset is their home, and those with something less than an advanced degree—are faring much worse. Housing values in 2011 were down about 30 per cent from their peak in 2005.

Discretionary service spending (including non-housing, energy, food, transportation, education, entertainment, restaurant meals, and insurance spending) fell by 6.9 per cent in the current recession, after never falling more than 2.9 per cent in any previous post-war recession. Without a revival in consumer spending, employment growth will remain weak, and the incomes of those relying on earnings will continue to suffer. The large overhang of household debt from before the Great Recession, though, continues to put considerable pressure on households.

This extended period of high unemployment threatens to have long-term consequences. Rising poverty, especially among young jobless adults and families, may permanently scar the futures of millions of unemployed younger (under age 30) unskilled adults. Over the longer term, traditional upward routes to the middle class in manufacturing and construction jobs will continue to disappear as high school-and-below wages and employment drop. These individuals need more-productive skills than they have at this time, given their current levels of education and human capital.

In this context, it is worth emphasizing the weakness of organized labour as an economic and political force in the United States. Output per capita in the United States in 2012 is above pre-recession 2007 levels, but these goods and services are being produced with 5 million fewer workers. Unionization is at all-time low levels, and even the public sector, among the most heavily unionized sectors in the United States, has lost 700,000 jobs since the beginning of the recession. The reasons for the long-term decline of US unions are complex, but any reckoning of the labour market and the Great Recession's effects on employment, wages, and incomes must recognize this reality.

3. Inequality's Social, Political, and Cultural Impacts

We consider two potential effects that rising income inequality may have on social, political, and cultural outcomes. The first is a change in the aggregate, or average, level. For instance, an increase in income inequality may contribute to an increase in the rate of lone parenthood. The second is a change in the degree of inequality in the outcome—in the 'social gradient'. For instance, an increase in income inequality may produce a larger increase in lone parenthood among those with less income or education than among those with more.

In assessing aggregate effects, we focus our attention on the impact of post-transfer-post-tax household income inequality (rather than inequality of wages, market income, consumption, or wealth). We summarize the trend in income inequality as follows: no change in the 1970s, a sharp rise in the 1980s, and then either a modest or a rapid rise in the 1990s and 2000s. If the top 1 per cent is excluded, as is the case with the data used for most (perhaps all) of the other countries in the GINI project, the rise in inequality in the 1990s and 2000s was fairly small. If we include the top 1 per cent, the rise in inequality in the 1990s and 2000s was nearly as rapid as in the 1980s.

In assessing the social gradient, we use education rather than income for reasons of data availability. In the American context educational attainment is a good stand-in for income, as earnings and incomes for Americans with different amounts of schooling have diverged sharply (Mishel *et al.*, 2012). For the most part we examine four groups: less than secondary school completion (0–11 years of schooling completed), secondary only (12), some tertiary (13–15), and four-year tertiary degree or more (16 or more).

Material Deprivation

The United States has various sources of data that could be used to create a multidimensional indicator of material deprivation, in particular the Survey of Income and Program Participation (SIPP). But the data do not yield a reliable time series. We therefore focus on two income-based indicators of deprivation: the relative poverty rate and the average absolute income of households in the bottom income quintile.

Relative poverty is in effect a measure of income inequality within the lower half of the distribution. We would thus expect the trend in relative poverty to more or less mirror that of income inequality within the bottom 99 per cent. That is essentially what has happened in the United States. Relative poverty increased between the early 1980s and the early-to mid 1990s, followed by little change.

An increase in income inequality may slow absolute income growth for households at the low end of the distribution, as a rising share of economic growth is captured by those at the top and/or in the middle. We see this in the United States. Apart from a brief period in the late 1990s, there has been little increase in absolute incomes for households in the bottom quintile since the 1970s.

The US government's official poverty rate is another indicator of absolute well-being at the low end of the distribution. It too has remained largely unchanged since the late 1970s. The trend differs markedly for different demographic groups. Among younger households, including those headed by individuals under age 35, poverty rates hit 30-year highs in 2009. For those between ages 35 and 64, poverty has not much changed since 1979. Indeed poverty rates were flat or ticked up for all types of units, except for those headed by a person 65 or over, across this period. Consistent with the other data reviewed above, poverty among elderly households which was about the same as poverty among persons under 25, largely children, at 18 per cent in 1979, has fallen to 10.3 per cent in 2009, hitting a new 30-year low. The rate of official poverty among households with children is typically several percentage points higher than it is among households without children. But over the last decade the gap has narrowed. Poverty rates fell dramatically for households (with heads aged less than 55) with children during the 1990s, while they declined only slightly among those without children. Among households without children, poverty rose by similar levels, but now exceeds high points from previous recessions by more than 25 per cent. By and large, the rise in poverty among households without children reflects the increasingly poor situation of younger less-skilled workers in the US job market.

Family and Friends

The chief hypothesis here is that rising income inequality will reduce income growth for people in the middle and lower parts of the distribution. This will produce greater financial strain, causing increased isolation, reduced child bearing (fertility) and marriage, and increased divorce and lone parenthood.

We have limited data on the degree of close personal connections among Americans. In 1985 and 2004, the General Social Survey asked 'Think back over the last six months and the people with whom you discussed the things most important to you. How many were there?' Though the rise in inequality would lead us to expect declining connections, the number was constant over those two decades (Fischer, 2009).

Nor do we find trends in family to be consistent with those of income inequality. The fertility rate in the United States fell sharply in the 1970s but then levelled off. This does not correspond to the trend in income inequality. The share of Americans age 25 to 64 who are married has been declining, but the decline predates the rise in income inequality. Divorce increased sharply in the 1970s. That followed a steady rise in the first half of the twentieth century that accelerated in the 1960s. At the end of the 1970s the upward trend stopped, and in the 1980s, 1990s, and 2000s the divorce rate declined. This does not correlate well with the trend in income inequality. Lone parenthood has risen steadily, a trend that is broadly similar to that of income inequality. But the rise in single parenthood actually began in the 1960s (not shown here), a good while before income inequality began to increase. And it slowed in the 1980s, 1990s, and 2000s, when the increase in income inequality occurred.

What of the social gradient? Marriage has declined more rapidly among those with less education. And the timing corresponds to the rise in income inequality: it begins in the

1990s, shortly after income inequality began to increase. Whether there is a causal link is not clear. The gap has widened for divorce and lone parenthood, too, but much of that occurred in the 1970s, prior to the rise in income inequality.

Health

There are three main hypotheses about why income inequality might have adverse effects on health. One is that the marginal utility of income in improving health declines as income rises. If we compare across individuals within a country, it is almost always the case that income is positively associated with health. But the degree of improvement per extra unit of income declines as we move up the income scale. Thus, taking some money from a rich person and giving it to a poor person should reduce the life expectancy of the rich person by less than it increases the life expectancy of the poor person. The second hypothesis is that larger differences in income within a society increase stress and anxiety due to heightened relative deprivation and/or status competition. The third hypothesized causal link is public policy. Greater income inequality may produce heightened opposition by the rich to higher taxes, thereby blocking expansion of public health care coverage or widespread adoption of new medical technology. If so, the quality of health care services and the quantity of its provision may improve less than they otherwise would.

Life expectancy in the United States has risen steadily since 1970. On the surface, this suggests no adverse health impact of rising income inequality. But technological advances in medical care, enhanced access to health insurance (via Medicare, Medicaid, and S-CHIP), and reductions in smoking surely have contributed to heightened longevity. What we need to know is whether life expectancy has increased as rapidly as it should have given these other changes. The rise in life expectancy slowed as income inequality began to increase in the 1980s, suggesting a possible adverse impact.

What of self-reported health? Since the early 1970s the US General Social Survey has asked 'Would you say your own health, in general, is excellent, good, fair, or poor?' The share responding excellent or good increased steadily in the 1970s, 1980s, and 1990s. But then in the 2000s the trend reversed. Neither of these patterns is consistent with what we would expect given developments in income inequality.

Another health outcome thought by some to be influenced by income inequality is obesity. The chief hypothesis is that rising inequality increases stress, which causes people to overeat (Wilkinson and Pickett 2009). Adult obesity in the United States jumped sharply in the 1980s, 1990s, and 2000s. Estimates for earlier years suggest that it was flat in the 1960s and 1970s. This trend correlates well with that of income inequality. However, there are plausible alternative explanations for this trend. One is rising economic insecurity. Another is weak regulation of food and restaurants and to the lack of a well-entrenched healthy eating culture. Large-portion restaurants, particularly fast-food ones, proliferated rapidly during this period. Junk food became more easily available in larger quantities at grocery and convenience stores. And there was a shift away from home cooking and limited snacking.

The social gradient by education is quite strong for life expectancy, self-reported health, and obesity. What little data we have are consistent with the hypothesis that rising income inequality has widened the social gradient, but the time series are too short to have much confidence in this conclusion.

Housing

Robert H. Frank (2005) argues persuasively that housing is a 'positional' good. That is, people's happiness with their home depends more heavily on relative comparison with other nearby homes than is true for many other goods (such as toothpaste or vacation time). Frank suggests that rising income at the high end of the distribution in the United States allowed the well-to-do to purchase increasingly large and elaborately-equipped homes. Because housing satisfaction depends on relative comparison, middle-class homeowners felt compelled to follow suit, leading to dramatic increases in home prices and housing expenditures and hence to a reduction in household saving.

According to the most commonly-used measure, the Case-Shiller index—US house prices' dramatic rise from 1997 to 2007 is readily apparent. This fits roughly with Frank's hypothesis, though the bubble began nearly two decades after the rise in income inequality commenced. Average household saving as a share of household disposable income has fallen steadily since the 1970s. On the surface, this might seem consistent with the Frank hypothesis. However, the timing is not consistent with that of the run-up in housing prices: the housing bubble began in the late 1990s, but household saving began falling long before that.

Crime

The relative deprivation approach to crime hypothesizes that income inequality will spur crime by increasing perceived deprivation, hopelessness, or envy. Given the sharp rise in income inequality in the United States in the 1980s, 1990s, and 2000s, we would expect to observe a rise in the violent crime and property crimes rates during those decades. However, that didn't happen. The violent crime rate rose in the 1960s, 1970s, and 1980s, but then fell sharply in the 1990s and 2000s. The property crime rate decreased steadily from the early 1970s through the end of the 2000s.

Income inequality may produce effective lobbying by the well-off for stricter punishment, as they may fear a rise in crime, have more to lose from it, and have greater political influence. This predicts a rise in incarceration. The incarceration rate rose steadily throughout the four decades beginning in 1970. This is broadly consistent with that of income inequality. But the fact that the increase in incarceration predates the increase in income inequality is problematic for the hypothesis.

Subjective Well-Being

A rise in income inequality should produce a decline in mean subjective well-being. Among individuals, life satisfaction and happiness increase linearly with income up to a point, but after that the gain per extra unit of income is less. There are diminishing returns, in other words. Thus, if the income share of the well-off increases at the expense of those in the middle and/or lower part of the distribution, the former's gain in subjective well-being will be more than offset by the reduction in the latter's.

Since 1972, the General Social Survey has regularly asked Americans 'Taken all together, how would you say things are these days: would you say that you are very happy, pretty happy, or not too happy?' Mean happiness was flat in the 1970s and 1980s and then declined slightly in the 1990s and 2000s. This is roughly consistent with the trend in income inequality, if we assume a lag time of about a decade.

The social gradient has widened beginning in the late 1970s, which is prior to the rise in income inequality. But much of the widening in the social gradient appears to have occurred beginning in the 1990s, which is a better fit in terms of timing.

Intergenerational Mobility

The standard approach to measuring intergenerational mobility looks at earnings or household income. To assess the trend over time in intergenerational mobility, we need a data set with reliable income information for parents and their adult children over three or more generations. The best US data set of this type, the Panel Study of Income Dynamics, doesn't go quite far enough back in time, and analyses using other data sets have yielded mixed conclusions (Harding, Jencks, Lopoo, and Mayer, 2005; Levine and Mazumder, 2007; Aaronson and Mazumder, 2008; Lee and Solon, 2009; Winship, 2012.) Moreover, there is recent evidence from a panel of US tax returns that incomes did not peak until age 50 in the US in 2007, and the peak was much higher for the more educated, suggesting that current estimates of intergenerational mobility that observe the younger generation at age 40 are downwardly biased (Auten and Gee, 2013, Figure 2).

We do have evidence on test scores of elementary and secondary students and on college completion, both of which are good predictors of earnings and income. According to data compiled by Sean Reardon (2011), the gap in average test scores between children from high-income families and those from low-income families has risen steadily since the early 1970s. (It is now much larger than the gap between white and black children.) Martha Bailey and Susan Dynarski (2011) have compared college completion rates of Americans who grew up in the 1960s and 1970s versus those who grew up in the 1980s and 1990s. In the earlier group, 36 per cent of those from high-income families and 5 per cent of those from low-income families got a four-year college degree. In the latter group the share rose to 54 per cent among those from a high-income family but only to 9 per cent among those who grew up in a low-income household. Given these widening gaps in test scores and college completion, the gap in earnings and income likely has expanded too, or will do so soon.

Participation in Civic and Political Activity

If rising income inequality causes stagnation or decline in the incomes of those in the middle or at the bottom, it may result in withdrawal from participation in civic and political activity. The causal mechanism can be financial (need to work longer hours or more than one job) or psychosocial (embarrassment, frustration, weakened sense of common interests). We consider voter turnout, union membership, and membership in civic organizations.

After falling in the 1960s, voter turnout in presidential-year elections stayed constant between 1970 and 2010. The fall in turnout in off-year elections continued through the 1970s, but it too then stopped. In neither case does the over-time pattern support the hypothesis of a negative impact of rising income inequality. Union density has decreased during the years of rising income inequality, but the drop in unionization began in the mid 1950s long before inequality started to increase. There are various measures of membership in civic organizations. Robert Putnam (2000, Figure 8) calculated average membership in 32 national chapter-based associations. This dropped steadily between 1970 and 2000 (the last year of data). Robert Anderson and colleagues (2006) used time diary data to calculate the extent of participation in civic associations. This too dropped steadily between 1975 and the late 1990s. While the overall pattern of change in these indicators is roughly consistent with the trend in income inequality, the timing does not square well. Putnam's measure actually begins declining around 1960 (not shown here), and the Anderson and colleagues measure's decline begins in the late 1970s. In both cases this precedes the rise in income inequality.

There is a huge social gradient in voter turnout; better-educated Americans are much more likely to vote. Unfortunately, we have comparable over time data only for the three presidential-year elections of 2000, 2004, and 2008; we see no change in the gradient during this brief time span. For union membership, the social gradient story is an interesting one. Among better-educated Americans, those with a college degree, union membership began low and has been flat since the early 1970s. In contrast, among the least educated, those with less than secondary school, union membership in the 1970s was somewhat higher but since then has plummeted. By the late 2000s, we observe the emergence of an education gradient. Was this due to rising income inequality? Probably not. It more likely owes to the shift from manufacturing to service employment and to the greater erosion of unions in the private sector than in the public sector.

Confidence in Political Institutions

To the extent rising inequality is viewed as a failure in the performance of government, it may reduce confidence in key governmental institutions. Since 1972, the General Social Survey has regularly asked the following question about the legislative, executive, and judicial branches of government: 'I am going to name some institutions in this country. As far as the people running these institutions are concerned, would you say you have a great deal of confidence, only some confidence, or hardly any confidence at all?'

The share of American adults saying they have 'a great deal' of confidence in the US Congress dropped sharply in the 1970s, reaching just 10 per cent in 1980, and since then has moved up and down depending on the state of the economy and on events such as the September 11, 2001 terrorist attacks. Given that the bulk of the rise in income inequality in the United States has occurred since the 1970s, it is difficult to see any impact of changes in income inequality on trust in the national legislature. The share expressing a great deal of confidence in the executive has varied between 10 per cent and 30 per cent since the early 1970s, with movement corresponding more to the business cycle than to the upward secular trend in income inequality. Similarly, there has been no noteworthy shift over time in confidence in the Supreme Court.

There is no indication of a social gradient for confidence in any of the branches of the US government, nor of a change over time that corresponds to the trend in income inequality.

Trust

To the extent that it increases people's perceptions of separation or social distance in the country, income inequality may reduce general trust. Since the early 1970s, the General Social Survey has asked American adults whether they feel 'most people can be trusted' or 'you can't be too careful in life'. The share responding that most people can be trusted has fallen steadily in the past four decades. Although this trend is broadly similar to that of income inequality, the fact that the decline in trust began before the rise in inequality calls into question the direction of causality. Indeed, Robert Putnam and Anant Thaker (2010) argue that the causality runs from social capital/trust to income inequality.

There is a sharp social gradient in generalized trust in the US, but it has not widened over time.

Tolerance

With a rise in income inequality, we may expect to observe an increase in selfishness and intolerance. This might result from financial pressures on those in the middle or at the bottom or from a reduced sense of societal cohesion and harmony. One useful measure of this in the American context is a Gallup polling question tapping the share of Americans who would prefer to keep immigration at its current level or reduce it (this does not necessarily mean stop all further immigration). The share actually decreased somewhat beginning in the 1990s and continued in the 2000s. This is not what we would expect given the rise in income inequality.

Desire for Government Action to Reduce Inequality and Poverty

A generation of public opinion research, using both standard survey findings and more in-depth qualitative investigation, suggests the following: Most Americans support capitalism and business. Many believe hard work, rather than luck or help from others, is the key to success. Many feel they have the opportunity to get ahead. Many believe income inequality is too high and that high inequality is not necessary for the country's prosperity. At a general level, many are sceptical about government's ability to help. There is limited support for enhanced redistribution as a remedy for high inequality. Yet Americans do support increased government spending on programmes perceived to enhance opportunity and economic security.

There is a growing literature on public opinion responses to the rise in income inequality in the United States (e.g., Bartels, 2008; McCall and Kenworthy, 2009; Page and Jacobs, 2009; McCall, 2013). The thrust of the conclusion is that Americans do appear to have noticed that income inequality has been rising, even before the Occupy Wall Street movement brought the issue to the forefront. But there has been little or no increase in support among Americans for programmes that directly address income inequality—for instance by increasing taxes on the well off or by increasing transfers to the poor. Indeed, the share saying the rich pay too little in taxes has tended to decrease rather than increase. Instead, the rise in inequality seems to have increased Americans' support for programmes perceived as boosting opportunity and economic security, such as education and health care.

Party Polarization

Party polarization refers to the fact that elected Republican legislators have moved to the right on key economic issues while Democratic legislators have moved to the left. Here the timing is a bit of a problem. According to the authoritative study of party polarization in the US, *Polarized America*, by Nolan McCarty, Keith Poole, and Howard Rosenthal, 'In both chambers [the House and the Senate], the Republicans became more moderate until the 1960s and then moved in a sharply conservative direction in the 1970s. The pattern for the Democrats is almost exactly the opposite. Consequently, the two party means [average party positions] moved closer together during the twentieth century until the 1970s and then moved apart' (McCarty, Poole, and Rosenthal 2006, p. 27). But income inequality between the top 1 per cent and the bottom 99 per cent didn't begin increasing until the 1980s.

Political Influence

Money matters a great deal in American politics. It can boost the election chances of a particular candidate, and it can get donors or lobbyists a hearing with an elected representative. With the richest getting a larger and larger share of the country's income, it is sensible to hypothesize that they would have greater success in swaying policy-makers to support their preferences.

Here too, though, supportive evidence is lacking. The most direct evidence comes from studies by Larry Bartels and Martin Gilens (Bartels, 2008; Gilens, 2012). Bartels examined the association between senators' votes on proposed policy changes and the opinions of people in the lower third, middle third, and upper third of the income distribution. He found that voting correlated much more closely with the views of those with higher incomes. Bartels' analysis covered the period from 1989 to 1994. Gilens extended Bartels' analysis by examining both the Senate and the House of Representatives and by covering the presidencies of Lyndon Johnson, Ronald Reagan, Bill Clinton, and George W. Bush. His finding echoed that of Bartels.

What we need to know, however, is whether this pattern of unequal influence has increased as income inequality has risen. According to Gilens' findings, the association between affluence and influence was weak during the Johnson presidency, strong during the presidencies of Reagan and Clinton, and relatively weak during the presidency of George W. Bush. This is not what the inequality hypothesis predicts, though there may be some confounding factors, such as the September 11, 2001 terrorist attacks, that skew the pattern during the Bush years.

This is by no means a full and complete test of the inequality hypothesis. After all, the well-to-do may exert their influence mainly by keeping proposed reforms from ever coming to a vote and by behind-the-scenes shaping of legislation that does pass. It's quite possible that their growing income share has enhanced their ability to pull these kinds of levers. But if this has in fact happened, it has yet to be effectively documented.

In their recent book, *Winner-Take-All Politics*, Jacob Hacker and Paul Pierson (2010) detail a litany of policy initiatives since the mid 1970s that in their view have had a significant influence—some because they were passed, others because they were blocked—on the degree of income inequality in the United States and on the living standards of ordinary Americans. But there is no indication in their account of a steady increase in the tendency for policy to favour the rich.

One final point on income inequality and unequal political influence: the influence of money in American politics occurs mainly via lobbying rather than campaign contributions, and lobbying is funded primarily by companies and other organizations rather than by individuals. The amount of money spent on lobbying has increased sharply in the past several decades. But much of that increase, if not all of it, might have occurred in the absence of a rise in income inequality.

Inequality's Impacts: Summing Up

Inferring from trends over time in a single country is problematic, because it is difficult to establish the counterfactual. For instance, income inequality rose steadily and sharply in the United States in the 1980s and also, if we include the top 1 per cent, in the 1990s and 2000s. During those same years, life expectancy increased. But we shouldn't necessarily conclude that income inequality had no impact (or a beneficial impact) on longevity, because life expectancy might have increased even more rapidly in the absence of a rise in income inequality. We need cross-country comparisons to establish causation.

With that caveat, here is what we can say about the association in trends and timing between income inequality and the *mean* level of social, political, and cultural outcomes in the United States: We observe the expected association for relative and absolute incomes of low-end households (poverty), obesity, and especially intergenerational mobility.

If we focus instead on the association between trends in income inequality and trends in *inequality* of social, political, and cultural outcomes (the social gradient), we find much more indication of a strong correlation. This is true for marriage, divorce, lone parenthood, life expectancy, subjective health, obesity, happiness, and perhaps political influence.

4. POLICIES

Relative to other affluent nations, the United States spends a small share of its GDP on public social programmes. Its total spending on social programmes is average, but a significant portion consists of private expenditures, particularly by employers for pensions and health insurance (Hacker, 2002; Garfinkel, Rainwater, and Smeeding, 2010). Public social expenditures rose between 1970 and 2007 from about 10 per cent of GDP to 16 per cent, with health care accounting for a good bit of this increase. In the Great Recession public expenditures then shot up, due to the drop in GDP, the rise in spending on automatic stabilizers such as unemployment compensation, and some increases in the generosity of programmes in the 2009 Recovery Act (Burtless and Gordon, 2011).

Government revenues are on the low end among the rich nations, at about 33 per cent of GDP. They have increased only slightly since the 1960s. Taxes on income and profits are the largest revenue sources, followed by taxes on payroll. The United States stands out among affluent countries in its limited use of consumption taxes.

Prior to the Occupy Wall Street movement in 2011, American policy-makers and journalists hardly ever made reference to the issue of income inequality, though concerns about very high CEO pay have occasionally received some attention (McCall, 2013). It is therefore unlikely that changes in tax and/or transfer programmes were aimed to any significant degree at addressing the growth of income inequality per se.

One exception is that in 1993 the newly-elected Clinton administration changed the tax rules for executive compensation, capping the amount that could be deducted at $1 million unless it was 'performance-based'. Ironically, this attempt to slow the rise in high-end incomes had exactly the opposite effect. Corporate accountants quickly figured out ways to classify pay above the threshold as performance-based (Epstein and Javers, 2006). Perhaps more important, the change encouraged firms to accelerate the shift toward compensation via stock options, which were the chief source of skyrocketing income for a number of American CEOs in the 1990s and 2000s (Jarque, 2008).

Nor, as we noted in Section 2, have actual changes in tax or transfer policy made any headway in stemming the rise in inequality. Redistribution achieved via federal taxes fell as a result of the 1981 Reagan income tax reform, which substantially lowered the top marginal tax rate. This was partly offset by a 1993 reform. The two other major tax reforms during these decades, in 1986 and 2001/03, produced little change in the redistributive impact of taxation.

Broadly speaking, government transfers merely kept up with inflation, rather than with the growth of the economy (Kenworthy, 2011). Hence benefit recipients, who tend to be in the lower part of the income distribution, fell further behind those at the high end whose market incomes were rising. Benefit levels for Social Security, the Earned Income Tax Credit, and disability rose in real terms. The benefit level for the Supplemental Nutritional Assistance Program ('food stamps') was flat. The benefit level for America's main social assistance programme, AFDC-TANF, declined steadily, and coverage too declined after the early 1990s.

Government-funded health insurance expanded somewhat through this period. Part of this owes to population ageing, which results in a larger share of the population being eligible for Medicare. Another part was due to expansion of access to Medicaid in the 1980s and then again in the late 1990s (S-CHIP). If fully implemented, the 2010 Affordable Care Act will further increase access to Medicaid. Up to this point, however, these expansions have been insufficient to offset declining health coverage from employers. As a result, the share of Americans without health insurance increased, albeit modestly, during this period of rising income inequality.

The minimum wage in the United States is a statutory one, determined by the government rather than through collective bargaining. Despite the steady rise in income inequality in the 1980s, 1990s, and 2000s, the minimum wage was allowed to fall in real terms in the 1980s and has remained essentially flat since then.

Much of the variation among Americans in cognitive skills and non-cognitive traits is already present by the time they enter kindergarten (Heckman, 2008). Universal public early education (childcare and preschool) might therefore help in reducing eventual inequality of wages and incomes, but thus far only a small number of states have introduced broad preschool coverage, and even then only for four-year-olds (Ermisch, Jantti and Smeeding, 2012). Government has also failed to respond adequately to the rise in the price of university education. In part because of the increase in college costs, the gap in college graduation rates between children from high-income families and those from low-income families has widened sharply in the past generation (Bailey and Dynarski, 2011).

Not only did policy changes do little to stem the rise of market income inequality in the United States; they may have been one of the key contributors to that rise. The large and sustained increase in inequality of pre-transfer pre-tax income has multiple causes, from technological shifts to heightened globalization and domestic competition to altered corporate governance structures to the emergence of winner-take-all markets to weakened unions and more. Jacob Hacker and Paul Pierson (2010) suggest that government policy was among the key contributors to these and other changes that produced the run-up in inequality.

They call particular attention to three aspects of government policy. The first is American labour law, which has made it difficult for unions to survive in the modern economy. In the 1980s and 2000s enforcement of labour law also weakened considerably. The second is financial deregulation, which occurred steadily through the 1980s and 1990s. This facilitated the stunning rise in pay for Wall Street traders and analysts. The third is a failure to require 'expensing' of stock options during much of the period of surging CEO pay in the 1980s and 1990s.

In the past three decades, the inequality of pre-transfer pre-tax income in the United States—already quite high relative to other affluent longstanding democratic nations—has increased sharply. We find no indication of action by US policy-makers explicitly aimed at ameliorating or reversing this rise. Consequently, redistribution achieved via tax and transfer programmes did not increase. And policy likely had a hand in contributing to the rise in inequality of pre-transfer pre-tax income.

5. CONCLUSION

In the 1970s, the United States had one of the most unequal (possibly *the* most unequal) income distributions among the world's rich nations. In the ensuing decades it has become even more unequal, and the pace of growth of inequality has been faster than almost anywhere else. If we exclude the top 1 per cent, as do the data for other countries in this project, income inequality rose rapidly in the 1980s and more slowly in the 1990s and 2000s. If we include the top 1 per cent, it rose rapidly in all three decades.

The causes of America's high level of, and rapid growth in, income inequality since the 1970s are multiple: weak and weakening unions; stagnant educational attainment; a surge in globalization; an increase in competition in mainly domestic industries; skill-biased technological change; a shift in corporate governance toward emphasis on 'shareholder value' and short-run profits; growing use of pay-for-performance; an increase in low-skilled immigration; a stall in the real value of the statutory minimum wage; deregulation (particularly in finance); growing use of stock options to reward CEOs coupled with a sharp run-up in stock values; the spread of winner-take-all markets in various industries; and reductions in effective tax rates for households at the top. There is no single culprit. Indeed, there is little agreement among scholars on even the top two or three causes.

What have been the social and political impacts? We hesitate to ascribe causality based on observation of trends in a single country. Instead, we call attention to outcomes in which the timing of change appears to be consistent with what we would expect if rising inequality did have a causal effect. For mean levels of social outcomes, in a few cases the trends are correlated but for many they are not.

What might we expect for the future of income inequality in the United States? We see no strong reason to expect a reversal or even a slowing of the upward trend that characterizes the past few decades. The drivers of that trend are many, and they look likely to continue. Economic shocks or changes in institutions and policies might intervene. But to this point they have not. Some hoped that the mid-to-late 1990s, when real wages began to grow in the middle and below, would mark the end of inequality's rise. But that didn't happen. Others viewed the 2008–11 economic crisis as the harbinger of profound shifts that might include a return to a more even distribution of the proceeds of economic growth. But after a brief pause, income inequality has returned to its upward path.

References

Aaronson, Daniel, and Mazumder, Bhashkar (2008), 'Intergenerational Economic Mobility in the United States, 1940 to 2000', *Journal of Human Resources* 43: 139–172.

Acemoglu, Daron, and Autor, David H. (2010), 'Skills, Tasks and Technologies: Implications for Employment and Earnings', in Ashenfelter, Orley and Card, David (eds.), *Handbook of Labour Economics* 4, Amsterdam: Elsevier.

Alvaredo, Facundo, Atkinson, Anthony B., Piketty, Thomas, and Saez. Emmanuel (2012), The World Top Incomes Database, <http://topincomes.g-mond.parisschoolofeconomics.eu>, accessed 30 December 2012.

Anderson, Robert, Curtis, James, and Grabb, Edward (2006), 'Trends in Civic Association Activity in Four Democracies: The Special Case of Women in the United States', *American Sociological Review*, 71: 376–400.

Atkinson, Anthony, Piketty, Thomas, and Saez, Emmanuel (2011), 'Top Incomes in the Long Run of History', *Journal of Economic Literature*, 49(1): 3–71.

Auten, Gerald, Gee, Geoffrey, and Turner, Nicholas (2013), 'Income Inequality, Mobility and Turnover at the Top in the US, 1987–2010'. *American Economic Review* 103: 168-72.

Autor, David H., Dorn, David, and Hanson, Gordon H. (2012), 'The China Syndrome: Local Labor Market Effects of Import Competition in the United States', *Working Paper* 18054, National Bureau of Economic Research, Cambridge, MA.

Bailey, Martha, and Dynarski, Susan, (2011), 'Inequality in Postsecondary Education', in Greg, J. Duncan and Richard J. Murnane, (eds.), *Whither Opportunity? Rising Inequality, Schools, and Children's Life Chances*, New York: Russell Sage Foundation, pp. 117–132.

Bartels, Larry (2008), *Unequal Democracy*, Princeton, NJ: Princeton University Press.

Bernstein, Jared and Baker, Dean (2003), *The Benefits of Full Employment*, Washington DC: Economic Policy Institute.

Blau, Fran and Kahn, Larry (2012), 'Immigration and the Distribution of Incomes', *NBER Working Paper* # 18515 at: <http://www.nber.org/papers/w18515>

Bricker, Jesse, Kennickell, Arthur B., Moore, Kevin B., and Sabelhaus, John (2012), 'Changes in US Family Finances from 2007 to 2010: Evidence from the Survey of Consumer Finances', *Federal Reserve Bulletin*, June, Vol. 98(2). <http://www.federalreserve.gov/pubs/bulletin/2012/PDF/scf12.pdf>

Burtless, Gary and Tracy, Gordon (2011), 'The Federal Stimulus Programs and Their Effects', pp. 249–293 in Grusky, David B., Western, Bruce, and Wimer, Christopher (eds.), *The Great Recession*, New York: Russell Sage Foundation, pp. 249–293.

Congressional Budget Office (2011a), 'Average Federal Tax Rates and Income, by Income Category, 1979–2007'.

Congressional Budget Office (2011b), 'Trends in the Distribution of Household Income Between 1979 and 2007', October.

Congressional Budget Office, (2013), 'The Budget and Economic Outlook: Fiscal Years 2013 to 2023', at <http://www.cbo.gov/publication/43907>

Davies, James B., Sandström, Susanna, Shorrocks, Anthony, and Wolff, Edward N. (2011), 'The Level and Distribution of Global Household Wealth', *Economic Journal, Royal Economic Society*, vol. 121(551), pages 223–254, March.

DeNavas-Walt, Carmen, Proctor, Bernadette D., and Smith, Jessica C. (2012), *Income, Poverty, and Health Insurance Coverage in the United States: 2011*, Current Population Reports, P60-243, US Census Bureau. September.

Epstein, Keith, and Javers, Eamon (2006), 'How Bill Clinton Helped Boost CEO Pay', *BusinessWeek*, 27 November.

Ermisch, J., Jäntti, M., and Smeeding, T. M. (eds.) (2012), *From Parents to Children: The Intergenerational Transmission of Advantage*, New York: Russell Sage Foundation, May.

Fischer, Claude, S. (2009), 'The 2004 GSS Finding of Shrunken Social Networks: An Artifact?' *American Sociological Review*, 74(4): 657–669.

Fisher, Jonathan, Johnson, David, and Smeeding, Timothy (2012), 'Inequality of Income and Consumption: Measuring the Trends in Inequality from 1985–2010 for the Same Individuals', Russell Sage Foundation Working Paper. <http://www.russellsage.org/research/reports/consumption-inequality>

Frank, Robert H. (2005), 'Positional Externalities Cause Large and Preventable Welfare Losses', *American Economic Review*, 95(2): 137–141.

Garfinkel, Irwin, Rainwater, Lee, and Smeeding, Timothy (2010), *Wealth and Welfare States*, Oxford: Oxford University Press.

Gilens, Martin, (2012), *Affluence and Influence*, Princeton NJ: Princeton University Press.

Goldin, Claudia, and Katz, Larry (2008), *The Race between Education and Technology*, Cambridge, MA: Harvard University Press.

Gordon, Robert, and Dew-Becker, Ian (2008), 'Controversies About the Rise of American Inequality: A Survey', *Working Paper* 13982, National Bureau of Economic Research.

Greenstone, Michael, and Looney, Adam (2012), *The Impact of Fiscal Cliff Negotiations on American Jobs: The Tradeoff Between Deficit Reduction and Economic Growth*, Hamilton Project, Brookings Institution. <http://www.hamiltonproject.org/papers/the_impact_of_fiscal_cliff_negotiations_on_american_jobs_the_tradeoff_/?utm_source=The+Hamilton+Project&utm_campaign=ff9a26e5e4-December+2012+Newsletter&utm_medium=email&ct=t(August_2012_Newsletter_8_21_2012)>

Hacker, Jacob (2002), *The Divided Welfare State*, Cambridge UK: Cambridge University Press.

Hacker, Jacob, and Pierson, Paul (2010), *Winner-Take-All Politics*, New York: Simon and Schuster.

Harding, David J., Jencks, Christopher, Lopoo, Leonard M., and Mayer, Susan E. (2005), 'The Changing Effect of Family Background on the Incomes of American Adults', in Bowles, Samuel, Gintis, Herbert, and Groves, Melissa Osborne (eds.)*Unequal Chances: Family Background and Economic Success*, New York and Princeton, NJ: Russell Sage Foundation and Princeton University Press, pp. 100–144.

Heckman, James J. (2008), 'Schools, Skills, and Synapses', *Working Paper* 14064, National Bureau of Economic Research.

Jarque, Arantxa (2008), 'CEO Compensation: Trends, Market Changes, and Regulation', *Federal Reserve Bank of Richmond Economic Quarterly* 94: 265–300.

Kenworthy, Lane (2011), *Progress for the Poor*, Oxford: Oxford University Press.

Lee, Chul-In and Solon, Gary (2009), 'Trends in Intergenerational Income Mobility', *Review of Economics and Statistics*, 91(4): 766–772.

Levine, David I., and Mazumder, Bhashkar (2007), 'The Growing Importance of Family: Evidence from Brothers' Earnings'. *Industrial Relations*, 46: 7–21.

Levy, Frank and Temin, Peter (2009), 'Institutions and Wages in Post-World War II America', in Brown, *et al.* (eds.), *Labour in the Era of Globalization*, 15–49, Cambridge: Cambridge University Press.

Machin, Stephen, and Van Reenan, Jan. (2012), 'Inequality and Opportunity: The Return of a Neglected Debate', *US Election Analysis No. 4*, October. Centre for Economic Performance, LSE.

McCall, Leslie (2012), *The Undeserving Rich*, New York: Cambridge University Press.

McCall, Leslie, and Kenworthy, Lane (2009), 'Americans' Social Policy Preferences in the Era of Rising Inequality', *Perspectives on Politics*, 7(3): 459–484.

McCarty, Nolan, Poole, Keith T., and Rosenthal, Howard (2006), *Polarized America: The Dance of Ideology and Unequal Riches*, Cambridge, MA: MIT Press.

Mishel, Lawrence, Bivens, Josh, Gould, Elise, and Shierholz, Heidi (2012), *The State of Working America*, 12th edition. Washington DC: Economic Policy Institute.

OECD (2011a), *Divided We Stand: Why Income Inequality Keeps Rising*. <http://www.oecd.org/social/socialpoliciesanddata/49170768.pdf>

OECD (2011b), *Education at a Glance 2011: OECD Indicators*, accessed at <http://www.oecd.org/education/preschoolandschool/educationataglance2011oecdindicators.htm>

Page, Benjamin, and Jacobs, Lawrence (2009), *Class War? What Americans Really Think about Economic Inequality*, Chicago: University of Chicago Press.

Putnam, Robert D. (2000), *Bowling Alone: The Collapse and Revival of American Community*, New York: Simon and Schuster.

Putnam, Robert, and Thaker, Anant (2010), 'Equality and Social Capital: What's the Connection?' Presented at the Tobin Project conference.

Reardon, Sean F. (2011), 'The Widening Academic-Achievement Gap between the Rich and the Poor: New Evidence and Possible Explanations', in Duncan, Greg J. and Murnane, Richard J. (eds.), *Whither Opportunity? Rising Inequality, Schools, and Children's Life Chances*, New York: Russell Sage Foundation.

Saez, Emmanuel (2013), 'Striking it Richer: The Evolution of Top Incomes in the United States', updated January; available at: <http://elsa.berkeley.edu/~saez>

Smeeding, Timothy M., and Thompson Jeffrey P. (2011), 'Recent Trends in Income Inequality', *Research in Labour Economics*, 32: 1–50.

Thompson, Jeffrey, and Smeeding, Timothy (2012), 'Inequality in the Great Recession—The Case of the United States', in *Income Inequality and the Great Recession*, Stephen P. Jenkins, *et al.* (eds.), Oxford: Oxford University Press.

US Bureau of Labour Statistics (2011), *Labour Force Statistics*, Table A15. Accessed at <http://www.bls.gov/webapps/legacy/cpsatab15.htm>

US Bureau of Labour Statistics (2011), *BLS Statistics of Unemployment and Employment*, <http://www.bls.gov/bls/unemployment.htm>

US Department of Commerce (2012a), *GDP and income per capita*, December. <http://www.bea.gov/national/index.htm#gdp>

US Department of Commerce (2012b), *Real GDP*, accessed 29 November at <https://www.bea.gov/newsreleases/national/gdp/gdpnewsrelease.htm>

Western, Bruce, Bloome, Deirdre, and Percheski, Christine (2008), 'Inequality Among American Families with Children, 1975 to 2005', *American Sociological Review* 73:903–920.

Western, Bruce and Rosenfeld, Jake (2011), 'Unions, Norms, and the Rise in US Wage Inequality', *American Sociological Review* 76: 513–537.

Wilkinson, Richard, and Pickett, Kate (2009), *The Spirit Level: Why Greater Equality Makes Societies Stronger*, New York: Bloomsbury Press.

Winship, Scott (2012), 'Has Economic Mobility Declined? Comparing Young Men Born Mid-Century and in the Early 1980s', presented at the National Tax Association Spring Symposium.

Wolff, Edward N. (2012), 'The Asset Price Meltdown and the Wealth of the Middle Class', *Working Paper* 18559, National Bureau of Economic Research, Cambridge, MA.

CHAPTER 30

....

CONCLUSIONS: LEARNING FROM DIVERSITY ABOUT INCREASING INEQUALITY, ITS IMPACTS AND RESPONSES?

....

BRIAN NOLAN, WIEMER SALVERDA, DANIELE CHECCHI, IVE

MARX, ABIGAIL McKNIGHT, ISTVÁN GYÖRGY TÓTH, AND

HERMAN van de WERFHORST

1. INTRODUCTION

....

IN this final chapter of the volume, we look back across the country case studies and bring out some key features of their findings when seen in the round. As highlighted in the introductory chapter, the point of departure for these country studies was a common template, used by country experts to produce in-depth country reports for 30 countries, covering a period of 30 years, on which the chapters in this book have been based. We encourage the reader seeking further detail and explanation to consult these at <http://www.gini-research. org>. The collection of countries is distinctive in including OECD countries from Europe, North America and Asia, and the thirty years, euphemistically labelled years of 'great moderation' in the richest countries until the outbreak of the financial crisis, witnessed growing inequalities in many places.

This common approach applied across very different settings provides a unique opportunity to assess how inequalities, social and political outcomes, and policies have evolved in these countries over this time period, casting new light on a number of central research questions. The common template allows for comparison between countries but also gave country experts the scope to use data sources that they felt were most reliable in capturing domestic trends, allowing for discontinuities and breaks in series, and to draw on national studies that are not always easily available for international comparison. In addition, country experts have provided their interpretations of what these series reveal and have drawn on available evidence about the factors that appear to underpin the observed trends, not least relating to the national context in terms of the macro-economy and of institutions and policies. This provided the basis for individual country chapters to map the evolution of income and educational inequalities, describe trends in a range of indicators in the social, political and cultural spheres against that background, and highlight what they regarded as key features of welfare state policies affecting inequality and its evolution.

In mapping the evolution of inequality over the period from 1980, a number of dimensions were examined, namely, income, earnings, wealth and education. Particular attention was paid to obtaining good quality series for inequality in household disposable equivalized income, central to other inequalities in society. The other domains—education, labour market and wealth—both contribute to differences in household income and also represent important aspects of inequality in themselves. Key drivers of trends in each country were also teased out. The potential impact of inequality on political, social, and cultural outcomes is at the core of the book's concerns, and the individual chapters used available data to describe levels and trends in key indicators which theory and previous research suggested might be affected by inequality. In the social domain these covered material deprivation, social cohesion, housing, health, life satisfaction, intergenerational mobility, and crime; and in the political and cultural domain they included voter turnout, political values, political and civic participation, trust, attitudes to migration, inequality and redistribution. In finally evaluating the role of policies, particular attention was paid to social spending, taxation, wage bargaining, and the minimum wage.

In this concluding chapter, the first and central point to be emphasized is the richness of the country case studies themselves. Anyone reading even a selection will be struck by just how varied country experiences have been, and convinced of the importance of understanding the national context in trying to explain them. All too often, the quest to identify over-arching trends and fundamental driving forces serves to shift the focus away from this variety, and runs the risk of both mis-characterizing and misunderstanding what is actually happening. So the first message of this concluding chapter is that it is no substitute for reading the individual country studies. Nonetheless, it is worth standing back and looking across the 30 countries covered, and in what follows we draw out some striking features, beginning with trends in inequality and then turning to its impacts and the role of policies, ending with some final reflections. A deeper comparative analysis that draws on the studies of this volume, their underlying reports, the relevant literature and a large number of comparatively-oriented project discussion papers is the focus of *Changing Inequalities in Rich Countries* (Salverda *et al.*, 2013), companion to this volume. It covers much the same ground, ranging from drivers of inequality to social impacts, political impacts and policies, studying in more depth certain issues such as the distribution of wealth and debt and educational inequalities, but adopts a more directly comparative mode of analysis. In this volume, by contrast, as stressed in the Introduction, the country studies are the core contribution, accompanied only by a transversal examination of the data on inequality and poverty in Chapter 2.

2. The Context of Inequality Trends

Over the last 30 years, many underlying trends potentially impacting on income inequality may be observed. The shift from industrial and/or manufacturing economies to service-based economies has been widespread, and with some exceptions (notably in the recent economic crisis), average living standards have been increasing. Educational attainment has continued to increase, at least at secondary school level, reducing dispersion in educational attainment, but not always keeping pace with the increase in the demand for skills. In some cases, policies aimed at increasing educational attainment have been biased towards improvement at the top rather than raising the bottom. Demographic and labour market shifts can be seen as drivers with both inequality enhancing and inequality dampening effects. These include increasing life expectancy and significantly more single-person or lone-parent households, increases in women's participation in the labour market and the demise of the male breadwinner model, and an increase in part-time employment. What were initially regarded as non-typical forms of employment—part-time working, temporary contracts and flexible forms of working—have now become part of the mainstream, at least in Europe, partly due to policy. Earnings dispersion has been affected by deep forces of globalization and skill-biased technological change, as well as policies with respect to, for example, regulation, wage bargaining, and minimum wages, which are often associated with a drive towards liberalization and privatization. Welfare state institutions have evolved at different paces and in different ways, with the 30 countries covered displaying a wide array of starting-points and evolutions. One significant tendency has been to lower tax rates on capital and top incomes in exchange for higher social security contributions and, especially in some Eastern European countries, for higher indirect taxes. The end of communism was followed by an increase of inequality in many of the countries affected in Eastern Europe, though their paths subsequently diverged quite markedly.

The over-arching analysis presented in Chapter 2 found that inequality in household (equivalized) disposable income increased over the period as a whole in many countries, but it was clear from that analysis and reinforced in the individual country chapters that, even where this was the case, the extent and timing of that increase varied a great deal, that some countries saw stable or declining inequality, and that each country has its own tale to tell. The extent to which countries have sought to temper the pressures they faced, or deal with their consequences, have varied quite widely. We see evidence that strong institutions can stave off upward pressures on wage inequality through widespread collective wage setting agreements (with Belgium being an example), and strong welfare states can successfully redistribute through taxation and cash transfers, although this has weakened in some of the usual exemplars, the Nordic countries. Some countries managed to keep inequality down but with poor fiscal discipline and expenditure levels that were not sustainable, as has come to light in the current crisis (an example being Greece). The scale and timing of increases in inequality have also reflected macro-economic fluctuations and shocks, political change (particularly, but by no means only, in Eastern Europe), and demographic factors. The recent economic crisis could well give rise to a further upward shift in inequality, witnessed on previous occasions in many of the cases, although this may not be immediately visible, as a result of the varying macro-economic impacts of recession, differences in the nature and intensity of 'austerity' measures, and uncertain medium-term prospects for both the macro-economy and for retrenchment strategies.

3. The Social Realm

Much has been written about the potentially harmful links between inequality levels and a range of outcomes, as exemplified in Wilkinson and Pickett's (2009) argument that societies with higher income inequality have lower levels of social cohesion, manifested in outcomes such as more social problems, higher crime rates, higher mortality rates, worse health, more educational inequalities, lower social trust, and lower political involvement. They highlight inequality's 'psychosocial' implications, relating to the effects of pronounced status differences in more unequal societies. Another possible causal channel, from a neo-materialist perspective, is that inequality is related to negative outcomes as a consequence of different levels and distributions of resources available to populations, both at the level of households and the nation (Lynch *et al.*, 2000). These two perspectives on the social impacts of inequality can be seen as complementary rather than competing (see also Elgar and Aitken, 2011). Due to both differential resources and the psychosocial consequences of them, income inequality may have a causal impact on the outcomes under study, even though empirically causality may be hard to assess.

Much of the empirical evidence that has been put forward in support of these hypothesized inequality effects involves cross-country cross-tabulations of an inequality measure on one axis (usually the Gini coefficient) and average outcomes for specific social outcomes on the other. One of the problems with this approach is that it concentrates on average outcomes, and information on averages can conceals a wide array of distributional outcomes. The evidence assembled here allows for such cross-country comparisons at a point in time, but also provides evidence on how relevant social indicators have changed over time as inequality changes, or after inequality has changed (since any effects may take some time to come through). This is not a conclusive basis for testing or assessing causal mechanisms, but seeing whether social outcomes have changed in a way that appears consistent with the thesis that increasing inequality leads to worsening outcomes is still a significant contribution, providing a useful inventory that may serve as a starting point for further analyses, especially where international comparison can make a highly valuable contribution.

Another important contribution from the country case studies is that where possible they have looked beyond average outcomes to examine social gradients in available indicators. While increases in inequality might affect average outcomes, for example where diminishing returns exists (that is where the returns to an incremental increase in income are lower for those on high incomes compared to those on low incomes), it is also possible that an increase in inequality might leave overall average outcomes unchanged but widen the differences between income groups or other socio-economic gradients. In that case average outcomes conceal significant information, and the evidence from the country case studies and elsewhere suggests that over the period covered these have been predominately affected by societal change, technological developments, and changes in real income, which dominate any perceptible effect of inequality. However, social gradients may widen as inequality increases, with inequalities in one domain accompanying or even producing inequalities in another. In addition, while some inequalities increase, others, e.g., female educational attainment or labour market success, may be diminishing.

Focusing on a number of social indicators, we can draw on the findings across the 30 countries and over the 30-year period to assess whether there appears to be an association between trends in inequality and trends in these outcomes, both at the average level and for social gradients where available.

Family Formation, Breakdown and Fertility

The hypothesized relationship between inequality and family formation and breakdown posits that where rising income inequality reduces income growth for households in the middle or lower parts of the distribution, this can lead to greater financial strain, acting as a source of pressure for falling fertility and marriage and increased divorce and lone parenthood. The 30 countries covered in this volume display major societal shifts in family formation and breakdown, with an increasing array of family structures, though the starting points and speed of change vary, and cultural differences are likely to continue to influence cross-country differences in this domain. Common trends across countries are falling marriage rates, increasing divorce rates, increases in cohabitation and extra marital births (except Greece), a growth in single-headed households and, in particular, single parent families, women starting families later and having fewer children. Most countries have seen a fall in fertility rates with evidence of a recovery towards the end of the period. These changes have to be assessed against the backdrop of increasing gender equality, female labour force participation, increased availability of contraception and, in Spain and Ireland, the legalization of divorce.

Rather than inequality being the main driver behind these social and demographic trends, the country case studies repeatedly draw out the relationship between economic hardship and family breakdown and divorce. For example, the Korean case study notes that unemployment of male household heads was found to significantly contribute to increasing crude divorce rates and, more generally, the Asian financial crisis in 1997 can be linked to increases in divorce rates and family breakdown. In addition, the Netherlands case study notes that divorce rates seem to be more sensitive to economic development than income inequality, and the Bulgarian case study observes that falling fertility is more closely related to changes in prosperity than changes in economic inequality. In Finland, the authors conclude that there is no clear trend in fertility and no clear connection to inequality, but there is greater sensitivity to changes in GDP growth rates, with fertility increasing during downturns and declining during booms. By contrast, falls in GDP across Eastern European countries following transition seem to be linked to falling fertility. It is frequently noted in the country case studies that the timing of changes in the family domain do not fit inequality trends. For example, the fall in fertility and increase in divorce rates in the USA started well before the increase in inequality in the 1980s, and the main increase in lone parenthood there occurred in the 1960s and in fact slowed from the 1980s.

In many countries, the growth of single-headed households and particularly single parent families explains part of the compositional changes at the bottom of the income distribution and increasingly also higher up the distribution, and therewith some of the increase in household income inequality. In fact, it seems likely from the evidence in the country case studies that these family changes have primarily acted as demographic drivers behind inequality change rather than being driven by it. As the Finnish chapter states, 'Rather than reflecting changes in inequality, these general developments are reflections of loosening of traditional family values, more individualistic values, establishment of a dual earner model in the labour market, and strong gender equality'. Belgium is another interesting case: over this thirty-year period, marriage rates fell and divorce rates increased, cohabitation and extra-marital births increased along with single parent families, there was a fall in average household size and an increase in single person households, all in a country where inequality remained stable. As the Ireland country chapter notes, patterns of household formation and composition are clearly relevant to poverty and inequality but the causal impact of trends in inequality on fertility and family structures has not been established.

Crime and Imprisonment

Rising inequality has been suggested as a factor increasing levels of crime, by increasing perceived deprivation, hopelessness or envy. Rising inequality may be associated with increasing imprisonment rates, even if crime itself is unaffected: as outlined in the US country chapter, the well-off with greater political influence could increase their political lobbying for an increase in imprisonment and harsher sentencing. There are problems with obtaining consistent series on crime rates, particularly where data relate to police-recorded crime as reporting and recording practices have a tendency to change over time. Overall this tends to mean that police-recorded crime understates the level of crime reported in victimization surveys (see for example Ireland and the UK). While there is a common trend towards greater imprisonment and increasing prison populations,[1] the picture for crime trends is more diverse. While policing policy, improvements in vehicle and property security, CCTV, even the deterrent effects of higher levels of detection and imprisonment are clearly likely to account for at least part of any trend in crime rates, there does appear to be some evidence in some countries that changes in crime rates have accompanied changes in inequality. For example, crime rates increased over the 1980s in the UK as inequality soared, and the evidence for Korea is that the high crime rates since the 1990s financial crisis are correlated with rising inequality. For Japan, total crime rates increased during the serious recession of the early 1990s, and studies find a positive relationship between increases in inequality and crime rates after controlling for time trends and changes in unobserved heterogeneity.

In the USA, violent crime rates increased in the 1980s as inequality increased, but declined in the 1990s and 2000s when inequality increased still further. In addition, violent crime rates also increased in the 1960s and 1970s, before inequality started to rise. Property crime rates also fell in the four decades from the 1970s to the 2000s. Imprisonment rates increased over the three decades of increasing inequality 1980s–2000s, broadly consistent with income inequality trends but they started to increase in the 1970s, predating the increase in inequality. In the UK, while the increase in crime rates over the 1980s is

---

[1] Poland is an exception with falling prison populations since transition in the early 1990s. This is the result of inflated prison populations under communism which tended to fluctuate following protests, martial law (1986–1989) and amnesties. The high prison populations in Poland under communism accompanied low crime rates.

consistent with increasing inequality, the substantial fall since around the 1990s is not in line with inequality trends. There is also contradictory evidence for the Netherlands, France, Poland (although clearly factors related to the transition were important here), Canada, Luxembourg and Greece. Interestingly, victimization rates increased in the late 1980s and late 2000s in Belgium, where inequality remained stable, although, as the authors carefully tease out, there were underlying tensions in Belgium which may have played a part.

Health and Health Inequalities

As Kenworthy and Smeeding outline in the United States chapter, three main hypotheses have been put forward to explain why income inequality might have an adverse effect on health:

1) If for health outcomes there are decreasing returns to income, that is the health return on a marginal unit of income is lower for a high-income individual than a low-income person, then redistribution of income from rich to poor would improve average health outcomes.
2) Wide disparities in income within a society increase stress and anxiety due to heightened relative deprivation and/or status competition.
3) Greater income inequality may produce heightened opposition by the rich to higher taxes, thereby blocking expansion of public health care coverage or widespread adoption of new medical technology. If so, the quality of health care services and the quantity of its provision may improve less than they otherwise would.

For health and health inequalities, we focus on trends in life expectancy although many other outcomes are reported in the country case studies.

Life expectancy. Across the 30 case studies we mostly observe upward trends in life expectancy (Romania being an exception), but the extent to which these trends can be related to changes in inequality is unclear, with perhaps some evidence in the USA, for example, that the rise in life expectancy appeared to slow as income inequality began to increase in the 1980s. While life expectancy is longer for women than men, in most countries the gap has narrowed since the 1980s (the exception once again being Romania). This convergence could be due to an equalization in labour force participation and the changing industrial structure of employment, with the shift from heavy industry and manufacturing (which were male dominated) to services which have lower occupational health hazards. These overall increases in life expectancy are primarily related to medical advances (improvements in early detection and diagnosis, drug treatments, surgical advances, etc.), increases in real incomes and living standards, improved access to health care, reductions in smoking, as well as the shift in industrial structure already mentioned, rather than the varied patterns of income inequality trends. It is clear that the huge shock to the former Soviet-led countries in Central and Eastern Europe had a negative effect on life expectancy but this appears to be temporary and was not uniform across all countries.

However, another common finding across the countries is that there are stark gradients in life expectancy. These gradients are delineated by income, education and social class. Evidence on gradients is not available for all countries or across the full 30-year time span for many countries, but where trends are available we find increasing social gradients in a number of countries, for example, the UK, Greece, Sweden, Luxembourg, Finland, the US, Slovenia, the Netherlands, Belgium and France. Not all of these countries are characterized by growing income inequality over the same time period but the exceptional cases such as Slovenia point to other explanations such as increases in privatization in health services allowing the better off to purchase better health care and avoid treatment delays.

Life Satisfaction

Assuming that an individuals' life satisfaction increases linearly with income up to a point, after which the marginal utility of income falls (i.e. there are diminishing marginal returns to income), then a rise in inequality with average income unchanged should lead to a decline in mean subjective well-being or life satisfaction. Any increase in the share of income of the well off at the expense of lower-income individuals will lead to a bigger loss in life satisfaction for the lower-income individuals than the well off would gain.

In Germany, it was shown that satisfaction with life in general and with different aspects of individuals' lives (health, job and income) generally followed the trends in net income. It was also found in Bulgaria and Romania that the low average levels of life satisfaction tended to follow the economic circumstances of the country rather than inequality trends, reflecting the poor living standards in both countries following transition. Also in Poland, the positive time trend in life satisfaction seemed to follow increases in living standards rather than the concurrent growth in inequality. In Ireland, too, average life satisfaction fell during periods of economic stagnation and increased in the economic boom rather than accompanying any inequality trend. Life satisfaction trends in Greece also appear to follow economic cycles rather than inequality trends.

In Finland, average levels of life satisfaction have been consistently high and do not appear to be related to changes in inequality (or economic conditions), but a bifurcation has occurred with both increases in 'very happy/very satisfied' at one end of the spectrum and increases in very 'unhappy/dissatisfied' at the other end. This highlights once again how the focus on averages can conceal important underlying changes. In Luxembourg, life satisfaction was also found to be high and the modest increase in inequality did not appear to affect the level of happiness or life satisfaction. However, a comparison between Estonia and Latvia does appear to suggest that the higher inequality in Latvia could partly explain the lower average relative levels of life satisfaction, compared with Estonia.

In the USA, life satisfaction could be regarded as roughly following inequality trends but with a long time lag (of about a decade), with mean happiness stable in the 1970s and 1980s but falling slightly in the 1990s and 2000s. There is also evidence that the social gradient widened in the 1970s, which was prior to the increase in inequality; but also widened in the beginning of the 1990s, which is more consistent with inequality trends. Gradients delineated by education were found in a number of countries. In the Netherlands, higher levels of education were found to be associated with higher life satisfaction, which increased over time. The authors of this country chapter speculate that this could be an indirect impact of increasing inequality since the late 1990s, due to the increasing role of education in determining success in the labour market alongside reduced labour market opportunities for those with a low education. An education gradient in life satisfaction was also found in

France, Belgium (the only non-CEE country in the study to be marked by falling life satisfaction from the mid 1970s to mid 1980s despite stable inequality) and Ireland.

4. POLITICAL AND CULTURAL REALMS

The possible impacts of economic inequalities extend beyond individual well-being. Outcomes in the realm of political behaviours and orientations are worth investigating too. Possible relationships between inequality and political outcomes have direct repercussions for the legitimacy of politics. If individuals (or particular groups of individuals such as the poor) refrain from political participation, or see their preference for redistribution ignored, or lose trust in their fellowmen, democratic governance may be threatened. Whereas other studies have demonstrated, using cross-sections of populations in many countries, that the level of income inequality in a society is associated with a number of political outcomes, the current volume enlarged our understanding of how, within countries, trends towards rising inequality have coincided with trends towards increasing problems in the realm of political representation and social trust. In this section results are summarized for three groups of outcomes: voter turnout; social trust; and popular opinions on income redistribution.

Voter Turnout

If inequality and relative deprivation leave those who are less well off feeling socially and economically excluded, this can lead to political disengagement. A general move to the centre ground in politics can exacerbate this problem leaving the disadvantaged feeling that the political elite are unable to empathize with the issues that are most important to them but, instead, focus on wooing the median voter. The well off can form a powerful political lobbying group and are able to persuade governments to protect their interests. The Netherlands chapter quotes Solt (2010) who makes a similar argument, 'As the rich grow richer relative to their fellow citizens, they consequently grow better able to define the alternatives that are considered within the political system and exclude matters of importance to poor citizens. Poorer citizens, less and less able to place questions of concern to them on the agenda, increasingly stay away from the voting booth'. The implication is that rising inequality will lead to falling voter turnout and differences across groups will widen. In a study of US States, Solt (2010) does find that where income inequality is higher (other US States and other points in time), citizens are less likely to vote. The authors of the Japan chapter choose to make a different argument. They suggest that an increase in inequality would lead to more people being willing to participate in political activities to redress deteriorating differentials in society. However, given the psychosocial effects of inequality and relative deprivation those who are economically disadvantaged may feel disempowered in other domains and will be less likely to vote but may ultimately express their views in different ways.

In Belgium, Luxembourg, and Australia voting in general elections is mandatory and consequently voter turnout is very high in all three countries. Elsewhere there is a common downward trend in voter turnout. Following transition from Soviet led systems, and the introduction of free general elections across the Central and Eastern European countries, voter turnout has decreased. Perhaps surprisingly, even the first free election in Poland in 1991 was marked by very low electoral engagement, with only 43 per cent of the electorate voting in this election. In Romania, voter turnout started higher at 86 per cent but has continued on a downward path to an all-time low of 43 per cent in 2012. Voter turnout in Bulgaria started reasonably high in 1991 at 82 per cent and although turnout has declined since then, in 2009 voter turnout was 61 per cent. Hungary also seems to have managed to retain fairly respectable voter turnout rates. In contrast the Baltic countries have some of the lowest voter turnout rates in Europe.

In Japan, voter turnout rates have fallen and important gaps between the voting behaviour of the older and younger age groups have been identified. There is some concern that the lower voter turnout rates among the younger age groups highlight the weak political power of this group. In Italy, a similar concern is raised. In Ireland, voter turnout rates have fallen since 1980, and were lowest towards the height of the economic boom in 2004. In other countries there appears to be a closer link between falling voter turnout and increasing inequality. For example, in Canada, voter turnout fell from 65 per cent in 1980 to 55 per cent in 2010 but the largest decline occurred in the 1990s at approximately the same time as the largest increase in income inequality, suggesting a negative effect of inequality on democratic engagement. In many countries, rising inequalities have coincided with lower turnout at elections, in particular in a number of Central and Eastern European countries (the Czech Republic, the Baltic States, Poland, Romania, Slovakia), but also in coordinated market economies in Western Europe (Finland, Germany, Sweden, the Netherlands).

Two exceptions to this general trend are the US, where voter turnout in presidential elections and off-year elections have remained fairly stable since 1970, despite the large increase in inequality, and France where voter turnout has remained fairly stable at around 70–80 per cent. Spain is also an exception, with turnout rates remaining stable, but, as the country chapter makes clear, for historical reasons the political context remains very important there.

Most countries exhibit marked differentials in voting patterns between education and social groups. In Sweden, voting is very stratified by education groups, where individuals with higher levels of education are more likely to vote than individuals with lower levels of education, and there is evidence that the gap widened from 8–9 percentage points to 15 percentage points. Despite stable voter turnout rates in the US, there is a steep social gradient with higher educated Americans much more likely to vote. This is also the case in Italy, with both an age and education divide, where there is concern that young less educated people are losing political weight by staying away from the voting booth. In the UK there is evidence of a social gradient, which widened in 1997 and increased substantially in 2005. Available evidence for the 2010 general election suggests that this wide divide has remained and may even have deteriorated further. The fall in voter turnout in the UK from 78 per cent in 1992 to 66 per cent in 2010 was driven by plummeting turnout among lower social classes. As the main increase in inequality occurred during the 1980s this looks to have been a lagged effect although it could be influenced by the fact that the top continued to increase their share of income even after the Gini coefficient levelled off. Exceptionally, in Spain, voter turnout among the lowest education/income groups is marginally higher than the top income group, reflecting again the importance of the political context in Spain.

Trust

Two dimensions of trust are examined, trust in institutions and trust in other people (also called generalized trust). Trust in institutions is said to indicate a system's legitimacy and confidence in institutions to perform efficiently and fairly. Where inequality is high, trust can break down between individuals and institutions. Although the evidence in the country chapters is rather limited concerning institutional trust, some relevant patterns emerge.

There appear to be a greater range of trends for trust in institutions than is observed for a number of other variables. It is clear that economic crisis and political scandal led to a reduction in trust in political institutions (government, parliament and political parties) and trust tends to follow an electoral cycle with trust higher at the start of a parliamentary term than mid term or towards the end of a term. Trust in the police and the judicial and legal systems tends to be higher, more stable and less affected by economic cycles. Trust in financial institutions is affected by crisis and periods of deregulation. There are generally lower levels of trust in Central and Eastern European countries, which seems to be a legacy from the Soviet era. This is perhaps most visible between East and West Germany. Latvia shows one of the lowest levels of trust in Europe and the most unequal distribution of income. By, contrast, Estonia has seen falling inequality over the last decade and increasing levels of trust. In Poland, a clear relationship is noted between the level of income inequality and the level of generalized trust.

On the whole, though, the relationship between inequality and generalized trust is rather weak. If the figures appearing in the country chapters are examined together, there is no relationship between the level of inequality and the level of generalized trust once GDP per capita is controlled for. This is an important finding, because one important factor in why inequality is held to be harmful to society is that it lowers trust: to the extent that inequality is related to 'societal ills', the findings presented here suggest that it is not significantly through reduced trust that this comes about.

Nevertheless, it is important that strong social gradients in trust are found in many countries where this information is available (France, Spain, Poland, the UK, US, Finland, Sweden, Luxembourg) but the gaps have not widened everywhere. For example, in the UK they appear to have narrowed as a result of falling trust of others among the highest educated group, stayed the same in the US but widened in Poland, Finland, Sweden. Bulgaria is an outlier, where it is reported that the least educated report higher levels of trust than those with higher education. Individuals with degree level qualifications in Bulgaria appear to be most critical of parliament, the judiciary and the government.

Attitudes to Inequality and Redistribution

In this section we assess the evidence across countries and over time for individuals' perceptions of inequality in their own country, and whether or not they agree that their government should redistribute income from those who are well off to those who are less well off.

While tolerance towards inequality, or the more active 'taste' for equality (Roemer, 2009), does vary across countries, perhaps due to cultural differences or arising from historical experiences, negative or positive, it does appear to respond to changes in inequality over time.

Slovenia, for example, was shown to have a low tolerance for inequality and there was an increase over time in the share of individuals who perceive inequalities to be too large, despite being one of the lowest inequality countries. In Sweden, it was found that dissatisfaction with present economic inequalities increased over time (along with increases in inequality) and underpinned support for a universal and generous welfare state with redistribution. Austrians too express a strong dislike for inequality but, interestingly, when inequality increased a little during the 1990s, Austrians became more accepting of inequalities and there was a fall in the share who thought that governments should redistribute. Since the 1990s, both of these shares have increased again. In Canada, as inequality increased, opinion reacted against this trend and there was an increase in the share of Canadians who felt that incomes should be more equal. In addition, there was an increase in the share of Canadians who thought that governments should act to reduce income differences. Across the Baltic States, most residents thought that current levels of inequality were not justified, while there was less support for redistribution in Estonia where inequality is lower.

In the UK, the vast majority of people think that inequality is too high and the trend in this share mirrors the trend in income inequality, but lower shares believe that the government should redistribute more. It is interesting to note that individuals with the highest and lowest educational levels are most likely to agree with government redistribution: that is the individuals most likely to gain and the individuals most likely to 'lose' (in terms of income) through increased government redistribution. In the US, while many Americans believe that inequality is too high there is limited support for enhanced redistribution through taxes and transfers. Instead Americans are more likely to support increased government spending on programmes designed to enhance opportunity and economic security, such as education and health care.

It is fair to conclude that across these rich countries populations are averse to high income inequality, that aversion tends to go up as inequality rises, and that there is evidence that tolerance varies across countries reflecting historical contexts and ideologies. There is generally less support for government redistribution but it is often still high.

One important question is why trends in inequality do not mirror public opinion on government intervention focused on the income distribution. Why is it the case that, despite the fact that large proportions of the population want more equality, and want more government involvement to achieve this, inequalities have often risen rather than fallen? A first answer to this question is that inequality results from external forces that can only partially be affected by social policies, such as globalization and skill-biased technological change. However, as the next section will discuss, policies do have pronounced impacts on income distributions, so this answer is not entirely satisfactory. Another answer may be more convincing, which is that popular opinion may not affect political decision-making and policy change because opinions on inequality are not salient enough in the political sphere. As described in Salverda et al., (2013), a lack of salience in politics results from, first, socially divergent turnout rates at elections. If the poor, or the uneducated, refrain from political participation, their views are under-represented in the political arena (Pontusson and Rueda, 2008). Second, inequality attitudes themselves may be of decreasing importance in choosing a political party in the election booth. Other issues have gained weight in politics between the 1980s and early 2000s, replacing concerns with equality. As of today, in an era showing increased concerns with inequality in the public discourse (particularly in English-speaking high-inequality countries such as the USA and UK), it is plausible that inequality attitudes may become more important again in electoral choice.

5. Effectiveness of Policy

Institutions and Welfare State policies are repeatedly highlighted as playing a prominent role in shaping and dampening background inequalities across the country case studies. Background inequalities across rich countries have been affected by economic globalization and a general shift from heavy industry and manufacturing towards increasingly service-based economies. This economic restructuring has largely led to an increase in demand for high-skilled workers, putting pressure on background inequalities, in some cases amplified by socio-demographic and sociological trends like educational homogamy. At the same time, and usually as a result of concerted policy efforts, educational attainment has increased across rich countries. To some extent this has dampened increasing returns to education.

Countries that appear to have been most successful in tempering increasing background inequalities have a combination of strong labour market institutions with coordinated wage-setting agreements (effectively preventing background inequalities from feeding through to market income inequality) and strong Welfare States which redistribute income through the tax and benefit system (equalizing differences between market income and disposable income). Some of the country case studies emphasize that it is the absence of these policies and institutions that has had an impact on inequality (in for example the US and Korea). There are many others where the weakening of institutions and Welfare States is linked to increases in inequality (Sweden, Canada, UK, Australia, Germany, to name just a few).

The chapters on the CEE countries bring to life how closely observed inequality trends can be linked to regulatory and structural reforms. After the collapse of the Soviet Union, the CEE countries experienced a major transition shock, marked by massive labour shedding and declining wages. Moreover, during the 1990s, many CEE countries started to restructure their economies and Welfare States, taking a turn towards liberalization. However, the extent and phasing of liberalization differed. In the Baltic States, for example, Estonia was very quick to implement market reforms, while Latvia and Lithuania first lagged behind and then also took a radical turn towards market-conforming reforms. The increases in inequality these countries saw clearly reflect these differences in phasing.

There are also a few instances where institutions have been strengthened or Welfare States have increased the extent to which they redistribute income—notably the UK under New Labour, to a limited extent, Greece (although poor fiscal discipline meant that this was not sustainable), Portugal, and Spain. Interestingly, newly industrialized countries such as Korea seek a strengthening of the public social safety net as this can no longer be provided by the rapid expansion of employment, which in practice drew in many at the bottom of the educational and income pyramid in recent decades. However, for many other countries these appear to be exceptions to a more general pattern of Welfare State retrenchment.

Collective Wage Bargaining Systems, Labour Market Regulation and Minimum Wages

Some of the most extensive and coordinated collective wage bargaining systems are found in Belgium, Austria, and Luxembourg: all enjoyed low and relatively stable inequality. The chapter on Belgium, for example, sees the stability of its strongly centralized and coordinated wage setting system as a key factor in stable income inequality. In contrast, countries which experienced a decline in collective wage bargaining systems also experienced rising inequality, for example Germany, Finland and Australia. For example, the chapter on Australia sees changes to Australia's wage-fixing institutions as contributing to increasing wage disparities and, in a similar vein, the chapter on Italy discusses at some length labour market regulation as a key driver of inequality patterns there.

Some chapters focus on particular elements of labour market regulation. The chapter on Bulgaria details the role of the minimum wages in observed inequality trends. Estimates presented in the UK chapter suggest that the minimum wage introduced there in 1999 helped to reduce inequality. In the Ireland chapter it is reported that the minimum wage introduced in 2000 has effectively underpinned the bottom of the earnings distribution. The Luxembourg country case study states that a high statutory minimum wage provided a floor that compressed the bottom of the wage distribution. Where real minimum wages have stagnated or declined, this has been associated with growing income inequality in countries such as Canada, Australia and Portugal. Real minimum wages in Canada (set by provincial governments) either stagnated or declined in the mid 1990s—the period of greatest growth in income inequality. The chapter on Portugal details how the steady devaluation of the minimum wage relative to the average wage, the considerable drop in union density, and the deregulation of the labour market all contributed to the increase in wage inequality. The Netherlands lowered the minimum wage and social benefits very significantly in real terms and even more so relative to trends in earnings and other incomes.

Cash Transfers and Taxes

Without a doubt, the policy sphere receiving most attention across the country case studies is the effectiveness of cash transfers and tax revenue in reducing inequality. A number of countries which experienced a retrenchment of their Welfare States discuss the links with rising inequality. In Australia, the cash transfer system became increasingly targeted but income inequality continued to rise as the size of the Welfare State shrank. The Australia chapter also highlights how policy drift can affect outcomes. That is to say incremental, not easily observable policy-related processes can accumulate into sizeable changes. The example is given of unemployment benefits, which are indexed to prices and therefore did not keep pace with rising wages and household incomes. The result has been that working-age social security recipients fell further and further behind community living standards in Australia.

Canada and Sweden effectively reduced cash transfers following recessions in the 1990s and this is thought to have had an effect on rising income inequalities. The underdevelopment of the welfare state in Romania is seen as a weakness in the fight against inequality and poverty with people forced to rely on kinship and subsistence agriculture during times of need. The lack of a national poverty strategy or universal income support programme plays a significant role in the high levels of income inequality in Italy, with the family still regarded as the main provider of welfare. In contrast, the Austrian case study concludes that a major explanation for the moderate increase in household income inequality is the largely intact redistributive function of the Austrian welfare state.

The introduction of dual tax systems, where different tax rates apply to capital and labour income across a number of countries, has been highlighted as a factor that has contributed to rising inequality, and to increases in top income shares in particular. Capital is generally given preferential treatment under tax regimes and due to the very unequal distribution of capital and the fact that capital income is highly skewed to top income households this tends to exacerbate inequality. In Sweden, the introduction of a dual income tax system, differentiating between labour and capital income to the advantage of the latter, is seen as an important factor behind the rise in income inequality, likewise in Germany and France. In many countries taxes on wealth, capital gains, and inheritance have been reduced or even abolished. In France, the country case study highlights the fact that the French tax system is not progressive since people at the top of the distribution pay proportionally less tax than people at the bottom. The fact that this was reinforced during the 2000s is put forward as an explanation for the rise in inequality and especially the growth of top income shares.

In looking across the various country case studies, then, it is striking that country experts in assessing inequality trends emphasize the major role played by policy changes and changes to the broader institutional environment.

6. Concluding Section

In this concluding chapter we have summarized some key features of the findings across the 30 country case studies in relation to the evolution of income inequality, and a range of outcomes in the social, cultural and political realms that might potentially be affected by it. We have also summarized what the country studies suggest about the effectiveness of policies in mitigating or exacerbating background inequalities and the extent to which these inequalities can be linked to further divisions between individuals, families and social groups. Chapter 2 of this volume documented trends in inequality and relative poverty over the last 30 years, a period of time that spans major developments across all 30 countries, politico-economic transition in some, expansive commodification and financialization in others, deep cultural and demographic change in most. For the Central and East European countries this was most pronounced, with the period straddling the transition from Soviet-led to independent market-led economies. Not surprisingly, as these were heterogeneous countries at the outset, their pathways through transition have been extremely varied. Economic cycles have been a feature across all countries, through neither their timing nor their causes or effects were uniform. The transformation of large-scale industrial and manufacturing based economies to service based economies continued throughout this period at the same time as revolutionary developments in technology in the form of computing and information and communications technologies. Europe saw the European Union reach 27 member states, and deeper economic union was accompanied for many by monetary union with the creation and expansion of the Eurozone. There have also been substantial demographic and societal shifts in family formation, family configurations and gender roles with greater diversity and movement away from the male-breadwinner nuclear family model. This has provided new challenges for

Welfare States and has been a demographic driver behind some of the changes in inequality that we have observed.

The evidence and narrative embedded in these country chapters is suggestive of an ideological shift across many of these rich countries towards freer markets, smaller Welfare States, less regulation and less institutional power for unions, although this was not universal. Such Welfare State retrenchment could be accelerated during the current economic crisis as countries grapple with balancing budgets and reducing public debt. The neo-Conservative governments of the 1980s, in particular the UK and the USA, reacted to the 'threat' of globalization and increasing trade with low wage economies in the global south by large-scale privatization of state-owned enterprises and utilities, accompanying efficiency drives, rolling back the Welfare State, reducing the power of institutions such as trade unions and embracing monetarist supply-side economics. Perhaps further fuelled by the collapse of Soviet-led communism, these policies, which some refer to collectively as the 'Anglo-Saxon model', found favour with many governments. Elements of them can be seen in the way governments reacted to the 1990s recessions that hit the Nordic countries and Canada and to a certain extent Japan and Korea following the Asian financial crisis.

While Welfare State retrenchment and deregulation may be reflected in an increase in inequality across the income distribution, it may also over time underpin the growth in a powerful elite (including the 'supra-national super rich') with an increasing share of income and wealth, sometimes accompanied by a disengagement of less powerful more disadvantaged groups from the political process, as seen in plummeting voter turnout in a number of countries.

There are global forces at play that have put pressure on earnings inequality across rich countries, but the evidence in this volume clearly demonstrates that governments can react to these pressures in different ways, substantially affecting the extent to which they lead to increasing inequality in household incomes.

Income inequality has far-reaching consequences for peoples' lives, and for society as a whole. We did not find strong evidence that increasing income inequality is associated with such negative social outcomes as more crime, more family breakdown, less trust and greater social immobility, at least in the relatively short term. The long-term effects of greater inequality remain to be seen, and will need to be carefully studied and monitored. In any case, it is been repeatedly demonstrated across the country studies that inequality in income is strongly associated with inequalities in other dimensions, including health, and these deep-seated social gradients are in themselves highly undesirable.

The country case studies provide evidence of a plethora of welfare policies both in the raising of revenue and its expenditure that are designed to (sometimes indirectly) reduce such differences between individuals and families. Cash transfers are used directly to assist those in receipt of low market incomes and the taxes funding these transfers and other public spending to varying degrees reduce market income inequality. In terms of broader social policies, publicly funded health and education are designed to raise population health and education, and to limit the extent to which income determines the level of health and education that people enjoy. These policies, and the welfare state more broadly, collectively create a corrective buffer, smoothing out differences between people and weakening the link between income from the market and other outcomes. The extent to which countries are successful in achieving this will also be reflected in the relationship between income inequality and negative social consequences. The depth and breadth of the material presented in this volume represent a valuable resource on which further research can and will build, demonstrating the importance of properly understanding the national and institutional context and the role of policies in seeking to describe and understand the way inequality broadly conceived has evolved and is evolving.

REFERENCES

Elgar, F. and Aitken, N. (2011), 'Income Inequality, Trust and Homicide in 33 Countries', *European Journal of Public Health*, 21(2): 241–246.

Lynch, J. W., Smith, G.D., Kaplan, G. A., and House, J.S. (2000), 'Income Inequality and Mortality: Importance to Health of Individual Income, Psychosocial Environment, or Material Conditions', *British Medical Journal*, 320: 1200–1204.

Salverda, W., Nolan, B., Checchi, D., Marx, I., McKnight, A., Toth, I.G. and van de Werfhorst, H.G. (eds.) (2013), *Changing Inequalities in Rich Countries: Analytical and Comparative Perspectives*, Oxford: Oxford University Press (forthcoming).

Solt, F. (2010), 'Does Economic Inequality Depress Electoral Participation? Testing the Schattschneider Hypothesis', *Political Behavior* 32(2): 285–301.

Wilkinson, R. and Pickett, K. (2009), *The Spirit Level*, London: Routledge.

INDEX